Praise for T. J. Stiles's

The First Tycoon

"Stiles, a superb researcher, has unearthed quantities of new material and crafted them into the illuminating, authoritative portrait of Vanderbilt that has been missing for so long."   —*The Washington Post*

"Very absorbing. . . . Much more than a biography. The book is filled with important, exhaustively researched and indeed fascinating details that would profit every student of American business and social history to read."   —*San Francisco Chronicle*

"Stiles writes with both the panache of a fine journalist and the analytical care of a seasoned scholar. And he offers a fruitful way to think about the larger history of American elites as well as the life of one of their most famous members."   —*The New York Times Book Review*

"Vanderbilt's story is indeed epic, and so is *The First Tycoon*. . . . Stiles is a perceptive and witty writer with a remarkable ability to paint a picture of the America in which Vanderbilt lived."   —*The Christian Science Monitor*

"Fascinating. . . . A reminder that Vanderbilt's life and times still have much to teach us."   —*Newsweek*

"Gracefully written. . . . [Vanderbilt] was the right man in the right place at the right time, and the meticulous Stiles seems to be the right man to tell us about it."   —*St. Petersburg Times*

"Stiles has given us a balanced and absorbing biography of this colorful and often ruthless entrepreneur."   —James M. McPherson, author of
Battle Cry of Freedom: The Civil War Era

"Monumental. . . . Arresting. . . . Stiles has a gift for making readers admire unsavory characters. . . . [*The First Tycoon*] resembles a five-course meal at a three-star restaurant: rich and pleasurable." —Bloomberg.com

"Engrossing and provocative. . . . Stiles draws on exhaustive archival research to clear away the apocryphal and celebrate Vanderbilt as an American icon."
                                                          —*Tulsa World*

"*The First Tycoon* has been widely praised, and rightly so. . . . [An] epic biography."
                                                          —*The New York Times*

"At long last a biography worthy of the Commodore, meticulously researched, superbly written, and filled with original insights."
                    —Maury Klein, author of *The Life and Legend of Jay Gould*

"Stiles writes with the magisterial sweep of a great historian and the keen psychological insight of a great biographer. . . . With panache and admirable ease, Stiles maps the financial and political currents on which Vanderbilt buccaneered and shows that it was Vanderbilt, more than anyone else, who enabled business to evolve into Big Business."
                    —Patricia O'Toole, author of *When Trumpets Call:*
                    Theodore Roosevelt After the White House

"A brilliant exposition of the life of Cornelius Vanderbilt and the entrepreneurial environment that he shaped. Readers will look at Grand Central Station and much else in American life with fresh eyes."
            —Joyce Appleby, author of *The Relentless Revolution: A History of Capitalism*

"The definitive biography of Commodore Vanderbilt. Both as portrait of an American original and as a book that brings to life an important slice of American history long neglected, this is biography at its very best. A magnificent achievement."   —Arthur Vanderbilt II, author of
                    Fortune's Children: The Fall of the House of Vanderbilt

"Stiles brings the Commodore, warts and all, to life in this new study, which is at once up-to-date in scholarly terms, analytically incisive, and lucidly written."   —*Raleigh News and Observer*

"Sweeping. . . . [A] magisterial, exemplary work . . . [that] offers entry into the storm-tossed world of our current tycoons and the rough waters they have piloted us into."   —*American History Magazine*

"Superbly researched and elegantly written. . . . Stiles's will likely prove to be the definitive biography of this epic entrepreneur."
                                                          —*Philadelphia Weekly*

T. J. STILES

THE FIRST TYCOON

T. J. Stiles has held the Gilder Lehrman Fellowship in American History at the Dorothy and Lewis B. Cullman Center for Scholars and Writers at the New York Public Library, taught at Columbia University, and served as adviser for the PBS series *The American Experience*. His first book, *Jesse James: Last Rebel of the Civil War*, won the Ambassador Book Award and the Peter Seaborg Award for Civil War Scholarship, and was a *New York Times* Notable Book. *The First Tycoon* won the National Book Award in 2009. He has written for *The New York Times Book Review*, *Salon*, *Smithsonian*, and the *Los Angeles Times*. He lives in San Francisco.

www.tjstiles.com

ALSO BY T. J. STILES

Jesse James:
Last Rebel of the Civil War

THE

FIRST

TYCOON

*The Epic Life
of Cornelius Vanderbilt*

T. J. STILES

VINTAGE BOOKS
A DIVISION OF RANDOM HOUSE, INC.
NEW YORK

FIRST VINTAGE BOOKS EDITION, MAY 2010

Copyright © 2009 by T. J. Stiles

All rights reserved. Published in the United States by Vintage Books, a division of Random House, Inc., New York, and in Canada by Random House of Canada Limited, Toronto. Originally published in hardcover in the United States by Alfred A. Knopf, a division of Random House, Inc., New York, in 2009.

Vintage and colophon are registered trademarks of Random House, Inc.

The Library of Congress has cataloged the Knopf edition as follows:
Stiles, T. J.
The first tycoon : the epic life of Cornelius Vanderbilt / T. J. Stiles.—1st ed.
p.   cm.
Includes bibliographical references and index.
1. Vanderbilt, Cornelius, 1794–1877.   2. Businessmen—United States—Biography.   3. Millionaires—United States—Biography.
4. Railroads—United States—History—19th century.
5. Steamboats—United States—History—19th century.   I. Title.
CT275.V23S85 2009
973.5092—dc22
2008047879

Vintage ISBN: 978-1-4000-3174-0

Author photograph © Joanne Chan
Book design by M. Kristen Bearse
Cartography by Mapping Specialists, Madison, Wisconsin

www.vintagebooks.com

Printed in the United States of America
10 9 8 7 6 5 4 3 2 1

To Jessica and Dillon,
for giving me the future

To understand just one life, you have to swallow the world.

—SALMAN RUSHDIE,
Midnight's Children

Contents

Illustrations

Maps

Part One

CAPTAIN

1794–1847

He is striking at everything. I am afraid of this man.
—THOMAS GIBBONS, December 12, 1822

I'd sooner have *him* with us, than against us.
—WILLIAM GIBBS MCNEILL, November 14, 1840

That Vanderbilt is a great ____ (you must fill in the blank).
—COURTLANDT PALMER, December 16, 1841

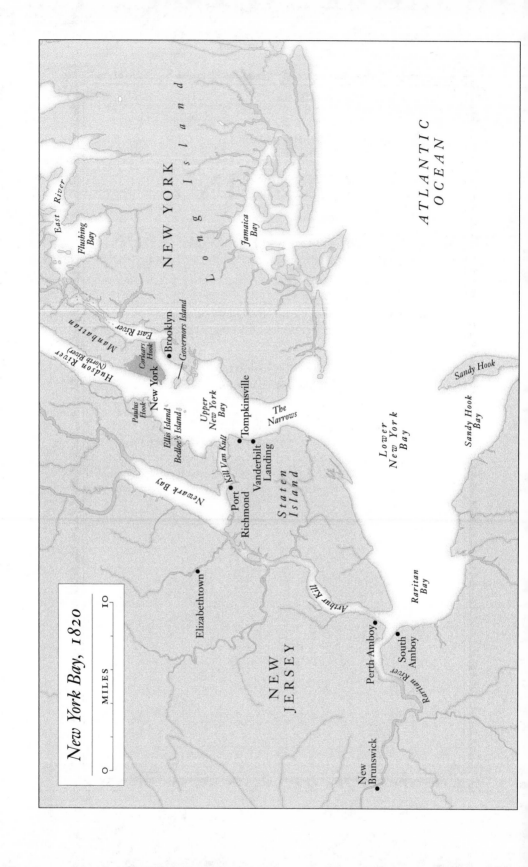

New York Bay, 1820

MILES

0   10

ATLANTIC OCEAN

East River

Flushing Bay

NEW YORK

L o n g   I s l a n d

Jamaica Bay

Hudson River (North River)

Manhattan

East River

•Brooklyn

Corlaers Hook

Governors Island

New York

Paulus Hook

Newark Bay

Ellis Island

Bedloe's Island

Upper New York Bay

•Tompkinsville

Kill Van Kull

•Port Richmond

Vanderbilt Landing

The Narrows

Staten Island

•Elizabethtown

Arthur Kill

Lower New York Bay

Sandy Hook

Sandy Hook Bay

NEW JERSEY

•Perth Amboy

Raritan Bay

•South Amboy

Raritan River

•New Brunswick

Chapter One

THE ISLANDER

They came to learn his secrets. Well before the appointed hour of two o'clock in the afternoon on November 12, 1877, hundreds of spectators pushed into a courtroom in lower Manhattan. They included friends and relatives of the contestants, of course, as well as leading lawyers who wished to observe the forensic skills of the famous attorneys who would try the case. But most of the teeming mass of men and women—many fashionably dressed, crowding in until they were packed against the back wall—wanted to hear the details of the life of the richest man the United States had ever seen. The trial over the will of Cornelius Vanderbilt, the famous, notorious Commodore, was about to begin.

Shortly before the hour, the crowd parted to allow in William H. Vanderbilt, the Commodore's eldest son, and his lawyers, led by Henry L. Clinton. William, "glancing carelessly and indifferently around the room, removed his overcoat and comfortably settled himself in his chair," the *New York Times* reported; meanwhile his lawyers shook hands with the opposing team, led by Scott Lord, who represented William's sister Mary Vanderbilt La Bau. At exactly two o'clock, the judge—called the "Surrogate" in this Surrogate Court—strode briskly in from his chambers through a side door, stepped up to the dais, and took his seat. "Are you ready, gentlemen?" he asked. Lord and Clinton each declared that they were, and the Surrogate ordered, "Proceed, gentlemen."[1]

Everyone who listened as Lord stood to make his opening argument knew just how great the stakes were. "THE HOUSE OF VANDERBILT," the *Times* headlined its story the next morning. "A RAILROAD PRINCE'S FOR-TUNE. THE HEIRS CONTESTING THE WILL. . . . A BATTLE OVER $100,000,000." The only item in all that screaming type that would have surprised readers was the *Times*'s demotion of Vanderbilt to "prince," since the press usually dubbed him the railroad *king*. His fortune towered over the American economy to a degree difficult to imagine, even at the time. If he had been able to sell all his assets at full market value at the moment of his death, in January of that year, he would have taken one out of every twenty dollars in circulation, including cash and demand deposits.[2]

Most of those in that courtroom had lived their entire lives in Vanderbilt's shadow. By the time he had turned fifty, he had dominated railroad and steamboat transportation between New York and New England (thus earning the nickname "Commodore"). In the 1850s, he had launched a transatlantic steamship line and pioneered a transit route to California across Nicaragua. In the 1860s, he had systematically seized control of the railroads that connected Manhattan with the rest of the world, building the mighty New York Central Railroad system between New York and Chicago. Probably every person in that chamber had passed through Grand Central, the depot on Forty-second Street that Vanderbilt had constructed; had seen the enormous St. John's Park freight terminal that he had built, featuring a huge bronze statue of himself; had crossed the bridges over the tracks that he had sunk along Fourth Avenue (a step that would allow it to later blossom into Park Avenue); or had taken one of the ferries, steamboats, or steamships that he had controlled over the course of his lifetime. He had stamped the city with his mark—a mark that would last well into the twenty-first century—and so had stamped the country. Virtually every American had paid tribute to his treasury.

More fascinating than the fortune was the man behind it. Lord began his attack by admitting "that it seemed hazardous to say that a man who accumulated $100,000,000 and was famous for his strength of will had not the power to dispose of his fortune." His strength of will was famous indeed. Vanderbilt had first amassed wealth as a competitor in the steamboat business, cutting fares against established lines until he forced his rivals to pay him to go away. The practice led the *New York Times*, a quarter of a century before his death, to introduce a new metaphor into the American vernacular by comparing him to the medieval robber barons who took a toll from all passing traffic on the Rhine. His adventure in Nicaragua had been, in part, a matter of personal buccaneering, as he explored the passage through the rain forest, piloted a riverboat through the rapids of the San Juan River, and decisively intervened in a war against an international criminal who had seized control of the country. His early life was filled with fistfights, high-speed steamboat duels, and engine explosions; his latter days were marked by daredevil harness races and high-stakes confrontations.

It was this personal drama that moved that crowd of spectators into the courtroom eleven months after his death, but more thoughtful observers mulled over his larger meaning. Vanderbilt was an empire builder, the first great corporate tycoon in American history. Even before the United States became a truly industrial country, he learned to use the tools of corporate capitalism to amass wealth and power on a scale previously unknown, creating enterprises of unprecedented size. "He has introduced Caesarism into corporate life," wrote Charles Francis Adams Jr. "Vanderbilt is but the precursor of a class of men who will wield within the state a power created by it, but too great for its control. He is the founder of a dynasty."[3]

Adams did not mean a family dynasty, but a line of corporate chiefs who would overshadow democratic government itself. Rockefeller, Carnegie, Gould, Morgan—all were just beginning their careers when Vanderbilt was at his height. They respected and followed his example, though they would be hard-pressed to match it. Few laws had constrained him; few governments had exceeded his influence. In the 1850s, his personal role in Central America had been more important than that of the White House or the State Department. In 1867, he had stopped all trains into New York City from the west to bring the New York Central Railroad to its knees. In 1869, he personally had abated a panic on Wall Street that threatened to ring in a depression.

His admirers saw him as the ultimate meritocrat, the finest example of the common man rising through hard work and ability. To them, he symbolized America's opportunities. His critics called him grasping and ruthless, an unelected king who never pretended to rule for his people. Still worse, they saw him as the apex of a vulgar new culture that had cast off the republican purity of the Revolution for the golden calf of wealth. "You seem to be the idol of . . . a crawling swarm of small souls," Mark Twain wrote in an open letter to Vanderbilt, "who . . . sing of your unimportant private habits and sayings and doings, as if your millions gave them dignity."[4]

Perhaps there were those who understood that Vanderbilt's true significance was more complex, even contradictory. How could it not be? His life spanned a period of breathtaking changes, from the days of George Washington to those of John D. Rockefeller (with whom he made deals). He began his career in a rural, agricultural, essentially colonial society in which the term "businessman" was unknown; he ended it in a corporate, industrial economy.[5] Neither the admirers nor the critics of his later years had witnessed his role during the tumultuous era of the early republic and the antebellum period. They could not see that Vanderbilt had spent most of his career as a radical force. From his beginnings as a teenage boatman before the War of 1812, he had led the rise of competition as a virtue in American culture. He had disrupted the remnants of the eighteenth-century patricians, shaken the conservative merchant elite, and destroyed monopolies at every step. His infuriated opponents had not shared his enthusiasm for competition; rather, the wealthy establishment in that young and limited economy saw his attacks as destructive. In 1859, one had written that he "has always proved himself the enemy of every American maritime enterprise," and the *New York Times* condemned Vanderbilt for pursuing "competition for competition's sake."[6] Those on the other end of the spectrum had celebrated the way he had expanded transportation, slashed fares, and punished opponents who relied on government monopolies or subsidies. To Jacksonian Democrats, who championed laissez-faire as an egalitarian creed, he had epitomized the entrepreneur as champion of the people, the businessman as revolutionary.

But the career that started early ended late, and the revolutionary completed his days as emperor. As he had expanded his railroad domain from the benighted New York & Harlem—annexing the Hudson River, the New York Central, the Lake Shore & Michigan Southern, and the Canada Southern—he had seemed not a radical but a monopolist. His role in the Erie War of 1868, with its epic corruption of public officials, had made him seem not a champion but an enemy of civic virtue. He played a leading part in the creation of a new entity, the giant corporation, that would dominate the American economy in the decades after his death. The political landscape had changed as well. With the rise of large railroads and the expansion of federal power during the Civil War, radicals began to think of the government as a possible counterweight to corporate might. Vanderbilt had remained as committed to laissez-faire as ever; as he told the newspapers more than once, his guiding principle was "to mind my own business," and all he asked from government was to be left alone.[7] He never acknowledged that, as Charles F. Adams Jr. wrote, the massive corporations he commanded gave him power to rival that of the state, and that he became the establishment against which populists armed themselves with government regulation.

Probably no other individual made an equal impact over such an extended period on America's economy and society. Over the course of his sixty-six-year career he stood on the forefront of change, a modernizer from beginning to end. He vastly improved and expanded the nation's transportation infrastructure, contributing to a transformation of the very geography of the United States. He embraced new technologies and new forms of business organization, and used them to compete so successfully that he forced his rivals to follow his example or give up. Far ahead of many of his peers, he grasped one of the great changes in American culture: the abstraction of economic reality, as the connection faded between the tangible world and the new devices of business, such as paper currency, corporations, and securities. With those devices he helped to create the corporate economy that would define the United States into the twenty-first century. Even as he demonstrated the creative power of a market economy, he also exacerbated problems that would never be fully solved: a huge disparity in wealth between rich and poor; the concentration of great power in private hands; the fraud and self-serving deception that thrives in an unregulated environment. One person cannot move the national economy single-handedly—but no one else kept his hands on the lever for so long or pushed so hard.

The spectators in that courtroom, then, could mark Vanderbilt down as complicated indeed, even before the first witness spoke. Yet what pulled them there was perhaps not so much his national significance as his strange, powerful character, his mysterious personal life. Public rumor depicted a home wracked by intrigue, spiritualist séances, and Vanderbilt's controversial sponsorship of the feminist Victoria Woodhull and her voluptuous sister, Tennie C. Claflin. What the public did not see was his emotional complexity: his patient business diplomacy, his love for his first and second wives (as well as his selfishness with them), and his conflicting feelings about his often difficult children—especially Cornelius Jeremiah, who struggled with epilepsy and an addiction to gambling. Contemporaries and posterity alike often would overlook the very human, even sympathetic, side of the imperious Commodore, attracted instead to the most salacious, scandalous, and overblown reports.

It was his final act that brought everyone into that courtroom, an act that combined the personal and the corporate. He had built something that he meant to last and remain in the hands of his own bloodline—to found a dynasty in the most literal sense. To that end, he had drafted a will that left 95 percent of his estate to his eldest son, William. William's sister Mary meant to break that dynasty by breaking the will, to force a distribution of the estate equally among the ten surviving children.

Would she succeed? Each side would fight to define Vanderbilt; each side would seek out its own answer to the enigma of a man who left few letters and no diaries. Lord began to speak, and the crowd bent forward to listen, straining to learn who the Commodore really was.

A CHILD, IT IS SAID, CHANGES EVERYTHING. For Phebe Hand Vanderbilt, another child meant more of the same. In May 1794, during the last month of her fourth pregnancy, her first three children, Mary, Jacob, and Charlotte, ran about their humble house. Knowing the Vanderbilt tradition, she could expect many more to follow the unborn infant in her womb. Continuity, not change, defined everything about her existence, an existence that differed little from that of her parents, grandparents, or great-grandparents. She sat in wooden furniture hand-cut from hand-hewn lumber. She wore clothes hand-sewn from hand-spun wool. She washed cups and plates that had been spun on a wheel, and bottles blown by a craftsman's mouth. Looking out a window, she would see hand-built wagons harnessed to teams of horses. Peering a little farther, she could watch the sloops and ships that sailed by the shore just steps from her door. And at night she would light the room with a mutton-fat candle or a whale-oil lamp.

Phebe lived in a close wooden world made by human hands, powered by winds and horse and human strength, clustered at the water's edge. Most of the technology she knew had been first imagined thousands of years before. Even the newest inventions of her time—the clock, the printing press, the instruments of navigation—dated back to the early Renaissance. The "Brown Bess" muskets stored in U.S. arsenals and carried by British redcoats had been designed in the 1690s, a full century before. Revolutions were a matter for politics; the constructed world merely crept ahead.[8]

Phebe lived in Port Richmond, that most ancient kind of community— a farming village, its air pungent with the smell of animal manure and open fires, its unpaved paths sticky with mud from the season's rains. It sat on the northern edge of Richmond County, better known as Staten Island, a sprawling, sparsely occupied landscape of not quite four thousand souls who still governed their affairs with town meetings. The islanders tilled the steep green hillsides, let pigs wander and forage for themselves, and built their houses close to the soft, swampy shores that crumbled into the kills—the tidal creeks that wrapped around the island's edges. Staten Island sat like a stopper in the mouth of New York Harbor, separated from Long Island by the two-mile-long Narrows, where the ocean decanted into the bay. West of Staten Island stretched the mainland of New Jersey, and across the length of the harbor sat Manhattan, a long and narrow island that extended between the deep East and Hudson (or North) rivers like a natural pier of bedrock.

An island is defined by its edges. Phebe looked across the water for her husband's return whenever he was gone, until he sailed up in his boat and tied it fast. His name was Cornelius. It was a solid Dutch name, as was Vanderbilt, and both were common around New York Bay. The first of his family had arrived in America in 1650, when Jan Aertsen Van Der Bilt settled in the Dutch colony of New Netherlands. In 1715, long after the English had conquered the province and renamed it New York, one of Jan's descendants had crossed the water to sparsely populated Staten Island. That one move was change enough, it seems, for the family that dispersed and multiplied there. The ensuing generations lived out their lives as farmers or tavern keepers, unmoved by the climactic North American war with France in the 1750s, the outbreak of revolution two decades later, the British occupation of their island, the triumph of independence, the ratification of the Constitution, and the swearing in of President George Washington in Manhattan.

On May 27, 1794, Phebe gave birth to her fourth child. She underscored the sense of continuity by naming him Cornelius, too, though they called the boy Cornele. She cooed over him in English. Phebe had first met her husband in Port Richmond, a heavily Dutch village, where she had been working as a servant in the home of a minister, but she herself came from an old English family in New Jersey.

In the town of New York this sort of intermarriage surprised no one. There the Dutch had fallen to less than half the population as early as 1720; now they were less a minority than an interbred strand among its 33,000 residents. As early as the rule of Petrus Stuyvesant in 1647, the village then named New Amsterdam had grown into a rather cosmopolitan place. Stuyvesant governed under the authority of the Dutch West India Company, created to mobilize merchant capital to advance Dutch interests in the New World. Under his administration, the little seaport came to reflect the commercial orientation of the Netherlands, the most industrious nation of seventeenth-century Europe. As in the mother country, the primacy of trade, foreign trade in particular, had fostered a tolerance of strangers and disparate creeds (at a time when being a Quaker was a hanging offense in Massachusetts), and that tradition persisted.[9]

On Staten Island, a slightly different legacy prevailed. Most of the original Dutch settlers in New Netherlands, including Jan Aertsen Van Der Bilt, came to farm. They spread out on either side of New York Bay and the Hudson River (known as the North River well into the nineteenth century) from Staten Island to Albany. Theirs was an inward-looking, rural society, and Americans of British descent often viewed them with distaste. "Nothing can exceed the state of indolence and ignorance in which these Dutchmen are described to live," wrote traveler William Strickland in the 1790s. "Many of them are supposed to live and die without having been five miles from their own houses." Outsiders generally considered the Dutch rude; one English-speaking Hudson Valley resident, for example, complained about "what I call Dutch politeness." At times suspicion boiled over into blows.[10]

These great-great-grandchildren of the Netherlands carried on old customs for decade after decade. As late as 1836, a diarist wrote, "It is difficult to turn the Dutch population from their old established ways." Women in high caps continued to serve "oely-coeks," sweetened balls of deep-fried dough; men often went about in traditional clothes, including the broad-brimmed beaver hat. And they preferred to speak "Laeg-Duits," or "Low Dutch." By 1790, this dialect had evolved into a tongue that was incomprehensible to natives of the Netherlands, but it was heard all along the North River and New York Harbor. In one telling measure, three-quarters of 1,232 runaway slaves in the region at the beginning of the nineteenth century spoke Low Dutch.

Those slaves point to another difference between the Dutch and their English-speaking neighbors. In 1799, the state of New York passed the Gradual Manumission Act, phasing out slavery over twenty-eight years. Opposition to the law came largely from rural Dutch areas. In 1790, only 11.3 percent of English families owned slaves, compared to 27.9 percent of the Dutch—and one out of every three families in northern Staten Island. As international merchants, the Dutch had played a central part in introducing slavery to North America; as New York–area farmers, they carried on the institution to the last.[11]

Slavery, in addition to being an oppressive social system, was a commercial institution, providing both labor and property. Its presence revealed another distinctive feature of the rural Dutch: they farmed for profit. In the seventeenth and eighteenth centuries, this was a notable fact. Even into the 1800s, many English-speaking farmers in New York and New England devoted much of their effort to subsistence—though not necessarily by choice—whereas Dutch farming "was market-oriented," in the words of one historian, "and derived its distinct regional characteristics from Dutch tradition."

The rural Dutch, then, shared much of the commercial consciousness of their urban brethren. They clattered their wagons into Albany, New Brunswick, and New York to sell their produce with a savvy that became proverbial. When a cobbler refused to return a man's shoes until he made full payment, for example, the frustrated customer wrote in his diary, "He is too Dutch by half." These perceptions led to such coinages as "Dutch treat." A more charitable observer linked this shrewdness, this market orientation, to a detachment from public life. "The low Dutch are a quiet, frugal people," he wrote in 1786, "possess considerable property, are afraid to run into Debt, without being fond of law, or Offices of Government."

There was, perhaps, one more inheritance from the land of dikes and tulips for the newborn boy on Staten Island: independent women. Dutch law extended substantial autonomy to women, compared to British custom, and the fact was reflected in society. "Strong and assertive Dutch wives were commonplace," observe two historians of New York City. Even after the English conquest, the tradition persisted, and Dutch women conducted business in their own names.[12]

Cornelius and Phebe Vanderbilt carried on these folkways faithfully, giving them no more thought than Staten Island's trails and landings, established long ago by their ancestors. Cornelius's own parents had died when he was young, leaving him no estate worth the name. Within a few years of the birth of his namesake, he achieved sufficient prosperity to move his family—little Cornele and his three older siblings, along with younger sisters Phebe, Jane, and Eleanor—to a roomier house east of Port Richmond, in what would become the village of Stapleton. This two-story wooden structure, with a steep-sloped roof, chimneys at either end, three dormer windows, and a porch that ran its width, sat amid pear and cherry trees, just two hundred feet from the shores of the Narrows.

They were pulled to the water's edge by the gravity of commerce. Living across the bay from New York, the Vanderbilts enjoyed a year-round market for their produce, something rare for American farmers. The longstanding trade between the crowded town and its neighboring shores had led the Dutch to develop a specialized vessel, a large, two-masted boat known as a periauger (or pettiauger).[13] In an act that spoke volumes about Cornelius's commitment to accumulation, he built or bought his own periauger and began to sell his services, ferrying his neighbors and their produce across the bay. As other work for the boat presented itself, he began to attend to the water as much as to his farm.

In some ways, it would be Phebe who would prove to be the more Dutch of the two. Like the classic wife of New Netherlands tradition, she radiated strength of personality. "She was not only the family oracle," one nineteenth-century writer declared, "she was the oracle of the neighborhood, whose advice was sought in all sorts of dilemmas, and whose judgment had weight." She was also as much a creature of the marketplace as her husband, as she sent her vegetables and sewing and whatever else she produced to town in her husband's boat. When cash came in, she would count the silver coins, march to her tall grandfather clock, and stow them within. Her shrewdness outshone that of her husband at times. According to tale, Cornelius once mortgaged the farm to finance a deal that then failed utterly. Phebe heard his confession, went to the clock, and came back with the entire amount. It was a legend, but one with a basis in fact: later court records show that she lent money at commercial rates of interest, and once foreclosed on a widow's mortgage—the widow being her own daughter. It seems that silver rarely stayed in the clock for long before Phebe found a better place to invest it.[14]

Ambition and inventiveness, practicality and toughness: the mixture of virtues that emerged from the marriage of these two people lifted them out of the poverty in which they had begun their lives together. They created a household where, far earlier than in more remote communities, the marketplace strode in the door and shaped their lives. Farmers living up the Hudson straggled along with much more haphazard connections to the world of commerce; one study found that the average household made just one delivery of crops and handicrafts to riverside merchants in an entire year. How different it was in the Vanderbilt house, where daily life was filled with buying and selling, borrowing and lending, earnings and debt. "The desire of riches is their ruling passion," a French observer wrote of Americans at this time, "and indeed their only passion." He could easily have been describing Phebe and Cornelius.[15]

But where would their passion take them? The future they could envision was in keeping with past generations of Vanderbilts, a set of possibilities confined within the water's edge that wrapped around them: a farm, a boat, perhaps a tavern, perhaps more land. The thin dispersal of people in a rural landscape dispersed opportunity as well. But unlike most country folk, the Vanderbilts lived within sight of the place of the most densely concentrated possibilities in North America: the city of New York.

THE DUC DE LA ROCHEFOUCAULD-LIANCOURT stared in wonder across the bay. Standing at the Battery, the plaza marking Manhattan's southern tip, he gasped at the view. "In this promenade," he wrote, "the eye embraces at once all the outlets of this great port, and sees all its shipping come in and go out." In a glance, he saw the marshy shores of New Jersey, the bluffs of Brooklyn, and directly across the green hillsides of Staten Island, looming above the Vanderbilt farm. In between billowed the sails of ships and sloops passing up and down the rivers, sailing to and from the ocean, mooring and unmooring from the piers that fingered the water. The scene, he sighed, made the Battery "incomparably the most delightful public walk anywhere to be found."[16]

In 1795 he had sailed across the ocean to North America, where he wandered as an exile for three years. They were years spent very much on the edge of civilization. The United States was a nation with grass between its toes. Only five cities held more than ten thousand residents; the percentage of the nation's four million citizens who lived in towns of at least 2,500 people languished in the single digits, and would linger there for decades to come. Most lived in farms, villages, and landings scattered along the long Atlantic coast.[17]

Across the Atlantic, Europe burned. In France, the king had been executed, thousands more had been guillotined during the Terror, and the massed armies of the surrounding monarchies marched in to crush the revolution. How different the United States was: during Rochefoucauld-Liancourt's three years there, the nation's military hero, George Washington, voluntarily stepped down from the presidency, declining to stand for a third term. Despite some pointed political debate, no heads rolled when

John Adams assumed the office in 1797. Here was a peaceful, stable republic, whose white-wigged leaders spoke of honor, service, and the example of classical Rome.

What captured the Frenchman's imagination, as he looked out over the ships crowding New York Harbor, was not politics but economics. Again and again, Rochefoucauld-Liancourt had observed the Americans' "ardour for enterprise." When he turned and strolled up Broadway, past bustling stores and workshops, under the ringing hammers and shouts of workmen erecting new buildings, he marveled that every inhabitant seemed to cherish "the project of making an ample and rapid fortune. . . . Few of them are contented with what they have."

It was that sense of the public mood, of the emerging American character, that illuminated Rochefoucauld-Liancourt's vision of this country. The United States, he wrote, "is destined by nature for a state of strength and greatness, which nothing can prevent her from attaining." The prophecy was far from obvious: despite the enormous geographical size of the republic, it was desperately underpopulated, with only a skeletal military establishment. And yet Rochefoucauld-Liancourt boldly predicted that it would attain "a degree of prosperity, which must in future render this part of the world the rival, perhaps the fortunate [i.e., more successful] rival, of Europe."

There was, however, an obstacle standing between the young republic and its destiny. A sophisticated as well as inquisitive traveler, Rochefoucauld-Liancourt saw that New York's busy harbor spoke of weakness as well as strength. A momentary disarrangement of the world—the war between France and its enemies—had allowed American merchants to step in as shippers to all nations. European ports once closed to Americans now stood open; competing merchant fleets now sat at their piers or were impressed into naval service. But Americans traded comparatively little with each other; merchantmen sailed from New York for Europe or the Caribbean rather than Baltimore or Boston. And fully half of American exports, in terms of value, were *re-exports* of goods arriving from overseas, rather than sales of U.S. products.

"The prosperity of a nation's commerce cannot be durable, unless it be founded upon a solid basis," Rochefoucauld-Liancourt warned; "and the solid basis of a nation's commerce is the produce of its soil, of its manufactures." But Americans manufactured little that they could sell to each other, beyond the confines of a local community. For a century and a half, London's imperial policies had molded the North American colonies into suppliers of raw materials and consumers of British manufactured goods. As a result, foreign trade had been at least four times greater than domestic during the colonial era, as each port gathered in crops and raw material from its immediate hinterland and shipped them abroad. Even now, foreign trade remained two or three times greater. The ports of the United States were an unstrung line of pearls, shining with Europe's trade but with little to hold them together when peace returned.[18]

If there was any place where that would start to change, where the republic would begin to grow into a cohesive *nation* and so grow great, it must be New York. When Rochefoucauld-Liancourt arrived in August 1797, the advantages of its location could hardly be missed. "The situation of this city in point of commercial importance," observed a foreign visitor, "is surpassed by none in the United States." Centrally placed between New England and the rest of the states, sitting on a large and sheltered deep-water harbor at the junction of the Hudson River, Long Island Sound, and the sea lanes to Europe, New York drew an ever-greater portion of American trade. By 1807, an Englishman could describe it as "the first city in the United States for wealth, commerce, and population."

And yet, New York remained in the moment of its dawn. In 1790, it remained the second city in population in the United States, with only 33,131 to Philadelphia's 54,388. New York nearly doubled by 1800 to 60,515, but even then it was hardly a grand affair. In 1811, one visiting Scotsman dismissed it as an "overgrown sea-port village." Like a rock in a sock, New York sank into Manhattan's toe, leaving most of the island to pastures, fields, and swamps. Much of the city's growth was not upward but seaward. South Street, for example, was constructed in the first decade of the 1800s on landfill dumped along the East River shore.[19]

But then, the waterfront was the very reason for New York's existence. "Belted round by wharves as Indian isles by coral reefs," Herman Melville would write, "commerce surrounds it with her surf." Every visitor, it seems, felt compelled to comment on the teeming scene. "The wharfs were crowded with shipping, whose tall masts mingled with the buildings," wrote John Lambert, after seeing it all in 1807, "and together with the spires and cupolas of the churches, gave the city an appearance of magnificence."[20]

Closer inspection tended to ruin that impression. To be blunt, the city stank. The docks consisted of solid masses of stone and dirt packed into wooden cribs, creating enclosures called slips. The water within the slips, observed a traveler, "being completely out of the current of the stream or tide, are little else than stagnant receptacles of city filth; while at the top of the wharves exhibits one continuous mass of clotted nuisance, composed of dust, tea, oil, molasses, &c., where revel countless swarms of offensive flies."

Within the belt of wharves, this overgrown seaport village swarmed with men rushing to make money. "Every thought, word, look, and action of the multitude," Lambert observed, "seemed to be absorbed by commerce." The impression deepened with each step along South Street. "Every thing was in motion; all was life, bustle, and activity," he wrote. "The carters were driving in every direction; and the sailors and labourers upon the wharfs, and on board the vessels, were moving their ponderous burthens from place to place." Penetrating a block or two deeper into town, one wandered through the twisting corridors of Pearl, Water, and Front streets, narrow lanes that were home to most of the city's "countinghouses," or merchants' offices and warehouses. A frenzy of construction was replacing old wooden houses with new brick buildings, standing shoulder to shoulder under slanting tile roofs, along new brick sidewalks lit by whale-oil lamps at night and bustling with business by day. "The Coffee-House Slip, and the corners of Wall and Pearl streets, were jammed up with carts, drays, and wheel-barrows," Lambert wrote; "horses and men were huddled promiscuously together, leaving little or no room for passengers to pass."[21]

Thirty years earlier, John Adams had expressed other reservations. "With all the opulence and splendor of this city, there is very little good breeding to be found," he had noted in his diary. "They talk very loud, very fast, and all together. If they ask you a question, before you can utter three words of your answer, they will break out upon you again, and talk away." These habits would never really change. But at least one visitor found New Yorkers' directness refreshing. "The people of Philadelphia are stiff in their manners," he noted by way of contrast, "& not so hospitable as those of New York." This was a more cosmopolitan place, he observed, thronging with an "immense number of foreigners established in N. Y., attracted thither by the advantages of its commercial importance."[22]

Commercial importance brought luxury, best seen on Broadway, the most fashionable street in North America. It flowed north from the Battery, glistening with enough elegance to impress even Rochefoucauld-Liancourt. "There is not in any city in the world a finer street than Broadway," he declared. Lambert marveled at the boulevard's "large commodious shops of every description . . . exhibiting as splendid and varied a show in their windows as can be met with in London. There are several and extensive book stores, print-shops, music-shops, jewelers, and silversmiths; hatters, linen-drapers, milliners, pastry-cooks, coach-makers, hotels, and coffee-houses." At the northern end of Broadway rose the new marble-clad city hall, presiding over an eponymous triangular park.

Still, with every mark of sophistication came a reminder of New York's rustic immaturity. Beyond City Hall Park steeped a stinking pond called the Collect. Surrounded by a nauseating cluster of tanneries and slaughterhouses, the Collect was rapidly filled in after 1802, but the area was avoided by all who could help it. The back of the city hall was left undressed with marble because contemporaries thought "it was not likely to attract much notice." But even the best neighborhood had its woes.

"It is remarked on all hands," admitted the author of a guide to New York in 1817, "that the streets of New-York are the dirtiest in the United States." There were the backyard lavatories, for one thing, that over-flowed with every heavy rain. And then there were the roaming herds of "innumerable hungry pigs of all sizes and complexions." Because of the swine, a petition of laborers explained, "many poor are able to pay rents and supply families with animal food during the winter." The pig was "our best scavenger," because it ate "fish, guts, garbage, and offals of every kind," and was smart enough to find its way home each night. But the hogs perpetuated the habit of strewing rotten waste into the gutters. "So long as immense numbers of swine are allowed to traverse the streets," wrote the travel-guide author, "so long will the inhabitants think themselves jus-tified in throwing out their garbage to them for food; and so long will the streets of New-York remain proverbial for their filth."[23]

The same tension between sophistication and simplicity—if not exactly squalor—could be felt off the streets as well, in the countinghouses, where clerks perched on high stools and scratched with quills in copy books, where porters lumbered in and out with sacks, crates, and barrels. A quar-ter of a century had passed since Adam Smith had explained the division of labor in *The Wealth of Nations;* yet this commercial community remained a city of the unspecialized. Apart from artisans who sold merely what they made, the economy belonged to general merchants.

"Their activities," writes historian George Rogers Taylor, "compre-hended almost every aspect of business." Each master of the counting-house (perhaps with two or three partners) bought and sold cargoes of goods, owned the ships that carried them, and warehoused them in the same building with his office. He distributed these goods to smaller gen-eral merchants in towns and villages, and perhaps retailed them from his own storefront, and spun out a web of credit to his customers. He made no specialty of any particular product, but bought and sold what he could.[24]

He also traded in promissory notes and bills of exchange. Cash was scarce. British law had banned exports of specie (precious-metal coins, worth their face value in gold or silver) to the colonies and prohibited them from minting their own. Americans mostly used foreign coins acquired in their trade with the Caribbean—especially Spanish dollars (the legendary "pieces of eight") and their constituent eighth-dollar coins. As the United States began to mint its own coins, Congress made the new

American dollar equal to the Spanish in silver content, for an easier transition. In New York slang, the eighth-dollar coin, worth twelve and a half cents, was known as a "shilling" well into the nineteenth century.* (Spanish pieces of eight continued to circulate in the United States as legal tender until 1857.)[25]

By any name, silver was hard to come by, so Americans made do with informal devices. A bill of exchange, for example, was a certificate of debt written up by a merchant who was owed money by a party in a distant place—London was a common case. It would be purchased by someone in New York who owed money in London. The buyer would then send it across the Atlantic with instructions for the seller's debtor to pay his own creditor. In this way, the movement of coin and final settlement of credit took place locally, at either end of these long-distance transactions. But the system was highly personal and unpredictable; it depended heavily on how well individuals knew and trusted each other. Because of the risks, the buyers of bills usually paid less than face value for them, driving up costs for everyone.

Locally, merchants usually paid each other with promissory notes, pledging payment with interest on specific dates. The recipient of one would endorse it, then use it to pay his own debts. But if the person who first issued it refused to pay when it came due, the endorser could be sued for payment, "according to the usage and custom of merchants," as the standard legal form read. It's notable that there *was* a standard legal form (in New York at least), indicating just how common unpaid notes were. And yet, promissory notes would remain a primary method of payment for decades to come.[26]

If this unspecialized, informal economy were to change, it would first be through organization, by institutions that would replace these messy personal dealings. And it was in New York where just such institutions began to rise. It was there that the merchants' patron saint, Alexander Hamilton, helped to found the Bank of New York, one of the nation's first commercial banks. Commercial banks concentrated money for bigger loans; as specialized, professional lenders, they tended to make better choices about borrowers than individuals did, so their loans were more productive. Banks also eased the cash shortage. They began to experiment with checking early on, and they also made loans by issuing banknotes— paper money—that could be redeemed at the bank for gold or silver coin.

Hamilton's role in the Bank of New York was nothing compared to

---

* The eighth-dollar coin (also known as a "bit") was so pervasive that stock prices were given in dollars and eighths, a custom that lasted until the end of the twentieth century.

what he accomplished as secretary of the treasury in Washington's first term, when the federal capital was temporarily located in Manhattan. In 1790, he presented a plan to have the federal government assume the states' Revolutionary War debts, paying for them with interest-bearing federal bonds, backed by a tariff and an excise tax on whiskey. Despite fierce resistance by Thomas Jefferson and James Madison, Congress enacted the program. The new federal bonds—known as "the Stock"—essentially created the securities market in New York, and by extension in America. The Stock's interest payments funneled federal revenue—those hard-to-come-by silver coins—to merchants, who invested the money in their enterprises. More important, the federal bonds provided a universal form of payment and collateral. The first, cautious banks in America unhesitatingly loaned money to merchants who mortgaged them; the Stock also provided a convenient means of payment over long distances, as they held their value anywhere in the country, even overseas in the British and Dutch markets.

The Stock was soon joined by shares in two banks: the new, federally chartered Bank of the United States (the second part of Hamilton's financial plan), and the older Bank of New York, which acquired a state charter and issued shares that year. Investors in New York began to meet six times a week for formal stock auctions at the Merchants' Coffee House on Wall Street; between sessions, they clustered outside under a buttonwood tree to trade informally. In 1792, they formalized the stock market with the Buttonwood Agreement, setting fixed commissions for brokers (or "stock-jobbers") and establishing the Tontine Coffee House at the corner of Wall and Water streets as a physical exchange (though the informal "curb market" continued to thrive).[27]

These new institutions laid a foundation that was absolutely essential for the future. But their immediate scope and impact should not be exaggerated. The stock market remained small for many years, because there was little stock to trade. In 1792, the New York stock exchange publicly quoted the price of just five securities, including three federal bonds; by 1815, the number had grown to only twenty-three. The vast majority of businesses remained partnerships or personal proprietorships. As a business historian notes, a corporation was "considered appropriate only when the enterprise was intended to perform a public service," such as the construction of a bridge or turnpike. A special act of the state legislature was required for every corporate charter. Few corporations had widely traded shares, and many were small, with a handful of investors, serving essentially as a new form for the traditional partnership.[28]

Every place, of course, is the scene of continuity. But not every place is equally a fulcrum of change. New York's geographical advantages—

its deep-water port at the end of a long river into the interior of the country—had attracted first imperial planners and then private merchants. Its density of merchants in turn gave rise to innovations in finance and business methods. A self-feeding cycle began to emerge, a multiplication of people and commerce, and needs and solutions, that was already starting to magnify New York's significance for the country as a whole.

Of all the accidents that would make the little boy Cornele into the man he would become, perhaps the most important was the location of his birthplace. From his waterside farmhouse hard by the Narrows, the future flowed in only one direction—toward the steeples and masts that marked the city across the bay.

A THIN LINE SEPARATES destiny from coincidence. A child's passion may begin a lifelong obsession; or a momentary interest, no more vehement than any other, may be remembered as an omen, thanks to the exaggeration of hindsight. For Cornele, the defining moment was a race. He was only six, he later recalled, when he rode a horse through the surf against another ridden by a neighbor's child slave. It would seem absurd if his rival had not returned decades later to publicly confirm the story. But what matters is that Cornele's earliest memory, the beginning of his self-image, was of competition—and victory.

A taste for competition may have been the natural result of growing up in a household filled with children. Certainly he never lacked confidence. With long limbs, a head of sandy hair, full lips, and a strong chin, he boasted a pair of penetrating eyes set between a high forehead and a long, sharp nose like the prow of a ship. A strong swimmer, he quickly grew tall and athletic, capable of immense labors and endurance.[29]

Farm life has always tended to erode the line between childhood and adulthood. Cornele lived a life of work and responsibility, hoeing and milking, piling and shoveling. There was church, too—Moravian services, the legacy of a conversion generations before that had taken the Vanderbilt family out of the Dutch Reformed tradition. But the sermons and hymns left no mark on him. He went to school briefly—for a mere three months, by one account—and would recall it as an agonizing process of rote memorization, drill, and punishment. Though he learned to read well enough, he manifested a lasting contempt for the conventions of written English. The handwritten letters that survive from his early twenties—the ink that flowed from a split nib, freshly dipped in an inkwell, now faded on brown, crumbling paper—show an alarming level of innovation in spelling. "See" became "sea" or even "se"—all in the same letter. To "know" was to "no." And he wrote "wrote" as "roat." His casual writ-

ten diction stood in sharp contrast to the formality of the letters of contemporaries, even of those who also had little education.

Indeed, Cornele wrote so phonetically that it is possible to reconstruct
his pattern of speech. Some of his quirks are not surprising. A man who
has returned home, for example, "is got home"; if he was forbidden, he
was "forbid"; if he ought to have been, he "aught a bean." Cornele's conversations featured now unusual or long-lost pronunciations (such as
"ginerally" for "generally"), including the frequent use of a long "a": "air"
for *are*, and "wair" for *were*. He also said "git" for *get*, "sence" for *since*, and
he did not *remember*, but would "recollect." And, like many others around
New York Bay, he would add "a" before a verb ending in -ing, as in "Mr.
Jones is agoing to Albany."[30]

When he was eleven, his older brother Jacob died. The event, scarcely
mentioned in later years by Cornele or his chroniclers, surely shook this
young boy's life. Already the family had lost a child—Phebe, born next
after Cornele, had died very young—but Jacob died as a teenager, at an
age when he no doubt served as his father's closest assistant in his operations and ambitions. Even apart from the emotional trauma of the loss of
a brother, the event turned Cornele from a middle child into the oldest
son. Small wonder that he left the schoolroom so young.[31]

Few traces remain of Cornele's childhood, such as it was. What is
known is a mirage, a hazy image floating above the real childhood. It
consists of stories repeated by the man the boy became, solidified into a
portrait with frequent retelling, colored by admirers. The haziness, the
distance, and the repetition not only cast doubts on the accuracy of the
image, they raise questions about what it really means.

The mirage tells us that, as early as 1805, during the presidency of
Thomas Jefferson, the eleven-year-old boy began to work alongside his
father in the periauger. Taking the place of his dead brother, he learned to
man the tiller, to raise and set the sails, to tack into the wind. He grew
comfortable with the vessel heeling steeply in a stiff breeze, the masts dip-
ping toward the waves, or crashing through a rising storm. One morning,
the story goes, the boy awoke to a day he had been looking forward to. His
father had promised him a reward for a particularly exhausting chore of
hoeing a potato field: Cornele could take his friend Owen in the periauger
to New York and spend the day. Cornele gathered Owen and ran down to
the shore, where his father stood beside a stack of hay he had contracted
to deliver to the city. "Now, Cornele, there's the periauger for you," Vanderbilt recalled his father saying. "I've pitched on more than half the
hay, you and Owen can just pitch on the rest, and take it up and unload it
at the wharf as usual, and you can play on the way." He tossed his son
a few pennies, and left him to do the work. "A boy can get fun out of

most anything," Vanderbilt later grumbled, "and we got some fun out of that; but I remember we were just as tired that night as if we had been working."

But what does the story mean? That the eleven-year-old was trustworthy enough to make a delivery across several miles of open water to what was now the biggest city in the country? That he resented his father's total control over his life? Probably something in both these explanations sealed the tale's place in Cornele's memory. But, observed across the chasm of two centuries, the story seems to demonstrate how the nearness of New York overshadowed this family, filling their lives with commerce, turning even a boy's play into a chance for profit. It is a story that could not be told about the more distant reaches of rural America.

The mirage expands. The next year, it tells us, Cornele's father took a contract to retrieve the cargo from a ship that had run ashore at Sandy Hook, the great sandbar that extends from New Jersey outside of Staten Island. Cornelius marshaled some laborers, three wagons, and a few rowboats to do the work. He put his son in charge of the wagons as they shuttled the cargo from the beached ship across the sandbar to the boats on the other side. Cornelius departed with the scows, leaving Cornele to lead the wagons and teamsters on the long drive to the ferry at South Amboy. By the time the boy and his men arrived, he had spent all his money on food and feed—but the ferryman demanded $6 for the crossing. Thinking quickly, Cornele went to a tavern and asked to borrow the money from the proprietor, offering to leave one of his horses and promising to redeem it with cash within twenty-four hours. The innkeeper agreed. They crossed, and the boy soon returned to give the innkeeper his money back.

The story would later be told as an example of Cornele's resourcefulness, but (if true) it too contains signposts that point to larger matters. For one thing, his family had so immersed him in business that, at the age of twelve, he already understood the principle of borrowing on collateral security. And the entire enterprise of salvaging a wreck further highlights the way the port of New York defined their lives.

There was another aspect of this tale that surely made an impression on the boy: the ferryman's ability to demand his own price. As an islander, Cornele could not help but feel that power in his bones. Living across the water from Manhattan and the mainland, he developed a sensitivity to the spaces between, to the significance of the crossing, to the strategic importance of the vessel that conveys from shore to shore. This knowledge, formed early in his mind, would serve him all of his life.[32]

But he was still a boy. Though it is reasonable to believe that he knew the marketplace better than the typical child, it is just as reasonable to believe that he reveled in his physicality—that he was moved by a "pride in action for action's sake" that a later friend attributed to his youth. That trait drew him to New York's waterfront, with all its furious activity: the strutting captains and mates; the insolent pilots, idling as they waited to take vessels back out to the ocean; and the packs of free-living sailors—many of them black—pushing into saloons or staggering drunkenly under the bowsprits that thrust like rafters over South Street. These were men whose lives were all action.[33] Cornele learned this scene well as he entered his teenage years, for he took on more and more responsibility for his father's periauger. As he sailed past fat merchantmen or sleek navy frigates, as he talked with ships' officers along South Street, he began to dream of possibilities beyond those on Staten Island.

At the end of 1807, the possibilities grew smaller. The city's frenzied trade abruptly halted when Congress passed the Embargo Act, at President Jefferson's urging, in a vain attempt to force Britain to lift restrictions on American ships and cease the impressment of American sailors amid its long war with France. The act prohibited the nation's vessels from sailing for foreign ports. "Not a box, bale, cask, barrel, or package was to be seen upon the wharfs," John Lambert observed. "The few solitary merchants, clerks, porters, and labourers that were to be seen were walking about with their hands in their pockets."[34] In March 1809, when Congress finally repealed the act, joy swept New York, and ships were again readied for distant ports.

After James Madison assumed the presidency in 1809, Congress continued to tinker with the idea of using trade to influence Britain and France—especially Britain, so detested by Madison and most Republicans. The Royal Navy, meanwhile, swept down on American ships with rising ferocity, seizing vessels and sailors under the notorious Orders in Council, which required neutral vessels to abide by Britain's blockade of Napoleon's empire. A crew could make enormous profits by running a ship to continental European ports, but at a tremendous risk that grew almost by the day.

In that tense and warlike world, young Cornele made a momentous decision. Early in 1810, after bringing passengers and goods to the city, he strode down South Street to see a captain he knew. The captain's ship was a fast-sailing merchantman, about to make the dangerous run to France with a cargo of silks—a luxury that would sell for a high price in the blockaded ports of Napoleon's Europe. Cornele was just fifteen, but he was tall and strong and an able sailor; when he applied for a place, the captain agreed to take him on as a member of the crew, with a regular share of the fortune they would gain. The act marked an abrupt end to Cornele's already tenuous childhood. Once he stepped onto that ship, he would depart the gritty marketplace and enter into a life of action for action's sake. He sailed the boat home that night, determined to tell his parents that he would be leaving Staten Island for good.[35]

"IT IS AS IF WE ALL CARRY in our makeup the effects of accidents that have befallen our ancestors," writes V. S. Naipaul, "as if we are in many ways programmed before we are born, our lives half outlined for us."[36] For a farm-born fifteen-year-old in 1810, it was nearly impossible to shrug off the weight of time. Cornele had acted forcefully when he signed on to that blockade runner, yet he still faced a formidable obstacle: his mother. She "found out," he later said, "and begged him so earnestly not to go."

There were dangers enough to startle her, from storms and disease to the threat of impressment into the British navy. More to the point, Phebe and her husband relied heavily on their oldest son as she continued to bear children. Cornele, who would become legendary for his ruthlessness, listened to his mother's pleading and was moved. He reluctantly told his father, he later recalled, "If he could get him honorably released from his engagement he would remain." The senior Cornelius promptly went to see the captain and settled the matter. It was a fortunate decision. Cornele later learned that the British captured the ship in the English Channel on that very voyage.[37]

The weight of the past pushed him back onto Staten Island, but it also subtly bent this would-be turning point in another direction. Cornele would return to the periauger as his own commander. But here, as so often in his childhood, the truth has been polished. According to an oft-repeated account, he learned of a periauger for sale at Port Richmond and agreed to purchase it for $100. Phebe would loan the boy the money if he cleared, plowed, and sowed an eight-acre lot that belonged to the family, a plot "so hard, rough, and stony," according to nineteenth-century biographer W. A. Croffut, "that it had never been ploughed." And he had to do it by his sixteenth birthday.

They agreed to the terms on May 1, so he had little time to spare. He gathered his friends and promised them a summer on the water in his boat, filled with fishing, sailing, and excursions to the city, which induced them to help him finish the job in the allotted time. His mother inspected the plot, then went to her clock and drew out the hundred dollars. Her son hurried down to Port Richmond, silver jingling in his pocket, knowing that he would not use the boat for fun, as he had told his friends, but for profit.[38]

Here again we have a tale from Vanderbilt's early life offered to us by his later admirers as a record of his virtues, a parable of the enterprising American spirit. But the earliest published account of his life, in an 1853 issue of *Scientific American*, puts the same events in another light. "He found himself with a growing desire to make his livelihood by following the sea," the story ran. "He therefore left the farm, and commenced running a small sail boat between Staten Island and New York, which was owned by his father."[39] This simpler version makes more sense than the legend. Cornele's parents told him that he could run his own boat, but it would belong to them. They grudgingly allowed him to keep half of what he earned after dark.

It would not be wise, then, to exaggerate Cornele's sixteen-year-old sophistication. But both versions of the story reveal something important: at the very beginning of his working life, he sought to be his own master. Through all of his later achievements, Vanderbilt recalled, "I didn't feel as much real satisfaction . . . as I did on that bright May morning sixty years before when I stepped into my own periauger, hoisted my own sail, and put my hand on my own tiller." He pulled away from the dock and immediately heard a sickening crack. The boat had collided with a large rock under the surface. He barely had time to run the boat ashore before it foundered. He soon repaired the damage.[40]

Eighteen cents per passenger, or a quarter per round trip: that, tradition has it, was the fare Cornele charged between Staten Island and New York. More likely it was a shilling each way (twelve and a half cents), the customary ferry charge in New York Harbor. At that price, in a boat that seated just twenty people, with only half of the nighttime fares going into his own pocket, revenue piled up slowly. Yet in those daily handfuls of silver shillings he discovered his hunger for money, an ache that would mingle with his pride and longing for control to shape his life at every turn.

Despite his youth, there was nothing childish about the trade he had entered. Cornele faced bare-knuckled competition—literally bare-knuckled. On the harbor's waterfront, he would find few boundaries to define a fair fight; and if no other means of beating a rival would do, then a beating it would be. Ten years earlier, Rochefoucauld-Liancourt had observed that absolutely everyone in America called himself a *gentleman*—"except," he had added, "the laborer in ports, and the common sailor."[41]

Cornele seemed suited to the battle. As he grew to his adult height of around six feet, he stood far taller than the average man (sixteen-year-olds then averaged perhaps five feet six, and full-grown adults about five feet eight). Above his strong chin and prow-like nose, under his high forehead, his eyes acquired a peculiar sailor's squint, the outer edges sloping down to dim the sun reflected on the water. His sandy hair swarmed on his head, and he began to cultivate thick sideburns that crawled down to his jawline.

"There are many still living who remember 'Corneil the boatman,' " declared *Harper's Weekly* in 1859, "how skillful he was in managing his craft; how daring in encountering the roughest weather; how perfectly reliable in every respect." Such references to common knowledge hint that the mirage of anecdotes was not merely an illusion. It would be said that he approached his work with the eye of a strategist. Rather than waiting for a full load before sailing, as most boatmen did, he ran on a schedule—operating a "packet" ferry, to use the technical term. "His life was regulated by self-imposed rules," claimed one admirer in 1865, "and with a fixedness of purpose as invariable as the sun in its circuit. Among other things he determined to spend less every week than he earned." Even allowing for exaggeration, it seems clear that the boy boatman did credit to his early education in the ways of business.[42]

Legend has it that he developed a reputation for an especially Dutch temper as he cursed at passengers who got in his way. One morning, the story goes, he was enraged to see his main rival, from the neighboring Van Duzer family, pull slowly ahead on the run to New York, as Cornele sat becalmed in shallow Buttermilk Channel between Governors Island and Brooklyn. Cornele ran out his long setting pole, pressed the end to his chest, and leaned into it to force the craft ahead, again and again. By the time he reached New York—ahead of his rival—the wooden pole had torn through to his breastbone, leaving a permanent scar.

Between and after his scheduled ferry runs, Cornele looked for whatever work he could get, even sleeping in his boat at Whitehall Slip in order to be on hand when a job came up. When autumn arrived and blinding sheets of sleet and snow crashed across the harbor, many nervous merchants who hurried from Pearl Street countinghouses to the waterfront trusted the boy to deliver messages to their vessels out in the bay.

But the image of young Vanderbilt as a cursing, isolated water rat cannot be entirely accurate. If he had learned anything from his parents, it was that business was a matter of relationships. Though he developed callused hands from hauling the spun-hemp sheets and twisting the wooden tiller, the work also brought him friendships. As he accumulated his modest portion of the periauger's earnings over the course of 1810, 1811, and 1812, he purchased shares in other boats, whose profits he did not share with his parents. This small act says as much about the boy as any anecdote. He had become an investor—or, to put it another way, a capitalist.[43]

WAR WAS COMING—so went the talk along South Street. As Britain's war with Napoleon moved toward a climax, the pace of impressments of American sailors accelerated, and the Royal Navy's seizures of American ships under the Orders in Council seemed to take on added brutality. In 1811, the USS *President* traded broadsides with the Royal Navy's *Little*

Belt, and workmen completed a series of fortifications around New York Harbor.[44] In February 1812, President Madison reimposed the ban on imports from Britain. On June 18, Congress declared war.

For a time the war seemed to go well. America's oversize frigates (carrying forty-four guns to Britain's standard thirty-eight) won a series of small but dramatic victories against the fabled Royal Navy. On January 1, 1813, the triumphant *United States* sailed into New York Harbor with the captured *Macedonian,* to the cheers of immense crowds. Cornele may even have found additional work in the first two years of the war. Britain imposed a blockade on American ports, and masters of coastal merchant craft feared capture if they sailed along the New Jersey coast. Instead, cargoes shipped between New York and points south passed along Cornele's accustomed route between Manhattan and Staten Island, then down the Arthur Kill and Kill Van Kull, where the British fleet did not penetrate. (Goods passed overland across New Jersey and along the protected waters of the Delaware River.) In November 1813 alone, some 1,500 wagons plied the route, offering abundant work for New York's boatmen.

Generally speaking, however, 1813 brought setbacks both military and commercial. In May, the Royal Navy tightened the blockade, and even landed a raiding party at Sandy Hook. The U.S. Army suffered reversals all along the frontier with Britain's colony of Canada. Some rare good fortune—the grand victory over the British fleet on Lake Erie on September 10—sparked a citywide outburst of joy. A celebration on October 4 saw candles in every window, a band playing on the balcony of city hall, and gunboats in the harbor swinging colored lanterns and firing rockets into the night sky.[45]

During this time Cornele was said to be unstintingly courageous, unfailingly skillful, and unflinchingly competitive. According to one of the flattering tales, he was hired to transport troops from Fort Richmond to Manhattan. A competitor's boat pulled alongside, and an army officer stepped out into Cornele's hull. The officer ordered all of the troops into the other boat "for inspection." Cornele, believing it to be a trick to steal his business, refused to let them go. Enraged, the officer began to draw his sword. The boy smashed his knuckles into the officer's face, chucked his limp body into the other boat, and continued on his way.

This story depicts a lad who was cunning and combative—traits later seen by all the world—and so it was readily believed when it circulated decades later. Other tales are more questionable. One describes the Royal Navy's attempt to sail past the outer fortifications of the harbor in the fall of 1813. A raging storm swept down on the bay, but Fort Richmond's commander felt it was urgent to notify the headquarters in New York of a skirmish that had taken place. Knowing Cornele's reputation, he took a few men to see him. Can a boat get through this storm? he asked. "Yes," the young man replied, "if properly handled," adding, "I shall have to carry them underwater part of the way." He made it through.[46]

Less than five years later the press would testify to Cornele's skill and courage when sailing into another storm, but the tale does not quite ring true. For one thing, the British navy did not attack New York in 1813. For another, Cornele was still a boy in a harbor full of skilled sailors—sailing a boat that was legally his father's property—and the idea that his reputation outshone all others' is hard to believe. If anything, he was then struggling to emerge from his father's shadow, to *start* to build a reputation.

By 1813, he took the steps that would finally establish him as a boatman in his own right. First, he ordered his own periauger, to be built in New Jersey, using the money he had so painstakingly saved. On Sundays, he often sailed up the Passaic River to the boatyard to examine the construction with the girl he was courting, Sophia Johnson. She was his pride, the realization of his hopes—the boat, that is; the girl was another matter. A nineteenth-century writer described this quiet woman as "lovely and industrious," a hint at her beginnings as a common servant. For young Cornele, neither her loveliness nor her industry was so important as her ring finger, for marriage was the essential second step in his plan to go out on his own.

He had not gone far to find a bride. Sophia was his cousin, granddaughter of his father's oldest sister *and* his mother's niece. She "was more typically Vanderbilt than Cornele himself," according to a later biographer. She, too, belonged to a large family and had little education. She had grown up nearby in Port Richmond, and Cornele had known her from early childhood; given his working habits, one must wonder if he had ever had the chance to meet anyone else. When he spoke of marrying Sophia, however, his mother reportedly objected, primarily because she would no longer be able to demand a share of the boy's earnings if he married.

To Cornele, that was much the point. How deeply he loved Sophia can never be known; how much he needed her, financially speaking, could not be more clear. On December 19, 1813, the couple married, then retired to the ferry dock to a small house that Vanderbilt had rented. There they began a life of suppressed turmoil and muffled intimacy. Within a year Sophia gave birth to the first of many babies to come, and one of her sisters moved into the household to help during the weeks that followed. In these early days, Vanderbilt relied heavily on Sophia's capacity for hard work and her tolerance for living lean; but legend has it that he often turned to his shrewd mother to discuss his plans, leaving his wife to wonder what he was thinking. He even insisted to Sophia that they name their first child Phebe.[47]

IN 1814, THE UNITED STATES stood on the brink of losing the war. On April 6, Napoleon abdicated the imperial throne of France, allowing Britain to reinforce its armies in North America. Of particular concern for New York was a possible thrust down the Hudson from Canada, an attack that would avoid the heavy fortifications on the harbor. On July 15, Brigadier General Joseph Swift began construction of a line across upper Manhattan and the western end of Long Island. On August 26, terrified New Yorkers snatched up copies of a special edition of the *Evening Post*, announcing that Washington had been captured and sacked by a British force. "Your capital is taken!" the press declared. "In six days the same enemy may be at the Hook! . . . Arise from your slumbers!" Thousands of residents took up shovels to dig trenches as 23,000 militiamen reported for duty.[48]

Military disaster meant economic windfall for the strapping twenty-year-old Vanderbilt. One of the canonical stories of his early life describes a moment of great excitement among the harbor's boatmen, as the military headquarters offered a contract to carry supplies to the forts and construction sites. Vanderbilt, at his father's urging, put in a bid at a price that he considered fair, but was far from the lowest. He was startled when he learned he had won. "Don't you know why we have given the contract to you?" the officer reportedly asked. "It is because we want this business *done*, and we know you'll do it." No evidence has ever surfaced to support the tale, but, if true, it hints at the moment when a subtle transition began, when he started to acquire a reputation in this slippery, low-caste society.[49]

That year Vanderbilt took his wife from their rented house in Staten Island to the city of New York, settling into rooms at 93 Broad Street. Their new home spoke eloquently of the young man's social standing: it was an artisans' boardinghouse, where there also lived a carpenter and a gunsmith, along with their wives and children. Broad Street boasted some countinghouses, but it was also home to grocers, drapers, and cabinetmakers, along with other boatmen—craftsmen and shopkeepers all.[50]

How alarming it must have been for Sophia to move from a country village on a broad green island to this crowded street. Cornelius expected her to raise their infant girl in a house shared with three other families, emptying the chamberpots in a backyard privy, dodging horses and wagons and grunting pigs on muddy streets to fetch water or bring home food from crowded open-air markets. Her transition calls to mind the observations of Frances Trollope, mother of novelist Anthony Trollope, who visited America a decade later. "The women are doggedly steadfast in their will," she wrote, describing a crowd jostling for seats in a boat, "and till matters are settled, look like hedgehogs, with every quill raised, and firmly set, as if to forbid the approach of any one who might wish to rub them down. In circumstances where an English woman would look proud, and a French woman *nonchalante,* an American lady looks grim; even the youngest and the prettiest can set their lips, and knit their brows, and look as hard and unsocial as their grandmothers."[51] Lovely and industrious Sophia may have been; now she had to learn to be hard as well.

She and her husband occupied a distinctly subordinate rank in a society shaped by eighteenth-century notions of social status. The craftsmen they lived with on Broad Street—the carpenters, coopers, and cabinetmakers, the gunsmiths, grocers, and fellow boatmen—were "middling sorts" who made a living with strength and skill. Such fellows affected "a sort of rough independence, which appeared to me manly," one genteel New Yorker wrote. "They . . . filled their parts in society with reputation and respectability." But even artisans who owned shops and employed assistants were men of labor. "The culture of rank," notes historian Stuart Blumin, "degraded those independent businessmen who worked with their hands."

Cornelius and Sophia lived only steps away from lower Broadway, where luxurious private houses were "occupied by the principal merchants and gentry of New York," as John Lambert observed. Lambert's travelogue frequently referred to this class, noting that their "style of living in New York is fashionable and splendid." They looked down on "the inferior orders" with contempt. In 1811, a memoirist wrote of how he and his friends had aspired "to be merchants, as to be mechanics was too humiliating."[52]

Vanderbilt could have remained on Staten Island, enjoying the fresh sea air at a fraction of the cost of living. But he and his fellow middling sorts were looking to rise. With the oceangoing ships of the "principal merchants" locked up in port, with wartime shortages rampant, craftsmen became entrepreneurs, breaking down longstanding methods to increase productivity. Vanderbilt's move to New York was itself an entrepreneurial act. It was in the city that information moved most quickly, through word of mouth or the many newspapers that published prices of important goods, news of ship arrivals and departures, and prices of stocks and commodities. It was in the city where the exchanges were located, where auctions of goods were held, where informal, curbside trades of bonds and shares went on each day. It was in the city where one acquired a reputation—and reputation was the axle of this informal, personal economy.

Vanderbilt could hardly avoid noticing that, despite the innovations and energy of his fellow artisans, most of New York's wealthiest citizens were general merchants. Even banks and securities markets largely remained merchant clubs. When the federal government needed to sell millions of dollars' worth of bonds to fund the war, for example, it turned to two ship-owning, international merchants, Stephen Girard of Philadelphia and John Jacob Astor of New York, who brokered the sale and took bonds for themselves. Vanderbilt would never forget that the richest men traded in cargoes.[53]

But for all of his success during the war years, his wealth could only grow so much as long as British ships-of-the-line shadowed Sandy Hook, the president embargoed trade, and the citizens of New York dug trenches that everyone hoped would never be needed.

SNOW FELL ON THE EVENING of February 11, 1815. The New York waterfront sat silent, the thousands who depended on the port lingering at home, many of them desperate. Chunks of ice descended the North River into the bay—ordinarily a problem for schooners and square-riggers, now a concern only for the few boatmen at work. Shortly before eight o'clock, a small craft steered up to Manhattan's slips. It was a swift pilot boat, one of those that used to race to meet incoming merchantmen from Europe and the Caribbean. As its hull scraped the dock, two men leaped out and raced across South Street to the offices of the city's newspapers. They burst in and gasped, *"There is peace."*

The pilot boat had met the British sloop-of-war *Favourite*, carrying an American and a British diplomat coming to announce the seven-week-old Treaty of Ghent. Within an hour the city burst into celebration. In every house residents put candles and lamps in the windows. Trinity Church rang its bells, over and over, as the batteries on the harbor fired off cannons. Men and women packed the freezing streets in impromptu torchlight parades, cheering "Huzza!" and "A Peace!" until midnight.[54] The next morning, crews began to scour the docks to prepare ships to sail again. They shoveled out salt that had been thrown into bottoms to preserve timbers, removed the tar barrels (nicknamed "Mr. Madison's night caps") thrown over mastheads, and prepared new sails and lines. On March 1 the first ship cleared the harbor—the *Diamond*, bound for Havana.

The incoming ships may have mattered more. British merchants, themselves suffering from the years of war, selected New York as their favored port for dumping their large inventories of manufactured goods. In 1811, New York had run behind Massachusetts in imports, and only slightly ahead of Pennsylvania; in the year ending September 30, 1815, it took in more than both combined. The resurgence of trade lifted New York's imports from $2.4 million in 1811 to $14.6 million in 1815.

It was merely the first act in a startling revival of the long-closed port over the next few years. On October 24, 1817, came the formation of the first transatlantic packet line (a regularly scheduled service, as opposed to the old custom of ships sailing when they were full), a major contribution to New York's growing dominance over other American ports. Also in 1817, the state passed new legislation that fostered auctions and made the city the most favorable place for merchants from across the republic to buy foreign goods, helping to seal New York's lead as the nation's import center. It began to emerge as the premier distribution hub for the entire country, and as a financial center as well, as money clattered in and credit poured out.[55] The result was a revolution in New York's trade, not only with the interior, but with the Atlantic seaboard. Its long-suppressed coasting trade burst out again as merchants made contact with isolated communities. Much of the nation was, in essence, a new market—a vast, untamed economic frontier.

After the long stagnation of embargo and war, the air on South Street vibrated with opportunity, with the concussion of hogsheads on ship decks and the snap of canvas filling with wind. A race began to be the first to reach new customers and find new suppliers. In this frenzied atmosphere, Vanderbilt's actions spoke both to his unending hunger for wealth and his close reading of the world around him. For one thing, he was bold: just twenty years old when peace arrived, he now reached far beyond the familiar New York Harbor to distant ports and landings along the Atlantic coast. For another, he was shrewd, as he looked for partners with expertise and financial resources greater than his own. His brother-in-law and fellow Staten Islander John De Forest joined with him first. A highly regarded mariner, De Forest was the master of a fast schooner, the *Charlotte* (named for Cornelius's sister and De Forest's wife), which he had run to Virginia and beyond before the war. In 1815, Vanderbilt purchased a share in the ship. The partners used it to haul goods from New York to Charleston and other Southern ports, where they filled the hold with fish and produce for the return voyage. Before long, Vanderbilt bought full ownership of the schooner. Slowly and steadily, he was making himself into a general merchant. Nothing better illustrated his careful study of the riches that poured into New York.

He also took on his father as a partner. Cornelius the elder put up some of the money for large new periaugers, big enough for open water. So too did James Day of Norwich, Connecticut, a shipwright who constructed or rebuilt Vanderbilt's vessels, all two-masted boats ranging from twenty-two to thirty-two tons* and costing around $750 each (at a time when a successful artisan in New York earned about $3,200 a year). Though patterned after the harbor-bound boats of New York Bay, Vanderbilt had them built for longer voyages, and registered them for the coastal trade with the New York Custom House. The first was the twenty-seven-ton *Dread*, registered on January 24, 1816. It measured forty-nine feet by fourteen and a half, with little more than a four-foot draft.

In his small fleet of the small and fleet, Vanderbilt swept down on coastal and riverside communities around New York, seeking out new customers and cargoes. Soon after the war ended, he raced ahead of a cluster of rival schooners to the Virginia oyster grounds to fill his hull with New York's favorite food. He began to sail the *Dread* around Cape May and up the Delaware River, where he bought shad by the slippery thousands, then sailed up New Jersey's Raritan River, where he learned to hire horsemen to spread the word that he had fish to sell. In New York Harbor, he paid boatmen to sail out to meet incoming ships to peddle food or liquor, while he haggled on South Street over the *Charlotte*'s cargo of fish, produce, and goods.[56]

As he struggled into the lowest tier of merchants, he conducted his business with an elbows-out aggressiveness. On October 2, 1816, he had one Daniel Morgan arrested for failing to pay De Forest and himself for a cargo, claiming $200 for goods delivered. The Mayor's Court, located in the city hall, ruled in Vanderbilt's favor, but decided that he had overstated the bill by $100. A few days later his lawyer John Wallis argued in the same court that merchants Phineas Carman and Cornelius P. Wyckoff owed Vanderbilt and his father the substantial sum of $900 for "divers quantities of fish and goods, wares, and merchandize before that time sold and delivered." Three merchant referees examined the books. In April 1817, they reported that the true debt was only $189.[57]

Americans had long been comfortable with the commercial marketplace, but for centuries many had lived in rural isolation or labored under British commercial restrictions. Now they encountered a new world, with the promise of new, better, *more*—as well as changes that no one could predict. The war had planted the seeds of manufacturing across the North, as workshops were established to produce things no longer available from Europe. New commercial institutions and mercantile houses opened for business. In 1815 alone, the number of American banks rose from 208 to 246, and the value of their circulating notes from $46 million to $68 million. That year marked the start of Vanderbilt's rise as well, as

---

* Tonnage represented not the vessel's weight (except in the case of warships), but its carrying capacity.

he both rode and added to this rising tide. As a decidedly minor, boat-owning merchant, he could not share in the lucrative transoceanic trade. His very limitations, then, forced him to seek out opportunities on the domestic frontier—to tie together distant marketplaces and introduce trade in places that had been wilderness when it came to commerce.[58]

Commerce, of course, consisted of the physical movement of people and goods; it only flowed as smoothly as transportation technology and infrastructure would allow. And transportation was a problem that deeply troubled merchants and lawmakers alike. The nation's road network could best be described as barely in existence. In 1816, a Senate committee found that it was as expensive to move a ton of goods thirty miles overland as it was to bring the same ton across the Atlantic from Europe. John Lambert described how in upstate New York goods were carried in nar-row, four-wheeled wagons, each drawn by a team of two horses. "It is a very rough method of riding," he complained, "for the waggon has no springs, and a traveller ought to have excellent nerves to endure the shak-ing and jolting of such a vehicle over bad roads." A movement emerged, a rush to build turnpikes—solidly engineered roads, financed by tolls. Turn-pikes, Lambert observed, "have tended greatly to improve the country; for as soon as a [turnpike] is opened through the woods . . . the country which was before a trackless forest becomes settled."

Even the best turnpike was suited only for short distances, and it was cheaper to move goods by water under any circumstances. But shipping had its own limitations. The coastwise trade traveled mostly in sloops and schooners, small vessels with limited capacity. And a journey upriver against the current was sometimes impossible under sail. The 150-mile, straight-line voyage from New York to Albany could take several days. In New Orleans, boats that arrived with goods from upstream were simply broken up for lumber in many cases.[59]

The speed of transportation largely determined the speed of *information*, which set limits on long-range commerce—the emergence of finan-cial markets, the efficient movement of capital, the transactions between distant regions. News traveled only as fast as people, whether by messen-ger, the mail, or the shipment of newspapers. When George Washington died on December 14, 1799, for example, the news took seven days to travel the 240 miles from northern Virginia to New York. Under these conditions, few institutions straddled state lines or operated across long distances—even as Americans began to cross the Appalachians by the thousands.[60]

Americans naturally looked for a revolution in transportation. In 1817, New York State began to construct an enormous canal, 363 miles long, between Albany and Buffalo, a village on Lake Erie. Equally important, a dramatic technological breakthrough had appeared on the North River: a vessel that provided its own motive power, independent of wind and muscle and current. They called it the steamboat.[61]

It can never be known how much thought Vanderbilt gave to these changes and challenges. He was a rough, ambitious young man, striving in his undersize schooners to match the international traders who strutted past in the stiff top hats, swallowtail coats, and trousers that had replaced the eighteenth century's powdered hair and knee breeches.[62] It probably never occurred to him that, in aspiring to their position, he was moving backward. He had started out as a specialist—one in transportation, no less, the field where a revolution was sorely wanted, where businessmen and legislators were looking to invest millions. But at this moment he surveyed the world as it was, saw that the general merchant reigned, and methodically became one himself.

AN OFT-REPEATED BUT APOCRYPHAL TALE portrays a thoughtful Cornelius in December 1817, tallying his wealth. Just twenty-three years old, he was now supposedly worth $15,000, including $9,000 in cash. But the Vanderbilt of legend was always one step ahead of everyone else. He shrewdly concluded that the economy was about to change, and so he abandoned his enterprises to ride the incoming wave.

In reality, he saw nothing special about the end of this particular year. To all appearances he planned to carry on as before, adding the *General Wolcott* to his tiny fleet in July.[63] He had established a solid reputation as a skilled sailor and merchant—albeit a small one, a shopkeeper of the sea. When men approached him on the docks, they now spoke to him not as Cornele, but as *Mr. Vanderbilt*, or even *Captain Vanderbilt*.

On November 24, 1817, he turned at the sound of those words and saw a well-dressed sixty-year-old man looking at him with sharp, hard eyes. The fellow's dark hair was combed forward in the style of the classical Romans, and when he spoke his puffy double chin wobbled. He introduced himself as Thomas Gibbons. He was a staggeringly rich rice planter from Georgia, now of Elizabethtown, New Jersey; recently he had started a ferry to New York from there. Emphatic and direct, Gibbons said that Ebenezer Lester, captain of his ferryboat *Stoudinger*, "has suddenly left my employ." Given "my present embarrassment," he said, he needed someone to take charge of the boat "on this day, and, I expect, for a few days to come." Would Vanderbilt do it?

As a past master of all things related to the port, young Vanderbilt knew the *Stoudinger* well. It was secondhand and small (smaller, at forty-seven feet, than the *Dread*). It was so tiny, in fact, that it went by the nickname

Mouse of the Mountain, or simply *Mouse*. But Vanderbilt also knew the critical difference between the *Mouse* and all his own vessels—or, for that matter, almost every craft on the surface of the earth: it ran on steam. And that made it the focus of a legal and business war that was the talk of the waterfront. Perhaps he grasped, in a flash of insight, that his future would pivot on the fate of Gibbons's little boat. In any case, he agreed to take command of the *Mouse*. After all, it was only for a few days.[64]

Chapter Two

THE DUELIST

The twenty-three-year-old Cornelius Vanderbilt who took command of the *Mouse* on November 24, 1817, had no way of knowing he was making the most important decision of his life. Then again, not even Thomas Gibbons, who saw a good deal, could foresee how far-reaching their collaboration would prove to be—how it would help unlock the potential of the steam engine, recast the Constitution, and contribute to the remaking of American society. Gibbons had his hard eye fixed on his enemies, unaware that his struggle would inexorably link his own name to Vanderbilt's for the rest of time.

Even as an impulse, Vanderbilt's snap decision to take orders from Gibbons must have mystified his friends and associates, for the brusque sailor was nothing if not commanding. Vanderbilt was proud, of course, and filled with "the desire of riches" that Rochefoucauld-Liancourt had identified as the essential American trait. His sense of physical power, too, should not be underestimated. He was a big man who lived by his strength, straining daily against the wind and current. His combative manner had been hardened in a fringe of society marked by "rough independence," where confrontation was the stuff of daily life. He sneered with that contempt for weakness that comes naturally to a man who has beaten and cowed other men.

What's more, the engagement with Gibbons set him back a step in his plans to build his fortune. A thriving ferryman, he aspired to more, as he used his boats to embark on the only obvious voyage to wealth in the new republic, setting up as a general merchant. Even as he stepped aboard the *Mouse* and inspected its copper boiler, he kept his periauger plying between Staten Island and Whitehall Slip with passengers and produce, and his schooner nosing along coastal waters with cargoes of fish and woolens.[1]

And yet, he clearly saw the advantages of the connection he had made. Having formed partnerships with his father and his brother-in-law, he recognized that few men in the entire nation commanded greater resources than Thomas Gibbons. Even more important, Vanderbilt and his contemporaries understood that the steam engine (or, to put it more broadly, motorized transportation) was the most dramatic technological breakthrough since the advent of the printing press at the dawn of the Renaissance. To move on water at will, against wind, tide, and current, was to transform a fundamental fact of life; to say that it marked a revolution is to give an overused word its proper weight. A practical education in steam would be worth a few days of taking orders.

What he did not reckon on was how well he would get on with Gibbons. "I always thought Thomas Gibbons a very strong-minded man, the strongest I ever knew," he said later. "I don't believe any human being could control him; he was a man that could not be led."[2] He could just as easily have been describing himself. And there, ironically, in this meeting of iron wills, lay the seed of an alliance that would force the freedom of commerce within America's borders and tear down one of the last bastions of the eighteenth-century world—a culture of deference, privilege, and rank already groaning under the pressure of the times. And it all started with the most aristocratic of rituals: a challenge to a duel.

"DUELLING IS AN ABOMINABLE CUSTOM introduced by the depravity of man," Thomas Gibbons scratched out on a piece of paper, pausing now and then to dip the nib of his quill into an inkwell. "And good men sometimes are dragged into it by the wicked, thoughtless part of the community." It was the evening of September 15, 1786; Gibbons was composing a letter to his eldest son, a letter that he believed might be his last. The next morning, he planned to engage in the "abominable custom" with characteristic righteous wrath. As he counseled his son, "Should your character be wantonly sported with, with deliberate caution arm yourself."

The next day, he and his opponent faced each other with pistols in hand, bellowing their firm intention to kill each other—until their seconds arranged a compromise. Gibbons had been entirely earnest; the essence of the art of the duel, he knew, was a sincere willingness to stake *everything* on the outcome. Killing the foe was entirely secondary; the point, rather, was to bravely expose oneself to deadly gunfire, thereby proving to the world a quality that lies hidden in a man's heart: his honor. In his own case, however, he may have confused honor with ruthlessness, for no trick or ploy was beneath him when he had a goal in mind.

Gibbons came into the world in 1757 as heir to an army of slaves, and a large rice plantation in Georgia, and he never forgot it. In adulthood he opened a thriving law practice in Savannah, and eventually bought more plantations. He accumulated and consumed until he himself had swelled to almost three hundred pounds. Cunning and commanding, he had, his daughter dryly noted, "a particular and singular mode of doing . . . business." In other words, he was almost pathologically contentious.[3]

In the Revolution, he alone in a family of patriots stood by the king. Imprisoned for treason, he called the sheriff a "damned scoundrel" and accused him of asking for a bribe. Remarkably, he was able to have his conviction overturned after the war, managed General "Mad Anthony" Wayne's campaign for Congress, then fought a duel with the losing candidate, who had accurately denounced him as a man "whose soul is faction . . . who never could be easy under government." The two faced off in 1791; they blazed away at each other three times before they settled their quarrel. Gibbons went on to serve as the Federalist mayor of Savannah off and on until 1801.[4]

That year he established "bachelor quarters," as he called them, in Elizabethtown, New Jersey. Perhaps he was driven out of the South by tense relations with the wife he left behind (he soon impregnated a young maid in his new home). In any case, it was a financially astute move. New York was just beginning its climb to a predominant role in the South's overseas trade. Living in the North, Gibbons served as his own middleman, and he had ample opportunities for reinvesting his profits in real estate, rapidly multiplying banks, and turnpike corporations that constructed solid new toll roads across New Jersey.[5] He also discovered a culture surprisingly familiar to him.

Three years after Gibbons's arrival, in that ritual he knew so well, Vice President Aaron Burr shot Alexander Hamilton dead in nearby Weehawken, in the culmination of Burr and Hamilton's long and bitter political rivalry. The duel led to a quixotic turn in Burr's life, sending it on a winding path that led to a trial for treason and an eventual return to a prestigious law practice in New York. It also showed that dueling (which first appeared in America among military officers in the Revolution) was far from the specifically Southern institution that it would eventually become. In the early years of the republic, politicians issued challenges to each other with alarming frequency. They did so in part because the first parties of the early republic were, to a great extent, factions of notables; political disputes quickly became matters of personal honor.[6] But the importance placed on honor reveals something deeper: the persistence of an eighteenth-century culture of deference, dominated by an American aristocracy.

The word "aristocracy" tends to be used rather loosely. In the modern world, it is calculated by multiplying wealth by snobbery. During the early republic, on the other hand, it reflected the division of society into distinct ranks. Until the Revolution, wrote historian Bernard Bailyn, Americans had assumed "that a healthy society was a hierarchical society, in which it was natural for some to be rich and some poor, some honored and some obscure, some powerful and some weak." Perhaps most important, "it was believed that superiority was unitary, that the attributes of the favored— wealth, wisdom, power—had a natural affinity to each other, and hence that political leadership would naturally rest in the hands of social leaders." In New York in particular, these natural leaders came from a closed set of families, distinguished by an inherited prestige. A full century before Gibbons moved north, the aristocrats of his day had already emerged—the Livingstons, Van Rensselaers, Schuylers, Beekmans, Jays, Bayards, Morrises, and others—in a self-perpetuating circle of intermarried clans.[7]

The patricians owed much of their status to their particular kind of wealth. New York's aristocrats were classic landed gentry, owners of vast manorial estates along the Hudson River that were populated by tenant farmers (a rarity in land-abundant America). Philip Schuyler, for example, held some six thousand acres, while the Van Rensselaers reigned over an enormous "patroonship" established by the Dutch in the seventeenth century. Their relationships with their inferiors were defined by vertical chains of deference and dependence. "As late as 1828," writes historian Martin Bruegel, an English observer was amazed by the "immense influence" of these manorial lords over their tenants and neighbors. And landed wealth was *proprietary* wealth, the kind that originally defined a "gentleman." The gentry did not work for their income, and so had the leisure to educate and improve themselves. Strikingly, they neatly adapted to, and even championed, the Revolution: they saw themselves as a refined, disinterested ruling class for a virtuous, classical republic.

Property requirements for suffrage under New York's constitution of 1777 hardened the culture of rank into law. Two distinct levels of wealth were required to vote: one for the state assembly, and a second and higher level for the state senators and governor—establishing a "three-tiered scaffolding of society," as Bruegel writes. In 1790, four of ten adult white men could not cast a ballot of any kind; in some places, only one out of four could vote for the assembly, and one out of five for governor.[8]

It was in this environment that the duel flourished. In the aristocratic culture of deference, little distinction was made between the person and his position. A leader could only function if he maintained his personal authority; upholding his "character" (as reputation was called), by the duel if necessary, was essential to all aspects of his life. So too in an economy with limited currency and few formal institutions, where transactions were highly personal and usually sealed by an exchange of promissory notes. A lofty character allowed one's notes to "pass current," to be circulated in the marketplace at little or no discount. The patricians literally could not afford to be defamed, to allow insults to their authority to go unchallenged.

The Revolution marked a decisive turn against the culture of deference. By the time Gibbons settled in New Jersey—the year Thomas Jefferson took office as president, after campaigning against patrician rule—assertiveness as well as deference was visible in the lower layers of society, swelled chests as well as bowed heads. Rochefoucauld-Liancourt noted the progress of this transformation in two telling observations in the 1790s: "They deceive themselves very much who think that pure republican manners prevail in America," he wrote, pointing out how the citizens painstakingly differentiated between the ranks of society. "In balls, concerts, and public amusements, these classes do not mix; and yet," he added in amazement, "every one calls himself, and is called by others, a gentleman."[9]

It is the image of a society in the midst of tectonic change. An older, stratified idea of the world was being torn up by political radicalism erupting out of the Revolution, and by a new social dynamism linked to the surging economy. Once-deferential artisans wanted to serve in public office themselves. Average Americans were less and less willing to passively follow the old elite, as they had for so long.[10]

Thomas Gibbons, by contrast, settled comfortably into that old order—or, at least, as comfortably as a cantankerous tyrant could—as he passed his promissory notes among New York's elite, and formed business partnerships with his neighbors Aaron Ogden and Jonathan Dayton, the Federalist senators for New Jersey. He could hardly have been a less likely champion of Jeffersonian ideals. Ironically, a chain of events had already been set in motion that would turn his famously hard head into a battering ram against the citadel of aristocracy. That chain of events—and that citadel—were the work of the most patrician of patricians, Chancellor Robert R. Livingston.

No one better exemplified the culture of deference than Chancellor Livingston. Peering out of serious eyes set between the arching eyebrows and long nose of his bloodline, he looked every ounce the aristocrat. As leader of one of the richest and most prestigious families of Hudson Valley gentry, he presided over a vast manor, serving as patron to hundreds of tenant farmers who came to him, hats clutched to their chests, to ask for favors or pay their rent. In keeping with his family's tradition of leadership, he played a prominent part in the Revolution, serving alongside Jefferson on the committee that drafted the Declaration of Independence, and he later became New York's first chancellor (a chief judge in the state court system). Livingston allied with Jefferson and his Republicans, proving that, under the state's restrictive constitution, the aristocrats and their values crossed party lines, despite the Federalists' reputation as the party of the elite. In 1802, the *New York Evening Post* referred to the Livingstons as a "house of republican nobility," and quoted a junior member of the clan as saying, "To be born with their family name is a fortune to any man."

Unlike the stuffy, fictional aristocrats of Jane Austen's novels, Livingston and his fellow patricians felt no disdain for trade. They maintained countinghouses in the city, invested in urban real estate, and had careers as lawyers and merchants. They embraced Hamilton's financial program, with its stocks, financial markets, and banks. Schuyler, Hamilton's father-in-law, sought to rationalize his tenants' leases for greater profits, and the patricians led the drive to build a canal to Lake Erie. Livingston organized a state agricultural society and promoted merino sheep and gypsum fertilizer. To quote George Washington, they were decidedly a "monied gentry."[11]

Those very activities, however, separated the commercial vision of aristocrats such as Livingston from the emerging ideals of rank-and-file Jeffersonians. He believed in economic development, but in an ordered manner, directed from above. After the Revolution, the seeds of a different notion began to sprout—of an individualistic, competitive economy where one could go as far as his ability and energy could take him. "Adam Smith's invisible hand," writes historian Joyce Appleby, "was warmly clasped by the Republicans." They criticized the patricians for using their political power to grant themselves special privileges. Corporate charters usually went to the well-connected. Many early banks extended credit only to a closed network of relatives and cronies. Government intervention in the economy largely consisted of special rewards to officeholders and favored men.[12]

The aristocrats saw no conflict of interest in using public office to enrich themselves. As society's natural leaders, they reasoned, they should be entrusted with economic stewardship as well. This outlook, this merging of the private and public roles of the elite, was the essence of mercantilism, in which the state empowered private parties to carry out activities thought to serve the public interest.[13] The standard reward for such an undertaking was a monopoly—just what Chancellor Livingston sought when he offered to meet a most pressing public need, the need for steamboats.

Even before Americans learned of James Watt's work with the steam engine in England in the 1760s, they had dreamed of bolting it to the hull of a boat to speed themselves across the vast stretches of water that linked their scattered communities. Experiments abounded: paddlewheels, early propellers, even a water jet and mechanical oars.[14] Chancellor Livingston dreamed and experimented as ambitiously as anyone. In 1798, he convinced his friends in the legislature to give him a monopoly on steamboats in New York State waters. Unfortunately, he failed to produce a working design of his own, and his monopoly remained unused.

In 1801 he arrived in Paris as Jefferson's minister to France, where he met an émigré American artist and inventor named Robert Fulton. As Livingston helped to negotiate the Louisiana Purchase, he financed Fulton's prototype steamboat, which ran on the Seine in 1803. They returned to New York, where Fulton tinkered with his designs. Finally, on August 17, 1807, the sixty-year-old Livingston invited New York's dignitaries aboard Fulton's final effort, a clanking, 150-foot-long vessel prosaically named *Steam Boat*. Crowds lined the shore to watch the amazing spectacle: a boat moving by mechanical power. It churned up the Hudson at five miles per hour to Livingston's manor, Clermont, where Livingston declared that his cousin Harriet and Fulton were to be married. The steamboat—and Fulton—had arrived.

Fulton created a line between New York and Albany while Livingston maneuvered an extension of the monopoly through the legislature—"a veritable model of state munificence," as legal scholar Maurice G. Baxter writes—that gave him the right to seize steamboats that entered New York waters from other states.[15] But Livingston had overreached. With so many inventors and investors interested in the steamboat, the monopoly only served to limit its widespread adoption. The new technology was simply too important for the monopoly to remain unchallenged.

In 1813, Chancellor Livingston died. That same year, Gibbons's neighbor and business partner Aaron Ogden took office as governor of New Jersey, and promptly launched an attack on the steamboat grant, both as chief executive of the state, fighting New York's claims to the waters shared with New Jersey, *and* as a private steamboat entrepreneur. In a bitter battle Fulton successfully defended his monopoly, though at the cost of his own life, after he fell ill from exposure when crossing the frozen Hudson on his return from a lobbying trip to New Jersey. The monopoly lived on in the hands of Livingston's heirs, who came to terms with Ogden. On May 5, 1815, a little over two months after Fulton's death, the Livingstons gave Ogden a license to run his own steamboat between Elizabethtown and New York. Ogden had begun as the monopoly's most potent challenger; he had ended as its ally.[16]

Enter the irascible Thomas Gibbons. On the surface, he and Ogden had everything in common: they were of the same party, profession, and patrician status. In temperament, however, they were virtually destined to clash. Gibbons was arrogant and explosive; Ogden, wily and sanctimonious. And both were men of infinite calculation. With all the force of a Greek tragedy, their respective traits drew them into an epic conflict, one that would decide the fate of the Livingston steamboat monopoly.

At the height of Ogden's battle against the Livingstons, he and Gibbons fell into a dispute over the renewal of a lease for his steamboat pier, which he rented from Gibbons, who characteristically made things difficult. Ogden tried to apply pressure by involving himself in Gibbons's ongoing dispute with his wife, daughter, and son-in-law over Gibbons's will, suggesting strategies to the disinherited family members. This only enraged the easily enraged Gibbons. To make matters worse, Ogden acquired a past-due promissory note that Gibbons had made out to a third party; Ogden deposited it with his banker in New York, who had Gibbons arrested for nonpayment on May 30, 1816 (on Ogden's steamboat, no less). Gibbons bailed himself out and stomped home, steeped in a hatred that soon took on a life of its own. "As we reside within half a mile of each other," he wrote to Ogden, "and your never intimating to me, nor any of my friends, any claims or cause of action you had against me, I pronounce your conduct *rascally.*"[17]

For Gibbons, it had become an affair of honor. On July 25, 1816, he stormed over to Ogden's house, horsewhip in hand. He pounded on the door as Ogden ran out the back and scrambled over a fence. Gibbons tacked up a challenge that read, "Sir—I understand that you have interfered in a dispute between Mrs. Gibbons and myself. . . . My friend Gen. Dayton will arrange with you the time and place of our meeting." He later testified in court that "if he had found him at home he meant to have whipped him within an inch of his life in his own house, for he knew he was a coward."

Ogden, who had no intention of exchanging shots at dawn, had Gibbons arrested for trespass and for dueling. Gibbons decided to get revenge another way, one that stood to increase his own wealth even further: he would drive Ogden out of the steamboat business by running his own paddlewheeler between Elizabethtown and New York. And that—against all logic of politics, social position, and personal conviction—pitted him directly against the New York steamboat monopoly.

In taking on Ogden as an ally, the Livingstons had unwittingly acquired their deadliest enemy yet.[18]

WHEN THE STORM HIT on the morning of February 3, 1818, Vanderbilt stood in the rocking hull of the *Dread*, which he ran on a strict schedule between Staten Island and New York's Whitehall Slip. Scanning the skies from within the grip of Manhattan's piers, he could see what little time he had to secure his boat. The winds began to howl through the bare masts of the ships that nursed along South Street, driving hail, then rain, then snow down New York's narrow ways.

Then the little steam ferry *York** came drifting past the Battery, just off Manhattan's southern tip. The boat had no business there; as Vanderbilt knew, it made its 10:30 run from Paulus Hook (later the site of Jersey City) to the foot of Courtlandt Street, over on the North River waterfront. What he did not know was that it carried a full load of thirty passengers and three wagons, each with a two-horse team; that the storm had smashed the boat like the butt of a rifle, halting its progress across the Hudson; and that the pilot had decided to seek the shelter of Whitehall Slip. On rounding the Battery, it had met a ruthless ebb tide pouring out of the East River, which ripped the *York* out of control. Waves crashed over the rails, sending tons of freezing seawater knee-high across the deck.

As Vanderbilt stood in the *Dread*, a single glance would have revealed hundreds of masts in the harbor—of boats, barks, and brigs, all anchored or moored against the gale. With the storm rising to its height, none dared to go to the aid of the *York*. Undeterred, he cast off and hoisted sail. Running before the wind, he bore down on the spinning *York*, bringing the *Dread* alongside amid the snow and hail. The two vessels drifted together in the worst of the storm; one by one, twelve passengers clambered over the gunwales into the *Dread* before Vanderbilt had to cut loose. He later tied up safely at Whitehall. Now out of reach, the *York* drifted on with the rest of the passengers, all the way to the Narrows, until it finally landed six hours later.[19]

After the rescue, Vanderbilt returned immediately to work, repairing his ravaged boat, preparing to resume his scheduled runs. If anything, his moment of glory only underscored the distance between himself and the merchants, who read about his exploit in the *Evening Post*.

It is often thought that youth is the time of grand horizons, of great dreams and bold plans. In fact, the reverse is often true: how little the young have experienced, how little they know of what might be. Vanderbilt daily glimpsed the emporium of New York, but he saw it strictly from sea level. He may have begun to buy and sell his own small cargoes of fish and fabrics, but he was removed from the countinghouse kingdom on the far side of South Street—the merchants who endorsed bills of exchange with glasses of sherry in hand, the auctions of federal bonds and British imports. His was a gunwale-to-gunwale existence of weather in the

---

* The *York* and all other steamboats operating in New York waters that will be mentioned in this chapter, apart from those owned by Gibbons, were run either by the Livingstons or under a license from them.

face and physical strain. He encountered the Anglo-Dutch elite only when they called on his sailor's skill and knowledge—as they did again just three weeks after the storm.

Late on the night of February 23, the British ship *Neptune* ran aground at Sandy Hook. Twenty-two days out of Jamaica, the merchantman carried $404,000 in gold and silver, of which $339,000 belonged to the New York branch of the recently refounded Bank of the United States. That precious metal formed the very foundation of the most important branch of the nation's central bank; every note, every record of deposit, every check it issued was considered a promise to pay in specie. Though no lives were at risk, the loss of the cargo might have a devastating effect, sparking a panic. None of the bay's boatmen had been able to salvage it, as waves battered the helpless vessel. So on February 26, Vanderbilt piloted the *Dread* down to Sandy Hook to see the stranded ship for himself. Two boats were luffing uselessly around its inert hull. Vanderbilt neatly steered his craft alongside and began to haul the specie across the gunwales. Later he met the federal revenue cutter *Active* and transferred the cargo. A possible financial catastrophe had been averted.[20]

By the time of this second rescue, Vanderbilt had already begun his foray into the world of wealthy men. When the *Mouse* was laid up for winter refitting, Vanderbilt had returned to his sailboats. But he seemed to sense that there was more to be made of his relationship with Gibbons; so when Gibbons asked him to check on the work being done to the *Mouse*, he agreed.

On the day the *Neptune* ran aground, Vanderbilt hurried over to the shipyards of Corlears Hook, the southeastern bulge of Manhattan island, and marched into the sprawling steam-engine works of James P. Allaire. A friendship quickly grew up between these two men, who both valued tough-minded competence, and Allaire willingly tutored Vanderbilt in this new world of steam. Few knew more about it. Allaire had worked on Fulton's first boats, then leased the inventor's engine works after his death and moved the machinery to these yards on Cherry Street. Allaire had built the *Mouse* himself, in fact, to test a paddle design. He walked Vanderbilt through the yard, pointing out the replacement parts for the boiler, the new toilet (or "necessary"), and the boring mill where the piston cylinder would be prepared.

Vanderbilt moved on to the shipyard of Lawrence & Sneden. There, beneath a swarming crew of caulkers and carpenters, glistened an entirely new hull ordered by Gibbons, for a vessel provisionally called the *Violin*. This sleek steamboat-in-creation stretched twice as long as the *Mouse* and would soon be fitted with Allaire's newest machinery. "I have saw the Violine," Vanderbilt reported, in his characteristically direct style, "and think she will be a fine Boat." It soon received a new and lasting name: the *Bellona*, after the Roman goddess of war. It would prove a fitting title indeed.

When Vanderbilt next sailed up the narrow Kill Van Kull to Gibbons's Rising Sun Landing, where a crew of workmen hammered together a pier and buildings to serve the *Mouse* and the *Bellona*, Gibbons greeted him with a demanding air. Obese and diabetic from a life of rapacious eating and drinking, Gibbons constantly grumbled about "the agonies of my frail body" that often left him housebound in Elizabethtown. Gibbons needed someone to help run his new steamboat enterprise; his first preference, his son William, spent much of his time overseeing the family's plantations. Gibbons observed that Vanderbilt stood in marked contrast to the "worthless fellows" who ran so many of the harbor's boats; his manner and conduct earned as much trust as Gibbons was grudgingly willing to give. He asked Vanderbilt to become his permanent captain, and move to Rising Sun Landing—directly under his hard eye.

Vanderbilt agreed, but only up to a point. He would take command of the *Mouse*, then the *Bellona* when it was launched, but no more. He looked over the rooms at Rising Sun Landing and begged off, explaining, "I would prefer living in N. York." He had his own ferry to run, after all, and a schooner to ready for the spring coastal trade.[21]

Gibbons put him in charge of the refurbished *Mouse* for several weeks before they settled on an employment contract, the only one Vanderbilt would ever sign.

> Memorandum of agreement made this 26 June 1818 between Thomas Gibbons and Cornelius Vanderbilt,—The said Cornelius Vanderbilt agrees to serve as master and commander of the Mouse, and when the Bellona shall run of the Bellona Steamboat until the present season is over, or until the ice shall block up the boat at the rate of Sixty Dollars a month and the privillege of half of the bar—Gibbons finding the bar furniture and Vanderbilt preserving the furniture and making the whole good at the end of the season. Vanderbilt will do all the duties required of him as commander, to run to and from Elizabeth Town at the landings of the said Thomas Gibbons.
> Th. Gibbons
> Cornelius Vanderbilt

It was a typically hard bargain for the stony Gibbons—though the bar would swell Vanderbilt's earnings. As one historian has put it, America was an "alcoholic republic"; early steamboats were motorized taverns, dispensing wine, whiskey, and brandy in enormous quantities. Once the *Bellona* was launched, Vanderbilt could expect anywhere from $60 to $110 a month from the bar alone.[22] More important was Vanderbilt's limitation of his commitment to the "present season" as he continued to pursue an independent course. He carried on with his ferry, of course, and even laid plans for a new schooner, the *Thorn*.[23]

Gibbons was focused on crushing Aaron Ogden. Vanderbilt listened to endless outbursts at "this fallen Shylock," as Gibbons called him. "He will if he can ruin me," he claimed, in a fit of projection. "Indeed he would ruin the whole world to enrich himself and family." Unfortunately, his enemy now sheltered inside the fortress of the New York steamboat monopoly. Ogden and the Livingstons, Gibbons wrote to John Randolph, "have no merit; they have no claim to useful invention. They are mere locusts and blood suckers in this part of the union. We cannot get to New York without their consent and at their price."[24]

In his employer's presence, Vanderbilt caught his first insider's glimpse of how business affairs were of one flesh with the law and politics. Despite Gibbons's physical infirmities and extravagant self-absorption, he possessed a legal mind of Damascus steel—sharp, hard, and penetrating. In the glare of his own self-righteousness, he readily saw the vast repercussions of his vendetta. To bankrupt Ogden, a ruthless business war was necessary, but insufficient; he had to convince the courts to overturn the Livingston monopoly itself. "The present is not a question of pounds shillings & pence," he later wrote; "it is the great question of sovereign rights—the right of navigating your own waters, under the laws and constitution of the U. States." At stake was the notion that the United States should be a common market, that the individual states should have no power to erect barriers to trade at their borders. The outcome of such a case could hardly be clear; indeed, if it did reach the Supreme Court, it would be the first in the Constitution's three-decade history concerning the commerce clause.[25]

In their frequent conversations, Vanderbilt learned of Gibbons's careful preparations for the legal battle to come. Aaron Burr had assured Gibbons that "any judge of the Court of the U.S." would find the steamboat grant "unconstitutional . . . highly absurd & tyrannical." Gibbons intended to obtain federal licenses under the Coasting Act of 1793, violate the monopoly to trigger a legal response from Ogden, then move the case to federal court. There he would argue that the commerce clause gave Congress sole authority over interstate commerce.[26]

Ogden, of course, merely held a license; behind him loomed the rich and powerful Livingston family. They were certain to fight back, for their monopoly was tremendously lucrative. In 1818, for example, the gross receipts of their North River Steam Boat Company reached $153,694, leaving a profit of $61,861 and dividends of $49,000. These sums were astronomical for the economy of the day. (In 1812, Fulton had described an income of $34,000 as "such immense profits.")

But the Livingstons were a divided clan. The chancellor had left to his heirs, Robert L. and Edward P. Livingston, the North River Steam Boat Company and its line to Albany. In 1808, however, he had sold to his brother John R. Livingston the rights to the waters between New York City and New Jersey, Staten Island, and Long Island. Intensely belligerent, eternally suspicious, and underhanded, John was aggravated by gout in both feet, and he aggravated his monopoly partners in turn. One of his many slippery maneuvers had led Fulton to erupt, "Never shall he edge himself into any other enterprise which I can control."27

On December 5, 1817, Gibbons had approached John R. Livingston to test his reaction to the news that he was building the *Bellona* to compete with Ogden's new ninety-five-foot *Atalanta*. Livingston had never liked Ogden; he had agreed to grant him a license only because of intense family pressure. So he slyly replied that he would not stop Gibbons from waging his vendetta.28

So far, so good: Gibbons had made every preparation for the legal fight to come. But the courtroom struggle would only be half the war. He still needed to win the business battle. After all, the ultimate goal was not to take away Ogden's license, but to send him to debtor's prison through direct competition. And that was Vanderbilt's job.

IN THE PARLOR OF THOMAS GIBBONS, Vanderbilt found a portal into the world of New York's wealthy patricians. Surprisingly, he found a second one through his own family. His introduction came through his brother-in-law, John De Forest, who now commanded the *Nautilus*, a steamboat that ran between New York and Staten Island. The craft belonged to the Richmond Turnpike Company, a corporation that was itself the property of Daniel D. Tompkins. Tompkins, a former governor of New York who had married into an aristocratic family, pursued expensive plans to develop his estate of Tompkinsville, Staten Island, even as he served as vice president of the United States. Thanks to De Forest, Vanderbilt became a regular guest at Tompkins's imposing marble mansion. There he learned that Tompkins, like all of patrician New York, was terrified by Gibbons's vendetta against Ogden.

An air of desperation hovered over Tompkins, who swayed under the weight of alcoholism and heavy debts. He owed a great deal of money to Gibbons, and ran the *Nautilus* under an expensive license from the Livingstons; he stood to lose heavily if the monopoly was overturned. Indeed, Gibbons's assault on the steamboat monopoly was also an attack on aristocratic privilege, as represented in Tompkins's own Richmond Turnpike Company. Whenever Vanderbilt stopped at the Tompkinsville dock and knocked on the doors of the mansion, the vice president urged him to press Gibbons to compromise, to make peace "with honor & propriety."[29]

What a universe was captured in that phrase—one that Tompkins's young guest could never grasp. For all of the vice president's Jeffersonian political affiliations, he picked his way through this changing society with an eighteenth-century mental map, written in the ink of deference and rank, drafted with mercantilist principles that placed the orderly direction of the economy in elite hands. To New York's patricians, Gibbons's insistence on competition was scandalous. Shortly after Vanderbilt took command of the *Bellona*, the aristocrat Rachel Stevens wrote in alarm, "Gibbons runs an elegant Steamboat for half price . . . purposely to ruin Ogden, and as he has a very long purse, I expect he will do it. Ogden has lowered his price and now Gibbons says he will go for nothing. Did you ever hear of such malice in this enlightened age?" *Malice* may seem a curious term for the offering of better service at lower rates, but it was malice indeed. Perversely, it was an obsession with honor that drove Gibbons to a kind of competitive capitalism that respected profits, not persons.[30]

In Vanderbilt's world, crowds were thicker, elbows sharper, confrontations cold and raw. He had grown up in a market-centered household outside the shadow of aristocrats; his was the individualistic society still emerging in America, guided not by honor but by calculation. He was angered but not scandalized when Ogden's men tore down signs to Rising Sun Landing, when the captains of Ogden's periaugers blocked the *Mouse*'s dock—to "plague" Gibbons, as one declared.

The twenty-four-year-old Vanderbilt took command of the 116-ton *Bellona* in October 1818. He brought it through the broad bay and narrow creek of Kill Van Kull less than a dozen times before he was met on the New York docks by a process server. Ogden had been content merely to harass the *Mouse*, but the large and powerful *Bellona* prompted him to seek an injunction from New York's Chancery Court, charging Gibbons with violating the monopoly. For Gibbons, it was all according to plan, and he began work on an appeal.

The vendetta played out in parallel battles of high and low. In September 1818, Gibbons stood trial for trespass, stemming from his attempt to challenge Ogden to a duel. (The charge for dueling was dismissed, as there had been none.) "The celebrity and high standing of the parties," the *Newark Centinel* reported, "excited considerable interest in the public mind." Each day, "a great number of respectable ladies" attended the trial, which ended with a $5,000 fine for Gibbons. It was far less decorous down on the waterfront, where the rival steamboat crews stooped to stealing fuel from each other's woodpiles. When Gibbons's own process server approached the engineer of the *Atalanta*, Ogden's man started punching and kicking, shouting, "Damned rascal, infernal villain, damned son of a bitch."[31]

Vanderbilt resorted to his own brazen and bewildering maneuvers to keep the *Bellona* running to Manhattan in the face of the court order. On June 4, 1819, as he chatted with De Forest and Tompkins at the vice president's mansion, he received another injunction barring the *Bellona* from New York. Nevertheless he went, was arrested, and was bundled off to Albany to see Chancellor James Kent, a man decidedly sympathetic to the monopoly. There Vanderbilt explained his insolence: Tompkins had hired the boat on the day he was taken into custody. The chancellor had no choice but to release him. Sometimes Vanderbilt simply ran the *Bellona* to the city, deftly avoiding the authorities who tried to impound it. When Ogden presented evidence of these violations, Gibbons blithely told the court that he had "misunderstood" its orders.[32]

With Vanderbilt managing the tactics of the struggle, Gibbons gave thought to strategy. His ferry service, he realized, was lucrative because it was a link in the most important commercial corridor in the burgeoning economy—the route between New York and Philadelphia, the young republic's financial centers and largest cities. Each year, more and more people passed between them, carrying information, capital, credit, and new business relationships. Gibbons constructed a consolidated line in early 1819 by forming a partnership with the Stevens brothers (aristocratic nephews of Chancellor Livingston, no less), who had a steamboat on the Delaware River, and with a group of stagecoach owners who provided transit by turnpike across the thirty-mile neck of New Jersey. The *Bellona* connected with the stages at New Brunswick, the farthest navigable point on the Raritan River. They called it the Union Line.[33]

There was already a steamboat that sailed between New York and New Brunswick. Perversely named *Olive Branch*, it belonged to John R. Livingston. He had eyed Gibbons's war against Ogden with unease that simmered into anger as Gibbons looked increasingly likely to succeed. Now that Gibbons competed directly against his own boat, his shallow patience boiled away, and he swept down on the *Bellona* with an injunction on April 24, 1819.[34]

Vanderbilt kept the business running, passing passengers through to New York by connecting with the *Nautilus* in New Jersey waters or simply by dodging process servers in Manhattan. Meanwhile Gibbons proceeded with his appeal to the Supreme Court of what was now called *Gibbons v. Ogden*. On December 13, 1819, he wrote to Daniel Webster, former congressman and future secretary of state. Webster already had a formidable reputation for his national vision, his championing of enterprise, his arguments before the high court—and his godlike vanity. A case that could tear down state barriers to national commerce, Gibbons thought, would suit Webster perfectly.[35]

THE ICE FROZE the *Elizabeth* in port. In February 1820, it sealed shut New York's North River piers and prevented the tall-masted vessel from departing. No one could free it. On board, Dr. J. M. Scott McKnight tended to the shivering passengers: some fifty black men and women, all skilled artisans bound for Africa to prepare settlements for rescued slaves. Technically a federal expedition against the transatlantic slave trade, it was a thinly disguised project of the American Colonization Society, which planned to ship freed slaves to Africa.

Vanderbilt stepped forward and said he could cut the *Elizabeth* loose in one night, and he'd do it for $100. With the *Mouse* and the *Bellona* undergoing winter refitting, he had been spending much of his time in New York, where he and Sophia still lived (now in a low wooden building at 58 Stone Street, a twisting, crowded lane close to the waterfront). The ship's agents agreed to Vanderbilt's price. He then took three sailors from the USS *Cyane*, the ship's escort, in a small boat alongside the trapped vessel. He balanced an anchor on the end of a long board and pushed it out onto the ice, then used another board to push it farther, then another, until the anchor sank on the outside edge. He and his men hauled on the anchor line and cut a path through the ice. De Forest brought the *Nautilus* around and swiftly towed the ship out.[36]

The city itself felt frozen in as 1820 began. The previous year, a devastating financial panic had cut short the heady expansion that had followed the peace of 1815, depopulating the countinghouses faster than a plague. Politics still sank beneath the weight of the old order—the limited franchise, the mercantilist monopolies, the political favoritism bestowed upon the privileged few. And Gibbons's boats were barred from New York by Ogden and Livingston's injunctions, a matter of rising gossip and debate.

As the year progressed, the frozen crust began to crack. A state constitutional convention convened, holding out hope for a more democratic government. In Trenton, the New Jersey legislature passed a retaliatory act that allowed Gibbons to impound the boats of anyone who impounded his own under the New York monopoly law. He promptly seized Ogden's and Livingston's vessels, which forced them to allow the *Bellona* to run to New York while his appeal crept toward the Supreme Court and the business war raged on.[37]

Vanderbilt fought this war at water level, lashing his crew ahead in a literal race for business. On the Delaware River landings, stages for Gibbons's and Livingston's lines swallowed passengers from Philadelphia, then pounded up the turnpike in a bouncing, careening charge to New Brunswick. Frances Trollope later described one such chaise as "the most detestable stage-coach that ever Christian built to dislocate the joints of his fellow men. Ten of these torturing machines were crammed full of the passengers who left the boat with us. . . . Every face grew grim and scowling." At New Brunswick, riders poured onto the pier as porters hurled their luggage onto associated steamers. "No sooner were we in the boats," wrote passenger Anne Royall, than "the steam was liberally plied to the wheels, and a race . . . commenced for New-York."

Down the Raritan and into the kills the *Bellona* and the *Olive Branch* plunged, paddlewheels beating the water, smoke trailing behind, as their pilots fought for any advantage. "It was quite an interesting sight to see such vast machines, in all their majesty, flying as it were, their decks covered with well-dressed people, face to face, so near to each other as to be able to converse," Royall thought. "It is well calculated to amuse the traveller." Speed was indeed everything: in a world where news generally traveled only as fast as people, first access to information from Philadelphia might mean a fortune to a speculator in New York. More than that, Americans were discovering a love of speed entirely for its own sake.

The daily race did nothing to mar the beauty of the Raritan. "For two or three miles the banks are pretty high," wrote *Bellona* passenger Sam Griscom, "and covered mostly with shrubs of pine and cedar with here and there a neat farmhouse to vary and give greater beauty to the scene. Beyond this the salt marsh commences. . . . The river winds its way thro this to the Bay." After more than an hour on board (with some three more hours left in the journey), Griscom sat down to "an excellent dinner," noting with curiosity that New Yorkers referred to their change as shillings and sixpence. Then the passengers rushed back on deck as they steamed out of Kill Van Kull into the bay.

"In a short time, the numerous spires of New York suddenly make their appearance," Griscom observed. "All around us the Bay is crowded with sails and Steam Boats with their long trails of smoke, crossing the Bay in all directions. . . . Directly ahead is the Battery . . . with the numerous masts of the shipping that line the wharves on each side of the city, the whole conspiring to render it the most delightful scene imaginable." The view took away the breath of the most cosmopolitan passenger. "I have never seen the bay of Naples," wrote Trollope, "but my imagination is incapable of conceiving any thing of the kind more beautiful than the harbour of New York."[38]

The *Bellona*—unlike the wedding-cake paddlewheelers that would soon teeter down every western river—ran low, sleek, and slender through the water. Ninety feet long and twenty-two wide, it had a low foredeck covered in an awning and dominated by a boxy pilothouse. Amidships loomed the paddlewheels sealed in arching wooden housings, a clanking working beam overhead that transmitted power from the piston, a pair of smokestacks, and dual copper boilers with blazing fireboxes, plus mounds of pine wood. Aft sat the main cabin, with its kitchen, dining room, and lounge.[39]

Lean and muscular, the twenty-six-year-old Vanderbilt remained very much the man of action, as the *Elizabeth* incident showed; but this enormous machine elevated him to another level of command. He presided as chief mariner, mayor, and magistrate of a temporary town, as he dealt with difficult passengers, tended to technical matters of the engine and hull, gave orders regarding navigation and speed, secured stocks of food and fuel, negotiated with harbormasters and customhouse officials, and coordinated with stagecoach drivers.

Then there were the lists he drew, the ledger entries that laid out line by line the complexity of this operation: the monthly payments made to the pilot, engineer, three firemen, four deckhands, "boy," cook, steward, chambermaid, three waiters, and "bar boy"; the equipment for the kitchen, the dutch oven, fish steamer, a pair of forty-gallon water casks, coffee boilers, frying pans, milk pails, and meat skewers; the payments for the lobsters, oysters, duck, and salmon, the veal, lamb, pork, and beef, plus fruits and roots and vegetables. Indeed, the *Bellona* was a floating restaurant serving nearly fifty diners at a time, who ordered glasses of brandy, claret, madeira, and gin from the bar. Trollope, writing later in the decade, marveled at this mobile social scene, describing the "gentlemen who . . . lounged on sofas, and balanced themselves in chairs . . . with all the conscious fascinations of stiff stays and neck-cloths . . . while doing to death the rash beauties who dared to gaze" from under "expansive bonnets."[40]

And so the few days that Gibbons had asked for multiplied into a year, and then two, and then another. Vanderbilt's service, rather than compressing him into another's lackey, stretched his stature and business knowledge. And with knowledge came ambition. That same year he built the *Thorn*, described in the press as a schooner, and began construction of his own little steamboat, the *Carolina*, as a speculative venture. When Gibbons could not find a buyer for the *Mouse*, Vanderbilt decided to take it himself and sell it at a profit, handing Gibbons two promissory notes for a total of $1,500 (signed "Van Derbilt," as usual, to contrast himself with his father).[41]

More and more, Vanderbilt acted as Gibbons's general agent, wandering the streets of New York to pay bills, collect intelligence, and visit lawyers. The experience lifted him from the world of deckhands, tides, and machinery breakdowns to that of quills and cravats, and he studied it carefully. Indeed, he now demonstrated an intensity and quickness of intellect that belied his coarse exterior. "Capt. V. is well acquainted with my case," Gibbons tellingly wrote to one of his lawyers.[42] In February 1821, Vanderbilt volunteered to go to Washington to hire the attorneys who would represent Gibbons before the Supreme Court: Daniel Webster and William Wirt, the attorney general of the United States. (In yet another example of the blurring of private interests and public office, Wirt maintained a private practice before the high court.) "I do not know a better way to present the fees . . . than by a special messenger," Gibbons wrote, "and C.V. has a desire to hear the argument."

Barely schooled but keen and shrewd, this blunt, bare-knuckled sailor rushed off to Washington to meet Wirt and Webster, two of the republic's foremost figures. He spent a couple of days going from one plush office to the next, shoving a meaty fist containing $500 into the hands of each man. The long-awaited day came on March 8, when the Supreme Court finally took up the steamboat case. The result was a crushing setback: the justices turned down the appeal on the grounds that New York's Court of Errors had not yet delivered a final verdict. Afterward Vanderbilt chatted with Webster, who promised to report to Gibbons about the case. The final battle would have to wait.[43]

VANDERBILT RETURNED TO NEW YORK to his wife and the daughters who multiplied in their rooms on Stone Street. Phebe Jane had been born in 1814, Ethelinda in 1817, and Elizabeth (or Eliza) in 1819—and Sophia waddled under the weight of yet another pregnancy, which she no doubt planned to see to term with family on Staten Island.[44] What passed between the captain and his cousin wife on his homecoming went unrecorded, whether it was tenderness, a stern insistence on a son, or simple neglect. What is known is that he once again began a frenzy of activity.

Soon afterward he launched the *Bellona* on a new season of high-speed competition, powered by another cut in the fare to Philadelphia. The repeated price reductions were a stark departure from the past. They delivered a competitive advantage, of course, but also showed that Gibbons and Vanderbilt believed in a growing market—that more and more people wanted to travel between the two cities, and would do so by steamboat if rates were cheap enough. This notion of an expanding economy was surprisingly new. The Livingstons' North River Steam Boat Company had kept the same number of boats running to Albany at the same fare for years, and saw ridership steadily *drop*. They believed there was a natural number of passengers, and that competition was destructive, robbing them of their due.

Increasingly, the belligerent John R. Livingston shoved aside Ogden as Gibbons's chief opponent. He seethed at the "mortification, trouble, & expence" resulting from the attack on the monopoly. "My right," he stormed, using consummately patrician language, had been "invaded." His son, R. Montgomery, felt the need to ask Ogden to "lend your aid" against Gibbons, writing, "We can destroy him."[45] Unable to impound the *Bellona* without having his own boat seized in New Jersey, Livingston came up with a new strategy: to file a lawsuit against Vanderbilt directly in the Marine Court, a minor bench limited to suits for $100 or less.

On May 29, 1821, two days after Vanderbilt's twenty-seventh birthday, the lanky captain squinted from the deck of the *Bellona* up the North River pier where his boat was docked, and saw High Constable Jacob Hays approach. Hays announced that he had an arrest warrant from the Marine Court, and Vanderbilt erupted. "I was mad enough to defy the whole Livingston tribe, Old Hays included," he later recalled, "but when I caught a glimpse of his calm and smiling face, and a twinkle in his eye, which . . . said as plain as words could express it, 'If you don't obey the order of the court, and that damn soon, I'll make you do it, by God,' I concluded to surrender."

Forty-nine years old, stout, and quite bald, the heavy-eyed Hays had earned a fearsome reputation as the city's calm but inexorable chief law enforcement officer. He possessed considerable skill in subduing criminals; rather than tussle with a brawler, for example, he would knock off the offender's hat with his staff, and then send him sprawling on the ground the moment he bent over to retrieve it. "I didn't want to back down, however, too hurriedly," Vanderbilt explained, "and I said that if they wanted to arrest me, they should carry me off the boat; and don't you know old Hays took me at my word, and landed me on the dock with a suddenness that took my breath away."

The Marine Court quickly found Vanderbilt guilty of violating the monopoly law, and he appealed. Heady with the experience of meeting Webster and Wirt, flushed with anger at Livingston, he decided to take his own case to the Supreme Court. If Gibbons did not destroy the monopoly, then he would.[46]

If Livingston didn't destroy him first, that is. Just as the fare cuts heightened the competition, this legal clash intensified the animosity of the daily race, adding a growing sense of danger that soon became evident. On October 27, the *Bellona* churned up the Raritan at top speed alongside Livingston's *Olive Branch*, engines straining, paddles battering the water. Suddenly the *Branch*'s captain spun the wheel. The vessel smashed into the *Bellona;* the sound of cracking wood reverberated as rails snapped off and part of the superstructure collapsed. Vanderbilt himself may have been at the helm, for his boat came through the harrowing collision with no serious damage.[47]

His response reflected a combination of technical and tactical mastery. One of the key problems for both competitors was the shallowness of the Raritan at New Brunswick; at low tide the rival steamboats had to row their passengers to the dock in scows. He could fix that, he thought, if the *Bellona* were cut in half and extended. "You will reccolect the Bellona must be halled up weather you have hir 12 feet longer or no, in order to repair hir bottom; that is, if you do hir justice," he told Gibbons. Lengthening the boat would give it a proper forward cabin and reduce its draft, "which will enable us to go to the dock at all times. . . . That will do over all that besides a number of othair advantages we would gain." Gibbons agreed.[48]

Then there was the matter of Livingston's lawsuits. To escape his reach, Vanderbilt decided to move to New Brunswick. At Gibbons's urging, he and Sophia settled into a house and stables that Gibbons had rented just a block from the river. The move to this old Dutch country town was a relief for Sophia, who had never taken to New York; it also gave her more responsibility than she was to have through all their years of marriage. The house was a small inn for overnight travelers, now dubbed Bellona Hall. She took charge and earned a reputation as a gracious innkeeper who provided good food and small courtesies such as heated stones to warm the feet of passengers on the stage ride to Trenton. And she did all this while caring for yet another baby—a boy named William Henry. Indeed, her husband left management of the children entirely to her. He even demanded that she feed, clothe, and educate them out of her income from the inn.[49]

THEY WERE WINNING. In early 1822, Vanderbilt and Gibbons talked matters over with the Stevens brothers and their stagecoach partners, then slashed the Philadelphia fare yet again, to $2.50. The move diverted even more traffic to the *Bellona*—and drove Ogden to the edge of bankruptcy. He pleaded vainly with Gibbons for a truce. In March, he put the *Atalanta* up for sale, though he found no buyers.[50]

Even the wealthy Livingstons began to panic. On one side, Gibbons squeezed John R. in business; on another, the monopoly right of the entire clan remained in danger as the appeals of Gibbons and Vanderbilt marched ominously toward the Supreme Court; on still another, the state constitution had been revised in 1821, peeling the aristocrats' last fingers off the wheel of power. In the face of fierce conservative opposition (headed by Chancellor James Kent, who wrote a decision upholding the steamboat grant), politician Martin Van Buren had led the Bucktail faction to triumph in the convention, expanding the electorate to 80 percent of white men and radically democratizing the institutions of government. (In 1826, the vote would be extended to all adult white males.) Real political parties could now emerge, with mass participation from people of all walks of life.[51]

The old order was collapsing on the aristocrats, following inexorably from the Revolution their fathers had helped lead. More and more, the scions of great families accepted their declining influence and devoted themselves to business. But the Livingstons clung desperately to their monopoly, that most lucrative relic of the age of privilege. In a telling moment, R. Montgomery Livingston appealed to Gibbons, his fellow patrician, for an accommodation in the face of all these challenges. "It has long been a matter of astonishment that you & the Mssrs Livingston have been so long at war," he wrote. Gibbons brusquely rebuffed him.

Afterward R. Montgomery ran into Gibbons's son William on the streets of New York and began to rage about seeking "personal satisfaction." As William related the conversation to his father, R. Montgomery declared that it was common knowledge that Thomas Gibbons had "declared you would ruin [John R. Livingston] as you had Col. Ogden and that you would have $200,000 to give means for that purpose if you could not succeed in your lifetime." The outburst led the senior Gibbons to demand a duel with young Livingston—indoors at five paces, supporting himself with a cane behind his back, due to his poor health and failing eyesight. Livingston indignantly declined.[52]

This farce abruptly ended when William Gibbons disappeared amid a yellow fever epidemic that swept New York. "Well-founded alarm prevails through every part of this city," the *New York Evening Post* reported on August 26, 1822, as hundreds grew sick and died. Though none knew it at the time, it was the natural scourge of a primitive city of backyard wells and privies, of filthy streets of standing water where mosquitoes bred and fed. Scores of businesses relocated outside the city, and Vanderbilt began to run the *Bellona* to a dock far up the North River. Every day he went into town to search for William, who finally surfaced, sick but recovering, like the city itself.[53]

The epidemic threw more light on Vanderbilt's character in these changing times. During the outbreak, a new crewman named Willett died after a few days on duty. "I want and will go to sea Mrs. Willit as quick as I can get Leasure," Vanderbilt wrote to Gibbons. "I take it we owe Mrs. Willitt nothing. Yet we conceive it to be a generous act to help this Lone widdow through the winter and bestow upon her something." The crew collected $90 for her, a third of it Vanderbilt's.

This ambiguous act of charity reveals the captain as a revolutionary of the world within. Though he worked for a patrician, he himself was the ultimate anti-aristocrat, a man who never felt the tug of noblesse oblige. He was hypermasculine, yes—he might beat down a man who defied his will—but he would never think to defend his honor in a duel. Nor was he a man "of sentiment," a man of feeling, a part of the Romanticism that was now replacing the culture of deference. Vanderbilt represented a far more radical departure than that. He was an early example of that most modern of characters: the economic man. His charity was real—a trace, perhaps, of his Moravian upbringing, even his fundamental sense of decency—but cold calculation also marked his thinking ("we owe Mrs. Willitt nothing"). That calculation extended even to his own family, with his insistence that his wife pay for his children's upkeep and education. Truly a creature of the market, Vanderbilt made the most intimate relationship a line in his ledger book.[54]

Law, rank, the traditional social bonds—these things meant nothing to him. Only power earned his respect, and he felt his own strength gathering with every modest investment, every scrap of legal knowledge, every business lesson taught by the irascible but brilliant Gibbons. He had little regard for legal formalities or public office, and bitterly resented any hint of condescension. After clashing with the Perth Amboy customs collector about registering the *Bellona*, for example, he declared that the man "puts on great airs. . . . I think if it was my case I would not get papers and let him stop her. I think it more than he dares to do." The collector complained that Vanderbilt had treated his staff "with a kind of contempt."[55]

Even Gibbons began to suspect that he had created a monster. By adding a broad and sophisticated vision to Vanderbilt's innate shrewdness and ferocious will, he feared that he had unlocked an unstoppable ambition. The young captain began to amass a stable full of thoroughbreds—the aristocrats' own hobby—and purchased a pair of exceptional gray mares for the astoundingly steep price of $220. He designed an elegant new steamboat of more than one hundred tons, named the *Fanny*—another speculative venture financed with the help of James P. Allaire. And yet, he deeply respected Gibbons. According to legend, the Livingstons offered to hire him, but he turned them down on the grounds of loyalty to his master. "He was a man that could not be led," Vanderbilt admiringly described Gibbons, "but some persons had influence with him to a certain extent." He added, with uncharacteristically modest pride, "I had some with him."

The suspicious Gibbons took no comfort in Vanderbilt's respect. It was clear to him that his gladiator was outgrowing this arena, that he would not be content forever in his position. "He will do nothing for me in Winter," Gibbons fretted to his son. "He is building a new steamboat the size of the *Bellona* before she was lengthened. Vanderbilt has commenced horse racing too. Tomorrow he runs his brown colt in a match race. He is striking at every thing. I am afraid of this man."[56]

AT EIGHT O'CLOCK IN THE MORNING on March 30, 1823, snow began to pour over New York Bay like an avalanche. Branches snapped off; then entire trees crashed to the ground; even chimneys blew apart in the gale, scattering bricks. A flood tide tore across the Battery and the slips, "causing the most alarming apprehensions," the *Evening Post* reported, "for the fate of vessels of all descriptions, either at sea or on the coast, in our rivers and harbors, or even at our wharves."

The *Bellona* started from New Brunswick at six that morning. At nine o'clock, it reached the mouth of the Raritan, where the pilot began to have trouble. "The storm was tremendous," Vanderbilt reported. In the roaring blizzard, faced with a flood tide, the *Bellona* "became unmanageable. She would not mind her helm at all." As the boat began to drift out of control, he concluded that it was useless to fight the storm—they would have to run with it. Somehow he managed to come about and steam back to New Brunswick. There he found the waves crashing over the pier. He dropped anchor and sat out the storm all night. He finally returned his passengers to shore at four the next afternoon, ferrying them over in rowboats. Elsewhere four ships sank in the storm as the torrent drove scores of vessels ashore, including Ogden's *Atalanta*.[57]

Self-assured in the face of nature's fury, he felt far less certain of himself with mercurial humanity. "Last evening New Brunswick wais in an uproar," he wrote to William Gibbons, five days before the storm. Some passengers had been detained in town; Robert Letson, a stagecoach driver, "toald the passengers that retaining them their was all my falt, that all I did it for was to get their supper and lodging from them." The trouble left Vanderbilt deeply distressed. "Cannot you stop Letson mouth by a letter," he begged. "I wish you would rite to Letson. I continuly beg of him to keep still."[58]

His uncertainty may not be as uncharacteristic as it appears. The creature of a commercial, individualistic, competitive generation, he saw every relationship as a business transaction; he simply didn't know what to do with this very human entanglement with a man who was less a rival than a blowhard. He had made himself into a supreme man of force, but now he showed how vulnerable he could be to a simple social interaction—one that could not be solved with his fists. His only solution was financial: he suggested that they pay Letson to keep him away from the dock.

It was almost with relief that he returned to the clarity of battle. By now, all sides knew the Supreme Court would decide the fate of the monopoly. Ogden and John R. Livingston had good reason to expect success, for the steamboat grant had been upheld repeatedly by lower courts. But Livingston wanted to crush his enemies before the case reached the high bench. Starting on May 1, he renewed his legal assault in Marine Court against Vanderbilt and his crew. The damages were limited to $100, but he filed a fresh suit every day, dispatching an officer to arrest them when the *Bellona* docked.[59]

"I could not leave the boat as J. R. would take all the men if I am not their," Vanderbilt wrote to Gibbons. "I now keep all my men out of the way so that they cannot take them and wile I am agoing in & out to the dock in NY I work the boat myself and let them take me but I will not let them take them as it is intended with some difficulty to get bail for the men." According to anecdotes told later, he grew increasingly ingenious at avoiding the arrests. He built a secret compartment and hid on board until the deckhands had cast off again; when the officer found him, Vanderbilt offered the man a choice of leaping to the wharf or spending the day in New Jersey. At one point he trained a young woman to steer the boat into dock, and hid as the officer stormed aboard, only to be left stuttering and embarrassed in the face of a female pilot.

Gibbons, on the other hand, began to panic. Bedridden with gout, diabetes, and possibly cancer, he had had a stroke in April, leaving him isolated at home. "J. R. L. is waging a dreadful war against us, ruinous in the extreme," he wrote. "Vanderbilt is not capable of defending such suits. I can't see him, he won't write. I am left like a dead man in the midst of a sanguinary war. I have submitted questions to V. Whether we must stop the Boat, run to Powlis Hook, or the Nautilus? I can get no answer."[60]

In fact, the possibility of failure never occurred to Vanderbilt. When he wasn't dodging arrest, he gleefully plotted traps for Livingston. He secretly obtained the lease to the *Olive Branch*'s dock, for instance, and waited until the season was under way to evict his foe. He had its crew arrested in New Jersey in a retaliatory lawsuit and taken "6 miles in the woods from N. B. before a magirstrate and make them give bail," he bragged. "It will give them more trouble than I have in N. Y." Far from fretting about the future, he brought his sixteen-year-old brother Jacob and his old partner, James Day, into the business.[61] But Gibbons was a lawyer who understood very well the uncertainties of the courtroom. After all the expenditures on boats, docks, and inns, after the fare cuts and steamboat races, everything could be destroyed by a few words from the Supreme Court.

———

AT ELEVEN IN THE MORNING of February 4, 1824, six justices of the Supreme Court of the United States, led by Chief Justice John Marshall, filed into their basement chamber beneath the Capitol and settled under the high windows on the eastern wall of that dim, semicircular room. Even in the February chill the space must have been sweltering, for it was packed with bodies—lawyers and congressmen, men and women—crowded in to witness what everyone knew would be a most important case. *Gibbons v. Ogden* was about to be heard at last.

Two lawyers for each side sat at the single counsel table. Representing Ogden were Thomas Jackson Oakley and Thomas Addis Emmet. Emmet had long defended the monopoly; in 1815, Fulton had given his life to rescue him from the freezing waters of the Hudson. As Attorney General William Wirt noted, "Emmet's whole soul is in the cause, and he will stretch all his powers." Wirt himself sat for Gibbons, alongside Daniel Webster. "Webster is as ambitious as Caesar," Wirt had written a few days earlier. "He will not be outdone by any man. . . . It will be a combat worth witnessing." With everyone in place, the marshal of the court intoned, "God save the United States and this honorable Court!" Then Webster rose to begin his argument.[62]

In far-off New York, the Livingstons were worried. For more than a decade they had fought off or bought off successive rivals; more recently, the New York Court of Errors had given them a resounding victory over Gibbons's challenge. Yet Gibbons had persevered, and Vanderbilt had his own case against them next on the docket. The Livingstons had decided to make one more appeal. After all, the political future looked grim; New York was no longer governed by factions of landed families, but by Martin Van Buren and his plebeian Albany Regency. And Gibbons and Vanderbilt had outmatched John R. Livingston, who warned his family of "an immense loss" if the court overturned the monopoly. It was a risk they could not afford to take.[63]

On January 27, 1824, the great clan had sent an emissary, Walter Livingston, to Elizabethtown on one last mission. I have "come on the old business," he said to William Gibbons. The monopoly had a final offer: Thomas Gibbons would discontinue his case, in return for the Livingstons' "letting T. G. participate in their rights & throwing open the Jersey runs to him."

William shook his head. "It was too late," he replied. Livingston said it could be settled in an hour—did his father agree with him? William entered the darkened sickroom and spoke quietly to the suffering old man. Thomas Gibbons glared up at his son and tersely refused. Livingston said "he was very sorry nothing could be done," William wrote, "& then immediately withdrew."[64]

The risk was at least as great on the other side. For Vanderbilt, defeat in the high court would virtually doom his future in shipping, forcing him to either buy an expensive steamboat license (assuming John R. Livingston would sell him one) or fall back on his far less lucrative sailboats. If he could avoid debtors' prison, that is: the Marine Court lawsuits had piled up remorselessly, threatening him with bankruptcy. His own case looked doubtful if Gibbons lost. And victory was far from certain. Chancellor Kent, the author of the New York decision upholding the steamboat grant, was one of the most highly regarded jurists in the country. And a new justice had just been appointed to the Supreme Court who had repeatedly ruled in favor of the monopoly: Smith Thompson, a relative of the late Chancellor Livingston.

But Thompson was so new to the Court that he had not yet arrived on February 4, when Webster rose to speak. "With Webster there was also a thin veil of hauteur," writes biographer Robert V. Remini. "He was a snob about many things: his New England breeding, his education, his legal, linguistic, and literary talents, the fact that . . . he was the foremost constitutional authority in the United States."[65]

The monopoly lawyers would argue, as they successfully had before, that the government of New York had created a valuable property right and the Court was bound to protect it. The public, on the other hand, grew ever more hostile to the idea that the state could carve up the economy and assign a portion to a prestigious family. By 1824, more and more Americans demanded a market open to any who dared to venture in, an economy as democratic as the political arena increasingly was.[66] Ogden's attorneys were also to assert a state's authority to interfere with interstate commerce. The claim affronted both Webster's nationalism and his economic vision. If it prevailed, it would establish a constitutional rule that would turn the United States into a collection of feuding principalities, each erecting its own barriers to trade.

And there Webster struck, in one of the most important speeches of his long career. He pointed out the "extreme belligerent legislation" that New York, New Jersey, and Connecticut had enacted, barring each other's steamboats. "It would hardly be contended," he intoned, "that *all* these acts were consistent with the laws and Constitution of the United States." The Constitution had been written to create a commercial "*unit* . . . complete, entire, and uniform. Its character was to be described in the flag which waved over it, E PLURIBUS UNUM."

Webster's rivals responded over the next three days, until February 7. Their arguments reflected a social and economic vision that had not kept pace with the growth in domestic trade, the increasing economic integration of the country, the new American outlook. Commerce was the buying and selling of goods, they argued, not the transportation of passengers, and so the commerce clause did not apply; in any case, the states retained powers over commerce that they had had before the Constitution. Wirt concluded for Gibbons with an appeal to national unity, warning of civil war.

For three weeks, they waited—Webster and Wirt in Washington, the Livingstons on their manors or the streets of New York, Ogden in Elizabethtown, Gibbons in his sickbed, Vanderbilt in his stables at Bellona Hall. The anticipation could be felt throughout the United States, for everyone sensed that this was a case that would help to define the age. Newspaper editors stood by, day after day, hoping to be the first to publish the result of the "celebrated Steam Boat controversy," as the *National Intelligencer* called it. On February 19, Chief Justice Marshall dislocated his shoulder, further delaying a decision. On February 23, William Gibbons wrote to his father from Washington that Webster had told him "*confidentially*" that one of the justices had said that his argument had convinced them "that it is a broad constitutional question upon which scarcely any doubt exists."

On March 2, Marshall led the associate justices into the courtroom and began to read the majority opinion—his own opinion—to the crowd that packed the basement, straining in utter silence to hear every word. He began by paying tribute to the immense authority of the New York courts, whose decision was now at issue. Then he struck at the heart of the matter. "Commerce, undoubtedly, is traffic," he said, "but it is something more; it is intercourse." Hardly another word was necessary. As the *Evening Post* succinctly put it, "The Steam Boat grant is at an end."[67]

Chapter Three

A TRICKY GOD

The tablespoon glittered in the craftsman's shop. As new silver, it would have been heavy and untarnished in Vanderbilt's hand. Looking into it on March 31, 1824, two months short of his thirtieth birthday, he would have seen himself in his prime: full lips, a long nose, and a high forehead, growing higher by the day as his hairline ebbed. It was the reflection of a man who had just won the biggest victory of his life.

The craftsman had engraved the spoon with a single word: *Thistle.* For Vanderbilt, it was the name of the future. The tablespoon was one of twenty-four specially prepared for the newly launched *Thistle,* along with sets of sugar tongs, mustard spoons, and five dozen teaspoons. Vanderbilt found them acceptable, paid for them, and carried them down to the dock. The *Thistle* belonged to his employer, Thomas Gibbons, but he attended to the boat's every detail himself, from bell covers to block straps, as it was built in a New York shipyard. At more than 123 feet long, twenty-three wide, and 210 tons, it was an "elegant Steam Boat," in the words of the *New York Evening Post.* On her first trial, it made thirteen miles per hour against the tide—truly a marvel of speed.

On April 19, Vanderbilt commanded it on its initial run to New Brunswick, where an enthusiastic crowd swarmed the dock to meet him. He piloted the *Thistle* to its moorings under the echoing boom of a small cannon, fired by a local merchant and two others to welcome the flagship of the new era of free competition. Then the cannon exploded, blasting off the fingers of two men and scorching the face of the third.[1]

In later years, many observers would ponder the gargantuan figure that Cornelius Vanderbilt had become and wonder if the unchecked marketplace had not blown up in everyone's face. In the immediate aftermath of *Gibbons v. Ogden,* however, no one doubted that the world had become a better place. The Livingston monopoly could not stop steamboats from entering New York waters from other states, the Supreme Court ruled; to the public, this was a blow for freedom.

Chief Justice Marshall's decision provided one of those rare turning points in history that is recognized as one at the time. Newspapers across the country greeted the ruling with lengthy coverage. "The interest excited by the decision," wrote the *Washington Republican*, "has induced us to . . . gratify our readers." *Niles' Register* reprinted the decision in full, filling almost eight pages.

"It is the fashion to praise the Chief Justice's opinion," John Randolph of Virginia observed. Indeed, it proved to be almost universally popular, perhaps the most popular of his long career. The *Evening Post* captured the mood when it called the decision "one of the most powerful efforts of the human mind that has ever been displayed from the bench of any court." It represented "a forecast, in relation to the destinies of our great confederacy." John Marshall foresaw a destiny of commerce, free and abundant, and the people wholeheartedly agreed.[2]

"Chief Justice John Marshall's great disquisition on the commerce clause," writes legal scholar Leonard W. Levy, "is the most influential in our history." In constitutional terms, it completed his great nationalist project, the establishment of federal supremacy. It struck down the New York steamboat monopoly as an affront to Congress's exclusive jurisdiction over interstate commerce, refuting the claim that the states shared power in that area. In practical terms, it threw the high court's weight behind the gathering momentum of competitive individualism—of laissez-faire—in American law and culture. "Marshall's nationalism," writes R. Kent Newmeyer, "aimed to create not a nation-*state* but a national market, an arena in which goods and credit moved without hindrance across state lines." Though the decision said nothing about the legality of government-granted monopolies as such, it added to a growing sense among many that they ran against the natural law of economics and the principle of equality. And Marshall fully recognized the need to expand transportation to develop (and unify) the sprawling republic. (After the Court adjourned at the end of March, he ruefully decided to return home by taking his first trip in a steamboat.)[3]

A century after *Gibbons v. Ogden*, legal historian Charles Warren hailed the decision as "the emancipation proclamation of American commerce." Marshall's admiring biographer, Albert Beveridge, claimed that it "has done more to knit the American people into an indivisible Nation than any other force in our history, excepting only war." More recent legal scholars have stepped back from such extravagant praise, noting the ways in which this sweeping decision was soon hemmed in.[4] And yet, there is much truth in these earlier assessments, especially when the case is set in a context larger than constitutional law. Marshall captured and codified a new mood in the country, after nearly fifty years of independence. Commerce, interstate commerce in particular, was the stuff of daily life as never before. The chief justice proclaimed that, yes, the United States was a common market; no matter how the states would later eat away at the edges of his ruling, he gave voice to what most Americans now believed—that freedom of movement and trade across state lines was a basic right.

Gibbons v. Ogden came at an extraordinary moment. Within a year, the most important work of public engineering of the era, the Erie Canal, would be complete from Albany to Lake Erie. The unleashing of steamboats in New York waters and the opening of the canal that connected the nation's interior to the Atlantic coast would integrate markets and open the way for new economic growth. They would also guarantee New York City's dominant position in the American economy, and make way for Vanderbilt's rise.[5]

The results could be seen almost at once. The *Thistle* was only the first of many new vessels to be launched after the death of the monopoly. The steamboats registered at the New York Custom House jumped from one or two per year to twenty-two. Even more churned in from neighboring states. In November 1824, *Niles' Register* reported, the number of paddle-wheelers in New York had increased from six to forty-three. New York went from stumbling block to keystone in the American economy.[6]

Aaron Ogden—hero of the Revolution, former New Jersey governor, former United States senator, hated by no one but Thomas Gibbons—went bankrupt. Gibbons had the great satisfaction of seeing his old foe descend into the indignity of debtors' prison. He went free thanks to the aged but still-influential Aaron Burr, who lobbied the New York legislature to enact a law to spare all Revolutionary veterans from imprisonment for debt. Ogden moved to Jersey City in 1829, received an appointment as collector of customs there, and died on April 19, 1839. A man who merely played by the rules of the day, he paid for the sins of the entire system, and was sacrificed for its transformation.

The Livingston clan was stunned by the Supreme Court's decision. "I had no idea of the court's going to the extent it has," mused a troubled Edward P. Livingston. "It seems to have adopted opinions which I had thought settled long ago." He and his brother Robert L. felt insulated, however; their North River Steam Boat Company operated entirely within New York State boundaries, where the monopoly still prevailed. The defeat really belonged to their uncle, John R. Livingston, whose rights covered the waters shared with neighboring states. But the ill-tempered John was determined to make his nephews suffer just as he did. Bitterly admitting failure in his battle against Vanderbilt, he took the *Olive Branch* off the line to New Brunswick and sent it to Albany to compete against his own family. In the resulting court case, the now more democratic state courts overturned the monopoly entirely. John R. Livingston, one of the oldest survivors of the culture of deference, had destroyed its last remnants. Like the rest of the old patricians, the Livingstons had become merely rich men in an economic war of all against all.[7]

For the man who sat in the office of the *Thistle* as it floated at its New Brunswick dock, counting out shillings and scratching entries in ledgers, the courtroom victory posed an entirely different conundrum. As the commander of Gibbons's forces, Vanderbilt had fought loyally under his chief in a great campaign. But his service had been a whetstone to sharpen his ambition. Now, with Ogden crushed, the Livingstons dispersed, and the monopoly in ashes, what was there to keep him in his master's pay? If even the aging chief justice had caught the rising spirit of the times—a rough, combative individualism—what would restrain the mariner-businessman who best embodied it? In Gibbons's dark, suspicious heart, he knew it was only a matter of time before his iron-willed captain fought his battles for himself.

WORKMEN BUSTLED AROUND BELLONA HALL, hammering together an extension on the building, laying a new terrace, making improvements to the stables. Vanderbilt urged them to finish by the end of May, when traffic between New York and Philadelphia would pick up dramatically.[8] His mind raced with ideas for the months ahead, searching for any competitive advantage for the Union Line. The Supreme Court had eliminated Ogden and the Livingstons as competitors, but in so doing had unleashed anarchy upon a business long restrained by law and custom. Already a new rival had appeared: the Citizen's Line, which ran the steamboat *Aetna* (or "Etney," as Vanderbilt typically chewed up the name). The war of all against all had begun.

As if to underscore the uncertainties of the age, the *Aetna* erupted in a massive boiler explosion on the waters of New York Harbor on May 16, 1824. The spectacular accident created a new anxiety—"the lurking fear that we might burst the boilers," as one passenger called it. Though Americans were still entranced with the technology of steam, the *Aetna* disaster planted a seed of that most modern awareness: that progress marches with tragedy, that new capacities breed new horrors. At the time, the press merely focused on the choice of machinery, angrily denouncing the *Aetna*'s owners for using a high-pressure engine. "*Let no such boats be trusted,*" the *Evening Post* fumed. Vanderbilt swiftly took advantage by notifying the newspaper that all of the boats on the Union Line "are propelled by the low pressure Steam Engines."[9]

Time would show that the difference between high- and low-pressure engines barely mattered when opposing captains strained their boilers beyond their limits. It was not merely the technology but the new culture of economic conflict that made the steam engine so dangerous to the public. Yet competitive zeal was what powered Vanderbilt in those weeks after *Gibbons v. Ogden;* rivalry seemed to make his mind ever more nimble, ever quicker, in these rapidly changing times.

At the end of May, he spent his thirtieth birthday consumed by the threat of a new and more dangerous foe, "the elegant Steam Boat *Legislator,*" as the *Evening Post* hailed it. "The *Legislator* has a large and airy centre dining cabin," the paper reported, "finished off with mahogany and curled maple; a ladies' cabin richly and beautifully furnished; beside a large and convenient forward cabin containing a bar for refreshments, &c. and is in reality a splendid floating Hotel."

Vanderbilt informed Gibbons that the *Legislator* belonged to a corporation based in New Brunswick; the shares were selling below par, he noted, and soon they might be able to buy enough to take control. (The par value was the official price which the original incorporators were technically obligated to pay.) It was a remarkable piece of creative thinking. In 1824, the corporation was a mysterious abstraction to most Americans, but Vanderbilt already grasped its nature and the market in stocks.[10] Indeed, the proposal offered an early hint of methods that would later define his career.

But it went nowhere. Instead, he and Gibbons met the *Legislator* with a fare war that drove the cost of the forty-mile journey from New York to New Brunswick down to a shilling. "But within a few days past the fare has been still farther reduced," commented the *New York Daily Advertiser* on June 4, "and they now carry for nothing; in some instances a good dinner has been given to all who would accept it." Vanderbilt—always alert to his personal interests—touted his inn in Union Line advertisements. "The elegant hotel, Bellona Hall, is connected with these boats," he boasted, "where travellers can be well accommodated, and horses kept at low rates."

The *Legislator,* meanwhile, suffered from its crew's inexperience. Several days after it began to run, schoolteacher Sam Griscom boarded it in New York. "We were getting along very fast, and were in hopes of getting to New Brunswick nearly as soon as the other Boat," he wrote in his diary; "then thro want of skill the pilot ran the boat on a bar in Raritan Bay. . . . The captain was very much mortified. I believe that neither he nor his pilot was acquainted with this passage; to add to his mortification, a steam boat passed us, which would carry the tidings of our disaster to N. York."[11]

As a teacher, Griscom had no reason to fret about a few minutes' difference in the journey to Philadelphia, but he was caught up in the craze for competition. "The sport arising from 'boat racing,' " the *Evening*

Post observed, captured the public imagination, as each vessel attracted dedicated adherents. English actress Anne Royall witnessed a race from aboard the *Legislator;* referring to the boat as "our heroine," she recounted the chase with breathless excitement. "Although she seized upon the middle of the channel, her rival drew up alongside somewhat boldly, and sometimes had the presumption to run ahead," she wrote, with a fan's attention to technical detail, "which her ability to sail in shoal water enabled her to do." Here was everything exciting about the age, captured in a moment: the power of the new machines, the ease and rapidity of travel, the thrill of the daily duel. And the benefits of this competition were clear to see: the passage between Philadelphia and New York shrank to less than ten hours, and fares had never been cheaper.[12]

To Vanderbilt's consternation, the *Legislator*'s captain, Lawrence Fisher, rapidly got better, and soon began to beat the *Thistle* with alarming frequency. On September 3, Vanderbilt won the race to New York; as the *Thistle* churned up to the pier that was used by both vessels, he ordered his deckhands to tie up in the middle, leaving no room for the enraged Fisher. Harbormaster John Minugh ran out on the dock and ordered Vanderbilt "to haul ahead in order to accommodate the . . . *Legislator.*" With characteristic contempt for empty authority, Vanderbilt "refused so to do," Minugh reported. Vanderbilt continued to block out Fisher whenever he could, snorting at the threat of a $250 fine. The battle was all that mattered.[13]

Shortly before six o'clock on the morning of June 2, 1825, Vanderbilt and Fisher ordered their engineers to build up steam for the morning race to New Brunswick. Men and women bound for New Jersey and Philadelphia lined up on the dock, boarding the boats at their berths. Vanderbilt glowered at his rival as Fisher strutted on his deck with pride. "He had beaten the *Thistle* yesterday," a passenger remembered Fisher saying, "and [he] intended to go ahead of her still farther today." The *Legislator*'s engineer was new, but he understood his mission well. "She *must beat the* Thistle," he told his assistant (one of many black men who worked the harbor's ferries), who accordingly held down the safety valve to build up extra pressure. The two captains ordered their deckhands to cast off the lines.

An enormous roar split the air. In the center of the *Legislator,* the superheated boiler exploded, disintegrating into a shock wave of scalding steam and metal fragments that shattered decks, windows, wheels, bulkheads, and bodies. In horror, Vanderbilt and his passengers watched splinters of the rival vessel shower the water and the dock amid the screams of the wounded. Four died in the blast: two black men (one a slave), one white man, and a boy who worked as a waiter. The new American ethic, to win at all costs, was proving costly.[14]

THE TIME HAD COME to say farewell to the age of the Founders. The Jubilee—the fiftieth anniversary of independence—approached, and the ever forward-moving Americans chose to look backward. "It is a moment that American history has forgotten," writes Andrew Burstein, "a moment when two critical generations reaffirmed their connection." It was a moment of tribute to the last few survivors of that founding generation, in a world that had changed radically since 1776, and changed still more with each passing day.

The long good-bye began two years early, with the arrival of Marquis de Lafayette, the French nobleman who had thrown himself into the cause of American independence. At the invitation of President Monroe, he sailed to the United States in 1824, making landfall on Staten Island on Sunday, August 15. The *Nautilus* steamed out to greet him, and he spent his first night in Vice President Tompkins's mansion. The next day Lafayette sailed to Manhattan, where the entire city turned out to welcome him. "It is impossible to describe the majesty of this procession," wrote one of his companions. "The water was covered with vessels of all descriptions, elegantly decorated. . . . At length we could perceive the crowds which everywhere covered the shore." The mayor of New York led squads of troops and public officials in making a formal salute. Lafayette, once the symbol of youthful rebellion, had become the aged emblem of the venerable past to a nation that was joyously sentimental about the Revolution.[15]

Even calculating Cornelius found himself swept up in the enthusiasm over the hero's visit. On September 24, the mariner joined a delegation of New Brunswick's dignitaries that awaited Lafayette's arrival at the bridge into town, along with a crowd of some eight thousand citizens. At length the old soldier appeared, and a battery of artillery fired a sixty-nine-gun salute. Vanderbilt presented a fine carriage pulled by four white horses, and personally drove Lafayette on a parade through the streets.[16]

Curious, this regard for the past: in so many other ways, Vanderbilt disdained the delicacy of cultured men, the sentiment that caramelized in the diaries and letters of the literate. "I love you? dearest—Ay, do I love you—and when I love you not, chaos is come again," Attorney General William Wirt wrote to his wife, in a typical note of the era. Vanderbilt would sooner start writing in Russian than write such things. He was the most commercial creature of a society that was throwing away the traditional social bonds—a self-made man, where the Founders themselves mostly had been old patricians. And yet, his patriotism was sincere, his veneration authentic. His heroes can be identified by the names he gave to his sons:

William Henry (after General William Henry Harrison, hero of the War of 1812), George Washington—and Cornelius.[17]

As Vanderbilt rose, Thomas Gibbons declined. The old Tory who had helped unlock the "radicalism of the American Revolution," in Gordon Wood's phrase—the dueling aristocrat who had overthrown aristocratic privilege—faded in the twilight of his generation. His sense of purpose seemed to evaporate in the heat of victory, and the flood of letters that poured from his pen dwindled. His chronic ailments overcame him, and he moved to the elegant patrician enclave of St. John's Park in New York. Vanderbilt largely ran Gibbons's steamboat enterprise, tracking income and expenses on large spreadsheets, boat by boat, month by month. Tension rippled through their relationship as days, even weeks passed between the captain's visits to his employer. "I used to do some things without his knowledge," Vanderbilt later testified, "and he used to bear me out in them, though sometimes he said he would not do so."[18]

And yet, despite their equally headstrong personalities, the seemingly inevitable conflict between the two never came to pass, thanks in large part to Vanderbilt's admiration for Gibbons. His regard for this impossible old man seemed to run together with his reverence for the Founders, mingling his esteem for the men who had made the nation with that for the former Tory who had helped reshape it.

Often bedridden, Gibbons played no part in the festivities of those years, in the farewell to the old and the heralding of the new. He shriveled as John Quincy Adams, son of John Adams, entered the White House in March 1825, in a literal transition to the Founders' children. He remained out of sight for the eventful week between October 26 and November 4, 1825, the grand celebration of the completion of the Erie Canal, that final gift from the aristocrats who had launched the project back when they still ruled the state. This historic achievement of engineering, cutting through a curtain of mountains, was all the more important for Gibbons's courtroom victory, yet his name was left unsaid throughout the ceremonies. Finally, on the afternoon of May 16, 1826, he wobbled out of his house to the corner of Hudson and Beach streets, where he collapsed and died.

Though the public scarcely noticed, Gibbons's death was also part of the passing of the founding generation. For all his acquisitive, competitive fervor, he was, to the end, an aristocratic, slave-owning Southerner who was obsessed with honor. A little over a month later came the deaths of both Thomas Jefferson and John Adams—on July 4, 1826, the very moment of the Jubilee.[19]

Gibbons's vast estate now passed into the hands of his son, William. But where the whip-wielding Thomas had effortlessly straddled the eighteenth and nineteenth centuries, his son remained somewhat ill at ease in these new times. Given to quarreling with his partners and dimly suspicious of competition, he seemed even more a product of the plantation South than his father.

In many ways, William represented the opposite of generational change—and therein lay a serious problem. When he inherited the *Thistle*, he also inherited its hard-driving captain; but Vanderbilt brusquely dismissed William's business acumen and, even more important, his strength of will. "I do not know that William Gibbons ever started a project which his father did not originate," he later claimed. "When they disagreed, the old man would have his own way." By contrast, Vanderbilt himself often had carried his point with "the old man."

The undertone of sibling rivalry is unmistakable. Cornelius had fondly sent Thomas Gibbons bushels of oysters and other tokens of affection; for the son (who was a year younger than himself) he felt no such admiration. Rough-edged, hard-muscled, and self-made, Vanderbilt couldn't quite bring himself to hate William, but he seemed to suspect that this rich boy lacked the drive, even the mental machinery, to cope with the age of commerce. Was it not Cornelius himself who best resembled Thomas Gibbons, in his energy, his entrepreneurial creativity, his sheer force of personality?[20]

Vanderbilt seemed to be nothing but energy as he burned through the year on the hunt for every possible source of profit. On summer Sundays, when William had the *Thistle* sitting idle, Vanderbilt leased the *Bellona* to take New Yorkers to the Union Garden on Staten Island. He even arranged to sell the manure from Bellona Hall's stables to James Neilson, a self-styled gentleman farmer. Meanwhile he supervised the construction of a new vessel for the Union Line. Christened the *Emerald*, it was a "splendid new steam boat," as it was advertised, and he proudly took command. But not for long.[21]

At half past one o'clock in the morning on November 5, 1826, Vanderbilt awoke in his bed at Bellona Hall to the cries of his crewmen. The *Emerald* had caught fire. He raced out the door to the wharf, where "the vessel was found to be one enormous sheet of flame," the *New York Gazette* reported. The captain sent for help and hurried with his men to set up pumps to hose down the fire. They accomplished nothing. The flames crackled and burned along the length of the boat, eating down to the waterline. Seeing that the cause was hopeless, Vanderbilt ordered the men to cut its lines and set it adrift, lest a sloop at the dock catch fire as well. As the enormous torch floated into the current, he helplessly watched the destruction of much more than his employer's asset. "Capt. Vanderbilt lost considerable property in papers, &c.," the *Gazette* reported, "and every article of clothing."[22]

A shame, to be sure—almost a tragedy, in fact, though no lives were lost. But the press report begs a fistful of questions. *Every* article of clothing? Was he living entirely on the boat? What about Bellona Hall? What about his wife and children? Thomas Gibbons had largely abandoned his family in his self-absorption and his greed; was Vanderbilt doing the same?

FIFTY YEARS LATER, in a courtroom packed with spectators and reporters, in a city home to more than a million, "a gentleman with silvery white hair and iron gray moustache" took the stand, the *New York Times* reported, and testified about Vanderbilt's wife, Sophia. The witness was Daniel B. Allen; he was married to Sophia's second child, Ethelinda, and had heard hours of conversation among the siblings who had lived in Bellona Hall— Phebe (born in 1814), Ethelinda (1817), Eliza (1819), William, or Billy (1821), Emily (1823), and Sophia (1825). Their reverence for their mother knew no bounds. "The fact that Mrs. Vanderbilt had fulfilled the duties of a mother more completely than any woman they had ever known, had been talked over," he testified. "In everything that interested her children she had full control. During a considerable portion of her life she had not only taken care of them, but fed, clothed, and educated them at her own expense, without getting a cent from [Cornelius]."

But what did they know of their father? As the *Emerald* disaster showed, he lived on his boats, starting his runs as early as six in the morning, sometimes even working on Sundays. He spent his leisure hours in the stables with his horses, training them for future races. He did spend enough time at Bellona Hall that his wife was with child for nine months out of every twenty-four through the 1820s and '30s. Baby Sophia was followed by Mary in 1827, Frances in 1828, Cornelius Jeremiah at the end of 1830, George Washington in 1832, Mary Alicia in 1833, Catherine Juliette in 1836 (the year George died), and a second George Washington in 1839. All the children eventually found their father remote, stern, at times antagonistic. As Allen recalled, they later asked each other "what the children would have been, or even [their] father, had it not been for the exertions of [their] mother."[23]

The trial that brought Allen to the stand in 1877 was staged to settle the fate of the Vanderbilt fortune, so his testimony ranged far beyond those early days in New Brunswick. But one more thing he said shed light on the man his father-in-law was back in the 1820s. "The Commodore was determined to have his own way, always, to a greater extent than any man I ever saw," Allen asserted, using a title as yet undreamed of in 1827. "It was his most prominent characteristic." In Bellona Hall, Vanderbilt's busy, harried, and pregnant wife could only have agreed, for she saw that trait expressed in every relationship, public and private.

During these years, the health of Vanderbilt's own father began to decline; he had accumulated a good-sized estate, worth some $40,000, and his will came under discussion whenever the family gathered on Staten Island. Cornelius senior wanted his wife to inherit everything. Cornelius junior, however, insisted on a particular provision: if his mother remarried, the estate would be divided immediately among the children; only if she remained single would she have the property for the duration of her life. "That feature of the will, Mrs. [Sophia] Vanderbilt said, had been a source of great discomfort to the Commodore's mother," Allen reported.[24]

A day would come when Vanderbilt's love for his wife and children would become apparent, suggesting that he had always harbored affection for them out of historical view. In the early hours of his rise, though, his ambition seems most striking, defining both his personal and historical role. Alexis de Tocqueville later would observe that the "respect, attachment, and service" that held men together in aristocratic societies had disappeared in America; now they were bound by "money only."[25] In Vanderbilt's case, that ever-present calculation, and competition, seeped into his own family relations. In place of the duel, the elaborate ritual for protecting the honor that defined a patrician society, he substituted brute force—emotional, and sometimes physical.

On the morning of May 9, 1827, the thirty-two-year-old Captain Vanderbilt started the new Union Line steamboat, the *Swan*, on its morning run; satisfied that the pilot had matters well in hand, he retired to the dining room for breakfast. In his customary chair sat Patrick Rice, whom he knew to be a difficult passenger. Vanderbilt tersely ordered him out. Rice refused. With the swing of a meaty hand, he sent Rice flying. The next morning, court papers dryly report, "without the permission of [Vanderbilt], and without any right to do, [Rice again] took possession of the seat of [Vanderbilt] at the breakfast table." In the hilariously understated legal language of Vanderbilt's account, he "gently laid his hands upon the said plaintiff to remove him." Too gently, it appears, for Rice (possibly drunk) sneaked back into the chair. At that, Vanderbilt curled his fingers into a pair of practiced fists "and did then and there beat, wound, and ill treat him so that his life was greatly despaired of," as Rice complained. The infuriated Vanderbilt dragged the apparently unconscious Rice up to the pilothouse, hurled him onto the floor, and locked him inside. Rice not only lost his ensuing lawsuit, but had to pay damages to the man who had pummeled him.[26]

In the year since Thomas Gibbons's death, Vanderbilt's aggressiveness—

his will to dominate—had grown fierce to the point of danger for those around him. At the same time, William Gibbons seemed to contract. In 1827 he leased to Vanderbilt the ferry rights to Elizabethtown Point (once rented by Aaron Ogden). In early 1828, Vanderbilt launched the first steamboat that was entirely his: the *Citizen*, a speedy 106-foot, 145-ton sidewheeler. With cousin John Vanderbilt and little brother Jacob alternating as captain, the *Citizen* connected Elizabethtown to New York with stops on Staten Island's northern shore. Cornelius also bought shares in the New Brunswick Coal Mining Company (a hint that he was interested in new sources of energy for steamboats), again demonstrating his ease with the complexities of the new economy.[27]

Gibbons, on the other hand, had difficulty adjusting to the world that his father had helped make. He fell into a series of squabbles with the Stevens family of Hoboken, who owned the Union Line boats on the Delaware River. He reacted with exaggerated alarm to the appearance of competing lines. Unlike Vanderbilt, he feared that still-uncommon, still-mysterious form of business organization, the corporation; when rival lines obtained corporate charters from the New Jersey legislature, he protested wildly. It was a "swindle," he complained, that would "check individual enterprise." Gibbons was hardly alone in such suspicions. Indeed, his response reveals how unfamiliar the corporation remained to the American mind in general, even as it shows how unsophisticated he himself was as a businessman.

On July 8, 1828, Gibbons gave in to despair and offered for sale his three vessels (the *Bellona*, the *Thistle*, and the *Swan*). Then he thought better of it—then he gave up again. The final blow was the incorporation of yet another rival company. With that, Gibbons abandoned the field with all the dispatch of Darius in his chariot, fleeing before Alexander's army. "I intend to retire from the employment of steamboats," he wrote on February 6, 1829, "as soon as I can dispose of my boats." Before the end of the month, he had sold his paddlewheelers, rented out his docks, and ended the enterprise that had sealed his family name in history.[28]

So began Vanderbilt's career as an independent steamboat entrepreneur. It was probably a relief. He had never been comfortable working for this younger, less acute man. Vanderbilt leaped into the race that William Gibbons had abandoned, sending the *Citizen* on shilling-a-head runs to New Brunswick. But the stress he now faced was unmistakable. It is not too much to say that Thomas Gibbons had been a second father to him, complete with father-son conflict. No matter how many businesses Vanderbilt had kept going for himself, he had remained within Gibbons's house, which gave him both shelter and a sense of purpose. Now the old man was dead, the house closed up. Vanderbilt would have to find his own

way forward, to use what he had learned from Gibbons to shape his enterprises, to develop his own vision of his future. In his solitary steamboat, he
sailed off to fight the economic war.[29]

ON THE EVENING OF APRIL 24, 1829, the *Citizen* pulled into its berth on
New York's North River shore, at the hour when the glow of the setting
sun reflected in a thousand orange points off the rippling waters. The
deckhands tied up the boat, and the passengers began to debark. Vanderbilt joined them, as did Sophia, and together they walked into the
crowded, dirty streets that ran between the low brick and wooden buildings of lower Manhattan. The Vanderbilts still lived in Bellona Hall, but
had come to spend a Friday night in the city.

Someone bumped against Vanderbilt's side, then disappeared into the
river of people pouring off the dock. Vanderbilt jammed his hand into his
coat pocket. His wallet was missing. He pushed through the crowd, then
sprinted after the man he believed to be the thief. In a moment he tackled
him and held him fast as he searched his coat. The pocketbook contained
"about $200 in money," the press reported, "and certificates for several
thousands in [New] Brunswick Bank stock." None of it appeared in the
man's pockets. Regardless, Vanderbilt hauled him off to High Constable
Jacob Hays.

The high constable must have rubbed his bald head in delight when his
former rival burst into his office. The man Vanderbilt dragged along was
"identified there by Hays as one of the most noted pickpockets in the
country," the *New York Gazette* explained. "Hays says he has passed by the
name of Henry Baptiste Lambert, and he graduated in the Pennsylvania
State Prison. It is probable that he had an accomplice, to whom he handed
Captain V.'s property, as soon as he got out of his reach. The Captain is
positive he is the thief." The now-incarcerated criminal had the perverse
fortune to have picked a rich target—a rapidly rising businessman—who
was also as big and tough as any thug on the waterfront.[30]

The city where his pocket was picked was far from the "overgrown seaport village" that he had moved to from Staten Island during the War of
1812. It swarmed with people, swelled with people, was bulging from
every door and window with people who poured in from the schooners,
steamboats, and ships that clogged the slips. "New York was changing
with disruptive speed," writes historian Allan Horlick. "It was becoming
strange where it had been familiar, and mysterious where it had been predictable." At mid-century, Joseph Scoville looked back to his youth and
recalled a time when an average New Yorker "of no very extended
acquaintance" could point out all the leading merchants, even direct a vis-

itor to their homes.[31] That memory faded rapidly as new faces arrived daily to rent apartments, find work, or start businesses.

The most popular story of the day, Joyce Appleby notes, was *Peter Rugg, the Missing Man*, about a farmer who disappeared before the Revolution, only to reappear in the mid-1820s. "Poh, New York is nothing," Rugg scoffs to his contemporary guide. "No, sir, New York I assure you is but a sorry affair, no more to be compared to Boston than a wigwam to a palace." Then Rugg wanders down Broadway, and he cannot believe his eyes. "There is no such place as this in North America," he stammers. "Here is seemingly a great city, magnificent houses, shops and goods, men and women innumerable, and as busy as real life, all sprung up in one night from the wilderness."[32]

It virtually had. In 1790, Manhattan's population had barely topped 33,000; in 1820, it reached 123,700; by 1830, it would pass 202,500. In just another five years, seventy thousand more people would cram into the city, pushing the population density to more than 25,000 per square mile. New York, then, remained tightly packed, but it was obviously expanding geographically as well. In 1811, the city extended only to Houston Street; by 1828, Broadway reached Tenth Street, and work began on Fourteenth Street from river to river. "Here the earnest merchant steps," observed Anne Royall in the mid-1820s, "there the gay cook and merry chambermaid, with some scores of honest tars, hucksters, rude boys, and chimney sweeps, with the rolling coaches, the rattling carts, may give some idea of this life-inspired city." As with every visitor, she reserved most of her astonishment for the island's watery edges, where the city met the world:

> But all that is only a drop in the bucket compared to that on the wharves or slips (as they are called here), the warehouses, docks, ship-yards, and auction stores, which occupy South, Front, and Water streets, pouring a flood of human beings. Here the sound of axes, saws, and hammers, from a thousand hands; there the ringing of the blacksmith's anvil; hard by the jolly tar with his heavo; the whole city surrounded by masts; the Hudson, East river, and the bay covered with vessels, some going out and some coming in, to say nothing of the steam-boats; in short, imagine upwards of an hundred thousand people, all engaged in business; add to these some thousand strangers which swarm in the streets and public houses; such is New-York.[33]

They were coming not so much from the impoverished districts of Europe (not yet, at least) as the fields and towns of the United States itself, especially New England and rural New York State. And that, to some small degree, was Vanderbilt's doing, for he had stood on the barricades of the transportation revolution and commercial expansion that were transforming American life. The northeastern states felt the effects first, due to both their access to tidewater and their proximity to capital-rich merchants of the seaports, who bought produce from farmers, sold them goods, and built the first cotton and woolen mills in their villages. Semi-subsistence farming disappeared; country folk left home as never before, looking for opportunities or simply some kind of cash income. Between 1820 and 1850, the percentage of the U.S. population living in towns and cities rose from 7 to 18 percent, and the absolute numbers increased five-fold. Uprooting oneself to find one's fortune became a new way of life; one Bostonian described his move to New York in 1833 as the product of "the general principle of Yankee roam-all-over-the-worlditiveness."

Now all depended on the marketplace, which linked together once-isolated communities. "Ten years ago we had *nothing*," exclaimed the *Catskill Recorder* in 1828, "now we have *everything*." In 1826, the *New York Evening Post* announced—in the same issue that marked Thomas Gibbons's death—the first shipment of Michigan pork through the Erie Canal. With such humble items new eras are made.[34]

Newly mobile, self-interested, unbound by the old culture of deference, this emerging nation of strangers gave rise to an aggressive spirit of enterprise. They called it "go-ahead." It became a New York catchphrase, for this business-minded city began to overflow with the chosen people of go-ahead, the New England Yankees. From farmboys to clerks to merchants, they invaded Manhattan and made it the capital of "the universal Yankee nation," as P. T. Barnum called it.

Fiercely calculating, afloat in a sea of drifting people who knew nothing of each other's character, the Yankees of New York and New England crafted new values to suit the age of the marketplace. To outsiders— English aristocrats, for example—they seemed to be "uncouth and curious rustics," one historian writes, "whose energies were exclusively given over to the pursuit of the main chance." In the course of two years in America, Frances Trollope learned the Yankee character well, and concluded that they cherished no attribute more highly than sharp dealing, better known as being "smart."

"I like them extremely well," she wrote of Yankees, "but I would not wish to have any business transactions with them, if I could avoid it, lest, to use their own phrase, 'they should be too smart for me.'" On her first visit to New York in the late 1820s, she "neglected" to strike a deal with a carriage driver before the ride, and was forced to pay an exorbitant sum. "When I referred to the waiter of the hotel, he asked if I had made a bargain. 'No.' 'Then I expect' (with the usual look of triumph) 'that the Yankee has been too smart for you.'" Americans from other regions, she wrote, described them "as sly, grinding, selfish, and tricking. The Yankees . . . will avow these qualities themselves with a complacent smile, and boast that no people on earth can match them at over-reaching in a bargain." It was a curious kind of vanity, she observed; if you listened to a Yankee describe himself, "you might fancy him a god—though a tricky one."[35]

Cornelius Vanderbilt needed every ounce of shrewdness in the enterprise he now embarked on. In May 1829, he sealed an arrangement with some stagecoach men and Captain Wilmon Whilldin on the Delaware to form the Dispatch Line, providing through service between New York and Philadelphia via New Brunswick and Trenton. The gatekeeper on the turnpike tracked the line's rising tolls as the *Citizen* carried ever more passengers: $19.30 in May, $73.75 in June, $126.22 in July, $157 in August. Vanderbilt stretched his resources to the limit to purchase more steamboats: his old favorite, the *Bellona;* the rebuilt *Emerald* (which he sent around Cape May to run on the Delaware); and the *Baltimore* and the *John Marshall* in early 1830. Now the master of a mostly secondhand fleet, with his brother Jacob and cousin John as captains, Vanderbilt carried the battle to the competition—who were none other than the new owners of the Union Line. A rate war broke out; the fare to Philadelphia plunged to a dollar, including free meals on board.[36]

Then, at the start of the 1831 season, the Dispatch Line would take a startling turn.

NOTHING ENTIRELY DISAPPEARS in history. The threads of tattered old fabric—especially social fabric—are ever woven into new tapestries. While Vanderbilt wrestled with his pickpocket in New York, his competitors plotted in their gardens to remake the culture of deference—or, at least, to maintain some sort of continuity, to impose some kind of order on the chaos of the marketplace.

Their gardens could be reached from New York only by boat, a special steam ferry that carried world-weary city folk across the Hudson to enjoy their splendor. Indeed, the name of this resort became a synonym for tranquil beauty: *Hoboken.* All 564 acres of the place belonged to Colonel John Stevens, who with his sons had long been Vanderbilt's allies, and now were his rivals.

The Stevenses were what the Livingstons might have been—patricians who successfully made the transition to this more individualistic, commercial, and ruthless age. Colonel Stevens, in fact, was the late Chancellor Livingston's brother-in-law. Like the chancellor, he dabbled in the sciences; and like the chancellor, he dabbled with little real ability, though he freely appropriated the inventions of those who worked for him. The Livingstons' monopoly had forced him to send his first steamboat to the

Delaware; his sons (John, Robert, Edwin, and James) soon dominated that river with more and better boats, and collaborated with Gibbons on the Union Line.

The sons inherited the colonel's technological interests, but with actual mechanical talent. Robert L. (for Livingston) Stevens proved to be one of the great engineers of the day, repeatedly improving steamboat design. The brothers mastered business competition as well, in sharp contrast to the Livingstons, whose North River Steamboat Company failed in 1826—whereupon the Stevenses immediately began to run their own boats from New York to Albany. In New Jersey, they took over the Union Line from William Gibbons, purchasing the *Thistle* and the *Swan*. In 1829 they drove the Citizen's Line into extinction. They intended to do the same to Vanderbilt's upstart Dispatch Line.[37]

Their strategy involved far more than free meals and discounted fares: they intended to make the stagecoach obsolete. As far back as 1812, the colonel had published a pamphlet proposing that a steam engine be put on wheels and pull a train of carriages on a road of rails. By the late 1820s, the "rail road" had become reality on such lines as New York's Mohawk & Hudson. The Stevenses reasoned that it was the perfect replacement for the bone-rattling stagecoach ride across New Jersey's turnpikes, and so they collected investors to build one. And, along with capital, they sought something the chancellor would have approved of: a legal monopoly.

This was not the eighteenth century, however, and this would not be a copy of the Livingston monopoly. For one thing, the family worked through a corporation chartered by the state legislature—the Camden & Amboy Railroad—with publicly traded shares. For another, the Stevenses faced fierce opposition from other interests, including the organizers of the Delaware & Raritan Canal, led by Robert F. Stockton, a wellborn navy lieutenant who was a swashbuckler at sea and in business alike. Stockton maneuvered the Stevenses into merging their well-financed railroad with his undercapitalized canal on February 15, 1831, creating the "Joint Companies," as the enterprise was known. The immense size of this new entity gave it the leverage to extract a remarkable bounty from the legislature: "That it shall not be lawful . . . to construct any other railroad or railroads in this State, without the consent of said companies." By signing over such a valuable piece of its sovereignty to a consortium of wealthy men, New Jersey earned the snide nickname "the Camden & Amboy State." The price for its virtue was an annual fee of $30,000 and a limit of $3 on the through fare (three times what Vanderbilt charged). The Stevenses had finally brought order out of the anarchy of competition—or *bought* order, to be precise.[38]

At just about this time the Dispatch Line disappeared. The standing

Tough, shrewd, and frugal, Phebe Vanderbilt strongly influenced her son Cornelius, who revered her. Of English descent, she married into an old Dutch family on Staten Island. Her husband ran a small farm and a sailboat ferry to Manhattan; she earned her own money, which she lent out at commercial rates of interest. *Collection of the New-York Historical Society*

The Staten Island of Vanderbilt's youth was a rural landscape at the mouth of busy New York Harbor. This 1833 view from the Narrows captures both the shipping and the undeveloped hillsides behind the Quarantine, the state hospital for immigrants. Young Vanderbilt ran a sailboat ferry like the one shown here. *Library of Congress*

Hardworking, modest, beloved by her offspring, Sophia Johnson Vanderbilt was Cornelius's first wife and cousin. Their early years
together weren't always easy, yet their intimacy grew over time, as they traveled together
and grappled with family turmoil. *Biltmore Estate*

New York Harbor, as seen in 1830 from the Battery, the promenade at the southern tip
of Manhattan. Staten Island lies directly across the bay; to the right is the curved bat-
tlement of Castle Clinton, just offshore, later enclosed by landfill. The abundant shipping and display of fashion depicted here drew much comment from visitors. *Collection
of the New-York Historical Society*

The open-air Fly Market, shown here in 1816, represented the sphere that Sophia Vanderbilt occupied after the young couple moved to New York during the War of 1812. As seen here, women both sold and purchased goods amid the densely built-up city, where packs of pigs and dogs roamed freely. *Collection of the New-York Historical Society*

Young Vanderbilt inhabited the lower social and economic tiers of a world captured in Francis Guy's 1820 painting of the corner of Wall and Water streets. To the right, the ships can be seen moored along South Street. On the left, with flag, is the Tontine Coffee House, the city's first financial market. *Collection of the New-York Historical Society*

An aristocratic Southern planter who settled in Elizabethtown, New Jersey, Thomas Gibbons was Vanderbilt's mentor and only employer. He turned a personal dispute into an attack on the Livingston family's monopoly on steamboats in New York waters. That culminated in *Gibbons v. Ogden*, the U.S. Supreme Court's first commerce-clause case and a legal landmark to this day. *Drew University*

Legal complications stemming from the battle against the steamboat monopoly led Vanderbilt to move his family to New Brunswick, New Jersey, the southern end of the ferry line he operated for Gibbons. His wife Sophia managed an inn in their home, dubbed Bellona Hall, through the 1820s. She used the proceeds to feed, clothe, and educate the children, without her husband's aid. *Library of Congress*

Vanderbilt emerged as one of the leading maritime architects of the paddlewheel era, a distinction perhaps first earned in 1835 with the revolutionary *Lexington*. Faster and more fuel-efficient than any steamboat afloat, it inaugurated his competition in the combined steamboat-and-railroad routes between New York and New England. On January 13, 1840, cotton bales piled on the deck ignited and started a tragic fire. *Library of Congress*

In the late 1840s, at the height of Vanderbilt's career as a steamboat entrepreneur, New York swelled with immigrants and bustled with commerce as the city became the nation's primary seaport and emporium. Vanderbilt's most famous steamboat, the *Cornelius Vanderbilt*, is seen here behind the rival *Bay State*. *Museum of the City of New York*

One of the earliest daguerreotypes of Cornelius Vanderbilt, made in 1845. At the age of fifty or fifty-one, he now dominated steamboat traffic on Long Island Sound. Within two years of the making of this image, he would engineer his election to the presidency of the Stonington Railroad. *Library of Congress*

Famous as Vanderbilt's enemy in the Erie War of 1868, an epic fight over the Erie Railway, Daniel Drew spent most of his life as Vanderbilt's secret partner. Drew used his experience with street-level finance to become a steamboat entrepreneur, financier, and stock operator. He went bankrupt shortly before Vanderbilt's death. *Library of Congress*

Canal contractor, steamboat entrepreneur, and political manipulator, George Law represented both the business energy and corruption of the antebellum era. For twenty years he loomed as one of Vanderbilt's most notorious enemies. In 1847 Law's steamboat *Oregon* defeated the *Cornelius Vanderbilt* in a famous race on the Hudson, watched by thousands of spectators. *Library of Congress*

William Henry, Vanderbilt's oldest son, was born in 1821. As a young man he went to work in the Wall Street office of Daniel Drew. William suffered an emotional breakdown, and his father sent him and his wife, Maria Kissam, to live in this farmhouse near New Dorp, Staten Island. Vanderbilt took notice as his son built his farm into a successful operation. *Library of Congress*

Nathaniel Jocelyn of New Haven painted this portrait of Vanderbilt in 1846, when the entrepreneur was starting to look for social respectability. That year he moved to Washington Place, in the heart of New York's most aristocratic district. The merchant elite trusted and feared him, but did not yet accept him as a social equal. *National Portrait Gallery, Smithsonian Institution*

No sooner had the thousand or so residents of Yerba Buena renamed their village San Francisco than the gold rush began. This 1848 engraving shows the sleepy town on the eve of the deluge, looking into San Francisco Bay. *Library of Congress*

assumption has always been that the Stevens brothers bribed Vanderbilt. According to an old New Brunswick mariner, "It was said they bought him off here and yonder and made him rich." The payoff was motivated by fear, the man claimed; Vanderbilt "fought 'em so hard that he left here with a reputation that scared people."[39]

If the Stevens brothers did bribe him, then he proved himself a tricky god indeed. He never intended for the Dispatch Line to last. He knew all along that the railroad, when complete, would destroy rivals who depended on stagecoaches. (This threat had weighed heavily on William Gibbons as early as January 1829.) Hardly had he launched his line than he began to plan a full-scale assault on an entirely different route, to the coastal towns of Westchester County and western Connecticut. Charles Hoyt and Curtis Peck currently ran a boat there with little or no opposition, making them vulnerable to an attack by a hardened fighter like Vanderbilt.

He carefully scouted the passage, and spotted a strategic spot for a new landing—an outcropping known as Jay's Rock near the shore of Sawpits, a cluster of lumber mills on the Westchester border with Connecticut (later dubbed Port Chester). On June 8, 1829, when the Dispatch Line had just started, he signed a ten-year lease to the rock with Mary De La Montaigne and Susan Moore, "for all docking privileges . . . ; the said Vanderbilt is to [bear] all the expense of building such wharf or wharves as he may think proper from said rock to the mainland for steam boat purposes." Soon he had a crew of workmen driving in piles and pouring in cartloads of dirt to build a dock to Jay's Rock. He put the *Citizen* and his old *Fanny* on daily runs between New York and Norwalk, Bridgeport, and New Haven with a stop at his Sawpits pier.

In early 1830, with the Dispatch Line's fare war still raging, Vanderbilt began his retreat from New Jersey. He and Sophia packed up Bellona Hall and loaded one of the steamboats with their belongings, their horses, and their children. They debarked in New York and made for a narrow townhouse at 134 Madison Street, near gritty Corlears Hook.[40]

The disappearance of the Dispatch Line, then, should be no mystery, bribe or no bribe. Vanderbilt did retain an interest in New Jersey, however, with his lucrative ferry to Elizabethtown. Nor was his brief fare war his last contact with the Stevens brothers. He would encounter them again—and next time it would end in bloodshed.

"I HEARD AN ENGLISHMAN . . . declare," reported Frances Trollope in 1832, that "in the street, on the road, or in the field, at the theatre, the coffee-house, or at home, he had never overheard Americans conversing without the word DOLLAR being pronounced between them."⁴¹ Who better exemplified this mania for money, this frenzy for calculation, than Vanderbilt? And yet, as he acquired more boats and hired more employees, as he grappled with the growing complexity of his business, he faced the fundamental problems of this new nation of self-serving strangers. How could a man earn a profit in a world where anything could come under attack at any time? How could you know whom to trust?

The anarchy of the new competitive culture naturally prompted a reaction. The Stevenses, by securing a legal monopoly for their railroad, had refashioned some of the tools of the culture of deference to bring order to their world. Vanderbilt drew on far more ancient concepts: family and reputation. As his stature grew, he made a determined effort to polish his image as a man who stayed true to his word. And as his business grew, he spent more and more time thinking about how he could find trustworthy people, and bind them to himself.

On his steamboat trips to Norwalk in 1830, he fell into conversation with an earnest twenty-five-year-old man from Danbury, Connecticut, named Hiram Peck. Peck, Vanderbilt learned, was intensely devout, an eager participant in a wave of religious fervor known as the Second Great Awakening. Being a good Yankee, Peck also intended to make his fortune; for that, he was moving to New York to open a shop. Vanderbilt (himself just thirty-six) gave Peck a temporary home until he found permanent quarters; afterward he frequently invited him to his house for tea or supper. There Peck mingled with Vanderbilt's family and senior employees, such as John Brooks Jr., captain of the *Citizen*.

The robust social scene in New York among such men of go-ahead startled the pious Peck. An oyster dinner hosted by his landlord, for example, featured "wine, some songs, & some stories," he reported to his diary. "I left about 11:00. Some staid much later. I do not enjoy myself well in such places. I prefer solitude with my book or some few included in company which we can be social without indulging in those love songs and dirty stories some of which would be debasing for a beast to express in language." He found Vanderbilt's company more agreeable, but the captain's energy pointed up a contrast with himself. "Called at Mr. V's in the evening with Sister Harriet & husband," he wrote on September 22, 1830. "I often have to regret that I have not more perseverance in doing any kind of business because I almost daily see that a man may attain to almost anything with sufficient application."

Vanderbilt kept his eye on Peck. The young man's earnestness marked him as a useful tool, should an appropriate use present itself. Peck observed him in return as he played father to his children, a role Vanderbilt had long neglected. In the heat of August, Vanderbilt invited the young man to join them on an outing to the shore. "I have been down to the Steam Boat to see Mr. V & his family. . . . It is a very pleasant thing to have a pleasant companion and a little group of lovely offspring," Peck scribbled in his diary. "To be sure there is much trouble with them some-times. But then there is I can well conceive a satisfaction which repays for all four fold and whatever I may argue in favor of a life of celibacy my own feelings do not at all respond to it."[42] The "trouble" with the children was obvious, and Peck had to talk himself into believing that there must be emotional compensation for it all.

Indeed, there must have been some, as the couple had still more chil-dren. In 1830, Sophia returned to Staten Island, pregnant, to lie in with her family, and gave birth to Cornelius Jeremiah. For Vanderbilt, the role of patriarch was hardly at odds with that of the clever businessman. There was, perhaps, no better way to exert control in a city of strangers, a city of tricksters, than through friends and family. As Vanderbilt cast his eyes across the dinner table, he saw more than a pious companion and various relatives—he saw assets.[43]

WAS THERE EVER A PRESIDENT like Andrew Jackson? This lean and predatory Tennessean, with his bristling mane of gray hair, resembled nothing so much as a hungry wolf, a creature of ferocious passion and ter-ritorial instincts, whether defending his inner landscape of honor or the physical boundaries of the United States. The only chief executive to have killed a man in a duel, this former general had defeated the British at New Orleans in 1815, crushed Indian tribes, and essentially conquered Florida. His presidency saw the last conflict with Native Americans in the Old Northwest (the Black Hawk War in 1832) and the forced removal of five Indian nations on the infamous Trail of Tears. A cloud of danger hung about the age of Jackson.

There was also a scent of triumph. When the general took the oath of office in 1829, at the age of sixty-two, he and his followers saw it as a vin-dication. Four years before, he had won the popular vote but been denied the office by maneuvers in the House of Representatives (which decided the election in the absence of an Electoral College majority). His sweep-ing victory in 1828, they thought, rang in what would be hailed as "the era of the common man"—a romantic and partisan title, to be sure, but one that reflected his supporters' fervent beliefs. To them, Jackson's rise epito-mized the rise of the West, the triumph of the millions who had poured across the Appalachians; Jackson represented the victory of an expanded electorate, a rebuke to the old elite. In a famous and telling incident, aver-age folks mobbed the White House for his inaugural reception, spitting tobacco and trampling on the furniture.[44]

To many Americans, the president embodied the energy, mobility, and enterprise that they believed defined their nation. So it makes perfect sense that the name *General Jackson* appeared on the side of the Hudson River steamboat commanded by Jacob Vanderbilt, Cornelius's younger brother. At 175 tons, it was fast and successful on its route between New York and the Westchester town of Peekskill. Jacob, just twenty-four, had bought a half share at the end of 1830 and took over as captain. He would continue to loyally aid Cornelius's enterprises, but he, too, was in business for himself. A broad-faced man with a wide smile, a round nose, and friendly eyes, he made a stark contrast with his brother (though they shared a receding hairline and abundant, cheek-filling sideburns). Jacob seemed to be warm where Cornelius was brusque, collegial as much as commanding. He rapidly became a popular figure in Peekskill.[45]

That changed abruptly at half past three in the afternoon on June 7, 1831. Coming down from Peekskill, the *General Jackson* chuffed across the river to Grassy Point, where the Hudson begins to widen into the expanse of Haverstraw Bay. The pilot guided the vessel to the crowded pier and Jacob jumped ashore to help load the luggage and boxes of merchandise. Then the engine detonated. "Such was the force of the explosion," noted one newspaper, "that the boiler was blown entirely from its place." The hot, expanding gas turned the boiler into a rocket. A wave of steam blasted through the hull as the apparatus roared into the air, then splashed heavily into the space that opened between the boat and the dock. The explosion "shivered to splinters" the bow and upper decks, the press reported. "In about 20 minutes the boat sank, the stern only being visible above the surface of the water."

Shattered pieces of wood, metal fragments, and shreds of clothing showered the water and the dock as some forty passengers screamed in panic or pain. At least nine would die from the scalding shock wave of steam, and two more were sealed in the sunken hull. Jacob was knocked to the ground, miraculously uninjured, with the dead and dying all around him. He then boarded a passing steamboat, the *Albany*, and left the bloody scene for New York. It was a public relations disaster.

"The public mind is painfully aroused to the subject of steamboat explosions," observed the *New York Evening Post*. The urge to "go ahead" as rapidly as possible increasingly strained against the daily fear of a horrible death. "I had never been on board a steamboat before," a New Englander recalled, describing his move to New York around that time. "As I heard the whizzing and puffing of steam, and the splashing of water— 'Heavens!' thought I, 'sposin' the *biler* should *bust*, what in the deuce would become of me?' So I stationed myself at the extreme bow of the boat, as far, I thought, as I could get from the boilers." After disasters, safety barges would proliferate, allowing nervous passengers to ride in a raft towed behind the steamer.

But nothing could quell the fury of the victims and their families. As outrage spread, Jacob defended himself in a letter to the New York newspapers. "I was one half owner of the *General Jackson*," he wrote, "and by her destruction found myself in one moment stripped of my property and ruined in my prospects." He only went to New York to get help, he said. He anchored his defense with one of the best-respected men in the business: his brother Cornelius. The engineer, he wrote, had been "strongly recommended by the owner of the steam boat *Citizen*, whose great experience in steam navigation is well known to the public."[46]

No one knows where Cornelius was at the time of Jacob's narrow escape from death, but it would not be surprising if he was in Huntington, Long Island, where his prize horse Bullcaff ran the races on these cool June days.[47] With his customary hard-eyed calculation, he saw an opportunity in his brother's misfortune, a chance to seize for himself the market that Jacob had lost. The endeavor would open a window on the customs that steamboat entrepreneurs were devising to bring order to the new chaos of the marketplace.

Six days before the *General Jackson* sank, Cornelius had received an influx of capital from his competitors on Long Island Sound, Charles Hoyt and Curtis Peck. The pair had desperately wanted him to go away, and eagerly accepted the deal he offered. On June 1, they agreed to buy the *Citizen*, along with the rights to his Sawpits pier and wharves at Stamford and Catherine Street in New York, for the inflated price of $30,000.

As they closed the deal, a visibly irate Hoyt snapped that he and Peck "were paying [Vanderbilt] a large sum of money for the route." Vanderbilt shook his head, and "distinctly requested . . . Hoyt to understand that all [he] sold them was the steam boat with the leases and docks." It was *understood* that he would not compete against them, he told Hoyt. They needed no formal deal on that score, because it was part of the steamboat man's code of conduct, the unwritten rules that had arisen to regulate competition after *Gibbons v. Ogden*. As Vanderbilt told a court, "In cases of sales of steamboats which are expected to run on a particular route, it is generally understood that the vendor would be considered as acting unfairly were he to oppose the purchaser with steamboats on the same route, except and unless in self defense."[48]

Monopoly on a line was the standard, the assumed state of affairs, and a sale by a competitor confirmed it. If the seller violated the code, the buyer could fairly counterattack against one of the seller's other routes. Vanderbilt made it a point of pride to refuse to make any formal agreement. Tellingly, Curtis Peck, an experienced steamboat man, "did not consider it worth his while to require or exact any stipulation . . . on the subject." Vanderbilt, he believed, would keep his word.

Vanderbilt claimed that he was abandoning "the run between the city of

New York and Norwalk because he considered it a hazardous run and not desirable in itself." There was some truth to this: in April, the *Citizen* had struck a rock off New Rochelle, sank, and had to be raised. But the money came at a critical moment.

With the *General Jackson* sitting on the bottom of the Hudson, Vanderbilt quickly leased the *Flushing* to take its place. Meanwhile he built a new steamboat, the *Cinderella*, to take over the route permanently. It seems he chose the name to charm a public disenchanted with the Vanderbilt family. "A fine little steamboat, of the fairy order, and appropriately ycleped [called] the 'Cinderella' was tried in our waters," the *New York Gazette* reported in September. "She sat buoyantly on the stream, gaily decked out in her best attire, and . . . she is 'swift as the flash.' The new Cinderella is decidedly in the field as a resolute competitor."[49]

By the time the *Cinderella* began to run, she already faced a rival, and a big one: the 207-ton, 134-foot *Water Witch*. Even more dangerous than the boat was the leading spirit behind it. He was a grim-faced man of thirty-four, with dark hair parted on one side, narrow eyes, and such a crimped jaw and sharp cheekbones that it looked as if his collar had compressed the lower half of his head—but then, he did make an art of keeping his mouth shut. His name was Daniel Drew.

A native of landlocked Carmel, New York, Drew had started his working life by driving cattle down to the meat markets of Manhattan. It would later be said—inaccurately—that he invented the "watering" of livestock, the trick of preventing them from drinking on the drive to market, then encouraging them to gorge, once they arrived, to inflate their weight. Incorrect as the attribution was, it speaks to the formidable reputation Drew developed for sharp dealing—which stood in odd juxtaposition with his eventual standing as a devout Methodist in an age of revivalism. Drew was "shrewd, unscrupulous, and very illiterate," Charles F. Adams Jr. would later write, "a strange combination of superstition and faithlessness, of daring and timidity—often good-natured and sometimes generous." Sly, silent, and stoop-shouldered, he seemed to take pleasure in passing down the street unnoticed by the crowd. One man thought that he resembled "a cross between a cartman and a small trader." But if you should catch his eye, "you will observe a sharp, bright glance in it, with a look penetrating and intelligent." As a another writer later remarked, "We have said his intellect was subtle. The word *subtle* does not altogether express it. It should be *vulpine*."[50]

Drew's peculiar character, and his background in cattle, led to his rise as a figure of street-level finance. In 1830, he took over the Upper Bull's Head Tavern, located on Third Avenue at the Two-Mile Stone (according to the street grid plotted in 1811, this was at Twenty-fourth Street, still far

above the settled portion of the city). A large three-story wooden building, the Bull's Head was described by one stagecoach driver as "the common resort for all travellers (and particularly drovers)" on the main route
down Manhattan. Drew became a central figure in the cattle business,
trading promissory notes and lending money, establishing himself as "a
man of sufficient and ample means," in the driver's words.[51] It was natural
enough, then, that an old friend, circus proprietor Heckaliah Bailey,
should approach him in the summer of 1831 to ask him to buy a share in
the *Water Witch*, and to take charge of its affairs on behalf of himself and a
group of Westchester investors who had built it.

Vanderbilt soon realized that he faced a worthy foe in Drew. Inevitably,
a rate war erupted, driving fares down to a shilling—only now, unlike his
war against the Livingstons, the public was against him. "In the midst of
the storm of indignation" over the *General Jackson*, "the very name of Vanderbilt aroused execrations deep and loud all along the North River,"
declared *Harper's Weekly* in an 1859 profile. "The exasperated river towns
and villages . . . would not allow his boat to make fast to their piers. . . .
When he ran to a wharf he could get no hand to take the ropes he threw
ashore to make fast. As to business, it is recorded that more than once his
daily receipts did not exceed $0.12½. When a solitary passenger did take
passage in his boat he hid himself from the public gaze, as though he had
been doing a guilty thing." The *Water Witch*, on the other hand, "was welcomed daily with huzzas and uproar from the thronging crowds at the
landings," according to another 1859 profile—this one of Drew.

Drew, it was later said, often slouched on the dock as the *Cinderella*
steamed up, Vanderbilt looming tall at its bow, confidently riding out the
public's rage. "You have no business in this trade," Vanderbilt told him.
"You don't understand it, and you can't succeed." But Drew understood it
all too well. He didn't need to make a profit; he simply had to make his
opponent suffer to the point that he was willing to make a deal. The same
tactics that Vanderbilt had employed against Hoyt and Peck—to drive
down fares until the established line bought him out of the market—now
worked against him. If he wanted the *Water Witch* to go away, he would
have to purchase it at a hefty premium. And so, in 1832, the people of
Westchester were startled to discover that their champion boat had been
bought by Vanderbilt, who promptly raised the fare again.

It was the beginning of a long and peculiar friendship. For the first time
in Vanderbilt's life, he had been forced to pay for what was already his, and
he couldn't help admiring the man who had done it to him. Over the
course of their lives, these starkly contrasting businessmen would mix
partnership and rivalry in a bewildering dance of mutual respect and self-
interest.[52]

ON MAY 20, DEATH HAUNTED the Vanderbilt family. Three years before, on May 20, 1829, Cornelius's brother-in-law and old partner, Captain John De Forest, had died, leaving his sister Charlotte a widow. Now, on May 20, 1832, Cornelius Vanderbilt senior died, pulling his son back to Staten Island for the Moravian Church funeral, the settlement of the will, and attendance on his bereaved mother.

Death defined not only the date, but the year as well. Rumors began to spread of an epidemic. "Some considerable said about the Cholera," noted Hiram Peck in his diary on July 5. Soon the newspapers began to track the disease's daily harvest—one hundred dead on July 20, 104 on July 21, ninety on July 22—as quarantines and a general panic shut down intercity travel. Then a fever struck Vanderbilt himself in September. Dr. Jared Linsly treated him with quinine, but the "ague," as the doctor called it, forced him to bed repeatedly for three months.[53]

Bankruptcies shadowed Vanderbilt as well—though this was not entirely a bad thing. Like Drew, he lent money to his fellow businessmen, drawing on reserves created by his cash-based steamboat trade; bankruptcies brought him collateral. In September, one debtor handed the keys to a store over to Vanderbilt, who thought of young Hiram Peck. For two years he had cultivated the friendship of this earnest churchgoer; now he had just the right use for him. "I have also today been negotiating with Capt. C. Vanderbilt to take charge of the business assigned to him by Mr. John Coten," Peck wrote in his diary on September 12. "Was at his house at noon and down to the store in the afternoon and at his house in the evening." Three days later he added, "Attended at the store again and came to the conclusion to have the business transacted in my name and Capt. Vanderbilt is to endorse for me. I am to get books and such things as necessary. I have not quite finished bargain about my salary but am to be liberally paid. . . . We commence taking an inventory this afternoon." Ultimately Vanderbilt granted him a salary of a thousand dollars a year, plus $250 if he returned "a good profit."[54]

Peck, then, served as the front man, while Vanderbilt lurked behind as the silent partner. It was hardly an unusual arrangement, but it underscored the uncertainties and suspicions that now ran through every business transaction. On March 29, 1833, for example, Vanderbilt sold his steamboat *Westchester* for $30,000 to John Brooks, former captain of the *Citizen*, and two other men; they put the boat on Vanderbilt's old line to Connecticut. The move outraged Charles Hoyt, who believed that Vanderbilt was using Brooks as a front man. Even Curtis Peck was ready to think the worst of the man whose word had been good enough a year before. The two filed a lawsuit, asking the court to enforce their unwritten understanding that Vanderbilt would not compete against them on this route.

Vanderbilt indignantly denied that he was behind Brooks's move, but it is difficult to know the truth. He proudly imagined himself to be a man who stood by his agreements, but he also possessed a Gibbons-like streak of self-righteousness that looked suspiciously like duplicity to others, when he interpreted agreements in what appeared to be self-serving ways. Was he a force for businesslike order or competitive anarchy? Even his contemporaries struggled to understand him.[55]

Vanderbilt's proud idea of himself soon clashed again with his public image. On June 12, 1833, President Jackson visited New York, sparking what the *Evening Post* called "one of the most striking public ceremonies ever witnessed by the people of this city. . . . The inhabitants of the city seemed to have deserted all the other quarters for the Battery and Broadway." On June 14, he toured northern New Jersey, and returned to New York on the *Cinderella*, commanded by Vanderbilt himself.

It was a striking moment, this convergence of two iron-willed men, one who gave his name to the age and the other who in many ways typified it. But Vanderbilt was merely Jackson's pilot, not his peer. In New Jersey, the president met with the still-famous Aaron Ogden, and most likely with Colonel Stevens and his sons, but he probably had no idea who Vanderbilt was.

Pride is often the door to humiliation. The contrast between the captain's ambitions and his actual status must have scraped his thin skin like sandpaper. Frances Trollope had come away highly impressed by New York's refined, wealthy elite—the "Medici of the Republic," as she called them—but Vanderbilt was not one of them. Though always unpretentious, he sorely wanted respect. On October 30, for example, he entered a four-year-old colt in races at the Union Course in Long Island against horses belonging to the patriarchs of transportation, past, present, and future: William Gibbons, Robert L. Stevens and his brother John, and Robert F. Stockton. It was a symbolic race—and Vanderbilt's horse was disqualified.[56]

If he had been disposed to dwell, he might have stewed gloomily on all that had happened in the previous two years: the death of his father, his defeat by Drew, his humiliation at the racetrack. By temperament and necessity, however, he was given not to reflection, but to movement. The *Legislator* had exploded in his face, and he had gone ahead; his brother had barely survived a steamboat explosion, and he had gone ahead; he himself had narrowly overcome a deadly fever, and he had gone ahead. He saw no point in mulling over dangers when a world of competition demanded that he seize the next opportunity. Like one of his paddlewheelers caught in the currents of Hell Gate, he had to drive forward or be wrecked.

Fortunately for Vanderbilt, whose entire business was transportation, transportation was precisely where the next opportunity appeared. The first rattling, chuffing, clanking trains of steam-drawn railway cars captured the public imagination—and no better example could be found than the Camden & Amboy, the special project of the Stevens family. It set off what one magazine called a "fever," for both the faster travel and the rich profits it promised to bring. "If any doubt existed as to the excitement about railroads," it argued in 1831, "it could have been removed by a view of the crowds thronging for stock to the . . . Camden." With the line now complete, the national press breathlessly reported that it carried passengers thirty-five miles in one hour and forty-six minutes, cutting the passage from New York to Philadelphia to just seven hours and forty-five minutes.[57]

On November 8, 1833, Vanderbilt sailed over to South Amboy to examine it for himself. The locomotive resembled an oversize barrel with a smokestack in front; the engineer and fireman stood on a rear platform with no shelter from the elements. Three passenger carriages trailed behind, linked by heavy chains. Each car looked as if three stagecoaches had been fused together, with three compartments, each of which had a side door, topped by one continuous flat roof for baggage. The whole rested on a leaf spring, set high above the large cast-iron wheels with wooden spokes—two pairs of wheels connected by iron axles. Vanderbilt stepped up into the middle car (the last being reserved for baggage). The engine began to chug, building to twenty-five miles per hour.

For Vanderbilt, as for almost all of the twenty-four passengers in his car, this was an entirely new sensation. The startling speed and relatively smooth ride (compared to stagecoaches) must have thrilled them—the woman from Washington, D.C., who cradled her baby, the minister from Pennsylvania, the gentleman from North Carolina. Just the day before the railroad had broken its own record, cutting the time between New York and Philadelphia to six hours and thirty-five minutes. The countryside slipped past them in a blur as they moved at a rate never known on land before.

Without warning, an axle broke in the lead car. With only two axles per car, the result was catastrophic. The lead car jumped off the tracks; sitting in the one behind it, Vanderbilt saw its roof and walls suddenly spin. His car pitched down the embankment, then tumbled and bounced heavily on its side as the locomotive dragged it farther before the engineer could stop the train.

Vanderbilt found himself at the bottom of the embankment. His clothes had been shredded, and his knees oozed blood where the skin had been torn off. He took a breath, and stopped at the knifing pain where his ribs had pierced his lungs, then suffered even greater agony when he convulsively coughed, blood filling his mouth. His body felt crushed, his back broken. Turning his eyes to the bodies splayed around him, he saw a man's thigh bone jutting through his pants; the woman from Washington, her arm broken, her baby motionless; a man with arms and legs mangled; and the North Carolina fellow, his rib cage driven over his face. The uninjured staggered past—including former president John Quincy Adams, who had been in the lead car.

As Vanderbilt lay at the bottom of the ditch, unable to move, one thought overwhelmed all others: He was going to die.[58]

Chapter Four

NEMESIS

On November 9, 1833, a messenger arrived at the home of Dr. Jared Linsly, a young physician who lived and worked in the four-story forest of buildings that was New York City. There had been an accident; the cars of the Camden & Amboy Railroad had overturned. One of the doctor's patients had been severely injured—a Captain Vanderbilt.[1]

Linsly pulled on his coat, gripped his bag, and rushed to the steamboat pier. The doctor had treated Vanderbilt's intermittent fever the year before, but he did not exactly look forward to seeing this difficult patient again. Linsly thought him "constitutionally irritable" and "dyspeptic." He found Vanderbilt to be an overbearing man under the best of circumstances—as Linsly later put it, "He never would take direction from anyone." And then there was the flatulence. "A great trouble," he would muse, and "apparently constitutional, as others of his family had it."

After crossing the bay, Linsly found his way to the crash site and was directed to a small cottage nearby. There he discovered two other doctors already in attendance. Edging his way to the bed, he saw the familiar leathery face of the thirty-nine-year-old Vanderbilt. His body had been shattered. Linsly noted the injuries as he examined his patient: "External bruises and the ribs badly fractured in the front and back on the right side. The knees were torn and bruised." Then the captain began coughing, an act that clamped him in pain; when somone wiped his mouth, the cloth ran red. "The ribs penetrated the lungs, as I knew by the escape of air under the skin and from his coughing up blood," Linsly explained later. "He suffered very much at that time trying to clear his lungs from the clotted blood."

Then Vanderbilt spoke, calmly, evenly. "Rational," the doctor noted. Rational indeed, from the very moment Vanderbilt had opened his eyes at the bottom of the embankment the day before, with boiling water and steam still spilling out of the overturned locomotive, the cars upended and broken, the people who had sat next to him almost all dead and mangled. Vanderbilt explained to Linsly that he had not wanted to die anonymously, so he had called out to a bystander and told him his name. That simple act of self-assertion had seemed to clear his brain. He noticed the cottage they were now in, and had choked through his mouthful of blood to order the fellow to carry him here. Then he had sent for help.

The thirty-year-old Linsly was just four years out of the College of Physicians and Surgeons, but it occurred to him that he had never seen anyone with such self-possession while in the gnawing jaws of pain. Lying in the mud with shattered bones and a punctured lung, Vanderbilt had organized his own rescue, taking command of those around him as surely as if he were ordering about the crew on the *Cinderella*.

Close encounters with death have a reputation for transforming lives, for starting dramatic new departures. Vanderbilt's near extinction concentrated his existing qualities—his decisiveness, his will to dominate, his ability to rapidly assess a chaotic situation. Indeed, it could be argued that this gruesome accident had nothing to do with the transformation that he would undergo in the next decade, from obscure captain to fearsome commodore, whose name alone would terrify hardened businessmen. But as he lay there impatiently in that cottage over the next four weeks, slowly healing under Linsly's care, the incident took on iconic significance for him. For one thing, Vanderbilt became an ardent admirer of the young doctor. You saved my life, he would often tell him. "If I had died in Jersey in 1833," he would add, decades later, "the world would not have known that I had lived. But I think I have been spared to accomplish a great work that will last and remain."[2]

AS THE CAPTAIN SLEPT IN HIS BED, the general waged war on the monster. Not just any monster—the Monster, as President Andrew Jackson called it. Without a doubt, General Jackson (as everyone called him) saw himself as St. George in arms against the dragon, an infernal, demonic entity that must be destroyed. The Monster, he told Martin Van Buren, "is trying to kill me, but *I will kill it*." This political battle would define not only American politics for the next generation, but also Vanderbilt's new and increasingly public role as a businessman. Coming at the moment of his brush with death, it would prove to be, in many ways, his resurrection.

The Monster, formally known as the Second Bank of the United States (and more commonly as the Bank), originated as the brainchild of Alexander Hamilton. He had desired a counterpart to the famed Bank of England: a federally chartered but privately owned institution to hold the government's funds, extend loans to private merchants, facilitate long-distance transfers of money, regulate the flow of credit from state-chartered banks, and provide a stable national paper currency. Jeffersonians had

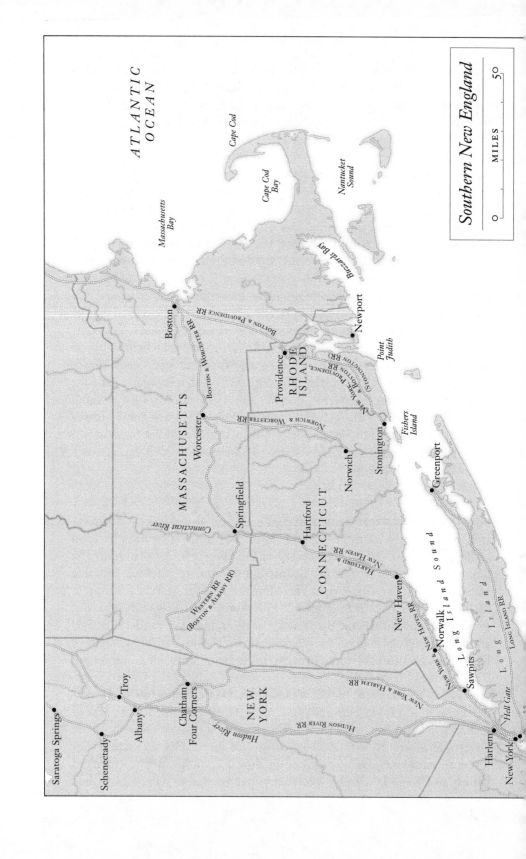

Southern New England

MILES

0   5°

thought a federal bank unconstitutional, and had destroyed the original Bank of the United States in 1811, only to revive it under the fiscal strain of the War of 1812. Jackson despised it. On July 10, 1832, he had vetoed a bill to recharter the Bank, and had run for reelection that year on the promise to permanently eradicate it.[3]

So began the Bank War, the result not merely of Jackson's obsessions, but the cultural crisis of the times. It broke out because two great waves now crashed into one another: the individualistic, anti-aristocratic, competitive impulse fostered by the Revolution, and the instinct to organize, amalgamate, develop, and bring order to the chaos of the marketplace. The first impulse was both radical and traditional, combining a suspicion of the wealthy elite with an outlook shaped by this world of small farms, stores, and workshops, where factories were few and self-employment was the standard. The second was both commercially advanced and highly conservative, as wealthy men both organized banks and corporations and tried to tamp down competition. Neither impulse was hostile to the market economy itself; indeed, out of this conflict would emerge a new American economic outlook, a culture that embraced equality of opportunity and fierce competition, as well as sophisticated business institutions.[4]

But not yet. The Bank War revealed the vast distance still between these two views of the world. When Jackson vetoed the recharter of the Bank, he complained that it "enjoys an exclusive privilege of banking under the authority of the General Government, a monopoly of its favor and support." But it was a very useful monopoly, protested Senator Daniel Webster. "In the absence of a Bank of the United States, the State banks become effectually the regulators of the public currency. Their numbers . . . give them, in that state of things, a power which nothing is competent to control." Where Jackson saw danger in a government-granted monopoly, Webster saw the danger of an unregulated marketplace, the anarchy of unchecked competition.[5]

To the president, Webster missed the entire point. As he wrote to Nicholas Biddle, the Bank's gifted chief, "I do not dislike your Bank more than all banks." Jacksonians condemned banks, and corporations in general, with a particularly damning word: they were "artificial." After all, what did banks do? In the best cases, they accumulated reserves of gold and silver coin, paid in by their shareholders, and made loans by issuing paper money, printed by the bank itself. The notes could be redeemed at the bank for gold and silver, but it was more convenient for people to continue to pay each other with the paper, keeping it in circulation. Even a conservatively run bank would issue notes worth at least three times its holdings in precious metals.

To Jacksonians, this was a fraud: banks were loaning what they did not have. Paper money was a dangerous shell game that only worked as long as everyone agreed not to look for the pea. "Real money," wrote William Gouge in an influential book of 1833, "is a *commodity*." Gold and silver had intrinsic value; no special trust had to be placed in anyone before precious-metal coin was accepted in payment. By contrast, paper money had replaced "the old standard of value" with "the new standard of bank credit," one that was subject to bank failures, to counterfeiting, to deliberate manipulation by greedy corporate officials. By 1833, Americans had already suffered panics in which note holders rushed to a bank all at once, forcing it to suspend specie payments, thus rendering its paper money virtually worthless.[6]

Even worse, banks could only perpetrate this supposed fraud because of their government-granted monopolistic powers. Most states outlawed private banking; to issue paper money, a bank had to obtain a charter from a state legislature—"by certain arts of collusion, bribery, and political management," declared William Leggett, radical editor of the *New York Evening Post*. "It is a matter of utmost notoriety that bank charters are in frequent instances obtained by practises of the most outrageous corruption." And that struck at the heart of the Jacksonian ideal: the equality of opportunity for every individual, and the hatred of any government-favored class (or aristocracy, in the rhetoric of the day), especially men with corporate charters.[7]

"Equality of talents, of education, or of wealth can not be produced by human institutions," Jackson observed in his veto message. "But when the laws undertake to add to these natural and just advantages artificial distinctions . . . the humble members of society . . . have a right to complain of the injustice of their Government." He and his followers accepted natural inequality—even celebrated the rise to wealth through hard work and intelligence—but hated anything that smacked of the *artificial*.

In the Jacksonian mind, the fear of monopoly and aristocracy was intertwined with a deep anxiety over the mysterious abstraction of commercial institutions. Features that were gradually emerging as standard for all corporations—their legal character as artificial persons, immortality, and limited immunity, which protected shareholders from liability for a corporation's acts—they saw as strange and alarming special privileges granted through political favoritism. "All corporations are liable to the objection that whatever powers or privileges are given to them, are so much taken from the government or the people," wrote Leggett. And so government had given rise to a race of man-made monsters, with the Bank merely chief among them. "If a man is unjust, or an extortioner, society is, sooner or later, relieved from the burden, by his death," glowered Gouge. "But corporations never die." The implications were frightful. Since they "live forever," fretted Massachusetts governor Marcus Morton, their property was "holden in perpetual succession"—unlike individuals, whose estates were divided upon death. Eventually corporations would own everything.[8]

This idea rested on the notion that the amount of property was constant (rather than growing in a growing economy), and that only physical things—land, goods, animals—could be property, never shares in corporations. Stock and paper money had no value of their own, Jacksonians believed; they were a conjuration that transferred wealth from real producers to stockjobbers who made nothing (except potentially money). Such a fundamentalist mind-set deeply frustrated the president's opponents, especially the Yankee businessmen who were learning to use the sophisticated devices of commerce. Daniel Webster argued that banknotes *were* money, that the definition of "currency" should include "all that adjusts exchanges and settles balances in the operations of trade and business," from precious metals to bills of exchange. The corporation was a "truly republican institution," declared John Quincy Adams, "of which every class of the community may share in the benefit, proportionate to their means and their resources." Jacksonians saw corporations as the grasping of rich men for special privileges; but one bank president argued that America's "*absence* of large capitalists [had] been remedied by corporate associations, which aggregate the resources of many persons."

This was the birth of a kind of abstract thinking never before required in everyday life. It sparked a fierce resistance. On a daily basis, most Americans rarely interacted with corporations; they still lived in a society of farms, small businesses, and independent proprietors. Jacksonians viewed corporations in much the same way that the evangelists of the Second Great Awakening saw the Masons or popery: as a corrupt conspiracy, a mysterious encrustation on the beautiful simplicity of the true religion. As artificial beings, Gouge intoned, "corporations have neither bodies to be kicked, nor souls to be damned."[9]

Jackson's veto of the Bank recharter marked only the beginning of the Bank War. The Bank still had six years left under its original authorization; its president, Biddle, still hoped to survive. He elected to systematically corrupt Congress by handing out loans and legal fees, and even bribed newspaper editors for friendly articles. Furious, Jackson launched a plan to withdraw the federal government's deposits and place them in friendly state banks, nicknamed the Pet Banks. Biddle retaliated, calling in loans, returning state banknotes for specie, and curtailing new credit. "All the other Banks and all the merchants may break," he growled, "but the Bank of the United States shall not break."

"The subject of the removal of the bank deposits increases daily in interest," wrote a New York merchant on January 11, 1834. "Nobody talks or thinks of anything else." Nobody, of course, but Vanderbilt, lying broken in that Jersey cottage, spitting up blood within earshot of the trains of the Camden & Amboy. They were weeks of torment for the country and himself. As merchants and brokers along Wall Street pushed back their top hats and worried aloud, he had himself carried up to the railroad tracks, then placed in a special horse-drawn car he had ordered. Each rattle along the rails must have been agony, but it was better than one of the famously uncomfortable carriages that bounced down the turn-pike. At South Amboy his crewmen lifted him out and placed him in one of his steamboats for the return to New York.

There the city's businessmen fretted over their own casualties. One of those worriers was Philip Hone, a former mayor of New York, a wealthy merchant, and a member of the old Anglo-Dutch elite. His life would repeatedly intersect Vanderbilt's, despite their sharply contrasting social backgrounds. Most nights he sat at his desk and wrote in his diary in a tidy cursive script, recording the events of the day in eloquent, highly opinion-ated prose that makes him an ideal witness to Vanderbilt's world. "Wall Street was thrown into consternation this morning by the failure of John G. Warren & Son," Hone wrote on January 31. Like most of the city's conservative merchants, he blamed the president, not Biddle. "If Gen. Jackson had visited Wall Street this morning, he might have been regaled with a sight similar to that of the field of battle at New Orleans. His killed and wounded were to be seen in every direction, and men enquiring with anxious solicitude, 'Who is to fall next?' "[10]

The Bank War spun American politics in a centrifuge, concentrating the two impulses of the day into distinct parties. On one side were Jack-son's followers, the Democratic Party—or the Democracy, as they called it—the party of individual equality and limited government. Under the slogan "Jackson, Commerce, and Our Country," they celebrated a market economy of real persons and republican simplicity. In opposition arose the Whigs, who were more trusting in the beneficial role of active govern-ment. At the time, the division between the two seemed as natural as a canyon. The Democrats had emerged out of the resistance to the eighteenth-century patricians and their culture of deference, out of battles against the limited franchise, aristocratic privileges, and mercantilist monopolies. Though their elected leaders often would make use of the government's economic power, the most radical among them—especially New York's "Locofoco" faction (nicknamed after the brand of matches they used when their rivals at a tumultuous party meeting doused the lights)—championed laissez-faire as their definition of equal rights. The Whigs (such as Hone) inherited some of the ordering, top-down outlook of the old elite, and a deeply moral vision of the role of the state. They believed that measures to assist the most enterprising, such as corporate charters or public works, would grace everyone; as historian Amy Bridges writes, they believed "the state should guide interdependent interests to a common good." As development-minded modernizers in a young and growing country, they saw competition as a destructive force that punished entrepreneurship.[11]

For months the nation endured the crisis, as Biddle squeezed, bankers and merchants gasped, and Jackson grimly held to his plan for removing federal deposits. Vanderbilt followed the war through the newspapers in his bed at 134 Madison Street, confined under Dr. Linsly's orders and the necessities of pain. Meanwhile Whig congressmen came to the painful conclusion that Biddle had gone too far. His retaliation against Jackson seemed to have proved the president's argument that the Bank threatened democracy.

As spring wrestled loose from the grip of winter, scooping the ice from the harbor's waters and snow out of the streets, Americans realized that they had survived the Bank War. Biddle was beaten; in the end, he was forced to obtain a state charter from Pennsylvania for the Philadelphia-based Bank. And, by the end of 1834, Americans would discover that the prospering, dyspeptic, overbearing Vanderbilt had become a champion of the radical Jacksonian creed.[12]

IN THE SUMMER OF 1834, not many weeks had passed since Vanderbilt had first emerged from his house on Madison Street, his skin pale from lack of sunlight, his legs shaky from lack of use. It had been a difficult winter. He was a man who charged ahead by instinct, by calculation, by the metaphor of the time; instead he had been confined to a single room until the onset of spring, struggling to simply hold steady as he managed his boats from his sickbed. He had ordered the new *Union*, for example, to be put on his lower Hudson River line, but Heyward, its captain (a "blockhead" or "blatherskite" or worse in Vanderbilt's extensive vocabulary of abuse), had allowed a shipment of thirty-eight crates of cotton prints to get so wet that the colors ran. Now Vanderbilt faced a lawsuit that would eventually cost him $5,000, plus $360 in court costs. At least his reliable brother Jacob had managed the *Water Witch* well on its route to Hartford.[13]

Now there was this *Westchester* business. Three men confronted Vanderbilt in his office, angrily reminding him that, on March 15, 1834, the boat, which he had sold the year before, had started to run between New York and Albany at a fare of $2 per person. The men believed, as Hoyt and

Peck had previously, that Vanderbilt was the real owner of the *Westchester*, and it infuriated them. They had taken pains to put the fare up to $3 on their own Albany-bound boats, and were grimly determined to do whatever was necessary to keep it there.

When Vanderbilt later discussed this meeting in the press, he neglected to mention the names of his visitors. No matter—the public would not have recognized them. They were all-but-anonymous members of the Hudson River Steamboat Association, an organization of businessmen who maintained a monopoly on traffic between New York and Albany. The most famous among them, Robert L. Stevens, had sold out to the rest in 1832. They had paid Stevens the enormous sum of $80,000 for his boat, the *North America*, but the physical vessel was only one part of the purchase. They also had bought his agreement to not run any boat on the Hudson for ten years.[14]

The stiff price—probably double the original construction cost— showed how difficult it was to maintain a monopoly on the Hudson, and how lucrative that monopoly proved to be. After the opening of the Erie Canal, traffic had boomed between Albany and New York, thanks to the passengers and freight coming from the West and the fast-growing towns along the Hudson and the canal. More and more entrepreneurs jumped in to meet this demand, forcing the monopoly to either buy them off or include them. By 1834, it had swollen to an overstretched alliance of three steamboat companies: the Hudson River, the North River, and the Troy.

This confrontation, Vanderbilt recognized, was a dangerous moment. In this age of the cunning Yankee, of strangers and professional thieves, suspicion reigned; no one knew how far to trust appearances. He insisted (quite truthfully) that he no longer had anything to do with the *Westchester*. "As further evidence of my unwillingness to appear as if joining in or promoting an opposition to the combined companies," he explained shortly afterward, "I [had] refused a liberal offer for a charter of my steamboat *Union*, to run as an opposition boat between New York and Albany, and this I did for the purpose of keeping myself entirely aloof from all contest and competition." The monopoly men didn't believe him. The question was settled: it would be war.[15]

The problem was, it was war by proxy. A competitor soon appeared on Vanderbilt's lower Hudson route—his old *Citizen*, captained by Curtis Peck, steaming to Sing Sing at what Vanderbilt called "the paltry and pitiful price of 12½ cents." Like his enemies, he saw a hidden hand at work— their hand. "It may be said that the *Citizen* does not belong to the combined companies," he announced in the press. "To that I answer—she has been started in opposition to me at their suggestion, and is running under their sanction, protection, and patronage, and therefore the act is theirs." The language was a bit too orderly to have come straight from his mouth, but the ferocity was pure Vanderbilt.

His language was also pure radicalism. It appeared on the front page of the *New York Evening Post*, in an announcement of his retaliation against the monopoly.

TO THE PUBLIC.—Having established a line of Steamboats on the North River, for the conveyance of passengers between New York and Albany, called the *People's Line*, in opposition to the *great triangular monopoly* composed of the North River Steamboat company, the Hudson River Steamboat company, and the Troy Steamboat company, I deem it proper to say a few words by way of appeal to a generous public, which, I feel persuaded, will sustain a single individual in an attempt to resist the overbearing encroachments of a *gigantic combination*. Competition in all things promotes the public convenience; and although the step I have taken may prove advantageous to the public, yet to me it may be far otherwise.[16]

The brilliance of this appeal could be heard in its echo of the *Evening Post*'s radical brand of Jacksonianism, as advocated by editor William Leggett. Two days before, Leggett had attacked corporations for "combining larger amounts of capital than unincorporated individuals can bring into competition." He had called for laissez-faire to allow individuals to defeat "the grasping, monopolizing spirit of rapacious capitalists," as expressed in corporate charters. "Even now, how completely we are monopoly-governed!" he had written. "How completely we are hemmed in on every side, how we are cabined, cribb'd, confined, by exclusive privileges!"

Vanderbilt's declaration mimicked this rhetoric, which celebrated commerce and entrepreneurship but blasted corporations. He went on to explain how the monopoly had instigated the *Citizen*'s run against him, and concluded:

Thus, fellow citizens, has this aristocratic monopoly, secure as they think themselves in wealth and power, wantonly attacked an individual whose constant endeavor has been to avoid a contest with them. The gauntlet has been thrown by them, and not by me; and the question now is, will the public countenance the combined companies in an act of overbearing oppression, or will they patronize and encourage one who is determined to resist aggression and injustice, although the odds is vastly against him. The North River is the great highway of the people, and does not belong exclusively to the Monopolists.[17]

Leggett himself could not have written a more vehemently Jacksonian statement.

A more deliberately manipulative man probably would have been more careful in his argument. Vanderbilt praised the benefits of competition, for example, then wrote that he was challenging the Hudson River association only after trying to *avoid* "all contest and competition." He attacked his enemies for being monopolists, but his outrage stemmed from their attack on *his* monopoly between New York and Peekskill. This inconsistency speaks of inflamed self-righteousness as much as cold cunning. He was undoubtedly opportunistic, and there is no evidence he was a Democrat (or a Whig, for that matter). But the political debate over monopolies and corporations went to the heart of his existence, leaving a deep impression that he believed his rhetoric: he was the people's rebel, a challenger of the mighty.

And the people loved it—the drama, the slap in the face of the monopoly, and, especially, the low prices. Vanderbilt put the *Nimrod* and the *Champion* on the line to Albany for a $1 fare. "Our river-boats are long, shallow, and graceful," wrote one passenger, "and painted as brilliantly and fantastically as an Indian shell. With her bow just leaning up from the surface of the stream, her cut-water throwing off a curved and transparent sheet from either side, her white awnings, her magical speed, and the gay spectacle of a thousand well-dressed people on her open decks, I know of nothing prettier." Serving fine food and abundant alcohol, these incessantly churning sidewheelers traveled a river renowned for beauty, slipping between the wooded bluffs of upper Manhattan and the stunning cliffs of the New Jersey Palisades. On reaching West Point, the same writer found it almost impossible "to give an idea of the sudden darkening of the Hudson, and the underground effect of the sharp, overhanging mountains as you sweep first into the Highlands."[18]

Vanderbilt's mind was not on beauty, but the pain he inflicted on his opponents. Even a fare of $1—half that charged by the *Westchester,* the ostensible cause of this war—did not strike him as ruthless enough. Within days, he reduced it to fifty cents. Meanwhile he ordered his captains to beat the monopoly's boats at all costs.

Philip Hone witnessed the resulting struggle on the Hudson. "We left Albany at ½ past 6 this morning in the Steam Boat *Champlain*," he wrote in his diary on September 14. "There is a violent opposition between two lines of boats." He meant *violent* literally. The rival crews hated each other, and public opinion was inflamed. "We were contending with the *Nimrod* all the way down, and for five or six miles before we reached Hyde Park Landing, the boats were in contact, both pushing furiously at the top of their speed. And we and our trunks were pitched ashore like bundles of hay. The people at the landing being all in favour of the opposition . . . nobody would take a line, and we might have drowned without an arm being reached to save us."

Hone was a commercially savvy merchant, yet he loathed such cut-throat competition, even when he had no personal interests at stake. Two days later, he took Vanderbilt's *Champion* to New York; the experience caused his social prejudices to rise up in his throat like bile. "Our boat had three or four hundred passengers, and such a set of rag-tag & bobtail I never saw on board a North River Steam Boat—the effect of the 50 cent system," he sniffed into his diary. "If the people do not rise in their might and put a stop to the racing & opposition it will be better to return to the primitive mode of travelling in Albany sloops."

If the people do not rise? Against what—cheap travel? Hone saw firsthand the popularity of Vanderbilt's fierce competition, but he did not believe his own eyes. Indeed, his visceral distaste illuminates America's social and political divisions. The Democrats derided Hone and his fellow Whigs as "aristocrats," and not entirely without cause. Though political and economic institutions no longer depended upon distinctions in social rank, New York's old patrician families had carried on into this more competitive, egalitarian era, carrying their wealth and prejudices with them. Their elitism blended with the Whig faith in an entreprenurial but orderly economy. Hone's disgust at being forced to mingle with his social inferiors was inseparable from his disaste for competitive anarchy. After complaining of the "rag-tag and bobtail," he added, "I would rather consume three or four days in the voyage than be made to fly in fear and trembling, subject to every sort of discomfort, with my life at the mercy of a set of fellows whose only object is to drive their competitors off the river."[19]

Vanderbilt pressed the war into November. He added the *Union* to the line. He offered overnight service. He ran ads in Albany newspapers headlined "PEOPLE'S LINE.—FOR NEW-YORK.—NO MONOPOLY." He battled on until fingertips of ice began to poke down the Hudson, until finally the freeze clasped its hands shut over the river.[20]

In the spring, steamboats began to churn again to Albany—and again charged $3 per person. The war was over; Vanderbilt had withdrawn. The public, which had cheered Vanderbilt's boats at every dock and landing, must have been mystified. Where had he gone? The answer would not come for another five years, when a careful investigation by the *New York Herald* revealed that Vanderbilt had fought not for a principle, but for revenge. On those terms, he had won a resounding victory. He had forced the "odious monopoly," as the *Herald* called it, to call Peck off the Sing Sing route and to pay Vanderbilt the astronomical fee of $100,000 to leave the line to Albany, plus an annual payment of $5,000 to stay away.[21]

It was becoming a pattern with him. In the emerging code of conduct for steamboat men, the first proprietor to occupy a line assumed a sort of natural right to the route. A challenger who lasted long enough could expect an offer of a bribe to abandon the market and, should he accept it, would be expected to abstain from further competition. Vanderbilt had now repeatedly preyed on existing lines—to New Brunswick, to western Long Island Sound, and now to Albany—and each time had taken money to stay away. Like his late mentor Thomas Gibbons, he often acted out of a sense of self-righteous outrage, but always in ways that suited his material interests. To say that his Jacksonian rhetoric was deliberately deceitful is, perhaps, to suggest that he was more self-aware than he actually was. He made himself his first and last cause, but never the subject of study.

The public, however, had no inkling of who Vanderbilt was as a man, or why he had left the Albany line. The people looked for his next fare-cutting offensive as he unerringly hunted out the next great channel of commerce. To them, he was not a self-serving capitalist, but a lone proprietor, an avenging entrepreneur, the monopolists' nemesis.

VANDERBILT PRESENTED THE MODEL to Joseph Bishop and Charles Simonson in their office down by Corlears Hook. The two men were among New York's most experienced shipbuilders, but—as Bishop remarked as he pored over the model—they had never seen a design quite like it. On this winter day of early 1835, Vanderbilt could boast of seventeen years in the steamboat business. He had built or owned perhaps fifteen paddlewheelers, and had worked closely with almost every steamboat man but Fulton himself. All his experience had led him to this new departure—the first of "an entirely new class of steam vessels," as one expert would declare.[22]

"Make her as strong as possible," Vanderbilt ordered. Bishop and Simonson could only nod; it would have to be very strong indeed. The captain wanted the twin paddlewheels enlarged dramatically from any previous design, to twenty-four feet in diameter. To drive them, he would have a new engine constructed, more powerful than any ever put into a steamboat. The piston in the North America, Robert L. Stevens's famous "rather-faster-than-lightning steamer," pulsed at a rate of 384 feet per minute; Vanderbilt envisioned one that would pound away at six hundred feet per minute. He foresaw a single engine that could do the work of two, saving as much as 50 percent on fuel while driving the wheels around at twenty-three revolutions per minute.

"Her shape was very peculiar," Vanderbilt later remarked. The hull was unusually long and narrow—205 feet from stem to stern post, with a beam of only twenty-two feet, less than the diameter of her wheels (though the guards outside the wheels extended her deck to forty-six feet). She was literally built for speed. The problem was that such a narrow, extended hull would "hog," or bend in the middle. To correct it, he called for an arched deck, "built on the plan of [a] patent for bridges," as he explained his inspiration, to shift the pressure to the ends of the deck planks.

Bishop and Simonson agreed to build it. "There was no written contract, no price agreed upon beforehand," Bishop recalled. Simonson was Vanderbilt's brother-in-law, and the three trusted one another implicitly. In the days that followed, as Bishop erected the gallows frame in their shipyard, Vanderbilt decided on a name: the *Lexington*, after the place where the Revolution began.[23]

He ordered the *Lexington* for a very simple reason: cotton. As the 1830s rushed past, cotton powered the American economy forward. Demand from British textile mills had already caused a westward-moving land rush across the South by cotton planters, dramatically expanding slavery into new territories. Slave-owning Americans had even settled the Mexican province of Texas. "Funds from the Northeast and England financed the transfer of slaves, purchase of land, and working capital during the period of clearing the land," writes economic historian Douglass C. North. Once cultivated, harvested, and pressed into bales, the cotton enriched not only the planters, but also the merchants, shippers, and financiers of New York. Much of it was transshipped to Britain through Manhattan; even after most of it came to be exported directly from the South, it was in New York–based ships that would return to Manhattan with cargoes of British goods. Then there were loans, commissions, and insurance charges, until one committee of Southern legislators concluded that one-third of each dollar paid for cotton went to New York—a percentage that continued to rise.[24]

But not all of it crossed the Atlantic. Every year, ever more thousands of dirty white bales were unloaded on New York's slips, then reloaded onto vessels bound for New England. That cotton fed the first real factories in the United States, the waterwheel mills that increasingly crowded the rivers and streams of Massachusetts, Rhode Island, and Connecticut, in a great arc centered on Boston. New York took back much of the finished fabric, to be made into clothing in the city's workshops and distributed by the city's merchants. By the time the *Lexington* took shape in its shipyard, New York had emerged as capital of the commercial revolution, Boston as capital of the industrial. Businessmen, craftsmen, and messengers, cargoes of cotton and kegs of gold, all passed between them in rising numbers. It was the aorta of the American economy.[25]

The question of transportation between the two cities attracted the attention of the nation's greatest minds and richest men. In 1830, those rich men organized corporations to construct railroads radiating out of Boston. If ever corporations were necessary, it was now, for railways were far more costly and far more complex than textile mills (almost all of which were owned by individual proprietors or partnerships). Curiously, their organizers never wanted to create those corporations in the first place. Historian John Lauritz Larson argues that New England's first railroad promoters initially planned their lines as public works, to be built and owned by the state (as they sometimes were in other regions, as in the case of the Michigan Central). But the state governments refused, due to the failure of various canals and turnpikes to replicate the success of New York's Erie Canal. "Thus it was in frustration (not appreciation for the corporate form) that Massachusetts's railroad pioneers turned to private corporations," Larson writes. This very specific political history set the pattern for American railroads nationwide. Though they were public works in the broadest sense—increasingly important as the common carriers of commerce—they were also private property, owned by individuals who pursued their own interests. In the end, these circumstances would define Vanderbilt's historical role as public figure and private businessman.[26]

A group of influential New Yorkers organized one of the first of these pioneering railways: the Boston & Providence Railroad, a forty-three-mile line that would link its eponymous cities and allow passengers and freight from Boston to connect to Long Island Sound steamboats, bypassing the long sea trip around Cape Cod. It would prove typical of New England's railroads: short, and specifically designed as part of a combined land-sea route to New York. A continuous railway between Boston and Manhattan was just too expensive to build with the available capital.

In early 1835, the construction crews on the Boston & Providence worked steadily southward. Their destination was the India Point dock in Providence, where the trains would meet the steamboats of the Boston & New York Transportation Company. "The stockholders in both are principally the same," Philip Hone observed in his diary; he himself owned $6,000 in shares in the railroad, and $5,000 in the Transportation Company. The railway connection would cement the latter's near monopoly on steamboat traffic down the length of Long Island Sound.[27]

The *Lexington* threatened that imperium. With the sleek vessel nearing completion, the Transportation Company's directors decided to build a new steamer, the *Massachusetts*, in order to defeat it. They also dispatched Captain William Comstock, their general agent, to examine the *Lexington* more closely. A tough-minded forty-eight-year-old veteran of the trade, Comstock had to be careful in sneaking aboard, as Vanderbilt himself constantly prowled the yard. ("My instructions in building the *Lexington* were given from day to day," Vanderbilt explained. "All my boats were thus built under my directions.") Comstock waited until just after the engine was installed, then slipped in to take a quick look around.

He viewed the *Lexington* with skepticism—"I did not like her build," he said—but he had to admit that it represented a remarkable departure. "I had no doubts of her strength and of the plan of securing her deck," he confessed. "In the structure of her keelsons [beams lining the hull to strengthen it], I think them stronger than any boat I ever saw." It was perfectly suited to the rough seas around Rhode Island's Point Judith. Hurrying back to the shipyard of Brown and Bell, Comstock modified the design of the *Massachusetts* accordingly. The new boat would be the same length as the *Lexington*, but far bigger (676 tons to 488), and he wanted it just as strong and fast.

That would prove difficult. When the *Lexington* finally slid into the East River in April 1835, Vanderbilt had good reason to exult. He had spent some $75,000 on it, to brilliant effect. He had insisted on "first-rate materials—chestnut, cedar, oak, yellow and white pine," he boasted. "I think she has 30 percent more fastenings than any other boat." Bishop, who was well acquainted with the Transportation Company's steamers, thought "none of them are stronger than the *Lexington*." Theodosius F. Secor said, after helping to install the vast new piston (measuring eleven feet by two), "I consider her as perfect an engine as ever was built." Vanderbilt put it simply: "I should have thought her one of the best boats in New York. . . . I had so much confidence in her strength, that I always instructed my captains never to stop for foul weather, but if they could see to go ahead, to always go."[28]

On June 1, the *Lexington* embarked on its maiden voyage with streamers flying, its enormous wheels thrashing at the water on either side, its sharp nose slicing through the turbulent currents of Hell Gate into Long Island Sound. It made the 210-mile voyage to Providence in twelve hours—a marvel to travelers who regularly devoted eighteen hours or more to the trip. "FASTEST BOAT IN THE WORLD," announced the *Journal of Commerce*. Though "elegantly fitted up," the paper commented, "her superiority is in her firmness and ease in the water, and above all, in her speed, in which we suppose it is safe to say, she surpasses any boat in the world, and has in fact reached a degree which was supposed two years ago impossible." The *Journal* voiced a broad consensus that Vanderbilt had achieved one of the great technical triumphs of the day. "Her construction exhibits great knowledge of mechanical principles," it reported, "and a peculiarly bold and independent genius."

The envious Captain Comstock watched it churn up the East River at the astonishing rate of twenty miles per hour. But his company had an advantage that Vanderbilt could not match. On June 15, precisely two weeks after the *Lexington*'s first trip, the Boston & Providence Railroad began service. It promptly gave the Transportation Company exclusive rights to land at the railroad dock in Providence, and established coordinated through fares and schedules. The contract was signed by Charles H. Russell, president of the steamboat company, and William W. Woolsey, president of the railroad. Both men were directors of both companies. As Comstock would say, the Transportation Company had "done up" Cornelius Vanderbilt.[29]

Except it hadn't. Vanderbilt prospered by drawing freight from the factories in and around Providence, but passengers were the most lucrative part of the trade—and passengers demanded speed, speed the *Lexington* had like no other boat. He slashed the fare, once as high as $10, to $3, and timed his arrivals in Providence to allow his customers time to walk from his dock and buy tickets for the Boston train. Philip Hone himself put the railroad together with Vanderbilt's boat as he marveled at the new swiftness of travel. "The time [of the first train trip] was 2 hours and a half, and the *Lexington* steam boat goes from New York to Providence in 12 hours," he wrote in his diary, "so that persons leaving this city at 6 in the morning can unstrap their trunks at their lodgings in Boston by daylight on a summer day."[30]

Cheap fares and breathtaking speeds made steamboat travel on Long Island Sound a widely shared experience in the 1830s. The docks and decks of paddlewheelers began to turn up in stories, novels, and anecdotes. "The boat was ready to start—the second bell was ringing—every thing was in confusion," went a typical tale, from the *Providence Journal* in 1836. "Disconsolate old gentlemen were searching in vain for their baggage, and terrified young ladies were trembling, lest half their party were left on shore. Porters were flying backwards and forwards with trunks and band-boxes, and stumbling over nursery maids, with children in their arms. The heavy arms of the engine moved slowly up and down, and the boat, impatient of restraint, swayed to and fro, gathering up her energies for a mighty plunge."[31]

"Directly you have left the wharf, all the life, and stir, and bustle of a packet cease," wrote Charles Dickens a few years later, after taking a Long Island Sound steamer. "The passengers, unless the weather be very fine indeed, usually congregate below. . . . There is always a clerk's office on the lower deck, where you pay your fare; a ladies' cabin; baggage and stowage rooms; engineer's room; and in short a great variety of perplexities which render the discovery of the gentleman's cabin a matter of some difficulty. It often occupies the whole length of the boat (as it did in this case), and has three or four tiers of berths [bunks] on each side." The more commonplace steamboat travel became, the more that customers demanded creature comforts. "Passengers are now-a-days expected to have every thing extravagant," grumbled Comstock. During the day, the crew set up two rows of long rectangular tables where stewards served drinks and luxurious meals.[32]

Transportation, not fledgling factories, captured Americans' imagination. It seemed to be the most strategic sector of the economy in this sprawling country, and Vanderbilt took a strategic view of it. His attack on the Transportation Company was only one part of an emerging campaign all along Long Island Sound. In the fall of 1835, for example, he shifted the *Lexington* to the run to Hartford to reinforce his assault on Menemon Sanford, another hard-edged steamboat captain who largely dominated shipping to New Haven and Hartford. Vanderbilt instinctively despised him, for he had a particularly untrustworthy reputation. "As to Sanford," Comstock declared, "I believe him to be a person void of truth and character." Vanderbilt advertised his offensive against him under the Jacksonian headline "OPPOSITION TO IMPOSITION: NO MONOPOLY — FREE TRADE & EQUAL RIGHTS."

With two business wars raging on Long Island Sound, he began to concentrate all his resources there. On August 27, 1835, he sold off the *Water Witch* and the *Cinderella*, along with his lucrative Elizabethtown ferry, to a group of six men for the hefty sum of $74,000—enough to build a fast and luxurious steamboat on the model of the *Lexington*, which he would christen *Cleopatra*.[33]

In 1836 he again sent the *Lexington* to Providence under the command of his brother Jacob. The Transportation Company retaliated with the *Rhode Island*, the new *Massachusetts*, and in October the *Narragansett*—all bigger but none so fast. Vanderbilt slashed his fare to $1 and added the beautiful new *Cleopatra*. But the *Lexington* remained the popular favorite. "The speed and excellence of this boat require no comment from us," the *Providence Journal* observed. The *Providence Courier* called it "this far-famed water witch, which measures distances as fast as one can keep account of the miles." Even Comstock grudgingly allowed that it was "the fastest boat on the route."[34]

Not everyone celebrated the *Lexington*. Philip Hone, for one, went aboard Comstock's prize *Massachusetts* and was moved to write, "She is decidedly the finest vessel I ever saw." He owned a large amount of stock in the Transportation Company, of course; but he was also a Whig. He and his party feared the destructive power represented by the *Lexington*. "The proprietors of steamboats . . . not unfrequently carry the spirit of competition to a ruinous and ridiculous extent," wrote another Whig, the editor of the *New-York Mirror*. "Mr. Vanderbilt, a large capitalist, and doubtless an enterprising man, with a view of breaking down what has been denominated the 'odious eastern monopoly,' has placed several swift and commodious steamers on the Boston line, and you may now take a trip from New-York to Providence for the trifling consideration of one dollar, lawful currency!" The editor feared that Vanderbilt would wipe out the established Transportation Company—annihilating its hard-to-come-by capital—and replace it with a chaotic world without social distinctions.

> In a crowded steamer . . . whose deck and cabin are thronged with what the great bard calls "all sorts of people," there is no more comfort than there is said to be in a badly governed family . . . when, the old ballad tells us, all is topsy-turvy and most admired confusion. Yet we would not be understood as raising our feeble voice in defence of any monopoly under the sun; but more especially that of steamboats. Far be it from us.

A feeble voice indeed. Conservative Whigs felt themselves losing their struggle against laissez-faire, as both an economic *and* a social phenomenon. As one paper declared, "OPPOSITION *is the very life of business.*"[35]

But the Transportation Company still had its exclusive contract with the Boston & Providence Railroad. During the winter of 1836–37, Vanderbilt's agent in Providence, a popular businessman named John W. Richmond, devised a plan to destroy that advantage. Richmond detested monopolies with the passion of a full-blooded radical Democrat. He believed that he could convince the Rhode Island legislature that the contract violated the railroad's state charter, and he eagerly shared his ideas with Vanderbilt.

The no-nonsense captain responded in November 1836 in his hasty, erratic scrawl. "Your application to your legislator is received," he wrote; "it looks well." But he was more concerned with securing fuel supplies for the coming season. "In speaking about pine wood think you may ingage from 1 to 2 thousand cords for next season only let us have as good contracts as our *oponants*," he scratched. Obsessed with information and control, he bombarded Richmond with a typical barrage of questions. "What progress have you made with your Legislator—how does the passengers get through on Sunday . . .—how does matters go ginerally—you did not say my preasance wood be nessessary theirfour I have made no calculation to go to your Place."[36]

In January 1837, a committee of the legislature reported that, "by giving a preference to a line of steamboats, in which directors of said Rail Road company owning a controlling portion of the stock . . . [the Boston & Providence Railroad] departed from the spirit of their Act of Incorporation." Richmond fired off a joyous account to Vanderbilt, telling him that he would now "enjoy . . . a location at the depot, & also the same rights of having passengers taken in the cars."

Richmond saw the episode as part of the struggle against the tyranny of monopolistic corporations. The hearings attracted "an immense crowd of spectators," he wrote proudly. He hailed the result as "a great victory. It is not only so in the consequences to you, but there is also some pride in the manner & circumstances of its attainment. It is the result of individual exertion against a mass of corporate wealth. . . . You will now stand on ground of fair competition."

Vanderbilt's reply marked a subtle but profound turn in his life. It appeared in the careful penmanship of a clerk; its praise for Richmond's triumph marched in formulaic phrases that had the air of having been inserted by a more literate assistant, phrases that distanced the entire episode from Vanderbilt himself. "It must be extremely gratifying to you to succeed in spite of all the force of such a powerful combination of companies against you," it began. "It will be a stroke that your opponents will not forget shortly."

So much for Jacksonian platitudes. The rest of the letter was dedicated to practical business issues; though written in the clerk's hand, it breathed Vanderbilt's authentic voice. "I have not had any communication with the [Transportation Company] since my boats laid up [for winter], nor do I wish to have anything to do with them," he said. "I am now repairing my boats, fitting them with state rooms. . . . I do not wish to start my boats until wood [for fuel] can be procured by the cargo. This single cord business will not answer." The enemy, preparations for battle, logistics: these were Vanderbilt's obsessions. With the legal battle won, he brusquely dismissed it as Richmond's personal affair. When the lawyer who had argued before the legislature billed him, he refused to pay.[37]

"Vanderbilt is building a splendid steamer to run on the Sound in opposition to the Transportation Company's boats to commence on the 1st of March," announced the *New York Evening Post* on February 10, 1837. "He is the greatest *practical* anti-monopolist in the country." High praise, coming from William Leggett, the radical Jacksonian prophet— but he was wise to stress *practical*. In the case of Cornelius Vanderbilt, circumstances made the idealist. When launching a high-speed raid on a fortified, established enemy, he very easily and naturally imagined his battles in the political terms of the day. It suited him to denounce his foe as an "aristocratic monopoly," to sail under the banner of "Free Trade & Equal Rights." He clearly believed it. But circumstances would change.

HE REALLY WAS GOING TO DIE THIS TIME, Linsly thought. Seated at the side of Vanderbilt's bed in his house, now at 173 East Broadway, in December 1836, the doctor observed his shallow breaths and intense pain. The ailment had seized him abruptly; but the doctor believed it had been lying in wait since the railroad accident three years before. He diagnosed "pleuro-pneumonia" in the lung that had been punctured then. Most likely it was an infection of the pleura, the membrane outside the lung, or else pneumothorax, an air pocket there that constricted or collapsed the lung. In any case, Linsly believed it would be fatal.

"I advised him to settle up his business, as I thought he could not live," the doctor later said. Vanderbilt sent for his attorney, and turned to Sophia. These were dark hours; a few weeks earlier, on November 16, their four-year-old son George had died. Nineteen-year-old Ethelinda was in the room with them as well, along with Daniel B. Allen, her husband of two years; the young couple had lived in the Vanderbilt house since their marriage. Allen listened to them discuss the will of Vanderbilt's late father, and saw them nod approvingly over its "equal distribution of property." But there was one provision of the will that Sophia did not approve of: the punitive one stipulating what would befall the widow if she remarried. Nonetheless, Vanderbilt would have the same terms in his own will.

Elsewhere in the house, James M. Cross waited anxiously with his wife, Phebe (Vanderbilt's eldest child), and their two-year-old son, Cornelius. They sat with the swarm of Vanderbilt's younger children and fretted. "We thought he would die," Cross said. Vanderbilt's lawyer arrived and hurried into the sickroom. When he left, they were all called to Vanderbilt's bedside. The prostrate patriarch confirmed their fears; he said he would not live long. "Don't be too anxious to make money," he told them. "There's enough for you all." As Cross recalled, "That was the whole of his conversation."[38]

It seemed as if the captain shared his flesh with his country—he quickened when it quickened, he struggled when it struggled. Just as three years before, he fell from a triumphant rise to a life-threatening illness as the country dropped from manic prosperity into crisis. From the East River to the Missouri River, from Boston to New Orleans, a financial panic now closed its grip on the nation. In Vanderbilt's house and out on the streets, no one believed in recovery. It appeared, as the evangelists of the Second Great Awakening had preached, that the end times had arrived.

It was so different a year earlier, when the island city was literally rising from the ashes. On December 16, 1835, a monstrous fire had burned out the commercial heart of New York. The ubiquitous Philip Hone saw everything. "When I arrived at the spot the scene exceeded all description," he wrote; "the progress of the flames, like flashes of lightning, communicated in every direction, and a few minutes sufficed to level the lofty edifices on every side." Afterward looters prowled the smoking ruins, getting drunk on recovered wine. "This will make the aristocracy haul in their horns!" they shouted. "Ah! They'll make no more five per cent dividends!"[39]

By the afternoon of December 17, though, gangs of workmen were "clearing the still warm rubble," historians Edwin Burrows and Mike Wallace write. Rebuilding began at once. Banks, insurance companies, brokers, and merchants in the "burnt district" demolished brick shells and raised columned, classical structures along Wall Street. And so, Burrows and Wallace record, "the value of Manhattan real estate, registered at $143 million in 1835, mounted to $233 million within ten months."

Stock and bond trading continued undisturbed in the aftermath of the great fire; in fact, it scudded ahead on a surge of speculation. Booming British textile mills boosted America's cotton-dependent economy; land prices soared, especially in the South. The number of banks exploded. Buoyed by specie and bountiful credits from Britain (itself enriched by exporting opium to China), giddy with optimism and the demands of capital-hungry borrowers, bankers radically expanded their loans. In the most extreme cases, western "wildcat" banks (named after the design on the notes of a particularly reckless Michigan institution) issued notes with little or no coin in reserve. The money supply inflated from $172 million to $276 million in just two years. The nation was on a winning streak, and it kept on spinning the wheel.[40]

Spinning the wheel was a connection that seemed more than a metaphor even at the time. " 'Sporting houses' are in every part of town," observed the *New York Herald* on October 5, 1836. "Several faro banks* have just opened, which are much more replenished with real capital than half the banks in Michigan." Gambling preoccupied society from high to low in this year of exuberance. "Literature, philosophy, and taste, are beginning to frequent the faro bank, and woman also has found an *entree*," the *Herald* noted.

Prostitution flourished openly, and it, too, seemed stitched into the fabric of the times. When courtesan Helen Jewett was murdered that year, the *Herald* called her "the goddess of a large race of merchants, dealers, clerks, and their instruments," who hired whores to entertain clients. Her brothel, intriguingly, was in a building owned by John R. Livingston.[41]

Livingston's social equals might not have frequented brothels, but they certainly were sporting with their money. Many entered their horses in the Union Course races on Long Island. John C. Stevens and Samuel L. Gouverneur offered a thousand dollars to any man who could run ten miles in an hour. On Wall Street, Hone observed "the gambling in stocks"

---

* Faro is a card game in which players bet against the dealer, or "banker," who draws two cards per turn.

as a fever for canals and railroads that seized men with capital, or simply access to someone else's capital—Vanderbilt's, for instance. Throughout 1836 the buoyant captain extended credit to New York's eager businessmen. On April 5, he loaned two Staten Islanders $8,000; on May 3, he loaned a city merchant $15,000; on October 29, he and James Guyon loaned another Staten Islander $35,000. These were large sums (Hone gloated about selling his prime Broadway lot for $60,000), and he probably loaned more. It revealed the demand for credit on one hand and the captain's prosperity on the other—for this was merely a sideline, a way to keep his surplus cash busy earning 6 or 7 percent. Yet he was careful in his agreements, demanding valuable real estate on Staten Island, Coenties Slip, and Warren Street as collateral.[42]

All this told Andrew Jackson that he had caged the Monster only to spawn a nation of speculators. "The present bloat in the paper system cannot continue," declared his ally, Senator Thomas "Old Bullion" Benton. "I did not join in putting down the paper currency of a national bank, to put up a national paper currency of a thousand local banks. I did not strike Caesar to make Anthony master of Rome." On July 11, 1836, Jackson issued the Specie Circular, requiring coin, not banknotes, in payment for federal lands. Westward-moving settlers began to demand gold for their banknotes, making everyone worry about how long the shell game could go on.

On November 12, four days before the death of Vanderbilt's son George, Hone made a nervous entry in his diary. "There has been for some time past a severe pressure for money," he wrote, "which continues, and I feel the effects of it. Stocks have fallen very much." Jackson's redistribution of federal deposits was about to begin. "By this unnatural process," Nicholas Biddle reported, "the specie of New York and other commercial cities is piled up in Western States . . . and while the West cannot use it—the East is suffering from the want of it. . . . Europe is alarmed and the Bank of England itself uneasy at the quantity of specie we possess." The Bank of England began to restrict credit in order to reserve more silver in its vaults, and the tightening soon squeezed the United States. The bottom of the bag was beginning to tear.[43]

As the grim, gray new year dawned in 1837, Vanderbilt planned for death. For the previous three years he had begrudged various clerical tasks to his son-in-law, Daniel Allen; now he had to delegate a few basic responsibilities. He called Allen to his bedside and gave instructions. Allen went out into the winter air to Vanderbilt's office on South Street, then sat down to write letters, asking for an accounting from his father-in-law's agents. "Mr. Allen wrote a week or ten days since for the bills to be forwarded to him," John W. Richmond informed Vanderbilt on January 24,

1837. "I have sent him a detailed statement of them." He promised to deliver the originals at "the first interview with you or him."[44]

For six weeks Vanderbilt was struggling, gasping, inert. Then there occurred something perhaps as straightforward as the response of his immune system, or the seeping of air out of the pocket outside his lung. Or perhaps the cliché applies—that he simply refused to die. There is no underestimating his force of will. Whatever the explanation, for the second time in three years he had avoided seemingly certain death. After a month and a half in bed, he found his feet again and wearily reentered the world of the living. There he discovered that the bottom had ripped out.

On February 25, a Wall Street broker named Joseph Hoxie visited Vanderbilt at his South Street office, where he sat, still weak, beside Daniel Allen. Hoxie explained that he came as an envoy from Nestor Houghton, one of the purchasers of the Elizabethtown ferry. Vanderbilt had just "lodged" (deposited for payment) Houghton's last promissory note for that transaction with his bank. There was a problem, however: Houghton couldn't pay it. Would the good captain be willing to renew the note?

Houghton's desperation marked a troubling shift in the wind. One by one, Vanderbilt's debtors began to default, forcing him to file lawsuits to seize the property they had mortgaged. Then, on March 13, the imposing new marble office building of I. & L. Joseph physically collapsed; at the end of the week, the firm stopped paying its bills, which "occasioned great consternation in Wall Street, for their business has been enormous," Philip Hone recorded on March 17. "The great crisis is near at hand, if it has not already arrived."[45]

That same day, Vanderbilt advertised the resumption of service on his People's Line to Providence, with his brother Jacob in command of the *Lexington*. On March 20, with its machinery repaired, galley stocked, and dishes replaced, the "far-famed" steamer eased out of Peck Slip, churned through Hell Gate, and sliced through the heavy seas of Long Island Sound. The *Providence Journal* announced its arrival, then went on to observe, "The *money market* in New York is still in a very precarious state." This was an understatement. As the *Lexington* tied up at the India Dock in Providence, Hone wrote in his diary, "The prospects in Wall Street are getting worse and worse. . . . The accounts from England are very alarming; the panic prevails there as bad as here. Cotton has fallen. The loss on shipments will be very heavy, and American credits will be withdrawn. The paper of the southern and western merchants is coming back protested."[46]

Hone's analysis was sound. Americans had climbed upward on a pyramid of debts that ultimately rested on high expectations for cotton prices. Instead, the restriction of credit by the Bank of England had been followed by a collapse of the cotton market. It was a classic speculative bubble. Hone had invested hope, and his supply of hope was gone.

"Philip Hone has gone to the d——l, figuratively speaking, having lost pretty much everything by his son . . . and by some speculation moreover, all of which have eased him out of not much below $200,000," wrote another Wall Street diarist, the pious George Templeton Strong, in April. "Confidence annihilated, the whole community, big and little, traveling to ruin in a body." On May 3, he exclaimed, "So they go—smash, crash. Where in the name of wonder is there to be an end of it? Near two hundred and fifty failures thus far!"[47]

"We are in the midst of a great revolution," the *New York Herald* proclaimed. "Wall street, and its business neighborhood, from river to river, has been for a week in a terrible convulsion. The banks—the merchants— the brokers—the speculators, have been rolling onward together in one undistinguishable mass, down the stream of bankruptcy and ruin." A desperate mob attacked a warehouse where flour was stored, as radical Democrats rallied in the streets. "A deep and radical revolution for a year past has been ripening and ripening in politics as well as commerce," the paper added. On May 9, the Dry Dock Bank locked its doors and refused to redeem its notes in gold and silver coin. "Crowds of exasperated creditors collected and great alarm prevailed," Hone recorded. The other banks followed suit.[48]

Vanderbilt slithered unsinged through the financial fire. He had no speculative embarrassments, no debts pledged against consignments of cotton. True, the stocks he owned may have lost some of their market value; their dividends may have been suspended; the promissory notes he held may have gone unpaid. But he had demanded premium real estate as collateral; his property consisted largely of state-of-the-art steamboats; and his was a business that remained in demand. Indeed, he had an abundance of that most valuable item in a deflationary panic: cold, hard cash— piles of silver shillings and gold dollars paid for fares.[49]

Even weakened by illness, Vanderbilt remained an instinctive predator, and, like every predator, he was drawn to the scent of the sick and the vulnerable. To him, the great Panic of 1837 was a time for the hunt. He left his son-in-law Allen to manage the humdrum daily affairs of the steamers. Allen ordered supplies and paid bills, coordinated with captains, and met with merchants who had freight to ship. The nature of a maritime business fortuitously gave the enterprise a neatly compartmentalized structure. With each captain managing the personnel and daily affairs of his boat, the rest of the operational details could be handled by Allen in New York and a single agent in each port.[50]

Vanderbilt also hired a personal clerk in 1837: a native of Shrewsbury,

New Jersey, named Lambert Wardell, who would stay by his side until his death. Looking back decades later, Wardell vividly remembered the day when, as an inconspicuous, unambitious twenty-two-year-old, he began to work for Vanderbilt. Like everyone else, he was overwhelmed by Vanderbilt's physical presence. His new employer "was a man of striking individuality," he recalled, "as straight as an Indian, standing six feet in his stockings and weighing about two hundred pounds." By the time Wardell started work, Vanderbilt had recovered from his near-fatal ailment; the new clerk found him to be "very strong" with "great powers of endurance," a man who exuded raw energy. "His personal appearance was very neat. . . . He was very abstemious, being a light eater and never drank to any extent, not even at his meals, taking liquor only as medicine." His only vice was smoking; he "always had a cigar in his mouth, either lit or unlit." That iron self-control proved to be as important to his success as his ruthlessness; never did he let his emotions, or ambitions, get the best of him. "He never had a debt and never bought anything on credit," Wardell declared (with some exaggeration). "He was economical almost to extremes."[51]

Frugality was one of Vanderbilt's most potent weapons as he hammered his opponents in this year of desperation. The *Lexington* now formally connected with the trains of the Boston & Providence Railroad, which hit the Transportation Company hard. He dispatched two boats to smash Menemon Sanford at Hartford and New Haven. Not content to name merely a son after himself, he launched "the new and fast sailing Steam Boat C. VANDERBILT," as he advertised it.

As he added vessels, he pioneered new routes. "The mode of arriving at the eastern part of Long Island has hitherto been by means of small sailing vessels, or by stage coaches," the *New York Evening Post* observed on July 15. "A more rapid and direct means of conveyance is now provided. Captain Vanderbilt has made arrangements for running the fine steamboats *Cleopatra* and *Clifton* from this city to Oyster-Pond Point and Sag Harbor." The paper helpfully noted, "The east end of Long Island offers a quiet and agreeable retreat from the noise, heat, and polluted air of the town."[52]

He also scanned the map for more distant targets. The panic may have disrupted the South's economy, he realized, but it would soon recover. Now was the time to strike at its coastal trade, while the market was vulnerable to a newcomer. "The new and elegant steam packet *North Carolina*, Capt. Reynolds, recently built in New York, and owned by Commodore Vanderbilt, arrived here on Saturday night from that city, on her way to Wilmington, N.C., between which place and Charleston she is to run," declared the *Norfolk Herald* on November 26. "The *North Car-*

olina is 170 feet in length. . . . Her furniture, accommodations, and equipments, are all of the best description, and admirably arranged for the comfort and convenience of the passengers."

The *Norfolk Herald* was the first newspaper to give him the honorific title of "Commodore." At the time, it was the highest rank in the United States Navy, and had been given before to notable steamboat men. The nickname made little impact at the time; though reprinted in New York's *Journal of Commerce*, it came and went, a passing tribute to Vanderbilt's aggressiveness. Yet it was also a sign of a change in his disposition.[53]

The captain had always played a double role—that of creator and destroyer, provider and plunderer. He had built his wealth through piratical raids, scourging monopolies with a mastery of tactics and "an economy not known to your opponents," as John W. Richmond put it, until they paid him blackmail. He also had established his own lines, which he fiercely defended. But the balance within him subtly began to shift, as he formulated the words he would later say to Dr. Linsly: "I think I have been spared to accomplish a great work that will last and remain." His buccaneering days were far from over, but he rather liked the title of commodore. It spoke of a commander, not a despoiler. By the end of the next decade, it would be a title associated with no one else.

Chapter Five

SOLE CONTROL

O n March 8, 1878, the murmuring and rustling of a crowded court-room in lower Manhattan suddenly fell still. Eighty-year-old Daniel Drew rose from his seat and cautiously ascended to the witness chair. He had been in court more than once that winter, his fragile bones and papery skin "wrapped up in sealskins and mufflers," the press reported, lips tight and pinched as if they had been sewn shut. He sat slowly, settled his hands on the armrests, and "looked shrewdly at the lawyers with his small gray eyes." He had been called to testify in what newspaper headlines called "THE GREAT WILL CONTEST."

When prompted, he tersely admitted "that he knew Commodore Van-derbilt very well," according to the *New York Sun*. He knew his sons, too, who now sat across the aisle from one another: William Henry Vanderbilt, plump and content, wearing a slight smile between the huge sideburns that clung to his cheeks like frightened monkeys, having "apparently inherited good health as well as nearly all the wealth of his father," a reporter commented; and Cornelius Jeremiah Vanderbilt, "looking pale, thin, and meek," disinherited, epileptic, and unhappy. "Occasionally Cornelius cast a furtive glance at William, but William never noticed Cornelius."

Drew could have told stories of his secret cooperation with Vanderbilt over the decades, a partnership that had first blossomed at the end of the 1830s. But he did nothing of the sort. Yes, he told the court, he had had many conversations with Vanderbilt; unfortunately, he could not remem-ber the substance of a single one of them. As the *New York Times* put it, "His testimony was of no importance." Vanderbilt would have been proud. If there was one trait that had led him to trust Drew, a man notori-ous for self-interest, it was his silence. And in the aftermath of the Panic of 1837, there had been much to be silent about.[1]

THE STONINGTON COULD CHANGE everything. On November 10, 1837, the first train had passed down its full fifty miles of track from Providence, where it connected to the Boston & Providence by ferry, to Stonington, Connecticut, a village seaport on Long Island Sound. Officially called the New York, Providence & Boston Railroad, and better known as the Stonington, it cut inside dreaded Point Judith, where steamboats ran into rough seas, which eliminated three hours and much seasickness from the trip between New York and Boston.

Soon after that first locomotive opened the route, Cornelius Vanderbilt investigated the line for himself. His nearly fatal accident four years earlier had not made him hostile to trains, as some later claimed; he keenly understood that control of traffic on Long Island Sound lay in the strategic balance between steamboats and railroads—and between rival railroads, as this and other lines neared completion. So he took a steamer to Stonington, boarded a train, and rode up the line to Providence. "There's nothing like it," he told the line's chief engineer three years later. "The first time I ever traveled over the Stonington, I made up my mind." It was the fastest route to Boston, potentially the key to the entire battle for the Sound.

And yet, the Stonington was a crippled giant. Its exorbitant construction costs "were a scandal," according to one railroad historian. "Its fifty miles, through a far from forbidding territory, had taken $1,300,000 in stock and $1,300,000 in bonds." Everyone who looked into its affairs could see that the interest on that staggering debt would weigh heavily for years to come.[2] Strategically situated, financially vulnerable, the Stonington gave Vanderbilt much to think about as he returned to New York.

Back at his office, now at 169 South Street, he found Daniel Allen and Lambert Wardell waiting for him with bills and correspondence. His brother Jacob needed to speak to him concerning his plan to burn coal in the *Lexington* in an attempt to save fuel costs and deck space; the engineer had no experience with coal and had to be fired.[3] But perhaps most pressing of all was the problem of Billy.

Vanderbilt's oldest son, William, had now passed sixteen, the age when both Cornelius and Jacob had started out in life. Vanderbilt thought it was time for Billy (as he always called him) to make his own way. But the contrast between himself and his son distressed him. Vanderbilt radiated strength, and he grew more imperious every year. Wardell could not recollect a single instance of him admitting that he was wrong. "If he was interrupted when he was relating something," noted Dr. Linsly, "he would stop and never say another word—never resume the subject." Allen later recalled, "He was always censorious towards people who differed with him."

Billy could not have been more different, Allen explained. "We were acquainted in our boyhood days, and the intimacy increased after I married his sister," he said. "He never in all that time made, to my knowledge, a single objection to anything his father suggested, either in business or in other matters. His father's will with him was absolute." Billy's lack of spine aggravated Vanderbilt, who expected more of his blood. He often pressed his "delicate" son, calling him a blatherskite and a blockhead. When he did, Allen saw Billy's face collapse into "a peculiar sort of expression—an expression peculiar to him—a falling down of his jaw, a sorrowful look and a whining sort of noise."[4]

After a brief education at the Columbia College grammar school, Billy had taken a job with a ship chandler, but the hard labor did not suit him. So Vanderbilt turned to Daniel Drew. This pious, deceitful, inn-keeping, cattle-dealing moneylender had adopted the People's Line name and competed against the Hudson River monopoly until he secured his own payoff in 1836. But Drew soon revived the line and assumed control of the monopoly himself. And that was why Vanderbilt and Drew grew so close, after so much enmity. They made an unwritten agreement to invest in the other's steamboats, precisely because neither had met a more dangerous opponent; giving a share to the other would make it in the interests of each to avoid competition.[5]

Vanderbilt wanted Billy to have a post in Drew's brokerage house. Together with Nelson Robinson and Eli Kelley (and later Kelley's son Robert), Drew worked at the center of Wall Street, trading stocks and bonds and serving as a "banknote shaver." The firm facilitated long-distance financial transactions by buying notes and bills of exchange of far-removed banks and merchants at a discount, securing payment from the issuer or reselling them at a profit. It was an extremely risky business, especially in the aftermath of the panic. "The banks *will not* discount under present circumstances freely to good and safe men. They are afraid of each other," declared the *New York Courier and Enquirer.* "Nearly every transaction is for cash." Drew, Robinson, & Co. were willing, but they demanded a stiff premium for their services.

This kind of financial tightrope act would make a man out of Billy and teach him the value of money, his father seemed to think. Drew accepted the teenager as his clerk, but wanted something for himself: the use of the speedy new *C. Vanderbilt* for his People's Line on the Hudson, to run at the start of the season, in March 1838. Vanderbilt gladly let his secret partner use it, for he now took a share in the ownership of the People's Line as Drew established himself as the river's new monopolist. These former rivals were becoming close allies and friends. But Billy's fate was another matter entirely.[6]

"I DID SUPPOSE THAT ALL NAVIGABLE WATERS were public highways, and open to all," Vanderbilt declared; "therefore I do not complain at any gentlemen running their boat against those that I may see proper to run." The signed statement appeared in the *Boston Daily Advertiser and Patriot* in July 1838. By now there was nothing surprising about his Jacksonian rhetoric. In this case, he was replying to advertisements "signed by the Directors of the Steam boat *Huntress* . . . [which] seem to aim at me and my boat, the *Augusta*," he explained. "And why? because of my having chosen to put a boat on the route between Boston and Kennebec River [in Maine]. Of this newspaper controversy between the *Directors of incorporated Steamboat Companies*, and individual owners of other boats . . . I leave the public to judge." Once again, he championed the lone individual against amalgamated wealth with special corporate charters.

But the rhetoric was wearing thin for those who glimpsed a self-serving opportunism beneath it. "We have had a great fuss here about Vanderbilt's boats," wrote a college student from Maine. "Vanderbilt's undisguised end is to drive the *Huntress* off the line and control it entirely himself." Wherever Vanderbilt had a chance to dominate a route, in fact, he tried to destroy his rivals.[7]

In April, for example, he had sat down with the president of the Stonington Railroad, Courtlandt Palmer, to offer his advice on how to defeat an opposition steamboat. Vanderbilt had put aside his competition on the Providence route to supply the railroad with the *Lexington* as a connecting boat, alongside one provided by his old foe, the Transportation Company. Now the *Kingston*, owned by a party in Boston, was undercutting the fare, and he wanted to fight them face-to-face. "Capt. Vanderbilt is in favor of breaking up the regular line and leaving at the same hour with the opposition," Palmer wrote to William D. Lewis, senior officer of the Girard Bank in Philadelphia, a major holder of the company's stocks and bonds. "Capt. Vanderbilt, who has more experience than all of us united, says he is sure his plan is the right one for the interest of all concerned."[8]

Vanderbilt agreed with Palmer. In his July newspaper appeal, he saluted himself for his "20 years experience in steamboats;—it has been my whole study, and I have built and owned some twenty, and can say, without any intention of boasting, *that not one life has ever been lost in any of the number.*" (Only a steamboat owner in 1838 would make a point of pride out of never having killed anyone in the ordinary course of business.) It was getting difficult to think of this forty-four-year-old as an outsider.

Vanderbilt ruthlessly pursued his interests at the expense of his would-be partners. He even used his old enemy as a foil. When the Transportation Company canceled its contract with the Stonington at the end of April, he followed suit. Instead, he offered to lease the *Lexington* for

$4,000 a month (plus the income from meals and the bar), the same deal offered by the Transportation Company for its steamer, the *Narragansett*. "His terms . . . are ruinous," Palmer wrote to Lewis. "Vanderbilt is anxious to sell the *Lexington*, and offers her for 70,000 dolls.," he added. "It is very desireable if we separate from the Transportation Co. to get Vanderbilt with us. If we do not take him, they will, & if we fight, we shall have to oppose both. But to pay 70,000 dolls. for the *Lexington* is buying him off at a price which is out of all reason."

It was "exorbitant," as Palmer put it, to demand $70,000 for a steamer that had cost $75,000 to build—before it had endured three years of battering and erosion on the rough, salty seas around Point Judith—especially now that steamers 25 percent larger had become the standard on the Sound. But Vanderbilt read his target well. Courtlandt Palmer was weak. This thirty-seven-year-old native of Stonington cringed and fawned before Lewis, the elite Philadelphia banker. He often made marvelously brave noises and then collapsed under pressure. When presented with the lease terms offered by Vanderbilt and the Transportation Company, he roared, "We had better however shut up the road than to accede to either proposal." Eleven days later, on May 3, he squeaked, "I think it for our interest to close with them [Vanderbilt and the Transportation Company] on the [lease] terms proposed. By doing so we avoid a collision."[9] No man afraid of a collision could withstand Vanderbilt.

The Stonington sank ever lower. During the summer, Vanderbilt's old agent, John W. Richmond, ran an opposition boat at reduced prices. "She is a sure scourge to us, causing us to lose heavily," Palmer noted. In October, Palmer negotiated a disastrous new contract with the Transportation Company, giving it 70 percent of the through fare between New York and Boston. Meanwhile the line issued more bonds, going deeper into debt.

In the middle of November, with the leasing agreement terminated, Vanderbilt approached Robert Schuyler, the president of the Transportation Company. If the company did not buy the *Lexington*, he declared, he would run it to Providence at a fare of $1. Even adding the cost of a ticket on the Boston & Providence Railroad, this would allow travelers to go from New York to Boston for far less than the $5 (or more) that the Stonington demanded. "Our losses will probably be $30,000 in consequence," Palmer fretted, "while the Trans. Co. would lose twice that or more." He and Schuyler immediately opened negotiations. All the while turmoil reigned within the Stonington, as stockholders angrily protested the extraordinary debt that would soon place the corporation in the bondholders' hands (as they held a mortgage on the railroad's physical stock of rails, locomotives, cars, and depots).

At the beginning of January, the Transportation Company agreed to pay $60,000 for the *Lexington*, and the Stonington added a $10,000 bonus, thus matching the original demand. No one had any illusions about the reason for the purchase. They were "buying off Vanderbilt," wrote banker Joseph Cowperthwait, a Stonington trustee. As Palmer put it, they were paying for the *Lexington* "to get rid of her as an opposition boat." He estimated her worth at $30,000, making a bribe, or "bonus," of some $40,000. "We found it unprofitable [to fight Vanderbilt]," explained Captain William Comstock, the Transportation Company's general agent, "and concluded that it was better to be at peace than at war, on any terms."[10]

Such was Vanderbilt's reputation that he not only forced his enemies to buy his too-small boat, but extracted $10,000 from a railroad even as it went bankrupt—and all without a single trip at a reduced fare. But a reputation is a slippery thing. "Before paying it, I sent for Mr. Vanderbilt and received from him a most positive *pledge* that he would never again in any way interfere with the Line," Palmer wrote. "I asked it in writing but this he declined to give, remarking that I knew his verbal promise could be fully relied on." The hard-bitten Captain Comstock, on the other hand, had "no confidence in him," as he told Schuyler. He was sure that, before long, Vanderbilt would be back.[11]

ON THE WARM SUNDAY AFTERNOON of September 2, 1838, a very angry man with the very peculiar name of Oroondates Mauran stepped aboard the *Samson*, a steam ferryboat as large and powerful as its namesake. The fare collector greeted him respectfully, perhaps with the salutation "Commodore." The *Samson* belonged to the Richmond Turnpike Company, and Mauran was its president and largest stockholder, as he had been for the previous seven years. "We always understood him to be the general agent as well as the President," the collector explained. "That is what we call 'Commodore.' His word was will there."[12]

Shrewd and tough, Mauran was a merchant with a long history at sea. Twenty years earlier, when Vanderbilt first had met Vice President Daniel D. Tompkins, the founder of the Richmond Turnpike Company, Mauran had owned a three-masted ship, the *Maria Caroline*, and he still invested heavily in the Havana trade. But most of his money was in the Richmond Turnpike corporation, which ran a ferry between Staten Island and Manhattan's Whitehall Slip—as it had when John De Forest took command of the *Nautilus*, the first steam ferry between the two islands, in 1817. Now he was having trouble with another of Vanderbilt's relatives: his cousin Oliver Vanderbilt.

Mauran stood on the deck of the *Samson* as it floated at its Staten Island dock, and gave some last-minute instructions to its master, Captain Braisted. He wanted the boat to get an early start that day. Usually Oliver took the lead with his own ferryboat, the *Wave*, and delighted in taunting the *Samson*. "She generally started first and she would often stop opposite our dock and ring her bell to coax us off," explained Braisted's son. "We would sometimes wait 15 minutes to let the *Wave* get off."

The harassment enraged Mauran—but then everything about Oliver Vanderbilt enraged him. Oliver had once been a Richmond Turnpike ferry captain and shareholder; on October 19, 1835, he had sold his stock with the explicit understanding that he would not compete against the corporation. "He meant to live on a farm," Cornelius remembered him saying, "and have nothing more to do with a life on the water on account of his health." Instead, Oliver had launched the *Wave* and began carrying passengers for sixpence, half the company's shilling fare. The rivalry had rapidly escalated to much more than the typical racing, as the boats crowded and nudged each other. "It was a common occurrence for the boats to come together 3 or 4 times a day," one man observed.

The collisions had grown more dangerous. In late August, just three or four days before this particular Sunday afternoon, Captain Braisted had come down to the deck to tell Mauran that the *Wave* was "crowding him out of his course. . . . She was a much smarter boat than the *Samson*." Mauran had glared back at him. "If she ever does that again," he had barked, "damn her, run into her, sink her."

On this day, September 2, Braisted took the *Samson* out with a good head start, but the *Wave* came up fast on her starboard side. Belowdecks, the bartender heard an enormous crack; he ran out and discovered that Oliver had nosed his boat against the side of the *Samson*, buckling wood for twelve feet behind the starboard paddlewheel. "This made the captain of the *Samson* much excited," he blandly observed.

On the return trip from Whitehall, Braisted angrily ordered his engineer to put on all the steam he could. As the *Wave* passed Governors Island, passenger Stephen W. West looked over at the *Samson*'s pilothouse. "The *Samson* was about twice her length ahead of the *Wave* when I noticed the Captain throw her wheel around," he recalled, "and the *Samson* run directly into the *Wave*." The *Wave* was packed with passengers, including numerous women and children, who began screaming in terror as wood splintered in the collision. Only a last-minute maneuver by Oliver Vanderbilt prevented the blow from striking square amidships and likely sinking his boat. "The *Samson* turned round again and came for another attack," West added. "I saw he was determined to destroy the boat I was in. . . . I told the captain of the *Samson* he would have company in the wheelhouse if he came near enough to us. Myself and some 15 or 20 others made preparations to attack. We got hold of sticks of wood and what loose things we could, 15 or 20 of us to get aboard of her."

The *Samson* sheered off before West and his boarding party could capture it, but on landing at Staten Island the *Wave*'s frenzied passengers stormed the ferry house of the Richmond Turnpike Company. "Mr. Mauran was on the dock when the people were destroying the property and he was much excited as were also the people," declared the fare collector, "and I think if he had gone 10 feet further he would have been killed or thrown into the water."

"Immediately after landing," West said, "when on the wharf at Staten Island, I asked Mr. Mauran whether he did not think it was unpardonable to allow his boat to run into and try to sink the *Wave*, when so many people were on board of her." Mauran replied, "Damn him I wish he had sunk him." West had had his young son aboard the *Wave*, and Mauran's heartlessness infuriated him.[13]

The steamboat trade had always been the most aggressively competitive business in America. Its fare wars, populist advertising, and high-speed racing embodied the nation's individualistic, unregulated society. It also embodied its mechanized, unregulated violence, with its deadly boiler explosions and reckless desperation to defeat the opposition. "ANOTHER, AND YET ANOTHER," declared one newspaper in late 1837. "It is hardly worthwhile to attempt keeping any account of the steamboat disasters which are daily and almost hourly occurring, for no one seems to feel any interest in the subject." Conservative Whigs such as Philip Hone found the mayhem "shocking in the extreme, and a stigma on our country. We have become the most careless, reckless, headlong people on the face of the earth," he wrote. " 'Go ahead' is our maxim and password; and we do go ahead with a vengeance, regardless of consequences and indifferent about the value of human life." It was the Democratic newspapers that made a point of praising "the incalculable benefits of competition" which helped "the people at large, by causing great and permanent reductions of fare on several of the most important routes." The Whig press, on the other hand, warned that it could go too far, and lead not only to bloodshed, but to "the utter ruin of one or both the competitors. When this occurs, the community must of course suffer in turn."

Yet the Whigs were coming to terms with competition. In 1838, they won control of New York's state government under the leadership of a triumvirate composed of Governor William H. Seward, newspaper editor Horace Greeley, and Albany party boss Thurlow Weed, who sought to wed active government with equality of opportunity. In an Independence Day address in 1839, Seward attacked special privileges, saying it was the Whigs' mission to "break the control of the few over the many, extend the largest liberty to the greatest number." In other words, government would aid the enterprising but not protect the elite. Even the Whiggish *Niles' Register* admitted, rather reluctantly, that competition "has its advantages. Community is generally benefitted—monopoly is suppressed, and the utmost perfection and economy is insured."[14]

Cornelius Vanderbilt, on the other hand, took a step in the other direction. He heard of the disastrous ramming of the *Wave* almost immediately, for he maintained close ties to Staten Island, where his mother still lived and where he had many friends and business associates. He learned that Mauran's fellow stockholders—principally Dr. John S. Westervelt, a son-in-law of Daniel Tompkins—wanted out. Oliver's opposition and the terrible publicity had destroyed the value of their shares. Vanderbilt snapped them up, fully half of the total, "upon the express condition that he should have the sole control and management," according to Oliver.

Sole control. It would be a recurring theme in Vanderbilt's life. Always dominating, he increasingly lost interest in investment unless he had power over what was done with his money. *Sole control.* Oliver differentiated it from "management," and for good reason. Cornelius wanted independence, not only from Mauran and the other directors, but from legal obligations and political authorities. The Richmond Turnpike Company's special charter was a relic of mercantilism, requiring it to provide ferry service at uneconomical times—a requirement Oliver, as an independent competitor, did not have to meet. Cornelius chose to ignore the mandate. "Cornelius Vanderbilt has frequently given out that he intends running the boats upon said ferry with the sole view of profit," Oliver complained, "and without regard to the rights or convenience of passengers."

And what was more convenient for passengers than competition? Oliver had cut the fare in half and doubled service. Cornelius got a bargain on the stock because of that competition, which he now meant to snuff out. On July 2, 1839, he filed suit against his cousin. The Richmond Turnpike Company owned the Staten Island property where Oliver kept his dock, he argued, and had exclusive rights to the "bridge, ferry house, and bulkhead" on Whitehall Slip that he also used. The company had "accepted and took the said lease [at Whitehall] with full confidence that no person was to be allowed to interfere with their right, immunities, & privileges." In short, "the greatest *practical* anti-monopolist in the country" claimed a legal monopoly.[15]

WHEN VANDERBILT STRODE through the portico, he passed between six fluted columns into the interior of his new mansion. Workmen crisscrossed the floor carrying mantels of Egyptian marble and balustrades of solid mahogany on their shoulders. A special crew of craftsmen from England hammered away at a grand spiral staircase recessed into an oval well, spinning upward forty feet to the top floor. The hustle resembled the bustle around Bellona Hall fifteen years earlier, but this grand house was a world away from that humble inn, even if it was just on the other side of Staten Island from the Raritan River. Here was French plate glass, rosewood parlor doors with silver knobs, and a stained-glass skylight at the top of the stairwell. Another English artisan placed a sheet of glass, painted with the steamboat *Cleopatra*, over the front door. The captain was building a home fit for a commodore.

He had been a very young man when he purchased the property from his father. "Cornele's lot," the locals had called it. His mother lived just a three-minute walk south of here. When he looked out the door of the house, he gazed out atop a hill that gave him a commanding view of the bay, over the terraced landscape and ferry dock below him.[16] "It is not possible to conceive a more extended or beautiful prospect," wrote Philip Hone that summer of 1839, after visiting Vanderbilt's neighbors, the Anthons. "Situated on the summit of the hill back of the Quarantine ground [the state hospital for sick immigrants], it commands a view of the ocean and bay, with all that enters or leaves the port, Long Island, the city, North River, the Jersey shore, the Kills, Newark, and Elizabeth." The island was becoming a fashionable summer destination, and even Hone toyed with the "plan of having a seat on Staten Island."[17]

Francis Grund, a wry observer of New York's social elite, took the ferry that same season. "A fine brass band was stationed on deck," he wrote, "and the company consisted of a great number of pretty women with their attendant swains, who thus early escaped from the heat of the city in order to return to it at shopping-time." These visitors went to the Brighton Pavilion, which "offers really a fine and healthy retreat from the noise and dirt of New York," thought Grund. "The busy bar-keeper was preparing ice-punch, mint-juleps, port and madeira sangarie, apple-toddy, gin-sling, &c. with a celerity of motion of which I had heretofore scarcely seen an example. This man evidently understood the value of time, and was fast rising into respectability; for he was making money more quickly than the 'smartest' broker in Wall street."[18]

Grund's sly joke applied to the captain overseeing construction of his mansion farther down Staten Island, only in his case it wasn't funny. In the midst of economic hardship, when Hone found "money uncome-at-able, and confidence at an end," the uneducated Vanderbilt rapidly rose in wealth, and so too in social stature, if more slowly. When Charles Dickens visited the United States in 1842, he marveled at the American "love of 'smart' dealing, which gilds over many a swindle and gross breach of trust." He often pointed out a man who was getting rich "by the most infamous and odious means," yet was "tolerated and abetted" by the public. He always asked, "In the name of wonder, then, what is his merit?" Back came the invariable reply: "Well, sir, he is a smart man."[19]

Vanderbilt, however, won respect for more than simply being smart. Americans, and Democrats in particular, distinguished between "stock-jobbing" speculators, whom they saw as little more than gamblers or tricksters, and "enterprising" men, who built businesses and created wealth. In 1842, editor Moses Beach added Vanderbilt to his annual list of "the Wealthy Citizens of New York City," alongside Philip Hone, Oroondates Mauran, Daniel Drew, and John Jacob Astor. Beach curtly described Drew as "a shrewd, money making man," but he lavished praise on Vanderbilt as a productive entrepreneur. "Cornelius has evinced more energy and 'go aheaditiveness' in building and driving steamboats, and other projects, than ever one single Dutchman possessed," he exclaimed. "Put on the coals and steam and flare up for Stonington!"[20]

When the mansion was completed in 1840, Vanderbilt moved his large family there, onto his ancestral lands, close to his mother, hard by the dock served by the ferry he now controlled. He now enjoyed spacious comfort commensurate with his wealth. But the newly fashionable status of a country seat on Staten Island certainly appealed to him as well, as he began to mingle with the rich and influential. "Vanderbilt . . . is now at Saratoga," wrote Courtlandt Palmer one August around this time; by habituating the little resort town of Saratoga Springs, just north of Albany, Vanderbilt moved in society's loftiest circles. "All the world is here," wrote Hone in Saratoga, referring to perhaps two thousand of the nation's elite, "politicians and dandies; cabinet ministers and ministers of the gospel; officeholders and officeseekers; humbuggers and humbugged; fortune-hunters and hunters of woodcock; anxious mothers and lovely daughters."[21]

On his Staten Island estate, the self-made, would-be dynast gathered his family about him rather like a royal court. He built a three-story Tudor house just south of this property for Ethelinda and her husband.[22] Vanderbilt's primary attorney was William K. Thorn, newly married to his daughter Emily. And his nephew, Jeremiah Simonson, worked for him as well.

And then there was Vanderbilt's younger brother (and neighbor) Jacob, who maintained a powerful bond with Cornelius even as he pursued his own business interests. After the Transportation Company purchased the *Lexington*, for example, Jacob continued to serve as its captain, faithfully carrying out repairs and reconstruction under the orders of Captain Comstock. Though he labored in his older brother's shadow, Jacob won renown on Long Island Sound. In December 1837, a New Englander wrote (using phrenological jargon) that Jacob, "as it is pretty well understood, has the 'go ahead' bump pretty strongly developed." That month he brought the *Lexington* safely through a ferocious storm that snapped the rope controlling the rudder.[23] He became famous for his "unsurpassed energy and decision of character, wonderful quickness, and reach of judgment," as the monthly *Ladies' Companion* declared, "and imperturbable calmness and resolution in the moment of danger." Had he not taken ill on January 13, 1840, the editors reflected, "many lives might have been saved."

At two o'clock on the afternoon of January 15, wrote Philip Hone, "the city was thrown into an awful state of consternation and alarm." Chester Hilliard of Norwich had arrived with terrible news: the *Lexington* had been destroyed in a horrific fire two nights before on its way from New York to Stonington. Cotton bales piled around the smokestack had caught fire; the crew had fumbled its attempts to fight the blaze, and had swamped the lifeboats by lowering them while the steamer was still at full speed. Hilliard and another man climbed onto a floating cotton bale; Hilliard strapped himself to it, but his companion did not. After a night adrift in the freezing seas, only Hilliard remained on the bale. Just four of some 125 men, women, and children survived. At least $20,000 in gold and silver disappeared into the Sound. It was, as the newspapers put it, an "appalling calamity."

Perversely, the horrific accident may have enhanced Cornelius Vanderbilt's stature. The press reprinted the testimony at the coroner's inquest, held a week after the tragedy. The public read of how Vanderbilt had personally designed the boat, how it had been built with the best materials, how even his enemies had admired its strength and speed. Charles O. Handy, the new president of the Transportation Company (now incorporated as the New Jersey Steam Navigation Company), and Captain Comstock hinted that Vanderbilt had coerced the company into buying it.[24]

Fear and admiration, admiration and fear—always they arose in pairs, a spiral helix of emotion, when other businessmen spoke of him. "I have seen Vanderbilt today," wrote R. M. Whitney of the Stonington on November 12, 1840. "I had much rather have the opposition of the Trans. Co. to contend with than his. . . . He and Mauran are determined, persevering men who will carry through all they undertake." (Whitney obviously believed, perhaps correctly, that Vanderbilt's partnership with Mauran went beyond the Richmond Turnpike Company.) Courtlandt Palmer reflected, "He is so powerful (worth at least half a million of dollars) that we do not wish to war with him if we can possibly avoid it." The railroad's chief engineer, William Gibbs McNeill, echoed these sentiments in an emphatic assessment he wrote after a lengthy interview with Vanderbilt: "Capt. V. has risen by his merits—a *very* enterprising, indefatigable, intelligent (of his business) man. His frequent practice—to build boats—run opposition—make money despite of opposition—then sell at a premium to leave the route. Possible that he may (in the count of not being connected with us) serve us the same way."

McNeill was a graduate of the two great schools of America's early railway engineers, West Point and the Baltimore & Ohio Railroad, and was hardly a soft touch. Yet his respect for Vanderbilt verged on awe. He concluded, "I confess if we are to be opposed I'd sooner have *him* with us, than against us."[25]

Vanderbilt was a man defined by enterprise, but he had handed his son over to Daniel Drew, the furtive master of speculation and subterfuge. As one of Drew's clerks, Billy entered the eternal dusk of Wall Street, where the dim light perfectly suited his boss. In New York's early, unregulated stock market, insider trading was the norm. Courtlandt Palmer and William D. Lewis, for example, often wrote about plans for an "operation in our stock," as they tried to profit through their access to inside information, or attempted to manipulate the share price up or down.

At one point the refined Lewis built a steamer, the *Eureka*, for the Stonington line. In a Vanderbiltesque maneuver, its captain tried to extort money from the Hudson River monopoly by threatening to run it to Albany. "Under the circumstances," Palmer advised Lewis, "perhaps it would be judicious for you to [put] the stock you have bought in the name of someone else, that you are not to be known as an owner of the *Eureka*." Unfortunately for them, the leading figure in the monopoly was now Drew, who saw through the deceit and sent a stark warning to the Stonington men. Soon Palmer glumly reported that the *Eureka*'s captain had been "tampered with" by Drew and his partners, adding, "he has been in their pay."[26]

"All visible objects, man, are but as pasteboard masks," Captain Ahab declares in *Moby-Dick*. "Some unknown but still reasoning thing puts forth the mouldings of its features from behind the unreasoning mask." Herman Melville's sense of the world as untrustworthy, as a shroud over a deeper reality, captured something essential about this time and place. For such was the world that swallowed Billy Vanderbilt: a netherworld populated by those artificial persons called corporations that masked the real persons behind them; by paper money, that masked real gold and silver; by whispered rumors, that masked the manipulations of self-serving men. Paper currency, the *North American Review* piously intoned, was "a consequence of the increased confidence of man in his fellow man"; but it could also be seen as a *demand* for confidence that raised suspicions all the higher. Melville's later novel *The Confidence-Man* consists largely of elo-quent appeals for trust in others, appeals made by the trickster of the title in the service of fraud. Legitimate banknotes were rarely accepted at face value, for fear that they could not be redeemed for the full amount of specie promised, and thousands of counterfeit varieties circulated. In *The Confidence-Man*, a hapless fellow tries to use a counterfeit detector (a list of identifying marks on legitimate bills) that itself is counterfeit. By the 1840s, it seemed that these mysterious abstractions, these false fronts, these outright lies, had layered over the direct, natural economy of people and things that Americans had always known. It is telling that Melville's talisman for the white whale, the ultimate, unreachable reality, is a gold coin.[27]

"Delicate" was the word that later popped up whenever Billy's youth was mentioned—but life in Wall Street's shadow world required iron nerve. It would be said that he worked hard, too hard, as he married Maria Kissam, daughter of a prominent Brooklyn minister, and settled into an East Broadway house (most likely rented from his own father). But the daily risks, the tensions, the double-dealing weighed on him.[28]

Then came the Indiana bonds. Like many states (including New York), Indiana embarked on a "Mammoth System" of public works during these years of depression. It issued millions of dollars' worth of bonds to finance canals, roads, railroads, and other "internal improvements." Many of these securities were entrusted to Commissioner Milton Stapp to sell in London. Unfortunately, the printing of the bonds did not meet the stan-dards of the London market; new bonds were issued, and Stapp was directed to cancel the old ones. Instead, he met with Drew and Robinson in late 1840. Drew's firm sold both the old and the new bonds in New York in January 1841, bringing a windfall of $134,000. A new commis-sioner, sent to investigate, stormed into the office and demanded an accounting. Robinson flatly refused to provide one, and Indiana filed suit. For the state government, it was part of a financial catastrophe. For the nation, it was part of a growing disgust with public works that failed to produce public benefits—a disgust that would open the way for Drew, Vanderbilt, and others to build fortunes in railroads. And for Billy, it was a shocking education in the underhanded ways of Wall Street.[29]

Billy suddenly quit Drew's firm. "He was a delicate young man," the *New York Times* would say, "and the hard work he had done proved too much for his constitution." More likely, he could not bear the stress of risky, even illegal maneuvers. Cornelius grudgingly purchased a farm for his broken son and his new wife near the village of New Dorp on Staten Island, not far from his own palatial estate. "Billy is good for nothing but to stay on the farm," he told Hosea Birdsall, one of his employees. As Birdsall recalled, "He said he would try to make a good farmer of him."[30]

Meanwhile, Vanderbilt returned to the war for control of Long Island Sound.

"THE STONINGTON IS THE *KEY*," wrote William Gibbs McNeill on November 13, 1840. The line's chief engineer never wavered in his belief that the railroad must become the primary artery of transportation between New York and Boston. But it faced a grave problem. "The company being embarrassed—involved in debt—with an impaired credit," he wrote in an official report, "could not procure steamboats of their own, and of course were dependent on those who did own them. To their terms we were compelled to submit, and we did submit." The Transportation Company had the upper hand. To change that, McNeill wanted to forge an alliance with Vanderbilt.[31]

On November 13, Vanderbilt strode into McNeill's rooms in New York, where the sick engineer was confined to his bed. A daguerreotype of Vanderbilt from this time calls to mind a description of a typical wealthy New Yorker by Francis Grund in 1839:

His stature was straight and erect; his neck . . . was, by the aid of a black cravat, reduced to a still narrower compass; and his hat was sunk down his neck so as to expose half his forehead. His frock-coat . . . was buttoned up to the chin, and yet of such diminutive dimensions as scarcely to cover any one part of his body. His trowsers were of the same tight fit as his coat, and the heels of his boots added at least an inch and a half to his natural height.

But Vanderbilt was no dandy. A viscerally physical presence, he was worth as much—and probably far more—than the entire Transportation Company (capitalized at $500,000). Even as he took control of the Richmond Turnpike Company, he had bought out the New Haven Steamboat Company and added the powerful *C. Vanderbilt* to his Southern coastal line. McNeill spoke bluntly to him, and made the only contemporary verbatim record of a conversation from the first fifty years of Vanderbilt's life.[32]

"Captain Vanderbilt," he began, "my usage and preference is, in a matter like the present, to be explicit and unreserved. You are aware of our present connection [with the Transportation Company] and the reasons its continuance is to be preferred. . . . They have suitable boats . . . and although it would be a loss to them, yet if not employed *by* us they as probably be run in opposition *to* us. . . . You know them?"

"Yes."

"We are in negotiation *now* and we await their terms. You have read my report?"

"Yes."

"Then you know my views," McNeill concluded. "What are yours?"

More than ten years earlier, Frances Trollope had observed the shrewdness of the Yankee businessman in conversation—his gift for indirection, his ability to avoid giving away any useful information—and Vanderbilt now displayed his talent at that fine art. After praising the railroad, he haltingly remarked, "To be candid with you, as you've been with me—I—couldn't—be in anything—with Mr. Palmer for president."

"Well, suppose you had it all your own way—whom you please for president and directors—O. Mauran? Or anyone else?"

"Anybody else and what board you please—anybody but him." Vanderbilt had nothing but contempt for the spineless, technically ignorant Palmer.

"Well," answered McNeill, with rising frustration, "suppose that settled—your terms?"

"Why—if the route were open I wouldn't ask a better business than one-half," Vanderbilt replied, meaning half the through fare between New York and Boston.

"That is my idea—but the route is not open," McNeill said, referring to the Stonington's ties to the Transportation Company. But he wanted to know if Vanderbilt planned on launching a rate-cutting war on the route. "By the bye," he asked, "do you think of coming on it *anyhow?*"

"Have not made up my mind."

Blunted in this probe, McNeill took another tack. "Would you propose to throw in your boats for stock—we have the privilege of owning boats under a very advantageous charter." In other words, would Vanderbilt consider selling the railroad some steamboats in return for shares in the Stonington, and a post as a director?

"I've heard of that, and think it might be made to answer." Vanderbilt warmed to the topic, pondering aloud how the railroad might run if he joined its management. "It might take one—or two—years to do any opposition up," he mused, using the slang "do up" for *destroy*. "Steamboats would both lose."

"Yes, and we pay expenses only."

"You'd do more than *that*," Vanderbilt snorted. A master of economy, he had a reputation for making a profit even in a rate war. "And—after two years—would have it all our own way. *I* shouldn't care to make money in that time. I know the route—there's nothing like it."

"Well—we agree in that—but as you can understand *me*—I should be glad at your convenience to know what you will do," McNeill stated.

The conversation displayed Vanderbilt's peculiar combination of wiliness and directness, of intense personal dislikes (in this case for Palmer) and sly concealment of his intentions. It also included one revealing exchange that McNeill mistakenly dismissed as mere bravado. Frustrated with Vanderbilt's refusal to commit himself, he asked at one point, "What do you think would be to your *interest* to offer?"

"If I owned the road," Vanderbilt answered, "I'd know how to make it profitable."

"Oh!" McNeill exclaimed sarcastically. "I suppose you'd *own* the boats too."

"Yes," Vanderbilt replied, and said nothing more about it. McNeill paid no attention. He could not take seriously the idea of one man buying control of a railroad. The Stonington was some fifty miles long, worth millions in fixed capital. It was also "embarrassed" by debt, as he put it, and in the hands of its creditors, the Philadelphia banks. Vanderbilt as master of his railroad? The idea was ridiculous.[33]

Chapter Six

MAN OF HONOR

arx says somewhere that men make their own history, but they
do not make it just as they please; they do not make it under circumstances chosen by themselves.[1] He forgot to add that great
plans often come about by accident. How many times had Vanderbilt
embarked on important enterprises only because of chance? His start in
steamboats under Gibbons, his Dispatch Line to Philadelphia, his lower
Hudson route, his People's Line to Albany, all originated in the unexpected. He was quick to turn trouble to his advantage, and to prey on the
weak and vulnerable.

In the 1840s, the strategic balance in the transportation network of
Long Island Sound destabilized as new railways were constructed alongside the Boston & Providence and the Stonington. The decade began with
the completion of both the Hartford & New Haven and, more important,
the Norwich, a line that descended from Worcester, Massachusetts, to the
Connecticut seaport that gave it its name. And the Long Island Railroad
advanced eastward by the hour. Though it would one day become a com-
muter line, it was designed to connect New York and Boston by way of a
steamboat ferry from its eastern terminus to New England's railways.

Even among these competitors, the Stonington should have throbbed
with traffic and profits, for it was still the fastest route between New York
and Boston. Instead it writhed in bankruptcy—mercilessly exploited by
the Navigation Company (formerly the Transportation Company) and
tormented by a feud between its angry stockholders and the Philadelphia
bankers who held its bonds.[2]

Vanderbilt entered the 1840s with no particular plan to take advantage
of the Stonington's weakness, despite his conference with McNeill. His
enemies, on the other hand, embarked on a game of deep subterfuge and
indirect pressure. It began in May 1841 with the appearance of Curtis
Peck, the captain who had purchased the *Citizen* from Vanderbilt exactly a
decade earlier. Peck advertised discounted fares from New York to Providence with the steamer *Belle*. This was now called the "outside" route; the
Stonington and the Norwich were "inside" lines, since they cut inside

Point Judith. Though the outside route was slower and rougher, passengers readily switched to it when fares went low enough. "Knowing the Yankee character, & how highly they value the sixpence," Palmer, president of the Stonington, worried that the railroad's passengers would start to take the *Belle*—as indeed they did.[3]

Vanderbilt followed this gambit with intense suspicion. It was not like Peck to run on the outside route; he operated short lines from New York to Flushing, Long Island, and Norwalk, Connecticut. But Peck was something of a mercenary. In 1834, for example, he had sailed the *Citizen* to Sing Sing, New York, in opposition to Vanderbilt, at the behest of the Hudson River monopoly. Was he acting now as a front for someone else?

As Vanderbilt hunted out intelligence on the stinking docks and in gaslit offices, he had a very short list of suspects. There were three major forces controlling Long Island Sound's steamboat business: first was the Navigation Company, which dominated the outside route to Providence and the inside to Stonington; second was Vanderbilt himself, who ran to the Connecticut River and New Haven, where he connected with the Hartford & New Haven Railroad; and third was Menemon Sanford, who connected to the Norwich Railroad with his *Charter Oak*, along with W. W. Coit, who commanded the *Worcester*.

Clearly the Navigation Company was not backing Peck, since it suffered badly from this maneuver. Comstock, its outspoken agent, denounced Peck's attack as "the most outrageous and unprovoked on record." The culprit, then, was most likely Sanford. Vanderbilt had long been a deadly enemy of Sanford's, and had recently driven him off the Connecticut River route to Hartford; he could easily believe that his old foe was to blame. Comstock came to the same conclusion. "I believe Sanford has an understanding with Peck," he wrote to the Navigation Company president, Charles Handy. "I have been suspicious of Sanford since last winter." But what could Sanford possibly gain from a fare war on the outside route—one that pulled traffic away from his own Norwich line?

By the end of July, Vanderbilt believed he had the answer. Under the financial pressure of Peck's opposition, the Stonington and the Navigation Company agreed to a proposal by Sanford and the Norwich to pool all their revenue from the through travel between New York and Boston, and divide it according to a fixed formula. Ordinarily it would have been a foolish move for the Stonington, as it usually garnered the greatest share of traffic. But its executives concluded, as chief engineer McNeill wrote, that "it is better even to waive a portion of our advantages over the Norwich route . . . than continue to lose money." A few days after they sealed the deal, Peck took the *Belle* off the outside route—and ran it instead to New Haven, in opposition to Vanderbilt.[4]

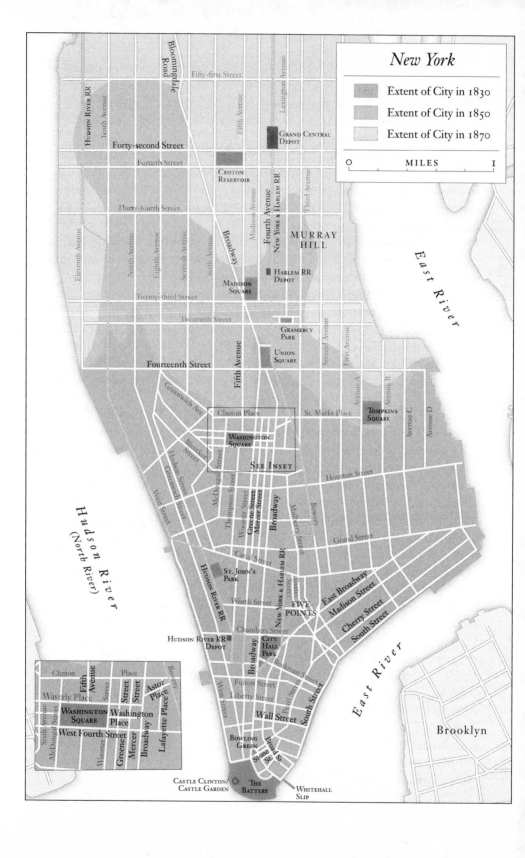

Bloomingdale Road

Fifty-first Street

HUDSON RIVER RR
Tenth Avenue

Forty-second Street

Fortieth Street

Fifth Avenue

GRAND CENTRAL DEPOT

CROTON RESERVOIR

Madison Avenue

Fourth Avenue
NEW YORK & HARLEM RR

Third Avenue

Thirty-fourth Street

Broadway

MURRAY HILL

Eleventh Avenue

Ninth Avenue

Eighth Avenue

Seventh Avenue

Sixth Avenue

HARLEM RR DEPOT

MADISON SQUARE

Twenty-third Street

East River

Twentieth Street

GRAMERCY PARK

Fifth Avenue

Second Avenue

First Avenue

UNION SQUARE

Fourteenth Street

Greenwich Ave

Clinton Place

St. Marks Place

Avenue A

Avenue B

TOMPKINS SQUARE

Avenue C

Avenue D

Bleecker Street

McDougal Street

WASHINGTON SQUARE

SEE INSET

Houston Street

Hudson Street

Greenwich Street

West Street

Thompson Street

Wooster Street

Greene Street

Mercer Street

Broadway

Mulberry Street

Bowery

Grand Street

Canal Street

HUDSON RIVER RR

ST. JOHN'S PARK

Worth Street

Hudson River RR

NEW YORK & HARLEM RR

FIVE POINTS

East Broadway

Madison Street

Cherry Street

South Street

H u d s o n   R i v e r
(North River)

Chambers Street

HUDSON RIVER RR DEPOT

CITY HALL PARK

Broadway

Beekman Street

Pearl Street

South Street

East River

Fulton Street

Liberty Street

West Street

Wall Street

South Street

Brooklyn

BOWLING GREEN

Broad St.

Stone St.

CASTLE CLINTON/ CASTLE GARDEN

THE BATTERY

WHITEHALL SLIP

Clinton

Fifth Avenue

Place

Astor Place

Bowery

Waverly Place

Wooster Street

Greene Street

Mercer Street

WASHINGTON SQUARE

Washington Place

Sixth Avenue

McDougal Street

West Fourth Street

Broadway

Lafayette Place

Vanderbilt was incensed. Using Peck as a decoy, Sanford had played the Stonington and the Navigation Company for fools, arranging to skim their profits and build a united front that excluded Vanderbilt. Then Sanford pitted Peck against Vanderbilt's own line. It was a masterful piece of indirection that demanded retaliation.

Too late, Comstock realized that his corporation had been duped. "Sanford, etc., have cheated you into the Norwich contract by false means," he told Handy. But he seethed with fury at Vanderbilt's response—to run a small steamboat, the aptly named *Gladiator,* to Providence at a very low fare. This struck Comstock as a flagrant violation of the verbal non-competition agreement made when the *Lexington* changed hands. "I . . . expected it from Vanderbilt as he has avowed it more than once," he remarked bitterly.

Vanderbilt received a message from Courtlandt Palmer, asking him to come and explain his move. Vanderbilt only had to stalk a few blocks from his office through the crowded, narrow streets of the Wall Street district to reach the Stonington's door. As he sat down in Palmer's office, the tall, powerful Vanderbilt could hardly have concealed his contempt for the officious weakling who ran the Stonington. He explained what had really happened that summer, how Sanford had tricked them and thrown Peck against Vanderbilt's own New Haven line. "To punish Sanford for this he runs the *Gladiator,* charging \$2 fare to Providence and \$3½ to Boston to draw the long travel from the Norwich route, where (with us) they charge \$5," Palmer wrote to the banker Lewis. "He states that the opposition is to the Norwich line, not ours."

Within the Navigation Company and the Stonington, this logic was angrily dismissed. "Vanderbilt's excuse is a miserable one indeed," Comstock thought. Palmer called the explanation "a mere pretext. He puts his boats on to make money, and a more outrageous violation of his pledged faith to us . . . could not be made." Vanderbilt, of course, had a different view—and, as usual, he was sure he was right. "Vanderbilt says he recognizes all his pledges to us," Palmer continued, "but says we have, in our arrangements with the Norwich Company, absolved him from them, and to satisfy us, he proposes to refer it to arbitration whether he shall pay us damages or we, him."[5]

As Palmer and Comstock dipped pens in inkwells and scratched out letters to their respective masters, their outrage soaked through the paper. They each took particular aim at Vanderbilt's reputation as a man of his word. Comstock sarcastically referred to him as "the *Honourable* Capt. C. Vanderbilt." Soon he simply abbreviated his views. "As to C.V.—you know my opinion of his word and honour," he told Handy. The humorless Palmer was more ornate: "I think Vanderbilt ought to be exposed to the public for the violation of his pledges to us, as nothing was ever more gross or unprovoked. This exposure would annoy him more than anything we could do, as he is very desirous of being considered a man of honor and integrity, and would be severely mortified to have his baseness trumpeted forth to the world."

Wisely, the railroad did no such thing. As Vanderbilt surely knew, the public hardly would be upset because he ended an agreement that protected the Stonington and the Navigation Company ("that vast and overshadowing monopoly," in the words of the *Brooklyn Eagle*). What is curious is that Palmer did not see that; it showed the persistence of an older elitism and Whiggish disdain for economic anarchy. McNeill, on the other hand, understood their precarious public position. "In our political climate," he sarcastically explained, "*corporations* must subsist on a very spare diet & practice very *fascinating* manners, or the Sovereign People will crawl them all over."[6]

In this conflict, both Vanderbilt's power and his self-righteousness would prevail. He forced Sanford and Coit to pay him one-third of their steamboat profits for as long as Peck competed with him. The dispute went to arbitration, and the panel (which included William Gibbons, at Vanderbilt's request) ruled against the Stonington and the Navigation Company, and awarded Vanderbilt $1,733.33 in damages. With the judgment of his peers to justify his aggression, Vanderbilt laid siege to the two corporations. Under the name "Vanderbilt's Independent Line," he sent his *New Haven* to Providence in December 1841. "That Vanderbilt," the prim Palmer exclaimed to Lewis, "is a great ____ (you must fill in the blank.)"[7]

Now committed to full-scale warfare, Vanderbilt battered his opponents with his grasp of both tactics and strategy. His main strength was, in a word, everything; the attack was nothing less than an all-enveloping onslaught, omitting no possible competitive advantage. He was better capitalized than his opponents, which enabled him to absorb losses. But he also could make money even in a fare war, thanks to his ability to control costs. In part, this was a technical advantage: the *Lexington*'s engine and hull design had saved an estimated 50 percent in fuel expenses, by far the largest operating cost, and all his later boats followed its plan. He kept personnel expenses down by shifting them to his customers; passengers began to complain that they were expected to tip for almost everything. And Comstock's letters to Handy bemoaned the way that Vanderbilt outmatched them in everything from pricing to renting office space to distributing handbills. "Vanderbilt has several agents in Boston making great efforts to obtain freight and passengers," he wrote. "The *New Haven*'s passengers and freight increases daily," he noted on another occasion. "We are losing some of our regular freight customers."[8]

Vanderbilt reached an agreement with the Boston & Providence Railroad—the erstwhile ally of the Navigation Company—that gave him a 25 percent rebate on freight charges. He put the *Cleopatra* on the line, which became very popular. ("She proves to be very fast," Comstock admitted.) He even hired a lobbyist to petition Rhode Island's legislature to stop the Navigation Company from having exclusive rights to its dock. "V. is determined to put us to as much trouble and expense as possible," Comstock said. "There is a great disposition here [in Providence] to assist him."

On the strategic plane, Vanderbilt shifted the Sound's travel patterns as he drew thousands of passengers away from the Norwich and Stonington railroads. Palmer was utterly flummoxed. "To the astonishment of everybody he has not lost money & it is supposed that he has made," he wrote to Lewis. "We have made every effort in our power during the winter to induce Vanderbilt to withdraw from the line but to this day have been entirely unsuccessful. . . . He is a very hard & troublesome customer."

As the spring of 1842 came and went, Palmer verged on a breakdown under the pressure. "His great wealth & tact in the management of steamboats renders him the most formidable opponent that could come in opposition," he moaned on March 6. A few weeks later he whimpered, "Vanderbilt's boat (the *New Haven*) lessens our receipts nearly one half. We are barely paying expenses." In June, he wailed, "Vanderbilt is pushing his opposition against us with great vigor, & as you must have perceived by our weekly returns is ruining our business." McNeill put it more graphically. Vanderbilt, he warned, "is gnawing at our very vitals."[9]

WHATEVER HUGH MCLAUGHLIN SAID OR DID, Cornelius Vanderbilt didn't like it. On Staten Island on December 1, 1843, Vanderbilt flared in rage at McLaughlin, and bashed him with his knuckles until he reduced him to a bleeding wreck. What's remarkable about the story is not the beating, but McLaughlin's nerve in then suing him for $1,000. Vanderbilt's reputation usually terrified people.[10]

On January 27, 1842, for instance, a committee from the Elizabethport & New York Ferry Company met him to discuss his proposal to sell them some waterfront land in Port Richmond, Staten Island. Coming from Vanderbilt, the most innocuous offer sounded like a threat. If they bought the land, they asked, would he sign an agreement to not compete with their ferry? "Capt. Vanderbilt would not agree to bind himself by any written agreement," the committee reported, "but said his word was better than his bond & that he has no intention of running an opposition to us any more than he should think of running a boat to Quebec." The delegation didn't believe him, but finalized the deal just the same, "believing that he will not interfere with us, if we make the purchase," as the committee put it. It was an offer they couldn't refuse.[11]

They did not have to look far for examples of Vanderbilt's ruthlessness. After taking over the Richmond Turnpike Company, he had pummeled his cousin Oliver—matching his fare cuts, filing lawsuits, even fencing in his dock and dumping gravel on it. And Vanderbilt insisted on a $20,000 bribe from the Navigation Company to leave the outside line. "Sooner than pay him one dollar tribute," Comstock sputtered, "I would die in a ditch. . . . In fact I protest as an owner to paying him one dollar, directly or indirectly." The company paid.

But this was not the usual sort of extortion. It formed part of a larger deal in August 1842 that forced Sanford off the Sound and gave Vanderbilt the right to connect to the Norwich Railroad. Sanford retreated to lines between Boston and Maine, and Coit sold his *Worcester* to Vanderbilt. Daniel Allen began to sell through tickets via the Norwich on the "New York and Boston Railroad Line" for the *Worcester* under Jacob Vanderbilt and the *Cleopatra* under Captain Isaac Dustan.[12]

The Norwich maneuver was the first of a series of strategic moves that would transform Vanderbilt from a spoiler to the ultimate insider. He began to systematically seize power in the companies that provided transportation around New York. On November 20, 1843, he bought 490 shares (out of 998 total) in the Elizabethport Ferry Company, which effectively gave him control of the second major ferry service to Staten Island (the company's boats stopped at Port Richmond on their way to New Jersey). On March 1, 1844, Vanderbilt became a director and treasurer; in July, he had Allen named secretary, and moved its offices in with his own, now at 34 Broadway.[13]

Also in March, another corporate delegation visited Vanderbilt—this one from the Long Island Railroad, now nearing completion to its eastern terminus, the village of Greenport. They had discovered, they told him, that the New England railroads across the Sound refused to supply a connection to Boston "without the concurrence of the steamboat proprietors connected with such railroads." As negotiations wound on, the corporation invited him to join the grand festivities that marked the opening of the line on July 29 and 30. Vanderbilt and some five hundred dignitaries, including the mayors of New York and Brooklyn, rode in the first set of trains to make the ninety-five-mile journey from Brooklyn to Greenport. In August, he closed a deal to sell the railroad the *Cleopatra*, the *Worcester*, and the *New Haven* for $120,000 in railroad stock and $125,000 in bonds. He joined the board of directors, and was named to the three-man committee that managed its steamboat affairs.[14]

In all these moves, Vanderbilt bracketed the Stonington with his attacks. First, as an individual proprietor he had drawn traffic to the outside route. Then his agreement not to compete with the Stonington and the Navigation Company in return for $20,000 had only bound him as an individual proprietor, not as a corporate director. So he operated through those corporations, undermining the Stonington through the railroads that ran parallel to it. He undercut it on both sides, by selling $2 tickets to Boston via the Norwich and, in 1845, arranging for the Long Island Railroad to switch its steamboat connection from Stonington to Providence.[15]

The Stonington, however, transformed from a bankrupt enterprise into a potential fountain of profits and dividends. It began with the rise of Elisha Peck to the board of directors in January 1843. This was a powerless position; with the Stonington in the hands of its bondholders, led by William Lewis of the Girard Bank, the stockholders had no influence. But Peck had a plan to reduce the crippling debt by half and regain control: the railroad would take back the existing bonds in exchange for new ones worth 50 percent less. He argued that it was better for the creditors to accept half than to hold title to a whole that would never be paid. The deal would allow the company to resume its interest payments and therefore restore its financial health.

Elisha Peck (apparently of no relation to Curtis Peck) was an ill-educated, hardheaded man, much like Vanderbilt. The polished and aristocratic Lewis mocked his unorthodox grammar and the sharp scrawl of his handwriting. But Peck proved that he understood his business very well indeed. He assembled a block of stockholders dedicated to "the work of regeneration & reform," as broker Samuel Jaudon put it—a reform in administration as well as debt. Peck maneuvered to remove Courtlandt Palmer as president.[16]

Peck pulled off his coup—assisted by Lewis, who literally sold out Palmer. Lewis arranged to have the Girard Bank sell the old bonds to a consortium of speculators at twenty-five cents on the dollar. Then the consortium swapped them with the railroad for its new bonds, as Peck had proposed, at a rate of *fifty* cents on the dollar, doubling the speculators' money. That consortium of lucky men included Peck, his faction of stockholders, and Lewis himself, who blithely profited at his own bank's expense. Peck ascended to the Stonington's presidency, and the railroad, with its debt reduced by half, finally emerged out of bankruptcy.[17]

But hardly had Peck assumed the presidency than he confronted the same problem that had wrecked Palmer. At the end of 1845, Peck wearily explained it in the railroad's annual report. "The receipts of the Company, it will be seen, have fallen off materially, compared with those of the former years," he wrote. "This has been caused by the very low rate of fare produced by an active opposition."

That opposition came from Cornelius Vanderbilt, of course, in conjunction with an old friend. "It appears that Vanderbilt, Newton, & Drew are all connected in their steam boat operations," Comstock wrote Handy. (He was referring to Isaac Newton, Drew's partner in the People's Line on the Hudson.) "I have it from pretty good authority that Mr. Newton & Drew are both interested" in Vanderbilt's operations on the Sound.[18]

And so they were. In recent years, Drew and Vanderbilt each had done his best to keep the other, a potentially deadly enemy, as close as possible. When Drew and Newton (an expert in the field of steamboats, unlike Drew) reorganized the People's Line as a joint-stock association in July 1843, Vanderbilt bought $11,500 worth of shares in the business, out of a total capitalization of $360,000, and took a seat on the board as one of five directors. (Drew owned $108,500, and Newton $52,000.) In December 1844, Daniel Allen became a partner in Drew's banking and brokerage firm, Drew, Robinson & Co.[19]

When Allen entered Drew's office, he learned that the latter had concocted a scheme to buy control of the Mohawk & Hudson, New York State's pioneering steam railroad, which offered a shortcut between the Erie Canal at Schenectady and the Hudson River at Albany. Starting on September 16, 1844, Drew's partner Nelson Robinson, a man renowned for his cunning as a broker, set out to acquire the necessary shares. He regularly would pass under the colonnaded facade of the Merchants' Exchange, a large building between Wall and William streets, and between Exchange Place and Hanover Street, completed in 1842. The edifice housed the long room where mere handfuls of brokers gathered in front of a table where the few publicly traded stocks were called in a daily auction. By June 11, 1845, Robinson had purchased enough shares to elect Newton as the Mohawk & Hudson's president, and both Allen and Drew as directors.[20]

With a man inside Drew's firm, Vanderbilt came to understand these operations intimately. They offered a promising model for his own offensive on the Sound. Barred by agreement from competing personally with the Stonington Railroad, he arranged in 1845 for the People's Line to take a steamboat off the Hudson and throw it on the outside route to Providence. Meanwhile, he used his position within the Norwich and Long Island railroads to further slash fares to Boston.

"All of these lines are probably run for the pleasure of doing an active business," the *Boston Advertiser* joked, for it seemed impossible that they made enough money to pay expenses.[21] This fare-cutting assault marked the final offensive of Vanderbilt's long war on the Stonington and the Navigation Company. This time, however, he had his eye not only on the movements of passengers on the Sound, but on the movements on Wall Street. He did not want a bribe—he wanted possession.

On July 4, 1845, the *New York Herald* published a lengthy analysis of Vanderbilt's attack, without mentioning his name. "The parties engaged in the running of the opposition boat, are perfectly indifferent about its earnings—they do not look for a single cent in return for the outlawry in that quarter," the paper stated, using the revealing term "outlawry" for the ruthless reduction in prices.

> The support of the opposition is purely a Wall Street stock operation, and so long as it suits the interests of these brokers cornering Long Island, Norwich and Worcester, and Stonington Railroad stock, the boats will be regularly employed on the route. . . . The stock of the Stonington Railroad Company has thus far been more seriously affected than any other. That road having no local travel of consequence, depending almost entirely upon the receipts from through travel, its income has been badly reduced by the attraction of passengers to other routes.

Perversely, the very reforms that Peck had carried out now made the Stonington a desirable property, and thus a target of attack. Vanderbilt waged his ferocious fare competition in order to drive down its stock price, in order to gain control. With Drew's firm (and most likely Nelson Robinson personally) handling the trading, Vanderbilt bought up large blocks of shares. He convinced Drew and his partners to buy shares as well, on the promise of a large rise in price once he assumed control of the corporation. As the annual meeting approached, Vanderbilt tried to rally support among the other investors. "A meeting of the stockholders of the Stonington Railroad is to be held at the Astor [House hotel] this evening," the *Herald* reported on September 26, 1845. "The late movements which have taken place in this Stock are said to be for the purpose of producing a change in the Direction."

A few days later, the old board of directors won reelection.[22] But the steady pressure Vanderbilt exerted on the railroad's business allowed him to acquire more and more shares. To that end, he next moved into the Hartford & New Haven Railroad. For its first few years, the line had staggered along with only local traffic; then, in December 1844, it completed a connection to Boston through an extension to the Western Railroad at Springfield, Massachusetts. "The result has produced a complete renovation of the affairs of the company," the *American Railroad Journal* reported, as revenue more than doubled. On June 1, 1846, Vanderbilt sold to Hartford & New Haven three modest steamboats in return for $180,000 in stock at the par value of $100 per share (which paid a dividend of 7.5 percent, or $7.50 per share). This made him a major shareholder and a company director. It was another route on which he could cut fares to Boston—another finger in his grip on the Stonington's throat.[23]

In September 1846, he seized Stonington directorships for himself, sons-in-law Allen and William Thorn, and Drew and his partner Eli Kelley. The Navigation Company succumbed as well, as Drew bought control of the old foe in early August 1846 (undoubtedly with Vanderbilt's assistance). Finally, in 1847, Vanderbilt and his partners forced Peck off the Stonington's board, replacing him with Nelson Robinson, and Vanderbilt assumed the presidency. "The road never was under better management or more prosperous condition," the *Herald* reported. The monopolists' nemesis, the champion of the people, was now the prince of Long Island Sound.[24]

"NO ONE WHO SAW IT WILL DENY that the Whig Procession yesterday surpassed anything of the kind ever seen in this country," the *New York Tribune* exclaimed on October 31, 1844. "The Procession occupied two hours and a half in passing Canal street, while it was half an hour longer in wheeling into Broadway from Marketfield st." Brass bands, columns of banner-wielding marchers, and formations of mounted men demonstrated in favor of Whig presidential candidate Henry Clay—and against Democrat James K. Polk, derided by the *Tribune* as "the creature and heir of the Annexation Conspiracy!"[25]

The intended insult spoke of an ominous shift in American politics. The old political debates still smoldered, but had cooled somewhat. Many Whigs remained unhappy with cutthroat competition, and many Democrats with banks and corporations, but they were learning to endure them. Policy makers from both parties often proved more pragmatic than ideological. In 1838, for example, New York's Whigs had introduced free banking, which allowed anyone who met certain requirements to obtain a charter for a bank; the Whigs had intended to end the political abuse of bank chartering by Martin Van Buren's Albany Regency, but the result was to open the field to all who wished to compete. And the Democrats generally embraced the largest and most active part of the federal government, the Post Office, which subsidized newspaper delivery and (until 1845) many stagecoach lines. Meanwhile a wave of defaults by state governments on their bonds after the Panic of 1837 had tempered the enthusiasm for internal improvements, and President Van Buren's creation of the independent treasury system (removing federal money from private banks) had settled the Democrats' gravest complaints with the banking system.[26]

But politics still generated searing heat, thanks to slavery. For the previous decade, abolitionists had been organizing and agitating, particularly in pious New England. On the other side, Democrats in particular wanted to annex Texas, where slave-owning settlers from the United States had won their independence from Mexico in 1836. Candidate Polk craved an expansion of the republic, hungrily eyeing Oregon, California, and New Mexico. But it was his enthusiasm for Texas that sparked the fury of many Northern Whigs. The idea of absorbing a territory where slavery actually existed upset even conservatives who frowned on the rabble-rousing abolitionists. And Mexico refused to accept Texas's independence, raising the danger of war. "It would ill become this nation, so boastful of its love of freedom," declared Horace Greeley, the *Tribune's* editor, "to embark in a foreign war, assume a foreign debt, and involve itself in a web of responsibilities the end whereof no man can predict, for the clearly discerned purpose of extending and fortifying slavery."[27]

And so the mammoth parade proceeded through New York's streets on October 30, 1844. It is too simple to say that passions ran high; the cliché conjures up none of the anger that vibrated between the watching crowds and the columned marchers, none of the hate in the eyes of the union members, the Irish immigrants who had flooded into the city since 1830, the expansionistic Democrats who saw the Whigs as aristocrats who conspired to hold them down. First came the shouts and insults, then pushing, and finally punching. All along the route, skirmishes erupted, in a daylong moving battle.[28]

Of all the Irish Democrats who smashed Whig cheeks and broke Whig teeth, perhaps the most feared was Yankee Sullivan. Born in Ireland in 1813, he had been transported by British authorities to Botany Bay, Australia, for an unknown felony. In 1839 he had stowed away on a ship to the United States, where he rose to fame as a bare-knuckle prizefighter. He had opened a tavern, the Sawdust House, in the infamous Five Points slum and became an enforcer for the Democratic Party in the city. Sullivan was flamboyant, crafty, and merciless. In one fight, he was losing badly until he broke his foe's arm; Sullivan then punched the broken arm relentlessly until the opponent gave up. In another, he got caught in a headlock, gasped that he was done for, and went limp. When the enemy let him go and turned toward his corner, Sullivan leaped up and hammered his head behind the ear.[29]

"Vanderbilt . . . was an ardent supporter of Henry Clay," an old Staten Islander told the *New York Times* in 1877, "and organized and commanded a magnificent troop of horsemen composed of about 500 of the finest men in the Whig Party on the Island. When the grand . . . procession took place in New-York, Commodore Vanderbilt and his troop of horsemen occupied a very conspicuous position in it." Yankee Sullivan, the man recalled, was drinking in his bar with "a gang of roughs" as Vanderbilt rode by. "Rushing out, he [Sullivan] seized the reins of his horse and tried to compel him to alight. The horse reared, the Commodore cut 'Yankee' Sullivan across the back with his whip, and then, leaping to the ground, so badly beat him that his friends took him [Sullivan] away in a nearly sense-less condition."

The story is too good not to repeat: one of the richest men in the city, now fifty years old, bludgeoning the greatest boxer of the day in a street brawl. Vanderbilt loomed over six feet tall, and he was a seasoned fighter; he suffered none of the hesitation, the muscle-tensing slowness, that an inexperienced man feels when an exchange of blows is imminent. Less than a year earlier, he had beaten a man down on Staten Island. And the details the old Staten Islander provided fit perfectly with the events of the day. Unfortunately, there is no evidence for the fight beyond this anec-dote, which first appeared decades later. Yankee Sullivan was a celebrity, and the newspapers covered him closely. A beating at the hands of a prominent capitalist surely would have found some mention in the press. There were none. It most likely never happened.[30]

But the symbolism of the story says more than the facts. Despite ten years of lavishing Jacksonian rhetoric on the public, Vanderbilt would be remembered as a Whig. Long the darling of the Democratic press, he would be depicted as thrashing a working-class Irishman of Five Points— a Tammany Hall operative, no less. In memory, at least, the champion of scrapping, competitive individualism ascended into Whiggery, into the party of social prejudice and Wall Street insiders. It is not an accurate por-trait (in no other case was Vanderbilt portrayed as seriously engaged with either party), but this anecdote can be seen as a reflection of his slowly changing social status.

In later years it would often be said that New York's social elite snubbed Vanderbilt. Not only is this biographical cliché misleading, it also over-simplifies the extreme instability of fashionable society at this time. In the eighteenth-century culture of deference, the differentiations of rank could not have been more clear: wealth, social status, and political power had been wrapped in a bundle as tight as the leases that bound tenant farmers to manorial lords. But the destruction of that culture wiped out the rules of hierarchy, replacing them with a mad scramble for standing. The com-petitive individualism of the economy found its reflection even in Sara-toga Springs.

"In this country, where a democracy on the broadest scale is supposed to exist, we discover at our watering places an eternal struggle for ascen-dancy," the *Herald* observed in 1845.

> Exquisites in broad-cloth and patent leather, and female miracles of ele-gance and taste—the posterity of some Irish washerwoman, turn up their

noses at Mrs. Smith and Misses Smith, because their papa keeps a hardware store in Pearl street; and an effeminate and deteriorated specimen of humanity, descended from the loins of some poor porter, pronounces the whole company "decidedly vulgar, and shockingly low."

The phenomenon of the newly rich caught the attention of many observers, as those who came into fortunes fought for social respect. Francis Grund derided them as "the mushroom aristocracy of New York" to underscore their lack of lineage, their reliance on mere wealth and pretension. "Do you observe that gentleman in tights, with large black whiskers?" he snidely asked. "He is one of the most fashionable and aristocratic gentlemen in the city. I believe he served his apprenticeship in a baker's shop, then went into an auction-room, then became a partner in the firm, and lastly took a house in Broadway, set up a carriage, and declared himself a gentleman."

The *Herald* mocked these rivals in snobbery, who "calculated to a nicety the number of dollars which may enable them to 'astonish the Browns' at the Springs." Few of the striving new toffs were truly self-made, despite the rhetoric of these observers; the point, rather, is that they struggled to invent social status in a culture that no longer depended upon hierarchy to function. A Livingston of 1800 did not *desire* distinction; she simply had it. But these latter-day climbers had to conjure up artificial ranks now that the organic ones were gone.[31]

This was the class that Vanderbilt *never* belonged to: an affected aristocracy, the patricians of puffery. And yet, he was a first-generation entrant into the ranks of the wealthy. To that extent, he had a fraught relationship with a distinctly different fashionable set—the remnants of the old knickerbocker elite, the descendants of those who had once stood atop the culture of deference. The onslaught of recently rich outsiders caused this group to rally around each other, to construct elaborate new forms of social exclusivity. They had launched this campaign on February 27, 1840, with a "grand fancy dress ball at Brevoort Hall," as the *New York Herald* called it. It was the first fancy ball held in a private residence in New York; it took place on Fifth Avenue and Ninth Street, at the grand home of Henry Brevoort, "a lineal descendent of the celebrated Dutch merchant, who . . . first settled Dutch colonies in North America." More than five hundred of the oldest and most prestigious families in the country came in costume. "The dresses worn on this occasion must have cost, we verily believe, nearly half a million of dollars," the *Herald* reported. The ball, the paper observed, marked the beginning of a new era, "as it is the first of its kind."[32]

All this—the affectations of the newly rich and the closing of the ranks of the old patrician families—reflected the same phenomenon. For centuries, the social, political, and economic elite had been one and the same; power and influence had gone together with social standing and family prestige. The democratization of politics and the unleashing of the market, however, had destroyed the functional purpose of social standing. One no longer had to be a Jay, a Colden, or a Beekman to dominate business or politics. Money was no respecter of persons, and neither were voters any longer. Though the old patrician families still carried on in wealth and, to a lesser extent, in politics as well, they had no choice but to make room for those who could clamber up, now that family connections ceased to be a requirement for success.

In the early nineteenth century, for the first time, a distinction emerged between the social elite and the elite of true power and wealth. They overlapped, of course, but they also existed in a state of tension. Vanderbilt went to Saratoga Springs each August; he built a palace on Staten Island; he bought teams of expensive horses. These activities reflected his sense of his own importance, and they were necessary, to a certain extent, to allow him to engage in highly practical socializing. But he did not go to the balls at Brevoort Hall, nor did his children marry the Livingstons and Van Rensselaers. Instead, he moved in a special zone established by fashionable society, one that allowed the elite to engage social outsiders such as himself. In 1844, for example, John C. Stevens of the patrician railroad-and-steamboat family organized the New York Yacht Club, which immediately attracted the likes of Philip Hone, Moses Grinnell, Oroondates Mauran, Peter Schemerhorn, William H. Aspinwall, and August Belmont, among others, a mixed group of men from old and new families, united only in wealth and influence. And on July 2, 1846, they welcomed Cornelius Vanderbilt into the club.[33]

VANDERBILT MIRRORED THE CITY'S own struggle for respectability as its wealth and reputation for enterprise grew. It had long suffered from polluted water and runaway fires, but on June 23, 1842, it opened the Croton Aqueduct, carrying millions of gallons of pure water down from Westchester County. Other moves were less successful. In April 1844, a nativist movement played on fears of Irish Catholic immigrants (and the rampant violence of street gangs) to elect James Harper mayor. He tried to both close businesses and stop the sale of alcohol on Sunday, the only day most workers had free. "In less than two months," writes historian Edward K. Spann, "the crusade had broken down in a cloud of protest, recrimination, and frustration." But 1844 also saw the birth of a professional police force that replaced the amateur constables and night watchmen who had worked under the venerable Joseph Hays.[34]

In the 1840s, New York rebounded from depression. One writer wryly called it "that town which it is the fashion of the times to call the *Commercial* Emporium of America—as if there might very well be an *emporium* of any other character." As Vanderbilt took the ferry daily between his Staten Island mansion and Manhattan, he saw the buoyant scene that Dickens described in 1842, the "confused heaps of buildings, with here and there a spire or steeple, looking down upon the herd below; and here and there, again, a cloud of lazy smoke; and in the foreground a forest of ships' masts, cheery with flapping sails and waving flags." Every time the *Sylph* or the *Staten Islander* chuffed closer to Whitehall Slip, Vanderbilt heard "the city's hum and buzz, the clinking of capstans, the ringing of bells, the barking of dogs, the clattering of wheels." Walking up to his office at 34 Broadway, he entered a daily parade of fashion. "Heaven save the ladies, how they dress!" Dickens exclaimed. "What various parasols! what rainbow silks and satins! what pinking of thin stockings, and pinching of thin shoes, and fluttering of ribbons and silk tassels, and display of rich cloaks with gaudy hoods and linings!" Young clerks turned down their collars and grew whiskers under their chins, while Irish laborers marched by with "long-tailed blue coats and bright buttons."[35]

As Vanderbilt thrived, the city thrived; as he conquered corporations and lines of travel, the republic looked to conquer as well. Polk defeated Clay and entered the White House in 1845, and territorial expansion became a national mission. "The movements for the annexation of Texas by the government of the United States, and the extraordinary sensation which it has produced," the *New York Herald* wrote on July 2, 1845, "is only a strong manifestation of the spirit of the age. . . . At all hazards Texas will be annexed to this country. California will follow—Oregon will be occupied."

Signs of trouble appeared, of course. "On all hands, you hear the question, will Mexico make war against the United States?" the *Herald* observed. "The merchant, the manufacturer, every man at all interested in the affairs of the country is asking. . . . Will there be war?" But Polk's plans proceeded heedless of such worries. So, too, with Vanderbilt, who rammed through all obstacles. On July 19, 1845, a huge fire destroyed some three hundred buildings along Whitehall and Broad streets, "occupied principally by importing and other merchants," the press reported. The blaze burned down Vanderbilt's office, wiping out such records as the stock ledgers of the Elizabethport Ferry Company. He steamed ahead regardless, opening a new office at 8 Battery Place and re-creating the lost books, as he built a vast new ferry dock on Staten Island.[36]

Even before the fire, Vanderbilt decided to make a declaration of his rising status by moving into the heart of the great city. He purchased two adjacent lots that stretched the width of the block between Washington

Place and Fourth Street, between Mercer and Greene streets east of Washington Square Park, for $9,500. Just a short distance away from the site where New York's social elite were building Grace Church, not far from the foot of Fifth Avenue, this was the heart of the most fashionable district. Typically, Vanderbilt dictated to mason Benjamin F. Camp every detail of the mansion to be built on the site. He called for stables and a carriage house in the back, facing Fourth Street; a paved courtyard; and a four-story, double-wide house of "red brick, with brown-stone trimmings," as the *New York Times* later described it, sixty-five feet deep and forty feet wide, with an entrance at 10 Washington Place. Camp went to work in May 1845. Rumors flew around the "splendid house," as one newspaper called it, being built for "the well-known steamboat proprietor." One account put the cost at an astronomical $180,000. Three decades later, the *Times* reported a figure of $55,000, noting, "It is reckoned to be one of the strongest and best constructed buildings in the City."[37]

On Staten Island, the house of Vanderbilt echoed with conspiratorial whispers and angry shouts. In April 1844, Vanderbilt's hard-nosed mother, Phebe, foreclosed on a mortgage she had taken for a loan to her son-in-law, Charles Simonson (one of the builders of the *Lexington*). Charles had died a year earlier, so the property she seized belonged to her own widowed daughter. On May 10, Vanderbilt bailed out his brother Jacob and cousin John, who had been arrested for missing mandatory payments to the disabled sailors' fund. And Vanderbilt's daughters rallied around his son Cornelius Jeremiah, who aroused his wrath and scorn. Shortly before the move to Staten Island, the boy had suffered an epileptic seizure; though the condition had not reappeared, he lingered at home, thin and aimless, in the shadow of his robust patriarch. "My treatment by my father was rather rough," he dryly recalled.

Vanderbilt was equally hard on Billy. He spoke to his elder son daily, often with "offensive" language, as Daniel Allen recalled. "The substance of the Commodore's remarks was that William was deficient in brains." Afterward, Billy would stop at Allen's home to complain of his abuse by "the old man."[38]

In 1846, Vanderbilt's children began to suspect that he had designs on the governess, a young woman who cared for the youngest siblings. He often took her on carriage rides as his offspring whispered about the "impropriety" of the relationship. Then, in June, the "old man" pulled Allen aside and suggested that he and Ethelinda take his wife on a trip to Canada. "She was at the change of life," Allen remembered, "and had been afflicted with the ailments incidental to that period for about a year, although she was naturally a woman of strong mind and body." She must have had a very strong body indeed, to have endured an unbroken string of pregnancies up to the start of menopause. Allen agreed to the proposal. Mrs. Vanderbilt "was more excitable than usual," he thought. "The Commodore told me that her physician advised a change of scene."[39]

With his wife away, Vanderbilt undertook the construction of the largest steamship ever built in the United States: the *Atlantic*, a 321-foot monster sidewheeler commissioned by the Norwich Railroad. Perhaps the most telling aspect of the vessel was not its size, but its aristocratic luxury. "On ascending the stairs, and reaching the upper saloon, one is almost bewildered with the variety of magnificent adornments which dazzle the eye," the *New York Herald* reported. Elegant staterooms, "furnished like the chambers of European hotels," surrounded the saloon, which featured "soft carpets, original settees, and courting couches . . . magnificent mirrors and rich curtains." On the distant Rio Grande, war with Mexico began—"the war for the extension of slavery," as the *Tribune* denounced it—but Vanderbilt abstained from politics, concerning himself with the Stonington, his liners, and his governess.[40]

After six weeks, Sophia returned and the governess left, to Vanderbilt's distress. Allen told him that the vacation had not improved Sophia's disposition. "During that journey she exhibited great excitability; her nervous system was apparently much shattered." It is impossible to specify the cause of her anguish, but perhaps her husband's wealth did not compensate for the stress he strung like cobwebs across every open space in their household. With the mansion at 10 Washington Place nearly complete, Vanderbilt mused openly about sending Sophia to an insane asylum.

Perhaps he was simply unable to cope with her distracted state. Or perhaps he wished to make room for the return of the young governess, a prospect he discussed as the move to Manhattan approached. Billy told Allen "that the 'old man' had induced some of his daughters to write to the governness and ask her to come back there."

Asked his daughters to write her? The maneuver seems strikingly uncharacteristic of an overweening titan who took what he wanted. Indeed, it is a rare glimpse of the vulnerability within the warrior. Though he blasted his eldest son—who only tried to please him—as a weakling and a "sucker," he found himself unable to express his tenderness and need for the young woman who cared for his children. From his earliest days, navigating the subtleties of the inner life escaped him, even if he could not escape its swirling emotions and compulsions. What attracted him to the governess? Was it sexual desire, a longing for youth, mere affection for a sweet girl his children loved? The unknowable answer may be less revealing than his response to her loss. He could not bring himself to demand her return, nor could he approach her directly and simply ask, so he delegated the emotional burden he found so bewildering.

Allen and Billy met to discuss the worsening family situation. They spoke as childhood friends and, in a way, as rival siblings. Allen cultivated a dignified air of efficiency and moral uprightness. He managed the details of Vanderbilt's businesses and served as his agent within Drew's brokerage firm. The blood son Billy, on the other hand, had been exiled from Wall Street to a farm. Slumping, sometimes whining, he had the disposition of someone accustomed to being beaten down. There is little sign that Billy resented Allen, but he had learned to be guarded in his dealings with his overbearing father.

"The old man was bound to have his way," Allen remembered him saying, "and it was useless to oppose him. He (William) had made up his mind not to do so, as he thought his own interests were too much at stake." Allen pointed out how angry Billy's sisters were. They had kept their mouths shut about their mother's forced vacation, but "her removal from home" would be too much. "The fact that Mrs. Vanderbilt had fulfilled the duties of a mother more completely than any woman they had ever known, had been talked over," Allen recalled. He told Billy that Ethelinda had denounced, directly to Vanderbilt's face, the plan to send her mother away and bring back the governess. Even Corneil, the younger brother, had spoken out "manfully."

Billy shook his head. He couldn't "justify the act," he told Allen. "He had a great deal of sympathy for his mother." And yet, "opposition would only provoke the old man's enmity. . . . The 'old man' would be 'down on him' forever and had at one time threatened to break up his family and go to Europe if his wishes were opposed." It was better to approach the problem indirectly, Billy argued. Take the departed governess, for example. "If she don't come back I'll find some woman to take her place," he said. "The old man is bound to fall under some woman's influence, and I'll have that influence."

A month after Sophia Vanderbilt's return from Canada, her husband dispatched her to an insane asylum run by a Dr. McDonald in Flushing, Long Island. Shortly afterward, in November 1846, Vanderbilt and his family settled into the house at 10 Washington Place—along with a new governess, the twenty-five-year-old cousin of Billy's wife.[41]

The meaning of all this should not be overblown. It is doubtful that Billy actually exerted any dire "influence" on the old man through the new governess. Allen saw no impropriety in their relationship; indeed, Billy may well have intended to flush scandal out of the household by replacing his father's mistress with a pious minister's niece. What's more, Sophia joined her family on Washington Place after her discharge from the asylum a few months later.*

---

* Edward J. Renehan Jr. claims, in his book *Commodore: The Life of Cornelius Vanderbilt* (New York: Basic Books, 2007), 155, to have discovered the privately held diary of Dr. Jared

And yet, the children's byzantine plotting does illustrate the strain placed on the family by its patriarch, a man who grew more imposing with every million. This unhappy family was unhappy in a way that only wealth and power (more specifically, a will to power) could bring. The very qualities that made Vanderbilt a formidable businessman—his ferocity, his obsession with control—left him unable to manage the murkier negotiations of love, affection, and fatherhood.

AT THE SAME MOMENT THAT Vanderbilt moved to Washington Place, the finest boat he had ever built was swallowed by the Sound. Shortly after midnight on November 27, the *Atlantic* picked up the Norwich Railroad passengers at its Allyn Point terminal and set out for New York. Then the boiler burst just as a "perfect gale" blew in, seizing the vessel from Captain Isaac Dustan. For long hours he made frantic efforts to save it. He put out multiple anchors and pulled down the smokestacks to reduce wind resistance, but nothing worked. The howling storm drove the steamer upon the rocks of Fishers Island, killing at least fifty of perhaps seventy passengers and crew, including Captain Dustan, a Staten Islander and past commander of many of Vanderbilt's boats.[42]

There is no evidence that Vanderbilt paid attention to the wreck of his creation, any more than he noticed the agonizing within his household. Ever awkward in his own home, he did not dwell in the domestic interiors of family, but rather in the outer world of men of affairs. It was said as a teenage ferry master that he slept in his periauger; as captain of the *Bellona,* he rose before dawn and returned after dark; as a "well-known steamboat proprietor," he spent his life in his office, shipyard, or on the docks, when not in the stables with his horses. What his family thought of him apparently mattered little to him; but among his business peers, Courtlandt Palmer had observed, "He is very desirous of being considered a man of honor and integrity."

In early 1847, he launched a new steamer—the second craft he named *Cornelius Vanderbilt.* "She is a magnificent structure," the *New York Herald* declared. "The model of the *Vanderbilt* differs from all others, and it is pronounced, by old and experienced shipmasters, peculiarly adapted to rough navigation." It became the very embodiment of his reputation.[43]

On May 25, 1847, Vanderbilt joined his brother Jacob on the *Bay State* for a social gathering of the leading steamboat men of New York. The *Bay*

Linsly, asserting that it shows that Vanderbilt contracted syphilis in 1839. In light of significant contradictory evidence and subsequent developments that cast doubt on Renehan's credibility, I must discount the validity of such a diary and Renehan's claims for it. See the bibliographical essay, pages 581–4, for a full discussion.

State itself was a beautiful new Long Island Sound steamer belonging to the Navigation Company; the host of this little party was Captain Comstock, the corporation's gruff general agent. But who wasn't gruff in this gathering? In addition to the notoriously rough-edged Vanderbilts, Isaac Newton was there, along with George Law, owner of the extraordinarily fast *Oregon*. The only missing men were Drew himself and Charles Handy, the Navigation Company's outgoing president.

No body of men could have better exemplified the ironies of the American economy in the 1830s and '40s. Steamboat proprietors were famous for their competitiveness, symbols of a hotly individualistic society in which hatred of monopoly was a pillar of politics. On the other hand, perhaps no other businessmen had worked so hard to construct mechanisms to limit or even eliminate competition. They made agreements to divide up routes, split profits, and punish those who violated their unwritten code. The business culture they created demonstrates how the impulse to stifle competition arose inseparably from competition itself in the American economy, with sometimes bewildering consequences. The banker William Lewis, for example, was exasperated when he tried to sell the *Eureka* because he was told that, if it went into opposition on some line, her sale would be considered a hostile act and lead to retaliation. "But whither would this doctrine lead?" he asked. "If the boat is only to be sold so as to interfere with nobody's route, who then would like to buy her?"[44]

The contradictory fact was, if one wanted to enforce monopolies, one had to be a master of competition. Such was each of those who sat in the saloon of the *Bay State*—good businessmen who divided markets to maximize profits, and ruthless warriors who savored triumph. And Jacob Vanderbilt spoke proudly of the most ruthless of them all, his older brother, and that brother's greatest achievement, the *Vanderbilt*, "new, strong, and elegant," as *Scientific American* called it, "first rate in every respect." Jacob suggested a race against the others' fastest steamers, Newton's *Hendrick Hudson*, Comstock's *Bay State*, and Law's *Oregon*. They could start at the Battery, he suggested, run up the Hudson to Haverstraw Bay, where the river widened enough for four large boats to turn, then drive back to the city. He suggested a wager of $500.

Why only $500? Cornelius asked. "I say, I will run the *C. Vanderbilt*, untried as she is, against any boat afloat to any place they name where there is sufficient water to float her, for any sum from $1,000 to $100,000." Newton sat silent, and Comstock said something about consulting with Handy first. But George Law took the bet. Twice before he had challenged Vanderbilt steamers (most recently the *Atlantic*) to race his *Oregon*. Now he would get his wish. The prize would be $1,000. They agreed to June 1, during the regatta of the New York Yacht Club.[45]

Law had emerged as a leader in transportation only three years earlier. Like Daniel Drew, he had no practical experience in navigation, and had moved into steamboats purely as an investment. Born near Saratoga in 1806, he had started his career by digging canals, working as a contractor on several major projects. From 1839 to 1842 he had built the mighty High Bridge over the Harlem River, the most impressive piece of the most important work of civil engineering in a generation, the Croton Aqueduct. He had proved as gifted at finance as at construction; he had set up a retail canteen for his bridge workers, for example, and soon put many of them in his debt. In 1842, he had taken over the troubled Dry Dock Bank, where he now made his office, as well as the nearly worthless Harlem Railroad; in short order, he had turned both businesses around. In 1843 he had bought his first steamboat; two years later he had launched the *Oregon* and begun to compete on the Hudson (where he forced Drew to pay him $4,000 to leave the river) and Long Island Sound.[46]

War filled the columns of the newspapers on June 1—detailed accounts of the American triumph over the Mexicans at Buena Vista three months earlier. Though that new invention, the telegraph, could carry news as fast as light, the wires had been strung only as far south as Maryland, so information from the battlefield trickled back slowly. Between the victory and the race, a holiday air breezed through the city. Crowds began to gather at ten o'clock in the morning, filling the Battery, the piers, and "every elevated position in the neighborhood of the Battery, as well the rigging of the various vessels lying at anchor," according to the *New York Evening Post.*

> At eleven o'clock the *Oregon* and *Vanderbilt* were seen opposite Castle Garden, near the Jersey shore . . . and then both started off on the race. For a few moments they kept side by side, and neither boat appeared to have the advantage of the other, but soon the *Vanderbilt* sheered off for the east shore, and the *Oregon* took the western side of the river, so that it was impossible to tell whether either boat was ahead of the other.

Vanderbilt commanded his steamer in person as the two great vessels, each more than three hundred feet long, thrashed up the Hudson, smoke trailing from their funnels, the furious splashing of the enormous sidewheels echoing inside their arching wooden cases. For thirty-five miles they raced bow by prow with no discernible lead. At one point, the *Hendrik Hudson* drew close with a boatload of spectators; Vanderbilt ran to the rail and shouted at it to "fall back." He returned to the pilothouse, only to see the *Oregon* pour on steam and gradually pull ahead. As they drew near the designated turning point, the "flag-boat" anchored in Haverstraw Bay,

Vanderbilt ordered a cut in speed in order to make a short, inside turn. His steamer promptly smashed its bow into the starboard paddlewheel housing of the *Oregon*.

Then the *Vanderbilt* suddenly slowed to a near dead stop. It would later be said that her anxious proprietor interfered with the pilot, but the *Herald* reported that "the engineer of the *Vanderbilt* made a mistake in answering the bell from the wheel house, and instead of reducing the speed so as to allow the boat to turn quicker, stopped the engine entirely, which retarded her progress very materially." The *Oregon* kept up its velocity, taking a wide turn of a full mile, but precious minutes passed as the *Vanderbilt* painfully regained its momentum. The *Oregon* pulled ahead and kept the lead down the river as they approached the northern tip of Manhattan.

Just as Law's boat passed the mouth of the Harlem River, its engine room ran out of coal. Desperate to win, Law ordered his crew to burn anything at hand. The firemen ripped out berth slats and doors, broke apart settees, tables, and chairs, and threw it all into the fire. The *Vanderbilt* rapidly gained on her—but it was too late. The *Oregon* steamed over the finish line two minutes ahead. "The river as far as Yonkers was crowded with people," the *New York Tribune* reported, "and when the boats hove in sight on their return the wharves of the city were a mass of spectators. As the *Oregon* swept in she was greeted with a continuous huzza from Hammond st. to the Battery."[47]

"Captain Vanderbilt was beaten for once," Philip Hone wrote in his diary. Hone's tone of surprise underscores the formidable reputation that Vanderbilt had made for himself. The "enterprising proprietor," as Hone called him, was expected to win. Indeed, the race only seems to have enhanced his stature. At the end of the month, President Polk began a triumphal tour of the northeastern states, a kind of political counterpart to the military thrust that General Winfield Scott was making from Veracruz to Mexico City. For the journey from South Amboy, New Jersey, to New York, the presidential party traveled in the *Vanderbilt*, dubbed "the pride of the rivers" by the *Herald*. "She was in charge of Capt. Vanderbilt himself, who performed the double duty of commander and pilot. Every subordinate was in his place, and every waiter punctual in the performance of his duty. . . . Nothing could exceed the completeness of the arrangements on board." Despite his admiration for Clay, Vanderbilt had laid any partisanship aside after Polk's victory in 1844—though throughout the president's speech at South Amboy, the vessel loudly let off steam, "rendering it almost impossible to hear a word of what was said at two paces distant from the speakers."[48]

This was the year that the general public promoted Vanderbilt from the rank of captain. In court testimony taken in September, a man casually referred to him as "Commodore Vanderbilt," a title even his family began to use in everyday conversation. When not escorting presidents, he hobnobbed with Philip Hone's set at the yacht club and bought up Manhattan real estate. In business, he continued to display his ability. He sold his Long Island Railroad shares shortly before it became obvious that the railroad suffered grave difficulties. After taking over as president of the Stonington, he immediately set to work to improve the long-troubled line's prospects. Soon he launched a new steamer to run to Stonington in conjunction with the *Vanderbilt*. He called it the *Commodore*.[49]

At almost the same moment that Vanderbilt ascended to the presidency of the Stonington, General Scott occupied Mexico City. On March 10, 1848, the Senate would ratify the Treaty of Guadalupe Hidalgo, which would strip 500,000 square miles from Mexico (roughly a third of that republic) and annex them to the United States, in return for $15 million. Even in the clamor of joy over the great victory, however, hints of future trouble could be heard. As popular as the war was, a significant group of Northerners—from Congressman Abraham Lincoln to Lieutenant Ulysses S. Grant—had opposed it, fearing that it would primarily enlarge the territory of slavery. Hardly had the fighting started in 1846 when Representative David Wilmot of Pennsylvania attached an amendment to an appropriations bill prohibiting the expansion of the "peculiar institution" into any land acquired from Mexico. Though the "Wilmot Proviso" failed to pass, it sparked abiding outrage across the South.

Perhaps Vanderbilt little imagined that the war and its foreboding aftermath would ever affect him. And yet, he had always existed in curious synchronization with the republic, living the larger struggles of the day in pursuit of his selfish interests. In his youth, he had helped to throw down the culture of deference, with its aristocratic privileges and mercantilist policies. He had risen to wealth and power by battling monopolies on the primary lanes of commerce as he vocally championed competitive individualism. Now he was coming to embody the rise of corporations in his railroad directorships and presidency of the Stonington. He worked toward a kind of synthesis between competition and incorporation that reflected gradual changes in the nation's culture. In early 1848, the *American Railroad Journal*, a periodical devoted to an industry consisting entirely of corporations, would declare, "It would be much more for the prosperity of business—much more for the credit of the people, and much more in accordance with the *spirit of the age*—to allow and encourage *competition*."

Even his ambiguity—his stubborn, irreducible ambiguity—mirrored these trickster times, the eternal ambivalence of the free market: he who drove down fares and improved service, yet demanded bribes to abandon competition; who praised free trade yet enforced his own monopolies; who celebrated the people yet summered in Saratoga and knocked knees with old knickerbockers. Dickens had noted with irritation the smug self-satisfaction of most Americans; the Commodore must have shared it when he contemplated his kingdom from his castle on Washington Place. He was "reputed to be worth some millions," the press reported. Almost everyone who traveled between New York and Boston took a Vanderbilt boat or a Vanderbilt train.[50]

An observer on December 31, 1847, would have found it absurd to think that all this would one day be half forgotten, that obituary writers would dismiss in a few sentences these fifty years of fistfights and Supreme Court cases, steamboat races and stock market machinations. But already forces were in motion that would upend the population of the continent, launch the nation toward civil war, and unleash an ambition in Vanderbilt greater than anyone could have imagined.

Part Two

COMMODORE

1848–1860

Commodore Vanderbilt's character for energy and go-aheadativeness is well known in this community. . . . He is a man whose resolution is indomitable, and before whose determination obstacles, no matter how great, disappear as the morning dew before a July sun.

—*New York Herald*, March 6, 1851

He is illiterate & boorish, [very] austere & offensive.

— THE MERCANTILE AGENCY, May 26, 1853

It is said that I am always in opposition, and that the same spirit of resistance which has often hitherto governed my action has influenced it now. . . . I have only to say, that this is the same spirit which founded this great Republic, and which is now drawing the commerce of the world to our shores. It was the same spirit which unchained the fetters which legislation . . . once fastened upon the Hudson. Repress it if you dare. . . . The share of prosperity which has fallen to my lot is the direct result of unfettered trade and unrestrained competition.

— CORNELIUS VANDERBILT, *New York Tribune*, March 8, 1855

If anything could make our mercantile community pause to look the curse of competition fully in the face, and measure the mischief which its unrestrained sway has done and is doing to the moral tone of the age in which we live, it ought to be the character and career of such monopolists as Mr. Cornelius Vanderbilt.

—*New York Times*, July 13, 1860

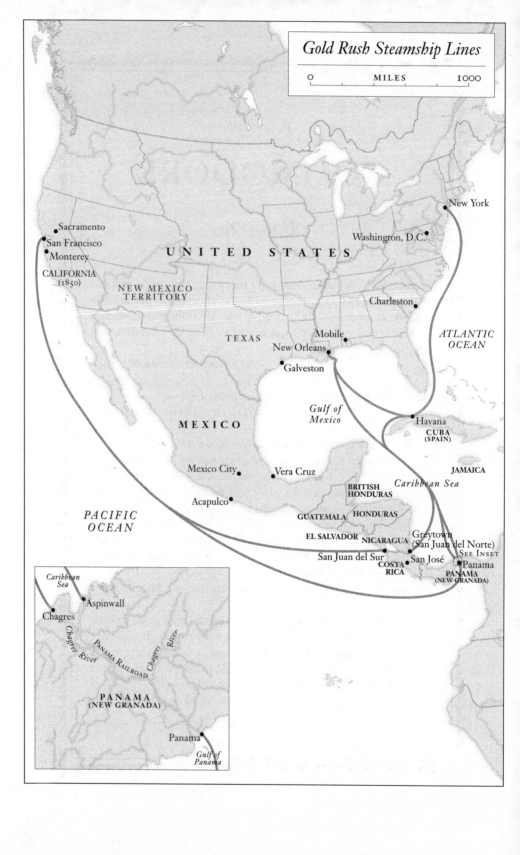

Gold Rush Steamship Lines

0   MILES   1000

Sacramento
San Francisco
Monterey
CALIFORNIA
(1850)

UNITED STATES

Washington, D.C.

New York

NEW MEXICO
TERRITORY

Charleston

TEXAS

Mobile

New Orleans

Galveston

Gulf of
Mexico

ATLANTIC
OCEAN

MEXICO

Havana

CUBA
(SPAIN)

Mexico City

Vera Cruz

JAMAICA

Caribbean Sea

Acapulco

BRITISH
HONDURAS

GUATEMALA   HONDURAS

PACIFIC
OCEAN

EL SALVADOR   NICARAGUA

San Juan del Sur

Greytown
(San Juan del Norte)

COSTA
RICA

San José

SEE INSET

Panama

PANAMA
(NEW GRANADA)

Inset

Caribbean
Sea

Aspinwall

Chagres

Chagres River

PANAMA RAILROAD

Chagres River

PANAMA
(NEW GRANADA)

Panama

Gulf of
Panama

Chapter Seven

PROMETHEUS

Prophets, it is written, find no honor in their own countries. Certainly Lieutenant William Tecumseh Sherman paid little heed to the two emissaries who loomed over his desk, carrying with them a sign that the earth was about to open and swallow them all. What they held in their hands would even transform the life of a steamboat proprietor and railroad president now three thousand miles away.

It was March or April of 1848, in the Pacific coastal village of Monterey, in the recently conquered Mexican province of Alta California. The two men had ridden down from the settlement of Johann Augustus Sutter to speak to California's military governor, Colonel Richard B. Mason. They had found their way to this simple two-story adobe building, climbed the exterior staircase, and stepped into the upper level, where they now spoke to Lieutenant Sherman in the North American accents of U.S. citizens. Sutter had sent them, they announced, "on special business, and they wanted to see Governor Mason *in person*," Sherman recalled. He waved them into Mason's office; before long the governor came to the door and asked Sherman to join them.

On Mason's desk, in the wrinkles of some sheets of paper that had been folded and unfolded, sat a few yellow, metallic lumps. Mason gestured to them and asked of Sherman, "What is that?" The young lieutenant picked up a couple of the larger pieces, unusually heavy for their size, and turned them over, peering closely at them. "Is it gold?" he asked in return. The governor responded with yet another question: Had Sherman ever seen "native gold"—that is, unrefined gold ore?

He had, in fact, though never in such large chunks. He polished a piece—"the metallic lustre was perfect," he remembered—and bit down on it. It yielded, as gold would. Shouting through the door to his own assistant, he called for a hatchet from the backyard. When the soldier returned with one, Sherman raised it up and with the blunt end proceeded to hammer the biggest lump flat. Without question, it was gold.[1]

Sherman saw little significance in the nuggets he battered down on Governor Mason's desk. He was a tall twenty-eight-year-old, his head bristling with red hair, not to mention ambition, as might be expected of an intelligent West Point graduate. A little over a year earlier, he had landed at Monterey Bay after 198 days at sea, eager to win glory. He would not win it in California. The province had fallen to U.S. forces almost without resistance. When his academy classmates would tell one day of their bravery in the war, he wrote, "I will have to blush and say I have not heard a hostile shot."

He did enjoy hunting "deer and bear in the mountains back of the Carmel Mission," he wrote years later, "and ducks and geese in the plains of Salinas." He also mingled with the residents of Monterey who, like Californians as a whole, were few—a mix of Mexicans, white emigrants from the states, and Indians. He joined in fandangos, poked his head into Mass at the Catholic church, and explored the countryside. On the whole, he found California to be "dry and barren," poor and unpleasant, not equal to two counties of Ohio or Kentucky. He hardly expected it to produce more gold than he had just seen. As he wrote at the time, "California is a humbug."[2]

Mason handed Sherman a letter from Sutter that explained matters. A man named James W. Marshall had found the gold in a tailrace, or water chute, for the wheel of a sawmill that he had been building for Sutter on the edges of the Sierra Nevada Mountains, forty miles above Sutter's settlement. Sutter had sent the messengers with a request for title to the mill land. At Mason's request, Sherman wrote that the governor could not help; California was still technically Mexican territory, and the laws of the United States did not yet apply. But, he added, "as there were no settlements within forty miles, he was not likely to be disturbed by trespassers."[3]

Rarely has a prediction of the future been so utterly wrong.

NEW YORK'S NEW YEAR IN 1848 began as it always did, with one of the annual traditions that marked the march across the calendar in the island city. Moving Day, for example, arrived on May 1, the day when leases expired, as they had since Dutch times, the day when furniture-laden wagons rattled and cracked against each other in dense herds on almost every street. Evacuation Day, the celebration of the British army's departure from Manhattan on November 25, 1783, saw parades, thirteen-gun salutes, and mobs of revelers. And the first of the year brought the tradition of the New Year's Day call, a custom practiced in New York by the elite—the wealthy *and* respectable—who debarked from private carriages before the brownstone townhouses that shouldered together in the streets radiating from Washington Square, and that increasingly lined Fifth

Avenue north, reaching nearly to Twentieth Street. To meet the torrent of visitors, women fortified themselves in their parlors amid rosewood and red satin, dispatching servants to usher in the gentlemen who raced up the steps to make their calls, stopping long enough to hand off their hats and remark on the weather. George Templeton Strong, a rising young lawyer in Wall Street, informed his diary that he made eighty calls by six o'clock one New Year's Day, "and got home at last, tolerably tired."[4]

Neither Strong nor any other wealthy *and* respectable diarist is known to have recorded a visit to 10 Washington Place, to the parlor of Sophia Vanderbilt. That was her husband's fault. When the Mercantile Agency, the nation's first credit bureau, first reported on Vanderbilt in 1853, it examined his character as much as his finances (since it reported on businessmen, not consumers, it attempted to assess the general trustworthiness of its subjects). The result says much about the attitude of New York's establishment toward the self-made Vanderbilt. "Started early in life as master of a [small] sailing craft between Staten Island & New York City. Manifested great ability & enterprize, & was taken hold of by the [late] Wm. [sic] Gibbons of New Jersey," observed its reporter. "From this position Vanderbilt has risen to great prosperity in his way. He has a [large] fortune." These words were honest, respectful, and only slightly snide. Unfortunately for Vanderbilt, it was a long report. After the commercial judgment came the social, and it was blunt: "He is illiterate & boorish, [very] austere & offensive & has made himself [very] unpopular with the inhabitants of Staten Island, so much so that his leaving there is subject of great rejoicing by the inhabitants & was manifested by a public jubilee." Among the Astors and Aspinwalls, the Schuylers and Grinnells, Cornelius Vanderbilt did not belong. He had no place in their traditions.[5]

Outwardly, Vanderbilt seemed impervious to the snickers from those who drove their carriages past his new home on their way to the Astor Place Opera House.[6] In many ways, he was destroying tradition as rapidly as possible. His career had disrupted ancient ways of life by facilitating a new mobility in society, breaking down barriers between markets, and introducing a fierce competitiveness that had become central to American culture. Now he had taken in hand the most important kind of business of the nineteenth century, the railroad.

In 1840, he had prophesied to the chief engineer of the Stonington, "If I owned the road, I'd know how to make it profitable." As president of the line he brought his prediction to fruition. He expanded local traffic and dramatically improved its financial position. On May 1, 1848, he completed a new set of tracks that eliminated the ferry in Providence that had been such a bottleneck. In June, the railroad hosted a party for the leading businessmen of Boston to herald a new junction with the Boston & Providence. In December, the Stonington won lavish praise in the press. "This route is, without question, the shortest, directest, and easiest now in use" between Boston and New York, commented the *Independent*. "The cars are comfortable, and their motion equable and noiseless. The boats to Stonington are magnificent. . . . Throughout the whole route there is full proof of care, energy, and competency, which justify the rapidly growing popularity of this route." Perhaps most important, under Vanderbilt's management the long-bankrupt line paid $65,000 in dividends that year.[7]

"Mr. Vanderbilt, the well-known Admiral of the Sound," in the words of one newspaper, had held on to his interests in the "magnificent" boats that steamed between Stonington and New York's teeming slips.[8] As he had assured the Stonington's chief engineer, when he finally owned the road, he owned the boats, too—though they were managed by Daniel Drew through the New Jersey Steam Navigation Company.

The year 1848 marked a high point of the partnership that Vanderbilt and Drew formed in the aftermath of their collision on the Hudson in 1831. For seventeen years each had taken a stake in the other's enterprises, neatly insuring against competition from the man he most respected. On Long Island Sound, they carried their cooperation beyond mere mutual nonaggression. With control of both trains and boats, they had eliminated the adversarial relationship between land and sea that had bedeviled the Stonington during the presidency of the hapless Courtlandt Palmer.

Vanderbilt and Drew took their partnership from business operations to the stock market. The model for what they now did with the Stonington took shape no later than 1844, when Drew had joined Isaac Newton and Nelson Robinson to buy control of the Mohawk & Hudson River Railroad. They had planned to divert its passengers and freight onto the People's Line boats, and to acquire (as they would explain in court in 1848) "the profits to be derived from the purchase and sale of stock." Once they took control of a corporation, Drew and his partners gained first access to information that would drive the price of its stock, from potential problems to impending deals to the number and disposition of its shares in the market. They could also manipulate the share price, so they could buy or sell in advance of a manufactured rise or fall in the stock. Drew's passion for insider trading (as dealing in the stock of one's own corporation came to be known) made him a good credit risk in the eyes of the Mercantile Agency. Writing a decade later, in reference to another railroad that Drew controlled, an agency reporter observed, "He is inside & knows its fluctuations & bearings, & he is shrewd [enough] to take [good] care of himself. He may therefore be regarded as reliable [for his debts]." It was all perfectly legal. When Drew had to explain his behavior in court, it was not in a criminal case, but in a civil lawsuit filed by a junior partner of Drew, Robinson & Co., who felt that he had been cheated out of his share of the profits. That junior partner was Daniel B. Allen.[9]

Drew made few such revelations. He, Vanderbilt, Newton, and Robinson profited by keeping their operations and arrangements to themselves. "It would be difficult to find the real wealth of [Vanderbilt]," the Mercantile Agency observed. "It must, however, be great." When their names came up for discussion, the same adjectives appeared again and again: "smart . . . shrewd . . . cunning."

Of all this cunning crowd, no one, not even Vanderbilt, was sharper than Drew's senior partner in Drew, Robinson & Co. Though both Drew and Vanderbilt understood the dynamics of the stock market exceptionally well, it was Nelson Robinson who worked "the Street," as Wall Street was called. ("Wall Street" was itself a nickname for the stock exchange, formally called the New York Stock and Exchange Board.) There he won a reputation as "one of the shrewdest and keenest operators," as he made trades among the crowd of unlicensed brokers who gathered on the curb outside the Merchants' Exchange and inside on the floor of the great hall where formal transactions took place. He mastered the brokers' arts—not simply buying and selling at the right price, but also managing the terms, such as the number of days allowed to close a transaction, and whether the buyer or seller would be able to select the day within that window to make payment or delivery. Perhaps most important, Robinson understood the magic of perceptions—the whispered rumor to shape the mood of the market, the daily feat of acting to fool the brokers who studied his face, the trades conducted anonymously through other brokers to mask his real movements.[10]

Secrecy in such operations served a political purpose as well. Many Jacksonians had never fully reconciled themselves to corporations, let alone to "stockjobbing" and "speculation," two of the worst insults an orator or editorialist could imagine. Even at the half century, the notion of dividing a company into shares, treating each share as property, and then allowing its value to fluctuate, just seemed wrong, even immoral to them.[11]

The rabble and their rousers were not the only Americans who had difficulty grasping the abstractions of the new economy. Most of those merchants and lawyers who paid New Year's calls on Fifth Avenue—not to mention the businessmen in smaller towns and villages around the country—still worked in personal enterprises, owned by single proprietors or small partnerships. Corporations remained so few that the stock exchange traded shares—and bonds—one at a time. The vice president of the Stock and Exchange Board called each one from the chair, brokers on the floor shouted bids and offers, and clerks recorded the trades on a large blackboard. Then they had lunch. Then they ran through the entire list once again.

As early as 1819, Chief Justice John Marshall had expounded on the corporation as "an artificial being, invisible, intangible," but even corporate officials had difficulty with such abstract thinking. They used "company" as a plural noun, as in, "The company are in renewed trouble for their floating debts." They saw the corporation as a gathering of individuals, as a kind of partnership—which it usually was, since few were very large or had widely traded stock.[12] They placed great emphasis on the "par value" of stock, usually set at $100 per share. This represented the original investment in a company; it was expected that the total value of all its shares would equal the cost of the physical capital—land, buildings, machinery, livestock. A stock certificate might be a slip of paper, but it was thought to represent something real, much as paper currency represented cold, hard gold that could be retrieved on demand from a bank's vault.

With this physical, tangible basis for the price of stock, most investors did not buy in hopes that values would consistently rise, as they would in later centuries; that would have made no sense, since share prices ultimately rested on what it had cost to physically create the company, not how much it earned. They looked instead to a return on that cost in the form of dividends—often referred to as "interest on capital." Share prices fluctuated, of course, but the most important factor driving them was the size and regularity of dividends. A price over par—above $100—was a premium paid for the certainty of a reliable return. A price below implied risk, uncertainty, even a dread conviction that dividends would never come. (Speculators did gamble on the prices of highly volatile, "fancy" stocks, but these were expected to go up and down, rather than rise steadily and permanently.)

It is easy to dismiss Vanderbilt and Drew's stock operations as mere corruption, as corporate profiteering of a type all too familiar to later generations. Indeed, they *were* corrupt, even by the broad social standards of their own time. When such dealings surfaced, contemporaries scorched these men with abuse, even though no laws prohibited their behavior. Social disdain for Vanderbilt, "illiterate & boorish," and Drew, the former cattle drover, suffused such commentary.

But it is a mistake to simply adopt the condescension and derision of the contemporary social elite. This view ignores a critical fact: Vanderbilt and Drew's business careers, coming in the first half of the nineteenth century, were acts of imagination. In this age of the corporation's infancy, they and their conspirators created a world of the mind, a world that would last into the twenty-first century. At a time when even many businessmen could not see beyond the physical, the tangible, they embraced abstractions never known before in daily life. They saw that a group of men sitting around a table could conjure "an artificial being, invisible, intangible," that could outlive them all. They saw how stocks could be driven up or dropped in value, how they could be played like a flute to command more capital than the incorporators could muster on their own. They saw that *everything* in the economy could be further abstracted into a substanceless something that might be bought or sold, that a banknote or promissory note or the right to buy a share of stock at a certain price could all be traded at prices that varied from day to day. The subtle eye of the boorish boatman saw this invisible architecture, and grasped its innumerable possibilities.[13]

It is important to remember that the corporation originated in mercantilism. Legal historian Morton J. Horwitz describes it as "an association between state and private interests for public purposes." (The mercantilist character of early corporations led Adam Smith to denounce them as "a sort of enlarged monopolies.") Over time it changed character until, Horwitz writes, "the corporate form had developed into a convenient legal device for limiting risks and promoting continuity in the pursuit of private advantage." Eventually it became just another way of organizing a business.[14]

But not yet. In 1848, the corporation was still emerging out of a political conflict over the best way to create commercial facilities for the public good (namely banks and transportation infrastructure—turnpikes, canals, and railroads). Whigs had favored direct government action, from the Bank of the United States to state-owned railroads such as the Michigan Central, or else public-private partnerships, as in the Camden & Amboy Railroad. Jacksonians had wanted to limit government, fearing that "the money power" would capture it to enhance the advantages of the wealthy over their fellow citizens; like Adam Smith, they viewed corporations with a jealous eye. The Panic of 1837 had proved decisive in resolving this debate. In its wake, canals and railroads had failed, discrediting state-owned "internal improvements." But the need for such public works remained. And so, for all the Jacksonian dread of "stockjobbers," the task of building railroads and other large projects fell to privately funded business corporations. That created a paradox: the nation's public works, the carriers of commerce and means of travel, were owned by private parties, who operated them for personal gain.[15] Because of this, Vanderbilt's position as a corporate executive gave him an increasingly public role, one that would grow over time until he became the foremost symbol of this public-private paradox. In the popular mind, that role began not with the Stonington Railroad, but with a far more ambitious enterprise yet to come.

At fifty-four, Vanderbilt could look back on a career of breathtaking leaps of imagination. Steamboats and railroads, fare wars, market-division agreements, and corporations: all were virtually unknown in America when he mastered them. He understood the emerging invisible world far better than those who condescended to him. And this knowledge was about to serve him better than he could have dreamed. He was about to imagine a work of global significance—to create a channel of commerce that would help make the United States a truly continental nation. In the process, a most perplexing collision of public and private interests would embroil him in great-power diplomacy, international finance, and a bitter war between a half-dozen sovereign nations. And it was all because of a frenzy that now began three thousand miles from 10 Washington Place.

IN APRIL 1848, in the northeastern corner of the great peninsula that extended like a thumb to enclose San Francisco Bay, some two hundred buildings could be counted in the village of Yerba Buena. They included some 145 houses, a dozen stores, and perhaps thirty-five shanties. Clustered in a sandy basin beneath steep hills and ridges, the town formed a convenient port close to the Golden Gate, with the promise of steady growth as Americans trickled into California. To assist that growth, the leading citizens had decided to change Yerba Buena's name to that of the bay—San Francisco. Already the population had risen from around two hundred in 1846 to as much as a thousand.

By the end of May, they were gone. Sand blew through deserted streets. Ships sailed through the Gate, rounded the northeastern corner of the peninsula, and dropped anchor in front of those two hundred empty buildings; then their crews scurried overboard, never to return. Over the previous few weeks, visitors from the upper country had brought rumors of gold near Sutter's settlement of New Helvetia; then men who had panned and dug for gold themselves had brought the yellow evidence to town. "The inhabitants began gradually, in bands and singly, to desert their previous occupations, and betake themselves to the American River," wrote a resident. "Soon all business and work, except the most urgent, was forced to be stopped. . . . About the end of May we left San Francisco almost a desert place."[16]

The craze soon struck Monterey. "As the spring and summer of 1848 advanced," William T. Sherman recalled, "the reports came faster and faster from the gold-mines at Sutter's saw-mill. Stories reached us of fabulous discoveries, and spread throughout the land. Everybody was talking of 'Gold! gold!!' until it assumed the character of a fever. Some of our soldiers began to desert; citizens were fitting out trains of wagons and pack-mules to go to the mines."[17]

Nothing could have been more predictable than the rush to the "diggings," as they were called. Gold was not simply *worth* money—it *was* money. Anyone could take refined gold (and refining was a relatively simple process) to the United States Mint and have it poured into coin. The earth was spitting up cash. Who wouldn't have gone?

In late June, Lieutenant Sherman convinced Colonel Mason that they must visit the diggings in order to report on the find. With four soldiers, Mason's black servant, "and a good outfit of horses and pack-mules," they journeyed up to the mines. "I recall the scene as perfectly today as though it were yesterday," Sherman wrote decades later. "In the midst of a broken country, all parched and dried by the hot sun of July, sparsely wooded with live-oaks and straggling pines, lay the valley of the American River, with its bold mountain stream coming out of the snowy mountains to the east." Along a gravel floodplain adjacent to the river, "men were digging, and filling buckets with the finer earth and gravel," which they poured into roughly made sifters. Sherman estimated that about four men worked each sifter, and each man earned an average of an ounce of gold—$16— per day, though they often pulled in twice as much. "The sun blazed down on the heads of the miners with tropical heat, the water was bitter cold, and all hands were either standing in the water or had their clothes wet all the time; yet there were no complaints of rheumatism or cold."

When Mason and Sherman returned to Monterey, they learned that the Mexican War had ended, and California would remain American territory. The troops began to desert by the company, riding to the mountains to take raw money out of the water and the dirt. "Nearly all business ceased," Sherman wrote, "except that connected with gold."[18]

It soon became clear just how much business could be connected with gold. Well before the end of the year, men began trickling back to San Francisco to start businesses to serve the thousands who poured off ships that sailed in growing numbers through the Golden Gate. California was one of the most remote parts of the new American empire—as much as six months' voyage from the Atlantic coast around Cape Horn—yet already its residents could see that something enormous had started there, something that would have repercussions far beyond the mountains and the bay.

IN MARCH 1847, *Merchant's Magazine* had published a survey of the commercial potential of the recently conquered territory of Upper California. "The Indians," the writer added, "have always said there were mines, but refused to give their locality."[19]

Cornelius Vanderbilt, like most New York businessmen, paid little attention to reports of secret Indian gold. He had other concerns. In 1848, he took over the presidency of the Elizabethport Ferry Company, now paying a 20 percent dividend (that is, $20 per share).* That same year, Oroondates Mauran died. On March 1, Vanderbilt bought Mauran's shares of their joint enterprises from his estate, buying full control of the Staten Island Ferry for $80,000, along with various parcels of real estate.[20]

Before the end of the year, Vanderbilt developed his own health problems. He began to suffer heart palpitations. His heart started beating faster and faster, until "it was impossible to count its pulsations," Dr. Linsly recalled. "At first these attacks lasted a few hours only. They increased at last to twenty-four hours' duration, and in 1848 Dr. Edward Johnson and I were with him sometimes all night and he was a great sufferer." Given the state of medical knowledge, Linsly and Johnson likely made things worse. George Templeton Strong for one seriously considered homeopathy as an alternative to conventional medicine, "with emetics and cathartics and blistering and bleeding and all the horrors, the anticipation of which makes the doctor's entry give me such a sinking of spirit."[21]

Vanderbilt survived his beating heart, blistered skin, and bleeding veins, only to learn that something strange was going on in the world. Rumors circulated of gold in California—real gold, not a figment of Indian legends. The rumors quickly found their way to the stock exchange, where brokers sucked in all commercial information, good or bad. With his ear to the Street, or at least to Nelson Robinson's lips, Vanderbilt would have heard the stories early on. On December 5, 1848, President Polk formally announced the discovery in his annual written message to Congress. "The accounts of the abundance of gold in that country are of such an extraordinary character as would scarcely command belief," he reported, "were they not corroborated by the authentic reports of officers in the public service." Horace Greeley proclaimed in the *New York Tribune*, "We are on the brink of the Age of Gold."[22]

Many wealthy New Yorkers feared an age of inflation. "This California business worries me sadly," Strong wrote on January 25, 1849. "Suppose . . . the circulating medium of the world should suddenly be increased by a third or a quarter? Where should I be then? Of course, without any loss whatever, one-third or one-fourth poorer." On January 22, the venerable merchant James G. King voiced the same concerns to Baring Brothers, the esteemed London bankers. "The news from California . . . cannot fail to have much effect here upon prices, inducing speculation, &c.," he wrote from New York. "Meanwhile, there is quite an

---

* Since stock usually had a par value of $100, per-share dividends were described in percentages.

emigration from this country to that region, although the journey is long and perilous."

As King observed, greed, rather than fear, seized most Americans. One by one, Strong counted friends who organized partnerships of a dozen or more men to buy supplies, outfit a ship, and sail around Cape Horn for the Golden Gate. "The frenzy continues to increase every day," he observed on January 29. "It seems as if the Atlantic Coast was to be depopulated, such swarms of people are leaving it for the new El Dorado. It is the most remarkable emigration on record in the history of man since the days of the Crusades." In the twelve months following President Polk's announcement, no less than 762 vessels departed North American ports for California; by April 19, 1849, 226 would sail from New York alone, carrying nearly twenty thousand people.[23]

The calculation in Vanderbilt's set was much too cold for either fear or frenzy. Clearly this extraordinary development offered new opportunities. Daniel Allen seems to have concocted the group's first gold-rush scheme. On February 2, he convened a meeting of twenty-one men, including himself, to organize the California Navigation Company of New York. Vanderbilt attended, as did nearly his entire circle, including Drew, Jacob Vanderbilt, shipbuilder Jeremiah Simonson, steam-engine manufacturer Theodosius F. Secor, Staten Islander Daniel Van Duzer, Allen's brother William, and Vanderbilt's son Billy. They paid in a total capital of $21,630, divided into twenty-one shares. With this sum they purchased a schooner, the *James L. Day*, and built a seventy-foot steamboat named *Sacramento*. The completed steamer was cut into three pieces and placed on the schooner; they planned to have it reassembled in San Francisco, in order to steam between that port and the Sacramento River landings that served the diggings.

It was an ingenious plan, though it followed the model of many small emigration companies. For example, the agreement obliged each of the shareholders to serve as a crewman on the schooner and steamboat or provide a substitute. Vanderbilt had no intention of going, but he thought the expedition offered a suitable start in life for his disappointing son, Cornelius Jeremiah, now eighteen years old. On March 4, 1849, Corneil (as he was called) shipped out under the billowing canvas of the *James L. Day* as it sailed out of New York Harbor, on a voyage that would change him forever.[24]

Did Vanderbilt stand on the dock and wave good-bye to his son? He gave little sign to his associates of sentimentality, and his daughter Mary would recall his "ill-treatment" of Corneil at this time.[25] Yet the day would come when he would quietly confess his concern, even his compassion, for the boy.

In business, his mind was occupied by larger matters than his single share in the California Navigation Company. At each stage of his career, he had seized control of the most important channel of transportation in the young country's growing economy. Now tens of thousands proved desperate to travel to San Francisco, an enormous journey that commanded equally enormous fares. If he were to enter this market, he faced fierce competition from both familiar and unfamiliar rivals.

Two men—two utterly contradictory men—stood in his way, thanks to a confluence of forces so unusual as to verge on the bizarre. Long before anyone had heard of Sutter's mill, George Law, the canal contractor, and William H. Aspinwall, a merchant at the pinnacle of New York society, had joined with the federal government and a pair of political fixers to establish steamship lines to the Pacific coast. Purely by coincidence, they put their first ships in place just as the gold rush began.

The project originated, in a sense, with a slogan: "Fifty-four forty or fight," battle cry of expansionist James K. Polk in the presidential election of 1844. He came into office determined to annex Oregon, a task he completed in 1846. The next question was how to establish mail service to this distant territory, separated from the organized states by thousands of miles of wilderness. A glance at the map suggested the sea, with a land crossing at the narrowest point in Central America, across the Isthmus of Panama.

But who would pay for such a line? Who would operate it? This was the golden age of laissez-faire Democrats who believed in competitive private enterprise rather than government rewards for a favored few. In 1846, for example, President Polk vetoed a bill to improve harbors and river navigation, calling it an inappropriate and extravagant use of federal money. Unfortunately, businessmen saw no profit in sailing thousands of miles to carry a handful of letters for a few thousand settlers; maintaining a strong link to the Pacific was a matter of national, not private, interest. But there was no public institution capable of carrying out the massive operation. With the extremely important exception of the Post Office, the federal government boasted only a few hundred civilian employees, and played a less active role in the economy than many states. Jacksonian Democrats faced a conflict between their laissez-faire dogma and their territorial expansionism. Expansionism won. Polk's Democratic administration embraced Whig notions as Washington embarked on a scheme to subsidize private enterprise on an unprecedented scale.[26]

Congress and the State Department prepared the way. In 1846, the South American republic of New Granada (later called Colombia) agreed to a treaty that guaranteed Americans free and safe passage across its province of Panama. Congress passed legislation that offered public funds for private carriers to establish a line to the Pacific coast. In 1847, it directed that the contract for the Atlantic passage (between New York, New Orleans, Havana, and the Panamanian port of Chagres) be given to "Colonel" Albert G. Sloo; the contract for the Pacific (from Panama to points in California and Oregon) went to Arnold Harris.[27]

These were curious choices. Harris was a resident of Nashville and Sloo of Cincinnati—cities not generally thought of as ocean ports. Rather, the two men represented a new creature in American life, at least at the federal level: they were "dummies." In some cases, dummies served as front men for other parties; more often, they were political connivers who used their contacts to obtain government privileges which they had no means—or intention—of using themselves, but promptly sold to real entrepreneurs. On August 17, Sloo essentially sold his contract to a group headed by George Law (including Marshall O. Roberts, Prosper M. Wetmore, Robert C. Wetmore, and Edwin Croswell). The federal government would pay these gentlemen $290,000 a year in return for two steamship voyages per month to Chagres. From there the mail would be carried by canoe and mule over the isthmus to the city of Panama, where it would be taken by steamships constructed by William H. Aspinwall, the merchant who bought the Pacific contract from Harris on November 19, 1847, three days after he had received it. Aspinwall would be paid $14,510 per voyage, or $348,250 per year, for his services. In some respects, these deals validated the Jacksonian critique of government largesse, offering a foreshadowing of the corruption that would creep into government in the aftermath of the Mexican War.[28]

Law's role in this contract-flipping subsidy speculation did not exactly shock political insiders. With his large, blunt head, his thick, wavy hair piled above overhanging brows, hard eyes, and a long, heavy nose, he resembled nothing so much as a prizefighter—and he spoke like one, too. "I ain't a-going to give you the money today," he snapped on one occasion, with regard to a disputed bill. "I have nothing to do with that 'ere account. It belongs to the company to pay." The Mercantile Agency, that mouthpiece of establishment opinion, later observed, "He is reported to be sharp & over-reaching in his transactions & dealt with accordingly. . . . Knows how to take care of his money but [has] little regard for the feelings or interests of others."[29]

Law, of course, had defeated Vanderbilt in the famed steamboat race of 1847; but it was conniving rather than racing that defined his career. As a contractor on the Croton aqueduct and other projects, Law had learned the craft of lobbying—or simply bribing—public officeholders. He also knew how to arrange deals. With such talents, he easily gathered more highly esteemed businessmen—notably Marshall Roberts and the Wetmores—to form the United States Mail Steamship Company to build and run the five steamships demanded by his contract with the federal government.[30]

Aspinwall's role, on the other hand, surprised many. Born in 1807 into a family of prominent New York merchants, he rose to become senior partner of the esteemed firm of Howland & Aspinwall. Unlike Law or Vanderbilt, he received countless callers each New Year's Day at his richly appointed house. "Made a very satisfactory call there," recorded the snooty Strong on January 1, 1846. "His arrangements, by the by, house and furniture both, are really magnificent." Aspinwall was, Strong later wrote, "a merchant prince and one of our first citizens."[31]

Aspinwall's overseas mercantile business revealed possibilities that his Manhattan-bound peers did not see. In 1847, with the federal subsidy in hand, he created the Pacific Mail Steamship Company to operate his half of the mail route. His corporation outpaced Law's U.S. Mail, building larger ships faster, and positioned its first vessels on the Pacific just as the torrent to California began to gush. When the scope of the rush became clear, Aspinwall helped organize the Panama Railroad to span the isthmus. Ticket buyers besieged the office of Pacific Mail as it continued to bank its huge federal subsidy. It is worth noting that, despite the romantic image of the gold-rush wagon train and dust-covered stagecoach, the steamship lines provided the primary means of travel and commerce between California and the East. They immediately became a very big business, one that would continue for two decades.[32]

To seize that business for himself, Cornelius Vanderbilt conceived perhaps the boldest plan of his entire career. It would require the help of his old associates, his family, the mercantile establishment, and still others. It would require his own political fixer—not as a dummy, but as an insider who could negotiate as an equal with officeholders at home and abroad. He planned to divert that golden torrent from Panama to a channel of his own making: a canal across the republic of Nicaragua.

Vanderbilt never revealed where his idea originated. Others had proposed much the same plan before. Louis Napoléon Bonaparte (Emperor Napoléon I's nephew) had championed a canal a few years earlier, though escape from imprisonment, the tumult of a revolution, and winning election to the French presidency had left him otherwise occupied. In the waning days of the Mexican War, even before gold had been discovered in California, American newspapers and magazines had frequently reported on a possible canal and transit route across Nicaragua.[33] As was often pointed out, there seemed to be an obvious route, following natural waterways: up the San Juan River, which ran some 120 miles from the Atlantic up to Lake Nicaragua; across the lake's 110-mile width; then down a short twelve-mile land excavation to the Pacific, or a channel northwest through Lake Managua.[34]

But perhaps something deeper than maps and magazine articles drove his thinking. Vanderbilt had yet to hit upon a grand work he believed he was meant to build; no line of steamboats, not even the Stonington Railroad, loomed large enough. But an interoceanic canal—that would be a monument to enshrine his name in glory forever.

VANDERBILT'S SON CORNEIL first saw the Golden Gate from sea. The name (which predated the gold rush) appeared obvious to anyone sailing the rugged coast to where it suddenly broke open to reveal the great bay—"the glory of the western world," as one man called it. Sailing through the Gate, the thin and sickly eighteen-year-old passed between mountains that rose straight up from the water, "the little stream tumbling from the rocks among the green wood," in the words of a traveler, "and the wild game standing out from the cliffs or frolicking among the brush, and the seal barking in the water."[35] It was a fittingly grand entrance to the greatest treasure trove in history.

For five months, Corneil had blistered his hands as a crewman on the *James L. Day*, sailing down tropical coasts, crashing through the titanic storms of Cape Horn, sailing up the Chilean shore. Two of the twenty-one aboard had died. Finally, on August 5, 1849, Captain John Van Pelt gave the order to drop anchor at San Francisco. Where once had been a sleepy village, Corneil now saw bedlam. Workmen milled about the shore, leveling the countless sand hills, dumping the dust and dirt into the bay, pounding in pilings and planking down piers. Tents pimpled the flats all about the town, tents of all descriptions—canvas, blankets, and branches stripped from trees. Some served as homes and some as shops, with bags of coffee, barrels of foodstuffs, and stacks of bricks and lumber on display. Men, mules, horses, and carts lumbered up and down ungraded dirt streets, fighting through clouds of dust—or, after heavy rains, through quicksand that sucked horses down to their ears, along with the drays they pulled.

And everywhere Corneil saw men—almost only men—all eager to head for the mines or make money from those who were going. At the time the *James L. Day* sailed through the Gate, one resident counted some two hundred ships in the bay, from virtually every nation with a port on the Pacific. Russians and Australians, Peruvian Indians and Indian Brahmins, Japanese, Mexicans, and Maori, all passed up and down on urgent business. The town was "crowded with human beings from every corner of the universe and of every tongue—all excited and busy, plotting, speaking, working, buying and selling town lots, and beach and water lots, shiploads of every kind of assorted merchandise, the ships themselves, if they could."[36]

No sooner had the *Day* pulled into port and the crew begun to unload the disassembled hull of the steamboat than Corneil deserted. Three others abandoned ship with him. He slipped into a town populated largely by young men awash in money, with no authorities to inhibit their impulses. Making his way past the tents and shanties into the city's center, he discovered the finest buildings in San Francisco: "Gambling saloons, glittering like fairy palaces," as a citizen wrote a few years later, "studding nearly all sides of the plaza, and every street in its neighborhood. . . . Monté, faro, roulette, rondo, rouge et noir and vingt-[et-]un, were the games chiefly played. In the larger saloons, beautiful and well-dressed women dealt out the cards or turned the roulette wheel, while lascivious pictures hung on the walls. A band of music and numberless blazing lamps gave animation and a feeling of joyous rapture to the scene." All night the gambling went on, with runaway sailors and runaway slaves elbowing between wealthy merchants and ministers of the gospel, all drinking, eating, smoking, gaming.

Gold was everywhere, in solid lumps or bags of dust, thrown about carelessly, measured indifferently, won and lost at the tables with stunning rapidity (as much as $20,000 riding on a hand, it was said). And with the money and the revelry came violence—a flashing knife over a contemptuous word, the crack of a revolver over an attempted theft, a flurry of fistfights and formal duels. *"And everybody made money,"* wrote our San Franciscan, *"and was suddenly growing rich."*

It is difficult to know how all this affected young Corneil, because we know so little of his childhood—just a fleeting image of a furtive second son, overshadowed by his overbearing father, occasionally seized by epileptic fits. But he landed in this most impressive place at an early and impressionable age. By every indication, the San Francisco of 1849 stamped him with its image—a city of gamblers and speculators, confidence men and killers. Cornelius J. Vanderbilt stood in the saloons that remained open all night, swam through cigar smoke and shouted over blaring music, smiled at female card dealers and calmed belligerent miners, learning to talk, learning to charm.

The fever of the place infected even Captain Van Pelt of the *James L. Day.* He and his crew reassembled the steamboat *Sacramento* and started to run it up the eponymous river on September 14; meanwhile his second-in-command, James S. Nash, took command of the schooner and entered the carrying trade on the bay. And they made money, and suddenly grew rich. Within two months, the *Sacramento* earned a profit of $40,000, and the *James L. Day* another $10,000. Unfortunately for Vanderbilt and the other owners, Captain Van Pelt allied himself with a San Franciscan, James H. Fisk of Turner, Fisk & Co., who saw no reason to remit such earnings all the way across the continent. Fisk and Van Pelt decided to auction off the two boats, even though they had no authority to do so. They named a time just before the departure of a Pacific Mail steamship from San Francisco, an hour when the city's merchants were frantically busy with correspondence and consignments of gold for the Atlantic coast. Then Fisk held the auction fifteen minutes ahead of schedule. With no other bidders, he bought the boats himself at ridiculously low prices. He soon sold them, winning a very large profit.

Corneil, on the other hand, did not do so well. Not long after abandoning ship, he ran out of money, most likely at the tables, and issued a draft on his father—a draft his father refused to honor.[37] But it was the excitement rather than the bad debt that endured in his memory. It is impossible to contemplate the Corneil of later years without imagining that he carried with him those heady days of utter abandonment and strained to his utmost to recapture them. "Happy the man who can tell of those things which he saw and perhaps himself did, at San Francisco at that time," wrote our witness. San Francisco would haunt Corneil to the end.

THEY CALLED HIM "INDIANA WHITE," though the records of the House of Representatives name him Joseph L. White. Curiously, his contemporaries never described his physical appearance; he seems to have cut an eminently forgettable figure. It was his voice they remarked on, his gift for rhetorical explosions and diamond-cutting logic. In 1840 he emerged from an obscure youth in upstate New York, where he had studied law, to become a powerful speaker in Indiana for presidential candidate William Henry Harrison. White was "the most fascinating orator that ever mounted a stump in the state," in the words of one newspaper. "Probably since stump speaking was invented no effort was ever received with such unqualified and extravagant delight, not merely by the 'roughs,' who could appreciate its 'hits,' but by cultivated men, who could penetrate its arguments." He won election to the House that year as a Whig. In Washington he withered, much to everyone's surprise. He possessed "a genius," the same writer observed, "that only lacked the balance of character to be one of the most powerful men in the nation." Perhaps, in his only term in Congress, his unbalance began to reveal itself.

Still, White was smart, in every sense that word carried in 1843, when he moved to New York and started to practice law. "He was one of the most social and genial men I have ever met, and a most engaging and eloquent conversationalist," remarked one New Yorker. "His apropos speeches, his witty and good-humored repartees, were inimitable." He emerges from these accounts as a highly confident man of sharp wit, a sophisticated and well-connected charmer, a master of both courtroom histrionics and backroom negotiations. As a former politician, he also had ties to the new Whig administration of Zachary Taylor, elected president in 1848. He was, in short, a fixer.[38]

How and when Vanderbilt first approached White remains uncertain, though two dates suggest the moment when they joined in the Nicaragua canal project. On March 24, 1849, Vanderbilt resigned the presidency of the Elizabethport Ferry Company, as if to concentrate his efforts on something else. On March 29, White sent a letter from a hotel in Washington, D.C., to the new secretary of state, former Delaware senator John M. Clayton. "I have come from *New York* expressly to see you *on business of importance*, & which admits of no delay," he wrote. "Will you oblige me by writing a note, informing me at what hour to day or tomorrow I can see you *privately*. . . . I have come on behalf of *seven* New York gentlemen & on their errand. I know something of your engagements, & would not press for an interview under *ordinary circumstances*."[39]

Clearly White was an *emphatic* man, impressed with his own importance. In this case, though, he understood his audience. Back in 1835, Senator Clayton had sponsored a bill to encourage Americans to dig a canal across Nicaragua. Now he came into office as secretary of state with U.S. territory on the Pacific, massive quantities of gold coming out of California, and tens of thousands of Americans migrating there. The canal idea had grown dramatically more important for American foreign policy. Clayton listened with great interest as White told him that Vanderbilt had organized the American Atlantic & Pacific Ship Canal Company, and had dispatched David White (Joseph's brother) to Nicaragua to negotiate with the government there.

Not many days later, Clayton appointed Ephraim G. Squier the chargé d'affaires to Guatemala (the chief diplomatic post in Central America). "Considering the motive which influenced you to make this appointment *so speedily*," Joseph White wrote to Clayton on April 3, "those with whom I am associated & myself . . . express their & my very sincere acknowledgments to you; and I beg you to examine this *written assurance, that under no possible combination of circumstances will I fail to reciprocate this great favor in any mode which you may designate*."

This curious letter reveals White as not only emphatic, but insinuating as well—not to mention vain. He assumed Squier's appointment had been a favor, to be repaid on demand. It was an assumption that came naturally to the scheming brain of a political fixer. Clayton, by contrast, was a very high-minded man, focused not on rewarding friends but on public policy. Ignorant of this, White blustered on, listing orders that should be given to Squier to assist in the canal intrigues—"instruct him *to avoid my brother* (now in Nicaragua) in securing the grant"—and assuring Clayton that the company's tolls would discriminate against the British in favor of American ships.

If he thought this would prove appealing, he was mistaken. Clayton believed that any canal must be neutral, or it would lead to "more bloody and expensive wars than the struggle for Gibraltar had caused to England and Spain." Yet he seems to have tolerated White's insinuations in order to accomplish the larger goal. As he wrote in his instructions to Squier, "A passage across the isthmus may be indispensable to maintain the relations between the United States and their new territories on the Pacific; and a canal from ocean to ocean might, and probably would, empty much of the treasures of the Pacific into the lap of this country." Clayton thought that the canal was essential to the national interest, but he also knew that Congress would never fund its construction. He needed Vanderbilt and his backers as much as they needed him.[40]

Joseph White happened to reveal to Clayton the names of those backers, who have previously escaped historical notice. The original organizers of the canal company included Cornelius Vanderbilt, of course, along with White and his brother David, merchants Nathaniel H. Wolfe and Edmund H. Miller, and three Wall Street firms: Livingston, Wells & Co.; Hoyt & Hunt; and Bowden, Groesbeck & Bridgham. The last-named firm suggests the disguised involvement of Daniel Drew, for David Groesbeck was one of Drew's personal brokers and close allies.[41]

They were not the only American businessmen seeking the rights to a crossing in Nicaragua. No sooner had Squier arrived there than he learned that another firm claimed to have signed an agreement with the government that granted them monopoly rights for a canal or railroad across the isthmus.[42] Vanderbilt's canal project had scarcely begun, and already it was mired in the political jungles of Central America.

ON AUGUST 26, DAVID WHITE signed a contract with the Nicaraguan government. It gave the exclusive right to build a canal to Vanderbilt's American Atlantic & Pacific Ship Canal Company in return for $10,000 a year, 20 percent of the annual profits, and a stake in the business. "It will also be observed that the grant is not only for a canal, but for a rail or carriage road," Ephraim Squier wrote to Clayton, "a provision which will enable the company to open a route at once across this isthmus, more rapid, easier, cheaper, safer, and more pleasant, than that by Panama. In distance, this route will save 300 miles on the Atlantic and upwards of 800 on the Pacific."[43]

For Vanderbilt, the transit route promised to make his Nicaragua adventure profitable during the prolonged canal construction by allowing him to carry passengers across the isthmus. But he may not have realized how lucky he was to get any contract at all. White negotiated it during a rare moment of peace and unity in a country whose divisions would plague Vanderbilt in ways he scarcely imagined in 1849.

The Spanish built cities in Nicaragua a century before Squanto taught the Pilgrims to plant corn, but they left an inheritance of perpetual civil war. When Spain's empire collapsed in 1821, Nicaragua briefly fell under Mexican rule; then it joined the United Provinces of Central America from 1823 to 1838, when it finally assumed full sovereignty. Independence, unfortunately, brought little sense of national cohesion. Unlike virtually every other former Spanish province, it lacked a single metropolitan center. Two cities—León and Granada—fought for dominance. As in other Latin American nations, two parties, generically known as the Liberals and the Conservatives,* dominated politics, but here they were identified with the two cities: the Liberals made a bastion of León, while the Conservatives were entrenched in Granada. The cities' patricians waged war without end, fighting less out of ideology than geographical rivalry, commanding armies of unmotivated Indians and mestizos who were dragooned out of the sparse population of only 275,000 or so. In 1849 alone, no less than three men declared themselves the supreme director, as the Nicaraguan chief executive was called. "Nothing exists but our misfortune," declared a government report. "One man fights another, one family opposes another, one town attacks another, all with such a variety of different interests that we will never be able to form a state."[44]

Fortunately for Vanderbilt, a popular uprising united Nicaragua's warring elite in 1849. They joined forces to suppress the rebellion, and executed its bandit leader a month before they signed the canal contract (superseding the agreement with the rival company, which had been negotiated before the settlement of the civil war). The unity government embraced Vanderbilt's proposal; for centuries, Nicaraguans had dreamed of a canal that would bring the riches of the world through their borders. "Where is . . . the patriot, the wise man," asked one Nicaraguan newspaper, "who does not want to see this productive project carried out?" Enthusiasm for the North Americans swept the country, as Squier arranged a treaty that promised U.S. protection to Nicaragua.[45]

The enthusiasm was mutual. "Certain American citizens, whose judgment, energy, and pecuniary responsibility need no better voucher than the designation of 'Cornelius Vanderbilt and others' . . . have chosen that [canal route] which follows the river St. Juan and crosses the Nicaragua

---

* In Nicaragua these parties were also called the Democrats and the Legitimists, respectively.

lake," rejoiced the *United States Magazine and Democratic Review*, an influential Democratic Party journal. "But," it added, "suddenly there arises a lion in the path—that is to say, a sort of lion."

Yes, a lion. Vanderbilt had slipped through the shoals of Nicaragua's civil wars through sheer good luck, only to confront the opposition of America's most persistent European rival: Great Britain. As soon as he secured his contract with Nicaragua, the British consul in New York published a warning, forbidding him to begin work on the canal.[46] What had begun as a simple business venture was fast becoming the epicenter of dangerous tensions between Washington and London. If ever Vanderbilt needed the services of Joseph White, it would be now. The Anglo-American conflict over Nicaragua would require intensive diplomacy at the highest levels, and more than once it would threaten to descend into war.

Ever since the War of Independence, a significant proportion of Americans had nursed a resentment of Britain as the monarchical antithesis of republican ideals. More to the point, tensions between the two nations had flared over their influence in Latin America after the collapse of the Spanish empire. Despite the promulgation of the Monroe Doctrine in 1823, Britain had largely filled the vacuum left by Spain in Central America. Leapfrogging from the colonies of Jamaica and British Honduras (later Belize), English merchants had come to dominate the region's trade. In 1841, the British had extended their sway by proclaiming a protectorate over the "kingdom" of the Miskito (corrupted to "Mosquito" by the British) Indians on Nicaragua's sparsely populated Atlantic coast. The Nicaraguans regarded it as an insult to their sovereignty—an insult the British had compounded in 1848, when they had occupied San Juan del Norte and renamed it Greytown to block any canal or transit route. In the United States, where the burning of Washington in the War of 1812 remained a living memory, the sight of the Royal Navy guarding the mouth of the San Juan River looked like an act of war. "Better by far to lose California and Oregon," the *United States Magazine and Democratic Review* wrote, than "Britain or any other great power should . . . stand in the way between us and our own."[47]

Not all Americans breathed fire and steel. Secretary of State Clayton, for one, wanted an accommodation. The canal was a strategic imperative, he wrote to Abbott Lawrence, the United States minister to Great Britain. "Without some such ship navigation, it may be difficult, at some future period, to maintain our government over California and Oregon." He instructed Lawrence to offer a neutral canal, open to all on equal terms.[48]

Clayton's initiative was complicated by a common problem in nineteenth-century global diplomacy: the independence of local agents, who operated for weeks or months without instructions from their capitals. The seizure of San Juan del Norte (to be called Greytown hereafter) was the work of the intrusive Frederick Chatfield, Britain's man in Central America since 1834, who worried that Nicaragua would be "overrun by American adventurers." He recommended that the entire country be put under "a protectorate . . . favorable to British interests."[49] Lord Palmerston, the foreign secretary, took a dim view of the often-belligerent United States and generally supported Chatfield. But the rest of the British government feared the consequences of being too belligerent over too little of consequence. Prime Minister Lord John Russell declared that the Mosquito protectorate was "not worth a barrel of gunpowder on either side."[50]

London responded to Clayton's overtures by sending a new minister, Sir Henry Lytton Bulwer, who presented his credentials in Washington at the end of November 1849. Palmerston had given him the mission of making a comprehensive settlement. He was to agree to an American-built canal in Nicaragua, but without ceding the Mosquito protectorate. The sly and polished Bulwer would prove more than equal to the task.

Joseph White checked into the Thomas Irving House in Washington just as Bulwer arrived in the capital. With the future of the canal company resting on these negotiations, he called on the new British minister. Bulwer, by definition, was a man of the world; he realized that he could take advantage of White's vanity and taste for intrigue. "In America nothing is done with the Govt.," Bulwer wrote. "One must influence the people who influence the Govt." He subtly cultivated White, in part by letting White cultivate *him*. Knowing the huge cost of building a canal, Bulwer dangled the bait of British capitalists, hinting that they wanted to buy a large stake once a treaty had been signed. White abruptly abandoned his anglophobic rhetoric of the year before. Why, he and his associates had been surprised that Nicaragua should give the United States special advantages over Britain. The canal contract would be amended at once![51]

As 1850 began, Clayton and Bulwer threw themselves into crafting a politically viable agreement. The American public would not accept a permanent British presence on the Mosquito Coast, and with the South in an uproar over California's request to be admitted to the Union as a free state, President Taylor could not afford to look weak. But imperial pride would not allow the British to recede. "Sir H. L. Bulwer & I am again at variance," Clayton wrote on February 10. "The Nicaragua question . . . *may* be settled—but will not be *unless* he agrees to abandon the Mosquito claim. I have many forebodings about this matter—yet I shall try hard to settle it."[52]

THE FATE OF THE CANAL depended on this intricate international state-craft, but Vanderbilt had little choice but to go ahead as he awaited the outcome. He threw himelf into the task of turning the American Atlantic & Pacific Ship Canal Company into a functioning corporation. For the moment, that required him to start up the transit business, the carrying of passengers across Nicaragua by steamboats on the San Juan River and Lake Nicaragua and a short carriage road to the Pacific. It was an integral aspect of the canal project (engineers and supplies had to be moved into the interior), but it also promised immediate profits once it was linked with a steamship line on both oceans. The demand for steamer berths from New York to San Francisco remained so high that the Pacific Mail and U.S. Mail Steamship companies began to compete against each other on both sides of Panama. Other lines were entering the fray as well.[53]

On May 14, 1849, Vanderbilt had resigned the presidency of the Stonington Railroad, a step that reveals how central Nicaragua had become to his career.[54] That year, as cholera swept New York, he attended to both the corporate and physical vessels of the canal company. He divided into 192 the shares held by the eight partners, for ease of trading. Then he went to the shipyard of his nephew Jeremiah Simonson, near Corlears Hook on the East River.

Simonson had inherited the firm Bishop & Simonson, which now faced bankruptcy. According to rumors in the shipbuilding trade, its chief problem was the spendthrift ways of Vanderbilt's "prodigal" nephew. "He lives in first rate style," the Mercantile Agency observed, "keeps a fast horse and spends his money freely with his associates." When he asked for credit, lenders turned to Vanderbilt to cosign the notes. With Simonson's failure looming, Vanderbilt decided to purchase the shipyard, though he would leave it in the care of his nephew, who, for all his faults, knew how to build boats. Vanderbilt also sketched plans for an oceangoing steamship. At some 1,200 tons, it would be one of the largest and fastest of its kind in the world. He would call it *Prometheus*.[55]

His next step would be a firsthand inspection of the canal and transit route. At three o'clock in the afternoon on December 13, 1849, he boarded the steamship *Crescent City* at Pier No. 2 on Manhattan's North River waterfront, accompanied by his brother Jacob and David White. It was a brisk winter day, yet thousands of spectators crowded onto the docks, even clambered aboard schooners and brigs moored in the slips. They came to witness the "singular sight," as the *New York Herald* called it, of four steamships departing at the same time. Three of these enormous vessels—the *Crescent City*, the *Ohio*, and the *Cherokee*—were headed for Chagres, Panama, carrying hundreds of California-bound passengers. The Vanderbilts and White had to fight a crowd on the gangway and the deck that loomed high above the pier, and push through "a large number of female friends of the passengers," as the *Herald* observed, "promenading the decks, viewing the cabins, sitting around the stoves, or taking a last fond farewell, with a merry, ringing laugh, or with streaming eyes, according to the disposition of each."[56]

Many women remained aboard as passengers when the crew let slip the hawsers that held the *Crescent City* to the pier. "Going to California has ceased to be regarded as the formidable undertaking it once was," the reporter noted. On shore, fewer watchers waved hats and cheered as the multistory paddlewheels churned against the Hudson, smoke surging out of the great stacks that rose amidships between supplementary masts and rigging. To a businessman such as Vanderbilt, all this was telling. The very ordinariness of the event, the abundance of female passengers, and the fact that three steamships could be packed full of California passengers on the same day confirmed the size and endurance of the gold rush. It would not end soon.

Those steamships also revealed the fact that New York was the primary point of departure for voyages to San Francisco. Though far up the Atlantic coast from Panama, it was the most important city in the United States, easily reached by rail or steamboat from elsewhere in the Northeast. As one historian notes, New York had a "unique position as the national city-system's hub." Travelers to California came from across the settled states to New York to make their departure.[57]

It was inevitable that Vanderbilt should go to survey the route for himself. In nineteenth-century terms, he was a "practical" businessman who attended to technical details to organize and direct the operation. As the *Crescent City* sailed south, he would observe weather, currents, and other aspects that could add or subtract days from each voyage. But he had a specific task at hand: to fetch the newly purchased *Orus*, a river steamer now in Panama, tow it to Greytown, and pilot it up the San Juan River. More intriguing than his task was his choice of company. Along with his brother and David White, he rode with the man who owned the *Crescent City*, one Charles Morgan.

At fifty-four, Morgan was a year younger than Vanderbilt, though with his thinning hair, wrinkled jowl, and bulbous nose that hung like a ripe pear between two large, cautious eyes, he made a decidedly poor contrast with his tall, athletic guest. In 1809, at the age of fourteen, Morgan had moved to New York from Long Island and had gone to work as a clerk. Ten years later, he had accumulated enough money to buy a share in a sailing ship; he eventually bought stakes in eighteen packet ships on ten lines, as well as some fifteen merchant vessels that plied European and Caribbean ports. He had moved into coastal steamers through James P. Allaire, Vanderbilt's own tutor in steamboats, and established a line on the

Gulf of Mexico upon the annexation of Texas. He purchased Theodosius F. Secor's machine works in New York, built his own steamships, and now competed in the California traffic, making him a potential rival.[58]

But Morgan's position also made him a potential ally and investor. Indeed, his biographer believes he was one of the original partners in the canal company—unlikely, but possible, since he could have disguised his share. In the small world of New York's steamboat entrepreneurs, he and Vanderbilt surely knew each other well. Unfortunately for their planned visit to Nicaragua, four days out of New York the cross rail supporting the engine of the *Crescent City* snapped. Powerless, the ship drifted on the ocean swells until a brig, the *Roscoe*, happened by. The *Roscoe* took on board Morgan and the Vanderbilt party and carried them to Havana. On December 30, Morgan took a sailing ship to New Orleans, and the Vanderbilt brothers boarded the *Ohio* to return to New York, abandoning their journey to Nicaragua. White took passage to Chagres to fetch the *Orus*.[59]

If Vanderbilt failed at one task, he succeeded in another. In his search for investors in the canal, he appears to have aroused Morgan's interest. Certainly the two respected each other as businessmen. Morgan shared Vanderbilt's instinctive understanding of when to take a risk, as well as his discipline and caution. (Like Daniel Drew, Morgan was highly reticent about his business, and committed little to paper that would survive his lifetime.)[60] The would-be rival was becoming a friend. If only Vanderbilt knew how costly that friend's ultimate betrayal would prove to be.

EVEN AS JOSEPH L. WHITE told lies to Sir Henry Lytton Bulwer, Vanderbilt searched out the truth for Governor Hamilton Fish. On his return to New York from Havana, he had traveled to Albany on mysterious business—though most of what he did was mysterious, for secrecy was one of the highest business virtues. But secrecy was quite a different thing from falsehood. Vanderbilt continued to cultivate his reputation as a man of his word, even if his words were few. This aspect of his character helps explain why New York's social elite continued to work with him, even seek him out, though they would never invite him to their houses for dinner. Austere and offensive Vanderbilt may have been—benevolent and polished he was not—but Fish knew that he was honest. And so, when the Commodore entered Fish's office on that mysterious errand, the governor brought up another, rather delicate, matter.

Fish boasted a head of thick, dark hair, along with an elaborate swell of cheek whiskers and a wide, heavy-lipped mouth that made him look rather like a grouper. He also laid claim to leadership of one of the first families of New York. His father had been a Federalist and a close friend of Alexander Hamilton, his namesake; he himself had served in the U.S. House of Representatives as a Whig, and had won the gubernatorial election in 1848. His problem now was that someone had told him that Addison G. Jerome, a prominent Wall Street figure, had spoken ill of him. The reported insult forced Fish to rethink some of his business or political plans. But was the story true?

Vanderbilt promised to look into it. "Upon investigation of the conduct of Mr. Jerome," he wrote, "I have come to the conclusion that your mind has been abused. I am satisfied that every charge made against him relative to his conduct towards you is *false*." The rumor's substance remains unknown, but Vanderbilt was unforgiving toward such intrigues. "It is extremely hard," he added, "that an upright, honourable man should be put down by the base fabrications of foul and designing men."[61]

He already may have grown uncomfortable with the highly designing Joseph White. On February 21, Vanderbilt stayed away from a formal dinner given by the canal company in honor of Eduardo Carcache, the Nicaraguan minister to the United States. White made the keynote toast; glib as ever, he boasted of his intimacy with Bulwer and insinuatingly alluded to matters of state that he could not discuss "without violating confidences." It was the sort of self-important performance that Vanderbilt despised.[62]

As events swept forward in 1850, White's personality began to create problems for Vanderbilt's company. True, the year began well enough: on February 24, under headlines that announced Daniel Webster's intent to forge a compromise to settle the disputes between North and South, the *New York Herald* declared that Bulwer and Clayton had reached a settlement, to be ratified later as the Clayton-Bulwer Treaty. It guaranteed the neutrality of the canal and barred Greytown's authorities from interfering with the company, though the British officials and fleet remained. The next good news came on March 9, when Nicaragua incorporated the American Atlantic & Pacific Ship Canal Company. But then some of White's letters fell into the hands of Nicaragua's leaders.[63]

"The letters from Mr. Joseph L. White," Squier wrote to Clayton from Nicaragua, "were past all precedent egotistical, and calculated to leave the impression that the individual above named was charged with the *entire* business of arranging affairs with Sir Henry Bulwer.... 'I stipulated this,' and 'I did that' are the burthen of every sentence. Mr. White," he added, "is unquestionably what the Yankees term a 'smart' man, but a most inveterate, indiscriminating, and indiscreet talker.... The General-in-Chief of the State, and other leading men, have openly expressed to me their disgust."[64] It was only a hint of the trouble White would cause.

Still, the treaty had been completed, allowing the canal to go forward. If White was, in Squier's judgment, "fitted for little beyond talking," at least his talk had accomplished what Vanderbilt had required of him. As the company's counsel, his verbal dexterity soon would be needed for one more essential task: to open the bank accounts of those British investors who Bulwer had promised were eager to invest.

In the meantime, Vanderbilt moved the work of the company forward. He called a meeting of the board on April 24, and directed the incorporating partners to pay the first installment on the stock they had taken, to pay for the *Orus* and the riverboats now under construction. When the first new boat, the *Director*, was completed on July 1, he had it sent down to Nicaragua with a corps of engineers who would survey the canal route. He hired Orville Childs, the former chief engineer of New York State, to lead this team. Newspaper editors began to puff up the project, listing its advantages in distance, speed of crossing, and climate over the Panama route.[65]

Vanderbilt kept his hand in numerous other enterprises, of course, from the real estate he owned on Coenties Slip and Warren Street, to the Staten Island Ferry, to his post as a director of the Hartford & New Haven Railroad, now paying 10 percent annual dividends (with an extra 5 percent in the fall). But he let go of his last link to the Stonington, resigning the seat on the board he had held after stepping down as president.[66]

Another event occurred that year that had far more obvious repercussions. On Independence Day, President Taylor fell ill after a ceremony in extremely hot weather at the Washington Monument. Less than a week later, he was dead. A victorious general in Mexico, the popular Taylor had been an implacable nationalist who had refused to bend to pressure from his native South during the still-unresolved California admission crisis. "He was a good and upright man, such as is uncommon in high office," George Templeton Strong wrote in his diary, "[and] everybody North and South had a vague sort of implicit confidence in him, which would have enabled him to guide us through our present complications." He left the White House to Millard Fillmore, an unknown quantity, in the midst of the ongoing crisis.[67]

At the end of September, the *Prometheus* slid down the rails at Simonson's (that is, Vanderbilt's) shipyard, splashing into the East River. It was Vanderbilt's first oceangoing steamship, and perhaps his finest vessel to date. "V. has superintended her construction himself," the *New York Tribune* wrote on October 1, "and the builder has made her a first-class vessel." Measured at more than 1,200 tons and 230 feet, with clean lines and enormous sidewheels, it promised to be the swiftest ship in the California trade.[68]

Everything seemed to be in place. Nicaragua had signed the contracts and issued the corporate charter; the United States and Great Britain had come to terms; riverboats were on the scene or on their way; and now Vanderbilt had launched the first ship for the Nicaragua transit line. Only one thing was lacking: money. And there was only one place where it would be found. No sooner had the hull of the *Prometheus* been towed to the Allaire machine works for the installation of its boilers and pistons than Vanderbilt and Joseph White boarded a different steamship, bound for London.

IF ANYONE DOUBTED that progress could serve to obscure the world, a carriage ride through London might have been proof enough. Here were all the wonders of civilization, from the cupolas of St. Paul's Cathedral to the crowded docks, where laborers swarmed over ships to unload goods from around the globe. Unfortunately, those wonders often were invisible, thanks to innumerable hearths of burning coal. When White and Vanderbilt rode in a coach through the crooked lanes of the great metropolis in October 1850, they, like characters in Charles Dickens's *Bleak House*, might well have asked "whether there was a great fire anywhere? For the streets were so full of dense brown smoke that scarcely anything was to be seen."

For Vanderbilt, on a personal level, the impact and implications of this transatlantic journey remain as obscure as London itself. We can only guess. For one thing, the sheer size of the imperial capital must have been a revelation. Millions milled through "the dirtiest and darkest streets that ever were seen in the world" (in Dickens's words), down lanes lined with ancient monuments and architectural marvels unknown in the United States. This transatlantic voyage was Vanderbilt's first; for him, as for so many other Americans who crossed the ocean, to discover London was to discover the world.

His very presence on this mission speaks of a particular, perhaps growing, confidence. Three more years would pass before the Mercantile Agency pronounced him "boorish" and "offensive," suggesting that he retained the crude manners of a Staten Island mariner. Yet no longer would he let White serve as sole interlocutor for the canal company. He conferred with Lord Palmerston himself during this visit—though it is unknown whether Vanderbilt kept his ever-present cigar clamped between his teeth, or spoke in curses and double negatives, as had been his wont.[69]

Vanderbilt and White journeyed from their hotel through the streets of the City, the heart of the metropolis and the financial capital of the globe, to a building around the corner from the Bank of England, at 8 Bishopsgate Street: the grand offices of Baring Brothers & Co. The firm was perhaps the foremost merchant bank in the world, rivaling the combined wealth of the international Rothschild clan. After ninety years in business, Baring Brothers carried such weight in world affairs that a common saying counted the company as one of the great powers of Europe, alongside Britain, France, and Russia.

Vanderbilt and White were ushered in and conducted past "a hollow square," as one historian described the central office, wherein worked a "corps of bookkeepers, clerks, copyists, and accountants, almost all perched on high stools facing the grillwork topping the high, continuous desk." They passed from this chamber into a conference room, perhaps, or into the office of Thomas Baring or one of the other managing partners.[70] In those private quarters, Vanderbilt and White explained the Nicaraguan grant, the treaty, and Bulwer's promise that English capitalists would invest. They offered Baring Brothers an equal stake in the canal company—a 50 percent share.

In this office, as at Rothschild & Sons, as with Sir J. H. Pelly, as elsewhere, Vanderbilt and White met with raised eyebrows. A Baring Brothers partner wrote that the hastiness of the proposal surprised them: "There appeared no information that could be used as to the profitability of making a canal or of the cost of constructing it."

The Americans went back to their hotel as the various merchant bankers they had approached put together a joint position on the canal, which they communicated in a letter on October 14. "If, after organisation, surveys, & estimates, it shall appear that a canal can be made at a cost that would offer a fair return for the capital needed," they declared, "we will endeavor to get English capital to join in completing it." As one of the financiers summarized their response, "The matter is not ripe for the present."[71]

The next day, the Baring partners read with surprise a gross distortion of their position in the financial columns of the London *Times*. "The junction of the Atlantic and Pacific may almost be regarded as a work commenced," the story began. White's hyperbole and insinuations echoed throughout the piece. "It is the grandest physical work the world can witness. . . . A promise was given to Sir Henry Bulwer that an equal participation in the enterprise should be offered to this country on reasonable terms. To fulfil that pledge two commissioners from the company, Messrs. White and Vanderbilt, arrived in London . . . and after a short period of negotiation a satisfactory arrangement was completed this afternoon." It was a planted story—White's own London fog.[72]

"*C. Vanderbilt & Joseph L. White* of New York have been here in regard to the Nicaragua Ship Canal," Baring Brothers wrote to Thomas W.

Ward, the firm's agent in Boston. "We see in the *Times* and [*London*] *Globe*
that they would make more of [what was agreed] than [was] said here. . . .
We don't think anyone knows at present whether the canal is practicable
or not, therefore these newspaper puffs are all absurd."[73]

Who were these Americans, with their grand plans, empty estimates,
and deceitful boasts to the newspapers? The English financiers were hardly
ignorant of the United States; the Rothschilds, for example, employed as
their agent August Belmont, who since his arrival in New York in 1837
had inserted himself into the center of that city's politics and society. Days
before Vanderbilt's visit, Baring Brothers and two other London houses
each had agreed to purchase $25,000 in stock in the Panama Railroad,
because the project was backed by William H. Aspinwall, whom they
knew and respected as an aristocratic merchant. They perceived that Vanderbilt and his associates had connections to the U.S. government, but
they knew little else about them. On October 15, one of the Baring partners penned a letter to James G. King of New York. "I should be glad if
you can give us any information respecting the partners forming the
Pacific Canal co.," he wrote, "and about support it is likely to meet with
on your side."[74]

James King had been born in Manhattan only three years before
Vanderbilt, yet he belonged to a completely different world. His father
was Rufus King, one of the first two U.S. senators from New York and
a friend of Alexander Hamilton's. James graduated from Harvard and
served as a congressman, president of the Erie Railroad, and president of
the New York Chamber of Commerce. He occupied the very peak of New
York society, and often might be found as a dinner guest in homes, as
Philip Hone observed, known for "excellent taste" and "the utmost good
breeding."[75]

King did not know Cornelius Vanderbilt. "To your enquiry respecting
the partners connected with the Pacific Canal Co., we can give you only
general information," he wrote to Baring Brothers on October 29, 1850.
"Some of them, we hear of as large owners of steamboats employed in our
neighboring routes, the success of which we have no means of estimat-
ing—large means, certainly, and so employed. And with the public, they
have more credit for sagacity and enterprize, than for caution."

Sagacity and enterprize, not caution: this distinction offers fascinating
insight into the differences between the business milieus of the merchant
banker and the steamboat entrepreneur in 1850. The competitive spirit
that moved Vanderbilt to strain every resource in battle against an opponent remained suspect in King's eyes. Most of all, though, King's assessment spoke to the social gap that still yawned between Vanderbilt and the
mercantile elite. "Altogether," he concluded, "they do not possess, so far

as we can judge, the confidence or cooperation of our prudent people. And they must join with them names better known and more widely confided in before they are able to command support here. And that, with other motives of more abundant capital abroad, is probably the reason of the plan being presented in London—before it was here."[76]

Vanderbilt and White boarded the steamship *Pacific* for the return voyage home. They carried with them nothing to show for their efforts but White's puffery in the *Times*. They docked on October 31; two weeks later, the real story of their reception in London leaked out in the press. The canal company was a mere "speculation," the *New York Herald* wrote. "No stock had been taken—no stock books opened—not one cent of capital subscribed or paid in." For Vanderbilt, the scathing *Herald* story marked a low point in his long career. The scheming White had become the image of the canal company; Vanderbilt was lumped in with him, and cast as a political dummy hoping to flip the canal rights. "The whole affair was an experiment," the *Herald* concluded, "in which a few lawyers in Wall Street were the principal movers, their original purpose being to obtain a charter, and afterwards dispose of it at any good price."[77]

What remained now for Vanderbilt was to make real what his critics thought was a vaporous fraud.

Chapter Eight

STAR OF THE WEST

Threading, the air of crisis seemed to turn Americans' minds toward death. All through 1850, the South had made increasingly loud noises about seceding from the Union. The issue was whether slavery would be allowed in the vast swath of territory conquered from Mexico. Southerners saw attempts to block the spread of the "peculiar institution" as an assault on their labor and property system, as an unfair discrimination against their section. Most Northerners saw any extension of slavery as unfair competition with free labor, and the relatively few but vocal abolitionists denounced the institution itself. The crisis persisted throughout 1850, as Henry Clay and Daniel Webster, the Senate's aging statesmen, labored over a compromise. The price of failure, many believed, would be the nation's extinction.

The dead literally haunted New York that summer, as the famous teenage sisters Margaret and Kate Fox came down from Rochester to perform séances. The pair appeared to have the gift of speaking to spirits of the deceased, who would answer with a rapping noise that a less credulous public might have recognized as the cracking of toes. "I've attended twice," George Templeton Strong informed his diary. "I'm mystified." The girls proved a sensation. The spirits they conjured answered questions with remarkable accuracy—though Strong complained about "the trifling and undignified demeanor of these ghosts."[1]

The People's Line on the Hudson died that year, in a way. For complicated legal and business reasons, Daniel Drew sent it to the cross. Just before the new year, Drew attended the auction of its steamboats at the Merchants' Exchange and purchased the best ones in his own name, in order to resurrect his monopoly. He attended to his own immortality as an avid member of the Mulberry Street Methodist church, one of only two churches in the city "built with no design of renting the seats [to rich congregants], though several have adopted the plan since their erection," as a religious journal wrote.[2]

When Vanderbilt returned from London, he found that the crisis had lifted. The four bills comprising the Compromise of 1850 had passed through Congress. They admitted California as a free state, settled a boundary dispute between Texas and New Mexico, paid a large sum to Texas, and organized Utah and New Mexico as territories open to slavery. The deal also enacted a new fugitive slave law, requiring federal marshals to assist in recapturing escaped slaves. It restored calm to politics, but gave new energy to abolitionists. Still, they remained a small minority, loathed by many merchants in New York, a city made rich by Southern cotton.[3]

"Now, however, there is no quarter of the world to which attention is more actively directed than Central America," declared a newspaper on November 2, 1850. For all the talk of disunion, Americans had continued to flock to and from San Francisco as gold emerged from the mountains in vast quantities. Most of the migrants—and all of the gold—traveled by steamship, crossing the isthmus at Panama. Miners, merchants, and bankers longed for a faster route. "The Nicaragua route must command the entire traffic to California, the moment it shall be rendered practicable, even by a mixture of water and land conveyance," the press asserted.[4]

Vanderbilt threw himself into making that route practicable. He prepared the *Prometheus* for its first voyage, and ordered his lawyers to prepare a petition to Congress, offering to carry the California mail for $180,000 a year, a mere fraction of what the government currently paid. In a formal proposal, delivered in December, he offered to build six first-class steamships *"at his own proper cost"* to transport the mail via Nicaragua, "which transit route will be opened . . . probably within six months." Joseph White played no part in this appeal, for an important reason: the steamship line Vanderbilt now organized was entirely separate from the canal company. Years later, his assistant Lambert Wardell vividly recalled how important it was to Vanderbilt that he personally owned the *Prometheus.* "She was the only [steamship] owned entirely by one man, up to that time at least. When she started out there was not a cent owing on her, he remarking that he wanted her to 'go out on her own bottom.' "[5]

As with the ship, so with the man: Vanderbilt himself would finally go to Nicaragua. It would be the first of three remarkable voyages to that distant republic, a land virtually unknown to his fellow countrymen. There were practical reasons to go, of course; as a master of the transportation business, he could best judge for himself the technical considerations of a canal or transit line. That was why he had set out to go there once before. But there was something Homeric in this uneducated man's conception of himself. Like Achilles, he would lead the charge himself; like Odysseus, he would face ocean storms, river rapids, tropical fevers, and the crocodiles and sharks of Nicaragua's waters. These trips would further open his eyes to the world and enhance his heroic reputation.

At ten o'clock in the morning on December 26, Vanderbilt stood on the

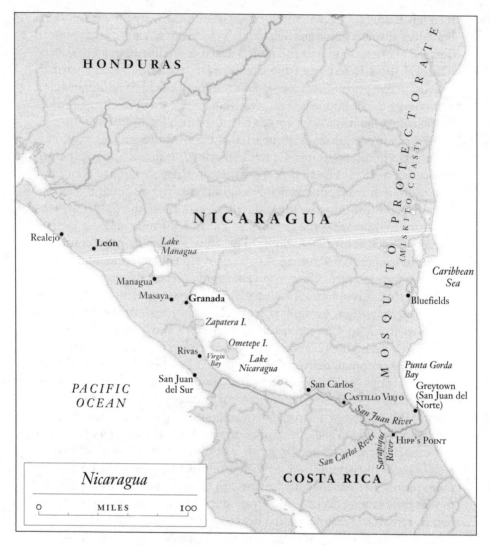

deck of the *Prometheus* as it churned through New York Harbor on its maiden voyage. Packed with passengers and freight, it would stop at Greytown and then Chagres, where most passengers would debark, since the canal company was not yet carrying travelers across Nicaragua. The *Prometheus* cut a fine figure of a ship as it steamed for the Narrows, with its distinctive vertical bow rising three decks in height, twin smokestacks, and enormous sidewheels—though it had to cut power in minutes to clear a rope caught in a paddlewheel. But this time Vanderbilt would not be stopped.[6]

The *Prometheus* proved itself. "Ship performing admirably," wrote Joseph N. Allen in his diary, "riding the seas like a duck and though very rough not a drop or spray even on deck." The forty-seven-year-old Allen was a merchant in New York and one of Vanderbilt's closest friends; he had agreed to help the Commodore establish the transit business in Nicaragua.[7] He noted that some of the "rich" passengers grew "very much excited" when the ship hit heavy cross seas, causing its 230-foot hull to plunge and roll. Three days out of port, a crewman fell to the deck from the mainmast (like all steamships in this era, the *Prometheus* had supplementary sails), dying on impact, leading to what Allen called "the solemn scene of a burial at sea." The ship made a New Year's Day call on Havana, and arrived at Greytown on January 4, 1851.

Greytown nestled on the inside of a harbor formed by the outlet of the San Juan River into the Atlantic. A sandy spit of land, Punta Arenas, enclosed the bay, in which porpoises frolicked among dugout canoes, called bungos, and canal-company steamboats. (Vanderbilt chose Punta Arenas as the location for machinery works, warehouses, and an office.) The town consisted of some sixty thatched huts, pushed nearly into the water by the great tropical forest that pressed up to the Atlantic shore. "There were no clearings, no lines of road stretching back into the country," wrote Ephraim Squier; "nothing but dense, dark solitudes, where the tapir and the wild boar roamed unmolested; where the painted macaw and the noisy parrot, flying from one giant cebia to another, alone disturbed the silence; and where the many-hued and numerous serpents of the tropics coiled among the branches of strange trees, loaded with flowers and fragrant with precious gums." Going ashore, Vanderbilt found a shanty port populated by three hundred Americans, Miskito Indians, mestizos, and "the English authorities," as Squier wrote disapprovingly, "consisting chiefly of negroes from Jamaica. . . . All mingle together with the utmost freedom, and in total disregard of those conventionalities which are founded on caste."[8]

At eleven in the morning on January 8, Vanderbilt and his party (including engineer Orville Childs) boarded the steamboat *Orus* and chuffed into the San Juan River. A heavy tropical rain fell as the paddles beat against the increasingly swift current, carrying them between high, vertical banks and dense, dark forest, past islands in the broad river. Now came the moment of greatest danger. On January 11, they spent an hour and forty minutes battling the torrent of water crashing through the Machuca rapids. Vanderbilt shoved the pilot aside and took the helm, an engineer recalled, "tied down the safety valve [and] put on all steam." With the boiler pressure building dangerously, the paddles whirling at furious speed, the boat shot through, Allen wrote, after "a tremendously hard struggle and grating . . . on the rocks."[9]

The next day they reached the ruins of Castillo Viejo, the ancient Spanish fortress that Horatio Nelson had stormed as a young man. On January 13, the *Orus* spent two hours fighting the raging Toro rapids, twice getting stuck on the boulders in the stream. Once again it appeared that the boat would be wrecked, deep in the Nicaraguan rain forest. This time Vanderbilt ordered ropes to be tied to trees on either bank, and had the boat painfully winched up over a hundred feet of water-swept rocks. *Harper's Weekly* later reported that one of the party, "a tough old sea-captain, declared he would not go through such work again for all Central America." Finally, on January 14, they landed at the village of San Carlos, where the San Juan River poured out of Lake Nicaragua.

The *Director*—the riverboat that Vanderbilt had sent down in July 1850 and that had steamed up to the lake on January 1—was nowhere to be seen. The Commodore told Allen to wait for its return at San Carlos, in the care of the town's governor, Patricio Rivas; then he set out for Granada in the *Orus* with Childs and the other engineers. Allen remained behind with mixed feelings. On one hand, he studied Spanish with "a very pretty and very obliging daughter" of Rivas; on the other, he slept on an animal-hide cot, with rats skittering along the rafters, various lizards and "enormous spiders" scurrying across the walls, and hogs rooting outside.[10]

Vanderbilt and party, meanwhile, crossed Lake Nicaragua. Home of a rare species of freshwater shark, this enormous expanse could switch in an instant from calm to violent, throwing the shallow-draft steamboat into swells far more alarming than the ocean storms encountered by the *Prometheus*. The boat chuffed past the island of Ometepe, with its twin volcano cones covered in greenery, nosing thousands of feet into the clouds. On the approach to Granada's landing, the waterfront could be seen teeming with poor Nicaraguans, splashing and bathing, "without regard to sex or age, all mixed up indiscriminately," as Allen wrote after he caught up with Vanderbilt, "a sight to make a northerner open his eyes."[11]

To reach Granada, the group made their way past wandering, pecking chickens and outlying cane-and-mud huts with thatched roofs. Then they entered the streets of the city proper, lined with tile-roofed adobe houses decorated with window balconies, ornamental archways, and heavy wooden doors that guarded elegant courtyards. They finally reached the plaza, with its decaying cathedral. Even for the increasingly worldly Vanderbilt, it was all strange, far more alien than London. On Sunday, January 19, for example, a religious festival erupted. "Such a din," Allen complained. "The streets were thronged with people. . . . In those occupied by the lower classes thousands of flags and streamers are fluttering in the wind. . . . As the morning advanced the people assembled in the neighborhood of the plaza and attired themselves in a variety of ways, among others by assuming masks and uncouth costumes."[12]

Vanderbilt and Childs consulted with the Nicaraguan authorities, sur-

veyed the canal route (through neighboring Lake Managua, up to the
Gulf of Fonseca), then headed south to scout the transit route. The transit road would cut through roughly twelve miles of land from the western
edge of Lake Nicaragua to the Pacific coast. The Commodore led his
men sixty miles south toward Rivas, through a still more alien landscape.
They passed scattered haciendas (mostly cattle ranches), seeing monkeys,
armadillos, and fences made by lines of cactus and prickly-leafed aloe
plants. In the immediate vicinity of Rivas, where some ten thousand people lived about three miles inland from the lake, innumerable fruit trees
gave the area the feel of "an immense and beautiful garden," as one
observer thought.

Vanderbilt and Childs rode a rough nine miles from Rivas to the
Pacific, through steep hills, trees, and brush, a route described by one
reporter as "dangerous and even impassable during the rainy season."
Fortunately, the fifty-six-year-old Commodore was an excellent horse-
man. He and the engineers marked out the best path for the road, down to
the virtually uninhabited little horseshoe harbor of San Juan del Sur, "one
of the prettyest bays I ever saw," as Allen described it. "I must say that with
a moderate outlay of money it can be made as safe a harbor as is to be
found anywhere." Creating a harbor on the lake, on the other hand, would
be more costly, as the western shore was exposed to swells that beat upon
the beach from the southeast. The engineers selected Virgin Bay for the
primary landing, but they would have to build a breaker and pier.[13]

Vanderbilt visited Granada once more. In that city, as elsewhere in
Nicaragua, he saw that the people "hate Englishmen with an inveterate
hatred, and hold Americanos Del Norte in high esteem," in Allen's words.
"Americans are welcomed in Nicaragua," a reporter wrote. "At balls and
public festivals the flag of the United States is seen wreathed together with
that of the country." At the end of the month, Vanderbilt descended the
San Juan to Greytown amid pouring rain. Before leaving the harbor, he
spoke to a reporter for the *New York Herald*. "He stated that the practica-
bility of this route is no longer problematical," the journalist wrote. "By
the first of May next, Mr. V. is sanguine that a speedy and expeditious
transit will be opened between this port and the Pacific; the motto is go-
ahead."[14]

As Vanderbilt and his entourage returned to New York (by way of
New Orleans) in the *Prometheus*, they again encountered ferocious seas,
and Allen came away impressed with how the vessel rode them. "The
Prometheus is without doubt the finest sea steamer ever afloat," he told his
diary, "and in all respects and as for speed her equal is yet to be built. Anything that may start with the idea of catching her, in order to make the
thing certain, must start at least two hours ahead."[15]

The *Prometheus* convinced Vanderbilt of his own genius. It differed from other steamships in many respects, the most important being the engines. When oceangoing steam vessels were first built, engineers decided that the machinery should be as low in the hull as possible, to avoid exposure to the elements and give the ship a low center of gravity. They came up with the "side-lever engine," which had elaborate gearing from the piston to the paddlewheels to keep the entire works belowdecks. The problem, Vanderbilt concluded, was that the multiple arms of the side lever made the engine inefficient, causing it to consume additional coal. Furthermore, side-lever engines had very narrow tolerances, and could not accommodate a ship's natural tendency to "hog," or bend lengthwise, at sea. That mandated a strongly reinforced engine compartment that made a ship heavier and more expensive. Refuting conventional wisdom, Vanderbilt went back to the walking-beam engine used in steamboats. The exposed arm that rocked up and down above the deck allowed for simpler gearing, which meant greater fuel efficiency, a lighter and cheaper engine, and a lighter and cheaper hull. He calculated that exposure and a higher center of gravity would not prove much of a problem. The *Prometheus* proved him right.[16]

"A most extraordinary passage," the *New York Herald* announced upon the *Prometheus*'s return to New York on February 22, 1851. Vanderbilt published a long letter describing the ship's remarkable speed and fuel efficiency. It ran 5,590 miles in just over nineteen days, consuming 450 tons of coal—a third less than any steamer of its size. "I consider the *Prometheus*, in her combination of qualities, far superior to anything afloat," he said. "I will venture a large wager that there is no ship afloat, and none that can be built within twelve months, having any other plan of engines of the same size in proportion to the capacity of the ship, that can make a winter passage in the same time, with the same quantity of fuel." The bet he proposed was $100,000.[17]

This same intense pride pulsed through his drive to win the California mail contract. He dispatched Daniel Allen to Washington with letters for Postmaster General N. K. Hall and Secretary of the Navy William A. Graham, saying that he could carry the mail via Nicaragua in twenty-five days, faster than any other route. "I am willing to pledge my reputation," he declared, "and it is well known to those who know me (and among those is the present Secretary of State), that I will make no such pledge unless certain of its fulfillment." That new secretary of state was Daniel Webster, whom Vanderbilt had known since he first traveled to Washington in 1821. Henry Clay himself presented Vanderbilt's bid to the Senate. "I dare say it is well known to every Senator, as it is to almost every person in the United States, that Mr. Vanderbilt has been one of the most successful and enterprising persons engaged in that description of navigation," Clay said. "All this is offered by this liberal, enterprising, and distinguished gentleman, without asking for one dollar of present appropriation."[18]

Vanderbilt seems to have bounced back fully from the humiliation of the London trip. With a little prodding on his part, politicians and the press hailed his reputation. On March 6, the *New York Herald*, the same paper that had derided the canal as a mere "speculation," effusively praised the Nicaragua route—and Vanderbilt himself.

> Commodore Vanderbilt's character for energy and go-aheadativeness is well known in this community, and apart from other considerations, the fact that he is connected with this enterprise is a guarantee to the public that both of these great projects—the construction of an ocean ship canal, and that of a transit route—will be finished at the earliest moment practicable. He is a man whose resolution is indomitable, and before whose determination obstacles, no matter how great, disappear as the morning dew before a July sun.[19]

It was not the first time Vanderbilt was titled "Commodore," but afterward his name rarely appeared in print without this honorary rank. He was becoming a cultural icon.

Despite the support of Webster and Clay, Vanderbilt failed to convince Congress to alter the existing mail contracts. Against George Law's skill at lobbying and William H. Aspinwall's aristocratic connections, he could make no headway—particularly after the U.S. Mail and Pacific Mail Steamship companies agreed in January to cease competing with each other, the first retreating to the Atlantic and the latter to the Pacific.[20] But Vanderbilt had delivered a clear warning that he was going to fight for the California trade, with English capital or not. And when he fought, he usually won.

ONE DAY IN THE FUTURE there would be a name for it: vertical integration. Late in the nineteenth century, John D. Rockefeller and Andrew Carnegie would emerge as leading exponents of this form of organization, in which a single owner takes control of businesses at every step of the manufacturing process, from mining raw materials to production of finished goods. A vertically integrated company captured profits (or reduced costs) at every point. Perhaps more important, in an age when few industries existed it helped ensure supply that otherwise might be diverted to a competitor.[21] Ship owner Charles Morgan understood the principle as early as the spring of 1851, when he bought control of a leading engine manufacturer in Manhattan, T. F. Secor & Co., and renamed it the Morgan Iron Works.

Ironically, Morgan's move quickened Vanderbilt's own steps toward a vertical integration of his budding steamship business. Already he had taken direct control of the Simonson shipyard, which constructed hulls; now he joined with the men whom Morgan had bought out, T. F. Secor and John Braisted, along with Daniel Drew, to purchase New York's other large steam-engine plant, the Allaire Works. "The works are immense," remarked the Mercantile Agency, "one of the most extensive in this city." Located at 466 Cherry Street on the East River near Corlears Hook, the Allaire Works would now be run by a corporation, commanded (not surprisingly) by Vanderbilt's sons-in-law: Daniel Allen as president, and James Cross as treasurer. The purchase hinted at the size of both Vanderbilt's means and his ambition.[22]

By the time the Mercantile Agency took note of all this, Vanderbilt's preparations for opening the Nicaragua route were advancing rapidly. Already the *Prometheus* carried California passengers—to Panama for now, until the transit route was ready. The steamboat *Director* plied Lake Nicaragua, carrying enterprising migrants who found their own way overland and down the San Juan River. The boat grossed $32,000 for the canal company in January alone. (The canal company owned the boats and infrastructure within Nicaragua, though not the oceangoing steamships.) The *Orus* had smashed onto the rocks of the Machuca rapids, but Vanderbilt sent down two specially constructed, shallow-draft, iron-hulled steamboats, the *J. M. Clayton* and the *Sir H. L. Bulwer*.

Meanwhile, he pushed ahead with his efforts to put steamships on both sides of the isthmus. He had two under construction in New York, the 1,000-ton *Daniel Webster* and the 1,800-ton *Northern Light*; both would receive Vanderbilt's customary walking-beam engines from the Allaire Works, and would run on the Atlantic, along with the *Prometheus*. For the Pacific, he fittingly bought the 900-ton *Pacific* (while it was en route to San Francisco) and the 600-ton *Independence*. It was still not enough tonnage.

On June 17, passengers on the big new *North America*, which already had its steam up for a voyage from New York to Galway, Ireland, were startled to learn that the ship would sail to California instead. Vanderbilt and Daniel Drew had bought it from P. T. Barnum. Barnum recalled the Commodore's amusement when they first met. "Why, I expected to see a monster—part lion, part elephant, and a mixture of rhinoceros and tiger," Vanderbilt exclaimed. "Is it possible that you are the showman who has made so much noise in the world?" Like more than one businessman in the 1850s, Barnum had dangled his feet in the ocean and found the waters too cold.[23]

"We are happy to have it in our power to announce the opening of the new route to the Pacific," the *New York Evening Post* declared at the end of June. "Cornelius Vanderbilt is the principal proprietor of this line, which is sufficient guaranty [sic] for the superior speed and equipment of the vessels." Passengers thronged to the upstairs office at 9 Bowling Green, next to the offices of other lines on "steamship row," to buy tickets. "The Vanderbilt line was then the rage," recalled passenger William Rabe.

On July 14, Rabe boarded the *Prometheus* at Pier No. 2 on the Hudson River for the inaugural voyage of the Nicaragua transit route. "On board I found . . . Mr. Vanderbilt himself," Rabe wrote a few weeks later. Rabe pressed the Commodore about whether the Nicaragua transit truly was in working order; otherwise Rabe and some of the other passengers might go on to Chagres and cross Panama. "Mr. Vanderbilt said that we would get through before any other passengers who had started about the same time for California, and insisted upon our going."[24]

Unknown to Rabe and the other passengers, Vanderbilt accompanied them because he had a mission to perform. He embarked on this journey to Nicaragua to meet a political threat, one that endangered his entire canal-and-transit enterprise. Due to the nature of the problem, he brought Joseph White, the company counsel and fixer. Before they returned to New York, Vanderbilt would have reason to wonder if White himself was not a greater danger than any problem in Nicaragua.

Government and nature seemed to conspire against Vanderbilt and his inaugural passengers at every step. After ten days at sea, the *Prometheus* anchored at Greytown, where they boarded the *Bulwer*, one of the iron-hulled riverboats. The first sign of trouble was a demand from the town's officials that the boat obtain their permission to ascend the San Juan River, in clear violation of the Clayton-Bulwer Treaty. White haughtily replied that "the only way to prevent us was to blow us out of the water." On they went—only to run aground. Most of the passengers leaped into the river "to drag her over, trying to lift her up, or pull her along," in Rabe's words. Humiliatingly, it took a boatload of sailors from the *Bermuda*, a British warship, to lift the steamer over the bar.

The next day, the tightly packed little paddlewheeler steamed to the Machuca rapids, where the passengers stared at the ominous wreck of the *Orus*, rusting on the rocks. As the pilot scraped the hull of the *Bulwer* helplessly into the rapids, it seemed likely that the boat would follow the *Orus*'s example. Once again, Vanderbilt took the wheel. At fifty-seven, he already could be considered somewhat elderly by the standards of the day. Yet he radiated power, both physical strength and force of personality. And so, deep in the wilds of Nicaragua, on a treacherous jungle river, Vanderbilt poured on the steam and piloted his first passengers into the rapids. "Back we were swept," wrote another traveler. "At it again; the boat's nose was brought out of the current, and all our steam applied. 'Now she moves,' cried one. Now she nears the rocks; puff, puff—up, up—not a word—all silent—how we gazed silently at the shrubbery fringing the water's edge, marking our headway. At length we passed the peril, and gave three hearty cheers, shot through one set of rapids, then ran aground on the next."

After spending a night trying to run the mighty Castillo rapids, again using ropes, chain, and a winch to haul the boat over, Vanderbilt had to give up. The passengers piled into Nicaraguan bungos and were paddled up to San Carlos, where they boarded the *Director*. "To my astonishment I found the lake a boisterous expanse of water, running as high as the angry Atlantic," Rabe wrote. Hungry, sopping wet, and seasick, the passengers finally arrived on the western shore, where they were ferried to land in canoes or carried on the shoulders of Nicaraguan porters. The passengers went on to California, some happy, some convinced that the transit was not really ready. Vanderbilt mounted a horse and galloped off to Granada, together with White, to complete his mission.[25]

Rumor had it that the Nicaraguan government, disturbed at the lack of progress on the canal, planned to revoke the company's charter. Vanderbilt knew that the canal would take far longer than originally envisioned, while the transit business offered immediate profits. To protect the latter from delays to the former, he wanted to separate the two enterprises by chartering a transit company.[26] But on his arrival in Granada, he learned that Nicaragua had once again descended into civil war. The unity government of 1849 had collapsed. The Liberals had risen in revolt; two hostile governments now faced each other, a Conservative one in Granada and a Liberal rival in León. It was a moment that called for great prudence.[27]

No one ever accused Joseph L. White of excessive prudence, or perhaps any prudence at all. Believing the Conservatives to be the friendliest government, he "promised to send men and arms to their support, assuring them at the same time that all resident foreigners were on their side," a reporter wrote. He said he could help wrest control of Greytown from the British. He also paid out $20,000 in bribes.[28] On August 14, the Conservative government agreed to charter the Accessory Transit Company, transferring to it the canal company's crucial monopoly on steamboats in exchange for 10 percent of its profits and $10,000 per year.

All this alarmed the Liberals. On August 25, John Bozman Kerr, the (notably bigoted) chief U.S. diplomat in Nicaragua, sent a warning to Secretary of State Daniel Webster from León. "Mr. White seems very naturally to have regarded these people as mere children, who could be led or driven any way he might be disposed," he wrote; "but I fear he may have carried his contempt for their intellect somewhat too far." One cynical journalist expressed ironic admiration: by dangling the false promise of a canal, the company had won a monopoly on the transit—"in my humble opinion, the most clever speculation which ever came into a Yankee's head."[29]

Too clever, perhaps. On August 22, the rival Liberal government in León addressed an angry letter to White and Vanderbilt. By choosing sides, the Liberals declared, "you have lost the neutrality of a foreigner." The Accessory Transit Company was created under a curse. White had been true to his nature, and so put the enterprise on the path to destruction from the start.[30]

For the time being, White's gamble seemed to pay off. The Conservatives remained safely entrenched in Granada, where they were well placed to protect the transit route. Rumor had it that the *Prometheus* carried a shipment of two thousand muskets to them in the fall of 1851. And Vanderbilt's new company flourished. Workers blasted rocks from the San Juan's rapids, and a steam sawmill arrived for construction of a plank road to San Juan del Sur. The creation of Accessory Transit as a separate corporation gave it access to the power of the stock market to gather capital through sales of bonds, issues of new stock, or calls for additional payments from the shareholders. The Commodore's sidewheelers now sailed the Atlantic and Pacific oceans, packed with passengers attracted from the Panama route by lower fares. Vanderbilt earned vast sums from his ships, and as agent of Accessory Transit he kept 20 percent of each $35 ticket for the Nicaragua crossing.[31]

The success of Vanderbilt's Nicaragua venture had national consequences. Simply put, he helped transform a rush for gold into the lasting establishment of American civilization on the Pacific. By steeply reducing fares and offering faster service, Vanderbilt sped up the flow of migrants to the West and gold to the East, where it had a significant impact on the economy. And he did it not only without a federal subsidy, but in competition with the subsidized line.

Thanks in large part to reduced transportation costs, San Francisco matured from a dust-blown, mud-lined tent camp with gambling saloons into a brick-walled, warehouse-filled commercial center with gambling saloons. Numerous devastating fires in the city's first few years destroyed the shanties and rough wooden buildings thrown up by the first settlers; by necessity, sturdy masonry structures went up along the orderly streets that stretched from the bay up the steep hills. "The characteristics of a Spanish or Mexican town had nearly all disappeared," wrote one resident. "Superb carriages now thronged the street, and handsome omnibuses regularly plied between the Plaza and the Mission. . . . The old stores, where so recently all things 'from a needle to an anchor' could be obtained, were nearly extinct; and separate classes of retail shops and wholesale warehouses were now the order of business. Gold dust as a currency had long given place to coin." It was still a fast town, but it also became a place of aristocratic display. "A striking change was observable everywhere and in everything. The houses were growing magnificent, and their tenants fashionable."[32]

The pulse of commerce between the Atlantic and Pacific coasts beat twice a month, a pace set by steamship departures. Every two weeks, "steamer day" sent San Francisco into a frenzy, as bankers prepared shipments of gold to New York houses, merchants called in debts to make payment to eastern suppliers, and everyone prepared letters and packages to mail to the "states."[33] When steamers were expected, all eyes watched the tower atop Telegraph Hill, where signalmen would announce the approach of a paddlewheeler by running out oversize wooden semaphore flags—two long black boards, hanging down on either side of a tall pole. The signal's centrality to life in the city was seen during a performance by a visiting theater company. At a climactic point in the play, an actor flung out his arms, the sleeves of his black robe hanging down, and asked, "What does this mean?" A wag in the audience shouted, "Sidewheel steamer!" The knowing audience erupted in howls of laughter.[34]

As the owner of one of the two primary steamship lines, Vanderbilt emerged as a powerful presence in San Francisco, where he never had and never would set foot. Railroad and newspaper promoters there besieged him with requests for investment. "If you knew of the hundreds of applications that we have daily for the same thing," he replied to one, "you would at once see that it would be ruinous to grant them."[35]

Rather than send money to California, Vanderbilt needed it close to home. His Nicaragua line posed a serious threat to the established interests on the Panama route, and those enemies had decided to strike back.

THE GHOST OF VICE PRESIDENT Daniel D. Tompkins bedeviled Cornelius Vanderbilt. When Tompkins had sought state assistance to develop Staten Island during the War of 1812, the New York legislature had chartered the Richmond Turnpike Company. Under the company's aegis, Tompkins started the first steam ferry to the island, which became known simply as the Staten Island Ferry. When Vanderbilt took over the ferry in 1838 it was still technically the Richmond Turnpike Company, the creature of eighteenth-century mercantilist philosophy. As such, it differed from later corporations in one important respect. This artificial person existed for a fixed term of years, after which its charter would expire. Just before it perished on April 1, 1844, its chief officers—Vanderbilt and Oroondates Mauran—assigned its leases and real-estate titles to two private citizens, Cornelius Vanderbilt and Oroondates Mauran. When Mauran died in 1848, Vanderbilt, as we've seen, purchased his stake, and was immediately forced to defend his title to the corporation's lands. New York's attorney general argued that the dead company's property reverted to the state. Vanderbilt battled back in court, where he repulsed the state's assault year after year. The ferry was worth defending, and it could pay for a few lawyers: the *New York Times* estimated its annual profits at $50,000.[36]

George Law never showed much interest in Staten Island. From his office in the Dry Dock Bank, he turned his eye toward Albany and Washington, where he bribed and bargained his way into government contracts, or to Panama, where his U.S. Mail Steamship Company connected to Pacific Mail, and where he had invested hundreds of thousands of dollars in the stocks and bonds of the Panama Railroad. By mid-1851, he had taken a number of steps to restore the original steamship monopoly. He had reached an agreement with Pacific Mail to divide the oceans (as noted earlier); he had purchased Charles Morgan's rival steamships, the *Empire City* and the *Crescent City*, along with Morgan's agreement to abandon future competition; and he had driven off or intimidated most of the lesser steamship owners who dared oppose him.[37] And then Vanderbilt opened the Nicaragua route.

As coarse and conniving as Law was, he lived under the same informal code of the transportation business that Vanderbilt had defined in court twenty years earlier. It was a code honored in the breach as often as the observance, but it was recognized nonetheless. If a man had a steamboat line, he was entitled to enjoy it in peace. If a competitor moved against him, then the competitor's other lines were fair game for a counterattack. They called it "self-defense." And so, with Vanderbilt cutting into profits on one of the most lucrative lines of transportation in American history, Law struck back on the route Vanderbilt had plied since childhood.[38]

Shortly before the Commodore went aboard the *Prometheus* to inaugurate the Nicaragua line, he gave orders for the construction of a ferry house on Staten Island, on a lot he had acquired through the late Richmond Turnpike Company. A crew went to work on the structure, only to discover that Henry M. Western claimed the property as his own, and had leased it to the New-York & Staten Island Steam Ferry Company.

The moving force behind the new ferry company was Law, who had joined with Western and other Staten Islanders who were eager to break Vanderbilt's monopoly. With the Commodore away, his men worked warily alongside Law's employees, who built a dock for the new ferry on the same lot. Law's men started to openly harass Vanderbilt's, throwing obstacles in their way and nailing up boards. One of Vanderbilt's subordinates went to court for an injunction, which briefly stopped the intimidation. But Law's workers still snarled threats, and violence hung in the air.

On the afternoon of July 26, as Vanderbilt piloted a steamboat through the far-off jungle, a mob of three hundred workers, armed with axes and crowbars, marched down the road toward the new building, led by Henry Western. "Tear it down," he bellowed. "It is on my land and I will be responsible." The mob rushed forward, swinging axes and shouting, "Down with the building!" Vanderbilt's foreman tried to stop them, telling them not to "cut" the structure. "They replied," the foreman later testified, "that if deponent did not get out of the way they would cut him too." They razed the building to the ground, then ran a wooden foot-bridge over the foundation to the dock, where the boats of the new ferry began to land on July 27. Law's men posted a guard, but Vanderbilt's men reportedly retaliated by cutting down the pier's pilings.[39]

Elsewhere Law took a more subtle approach to countering his oppo-nent. He worried that Vanderbilt's boast might prove true, that the Nicaragua route might consistently carry passengers between New York and San Francisco in twenty-five days, roughly a week less than the aver-age on the Panama route. On July 21, Law told the postmaster general that most of his ships would sail directly between New York and Panama to save time; a separate postal steamer would tag along behind, making the multiple stops mandated by contract. Yet passengers traveling by way of Nicaragua still arrived from California eight days ahead of those on the Panama route. So Law and his partners resorted to a whispering campaign, spreading accounts of the poisonous climate and long delays encountered on Vanderbilt's line. Even the London *Times* took note of "the constant attempts to depreciate its success and underrate its con-venience."[40]

The Nicaragua transit *did* suffer problems. After all, it ran through hundreds of miles of rapids-filled river and storm-tossed lake. Only small, shallow-draft boats could run the river, a guarantee of overcrowding. Droughts and heavy rains both made for delays. The route ran through a wilderness without amenities; it would take time before hotels and restau-rants could be built. Steamships arrived early or late. Cholera and tropical diseases plagued travelers in this era of dim medical knowledge. Passen-gers often complained, bitterly and publicly. But all this was true of the Panama route as well.[41]

Vanderbilt returned to New York to find that Daniel Allen already had filed a lawsuit against Law and his company for the attack on Staten Island. The Commodore prepared for a long war to keep his monopoly on the ferry. To fight the aspersions cast on the Nicaragua route, he served as his own publicist, writing letters to the press to tout his accomplishments. He constructed a new steamboat for Lake Nicaragua, named *Central America*. "When the expedition that has thus far marked the progress of this little vessel is taken into consideration I think it will somewhat astonish the world," he wrote. "I had her built in 27 days. . . . Let some one try to beat it."[42]

On October 22, 1851, Vanderbilt embarked on his final voyage to Nicaragua. His three trips neatly adumbrated the enormous effort he had put into his California line, for they were in turn geographical, political, and commercial—or, perhaps, maritime—in nature. First he had gone to scout the canal and transit route, next to create the corporate body of Accessory Transit, and last to crush his competitors. Unlike Law or William H. Aspinwall, the Commodore was a technical master of steam navigation, and it was to trumpet his prowess that he personally took the *Central America* to Nicaragua. The 375-ton steamboat trailed in the wake of the new *Daniel Webster*, sister ship to the *Prometheus*, sailing on its maiden voyage. It was another day of four simultaneous steamship departures; a huge crowd pushed onto the slips, and some of the onlookers even climbed wood piles and heaps of coal to get a look. "No sooner were the vessels observed to be moving from their berths," the *New York Tribune* reported, "than parting cheers began to be exchanged between the people on board and those on shore, which were heartily renewed and continued till the increasing distance . . . rendered them inaudible."[43]

Decades later, Vanderbilt's clerk, Lambert Wardell, would describe the Commodore as a man who couldn't be bothered with details. Clearly that was not true in 1851. The millionaire checked and double-checked the two stout hawsers that ran out over the stern to the *Central America*, as the *Daniel Webster* paddled through the Atlantic swell. Towing the boat onto the ocean was highly risky, as he had often been told before leaving New York. "All the 'knowing ones,' " Vanderbilt wrote, "and particularly those of the greatest experience of the seafaring part of the community, pronounced it to be impossible." The critics gave the *Central America* six hours before it swamped.

That evening, the water grew restless, then rough. After nightfall, the sea lashed out violently. Vanderbilt made his way across the tossing deck to the stern and learned that one of the hawsers had snapped. "This would have been the last of the tow had I not been here," he declared. As always, the moment of crisis—of physical danger—showed the Commodore at his finest. He ordered the *Daniel Webster* to slacken its speed and personally directed the crew as they attached a new cable in the darkness, amid crashing waves and a soaking spray. The *Webster* went ahead again, and the new line held. The crisis had passed.[44]

On November 2, Vanderbilt arrived at Greytown and piloted the *Central America* into the San Juan River. Now came the second moment of danger. "She is a large vessel to get up through this river, drawing about four feet of water," he wrote to a friend in New York, "when you know I never pretended, nor do I now, to navigate it with a greater draught of 20 to 22 inches, which is the draught of the small iron steamers now navigating it." After a hard struggle, he made it through on November 19, and the *Central America* began to carry five hundred passengers at a time across the rough waters of Lake Nicaragua. "The steamer will now always be in readiness on the Lake," he wrote to the *New York Tribune*, "which will hereafter remedy the former delays of the line."[45]

His mission accomplished, Vanderbilt descended the now-familiar river to Greytown. With the increasing traffic across the isthmus, Americans hoping to profit from the migration had swelled the village. They met with frustration. Few passengers stopped in town; most transferred directly between the steamships and the riverboats. Accessory Transit set up its facilities across the harbor, at Punta Arenas. Exasperated municipal officials began to pester steamship and riverboat captains to pay port fees, only to be ignored—in part because the officials were black Jamaicans and the captains white Americans, and in part because the British had stipulated, as Sir Henry Lytton Bulwer had informed Daniel Webster, "All vessels or goods connected with the Nicaraguan Canal Company going up the River San Juan should be admitted free of duty."[46]

On November 21, a well-satisfied Vanderbilt stepped aboard the *Prometheus* from one of the Accessory Transit Company's riverboats tied alongside. With him came some five hundred passengers traveling from California, who flocked through the ship, dropping bags in their cabins or claiming berths in steerage. At two in the afternoon, as Captain Henry Churchill was about to give orders for departure, a boat rowed over from Greytown and disgorged the port collector, Robert Coates. As on four previous occasions, Coates demanded port fees. This infuriated Vanderbilt; he had been assured by Lord Palmerston himself in London that his ships would be free from municipal interference. "I cannot nor will not recognize any authority here," he snapped, "and I will not pay unless I am made by force." The crew bundled Coates and his entourage off the *Prometheus*. Unnoticed by Vanderbilt, Coates notified the British consul, who dispatched a messenger to the British warship *Express*, anchored offshore.[47]

"I hove up my anchor and dropped down the harbor with the current, having alongside one of the river steamers, receiving from her the baggage of the passengers," Captain Churchill reported later that day. "The English brig-of-war, lying a short distance from us, immediately got under weigh, made sail for us, and when within a quarter of a mile from us fired a round-shot over the forecastle, not clearing the wheelhouse over ten feet."

Stunned, Vanderbilt and the passengers watched as smoke again billowed from the warship's gunports, and a moment later heard the cannon's boom and the dull whir of a second ball rocketing over the stern, "so near that the force of the ball was distinctly felt by several passengers," Churchill wrote. When he sent a boat over to ask the reason for the shots, "the captain stated that it was to protect the authorities of Greytown in their demands, and if we did not immediately anchor he would fire a bombshell into us, and ordered his guns loaded with grape and canister shot."

Some of the passengers, filled with fury at the bully Britain, demanded that they risk it. But Vanderbilt told the captain to steam back into the harbor and anchor, as the Royal Navy had ordered. (To pile on insult to American pride, the British sent over a detachment to see that the *Prometheus*'s boiler fires were extinguished.) Then the Commodore went ashore to pay $123 to the triumphant Greytown authorities.[48]

No sooner had the *Prometheus* returned to the United States than news of the affair prompted a national wave of indignation. Americans had a clear sense of inferiority toward Britain that, together with a belligerent pride in the superiority of their republican institutions, primed them for outrage. And it *was* an outrage. A British warship had shot at an unarmed American passenger ship, had threatened to destroy it and kill hundreds of civilians. The order to fire came from the British consul, James Green, in violation of treaty and explicit assurances from London.

Joseph White carried an official protest from the American Atlantic & Pacific Ship Canal Company to Washington (oddly, as the canal company was not involved). The United States government demanded an explanation from London, and dispatched the USS *Saranac* to Greytown. Newspapers across the country voiced anger, even a willingness to go to war with the British Empire. "The outrage upon the *Prometheus* demands the most ample apology and reparation," proclaimed the *New York Herald*, "or it demands the application of the Jacksonian doctrine of retaliation and reprisals."[49]

As luck would have it, the British cabinet was in a state of turmoil. On December 21, Lord Russell dismissed Palmerston from the Foreign Office; his replacement, Lord Granville, eventually wrote to Washington, "Her Majesty's Government have no hesitation in offering an ample apology for that which they consider to have been an infraction of Treaty engagements." The onus fell on the Greytown consul, James Green, but the ultimate victim may have been Frederick Chatfield, the British viceroy in Central America who had charted an aggressively anti-American course. London recalled him, even though he had not taken direct part in the affair. The real result of the near bombardment of Cornelius Vanderbilt, then, was a more stable diplomatic environment.[50] In his war with George Law, he had gained another advantage.

IF THERE WAS ONE RELIGIOUS RITE that Vanderbilt believed in, it was marriage. Weddings brought him sons-in-law—and sons-in-law made trustworthy assistants, which were hard to find in the treacherous business world at mid-century. Vanderbilt's own sons sorely disappointed him, but his daughters gave him a steady succession of replacements in the form of their husbands. In the end, he would rely on no son-in-law, not even Daniel Allen, more than Horace F. Clark.

Clark exuded ambition from every pore—ambition in politics, ambition in business, ambition in society. Born in 1815 to a respected clergyman in Southbury, Connecticut, he graduated from Williams College and began to practice law in New York in 1837. In 1848 he joined the firm of Charles A. Rapallo, the Commodore's attorney. Round-faced and wide-eyed, Clark pursued high-profile cases—demanding, for example, that famous writer Nathaniel P. Willis hand over letters written to Willis by a client's wife. Clark threw himself into Democratic Party politics alongside such luminaries as August Belmont. Above all, he tried to climb in social standing. George Templeton Strong derided him in 1851 as "that snob of snobs"—not in the sense of one who condescends, as the word would later mean, but one who sucks up insufferably. A dictionary of that era defined "snob" as "a person who looks up to his or her social betters and tries to copy or associate with them." So when Clark married Maria Louise Vanderbilt on April 13, 1848, on a Thursday evening several months before the California gold rush changed the world, it was undoubtedly a wedding in keeping with the customs of New York's social elite, even if that elite shunned the event itself.[51]

Years after the wedding, a story would circulate about Clark's request for the Commodore's permission to marry Louise (as she was called). Vanderbilt assumed the lawyer was after his wealth, and curtly refused. "The impetuous Horace, with more emphasis than elegance, told him to take his money and be d——d, he would have the girl anyhow," a newspaper later wrote. "Whereupon the Commodore, always an admirer of pluck and perseverance, quickly relented and consented to the union." The story sounds suspiciously like something that a self-admiring man like Clark might tell of himself. He was too smart a Yankee not to see, and take advantage of, his new connection; and Vanderbilt was smart enough to see how useful Clark could be to him. The new son-in-law boasted strengths in precisely the areas where Vanderbilt felt most vulnerable—those requiring great learning, such as the law, public speaking, and politics, areas in which his business increasingly carried him.[52]

If the Commodore felt a growing appreciation for his new son-in-law, he seethed at the son who bore his own name. When Cornelius Jeremiah came to the wedding in his father's house at 10 Washington Place, the father boiled over. In the midst of the reception, this finely calibrated social event, he lashed out at his son with his fists. "The Commodore tried to do something to Cornelius," son-in-law James Cross recalled, and Corneil "fled from the house." The specific cause is unclear. The incident occurred before Vanderbilt sent Corneil to California, but perhaps the boy already showed some of the character flaws that later became so pronounced.

Corneil returned from California in 1849 with something broken inside of him. It was the gear that connects labor with reward, diligence with satisfaction. Perhaps it had never worked properly in the first place, but the land of excitement and easy money had ruined it for good. Back on the Atlantic coast, he drew another draft on his father, which his father also refused to pay. He then agreed to seek treatment in an asylum. It did not help. He began to disappear into card and roulette-wheel saloons, only to emerge penniless. He developed a taste for fine clothes—a black silk tie, white watered silk vest, black frock coat, and kid gloves—but he neglected to pay for them, causing his creditors to pester the Commodore with the bills (unsuccessfully). Vanderbilt had given his own name to this boy, only to see him become everything he despised: sickly, weak, spendthrift, dishonest, dishonorable.[53]

William H. Vanderbilt—or Billy, as the Commodore still called him—had said nothing about his father's outburst at the wedding. He knew better than to try to fight such abuse, which he himself still received during his father's regular visits to Staten Island. Billy continued to complain to Daniel Allen about "the old man." Vanderbilt had exiled Billy to a farm, yet harshly rebuffed his requests to borrow money to improve the place. "He would say of his father that he was mean," Allen later recalled, "that he couldn't get anything out of him and couldn't get along without money." As a prosperous businessman as well as a brother-in-law, Allen was always willing to help, loaning a few hundred dollars here and there, which Billy repaid promptly. Very likely it was Allen who brought Billy into his first joint business venture with his father, the ill-fated California Navigation Company (under which they had shipped the disassembled steamboat to San Francisco at the start of the gold rush).[54]

Gradually—and almost unnoticed by the Commodore—the supposedly meek, soft son turned his farm into a profitable operation. "He was a hard master to work for," one field hand told W. A. Croffut, the nine-teenth-century biographer. Knowing that new workers tried to make a good impression on their first day, Billy "would count the number of rows of corn they had hoed, and then require them to do the same amount of work every day."[55]

Billy's stature rose steadily, lifted by his own success. On December 5, 1851, virtually the entire population of Staten Island poured down to the water's edge to see "the greatest living man," in the words of the *New York Herald:* Louis Kossuth, the Hungarian revolutionary who had nearly won his nation's independence from the Austrian Empire. Billy stood in front of the crowd as part of Richmond County's official welcoming committee; the other members included Daniel Allen and George A. Osgood, another of the Commodore's sons-in-law.

The next day, Kossuth took the *Vanderbilt* across the harbor to Manhat-tan. There the Commodore must have had trouble getting to his place of business at 9 Bowling Green, for an immense mob jammed into every crevice and climbed every ledge and pole to see the Hungarian hero.[56] When Vanderbilt did reach his door and climbed the steps to the second floor, he strode past Allen's desk on his way to his own office in the rear. Allen would present the affairs of the steamship business, discuss decisions tentatively made, and show him handbills and documents. The Com-modore would shift the cigar around in his mouth, put on his reading glasses, and give his approval or curtly say otherwise.

In late 1851 and early 1852, there was much for him to review. "That was a time of great emigration," recalled James Cross. "There was a great demand for passages." With the Nicaragua steamships sailing from Pier No. 2, just around the corner, ticket buyers packed into the office. Daniel Drew regularly stopped by to chat, discussing their joint ownership of the *North America* and Wall Street matters. And Vanderbilt often unrolled plans of various steamers, pondering which to buy to expand his fleet, especially on the Pacific, where he needed more tonnage. In the process, he built a partnership with Robert and George Schuyler, Alexander Hamilton's illustrious nephews, who helped settle a dispute between Van-derbilt and shipbuilder William H. Brown over the six-hundred-ton steamer *Independence.* "We came in and re-imbursed Mr. Vanderbilt his advances" for the ship, Robert testified, "and let the ship remain in the line, and took our chance for the earnings." That brief statement shows how thoroughly the aristocratic Schuylers trusted Vanderbilt. As always, though, Vanderbilt trusted his own family most. On January 21, he sent his son-in-law Cross to California to act as his new agent in San Francisco and Jacob Vanderbilt to Nicaragua to supervise the Accessory Transit Company's affairs.[57]

As master of one of the two primary channels of commerce and travel between San Francisco and New York, the Commodore emerged as a national figure with a public stature worthy of his informal title. But Washington continued to fund his rivals, a circumstance that offended both his quasi-Jacksonian outlook and his personal interests. In January 1852 he offered to carry the mail via Nicaragua for $250,000 per year, compared to the current annual payments of $638,000 to the Pacific Mail and U.S. Mail Steamship companies and $100,000 to the still-incomplete Panama Railroad.

Though Congress declined his offer, he redoubled his competition. He purchased the *Samuel S. Lewis* in February and the *Brother Jonathan* in March, as well as the *Pioneer* and the *Monumental City*. He ordered eighteen omnibuses for the carriage road from San Juan del Sur to Virgin Bay. He launched an 1,800-ton steamship, the *Northern Light*, from the Simonson yard, and began construction on another steamship. As if in tribute to the great turn in his career, it was named *Star of the West*. Bankers, merchants, and travelers all gained as he cut fares, added facilities, and put new hulls in the water.[58]

No one studied Vanderbilt's march more closely than George Law. In February, in seeming imitation of the Commodore's celebrated journeys to Nicaragua, Law sailed to Panama to inspect the progress of the railroad he had invested in so heavily. He inaugurated the Atlantic terminus of the line at Navy Bay, where he christened the new city of Aspinwall. He returned to New York in May and was welcomed with a public dinner at the Astor House hotel, hosted by Charles Morgan, Isaac Newton, Daniel E. Sickles, and an obscure Democratic Party functionary named William M. Tweed.[59]

Law took Vanderbilt's competition personally. One of Law's partners was Colonel Sloo, the original steamship "dummy"; alarmed at the "ruinous competition with the Nicaragua Company," Sloo accused Law of refusing an offer to set fares jointly with Accessory Transit "in consequence of an old grudge between Law and C. Vanderbilt." Law was full of grudgery, but he also faced a deeper problem: Nicaragua's greater proximity to the United States gave Vanderbilt a permanent advantage over the Panama lines. A faster passage was one result, of course, attracting both passengers and specie shippers (who lost money with every day gold remained in transit, and who paid a lucrative commission on consignments). But the biggest benefit was the savings Vanderbilt reaped in operational costs. "The route by the Isthmus of Nicaragua is decidedly the most economical route," declared John A. Buckman, a veteran of the California steamship business. Because of the shorter trip, a ship needed fewer provisions and, in particular, less coal, the biggest operating expense. On the Pacific alone, a Nicaragua voyage saved at least $5,000 over one to

Panama. Even if the rival lines agreed to charge the same fare, Vanderbilt would earn a larger profit.[60]

Law had the advantage of a federal subsidy, of course; he also counted on the Panama Railroad, when complete, to make the Panama route just as fast. At the moment, he had to cope with a small distraction: in March, the *New York Times* reported that the New York attorney general, under highly suspicious circumstances, had lobbied the board that was awarding contracts to widen the Erie Canal to set aside $1 million for Law. Small wonder Law left the country for Panama.[61]

Vanderbilt soon had his own problems. On March 27, he learned that the *North America* had run aground on the coast of Mexico, and was a total loss. "The owners"—meaning Vanderbilt and Drew—"might as well have thrown $400,000 into the sea as to lose her," remarked James Cross. The ship was also uninsured, as was Vanderbilt's custom. Still worse, it was the biggest ship on the Pacific side, with six hundred berths—though it usually packed in nine hundred passengers. In San Francisco, Cross frantically worked to charter and dispatch steamships to carry customers stuck in Nicaragua, but many remained stranded for weeks. Some eventually gave up and returned to New York.

One of the latter was Sidney Briggs. He went to 9 Bowling Green and introduced himself to Vanderbilt. "I asked him if he proposed to do anything" to provide compensation, Briggs recalled. "He said he proposed to do what was right. . . . I told him there was no other way but for us to return. He said he supposed not." Then Briggs asked why, *after* Vanderbilt had learned that he had lost his biggest Pacific steamship—when he knew Nicaragua was clogged with stranded travelers—he had let the *Northern Light* sail from New York, full of passengers. "His reply was that some of the tickets for the *Northern Light* were then in the hands of the passengers, that if he had kept back a part, it would have frightened the whole, and it was better for him to let us come back and settle with us and pay us our damages than to let the *Northern Light* go out empty."

Vanderbilt had added up the numbers, and calculated that it would be more profitable to strand dozens, perhaps hundreds, of passengers in a tropical country, exposed to diseases for which they had no resistance, in a region chronically short of shelter and amenities, than to hold his ship. Of all the things the Commodore would be accused of in his long career, it would never be said that he had gone soft.[62]

Claims for damages soon flowed in. To defend himself, Vanderbilt turned to his son-in-law Horace Clark. Clark faced a grueling task, but he was wise enough to see that it was an apprenticeship, or even a test. Vanderbilt would give him bigger assignments in the future—greater, perhaps, than anything Clark now imagined.

TRAGEDY, TREACHERY, AND ACCIDENT most often strike at home. On July 5, 1852, that lesson came on a crowded dock at Vanderbilt's Landing, the terminal of the Staten Island Ferry, just a short distance from the Commodore's old mansion. At four o'clock on that Monday afternoon, the *Hunchback* chuffed in, and a crowd of passengers on the pier pushed forward onto a hinged bridge at the end, held in place by heavy chains. The bridge was designed to allow the boat to dock no matter what the state of the tide; it was *not* designed for the weight now pressing upon it. When the arriving passengers surged off the boat, the chains snapped, sending dozens of men, women, and children into the water below, smacking on top of each other, pushing the first to fall down under the surface. In the end, seventeen bodies would be recovered, most of them women, most of them German immigrants returning to the city from a jaunt to breezy Staten Island. A grand jury convened; in mid-August, it indicted Cornelius Vanderbilt for manslaughter. He would need Horace Clark's services more than ever.[63]

One week before the indictment was handed down, Joseph White and Orville Childs stepped off the Atlantic steamship *Africa* onto one of New York's piers, having returned from a second attempt to convince British bankers to provide capital for the canal. Back in March, Childs had presented his full report to the directors of the canal company, making an eminently reasonable (if unreasonably precise) construction estimate of $13,243,099.47. This had caused the price of the 192 canal shares (or "rights") to shoot up on the stock exchange, from $1,800 to $3,250 to $3,600. Childs then had accompanied White and H. L. Routh to London to present the report to Rothschild, Baring Brothers, and the other British investment banks. The delegation returned with joyful news. At a meeting of the canal-company board, held on August 19, White announced that British capitalists had agreed to invest half of the amount needed to build the canal. Canal rights soared to $4,000 each.[64]

Then, mysteriously, the price suddenly collapsed. Someone was dumping the rights, in sufficient quantities to drop the price to $750. The press found it "striking," and baffling.[65] Who would be selling when construction of the canal now seemed assured? Close behind came a second surprise: a collapse in the stock of the Accessory Transit Company. "A transfer of 1,500 shares, it is stated, was made today by one of the strongest parties connected with the Company," the *New York Tribune* reported. (This was a very large percentage of the 38,700 Transit shares in existence.) "The street appears to be entirely in the dark as to the reason for the late decline in this stock."[66]

A war was playing out behind the scenes through the offers and bids of brokers at the Merchants' Exchange—a war between Vanderbilt and White. After White's return from London, the long-simmering tension between the two men had finally boiled over. It appears that White had betrayed Vanderbilt by withholding the real result of his mission to London. The great bankers of London had *not* agreed to put up half the money for the canal. On July 23, Joshua Bates, an American partner of Baring Brothers, had written a long letter to Thomas Baring that destroyed any chance of British investment in the project. "The proposed size of the canal strikes me as totally inadequate to the largest class of ships," Bates argued. "To make this increased depth would more than double the cost." At that price, the project would never pay for itself. The great Nicaragua canal project was dead. Back in New York, White had lied about his failure, loudly and long enough to dump his soon-to-be-worthless canal rights. It appears one of those who was burned by this brazen play was Vanderbilt.[67]

"An exceedingly bitter personal hostility existed between White and Vanderbilt, so much so that they were not on speaking terms at that time," Daniel Allen testified three years later.[68] Vanderbilt could do nothing to revive the now-lifeless canal rights, but he could go after White in his last stronghold: the Accessory Transit Company. For much of the previous year, White had been intriguing within the company, stealing influence from the Commodore. "Mr. Cornelius Vanderbilt," the *New York Times* reported on August 27, "has not had, for some months, as much control of the affairs of the Company as he had desired, nor as much as his ownership of the line of California steamers, from which the Transit Company derive their main profits, would seem to entitle him." As vain as he was treacherous, White was heard to boast, "I am the Nicaragua Transit company!"[69]

The corporate form had aided Vanderbilt in amassing capital and negotiating with sovereign governments to open the Nicaragua line; now it served him in a more personal way, as he used it as a weapon for revenge. As soon as he learned of White's deception, he launched a full-scale assault on the price of Accessory Transit shares—the bulwark of White's wealth—to impoverish his foe. "Vanderbilt advised [me] to divest . . . this stock," recalled Franklin Osgood, "and declared the stock worthless, as long as White remained in the company, for he was using the company to his own benefit." But in trying to drive the price down, Vanderbilt confronted a serious problem: the Accessory Transit Company was extremely profitable. The Commodore himself had talked up the stock in early 1852, when it had declared its first dividend. Since then, its competitive position had only grown stronger. Within Nicaragua, the friendly Conservative government had tightened its control, capturing León early in the year.

But Vanderbilt owned the all-important ships. He announced that his vessels would stop at Panama first before continuing on to Nicaragua. "The effect, of course, is to damage the Transit interest," the *New York Times* wrote. Instantly Nicaragua became the slowest route. Accessory Transit plunged from 40 to 24.* Vanderbilt suffered losses, but revenge mattered more. "Vanderbilt declared that he would rather sink his ships at the dock than that White should make money," Osgood reported.[70]

"Commodore Vanderbilt resigned the Presidency of the Transit Co., and with it the Directorship, which his colleagues promptly accepted," the *Times* reported on September 14. "The fight on the Stock, therefore, is not likely to end at present. The immediate relatives of Commodore V. have been selling and talking it down for some weeks past. It is said that he has never been beaten in a Stock or Steamboat contest of this sort." In all likelihood, his lead broker remained Nelson Robinson. Robinson recently had dissolved Drew, Robinson & Co. and moved into a luxurious home on fashionable Union Place, but he remained Vanderbilt's friend and a master of the game.

Then a strange thing happened. Four days later, on September 18, the *Times* reported that the "Vanderbilt" party were now *buying* Transit stock, and that White and his friends were selling. "It is a frisky game of late," the financial writer commented.[71]

On closer inspection, the turnaround appears less mysterious than brilliant. Vanderbilt used his "bear" campaign to pry shares out of the hands of White and his friends, and gain control of the company. How could selling lead to owning more? Most stocks, especially those in a "fancy" company like Accessory Transit (a volatile one that attracted speculators, who bought and sold rapidly), were bought "on margin." A broker would lend the purchase money to his client, who merely put up a margin—an amount sufficient to protect the broker against loss if the price fell. Such stocks were, to use the technical term, "hypothecated." When prices fell, the broker could either ask for a bigger margin from the client or sell the stock immediately to avoid a loss. The faster the price dropped, the more likely brokers were to dump hypothecated stocks, because they had less time to get more money from their clients. That drove the price down further, and eventually shook loose all the stock held on margin.

This was the secret behind Vanderbilt's bear attack on the Transit Company. Even before the end of August, the *New York Tribune* observed that the stock "has sunk so low that the margins on a large amount of

---

* The stock prices will be given without dollar symbols throughout the text.

hypothecated stock have been used up and this stock has also come upon the market." By September 18, the price fell far enough that Robinson stopped selling and began to buy, on his own behalf as well as that of Vanderbilt, his family, and a new ally, Charles Morgan.

But White was not going away. He could not be pried from the shares that he owned outright, those he had been given as one of the original incorporators of the company. So, as the battle raged, Vanderbilt dispatched Franklin Osgood (a large Transit shareholder) to offer terms to the man whom he could not bear to speak to himself. It was useless. "White declared," Osgood said, "that . . . Vanderbilt was a great scoundrel, and would cheat and rob any person he had any dealings with."[72]

For the vain and self-destructive White, it was another sign of that imbalance of character that had driven him from Congress. Even as he insulted the Commodore, a man with far greater resources and even more guile, he provoked the one force that he could not afford to alienate: the government of Nicaragua. The lack of progress on the canal had left even the Conservatives of Granada disgruntled. They had grown more upset when they learned that Accessory Transit had declared a dividend even though it had not paid the 10 percent of its profits that were owed under its charter. To investigate, the Nicaraguan government appointed two commissioners, who arrived in New York in August to inspect the books; after a long delay, they received a thin and highly suspect ledger that showed no profits. For all their frustration, the commissioners modestly concluded that Accessory Transit owed $30,000. White's astounding response was to deny their diplomatic powers. He claimed that Nicaragua had lost the "attributes of a sovereign state" when it joined the Central American confederation decades earlier—asserting, in essence, that the company existed, but Nicaragua did not. The Nicaraguans seized the lake steamboat *Central America* to enforce payment of the $30,000, "but she was subsequently released in consequence of the threatening attitude taken by our minister," the *New York Tribune* reported.[73]

Vanderbilt, meanwhile, learned that the *Pioneer* had been wrecked on the Pacific.[74] If anything, the loss made him more determined to bring his war with White to a satisfactory conclusion. He asked his son-in-law Allen to take over the negotiations. What Vanderbilt wanted was to sell his steamships to the Accessory Transit Company for $1.1 million. Allen refused. Considered "a high minded man" by his colleagues in business, he believed that the company's charter prohibited it from owning steamships. Vanderbilt dismissed the argument. He wanted his deal. With Osgood stymied, he thought only Allen (who had worked closely with White in the past) could achieve a settlement, so he pressured him until Allen finally agreed to open new talks.[75]

For several weeks, the stock market battle had fallen silent, with the Transit Company stock lying exhausted below 30. Just before Christmas, Vanderbilt and his friends began to buy heavily. Aroused by the large purchases, the bears came out of their caves. The bears—brokers who believed the Transit stock would fall again—began to sell it "short"; that is, they made contracts to sell shares that they didn't own. They would either borrow the shares in order to deliver, then repay the lenders with shares they bought later at a lower price, or—more commonly in this era—make contracts for sale that gave them weeks or even months to deliver, hoping to buy the shares in the interim at a lower price. Instead of buy low, sell high, the short strategy was sell high, buy low. The Commodore's heavy purchases in "sick Transit" (as brokers called the stock) offered the bears a seemingly perfect opportunity. Unaware of the progress of the talks, they believed the price was doomed to sink.[76]

On Christmas Eve, Allen concluded the negotiations. Vanderbilt now formally made the offer that had already been agreed to, in a letter to the board of the Accessory Transit Company. "I will sell to your company the steamships *Northern Light, Star of the West, Prometheus, Daniel Webster, Brother Jonathan, Pacific,* and *S.S. Lewis,* together with their furniture," he wrote, "for the sum of $1,350,000; payable $1,200,000 in cash, and $150,000 in the bonds of your company, payable in one year from the date of the bills of sale. All the coal bulks, and all other fixtures, your Company to take at cost, paying for them from the first earnings of the vessels." Three days later, the board accepted the terms. The directors decided to issue forty thousand new shares of stock to pay for the ships—to be sold to the directors themselves at 30. Vanderbilt would be the agent, managing the ships from his New York office, with a 20 percent commission on each transit ticket for the Nicaragua crossing. He would also take a 2.5 percent commission of the entire gross receipts.[77]

The deal sent Accessory Transit stock skyrocketing. "The shorts have fairly been caught," the *New York Herald* proclaimed, "and the probability is they will suffer some before they see the end of the present movement." The bears had to buy stock for as much as 40 to deliver the shares they had sold for less than 30. Even worse, it appears that Vanderbilt and his friends may have "cornered" the market by buying up the available supply (the new stock had yet to be issued). When caught without shares to deliver, the bears had to pay the buyers heavily to get out of their contracts. Thus Vanderbilt made money by buying shares that didn't even exist.[78]

In the end, the Commodore got all that he wanted. He had waged his wars on multiple fronts, under difficult conditions, against wily opponents, and won them all. He had battled the U.S. Mail and Pacific Mail Steamship companies, and made a great deal of money doing it. "The nett [sic] profits of his line of boats for the past season are figured up to

$1,150,000," the *New York Times* reported at the end of 1852. (Profits for the entire year, when added to those for 1851, must have been far more than that amount.) Then he had sold his ships on his terms, and at his price—indeed, for more than his initial price. His stock market campaigns had added enormously to his fortune. And he and his allies seized control of the Accessory Transit Company from the detested White (though that remained to be formalized).[79]

For the public the picture was far more ambivalent. On one hand, Vanderbilt wrought much good for his fellow citizens. Even though his canal scheme failed, he had created a new path of commerce and travel to California, one of great practical and strategic value to the United States. Falling costs and increasing speeds helped lift San Francisco from a trading outpost to a thriving metropolis—firmly rooting the republic on the Pacific—and improved the flow of gold to New York, pumping money into the national economy. Vanderbilt seemed to vindicate Jacksonian philosophy as he successfully competed against a government-subsidized line. He also revealed the beneficial role of the stock market by mobilizing capital to develop this critical new route. On the other hand, his battle against White demonstrated all too clearly the sometimes unhappy consequences of mixing private and public interests in a large enterprise. Travelers, merchants, and specie shippers fell victim to his vindictiveness as he disrupted the Nicaragua line to destroy its stock price; small investors fell victim to his bear campaign against White.

In pursuing his own interests, Vanderbilt acted as he always had, both creating wealth and punishing his enemies. But, as his businesses achieved a truly national scale, those who benefited and suffered from his decisions multiplied into the hundreds of thousands, and, eventually, millions. Like the marketplace itself, Vanderbilt was a paradox—both a creator and a destroyer.

From his own perspective, he was simply the victor. All in all, it was a remarkable new year that Vanderbilt celebrated in 1853. Small wonder that he decided to celebrate as no American had ever celebrated before.

Chapter Nine

NORTH STAR

"There is no friendship in trade." Lambert Wardell often heard the Commodore make the remark as he pitched letters into the office fire, "bundled his bonds and stocks in packages," or advised his sons-in-law. It was one of the few things he ever said. "He talked very little," Wardell recalled. Indeed, his wariness with words marked him in the public eye. "Vanderbilt, as is well known, is remarkable for terseness of expression, a compacted force of argument, and Spartan simplicity, rarely to be equalled," commented one newspaper. Standing six feet tall from the soles of his feet to his bristling grey hair, weighing a powerful two hundred pounds, he could be mistaken for a man of appetites; he was not (except, perhaps, for sex). Sparing with words, sparing with money, sparing even with food, "he was economical almost to extremes," Wardell reflected, as if Vanderbilt suspected that his own mouth might betray him, just as he suspected everyone around him. "He thought every man could stand watching," the clerk added, "and never placed confidence in anyone."[1]

As fancy carriages passed by 10 Washington Place on January 1, 1853, carrying the fashionable on their way to New Year's Day calls, Vanderbilt contemplated an end to his life of frugality and suspicion. A few months earlier, he had said to Franklin Osgood "that he was getting old, and had better close business."[2] And yet, even when brooding on his own mortality, he cast a jaded eye over those closest to him.

One day, in his office at 9 Bowling Green, he brought up the subject of his will with Daniel Allen. "Daniel," he exclaimed, "when I die, there'll be hell to pay!"

"Oh, no," Allen replied. "Commodore, I guess not."

"Oh yes there will; yes there will!" Vanderbilt insisted, as Allen later recalled, "in that peculiar emphatic way that I have no doubt he meant it to be so."[3]

At the time, Vanderbilt was reordering the hierarchy of his heirs apparent, his sons and sons-in-law. Allen, who had served him so well for so long, slipped inexorably downward. He had self-righteously opposed the steamship sale, and now resigned his directorship in the Accessory Transit Company in protest. Horace Clark, on the other hand, continued his climb in his father-in-law's favor. Vanderbilt had asked him to review the terms of the sale, and now referred to him as his "professional adviser."[4] Daniel Torrance and James Cross hovered nearby, but Vanderbilt treated them as middle managers rather than possible successors.

As for the sons by blood, Billy lurked in Staten Island obscurity, while George remained too young to be of much note—though he was strong and athletic, a favorite of his father. Cornelius Jeremiah continued to walk under the shadow of his addiction to gambling and his episodic epilepsy. His sister Mary later remembered how their mother confronted the Commodore in their home around this time. "Your hatred or dislike of Cornelius arises from the fret of his affliction," she insisted. "You intend to give all your money to William."

The old man said nothing, as usual.[5] Leaving a legacy grew increasingly important to him, but what he intended to do with his wealth remains a mystery. Frugality, suspicion, and silence guided his every step.

In contemplating his mortality and his fractious family, Vanderbilt embarked on a most un-Vanderbiltian adventure. Reports soon spread that he was building a new steamship larger than any of those he had just sold. "Various opinions were entertained as to his ultimate designs," reported Rev. John Overton Choules, a noted travel writer. "Many imagined that Mr. Vanderbilt . . . was to sell his ship to this monarch, or that government—or he was to take contracts for the supply of war steamers." Choules learned the truth from Vanderbilt himself. In February, the minister sat down with the Commodore in the library at 10 Washington Place. There Vanderbilt confirmed the wildest rumor of all: that the great steamship, named *North Star*, was to be his private yacht. He planned to take his extended family on a grand tour of the Old World, and he invited Rev. Choules and his wife to join them. "Mr. V. expressly informed me that his sole object was to gratify his family and afford himself an opportunity to see the coast of Europe," Choules wrote. "He observed that, after more than thirty years' devotion to business, in all which period he had known no rest from labor, he felt that he had a right to a complete holiday."[6]

It seemed out of character that this "boorish, vy. austere" businessman (as the Mercantile Agency would call him that May) would splurge on his family in such grand fashion, and on a grand tour of Europe, no less. But even so monomaniacal a moneymaker as Vanderbilt was capable of ordinary human complexity. In his own blunt fashion, he loved his wife and children. Indeed, the *North Star* was a sign that, as he attained public eminence, he paused, as it were, and looked fondly at the family he had pressed so hard for so long. Then, too, there was his brooding over his advancing age. Recently the leading men of his day had started to die off: John Jacob Astor, Philip Hone, Daniel Webster, and Henry Clay. Believing that he had limited time, he sincerely wanted a holiday.

This is not to say that Vanderbilt underwent a Scrooge-like conversion to Christian charity. He refused to bring along Corneil, for example. And two of his oldest obsessions, pride and patriotism, shaped his vision for the voyage. "I have a little pride, as an American, to sail over the waters of England and France," he wrote to Hamilton Fish, now a U.S. senator, on February 15, "up the Baltic and through the Mediterranean and elsewhere, under this flag without a reflection of any kind that it is a voyage for gain—with such a vessel as will give credit to the enterprize of our country." He wrote to Fish to learn if the *North Star* would retain the protection of the U.S. government, since Congress had not covered private yachts under the statute for American shipping abroad. "When the law was passed," he observed (or perhaps boasted), "they did not think at that time our yachts would ever sail to a foreign port."[7]

Vanderbilt made careful preparations for the smooth operation of his corporate interests during his long absence. Amid rumors that he himself would take the presidency of the Accessory Transit Company, he forced Joseph L. White and his clique to resign from the board of directors. Vanderbilt resumed his seat on the board and brought in two close allies, Nelson Robinson and Charles Morgan. The *Tribune* reported talk that other friends, including Robert Schuyler, would become directors as well.[8]

The Vanderbilt group also took steps to put the Pacific end of the business in capable hands. At the end of January, they called to New York Cornelius K. Garrison, a former Mississippi River steamboat captain who had established a successful bank in Panama. On February 1, Garrison agreed to an unusually lucrative two-year contract. As Accessory Transit's San Francisco agent, he could keep a 5 percent commission on receipts and 2.5 percent on disbursements, up to a maximum of $60,000 per year; or he could choose to limit himself to 2.5 percent all around, with no limit on his income. On February 19, Garrison departed New York to embark upon his new career in San Francisco.[9] With White out and such trusted men as Morgan and Garrison in, Vanderbilt could sail for Europe with peace of mind.

No other unfinished business was as important as Vanderbilt's indictment for manslaughter in Richmond County for the Staten Island Ferry's deadly bridge collapse. He showed no sign of concern, however, and for good reason: on February 26, the *Brooklyn Eagle* announced that the indictment had been quashed.[10] In all likelihood, the result surprised no one. Vanderbilt dominated Staten Island more thoroughly than any medieval baron did his manor. For all his wealth, his mansion off Washington Square, his international prominence, he remained very much a man of Richmond County, a son of the soil between the Narrows and the Kills.

Jacob J. Van Pelt brought up Vanderbilt's extensive Staten Island holdings in conversation one day early in 1853. For years, Van Pelt had sold timber to Vanderbilt for the construction of his ships; in recent weeks, they had begun to socialize, riding together on Vanderbilt's wagon as he whipped a pair of fast horses out of the narrow streets of New York and up through the rural stretches of upper Manhattan. "The Commodore asked me once what was the best thing to invest money in," Van Pelt recalled. "I told him I thought he ought to improve his Staten Island property."

"Oh, the Staten Island property?" Vanderbilt replied. "The title ain't worth a damn."

"I didn't think you bought property unless it had a good title," Van Pelt said.

"Well, I didn't pay much for it."[11]

Indeed he had not, for he had purchased his crucial waterfront real estate from the dying Richmond Turnpike Company. His control of key landings had sustained his monopoly with the Staten Island Ferry for years; but now his title was under siege by the state attorney general, and he faced two rival ferries. (In addition to George Law's, another had been started by Minthorne Tompkins, the son of the late vice president.)

With his departure looming closer, Vanderbilt had little time to rescue his imperiled fortunes on Staten Island. His ferry, once stripped of its landings, could well be crushed during his long absence overseas, and one of his most valuable businesses would become worthless. As the days ticked by, he simultaneously lobbied the New York legislature to pass a law confirming his title and opened negotiations with Law and Tompkins for a consolidation of the three ferries. Using his lobbying for leverage— along with Tompkins's anxiety over the value of his own Staten Island real estate—he achieved a triumph. In his most vulnerable moment, he convinced his rivals to buy him out for $600,000—$150,000 in cash, plus $50,000 a year (the annual profits on the ferry) for the next nine years.[12]

"I asked him if he had everything fixed," Van Pelt later reported. "He said yes." Vanderbilt had picked up his friend for another rattling fast ride shortly before his planned departure. The Commodore added, "Van, I have got eleven millions invested better than any eleven millions in the United States. It is worth twenty-five percent a year without any risk." Given the size of Vanderbilt's business operations, the $11 million figure rang true. It would have made him one of a half-dozen or so of the richest men in America; only William B. Astor and very few others could boast notably larger estates. The risk-free rate of return he cited was clearly hyperbole, but his point was clear: he had taken great care to put his affairs in order.

To Van Pelt, Vanderbilt seemed very much like a man preoccupied by his own death—and incapable of accepting it. "Commodore," he once asked, "suppose anything should happen, what are you going to do with your property?" (As Van Pelt added, "He never liked to have me say 'die,' so I always said, 'if anything happens.' ")

Vanderbilt replied, "They will all have plenty if they let things stay the way I leave them." He thought he knew best, and always would know best, even after he was dead.[13]

THE NATION WATCHED AS THE *North Star* approached completion. On March 10, it slid down the ways at Simonson's shipyard into the East River, to rousing cheers from a crowd of onlookers. It was towed to the Allaire Works dock, where a swarm of engineers spent the next few weeks installing its massive twin engines, attracting the notice of newspapers as well as technical experts.

The intense public interest that surrounded Vanderbilt's ship and trip stemmed from more than curiosity about the rich. "Although it is solely a personal matter," the *New York Herald* explained, "it partakes somewhat of a national character." Americans considered the regimes of Europe their ideological opponents. Monarchs ruled all of the Old World—even France, now that Louis Bonaparte had declared himself Emperor Napoléon III. In the United States, less than eighty years had passed since the Revolution, and the people thought of themselves as the guardians of a bold experiment in republican government and social equality. "The sovereigns of Europe," the *Herald* added, "have looked upon our increasing power with mingled surprise and alarm—surprise at our progress, and alarm lest the lesson which it silently inculcates might be learned by their own oppressed subjects." The *North Star* would bring them face-to-face with the superiority of American democracy. As *Scientific American* put it, "Queen Victoria, Czar Nicholas of Russia, and Napoleon III will get some of the conceit knocked out of them by a private citizen of New York."[14]

Of course, fascination with this fantastic display of wealth did account for much of the attention. It is important to remember that steamships were the largest, most complicated, and most expensive man-made objects in existence (apart from a very few buildings). Most of the vessels that plied the oceans were still sailing ships; even the U.S. Navy remained largely under sail, with only sixteen steam vessels of any description in 1852 (and only nine of those categorized as frigates or "first-class" steamers).[15] Now Vanderbilt had constructed, as a personal yacht, a steamship to rival the largest commercial liners—260 feet in length (at the keel; it stretched to 270 feet on deck) and 2,500 tons. The press lovingly described two mighty walking-beam engines, their pistons pumping a ten-foot stroke, fed by four massive boilers, each ten feet in diameter. The Commodore had designed the *North Star* himself; in keeping with his now-standard pattern, it boasted enormous thirty-four-foot paddlewheels and a straight stem (as the nearly vertical line of the bow was called).

The ship's luxuriousness attracted the most notice. A grand staircase led down to a reception area, with a large circular couch, which opened onto the main saloon. "The furniture . . . is of rosewood, carved in the rich and splendid style of Louis XV, covered with a new and elegant material of figured velvet plush," the *New York Tribune* reported. "Connected with this saloon are ten staterooms, superbly fitted up, each with a French *armour le gles*, beautifully enamelled in white, with a large glass-door. . . . The berths are furnished with elegant silk lambricans and lace curtains. Each room is fitted up with a different color, viz: green and gold, crimson and gold, orange, etc." Then there was the main dining saloon, paneled with polished marble and Naples granite, with tables boasting fine silverware and china with a ruby and gold finish. "The ceiling of the room is painted white, with scroll-work of purple, light green, and gold, surrounding medallion paintings of Webster, Clay, Washington, Franklin, and others."[16]

Vanderbilt—who paid close attention to his reputation—fully grasped the public impact of his grand holiday. Indeed, there is every reason to think that he planned the entire thing with an eye on his growing status as a cultural icon. He was not merely a businessman, but "one of our steamship nobility," as *Scientific American* wrote. Compared with his "magnificent steamship—his pleasure steam yacht . . . the yachts of the English nobility are like fishing cobles to a seventy-four gun ship."[17] He was no mere rich man; he was the Commodore.

When May 19, the date of departure, arrived, Vanderbilt encountered an omen of what lay before him in the year ahead—a jarring reminder that there was indeed no friendship in trade. All spring, labor trouble had wracked the docks. Firemen and coal passers, the crewmen who fed the fires under the boilers, had organized repeated strikes in April, forming angry processions from ship to ship along the waterfront. Just a week before the *North Star*'s departure, a mob of white dockworkers attacked their black counterparts when they learned that the black men received lower wages, which undercut their own pay.[18] The *North Star* had a picked crew of firemen and coal passers who had served on Vanderbilt's other ships, but they, too, caught the militant mood. One hour before departure, they (and some of the sailors) called a strike.

"Mr. Vanderbilt refused to be coerced by the seeming necessity of the case," Rev. Choules wrote. "He would not listen for a moment to demands so urged, and in one hour selected such firemen as could be collected; and many of them were green hands, and ill-adapted to give efficient service in their most important department." The action was so in keeping with Vanderbilt's personality, it scarcely needs comment. Rather than, accept his disadvantage, he fired the strikers and took his chances with untried men.[19]

At ten thirty in the morning, after the new firemen had been ushered down into the hold and handed their coal shovels, the crew cast loose the lines that held the ship to the dock at the foot of Grand Street. The side-wheels began to churn, and the immense hull of the *North Star* eased into the East River. Some four hundred guests milled about the deck with Vanderbilt and his family; the visitors were to sail aboard until Sandy Hook, where they would transfer to the *Francis Skiddy* for the return to New York.

Suddenly the happy crowd felt a jolt. The rapidly ebbing tide had caught the ship and smacked the stern into another pier. Vanderbilt shouted at the pilot to spin the wheel hard aport, to carry the *North Star* into the main channel, but the current was too strong. The ship struck hard on a hidden reef, and the alarmed visitors lost their footing as it keeled over onto one side, tilting the deck at a frightening angle. "For a moment," *Scientific American* reported, "there appeared danger of her capsizing." In a breath, the ship righted itself—but it was still "stuck fast."

The grand voyage had come to a halt 150 feet from the pier, with the near sinking of the celebrated yacht. But the Commodore knew how to manage a crisis. As the passengers returned to shore in another boat, he telegraphed Secretary of State William L. Marcy, asking permission to use the U.S. Navy's dry dock across the East River. Permission was immediately granted. As soon as the rising tide lifted the *North Star* free of the rocks, it steamed into the facility for inspection and repairs. That night Vanderbilt dined aboard ship (as it sat in the stocks of the dry dock), accompanied by broker Richard Schell, and the two men drank a toast to Marcy. The Commodore paid the not inconsiderable sum of $1,500 for use of the dock. To Marcy, the money mattered less than facilitating a voyage that would serve as a bit of informal public diplomacy.[20]

Vanderbilt's children and their spouses* fretted over a long delay; fortu-

---

* John Overton Choules, *The Cruise of the Steam Yacht North Star* (New York: Evans and Dickerson, 1854), 26–7, records the following passengers, in addition to himself and his wife: Dr. Jared Linsly and his wife; the wife of the captain, Asa Eldridge; Cornelius and Sophia Vanderbilt; and the Vanderbilts' children and their spouses, Phebe Cross, Kate Vanderbilt, George W. Vanderbilt, Maria and William H. Vanderbilt, Ethelinda and Daniel B. Allen, Eliza and George Osgood, Emily and William K. Thorn and their daughter Louisa, Sophia and Daniel

nately, the damage was superficial, and easily fixed. "At seven minutes to eight o'clock P.M. on the 20th of May," Choules wrote, "we left the gates [of the dry dock] amid the cheering of our kind friends who lined the dock; and, as we steamed down the river, we fired salutes and received them from various ships, and at the Battery, where a large party had gathered to give us a farewell greeting." As the *North Star* churned through the Narrows, past the home of Vanderbilt's aged mother, the crew fired off cannons and shot rockets into the clear night sky. The flinty old woman had taught the Commodore his shrewdness and frugality; now he saluted her from an emblem of extravagance, on a voyage that would prove shrewder than anyone could know.

At nine thirty in the evening, the *North Star* passed Sandy Hook and slowed to a halt to allow the pilot, John Martineau, to board a boat for the return to New York. Martineau may have been a bit dispirited after his highly public embarrassment of the day before, and perhaps more so when, as he was about to step off the ship, he was called to Vanderbilt's cabin. He encountered Horace Clark, the Commodore's "professional adviser." The Commodore, Clark informed Martineau, had sent a letter to the New York newspapers concerning his conduct. "He is entirely free from censure," Vanderbilt wrote. "I know Mr. Martineau to be as good a pilot as there is out of the Harbor of New-York." Then Clark dropped a "purse of gold" into Martineau's hand.[21]

The *North Star* steamed into the Atlantic, its paddlewheels churning the calm sea under bright moonlight. An unexpected act of generosity marked the departure; but then, the entire voyage was an unexpected act of generosity. More telling may have been Vanderbilt's choice of messenger. With nearly his entire family aboard, from his oldest son to those sons-in-law who had long served him as lawyers, managers, and agents, he chose Clark. It was a sign of things—and trouble—to come.

VANDERBILT HAD PREPARED as well as anyone could have for a long absence overseas. It would not be enough. "Ships are but boards, sailors but men," Shylock wisely observes in *The Merchant of Venice.* "There be land rats and water rats—water thieves and land thieves."

When Vanderbilt had resumed his place in the Accessory Transit Company, he had not, in fact, moved to take complete control. It appears that he acted merely to protect his interests, to ensure an income stream as agent during his prolonged absence.[22] As a result, the company suffered a power vacuum. It was filled, in part, by a man intimately familiar with the

---

Torrance, Louise and Horace F. Clark, Mary and Nicholas B. La Bau. Cornelius J. Vanderbilt and Frances Lavinia did not accompany them.

company's affairs, a man who still served as its counsel, if no longer as a director: Joseph L. White. Like a tapeworm, he had wound his way into the intestines of the Transit Company, and would not be removed until both he and it had been murdered.

White's influence persisted because it was of a particular kind, confined to the company's relationship with the U.S. and foreign governments. The board did elect a new president, James De Peyster Ogden, but, as White explained to Secretary of State Marcy, "He is new in the company, & hence not familiar with its antecedents." With characteristic arrogance and condescension, White took it upon himself to advise the new administration of President Franklin Pierce on Nicaraguan affairs. "I *know* the Central Americans quite as well, I think, as any man in this country," he told Marcy. "Firmness & determination will accomplish anything with them."[23]

White was not wealthy enough to become a dominant stockholder—but Charles Morgan was. Initially, at least, Morgan made no attempt to take power. He waited until the *North Star* steamed over the horizon, then began to buy up the company's shares. "The movement in Nicaragua is of such a decided character," the *New York Herald* reported on May 28. "A large party have taken hold of it." Soon a rumor ran through Wall Street that this was more than a short-term operation. Morgan, the brokers whispered, "is to take superintendence of the Company."[24]

As Morgan strengthened his grip on the stock, White wormed into his confidence. Each offered something the other lacked. White could handle political intrigue with slippery, insinuating skills that did not come easily to a self-made businessman like Morgan; Morgan, on the other hand, possessed the wealth, financial acumen, and large blocks of stock that White lacked. The two men, it appears, agreed on a new axis of power in the Accessory Transit Company. On Monday, July 18, they held a new election for the board of directors. White and his lackey H. L. Routh resumed their seats, and Morgan took office as president. Vanderbilt was out.[25]

Nelson Robinson survived on the board, but he could not protect the Commodore. Robinson's own interests were complicated enough. By March 1853, he had accumulated twelve thousand shares of the Erie Railroad. At a par value of 100, that made his holdings officially worth $1.2 million. There were few American businesses that, in their entirety, had a value equal to his stake in Erie. In the stock market, though, the share price was only 83, and it was falling. The stress proved to be too much for him. He declared that, as of May 27, he would retire from business. "The tremendous vicissitudes of stocks affected his nerves," a Wall Street observer later wrote. "His family implored, his doctor insisted. At last he yielded and retreated into the country."[26]

Vanderbilt's other long-standing ally, Daniel Drew, did nothing to help his absent friend. After the loss of the *North America*, he had abandoned all interest in California steamship lines. In any event, he was busy with his religious duties. For the past year, he had raised funds for a very special project of a Methodist charity, the Ladies' Home Missionary Society: to purchase the Old Brewery, the hulking warren that glowered over Paradise Square at the heart of the infamous Five Points, the most violent, impoverished slum in the city. Since 1837, the very poorest of the very poor had packed into the filthy and infested building, "creating a tenement so repulsive that it quickly became the most notorious in New York," writes historian Tyler Anbinder. "Here is vice at its lowest ebb," wrote the *National Police Gazette*, "a crawling and fetid vice, a vice of rags and filth." Drew collected the $16,000 to buy the structure, which was then ripped down. On June 17, the society celebrated the opening of a new four-story mission where the Old Brewery had long stood.[27]

With uncontested control of Accessory Transit, Morgan and White removed Vanderbilt from his post as agent, depriving him of his rich commission on tickets. "This payment was regularly made to Mr. Vanderbilt up to the time he left in his yacht for Europe," the *New York Herald* reported on July 29. "Since, the company have refused to make payments to Mr. Vanderbilt's agent." Morgan himself took over as agent. Brokers on Wall Street chattered anxiously about the act of treachery. As the *Herald* observed, "Trouble is anticipated upon the return of Commodore Vanderbilt."[28]

AS THE *NORTH STAR* CHURNED ACROSS unusually smooth seas, smoke billowing out of its twin black funnels, Vanderbilt instructed Captain Eldridge to cover no more than 250 miles every twenty-four hours. "As my journey would be a long one," he explained in a letter to a friend in New York, "and as I meant to have the ship in such order on our arrival in a foreign country as to be a credit to our 'Yankee land,' I did not wish to hazard this by making any attempt to obtain high rates of speed." Pushing a new engine too hard could damage it; steam engines generally had to be broken in before they could produce their best speed.

Stoking a fire, though, was no mere unskilled labor; keeping the heat under a boiler at just the right level required experience. And the untrained firemen Vanderbilt had plucked off the wharf when he fired the strikers had no experience. After the first day passed, Vanderbilt wrote, "I was somewhat astonished." Instead of 250 miles, the ship made 272. He went to the engine room to investigate, and found the green hands stoking away heedlessly, the great pistons and beams of the engines pounding up and down, turning the wheels at fourteen and a half revolutions per minute.

He complained about the firemen, but he found that his guests were, in fact, delighted by the ship's speed. And so the man who always knew better than everyone else did something unusual: he indulged them.

> The party were so elated and pressed so hard to let her make one day's run, that I finally told the engineer that he might let her engines make 14½ revolutions per minute for twenty-four hours, but no higher would I permit him to go. Whenever it rated a particle above this I compelled him to shut the throttle valve and confine her to the 14½. To my astonishment, at the end of twenty-four hours, she had made three hundred and forty-four miles, a greater distance, by twenty-four miles, than ever was made from New York to Europe.

It ran as fast as eighteen knots, a remarkable speed in 1853.[29]

Vanderbilt referred to his group as a party, and a party they had. Even the ignorance of the raw sailors amused them. At one point, the mate ordered one of the green hands to ring two bells, a traditional mark of time at sea. The mate grew annoyed when nothing happened. "He again called for two bells," Rev. Choules chortled in a letter home, "and the novice innocently said, 'Please, sir, I can't find but one.' " Most evenings, the guests—attired in their heavy broadcloth suits and elaborate dresses, and tended by a squad of Irish maids—gathered in the main saloon, where one of the men played a piano and the ladies sang. Sometimes the crew joined in. Some of the sailors were black, and, Choules claimed, "were decidedly fond of negro melody. One of them, who answered to the euphonious name of 'Pogee,' was, I think, quite the equal of the Christy Minstrels [a famous musical group that performed in blackface]."[30]

Now began the hour of Vanderbilt's glory. Southampton, Copenhagen, and St. Petersburg; Le Havre, Málaga, and Naples; Malta, Constantinople, and Gibraltar: the North Star sailed around Europe in triumph over the course of four months. The triumph was technical; at each port, marine experts pored over the ship. Commanders of the Royal Navy inspected its beam engines; officers of the tsar's fleet sketched its lines; pashas of the sultan's forces browsed through its cabins. And the triumph was patriotic: American newspapers published accounts of the North Star's progress, reporting its speed and fuel efficiency, describing the thousands of spectators who lined up at each port to visit the gigantic yacht. Editors across the United States reprinted lengthy articles from the English press. "In this magnificent trip to England by Mr. Vanderbilt," the Chicago Tribune quoted the Southampton Daily News as writing, "Brother Jonathan has certainly gone ahead of himself." ("Brother Jonathan" was a nickname for America in the 1850s, as common as "Uncle Sam" later would be.)[31]

And the triumph was social. When the North Star docked in Southampton, Vanderbilt, with his wife and guests, took the train to London, where the prestigious expatriate American banker George Peabody played host—tendering his box at the opera, for example, to the Commodore and his family. The U.S. minister to Great Britain, Joseph R. Ingersoll, held a formal reception for Vanderbilt. "The attendance was large," Choules wrote, "and the party a very fashionable one. The display of diamonds was very brilliant. General attention was directed to Mr. Vanderbilt, who was quite the man of the occasion; and all seemed desirous to obtain an introduction."[32] Lords and squires and millionaires crowded around the man from Staten Island, pressing him to bring his yacht up the Thames "and enable the fashionable world—then, of course, in London—to visit the *North Star*," Choules added. Vanderbilt begged off, lest he "take a step which might appear like ostentation"—as if anything could be more ostentatious than crossing the Atlantic in such a yacht. More likely he wished to save coal.

The lord mayor of London invited Vanderbilt to a soirée, where the Commodore and Sophia mingled with the Archbishop of Canterbury and Thomas Carlyle. Vanderbilt went away with a party to the races at Ascot, the most fashionable racetrack in the world. In St. Petersburg came chats with Grand Duke Constantine, second son of the tsar, and a visit to the Winter Palace. In Florence came a session with Hiram Powers, perhaps the most famous American artist of the age, who sculpted a bust of Vanderbilt's proud head (for $1,000) and then accompanied him around Italy. In Naples the royal government turned the *North Star* away, for fear that the ship carried antimonarchical arms or rebels, but Vanderbilt and his wife paid calls on the British governors of Malta and Gibraltar.[33]

On May 27, less than a week after the *North Star*'s departure from New York, the Mercantile Agency recorded its scathing judgment of Vanderbilt as "illiterate & boorish," not to mention "offensive." This judgment was wrong—or, at least, incomplete. Though he could still manifest a brutal demeanor when locked in combat, he had learned by 1853 to affect the sort of polish expected of a man of wealth and accomplishment. Men ranging from Hiram Powers to Lord Palmerston were struck by his confident, commanding air, an impression reinforced by his erect posture and neat appearance. Though Choules was no disinterested observer, he spoke for many when he reflected on Vanderbilt's "dignified reserve" and "dignified self-control." (After the journey, he would broadcast these judgments in a popular book on the trip.)[34]

Vanderbilt even came to terms with his old rival, the English language. Not that he conquered it; as Lambert Wardell later recalled, he "abominated papers of every description." The phonetic spelling and careless punctuation that marked the letters of his youth remained in those few notes he chose to write in his own hand. Usually he dictated to Wardell, who smoothed out the sentences.[35] More significant was the change in his speaking. Among cronies and underperforming subordinates, he still would spout profanity with fluency and enthusiasm; but he had learned to speak on something like equal terms with men of refinement. This was reflected in Vanderbilt's comments at a grand municipal dinner given to him in Southampton, which were articulate, if brief. After a very few remarks, he said, "Were I able to express the gratification we have experienced in passing through the country and your town . . . I am fearful you would construe it into an attempt to make a speech." Then he sat down.

Perhaps self-conscious of his lack of education, he avoided public speaking—a significant fact in that great era of oratory, when men and women passed the hours listening to long, elaborate speeches from politicians and ministers, lecturers and poets. But his recorded remarks show that he was capable of keeping his errant grammar under control in conversation. A more likely explanation for his reticence was given by those who knew him best: that he detested circuitousness, viewed loquacity as a kind of vanity, and distrusted the rhetorical flourishes expected in this culture of the word upon word. When dictating letters, for example, he expected Wardell to preserve the brevity, the concentrated force, of his language. As Vanderbilt said in his terse Southampton toast, "He had been accustomed, all his life, to go direct to a point."[36]

When he plumped back into his seat at that dinner, another of his party rose: Horace Clark. At the Commodore's request, the ambitious lawyer gave precisely the sort of speech expected on this occasion, the kind that Vanderbilt loathed, larded with such passages as, "a few days of unalloyed pleasure, passed in contemplation of the Great Creator in his broadest and most glorious field—a few nights of calm repose, undisturbed by danger or fear—and lo! your magnificent shores burst upon our view." Now that Vanderbilt was most emphatically a public man, he needed someone like Clark. He had thought he had found such an ally in Joseph White; but White's treachery had taught him to look within his own circle for someone more trustworthy.

Clark wanted to be more than Vanderbilt's mouthpiece, but others stood in his way. His most serious rival was Daniel Allen, who had shown himself to be a quiet, shrewd businessman more like the Commodore himself. But Allen's split with his father-in-law over the steamship sale to Accessory Transit continued to fester. So he and his wife, Ethelinda, decided to spend a year in Europe. They had a son and a brother-in-law currently residing on the continent, and perhaps they hoped the time abroad might improve Ethelinda's health. "Mrs. Allen came on board the yacht from a sick bed," Rev. Choules wrote, "and in a condition of extreme debility." The months at sea seem to have helped immensely, and she and her husband said their good-byes at Gibraltar.[37]

More ominous for Clark's future (though there is no sign that he thought of matters this way) was the thaw in Vanderbilt's relationship with Billy. The two had never spent so much time together; more than that, they socialized in a holiday setting overseen by Billy's eternally patient and kindhearted mother. Overshadowed by her domineering husband, Sophia's personality rarely flowers in the historical record, though a few suggestive comments come from Rev. Choules (however prone he may have been to praising everything and everyone, apart from the pope, whom he reviled). "Every day, everyone on board was made to see and feel the excellent qualities" of Sophia Vanderbilt, Choules wrote, "whose uniform amiable spirit was the regulator of the circle."[38]

Amiable patience marked William's manner as well. A story would later circulate that depicted father and son on the *North Star*'s deck as it churned toward home, both of them puffing on cigars. Vanderbilt cocked an eye at Billy and said, "I wish you wouldn't smoke, Billy; it's a bad habit. I'll give you $10,000 to stop it." The young man pulled the cigar out of his mouth and said, "You needn't hire me to give it up. Your wish is enough. I will never smoke again." With a flick of his wrist, Billy tossed the cigar over the rail and into the waves below.[39] The tale is utterly apocryphal, but it survived because it reflected two truths: Cornelius's relentless testing of his son, and William's steady display of loyalty—a dutifulness that slowly affected his father.

Onward the *North Star* sailed toward New York, cutting through clouds of flying fish, dredging through green Sargasso Sea islands of seaweed, and steaming into view of Staten Island. Back through the Narrows it went—firing another salute as it passed the home of Vanderbilt's mother—up to the Allaire Works, where the journey had begun. "On the dock were kind friends and beloved relatives," Choules wrote, "and I almost felt that the entire four months of absence was but a dream! But I soon learned a painful fact . . . that the sweetest joys of life are dashed with bitter waters."[40]

FOR THE FIRST SUMMER IN TWO DECADES, Cornelius Vanderbilt did not go to Saratoga Springs. He was, of course, on the far side of the Atlantic, so Saratoga went on without him. "Senators and members of Congress are abundant," the *New York Times* reported on August 12. Other notables included George Law; Thurlow Weed, the Albany newspaper editor and titan of the Whig Party; Edward K. Collins, head of a federally subsidized transatlantic steamship line; and Charles Morgan.[41]

In the summer of 1853, it was Morgan, not the Commodore, who went each morning to the little temple erected over the Congress Spring, inside the hollow square of the Congress Hall hotel, where a boy lowered a staff to dip tumblers full of mineral water, three at a time. It was Morgan who played hands of whist with other Wall Street warriors, or sat in the evening in the colonnade of the Congress or the United States Hotel, smiling at the passing girl in white muslin and a pink sash, daringly wearing no bonnet, who made her way to a fashionable ball or a more casual "hop."[42] It was Morgan who took a carriage up to the lake to eat a dinner of wild game at the Lake House restaurant, famous for its crispy fried potatoes (or potato chips, as they would come to be known), a wildly popular dish invented by "Eliza, the cook," in the 1840s.*

By September 23, Morgan was back in New York, where he could not have missed Vanderbilt's return in the *North Star.* Every newspaper published the news, as if it were a matter of national import to announce (as the headline in the *Times* read), "Com. Vanderbilt's Pleasure Party at Home Again." The *New York Herald* went further, notifying the Commodore that during his absence the Accessory Transit Company had fired him as agent and kept his money. It reprinted a letter from the corporation that had run on July 29. "It is quite true that since the departure of Mr. Vanderbilt the company have not paid him the twenty percent on the gross receipts of the transit route," the company had stated, "for the plain and simple reason that, in their belief, he is largely indebted to the company, it having found it impossible to obtain a statement of the accounts of the agency during the time he had acted as agent for the steamers of the company." The *Herald* added, "As soon as Commodore Vanderbilt gets fairly located again among us, it is expected he will furnish some exculpatory reply."[43]

Vanderbilt's discovery of this treachery provided the context for what is said to be one of the most famous letters in the history of American business: "Gentlemen: You have undertaken to cheat me. I won't sue, for the law is too slow. I'll ruin you. Yours truly, Cornelius Vanderbilt." This terse, belligerent note is pure Vanderbilt. It is also mythology. It first appeared decades later, in Vanderbilt's obituary in the *Times,* and its valid-

---

* A popular story attributes the invention of the potato chip to Vanderbilt. In 1853 he supposedly complained that his fried potatoes were not salty or thin enough; the Lake House cook, George Crum, retaliated by frying absurdly thin and salty slices, which Vanderbilt loved. (The *Washington Post,* May 19, 1917, credited Crum's half sister, Catherine A. Wicks.) There is no truth to the tale. The *New York Herald,* August 2, 1849, strongly suggests that the potato chip originated with the now-forgotten Eliza, no later than the summer of 1849. See William S. Fox and Mae G. Banner, "Social and Economic Contexts of Folklore Variants: The Case of Potato Chip Legends," *Western Folklore* 42, no. 2 (April 1983): 114–26.

ity is dubious at best. He never wrote "Yours truly," but usually he signed, "Your obedient servant." And it never would have occurred to him to give up legal redress. He had been suing his opponents since 1816; he knew that, even when the courts did not give satisfaction, legal action gave him leverage in negotiations.[44]

But reply he did. As soon as he had wobbled on his sea legs into his office, he ordered Lambert Wardell to pull out pen and paper; he wanted to dictate a letter to James Gordon Bennett, editor of the *Herald*. "The statement made in the name of the company," he wrote, "calls for a few words of explanation. To say nothing of the cowardice which, in my absence in a foreign country, dictated the calumnious statement referred to, it is none the less unfortunate that it was utterly false."

Cowardice and mendacity—the two cardinal sins in Vanderbilt's business code, and the two salient traits of Joseph White—drove him into a fury. He did not owe the Transit Company, he said; rather, it owed *him* some $36,000 for property (mostly coal and coal hulks) that he had sold along with the steamships, an amount that was to have been paid out of the first earnings of the ships. "My object in accepting the agency of the steamships . . . was chiefly to enable me to secure the amount of the company's unpaid indebtedness to me," he explained. "These earnings should come directly into my hands. I need not say that I would not have trusted the company for so large a sum of money upon any other terms." His man in New York, Moses Maynard, had made the books freely available for inspection at any time. And, far from decrying lawsuits, he concluded with this warning: "My rights against the company will be determined in due time by the judgment of the legal tribunals."[45]

On September 29, the day after the *Herald* published Vanderbilt's angry letter, the Commodore and Charles Morgan met to discuss their conflict. Where they spoke is unknown, though Morgan's office was at 2 Bowling Green, only a few doors from Vanderbilt's. The Commodore proposed to refer the dispute to arbitration. Morgan seems to have thought well of the idea, but he declined to make a commitment, and the meeting broke up without any settlement.

A split seems to have formed in Accessory Transit over how to proceed. On October 27, the *Herald* reported that it had agreed to arbitration; on the next day, the company refused, making petty excuses about the state of the accounts Vanderbilt had rendered. Indeed, it taunted him, in what sounds very much like the voice of Joseph White. "The company are desirous he should commence proceedings against them at once," said the official statement, "and are afraid he will do nothing but threaten." Vanderbilt's lawsuit, postponed to allow time for negotiations, would proceed.[46]

THE BATTLE SEEMED TO energize Vanderbilt, for he simultaneously embarked on a series of breathtakingly huge financial transactions. First, his friend Robert Schuyler—now president of the New York & New Haven, the Illinois Central, and other railroads—asked for help. He had overextended himself in his vast stock operations, and the *Independence*, the ship he and his brother George had purchased from Vanderbilt, had sunk in the Pacific. He needed money, a lot of money; fortunately, he could offer thousands of railroad shares as collateral. Vanderbilt took them, loaning Schuyler $600,000 in October to see him through his difficulties. This was a staggering figure: if a merchant's entire estate amounted to that sum, he would be praised as extremely wealthy by the Mercantile Agency.[47]

Next came a fresh campaign on Wall Street led by Nelson Robinson—who, it appears, could not bear to remain in retirement as long as he owned twelve thousand Erie shares, waiting to be bulled. In mid-October, Robinson won reelection to the Erie Railroad's board of directors, and took over as treasurer; he was joined by Daniel Drew, who was new to the board. The two organized a "clique" of investors to run up the price of Erie. Vanderbilt agreed to cooperate, though he demanded a bonus in the form of a discount on the stock. He purchased four thousand shares at 70 each, 2½ below the market price. (How Robinson and Drew arranged the discount is unclear.) "The removal of so much stock, even temporarily from the market, was calculated to improve it [the price]," the *New York Evening Post* reported.

With so many stock certificates sitting in Vanderbilt's office rather than circulating among brokers, Erie's share price immediately rose. Robinson made the most of it as he worked both the curb and the trading floor on Wall Street. "His name & influence put up the price," the Mercantile Agency reported. "It went as high as 92 in April [1854] & he sold out." Robinson made as much as $100,000 in this single operation. Vanderbilt garnered perhaps $48,000 in profit (less brokers' commissions), in a lucrative beginning to a long and ultimately tragic relationship with Erie.[48]

Success in this operation had been far from certain, but Vanderbilt "was a bold, fearless man," Wardell later explained, "very much a speculator, understanding all risks and willing to take them."[49] As Vanderbilt's notoriety as a speculator rose, so would the public's ambivalence toward him.

Ambivalence, but not simple loathing: the Commodore simultaneously remained the archetype of the economic hero, the productive, practical man of business, precisely the sort popularly depicted as the opposite of the speculator. Indeed, the key to understanding Vanderbilt is that he saw no distinction between the roles defined by moralists and philosophers. He freely played the competitor and monopolist, destroyer and creator, speculator and entrepreneur, according to where his interests led him. The real conundrum lies in how he saw himself. His public pronounce- ments reflected Jacksonian laissez-faire values, as he denounced monopo- lies and touted himself as a competitor. Did he detect a paradox, then, when he sold out to a monopoly or sought his own subsidies? Most likely no. Competition had arisen in America conjoined with customs and mechanisms to control it. Vanderbilt saw "opposition" as a means to an end—war to achieve a more advantageous peace. On a personal level, he was acutely aware that he had won all that he possessed by his own prowess. And whatever he won in battle, he was ready to defend in battle.

VANDERBILT'S COMBINATION of entrepreneurship and stock market gamesmanship also appeared in his elaborate plot to take revenge on Mor- gan and White. The first phase involved an attempt to drive down the Accessory Transit Company's share price. He faced long odds. In Decem- ber, Morgan fed information to the *New York Herald* that won him the support of its influential financial column (despite Vanderbilt's protest that the numbers leaked to the paper were "calculated to deceive"). Rumors of the company's rich profits and bright prospects sent its stock price up to 27⅝.[50]

Seemingly in defiance of reality, Vanderbilt deployed a platoon of bro- kers on the stock exchange to sell Accessory Transit short, starting on Jan- uary 5. "The bears made a dead set against it," the *Herald* reported. Vanderbilt shorted five thousand shares—that is, sold five thousand shares that he did not own—at 25, on contracts that gave him up to twelve months to deliver the certificates. He gambled that the price would go down in the interim, so he could buy the shares for less, thus making a profit when he delivered them. "This looks like a most determined oppo- sition," the *Herald* noted. Morgan started buying to keep the price up, making for a direct battle between the two titans.

The next day the *New York Times* reported, "The contest of *Bull* and *Bear* opened . . . on Nicaragua Transit stock, [and] was followed up with considerable spirit by the buyers for the rise. The large seller yesterday it is now confidently asserted is Mr. Cornelius Vanderbilt, and the buyer Mr. Charles Morgan, the President and managing man of the Company; both old heads on the Stock Exchange, and wealthy." The *Herald*, too, observed the "immense pressure from the bears," as Vanderbilt's brokers sold fever- ishly in an attempt to drive down the share price, but "Nicaragua" stub- bornly rose. "The enormous sales . . . had an effect quite contrary to that

The gold coming down from the mountains led to an international rush to California. In early 1849, Vanderbilt sent his son Corneil around Cape Horn in a schooner to work on a ferry in San Francisco Bay. He jumped ship, as did the gold-crazed crews of dozens of vessels, turning the San Francisco waterfront into a floating graveyard. *Library of Congress*

California's primary channel to the Atlantic coast consisted of steamship lines and a land crossing at Panama. Vanderbilt created a rival transit route across Nicaragua. This engraving shows a sternwheel riverboat in the harbor of Greytown on the Atlantic, having loaded passengers from a steamship in the background, as it enters the San Juan River, bound for Lake Nicaragua. *Library of Congress*

The San Juan River flows from Lake Nicaragua to the Atlantic through a dense rain forest. This 1880s photograph shows a steamboat in a wide, shallow section. Vanderbilt personally piloted the first passengers on his Nicaragua line up the river in 1851. *Library of Congress*

At the head of the San Juan River was the village of San Carlos. This photograph from the 1880s shows the great Lake Nicaragua in the background, along with typical thatched-roof huts. A fort also guarded this strategic point. *Library of Congress*

On leaving the San Juan River, passengers transferred to larger sidewheel steamboats that traversed Lake Nicaragua's 110-mile expanse. The western landing was at Virgin Bay, where a large pier was eventually constructed. This somewhat exaggerated engraving shows the twin cones of the island of Ometepe. *Library of Congress*

A twelve-mile carriage road connected Virgin Bay with the little Pacific port of San Juan del Sur, which was virtually uninhabited until Vanderbilt personally chose it as the terminus of the transit route. Passengers transferred between steamship and shore by means of launches. *Library of Congress*

By 1851, San Francisco had emerged as a major American city, nourished in part by Vanderbilt's steamship line to and from New York. This photograph looks east across the bay toward Yerba Buena Island. It reveals the shipping that thronged the new wharves and the dense grid of substantial brick buildings that were constructed in the wake of repeated fires. *Library of Congress*

This 1854 engraving shows the Narrows at the mouth of New York Harbor, with Staten Island in the foreground, Long Island to the right, and in the distance on the far right the cities of Brooklyn and New York. *Library of Congress*

The offices of Vanderbilt's various lines to California could be found next to those of his competitors on Steamship Row, the nickname for this stretch of buildings just to the left of the small oval park of Bowling Green. Vanderbilt maintained a personal office here, at the southern tip of Manhattan, until he sold his steamship interests during the Civil War. *Museum of the City of New York*

Shrewd, dashing, and more than a bit slippery, Cornelius K. Garrison became the San Francisco agent for Accessory Transit, the company Vanderbilt had started to carry passengers via Nicaragua. He was manipulated into opposing Vanderbilt in late 1855. *Library of Congress*

A small, quiet, intense man, Nashville-born William Walker emerged as a leading "filibuster"—a private citizen who launched armed invasions of foreign countries. In 1855, he landed in Nicaragua with fifty-six men to fight in its civil war. He won, formed a new government, and abolished Accessory Transit. He gave the transit rights to a friend, who resold them to Garrison. *Library of Congress*

Granada was the capital of the Conservative government that ruled Nicaragua when Vanderbilt established the transit route. He visited the city on two of his three expeditions to the country. William Walker captured Granada in 1855 and consolidated his power by executing Conservative general Ponciano Corral on the city plaza, shown here. *Library of Congress*

Vanderbilt resumed control of Accessory Transit just as Walker revoked its corporate charter and gave its property to Cornelius Garrison and his partner Charles Morgan. Vanderbilt made an alliance with Costa Rica to oust Walker. Walker's downfall began when Sylvanus Spencer, Vanderbilt's personal agent, led a force of Costa Rican soldiers in a surprise assault on a filibuster garrison at Hipp's Point on the San Juan River, shown here. *Library of Congress*

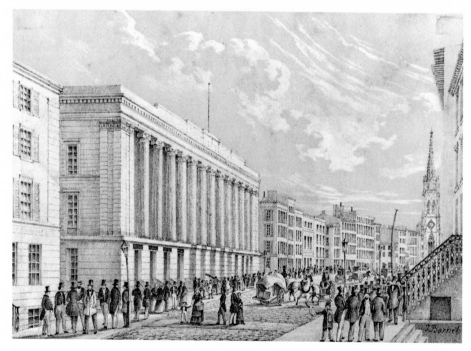

In the 1850s Vanderbilt emerged as a major force on the stock exchange, often working closely with Daniel Drew. During this period stockbrokers conducted formal trades of securities in auctions in the Merchants' Exchange on Wall Street, shown here in 1850. Informal trades took place among unlicensed brokers on the curb outside. *Library of Congress*

Vanderbilt's youngest son, George Washington Vanderbilt, entered West Point in 1855, graduated near the bottom of his class in 1860, and served briefly in the West. At the beginning of the Civil War, he was convicted by a court-martial of deserting his post. He died in France on December 31, 1863. *Library of Congress*

Vanderbilt's respect for his son William grew in the late 1850s, as he became an officer of the Staten Island Railroad. Vanderbilt made him vice president of the Harlem Railroad, and eventually operational manager of all his lines. A gifted manager, William proved far less diplomatic than his father. *Library of Congress*

Vanderbilt named the greatest vessel he ever constructed after himself. For a time the largest and fastest steamship afloat, the *Vanderbilt* shared the characteristics of all the steamships he designed: a nearly vertical bow, massive sidewheels, supplementary sails, and twin walking-beam engines adapted from steamboats. *Naval Historical Center*

The *Champion* was the first iron-hulled steamship constructed in the United States. Though not the largest in Vanderbilt's fleet, it was fast and fuel efficient. During the Civil War it ran between Panama and New York, as part of a monopoly on California steamship traffic that Vanderbilt helped establish. *Library of Congress*

The rampage of the Confederate ironclad *Virginia* (also known as the *Merrimack*) created a panic in Lincoln's cabinet. The *Monitor* rushed to the scene and battled it to a standstill, as shown here. But the *Virginia* survived. Its continuing threat led Secretary of War Edwin Stanton to ask Vanderbilt to equip the *Vanderbilt* to destroy it. *Library of Congress*

intended. The probability is that the same party [Vanderbilt] will not try the same game a second time. It was a desperate move, and must result in serious loss." Now firmly on Morgan's side, the *Herald* reporter cited the "present able management" of the company and its glowing annual report, concluding that it was "rash to bear the stock."[51]

Then the Commodore sprang his trap. On January 17, a headline in the *Times* announced, "NEW LINE OF STEAMSHIPS TO SAN FRANCISCO." He was going to compete against Accessory Transit. The move epitomized the paradox that was Vanderbilt, for it was motivated by a personal vendetta yet had wide public consequences. The resulting fare war would dramatically reduce prices on the corridor between California and New York, showering benefits on migrants and merchants. It would also destroy Accessory Transit's profits, lay low the share price, and thus enrich Vanderbilt at the expense of his enemy—and innocent stockholders.

All these months, the Simonson shipyard had been refitting the *North Star* as a passenger liner. The world-famous yacht was to serve as the flagship of a new steamship fleet, but it would take time to build more vessels. So Vanderbilt made an alliance with merchant Edward Mills, who owned the *Uncle Sam* and built the new *Yankee Blade* with Vanderbilt's help. "These vessels are all known as exceedingly swift and commodious," the *Times* reported; they would run on the Pacific, and connect to the *North Star* at Panama. Official notice of the "Vanderbilt Line for California" ran on January 23. With Daniel Allen in Europe, James Cross would manage the ships.[52]

Interestingly, it was the Washington correspondent of the *Times* who broke the story. Vanderbilt had gone to the capital to add a third role to those of speculator and entrepreneur—that of lobbyist, in pursuit of the California mail contract. As early as October 10 he had written to Secretary of State William L. Marcy on the subject. Vanderbilt likely knew Marcy personally, and undoubtedly found the jowly former governor of New York appealing. Historian Allan Nevins judged Marcy "blunt, humorous," and highly social. "A gentleman of the old school," he reportedly coined the phrase "To the victor belong the spoils," an apt summary of the Commodore's own code. Vanderbilt wrote to Marcy, "I feel some solicitude to enlarge my reputation by doing something valuable for the country," and suggested that a transit across Mexico, farther north even than Nicaragua, could save two weeks on the mail to San Francisco.[53]

Washington had been empty when Vanderbilt wrote to Marcy; in December Congress reassembled, and the capital came alive. "The hotels and boarding-houses filled up, the shopkeepers displayed a varied stock, and the deserted villages [that made up the city] coalesced into a bustling town," Nevins wrote—though it was still "a fourth-rate town." Since

Washington existed entirely for the seasonal gathering of Congress and a mere handful of year-round civil servants (the entire State Department staff consisted of eighteen men), it had few attributes of a true city. It lacked proper water or sewage works; parks remained undeveloped tracts, overrun by weeds; most government buildings were small, drab brick structures; even the Capitol and the Washington Monument sat unfinished. The most common business seems to have been the boardinghouse. "Music and drama were so ill-cultivated," Nevins noted, "that a third-rate vocalist or strolling troupe created a sensation."[54] This was the town that Vanderbilt traveled to in January to press his war on Accessory Transit.

And to win glory for himself. The triumphant voyage of the *North Star* had swelled his sense of importance. It also seems to have soothed his strained relationship with his wife. Sophia acompanied him to Washington, where they socialized with Joseph L. Williams, a former Whig congressman whom Vanderbilt hired to assist in his lobbying. "The Commodore and lady were in pleasant spirits when here," Williams wrote to a friend in New York. "I visited them several times at the hotel, and they went to see Mrs. [Williams] at our house, as she could not go out. I am to see the Secretary of the Navy for the Commodore by the time he comes back. Between you and I, he is anxious, or, rather, *ambitious* to build the government vessels." Vanderbilt offered to build a "first-class steam frigate" for the navy; unlike most such proposals, his demanded no money up front, but merely repayment of the cost should the ship be accepted into the fleet.

This was patriotism, yes, but Vanderbilt hoped the positive publicity would strengthen his attempt to capture the contract for the California mail, to carry it by the aforementioned transit over Mexico, via Veracruz and Acapulco. As lobbyist Williams added in his letter, "He has other wishes in respect to the Vera Cruz and Acapulco route to California, to succeed in which he has to break down the prejudices of the Postmaster General and the elaborate arrangements of Jo White as to Nicaragua."[55]

Inevitably, Joseph White dashed to Washington as soon as he learned of Vanderbilt's lobbying mission. "We are having some excitement indoors just now, relative to California mail contracts," the Washington correspondent of the *Times* reported on January 17. "Parties interested in the Ramsey [Mexico] route, the Panama route, and the Nicaragua route, are all upon the ground attending to their respective interests." (Ramsey was a figure in the company trying to open the Mexican land transit that Vanderbilt hoped to link to with his ships.)

White did what he did best: insult Vanderbilt. He desired the mail contract for Accessory Transit, of course, but he wanted most to deny it to Vanderbilt. Together with Senator James Cooper, White called on Postmaster General James Campbell "for the purpose of impressing him with the advantage of the Nicaragua route and the worthlessness of any other, and especially the Ramsey route via Vera Cruz and Acapulco," the *Times* wrote. "Postmaster-General Campbell says it is a waste of time to cry down the latter route in his presence, because his mind is decidedly and irrevocably made up against it, which of course is a great satisfaction to the Nicaragua people."[56]

The Commodore soon had more bad news. He returned to Washington in March with Sophia and daughter Phebe Cross, and discovered that his lobbyist Williams had fallen sick with tuberculosis—*"lung fever,"* as Williams called it. Vanderbilt carried on, one colleague recalled. "We wanted to see [Senator] John M. Clayton, and arranged to go and call on him on a certain evening. When night came . . . it rained pitchforks. I said to the Commodore, 'We can't go now; wait, and if it slacks up we will go over.'" When the weather cleared, the friend couldn't find Vanderbilt, so he took the stage to Clayton's house. "I went in and found him, and the Commodore with him, playing whist. . . . He [Vanderbilt] said, 'Between you and me, that's the way I got ahead of some of the other boys. I never failed to keep an engagement in my life.'"[57]

In this case, Vanderbilt would not get ahead of the other boys. He and White neutralized each other. Pacific Mail, U.S. Mail, and the Panama Railroad (a formidable lobbying bloc in their own right) would remain the official carriers for the Post Office. Stymied in politics, Vanderbilt carried on the business war, the one he knew best. His and Mills's ships continued to connect via Panama, rather than Mexico, but the Commodore's prowess at cutting costs would allow him to slash fares until he had cut open the very arteries of the Accessory Transit Company.

AS THE BUSINESSMEN BATTLED, the fixer left Washington to continue his work. In February 1854, Joseph White returned to Nicaragua to cope with the government's anger over Accessory Transit's failure to pay the required 10 percent of its profits. White, of course, preferred intrigue and corruption to simply paying the debt, as he freely admitted to Secretary of State Marcy. "I am fatigued with listening to the extortionate demands of this Govt. & bribing it into silence," White wrote from Nicaragua. "This process of securing the observance of chartered rights is too annoying and expensive."[58] Whatever Marcy thought of White personally, he supported the company. As Nicaragua surpassed Panama in popularity as a route to California, keeping the transit open became a strategic imperative for the United States, which would admit no fine points of morality.[59]

In the course of 1854, the company's profits suffered under the competition of Vanderbilt's Independent Line, as the Commodore slashed fares—by half, then to one-third of what Accessory Transit charged.[60] At Virgin Bay on Lake Nicaragua, an Accessory Transit launch shuttling passengers to a steamboat overturned, drowning twenty-one.[61]

In July, a murder carried out by one of the Accessory Transit riverboat captains brought to a head years of conflict with the people of Greytown. Together with Solon Borland, the belligerent U.S. minister to Nicaragua, White convinced Marcy to send the USS *Cyane* to destroy the town. White himself wrote instructions for the ship's captain, telling him not to "show any mercy to the town or people. . . . It is of the last importance that the people of the town should be taught to fear us. Punishment will teach them." On July 13, the *Cyane* bombarded Greytown for several hours; then a landing party burned the remaining buildings to the ground. Not for the last time, Americans had completely destroyed a Nicaraguan city.[62]

VANDERBILT FACED SWINDLERS of every description, in every direction. In June 1854, he sued William C. Moon for fraud. He had accepted a $3,000 promissory note from Moon, who claimed to represent a well-known mercantile house. Vanderbilt endorsed it over to August Belmont, who discovered the hoax. The Commodore promptly paid Belmont, though he is unlikely to have gotten his money back from Moon. In this case, the crime is less interesting than what it says about Vanderbilt's prolific small-scale lending. In 1854, he took numerous promissory notes for amounts ranging from $1,000 to $5,000. Years later, Lambert Wardell would claim that Vanderbilt had no time for small deals, observing, "An intimate friend of his once said that 'The Commodore was the biggest man in a big thing and the littlest man in a little thing that he ever knew.' " In 1854, that judgment was only half true, as Vanderbilt sought to invest every penny. He reportedly admitted all callers at his private office, and accommodated requests for minor loans rather freely (though he charged market rates of interest).[63]

But swindlers continued to haunt him; indeed, they would plague him in 1854 as at no other point in his life. The most heartbreaking, though not the worst, was his son Corneil. In March, Corneil's epilepsy struck him hard. "He is in feeble health," a friend wrote, "and visits Washington for pleasure & for the benefit of his health." The idea of anyone visiting the swampy city of Washington to improve his health would have struck most Americans as a bit strange. Stranger still were the identities of the friend who wrote this letter and the man who received it: John P. Hale, former senator from New Hampshire, and Charles Sumner, senator from Massachusetts, both leading opponents of slavery.

At the moment, Hale and Sumner were embroiled in a struggle against the Kansas-Nebraska bill, which threatened to overturn the Missouri Compromise's ban on slavery in the lands north and west of Missouri. It was a titanic battle, yet Hale found time to intervene for the "son of the celebrated Mr. Vanderbilt." He told Sumner, "If you can show him any attention, you will confer a favor on yours [truly]."

Corneil, who once had limited himself to drawing drafts on his unsuspecting father or skipping out on his bill at the haberdashery, had discovered a new method of acquiring gambling money: he charmed and flattered powerful men, playing on his father's fame to elicit loans. "Corneil was eccentric, and was possessed by some astonishing peculiarities that made him a genius in his way," said Henry Clews, a gossipy banker who knew Corneil in later years. That genius lay in "his ability to catch the ear of prominent men, who would listen attentively to his tale of woe, and some of them were so thoroughly under the spell of his persuasive powers that they would fork out the required amount without hesitation, to relieve his pressing necessities."[64]

As if this were not strange enough, Corneil managed to get himself arrested for forgery. His father, it seems, bailed him out of jail, then took him for a carriage ride.[65] What Vanderbilt said to his son is unknown, but clearly he was unhappy with Corneil's increasingly disturbing behavior—the behavior of an addict. And he had a plan to address it. Before he could put it into operation, however, he suddenly fell ill.

One day in late May, Dr. Linsly received an urgent message to come to 10 Washington Place. He rushed to Vanderbilt's bedside. Listening closely to his patient's heart, he heard the same rapid yet feeble beating that had afflicted the Commodore in 1848. It was "a severe attack," Linsly recalled. "He had had this trouble with his heart for eighteen days. He could not lie down, and the infiltration of water into his legs gave him dropsy." It was a "singular heart trouble," Linsly said. "There is no name for it." Nonplussed, he once again advised Vanderbilt that he would likely die, and should put his affairs in order.

"SERIOUS ILLNESS OF COMMODORE VANDERBILT," the *Times* announced on May 31. "We regret to hear that Cornelus Vanderbilt, Esq., lies dangerously ill at his residence in Washington Place." The children, including Corneil, took up vigil in the house, shrouded by a near certainty of their father's demise. As in 1836, Vanderbilt called for an attorney and dictated a will. "He told me he had given the bulk of his property to his two sons, William H. and George," Linsly reported. "He also told me he had left the house in Washington Place to Mrs. Vanderbilt, and, my impression is, with $10,000 added." Like an ancient dynast, the Commodore meant to keep his estate intact, and pass it on to his sons—the sons for whom he still had some respect, that is. Curiously, he drafted no special provisions for the sons-in-law who played such a large role in his businesses, not even for Horace Clark, who had just settled 128 lawsuits stemming from the *North America* disaster for just $61 each. For the daughters who fretted beside his deathbed, and for Corneil, the Commodore planned to leave comparatively little.[66]

On the very day the *Times* announced Vanderbilt's illness, he began to improve. The *New York Evening Post* reported "the favorable change to-day in the symptoms of the disease." His heart began to beat strongly and evenly, and the "dropsy" disappeared. By June 30, he had fully recovered. On Sunday, July 2, he had Corneil arrested. "Dear Sir," Corneil wrote to his lawyer, at four o'clock that afternoon, "I have this moment been arrested by two officers, on the charge of insanity, and am now on my way to the Asylum. Do what you can to release me at once."

Four days later, a judge ordered Corneil's release from the Bloomingdale Asylum, after its presiding physician testified that "he was perfectly sane."[67] The physician was correct. Corneil's problem was not insanity; it was addiction to gambling. The Commodore's heavy-handed intervention in Corneil's self-destructive course failed because the era lacked the language, let alone the science, for addressing the disease.

When Corneil went free, he found his brother Billy and lawyer Charles A. Rapallo waiting for him. Billy told him, Corneil later reported, "that the doctor had sworn to this commitment to keep me out of the State prison [for forgery], and I told him I had rather be considered a damned rascal than a lunatic. . . . After that I had no conversation with William H. for two years."[68] Corneil blamed his brother, but his father almost certainly gave the order. The incident speaks to Vanderbilt's exasperation with Corneil. George inherited his athleticism; Billy showed signs of his shrewdness and intelligence; but Corneil was a schemer, a talker, and a weakling, all things that aroused the Commodore's contempt. Characteristically, Vanderbilt tried to solve the conundrum with a decisive act; but family cannot be managed like a business. Like so many fathers, he would have to just muddle through.

On the day that Vanderbilt had his son arrested, he confronted a far more dangerous, and far less likely, swindler: Robert Schuyler. Vanderbilt's relationship with him reached back at least as far as 1838, when Schuyler had served as president of the New York & Boston Transportation Company, the steamboat monopoly on Long Island Sound. But the twisted tale that unfolded over Independence Day of 1854 may have begun even earlier.

The nephew of Alexander Hamilton, Schuyler was "no nameless money-making speculator," George Templeton Strong wrote in his diary, "but . . . one of our 'first' people in descent and social position and sup-posed wealth." And yet, according to one Wall Street source, he led a dou-ble life. As an unmarried man, he resided at a hotel downtown, and maintained an office with his brother on Wall Street. Yet he also had a small house in the upper reaches of Manhattan, where he kept a mistress. "Here he lived a part of his time, and reared a family, though the mother of his children was not his wife," the Wall Street insider wrote fifteen years later. Why he did not marry the woman is unclear—perhaps she was not considered a suitable match for the illustrious Schuyler scion. "The landlord, the butcher, the grocer, and the milkman transacted all their business with the lady. Bills were promptly paid, and no questions asked. The little girls became young ladies. They went to the best boarding-schools in the land."

His eldest daughter indirectly ended the masquerade. A minister of the gospel asked for her hand, insisted on meeting her family, and was stunned to discover that his prospective father-in-law was the rich and famous Robert Schuyler—and that his fiancée was an illegitimate child. At the minister's insistence, Schuyler agreed to marry the mother of his children, despite the likely scandal. To Schuyler's surprise, the elite of New York embraced his new family. "An uptown fashionable mansion was pur-chased, and fitted up in style. Crowds filled the spacious parlor, for there was just piquancy enough in the case to make it attractive. Splendid coaches of the fashionable filled the street; a dashing company crowded the pavement, and rushed up the steps to enjoy the sights."[69]

No other sources mention this tale; perhaps it was too delicate a subject for the newspapers, or perhaps it was just a rumor, an echo in the ruins of Schuyler's cataclysmic downfall. Tellingly, it suggested a personality steeped in subterfuge, an accomplished liar who saw deception as some-thing other than his last resort. As Vanderbilt soon discovered, this described Robert Schuyler with tragic precision.

On the morning of Saturday, July 1, New York's merchant community expected runners to spread through the streets of downtown New York from "the eminent house of Robert and George L. Schuyler," as the *Evening Post* called it, carrying payment for promissory notes and other debts now due. But instead of money, a message went forth that the firm could not meet its engagements; and Robert, the senior partner, had fallen terribly ill and could not leave his bed to manage his affairs.

Wall Street had known great failures before, but this one deeply trou-bled the city's businessmen. The Schuylers occupied the center of the emerging corporate economy. George served as president of the New York & Harlem Railroad, Robert of the Illinois Central, the New York & New Haven, and others. Even worse, the money market was already approaching a crisis. The capitalists of New York and New England had overextended themselves in lending to expanding railroads in the West, while the supply of credit from London had dried up because of heavy borrowing by the British and French governments to finance the Crimean War against Russia.[70]

When word went out of the Schuylers' failure, Cornelius Vanderbilt drove to Robert's mansion on Twenty-second Street. Schuyler owed him $600,000, of course, but Vanderbilt also feared a general panic in the wake of the bankruptcy. Sitting at Schuyler's bedside, the Commodore held out a check for $150,000, enough to see him through the next week or so. After a few arrangements, he said, he could provide still more help, as much as $3 million. Furthermore, he would go into Wall Street and start a bull campaign to drive the stock of the New Haven and Harlem railroads up to par, which would inflate the value of Schuyler's stock portfolio and allow him to settle with his creditors. All this and more he would do, the *Evening Post* reported, "if Mr. Robert Schuyler would only assure him that 'all was right.' To this Mr. Robert Schuyler made no other reply than shaking his head. No such assurance could be given."[71]

Perhaps this disturbing conversation had something to do with Vanderbilt's decision, the next day, to have his son arrested for lunacy. Certainly he saw something rotten in Schuyler's affairs—and others did too. On Monday, July 3, a director of the New Haven Railroad, Morris Ketchum, went to the company's office to investigate some unusual sales of the company's stock. "In a conversation with the book-keeper his suspicions were excited," according to the press, because Schuyler had given orders that no one should be allowed to examine the company ledgers. Ketchum seized the books, and the next day pored over them with the treasurer and two other directors.

When Schuyler learned of Ketchum's actions, he panicked. He sent for his brother, and "executed an assignment of all the property belonging to the firm, as well as his individual property," to his attorneys. The next day, as the directors examined the books, he boarded a train to Burlington, Vermont. There he took a Lake Champlain steamboat to Canada.

On Wednesday, July 5, Ketchum and his fellow directors announced the stunning news: Robert Schuyler had issued certificates for nineteen thousand shares of stock that legally did not exist—a fraud amounting to $1.9 million at par value. Since Schuyler was both president and stock transfer agent, he had thought he could hide his crime, because he had not sold the stock but used it as collateral for loans. He had hoped to ride out the crisis in his finances, repay the loans, and then destroy the fake certificates. Instead, he had gone bankrupt, leaving the railroad with an excess of nineteen thousand shares.[72]

"The business and money circles of New York were electrified, and the whole community in some measure shocked, by the sudden disclosure," one magazine reported. "Mr. Robert Schuyler, the person implicated, stood among the highest in the community, was the honored representative of one of the old aristocratic families of New York." As Strong wrote in his diary, "Wall Street all agog. . . . This swindle of Schuyler's is a great disaster and may well be the first crack that preludes a general crash and collapse." Stock prices swiftly fell as further failures ensued. One of the bankrupts, the aristocratic Gouverneur Morris, had borrowed $100,000 on Schuyler's behalf, with the fraudulent stock as collateral.[73]

Vanderbilt held more "spurious" shares than anyone—a total of 2,210, worth $221,000 at par value. The man scorned as "boorish" by New York's elite had done his best to save the most elite of them all, and had been repaid with treachery. To make matters worse, the New Haven Railroad soon announced that it would repudiate the spurious shares. Even the legitimate Harlem stock that Schuyler had given Vanderbilt as collateral proved a source of trouble when the now-struggling railroad refused to pay dividends on Vanderbilt's one thousand shares.[74]

Robert Schuyler fled across the Atlantic to Genoa, where his family followed, and lived "in the strictest incognita," a French reporter claimed. "Since his departure from America his health has been on the decline, and he finally died of grief and mortification" around the middle of February 1856. His widow returned to the United States and retired to an isolated cottage on Saratoga Lake, dogged by rumors that her husband was still alive, hiding himself with the woman he had once hidden from the eyes of society. "Fashionable New York, which could overlook twenty years of criminal life, could not excuse poverty," wrote Matthew Hale Smith, the aforementioned Wall Street insider. "It took reprisals for bringing this family into social position by hurling it back into an obscurity from which probably it will never emerge."[75]

NOTHING, IT SEEMS, WAS BETTER for the public than an angry Cornelius Vanderbilt. For all the distraction of Schuyler's fraud, the Commodore remained fixated on punishing Morgan and White—and the consumer profited. At the end of May 1854, he opened a second front by attacking one of the main sources of Morgan's wealth: his Gulf Coast steamship company. Vanderbilt established a rival line, running "three large first-class steamships" between Texas and New Orleans. "The avowed object," the *Indianola Bulletin* reported, "is to oppose Harris & Morgan—to the death." (Harris & Morgan, a New Orleans firm run by Israel C. Harris, Morgan's son-in-law, was the agent for his line.) Here, it seems, Vanderbilt's lobbying in Washington actually worked, for the Post Office took the Gulf mail contract away from Morgan and gave it to the Commodore. This pleased Texans who had grown tired of the "Harris & Morgan" monopoly. "Their uniform course was high-handed and despotic in the extreme," the *San Antonio Ledger* wrote. "It is not probable that they will succeed in running Messrs. Vanderbilt & Co. off the track."[76]

This attack began just as the California traffic slacked off for the summer. Accessory Transit share prices slid down from a high of over 27 in January to 20¼ on July 17. A company official would feel obliged to explain to stockholders, "For some time, the sharp competition of three lines caused heavy losses." That reference to *three* lines serves as a reminder that Vanderbilt's Independent Line hurt not only Accessory Transit but also the long-established axis of the Pacific Mail and U.S. Mail Steamship companies. Their revenues plunged as they tried to match Vanderbilt's reduced fares, which drew away passengers by the shipload. And that was the Commodore's intention, for he hoped the mail companies would put pressure on Morgan and White to settle.

U.S. Mail recently had undergone a change in management that boded well for Vanderbilt's strategy. On March 18, George Law had sold his shares to Marshall O. Roberts; on April 4, he resigned from the board. With the scratch of a pen, Vanderbilt's most intransigent foe had retired from the battlefield. Leadership now passed to Roberts, the president of the North River Bank, owner of vast amounts of prime real estate in Manhattan and New Jersey, and a wily operator on the stock market. On Wall Street, he was "not [very] popular," the Mercantile Agency reported that year. "Mr. Roberts, on the commencement of his mercantile life, was in [very modest] circumstances, & has risen to his present position by his industry, shrewdness, & perseverance." This sounded very much like a description of Vanderbilt. But Roberts had ascended into the sanctum of New York's most refined society. A former Whig candidate for mayor, a close ally of Moses Taylor and August Belmont (both wealthy social leaders), Roberts built a costly mansion on Fifth Avenue in 1854, and boasted that his net worth amounted to half a million dollars. He had no interest in pursuing Law's old vendetta or in bleeding profits merely to save Charles Morgan's pride.[77]

With steerage fares between New York and San Francisco as low as $35, passengers flocked to the Independent Line, only to see the ugly side of competition, the ferocious cost cutting that made such prices possible. As one popular song ran:

> *You are driven round the steerage like a drove of hungry swine,*
> *And kicked ashore at Panama by the Independent Line;*

Your baggage is thrown overboard, the like you never saw,
A trip or two will sicken you of going to Panama.

Despite this ruthless attempt to limit expenses, Vanderbilt, too, lost money on his California line, especially when traffic fell during the summer. And so did his partner, Edward Mills, who "was [about] ruined in consequence," according to the Mercantile Agency. Desperate to cut his losses, Mills sold his share of the *Uncle Sam* and the *Yankee Blade* to Vanderbilt. It did little good. Unable to pay his debts, he went bankrupt, ending a long career as a steamship entrepreneur.[78] Vanderbilt had carried him down to disaster. Truly there was no friendship in trade.

If Mills had been able to hold on for just a few weeks longer, the outcome for him would have been very different. On August 29, rumors began to circulate on Wall Street that Vanderbilt and his foes were meeting to discuss terms. Two days later, news broke of a final settlement. Driven to desperation, Morgan, Roberts, and Aspinwall decided to buy out Vanderbilt on his terms. The Accessory Transit, U.S. Mail, and Pacific Mail companies purchased his steamships for $800,000, an amount far exceeding their original cost ("a gd. price," the Mercantile Agency judged). The mail companies jointly paid half and received the *North Star*, which U.S. Mail would operate. Accessory Transit paid the other $400,000 and took the *Yankee Blade* and the *Uncle Sam;* it also agreed to give Vanderbilt $115,000 in compensation for "his claims of every sort, including his interest, past and prospective (say for two years), in the transit over the isthmus," as the company reported. The first payment of $60,000 would be made in December, with two more scheduled in early 1856. To add injury to insult, the *Yankee Blade* soon went ashore on a reef at Point Arquilla and proved to be a total loss.[79]

On top of that, the Accessory Transit share price slid still lower, allowing the Commodore to "buy in" and profitably "cover" the short-selling contracts he had made in January (to use the jargon of the time). He paid as little as 16¼ for each share that he now sent over to Charles Morgan, who had agreed to pay 25 whenever Vanderbilt chose to deliver them.[80] The Commodore had not only forced his foe to acknowledge he was right, he also had forced Morgan to pay him three times—in an inflated price for his steamships; in cash for his claims; and in the stock market.

Accessory Transit and the mail companies quickly made arrangements with each other to return fares to their previous high levels: $300 for first cabin, $250 for second, and $150 for steerage—three times or more what Vanderbilt had charged. But if Morgan and Roberts had paid any attention to the Commodore's long career, they must have been wary of his agreement to forgo future competition. "Vanderbilt is slippery," observed the *San Francisco Alta California*, "very much like the Irishman's flea, and we should not be at all surprised if a line of opposition steamers were puffing away in the course of six months, established at least indirectly through his means."[81]

The precise prediction would prove wrong, but the sentiment was entirely correct. In little more than a year, Vanderbilt would once again take his place as a major force in the steamship lines to California. And when he did, he would find himself embroiled in a war not only for business but for the very survival of Central America, as the United States plunged toward civil war.

Chapter Ten

ARIEL

"Billy, never underestimate your opponents." Lambert Wardell overheard the comment in one of Vanderbilt's increasingly frequent,
and increasingly fatherly, conversations with William. It is difficult to chart this father-son relationship, for it was entirely oral, yet it
seems that a warming continued after their months together on the *North
Star*. This particular piece of advice stuck in Wardell's memory because it
was so characteristic of his employer's thinking. "This was one of the
secrets of his success," Wardell later reflected. "He never underrated himself nor anybody else."[1]

These well-remembered words say much about how the Commodore
envisioned his business career. Wardell would add that he "detested
details. . . . He was very concise and gave general directions regarding
matters rather than dictating in detail." This statement seems not to apply
to this stage of Vanderbilt's career, considering the minute attention he
often lavished on his ships and various operations, until it is put into the
context of that comment about "opponents." He did not think of his businesses as machinery; rather, he saw them as military campaigns against his
enemies. When he could not avoid the merely mechanical aspect of his
enterprises he often expressed impatience; but when he was locked in
combat he paid attention to the tiniest detail. This helps explain why he
regularly sold out his steamboat and steamship lines after only a year or
two of competition: once he achieved victory, he lost interest. He devoted
little time to the businesses that he did operate year after year, such as the
Staten Island Ferry, which had attracted widespread complaints about its
condition.[2]

In the months and years that followed the *North Star*'s voyage to
Europe, Vanderbilt increasingly thought of himself in another way: as a
pillar of New York's mercantile community. That could be seen clearly in
August 1854 (the same time that he achieved victory over the Accessory
Transit Company), when he set out to rescue a bastion of New York's business establishment, the New York & Erie Railroad—or Erie, as it was
more commonly known. The Democrats who ran New York State had

chartered the company in 1832 with the Whiggish notion that it would be a private corporation with a public purpose, to bring the benefits of the newfangled railway to the southern tier of upstate New York counties. Even the radical *New York Evening Post* supported it, and prominent merchants subscribed to the stock. But building a line over the mountains from the Hudson River to Lake Erie proved far too expensive and time-consuming for private capital alone. The state stepped in repeatedly to keep the enterprise afloat as it grew ever more costly. Finally, in 1851, New York celebrated the completion of what was then the longest railroad in the world.[3]

After all the trials the Erie endured in construction, it began to make a great deal of money. In 1853, it earned $4,318,762, a 25 percent increase over the year before and well above expenses (at a time when only three or four dozen textile factories represented a total investment of $250,000 or more). When Nelson Robinson carried its stock up to 92, it was not simply because of his skills as a broker, but also because the Erie had bright prospects. But it seems that Robinson did not attend to his duties as treasurer quite as carefully as he should have. A massive cluster of debts fell due on September 1, 1854; when the railroad's officers tried to arrange short-term loans to cover the payments, they encountered the same tight money market that had brought down Robert Schuyler. The company needed a great deal of credit, very fast.[4]

The Erie towered over the economic landscape. Its stockholders numbered in the hundreds, and it boasted a capitalization larger than all but a few other giant railroads. Yet it was situated in a culture that still did not distinguish between the invisible corporation and its corporeal managers and shareholders. In this crisis, all eyes turned to its directors, who were expected to take personal responsibility for the corporation's debts. Panicked by the enormity of the payments coming due, they all declined. "Where are all the great financiers who used to congregate in the directors' room of this huge concern, and put forth their edicts with all the pomposity of the Grand Mogul?" asked the *New York Herald.* "Where are they now? We do not see them striding about the streets, annihilating all the little bears by a look. Verily, their occupation is gone, and they have given place to a set of hungry creditors."[5]

Robinson was nowhere to be found. As treasurer, he had seen the storm coming, sold all of his stock, and again went into retirement. Only his former partner, Daniel Drew, stood up to the challenge. Drew's connection to the road predated his election to the board of directors; as early as 1842, he and Isaac Newton had provided the steamboat connection between Manhattan and Piermont, the railroad's terminus on the west bank of the Hudson River. On August 30, 1855, the Mercantile Agency summarized his life and reputation in words that reflected the deep respect of Wall Street. "He is a self made man, of great energy, [prudence,] & integrity. Began his [business] life as a cattle dealer, in which he made considerable money. Was afterwards a broker in the firm of Drew, Robinson & Co. . . . until March '52, when he retired," it wrote. "Was then believed to be [worth] over a million & is probably [worth] that now. . . . He is [very] prompt in all his [business] transactions. Is in unquestioned [credit] & his [notes] are placed amongst the first-class paper."[6]

A day would come when the brokers of Wall Street would howl with laughter at the thought of Drew being described by the words "prudence" and "integrity." But in August 1854 he seemed like a savior when he undertook to rescue the Erie from bankruptcy. Not that he acted out of sheer nobility: he knew that the railroad would have to pay him enormous fees for credit it could get nowhere else. But it needed more credit than Drew alone could muster, and so the former drover turned to his old friend. "Mr. Vanderbilt has been called upon for aid after every member of the board of directors, except Mr. Drew, declined to come under for any further responsibility," the *New York Herald* reported, "and if he backs out we really do not know what will become of the once magnificent Erie Railroad Company."[7]

He did not back out. Vanderbilt endorsed the Erie's paper—that is, he accepted ultimate responsibility for its repayment of a six-month loan—to the sum of $400,000. For collateral, he took a mortgage on the entire rolling stock, all 180 locomotives and 2,975 cars. Drew endorsed notes for $200,000 (later even more) and took a mortgage on everything that was left. If the Erie didn't pay, it would become the personal property of Vanderbilt and Drew. The railroad's position was so precarious that a panicked sell-off of its stock broke out when it was rumored that Vanderbilt had been thrown from his wagon in Broadway and severely injured (it actually happened to his brother Jacob).

But the Erie paid back the loan. It also delivered a 10 percent fee to the two gentlemen, a neat $40,000 payoff for the Commodore on his bet that the Erie would survive.[8]

The incident reveals much about Vanderbilt's peculiar role in the emergence of the modern economy. The hallmark of a modern financial system is institutionalization—the emergence of banks and similar bodies to pool capital, assess risks, and provide credit. By 1854 such institutions had already sprouted on the American scene, but Vanderbilt the individual seemingly dwarfed them all. In rescuing the Erie, he (and Drew) accomplished what seemed beyond the combined might of New York's merchant class. He would have to battle that class again—as early as the beginning of October, when his spokesman faced down an angry meeting of New

Haven Railroad stockholders, marking the start of Vanderbilt's long war to force the corporation to accept responsibility for the spurious stock Schuyler had issued.[9] But his salvation of the Erie consolidated his position as a merchant prince in the Medici mold, both a relic of a bygone era and an aggressive leader of the new. And it contributed to a slow and subtle change in his social status.

At first glance, it seems impossible to decipher the contradictory signals sent by New York's great merchants in the 1850s. James King and the Mercantile Agency scorned him; Hamilton Fish and Robert Schuyler turned to him for help. But the signs of acceptance were growing more numerous. In 1855, for example, he received a dinner invitation from the socially prestigious merchant Cyrus W. Field, brother of the prominent lawyer David Dudley Field, denizen of fashionable Gramercy Park, and organizer of an attempt to build a transatlantic telegraph cable. Unusually, Vanderbilt personally wrote a reply. "I am extreamly mortified to be compelled to say it is out of my power to do so in consequinc of an ingagement previously made," he wrote.[10] This otherwise insignificant letter is less notable for Vanderbilt's continuing disregard for conventional spelling than for the formal tone that now suffused his language, as well as the fact of the invitation itself.

Did this creeping social acceptance give his wife Sophia equal satisfaction? "She was of simple tastes and habits, and never learned to feel quite at home amid the great and splendid city," wrote William A. Croffut a decade after Vanderbilt's death. Croffut was more a gossip than a biographer, but we have little other evidence. "She clung closely to the acquaintances of her youth, and used to tell . . . that the happiest days of her life were those spent in hard work in the halfway tavern at New Brunswick, and that she liked the house that her husband had built on Staten Island, with all the children romping on the lawn . . . far, far better than the prim mansion on Washington Place."[11]

WITH ALL HIS ENEMIES CHASTISED, Vanderbilt had to decide what to do next. No matter how significant he was as a financier, temperamentally he wasn't suited to merely play the money man. He was a builder of enterprises—more specifically, he was a competitor. He was accustomed to taking a leading role in transportation, which was by far the largest sector in the American economy; that meant he was accustomed to being a public figure, for transportation was the great meeting ground of public and private interests in the nineteenth-century republic. It is not surprising, then, that as soon as he closed up his California lines he launched an attack on the sea lanes to Europe.

The end of 1854 happened to be the perfect time for his entry into the transatlantic steamship business. The Cunard Line, the British steamship company, temporarily disappeared because of the intensifying war with Russia. "In response to the British government's need for support in the Crimea," writes maritime historian John A. Butler, "the line was . . . obliged to withdraw from the New York–Liverpool route and send its ships to the Black Sea with troops and mail." In addition, the primary American competitor, the heavily subsidized Collins Line, had recently suffered the sinking of its flagship *Arctic*.[12]

"There is room for more Atlantic steamships, and, just in the nick of time, we have the man to step in and fill up the deficiency," the *Herald* announced in December. "We understand that Mr. Cornelius Vanderbilt, who, as a shipbuilder and navigator has earned for himself the title of 'Commodore Vanderbilt,' is now building two fine steamers, upon the general plan of the *North Star*, to ply from New York to Havre or Liverpool, and that they will be ready for sea in the course of the coming spring." Though the *Herald* avoided criticizing the Collins Line, the political controversy surrounding its federal subsidies suffused its commentary. "Competition is the life of business," it wrote. "Commodore Vanderbilt has the necessary experience, both as a steamship builder and as a steamship navigator, to know what to do in the way of putting up a perfect steamer; and with a private fortune of some $7,000,000 or $8,000,000, he may undertake this great Atlantic enterprise with impunity."[13]

The *Herald* was right in one respect, but off the mark in two others. The Commodore did indeed have a steamship under construction at the Simonson shipyard, one specifically designed for the Atlantic. The *New York Post* lovingly described the three-deck sidewheeler: "*twenty-three* hundred tons burden, and named the *Ariel*, diagonally iron-braced throughout, and considered as strongly built as any steamship of her class afloat." But, according to Vanderbilt himself, the *Herald's* estimate of his fortune was short by several million—a margin larger than the estate of nearly any other wealthy man in the country. An associate later recalled how the Commodore asked him who he thought was New York's next-wealthiest merchant, after William B. Astor. When he guessed Stephen Whitney, with some $7 million, Vanderbilt snorted, "Hmmm! He'll have to be worth a good deal more than that to be the second-richest man in New York."[14]

A more significant oversight concerned Vanderbilt's attitude toward subsidies. He undoubtedly took a dim view of federal payments to private businesses—but he had no intention of operating at a disadvantage. He wanted for himself those federal dollars now flowing to Collins, though he was willing to take smaller helpings. To get them, he would embark on a dramatic new lobbying campaign in Washington.

Before he did so, he may have seen an opportunity to make a quick return on his investment in the *Ariel*. Sometime around January 1855, he reportedly called upon Collins in his office. The sixty-year-old Commodore bluntly stated his proposition: he planned to fight for the subsidy in Congress, but "he would refrain from doing so if he (Mr. Collins) would put back two of his ships to the Allaire Works for repair, and purchase the steamer *Ariel*, then on the stocks, for $250,000," wrote the *New York Times* some weeks later. "Mr. Collins declined, considering the *Ariel* worth not over $150,000, and that $100,000 was asked simply as 'hush money.' " If the story was true, Collins badly underestimated the *Ariel's* value. In conversations with friends, Vanderbilt reportedly shook his head over his foe's stupidity in turning down a very fair price (especially in light of his long history of commercial extortion). Then again, the story may have been false, as it was reported by the openly hostile *Times*. The newspaper surmised, "The fact is, the 'Commodore' has become so accustomed to bringing down his game, that it is not to be wondered at if he *does* expect it to fall the instant he points a gun."[15]

Collins himself brimmed with confidence. In the age that saw the great flowering of lobbying, he lobbied more effectively than anyone. In 1847, he had convinced Congress to pay him a subsidy for ten years in return for building five ships capable of conversion into military transports or men-of-war. He built four, all luxury passenger liners. The sums his company drew were staggering for the time. Its ships, each roughly 2,800 tons, cost an average of $736,035, an extravagance that Vanderbilt would never have tolerated—though he never had federal loans to cover his expenses. By 1855, federal payments to the line had risen to $858,000 annually, or $33,000 per trip; one congressman calculated that it had sucked $7,874,000 out of Washington since its formation. Collins lavished luxuries on his ships, built them to be very fast, and ran them hard. "They used twice the coal of other ships," writes historian Mark Summers, "and cost more in repairs after six years than the original outlay for construction."[16]

"A great deal is said about the excellence of these steamers," one congressman quipped. "They are certainly the deepest-draught steamers I have ever yet heard of—drawing thirty-three feet in the National Treasury." Collins secretly pooled earnings with the Cunard company, and earned an average annual profit of 40 percent per year, though inventive accounting made it seem that his line ran at a loss. "Any observer," Summers concludes, "could see how well it did by a glance at the Brussels tapestries, chandeliers, silver tea-services, and rosewood furniture on board."

To keep Congress from so observing, Collins marshaled the most effective lobbyists in Washington, including banker and gambling-house proprietor W. W. Corcoran and former House clerk Benjamin B. French. "While others got their thousands for aiding in the Collins steamer appropriation, I got $300," French complained in 1852. "True I worked only *one day*, but if I had not worked that day, their appropriation would have been lost, for my intimacy with a single member caused him to remain at home, & his vote against it would have defeated it. They ought to have given me ten times what they did." Another of Collins's "borers" (as they were called), a man notorious for his effectiveness in greasing money out of Congress, was described by a close friend as suffering from only one flaw: "He is such an infernal scoundrel." Collins worked the Capitol in person, bringing the lavishly appointed *Baltic* up the Potomac in 1852 to entertain congressmen desperate for amusement in backwater Washington.[17]

The borers, the Collins subsidy, and the lucrative mail contracts for the California lines all represented a simmering crisis in American politics, as the ideology of an earlier generation broke down in the face of economic and territorial expansion. Radical Jacksonians condemned both active government and business corporations; yet the growing nation clearly needed transportation enterprises on a vast scale. This contradiction resulted, perversely enough, in large public payments to private corporations to do the work, with an attending frenzy of corruption.[18] Ironically, these circumstances set up Vanderbilt to play the Jacksonian champion even as he reached new heights of stockjobbing.

In February 1855, Vanderbilt launched his attack on Collins's subsidy with a formal proposal to carry the mail to Liverpool for $15,000 per voyage—less than half of Collins's fee. "I have had some experience in ocean navigation," he wrote, "and am well satisfied that . . . the enterprise can be accomplished with great advantage to the country, and without loss to myself. I would not ask for the protection of $15,000 per voyage, were it not for the considerable compensation now allowed to the Cunard line by the British Government, and the still more stupendous protection afforded by our own Government to the Collins line." In conversation with the press, he won sympathy by directly appealing to Jacksonian values. "He considers that the large sums now paid by the American and British governments for carrying the mail blights individual enterprise, and defies individual competition," *Scientific American* reported.[19]

And so commenced the great congressional struggle over the Atlantic mail subsidy. It would be forgotten in later years, overshadowed by more ominous events. In 1854, the Kansas-Nebraska Act had passed, repealing the Missouri Compromise and throwing open the question of slavery to the settlers of those newly opened territories. An organized land rush was under way, as free-soil migrants from the North moved into Kansas, where they confronted heavily armed, pro-slavery "border ruffians" from neighboring Missouri. The collapse of the old sectional compromises undermined the Whig Party; out of its ashes were arising the nationalist, anti-immigrant Know-Nothings (formally the American Party) and the free-soil Republicans. The Kansas-Nebraska earthquake was tearing apart the political landscape; already many were talking about the secession of the South, should slavery fail to expand into Kansas.[20]

On February 15, 1855, however, it was Collins's "enormous appropriation" that dominated the floor of the House of Representatives. Though the principles at stake would later seem minor compared to secession, they went to the heart of American politics. Simply put, it was a struggle between the old Democratic belief in individual enterprise and limited government, and the patriotic conviction that the United States must assert its place in the world, at least to the extent of carrying its own mail—in speed and style. "We live in a fast age," declared Congressman Edson Olds of Ohio, chairman of the House Committee on the Post Office and Post Roads. "We have fast horses and pretty women [laughter]—and we want the fastest steamers in the world." Olds's enthusiasm aroused skepticism in a congressman who later became quite an expert in government extravagance, one William M. Tweed. But Olds was adamant in his defense of Collins. "His line of steamers have done more for the American name and skill on the ocean than all the Government [Navy] steamers put together," he claimed.

Olds spoke for a bill to lock in the Collins subsidy at its recently elevated level and eliminate Congress's option to cancel it with six months' notice. Congressman William Smith of Virginia stood up to interrupt him. According to the *New York Times*, Smith "said he listened with inexpressible surprise," because Olds had denounced the subsidy in 1852. "Mr. Vanderbilt offered to do the service for a very considerably less sum than Mr. Collins, tendering good security, but the proposition was rejected and duly disregarded, in order to continue the present monopoly," Smith thundered. He "declared himself opposed to the whole scheme, viewing it as a source of corruption." At that, Olds stood up and asked, "If the gentleman were so opposed to extras, how he got the name of 'Extra Billy?' [Laughter.]" Smith replied, "By extra and faithful service in the Democratic Party—not by dishonorable means or unworthy tricks. 'Do you,' he asked of Mr. Olds, 'understand that?' [Sensation.]"[21]

The House of Representatives passed the Collins bill. In the Senate, Democrat Robert Hunter of Virginia pointed to bribery as the explanation, noting that just seven months earlier the House had defeated the same measure, as had the Senate. "Now look at both Houses and see the tendency to the other side. What has produced this? Have any new features come up? Shall we say the change is attributable to outside influences? Mr. Vanderbilt proposes to do this service without the extra pay, and my constituents shall know that there is one Senator who is unwilling recklessly to squander the money of the people."

"I don't know nor care about Mr. Vanderbilt," said Whig George Badger. "I do know what Mr. Collins has done. He has accomplished a successful rivalry with Great Britain, and I think for the honor of the country he should be permitted to proceed."

"Mr. Vanderbilt is well known to us all," countered Stephen R. Mallory of Florida. "His reputation is second to nobody." But William H. Seward, the giant of New York's old Whig Party and an emerging Republican leader, came to Collins's defense. "It is said by some senators that this is an extravagant, a luxurious line," Seward announced. "Sir, this line of steamers is, in my judgment, the proper diplomatic representative of the United States to the Old World."[22]

The debate in the Senate raged on February 27 from one o'clock in the afternoon until nine at night. Finally the chamber passed the Collins subsidy bill. "Congress was *not* deluded—it was corrupted," the *New York Tribune* declared. "Where the money came from, we do not legally know—we can only give a Yankee guess—but that money passed this bill—money not merely expended on borers and wheedlers, and the usual oyster-cellar appliances of lobby legislation—but money counted down into the palms of Members of Congress themselves—this is as clear as the noon-day sun."[23]

At nine thirty a.m. on Saturday, March 3, the *Ariel* slid down the stocks into the East River. That same morning, President Franklin Pierce vetoed the Collins subsidy bill, denouncing it as a "donation" that would establish a monopoly and eliminate "the benefits of free competition." The reaction on Capitol Hill was violent. "The veto of the Ocean Steamer Bill produced the greatest excitement in Congress today," the *New York Herald* reported. "When it was read cries for impeachment were heard from different parts of the hall. Mr. Campbell of Ohio, with much vehemence, exclaimed, 'The time for revolution has come!' "[24]

"The veto was bought by the opposition," claimed one New York newspaper. "Vanderbilt is rich and bids high to carry his points, especially his enmities; and President Pierce has sold himself, and his friends, too so often, that his influence has become a marketable commodity. Fifty thousand dollars is supposed to be about the present price of a veto involving a million of dollars."

The accusation led Vanderbilt to respond, in one of the most distinct expressions of his philosophy ever to be printed. It may well have been crafted by Horace Clark or one of his attorneys, though Lambert Wardell would later claim that Vanderbilt dictated his correspondence with great skill; certainly the letter he now sent to the *New York Tribune* crystallized sentiments he had expressed for the last thirty years. He suggested that he might file a lawsuit over the libelous accusation that he had bribed the president, but for the moment, "I desire that the public should know all that I have done and all that I wish to do," he wrote. "After my return from my last visit to Europe, I became satisfied that the facilities of communication between the two countries were altogether insufficient." The Cunard Line's interruption had brought matters to a head.

> Now I have made no attack upon the Collins line, though I have never regarded, and do not now regard, any particular line of steamers as one of the institutions of the country . . . to venture to compete with which is treason. I am not inimical to that line, nor have I entertained aught of ill will toward the gentlemen who founded it. . . . I congratulate them on the prosperity which has hitherto attended their enterprise, and perhaps ought to applaud them for their ingenuity in its management. . . . They have succeeded in awakening a species of national fervor in favor of their enterprise till some seem to have considered that the measure of American patriotism is the extent of the public contribution to their treasury.

The tone of disdain hardly needs comment. But Vanderbilt went further, using impeccable Jacksonian language. "I assumed that the Atlantic Ocean was wide enough for two lines of steamers, and that if I saw fit to venture there, I encroached upon no private domain, and invaded no vested right," he wrote.

> But it is said that I am always in opposition, and that the same spirit of resistance which has often hitherto governed my action has influenced it now. In answer to this imputation I have only to say, that this is the same spirit which founded this great Republic, and which is now drawing the commerce of the world to our shores. It was the same spirit which unchained the fetters, which legislation similar in principle to that against which I now protest, once fastened upon the Hudson. Repress it if you dare, and before many centuries shall have passed away, your greatness and your glory, and your commerce will have gone still further west.
> My life has been thus far spent among a people who I supposed favored no such principles as these which sanction this kind of legislation, and the share of prosperity which has fallen to my lot is the direct result of unfettered trade and unrestrained competition.[25]

What is most remarkable about this letter is its complete consistency with his previous public pronouncements, going back to the early 1830s.

For all the apparent contradictions in his behavior, he envisioned his own career—his mission—in terms of a coherent philosophy: Jacksonian laissez-faire. Though the day was approaching when laissez-faire would be the conservative philosophy of a wealthy establishment, at this moment it lay on the populist—even radical—side of the spectrum. Vanderbilt had come of age in a society in which government intervention in the economy was seen as assistance for the elite. Even now, two decades after Jackson's day, the beliefs of that president pulsed through American politics, equating egalitarianism with individual enterprise and competition in a way that would make little sense to Americans of later centuries, after both government and the economy had grown larger and more intricate.

In Vanderbilt's mind, his commitment to competition kept alive the spark of the Revolution. He, Vanderbilt, represented the "spirit of resistance," whether to the odious Livingston steamboat monopoly or the obscene subsidy to the already-rich investors in the Collins Line. He, Vanderbilt, had "unchained the fetters" that held men and commerce and American greatness down. What is most notable about this self-image is how much truth it held. Between the stances of hero-worship and cynicism lies an honest assessment of Vanderbilt at half century, one that both recognizes his ambivalence as a historical figure and still gives him due credit. For all his contradictions over the years, he remained the master competitor, the individual who did more to drive down costs and open new lines in steam navigation than any other. More than that, he had helped shape America's striving, competitive, productive society. Waging war with his businesses, he had wrought change at the point of a sword. He was the selfish revolutionary, the millionaire radical.

What he did not realize was that the world in which he had made himself—the world that gave rise to these individualistic, laissez-faire values— was beginning to disappear, thanks in part to his own success. He helped create enterprises on a scale never seen before in the United States. Small proprietors could not compete against him. Still more profound, his businesses required large numbers of wage workers. Laboring for someone else had been seen as a temporary condition, until a man set up his own farm or shop; now lifetime employees began to appear on the American scene—still few in number, but significant nonetheless. The emerging importance of big business can be seen in the life of lawyer Abraham Lincoln. Lincoln's clients had always been individuals with small cases; but in the mid-1850s he began to devote most of his time to representing railroad corporations. Thanks to Vanderbilt, one day those corporations would grow far beyond any that employed attorney Lincoln.[26]

Despite the veto, Congress enacted the Collins subsidy through an amendment to a naval appropriations bill. The day after Vanderbilt's letter ran in the *Tribune*, the *New York Times* offered a closing commentary on his defeat. The *Times* supported Collins, and condemned the lack of "morality" in Vanderbilt's purported attempt to force him to buy the *Ariel*. " 'Commodore' Vanderbilt has returned from Washington in rather unfortunate spirits," it declared. "Possessing a large capital, upon which he is willing to draw freely to accomplish his ends, and endowed with a more than ordinary share of energy and perseverance, he is accustomed to succeed. Under these circumstances he submits to defeat with a very bad grace." The paper saw one likely result: "Judging from his past history, we shall expect soon to see the 'Commodore' setting up an 'opposition' Congress, at half price."[27]

As the *Times* foresaw, Vanderbilt would not give up. At the beginning of April, he announced the imminent start of his new Atlantic line, featuring the *Ariel* and his repurchased *North Star*, managed by another capable son-in-law, Canadian-born Daniel Torrance. Subsidy or no subsidy, he would fight Collins to the death.[28]

DURING THE BATTLE IN CONGRESS, Vanderbilt attended to another matter pertaining to Washington, one that involved his own family. George, his youngest son, wanted to attend the United States Military Academy. Though evidence about the boy is mostly apocryphal, by all accounts he was an outstanding athlete, a favorite of his father. On February 7, 1855, Congressman James Maurice of New York wrote to Secretary of War Jefferson Davis to name George a cadet at West Point, after a spot opened up due to a serious injury to a previous appointment. Five days later, President Pierce authorized the selection; a week after that, the Commodore sent Davis his formal permission for George's entry in the academy. On July 1, the boy began his training.[29]

George's appointment could only have been a matter of pride to the father who, of course, had named two of his sons after famous generals. Corneil, too, seems to have taken a step to untangle his unhappy life, by becoming a notary public in March. To all appearances, he began to work productively during this period, first in the law firm of Charles Rapallo and Horace Clark, then as a clerk in the leather store of Willliam T. Miller & Co.[30] For once the source of strife in the Vanderbilt family came from a different source—Daniel Allen, now returned from Europe.

About the time of the launch of the *Ariel* and the veto of the Collins subsidy, Allen filed a lawsuit against the Accessory Transit Company, claiming that its purchase of his father-in-law's steamships violated its corporate charter. "The street was full of rumors today about the proceedings instituted against the Nicaragua Transit Company," the financial column of the *New York Herald* reported. "Personal spite and prejudice has undoubtedly something to do with it." It was widely believed that the lawsuit was an attempt by short-sellers to drive down the stock price.[31] Indeed, twenty-two years later Allen admitted, "I was representative of parties who had an interest."

The problem was, that interest ran counter to those of his father-in-law. Vanderbilt had earned a large profit from the steamship sale. The lawsuit infuriated him, as Allen later acknowledged. "Our friendly relations were interrupted during that period," he would observe, rather drily. Vanderbilt delivered a damning affidavit to counter Allen's claims, and told Horace Clark to defend Charles Morgan and the company.[32]

Just as Vanderbilt believed friends could not be trusted, he was showing once again that enemies could be partners. Indeed, he seemed to view his prior battle with Morgan strictly as a matter of business. In January, they both had served on a committee appointed by the Chamber of Commerce to honor Commodore Matthew Perry's recent trade treaty with Japan. In May, both would publicly oppose the conversion of Castle Garden into an immigrant depot. (Fear of epidemics motivated resistance to the plan.) Business made strange bedfellows; before the end of the year, Vanderbilt would be driven into the arms of still another despised rival.[33]

AS SPRING TURNED TO SUMMER IN 1855, opponents preoccupied Cornelius Vanderbilt, as they so often did. There was Edward K. Collins, of course; but the Commodore also confronted his old rival George Law in an unlikely ring. Law had become a hero to many by defying the Spanish rulers of Cuba, who had tried to bar his steamships from docking in Havana because of an employee who had written tracts in favor of Cuban freedom. In 1854, a rumor had circulated that Law planned to use his private yacht, the *Grapeshot*, to smuggle to the island 200,000 surplus muskets that he had purchased from the federal government. Thanks to widespread American enthusiasm for seizing Cuba from Spain, this made Law a champion of expansionist nationalism.[34]

In March 1855, a movement began to build within the Know-Nothing Party to nominate Law for president. These anti-Irish, anti-immigrant ex-Whigs hailed him as "Live Oak George," in tribute to his steamships; "Live Oak Clubs" sprang up in New York and Pennsylvania. The *New York Herald* wrote, "He advocates the intermingling of all our adopted citizens in the homogenous mass of the American people, not as Irish Americans, German Americans, or American Catholics, but simply as Americans." The *Herald* stressed his "opposition to all sectional agitators, North and South."[35]

Law's candidacy reflected the chaos enveloping American politics. The destruction of the Whig Party, coupled with the growing crisis between North and South, left political activists scrambling to find new men and erect new parties. And the excitement around Law reflected his very public role as a creator of the U.S. Mail Steamship Company and stockholder in the Panama Railroad; in them he had owned and managed a vital piece of the nation's transportation infrastructure. It should not be surprising, then, that the next man spoken of as a suitable president should be another steamship tycoon. On March 30, ten members of the New Jersey legislature signed a letter to Cornelius Vanderbilt. "Recognized at home and abroad as an American citizen who, by ability and integrity, energy and enterprise, has practically illustrated the genius and character of our republican institutions," they wrote, "we desire to connect your name with the high office of President of the United States."

On April 12, Vanderbilt responded with a curiously ambivalent letter. "The earlier period of my life was devoted to unremitting toil, while my later years are severely burdened by the multiplied cares which my varied pursuits have engendered," he wrote. "I have never found the time to indulge one single dream of ambition; and I have already attained to that period of life when more simple realities take the place of the hopes and the anticipations of youth." Along with this apparent refusal to stand as a candidate, he announced some positions on public affairs. He declined to partake of the anti-immigrant fervor, for example, speaking in defense of "the large class of industrial emigration now flowing in upon our shores." And he recommended his personal approach to enterprise for the nation as a whole. "I am well satisfied that all the results that have attended the labors of my life are attributable to the simple rule which I early adopted, to mind my own business. . . . Nor can I suggest one more appropriate for the regulation and conduct of the foreign policy of the American people."[36]

The attempt to draft Vanderbilt, and his response, say a great deal about the man and his relationship to his times, albeit indirectly. The appeal to him was nonpartisan, which reflected the collapse of the old party system, of course, but also Vanderbilt's own lack of party affiliation. As noted earlier, the only evidence of serious political activity on his part is an apocryphal account of his parading for Henry Clay in 1844; before and after, he expressed no interest in public affairs unless they intersected with his own. Lambert Wardell later summarized, "He paid no attention to politics and was not a party man."[37] His lack of partisanship showed in the positions that he did take. Like a Whig, he looked askance at U.S. intervention abroad, and embraced corporations and the entire invisible architecture of modern commerce; like a Democrat, he championed immigration and free competition.

All of this was a bit remarkable in 1855. Politics saturated American life even more thoroughly than twenty years earlier, when Alexis de Tocqueville toured the republic and commented on the partisan passions of the people. To disengage from politics was, in some ways, to disengage from the substance of social intercourse.[38] So, too, was Vanderbilt's lack of ambition rather noteworthy. In New York, the tradition of political leadership by the mercantile elite lingered from the eighteenth century. True, it had become attenuated in recent decades, as professional politicians came to dominate the ballot, but men such as Hamilton Fish and various Livingstons still walked the halls of power; banker August Belmont occupied the center of the national Democratic Party organization; and wealthy merchants organized mass meetings and citizens' committees that declaimed on every aspect of public affairs. Vanderbilt, on the other hand, represented a new species of wealthy Americans. After his precedent, it would not seem strange that Andrew Carnegie or John D. Rockefeller should shun public office, choosing to quietly exert their influence behind closed doors.

Despite enthusiasm in the newspapers for the "steamboat candidates," neither went anywhere. Law being Law, he tried to corrupt delegates to the Know-Nothing convention. "A well-known agent of his attempted to bribe John H. Lyon of Jersey City with a certified check for $200," reported a New Jersey newspaper. "This fact was made known by Mr. Lyon, and thence [contributed to] Mr. Law's defeat." As for Vanderbilt, he never seriously considered running. It was a curious diversion in a year when business, not politics, drove his Washington agenda.[39]

The first order of business was his Atlantic line, scheduled to start on May 21. In April, he announced that he would slash fares to Europe from $130 to $110 for first cabin tickets, and from $75 to $60 for second cabin. "The magnificent steamship *Ariel*, lately built as a consort to the *North Star*, in Vanderbilt's direct New York and Havre line, will sail on her first voyage on Saturday noon next," the *New York Herald* announced on May 17. The newspaper lavishly praised the vessel, focusing in particular on the luxury of the grand saloon. "The wainscotting is of satin rose and other highly polished wood. The deck is superbly carpeted, and the walls are ornamented with beautiful mirrors; and easy chairs, ottomans, and lounges of the most luxurious description are profusely scattered about." Unlike the *North Star*, the *Ariel* had only one engine, a feature calculated to reduce fuel costs. And yet it proved fast enough, crossing the Atlantic on its first voyage in only twelve days.[40]

"Both the *Ariel* and *North Star* are fine steamships of great speed," the London *Times* observed on August 1. "Their voyages across the Atlantic have recently been performed with admirable regularity." It reported that "the well-known" Vanderbilt had arranged for the ships to stop at

Southampton. "What is the most interesting feature of the business is, that Commodore Vanderbilt is running his ships entirely unassisted by any Government grant or subvention whatever."

This was indeed international news. It may be that Vanderbilt conducted his campaign out of personal pique against the man who had snubbed him, yet his fast, well-run, *unsubsidized* line kept him at the center of the political debate. As the London *Times* concluded, "His ships have, therefore, to sail at every disadvantage against the heavily subsidized mail steamers of the various British and American lines. The Commodore appears to be convinced that good management and great speed of transit will enable his vessels to hold their own and to make a fair profit." Or, perhaps, he simply had to run his ships long enough, even at a loss, to undermine congressional support for Collins's subsidy.

As Vanderbilt pounded the Collins Line with his swift, luxurious ships and low fares, he prepared for a second assault: a ship nearly twice the size of the *North Star*, a steamship larger than any ever built. Construction began in the Simonson yard about the time the *Ariel* made its first voyage. It would prove to be the pinnacle of Vanderbilt's shipbuilding career.[41]

Collins began to see his company fall apart under the strain. He doggedly kept his fares up, only to see passengers flock to the Vanderbilt line. Pressing his ships' advantage in speed, he ordered his captains to run them so fast that their engines needed costly, time-consuming repairs on each return to New York. Soon a second transatlantic line, the Ocean Steam Navigation Company—a line that had run to Bremen for a decade—began to struggle under Vanderbilt's pressure.[42] Eventually all would come down to a test of will between Collins, with his bookkeeping tricks and political connections, and the fierce but savvy Commodore.

VANDERBILT'S SECOND ORDER of business for 1855 would be the Accessory Transit Company. It was rather like the business version of his son Corneil, a child with a kind of genius and a kind of curse, its great promise addled by an addiction to deceit, a child he was unable to simply shunt aside.

It was a ripe and vulnerable target. The company had continued to do "an exceedingly favorable business," according to the *New York Tribune*, but it faced seemingly grave difficulties: its unsettled debt to Nicaragua, its ongoing payments to Vanderbilt, its loss of the *Yankee Blade*, and, perhaps most important, competition with the Panama route. In February, workers completed the Panama Railroad, and trains began to run from Aspinwall on the Atlantic to the city of Panama on the Pacific. Passengers flocked to the Pacific Mail and U.S. Mail Steamship companies as the isthmus crossing dropped from a matter of days to only hours. And yet, these obstacles were all surmountable. Over the previous two years, Accessory Transit had improved its operations, and even now remained competitive in terms of speed between New York and San Francisco. The initial surge of business to Panama slacked off as passengers began to return to the Nicaragua route. And shorter steamship voyages meant that operating expenses still remained significantly lower for the Transit Company. It was under these circumstances—short-term trouble but long-term possibilities—that Vanderbilt made his return.[43]

He had never left, really, having retained shares in the company all along. In early November, he went to the company offices, where Charles Morgan presided over the annual stockholders' meeting. There were "many other anxious faces" among the shareholders, one man reported. Of particular concern to them was Morgan's practice, as New York agent, of letting the company's ships sit "idle for the need of trifling repairs," while Morgan put his own *Sierra Nevada* on the line, taking 60 percent of the earnings for himself. "Cornelius Vanderbilt said he had performed similar service for the Transit Company for 40 percent," the witness wrote. "Mr. Morgan apologized for the extra 20 percent, under a plea of a higher price for coal." The meeting broke up in suspicion over Morgan's conduct.[44]

Discontent within the company and worries without presented an obvious opportunity. On November 21, the day when newspapers published Accessory Transit's annual report, detailing its difficulties, certain brokers began to bid for large amounts of its stock. Within a few days, the mysterious "new party" behind the purchases bought 25,000 shares, nearly a third of the 78,000 shares in existence. Word went out on Wall Street of a secret plan, the *New York Tribune* reported, "to buy a majority of the whole, so as to control the company."[45]

Vanderbilt, of course, was behind the "movement," as it was called; but he had something larger in mind besides simply taking back the Accessory Transit Company. For some time, he had plotted the future of the California passenger business with Marshall Roberts of U.S. Mail and William Aspinwall of Pacific Mail. Nothing could have said more about Vanderbilt's rising status, for these men—both leaders of New York's social establishment—wished to place their fortunes in his hands.[46]

The three men crafted a multifaceted plan for both immediate profit and long-term dominance. First, after they acquired control of Accessory Transit they intended to have the company buy back forty thousand of their shares for several dollars more for each than they had paid. Second, Vanderbilt was to bring his ferocious cost-cutting skill to bear, to enable the company to pay a consistent dividend. Third, Accessory Transit would buy out the U.S. Mail Steamship Company, and then abandon the Pacific to Pacific Mail, which would become sole carrier for both Nicaragua and Panama. Accessory Transit ships would provide the Atlantic connection for both routes. Fourth, Accessory Transit would assume the Atlantic mail contract from the soon-to-be-dissolved U.S. Mail; as an incentive for Congress, Vanderbilt would carry the mail weekly instead of bimonthly, and for $90,000 less per year.

It was a remarkable turnabout. Not nine months after Vanderbilt publicly proclaimed his belief in "unfettered trade and unrestrained competition," he conspired to erect a monopoly over California's steamship lines. To all appearances, he saw no inconsistency in this curious juxtaposition, despite the fact that this new monopoly would be supported by government funds (if they succeeded in transferring the mail contract). Perhaps he felt himself justified, for unlike his intended partners he had arrived at this point—at the threshold of total market control—through his prowess in competition, and he would maintain it in the future only if he remained ready to fight against any challengers. In any case, he never engaged in competition purely for its own sake, but always as a means of achieving a satisfactory, and profitable, equilibrium.[47]

One thing is certain: he had grown accustomed to holding his fate in his own hands, whether whipping a team of fast horses through a crowded street or seizing the corridor between the Atlantic and Pacific coasts. Little did he realize that he recaptured Accessory Transit at the very moment when its fate—and the fate of Nicaragua itself—was falling into the hands of an international criminal.

ON THE AFTERNOON OF NOVEMBER 8, a company of soldiers drew up in formation on the grand plaza of Granada, Nicaragua. They stood at attention as a distinguished figure approached: General Ponciano Corral, a popular patrician of the city, a veteran of the republic's many civil wars, and the Conservative military commander. He strode beside a priest to the center of the plaza, sat down in a chair, and looked out over the city's tiled roofs and its massive cathedral, the volcano Mombacho in the distance. Then the soldiers raised their rifles and shot him dead.[48]

The man who ordered Corral's execution was William Walker. Vanderbilt would never meet Walker, but he would prove to be the most dangerous enemy of the Commodore's life so far. Walker was a small man, just five feet six inches tall, with a slender frame, thin mouth, thinning hair, and a freckled complexion. He had intense gray eyes that often drew notice. Commodore Hiram Paulding, one of the U.S. Navy's senior officers, remarked, "He listens to everything in a quiet way, says but little, speaks in a mild and subdued tone, and has rather the appearance and manner of a clerical gentleman than that of a warlike leader. He is said to be remarkable for his abstinence . . . and that wine and the society of ladies have no charm for him."[49]

Walker had landed in Nicaragua six months earlier, leading fifty-six rifle-carrying Californians hired to fight for León's Liberals in the most recent flare-up of civil war. In the United States, though, he was known not as a mercenary, but as a filibuster. "Filibustering" had entered the American vocabulary around 1850 as a name for armed invasions of foreign territory by private American citizens—generally with the hope of annexing those lands to the United States. The term had likely been imported from Spanish (*filibustero*), which had borrowed in turn from the Dutch word for freebooter. By any name, it dated back to the earliest days of the republic. In 1837, for example, the first steamboat constructed by Vanderbilt, the *Caroline*, went over Niagara Falls amid skirmishing between Canadian militia and American invaders. The current wave grew out of the fight for independence by American settlers in Texas and the Mexican War. Filled with that expansionist enthusiasm captured by the name "Manifest Destiny," small groups plotted expeditions into Latin America. In 1850 and again in 1851, scores of Americans made disastrous landings in Cuba. Walker himself had led an invasion of Mexico with a handful of men in 1853—a failure, but one that made him famous.[50]

In retrospect, filibustering can seem like a curious footnote to the antebellum era, a case of quixotic eccentrics racing down one of history's blind alleys. In reality, it was a significant element in the United States' slide toward civil war. Militants in the South embraced the movement in hopes of enlarging the territory open to slavery; the filibusters' focus on Cuba, for example, was due in part to the island's proximity to Florida and the fact that large-scale slavery already existed there. Perhaps most important, filibustering reflected the explosion of freelance violence as civil society and respect for political norms disintegrated in the fight over slavery's growth in the 1850s.

But filibustering was a complicated phenomenon, mingling nationalist expansionism with naked racism with a crusading belief in spreading Protestantism and free institutions to benighted Latin America. As one U.S. diplomat in the region wrote to Secretary of State William Marcy, "Catholicism and Military rule have charms for them, which my pen is inadequate to describe, while any other more rational form of religion or government appears to them, heresy and anarchy." After Walker landed in Nicaragua, Paulding wrote to his wife, "Central America will soon be brought into harmonious action by the introduction of our own beautiful system of government."[51]

Walker himself had no lofty goals in mind. Entranced with the power of his own star, he believed himself destined to become Central America's own Napoléon. Nicaragua, with its transit route, was simply a convenient place to begin his conquests.[52]

He did have his beliefs—chiefly in his own genius. Born in Nashville, he received a classical education, and later wrote a memoir in which he referred to himself in the third person, in imitation of Julius Caesar's *Commentaries*. Caesar he was not. He fought four pistol duels in his life, missing his antagonist every time. In Nicaragua he threw his men into headlong attacks against fortified enemy troops, suffering horrific casualties. But he was lucky. The Liberals' chief executive and army commander both died soon after Walker's arrival; by default, he emerged as León's senior military leader.

After some of his usual, costly blundering, he won the war with his only inspired maneuver: he commandeered an Accessory Transit steamboat at Virgin Bay on Lake Nicaragua, landed at Granada, and captured the city from the rear. He then took hostage the families of leading Conservatives, forcing General Corral to surrender. Walker dictated a peace treaty that established a provisional unity government nominally led by Patricio Rivas, former governor of San Carlos, a weak figure whom Walker easily dominated. Walker named himself commander of the army and Corral minister of war. Within days, Walker accused Corral of treason, had him tried by a court-martial of filibuster officers, then had him shot, thereby consolidating his own power.[53]

With his political position secured, Walker turned to the problem of the transit. If he were to survive as Nicaragua's strongman, he would need a steady supply of reinforcements from the United States; his fellow countrymen were his most reliable troops, but they died in large number in his frontal assaults. Walker was intensely aware of this dependence. As he later wrote, "Internal order as well as freedom from foreign invasion depended . . . entirely on the rapid arrival of some hundreds of Americans." Fortunately for him, his success created a wave of enthusiasm; thousands of young Americans proved eager to join his army—*if* they could get to Nicaragua. Walker, then, was as dependent on the Accessory Transit Company as he was on his American recruits.

But how to get Accessory Transit to respond to his dictates? His initial correspondence with the company was discouraging. Joseph White dismissed his demands, and Cornelius Garrison, the company's agent in San Francisco, did not reply at all. Frustrated, Walker turned to an aide, a one-handed confidence man named Parker H. French. Walker instructed Rivas to appoint French as Nicaragua's minister to the United States, then sent French to New York with orders to buy guns from George Law and bring Accessory Transit to terms. But Walker continued to mull over his relationship with the company.[54]

In every account of Walker's invasion of Nicaragua, from the 1850s to the twenty-first century, it has been said that Accessory Transit "willingly cooperated with Walker," as historian Robert E. May writes, "because company officials viewed him as a stabilizing influence on the country." This was neither true nor logical. It makes no more sense than a store-keeper, troubled by shoplifters, thinking of an armed robber as a "stabilizing influence." Most accounts cite as evidence a crate of $20,000 in gold bars that Accessory Transit donated to Walker upon his victory at Granada. In reality, a local company official named Charles MacDonald, overcome with enthusiasm for Walker, delivered the gold on his own initiative. The move infuriated Garrison, who fired MacDonald when he learned of it. Indeed, Walker and French had called on Garrison before departing San Francisco to ask for transportation on an Accessory Transit steamship. "Garrison not only refused to let us go on the steamer," French recalled, "but told us he would have nothing to do with the matter, for if he did, he would be blamed by the company." After Walker sailed, French had remained behind to forward arms and men to Nicaragua, smuggling them aboard Accessory Transit ships with the connivance of friendly captains to avoid Garrison's scrutiny. When French himself had left San Francisco, leading scores of recruits, he had hijacked the steamship *Uncle Sam*, forcing Garrison off the ship at gunpoint.[55]

Garrison's resistance is significant because he has consistently—and wrongly—been depicted as the mastermind who pitted Walker against Vanderbilt. Historians have not done well with Garrison; for example, they have named him as Charles Morgan's partner in throwing Vanderbilt out of Accessory Transit in 1853, even though Garrison had left for San Francisco shortly before the Commodore's departure in the *North Star*, and took no part in the ensuing battle from all the way across the continent. It was only *afterward* that Garrison and Morgan had formed a business partnership, establishing a bank in San Francisco and cooperating on the stock exchange. And in the story of William Walker, Garrison would be the manipulated one, not the manipulator.

Not that he was a man to be taken lightly: Garrison was wily, decisive, and personally courageous. An engraving from this period reveals a man of force, with a large head, a long, strong chin, a long nose that points downward between prominent cheekbones, large perceptive eyes lurking under a high forehead, and wings of hair tufting out above his ears, as if he were wearing fuzzy laurels. He wears a dignified gray double-breasted coat with large black lapels and a black cravat. But it was cunning, not dignity, that defined his career.

Born in 1809 on a farm near West Point, Garrison went from cabin boy on a Hudson River sloop to command of the Mississippi riverboat *Convoy*. In 1849, he followed the tide of the gold rush to the city of Panama, where he established a firm that was part bank, part mercantile house, part casino. On one occasion, he and a rival drunkenly agreed to a duel in the moonlight at no paces. They grabbed each other's lapels and one of the men shouted, "Fire!" As they raised their revolvers to shoot, the weapons collided, both bullets went astray, and the duel ended in laughter. In 1851, bandits robbed a mule train carrying a large consignment of gold across Panama; Garrison leaped onto a horse and led a posse into the jungle in pursuit. He rode back in triumph with two captured outlaws, one white and one black, both from New York.[56]

In Panama, Garrison had served as agent of Morgan's short-lived steamship line, which had led to his lucrative position as agent of Accessory Transit in San Francisco, where he had arrived on March 23, 1853. Over the course of three years, he would handle well over $3 million in revenues, and speculated in land, coal, and flour. A reporter for R. G. Dun & Co. would conclude almost two decades later that Garrison would "take an interest in almost any apparent successful venture . . . but is not consd. reliable. Antecedents not in his favor, and all transactions [with him] should be clearly defined." Or, as one writer put it, it took "twenty men to watch him." That made him an ideal leader for San Francisco, which elected him mayor six months after his arrival.[57]

At the end of 1855, Garrison did not know about Vanderbilt's campaign to buy control of Accessory Transit, which was just beginning to unfold on the far side of the continent. But he did know about Walker's victory. So he paid close attention when Edmund Randolph, one of Walker's closest friends, walked into his office on the southeastern corner of Sacramento and Leidesdorff streets in San Francisco. The thirty-five-year-old scion of one of Virginia's first families and an early California lawmaker, Randolph would become the link between Garrison, Morgan, and Walker—the man who would threaten Vanderbilt with financial disaster and throw into chaos one of the primary lines of communication with California. And he would do it all out of greed.

Randolph explained to Garrison, quite candidly, that he intended to profit from his friend Walker's conquest of Nicaragua. "I told him that it seemed to me inevitable that the Accessory Transit Company would be abolished," Randolph recalled; inevitable, that is, after Randolph spoke to Walker about the matter. But Walker would need a replacement company to bring arms and men from the United States. Randolph would later testify that he told Garrison, "I believed that I could obtain General Walker's influence with the new government to grant me the [new] charter in preference to anybody else." If Garrison threw his support behind the fili-buster movement, then Randolph promised to sell the transit rights to him, as a private individual. In essence, Randolph aspired to be Nica-ragua's own "dummy," in the proud tradition of the California steamship business.[58]

Garrison indignantly declined, but Randolph's insouciance gave him pause. "If things should take that twine," Randolph recalled him musing, "he did not wish to be involved in the ruin. . . . He would do nothing what-ever against the company, but if they fell wanted to save himself." Garri-son believed that Morgan remained in charge of the company, and he worried that Morgan would think that he had betrayed him if he gave in to Randolph's plot. But the wily Garrison was up to the challenge. When Randolph sailed for Nicaragua on December 5, Garrison sent along two agents (one of them his son, William R.). If Walker approved Randolph's plan, they were to buy the transit rights, and William was to go to New York to bring Morgan into the new line.[59]

Less than two weeks later, Walker welcomed his friend with joy. "The friendship between Randolph . . . and Walker," the filibuster wrote, "was of a character not to be expressed by words; but the existence of such a sentiment . . . is essential for an understanding of the perfect confidence which marked their acts in reference to the Transit."[60] Walker listened closely as Randolph outlined a case for revoking Accessory Transit's cor-porate charter. It existed to aid the original canal company, he argued, but the canal had been abandoned. It had failed to pay the state its $10,000 in dues for 1855. And it never had paid the 10 percent of its profits. Walker accepted the indictment without question.

There were solid arguments against these charges. Accessory Transit was a separate entity from the canal company (which had until 1861 to build a canal). It still had time to pay its 1855 dues; more than that, it had cause to withhold the money, since the legitimacy of the new government remained in question, and the United States refused to recognize it. Fur-thermore, the company was then negotiating with representatives of the old government over the unpaid 10 percent. Finally, Nicaragua previously had assigned all payments to Thomas Manning, a British merchant who had lent the state a great deal of money. Randolph, however, was not adjudicating—he was prosecuting. He freely admitted that he wanted "a grant for myself of a charter of a similar nature" so he could sell it to Garrison.[61]

By coincidence, Walker was looking for a legal justification for killing the company. He had just learned that White previously had sent a small armed force to aid the Conservatives against a completely different fili-buster. Curiously, this short-lived body of some fifty mercenaries would be overlooked in all the press coverage of this episode. In Walker's mind, it was decisive. Accessory Transit had taken up arms on the side of his enemies; even before Randolph's arrival, he had concluded to destroy it.[62]

By the end of December, William Garrison finalized negotiations for a new transit company. Walker would grant Randolph the exclusive right to carry passengers and freight across Nicaragua. Randolph would sell that right to Cornelius Garrison for an undetermined sum. Garrison would bring Morgan into the new line, and transport reinforcements to Nicaragua for free. Walker would seize Accessory Transit's steamboats, steamships, and other property, and give them to Garrison and Morgan. William left for New York to inform Morgan, and his fellow agent returned to San Francisco to secure Garrison's approval. Walker held off on the revocation of the charter until everything was in place.[63] News of a coup of this scale would be explosive; they had to time the announcement very carefully to deny the Accessory Transit officials any hope of stopping them.

The chief Accessory Transit official would soon be Vanderbilt, who purchased shares and drew up plans for a monopoly in happy ignorance of the looming disaster. As 1855 drew to a close, his world had suddenly become a very different place. He had grown accustomed to ruling his own fate, with money, guile, and force of will. Now his future was being driven by a quiet, fanatical man and his scheming friend, who wielded the one thing he lacked: armed force. To survive the impending conflagration, he would need armed force of his own.

Chapter Eleven

VANDERBILT

"To see a vessel handsomely launched, gives one a feeling akin to the enjoyment of a new poem," wrote a correspondent for the *New York Times*. "To stand close enough to feel the wind as she rushes past, especially if she is a magnificently large and beautiful boat, is like hearing the *Odyssey* from the mouth of an expert reader—only at the launch all the thrill and the enthusiasm and enjoyment are compressed into a single brief minute." New York was a great shipbuilding center, so its residents knew that experience well; but they had never seen a launch like the one the reporter described.

As nine o'clock in the morning on December 10, 1855, thousands crowded the waterfront near the Simonson shipyard (which had relocated across the East River to Greenpoint early in the year). Some had come great distances to see the spectacle that was about to unfold; even the Brooklyn ferry paused on its crossing to afford its passengers a view. They cheered in the cold winter air as an immense hull slid down the enormous wooden stocks into the dark waters.

It was the largest steamship ever constructed. A "gigantic steamer," the *Brooklyn Eagle* called it; a "monster," said the *Times*; a "leviathan of the deep," declared *Scientific American*. "Four tolerable sized tugs—two on each side—appeared beside her, like dog-fish beside a whale," and towed it to the dock where its hull would be coppered. Its statistics staggered the writers who reported them: with a length of 335 feet, a capacity of well over five thousand tons, and sidewheels of forty-two feet, it carried sixty tons of bolts and ninety-four of wrought-iron straps to bolster its massive wooden beams. Other Atlantic steamers had three decks, but this one had five, looming over every ship in the harbor. It was so enormous, so powerful, so threatening to its competitors, that its owner and builder named it after himself: he christened it the *Vanderbilt*.[1]

Of all of the *Vanderbilt*'s eye-rubbing figures, perhaps the most telling was its cost. The Commodore had spent some $700,000 on its hull, and by the time he installed the plush sofas, carved rosewood, and titanic twin engines, he would pay out more than $900,000. This sum suggests that the Mercantile Agency sorely underestimated his wealth when it guessed that he was worth $5 million—for not even the risk-taking Commodore would have devoted almost 20 percent of his entire fortune to just one ship.[2] But the great cost of the *Vanderbilt* does reveal his confidence. He constructed this ship to compete on the Atlantic; he was staking a huge sum on his ability to defeat the heavily subsidized Collins and Cunard lines. Then again, no one in the steamship business could calculate the costs, the risks, the profits as accurately as Vanderbilt.

As 1855 drew to a close, his calculations had grown intricate and vast, as he plotted to take control of America's steamship traffic to Europe and California. Soon he would launch a fresh lobbying campaign in Washington to strip Collins of his mail contract and subsidy. In the California business, he polished his arrangements with Marshall Roberts and William Aspinwall to create a consolidated monopoly that encompassed Panama and Nicaragua. Vanderbilt went to Washington to meet with Secretary of State Marcy, who endorsed their proposal to transfer the California mail contract on the Atlantic side to Accessory Transit after Vanderbilt took control and had consolidated it with the U.S. Mail Steamship Company.

Returning to New York, Vanderbilt continued to buy Transit shares, alongside Aspinwall and Roberts, until they controlled forty thousand—a majority of the total of 78,000. Charles Morgan could see his doom more clearly than anyone. On December 21, he resigned as director. Vanderbilt took his seat on the board, and planned to take over as agent after the new year. It seemed like he had accounted for everything.[3]

CHRISTMAS EVE GAVE VANDERBILT a rare gift: Joseph White on his figurative knees. At half past two in the afternoon, White burst into Vanderbilt's office (now at 5 Bowling Green) and begged for help. Not for the first time, the lawyer's mouth had gotten him into trouble. He had struck a deal with Parker H. French, William Walker's representative, to carry filibuster recruits to Nicaragua—as peaceful emigrants rather than armed soldiers, to avoid an infraction of the neutrality act, which barred private citizens from fighting against countries with which the nation was at peace. Each "emigrant" would count toward the company's debt to Nicaragua at a rate of $20 each.[4] On this point, it is difficult to find fault, even with the slippery White, for Walker literally held the transit route hostage. Little did White—or even French—realize that Walker had decided to destroy the company instead.

White's dealings with the federal government were less defensible. Because of the Crampton affair—an attempt by the British minister to recruit American citizens to fight in the Crimean War—the administration now enforced the neutrality act to the fullest. Despite sympathy in the cabinet for Walker, President Pierce refused to recognize Walker's government, or French as the Nicaraguan minister, and issued orders to block the departure of filibuster reinforcements.[5] U.S. Attorney John McKeon had written to White, asking him to prevent one hundred or so men whom French had recruited from boarding the Accessory Transit ship *Northern Light*. White had rebuffed him with words that stunned the cabinet. "The Transit Company is a corporate body, created by the law of Nicaragua," he had written. "We owe allegiance to the Government of Nicaragua." McKeon had then presented Pierce's order to hold the *Northern Light* in port. Arrogant as ever, White had snapped that he didn't "care a damn for the President of the United States, or his dispatches." In that case, McKeon had said, he would impound the ship.

And that brought White into Vanderbilt's office. Just two days before, the Commodore had returned to the Accessory Transit board of directors; though he had not yet assumed any management role, he clearly was taking control. In a state of panic, White presented his dilemma. If he was forced to stop the ship, he fretted, he would strand hundreds of paying passengers and damage the line's reputation. "No, you must not do any such thing," Vanderbilt replied. "Go down and ascertain the nature of the process exactly, and if I can assist you, I will."[6]

Mayhem reigned at the dock. A mob swarmed the ship and the pier—a mob of men who flocked to join Walker's forces in Nicaragua, a mob of desperate denizens of Five Points. Largely Irish and entirely poor, they reflected sweeping changes in the city over the past ten years, as it had filled with refugees from the potato famine. They came to New York because it had become the primary transportation hub of North America, thanks to geography, economic history, and the diligent efforts of Vanderbilt and other steamboat, steamship, and railroad entrepreneurs. Long gone was the Manhattan of unspecialized countinghouses and striving artisans that Vanderbilt had settled in during the War of 1812; in its place was rising a polarized island of the aristocratic and the laboring poor, who struggled to earn enough for tenement rent and to remit a few shillings back to Europe. French's promise of land, livestock, and wages in Nicaragua had brought them by the score to the *Northern Light*. When McKeon went on deck to search for arms, a riot erupted; at one point, the ship set sail only to be intercepted by a revenue cutter and forced back. In the end, Vanderbilt dispatched Horace Clark to post a $100,000 bond for the steamer, and it was allowed to depart.[7]

To Vanderbilt, the sailing of the *Northern Light* was a sign not of trouble, but of his ability to settle Accessory Transit's many difficulties. Starting on New Year's Day of 1856, he ticked through a number of steps to set everything right. He convinced his estranged son-in-law, Daniel Allen, to compromise his lawsuit, and advanced $70,000 to the company to meet a cash shortfall. On January 3, he took direct command as general agent. Two days later he finalized his monopoly-making agreement with Roberts and Aspinwall. Amid a howling blizzard that piled up snow in horse-high drifts in the streets, Vanderbilt left for Washington to press for the transfer of the mail contract to Accessory Transit. On his return to New York, he continued to buy shares. "The Commodore does not hesitate to predict that the stock will go as high, if not higher, than it was when he left it, say 32, and that it is worth much more," the *New York Tribune* reported. Morgan had been short-selling it, but Vanderbilt's bull campaign now forced him to cover his sales contracts at a loss.[8]

An intense cold followed the snowstorm. Horse-drawn omnibuses (their wheels replaced by sleigh runners) slid through the streets almost empty of passengers as temperatures plunged to two degrees below zero. But Vanderbilt thrived. On January 30, he assumed the company's presidency. He promptly sent a letter to U.S. Attorney McKeon, promising to prevent filibusters from going to Nicaragua. (He was sincere; though he inherited the agreement to carry "emigrants" at $20 each, the best-informed supporters of Walker believed him to be an intractable foe of the filibusters from the beginning.) And he renewed his appeal to Congress for the California mail contract.[9]

What Vanderbilt did not know was that William Garrison had arrived from Nicaragua in the middle of the month; that he had informed Morgan of the deal with Randolph and Walker; and that Morgan had agreed to join in a new line. Vanderbilt did not know either that, on February 18, President Rivas obediently revoked the Accessory Transit charter and granted the rights to Randolph; and that a copy of the decree was rushed to Morgan by a private messenger, who reached New York a little over a week later. Vanderbilt had walked into a gigantic trap.[10]

STARTING IN FEBRUARY, Charles Morgan began to act very strangely. He was never a man to repeat a failed strategy, yet again he began to short-sell Accessory Transit stock. He sold it for as little as 21, on terms that gave him up to four months to make delivery. Vanderbilt took every share that Morgan offered. The financial columns of the press found Morgan's strategy mystifying. "As the length of the Commodore's purse is proverbial," wrote the *New York Tribune*, "the result of such a contest can scarcely be doubted." Vanderbilt carried the share price back up over 23, but Morgan redoubled his campaign, selling ten thousand shares short on March 4 alone. He seemed to have gone insane. Vanderbilt's ring reportedly controlled 68,000 out of a total of 78,000 shares. Morgan, it seemed, had cornered himself.[11]

Early on the morning of Thursday, March 13, news reached New York that Walker had revoked Accessory Transit's corporate charter, seized its property within Nicaragua, and granted the transit rights to Randolph. It was rumored that a new line would be established by Garrison and Morgan. "The telegraphic despatches from New Orleans fell upon Wall Street like a bombshell," the *New York Herald* reported. Walker's "coup d'état," the *New York Times* observed, "has created a greater excitement in Wall Street, among stock jobbers, than any event of the past ten years." Everyone rushed to sell, instantly knocking the share price down by a third. At the head of the swarm that scurried off the ship was Joseph White. He had received a private telegram with the news that same morning, and had rushed out to find his broker. "White sold out about $100,000 of his Transit stock the instant he received news," the *Times* reported.[12]

Vanderbilt faced the gravest crisis of his life to date. No catastrophe—not the great fires of 1835 or 1845, not the Panic of 1837, not the Schuyler fraud—had been so sudden, so deliberate, so thoroughly beyond his control. And yet, he did not sell out. What distinguished him in the moment of crisis was his self-command; characteristically, he prepared a counterattack on multiple fronts. He began with a trip to Washington. He met with Secretary of State Marcy and urged the administration to intervene in Nicaragua to "sustain the rights of American citizens." He wrote a letter to Marcy for public consumption, refuting Walker's pretext, taken from Randolph, for annulling the Accessory Transit charter. He sent a similar letter to Senator John M. Clayton, the former secretary of state, who took to the Senate floor to denounce Walker and his high-handed acts.[13]

Despite Vanderbilt's personal lobbying, the administration chose to do nothing. In some respects, its inaction is difficult to understand. This was a national crisis: a private American citizen had seized control of a foreign country, attacked a major corporation, and temporarily shut down a strategically vital link between the Atlantic and Pacific coasts of the United States. But the cabinet was frozen by its divisions. Like so many other Southerners, Secretary of War Jefferson Davis supported Walker, hoping to increase the territory open to slavery. But even antifilibuster cabinet members refused to help Vanderbilt, because they suspected Accessory Transit of having assisted Walker. Most important, White's insolence remained "fresh in the minds of all," according to the *New York Times*. White had claimed that the company owed allegiance only to Nicaragua, the administration grumbled—so let it appeal to Nicaragua.[14]

Stymied in the capital, Vanderbilt embarked on what can only be called an independent foreign policy. In the months ahead, his negotiations with foreign powers and deployment of secret agents abroad would prove far weightier than the acts of the federal government.

First, the Accessory Transit board voted on March 17 to give him "full powers to conduct all such negotiations and do such acts as in his judgment might be necessary." Next, he announced the closing of this route to California. "THE NICARAGUA LINE IS WITHDRAWN FOR THE PRESENT," he wrote. "I do not consider passengers or the property of American citizens safe on the transit of the Isthmus." Then he went to see Aspinwall and Roberts. In place of their foiled plan for a monopoly, they reached a new agreement: as long as the Nicaragua route remained closed, Pacific Mail and U.S. Mail would pay Accessory Transit $40,000 a month to lay up its ships and forgo competition via Panama. The contract was strictly oral. It would spark outrage when it emerged, but it was in many ways merely an alteration of their existing plans.[15]

Most important, Vanderbilt opened talks with the republics neighboring Nicaragua. Alarmed by Walker's success—and the threat of further filibustering—they concluded to oust the usurper. Costa Rica's pro-British president, Juan Rafael Mora, proved particularly determined to overthrow Walker. Vanderbilt agreed to cooperate.

Now he had to save and recover the company's property. *Save* would be the operative word for the moment. Walker had seized only the boats and other material within Nicaragua's borders, but the steamships remained vulnerable. Vanderbilt had withdrawn the Atlantic steamers, but he still had to protect those on the Pacific. He ordered son-in-law James Cross to sail immediately for San Francisco to take them out of harm's way. He also sent engineer Hosea Birdsall to Greytown with orders to take possession of the steamboats on the San Juan River—a potentially decisive blow.[16]

For the moment, the fate of Vanderbilt's company rested in the hands of his two agents. They sailed off to war, armed only with their wits.

SOMEWHERE OFF THE WESTERN COAST of Central America, sometime near the end of March, James Cross intercepted the Accessory Transit ship *Cortez* as it steamed south toward Nicaragua. He hailed it from the deck of a Pacific Mail steamer heading north from Panama, and transferred over in a small boat. Once on board, he presented his orders to its commander, Captain Collins. He was to land his passengers at Panama, not San Juan del Sur, to prevent Walker from capturing the *Cortez*.

The trouble was, Cross and Collins still felt obliged to stop at San Juan del Sur. They probably needed to refuel, as the port was the company's only regular coaling station south of San Francisco. Cross also wanted to take that coal out of Walker's reach, for it was highly valuable in this remote region. And William Garrison was aboard the *Cortez*, returning to Nicaragua after reporting to his father; Cross did not want to awaken his suspicions. The trick would be to remove the coal without losing the ship.

On April 1, the 220-foot paddlewheeler nosed into the little horseshoe harbor. Captain Collins ordered the pilot to drop anchor near the two sailboats that held the coal. Garrison rowed to shore, where a hundred or so filibuster troops waited. From the other direction came a boat with four of Walker's officers. They boarded the *Cortez* and announced that they had come to seize the ship. Collins graciously escorted them down to his cabin, where Cross waited with a luxurious meal and "an unlimited supply of champagne," according to the *New York Express*. The filibusters popped cork after cork, believing that they were waiting for the passengers to land. As they drank with Cross, Collins ordered lines attached to the two coal hulks. The *Cortez* drifted silently out to sea with the ebb tide, its two consorts in tow. Once clear of the bay, the steam engines rumbled to life, and the drunken filibusters learned that they were trapped. The *Cortez* sailed to Panama, where Cross arranged for the passengers to complete their journey to New York in a U.S. Mail steamship on the Atlantic.[17]

Cross's coup infuriated Walker. Costa Rica had just declared war on his regime, and he had counted on recruits from among the *Cortez*'s passengers. William Garrison admitted that Cross had taken him by surprise, and that his father might not be ready to start the new line for another six weeks—a long time to wait for reinforcements.[18]

Cross steamed north in the *Cortez*, intercepting the *Uncle Sam* on the way and diverting it to Panama. In San Francisco, he delivered a letter from Vanderbilt to Cornelius Garrison. Vanderbilt offered to let Garrison continue as the San Francisco agent for Accessory Transit, "on the condition that neither Mr. Garrison nor any of his family should have anything to do with any other steamships running in a line between New York and San Francisco," Cross reported. Vanderbilt's attempt to co-opt Garrison was cunning. It remained unclear whether the rumors of Garrison's betrayal were true; the offer was meant to prevent his defection or force him to reveal himself.

Garrison's reply was equally shrewd. "He freely and without any reservation accepted the offer," Cross said, "and seemed to feel—and so expressed himself—very grateful for a continuance of the confidence which Mr. Vanderbilt placed in him when he first took the agency of the company in San Francisco." Thus Garrison bought time to put his new line into operation.

Before Cross returned home, he heard warnings about Garrison. "I was repeatedly cautioned by my friends in that city not to place too much reliance upon Mr. Garrison's professions," he wrote. "Yet . . . I left San

Francisco with the fullest possible assurances from him that he was and would remain faithful to the company."[19]

DESPITE GARRISON'S SUBTERFUGE, Cross succeeded in his mission. Hosea Birdsall did not. Even worse, by carrying out the Commodore's orders he nearly embroiled the United States and Great Britain in war.

Birdsall arrived at Greytown on the night of April 16 aboard the *Orizaba*, the first Atlantic steamship in Morgan's new Nicaragua line. As the passengers transferred to a riverboat, Birdsall rowed over to Punta Arenas to see the Accessory Transit agent, whom Walker had left in charge of the company's property. The agent was a burly fifty-one-year-old engineer who stood six feet tall and wore an iron-gray beard. His name was Joseph N. Scott. Birdsall had every reason to expect Scott's cooperation. In 1821 Vanderbilt had hired Scott as a deckhand on the *Bellona*, and had taught him the ways of steam engines over the succeeding decades. But when Birdsall demanded control of the machine shops, coal, and steamboats, he refused to give them up. Scott had a personal agenda. Years before, he had advanced nearly $20,000 of his own money to purchase a lake steamboat, *La Virgen*, for Accessory Transit; despite his repeated pleas, the company's management had never reimbursed him. Scott had no love for Walker, whose men had threatened to shoot him more than once; but, he told Birdsall, if he wasn't repaid he would never give up the property.[20]

Scott's recalcitrance would prove decisive for Nicaragua, its neighbors, and Cornelius Vanderbilt. Had he complied with Birdsall's order, Garrison and Morgan would have been unable to conduct the transit between the Atlantic and the Pacific. They never would have started a new line, cutting off Walker from any reinforcements.

But Vanderbilt had given Birdsall a means of hurdling this unexpected obstacle. Through talks with Costa Rican diplomats, the Commodore knew that Nicaragua's neighbors were planning to invade. So he had handed Birdsall a letter (over the signature of outgoing Accessory Transit president Thomas Lord), authorizing him to ask for help from the Royal Navy, should the filibusters attack Punta Arenas. "You are authorized to ask for the assistance of the commander of any man of war of her Britannic Majesty's Navy in the port," it read. "The object of the Transit Company is to prevent accessions of filibusters to Walker's force, pending his hostilities with Costa Rica, and to effect this purpose no pains must be spared, no effort left untried." The letter shows how well Vanderbilt had analyzed Walker's vulnerabilities, and how explicitly he had allied himself with Costa Rica. "Unless our boats are seized by the filibusters," it continued, "they cannot get into the interior—and without large accessions Walker must fail, and Costa Rica be saved."

Remembering these instructions, Birdsall rowed out to a British sloop-of-war, the HMS *Eurydice*, anchored nearby. At his urging, its captain, John W. Tarleton, boarded the *Orizaba*, stopped the unloading of passengers, and reviewed the waybook, which listed the passengers' destinations. He could identify no filibusters and refused to intervene. Birdsall had failed.[21]

For all of Tarleton's diffidence, the affair became an international incident. When it emerged that Vanderbilt had asked the Royal Navy to interfere with an American vessel, the *New York Times* called it "almost too incredible for belief." The outrage went to the top. At the time, President Pierce and Secretary of State Marcy were seriously contemplating war with Britain over the Crampton affair. The *Orizaba* incident, coming amid this crisis, embarrassed and angered them. "The President and Secretary," the *Times* wrote, "are much incensed at this conduct of Vanderbilt & White."[22]

To make matters worse, Pierce had just recognized Walker's government. It was U.S. policy to recognize the de facto government of any state, he declared; and Nicaragua did have a native president, Patricio Rivas. But politics played a role. A presidential election loomed in the fall, and Pierce wished to be renominated by the largely pro-Walker Democratic Party. He would never side with Vanderbilt.[23]

The aftermath of Birdsall's mission underscored the near impossibility of Vanderbilt's position. He found himself at the center of competing interests, perfectly aligned so that his every action offended every party. Federal officials found it almost impossible to differentiate between legitimate emigrants and volunteers for Walker's army, but they condemned Vanderbilt for the same inability. If the company had declined French's terms for carrying those "emigrants," Walker would have revoked the corporate charter; but when Walker revoked it anyway, the federal government refused to intervene.[24] Denied U.S. protection, Vanderbilt appealed to the British, only to be blamed for that act as well. The Commodore had learned early on in life that he had to protect his own on his own. Now that lesson was pounded painfully deep. Even in far-off Central America, Vanderbilt could rely on no one but himself.

IT WAS A YEAR OF REVOLUTION, insurrection, and mayhem.

On April 15, as the hapless passengers of the *Cortez* waited in Panama for a train across the isthmus, one of them got into a fight with a Panamanian outside a hotel. The quarrel sparked an explosion of rage and frustration among the native population at the U.S. presence. A mob of hundreds—including many policemen—attacked American citizens wherever they could, forcing them to take refuge in the Panama Railroad depot. U.S. consul Thomas Ward estimated that the rioters killed fifteen and wounded fifty.[25]

In Nicaragua, Walker launched a revolution against a revolution against his revolution. President Rivas, long his quiescent puppet, suddenly declared Walker "an enemy of Nicaragua" and fled to the protection of an antifilibuster alliance consisting of Guatemala, El Salvador, and Honduras. With Rivas's support, the allied army marched over the northern border and advanced on León. Walker responded with a rigged election for the presidency at the end of June. He won by a landslide.[26]

Bloodshed wracked the United States as well, as tensions over the extension of slavery boiled over in the Kansas Territory, where rival militias of free-soil jayhawkers battled pro-slavery border ruffians from Missouri. On May 21, 1856, David Rice Atchison—recently a U.S. senator from Missouri—led eight hundred of those ruffians in the looting of Lawrence, the jayhawker capital. On May 24, John Brown and his sons murdered five pro-slavery settlers. A low-level civil war broke out, eventually costing two hundred lives.[27]

And then there was San Francisco. In the few years since the gold rush began, the city's government had fallen under the control of David C. Broderick, a Democratic Party boss. He ruled through fraudulent votes, rampant corruption, and such enforcers as Yankee Sullivan, who (like many of Broderick's men) had relocated from New York. But the city's merchants had grown unhappy as municipal graft and debt damaged their own credit in the East. On May 14, after one of Broderick's men gunned down a crusading newspaper editor, the city's exasperated businessmen revived the Committee of Vigilance. They targeted Broderick's organization, hanging two of his men and banishing twenty-eight more in short order. Broderick escaped, but Yankee Sullivan hanged himself in his cell on June 1, shortly after his arrest.[28]

Cornelius Garrison thought that this was an excellent moment to leave town. He almost certainly had been elected to his term as mayor with the support of the Democratic machine, and he was not exactly a champion of reform. On June 21, after a political operative named Walter L. Chrysler attempted to blackmail him, Garrison departed for New York—just as the vigilance committee took full power.[29]

In July, all the leading players in the Nicaraguan transit drama, except Walker, had gathered in New York: Garrison, Morgan, Vanderbilt, and Randolph. Now came the ultimate absurdity in this theater of the absurd. On arriving from Nicaragua, Randolph tried to sell his transit grant twice. First, on July 16, he and Garrison agreed on a price: $10,000 in cash, 50 cents per passenger, and a 2.5 percent commission on nonspecie freight. (The steamboats and other property in Nicaragua, held by the state, would be paid for with credits for carrying filibuster reinforcements.) Ten days later, Randolph brazenly offered Vanderbilt the *same* transit contract, in return for various fees that amounted to $300,000. The *New York Tribune* aptly characterized Vanderbilt's reaction: "Give three hundred thousand dollars cash for a grant which Walker might find plenty of pretexts for revoking the next day, just as he had revoked the former one!"

Rebuffed by Vanderbilt, Randolph fell back on his original plan. Morgan agreed to take the Atlantic half of the transit contract, formalizing the arrangements already in operation. Walker approved all of Randolph's actions; as he wrote on August 20, "The transit business is well settled at last." But Vanderbilt had not yet begun to fight.[30]

IT WAS A YEAR FOR WILLPOWER. In 1856, the sixty-two-year-old Commodore had to muster all of his famous force of mind to master the crisis—or *crises*, for the Accessory Transit Company represented only one of his many operations. In 1853, for example, he and Marshall Roberts had purchased the Vallecillo silver mine in Mexico, originally discovered by the Spanish but abandoned after Mexican independence. They had put to work a corps of men to reopen it, and in 1856 it produced silver again— at least $1,000 worth per day, with expenses of only $50 per day.[31]

Vanderbilt needed such resources in this year of trouble and strife. On March 23, one of his oldest and most valuable allies, Nelson Robinson, fell dead as he left church. The stock exchange closed early the next day in his honor, and Daniel Drew served as executor of his estate.[32] Vanderbilt also suffered a setback in court in his fight to force the New Haven Railroad to acknowledge his "spurious" stock. And lawsuits against the Accessory Transit Company by empty-handed creditors multiplied. The Commodore took extreme measures to keep the company alive. He corresponded with Marcy and Pierce; he bought up $118,000 of the company's unpaid bonds (at ninety cents on the dollar); and he expended more than $400,000 of his own money to cover company expenditures.[33] Now president, Vanderbilt drove White off the Accessory Transit board and brought in his son-in-law Cross, ally Frank Work, and various other trusted men.

Troubles mounted. In June, after Garrison finally put his new Nicaragua transit line into operation, Pacific Mail halted its monthly $40,000 subsidy, refusing to pay for a monopoly that no longer existed. Then the U.S. marshal seized the Accessory Transit steamships in San Francisco for alleged indebtedness, forcing Vanderbilt to dispatch an agent to untangle that distant mess. He began to take personal ownership of the steamships as repayment for his advances, rather than let them fall into the hands of other creditors (which would have made them unavailable should he restart the line).[34]

Remarkably, even in the midst of the Accessory Transit imbroglio Vanderbilt pursued his campaign against the Collins Line on the Atlantic. There, too, he faced enormous obstacles—none larger than the *Adriatic*, launched by Collins on April 7. It was the biggest ship ever built, nineteen feet and eight hundred tons greater than the *Vanderbilt*, though late design changes would keep it out of service for over a year. As the *New York Times* wrote, it was "at once a source of pride and mortification."[35] By contrast, Vanderbilt gave almost daily attention to his namesake ship as cranes at the Allaire Works lowered into the hull the twin engines, each 2,500 horsepower, and four boilers weighing sixty-two tons apiece.

Late in July, the Commodore and several members of his family boarded his new steamship and set sail from New York. Despite the enormous size and power of the engines, "the one thing that struck us most strongly was the complete absence of all vibratory *jarring*," one observer wrote—a testimony to expert construction. "Twenty-four firemen, 18 coal-heavers, 4 engineers, and 3 water-tenders minister to her capacity for the production of steam," the *New York Times* reported, "while 8 cooks, 34 waiters, 3 porters, and an efficient steward" tended to the needs of its passengers. Apart from the family, the *Vanderbilt* carried no passengers, but it probably had its full compliment of cooks and waiters—for this was a lobbying trip.

On July 22, the *Vanderbilt* dropped anchor off Greenleaf Point, where the Anacostia River poured into the Potomac. The next day, William H. Seward stood on the floor of the Senate and invited his colleagues to inspect the ship, to judge whether they should give the Commodore the European mail contract. "Immense crowds visited her," the *Times* reported. Vanderbilt welcomed aboard representatives and senators, as well as President Pierce and his cabinet, who "were treated to a sumptuous entertainment on board." The ship steamed home on July 27 to receive its finishing touches; the Commodore remained behind to press his advantage with Congress.

The ship made a suitable impression. Congress was growing uneasy over the subsidy for the Collins Line, which failed to float the required number of ships. Collins alienated even his own lobbyists. "I am coming there in season to help *defeat* Collins this year," wrote former House clerk Benjamin B. French. In August, Congress gave Collins notice that in six months it would roll back the subsidy increase it had previously granted. It was far from a complete victory for Vanderbilt, but it was progress.[36]

BACK IN 1841, Captain William Comstock had observed that Vanderbilt wielded every possible weapon when in combat, that he strove for any

possible advantage. This was never more true than in 1856. The war over
the Nicaragua transit was proving more complicated, more perplexing,
than any he ever had fought or would fight—even more than the struggle
that had culminated in *Gibbons v. Ogden*. Cross had failed to prevent
Garrison's defection; Birdsall had failed to forestall Morgan's start of the
line; and Washington had refused his appeals for help. Indeed, this was
far more than a metaphorical war, but a real war of guns and bullets, and
it was not going well. Vanderbilt's Costa Rican allies had invaded, occupied the city of Rivas, and defeated another of Walker's frontal assaults on
April 11, only to fall victim to a cholera outbreak that forced them to
retreat.[37] But the Commodore planned counterattacks on both the international level and the personal.

On September 4, Garrison found himself under arrest. He was still in
New York, where Accessory Transit filed a suit against him "for alleged
frauds . . . amounting to over five hundred thousand" dollars (according to
the *Chicago Tribune*), committed when he was the company's San Francisco agent. In the evening, after he posted the bail of $150,000, Garrison
went to 10 Washington Place, where he tried to employ his wiles against
the Commodore.

"He insinuated that if I would participate with him and Charles Morgan . . . [in] the Walker grant . . . we could make a good business of it, to
the exclusion of the Transit Company," Vanderbilt reported. "My reply
was, that my action in this matter had been wholly for the benefit of the
Transit Company and its stockholders, and nothing could induce me to
swerve from that course. At this he recoiled, and observed that he did not
mean to make any insinuations of the kind." Vanderbilt's choice of words
says everything about his reaction to this proposition. To him, the word
insinuate distinguished the talk of a crooked businessman from a "smart"
but honest one. "I then told him he must clear up his character as regarded
his conduct towards the company," he wrote, "and when done, then I
would be willing to refer his accounts to arbitration."[38]

Vanderbilt's reponse deserves notice, for he has been misunderstood by
historians and contemporaries alike as an amoral creature, ready to seize
the main chance under all circumstances. "His over-reaching disposition
makes people shy of him," R. G. Dun & Co. noted four years later.
Undoubtedly he possessed immense personal force, and pursued his personal interests more aggressively than anyone; but he lived by a code, and
despised those who did not. As president of Accessory Transit, he held a
position of trust, and he drew heavily on his personal resources to fulfill
his responsibilities. In his own mind, at least, he was ever a man of
honor.[39]

What is surprising is that so few others understood that. Everyone, it seems, tried to make Vanderbilt buy what had been stolen from him—even a friend of his, Domingo de Goicouria.* The fifty-one-year-old Goicouria belonged to a community of Cuban exiles in New York who plotted to free the island from Spanish rule. He had supplied Walker with Cuban independence fighters; in return, Walker named him minister to Great Britain, and ordered him to raise money in New Orleans on his way to London. Goicouria went to New York instead, where he discovered that Vanderbilt's enmity had frightened the city's merchants away from any connection with Walker. So Goicouria tried to convince the Commodore himself to buy the transit back—only to learn that Randolph had sold it to Garrison, much to Goicouria's outrage.[40]

Walker completed the alienation of Goicouria on September 22, when he reinstituted slavery in a blatant attempt to gain money and recruits from the Southern states. The antislavery Goicouria retaliated by publishing Walker's letters in the *New York Herald.* They staggered Walker's supporters, who had always believed that Nicaragua would be absorbed by the United States; now they learned that Walker hoped to *forestall* annexation, not only of Nicaragua but of Cuba as well. "Oh, no! that fine country is not fit for those barbarous Yankees," he wrote of Cuba. "What would such a psalm singing set do in the island?"[41]

The revelations also estranged the Pierce administration. Already it had withdrawn its recognition, after Walker named himself president; now the letters eliminated any chance it would reverse course. All this was good news for Vanderbilt. But Walker continued to attract significant support. A famous British soldier of fortune, Charles Henningsen, went to fight for him; Morgan sent artillery and ammunition by sailing ships, which the authorities did not inspect; and hundreds of recruits, many now from the South, still flocked to Nicaragua. But the Commodore had one more weapon to wield, one designed to turn the course of the war itself.[42]

Throughout the autumn of 1856, this drama played out in newspaper headlines and closed-door cabinet debates, in speeches on the Senate floor and noisy rallies. The nation's attention was simply riveted on Walker. But the public did not see Vanderbilt, as he secretly crafted a strategy to bring Walker down. It did not see Vanderbilt, as he quietly met with Costa Rican diplomat Luis Molina. It did not see Vanderbilt, as he quietly interviewed a tall, lean, sharp-chinned young man in a Panama hat, Sylvanus Spencer. It did not see Vanderbilt, as he quietly wrote instructions for Spencer, as he quietly dispatched him on a steamship to Central America in October.

---

* The modern spelling is "Goicuria," but this book will follow historic sources, both English and Spanish.

On October 15, the public got one quick glimpse of what went on in Vanderbilt's office. He testified in a lawsuit, one of the many against the Accessory Transit Company, and he spoke of his efforts to restore the corporation to possession of its property and its rights in Nicaragua. "I have corresponded with the Secretary of State and the President on the subject. The correspondence has continued till within the last two weeks, and is still in progress," he said. "I think the property will come out right for the stockholders. . . . I have had but one opinion on the subject. I am devoting my own means to bring the matter out right."[43]

IT IS A REMARKABLE FACT that the only foreign conflict involving the United States during the fifty years between the Mexican and the Spanish-American wars was fought by a private army of American civilians. True, they claimed that they were the army of Nicaragua and that Walker was president of that republic; but the charade fooled no one. Indeed, this foreign interloper accomplished a feat that had eluded the victors of countless civil wars: he reconciled Nicaragua's Liberal and Conservative parties, when Tomás Martínez arranged for a unity government under Rivas to fight the filibusters. Their combined forces won their first victory at San Jacinto hill, where they captured and hung Byron Cole—the man who had first convinced Walker to go to Nicaragua.

In many ways, Walker had been fighting for survival from the moment he executed General Corral. But in the summer of 1856 his situation grew more desperate. The allied army of some eight hundred Salvadorans, six hundred Hondurans, and five hundred Guatemalans had seized León on July 12, the very day that Walker declared himself president. There the advance halted as the allies squabbled.[44]

Walker's own army consisted of the duped, the drunk, and the depraved. The troops lacked blankets, disease ran rampant, wages were nonexistent. Men who finished their terms of service were forced to remain. "Walker even posted sentries at the gangplanks of departing steamers to cut off the possibility of escape," writes historian Robert E. May.[45] Walker's survival rested on one thing: a steady influx of fresh cannon fodder.

In November, the Costa Ricans launched a second invasion in the south. This Walker saw as the paramount danger, since it threatened his access to reinforcements. As he later wrote, "It was all-important to keep the Transit clear." On November 18, he decided to abandon Granada and fortify Rivas, which dominated the transit road.[46] He left behind a force under Charles Henningsen with orders to destroy the city. When the destruction began, the allies stopped dithering and attacked; close-range fighting raged in the streets for two weeks as the filibusters pillaged and burned. Walker finally returned with a steamboat, landed a relief force, and evacuated the embattled garrison. "Granada has ceased to exist," Henningsen reported. On leaving the smoking metropolis, he erected a sign that read, *"Aqui fue Granada"*—"Here was Granada."[47]

By December 20, Walker had concentrated the bulk of his army at Rivas and garrisoned key points along the transit route: Virgin Bay, San Carlos, Castillo Viejo, and Hipp's Point, where the Sarapiqui River flowed into the San Juan. When he looked over his situation, he felt reassured. True, he had abandoned the northern provinces, but cholera had driven out an invading army once before. Most important, he was expecting large contingents of fresh troops, due at Greytown at any moment. "Walker, *keeping his forces concentrated*, can maintain himself in Rivas," reported a U.S. naval officer who visited his encampment. "I have no hesitation in saying that if the external aids he has hitherto relied upon do not fail him, he will repel his enemies."

The key, of course, was the "external aids," the filibuster recruits. On January 2, 1857, the steamboat *San Carlos* departed Virgin Bay, carrying passengers for New York; Walker expected it or *La Virgen* to return with his reinforcements from the east. "In a few days," Walker wrote, "uneasiness was felt on account of the non-arrival of the steamers from the river." There were any number of reasons why the boat might be late, he told himself, as he waited, and waited, and began to dread.[48]

THE MAN WHO MADE WALKER WAIT was Sylvanus Spencer, acting on Vanderbilt's orders.

Spencer was a man adrift on the tide of fortune. Orphaned when very young, he was taken in by a family in a tough part of New York's Thirteenth Ward. The *New York Times* would write, "His boyhood is presumed to have been a hard one—at least he came out of it a very hard boy." He went to sea early on and rose rapidly in the often brutal society of sailors. As mate, he frequently punched recalcitrant subordinates. He talked freely and often, in a bit of a Yankee accent, as he strode the deck in his customary dark clothes and Panama hat.

The tide that carried Spencer toward Vanderbilt began to rise back on April 25, 1855, at the very moment when Walker was preparing to embark on his invasion of Nicaragua. On that day, the square-rigged *Sea Witch* sailed out of New York Harbor. It belonged to Howland & Aspinwall, the mercantile house of William Aspinwall, and was bound for Hong Kong "to take a cargo of coolies for Panama," the press reported. Its captain, by the name of Frazier, commanded a crew of twenty-three, and Spencer served as first mate. Once at sea, Frazier abused his mate, picking petty quarrels, giving demeaning orders, and belittling him in front of the men. On June 4, Spencer snapped. "By God, I took more from you this morning at the breakfast table than I ever did from any other man," he shouted. "If I continue the voyage in this ship, or if you do not send me on shore out of this ship, either you or me will have to die." The next morning, Spencer announced to the crew that he had found Captain Frazier bludgeoned to death in his bunk.

On December 19, 1855, Spencer stood trial for murder in the U.S. District Court in New York. The jury found him not guilty, because no one had witnessed the crime.[49] But the incident seems to have made other ship captains reluctant to hire him, so he drifted to Greytown, Nicaragua. "He asked me if I had any employment for him," Joseph N. Scott recalled. "He told me he was a sailor and would turn his hand to anything." First Spencer labored as a stevedore; then Scott made him the mate on one of the river steamboats, the *Machuca*. As such, he learned the river and Transit Company operations well. After four months in Nicaragua, Spencer returned to New York.[50]

At some point in 1856, he went to see Cornelius Vanderbilt. Spencer would later claim that he did so because he had inherited Accessory Transit stock from an uncle, but he may simply have been swimming with fortune's current. The Commodore would say nothing about their talk, but his calculations upon meeting Spencer are all too clear. His strategic assessment of Walker's situation had not changed, despite the failure of Birdsall's mission. If he could seize the steamboats on the San Juan River, he would block reinforcements from the Atlantic side. That also would stop passengers from crossing the isthmus, forcing Morgan and Garrison to withdraw their steamers (as they were not running a charity). He would, with one stroke, cut Walker off on both oceans. In Spencer, he found precisely the man for the mission. He was physically tough, accustomed to command, and, most important, intimately familiar with the terrain, the fortifications, and the steamboat operations. So Vanderbilt placed all his hopes—the fate of millions of dollars, of a critical channel of commerce to California, of a war involving six nations—in the hands of an acquitted murderer.[51]

On October 9, 1856, Spencer departed New York for Costa Rica. He carried an agreement that Vanderbilt had made with Luis Molina, the Costa Rican chargé d'affaires in the United States. In San José, Spencer met with President Juan Rafael Mora and explained the plan that Vanderbilt had drafted—and how it would benefit them both. The Commodore would get his property back, and Mora would cripple Walker's army. Mora was no fool; such a plan had occurred to him before. But Spencer offered two things the Costa Ricans lacked: a detailed knowledge of the Transit operations, and $40,000 from Vanderbilt to pay expenses.[52] Mora agreed to give Spencer some Costa Rican soldiers to carry out the mission; if he succeeded, General José Joaquín Mora, the president's brother, would follow with 1,100 men. If he failed, it would cost Mora little.

Spencer marched north out of San José with a work detachment, crossing the mountains to the headwaters of the San Carlos River, which flowed northeast into the San Juan. He and his carpenters felled trees and lashed together several large rafts to carry his detachment. On December 3, President Mora formally placed 250 troops under the command of "Captain S. M. Spencer," writing that they were "under your orders to carry out the military operations as you will think proper."[53]

On December 16, Spencer ordered his men into the rafts. They pushed out into the stream, drifting down under the rain-forest canopy that rose some two hundred feet above them, through heavy rain and dense humidity. Finally the current carried them into the wide San Juan. On the morning of December 22, he ordered them to pull the rafts into the mouth of a creek near the location of his first target: the filibuster fort at Hipp's Point. Hearing a steamboat churning upstream, he told everyone to lie down flat and be still. The boat chuffed up to their hiding spot, then continued on its way.

Spencer led his men through the forest to the rear of the fort. A Costa Rican scout shimmied up a tree, and scooted back down to report. He saw forty to fifty men, with two cannons—more than enough to defeat an attack, if the Costa Ricans lost the element of surprise. Silently the troops filed into position and crept up behind the unsuspecting filibusters. Spencer drew his revolver to fire the shot that would launch the assault.[54]

THE MOST IMPORTANT EVENTS may well be the quiet ones, the private ones. On November 26, for example, Corneil finally did something right in his father's eyes by marrying Ellen Williams of Hartford, Connecticut. It remains unclear how they met, but the Commodore heartily approved of "our dear Ellen," as he called her, and showed genuine warmth for her family. He and Sophia attended the wedding in the Hartford home of Ellen's father, Oliver E. Williams.[55]

Vanderbilt's existence was divided into public and private, the carefully concealed and the loudly promoted. In November, Texas newspapers announced that he had formed a steamboat-and-railroad line from New Orleans to Galveston in competition with Morgan's most lucrative business. On December 10, Vanderbilt went to Washington to attend the opening of the new Congress. "Railroad and steamboat robbers crowd the lobbies," the *New York Times* wrote. The House postal committee duly reported a bill to grant him the Atlantic mail contract. "A provision of this contract is that, in the event of this line not making as quick time as the Cunard steamships, $1,000 shall be deducted for every twelve hours' deficiency," the *Times* noted.[56]

Some of the Commodore's secrets were meant to go public. On Christmas Eve he wrote a letter to the stockholders of the Accessory Transit Company to prepare them for an impending revelation. He noted that the *Prometheus* had been attached in one of the many lawsuits and auctioned off that very day, and that he had bought it for the bargain price of $10,011. But he purchased it in their interest, to be ready to reopen the line at a moment's notice. "Present appearances indicate a realization of my hopes," he wrote, "that the company will be speedily restored to their rights."[57]

THE CRACK OF SPENCER'S GUNSHOT echoed through the rain forest, sending the Costa Ricans surging forward with fixed bayonets. Panic swept the filibusters. They had posted no sentries, never imagining an attack from the rear. The Costa Ricans speared them and shot them as they scrambled over the breastworks and slid down the riverbank. Perhaps half a dozen escaped alive. Spencer detailed a platoon of thirty or forty troops to hold the works; then he and the rest returned to the rafts.

At around two o'clock in the morning on December 24, Spencer and his men drifted into Greytown harbor. Silently they boarded four Accessory Transit steamboats anchored in front of the company buildings, and crept onto Punta Arenas. "At daylight an alarm was sounded at Punta Arenas . . . that the Costa Ricans were there," recalled Joseph Scott. "All the hands were called together to defend ourselves. . . . We organized into a company, with firearms, to retake the boats."

Though outnumbered ten to one, the iron-bearded Scott organized a counterattack, only to be interrupted by Captain John E. Erskine, commander of a squadron of British warships in the harbor. Erskine announced that he would not tolerate any violence on either side— thereby confirming Spencer's possession of the steamboats—though he did convince the Costa Ricans to evacuate the point.[58]

After the troops returned to the steamboats, Spencer strolled into Scott's office. It was almost exactly a year since he had first set foot there, begging for work. Now he commanded an armed force that was changing the course of the war. "I asked him what he was going to do with the steamers," Scott reported. "He said he meant to take them up the river. . . . [He said] I could do no further harm with them, meaning that I couldn't carry any more filibusters up the river."[59]

Spencer ordered the little fleet to put on steam and head up the river.

At the mouth of the San Carlos, he directed the smallest boat to turn into the tributary and notify General Mora of their success. Then Spencer used his knowledge of transit operations to bloodlessly capture the remaining steamboats and Castillo Viejo, one by one, giving the standard signals until he was close enough to surprise the crews and garrison with his Costa Rican detachment. But one target promised to be more difficult: the heavily fortified battery at San Carlos, where the San Juan River met Lake Nicaragua. After Spencer seized *La Virgen,* he loaded it with troops and ordered its engineer, William Wise, to put on all steam for San Carlos. Wise recalled that he nervously remarked that he would rather be put ashore in the wilderness than "risk his life in front of the heavy cannon stationed at the fort. To this Spencer replied that it was useless for [Wise] to talk, that he must get up steam and go up the river."[60]

On December 30, Spencer stopped the boat just below San Carlos and detailed a detachment of sixty troops. He ordered them to sneak behind the fort, approach as closely as possible, and wait for a signal. He planned to trick the garrison, but if he failed they were to launch an attack. The men rowed to shore in boats, and *La Virgen* continued to San Carlos. Spencer piloted the steamboat to its usual anchorage and gave the customary blast from the whistle. The fort answered in kind. A boat rowed out with a few filibusters and the garrison's commander, Captain Kruger, to pick up mail.

As Captain Kruger's men tied up their boat alongside *La Virgen,* Spencer leaned over the rail. "Is that you, Kruger?" he asked.

"Yes," came the reply.

"Come on board," Spencer said.

Kruger followed him to the top deck, "and was immediately surrounded by Costa Rican officers," he later reported, "who had been lying down flat on deck, concealed from view. Mr. Spencer then told me that he had taken all of the steamers and was in command of all the river." Spencer declared that he had seized the boats in the name of Commodore Vanderbilt, and he demanded the surrender of the fort. Kruger balked, but the steamboat crew told him about the Costa Rican force hidden in the trees. "Mr. Spencer told me (when I hestitated) that the innocent blood of my men would fall on my head, as we would certainly be put to death by the Costa Ricans," Kruger recalled. "I concluded to surrender."[61]

Spencer's coup was almost complete. Mora's army arrived on December 31, whereupon Spencer and a detachment of troops boarded a small riverboat to go find the *San Carlos,* the largest and last uncaptured lake steamer. On January 3, the two boats encountered each other on the upper reaches of the San Juan River. The result was a repeat of his previous encounters: Spencer gave the correct signals, the boats came alongside, and the Costa Rican soldiers rose from hiding, rifles ready. The *San Carlos*'s captain surrendered without a fight. Spencer went aboard and read aloud a proclamation from President Mora, promising safe passage to the passengers. He also tacked up a notice. "Gentlemen: Do not be deceived or induced to enter into any combination to take this boat out of my possession. I am amply prepared for any emergency that may arise. Keep quiet, behave as gentlemen should, and I pledge you my sacred word and honor to see you safe through to Greytown." The Costa Ricans posted a guard in the main saloon, behind a barricade of piled-up trunks and baggage.

Spencer had carried out Vanderbilt's plan with exceptional skill and courage. Apart from the brutal storming of Hipp's Point, he had used speed and guile to achieve a sweeping—and bloodless—victory. As the *San Carlos* steamed down the river, Charles Morgan's son-in-law, Israel Harris, came forward. "We had you once, now you have us," he said to Spencer. "We are even."[62]

Chapter Twelve

CHAMPION

"This famous pretended experiment for the spread of Anglo-Saxon enterprise and civilization at the point of a bayonet," declared the *New York Tribune*, "and for introducing free institutions into Central America through the medium of a military despotism, has ended in blood, murder, rapine." With these words, Horace Greeley succinctly described William Walker's reign in Nicaragua. But it had not ended quite yet. On January 27, 1857, the day this editorial appeared, the final siege of Rivas began.[1]

After Spencer's capture of the steamers and forts on the San Juan River, General Mora loaded most of his troops onto the steamboats and crossed Lake Nicaragua, where he joined the allied army encircling the filibuster stronghold. Walker would receive no reinforcements or supplies from the Atlantic—or from the Pacific, because Garrison diverted his ships to Panama as soon as he learned of Spencer's exploits.[2] February, March, April—the siege of Rivas ground on. Finally an American naval officer, Lieutenant Charles H. Davis, intervened. He shuttled between the two camps and negotiated an agreement. On May 1, Walker surrendered to Davis, who conducted the filibusters through the allied lines. Walker departed Nicaragua.[3]

"The most disastrous blunder of Walker," observed the *New York Herald*, "was his *coup d'etat* against 'the house of Vanderbilt.' " The Commodore's role in Spencer's mission was suspected by the press as soon as the first reports reached New York in January. Then again, the newspapers imagined that the steamship tycoons were behind everything from the start. Ignoring evidence that Walker, Randolph, and the Central Americans had driven events, they called the conflict the "war of the commodores." They even claimed, mistakenly, that George Law intrigued for the Nicaragua route. (The most he did was to sell rifles to Parker French.) In Spencer's case, however, the press was correct. The filibusters themselves stressed Vanderbilt's importance. "Walker owes his defeat not to the natives of Central America, but to his own countrymen," one wrote in 1859, "and had it not been for the malice or revenge of Vanderbilt, he might have reigned in Nicaragua at this day."[4]

The filibusters based their entire movement on contempt for Spanish-speaking peoples, so they naturally underplayed the role of the "natives" in the war. In fact, the isthmian republics had fought hard and paid dearly. One British diplomat estimated that the war cost the lives of forty thousand Nicaraguans, Costa Ricans, Guatemalans, Hondurans, and Salvadorans. The Central American soldiers who survived filibuster gunfire and outbreaks of cholera carried disease home, causing epidemics. The war bankrupted Costa Rica (despite Vanderbilt's aid), which prompted murmurs of dissent against President Mora. But the greatest suffering was inflicted on Nicaragua, where one city embodied the death and destruction that Walker had strewed about him. "Granada . . . presents, with her demolished houses and masses of ruined citizens, a consummate picture of misery and distress," wrote a correspondent for the *New York Herald*. "Walker, in burning and in the destruction of Granada, has earned a notoriety which for ages to come the historian will chronicle with infamy and horror."[5]

And yet, it cannot be denied that Vanderbilt played a decisive role in Walker's downfall. He had found the filibuster's weak point, crafted the plan to strike it, selected the agent to carry out the operation, and paid its costs. The Central Americans likely would have won in the long run without his help—but with it, they won in the short run. "Mr. Vanderbilt . . . has shown the ablest generalship," the London *Times* observed. "Walker's most formidable enemy has conducted the campaign from New York."[6]

He exacted revenge on Garrison and Morgan as well. Even before Spencer struck, Morgan had complained of the "large expenditures made to organize a line." Morgan was so close-mouthed that it is difficult to know how much he had at stake; as the Mercantile Agency noted, with regard to the Morgan Iron Works, "The extent of their means is a *family secret* with Morgan." But once the line collapsed, he could no longer conceal his need for cash. In April, he mortgaged his iron works for $317,500. In 1859, clerk Benjamin Voorhees testified that Morgan and Garrison "suffered a loss of about $300,000. I have been so assured by [Garrison] and from my own knowledge of his affairs. I believe it absolutely true." This was a staggering figure—as large as the entire estates of many of New York's richest men. And Morgan continued to bleed as Vanderbilt competed against his Gulf Coast line, slashing fares by up to 90 percent.[7]

Vanderbilt had wrought his revenge by guiding the military operations of a sovereign nation, at a cost of dozens of lives, through the instrument of a murderer on a jungle river a continent away from 10 Washington Place. His blow had captured international attention, alerting enemies present and future to just how far he would go to punish betrayal. But revenge didn't pay the servants. As *Harper's Weekly* asked, just before the filibusters surrendered, "When we have got rid of Walker, what next?"[8]

ONE FRIGID EVENING IN JANUARY, Vanderbilt, his brother Jacob, and a third man boarded a rowboat in the Hudson River at Hoboken, New Jersey. It may not have been in January of 1857—it may have been 1856 or 1855 or 1854—but what is certain is that the third man circulated the story of what happened that night. They were returning to New York from a corporate board meeting in New Jersey. It was late, and Vanderbilt did not want to wait for a ferry. So he hired the craft and took a seat in the stern as two boatmen pulled on the oars. They rowed into a dense mat of slush. It was rapidly getting darker and colder. The slush was hardening. A chunk of ice floating with the current plowed through and cracked dangerously against the side of the boat.

"The Commodore had from the first sat quiet," reported *Harper's Weekly* in 1859, "and his companions, who looked to him as their leader, had followed his example. At length he sprang up. 'Boys,' said he, cheerily, 'this won't do. Give me an oar! Now you two,' he added, addressing his brother and one of his friends, 'take those oars and row.' " At first the boatmen refused to give up control of the boat. Vanderbilt glared at them and said, in a low voice, "You keep out of my way, or you'll maybe come to grief." Standing upright in the bitter cold, balancing on the gunwales, he plunged his oar in the water to serve as a rudder and guided the craft through the bombardment of ice floes until finally they docked, sometime around midnight. "One of the parties who shared the Commodore's society on that evening," *Harper's* wrote, "has been heard to declare that he grew ten years older in the five or six hours they spent in the boat."[9]

Cornelius Vanderbilt remained a powerful physical presence, even in his sixties, as he prowled the city, straight and tall, his cravat around his neck, a cigar swiveling around in his mouth, wearing an air of profound confidence even in crises that threatened his survival. A mastery of physical danger can breed character, or it can breed a bully; it seems to have done a bit of both in the former boatman. It certainly made him a man whom contemporaries found striking. "One's first impression of Vanderbilt is that he is a man of steel," one writer observed, fifteen years later. "There is a steely glint in his grayish-blue eyes that reinforces the impression."[10]

Character, judgment, self-possession—these rose in Vanderbilt's values as he gained eminence. More than that, he began to reveal strands of warmth and humanity in his soul; even strangers now remarked on "his extreme courtesy." Such strands were gently pulled into view by Ellen Williams Vanderbilt, Corneil's wife. On February 12, 1857, for example, Vanderbilt did something very unusual: he wrote a letter in his own hand, to the Williams family in Hartford. His fondness for them, especially for his daughter-in-law, overflowed the page. He had sent a letter to "our Dear Ellen," he said, by a messenger "who promised to deliver it with his own hand. . . . I am in hopes to spend an evening with you shortly when we can talk over matters & things. Please give my best regards to all the ladies. Tell Ellen to send her notes along. I like to read them."

But these threads of warmth were wound around the steel core of a demanding father. The impetus for this letter came from his frustration with his son. "I this moment received a long letter from Cornelius in which he complains of Mr. Bond," he wrote, "for something he dun on my account. All this looks like one of *Cornelius visions.*" This tantalizing choice of words hints that Vanderbilt still doubted his son's sanity, even after he had won his release from an asylum. The Commodore asserted that Mr. Bond felt great affection for the Williams family, "& if he did not he could not be a friend of mine for a moment. I think these few line should be all sufficient," he added. "They air for the purpose of your correcting Cornl as his judgemint seams not to be mature upon all points. A great fault of his is to take disputes without sufficient cause."[11]

This letter offers a flash of insight into Vanderbilt's own late-maturing notion of fatherhood. He flared with scorn for his son, yet also demonstrated genuine concern. He wanted to correct the troubled lad, to teach him judgment, coolness, character.

Soon after this note, the Commodore presented Corneil and Ellen with a "fine mansion," together with an orchard, vineyard, garden, and hayfield, on a ridge overlooking Hartford. "There are few country seats in the land possessing equal attractions," the *Hartford Courant* observed. "The rooms are uncommonly spacious. . . . The view of the city, of Hartford Rocky Hill, and of the valleys on both sides of the ridge is charming."[12] The Commodore still shook his head over Corneil, but he made sure that Ellen would live in comfort. In fact, he gave the estate not to his son, but to his daughter-in-law, whom he trusted more than his own flesh and blood.

ON MARCH 9, 1857, the *New York Tribune* announced the Supreme Court's decision in the Dred Scott case. "THE TRIUMPH OF SLAVERY COMPLETE," declared one of its many headlines. The enslaved Scott had sued for his freedom on the grounds that he had resided in the free Wisconsin territory; Chief Justice Roger Taney ruled against him. Negroes, he wrote, "had no rights which a white man was bound to respect." What shocked the majority of the Northern public was not the blatant racism, but the implication that free states had no power to bar slavery within their borders.[13]

What Vanderbilt thought of the decision—or if he thought of it at all—

is unknown. But his efforts to reopen the Nicaragua transit route would become entangled with the worsening sectional crisis, thanks in large part to two men: his son-in-law and advisor, Horace Clark, and the new president, James Buchanan. Just a few weeks shy of his sixty-sixth birthday, Buchanan was tall and portly, a deft Democratic politician who had leaped from the House to the Senate to posts as minister to Russia, secretary of state, and minister to Great Britain, winning the wry nickname "Old Public Functionary." From beginning to end, his presidency would be defined by slavery. In the election of 1856, the new Republican Party had captured the northernmost tier of states on the pledge to stop its expansion; Buchanan had won only with the support of a nearly solid South. No one knew it better than the president, who sought to appease Dixie at every step.[14]

Yet the "irrepressible conflict" hardly monopolized Buchanan's attention. The great question for any new administration was patronage—the doling out of federal offices to create a network that would support both the party and the president personally. The most lucrative and nearly the most powerful position he had to fill was the collector of the port of New York. When Buchanan turned to the city's Democratic Party for a candidate, though, he found it divided between the adherents and opponents of Mayor Fernando Wood. The ambitious Wood relied on the support of the infamous Dead Rabbits gang of Five Points, whom he richly rewarded. When a gang leader, Fatty Welsh, was shot in his bar at 7 Mulberry Street, for example, the *New York Herald* revealed that "he holds the office of Inspector of Manure, at a salary of $3 per day."

Wood assumed that he would control all federal patronage in the city, but Buchanan loathed him. So the president chose as collector one of Wood's opponents: Augustus Schell, a man with small, round glasses, a professorial air, and swarms of greasy hair that dripped down the sides of his otherwise bald head. An even-tempered native of Rhinebeck, New York—and brother of stockbroker Richard Schell—he lived a quiet bachelor life as a lawyer in Manhattan. He served as chairman of Tammany Hall and (like the Old Public Functionary himself) valued party loyalty above all else. He had another advantage: the vocal support of his law partner, close friend, and political ally, a newly elected Democratic congressman named Horace F. Clark.[15]

The fact that Clark was Vanderbilt's son-in-law may have mattered a great deal to Buchanan. Like every president since Polk, he believed that the United States had no greater strategic imperative than securing the Central American transit routes to California. "To the United States these routes are of incalculable importance as a means of communication between their Atlantic and Pacific possessions," he declared in his first annual message to Congress. A solid Jacksonian, he wished to restore competition with Panama. As he later wrote, reopening the Nicaragua route "is an object the accomplishment of which I have much at heart."[16]

As Walker's downfall played out in the siege of Rivas, a serious question arose: Who owned the transit rights—the transit steamboats and property, and even the geographical route? Costa Rica and Nicaragua both claimed the San Juan River, but after the war Costa Rica remained in possession of it, along with the steamers Spencer had seized. Vanderbilt's final struggle to reopen the transit would center on this simple but weighty question of ownership.

He even had to fight for the Accessory Transit property within the United States. As a major creditor of the bankrupt company, he forced the sale of its steamships to himself and his family, including son-in-law Daniel Torrance and son Billy, who remained a farmer on Staten Island. Vanderbilt was accused of stripping the corporation of its assets, but he argued that he was pursuing the stockholders' interests; if other creditors forced the sale of the ships at auction, they would be unavailable to restart the line. At the annual meeting on May 5, 1857, he assured the stockholders "of his design to re-establish the company and save the property," the *New York Herald* reported. "He expressed a confident belief that everything would work out in the most satisfactory way, and advised that no one should part with a share of stock."[17]

In his fight for the transit route and property in Nicaragua, Vanderbilt faced two opponents, one old, one new. The new adversary was an Englishman named W. R. C. Webster. Webster had met the talkative Spencer in Costa Rica, and drew out of him the details of his mission with the skill of a practiced confidence artist. Webster then passed himself off as Vanderbilt's agent. Vanderbilt repudiated his every act, but Webster fooled President Mora, convincing him of the riches the transit could bring.

On May 6, Vanderbilt sent Spencer back to Central America with written orders. "You will proceed to Nicaragua, and to Costa Rica, if necessary, in the name and behalf of the Accessory Transit Company," he wrote, "and . . . take possession of the steamboats and all other property." When Spencer met Mora in San José on June 5, the president refused to cooperate. "He thought it was better that said steamers and other properties should remain in the possession of the Costa Rican Government until they could consummate some arrangement with the . . . company in relation to the Transit," Spencer reported.[18] Once again, Vanderbilt had been betrayed. Faced with the staggering expense of the war, Mora had been swayed by Webster's talk of Yankee gold into holding the steamboats and transit route hostage.

Vanderbilt's other adversary would prove even more troublesome. He was Joseph White, the one consistent villain in the Nicaragua tale. Every time Vanderbilt drove him out, he found a way back to preen and pronounce with consummate arrogance. As the *New York Times* sarcastically wrote, "Great is the Transit Company, and White is its prophet!"[19] Now that he was truly locked out of Accessory Transit, he revived the dormant American Atlantic & Pacific Canal Company, drawing in the well-respected Henry G. Stebbins (a past and future president of the New York stock exchange) to serve as financier and president. Then he negotiated for a transit grant with Antonio Yrisarri,* newly designated as Nicaragua's minister to the United States. On June 19, they agreed to a contract; Yrisarri, it was rumored, received a large gift of stock in return. The document went off to Nicaragua for ratification.[20]

On one side, Vanderbilt was pressed by President Buchanan to reopen the Nicaragua route; on the other, he was obstructed by the conniving of confidence men and Central American authorities. Still the Commodore believed he would win out. What he did not count on was the most unpredictable factor of all: William Walker. For all the strategic interests of the United States and isthmian republics, for all the calculations of Vanderbilt and his enemies, Walker's megalomania would rule the day.

THE WAR VANDERBILT WAGED in Nicaragua made him feared on Wall Street, but did not garner him esteem. The merchants of New York were a provincial group in their own way; despite their sway over the national economy, they knew and respected best those businesses located in Manhattan, amid their homes and offices. In early 1857, the Commodore attended to two vast operations rooted in New York, operations that reflected his rising status and would raise it still higher.

First was his transatlantic line. He had laid up his European steamships for the winter, when weather was especially rough and passengers few. But his competitors began to disappear as well. Collins withdrew his company's steamships for April, claiming that the reduced subsidy of $19,000 per month to carry the mail to Liverpool was insufficient. And the Ocean Steam Navigation Company, the mail line to Bremen, trembled on the brink of failure under the Commodore's pressure.[21]

He prepared to start the year's operations with his enormous, luxurious *Vanderbilt*. On April 27, he threw the ship open to the public, and it "was thronged throughout the day by ladies and gentlemen," according to the

---

* A Basque name, Yrisarri is also spelled with an initial I in Castillian Spanish. I am following the most common contemporary spelling, which followed the Basque custom.

New York Times. On May 5, the great five-deck sidewheeler departed on its maiden voyage, carrying $445,000 in gold and 212 passengers, including Sophia Vanderbilt on her way to Paris. The *Vanderbilt* reached England in the fastest first crossing of any ship to date. "While the new steam frigate *Niagara* is eighteen days crawling from New-York to Liverpool, the new passenger steamer *Vanderbilt* skims over in nine," said the *Albany Evening Journal.* "The *Niagara* is the 'crack sailer of the Navy!' "[22]

"The verdict from all competent judges is, that the *Vanderbilt* is bound to win the prize of Atlantic ocean popularity," the *Hartford Courant* reported. The London *Times* wrote, "Great interest was excited in commercial circles on account of the size and power of this vessel, and the rapid passage she recently made from New York. . . . She is in many respects the finest steamship we have ever seen."[23] It regularly beat its fastest rivals, Collins's *Atlantic* and the Cunard steamship *Persia.* After its reputation for speed and luxury had been established, Vanderbilt slashed fares—and made a point of departing on the same day as the Collins Line. When the Le Havre and Bremen postal contract expired on June 1, Vanderbilt agreed to carry the continental mail for the postage alone. The Ocean Steam Navigation Company soon went bankrupt. As for the Collins Line, "The result is a very serious curtailment," the *New York Times* concluded, "and unless their ships also reduce the price of passage it must inevitably be broken down."[24]

When the *Vanderbilt* made its maiden voyage, the Commodore did not accompany his wife to Europe. He remained behind to look after his other operation of 1857, involving a venerable project of New York's mercantile elite: the New York & Harlem Railroad, organized in 1831 as the city's first railway. As workmen had extended the tracks up Fourth Avenue, across the Harlem River, into Putnam County and beyond, its directors had positioned the line inland from the Hudson River to avoid competition with steamboats. Unfortunately, the major towns between New York and Albany all lined the river, so the Harlem (as the railroad was called) had had difficulty attracting enough business to pay for its expansion. Finally, in 1852, it had connected to the Western Railroad, which provided access to through traffic from Albany and western New York. It also profited from a connection to the New York & New Haven, made in 1848, which allowed trains to run between Boston and New York at last. But heavy construction debts burdened the line.[25]

Fraud pulled together the troubled Harlem and the Commodore—the great fraud of Robert Schuyler in 1854. Schuyler's deep involvement in the railroad (his brother George served as its president until Robert's scandal bankrupted them both) enmeshed Vanderbilt in a pair of bitter disputes with it. First, there was a battle over the dividends owed on the one thousand shares of stock assigned to him by Schuyler. In October 1854, he had sued the railroad to force it to pay; on January 20, 1857, a jury found in his favor.[26] Second, there was an ongoing fight over a block of $1 million worth of the Harlem's first-mortgage bonds. Vanderbilt had pledged to buy them from the Schuylers in 1854, paying $100,000 as an installment; after the Schuylers went bankrupt the railroad had declined to refund the down payment, leading to an intractable dispute.[27]

Make no mistake: the money mattered to Vanderbilt. But the railroad's refusal to honor the acts of its agent struck at the heart of his commercial code. Over this matter, he did not sue; rather, he secured enough stockholders' votes and proxies to win election to the board of directors on May 19, 1857, along with son-in-law Horace Clark and Daniel Drew. Now he had a presence within the company—at a moment when it was highly vulnerable. In early 1857, the money market spasmed, and the company's floating debt (short-term loans, unstructured into bonds, that cost a high rate of interest) threatened to bring the corporation down.[28]

The railroad's precarious position made the other directors reluctant to meet Vanderbilt's demand—and also desperate for his help. Vanderbilt, too, was in a delicate position: he wanted his money back, but to get it he had to help restore the line to profitability. So the Commodore embarked on a subtle strategy of simultaneously frightening and sustaining the company. On June 15, he stood before the board and explained "the nature and circumstances of his claim," as recorded in the minutes, "after which he and Mr. Clark withdrew." On June 24, he tendered his resignation, terrifying his fellow directors. Yet he also arranged for Clark and Drew to make a large short-term loan to the line. Clark was not wealthy enough to have done so himself; he operated as a false front, disguising Vanderbilt's support for the company.[29]

The hidden carrot and very visible stick worked. The board refused to accept his resignation; instead, it appointed a committee to settle with him—and secure his aid in rescuing the road. A decade later, Vanderbilt recalled how president Allan Campbell told him that the line would go bankrupt; with its assets sold off, his claim might be paid at last. "No," he replied, "I will help you out and lend you what money you want, and am willing to do anything else than that. There will be a time, before a great many years, when this road's whole property will be worth par and it will be a stigma upon the man who will take this course [of bankrupting the company], and I won't take it."[30]

How intricately his financial calculations interwove with his sense of honor: he foresaw a great future for the benighted railroad, a time when its stock would rise on the exchange to its par value; he was willing to let the situation mature until he could profit from its strengths. Yet he also wanted the credit—and resulting social prestige—for rescuing an enterprise so closely identified with the ambitions of New York's elite.

Daniel Drew said he would join Vanderbilt in endorsing the railroad's notes to see it through the crisis. "We will do it for two and a half percent [commission]," Drew said. "Mr. Drew," the Commodore loftily replied, "I won't do it for two and a half percent! I will do it with you for one-half percent." Drew agreed. As Vanderbilt recalled, the railroad "made the bargain, and they drew up, and drew up, and kept drawing and coming with things to sign—notes, if you please, and acceptances—until we got some [seven] hundred thousand dollars."[31]

Thus the Commodore forced the Harlem to admit that he was right, even as he saved it from destruction. Within ten weeks, the railroad paid back his $100,000 with interest.[32] The line would face further crises in the months to come, but Vanderbilt would be there to meet them. Once in Harlem, he would never leave.

FIVE POINTS WOULD HAVE its say about William Walker. Despite the deception of his recruiters in New York, despite the scores who died of disease and blundering tactics in his army in Nicaragua, he remained the greatest purveyor of freelance violence of all, and a hero in Five Points. So when Walker arrived at Pier No. 1 on the North River on June 16, a mass of laborers and rowdies cheered him. They followed his carriage to City Hall Park, where he addressed a crowd of thousands.[33]

Walker's arrival troubled Vanderbilt, who feared that he was preparing a fresh invasion of Nicaragua. Shortly afterward the Commodore went to Washington to ask Buchanan if he would prevent it. Publicly the president made no comment; he wished to avoid antagonizing the South, which strongly supported the filibuster, especially after Walker had reinstituted slavery in Nicaragua (an act that did not survive his rule). In private, Buchanan seethed. "That man has done more injury to the commercial & political interests of the United States," he wrote, "than any man living." He said as much to Vanderbilt. If Walker moved he would be "crushed out."[34]

Less reassuring was Buchanan's refusal to commit to the cause of the Accessory Transit Company. Though the president was eager to reopen the Nicaragua route, he didn't particularly care who did it, which meant that Vanderbilt had to race to defeat White's maturing schemes. The Commodore corresponded with General José María Cañas, who commanded Costa Rica's troops on the San Juan River, in an attempt to regain Accessory Transit's steamboats. (Cañas hinted that he could carve out a new republic for the company along the transit route, but Vanderbilt thought that was going a bit too far.) He asked Goicouria to write to Nicaragua's new government to persuade them that White could not be trusted. He took Horace Clark on a visit to the White House in an attempt to convince Buchanan to refuse recognition of Yrisarri—White's coconspirator—as Nicaragua's minister. Finally he sent Daniel Allen to Nicaragua as his personal representative. Above all else, Vanderbilt had to secure the property and transit rights before Walker launched a second expedition.[35]

He failed. On November 25, Walker landed with 270 men on Punta Arenas.[36] All calculations regarding the transit route immediately became obsolete.

IN THE MID-1850S, George Templeton Strong contemplated the metropolis of New York—from Alexander T. Stewart's gleaming marble department store at Broadway and Chambers to the squalor of Five Points to the domed Crystal Palace up on Forty-second Street—and marveled about it all in his diary. "There is poetry enough latent in the South Street merchant and the Wall Street financier," he wrote;

> in Stewart's snobby clerk chattering over ribbons and laces; in the omnibus driver that conveys them all from the day's work to the night's relaxation and repose; in the brutified denizen of the Points and the Hook; in the sumptuous star courtesan of Mercer Street thinking sadly of her village home; in the Fifth Avenue ballroom; in the Grace Church contrast of eternal vanity and new bonnets.[37]

This was the New York that Vanderbilt had helped to create: commercial, mobile, and individualistic—yet increasingly polarized into rich and poor. The age of unspecialized merchants and skilled artisans began to fade as mills, factories, banks, and railroads rose in their place. Most Americans still worked on their own farms, in their own shops, or for small partnerships or personal businesses, but New York (and New England) presaged a future of industrialization and incorporation, of stockholders, managers, and wage workers. Unquestionably the new economy worked wonders, creating a highly productive, exceedingly wealthy society; but in 1857 the great self-directed orchestra of New York threatened to break apart into cacophony and chaos.

In the middle of June, New York's policemen divided into two camps: the Metropolitan Police, organized by the Republican-controlled state legislature, and the Municipal Police, under the control of Mayor Wood. Skirmishes broke out over station houses; then an all-out battle erupted on the steps of the city hall as the largely Anglo-American Metropolitans tried to fight their way through a phalanx of largely Irish Municipals in order to arrest the mayor. On July 4 and again on the 8th, the conflict drew in the city's leading gangs, the Irish Dead Rabbits and the nativist Bowery Boys, the first fighting for the Municipals, the latter for the Metropolitans. Finally the state militia marched into the city to suppress what appeared to be an insurrection.[38]

Scarcely had this mayhem died away than the nation fell into the greatest financial crisis in twenty years—the Panic of 1857. In retrospect, the warnings of a collapse look all too clear. There was railroad overexpansion: of the twenty thousand miles of line built in the 1850s (tripling the total length of track), 2,500 were constructed in 1857 alone. There was the end of the Crimean War: Russian wheat now flooded the international market, hurting American exports. There was France's need for money: French banks borrowed from those in England, which raised English interest rates, which led British investors to sell off their American securities and invest at home, which undercut stock prices in the United States. And there was the heady effect of nearly nine years of California gold, which had fed speculation and inflated credit. Since the start of the gold rush, the number of banks in America had doubled, to more than 1,500. The monetary expansion reached a peak in early August. "And then there came on a sharp money market," Vanderbilt recalled, "and everything broke down."[39]

On August 24, the New York branch of the Ohio Life Insurance and Trust Company announced that it could no longer pay its bills. "The high credit enjoyed by that concern, and the fact that its solvency had hardly been questioned, made the failure a matter of . . . importance," the *New York Herald* reported. It "opened the first great seal of the revulsion." Constantly borrowing and lending in New York's intricate web of banks and investment houses, it ripped the financial lattice apart when it failed.[40]

On September 2, Vanderbilt welcomed his wife back from Europe. It would be the only happy event for many weeks to come, as banks and merchants collapsed. On the 18th, word spread through the city that the U.S. Mail steamship *Central America* (formerly the *George Law*) had sunk in a storm on its return from Panama. It was a terrible blow for Vanderbilt's troubled friend and ally Marshall Roberts, who was president of the corporation; already the North River Bank, of which Roberts owned half the stock, had failed and gone into liquidation. Even worse, the *Central America* carried down $1.6 million in gold from California, desperately needed in New York's constricted money market. In the afternoon, Vanderbilt went in person to the U.S. Mail office and asked for the details of the disaster. "He expressed his deep sympathy for the passengers on the ill-fated steamer," the *New York Times* reported, "and commiserated with the Company [i.e., Roberts] for the heavy pecuniary loss entailed upon them by her loss."[41]

"All confidence is lost, for the present, in the solvency of our merchant princes—and with good reason," Strong wrote in his diary on September 27. "It is probable that every last one of them has been operating and gambling in stocks and railroad bonds." Perhaps because he was a Wall Street lawyer, the financial catastrophe brought out the poet in his soul. "O Posterity, Posterity, you can't think how bothered, bedeviled, careworn, and weary were your enlightened ancestors in their counting-rooms and offices and bank parlors during these bright days of September, A.D. 1857," he wrote, two days later.

> They are fighting hard for a grand, ugly house in the Fifth Avenue; for the gold and damask sofas and curtains that are ever shrouded in dingy coverings, save on the one night of every third year when they are unveiled to adorn the social martyrdom of five hundred perspiring friends. They are agonizing with unavailable securities, and pleading vainly for discount with stony-hearted directors and inflexible cashiers, lest they forfeit the privilege of inviting Joe Kernochan and Dan Fearing [two of the most prestigious leaders of elite society] to gorge and prose and stupefy over the barbaric splendors of an unwholesome dinner; that they may still yawn through the *Trovatore* in their own opera boxes; that they may be plagued with their own carriage horses and swindled by their own coachman instead of hiring a comfortable hack when they want a ride.

The *Times* echoed Strong's thoughts—in fact, it singled out Vanderbilt as a prime exemplar of what had brought the economy so low. "Commodore Vanderbilt, in his steam-yacht excursion, was just a type of the general Yankee who spends his money liberally and is as magnificent as his means will allow, and sometimes a good deal more so. That this extravagance can be carried much too far . . . a great many people have learned from their own experience."[42]

Vanderbilt survived the great disaster with no sign of suffering. He must have felt *some* pain, for he could not levitate entirely above the great river of credit that carried the economy along. Yet it appears that he possessed deep cash reserves, and never failed to pay a bill or debt even in the worst of the storm. In early 1858, when the Mercantile Agency reported on the Allaire Works—a corporation that operated virtually as an extension of Vanderbilt's personal business—it observed, "They are [said] to be in [good] condition & to [have paid] all thro the panic. Have done & are [doing] a [good] bus. & are sold to freely." No doubt all of his other agents, clerks, and companies also paid debts on time and in full.[43]

As the panic purged the city, Vanderbilt went to work each day as usual, down to his office on Bowling Green, behind the ticket desk to his private chamber in the rear, where he put on his reading glasses and reviewed letters and invoices and worried the cigar he kept clamped between his teeth. Sometime in September, Allan Campbell, the Harlem's president, came in to see him. The railroad could not pay its bills. Its own debtors refused to pay it, and its creditors would only take its acceptances (its corporate promissory notes) at the ruinous rate of 5 percent interest *per month*. "Commodore," he pleaded, "how will we get along?"[44]

At the time, the railroad had large short-term notes coming due, endorsed by Daniel Drew. With the panic at full force, Drew refused to endorse a renewal of the notes. If he didn't sign, the creditors would refuse to extend the time for repayment. "He won't?" Vanderbilt asked Campbell. The railroad president said no. "He will!" the Commodore declared. "Go away, and mind your business, and I will send you the bonds."

Twelve years later, Vanderbilt, with great relish, told a committee of the state legislature the story of what happened next. First, the board of directors put him in charge of managing the railroad's financial crisis.[45] Then he called Drew in for a meeting, one that resulted in the Harlem's salvation—and that exposed the stark difference in temperament between these longtime partners and friends.

"I sent for Drew and he came to the office," he recalled, "and I was signing these acceptances . . . and he says, 'Commodore!' "

"Mr. Drew," Vanderbilt replied, "how are you? Sit down there and sign these acceptances." Drew was to be the primary endorser, Vanderbilt the secondary.

"Not one of 'em! Not one of 'em!"

"You will sign them all!" Vanderbilt insisted.

"Not one of them!" Drew proclaimed. "Are you crazy?"

"And [he] went on in that kind of strain, you know," Vanderbilt recalled, "and I says, 'No, I am not crazy, Mr. Drew!' "

"My God!" said the distraught Drew. "What are you going to do?"

"I am going to sign all these things, and you are too."

"Where is the money to come from to pay it?"

"You and I will pay, if nobody else will," Vanderbilt said. "Didn't you agree to? You have got one-half percent on the $400,000 that you have already signed. You have had that money, hain't you?"

"Yes," Drew replied.

"I am going to do it, if it takes the coat off my back," Vanderbilt said. "I am going to live up to it." It was a moment that said everything about the Commodore at this stage of his life. His strict code of honor in business mattered more to him now than ever as he attained eminence among New

York's merchants. He had promised to support the Harlem's credit, and so he would—and he would browbeat Drew into doing the same. As for Drew, he was a curious fellow: bold when he had every advantage, timid at all other times, he was the sort of financier who tried to run ahead of the changing wind rather than fight it. "I worked him up so that he signed them," Vanderbilt recalled. "The old fellow was almost crying all the while."

"Mr. Drew," Vanderbilt said, when they were done, "you are one of the best receivers I ever knew, but about as bad a payer as I ever knew." In return for Drew's half-percent commission, he offered to indemnify Drew completely and take on himself all responsibility for paying, should the railroad fail. Drew agreed. "He did not dare cheat me!" Vanderbilt recalled.[46]

The combined names of Drew and Vanderbilt on the company's notes reassured its nervous creditors. The Commodore began to work on a plan to restructure the large floating debt of about $750,000, to allow the Harlem to put its finances in order, and bought a majority of $1 million in third-mortgage bonds (at a 50 percent discount). On February 10, 1858, the directors would pass a resolution, declaring "that the thanks of the Board are due and are hereby tendered to Cornelius Vanderbilt Esq. for the liberal aid afforded by him in the disposition of the new loans of the company."[47]

Vanderbilt carried the Harlem through the Panic of 1857 with the liquid power of his wealth, his formidable reputation, and his ability to coerce Drew. But he was a man of foresight. Most likely he had no specific plans in mind, but he could sense that the time was coming when he would make a great deal more out of the railroad than one-half of 1 percent.

"THANKSGIVING," a columnist for *Harper's Weekly* exclaimed on November 21, 1857. "The very word sounds like a blessing. The whole week seems to be covered with plums, and the smell of roast turkey and pumpkin pie. The boys have visions of snow and sliding, or coasting. The parents open their homes and hearts to the long absent. Business stops suddenly on a weekday." It was a traditional holiday, not a legal one, having spread across the country from New England in the 1820s and '30s. In hard-pressed New York, it offered a welcome respite from the Panic.[48]

This week, like most weeks, Vanderbilt went to his two-story brownstone stables at 21 and 23 West Fourth Street, at the rear of the block occupied by his double-wide mansion. Approached from Fourth Street, there was a door to the harness room on the right, and on the left a large arched carriage entrance, which led into a cobblestone passage equipped with hydrants for washing the horses and carriages. Passing through, he would enter an enormous room—a "hippodrome," as one newspaper called it—filling the building and rising to the roof, lit by sunshine from the great skylights above. Carriages, wagons, and sleighs were parked in a group in the center; young boys walked the horses around an oblong track on the outside of the room, on sawdust strewn across the cobblestones. Then the Commodore would descend a gradual winding stairway, designed with the horses in mind, to the well-ventilated stalls below, where his prize trotters were brushed and fed.[49]

This week, like most weeks, Vanderbilt ordered a pair of his fastest horses harnessed to a light, open-air racing rig, then climbed aboard, took the reins in hand, and smartly whipped his team down the cobblestone passage into West Fourth Street. A left turn, then another left onto Broadway, and uptown he went, past aristocratic Grace Church, past Union Square, out of the city to where Broadway became Bloomingdale Road. There "sporting men" liked to challenge each other amid the trees and pastures of upper Manhattan. On this day, as usual, they gathered at Jones's tavern, hoping to set up a race, when they saw Vanderbilt drive up behind his famously swift horses.

"Knowing, as all the sporting men do, that Commodore Vanderbilt likes a good brush, it is a very widespread ambition to pass him on the road," *Harper's Weekly* remarked. "But this is not very easily done." On this occasion, as so often, Vanderbilt came with his friend and broker Frank Work, who rattled alongside in his own rig. They pulled up in front of the tavern, but "everybody seemed to hold back. No one cared to lead off." Disappointed, the Commodore and Work whipped their horses onto the road and headed back toward the city.

Immediately ten to fifteen men grabbed their horses' reins and set out after them, hoping to pass them. "If there wasn't some trotting done at that time I never did see any," the correspondent wrote. "There was only one drawback—there were too many in the race, they kept too closely together, and the road was not wide enough." With dozens of horses sprinting down the lane, the spinning wheels cracked against each other, and three wagons were smashed to pieces, "and all tumbled together. The Commodore came out all right." Municipal policemen rushed to the scene from Mayor Wood's nearby home, but no one was hurt.[50]

In the year ahead, Vanderbilt would need all his coolness, dexterity, and speed in the race for the Nicaragua transit. Walker's landing at Greytown disrupted everything. Not that he remained for long: Commodore Hiram Paulding of the U.S. Navy rushed to the scene and forced Walker to surrender on December 8. Paulding's action caused outrage among Walker's Southern supporters; debate over whether to censure or congratulate Paulding tied up the Senate for weeks.[51]

Popular or not, Walker doomed all attempts to reopen the transit route with his latest foray. Nicaragua and Costa Rica abruptly settled their differences in order to present a united front against the filibusters. Fear of North Americans in general pervaded Nicaragua's national consciousness. "There is in all this country a deep-seated terror," wrote the U.S. minister, Mirabeau B. Lamar, "that, when the Americans are admitted into it, the natives will be thrust aside—their nationality lost—their religion destroyed—and the common classes be converted into hewers of wood and drawers of water." The most that Daniel Allen could do upon his arrival there was to file a protest over Yrisarri's contract with White's company. Not that he needed to: there was little danger that the Nicaraguans would open their borders ever again.[52]

As usual, it was White's bluster, not his deeds, that plagued Vanderbilt. White loudly proclaimed that his new line would start up on February 20, 1858, which led Pacific Mail to stop paying its monthly subsidy to Vanderbilt (who now pocketed the money, since he had taken possession of the steamships at issue). The Commodore, knowing that White was penniless, viewed this as a breach of their noncompetition agreement. In retaliation, he announced an opposition line via Panama, in partnership with none other than Cornelius K. Garrison. He made just one voyage before Pacific Mail surrendered, raising its payment from $40,000 to $56,000 per month. It could afford the increase: it paid 30 percent dividends in 1857 (that is, $30 per share), even while paying off Vanderbilt. Monopolies were lucrative.[53]

Vanderbilt's short-lived line was an early sign of a comprehensive reconciliation that he reached with Morgan and Garrison. The deal, which they finalized in April, required Vanderbilt to buy Morgan's share in Garrison's steamers on the Pacific, the *Orizaba* and the *Sierra Nevada*, and to buy a very large new steamship that Morgan was building in New York, the *Ocean Queen*. Morgan purchased Vanderbilt's Gulf Coast line, and he and Garrison promised to never again compete in the California trade. On April 20, Garrison wrote to Joseph Scott at Punta Arenas, ordering him to transfer all transit property to Vanderbilt's control. It seems that once Morgan and Garrison admitted defeat, the Commodore forgave their treachery. He even saved Garrison from the ongoing lawsuit that Accessory Transit had filed against him. The two sides agreed to William K. Thorn, Vanderbilt's son-in-law, as referee in the case. In September, Thorn would rule that Garrison owed nothing.[54]

Truly April was the weirdest month. On the 15th, the Commodore welcomed to his office Joseph White. A fortune had passed through White's hands since he first had met Vanderbilt. "What he has made has been within the past 6 yrs.," the Mercantile Agency reported at the end of 1853. "Was not [worth] much when he came here [to New York]." At his height, he had accumulated as much as $200,000, purchased a fine house on Madison Square for $40,000, bought the farm of novelist James Fenimore Cooper, kept a private box at the opera house, and rode "in a handsome carriage." But all that had come to an end. Ruined in the fall of Accessory Transit, he held on to the hope that he could convert the canal company's shaky transit contract with Yrisarri into a new pile. In the meantime, he had come to the end of all his resources. And so he asked his sworn enemy for a ninety-day loan of perhaps $10,000—offering as collateral twenty-five shares of the canal company, ostensibly worth $1,000 each. In all likelihood, White could find no one else with money to lend during the ongoing panic.[55]

Vanderbilt agreed. He certainly doubted that White would be able to repay him. And he couldn't have placed much value on the canal shares. But by lending the money he obtained inside information on White's finances and the state of the company. Perhaps he also took satisfaction in holding the debt over someone who had exuded arrogance for so long.

Another enemy succumbed in April as well. The Collins Line finally collapsed and sold off its last steamers—the *Atlantic*, the *Baltic*, and the *Adriatic* (larger than any ship except the newly launched English leviathan, *Great Eastern*). The *New York Times* blamed Vanderbilt for "driving too sharp a competition." That brought an anonymous friend to his defense. "I know him well, and am well satisfied that he asks the sympathy of no nation and of no man, beyond that to which his merit may justly entitle him," the advocate wrote. "I have always found him bold, energetic, upright, and honorable."[56]

Perhaps he was—but he could never claim to be omnipotent. His grand Nicaragua venture, the single most original enterprise of his long career, slipped irretrievably beyond his grasp. First, he lost control of the Accessory Transit Company. A lawsuit by the Pennsylvania Coal Company, one of many unpaid creditors, resulted in the appointment of a receiver, David Colden Murray, on May 31. Murray prepared to sue the Commodore over the steamships he had taken from the company, for a total of $261,541.36.[57] Next, "the inevitable W. R. C. Webster" (as the *New York Times* called the confidence man) arrived in New York, bearing yet another transit contract that he claimed to have negotiated in Nicaragua on Vanderbilt's behalf. Vanderbilt spurned him, but his claims led the Commodore to make one last grasp for the prize.[58]

In the middle of June he sent Daniel Allen to Nicaragua with a final proposal and $80,000 in gold. On arriving in Greytown, Allen encountered Joseph Scott, who still guarded the Accessory Transit ruins on Punta Arenas, refusing to let go until he was repaid his advances of years before. Scott was fierce: when one of White's agents had tried to seize a steamboat, he had forced him off. "Webster afterwards attempted to take possession," Scott recalled. "I prevented him by threatening to shoot him, and he retreated." He threatened to shoot Allen too, but Allen merely asked for a lift in one of the few functioning steamers. On his arrival at Managua, the new capital, President Tomás Martínez exploded any notion of reopening the transit. Allen returned home with the gold and without a contract.[59]

PRESIDENT BUCHANAN SENT WORD to Congressman Horace Clark that he would like to see him at the White House. Clark's political senses had been honed in a decade of infighting in New York's treacherous Democratic Party; surely he knew that the president wished to speak to him about Lecompton.

In the political jargon of 1858, "Lecompton" stood for the proposed constitution for Kansas, now petitioning to join the Union as a slave state. It was in the town of Lecompton that a convention of delegates had written the document, which had been submitted to the voters for ratification. The election of delegates had been "rigged," however, as historian James M. McPherson writes, to ensure a pro-slavery majority; and the referendum on the constitution had seen thousands of illegal pro-slavery ballots. Free-soil voters (who were a majority) had boycotted both elections, and Lecompton had passed, against the will of the electorate. Outrage swept the North. Senator Stephen Douglas, the author of the Kansas-Nebraska Act, railed against Lecompton as a rape of democracy. Even Kansas's governor Walker, a Southerner himself, denounced the constitution and its so-called ratification as "a vile fraud."

President Buchanan chose to make Lecompton a test of party loyalty. Southern Democrats insisted that Kansas be admitted as a slave state, and he believed that the survival of the Union might well depend upon appeasing them. On February 2, 1858, he asked Congress to accept Lecompton and admit Kansas as a slave state.[60]

Clark loudly opposed him. So he answered the president's call and endured the full weight of Buchanan's displeasure. In his high, thin voice, the president warned "that it would be *impossible* for Mr. Clark to be reelected if the federal patronage in his District were arrayed against him," it was later reported. Clark replied that he "was not a professional politician; that he was an independent man, not hoping for anything from place or patronage; and that therefore, if his Excellency wished to obtain his support, he . . . must use arguments more pertinent to the *merits* of the measure."[61]

Clark's principled stand made him one of a handful of influential "anti-

Lecompton Democrats" who blocked Kansas's admission as a slave state. But his claim to care nothing for patronage did not ring true. He stood at the center of an interwoven lattice of business and politics that trembled with every decision in Washington. Clark's rival in New York's Democratic Party, Congressman Daniel E. Sickles, wrote to Buchanan that Vanderbilt—in defiance of the president's wishes—wanted the Nicaragua transit to remain closed in order to retain the subsidy paid by Pacific Mail. "This interest is represented by his son-in-law H. F. Clark, one of my colleagues," he added.[62]

Clark's defiance also compromised his close friend and ally, Collector of the Port Augustus Schell. Schell steadily worked his way into Vanderbilt's circle (which already included his brother Richard), and was seen socializing with the Commodore at Saratoga Springs. The collector had allowed Clark to name many of the officers at the Custom House, which gave him a valuable patronage network. In the storm over Lecompton, though, Schell had to save himself from Buchanan's wrath, which required "the sacrifice of Horace F. Clark and his numerous appointees in the Custom House," the *Times* reported.[63]

Clark's alienation from the administration gravely complicated his father-in-law's life. Until this dispute, his political position and connections had been immensely useful to the Commodore. Vanderbilt's vast interests constantly intersected government affairs; he needed friendly relations with policy makers, but he also tried to remain above partisan politics. He took no part, for example, in Fernando Wood's fall from power in 1857, when Tammany Hall rejected him as a gang-connected rabble-rouser and replaced him with Daniel F. Tiemann. Yet Vanderbilt also called on the aid of the police in August 1858 to bring nonunion men onto his steamships.[64]

As if Vanderbilt's relationship with government were not delicate enough, his brother Jacob dragged him indirectly into a gruesome incident known as the Quarantine War. For years, the people of Staten Island had resented the presence of a hospital, near Vanderbilt's Landing, where sick immigrants were quarantined. In January, William H. Vanderbilt had served on a committee that petitioned for the Quarantine's removal. An outbreak of yellow fever on the island proved to be the final provocation. On the nights of September 1 and 2, a large body of Staten Island's most distinguished citizens—led by Jacob Vanderbilt, among others—burned the hospital to the ground. Jacob was arrested, and William and his father came to the jail to bail him out. Augustus Schell secured the services of one hundred U.S. Marines to stand guard on the island; Governor John A. King declared Richmond County to be in a state of insurrection, and dispatched militia to the scene. But no aspersions were cast on the Commodore; he was far too important a businessman for politicians to slight. When the governor began to look for a new location for the Quarantine, he asked for Vanderbilt's advice.[65]

For all his efforts, Buchanan would not be rid of Clark. Clark won reelection in 1858 as an independent, anti-Lecompton Democrat.[66] In time, the president would realize that he could not afford a grudge against Clark's father-in-law—not when the Commodore was needed to protect the strategic interests of the United States.

"TEN YEARS AGO," the *New York Herald* asked in 1859, "who would have said that San Francisco, when but seven years old, would on the score of tonnage rank as the fourth city of this Union?" With a population of nearly 57,000, San Francisco had grown into a true metropolis, thanks to the gold that poured out of California's mountains to the value of tens of millions of dollars each year. Loaded onto steamers at the city's piers, the precious metal flowed down to Panama and up to Manhattan, where it helped power the American economy and reinforce New York's dominance over the financial nation.

Vanderbilt had done much to build up both New York and San Francisco, but he had never attained the lucrative postal contract to California. That contract finally would expire on September 30, 1859. On April 7, Postmaster General John Holt announced that he would accept bids for a new, temporary contract, lasting only nine months. The federal subsidy was in play again at last.[67]

Unfortunately for Vanderbilt, he was barred from the bidding for it by his noncompetition agreement with Pacific Mail and U.S. Mail, which paid him $56,000 per month to keep his ships at their moorings. But the siren call of Nicaragua obsessed both President Buchanan and Joseph White, and that would force Vanderbilt to enter the business for the last time.

After all his calumnies and lies, White had finally started his Nicaragua line under the Yrisarri contract. On November 6, 1858, he had dispatched a creaking old steamship from New York for Greytown. Vanderbilt knew that it was just another fraud. For one thing, White was broke; he had never repaid Vanderbilt's loan, and he would never pay for the lease of the ship. For another, the Nicaraguans would never reopen the transit as long as Walker remained free to plot a fresh invasion. Most of all, they had learned to detest White. President Martínez told Alexander Dimitry, the latest U.S. minister, "that the government could not entertain any proposition from the 'White . . . company.' " Dimitry reported "that Nicaragua had been *hum bugueado*—the word is his—humbugged by them." Nothing could say more about the Nicaraguans' experience with White than their adoption of the slang verb "humbug"—to swindle. When his steamship arrived, they refused to let the passengers land.[68]

But Pacific Mail saw White's latest gambit as a reason to stop paying $56,000 per month to Vanderbilt. The Commodore disagreed; indeed, the dispute went to arbitration, resulting in an award to Vanderbilt of $30,000. But this time there would be no renewal of the subsidy. Rather, in March 1859, Vanderbilt launched his final war for the steamship traffic to California. In partnership with Cornelius Garrison, he dispatched the *Northern Light* for Aspinwall and readied the ships not otherwise occupied on the line to Europe: the *North Star,* the *Daniel Webster,* the *Uncle Sam,* the *Orizaba,* the *Sierra Nevada,* and the *Cortez.* He also ordered the first iron steamship ever built in the United States, the fittingly named *Champion.* The London *Times* saw "every prospect of the contest, owing to the wealth and tenacity of Mr. Vanderbilt, being carried to a most damaging extent." This war would not end until one side accepted the other's terms for good.[69]

By midsummer Vanderbilt's California line was operating at full capacity. Together with Marshall Roberts, Moses Taylor, sons-in-law James Cross and Daniel Allen, and his old enemy Charles Morgan, he incorporated the Atlantic & Pacific Steamship Company to conduct the business. The Panama Railroad happily sold tickets to his passengers, but it joined with Pacific Mail to form the North Atlantic Steamship Company to run against him on the Atlantic. Both sides slashed fares; despite a dramatic rise in the number of passengers, both sides lost money. But Vanderbilt lived up to his reputation for controlling costs, economizing in everything from coal consumption to amenities for the passengers. He lost less.[70]

White's gambit, then, drove Vanderbilt back into the California steamship trade just in time to compete for the postal contract. His beleaguered friend Roberts planned to shut down U.S. Mail upon the expiration of the old contract, so the Commodore put in his own bid—though he found himself at a disadvantage. With Nicaragua closed, his only means of crossing the isthmus was the Panama Railroad, but it shared many stockholders and directors with Pacific Mail and the railroad's directors refused to speak to him. Instead the railroad and Pacific Mail made a joint bid of their own.

In the end, the decisive factor in awarding this rich prize was Buchanan's intense desire to break the Panama monopoly. On May 9, to everyone's surprise, Postmaster General Holt gave the contract to Daniel H. Johnson, primarily because he claimed to possess a transit grant from Nicaragua. But who was Johnson? He owned no steamers and had no experience in shipping. And how did he get this supposed grant?

Vanderbilt quickly learned that Johnson was a dummy—the last dummy in the dummy-filled history of the California mail—of Joseph White. The Commodore must have found White's maniacal persistence infuriating; on a human level, though, it was pathetic. Nicaragua had given White his only real taste of wealth and importance. In a meteoric flash of success, he had enjoyed the confidence of ambassadors, cabinet secretaries, and presidents as he indulged in luxury, only to fall into irrelevance, poverty, and disrepute. And so he came back to Nicaragua again and again, long past the point of plausibility. For this latest ploy he formed a new company, the U.S. & Central America Transit, hoping that the mail contract (which Johnson duly assigned to him) would give him the credit he needed to obtain ships to restart the transit route, and trusting that his ties to Yrisarri would assuage President Martínez.[71]

Vanderbilt quietly explained all this to Holt, hoping to convince him that Johnson should not be allowed to flip the contract to White. His words carried great weight with the postmaster general. For one thing, the Commodore already had agreed to carry the mail to Europe, from April to November, for no more compensation than the sea and inland postage. (Not that the business was very lucrative: in June, Vanderbilt offered to sell his Atlantic steamships—the *Vanderbilt* for $800,000, the *Ocean Queen* for $500,000, and the *Ariel* for $300,000.)[72] And Vanderbilt enjoyed a direct connection to the White House. He negotiated personally with Buchanan, writing of "my willingness and desire to carry out your views as to opening Nicaragua," and blaming White for "keeping this much desired route closed."[73]

Vanderbilt knew that it would remain closed, of course, but he managed to get a conditional contract: if Johnson could not come up with ships of his own by October 5, then Vanderbilt would carry the mail instead. Encouraged, he bought Garrison's interest in the Pacific steamers for $450,000 and spent another $50,000 repairing them. In September, the *Champion* steamed to New York from the Delaware River, where it had been built. The great iron sidewheeler measured 1,850 tons and 250 feet in length, and could carry 738 passengers. Vanderbilt claimed that it could be run as cheaply as any other ship afloat. The Pacific Mail directors began to reveal their anxiety by spreading patently false rumors on Wall Street. They claimed to be making a profit, while Vanderbilt lost money, and said they would carry the mail after all on October 5.[74]

On the fated day, the Post Office loaded the mail onto Vanderbilt's *Northern Light*. White was left sputtering about "a certain damned old sea pirate" who had taken away the contract "by some hocus pocus." Vanderbilt would receive $187,500 for his nine months of postal service. And Pacific Mail continued to lose money.[75]

ON DECEMBER 18, 1858, Mrs. Nancy Dobley asked *Harper's Weekly* "to
say a word to the ladies *exclusively* . . . [in] reference to the mud—to
walking in the mud and slush—to crossing the streets in the mud and
slush. . . . Are we aware, ladies, that we have a habit, in these days, of lifting our skirts very high indeed when we cross the street?" All this flashing
of ankles was unseemly. "To watch a well dressed and careful woman wade
across Broadway is a favorite occupation of men whose admiration is not
flattering."[76] Of course, such extreme concern for modesty in public only
masked Americans' sexuality. On October 17, 1859, the *New York Herald*
reported on the prosecution of importers of "indecent stereoscopes" that
showed men and women in various states of nudity. "The sale of these
articles is immense, and New York bids fair to vie with France in the man-
ufacture of this description of artistic invention."[77]

Like those hidden stereoscopes, a vivid, three-dimensional world of
passion and appetites certainly played out in Vanderbilt's private, unseen
spaces. The inner lives of his wife and daughters in particular remain
invisible to us, as hidden as a respectable lady's knees. His girls were wives
and mothers now. They often gathered at 10 Washington Place, spending hours in parlors and dining rooms, waited upon by servants. They
attended concerts and went to the theater; they visited Saratoga and
Staten Island; they talked, they joked, they laughed; but they did not commit their experiences to paper.

What discussions went into the construction of a family vault in the
Moravian churchyard on Staten Island in 1857, with its Corinthian
columns, marble statue of "Grief," and a twenty-foot shaft inscribed
"VANDERBILT"? Did the women debate the likelihood of secession,
should the Republicans win the White House in 1860, or did they gossip
about Robert Schuyler and his wife? Did they order a driver to take them
through Central Park, now rapidly approaching completion? Did they go
out in the "close-quarter carriage," each costing $1,000 or more, so
favored by wealthy women? Or did they prefer an open-air coupé or
barouche, recently introduced from France? ("They are made large and
luxuriant, as lounging carriages," the *Herald* wrote of barouches, "and
seem to be all but indispensable in the present style of ladies' dresses.")[78]

The carriage was the great recreational institution of New York's rich.
Any afternoon would see expensive affairs pulled by fancy horses, carrying
William B. Astor, Hamilton Fish, Watts Sherman, or even Daniel Drew
through "the pleasant drives of the Central Park," as the *Herald* remarked
on December 5, 1859. Vanderbilt, of course, was one of the "fast men"
who held his own reins and hungered for speed. For decades, harness rac-

ing had been the plebeian alternative to the aristocratic sport of Thoroughbreds; but Vanderbilt led a rising elite, lacking any social pedigree, that championed trotters in both formal races at dedicated tracks and informal contests on the road. To garner respectability for the sport, he helped organize the Elm Park Pleasure Ground Association, a club "of many of the best people in the city," to race on or near Bloomingdale Road above Ninetieth Street. Four hundred men belonged, with a combined investment of nearly $1 million in horseflesh.

The Commodore's great rival was Robert Bonner, editor of the *Ledger.* He rarely beat the skillful Bonner—but it was Vanderbilt who drew the admiration of onlookers. "What fine looking man is that," the *Herald* rhetorically asked,

> with a segar in his mouth, who is passing all those roadsters on the right? He dashes past everybody but Bonner. His bays must be well trained; he handles the ribbons as though he was used to it. That gentleman with a white cravat on, you mean? Yes, sir. That is Commodore Cornelius Vanderbilt, who has four of the best horses that appear on the road, every one of them exceedingly fast. He never gives up to anyone but Bonner; is always in good spirits, and takes great comfort in his $10,000 worth of horse flesh; is one of the coolest drivers on the road.[79]

August Belmont and William Aspinwall created a stir in 1859 by opening the first private art galleries New York had ever seen—large, specially designed spaces for paintings by Europe's old masters, including Velázquez and van Dyck. By contrast, Vanderbilt's only notable work of art was a bust of himself.[80]

But there was another New York that arose in the 1850s—the New York of tenements and day-to-day earnings, of pushcarts and workshops and strikes and police batons. In 1857, *Harper's* looked back fifty years and remarked, "What was then a decent and orderly town of moderate size has been converted into a huge semi-barbarous metropolis—one half as luxurious and artistic as Paris, the other half as savage as Cairo or Constantinople." This polarization angered and depressed Herman Melville, who criticized it in *Pierre*, "Bartleby, the Scrivener: A Story of Wall Street," and the self-explanatory "Poor Man's Pudding and Rich Man's Crumbs." In the aftermath of the Panic of 1857, as many as 100,000 went jobless in New York and Brooklyn; in November of that year, thousands demonstrated at Tompkins Square, the city hall, and the Merchants' Exchange, sometimes in the face of hundreds of police and troops. In the winter of 1857–8, at least 41,000 went homeless in Manhattan.[81]

As majority shareholder of a shipyard, machine works, and a fleet of steamers, Vanderbilt played a direct role in shaping this second city. He earned his reputation for keeping costs low in part by paying his workers as little as possible. In August 1858, for example, he cut the monthly wages of his firemen and coal passers from $25 to $20 and $20 to $17, respectively. (Even at the higher wage, a fireman on the *Vanderbilt* earned in an entire year only 3 percent of what the Commodore spent on a team of horses.) When they went on strike, Vanderbilt called on the police to bring in nonunion men. In successive battles on the slips, the police beat back the strikers.[82]

Vanderbilt never acknowledged that conditions had changed since he had lifted himself up—that it was more difficult to attain self-sufficiency, let alone wealth, in this emerging new world. He expected everyone to make his own way, including Billy. As recently as 1856, Vanderbilt had derided his son as a "sucker." He knew that Billy had borrowed heavily to develop his farm, taking $5,000 from Daniel Allen alone. Jacob Van Pelt recalled how, when he had praised Billy's "splendid farm," the Commodore had reacted angrily. "Yes," he replied, "but he can't make a living off it. He has it mortgaged to a damned ——. He ought to come to me. I've got plenty of money to put out on mortgages."[83] But the dutiful son built up his farm successfully. He supplied great quantities of hay to the city's draft animals, and made independent investments. In 1860, for example, he became a director of the nearly complete Staten Island Railroad, and took over as its treasurer. He had emerged as a leader of Richmond County.[84]

Whether Vanderbilt's other sons would succeed remained an unanswered question. George was still at West Point. During the summer, he went on military maneuvers. "The boys are taught to sleep under the canopy of heaven, to dispense with all the luxuries and comforts of civilization, and to accustom themselves to the privations of actual warfare," wrote *Harper's Weekly* on September 3, 1859. "The strictness of West Point discipline has long been proverbial; during 'the encampment' it is severe indeed." In his leisure hours, he would have attended the frequent "hops" or dances organized by such cadets as Adelbert Ames, Wesley Merritt, and Horace Porter. But demerits or low grades hurt George's standing; as he neared graduation, he was ranked next to last in his class.[85]

Vanderbilt remained immensely fond of the clan Corneil had married into. In early 1860, the Commodore wrote to Corneil's father-in-law, Oliver Williams, promising to visit "your sweet home." In some of the most telling lines he would ever write, he added, "Your famally is the only one on earth that I ever say a word to on paper. I much dislike to write & never do out side of business matters."[86]

ON THE NIGHT OF OCTOBER 16, 1859, John Brown led eighteen men into the federal armory at Harper's Ferry, Virginia. A veteran of the fighting against border ruffians in Kansas, he now hoped to spark an uprising by slaves in the South. Instead, Colonel Robert E. Lee and Lieutenant J. E. B. Stuart arrived on the scene with a force of U.S. Marines, who stormed the arsenal on October 18, captured Brown and sixteen of his men, and killed two in the process. The abolitionist stood trial and died on the gallows on December 2. "His name may be a word of power for the next half-century," George Templeton Strong wrote in his diary. The Wall Street lawyer had no sympathy for the antislavery movement, but "Old Brown's demeanor" moved him. "His simplicity and consistency, the absence of fuss, parade, and bravado, the strength and clearness of his letters, all indicate a depth of conviction that one does not expect in an Abolitionist," he wrote. "Slavery has received no such blow in my time as his strangulation."[87]

John Brown's raid confirmed the worst suspicions among "fire-eaters" in the South. When the newly elected House of Representatives tried to choose a speaker in December, Southern Democrats and Know-Nothings blocked the Republican plurality from naming John Sherman, the moderate brother of William T. Sherman. But they could not elect their own man because Horace Clark and a handful of other anti-Lecompton Democrats stood in their way—though Clark refused to vote for Sherman. "Common report attributes the conduct of [Clark] more to the influence of his father-in-law, Mr. Vanderbilt, than any other," the *Chicago Tribune* reported. "Mr. V's mail steamship interests are too valuable to be sacrificed by a single vote for Speaker."[88]

Certainly the Commodore did not wish to alienate the Democratic administration. At the moment, though, both Clark and Vanderbilt were deeply enmeshed in an even more complicated negotiation. William Aspinwall—the merchant prince, the founder of the Pacific Mail and Panama Railroad companies, the man who had given his name to a city in Panama—had decided to give up. He had opened secret talks with Vanderbilt, and on November 25 he presented the Pacific Mail board with the results: a tentative agreement to shut down the North Atlantic Steamship Company, sell to Vanderbilt Pacific Mail's seven ships on the Pacific for $2 million, distribute the proceeds to the stockholders, and terminate the corporation. Despite some dissent, the board empowered Aspinwall to conclude the negotiations. Vanderbilt prevailed on Clark to remain in New York to finalize the talks alongside Marshall Roberts, despite Clark's eagerness to go to Washington.

At nine in the evening on November 29, Clark sent a one-line note to Vanderbilt: "I am quite satisfied that the proposed arrangement is wholly impracticable." The problem was that Clark and Roberts insisted on a guarantee that the directors of Pacific Mail would not go on to compete against Vanderbilt's company as individual proprietors, newly enriched with the Commodore's money. They insisted that Aspinwall give his personal word of honor that there would be no competition—which he "peremptorily declines to give," Clark and Roberts wrote on November 30. Aspinwall replied that this demand was a "new feature," that he could not possibly speak for the stockholders as individuals. "It is a great pity," Vanderbilt concluded.[89]

This argument reveals the culture of American business in a moment of transition. On the eve of 1860, after decades of experience with—indeed, mastery of—the abstractions of the new economy, Vanderbilt and his ring still saw little distinction between the corporation and its stockholders. Theirs was not an elaborately worked-out philosophical position; rather, it was the product of a long tradition of controlling competition with formal and informal agreements—as well as raw self-interest. Yet it demonstrates how even the most sophisticated businessmen held to a tangible understanding of the world of commerce. The financial columnist for the *New York Herald* found it astonishing that Aspinwall and his fellow directors refused the demands of Vanderbilt's representatives. "Without such a guarantee, in fact, Mr. Vanderbilt would have made the worst of bargains," the newspaper observed. "In ordinary cases, it is the vendor who guarantees his purchaser against competition; in this case the vendor was the Pacific Mail Company, which was going into liquidation and out of existence on the consummation of the bargain; the guarantee, therefore, was naturally sought from the individual directors, from whom alone opposition was to be expected."[90]

In January 1860, Joseph Scott, the guardian of the machine works and steamboats at Punta Arenas, walked into Vanderbilt's office on Bowling Green. "I had always expected there would be a line there [in Nicaragua], and that probably he would run it, and if I could sell the things then, I could receive enough to pay my services," he later testified. But the line never reopened, and the property fell into ruin. "I went to Mr. Vanderbilt for a settlement," Scott reported, "to see if he would take the things off my hands." Instead, he went to work for Vanderbilt as agent of the Atlantic & Pacific Steamship Company in Aspinwall, Panama.[91]

Pacific Mail felt the pain of continued competition. It lost a reported $100,000 in the last quarter of 1859 alone, and its prospects looked grim. In January, Vanderbilt's iron-hulled *Champion* arrived in San Francisco, and greatly impressed the city's cynical residents. "As far as we can ascertain by full inquiry the Commodore shows no symptoms of yielding," the *New York Tribune* remarked. The newspaper was correct. When Samuel L. M. Barlow, a key figure in Pacific Mail, suggested the possibility of a compromise to Horace Clark, Clark offered no encouragement. "The Commodore was here [in Washington] yesterday and I endeavoured to sound him [out] on the subject. He is more indifferent than I hoped to find him," Clark wrote on January 16. "Let me suggest to you that *you* go right straight to him and talk to *him* yourself."[92]

Clark's letter was a warning of Vanderbilt's determination, but also an invitation to further talks. Once again, Aspinwall and Barlow began to meet secretly with the Commodore. They soon arrived at a new agreement, one that obviated the need for guarantees of any kind. They would divide the business in half, Pacific Mail retreating to its eponymous ocean and Vanderbilt's Atlantic & Pacific Steamship Company restricting itself to the Atlantic. (This was the same basic agreement they had made in 1856, before Walker had disrupted everything.) Vanderbilt was to bring his new *Champion* back around Cape Horn, receive $50,000 to pay for the voyage, and sell the other, much older ships based in San Francisco to Pacific Mail for five thousand shares of stock and $250,000 in cash, to be paid in ten monthly installments. He would not be allowed to trade the shares for two years. (Vanderbilt owned the ships, so he took this payment himself.) The North Atlantic Steamship Company would be shut down. The two parties would split fares and postal payments according to mileage (giving Vanderbilt 30 percent). The plan would establish a new, more stable monopoly.[93]

There was only one problem: the Panama Railroad did not want a settlement with Vanderbilt. It profited enormously by carrying passengers for both sides, and it had enjoyed a record business during the fare war. A number of the railroad's directors sat on the Pacific Mail board, and they were certain to resist the agreement. So Aspinwall played a trick. He invited those directors to take a junket with him to Panama. He boarded the steamship in New York with his trunks, along with his guests; then, moments before the ship sailed, he announced that pressing business would keep him at home. When the directors returned from Panama, they discovered to their irritation that the treaty with Vanderbilt had been signed and ratified in their absence.[94]

As the 1860s began, Vanderbilt attained wealth and influence never before imagined for a private American citizen—"almost kingly power," as the *Chicago Tribune* said. He controlled American steamship traffic on the Atlantic Ocean, and stood as the largest shareholder in Pacific Mail.[95] (In 1860, Daniel Allen took a seat on the company's board of directors to represent his father-in-law's interests.) Vanderbilt arranged a lasting rise in fares (though not to their previous heights), and along the way prevented his friend Roberts from starting a rival line without paying him a penny. When the California postal contract expired after Congress adjourned without making arrangements for a new one, Vanderbilt refused to carry any more mail. This edict threatened to add weeks to communication between the two coasts by forcing the mail to be carried overland. The Commodore relented only after President Buchanan begged him to reconsider and promised to ask Congress to pay him retroactively. Vanderbilt expanded his role in New York's railroads as well. Already a director of Harlem, he helped Drew restructure the bankrupt Erie's debt (for a very large fee), and joined him on the Erie's board of directors.[96]

One by one, Vanderbilt's enemies lost, surrendered, or met with a violent death. Law had given up; Collins had failed; Morgan, Garrison, Aspinwall, and even Joseph Scott had accepted his terms. Others were less wise, or less fortunate. On August 14, 1859, an uprising in Costa Rica overthrew President Mora. He was executed on September 30, 1860. Even the irrepressible William Walker reached the end of his piratical career. The British captured him on his latest filibustering expedition, and handed him over to the Hondurans, the nearest Central American authorities. They unceremoniously shot him to death on September 12, 1860.[97]

And then there was Joseph White, who had plagued Vanderbilt from the beginning of the gold rush. In January 1861 White returned to Nicaragua, this time to buy exclusive rights to harvest rubber. As he swung in a hammock on the porch of a hotel, he began to talk with another American, Jonathan Gavitt. "It appears that this conversation was not of a very pleasant character, as Mr. Gavitt had been several months in Nicaragua on business of a similar nature to that of Mr. White's, and the former thought the latter was trespassing on his ground," the *New York Times* reported. Gavitt sent his servant to retrieve his revolver, then shot White in the leg. After seven days in tremendous pain, White died.[98]

ON NOVEMBER 4, 1859, VANDERBILT sued Henry J. Raymond, editor of the *New York Times*, for libel. The article in question—a patently false report that Vanderbilt had supported Walker's last expedition—was hardly the issue. After all, journalists of the day relied heavily on rumor and innuendo; newspaper reporting was inaccurate on a regular basis. The point, Vanderbilt argued in his legal complaint, was "that the said article in the *Times* is the result either of personal ill-will toward him or interest averse to his, which leads to the said newspaper being impelled to assail and if possible injure him." Personal ill will indeed. Raymond responded with insults the very next day. "We are at some little loss to understand the meaning of this sudden floundering of the Commodore—this explosion of blubber at the prick of a newspaper paragraph," he wrote. "We don't know whether it indicates that he is growing old and touchy, or that he is becoming ambitious of notoriety."[99]

But this attack was also a matter of politics. During the late 1850s, even into 1860, the *New York Times* waged a crusade against Vanderbilt. On February 9, 1859, Raymond published perhaps his most memorable assault, "Your Money or Your Line," berating Vanderbilt for forcing Pacific Mail to pay his monthly subsidy under the threat of his renewed competition. In this piece, Raymond crafted a lasting metaphor in American culture: the robber baron.

> Like those old German barons who, from their eyries along the Rhine, swooped down upon the commerce of the noble river and wrung tribute from every passenger that floated by, Mr. Cornelius Vanderbilt, with all the steamers of the Accessory Transit held in his leash, has insisted that the Pacific Company should pay him toll, taken of all America that had business with California and the South Sea, and the Pacific Company have submitted to his demand. . . . He has . . . devoted himself to the study of the steam navigation of his country—not with the object of extending its development, but for the purpose of making every prosperous enterprise of the kind in turn his tributary or his victim.

Though Raymond never used the exact phrase "robber baron," it entered the American lexicon as a term for an industrialist who wields his power unscrupulously, to the harm of others. Yet it is essential to note how the metaphor originated. Raymond criticized Vanderbilt for *preying upon* monopolists. He attacked him for, as he wrote elsewhere, "driving too sharp a competition."[100] In "Your Money or Your Line," Raymond derided "competition for competition's sake; competition which crowds out legitimate enterprises . . . or imposes tribute upon them." On July 13, 1860, he called on "our mercantile community to look the curse of competition fully in the face."

To later generations of Americans, Raymond's critique would make no sense. Vanderbilt was a robber baron because he was excessively competitive? Vanderbilt's enterprises were not "legitimate," even though they were more successful than those that supposedly were? Was competition supposed to have no winners or losers? And wasn't it Pacific Mail that was the monopolistic force that restrained trade by buying off competitors (a policy that made it immensely profitable)?

Raymond's arguments reflected a deep and persistent strain of Whig philosophy. The editor himself was a "reliably orthodox" Whig, and his newspaper was founded by "Whig bankers," as two historians write.[101]

When he tried to express his loathing for Vanderbilt, he drew on a political vocabulary, a political mind-set, now decades old, crafted in a younger America with limited capital and few large enterprises. The Whigs had strongly believed in economic development, and had championed legal devices such as corporations to assist wealthy men in concentrating capital for useful purposes. Pacific Mail, which originated in a federal plan to guarantee mail service to the Pacific coast, offered a perfect example of their ideals; more than that, the elite status of its incorporators appealed to social prejudices that lingered among old New York Whigs. Raymond even depicted corporations as fragile creations. In "Your Money or Your Line," he made the argument that "no joint-stock company . . . can ever be a match for a single man" who possessed a large sum of money. Raymond gave voice to a certain strand of Whig thinking that had always condemned the destructive tendency of free competition, casting it as piracy that annihilated capital.

"The idea of depicting Vanderbilt as a corsair because he establishes rival lines to successful steamboat companies is not consistent with experience or common sense," argued *Harper's Weekly*, in a direct counterblast to the *Times*'s famous editorial. "It is because competition is free—because it is encouraged in every branch of trade and enterprise—that this country has become rich and prosperous."[102] On March 5, 1859, *Harper's* published an adulatory profile of the Commodore in which it continued this argument. "It has been much the fashion to regard these contests as attempts on his part to levy black-mail on successful enterprises. . . . He must be judged by the results; and the results, in every case, of the establishment of opposition lines by Vanderbilt has been the *permanent reduction of fares*." It added, in a much-quoted line, "This great boon—cheap travel—the community owes mainly to Cornelius Vanderbilt."

This defense of the Commodore sounds more logical to the mind-set of later centuries, but it, too, drew upon an earlier generation's political rhetoric—that of Jacksonian Democrats. *Harper's* argued that he had championed the fight against the aristocratic elite, against those artificial monsters the Whigs loved so much: "powerful corporations, who enjoyed a monopoly of the traffic, and whose wealth and obvious soullessness were a terror to steamboat men." It praised Vanderbilt, on the other hand, specifically as an *individual*, in battle against such devils. "We have heard it said that no man in this country gives employment directly or indirectly to so many persons," the *Herald* wrote. "He began life by working to live, he now lives to work."[103]

The truth is that neither Andrew Jackson nor Daniel Webster, nor anyone else who had helped to create the Democratic and Whig parties, had imagined a man like Vanderbilt. Few previously had accumulated so much wealth, in either absolute or relative terms; and there was probably no one who had ever possessed such sway over public affairs—over the survival of a railroad, or a government, or over the great corridor to California. Nor did he exist in some kind of polar opposition with corporations and monopolies. By 1859, he operated almost entirely through corporations; he proved himself an expert at using the stock market to concentrate capital or avenge himself on his enemies, and emerged as a master of corporate structure. He saw the corporation as just another type of business organization. For many old Whigs and Democrats, on the other hand, the corporation remained a political animal. Whigs had approved of it as a means of harnessing private enterprise for the public good; since corporations remained few in number, they may not have imagined that they one day would become commonplace. On the other side, Democrats who praised Vanderbilt's competition failed to grasp that he was using the corporate form to create enterprises on an unprecedented scale, gaining control over vast channels of commerce. He represented a new creature on the American scene, and political language and logic had not yet come to terms with him.

Vanderbilt was clearly an unsurpassed competitor, and the good he thereby wrought was well described by *Harper's Weekly*. He was a fighter by nature, a cunning and proud warrior. He always felt that he could take care of himself, under any circumstances. He seems to have believed the Jacksonian rhetoric he so often repeated, a creed of laissez-faire individualism, a vision of a world in which any man might get ahead by his natural gifts rather than government favors. And yet, in pursuing his private interests wherever they took him, he felt no obligation to act in the public interest; when competition had served its purpose, he freely sold out or constructed new monopolies. As he operated on a vast new scale, he brought to a head the contradiction inherent in the private ownership of public works—a paradox that would grow starker when he moved from steamships into railroads in the climactic phase of his life.

Raymond's attack on Vanderbilt, for all its incoherence, spoke to a budding sense that this increasing concentration of wealth and power in the hands of one man posed a challenge to democratic, egalitarian society. Unions could not restrain Vanderbilt from slashing wages and firing strikers; no federal or state laws prohibited his inside trading on Wall Street; few taxes touched his wealth; no regulatory agencies examined his vast affairs or rendered them transparent. It is true that Vanderbilt created tremendous wealth in this environment; it is also true that the limited government deliberately crafted by the Jacksonians—staffed by political appointees, without any kind of professional civil service—lacked the means to check any abuse of his power. And his power would grow dramatically in the next decade and a half. But before Vanderbilt died, a new political matrix would begin to emerge.[104]

So much for the meaning; but there remains the man himself. In December 1859, a fierce Atlantic storm smashed the *Ariel*, threatening it with destruction. Its captain, a man named Ludlow, went out on deck to direct the construction of a drag, or emergency sea anchor, to save the ship. "A tremendous sea broke upon her forward deck," the *Times* reported. Ten feet of water swept over Ludlow, and "the heavy drag, composed of plank and timbers, struck him on the side." He lived long enough to gasp, "Tell the Commodore I died at the post of duty."[105]

Those words deserve to be the last about the Commodore as commodore. They call to mind Tolstoy's observation in *The Sebastopol Sketches*, a soldier's view of the Crimean War. Discipline and obedience, he wrote, ultimately depend upon "the subordinate's recognition that those placed in authority over him are possessed of a higher degree of experience, military prowess, or—not to beat around the bush—moral development."[106] But a superior who lacks real ability—or character—draws only scorn. In a quasi-military (or, more properly, quasi-naval) culture such as that of the merchant marine, a commander need not be sweet-tempered to be admired; rather, he had to be skilled, knowledgeable, fair, and preferably tough.

Beyond all analysis of Vanderbilt's historical role, it is worth remembering that men willingly followed this difficult, profane titan, even at the risk of their own lives. It was not because he was generous or kind, but because he was a man of genuine prowess. No one, they knew, understood steamships better; no one, they knew, was more willing to face personal danger; no one, they knew, was truer to his word. Vanderbilt was many things, not all of them admirable, but he was never a phony. Hated, revered, resented, he always commanded respect, even from his enemies.

Part Three

KING

1861–1877

I have about made up my mind he does not know what is right and what is wrong.
—HENRY KEEP, January 8, 1867

It is not according to my mode of doing things to bring a suit against a man that I have the power in my own hands to punish. . . . I am not afraid of my enemies, but, my God, you must look out when you get among your friends.
—CORNELIUS VANDERBILT, February 5, 1867

A strong friend, a mostly bitter enemy. . . . The ablest R.R. manager in this country, engaged in vast operations [which] he controls at will.
—R. G. DUN & CO., May 19, 1868, May 25, 1869

It is impossible to contemplate this vast aggregation of money power and commercial control in the hands of one man without feeling concern for the result. . . . In the past no Legislature in this State has ever dared to beard him. . . . It is, moreover, one thing to pass laws, and quite another to execute them against a man fertile in resource, energetic in action, obstinate in combat, and inexhaustible in purse.
—*Harper's Weekly*, July 26, 1873

An old sea captain who knew him well used to say it was fortunate that the Commodore was not educated; for had he been he would have been a god.
—*New York Sun*, April 14, 1878

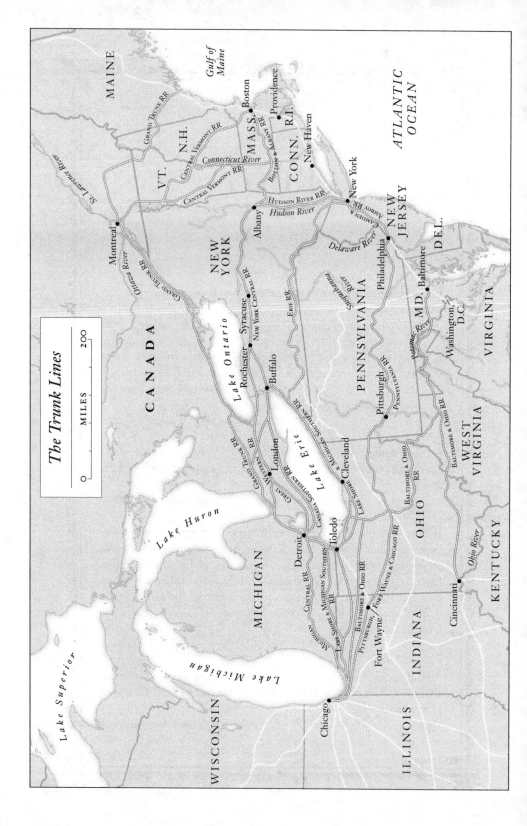

The Trunk Lines

Chapter Thirteen

WAR

They came to tell his secrets. Starting at the appointed hour of two o'clock in the afternoon on November 12, 1877, dozens of witnesses took the stand, one by one, week after week, in that courtroom in lower Manhattan. They included friends and relatives of the deceased Commodore, of course, as well as businessmen and acquaintances. But many of the men and women who took the stand were mediums, magnetic healers, and outright confidence artists. They told tales of séances, outbursts, and high emotion—and attorney Scott Lord tried to introduce even more, as he sought to undermine the last will and testament of Cornelius Vanderbilt. It was a burlesque parade of the marginal and untrustworthy (including one woman who had shot a druggist in Baltimore),[1] whose stories left a nearly ineffaceable imprint on Vanderbilt's image.

Most of the witnesses spoke of the Commodore's last years—years of triumph and of loss, years when he outlived so many of his contemporaries, years when he accumulated his greatest achievements. The testimony that best illuminated his final decade and a half, though, came on the first two days of the trial; and it was spoken not by a medium or mesmerist, but by Daniel B. Allen. He had managed the Commodore's businesses from the 1830s onward, tending to bills, organizing corporations, and relaying messages to presidents in Nicaragua and the White House. He was elderly now, and dignified. "A gentleman with silvery white hair and iron gray moustache," the *New York Times* described him; "a man who would be noticeable in any assemblage."[2]

As he looked out from the witness box at the high, inlaid ceiling, the fluted columns, the bearded faces of the attorneys, he named two years that defined the ultimate phase of Vanderbilt's life: 1864 and 1873. They marked the end of Allen's ties to the Commodore—first of their business, then of their personal relationship. Those two years also defined Vanderbilt's historical role and overarching significance.

The first was a year of transformation, the second of crisis. In 1864, at the age of seventy, Vanderbilt abandoned his lifelong career in shipping as he amassed a railroad realm. Nine years later, he faced the Panic of 1873, an economic cataclysm that forced him to call up all his aged strength and ingenuity to protect what he had built. How he handled these two moments defined his legacy. In the end, he would not only build an empire, he would found a dynasty. And his family would never be whole again.

OUTSIDE, THE MASSES WERE MARCHING. Inside, the Commodore mourned.

On the evening of November 2, 1860, a procession of young men advanced on Union Square. They carried torches, waved lanterns, and fired rockets and Roman candles into the night sky. They were Wide Awakes, members of Republican Party clubs that marched in towns across the North as the presidential election approached. As the parade approached the New York Hotel on Broadway, Southern guests gathered on the sidewalk to hiss and make catcalls; across the street, cheers echoed from the Lincoln campaign headquarters. "The din was deafening," an observer remarked.[3]

That single scene captured the times: a panorama of mobilization and mutual hostility, lit by fire. Everyone remarked on the gathering crisis, except when it seemed to require no comment at all. The Republicans had nominated the Illinois railroad lawyer Abraham Lincoln on a platform of firm opposition to any spread of slavery. The Democrats had splintered. The round-faced and wide-eyed Horace F. Clark stood by his friend, Senator Stephen A. Douglas, who infuriated Southern "fire-eaters" with his insistence on the right of settlers in Kansas to reject slavery; Douglas was nominated by a largely Northern fragment of the Democratic Party. Border-state Whigs and moderate Democrats had created the pro-slavery-yet-Unionist Constitutional Union Party, running John Bell for president. The fire-eaters demanded the right to carry slaves into any federal territory; they nominated John C. Breckinridge, who ran on less a platform than an ultimatum. His supporters warned that the South would secede if Lincoln won; as Senator Robert Toombs of Georgia declared, they would "never permit this Federal government to pass into the traitorous hands of the Black Republican party." But Northern resolve arose in turn, as seen by the torch-waving Wide Awakes.[4]

Away from conventions and parades, inside the four-story brick mansion with brownstone trim at 10 Washington Place, Cornelius Vanderbilt was up to date about the irrepressible conflict. The crisis posed serious questions for the future of his shipping lines between New York and New Orleans, Havana, and Aspinwall. But never far from the front of his mind was a sense of mourning, a sense of loss. It had been six years—nearly seven—since his mother had died on January 22, 1854.[5] Even for the steely Commodore, the pain endured.

"That irreparable change a death makes in the course of our daily thoughts can be felt in a vague and poignant discomfort of mind," Joseph Conrad writes.[6] This modest observation aptly describes Vanderbilt's response to the passing of the eighty-seven-year-old Phebe. Unquestionably he always had revered her, as shown by the rockets he fired in tribute from the *North Star* in 1853. But after her death a vague and poignant discomfort compounded in his mind like interest on a debt, piling up year after year, until his love publicly manifested itself as it rarely had during her lifetime. Writers who interviewed him began to note his adoration of the flinty old woman who had educated him in the ways of the market. Over a meal in the dining room at 10 Washington Place, Vanderbilt would tell of how, back around 1820, he had invited his mother aboard the first steamboat he had built and owned entirely on his own. "I escorted her aboard and showed her the gay decks and the engine, and the galley," he would recall. "I was mighty proud of her, I tell you!" (Meaning the boat, not his mother.) Then he took her down to the saloon for a celebratory banquet. "Cornele," she snapped, "where the devil did you git this dinner?" Even amid the grandeur of his very own steamboat, the food had struck her as an extravagant waste of money.[7]

Conrad also notes, "Action is consolatory. . . . Only in the conduct of our action can we find a sense of mastery over the Fates."[8] Perhaps it is not surprising, then, that the long-bereaved Vanderbilt—with all his battles seemingly won, with virtual ownership of the America's sea lanes to Panama and Europe—should undertake a project that took him back to Staten Island. Both his brother Jacob and his son William had taken an interest in the thirteen-mile Staten Island Railroad, in which Billy served as treasurer. "They had very bad accommodations to get to it," Vanderbilt testified in 1861. "I said I would build a ferry. . . . It was a kind of hobby of mine."

A hobby to the Commodore, of course, would have been a major investment to most other men. On June 1, 1860, he began construction at the Simonson shipyard of two new boats to connect with the railroad: the *Clifton* and the *Westfield*, costing roughly $90,000 apiece. By the end of the year he had them running from Whitehall Slip to a new railhead at Vanderbilt's Landing; soon he added a third boat, the *Southfield*. "They cost me an immense sight of money," Vanderbilt noted. "They run along and did very well; but I never made any money out of them. . . . The boats I built as a matter of pride."[9]

It was an inward turn of mind, this hobby of Vanderbilt's, for a man of transoceanic, transcontinental enterprises. It was, perhaps, the turn of a sixty-six-year-old mind increasingly attuned to family and home, to the places of birth and death. But the crisis enveloping the world around him would penetrate even here.

ON NOVEMBER 7, 1860, the *New York Herald* announced, "END OF THE GREAT NATIONAL CONTEST." Abraham Lincoln was elected by a plurality of the popular vote, though without a single ballot from the South in the electoral college. Of course, the great national contest had only begun. Immediately the slave states began to convene special conventions to consider the question of departing from the Union. South Carolina voted to secede on December 20, followed by Mississippi on January 9, 1861, followed in rapid succession by Florida, Alabama, Georgia, Louisiana, and Texas. On February 4, delegates gathered for a constitutional convention at Montgomery, Alabama, in order to form the Confederate States of America.[10]

Lincoln would not take the oath of office until March 4. In the meantime, attempts to hold the Union together centered in the outgoing Congress and, to a considerable extent, in the ranks of the great merchants of New York. On both counts Vanderbilt found the storm swirling around him. Horace F. Clark (who had not stood for reelection) argued for a constitutional amendment to protect slavery, "to bribe the slaveholders to remain" in the Union, as the *Chicago Tribune* scornfully remarked.[11] On January 7, 1861, Mayor Fernando Wood (who had returned to office after organizing Mozart Hall as a rival organization to Tammany) proposed that, if the South seceded, New York should too, and stand as a free city. No one of note supported him, but the very idea demonstrated how closely the city's economy was tied to the cotton trade, and why so many of its merchants and financiers fought for a compromise. In December, a group led by August Belmont, William Astor, William Aspinwall, Moses Grinnell, Hamilton Fish, and Richard Blatchford had gone to Washington to plead for appeasement. At the end of January, Aspinwall led another elite group to the capital, bearing a petition with thousands of merchants' signatures, asking that the South be placated. "We fear," Mayor Wood admitted, "that if the Union dies, the present supremacy of New York may perish with it."[12]

The division of the republic proceeded inexorably; but the question of whether it would result in war centered on Fort Sumter, a federal post on an island in Charleston Harbor. The South Carolinians wanted it. Soon after the new year, the aged General in Chief Winfield Scott dispatched men and supplies from New York to reinforce the slender garrison. The ship he chartered for the job was Vanderbilt's old *Star of the West.* On January 9, the rebels opened fire on the steamer and drove it out of the harbor. On March 4, Lincoln delivered his inaugural address, appealing to the "mystic chords of memory, stretching from every battlefield and patriot grave to every living heart and hearthstone." The next day, he learned that Fort Sumter had barely six weeks before its besieged men would run out of supplies.

General Scott and many in the cabinet argued that Lincoln should withdraw the garrison. Instead, the president decided to resupply the fort, but without blasting his way into Charleston. So far, no shots had been fired at Sumter; some border states still wavered between Union and secession. Lincoln wanted to force the Confederates to fight for the fort, but to place the onus of starting hostilities squarely on them.[13]

On April 5, New Yorkers observed an extraordinary bustle in the army and navy facilities around the harbor as the resupply expedition set sail. A week later, newsboys poured into the evening streets, crying, "Extra—a *Herald!* Got the bombardment of *Fort Sumter!*" Walt Whitman, George Templeton Strong, and countless others anxiously read the freshly printed sheets in the glare of corner gaslights. War had begun.[14]

War deserves its reputation as the most serious event in national life. It is a grimly wasteful enterprise: the expenditure of resources on materiel that can only destroy, not create, wealth; the termination of lives, usually of young men, at the moment of their greatest energy and potential; the gradual, bitter realization that, as Wellington famously declared, the only thing worse than a battle won is a battle lost. But the Civil War was more extraordinary than most, and more horrible. It brought to a head decades of animosity that had grown into suspicion and flowered into paranoia. Perhaps most important, it was a war for national survival. For the people of the North, the republic they loved had been torn in two. When Virginia joined the Confederacy (along with North Carolina, Tennessee, and Arkansas), the enemy stood across a river from Washington, D.C. Seemingly as one, Northerners decided this could not stand.

On April 15, the day after Fort Sumter was forced to surrender, Lincoln called 75,000 state militiamen into national service to suppress the rebellion. It soon became clear that he would get many more. In New York, once the scene of so much sentiment for compromise, a patriotic frenzy seized the people. Recruiting offices opened, tents popped up at the Battery, rough wooden barracks rose in Central and City Hall parks. "The city seems to have gone suddenly wild and crazy," one man wrote. On April 20, platoons of recruits practiced marching up and down Broadway to the cheers of onlookers, under flags that hung from almost every building. Some 250,000 citizens packed Union Square for a rally. On

Staten Island, Jacob and William Vanderbilt helped organize a mass Union meeting where Horace Clark spoke.[15]

But the seriousness of the crisis could not be denied. A panic seized Wall Street as stocks fell, banks called in loans, and depositors withdrew money and hoarded gold. "I believe my assets to be reduced fifty per cent, at least," Strong wrote in his diary. "But I hope I can still provide wholesome training for my three boys. With that patrimony they can fight out the battle of life for themselves."[16]

Soon the battle of life would seize Vanderbilt's own sons in ways that he could not have predicted in April 1861. For the time being, he had to attend in person to the battle with the Confederacy. Curiously, William C. Jewett (Cornelius Garrison's son-in-law) wrote to Vanderbilt about a "report you are disposed to aid the South."[17] Quite the opposite was true—but purely selfish interests, not patriotism, first propelled him into wartime affairs. After consulting with William Aspinwall, Vanderbilt wrote to Secretary of the Navy Gideon Welles on April 16, under the letterhead of the Atlantic & Pacific Steamship Company, 177 West Street. "The shippers of specie by our line," he observed, "are apprehensive that our steamers may be seized or robbed on their voyage from Aspwinall to New York, unless some special provision be made for their safety." Vanderbilt wanted the government to equip each of the company's ships with a cannon, along with one hundred rifles. "These arms, in the hands of passengers such as ordinarily travel over this route, will be a sufficient protection against any pirate or privateer," he wrote, thinking perhaps of the hardened Californians who had gone straight from the gold fields to Walker's army.

His concern was well founded. The next day, a group of New York's merchants and bankers begged Treasury Secretary Salmon P. Chase to place guns on Vanderbilt's ships, noting that they carried "$40,000,000 of gold annually from San Francisco to this port. . . . The capture of even one of these steamers," they argued, "would stop shipments of gold from San Francisco, or at any rate divert the flow of treasure from New York to foreign countries."

The Commodore's quick response to the crisis prevented the capture of one ship, the *Daniel Webster;* he diverted it from its voyage to New Orleans, where the rebels had planned to seize it on April 22. But the danger remained. On April 17, Confederate president Jefferson Davis authorized Southern privateers to attack Northern merchantmen. In June, Captain Raphael Semmes escaped the blockade of Southern ports in the CSS *Sumter,* the first Confederate commerce raider. It would not be the last. Indeed, Semmes would become a personal problem for Cornelius Vanderbilt.[18]

Meanwhile, New York's wealthy men took in hand the problem of mobilization. Before the end of April, they organized the Union Defense Committee, with an office at 30 Pine Street. The members comprised a roster of the city's patriarchs: John J. Astor, Moses Taylor, Moses H. Grinnell, Alexander T. Stewart, Samuel Sloan, William E. Dodge, and nineteen others, of both parties. They raised regiments of volunteers; purchased arms, uniforms, and supplies; issued passes for travel to Washington; and generally assumed governmental functions.[19]

To a great extent, this was inevitable. The limited government inherited by Lincoln's administration lacked the financing, the manpower, even the organizational capacity to undertake a major war. The federal budget for 1860 had amounted to just $63 million. (The annual figure would grow to more than $1 billion by the end of the war.) Only sixteen thousand men filled the regular army, and they were dispersed across the western frontier. The navy floated just forty-two ships, not all of them ready for service. Though the army boasted some highly professional quartermasters, they had never dealt with the demands now imposed on them; as James McPherson writes, "The War Department slumbered in ancient bureaucratic routine." States and private citizens *had* to assume responsibilities ordinarily reserved for the national government.[20]

Vanderbilt did not join the Union Defense Committee. He never joined civic organizations or loaned his name to charitable bodies. In part, he hated the formality of the proceedings; in part, he was too proud to be a rank-and-file volunteer. "When the rebellion broke out in 1861 and Mr. Vanderbilt was waited upon by Moses Taylor to take some government bonds," Lambert Wardell recalled, "he declined to do so, but later on was a large purchaser of the bonds, purely from the standpoint of speculation. It is believed that had the idea originated with him he would have taken the bonds in the first instance, but he was averse to playing second fiddle to Mr. Taylor."[21]

And yet, his patriotism remained as real and deep as on the day when he had driven Lafayette through the streets of New Brunswick. His opportunity to serve came as the Union prepared amphibious expeditions against the Southern coast. But he grew dissatisfied—even angry—as the War Department and navy began to charter his ships. "The moment a man comes to New York he is surrounded by a lot of thieves all the time, and in every shape and direction," Vanderbilt told a committee of the House of Representatives later that year. Ship brokers swarmed around the federal officials in charge of the charters, inserting themselves as middlemen for either the government or the private owners.

"I am to give a man, one of these outside thieves," Vanderbilt stated increduously, "two and a half percent commission on that charter."[22] The idea offended both his patriotism and his sense of commercial justice—but he had a solution. On April 20, he wrote to Navy Secretary Welles, "I feel a great desire that the government should have the steamer *Vanderbilt*, as she is acknowledged to be as fine a ship as floats the ocean, and, in consequence of her great speed and capacity, that, with a proper armament, she would be of more efficient service in keeping our coast clear of piratical vessels than any other ship." He suggested that the sale price be determined by any three men with the rank of commodore (still the highest in the navy), recommending the eminent Robert Stockton as one of them. "If this will not answer," he added, "will the government accept her as a present from their humble servant?" In addition, he offered to sell the *Ocean Queen*, the *Ariel*, the *Champion*, and the *Daniel Webster* on the same terms.[23]

"There is no such water craft afloat, and I know it," Vanderbilt later testified before Congress, speaking of the *Vanderbilt*. "But he [Welles] would not hear it, and did not answer my letter." Instead, Welles wrote a note on May 2 to Captain Samuel L. Breese, commandant of the Brooklyn Navy Yard, saying he did not want the *Vanderbilt*. "The complement originally ordered is full," he stated, and the great steamer was "of a larger and more expensive description than the service is supposed to require."[24]

Why turn down a gift—the most "princely and munificent" ever offered by an individual to the government, in the words of the *New York Herald*? Perhaps Welles expected the war to end soon, as many did, and did not want to be left with an unnecessarily large and expensive-to-run ship. The secretary was also a man with a great deal of pride. The idea that his fleet needed Vanderbilt's help may have insulted him. Perhaps most important, there was tension between the War Department and the navy. Much of the chartering of merchant ships was not conducted by naval personnel; and Welles seems to have viewed all transactions with commercial men with a bit of cynical distaste.

So the *Vanderbilt* would *not* be "at the head of the navy, where she ought to be," as its owner believed. Instead, it would be chartered as a mere transport, along with most of the sidewheelers run by the Atlantic & Pacific Steamship Company, as the "outside thieves" collected their 2.5 percent and drove up the price. Vanderbilt received $2,000 a day for his great ship; in the end, the federal government would pay him a total of $303,589.10 for the use of that vessel alone—approximately one-third of its original cost. Yet even this fee was not as unreasonable as it might seem. Vanderbilt paid all costs of operation, which could amount to $600 a day under ordinary circumstances, and bore all risks except for actual combat; the peculiar demands of wartime operations could raise that operating cost far higher. (Boiler fires had to be kept burning at all times, for example, to allow for a quick escape or to avoid collision in a dense fleet.) The charge of extortionate pricing would prove persistent, but it was not well founded. In any case, he never wanted to charter his steamers in the first place. "The fact is, I would rather sell every ship I have," he testified. "I, myself, am not a fair criterion for other men. I would rather sell my ships than let them remain in the government employ until they earn their whole value and then have the ships and the money too."

He did finally sell two boats to the navy in 1861—two boats he did not want to let go: the *Clifton* and the *Westfield*, of the Staten Island Railroad ferry, for $90,000 each. The navy's agent was George D. Morgan, cousin to Governor Edwin D. Morgan of New York and brother-in-law to Gideon Welles—who took his 2.5 percent. As Vanderbilt wisely observed, New York had thieves in every shape and direction.[25]

WAR BROUGHT George Washington Vanderbilt home.

On July 1, 1860, he had graduated from West Point after the standard five years. (George Custer graduated in 1861 in the first four-year class.) The regular army was stingy with promotions—so stingy that it did not even grant him the rank of second lieutenant, the very lowest for commissioned officers. Instead, it named him brevet (honorary) second lieutenant. He was dispatched to Fort Dalles in Oregon, where there recently had been hostilities with Indians. He had arrived on December 4, 1860, only to be recalled on January 28. Posted to Fort Columbus on Governors Island, he finally received the full rank of second lieutenant in the 10th Infantry Regiment on February 27, 1861. With the outbreak of war, the army assigned him to the unglamorous task of training the recruits who signed up by the thousands.[26]

Of the Commodore's three sons, George remains the most mysterious. William was dutiful, diligent, and dull, the colorless farmer and manager whose profile steadily rose higher without ever seeming any larger. Corneil flared fitfully into public view, with his epileptic fits, episodic gambling, and artful begging from prominent men. But George exists in the historical record as little more than a shadow, defined largely in contrast to his brothers. He was brave and strong and manly, legend tells us, the pride of a father who wanted so much to have a Vanderbilt to be proud of. This comes to us as more an impression than even an anecdote, but perhaps it is true; William named a son after his brother, after all. But hidden by the warm glow of the honored memory of a Civil War veteran is lurking disappointment.

For one thing, George clearly had struggled at the Military Academy, where he graduated thirty-ninth out of forty-one, only one step above his lowest point. Custer, of course, graduated last in his class and still went on to fame in the war. But the two Georges had different fates. Hardly had the hostilities begun than the Commodore's son found himself standing before a court-martial. On the afternoon of May 16, he had disappeared from his training duties at Fort Columbus. He had returned the next day, without explanation. At his trial on May 29, he made no defense, and was sentenced to one month of confinement to the fort, after which he returned to duty.

The conviction seems to have marked him. Though it is always difficult to understand why a military bureaucracy treats any individual the way it does, the army shunted him aside, despite its need for every regular army officer it could find, as it created hundreds of new regiments of U.S. Volunteers (temporary units for the duration of the war). Men such as Ulysses S. Grant and William T. Sherman, West Pointers who had retired after rising no higher than captain or lieutenant, returned to service and rapidly became generals. But the army sent George to Boston. There, on September 1, he took charge of the recruiting station, replacing an officer who was given command of his own regiment. It appeared that if the Vanderbilts were to gain any glory in the Civil War, the aged Commodore would have to win it for himself.[27]

IT HAD BEEN A YEAR of defeat upon defeat. Bull Run, Wilson's Creek, Ball's Bluff, and Lexington, Missouri: such was the legacy that Edwin M. Stanton inherited when he took office as secretary of war in January 1862. Overbearing, incisive, and fiercely honest, this former U.S. attorney general brought a determination to reform a department demoralized by the inefficiency and corruption that had prevailed under his predecessor, Simon Cameron. "Stanton impresses me and everybody else most favorably," wrote Strong. That ubiquitous observer met Stanton in Washington on January 29. "Not handsome, but on the contrary, rather pig-faced. At lowest estimate, worth a wagon load of Camerons. Intelligent, prompt, clear-headed, fluent without wordiness, and above all, earnest."[28]

As his secretaryship began, Stanton could count a rising number of victories and advantages. Even before he came into office, amphibious expeditions had captured key fortifications along the Southern coastline. In February, General Ulysses S. Grant won rousing twin victories at forts Henry and Donelson in Tennessee. And General George B. McClellan now commanded the Army of the Potomac, which he organized, trained, and equipped superbly. McClellan planned a new offensive against the Confederate capital, Richmond, Virginia. He would land his army at Fortress Monroe, at the tip of the peninsula that extended east from Richmond between the York and James rivers. From Monroe (still in federal hands), he would strike west. In March, swarms of men loaded dozens of ships with arms and supplies as the great expedition prepared for departure.

On March 8, it seemed that the Confederates would stop McClellan's Peninsula Campaign before it could begin—indeed, that they would anni-hilate Union maritime power at will. That day, a strange craft steamed out of Norfolk harbor at the creeping speed of about four knots. It resembled a turtle or, as someone at the time described it, the roof of a submerged barn. It was the salvaged hull of the *Merrimack*, a U.S. frigate scuttled at the Norfolk naval yard that the Confederates had salvaged, covered in iron plate, and renamed the CSS *Virginia*. (The Union persisted in calling it the *Merrimack*.) It steamed straight for the Union blockade squadron at Hampton Roads, the waters at the mouth of the James River, where it sank two ships. A third, the *Minnesota*, ran aground in shallows where the deep-draft *Virginia* could not go with its deadly ram. During the fight, solid shot ricocheted off its armor shell. The *Virginia* suffered internal damage, but outwardly it seemed invincible.[29]

"Stanton was the most frightened man that I ever saw," Gideon Welles afterward reflected in his diary. When news arrived of the *Virginia's* ram-page, "I called at once on the President, who had sent for me," he wrote a few years later. "Several members of the Cabinet soon gathered. Stanton was already there, and there was general excitement and alarm." The sec-retary of war, he recalled, "was almost frantic. . . . The *Merrimac*,* he said, would destroy every vessel in the service, could lay every city on the coast under contribution, could take Fortress Monroe—McClellan's mistaken purpose to advance by the Peninsula must be abandoned." Both Lincoln and Stanton, he added, "went repeatedly to the window and looked down the Potomac—the view being uninterrupted for miles—to see if the *Mer-rimac* was not coming to Washington."

Welles's spies had followed the progress of the *Merrimack* turned *Vir-ginia* all along. In fact, the navy secretary had multiple ironclads of his own under construction; one had just been completed in New York, and it departed immediately for Hampton Roads. It was a small, raft-like craft with a revolutionary rotating turret that mounted two guns. It was called the *Monitor*. On March 9, it battled the *Virginia* to a standstill.[30]

So ends one of the set-piece stories of the Civil War: the historic first clash of ironclads, the tale of the *Monitor* steaming onto the scene just in time to prevent the complete destruction of the Union fleet. Certainly that was the story that set itself firmly in the memory of Welles, who felt a deep antipathy toward Stanton. But history went on after the indecisive battle of March 9. The *Monitor* had not defeated the *Virginia*; it had

---

* *Merrimack* was commonly spelled without the final "k."

merely stood off the enemy. The rebel ironclad still lurked. If the *Monitor* simply suffered a breakdown—a commonplace occurrence in a newly launched ship—then nothing could stand in the *Virginia*'s way.

On March 14, five days after the clash between the two armored vessels, General John E. Wool, commander of Fortress Monroe, sent a frightened telegram to Stanton, arguing that the *Virginia* might "overcome the *Monitor.*" The next day, Stanton had an aide telegraph Vanderbilt in turn: "The Secretary of War directs me to ask you for what sum you will contract to destroy the *Merrimac* or prevent her from coming out from Norfolk—you to sink or destroy her if she gets out? Answer by telegraph, as there is no time to be lost."[31] Welles later mocked Stanton's anxiety. "He had no faith in the Navy officers nor me, nor anyone else," he wrote long afterward, "but he knew Vanderbilt had big steamers." Welles apparently forgot that, on March 14, he himself assigned Gustavus V. Fox, the assistant secretary of the navy, to get the *Vanderbilt* from New York.[32]

The Commodore seems to have been away from home, but William B. Dinsmore, president of the Adams Express Company, tracked him down. Vanderbilt wired Stanton, through Dinsmore, that he would come to Washington on March 17.[33] On that Monday morning, "I called at the War Department, where I saw for the first time Mr. Stanton, the Secretary of War," the Commodore wrote four years later. "He requested me to accompany him to the Executive Mansion." Vanderbilt and Stanton were similar men in many ways, both tough-minded, demanding, and immensely capable. They clearly got on well as they walked together to the White House, "where," the Commodore went on, "I was introduced to Mr. Lincoln, to whom I was then personally a stranger."[34]

Now approaching the age of sixty-eight, Vanderbilt experienced the rare sensation of meeting a much taller man. Lincoln asked if Vanderbilt could do anything to keep the enemy vessel from steaming out of Norfolk once more. "I replied to him," the Commodore wrote, "that it was my opinion that if the steamship *Vanderbilt* was there properly manned, the *Merrimac* would not venture to come out; or if she did, that the chances were ten to one that the *Vanderbilt* would sink and destroy her." Then the president asked his price. "I at once informed Mr. Lincoln that I was determined that I would not allow myself to do anything by which I could be ranked with the herd of thieves and vampires who were fattening off the Government by means of army contracts," Vanderbilt recalled, "that I had no vessels to sell or bargains to make, except one." He would give the *Vanderbilt* to the government on the condition that he, the Commodore, should control its preparations for battle. Lincoln replied, "I accept her."

"They asked what my plan was," Vanderbilt recollected, "and I said, to keep steam up and protecting my vessel as much as possible by various means; to run right into the rebel and drown him; that no vessel had been, or could be, made by the rebels that could stand the concussion or stand before the weight of the *Vanderbilt*." Lincoln asked how soon he could have the great steamship at Hampton Roads. "The *Vanderbilt* should be at Fortress Monroe properly equipped and officered, under my direction, within three or four days at the farthest," he answered. Vanderbilt then left immediately for New York. With the fate of McClellan's planned expedition in peril, with fears for the entire blockading fleet, he had no time to spare.[35]

During those rushed few days, Vanderbilt directed the refitting of his flagship in the Simonson shipyard at Greenpoint. His primary effort was to equip it as a ram. Treasury Secretary Salmon P. Chase inspected it soon afterward. "She was already strengthened [about] the bow with timbers," he wrote, "so as to be little else for many feet (say 50) from the prow than a mass of solid timber plated outside with iron." On March 20, the Commodore telegraphed Stanton to ask for formal authority to hunt for the *Virginia*. "The ship leaves to-morrow," he wrote. The war secretary promptly wired back to Vanderbilt's office at 5 Bowling Green, "The President and this Department are highly gratified at your promptitude, and that you are so far forward." In the formal order, Stanton wrote, "Confiding in your patriotic motives and purposes, as well as in your skill, judgment, and energy, full discretion and authority are conferred upon you to arm, equip, navigate, use, manage, and employ the said steamship *Vanderbilt*, with such commander and crew and under such instructions as you may deem fit." The next day, Vanderbilt departed for battle.[36]

"Commodore Vanderbilt," Stanton commented to General Henry Halleck on March 25, "is now at Norfolk to meet the *Merrimac*, and although not armor-clad, he is very confident of being able to run her down." Many observers shared his optimism. "The immense size, great weight, and speed of the *Vanderbilt* especially would seem to make her a terrible opponent in an encounter of that kind," remarked the *Journal of Commerce*. "An unwieldy floating battery, lying low on the water, could not survive many blows from a vessel of her weight." The *Vanderbilt* was "put in fighting trim," the London *Times* reported. "Her steam machinery has been protected by rails in the most ingenious way, and also by cotton bales and hay. Her prow has been armed with a formidable nose, with the intention to poke it right into the side of the *Merrimac*. . . . Its edge is made of steel, and very sharp."[37]

Vanderbilt steamed up to Fortress Monroe in his titanic vessel, its immense sidewheels churning the water, smoke billowing out of its twin funnels. On going ashore, he consulted with General Wool and Commodore Louis M. Goldsborough, commander of the squadron so badly beaten in the first battle with the *Virginia*. Goldsborough impressed Vanderbilt, who turned his ship over to the officer (under the immediate command of Vanderbilt's own captain), despite Stanton's wish to keep it in the War Department's control. Vanderbilt returned to New York, sick with a cold, and explained himself to Stanton. "As for Commodore Goldsborough," he wrote on March 31, "*he is a trump*. I think to be depended upon. He had given Captain Le Ferre directions, which accorded exactly with those that I had given him before leaving New York. So I left this matter undisturbed. My opinion is that the *Merrimac* will not venture outside of Fortress Monroe. If she does, I am quite certain she never can return."38

His enemies feared that he might be right. The rebels respected "the powerful steamer *Vanderbilt*, fitted with a ram expressly to attack the *Virginia*," as Confederate Flag Officer Josiah Tatnall reported on April 30. With its great speed, it could easily outmaneuver and run down the *Virginia* (which could do no better than five knots), and sink it with its enormous weight, even if the ram did not carve open the rebel ship. As one Confederate officer recalled, "We were primed for a desperate tussle."39

By now McClellan had landed the Army of the Potomac on the peninsula and proceeded to waste week after week besieging Yorktown. In early May, Lincoln himself visited the front, accompanied by Treasury Secretary Chase. One day, he and his party saw the telltale trail of smoke that indicated the *Virginia* was coming to fight. On May 7, Chase wrote to his daughter of how "the *Merrimac* came down & out—how the *Monitor* moved up & quietly waited for her—how the big wooden ships got out of the way, that the *Minnesota* & *Vanderbilt* [might] have fair sweep at her & run her down—how she wdn't come when they cd—how she finally retreated to where the *Monitor* alone cd. follow her." The *Vanderbilt* performed its task as Vanderbilt predicted: the Confederates refused to risk the *Virginia* against his ship. Lincoln personally ordered an attack on Norfolk, and the retreating rebels scuttled their ironclad.40

Vanderbilt did not win glory in battle, but he played a key role in bottling up the *Virginia*, allowing the federal authorities to regain their confidence and the Peninsula Campaign to proceed (though to ultimate failure in the Seven Days' Battles). His ship remained in the fleet, where he always had thought it belonged. It was indeed a magnanimous gift—and one that would be remembered by Captain Raphael Semmes.

IF WALL STREET HAD SAINTS, then the college of financial cardinals would surely canonize Elbridge G. Spaulding. Spaulding, chairman of a House subcommittee on emergency measures, performed a true miracle:

he conjured money out of nothing, and so contributed more toward the Union victory (and the future of New York's financial sector) than any single battlefield victory.[41] Though his eminently forgettable name is eminently forgotten today, he was one of the most important architects of the invisible world of commerce that emerged in the nineteenth century. In the nation's darkest hour, he took the increasingly abstract economy and completely abstracted the most solid thing of all: the dollar.

In the opening months of the Civil War, the financial markets staggered along in doubt and fear. These "financial markets" included not only the stock exchanges, but also farmers in Missouri and Michigan, merchants in Danville and Davenport, who clutched the paper notes and deposit receipts issued by local banks; which in turn deposited much of their reserves in New York banks; which in turn made their surplus funds available as call loans to stockbrokers; who in turn provided credit to clients for purchases of securities on Wall Street. The uncertainty of war caused many across the country to withdraw deposits or return notes for gold, ultimately draining reserves in Manhattan. Then, too, Secretary Chase borrowed heavily in New York to finance the war. Following Jacksonian treasury laws to the letter, Chase refused to open accounts with the banks; instead, he insisted that gold be carted from their vaults through the twisting streets of lower Manhattan to the federal subtreasury. The specie lingered there, out of circulation, for weeks or even months before it was spent.

As banks struggled with reduced reserves, the Union suffered the string of setbacks that marked the fall of 1861: the loss of Lexington, Missouri, in September; defeat at Ball's Bluff, Virginia, in October; and McClellan's long refusal to advance on Richmond. When the navy seized two Confederate diplomats at sea, on their way to London, it seemed that war with Britain might ensue. Banknote holders rushed to redeem their paper money for gold, which they hoarded; banks called in loans; stock prices fell, causing panicked selling, causing prices to fall faster, erasing their value as collateral for borrowers. In short, a panic ensued. The banks of New York had no choice but to do the unthinkable (indeed, the illegal under state law): by mutual agreement, they ceased to pay note holders and depositors in specie on December 30.[42]

"There is no such thing as gold and silver coin circulating in the country," declared Senator John Sherman. "It is stowed away." Hoarding threatened to strangle the North. Gold was the stuff that made Americans comfortable with the imagined devices of economic life; when it disappeared from circulation, the public began to give the emperor's wardrobe a second look. Sherman warned that the economy might break down, that the government might find itself unable to secure funds from the private sector. The war would be lost. "We must have money or a fractured government."[43]

Congressman Spaulding found a solution. A banker in private life, he drafted a law to issue federal notes that could not be redeemed for specie. They would be legal tender, which meant that they had to be accepted as payment for any debt; only customs duties and interest on federal bonds would be paid in gold. Lincoln signed the Legal Tender Act on February 25, 1862, and the Treasury began to issue $150 million in "greenbacks," as the new bills were nicknamed. (In July came $150 million more.)

"The new currency began to be seen in the Exchange brokers' offices early in April, first in large notes of $1,000, then of $500," recalled Wall Street speculator William W. Fowler. "In a fortnight, it was coming on in sums counted by the million. . . . From Washington, they came back to the sub-treasury in New York by the express-wagon load, in boxes and in bags, but generally done up in packages the size of small bricks, in brown paper, tied with red tape, sealed with the treasury seal, and numbered and marked; at the sub-treasury, they were paid out." The flood of money revived the markets, he wrote, "as if by magic."[44]

The greenback started a massive reconstruction and expansion of the invisible architecture of the economy, institutionalizing New York's existing centrality to the financial system. In 1863, the National Banking Act created a network of federally chartered banks, which were required to purchase federal bonds and to deposit their cash reserves with banks in reserve cities; banks in reserve cities had to deposit their own cash reserves with banks in New York. This sanctified in law the pyramiding of cash and credit in Manhattan that had occurred before the war, strengthening the mystic cord of money that stretched from the hearthstones of western farms to stockbrokers' offices in Wall Street. The act also allowed such banks to issue national banknotes, which were redeemable in greenbacks, not gold.[45]

The revolutionary nature of all this can scarcely be overestimated. On one hand, it suddenly overturned long-standing traditions concerning the role of the national government in the economy. Jackson had staked his presidency on the fight against the federal charter of one bank (albeit an enormous one); now Washington chartered hundreds of banks, dictated how they would structure and place their reserves, and even issued a national paper currency for the first time since the ratification of the Constitution. In addition, Congress enacted a federal income tax in 1861, also for the first time, extending the touch of the central government to individuals through an extensive new bureaucracy as never before. As one New Yorker wrote in his diary, "The direct tendency of all the acts of the administration and the great aim of the Republican party is toward a strong consolidated Govt overriding state constitutions or laws."[46] It was not a party platform but a war for national survival that drove this process, and radically redefined what Americans accepted as legitimate federal activity.

Perhaps the most revolutionary innovation of all was Elbridge Spaulding's greenback. The idea of "fiat money" (as economists call irredeemable legal tender) offended economists and businessmen, who believed that it would spark disastrous inflation. Old Jacksonians saw it as a dangerous step that opened the economy to political corruption and manipulation. Going deeper, the Legal Tender Act represented a direct attack on the ancient worldview that was rooted in the tangible and real, by declaring that mere markers, the product of imagination alone, would be the medium of exchange and store of value. Serious, knowledgeable men—men such as Hugh McCulloch, a future secretary of the treasury—argued, "Gold and silver are the only true measure of value. These metals were prepared by the Almighty for this very purpose." Now Spaulding made straight what God had made crooked.[47]

The greenback did lead to unforeseen complications. Since the Legal Tender Act did *not* eliminate the gold dollar, it created two currencies—both denominated as dollars. The supply and demand for each varied, so the value of the greenback fluctuated against the gold dollar. An improvised currency exchange soon emerged in New York, later transformed into a formal trading floor called the Gold Room. There brokers determined the "gold premium"—the price in greenbacks of one hundred gold dollars (e.g., a gold premium of 115 meant $115 in greenbacks would buy $100 in gold coin).* Gold stayed out of circulation within the country for the most part (due to the effect known as Gresham's law), but it remained the exclusive form of payment in overseas trade; the Gold Room, then, became the international currency exchange, and thus essential to American foreign commerce. But the value of the greenback also fluctuated with the fate of Union arms on the battlefield. As an abstract unit, created by law, it represented only the strength of public confidence in the federal government. Defeats damaged the greenback; victories brought the two dollars closer in value. Whenever a military campaign began, speculators would gamble on the result by buying greenbacks or selling them short. Essential or not, the gold market began to look seditious.[48]

"I never cared anything about your gold or paper money," Vanderbilt

* Writers often mistakenly describe the gold premium as the price of gold *per ounce*, which only would be true if the weight of a gold dollar was 1/100 of an ounce. (It was, in fact, more than five times that amount.) Setting the price of gold by the ounce emerged far later. The distinction is important, for it speaks to the true nature of the gold market in the 1860s as a currency exchange.

later testified. "I always considered it the same thing with me. If it had cost $1,000 in gold and I paid for it with $1,000 in paper . . . I say there is no difference."[49] He spoke after the end of the war, when the gold premium had grown smaller and less volatile; during the worst of the conflict, when a gold dollar commanded as many as three greenbacks, he undoubtedly paid more attention to the difference.[50] But his casual dismissal of this revolutionary development says much about his mind. After five decades on the forefront of economic change, he easily accepted this innovation. Flexible and pragmatic, he saw Spaulding's miracle as a minor change in the rules.

More important was the sudden acceleration of the pace of the game. In 1861, he had continued his business life much as before. At sea, he had withdrawn his European line, but he remained the guiding spirit of the Atlantic & Pacific Steamship Company. He had received his last payment of $105,050.67 from Pacific Mail, in which he remained the largest stockholder (receiving 15 percent, or $15 per share, in annual dividends). On land, he continued to serve on the board of the Hartford & New Haven Railroad (now paying annual dividends of 12 percent), and he held his seat as a director of the Harlem Railroad, though he rarely attended meetings now that he had helped reduce its floating debt to a manageable $43,789. He also indulged in his own version of charity when he agreed to pay off a mortgage held by a Mrs. Herndon, at the request of Chester A. Arthur, a politically active lawyer and future president. "This will save her from being annoyed with a mortgage," he had written to Arthur on October 8, 1861, "& can pay at her pleasure." And, in a curious echo of the war in Nicaragua, Parker French, William Walker's one-handed confidence man, was arrested in November as an organizer of the Knights of the Golden Circle, a shadowy pro-Confederate conspiracy in the North. Then, in 1862, everything began to move much faster.[51]

The old commercial heart of the city had pulsed with cotton, beating in time to Southern harvests and exports. Seemingly overnight, a transplant gave New York a new, industrial, Northern heart of coal and iron and rifles and tents and shoes and uniforms. Greenbacks and military purchase orders flowed into New York and quickly revived business. Factories, workshops, and warehouses could not meet demand, so new factories, workshops, and warehouses opened. The wave of investment and confidence sped up life on Wall Street dramatically. In early 1862, the Open Board of Stock Brokers organized in a dark basement room on William Street. Known as the "coalhole," it was a literal trading pit into which unlicensed curbside brokers flowed to buy and sell shares from each other with an abandon not seen in the auctions at the older New York Stock and Exchange Board. A financier reportedly said, "The battle of Bull Run makes the fortune of every man in Wall Street who is not a natural idiot."[52]

The turn of New York's economy perfectly suited Vanderbilt, the maker and driver of ships, the financier and rescuer of railroads. New construction and repairs kept his Simonson yard in Greenpoint filled to capacity. The Commodore's Allaire Works employed eight hundred men in constructing gun carriages for *Monitor*-style turrets; building engines for passenger steamers, navy frigates, an ironclad warship, and various gunboats; and repairing machinery on dozens of ships.[53]

Newspaper editors and political malcontents talked of making Vanderbilt the secretary of the navy or treasury, a chorus that grew louder whenever the Union had a nautical or financial setback. But the Commodore stuck to his long-standing policy, as he once put it, "to mind my own business." Perhaps he stuck to it a bit too closely. There was no sign of him when the income tax assessor of the new Internal Revenue Bureau made his rounds in 1862. At 38 Lafayette Place, the assessor found that William B. Astor owed taxes on three carriages, one billiard table, and 8,400 ounces of silver plate, in addition to an annual income of $617,472 (plus $64,850 in interest from federal bonds). At 10 Washington Place, he discovered nothing. The dry federal tax list reveals the bureaucratic equivalent of frustration; the assessor simply made up an income figure of $500,000 for Vanderbilt (on which he was taxed at the top rate of 5 percent), and added a 50 percent penalty, presumably for a failure to respond to inquiries. In fact, federal tax lists would prove to be a worthless source of information about him. His income increasingly consisted of stock dividends, which were taxed at the source. Even the most reliable individual income tax figure radically underreported his actual receipts.[54]

Perhaps he was at the Fashion Course on Long Island when the tax man knocked on the door, for it was there that Vanderbilt indulged in the latest phase of his rivalry with Robert Bonner, editor of the *Ledger*, for ownership of the fastest trotting horses in New York. After one race at the course in 1862, "it was whispered that Mr. Bonner would give his mares a trial of one mile," the *Atlantic Monthly* later reported, "and his appearance on the course in his road wagon, driving the well-known beauties, detained the whole assembled multitude." Bonner and Vanderbilt's informal heats on Harlem Lane and Bloomingdale Road remained a topic of fascination in horse-mad New York, a city all the more crazed for racing as the wartime boom multiplied the men of leisure. Vanderbilt offered to bet $10,000 that his finest pair could beat Bonner's, but Bonner refused to bet as a matter of principle. Instead, he offered to stage a public time trial.

After the jockeys cleared off the track, the audience watched the Commodore walk onto the turf with a watch in hand. "When Mr. Bonner brought out his team there was a murmur of admiration," the *Atlantic Monthly* wrote. He started his horses, Lady Palmer and Flatbush Maid, on a fast first mile round the track, then whipped them to an even faster second mile. As Vanderbilt kept time, his competitor drove the team to a speed of 2 minutes and 28¾ seconds per mile, and the crowd roared. "It was entirely unprecedented," the *Atlantic Monthly* observed. "After learning the time in which his horses had trotted, Mr. Bonner publicly declared that, while it was a rule with him never to make a bet, he would present ten thousand dollars *as a gift* to any gentleman who owned a team, if he would drive them in the time just made." Vanderbilt took his horses as seriously as he did his business; he would work very hard to earn that gift.[55]

There was nothing really new about Vanderbilt's day on the Fashion Course, but it hinted at how he and the world around him were coming into closer alignment. On one hand, the old mercantile aristocracy continued to treat him as a worthy business partner but a bit of a vulgarian. His status as a social outsider among the elite has been exaggerated—his poor manners and ignorant speech even more so—yet there was undoubtedly an inner sanctum of patrician life in which he was still not welcome. In April 1860, for example, Strong had informed his diary that he had been asked to join a "committee of twenty, which is hereafter to take charge of polite society, regulate its interests, keep it pure. . . . It is to pass on the social grade of everybody, by ballot—one blackball excluding." The other members included "Hamilton Fish, Anson Livingston, John Astor, William Schemerhorn, and others of the same sort"—but not, of course, Commodore Vanderbilt. "His wealth is unquestioned," R. G. Dun & Co. had reported in 1860, but "his over-reaching disposition makes people shy of him."[56]

On the other hand, Vanderbilt socialized with another set that came rapidly to the fore in the volatile atmosphere of the war years: the aggressive, enterprising, risk-taking "fast men" of Wall Street. These men—Vanderbilt's circle—raced trotters, played whist at Saratoga, and bought and sold stocks with an avidity never seen before.[57] The cultural appeal of exclusivity would persist; in some eyes, the social strength of old family names only grew stronger, and new families sought to mingle and marry with them. Still, the economic and cultural reorientation of the Civil War undoubtedly created a sense that new growth was crowding out the old. Dixiecentric cotton merchants declined, and the geographical center of business shifted north. What historian Sven Beckert calls an emerging industrial bourgeoisie was not so much a new class, perhaps, as the triumph of a new *outlook* among the wealthy, one that had long existed but now came to the fore. It was an ease with the abstract economy, the intangible commerce of stocks and bonds and clearinghouse transactions, the impersonal corporations that began to supplant old family firms. This was the mind-set of the rising generation of rich New Yorkers. To them, the aged Commodore would be seen not as a barbarian but as a hero, an esteemed elder who saw far beyond the men of his time. In 1870, for example, when William W. Fowler published *Ten Years in Wall Street*, a memoir of his decade as a player on the stock market, he dedicated the book to Vanderbilt.[58]

In 1862, the Commodore had not yet performed the miracles that would make him a messiah to many on Wall Street. Despite his past financial warfare, the new men who rushed into the "coalhole" where the Open Board met, who lurked in the offices of brokers on Broad Street or Exchange Place, hardly gave him a thought. A year would pass before he forced the entire financial community to rethink what a man could do with those stocks, bonds, and greenbacks with which their invisible world was built. In the meantime, the secretary of war called him back into the service of his country.

AT FIFTEEN MINUTES AFTER NINE in the morning on July 29, 1862, a sleek, bark-rigged sailing ship weighed anchor at the Laird shipyard in Birkenhead, England, and proceeded down the Mersey River on a trial trip. Various ladies and gentlemen, friends and relatives of the builders, enjoyed a party on deck to celebrate. It was a fine ship, 220 feet in length (210 at the keel), with two steam engines (horizontal, to remain below-decks); a propeller that could be raised or lowered, depending on whether it was powered by steam or sail; and, curiously enough, a collapsible funnel. Stranger yet, it had been fitted for cannons, though none were currently on board. Strangest of all, it was called simply "hull No. 290."

The "trial trip" and celebratory party were all part of a ruse. Thomas H. Dudley, the U.S. consul at nearby Liverpool, had spied on the 290 all through its construction, and learned that it was, in fact, a commerce-raiding cruiser being built for the Confederacy. Already he had taken legal steps to prevent delivery, forcing the South's naval agent in England, James D. Bulloch, to rush his ship to sea. The hastily planned trial run took place immediately after Bulloch received word that the British authorities were about to seize the vessel. "In the evening transferred our visitors to a steam tug," wrote sailor George Townley Fullam in his journal. On board came the full complement of crewmen for a long cruise in search of Union ships. To evade British law, the 290 sailed to the Canary Islands to receive its armament of eight guns.

Its commander was Raphael Semmes. The dashing Semmes had served in the U.S. Navy decades before going over to the Confederacy, seemingly training all the while to be the perfect pirate. Already he had shown his prowess as captain of the CSS *Sumter*, which had seized eighteen merchantmen before the Union fleet trapped it in Gibraltar. Now, in his custom-built cruiser, he embarked on a far more destructive voyage. He also gave the 290 a new, more resonant name: *Alabama*.[59]

ON JULY 17, 1862, PRESIDENT LINCOLN sent a formal message to Congress. "I have inadvertently omitted so long to inform you that in March last Mr. Cornelius Vanderbilt, of New York, gratuitously presented to the United States the ocean steamer 'Vanderbilt,' by many esteemed the finest merchant ship in the world," he wrote.[60]

Despite Welles's initial refusal to accept the great sidewheeler, many of the navy's senior officers now considered the *Vanderbilt* "the most formidable war vessel afloat in our waters," as *Harper's Weekly* reported. On July 31, for example, General David Hunter wrote to Stanton from Port Royal on the Southern coast, "I have just had an interview with Flag-Officer [Samuel] DuPont, who considers it extremely important to the safety of his fleet that the *Vanderbilt* should be sent here immediately." Admiral David D. Porter informed Congress after the war, "We never had a vessel that could run down a blockade-runner during the whole war, except the *Vanderbilt* and two others." Its combination of speed and size made it formidable.[61]

During the *Merrimack* scare, the untrusting Stanton had learned to trust both the ship and its builder. Accordingly, new orders went forth from the War Department to the office at 5 Bowling Green. "The *Vanderbilt* is to be fitted out for cruising in the West Indies to run down the privateers that our Navy cannot catch," Assistant Secretary of War Peter H. Watson wired the Commodore on September 3. "You are authorized to fit her up as well and as speedily as possible for the service. . . . Captain [Gustavus V.] Fox will correspond with you about fitting her out and arming her. The Navy are very anxious to obtain the aid of the *Vanderbilt*, for without it they cannot maintain the blockade against the *Nashville, Ovieta*, No. 290, and other fast vessels."[62]

Once again, the federal government gave this private individual great public responsibilities, as if the title "Commodore" were a formal rank. Once again, Vanderbilt carried out his duties swiftly and capably. "The *Vanderbilt* is now in first-rate condition," Lieutenant C. H. Baldwin reported to Fox from New York on November 7. Baldwin, the ship's new commander, wanted to sail to the Caribbean, where he thought the *Alabama* (or 290, as Union officials persisted in calling it) might try to capture the Atlantic & Pacific steamers as they returned from Panama, laden with gold. He hoped to meet the rebel cruiser in battle, writing, "I pray I may have the opportunity of doing something worthy of so splendid a command."[63]

While the *Vanderbilt* was still refitting, the Commodore received a telegram from Stanton, asking him to come to Washington. He arrived late in the evening and went directly to Stanton's office in the War Department, where the secretary was still at his desk. As was the custom with each of these two men—who were getting to know each other quite well—they immediately proceeded to business. Stanton peered through his little round glasses and said something about appointing Vanderbilt to a position as quartermaster in New York. "We'll stop right there, Mr. Stanton," the Commodore replied. "There is no position in this government that I want, and none that I will take; no place of emolument that I can take." This brought the secretary to a halt. "He was delicate on that point," Vanderbilt recalled. Given the late hour, Stanton said he would explain in the morning why he had called him to Washington.

At nine o'clock the next day, October 27, Vanderbilt returned to Stanton's office. "I have thought this thing over and made up my mind," the secretary said. "Come and get into the carriage." The two rode to see General Nathaniel P. Banks, a former speaker of the house turned unsuccessful general (against Confederate general Thomas T. "Stonewall" Jackson, against whom almost everyone was unsuccessful). Stanton spoke privately with Banks for a few minutes, then called in Vanderbilt. Stanton explained that Banks was to lead "a secret expedition, and no one else is to know it but us three."

"No one will know it from me," Vanderbilt replied. "I will assure you that."

"I want you to assist General Banks in New York in fitting it out," Stanton said. He asked Vanderbilt to charter steamships as transports and see that they were adequately prepared and supplied; he also briefly discussed with him a system of inspectors. ("His interviews were short," Vanderbilt recalled, much to his liking.) Then Vanderbilt and Banks took the afternoon train to New York.[64]

Banks went on to Boston to organize the new recruits who formed most of his expeditionary force, and Vanderbilt began to charter steamships. He tried to deal directly with ship owners to avoid brokers, and bargained fiercely to keep the cost as low as possible. "I believe religiously that he has saved the government fifty percent in fitting out these vessels," said Commodore George J. Van Brunt, the naval inspector assigned to the expedition. "My intercourse with Commodore Vanderbilt throughout this whole matter has been of the most pleasant kind; he was acting, as I thought, with great patriotism, in serving the government for nothing."[65]

Banks wired Vanderbilt from Boston that he would need transportation for fifteen thousand men, as well as a large number of horses. The Commodore chartered twenty-seven steamers, all that were available, and still he needed more. Transporting the horses was the real problem; sailing ships suited them best, he thought. "Then a man from down east came to me with a letter from General Banks," Vanderbilt later testified before Congress. He was a shipbuilder from Richmond, Maine, named Thomas J. Southard. "When he gave me this letter of introduction from General Banks I talked with him, and I found he understood more about a horse-ship than I did, a heap more. He said he had been in it a good deal in his life, fitting up different horse-vessels for the West Indies, &c." Vanderbilt thought to himself, "This is just the man I want."

"Mr. Southard," the Commodore said, "I want you to understand that I feel a strong interest in this controversy that we have got into, and I feel it to be a duty to my country to do it all the service I can. I am going to do it voluntarily, without any pay—how do you feel on that?"

Southard sat mute.

"Think it well over," Vanderbilt added. "We ought to find patriotism enough in our country to do something for it without everybody making money out of the funds of the government." Finally Southard agreed to take no pay. He assumed the duty of finding and fitting out sailing ships to carry the horses, chartering a total of thirty-five.[66]

Unfortunately for the Commodore, Southard did not leave ship owners with the impression that he would take no compensation. The Mainer seems to have been a very smart man, in the old Yankee sense. He had family ties to ship chandlers and brokerages in New York, and—without ever explicitly demanding it—he implied that the ship owners must do business with his relatives, at a rate of 5 percent per charter. When Congress learned of the charges, Vanderbilt's handling of the Banks expedition took on the dimensions of a scandal—one that grew larger when one of the twenty-seven steamers, the *Niagara*, turned out to have rotten timbers which had been disguised by new planking that had fooled the inspectors. An impression formed that the entire fleet consisted of unseaworthy vessels chartered at exorbitant rates. The Senate convened an investigation, and a motion was made to censure Vanderbilt.

The motion died with the so-called scandal. Southard may have fooled the Commodore (and Banks, who recommended him) with his indirect commissions, but Congress concluded that the affair had been handled economically overall. As for the *Niagara* and two other ships with boiler troubles, such mishaps were to be expected in a large military expedition that was organized and launched in little more than a month.[67]

Banks had no misgivings about Vanderbilt's conduct. On the afternoon of December 4, the general joined the Commodore, Mayor George Opdyke, and other prominent men in a celebratory excursion into New York Bay aboard a Treasury cutter, in tribute to Banks and his mysterious expedition. A toast was then made to Vanderbilt, who typically replied (according to the *New York Tribune*) that "he was not a speechifier; he would speak by proxy, through Gen. Banks." Banks informed the distinguished guests "that Commodore Vanderbilt was the only man who knew where the expedition was going." Vanderbilt kept the secret.[68]

Banks, it turned out, would not make a grand attack on a Confederate stronghold. He was bound for New Orleans, which the Union navy had captured earlier. There his army would be able to cooperate with Union forces under General Grant, now driving south toward Vicksburg. The secrecy, of course, served to keep the rebels in doubt about where he might land. But Stanton may have thought to protect Banks from a serious danger, one he had asked Vanderbilt to help thwart. Somewhere at sea lurked Captain Raphael Semmes and the CSS *Alabama*.[69]

ON THE MORNING OF DECEMBER 7, 1862, Captain Semmes went out on the deck of the *Alabama* and put his telescope to his eye. He looked every inch the pirate, in his long double-breasted coat with twin rows of bright brass buttons, his fierce moustache pointing to either side of his face like cannons run out of gunports on a man-of-war. He swept the horizon with his spyglass, looking for a wisp of smoke. Nothing. He turned and went back into his cabin, where he sat down to breakfast, "hopeless for that day of my California steamer," he wrote in his memoirs, "and my millions of dollars in gold."

For more than three months, the *Alabama* had burned or ransomed one Yankee merchantman after another. But what Semmes wanted more than anything else was to capture a Vanderbilt steamer on its way to New York, laden with California gold. The Confederate government would allow Semmes and crew to share in the prize; more important, such a capture might cripple the flow of gold to New York, just as specie shippers had warned the federal government at the start of the war. It would also saddle Vanderbilt's company with expensive claims for the losses.

"We had accurate time-tables of the arrivals and departures of the California steamers in the files of the New York papers that we had captured," Semmes recalled. He loitered now in the windward passage east of Cuba, where he expected the iron sidewheeler *Champion* to pass on its way from Aspinwall to New York. Today, Semmes thought, would not be the day. The boatswain ordered the crew into their white frocks and trousers for Sunday services on deck, as the captain sipped coffee in his cabin.

"Suddenly the prolonged cry of 'S-a-i-l h-o!' came ringing, in a clear musical voice, from aloft," Semmes wrote, "the look-out having at length descried a steamer." George Fullam, a sailor on the *Alabama*, recorded the ensuing frenzy. "Steam was immediately got up, the propellor lowered, sails taken in and furled," he wrote in his journal. "All hands called to quarters, the battery loaded with shell and run out. . . . Everybody in the best possible spirits and eager for a fray." Semmes knew that the steamships of the Atlantic & Pacific company were fast, so he hauled up a United States flag to lull suspicions until he got closer.[70]

From the deck of the Vanderbilt steamer, Captain A. G. Jones peered through his own telescope at the approaching steam sloop as it emerged out of the sun glare. He could see it flew the Stars and Stripes, but he surveyed it with suspicion. Suddenly he exclaimed, "If that isn't an English rig, you may shoot me!" He was certain it was the English-built commerce raider, the *Alabama*. He ordered the engineer to put on all steam in an attempt to outrun the predator.[71]

Jones's ship was not the *Champion*, but the *Ariel*. The aging sidewheeler had steamed out of New York Harbor on December 1, bound for Aspinwall, and it carried no chests of gold. "The boat crowded to capacity with human beings, and some scarcely human," wrote passenger George Willis Read. "The confusion and discomfort on board surpassed anything by far I have ever before experienced. The cooking was *filthy* beyond my powers of description. The smell and filth, with the rough sea, has kept me seasick most of the time." Read was so disgusted that he interrupted the story of the *Alabama*'s appearance to write that he ate only a baked potato that day. By the time he reached the deck, the *Alabama* had fired a blank cartridge and run up the rebel ensign.

"I knew it was the 290 at first sight," Read added. "When I first saw her she was coming up behind us, a mile and a half in the rear, as near as I could guess. She is a splendid ship, and could sail around us with ease. The Capt. put on all steam, and hoped he could get off, but she [the *Alabama*] turned broadsides, and shot two heavy balls. I stood on deck, close to the aft, or back, mast. Saw the smoke rise, the balls leave the guns and come tumbling and whizzing towards me." One round neatly severed the forward mast. At the urging of a marine officer on board, Jones surrendered.[72]

"I was very anxious to destroy this ship," Semmes wrote, "as she belonged to a Mr. Vanderbilt of New York, an old steamboat captain who had amassed a large fortune in trade, and was a bitter enemy of the South." After Captain Jones went aboard the *Alabama*, Semmes told him that "Vanderbilt had given one of the finest steamers in the world to the Government with which to run him down, and he would destroy everything of his he fell in with," according to the London *Times*. "Capt. Jones says the only ship that Semmes fears is the *Vanderbilt*," the *Chicago Tribune* reported. "He [Semmes] made many inquiries regarding her speed and armament, but obtained no information whatever. He laughs at all the other ships we have."

Semmes planned to burn the *Ariel* after landing the passengers in Jamaica, but reports of a yellow fever epidemic there caused him to change his mind. Instead, he had Jones sign a bond obliging Vanderbilt to pay $261,000 to the Confederacy thirty days after the United States extended it formal recognition. Then he let the steamship go. Not only had Semmes captured a Panama steamer headed in the wrong direction, his preoccupation with the *Ariel* caused him to miss the *Champion*, which arrived safely in New York with a million dollars in gold.[73]

The fate of the *Ariel*, on the other hand, remained unknown in New York. Vanderbilt and the specie shippers waited with growing anxiety for its return from Panama. A report that it had encountered the *Alabama* reached the city, but not word of the ultimate outcome. As the *New York Times* reported, they were "prepared to mourn her." Then, on December 28, it finally arrived unharmed, "and cut short the several obituaries that were in preparation for the occasion."[74]

"It strikes me that the rebel steamer *Alabama* is now looking for a homeward-bound California steamer," Vanderbilt wrote to Welles the next day. "If the steamer *Vanderbilt*, or some other of sufficient speed, could be placed in the Caribbean Sea to convoy the steamers on leaving Aspinwall for two and one-half or three days up to the west end of Cuba, then returning to Aspinwall to be ready for the sailing of the next steamer, which is ten days apart, it would give ample security and would give her a better chance to fall in with the 290." He said he would order his ships to sail by way of the western end of Cuba; he anticipated little trouble north of the island, given the presence of a U.S. blockading squadron in the Florida Keys. Welles agreed, and forwarded Vanderbilt's letter to the captain of the USS *Connecticut* with orders to carry out his instructions.[75]

Semmes considered Vanderbilt not only a symbol of Union power and resolve, but a major force in his own right for the South's defeat. The rebel captain would not get a second chance at the Atlantic & Pacific liners, now that the Commodore had arranged for a naval convoy, but he did see a chance to strike at another enterprise organized by "the bitter enemy of the South." From the newspapers he captured, he learned about Banks's expedition. The press did not know where it was headed, but Semmes sifted through the various guesses and came to a wise conclusion. He accordingly set his course for the Gulf of Mexico; with any luck, he would descend on the vulnerable transports and blow them out of the water, along with their thousands of Union troops and countless tons of arms.

On the evening of January 11, 1863, Semmes closed in on a line of ships

off the Gulf Coast. It turned out not to be Banks's expedition, but a blockade squadron. Semmes had guessed wrong, sailing to Galveston, Texas,
rather than the mouth of the Mississippi. One of the Union ships, a sidewheeler named *Hatteras*, pulled out of formation and gave chase. Semmes
ordered the *Alabama* about and ran, firing all the while with a large gun
mounted on a pivot at the stern, throwing eighty-five-pound explosive
shells. In a battle of just fifteen minutes, the *Alabama* sank the *Hatteras*.

It was, in many respects, a lucky victory. Semmes's business was to avoid
Northern warships, not fight them. And the hardest to avoid was the
biggest and fastest, the one specially assigned to hunt him down. "He
thinks the *Vanderbilt* much too heavy for him," a South African newspaper
reported on September 13, 1863. "In commenting upon the probable
consequences of an encounter with the *Vanderbilt*, Captain Semmes spoke
with much modesty about the power of his own ship. . . . His opinion is,
that the *Vanderbilt* has much greater speed than the *Alabama*, and that it
will be impossible for him to get away from her." Referring to each ship's
broadside, Semmes fretted that the *Vanderbilt* "threw twice my weight in
metal."

For a few days near the Cape of Good Hope, the *Vanderbilt* came close
to catching the famous Confederate commerce raider—even passing close
by in a fog bank—but the prey slipped away. In June 1864, the USS
Kearsarge finally destroyed the *Alabama* in battle off the French port of
Cherbourg. By then, the rebel cruiser had captured or destroyed sixty-
four merchant ships, nearly crippling the U.S. commercial fleet.[76]

VANDERBILT'S INSTRUCTIONS for convoying the Panama steamers
marked a virtual end to his direct involvement in the Civil War. Cynicism
would color later assessments of his efforts, growing out of the deep suspicion of nineteenth-century Americans—particularly newspaper editors—
toward wealthy and powerful men. Cynicism, of course, always seems to
be the most sophisticated position to take; yet it is also the laziest (along
with hero-worship, its direct opposite).

An honest reading of the evidence shows a proud, prickly, and highly
capable man of immense personal force—one who was also deeply patriotic. Welles's refusal to accept the *Vanderbilt* as a gift, or any of Vanderbilt's
steamers at a fair purchase price, essentially forced the Commodore to
take enormous sums of money from the federal government in charters
fixed by brokers who had every interest in running up the rates. When
given the chance, he served his country to the utmost while refusing any
remuneration. The notion of a scandal surrounding the Banks expedition
does not stand scrutiny. Just one ship out of the entire fleet slipped

through inspection when it clearly should not have—and this at a time when Vanderbilt was chartering every steamer available in New York under a tight deadline. Southard exacted a commission (on the sailing ships only) through methods so indirect that Vanderbilt can hardly be blamed. Furthermore, Southard did his job, fitting out the vessels with the expertise expected of him. Vanderbilt's prompt and capable response to the *Merrimack* scare throws new light on this oft-told tale, for he played an important part in a strategic victory that usually is credited to the *Monitor* alone. And the gift of his eponymous steamship was an unprecedented act of patriotic charity, worth nearly $1 million.

Vanderbilt needs no special pleading. A man of his unfathomable wealth, obsessed with maintaining the power to defend himself against his enemies, could (and did) withstand a great deal of cynicism. But perhaps his elemental humanity requires a few words of defense. Derided by the most sneering of his contemporaries, he remains unreasonably fixed in the historical imagination as lacking all sensitivity, as an iron-hearted man of money. A man of money he most definitely was, often harsh and profane. But he possessed a tenderness that had become more and more visible in the years after the cruise of the *North Star* in 1853. Here we read a comment of how he and Sophia enjoyed their trip together to Washington; there we read Vanderbilt's truly warm letters to the family of his daughter-in-law, Ellen Williams Vanderbilt. Such signs would continue to accumulate.

This emotional inner life was certainly affected by the fate of that other member of his immediate family who was called to national service during the Civil War. Lieutenant George W. Vanderbilt commanded the inglorious recruiting station in Boston until April 1, 1862. On April 17, the regular army promoted him to the rank of captain, and named him aide-de-camp to General John C. Frémont, commander of the Mountain Department. But it seems unlikely that George ever saw duty beyond the Back Bay. He fell sick and went on a leave of absence even before his promotion. The illness—consumption, by one account—was clearly serious. At some point in 1862 or 1863, he traveled to Nice, France, to recover his health. Curiously, another George W. Vanderbilt from New York fought in the war, a doppelgänger to the Commodore's son, winning glory as a cavalry officer that the George of West Point and Washington Place would never earn.[77]

It was a bitter twist for Vanderbilt, who dearly loved both his country and his youngest boy. He offered his son as a sacrifice to the nation in its hour of greatest need, and the nation took it. But the sacrifice was wasted, without purpose, without honor, leaving George only the pain and humiliation of a body that refused to function.

If Vanderbilt suffered as his son departed for Europe with a doubtful future, he also maintained that single-minded strength of will that had carried him to such heights. As the Civil War continued to rage in 1863, he went into battle to protect his private interests with a cunning and ferocity that would astonish the world—and seal his place in history.

Chapter Fourteen

THE ORIGINS OF EMPIRE

F ew men in wartime New York were better known than Cornelius
Vanderbilt—or so often misjudged. Thousands recognized him as
he drove his fast horses through the streets each day, sitting erect on
a light racing wagon with reins in hand, long white sideburns flowing
down his cheeks, keen eyes squinting ahead. The fastidious Commodore
always dressed in black and wore a white cravat typical of a passing generation, now affected largely by clergymen. One afternoon he left his office
on Bowling Green and caught a stage headed north on Broadway. In front
of him sat two young men dressed in the street finery favored by New
York thugs. "I looked them over rather sharply, as I am accustomed to do,"
Vanderbilt recounted to a friend. One of the pair turned and looked back;
he did not recognize the dignified old man in the white cravat, but
assumed that he was a minister of the gospel. "I suppose you think I'm
going to hell?" the rough asked. "No," Vanderbilt replied. He told the
youth (as he later related) that "he seemed pretty badly off just then, but
he appeared to have good stuff in him, and I guessed he'd come out all
right." The stranger turned to his friend and exclaimed, "Universalist, by
God!"[1]

Individuals far better informed than this one came to wrong conclusions about the clerical-looking Commodore (who spent very few of his
many days in any kind of church, Universalist or otherwise). They still do.
Even in retrospect, it is difficult to appreciate the true dimensions of his
wealth and the power it gave him. The American economy grew rapidly,
but unevenly. New York towered over the rest of the developing nation as
would be impossible in later centuries; wealth concentrated there, and
financial markets matured there, far faster than anywhere else. It was the
preeminent American port, the preeminent banking center, the home of
the preeminent stock exchange. Securities held in New York could be liquidated or hypothecated rapidly. Vanderbilt was not only far richer than
most rich men, he also occupied a strategic location in which he could use
his fortune as a lever to move even greater masses of wealth and personally
affect the economy nationwide.[2]

Vanderbilt himself struggled to describe his role as his financial capacities grew. "I . . . am connected with shipping," he vaguely told a Senate committee on December 30, 1862. Then he felt obliged to add, "I run steamship lines." Then he qualified again, observing, "Some would call me a merchant." In some ways, this old-fashioned and highly general term remains the best description. Shipper? Financier? Industrialist? Railroad director? He was all these things. He guided the Atlantic & Pacific Steamship Company, and managed its strategic relations with Pacific Mail. His engine works and shipyard produced pistons, boilers, and steamers. He purchased half a million dollars in Connecticut state bonds. He served on the boards of the Harlem, Erie, New Jersey Central, and Hartford & New Haven railroads.[3]

The very diversity of his activities makes it difficult to understand his true significance, for it is often impossible to know where he placed the lever of his fortune. He made an art out of hiding his hand, having risen with the original generation of New York and New England's smart men, the wily pioneers of free-for-all commerce who knew how to speak and say nothing. He would make this connection himself in dodging an inquiry from a New York State Assembly committee. "Let me answer your question by asking another," he would say, "as the Yankee does."[4]

In 1863, much of the mystery would disappear. That year he embarked on a new course, the last in his long business career. The results would cast a shadow over millions of people, if not the entire nation; indeed, Vanderbilt's historical importance would become apparent to all, rising above his furtive methods like a mountain peak above the clouds. In step with an increasingly specialized economy, he would concentrate his resources in a single industry, the most important of the nineteenth century: the railroads. So great would be his impact that a leading business journal could eulogize him, without fear of contradiction, as "the most striking figure in the American railroad world."[5]

Vanderbilt was striking enough already, with his vast wealth and control over major steamship lines, but his transformation from Commodore to railroad king would give him a significance that was cultural as much as economic. He would lead a revolution in American life, one that was terribly obvious to his contemporaries but perhaps less so to later generations. The lingering image of post–Civil War railroads is one of construction—think, for example, of the Chinese and Irish work crews who laid the transcontinental lines through mountains and wilderness—and it is an image with a solid basis in fact. After a wartime pause in new building, U.S. railroad mileage would more than double, from about thirty thousand in 1860 to seventy thousand by 1873, as the loose net of tracks that overlaid the American map became a fine mesh. But Vanderbilt would play little role in this process. Though he would build critical (and lasting) new infrastructure, he would lay few new lines and take no interest in the West, where construction through virgin land was most pronounced.

Vanderbilt, rather, would pioneer the rise of the truly gigantic business corporation. This process would leave an imprint on American society every bit as deep as the expansion of the physical railroad network itself. His role in this revolution would prove more startling in his own day than the mere fact of his riches. As the *Railroad Gazette* would write of him in 1877,

> His early career as a railroad manager [i.e., starting in 1863] was distinguished by a series of bold, startling, revolutionary measures which attracted universal attention and had an effect reaching far beyond the lines and companies with which he dealt directly. The Vanderbilt era was the first great era of consolidations. That it was created by Vanderbilt would be too much to say; but he was the first great actor in it, and apparently hastened its coming.[6]

Consolidations. The word seems quaint, an old-fashioned version of the eye-glazing phrase "mergers and acquisitions," yet it was fraught with portentous meaning in the 1860s. Vanderbilt's consolidation of one railroad company into another into another into an empire would mark a profound change in the nature of the corporation itself. As late as the Civil War, a strong sense lingered that corporations were public bodies, chartered to channel private capital toward public ends—specific, limited ends. Early business corporations even operated under time constraints. The Richmond Turnpike Company had expired on schedule, and even the New York & Harlem Railroad had had to renew its charter in 1859 before it lapsed. Most corporations had come into existence during the lifespans—indeed, the active careers—of their stockholders and managers, who did not necessarily imagine that their companies would outlast their own involvement in them. The Pacific Mail directors had tried to sell out to the Commodore in order to pay off the stockholders and shut down permanently.

Starting in 1863, Vanderbilt would progressively destroy the last vestiges of this long-held conception. Drawing on his extensive experience with the corporate form, he would strip it of its remaining public character as he finished the long process of converting it into a vehicle for private gain alone. His consolidations would submerge older railroad companies into a behemoth to serve the requirements of efficiency and profitability; in so doing, he also would drown the original public purpose of these companies' charters, to serve specific localities over well-defined routes. Often these consolidations would prove highly beneficial for the public—though only incidentally, because it was good business. And his takeovers would heighten the growing distinction between corporations and their flesh-and-blood shareholders and managers. He would separate companies from the individuals originally associated with them, transforming them into impersonal and permanent, or very long-lived, institutions.[7]

Historian Alfred D. Chandler Jr. famously referred to the rise of the large business enterprise—a rise led by the railroad corporation—as a "managerial revolution" in American business. The demands of a geographically sprawling railroad with thousands of employees necessitated the creation of a bureaucracy of salaried, professional managers; these managers imposed a "visible hand" on economic decisions that remade the smaller, simpler market economy of old. By creating one of the largest railroad companies the world had ever seen, Vanderbilt would directly shape this business transformation. But the sheer size of his enterprises would give him a larger cultural significance. He operated on an unprecedented scale, amassing some of the first interstate corporations in American history, which gave him a chokehold over the nation's arteries of commerce. The gigantic entities he helped pioneer would overshadow forever after the old landscape of individuals and small partnerships. They would also infuse American life with an institutional, bureaucratic business culture—what scholar Alan Trachtenberg calls the "incorporation of America."[8]

Vanderbilt would emerge as the first great icon of this revolution. This self-taught native of the eighteenth century would masterfully play the instruments of the corporation to gather unparalleled power in his own hands and contribute to a stark polarization of American society. Yet his ascendancy can hardly be dismissed as a curse. He would also create vast new wealth and forge one of the most efficient, lowest-cost transportation routes in the world, speeding American economic growth and opening new opportunities for investors and consumers. His contemporaries would have good reason to mark his rise as the start of a new era—and to give his name to it.

How did he do it? *Why* did he do it? Observers typically have accepted the simplistic formula that he suddenly realized that railroads, not steamships, were the technology of the future.[9] In truth, what he started in 1863 emerged naturally from his earlier career. He had been embroiled in railroads since the 1830s, served as the Stonington's president in the 1840s, and his involvement in the industry had increased in the 1850s. But too often writers have credited him with deep-laid plans of conquest, a systematic scheme to build an iron Rome.[10] There is another interpretation that better fits the unknowability of the future before it becomes the past, an interpretation more complimentary, perhaps, of the Commodore's abilities. Though he was an excellent planner, he was still more accomplished as an improviser, a master of the unpredictable rough-and-tumble of business combat. He possessed a keen eye for strategic opportunities in his opponents' tactical errors, for turning successful skirmishes into full-blown campaigns. When he first started, he had little inkling of what he eventually would accomplish.[11]

The irony of this, the most successful phase of Vanderbilt's career, is that he would resist each of the battles that brought him to new heights of wealth. He would consistently pursue diplomacy with connecting railways, accepting war only as a last resort. Contented with his realm, he would conquer a neighbor in order to eliminate its harassment of his domain. New conflicts with new neighbors would follow, leading to further conquests, until he gained a vast, consolidated kingdom—much as the Caesars pressed their boundaries forward to pacify the barbarian tribes that always lay beyond.

These epic wars of conquest began humbly, with what might be called a hobby. In 1863, he cocked an eye at the most bedraggled railroad in New York: the Harlem, the benighted line that he twice had rescued from bankruptcy. His initial interest in the company need not have concerned the public at all, except that it led him into a conflict with one of the great perils that plagued American democracy in the 1860s, that of government corruption. The elected officials of New York flapped around what they assumed to be the mere corpse of a company, each looking to tear off a piece for himself. Vanderbilt would not let them. The origins of his empire, then, lay not in his godlike foresight, but in his determination to punish the greed of a few foolish men.

ON FEBRUARY 16, 1863, Cornelius Vanderbilt wrote to former governor Edwin D. Morgan to decline a request to stand as an incorporator of a hospital for invalid soldiers. "I feel it a duty I owe myself to keep my name aloof from any association with public acts granted by legislative bodies," he wrote, "inasmuch as whenever my name has appeared before such bodies, without any regard to the justice of the object, it has been looked upon as a speculation, and with an eye of jealousy." Vanderbilt's concern for his personal honor is striking, and his wish to reduce his visibility even more so. "At this late day," he added, "I am desirous of keeping myself aloof from any public transaction of any kind or nature."[12]

This sentiment typified the Commodore's attitude toward both charitable bodies and his public image; and perhaps it reflected his desire to avoid any connection with the disreputable state legislature. But this attempt to distance himself from speculation would prove highly ironic. Even as he dictated this letter, the current of events carried him into an operation that would launch his career as a railroad tycoon through the greatest speculation to date.[13] It would center on the New York & Harlem Railroad.

"It is not so big a road," Vanderbilt remarked six years later. "It is a small thing, with a little capital of only about $6,000,000" ($5,772,800, actually). A small thing! Only in comparison to other railways could a business worth several million in the 1860s be considered "not so big."[14] And only in comparison to the Commodore's fortune, of course. But Wall Street agreed with his judgment, on the grounds of Harlem's potential as well as its size. New York State's two largest railroads dwarfed it, the Erie having a capital stock of just under $20 million at par, the New York Central just over $24 million. Its business suffered grave weaknesses, for it carried almost no through freight from the West, apart from some cattle, due to steep grades north of Manhattan. Even though Vanderbilt had helped reduce its floating debt, it still had trouble meeting expenses. "Of all the active railway shares dealt in at the board, the Harlems probably possess the least intrinsic value," wrote the *New York Herald* on March 25, 1863. "The net earnings last year—which was an extraordinarily good one for all roads—were $473,401," about equal to the interest on its $6.7 million in bonds. "No one believes that the road can, for ten years to come, pay anything" in dividends.[15]

The Harlem was a peculiar line in many ways, in part because it had been chartered in 1831, when railroads were still regarded as an unproven experiment. For example, the par value of each share was set at $50, half the standard $100 for an American corporation (though the press still reported changes in its price as 1 "percent" for each dollar, as with other stocks). It was a hybrid road, both a horse-drawn streetcar line and a steam-locomotive railway. Trains ran down the Harlem 130 miles from Chatham Four Corners or came in from New England over the New York & New Haven Railroad, crossed the Harlem River on a bridge, and rolled down Fourth Avenue to Forty-second Street. They entered a tunnel dug under Murray Hill (and covered over with parks, all at the expense of the railroad), rolled out ten blocks south, and continued into the Harlem depot at Twenty-sixth Street, a structure with crenellated walls that rather resembled a castle. There the trains interchanged passengers with the horse-drawn streetcars, which went as far down as the city hall via the Bowery. For years the company had fought city ordinances, passed at the urging of wealthy Murray Hill residents, to stop the locomotives north of the tunnel. Fearing an uptown creep of this sentiment, on

April 16, 1859, the Harlem had secured from the state legislature the right to use steam engines as far south as Forty-second Street (though it was forced to haul its cars between the depot and Forty-second Street with horses).[16]

This undersize hermaphrodite road attracted the Commodore's renewed attention amid the Civil War boom in railway shares on Wall Street. "In 1862 he was known to be buying a large amount of the stock," recalled William Fowler. According to rumor, Vanderbilt foresaw a great day in Harlem. "The idea that he was buying it for *investment* seemed intensely funny to the brokers," Fowler wrote. Vanderbilt's purchases had no effect on the negative view of the railroad among financial men, even though he drove the share price from a few dollars a share to over 50. Most brokers said "the certificates were only good for wrapping paper."[17]

Wall Street was at all times a waterfall of rumors, few of them accurate. In this case, the tales muttered over fillet of sole at Delmonico's proved to be true: Vanderbilt was, in fact, buying because he believed in the Harlem's prospects. "I recollect . . . hearing him say that this railroad property, if properly managed," Horace Clark later remarked, "will be as good property as there was in the state."[18]

What did he see in it that no one else did? From the very beginning of Vanderbilt's career, he had focused on transportation routes that had decisive strategic advantages over competitors. The Stonington railroad, for example, ran from a convenient port inside Point Judith over a direct line to Boston with easy grades that he made into the fastest and cheapest to operate at the time of his presidency. Likewise, the Nicaragua route to California had possessed a permanent superiority in coal consumption over Panama, thanks to shorter steamship voyages. The Harlem's fixed strength was its penetration of the center of New York, down Fourth Avenue and through its streetcar line. This was something that no other railroad possessed—not even the only other steam railway to enter Manhattan, the Hudson River, which was restricted to the far west side. The Harlem provided the only portal for direct rail traffic with industrial New England, a rich trade that Vanderbilt knew well from his directorship of the Hartford & New Haven. And, as with the Stonington, he moved in *after* the company's debts had been starkly reduced. Once in control, he could reduce the Harlem's operating costs (a science he practiced most effectively), and then he thought it would prove very profitable.[19]

But there was something more personal driving Vanderbilt's interest in the Harlem. Perhaps the most important element in his character—even more than his economic calculation—was pride. We know he prized his reputation (as shown by his letter to Governor Morgan, among many other examples) and cherished his status as a man of honor. Most of all, he took pride in his abilities. Competitive to the core, he had spent his life outdoing other men, whether sailing New York Bay or navigating the Nicaraguan rapids; fighting with his fists or waging rate wars; racing his steamboats or running his four-footed trotters; designing steamships or planning sprawling enterprises. Now he would show the world that he could revive the most necrotic of companies. "Here is a man," the Commodore would remark in 1867, "who has taken a road when its stock was not worth ten dollars a share, and had not been for years. He has had a little pride; he said he would bring up that road, and make the stock valuable."[20]

Of course, Vanderbilt's pride mattered little to anyone else. He had been an important Harlem stockholder for almost a decade, and his slowly increasing stake changed nothing for the public (except those few who also owned stock and saw the value rise). But his purchases led him into a confrontation with one of the great evils that worried civic-minded New Yorkers: the corruption of their government.[21]

During the Civil War, Americans began to fear that rampant corruption threatened democracy itself. The head of the New York Custom House alone could scoop in as much as four times the salary of the president (which, at $25,000, was many times larger than that of railroad presidents or other extremely well-paid men). As the federal budget grew, the scope of graft seemed to swell as well. Profiteering off military contracts seemed to run rampant, particularly under Lincoln's first secretary of war, Simon Cameron, who did without competitive bidding. Manufacturers delivered cheap, flimsy shoes and uniforms made of recycled wool, or "shoddy," that soon fell apart. Conflicts of interest abounded as businessmen filled new government posts; for example, Thomas A. Scott, the superintendent of the Pennsylvania Railroad, served as assistant secretary of war with jurisdiction over military transportation.[22]

Crooked dealing within the federal government seemed almost tame compared to its rapacity in New York. George Templeton Strong, like many, complained of "our disgraceful, profligate legislature." *Harper's Weekly* reported late in 1863, "Last winter, it became evident to all discerning observers that a combination of adventurers had bought up a majority of both branches of the Legislature." And city government looked worse. At war's end, the Union League Committee on Municipal Reform would admit a "longing for a temporary dictator who would sweep these bad men from our municipal halls and cleanse this Augean stable of its accumulated corruption."[23]

As Vanderbilt steadily purchased Harlem stock, the company fell afoul of a past master of bribery, one of the Commodore's oldest enemies, George Law. New York's merchant community smelled sulfur wherever he went. "It is impossible for outsiders to estimate his worth, & it is doubtful if he can do it himself," R. G. Dun & Co. reported in 1859. The next year it added, "He is reported to be sharp & over-reaching in his transactions & dealt with accordingly." He had spread his money freely in the fallow fields of Washington during his years in the U.S. Mail Steamship Company and the Panama Railroad. Now he devoted himself to transportation in Manhattan, with a stake in various ferries and the Eighth Avenue Railroad, a horse-drawn streetcar line, so his bribes flowed upstream to Albany.[24]

Sometime around March 1863, Law reportedly began to twitch and tweak the state legislature into granting him a charter for a streetcar railroad down Broadway. "Reportedly" is as conclusive as any account can be; though the press blamed him for pushing this bill, direct evidence of his involvement is hard to find.[25] But no doubt exists over the furious reaction that erupted in late April when Manhattanites learned that the most famous avenue in America might be bound with iron rails. As the bill advanced toward passage, a long list of New York's patriarchs—among them William B. Astor, Moses Taylor, Peter Lorillard, and Royal Phelps—signed a petition to the new governor, Horatio Seymour, to protest "bestowing a franchise of immense value upon individuals, many of whom are unknown. . . . Its effect will be to injure immensely if not almost destroy the most beautiful thoroughfare on this continent." The *New York Herald* declared that New Yorkers were "wonderfully unanimous" in "disgust and anger at the shameless corruption of the Albany scheme."[26]

One might well wonder why the state should intervene in a purely municipal matter. The answer is that the Broadway bill, and the corruption that surrounded it, reflected a long-standing struggle for power between city and state, and within the Democratic Party. In 1857, in an effort to weaken then-mayor Fernando Wood, the Republican legislature had passed a series of measures to strip New York of authority over its own affairs. This had strengthened Wood's Democratic opponents more than the city's Republicans, as one of his leading rivals, William Tweed, gained an independent power base in the enhanced New York County Board of Supervisors. By 1863, the city's Democratic Party had divided into three fiercely alienated factions: Tammany Hall, Wood's Mozart Hall, and a splinter group led by former U.S. attorney John McKeon. Even Tammany itself was split between Tweed's crowd and the wealthy circle around Horace Clark, Augustus Schell, and August Belmont.[27]

The "George Law" bill threatened to further erode the city's power over its own streets, and deny it any revenue from a potentially lucrative franchise. City hall, torn by its internal feuding, looked unlikely to come up with an effective response. But there was one force that could unite the bitterest enemies in New York: money.

Someone conceived a plan to have the city preempt the Law company, by granting the Harlem the right to run a streetcar line down Broadway. If the city fathers must have a Broadway railroad, they thought, they should at least keep control of it—and its proceeds. According to *Harper's Weekly*, the aldermen and councilmen demanded that, in return for this gift, the Harlem pay roughly $100,000 in bribes. ("We don't pretend to know exactly," *Harper's* wrote.) What's more, rumors began to fly about unusual purchases—and purchasers—of Harlem stock. "Men with strongly Celtic faces were seen on Wall Street," recounted Fowler, with the unblushing anti-Irish prejudice of the day, "sixth-warders by the cut of their jib, and said to belong to the Ancient and Honorable Board of Aldermen."

On April 21, this farce turned into slapstick when a deputy sheriff appeared at a meeting of the aldermen, bearing an injunction on behalf of Broadway's stage and omnibus lines. "He was ordered to retire," the *New York Herald* reported, "but not seeming inclined to go, the President directed the Sergeant-at-Arms to remove him." Once the deputy had been wrestled out and the door locked, the honorable gentlemen voted to give the Harlem the Broadway streetcar franchise. Two days later the railroad's workmen began to lay tracks. Meanwhile the "George Law" company went to work on *another* section of Broadway, in anticipation of victory in the well-greased legislature.[28]

Even with General Grant attacking Vicksburg from the rear, with General Joseph Hooker in motion against Robert E. Lee, the people of New York could talk of little else but the battle of Broadway. "The *coup d'etat* of the Common Council" was "the great theme of conversation in the city yesterday," the *Herald* reported on April 24. "The deepest interest was expressed by all classes, and a high state of excitement prevailed in Wall Street, about the City Hall, and around the newspaper bulletins." Finally a fresh injunction halted both sides. Strong wrote that the "only visible sign" of the Harlem's Broadway line "is a strip of lacerated pavement between 13th and 14th Streets, and a few sleepers and rails lying out in the rain." Then Governor Seymour vetoed the George Law bill. The city—and the Harlem Railroad—had won.[29]

Where was the Commodore? True to his word, "at this late date" he chose to keep "aloof from any public transaction," particularly the mass corruption of New York City and State. Though he held a seat on the Harlem board, he did not bother to attend meetings with any regularity until the beginning of May (though Horace Clark helped fight the George Law bill in Albany). The first overt sign of Vanderbilt's intentions came on May 13. With the Harlem's annual election five days away, he asked Erastus Corning, president of the New York Central Railroad, to serve as a director on the new board.[30] (Corning declined.) On May 18, Vanderbilt swept the election, winning directorships for himself and his circle, including Clark, Daniel Drew, Augustus Schell, and a vice president of the Bank of New York named (appropriately enough) James H. Banker. The next day the board unanimously elected the Commodore president.[31]

The final phase of the Commodore's career now commenced. If the Harlem was "not so big a road," it was a beginning. And the measures he enacted upon assuming power set the pattern for what he would do with every railroad that later fell into his hands. "Mr. Vanderbilt replied that he would accept the office of President of the Co. upon the condition that he receive no compensation for his services," the secretary recorded, "& that the Board appoint a vice president who shall discharge the executive duties of the office." It was a declaration of a sweeping new policy of reform: he would save the company every penny—including the president's $6,000 salary—but he would not be an operational manager. Rather, he would be a railroad *leader*, a distinction critical to understanding his role.

The board ratified his terms, of course, and elected William E. Morris vice president. Other reforms appeared in swift succession. The same day, the board created an executive and finance committee, a tighter, more efficient group to act on behalf of the full board. It consisted entirely of Vanderbilt's assistants and allies: Clark, Schell, Banker, A. B. Baylis, and John Steward. The committee promptly restructured the company's debt by issuing $6 million in new consolidated mortgage bonds "for the liquidation, adjustment, & settlement of all debts & liabilities of the company." In a stark departure from past expediency, the bonds were not to be sold for less than par. It was a bold decision given the railroad's miserable reputation.[32]

By emerging from the shadows to publicly take charge of the Harlem, the Commodore staked his prized reputation on his ability to revive the ailing railroad. His failure to save the Accessory Transit Company had cut deeply into his muscular pride; he would never let the same thing happen again. But this personal project immediately came under attack. The two tales of Harlem—the comedy of public corruption and the heroic saga of its rescue—now converged.

Just as Vanderbilt assumed the presidency of the railroad, the Harlem came under attack by New York's corrupt officials. Those officials were *not* its original enemies, the state legislators, but its erstwhile allies, the city councilmen. The elected elders of Gotham had bought as many shares of Harlem as their good credit would allow before giving the railroad the Broadway franchise. As soon as Governor Seymour vetoed the George Law bill, the price of Harlem soared to 105—nearly twice the market price of 58 recorded when this affair began. "In comparison with the thousands thus made in a day or two," *Harper's* declared, "street-cleaning schemes, by which a few hundreds were filched, or the sale of votes at $100 a piece, seemed petty and contemptible." But their grand profit in this most inside of inside trading led them, en masse, to a grave miscalculation: "If they could create, could they not also destroy?"[33]

"The City Hall junta, like many other men, are smart in their own sphere, but children out of it," *Harper's* continued. "In a sweetly innocent way, they 'sold Harlem short' all the way from 85—to which point the Commodore let it drop—to 72." Their plan was simple: to sell Harlem short, *revoke* the Broadway franchise, then buy in at a profit after the price tumbled. They would use their official powers to destroy the share value of one of the city's largest companies and most important transit lines. The result would devastate the railroad's shaky credit as the price of its securities collapsed.

For Vanderbilt, the potential losses may have been less important than the attack on his pet project, the intended showcase of his abilities as a businessman. It was said that friends of the aldermen and councilmen informed Vanderbilt of the impending revocation of the Broadway grant. "Rumor states," the *New York Herald* wrote, "that the President of the Company, Commodore Vanderbilt, warned the members of the Council of the folly of their trick, and predicted that they would lose more than they would make by it."[34]

On June 25, the battle of Harlem began. The price began the day at 83¼, but orders to sell poured out of city hall. At four o'clock, the board of councilmen voted to repeal the Broadway grant, and Harlem fell rapidly to 72½ at the Open Board. But the Commodore had laid a trap. He intended to corner the market—to buy every share offered by the brokers working for aldermen and councilmen, even if they surpassed the total in existence. When the short-sellers went into the market to buy shares in order to deliver them to Vanderbilt's brokers, they would find none—and still less mercy.

The corner was hardly a new maneuver on Wall Street (Vanderbilt may have carried one out in late 1852), but the Commodore proposed to conduct this one on a far larger scale than ever before. The dangers were immense. He had to buy on credit, for he had to buy quickly. Anything short of complete victory would prove disastrous; he had to control *all* the shares or he would be unable to extort money from the short-sellers. But Vanderbilt, as Lambert Wardell later explained, "was a bold, fearless man, very much a speculator, understanding all risks and willing to take them."[35]

On the morning of June 26, news of a Confederate invasion of Pennsylvania filled the pages of the newspapers. On Wall Street, nervous traders expected Harlem's rapid retreat after the repeal and the losses of the night before. "Instead of declining, however, it advanced, rather to the astonishment of the shorts," reported the *Herald*. "It rose today to 97, a difference rarely witnessed in a single day, and a more severe punishment than the bears have suffered for some time." Vanderbilt's credit stretched as his brokers bought and bought, fighting the bears who sold in a desperate attempt to break down the price. Some of the short-sellers panicked and borrowed stock to deliver (rather than buy in at a loss); they paid interest of as high as 2 *percent per day* for its use. Still Harlem rose, to 101½ on June 27, then 106 on June 28. "The bear campaign in Harlem proves the most disastrous on record," the *Herald* observed.

As Harlem marched upward, the bears realized that they were borrowing stock, through third-party brokers, from Vanderbilt. He had slyly lent out his own stock for delivery to himself, to both fool and squeeze his opponents. Those opponents were cornered; they could not fulfill their contracts by delivering the stock they had promised. Each day that the situation persisted, they paid interest. "It is understood that the short sellers have acknowledged their defeat, and endeavored to make terms with their triumphant antagonists without success," the *Herald* wrote.[36]

The "triumphant antagonists," of course, were Commodore Vanderbilt and a tight clique of friends and advisers who wisely followed his directions. He had directed his campaign from his office at 5 Bowling Green without ever going near Wall Street, ruthlessly gambling his fortune on complete victory. It was a chilling display of nerve. According to *Harper's Weekly*, the councilmen called to beg for mercy, and the Commodore graciously replied that "he knew not who had sold the stock he had bought. If the gentlemen present were the sellers, he feared they had parted with valuable property at a low price. For his part he didn't see that he had had, or was likely to have, any dealings with them; and wished them a very good morning."

For New York's famously corrupt councilmen, Vanderbilt's vengeance proved a grand humiliation. He had caught them in their game of twisting public power to private ends, and drove them to the brink of bankruptcy. They "slunk back to Wall Street" and found that Harlem had risen $2 per share. Even more devastating, *Harper's* added, was that "the public had come to understand the game. . . . No member of the City Hall party could show himself in public without exciting a roar of laughter."[37] Finally Vanderbilt granted a (stiff) price to let them out of their contracts. On June 29, the humbled Common Council restored the Broadway grant. Vanderbilt let the price down after he had squeezed the most he deemed prudent out of his foes. "It may seem anomalous to outsiders that Harlem should rise 30 percent on the repeal of the grant and fall on the repeal of the repeal," the *Herald* wrote on July 1. "But people who sold the stock short understand the reason."

Two days later the Union army at Gettysburg held the line against

Pickett's charge. The battered Army of Northern Virginia retreated, leaving the battlefield to the Army of the Potomac. "A memorable day," Strong wrote on July 5, "even if its glorious news prove but half true. . . . This may have been one of the great decisive battles of history." So too on Wall Street, if the reporting was only half true. Vanderbilt enriched himself by forcing greedy men to pay for selling him what was his all along.[38]

The Harlem corner proved significant in many ways. For one, Vanderbilt's punishment of the famously corrupt city government resonated with disgruntled New Yorkers, especially the elite who resented the rise of the Irish to office. For another, the sheer volume of money in play attracted unprecedented attention to Wall Street. Some were charmed by the romance of this financial warfare; others were alarmed that the public highways should be gambled in financial markets that few Americans fully understood. Perhaps most important, the corner greatly increased Vanderbilt's stake in the Harlem Railroad. In a typical corner, the victorious bulls would try to unload the stock they had acquired; in this case, Vanderbilt held on to many of the additional shares he had bought, lifting his official holdings from less than one-tenth to almost one-third. He had pursued the corner to avenge himself, but it may have led him to make an even more serious commitment to the railroad. It transformed the Harlem into the foundation of his railroad kingdom.[39]

In July, the annual wave of heat and humidity and dirt and stench rolled over New York. It was time for Vanderbilt to move on, as he did every summer, to Saratoga. His victory secure, he could remove himself two hundred miles to the Springs. Everywhere people declared that Gettysburg had effectively ended the rebellion. "My cheerful and agreeable but deluded friends," Strong wrote in his diary, "there must be battle by the score before that outbreak from the depths of original sin is 'ended.' "[40]

MANY MYSTERIES SURROUND the Harlem corner. How much stock did Vanderbilt really keep in the end? How much did he make? Who were his collaborators? Perhaps most important, who were his enemies? The councilmen and aldermen? In the last case, this was petty, individual graft. The famously corrupt Tweed Ring did not yet exist. Nor was it a Tammany Hall operation. Contrary to historical myth, Tammany had never been an all-powerful machine, especially not now, when it comprised only one wing of the Democratic Party.[41]

Historian Mark Wahlgren Summers convincingly refutes the long-held idea that the Civil War gave rise to "exceptional rascality." It was not corruption that was new, he writes, but the corruption issue—a fever for reform that would grow with the coming of peace. As we've seen, graft arrived on the American scene long before 1861; as Summers notes, the "argot of corruption," with such terms as "borers," "strikers," and "dummies," first emerged in the antebellum years. The source might be traced back to the Jacksonian revolution in politics, with the rise of professional politicians who treated elections and officeholding as a business. Some were simply greedy, but even the most public-spirited needed money to fund campaigns, partisan newspapers, and party rallies. As Tweed ascended to power in the months ahead, he would not pioneer graft, but *rationalize* it to serve the purpose of governing the decentralized, anarchic city. In that sense, the Common Council's bear raid on Harlem represented a transitional moment in New York's rich history of corruption—a frenzy of profiteering before the rise of the more systematic (but equally greedy) Tweed.[42]

A more personal mystery surrounds Daniel Drew. The banker Henry Clews would later write in his influential memoir (*Twenty-eight Years in Wall Street*, updated later as *Fifty Years in Wall Street*) that "Drew was one of the great bears in this deal with the aldermen." Clews and other Wall Street men of the 1860s depicted Drew as Vanderbilt's natural rival—the bear who fought the bull, a skulking fiend who undercut stock prices and refused to fulfill his contracts when he lost money.[43] Unfortunately, Clews was a wildly unreliable rumormonger with a taste for the most colorful version of any story; his oft-quoted tales are mostly worthless as historical evidence. More than that, this dark picture of Drew was projected through the lens of events yet to occur. In 1860, by contrast, R. G. Dun & Co. had made a more nuanced report: "His stock firm stands high at the Board. Drew is pretty well liked & not very grasping in his disposition, but takes care that he gets his own. Altho he is [responsible], his contracts would be better interpreted in writing."[44] He was a bit slippery, then, but not dishonorable—quite popular, in fact, and well respected. True, he had a taste for short-selling (his inside trading in Erie stock had come to light as early as 1857), but that did not make him Vanderbilt's enemy. No evidence exists to indicate a departure from their long years of close cooperation in business operations and speculation, let alone their friendship. "Uncle Daniel" was far more likely to have joined the Harlem corner.[45]

A final enigma surrounds Vanderbilt's intentions, now that he controlled the Harlem. He had turned sixty-nine on May 27, an age generally associated with retirement—or death—rather than beginnings. He himself had written of "this late day" in his life. Yet he showed every sign of embracing his new role as chief executive despite his insistence on a vice president to run daily affairs. Over the ensuing months he would correspond with everyone from the Harlem's chief engineer to Edwin D. Stanton about everything from machine shops to individual locomotives.[46] His long-term plans, on the other hand, remain shrouded. More than likely, he had little notion of the epic wars to come.

THE HARLEM CORNER was perhaps the most spectacular sign of the vast quantities of wealth now being handled by the men of Wall Street. Vanderbilt kept his profits secret, but they surely ran into the hundreds of thousands of dollars. It was a harvest that reflected an increasingly stark polarization of society. When the income tax assessors drew up their lists that year, they found that the top 1 percent, a group of 1,600 families, earned 61 percent of the *taxable* income of Manhattan's more than 800,000 souls. Were dividends (which were taxed at the source) included, that percentage would prove far larger. Department-store magnate Alexander T. Stewart earned $1,843,637 in 1863; when one of his clerks was promoted that year, he received a salary of only $500, and many clerks received as little as $300. Wartime inflation punished the city's poor. Retail prices had risen 43 percent since 1860, and rents had climbed as much as 20 percent, but wages had increased only 12 percent. The resentment felt in such slums as Corlears Hook and Five Points began to boil.[47]

On Saturday, July 11, a typically suffocating New York summer day, the lottery for the draft began, as mandated by the Conscription Act, passed by a Congress desperate for men to fight the increasingly costly war. At the corner of Third Avenue and Forty-seventh Street, "an area of vacant lots and isolated buildings," as two historians of the city write, "the provost marshal read off names drawn from a large barrel." Some of the 1,236 men drafted belonged to Black Joke Engine Company No. 33. Largely Irish and working-class, the firemen had always enjoyed an exemption from the state militia; being called up for federal service enraged them. On Monday, when the lottery was scheduled to resume, the Black Joke men sparked a citywide inferno known as the Draft Riots. Mobs stormed buildings and battled police; arsonists started fires from river to river, from Fiftieth Street to the Battery. The violence took a savagely racist turn. Rioters attacked black-owned homes and businesses, lynched black men and women, and ransacked the Colored Orphan Asylum on Fifth Avenue and Forty-second Street, shouting "Burn the niggers' nest!" Troops rushed back from Gettysburg; they charged barricades and battled lines of armed and organized civilians. By Thursday night, six thousand soldiers patrolled the smoldering city. On Friday, the omnibuses rolled once again.

A man could avoid the draft by paying a $300 fee, a provision that inflamed class tensions—indeed, that drove much of the riot's fury. "There goes a $300 man!" the rioters bellowed when they spotted (and attacked) a prosperous-looking fellow on the streets. "Down with the rich men!" they cried, as they looted fine houses on Gramercy Park.[48] But the Commodore did not feel their wrath, nor did he have any feeling for it.

The city's response was typically divided. The Republican mayor Opdyke had appealed for troops. Democrats came up with a more sympathetic and expedient solution. With Tweed's guidance, the county board of supervisors created a committee to pay for exemptions and substitutes for the poor. Governor Seymour, a Democrat, also convinced Lincoln to reduce New York's quota.

Somewhere amid this crisis moved Horace Clark and Augustus Schell. Along with August Belmont, they led the "silk-stocking sachems" of Tammany Hall, a faction of wealthy Democrats who eyed Tweed warily as his influence grew in the wake of the riot. The time would come when Clark and Schell moved openly against Tweed, whom they considered a dangerous demagogue; but for the moment, they devoted themselves to the service of the Commodore as he worked to reform the Harlem Railroad. They would rebel against him one day as well, with disastrous consequences for all.[49]

ON AUGUST 20, 1863, a small, slender, reserved young man with a great black sack of a beard composed a letter on the stationery of the Rutland & Washington Railroad, addressed to Erastus Corning, president of the New York Central. "I was informed to day," he wrote, "that a party in intent with the Hudson River [Railroad] clique had been made up for the purpose of purchasing controll [sic] of the N.Y. Central." An "informant" in the office of the ring's leader, Leonard W. Jerome, had overheard a conversation among its members, "[and] I thought it proper to advise you."[50]

Curiously, the writer of the letter shared a birthday with Cornelius Vanderbilt, though he was born in 1836, making him only twenty-seven. A former surveyor and local historian from the heart of the Catskill Mountains, he had set up as a leather merchant in Manhattan, where he was not very popular. Recently he had purchased a large quantity of the securities of the little Rutland & Washington at a steep discount and had gone into railroading, albeit on a very small scale. His name was Jay Gould.[51]

Less than five years later, Gould would emerge as the most dangerous enemy of Vanderbilt's long life, but the plot that Gould now uncovered would bring them onto the same side. For Vanderbilt—only weeks into his presidency of the Harlem Railroad—Jerome's scheme posed a test: How would he conduct himself on the treacherous battlefield of New York's railways? The answer would prove surprising, given his reputation, but it would be characteristic of his career as a railroad executive. More than that, his handling of this plot spoke to the strategic geography of the nation's railways, a reality that would define the rest of his life.

If one word could describe the railroad system, it would be *fragmented*. By 1860, a total of 30,626 miles of track draped the American landscape; hundreds of companies made up that network, which had as many as seven different gauges (widths between tracks), from 4 feet 8½ inches (standard in New England, New York, and Pennsylvania) to 6 feet (used on the Erie Railway and some thirteen smaller lines). This confusion dated back to the origins of the system in the 1830s and '40s. Rather like the old turn-pike companies, railroad corporations had been created by the merchants of various cities and towns to funnel trade toward themselves. Local com-munities fiercely resisted the integration of the network for fear that busi-ness would roll right past them; they wanted breaks between railroads, despite the inefficiencies imposed on long-distance commerce. The origi-nal charter of the Erie actually prohibited it from linking to railroads that led into neighboring states. By the start of the Civil War, such legal restrictions largely had been eliminated, but the profusion of incompati-ble gauges and the fragmentation into scores of companies persisted, with consequent costs from "breaking bulk" (loading freight from one car into another) and outbreaks of hostilities between connecting lines.[52]

In the 1850s, four giant railroads rose to dominance over these mis-matched pieces. As early as 1854 they were dubbed the "trunk lines"— defined as the primary routes between the eastern seaboard and the West, reaching from the main Atlantic ports to the heads of river and lake navi-gation across the Appalachians. They were the Baltimore & Ohio, the Pennsylvania (often called the Pennsylvania Central), the Erie, and the New York Central.* The latter two were New York lines, though the Erie now terminated in Jersey City. The New York Central had emerged in 1853 from the consolidation of ten railways that paralleled the Erie Canal from Buffalo to Albany; it and the Erie were far larger, in capitalization and length, than any other line in the state.[53]

It was the New York Central that overshadowed the smaller lines run by Gould and Vanderbilt. The Erie ran through barren mountains, but the Central connected a chain of agricultural and manufacturing centers from Buffalo to Rochester to Syracuse to Albany. From its terminus in the latter city, it had a choice of three paths into Manhattan: Daniel Drew's People's Line steamboats, the Hudson River Railroad, or (through a short link) the Harlem. The Central's long-standing policy was to pit the three

---

* A "trunk line" would later be defined as an integrated line, under one management, from the seaboard to Chicago or St. Louis. This book will use the contemporary meaning of the term, as explained here.

against each other to keep down costs. It routinely gave most of its New York–bound freight to the steamboats, except when ice closed the river during the winter; then it delivered to the Hudson River line. Very little ever went over the Harlem.[54]

Vanderbilt sorely wanted the long-distance passengers and through freight that came from the West via the Central, no matter how little revenue he received. Unlike a steamboat and steamship line, a railroad suffered from high fixed costs. It was an immovable piece of infrastructure. Whether trains ran or not, the tracks, bridges, buildings, locomotives, and cars had to be maintained; conductors, engineers, firemen, and laborers had to be paid. At least two-thirds of a railroad's expenses remained constant no matter how much or how little traffic it carried. If the Commodore could get additional business, even at losing rates, it would improve the Harlem's outlook.[55]

To gain access to that rich flow of freight from the West, Vanderbilt decided to pursue diplomacy with the Central. He made this choice as a matter of policy, but he liked and respected the Central's president, Erastus Corning, whom he hailed as "a man of business and a gentleman." Corning, who was only a few months younger than the Commodore, also had risen to wealth through his wits. At thirteen, he had moved from Connecticut to upstate New York and set up as a merchant in Albany. Though he had served as the Central's president from its creation, he remained alert to his own interests, and ordered the railroad to buy its ironware from a foundry he owned. Corning was also a political power broker—a former congressman and leader of the state's Democratic Party (along with the Central's vice president, Dean Richmond of Buffalo). Corning had thin gray hair, a prominent lower lip, and large, dark, deep-set eyes. Clark and Schell knew him well; indeed, Vanderbilt took Clark with him when he opened talks with Corning in late summer. On September 16, Vanderbilt called on Corning again, and dispatched to him James Banker, who was emerging as a favorite subordinate.[56]

Unfortunately for Vanderbilt, Corning believed the Harlem offered the Central few advantages. But then came Leonard Jerome's plot to oust Corning from the Central's presidency, offering the Commodore an unexpected opportunity for leverage.

Jerome, the younger brother of Wall Street giant Addison G. Jerome, exemplified the flowering of wealth on wartime Wall Street and the resulting flourish of conspicuous consumption. Strong derided as "a sign of the times" Jerome's "grand eighty-thousand-dollar stable, with the private theatre for a second story." Social observer Matthew Hale Smith observed that Jerome became "the leader of fashions."* According to

---

* Leonard Jerome was to become the grandfather of Winston Churchill.

William Fowler, Jerome was "a tall man, fashionably but somewhat carelessly attired, having a slight stoop, a clear olive complexion, a tigerish
moustache, and a cerulean eye."[57]

Jerome's belligerence, like Vanderbilt's diplomacy, was a response to
the fragmentation of the railroad system. He had come onto the Hudson
River board only recently, and he and his fellow directors resented the
Central's custom of delivering its freight to Drew's steamboats. To solve
this conflict, he organized "a large combination . . . to control NY Central
RR affairs at the next election" in December, as banker Watts Sherman
warned Corning, with the aim of "forcing the immense eastward traffic
over the road of the [Hudson River]," according to Gould. The game
began on October 20 when the Hudson River directors voted to loan
Jerome $400,000 for his operation.[58]

Vanderbilt had personal ties to both Corning and the Jerome brothers,
but he calculated his strategic interests clearly and coldly. A takeover of
the great trunk line by his rival, the Hudson River Railroad, would permanently deny the Harlem any through freight and passengers from the
West. Furthermore, if Vanderbilt helped Corning he would put the Central's president in his debt. On November 11, Vanderbilt scratched a note
to Corning in his own hand, a significant fact for a man who loathed writing. "Is their any feair of their success," he asked, referring to Jerome and
his allies. "I feal a little anxious, if I can be of any servis say so." He wrote
that he just had purchased a thousand shares, and had had a total of 5,250
transferred under his name. He offered to obtain "proxys" for many more.
"If J. H. Banker ask you for information you can giv it to him he is true &
will not deceive us this is certain," he concluded—revealing how heavily
he relied on the honey-smooth vice president of the Bank of New York.
(As Watts Sherman told Corning, Banker was well known as Vanderbilt's
personal agent. "He holds a position here of great influence in many quarters & is class in all respects.")[59]

On Vanderbilt's orders, Banker ferreted out information about
Jerome's plot at brokers' offices and gentlemen's clubs. "They are making
great exertions," he wrote to Corning. "I believe they have gone to the
extent of sending to Geo. Peabody & Co. to influence foreign proxies,"
referring to the American banking house in London where many shares of
key railroads, including the New York Central, were held by British
investors. The fight for proxies (the right to the votes of those shares)
often was more important than stock purchases, especially in a big corporation in which it was prohibitively expensive to buy majority control.[60]
And the fight was fierce. The *New York Herald* wrote on November 19,
"The excitement has now reached a pretty high point, and hard words are
resorted to on both sides, instead of argument."[61]

"I sea by the New York Times of this morning that the opposition has used my name" on their ticket of proposed directors, Vanderbilt wrote to Corning on November 20. The letter that followed constitutes a piece of found poetry, a free verse of the Commodore's approach to Wall Street's shadow warfare.

> this is without athority
> They do not understand how
> I feal in this matter
> I keep them in the dark
> I in close you the two proxies
> I tell Mr Banker to keep
> you posted with what is
> doing here & get all proxy
> possible—let them say what
> they will I want you to
> understand I will have
> nothing to do with them
> in any form—over
>
> I want you to feal that
> you air at liberty to
> use me in this matter
> in any honorable way you
> may think adviseable[62]

Shrewdly, Vanderbilt declined Banker's suggestion that he stand for election to the board on Corning's ticket, for he wished to avoid alienating Jerome. Indeed, one week before the election, he met with Jerome in private to propose a compromise. "I don't believe it is worthwhile to say anything more about what we talked about last night," Jerome wrote to him the next morning. "I appreciate your views and feelings in the matter and in the main think you are perfectly correct. But you see I have been acting with other parties. . . . I guess we had better let the thing take its course."[63]

Was that a tone of resignation? Certainly the Commodore now acted as if he were certain of Corning's victory—and of the material benefits to flow from it. On December 2, for example, he convened a special meeting of the Harlem's stockholders. They approved the sale of the unissued $2,139,950 in stock authorized by the corporation's charter to double-track and extend the line to Albany. The stated reason was to accommodate "anticipated connections with other railroads."[64]

It was a dangerous game, especially now that Vanderbilt had revealed his position—dangerous because Jerome not only had taken power in the Hudson River, but also in Pacific Mail, the partner of the Commodore's steamship line. But Vanderbilt was as sure of his strength now, at sixty-nine, as he had ever been. On December 7, with the Central election two days away, he went down to his stables and ordered a fast team harnessed to his racing wagon. He drove up Broadway to where it became Bloomingdale Road, and looked for a "brush." He found one. He and a challenger rattled their rigs alongside each other at top speed, Vanderbilt whipping his horses ahead as he tried to edge out his rival. Then the Commodore's powers failed him, and the wagons cracked into each other. "His carriage was broken," the *Chicago Tribune* reported, "and the Commodore thrown over the dashboard to the ground"—more specifically, "head foremost and violently to the ground," according to the *New York Times*. "He was picked up insensible, but soon recovered consciousness, and was conveyed to a house nearby, where he received every attention."[65]

The Commodore overcame his injuries, but he could not go to Albany as he had intended. Corning and his party triumphed regardless. "No election of this kind has ever produced such an extended & warm excitement," longtime Central director John V. L. Pruyn noted in his journal. "The result has been most gratifying." Banker dined at Corning's house on December 11 as his patron's representative.[66]

In the first crisis of Vanderbilt's new career as a railroad president, he had displayed masterful statecraft, adroitly turning a battle between two far stronger companies to his advantage. As soon as he was able to go to his office, he addressed a letter to Corning. "In consequence of the severe fall I had I have been prevented from visiting you," he wrote. He then specified how the Central could repay him. "It would suit the Harlem Road to have your agents . . . make their tickets in such a form that the holder should be entitled to pass either, at his option, over the Harlem or Hudson River Rail Road. I can see no good reason why this should not be." Even more important, he insisted that his man Banker should have a seat on the Central's board. Corning obliged by forcing the resignation of one of his directors.[67]

Hardly had Vanderbilt secured Corning's hold on power than he attempted to collect the debt. But time would show how difficult that would be. The structural conflicts stemming from the fragmentation of the railroad landscape—the same problem that gave rise to this particular battle—would continue to grow. As the Commodore would learn, they had only one solution.

AT SEVEN O'CLOCK ON SATURDAY EVENING, December 19, 1863, a visitor who stepped out of a carriage in front of 10 Washington Place naturally might have paused in the cold winter air and looked up to the windows of the second floor. Scores of well-dressed people would be seen through the glass as band music drifted down from that nearly twenty-year-old mansion, twice the width of a regular brownstone. If a visitor proceeded up the stoop to the entrance, where one of the Irish servants would open the door, into the great hall where one's coat would be taken, then up the stairs and to the right, through the small library and into a large sitting room, twenty by twenty-five feet, the reason for all the revelry could be seen.[68]

There, surrounded by the Commodore's milling siblings and children and grandchildren and nieces and nephews, was a table filled with gifts in celebration of Cornelius and Sophia Johnson Vanderbilt's fiftieth wedding anniversary. "There was a profusion of bracelets, porte-mounnales [sic], gold plate, exquisitely carved chess-men, superbly bound Bibles, brooches, and feminine ornaments of every kind," wrote Mrs. Ann S. Stephens, a popular "authoress" and friend of the wealthy pair, who described the event for the *New York Tribune*. At the center perched the Commodore's gift to his wife, a miniature steamship crafted of gold, specially ordered from Europe. "It is twenty inches long and five wide, with exquisitely wrought revolving towers," Stephens wrote, "which filled the room with fairy music whenever the delicate machinery was set in motion." After a formal review of the ship, the bride presented the golden groom with "a collection of gold-headed canes [and] driving-whips, mounted in some costly manner." Then the party descended to the main-floor parlors, where Stephens observed two striking sculptures: the marble bust of Vanderbilt, carved by Hiram Powers in Italy in 1853, and in the opposite corner of the room—in line with the stone Commodore's stare—a statue of the son of William Tell.[69]

The family swarmed around Vanderbilt—dressed "in quiet black . . . unpretending and gentlemanly as he is everywhere"—and his wife, who wore "a head-dress of Brussels point, wreathed with gold-tinted roses and marabout feathers," perched on her "thick and scarcely silvered curls," as Stephens wrote. Sons-in-law all appeared: Nicholas La Bau, who had often served as Vanderbilt's attorney; George Osgood, a rising stockbroker who handled some of Vanderbilt's trades; Daniel Torrance and James Cross, who had helped to manage Vanderbilt's steamship lines; Horace Clark, growing ever more important as a lieutenant in all capacities; and Daniel Allen, the longest-serving of Vanderbilt's daughters' husbands. R. G. Dun & Co. would deem Allen "a high minded man of 1st rate [business] qualifications," an accurate assessment of the man who had learned how to run a shipping line in Vanderbilt's office, only to stand up to him when Allen believed he had violated the Accessory Transit Company's charter. Now, after nearly thirty years in business together, they began to sever their ties. On November 27, Allen and Cornelius Garrison had incorporated the Atlantic Mail Steamship Company, with an authorized capital of $4 million. Within a year, the new corporation would buy out the old Atlantic & Pacific Steamship Company, along with Vanderbilt's remaining stake in shipping. The Commodore was leaving the ocean behind.[70]

Despite the profusion and importance of sons-in-law, Vanderbilt's sons by blood—the Vanderbilt princes, as it were—stepped forward to take command of the celebration. The teeming family assembled in one of the parlors, in front of a grand floral display, and the murmur of conversation died away. "Here and there," Stephens wrote, "half-hidden by flowing robes of gossamer, tulle, brocade, or velvet, a little fairy child would peep into the front ranks to learn why all the stillness had come on so suddenly." Then the ceremony formally began with a speech by Cornelius Jeremiah.[71]

Corneil, the victim of disease and the degenerate gambler, had been the subject of concern and scorn poured out in unpredictable measure by his father. Once he collapsed in a severe seizure during a visit by his father. "While he was lying there," recalled Corneil's servant, Margaret Massy, who went to work in his Hartford house around 1862, "the Commodore came in, and, pointing his cane at the ship *Vanderbilt*, a picture in the room, said, 'I would have given that ship to have cured Cornelius if it were possible.' " In the moneymaking frenzy that came with the war, Corneil had fallen back into his gambling habit. "Many times," Jacob J. Van Pelt recalled, the Commodore "spoke very disrespectfully about him. He said he would lie and steal. He said, 'I wouldn't let him go into my office if there was anything there he could lay his hands on.' " This mix of compassion and disdain—what Sophia called her husband's "stubborn inconsistency" toward his namesake—made Corneil self-conscious as he stood before the gathering. But his mother had always been his defender.[72] And so, before his judge and his protector, Corneil began to speak.

"Kindred and friends," he said, "the joyful yet solemn anniversary to which we have so long and anxiously looked forward, has at length brought us together. Let us be thankful that it finds so many links in our family circle still bright and unbroken." After this auspicious beginning, Corneil's address took an awkward and painfully solipsistic turn. "For myself, having tested in a larger measure, perhaps, than others, the unwearying patience and unfailing love of those around whom we are gathered tonight," he continued, "I feel sure that they will yet remain with us for many years, if only that I may be enabled to prove, by devotion and watchful care, through the long bright autumn of their days, that their long-suffering goodness was exercised in behalf of one who is neither insensible nor ungrateful." A ripple of cringing around the room can be imagined at this wordy display of self-absorption and self-loathing.

As if to break the crust of discomfort, La Bau brought in a six-foot "tree" of ivy wrapped around a trellis that spelled out the names of Vanderbilt's children in tiny flowers. "The Bible tells us that to everything there is a season," he said. "I insist that it is not time in which to cast away stones, because, alas for poor humanity, we all dwell in glass houses." This was an appropriate occasion for such reflections. "Could you, sir, fifty years ago, have predicted that steam would have been encased in a steel jacket, placed on wheels, and sent off, puffing fire and smoke, through this land, upon iron roads?" La Bau asked. "And could you, madam, have predicted that men of this day, thousands of miles apart, would converse by lightning?"

The Commodore declined to speak, as always. Rather, he and Sophia thanked their offspring through their oldest son, William. Billy, as Vanderbilt still called him, had earned his father's almost begrudging affection during the *North Star* excursion and its aftermath, in large part by winning his respect. "He was slow and clumsy in his movements," the *New York Sun* later remarked. "His face was red and rough-skinnned and he had very small, dull eyes, so that he had the appearance, not justified by the facts, of a slow-witted man." Unjustified indeed. The former treasurer of the Staten Island Railroad became the bankrupt line's receiver, revived its fortunes during the wartime boom, and now served as its president. This dull-looking farmer had emerged as a leading man of Richmond County, and stood now as his parents' mouthpiece.[73]

At ten o'clock, after Billy spoke, the band played a march to accompany the family into the dining room, in a procession led by the Commodore and Sophia. They ate; La Bau sang; the grandchildren sang; the 7th Regiment Band marched up outside and serenaded the famous couple; and near midnight the band indoors played "Home, Sweet Home," as arms slid into coats and coachmen drove up carriages. It was a glorious evening for the Vanderbilts and their children—except for the two who did not attend. One was Frances Lavinia. She was described as an "invalid," a term so general and all-encompassing that it could have included anything from mental retardation to multiple sclerosis, though clearly her ailment had left her unable to care for herself since her birth in 1828. She lurked somewhere out of view, a vivid yet completely obscured fact in Vanderbilt's life.[74]

The other missing child was George. On September 19, the regular army had promoted him to captain of the 10th Infantry Regiment, but it appeared increasingly likely that it would be a purely honorary appointment. Soon after the horses pulling the last carriage had clopped away from the front of 10 Washington Place on the night of the golden anniversary, Billy resigned the presidency of the Staten Island Railroad to go to his brother in Nice. Whether he was prompted by news of his brother's decline is unclear. Whether he was prompted by news of his brother's death is unclear as well. George died on December 31, 1863. About the end of January, Billy returned to New York with his corpse.[75]

At half past ten in the morning on Thursday, February 4, not quite two months after the golden gathering, the family again assembled at 10 Washington Place, along with army comrades and friends of the deceased. By one report, George was engaged to a Miss Hawley, on whom the Commodore bestowed a house in upper Manhattan; most likely she attended as well. The funeral procession trailed in black behind teams of horses down to the Staten Island Ferry, rolled onto a boat that steamed across the bay, and drove up the drive from Vanderbilt's Landing to the cemetery, where the statue of Grief presided over the family tomb. "How wavering are the scenes of earth," wrote Rev. Samuel Kissam, Billy's father-in-law, "our kindred pleasures, too."

> *Now, now that circle we behold*
> *In sorrow deep and wide,*
> *Weeping o'er son and brother cold,*
> *Long, long their joy and pride—*
> *Embalmed, and ready for the tomb.*

Vanderbilt buried his youngest son. Now he looked to his oldest. William would speak for him not merely on ceremonial occasions, but with the full authority of the Commodore's tens of millions of dollars in his voice. At the next Harlem election in May, Vanderbilt made William vice president of the company. He brought him all the way into Manhattan, in fact, giving him a gift of a house on Thirty-eighth Street, on the west side of Fifth Avenue, two blocks south of the massive stone walls of the Egyptian-style reservoir between Forty-second and Fortieth streets. As dutifully as when William had left East Broadway for the farm twenty years before, he moved his family back to New York, into a house much like its new owner, substantial but unostentatious. "The interior was richly and not showily furnished," the *New York Sun* wrote, "and the drawing room was surpassed in elegance of decoration and furnishing by hundreds in the city."[76]

As for Corneil, he seems to have left George's funeral with a determination to plummet as swiftly as he could.

ON JANUARY 28, 1864, the Congress of the United States passed a resolution thanking Cornelius Vanderbilt for his "unique manifestation of a fervid and large-souled patriotism," the gift of the steamship *Vanderbilt* to his country. It further resolved that President Lincoln be requested to "cause a gold medal to be struck, which shall fitly embody an attestation of the nation's gratitude." Congress may have waited nearly two years before extending its thanks, but its timing was appropriate: it celebrated the finest act in the long career of perhaps the single most important figure in the history of American steam navigation, at the very moment he left the sea behind.[77]

On the rivers, bays, and oceans, he had acted like a Viking prince, taking his fleet wherever trade or plunder seemed most promising, freely abandoning markets for a price. Railroads, on the other hand, were fixed properties, geographical entities by their very nature—often compared to nation-states by contemporaries and historians. The Commodore understood this intimately, having been involved in the industry for three decades. Though famous as a warrior, he demonstrated statecraft in the New York Central election, offering no hint of aggressive intent.

Diplomacy, unfortunately, did not seem to work on the management of the Hudson River Railroad. "When I first went into the Harlem road, I did not want to have anything to do with the Hudson River," Vanderbilt said later. "I took the Harlem when it was down to nothing, and I got it up along by degrees; but I found that there was a continual clashing with the Hudson River. I said this is wrong; these roads should not clash." For one thing, competition between the parallel lines kept fares dangerously low.[78] For another, their friction could be felt in relations with their mutual partner, the New York Central. Even after the Hudson River's directors failed to oust Corning, they demanded preference in through traffic. It was a conflict made nearly inevitable by the fragmentation of the railroad net into multiple companies. "In a hundred miles," the *Railway Times* observed, "we have two or three corporations with their conflicting interests, conflicting time tables, and different organizations, likely at any moment to be at war with each other as interest or personal feelings may dictate."[79]

Now began the second phase of the founding of Vanderbilt's empire: his campaign against the Hudson River Railroad. He began with an attempt to undermine it by changing the physical railway net itself—by outflanking the enemy in a double envelopment. First, on January 27, the Harlem board authorized him to sell (to himself, if he wished) the additional $2,139,950 in stock approved by the stockholders for the purpose of double-tracking the line to Chatham Four Corners. Second, he threatened to build down the western shore of the Hudson River, filing for incorporation of a line from Albany to the vicinity of New York City. And he accepted Daniel Drew's proposal to build a short railroad from a point on the Central's line at Schenectady to Athens, a town on the Hudson River south of Albany where the People's Line steamboats would face fewer weeks of ice each winter. Officially known as the Saratoga & Hudson River Railroad (more commonly as the Athens road), it received a charter on April 15. Vanderbilt took a quarter of the $1.5 million in stock and went on the board with such well-known Wall Street figures as Henry Keep and Azariah Boody, with Drew as the president. The two lines would be weapons against the Hudson River Railroad, threatening to strip it of what little freight it received from the Central.[80]

The Commodore also had a spy among the enemy: John M. Tobin, whom Vanderbilt had hired years before as a fare collector on the Staten Island Ferry. Matthew Hale Smith reported a popular story that, when Tobin first went to work for the ferry, Vanderbilt strictly instructed him to allow no one to ride for free; the first time Tobin saw the Commodore come aboard, he demanded the fare, saying, "No dead-heads on this line" (using the common slang for those who rode boats and trains for free). "Tobin became the delight of the Commodore," Smith wrote. Tobin later had gone into the liquor business in Manhattan in the 1850s, and was considered to be "of gd [character] & [habits], hard-working & [industrious], careful & reliable," according to R. G. Dun & Co.

The thin, wiry Tobin turned to stock speculation during the war, and became a flamboyant broker at the Open Board. "He was known to be somehow mysteriously connected with Vanderbilt," William Fowler recalled. "His style of operating, too, was so bold and so dashing and even reckless . . . that it quite captivated 'the boys,' and they were all agog when Tobin got on his pins and commenced bidding."[81] Tobin's connection to Vanderbilt remains just as mysterious now as it was then, but a connection they clearly had; so when Tobin had taken a seat on the Hudson River board on June 8, 1863, Vanderbilt had gained either a puppet or an ally inside the rival corporation.[82]

One of the canonical stories of Vanderbilt's life, enshrined in myth by the banker-memoirist Henry Clews, is that he had masterminded a famous corner in Hudson River stock almost simultaneously with the Harlem corner of 1863.[83] There is no evidence for this tale, and it makes little sense. The leader of the Hudson River corner was Leonard Jerome, whom Vanderbilt simultaneously battled in the New York Central election. In December, the Commodore prepared to double-track the Harlem to Albany; why would he plan to pour money into a line with heavy grades if he was buying control of a parallel route, one better equipped and cheaper to operate?

The best explanation of his real actions, and calculations, would come from the Commodore himself on February 5, 1867, in testimony before a legislative committee. As quoted before, he would state that he had been frustrated and irritated by the railroads' conflicts. "I said this is wrong; these roads should not clash," he would say. "Then, step by step, I went into the Hudson River." Having weakened it with his outflanking moves, he slowly purchased its stock, quietly maneuvering for control.[84]

IN 1864, AS VANDERBILT stepped-by-step into the Hudson River, he continued to direct the Harlem's affairs—none of which were more pressing than the Broadway streetcar line. Despite the municipal grant (and the Harlem's plan to buy the Broadway stagecoach companies), no progress had been made. In October 1863, a judge had ruled that the city had no power to issue its grant. The Harlem would have to go to Albany.[85]

In early March, the railroad asked the state legislature for a bill to validate its rights to a railway in Broadway. Horace Clark led the lobbying effort, taking with him his fellow director, Daniel Drew. The committee seemed agreeable, and Senator John B. Dutcher, the Harlem's champion, prepared a report in favor of the bill. Harlem stock rose to 145. Then a vote was called. To Dutcher's (and Clark's and Vanderbilt's) surprise, the committee issued a negative report. Harlem plunged to 107.

Legislators on either side of the issue muttered charges of corruption against their foes. On March 25, Dutcher raised the issue openly on the Senate floor. "He . . . denied that those who were here urging this bill had been speculating in the stock, but the speculating in stock was on the other foot," the *New York Herald* reported. "Those who had been trying to kill this bill had been in Wall Street, to his knowledge, betting great odds that the report would be unfavorable, and had also been selling the stock short."

So they were. In fact, the inside trading on the committee report marked only the start of a massive attack by "a legislative clique" (as the *Herald* called the conspirators) on the stock value of the New York & Harlem Railroad Company. Following the example of the city councilmen the year before, they plotted to use their lawmaking power to make money by shorting Harlem. The corrupt legislators likely had an inside partner. Pervasive reports circulated in the press that Drew was selling Harlem short.[86]

Drew's betrayal of Vanderbilt marked a chilling turn in their relationship. Despite Drew's later reputation for treachery, there is no evidence that he ever double-crossed the Commodore over their decades of partnership and friendship. Indeed, they were so close that Drew named his own son after William H. Vanderbilt.[87] So why now? Perhaps most perplexing, why did the famously shrewd Drew believe that he could drive down the price of the very stock that Vanderbilt had recently cornered?

One motive is obvious: if he succeeded, there would be a great deal of money in it. But more telling is the fact that, for the first time in more than thirty years, the two men's strategic interests were diverging. As long as Vanderbilt controlled the Harlem alone, he and Drew had a common enemy—a common rival for the New York Central's through freight—in the Hudson River Railroad. But Vanderbilt's creep toward control of the Hudson River presaged a conflict with Drew's steamboat line.

As to why Drew thought he could succeed, there are four likely answers. First, he probably believed, like most of Wall Street, that the Harlem had no hope for prosperity without the Broadway line, and he knew that the legislature held the last hope for such a franchise. Second, the amount of Harlem stock had just increased, which would tend to depress the price. Third, the legislature was considering another bill to allow the Harlem to convert $3 million of its bonds into still more shares; this would cut its debt in half, but further add to the circulating stock.

Finally, in a reflection of the growing complexity of the financial markets, Drew had cunningly refined his method of operations. In addition to selling shares that he did not own, he sold *calls* on shares that he did not own. A call was a contract that gave the buyer the right to call on the seller and buy a certain stock at a certain price within a limited period of time. If Drew sold seven-day calls for Harlem at 125, but the price fell below that figure for the duration of the call, then the holder of the call was certain to forgo his right to demand the stock. Who would insist on buying stock for more than the prevailing price? Drew, then, could make money without having to provide anything. More important, short-sellers used calls as margins to protect themselves from an upturn in the market. (Should the price rise unexpectedly, they could limit their losses by buying in at a preset call price.) Drew's huge distribution of calls, in addition to his own short sales, added momentum to the downward movement in Harlem.[88]

Vanderbilt responded to Drew's campaign in characteristic fashion: he began to buy. With Tobin as his partner and agent, he took every offer of Harlem stock. Every day, Fowler recalled, Tobin could be seen at the Open Board or on the curb, "bidding for and buying thousands of shares, his face pale with excitement and his opalescent eyes blazing like a basilisk's. He grabbed at the stock with fury, for he had suffered by the decline." The market felt the weight of the Commodore's liquid millions pressing down on short-sellers, who were burdened also by the thousands risked by Clark, the Schells, and Tobin himself. By March 29, Harlem had stabilized at 126½. In a few days it climbed over 141, and it kept rising.[89]

The Commodore may have felt even richer than usual in the first week of April, when he was approached by members of the United States Sanitary Commission, a private charity devoted to the medical care of soldiers that had grown into an enormously important auxiliary to the Union army. The organization was about to hold a fund-raising fair in Union Square, and its leaders wanted a donation from the Commodore. Vanderbilt declined to make a pledge. Ever attuned to the marketplace, he said he would donate as much as any other man. The delegation later returned with a check for $100,000 from Alexander T. Stewart. "He found himself cornered," the press reported. "However, he was as good as his word. He covered Stewart's check with a check of his own for a like amount."

On April 4, the fair commenced with a military parade before perhaps half a million onlookers. Leonard W. Jerome contributed in his own way, hosting plays at his private theater. "Tickets are in great demand at five dollars, the whole transaction being highly distinguished, aristocratic, and exclusive," Strong recorded. "House was full and everybody in the fullest tog, men in white chokers and women in ball costume."[90]

On Wall Street, all went well. A great upward tide lifted all shares. In the general financial frenzy of that year, brokers decided to open an evening exchange in a room at the Fifth Avenue Hotel, to keep on trading after dark. But Harlem led all others. Drew and his followers in the stock exchanges fought to drive down the price—the legislators prepared to obliterate the Broadway bill—all to no avail. "The Harlem corner goes up vigorously," the financial correspondent for the *New York Times* wrote on April 15. Already Vanderbilt made money from frightened bears. "Heavy differences are said to have been paid to the leading *Bull* in the stock to close contracts," the *Times* added.[91]

The next day, disaster struck, at the hands of Treasury Secretary Chase.

Over the preceding months, congressmen and cabinet secretaries had grown increasingly angry at the gold market, seeing it as a den of treason. Speculators whistled "Dixie" as they sold greenbacks short before major battles, gambling that the Union would be defeated and legal-tender paper currency would lose value against gold. Chase pushed a bill in Congress that, with a spectacular lack of realism, would ban the trade in gold. Then he took direct action. On April 16, in an attempt to drive down the gold premium and undercut speculation, he went into the market and sold a large amount of federal specie; he took the greenbacks thus received and withdrew them from circulation. This moralistic act was a sharply deflationary blow, one that hit Wall Street hard. "The stock market was struck with a panic to-day," the *New York Herald* reported. Even as Chase "locked up" millions in currency, another $15 million was absorbed by a new loan by the banks to the federal government. The sudden drain on cash reserves caused prices to collapse across the board in what the *Evening Post* called "one of the severest panics recorded since 1857 on the annals of the

Stock Exchange." Drew's hour, it seems, had come round at last; he had sold calls at 140, and now Harlem slouched to 133. The slide drove Vanderbilt to the brink, forcing him to put up more and more cash as margins for his millions of dollars' worth of purchases.[92]

But Harlem rose again. Indeed, it rose relentlessly. On April 21, it reached 210. Five days later, it climbed to 235. Despite the immense strain on his resources—and the increasingly severe consequences should he fail—Vanderbilt kept up the pressure, buying still more. Short-sellers desperately waited out the terms of their contracts, hoping to buy in at a lower price before they ran out of time. They could not. Vanderbilt leaped every precipice (including a vicious attack on his management published in the *Herald*) in a splendid display of nerve, the most important virtue in a stock market battle. He carelessly attended the opening of the races at the Fashion Course while Tobin and his other brokers gambled his millions against the combined power of Daniel Drew, the New York State Legislature, and the desperate bears of Wall Street. On May 11, Harlem rose to 256. On May 14, it ascended to 275. Finally, it peaked at 285. One after another, the short-sellers crawled to the Commodore's myrmidons to buy their way out of their unfulfillable contracts. The legislators' attempted abuse of power cost them dearly.[93]

Drew, according to the press, refused to settle. He faced staggering losses on the tens of thousands of calls and whatever short sales he had made, so he announced that he would "squat"—litigate his contracts, rather than pay. The news shocked Wall Street. Should losers in transactions resort to the courts, the markets would break down in short order. If Drew carried out his threat, he likely would be shunned; few brokers, not even his longtime partner David Groesbeck, would do business with a man who did not fulfill his agreements. Once barred from the exchange, Drew never would recover his losses in the future. So Vanderbilt remained cool in the face of this intransigence, and icy cold to the mercurial Drew's pleas for mercy. In the course of further negotiations, Drew finally agreed to pay his old partner perhaps $1 million, roughly half of what the Commodore is believed to have gained in this second corner.[94]

The tens of millions thrown about in this abstract battle on Wall Street captivated—and repulsed—the public. For one thing, the incident demonstrated that Civil War–era corruption was far more complicated than the historical cliché of the rich buying off lawmakers; in this case, as in the previous Harlem corner, the officeholders abused their power to profit from the deliberate destruction of the value of a major corporation. Time would show that extortion by legislators and their hangers-on was as serious a problem as bribery by the wealthy. Such graft only reinforced Vanderbilt's long-standing laissez-faire beliefs.

Paradoxically, by punishing corrupt state legislators so thoroughly, Vanderbilt made it appear that the balance of power in society was shifting away from democratic government and toward wealthy individuals and corporations. "Think of the one-man power that could accomplish this wonderful feat and prevail against a whole Legislature," Henry Clews admiringly wrote in his memoirs. "Think of this, and then you will have some conception of the astute mind that the Commodore possessed, without education to assist it, in the contest against this remarkable combination of well-trained mental forces. There can hardly be a doubt that the Commodore was a genius, probably without equal in the financial world."[95]

The second Harlem corner marked the culmination of his move from steamships to railroads, for it forced him to concentrate his resources in this titanic battle. With victory in hand, he consolidated his power in the Harlem by driving Drew out of the board at the election on May 17 and giving his seat to Senator Dutcher. Out of 105,873 shares represented, the Commodore voted 29,607, though he likely hid the rest of his stock under the names of Horace Clark, Augustus Schell, James Banker, John Tobin (who voted 31,900 shares alone), and others. The next day, Vanderbilt hired his son William as the Harlem's vice president to manage the road's operations.[96]

One month later, Vanderbilt made a second move to solidify his holdings, by displacing the Hudson River Railroad board in a disputed election. Out went Samuel Sloan, Moses H. Grinnell, Addison G. Jerome, and other giants. In came Vanderbilt's captains: Clark, Schell, Banker, and allies Oliver Charlick and Joseph Harker. John Tobin survived from the old board, of course, as did Leonard W. Jerome, who (according to rumor) had cooperated with Vanderbilt in the second Harlem corner. The new board elected Tobin president and created a standing executive committee—a common device, but typical of Vanderbilt's desire to centralize power—consisting of Clark, Schell, Banker, Jerome, and Charlick, in addition to Tobin. On July 6, the committee voted to end the competition between the Hudson River and Harlem trains.[97]

Also in July, the Commodore sold his last sidewheelers to Atlantic Mail, which now supplanted the old Atlantic & Pacific Steamship Company. The step severed his business ties to his son-in-law Daniel Allen, who was a leading figure in Atlantic Mail alongside Cornelius Garrison. Curiously, Allen provided the only Vanderbilt to win glory in the war: his son Vanderbilt Allen, a West Point cadet appointed first lieutenant on June 13, 1864. The young officer soon found a place on General Philip H. Sheridan's staff.[98]

The second Harlem corner typified Vanderbilt's battles on Wall Street in the 1860s. It was a defensive campaign rather than a merely speculative maneuver, designed to avenge himself upon men who had betrayed him. But it proved to be far more than a personal affair. By the summer of 1864, the Commodore had definitively left the floating world behind to concentrate on railroads. In short order he had gained control of the only two steam railways that entered Manhattan and linked it to the world, and had ended their costly rivalry. This first year set the pattern for his long railroad career: diplomacy, defensive battle, acquisition, reform, consolidation. In pursuit of "a small thing," the bedraggled Harlem, he had begun to build an empire.

"YOU MIGHT AS WELL HIT A BRICK WALL as hit that man on the head," Yankee Sullivan declared in 1853. He spoke through the dripping blood of a badly battered face, and he spoke about John Morrissey, his burly foe in a fight for a $1,000 stake, after the brick-wall fellow had beaten him into submission in fifty-seven minutes. The triumphant Morrissey—a fellow Irishman by birth—was somewhere between twenty and thirty years of age at the time, yet already he had acquired a fearsome reputation. As a teenager he had led an Irish gang on the streets of Troy against nativist thugs, before setting up in the slums of New York as a prizefighter, Democratic Party enforcer, and saloon owner. Notably lucky with his games of chance, he expanded beyond Five Points. His gambling house on Fifth Avenue was considered one of the city's finest.[99]

Sullivan returned to San Francisco after his defeat, on a path toward ultimate suicide; the victor, on the other hand, went to Saratoga. Morrissey, the broken-nose prince of Paradise Square, aspired to fashion, and so he flowed with fashion's current to the Springs every summer. There his presence was unmistakeable, "in his white flannel suit, huge diamond rings, and pin containing brilliants of the first water," as Matthew Hale Smith described him. He was a man "of immense size; tall of stature, a powerful-looking fellow, walking quietly about the streets, or lounging at the hotels, but seldom speaking." During the Civil War he opened the Club House, a brick saloon on Saratoga's Matilda Street; as on Fifth Avenue, his place attained a reputation as the most elegant casino in town. But he remained a creature of the street, no matter how high he rose above it. In 1864, for instance, a crowd of con men from Manhattan—three-card-monte artists—stepped off the train at Saratoga. Morrissey sauntered up to them in his white flannel suit and quietly told them to leave town. They did.[100]

Morrissey himself had a taste for gambling, though he would never be seen at a roulette wheel; he understood that apparatus too well to risk his money there. Rather, he played the stock market. Rumor had it that he had joined with his Irish Democratic cohorts on the Common Council to short Harlem in 1863, forgetting the old rule that the house always wins. But he recovered his wits soon after. As the *Chicago Tribune* had observed, "no skull in the world" could absorb as much "pounding" as his and come back fighting. Poorer but wiser, he determined to join the house. For example, when the Commodore built a racetrack less than a mile outside of Saratoga, along with a group of Wall Street men (including his son-in-law George Osgood and William R. Travers) and a school of New York Central remoras (Erastus Corning Jr. and John M. Davidson, a partner of Erastus Corning Sr.), Morrissey agreed to serve as the track's manager.

He steadily gained Vanderbilt's friendship in the course of the Commodore's summer residence in Saratoga, during his days at the track and evenings playing hands of whist in the rooms at the Congress Hall or the United States Hotel. And when Vanderbilt returned to the Springs in August 1864 on a train carrying his fastest horse, Post Boy (valued at $22,000), and four other expensive trotters, the knowing ones whispered that at least one of them was a gift from Morrissey. Vanderbilt's reward to the fighter, they said, had been a "point" or tip on the second Harlem corner.[101]

For Vanderbilt's son Corneil, all the world comprised the house, yet he still bet against it. His gambling addiction continued to grow worse. He filched a gold cup from Horace Clark's house in Murray Hill before descending Broadway to bet and lose the money it brought him. Penniless again, he went into a pawnshop with a pair of gold sleeve buttons. They came from his dead brother George's dress uniform, and had been given to Corneil as a keepsake. When William learned they had been hocked, he redeemed them himself—and he never trusted Corneil with them again.[102]

Corneil responded by gambling on a far larger scale, on the gaming table of the war itself. As early as February 1864, he charmed his way into the confidence of Horace Greeley, editor of the *New York Tribune*, with that gift for manipulation that so confounded his closemouthed father. He borrowed money from Greeley, which he did not repay. He issued drafts that descended upon the famous editor unexpectedly.[103] Then Corneil brashly declared that he had a scheme to set things right. A frequent traveler to New Orleans before the war, he returned in 1864 to trade cotton across Confederate lines. There he befriended and beguiled General Nathaniel P. Banks, whom Corneil pronounced "a glorious fellow."

"Matters with me are progressing very favorably," Corneil wrote to Greeley from New Orleans on September 7, "and through the friendship of Gen. Banks & [Edward R. S.] Canby & the especial favoritism shown myself & friend in connection with a certain cotton transaction I shall soon realize a very handsome profit. I do hope & feel that I shall shortly relieve myself of the heavy incubus hanging over me by reason of my former misdeeds." It is a classic trait of the addict, of course, to admit his crimes and declare his intention to set them right just before a fresh round of lying and cheating. Corneil continued:

> I have been obliged to make use of some ready capital, & knowing of no earthly means to obtain it here I have drawn upon you for $1,700. I do beg that you will honor it, as a refusal to do so would of course involve me in dishonor & ruin. I shall leave here by the steamer of the 18th and shall bring home with me several thousands of greenbacks. I will call on you at once.... I beg Mr. Greeley that you will not desert me, just as my success is coming around.

Greeley never saw how transparently dishonest this was; he had been manipulated completely. But Corneil knew that not everyone would prove so gullible. He warned Greeley, "On no account give any information to Father or family in relation to the past & present."[104]

Greeley did his best to help. Corneil needed a permit to buy and sell cotton in occupied territory, so Greeley asked for one directly from Lincoln. "His father, the Commodore, is the largest individual holder of our Public Securities (to the extent of $4,000,000), has given outright more than any other man to invigorate the prosecution of the War, and his good will is still an element of our National strength," he wrote. "I know little of the business in question; but I feel confident that any favor shown to Mr. V. will redound to the advantage of the Union cause." For this reason, "as well as that of my personal regard for him," he begged that Corneil's application be approved.[105] Lincoln, however, did not act on the request, so Greeley began to badger William P. Fessenden, the new secretary of the treasury.

On October 8, the *New York Herald* reported a rumor that the Commodore stood behind the persistent lobbying on behalf of his son, which led him to write an angry letter that the paper published two days later. "I am at a loss to conceive how a report of this nature should have obtained currency," Vanderbilt declared. "I have remained perfectly passive [in terms of recommending appointments], feeling that the present condition of the country requires of its citizens other and more patriotic endeavors than those of self-interest and personal aggrandizement." Greeley sent the clipping to the Treasury Department as yet another reason to make Corneil a cotton-trading agent![106]

Stymied, Greeley wrote to Lincoln on November 23 to recommend that Fessenden be replaced as treasury secretary by the Commodore. He listed five reasons why Vanderbilt deserved the position, beginning with "1. He is the ablest and most successful financier now living, and has the largest private fortune in America." He stressed Vanderbilt's knowledge, his reputation at home and abroad, and concluded, "He is utterly and notoriously unconnected with any clique, faction, or feud among the Unionists of our State or of any other." It was all true, but Greeley admitted that he was not intimate with the Commodore, "whom I scarcely know by sight."[107]

The Commodore would have been appalled at Greeley's lobbying on his behalf. He never begged for public office; and when he wanted a corporate position, he simply took it. On September 6, he forced the resignation of two members of the Hudson River board (one of them William R. Travers, his partner in the Saratoga racetrack). He took one of the directorships for himself, and gave the other to Dean Richmond, the new president of the New York Central. At a board meeting in October, Vanderbilt ordered that the Hudson River's tracks be opened to the Harlem's trains between a junction at Castleton (now Castleton-on-Hudson) and Albany.[108]

So went the tale of dynastic struggles and railway statecraft. With his younger son conniving for petty favors, the Commodore brought the older into his new principality. He eliminated one rival, the Hudson River, by taking it over through quiet purchases and persuasion; with regard to the powerful New York Central, he clearly hoped that diplomacy would suffice. With a little decency on both sides, a few negotiations conducted with honor and propriety, he might manage that fraught relationship successfully for perhaps the first time in the history of those companies. All he sought, it appears, was to give Tobin and his son William a chance to reform their respective charges.[109] But Vanderbilt would closely watch his old friend Drew; after his unprecedented betrayal in the second Harlem corner, there was no telling what he might do next.

Unfortunately for Vanderbilt, betrayal, not friendship, would govern the future. What he had begun with diplomacy, he would bring to an end in a stunning act of revenge.

Chapter Fifteen

THE POWER TO PUNISH

On September 5, 1864, abolitionist William Lloyd Garrison wrote a letter to his wife. He had just arrived in Albany by train, which caused him to reflect on how the locomotive had changed the country since their wedding thirty years earlier. "Then there was no railroad conveyance; now the whole country is covered in rails," he wrote. "And through what enormous expenditure of money, and what incredible efforts of the human brain and hand!" Like many, he saw that railroads already were bringing a revolution—one that, as it spread beyond the Northeast, would foster national cohesion after the Civil War. As a devout Christian, he welcomed the prospect. "So may the modes of communication and the ties of life continue to multiply, until all nations shall feel a common sympathy and worship of a common shrine!"[1]

In late 1864, Cornelius Vanderbilt entered the third and most critical phase of his conquest of a railroad empire. It would drag out over the course of three frustrating years, because he doggedly tried to avoid a climactic war with New York's most important railway: the New York Central. As master of the lines that penetrated Manhattan, he depended entirely on the Central; it was the trunk line that connected his tracks to western markets. Year after year he would practice patient diplomacy with the Central's presidents in an effort to settle their persistent conflicts. In the end he would fail. His response would be a shocking demonstration of the nation's vulnerabilty to the railroads'—to *his*—power.

But what was that power? The importance of the railroad in the nineteenth century is a historical cliché; a cliché can be true, of course, but will have lost its force, its original meaning. Garrison's letter, on the other hand, speaks to the railroad's dramatic impact at the time of the Civil War. It was, one contemporary writer argued, "the most tremendous and far-reaching engine of social revolution which has ever either blessed or cursed the earth." It magnified the steamboat's impact, instilling a mobility in society that unraveled traditions, uprooted communities, and undercut old elites. It integrated markets, creating a truly national economy. It was so central to the development of the United States that this writer could reasonably claim (by including steamboats), "Our own country is the child of steam."[2]

In retrospect, this revolution had barely begun in 1864, yet already the railroad was central to American life. Everything went by rail, whether unmilled wheat or imported watches, an Irish immigrant or the president of the United States. Steamboats remained competitive for moving cheap, bulky goods (grain especially) or on particular passenger routes (notably the Hudson River), but even here trains gained rapidly on their aquatic competitors. The first all-rail shipments of grain from Chicago to Buffalo began in 1864; within a decade, they would surpass the volume carried by lake, river, and canal. The rise of cities that served as rail hubs was astounding. Kansas City was virtually nonexistent before the Civil War; afterward it rapidly sprouted as a cattle shipment center on the edge of the Great Plains, growing into a major city. The railroads had raised up Chicago even earlier, building on its status as a major lake port. Cook County, home to this midwestern metropolis, grew from 43,385 people in 1850 to 394,966 in 1870. Railways to the eastern seaboard allowed Pittsburgh to flourish as an iron and steel center; railways to the oil fields of Pennsylvania permitted Cleveland to emerge as a refining center; railways to the East brought farmers from Ohio to Nebraska into the global market. It is telling that the word "rail" was often dropped from "railroad"; the companies were, indeed, America's roads.[3]

The railroad sector surpassed all other industries combined, and individual railway corporations overshadowed any other kind of firm. Most manufacturing was still conducted in family-owned workshops and small mills; very few factories represented as much as $1 million of investment. (Historian Alfred D. Chandler Jr. counted only forty-one textile mills in the 1850s capitalized at $250,000 or more.) Even the largest commercial banks rarely boasted a capitalization of more than $1 million. By contrast, at least ten railroads had a capitalization of $10 million or more even before the war began. The stock of the New York Central alone stood on the books at about $25 million at par in 1865; even excluding its $14.6 million in outstanding bonds, this figure was equal to approximately one-quarter of all investment in manufacturing in the United States. Railroads connected American industries to sources of raw materials and to their markets—and were their most important customers, consuming vast quantities of products that ranged from coal, lumber, and iron to countless manufactured goods. Railroads were not simply the first big business, as Chandler famously called them; in Civil War America, they were the only big business.[4]

Size—geographical as well as financial—brought challenges faced by no other type of enterprise. The Hudson River Railroad, for example, was far smaller than any of the four trunk lines, yet it stretched 144 miles in length, with sixty-seven locomotives, twenty-nine baggage cars, 130 passenger cars, and 671 freight cars, not to mention twelve engine shops and numerous depots and stations; in 1864, it carried more than 2 million passengers and 600,000 tons of freight. The technical demands of managing such businesses were unprecedented. The best-trained minds in the United States grappled with the problem, developing new systems of organization, control, and accounting.[5]

The Commodore was surprisingly well prepared to serve as a chief executive in this emerging new world. He previously had served as president of the Stonington, of course, and had sat on the boards of a number of railroads since the 1840s. Perhaps more important was his experience in running far-flung steamship lines, involving multiple ports, transit operations in Central America, and a base on the far side of the continent. Not surprisingly, from his earliest days in railroads he demonstrated a comprehensive grasp of how to delegate authority. "Are you a practical railroad manager?" a state assemblyman would ask him in early 1867. "No sir, I don't manage anything," he would reply. "We have our superintendents, etc., who attend to those matters. All those matters of detail are done by our officers."[6]

What Vanderbilt did was set general policies, as well as the overall tone of management. Any corporation has an internal culture shaped by the demands, directives, and expections that rain down from above. The Commodore created an atmosphere of efficiency, frugality, and diligence, as well as swift retribution for dishonesty or sloth. As Lambert Wardell observed, "He thought every man could stand watching." Even though he disclaimed any interest in practical management, he tellingly remarked, "Now and then I get hold of a point that I have to look to. Smooth matters they never say anything to me about." Every employee knew he was watching.[7]

As the winter of 1864–65 set in, the end of the Civil War came into view—still a bloody distance away, but visible at last. Grant besieged Lee at Petersburg, and Sheridan had burned out the Shenandoah Valley. Railroads, which had grown little during the conflict, looked forward to peace with plans to lay new track, refurbish infrastructure, and generally reinvest their wartime profits. Lines short and long would soon burst out across the trans-Mississippi West, as seen in the famous example of the transcontinental Union Pacific. The Hudson River Railroad released its pent-up energies into the completion of a double track to the Albany bridge, an enormous span that it was building in conjunction with the New York Central and Western railroads.[8]

The railroads' massive demand for capital for new construction, even for ordinary maintenance and operations, drove another, subtler revolution. The financial world had long been ruled by generalized merchant capitalists such as Vanderbilt himself, but the railroads' appetite for money far outstripped the capacity of individuals to meet it. Financial institutions—investment banks—now aggregated and channeled the capital of American and foreign investors. The wartime nationalization of the U.S. financial structure, with the introduction of greenbacks and the national bank system, contributed to this development. The frenzy on Wall Street, so notable in Vanderbilt's Harlem corners, centered almost entirely in railroads, which provided by far the largest number of securities actively traded on the exchanges. This, too, played a role in the institutionalization of the economy. The identification of corporations with individuals, already waning when the war began, virtually disappeared in the 1860s, heightening the abstraction of the economic world. On the Pennsylvania Railroad, this process had gone one step further. This trunk line was managed by a professional staff rather than leading stockholders, with an engineer as president (J. Edgar Thomson) and a powerful vice president (Thomas A. Scott) who had risen through the ranks.[9]

Vanderbilt understood these financial changes; in part, that is why he relied so heavily on a vice president of the Bank of New York, James Banker. But he also represented a glaring exception to these trends. The Harlem was increasingly seen as his personal property, as the Hudson River would be before many months passed. He wielded financial might that surpassed that of the largest banks. The Hudson River estimated the cost of completing its second track to Albany at $900,000; Vanderbilt personally provided at least two-thirds of it, purchasing $600,000 in bonds at 105. This was Vanderbilt summarized in one transaction: maker and exemplar of his times, yet always standing apart, unique in his wealth and power.[10]

"The influence of one earnest, energetic life upon the world is scarcely appreciated," *Merchant's Magazine* declared in January 1865, in a front-page profile of the Commodore. His name was "inseparably connected with our commercial history. . . . Perhaps there are two or three men wealthier than he in New York city—but no more; and all of his vast wealth is the product of his own labor." The theme that ran through the article was the intersection of the broad current of history and the individuality of this man. The journal observed, just as Courtlandt Palmer had back in 1841, that the Commodore valued his reputation for honor, and rewarded "frankness and honesty of speech." His courtesy toward men worthy of respect was matched by mercilessness toward those who were not. "Deceit and underhand dealing," the magazine added, "he has ever quickly detected and thoroughly hated."[11]

ON DECEMBER 8, 1864, VANDERBILT AND HIS WIFE attended the wedding of their granddaughter, Sophia Cross, to Rev. J. B. Morse, at the home of the bride's parents, Phebe and James M. Cross.[12] As the saying goes, their granddaughter had her entire life in front of her, yet she would never witness changes as sweeping as those the Commodore had both experienced and helped to bring about. The biggest had been the advent of change itself—change as a nearly constant state in American society.

"When I was a boy," George Templeton Strong reflected in early 1865, "the aristocracy lived around the Battery, on Bowling Green." So it had been since New York was named New Amsterdam, two centuries earlier. Young Cornelius and Sophia Vanderbilt had lived on Broad and Stone streets, in buildings and circumstances that might have been recognizable to Pieter Stuyvesant himself. Then, in the 1820s, the transformation of New York began, as immigrants swarmed in from Germany, Ireland, and the American countryside. The elite relocated, and kept on relocating every decade or so. In 1864, Strong declined to serve as president of Columbia College, since it would require him to move from Murray Hill (the current center of fashion) "to a frontier settlement . . . on Forty-ninth Street." He little realized how quickly the city's center of gravity would shift to that very area.[13]

Each generation flatters itself with the thought that it is the vanguard of the new, sweeping away the stodgy ways of the past. Henry Clews imagined that he and his peers had introduced real cunning to the stock exchange in 1857—unaware that they could never surpass Nelson Robinson's skill at sharp dealing. The brokers who arrived on Wall Street during the Civil War told themselves that the aged Vanderbilt snorted at trains as "these steam contrivances that you tell us will run on dry land," until he finally bought the Harlem.[14] Much of it was nonsense, of course; but once upon a time the old had indeed been new for Vanderbilt and such contemporaries as Erastus Corning and Dean Richmond. These elder statesmen had grown up with the country, with the securities markets and corporations and mechanized transportation and rapid growth that were beginning to define the United States. Small wonder the venerable Commodore remained so quick to grasp possibilities, to accommodate change. Yet the world that they had created trapped them in an intractable conflict that defied even their most well-meaning attempts at compromise.

In April 1864, an exhausted Corning had resigned the presidency of the New York Central, passing the office on to his vice president, Dean Richmond.[15] A burly man, more than six feet in height, the sixty-year-old Richmond exuded power. He combed a layer of dark hair across his large, round pate, and peered at his (smaller) fellow directors through heavy-lidded eyes set between arching eyebrows and above a fat, mushroom nose and the permanently pursed lower lip so common to jowly faces. He had the look of a man who never moved quickly, for anyone. He, too, had risen from a poor childhood, having moved from Vermont to Syracuse to Buffalo, from clerk to salt manufacturer to commission merchant, before entering the business of railroads. A man of volatile temper, he had little education, with handwriting so abominable that even Corning regularly ordered a clerk to transcribe his letters. He had worked closely with Corning in Democratic Party politics as well as business. The two were recognized as heirs to Martin Van Buren's Albany Regency—though Richmond, unlike Corning, refused to stand for elected office, exerting influence instead as chairman of the Democratic State Central Committee.[16]

Politics remained uppermost on Richmond's agenda—not electoral but railroad politics. The lucrative business provided by the federal government had muted competition among the trunk lines, but peace threatened to break out. On December 15 and 16, the Union army under General George H. Thomas annihilated the rebel Army of Tennessee at Nashville. At the end of the same month, Sherman completed his March to the Sea. "I beg to present you, as a Christmas gift," he wired to Lincoln, "the city of Savannah." And on January 15, 1865, a division led by General Adelbert Ames stormed into Fort Fisher, North Carolina; its capture effectively closed Wilmington, the last rebel seaport. Richmond worried that victory in the South would mean war in the North between the trunk lines.[17]

As Richmond embarked on his presidency in these troubling times, he spent many of his dinner hours with James Banker, the special representative of Commodore Vanderbilt. Though the Harlem and the Hudson River were minor powers on the railroad landscape, they occupied a strategic position. They provided the Central with a direct rail link to New York, and Richmond had no choice but to pay heed to Vanderbilt (who was, in any case, a major Central stockholder, with some four thousand shares). Still, Richmond saw no reason to cease the practice of shifting the Central's passengers and freight to the People's Line steamboats from spring through fall, when the Hudson was clear of ice and navigable all the way to Albany.[18]

That infuriated John M. Tobin, the Hudson River Railroad president. "It was unjust to insist that the Hudson R.R.R. should form part of its [the Central's] trunk line during three months of the year and be excluded from the advantages of that traffic during nine months of the year," Horace Clark later explained. "There never has been a man connected with the Hudson River Railroad Company who has not protested against and felt the wrong that such a state of things brought about."[19] This was the issue that brought Vanderbilt's and Richmond's railroads into conflict—the result of the fragmentation of the railroad network, which forced long-distance traffic to pass through the hands of successive companies, each with its own needs and agendas.

The problem came down to a central feature of railroad economics: the difference between through traffic from "competitive points" and purely local traffic from stations where a railway had a monopoly. For freight shipped to New York, the Central could charge higher local rates in Syracuse or Rochester, where it faced no competition, than it could in Buffalo or Chicago, where rival trunk lines fought for the business (especially exports, which theoretically could be shipped from Philadelphia or Baltimore as easily as New York). The Central set the rates for this through freight, and prorated its revenue with the Hudson River on a mileage basis. Daniel Drew's People's Line, on the other hand, operated more cheaply than the Hudson River Railroad, so it accepted less than a pro-rata percentage. Why wouldn't the Central give its business to the steamboats? As Clark admitted, "Before the [Albany] bridge was built, and bulk had to be broken, it might as well be broken and the freight go by river, as the other way." For the Hudson River, however, this state of affairs brought "all the disadvantages of consolidation without any of its advantages."[20]

Tobin wanted compensation—to receive the higher local rates on through freight during the winter.[21] For Richmond, this was a frightening prospect. It would cripple the Central's ability to compete with the other trunk lines during the season of ice and snow. He anxiously asked Clark to arrange a meeting with Vanderbilt.

"Commodore Vanderbilt had a great admiration for Dean Richmond," attorney Chauncey Depew later remarked. "The Commodore disliked boasters and braggarts intensely. Those who wished to gain his favor made the mistake, as a rule, of boasting about what they had done, and were generally met with the remark: 'That amounts to nothing.' " As Depew's juxtaposition of these observations implies, the Central's president was much like Vanderbilt himself: authentic, honest, and direct. Vanderbilt agreed to intervene on his behalf. "After a severe struggle, Mr. Tobin's policy was overruled," Clark recalled, "and an agreement was made for that winter through Mr. Richmond and through Mr. Vanderbilt. That winter . . . the N.Y. Central R.R. Co. should fix rates such as they might see fit to fix, in accordance with their policy in competition with the other great trunk lines, and the Hudson R.R.R. Co. should carry them out."[22]

Vanderbilt had other interests that impelled him to cooperate with

Richmond—particularly the Athens railroad. He had helped Drew create it as a weapon against the Hudson River Railroad; now he needed Richmond's help to prevent it from being turned against himself. Nevertheless, he demanded a price for overriding Tobin: once the ice cleared from the river, the Central would make a permanent arrangement to either give the Hudson River a larger share of freight or pay it compensation.[23]

Time and again, Vanderbilt showed himself to be patient and diplomatic in his dealings with Corning and Richmond, as he sacrificed short-term profits in return for long-term stability. But the structural conflict between these lines would only get worse.

ON THE AFTERNOON OF February 6, 1865, a Wednesday, Vanderbilt climbed into his wagon outside his office on Bowling Green. He whipped his team of horses up Broadway until he reached Fulton Street, a block below City Hall Park. There he bowled over a woman named Caroline Walter; her fright and the ensuing confusion can only be imagined. An Officer Dodge arrested the Commodore and took him to the glowering, neo-Egyptian Tombs, the police court and city jail. Mrs. Walter did not appear to make a complaint, so the judge released Vanderbilt. The victim had not been seriously injured, and perhaps she thought it best to let the powerful man go about his business.[24]

One week prior to his brief imprisonment, the House of Representatives had voted to abolish slavery, by sending the Thirteenth Amendment to the states for ratification. It was both a revolutionary act and a practical recognition that the war had destroyed slavery as a functioning institution. In both senses, it demonstrated how thoroughly America's most costly conflict remade the nation.

But the war itself approached an end. In fighting that began on March 24, the Confederate position at Petersburg crumbled. On April 2, Grant launched a decisive attack that sent Lee's army fleeing to the west. The next day, Lincoln (who had been visiting the Army of the Potomac) entered the fallen Confederate capital.[25]

When the news reached Wall Street, the rector of Trinity Church began to ring the bell, over and over, joining a symphony of church bells that chimed all over New York. Crowds crowded the pavement. "All the cheers I ever listened to were tame in comparison," Strong wrote. The massed men—for they were all men on Wall Street—sang "John Brown's Body" and "The Star-Spangled Banner," and waved their hats in ecstasy now that the long nightmare had ended, and ended in victory. "I walked about on the outskirts of the crowd," Strong added, "shaking hands with everybody, congratulating and being congratulated by scores of men I hardly know even by sight. Men embraced and hugged each other, *kissed* each other, retreated into doorways to dry their eyes and came out again to flourish their hats and hurrah. There will be many sore throats in New York tomorrow."[26]

The war was not over yet. On April 7, Grant's troops caught Lee's army at Appomattox Courthouse, where a truce was called. Sheridan rode to meet Confederate general John B. Gordon, and complained that a South Carolina unit was firing on General Wesley Merritt's men. He asked Gordon to dispatch orders to cease fire. "He answered, 'I have no staff-officer to send,' " Sheridan wrote in his memoirs.

> Whereupon I said that I would let him have one of mine, and calling for Lieutenant Vanderbilt Allen, I directed him to carry General Gordon's orders to General Geary, commanding a small brigade of South Carolina cavalry, to discontinue firing. Allen dashed off with the message and soon delivered it, but was made a prisoner, Geary saying, "I do not care for white flags; South Carolinians never surrender." By this time Merritt's patience being exhausted, he ordered an attack, and this in short order put an end to General Geary's "last ditch" absurdity, and extricated Allen from his predicament.

The Commodore's grandson was one of the last prisoners of the Civil War, and, ironically, carried one of the last Confederate orders. On April 9, Lee surrendered.[27]

"We have the astounding intelligence of the assassination of President Lincoln & the attempt to assassinate Mr. Seward," New York Central director John V. L. Pruyn wrote in his diary on April 15. "The whole community has been stirred to its deepest depths by these events. Their results cannot be predicted. . . . Every face bears evidence of emotion. It is a terrible, a fearful tragedy." At the moment of victory, the great emancipator had been shot dead by John Wilkes Booth—on Good Friday, no less. Three days later, Pruyn observed in Albany, "All buildings in the city, almost without exception, are hanging emblems of mourning for the death of President Lincoln. Accounts from every part of the country show this to be the case everywhere. The grief seems to be universal & profound."[28]

Lincoln's death was one of an estimated 620,000 in the Civil War: 360,000 from the North and 260,000 from the South, not including civilian casualties. Statistics cannot do justice to the extent of this loss, but they are devastating enough. In perhaps the most commonly cited comparison, this figure, in absolute numbers, surpasses the *combined* toll in American lives from all of the nation's other wars, up to and including the Korean War.[29] The death count represented almost 2 percent of the nation's entire population as measured in the 1860 census. Nearly every family suffered.

Long after the Commodore had passed, this generation of the dead would continue to haunt the survivors. Statues would be erected, monuments built, and parades conducted through the end of the century. But for many veterans who lived through the fighting, the encomiums for their fallen comrades sounded bitterly empty. Unquestionably, the war accomplished profound good: it resolved a long-building conflict, freed 4 million slaves, and destroyed the peculiar institution of slavery forever. Yet the personal experience of the Civil War was often as dehumanizing, as poisoned by pettiness, random brutality, and stupidity, as in any other war.[30]

Out of the war emerged a corps of public intellectuals—Ambrose Bierce, Oliver Wendell Holmes, and Charles Francis Adams Jr., to name a few—with a dark sensibility shaped by such horrors. After Appomattox, these men would view the world with a grim realism that often overflowed into cynicism, stark and sometimes overblown. The outlook of this generation of writers and thinkers would influence historians, many of whom would picture the postwar years as a time of unrelenting self-aggrandizement, when vulgar, amoral tycoons and carpetbaggers corrupted a political process barely worthy of the name democracy.

There was another, more instinctive response to the war's death and destruction. It was a resurgence of a superstition that owed its modern origin to a pair of toe-cracking girls from Rochester, New York. With so many spirits to contact, Spiritualism became more popular than ever, attended by a general faith in the unseen. As Strong observed in 1865, "The tough, shrewd, unbelieving Yankee generally develops a taste for marvels—for infinitesimal homeopathy, magnetism, spiritualism." It was a cultural current that moved even the toughest, shrewdest, most unbelieving Yankee of all, Cornelius Vanderbilt. Mrs. Mary Augusta Smett would later claim that she visited the Commodore in his office, apparently during the second Harlem corner, to ask him to spare a friend who faced ruin. As she was about to leave, Vanderbilt asked her, "Did you ever see my son George?" He pointed out a picture and said, "That poor fellow is dead. Would to God he had lived." As Mrs. Smett recalled the moment, "His eyes filled with tears." For a man who had grown accustomed to controlling the world around him, the possibility of mastering even death itself must have been appealing.[31]

A few years later, Vanderbilt asked a minister what he thought of séances. "I expressed emphatically my disbelief in modern spiritualism," the preacher reported. "He said, 'I think so too.' He said nevertheless that there was skill and acuteness in it, and he felt interested." The subject may have been introduced to the Commodore by his daughter, Mary La Bau, a devoted spiritualist. Medium James B. Mansfield would later testify that Vanderbilt approached him as early as 1864. Vanderbilt would write questions for the dead and put them in sealed envelopes, and Mansfield would write replies without reading the inquiries. (According to the medium, Vanderbilt initially tried to contact his father and John De Forest; since the latter had died in 1829, the mention of his name lends credibility to Mansfield's account.) If the answers made any sense, they would have impressed Vanderbilt, who recognized skill and acuity when he saw it.[32]

If the mournful and curious Commodore tried to speak to the dead, he was hardly unusual in that age of empty chairs and missing men, but he gave no sign that the spirits influenced a single decision he made. And he had many decisions to make in the months after Appomattox, decisions that could affect the lives of millions. Peace had come to the nation, and war would inevitably come to the railroads.

ON JUNE 6, 1865, TOBIN INFORMED the Hudson River Railroad board of directors "that he could not under any circumstances become a candidate for reelection as President," the secretary recorded. Everyone at the table knew that Tobin was stepping down because Vanderbilt had undercut his authority—and that Vanderbilt would succeed him.[33]

One week later, after the annual stockholders' meeting, the board duly voted in the Commodore as president and his son William as vice president. But perhaps the ascension was not as predictable as it seems. The Commodore has been caricatured as a bloody-minded tyrant, yet his methods as a railroad executive often proved subtle. He preferred to hide his hand not only from his enemies, but from a public increasingly wary of the growing size and power of railroads. Vanderbilt put his son in operational control of both the Hudson River and the Harlem, but he kept the companies organizationally separate. Indeed, the two corporations— managed by a nearly identical slate of directors and senior executives— signed a contract under which the Hudson River paid the Harlem at least $10,000 a month in return for cooperation in setting rates. Perhaps it was simply a legal mechanism for subsidizing the weaker line; even if that was the case, it demonstrated the Commodore's caution as he widened his grasp.[34]

In his relations with other lines, too, he usually chose to exert influence quietly rather than resort to financial combat. In April, for example, he put James Banker on the board of the Michigan Southern & Northern Indiana, a key link in a chain of railways that gave the New York Central access to Chicago. Vanderbilt merely wanted a voice in its management, such as he had in the Erie and the Hartford & New Haven.[35]

In his role as railroad diplomat, the Commodore took a train to Albany less than six days after his election. By special invitation, he joined his friend Richmond and his lieutenant Banker on the directors' annual inspection of the New York Central line. In the afternoon of June 19, they boarded a special train amid thick heat for their westward journey. In cars outfitted with upholstered comforts and abundant food, they rattled through Syracuse and Rochester, visited Niagara Falls, inspected the Great Western of Canada, and chuffed back to Buffalo. "Commodore Vanderbilt," John V. L. Pruyn noted in his diary, "had not been west in thirty years. Seemed to enjoy the trip very much."[36]

That was good news for Richmond. He needed Vanderbilt's cooperation as he dueled with the other trunk lines. Despite the buoyant economy, tensions between the major railroads simmered. Richmond competed more aggressively than Corning had; at the same time, his relations with J. Edgar Thomson, president of the Pennsylvania Railroad, grew prickly, then broke down altogether. Desperate to keep rates low, Richmond again sent passengers and freight on Drew's People's Line. By summer's end, William H. Vanderbilt testified, "the Hudson River road felt itself very much aggrieved." The Commodore understood the pressure on Richmond, but he made clear "that it was impossible for them to continue under their arrangement." Richmond eventually agreed to give the Hudson River Railroad all of the "state freights" (those originating in New York, and not subject to competition from other trunk lines).[37]

As the Commodore engaged in these wearisome negotiations, he received news that Elizabeth Williams had died on August 31. "Libbie" was the older sister of his daughter-in-law Ellen, wife of Corneil, and a favorite member of a family that Vanderbilt loved deeply. Cheerful, even effervescent, she had liked to gossip about who was rising or falling in fashionable society, and had been openly jealous of her sister Ellen's invitation to the Vanderbilt golden wedding celebration. ("I trust mother will have her black satin dress converted into a fashionable one," she slyly had written to Corneil before the event.) She was only forty-two when she died.[38]

"The dispatch I received yesterday from Corneil stating the death of our *Dear Dear* and much beloved Libbie completely unmanned me," the Commodore wrote to Oliver Williams, Elizabeth and Ellen's father. "And I did not dare to say a word on paper, until this morning. And even now, I have no language to express my feelings; nor will I attempt it here." In the context of Vanderbilt's earlier writings to the family (those in his own hand), there can be little doubt that this letter reflected his sincere emotions. Indeed, it briefly opens a window into the way this man, who owned so much and ruled so many, grappled with loss. It left him desperately vulnerable, and grasping for the faith that he had largely relinquished for most of his life.

> It has pleased the great ruler of all things to take her away from us while in the enjoyment of *health, beauty* and *usefulness;* and as Christians we are bound to submit. But my dear Colonel I feel that I dare not trust myself to see her, for fear that my manhood may give way; therefore dare not attend the funeral.
>
> The moment I have recovered from the shock, I will make the family a short visit.
>
> Please give my love to all, and tell them to try and bear up with their irrecoverable loss.
>
> I can say so no more at this moment. I feel too much depressed.
> Truly Yours,
>
> C. VanDerbilt[39]

Vanderbilt's use of the words "unmanned" and "manhood" are significant. It is only natural, of course, that he should value a muscular masculinity; during his long career, he had gone from fistfighting sailor to boat-racing captain, from rapids-shooting Commodore to Wall Street warrior. But here he equated "manhood" with dignity, reserve, self-control. His refusal to go to the funeral for fear that he would not be able to maintain his mastery over his emotions is telling. This sort of manhood, this self-possession, he clearly saw as a social as well as a business virtue.

These few lines may not be proof of how Vanderbilt conducted himself in private, but they call into question the image of him as an unmannered brute. In this letter, we see the man who dined with Daniel D. Tompkins, negotiated with Lord Palmerston, cooperated with William H. Aspinwall, and consulted with presidents Buchanan and Lincoln. And we see him vulnerable.

But he was still combative. On October 24, this most manly old man drove his rig out for a brush on Bloomingdale Road, or perhaps nearby Harlem Lane, where the new generation of fast men preferred to race. Again, the wheels of his wagon cracked into those of a rival; again, he pitched headlong to the ground, and had to be carried back to his bed, where he lay, helpless, as his family gathered around. "He did not seem conscious. His head was cut," recalled his nurse, Margaret Cadwell. Then William, the diligent and trusted son, bent forward to fix the pillows, and his father snapped awake. "The Commodore told him to let them alone, that I would do them," Cadwell added. "I suppose he thought I would be more gentle."[40]

Perhaps he did—or perhaps family relations are simply more fraught than any other kind. His aggravation may have been all the worse because he was going to miss a special reception for General Grant at Dubois's Club House on Harlem Lane, on November 16, hosted by the owners of the fastest horses in New York. The general in chief, like the Commodore, was passionate about horses, and seemed to enjoy that afternoon far more than the "Gathering of the Wealth and Fashion of New York" that feted Grant at the Fifth Avenue Hotel, as the *New York Herald* reported, on the evening of November 20.[41]

Vanderbilt did eventually meet the general some weeks later. In February 1866, General Daniel Butterfield took Grant to 10 Washington Place. Vanderbilt descended the stairs from the second floor and exclaimed, "Why, General, you're nothing but a boy!" Grant and Vanderbilt, both direct and honest, struck up an instant rapport. Butterfield recalled, "The Commodore took him over the house, and then invited him out to lunch. Not long afterward they went down to the stables and . . . 'talked horse.' " Grant liked nothing better.[42]

Vanderbilt's social life centered on cards almost as much as horses—particularly whist, the ancestor of bridge, which he liked to play with other men of wealth, power, and influence. He spent countless hours at Saratoga playing cards, and soon would in New York as well. "Let the women wail, for another club-house is about to be opened on Fifth Avenue," announced the *Round Table* on November 25, 1865. "A company of gentlemen who combine democratic principles with aristocratic taste have bought one of the very few really handsome and well-built private houses of which . . . the Fifth Avenue can boast, and propose to install themselves therein, under the style and title of the 'Manhattan Club.' " It had been organized the year before by the fashionable Democratic Party leaders—the "silk-stocking sachems"—including August Belmont, Samuel L. M. Barlow, Horace Clark, and Augustus Schell. They intended to establish a rival headquarters to Tammany Hall, which increasingly fell under the sway of William Tweed and his circle. In the summer of 1865, the club founders purchased a palatial building at 96 Fifth Avenue, at Fifteenth Street, for $110,000. By the time the *Round Table* published its story, all the marble and dark wood was in place.[43]

Vanderbilt was a charter member. Though he belonged to the Union Club and others, he began to spend most evenings in the Manhattan Club with his friends, railroad directors, and sons-in-law, playing whist for money, always for money. Eight years later an author would record, "The club has always been the headquarters of the Vanderbilt coterie."[44]

The club's political tone served a valuable purpose. The Commodore, though thoroughly nonpartisan, could not avoid constant contact with the political world, for railroads remained the most political of businesses, constantly subject to criticism and legislation. The Manhattan Club gave him a social setting where he could interact with powerful Democratic leaders associated with his own followers, Clark and Schell, without seeming to be partisan himself. He soon would be talked of as a supporter of Grant for the presidency, for example, yet in December 1865 he asked the former secretary of state for New York, Democrat Chauncey M. Depew, to be the Harlem's attorney. President Andrew Johnson had nominated the thirty-one-year-old Depew to be minister to Japan, and the Senate had already confirmed him. "When I said this to the Commodore," Depew recalled, "he remarked: 'Railroads are the career for a young man; there is nothing in politics. Don't be a damned fool.' That decided me." It was a curious comment, if Depew remembered it accurately, because politics was a key reason for his selection. The lawyer was a rising Democratic leader, and Vanderbilt relied on his influence in Albany.[45]

On December 13, it seemed that the Commodore's patient politicking in the business world finally achieved success. On that day, Dean Richmond sealed their alliance in the New York Central's annual election of directors. With Richmond's support, Horace Clark now joined the board. Banker, meanwhile, continued to serve as Vanderbilt's personal envoy, and came to be seen as the most influential director. But Corning fell off the board entirely. A split emerged between the Central's current and former presidents as Richmond pursued his own path. Thoroughly marginalized, Corning went into exile and plotted his return.[46]

"I WAS IN THE HABIT OF entertaining a good deal at my house the public leading men of the country," Corneil would say, "and my expenses were very large, inasmuch as it was expected of me to sustain the honor of my family name as far as I could." When asked precisely which "name" he meant, he loftily replied, "The name of my father, which was also my own. I maintained the honor of it in the State and city where I lived."[47]

This statement revealed more than he probably intended. He equated "honor" with a lavish lifestyle, and the only one who "expected" it was Corneil himself. The Commodore gave him $100 per month, increasing the allowance to $150 after his marriage—more than the monthly salaries of many men, but hardly an income on which to entertain "the public leading men of the country." Corneil could not escape the hope that he might suddenly multiply that amount with a hand of cards or a spin of the roulette wheel. He returned again and again to an ever-lengthening list of saloons: Portland's, at 139 Broadway; Charley Ransom's, on Twenty-fifth Street; John Daly's, on Broadway between Thirteenth and Fourteenth streets; Zachariah E. Simmons's policy bank, on Broadway near Fourth

Street; and George Beers's place, on University Place at Thirteenth Street. At Beers's saloon, it was said, Corneil conveniently collapsed in an epileptic fit if he held a losing hand.[48]

And Corneil lost, and lost, and lost. He pawned his watch; he pawned his wife's rings; he pawned what self-respect remained to him. Like many addicts, he loathed himself, yet blamed his father for withholding his wealth. Corneil even forged the Commodore's name, to punish his father as much as to get money out of him. He wrote to Horace Greeley after he had finally struck bottom, "Discouragement, disgust, & an indicative desire to revenge myself upon my father by thus disguising his name forced me to everything vicious."[49]

He collided with said bottom in late November 1865. Shattered emotionally and physically—"a discouraged, abandoned, and well nigh God-forsaken wreck," as he described himself—he went to the home of his brother, whom he resented deeply. He handed over pawn tickets for his wife's jewelry and his own watch. Then he disappeared. "Corneil has now gone to Litchfield [Connecticut] to a private institution which receives but eight or ten patients," Ellen wrote to William on December 3. "He was admitted through the influence of my family physician. I have never known him during all the years of our married life so completely undermined in his general health as between the last two or three months."[50]

When Corneil went into the Litchfield asylum, he carried with him the love and support of two women who never turned away from him. He felt himself sustained, he wrote, by "many kind & encouraging letters that I have received from my dear wife & my noble, faithful *mother* (the only two in fact who had faith)." Greeley, too, maintained their friendship, despite Corneil's many unpaid loans; for good reason, Corneil called him "my truest & *only self-sacrificing friend* apart from mother & wife."

Yet even those family members who had rebuked Corneil now rose to help him as he sought to help himself. On December 25, as Ellen ate her Christmas dinner alone at her home in Hartford, a messenger from William knocked on the door. He handed her the rings that Corneil had pawned and William had redeemed. The Commodore himself took pity. On February 26, 1866, Corneil wrote to Greeley about "a few lines received . . . from my serious & well meaning father, congratulating me on my present course & urging me to persevere in well doing." This rare encouragement gave him "fresh ambition & determination to regain from him that confidence & esteem which my past recklessness so materially impaired." Corneil wrote to William of his resolve to abandon "my wild, reckless, and unprincipled conduct . . . and to avoid likewise all connection with the corrupt and demoralized associates who have hitherto so artfully sought to entrap me by their wily and infernal concoctions."[51]

But it is not easy to escape who we are. On December 27, Corneil had celebrated his thirty-fifth birthday in the Litchfield asylum. He was no longer at a formative or impressionable age. "I am sorry to state that our income is pledged by Ellen to joint creditors for five months to come," he informed William, implying that his brother should cover the debts. He also wrote that it was "seriously inconvenient to be without a timepiece," and glibly asked William to redeem his watch from the pawnshop, promising to pay him back later. Not long after he left the asylum, he returned to form, issuing promissory notes in August and September 1866 that he declined to pay.[52]

There is little doubt that the Commodore felt betrayed by his son's relapse. Corneil, desperate for love and money, often went to 10 Washington Place to see his father, but Vanderbilt sent him away. "The Commodore said he didn't want Cornelius J. around at all," recalled nurse Cadwell. When Corneil wrote a wordy appeal to his father, Vanderbilt thought it impressive—as a piece of sophistry. "I remember the Commodore receiving a letter once from Cornelius J.," Cadwell added, "and saying that fellow, or that scamp, could write a letter to the Queen." Sophia, on the other hand, could never bring herself to condemn her son. She let him into the house secretly, saw him privately, and kept him out of his father's sight.[53]

And yet, even Corneil, this creature of deceit, could not deny the truth about himself. He alternated his bombast with references to "my shame & mortification & sorrow." He was literally fatalistic about his hope of reform. He wrote to Greeley of his "determination to *humbly forfeit my life* as the penalty of further *vice*." It was the one prediction about himself that would come true.[54]

ON FEBRUARY 15, 1866, the locomotive *Augustus Schell* chuffed onto the Albany bridge and rolled westward along its 2,020-foot span, over a total of nineteen piers, across an iron turntable above the center of the river below, and rattled down into Albany itself. Following this symbolic inauguration, the first passenger train crossed one week later. After four years of construction (and many more of litigation), the bridge gave the New York Central a continuous, direct connection to the Hudson River Railroad, and thus to Manhattan. But its completed track became a lighted fuse.[55]

The Commodore's cold response to Corneil's backsliding revealed the icy judge who had always lurked behind the encouraging father. So, too, did the implacable warrior remain within the diplomat who had negotiated with Corning and Richmond. In December 1865, for example, the

New York Court of Appeals handed down final judgment in the long-running court battle between Vanderbilt and the New York & New Haven Railroad over the shares that Schuyler had fraudulently issued in 1854. Over the years, weary shareholders had settled with the company—but the Commodore refused. He had waged his battle until the court ruled that the company owed $900,000 to Schuyler's victims. "The great principle is now settled by the highest court in this State," wrote the *Commercial and Financial Chronicle*, "that railroad and other corporations are bound by the fraudulent acts of their own agents."[56]

It was, indeed, a great principle—but businessmen also saw a more personal lesson in the Schuyler fraud case. "The Commodore's word is as good as his bond when it is fairly given," wrote Matthew Hale Smith. "He is equally exact in fulfilling his threats." Vanderbilt "pursued his purpose for years with the instinct of an Indian. He attained his end at last." In a more nuanced way, the reporters for R. G. Dun & Co. drew much the same conclusion: that Vanderbilt was a good ally but a dangerous man to cross. "Is a bold operator, but does not [do] that [which] will hurt him much," they wrote in 1865. "Has so many resources at his command that it is hard to be caught." In 1867, they added, "Among the richest men in this country. Good as gold but sharp."[57]

His edge would be felt again after the completion of the Albany bridge. Vanderbilt expected that the Central would finally end its custom of shifting freight to Drew's steamboats, as it was now more efficient to send through trains over the bridge. But once the ice on the river dissipated, the People's Line boats again churned up to the Albany docks and began to load freight. Even worse, March saw the completion of the Athens railway, giving the Central a shortcut to the river and a pier that allowed cars to run right alongside the steamboats. "That was one of the foolish acts of my life," Vanderbilt would say of his investment in the Athens road, "but I don't cry about it."[58]

Instead, he tried to do something about it. As the *Railway Times* later reported, "Commodore Vanderbilt, who is an owner in the Athens line to the extent of half a million of dollars, is reported to favor the taking up of the rails and the abandonment of the route."[59] The struggle over the thirty-eight-mile line was convoluted and largely hidden, pitting Vanderbilt against Richmond, Drew, and Henry Keep, each with his own interests and agenda. "I will tell you a very sore grievance to us," Vanderbilt said to a state assembly committee several months later, speaking for the Hudson River.

> We could send up hundreds of car loads of freight, and they [the Central]
> would uniformly send our cars back empty. We cannot afford that. Not only

that, but they would take our cars that we would send up and send them over their road. . . . We would sometimes trace our cars to Athens. What business had they to send our cars to Athens?

Hauling empty cars back from Albany, of course, was a pure loss for the Hudson River Railroad, and the Central's appropriation of them was costly; but sending them *to Athens* was insulting. "I don't like your manner of getting our cars, running them to Buffalo, and then running them back to Athens," he told Richmond.[60]

If these disputes seem trivial, they were in fact the birth pains of a truly national economy. These railroad companies had been created for parochial reasons—to connect New York to Albany, to connect the Great Lakes with the Hudson River, to undercut the Hudson River Railroad— but now they were pressed into a continental transportation system. Freight and passengers moved by rail across distances scarcely imagined just ten or twenty years earlier. As far as the public interest was concerned, the fragmentation of the system was problematic, for the repeated transfers of freight from one company to another was inefficient and costly. But these conflicts between connecting lines raised even greater dangers: What if one company simply refused to cooperate, and closed its rails to its neighbors' shipments? The result could be catastrophic.

Another of those pains came at the end of the second week of April, in the form of a strike by the Harlem streetcar drivers. "They held a mass-meeting this afternoon around the Washington statue on Union Square and afterwards marched in procession up Fourth Avenue," Strong wrote in his diary. "I heard one of their orators, an unwashed loon. He spoke grammatically, fluently, and sensibly, and with good manner and action. Would that I enjoyed the same gift! I hear of no rioting yet and of but few cases of assault on newly enlisted drivers. The police seem wide-awake."

A fluent and sensible unwashed loon? Strong's apparent confusion over the union leader reflects how rapidly the times were changing. The wartime boom—and polarization of rich and poor—spawned a proliferation of labor organizations. In 1861, there were roughly fifteen unions in New York City; by 1864, there would be 157. "A larger proportion of the metropolitan working population enrolled in trade unions between 1865 and 1873 than during any other period of the nineteenth century," write two historians of New York. Between 1863 and 1873, workers carried out 249 recorded strikes. Of course, walkouts had occurred in previous decades, but the Harlem drivers' strike pointed to the future. The Harlem men were employees of a large, impersonal corporation. Most could anticipate working their entire lives for wages, rather than starting their own farms or shops as their fathers might have done. Strikes now broke out not simply over short-term grievances, but to rebalance the long-term relationship between capital and labor—as seen in the campaign for an eight-hour day. A labor *movement* emerged, mirroring the rise of the large business enterprise.[61]

The Commodore had never experienced such an existence as that faced by his employees. Even his relationship with Thomas Gibbons was more one of sponsorship than mere employment. From his perspective, labor represented a cost. His son William managed the workers under strict instructions to economize, even to the extent of hiring strike-breaking drivers. The fluent and sensible "spokesloon" for the strikers may not have appreciated it very much, but William carried out his task so well that the Harlem finally would pay a 4 percent dividend ($2 per share) in June.[62]

Wall Street and the railroad industry greeted the dividend with disbelief. "It has never been considered a paying road," judged the Central's superintendent, Harlow W. Chittenden. "Mr. Vanderbilt paid a dividend but most people doubt whether he had earned it. I think it was like taking money out of one pocket and putting it in the other." He and others saw it as an accounting trick, pulled by the man who owned most of the stock, in order to make his pet project look successful. But they were wrong.[63]

How do I make a profit? Vanderbilt would rhetorically ask in court in 1869. "I make it by a saving of the expenditures. If I cannot use the capital of that road for pretty nigh $2,000,000 per year better than anyone that has ever been in it, then I do not want to be in the road." He would elaborate at length on this approach. "That has been my principle with steamships. I never had any advantage of anybody in running steamships; but if I could not run a steamship alongside another man and do it as well as he for twenty percent less than it cost him I would leave the ship." His triumph in making the Harlem pay may well have been more satisfying to him than the award, on April 17, of the gold medal that Congress had authorized during the war.[64]

THE ATHENS RAILROAD, the Albany bridge, and the People's Line: this was the iron triangle in which the Central and the Hudson River railroads collided. And Henry Keep, Dean Richmond, and Daniel Drew were the three men whose interests and personalities shaped the conflict. In 1866, Vanderbilt would make one last attempt to reach an accommodation with each of them. His hope lay in the fact that Drew and Richmond, at least, had vulnerabilities that inclined them toward compromise.

Drew's were personal and pecuniary. In early 1866, he engaged in a massive short-selling campaign in Erie stock. Drew was treasurer of the railroad—but inside trading by corporate managers and directors had gone on for decades in America. Still, the *Nation* noted, the Erie had suffered more than most railroads. "It has been milked dry by parasites and hangers-on," it wrote on June 5. "Everybody has fattened except the company, which has grown poorer and poorer every year." Drew had grown fattest of all, and always off the Erie's financial weakness. "There has never been a time these ten years that the Company has not owed him money," *Harper's Weekly* later wrote. "It has borrowed of Mr. Drew—because no one else would lend it."[65]

In early 1866, the railroad again needed money. Drew offered it, but he demanded Erie securities as collateral. The Erie (that is, Drew in his role as company treasurer) gave him (that is, Drew in his role as private speculator) 28,000 unissued shares created under a state law of May 4, 1864, along with $3 million in bonds that could be converted into stock at the holder's option. In return, Drew loaned the railroad a little less than $3.5 million. He then sold huge quantities of Erie stock at 90, on contracts that required him to deliver around the beginning of June. He steathily converted his bonds into stock, and on May 29 took all 58,000 shares out of his safe and threw them on the market. What he had sold at 90 instantly fell to 57½. Erie stockholders sold off in a panic, and Drew bought back his collateral for far less than he had sold it. It was "an operation," Charles F. Adams Jr. later wrote, "which was at the time regarded as a masterpiece."[66]

Throughout this highly profitable maneuver, Drew had faced one potentially fatal danger: his friend and fellow director Cornelius Vanderbilt, who was a creditor of the railroad and very much wanted it to clean up its finances. (A year earlier the Erie board had voted a dividend "against the remonstrance of Commodore Vanderbilt," according to the *Chicago Tribune*.)[67] If Vanderbilt had turned his mighty fortune against Drew's bear campaign, it would have been far more risky, perhaps even catastrophic.

But Vanderbilt did not oppose his old friend. Did Drew make a bargain with him? It is impossible to know. What is known is that Drew suddenly called a halt to the battle between his paddlewheelers and the Hudson River Railroad on June 1. When John M. Davidson, one of Drew's partners, sent runners to the railroad stations to call out the lower fares on the boats, a messenger "call'd to see me," Davidson wrote to Corning, "and says, Drew says it must be stopped. Of course we understand Drew. He wants the fight to go on, but dares not show his hand, from fear of Vanderbilt." At some point in 1866, Drew also agreed to cease running his boats to Athens. Taken together, these two facts sound very much like Vanderbilt's price for leaving Erie stock alone.[68]

Richmond's vulnerabilities were strategic. He needed Vanderbilt's cooperation to settle a ruinous rate war with the other trunk lines. William Vanderbilt and James Banker joined Richmond in peace talks with the Pennsylvania, the Erie, and the Baltimore & Ohio on May 2 in Buffalo and May 22–23 at the St. Nicholas Hotel in New York. The negotiations produced a cartel—one of the "largest and most sophisticated cartels ever attempted in American business," in the words of Alfred D. Chandler Jr. The trunk lines agreed to a schedule of rates; to end the special pricing represented by drawbacks and rebates; and to put themselves under the authority of Samuel Sloan as trunk line commissioner. He would receive a salary of $10,000 a year and have the power to fire any employee of any company who undercut the agreed rates.[69]

Despite the happy cooperation between Richmond and the Vanderbilts in the creation of this cartel, tensions between them continued to rise. William, for example, discovered "hundreds of instances" in which freight specifically consigned to the Hudson River Railroad was reconsigned in the Central's offices to the People's Line.[70] Rather than continue to fight over these petty but intractable issues, Richmond proposed a bold solution. One day in May, he suggested to Horace Clark that the Central consolidate with the Hudson River into one super corporation.[71]

"I do not see how it is practicable," Clark said. "To propose a law to consolidate the Hudson River and the Central roads would shake the State to its centre, because everybody would say that it was an attempt to increase the power of the railroad monopoly." Clark's observation speaks to the political sensitivity that pervaded Vanderbilt's circle. Though railway corporations did indeed wield great influence (the Pennsylvania especially deserved its reputation for overshadowing its state legislature), they also operated under the eye of a cynical and suspicious public. In New York, they were influential, but not all-powerful. The Central labored under statutory restrictions on fares and faced repeated proposals in the legislature for further restraints. Many considered it to be dangerously large as it was.[72]

Richmond did not argue the point. He wryly observed, "Railroads can lease other roads. I wish you would talk with the Commodore about it, and see what he will do." Richmond and Vanderbilt met to discuss the matter in person. "Mr. Richmond expressed himself that he was very anxious that these roads should be one," Vanderbilt recalled. "We talked it over a number of times afterwards, and finally he got me to thinking of the thing. He talked then about a lease."[73]

He got me to thinking of the thing: what Richmond proposed would smolder in the Commodore's mind, until, under the right conditions, it would flare spectacularly into fruition. For the time being, he rejected consolidation for the reasons Clark enumerated. And yet, surprisingly, he agreed to consider a lease of the Hudson River and the Harlem to the New York Central. In retrospect, Vanderbilt's openness to virtually abandoning his railroad career—a career that later went on to such triumphs—is stunning. It obliterates any notion that he harbored long-term plans for monopolizing New York's railways. Rather, he thought he would be content if his business peers accepted that he had successfully reformed his two companies, especially the Harlem.[74]

With lease talks under way, Richmond made his own conciliatory gesture by agreeing to lease the troublesome Athens railroad. Thus Vanderbilt would receive a return on his "foolish" investment, along with the satisfaction of seeing the line shut down, its threat to the Hudson River road ended for good.[75]

So much for Drew and Richmond; but there remained Henry Keep. To him, Vanderbilt and Richmond's gestures of peace looked like acts of war. Bearded and brooding, Keep had kept silent during this intricate game, but he felt badly used by the Athens lease agreement. "A dispute or misunderstanding arose as to the terms upon which it should be leased, and out of that misunderstanding it is supposed that some of difference of opinion arose between Mr. Vanderbilt and Mr. Keep," Clark said. The Commodore himself remarked, "That Athens business is a matter which I suppose Mr. Keep does not feel well towards me about."

No, he did not. Keep coldly told Banker "that he would have revenge against Mr. Vanderbilt if it cost him half he was worth."[76]

SARATOGA, WROTE A CORRESPONDENT for the *New York Tribune*, was a place of "huge dining halls with long walls of staring white . . . ball-rooms with the same shadowless surfaces, with blinding glare of gas, and stifling atmosphere of odors." The writer thought the only remnant of the elegant Saratoga of old to be the aristocratic Cubans who flocked to the Springs each summer. The rest were vulgar climbers. "From 8 o'clock till 11 there streams into the dining room a constant procession of over-dressed women, of flippant and loud-tongued men," the reporter continued.

> These fashionable young ladies audibly comment on the costumes of their neighbors, audibly snicker—I beg pardon of a polite world, but it is exactly what they do—at a toilet a little less fashionable, at a complexion a little less fair, at manners a little more rustic than their own. They paint and powder to a degree which arouses in one a desperate longing to get all of them under a pump.[77]

How like the reporting of the 1830s and '40s this was. Saratoga had been the scene of social climbing since the collapse of the hierarchical culture of deference. The ladies' snickers were a testament to the triumph of democracy—for without inherited distinctions, social rank had become a battefield. Yet it was also true that, after the Civil War, a new elite was surpassing the old patricians in riches and in extravagance, and that Saratoga no longer remained the sole summer center of fashion. As the *New York Herald* had observed in 1865, "Newport seems to have become by common consent the watering place *par excellence;* and there wealth, fashion, rank, and beauty . . . have formed a colony, and consider it their summer home." In May 1866, in a symbolic bit of destruction, fire destroyed Saratoga's far-famed Congress Hall hotel, built in 1812.[78]

But the Congress Hall would rise again, for Saratoga had not yet lost its supremacy as the nation's premier summer resort. Vanderbilt returned in 1866, as he had for at least three decades. This year, Saratoga chattered about his latest purchase, a six-year-old trotter named Mountain Boy. "I thought him the best horse of his age I ever saw," Vanderbilt later wrote, worthy of his estimated price of $14,000.[79]

And Saratoga remained Wall Street's favorite haunt. "At other watering places, they *talked* stocks; at Saratoga they *bought* and *sold* them," William Fowler wrote in 1870. "Little knots of dealers stood in the piazzas of the United States Hotel, the Union, and the Congress, and traded in Erie and Harlem. The great pulsations of the heart-financial, 180 miles away, throbbed here through the telegraphic wires."[80] In the summer of 1866, these clusters of brokers murmured stories that the Commodore's and Richmond's enemies had formed a coalition to take control of the New York Central Railroad at the December election.

The first element in this alliance was Corning, who wished to return to power in the railroad he had helped create. The second element was American Express, as embodied by William G. Fargo, the Buffalo businessman who had founded it (in addition to Wells, Fargo & Co.). Express companies had existed for decades, carrying expensive, high-priority items—especially money, for this was an economy that relied heavily on cash. They paid railroads rent to allow their messengers and safes to travel in the baggage cars of trains, though they often secured their routes by giving railway presidents shares in their companies—shares that were not publicly traded and paid double-digit dividends. Vanderbilt, impervious to this bribery, squeezed them to pay more to the Harlem and the Hudson River. "The directors of the [American], Adams Co. & United States [express companies] held a meeting to devise some means to break down the present prices charged by Vanderbilt & Co.," John M. Davidson reported to Corning on June 19. "The whole thing may end in smoke, but at present it looks like a fight." Already Fargo, on behalf of American Express, was buying Central shares in preparation for the December coup.[81]

So was Henry Keep, the third and most important party in the plot against Richmond and Vanderbilt. Keep, who turned forty-eight on June 22, was a powerful, if silent, figure on Wall Street. Orphaned at the age of twelve, he had served as an apprentice to a Joseph Grimmonds in Adams, New York, near Lake Ontario and the Canadian border. After five years, Keep ran away; Grimmonds posted a notice in the local newspaper, announcing, "All persons are forbid trusting him." He became a teamster on the Erie Canal, then began to buy and sell bank notes and bills of exchange, and finally became a banker. He forged a connection with LeGrand Lockwood of the banking and brokerage firm Lockwood & Co., and together they manipulated the stock of the Michigan Southern & Northern Indiana, one of the Central's links to Chicago. Thickset with a thick beard, Keep rather resembled General Grant, not only in appearance but in his taciturn manner as well. As Fowler wrote, Keep kept "an open countenance but thoughts concealed, a still tongue but a busy brain."[82]

Keep served as leader of the alliance. He was a past master of stock market battles; more than that, he had a personal vendetta against the Commodore, whom he saw as the real power behind Richmond. Keep, too, traveled to Saratoga that summer, and though he famously kept his mouth shut, word of his plot found its way to the ears of John Morrissey. The prizefighter operated a kind of clearinghouse for "points" (as stock tips were called) in his Saratoga gambling saloon. "He (M) told us last night Keep and his party had control of all the Central stock here & they had arranged to carry it," wrote G. C. Davidson, brother of John, "and [Keep had] gone to Europe to be gone till the Fall. He says they are in earnest and want to out the present directors."[83] Translated from Wall Street jargon, this meant that Keep and his allies had bought a majority of the shares and proxies held in New York, and had done so on credit. (To "carry" a stock was to hold it on margin.) Keep sailed for Europe to deceive Richmond and Vanderbilt as well as to buy up proxies for shares held in London.[84]

Keep did not fool the Commodore, but Vanderbilt responded in two starkly different ways. As a private investor, he limited his personal exposure. "I said, 'I will not own any of this property where it is owned by such a set of men,' " he later testified. "I sold out." On July 30, after the payment of dividends, he sold all of his 6,500 Central shares. As a railroad president, on the other hand, he behaved as if it were irrelevant who ruled the Central. As he often said, "I think the Hudson River Road can take care of itself." Perhaps he thought that Richmond might survive after all. But he did not.[85]

"The announcement of the death of Dean Richmond creates a profound sensation in this city," wrote an Albany correspondent for the *New York Times* on August 27. The railroad president, so long a titan in New York business and politics, had fallen ill at the Manhattan home of lawyer Samuel J. Tilden, and unexpectedly died. "He was sometimes abrupt in his manners," the New York Central directors declared in their official tribute, but "he never betrayed a confidence reposed in him and never practised deception."[86] Those qualities explain why he and Vanderbilt liked each other so much.

Richmond's plan to lease the Hudson River and Harlem railroads died with him. In London, Keep received letters from his partners, warning "that there was great danger that the roads would be consolidated," as he recalled. With his encouragement, the pool secured an injunction that prohibited any lease. But Richmond's demise created a power vacuum on the Central's board that Vanderbilt exploited.[87]

On October 18, William traveled to Albany to see the Central board "on matters of general business," as he later said, and fell into a discussion over how the two sides could settle their problems. William wanted the Hudson River to have the Central's freight business all year round; the Central directors wanted to use the People's Line and set through rates as before. "It was urged that I should name a price—so much money" as compensation, William said. He had not been charged with the task of settling this great question; considering his father's temper—and need for control—he might well have begged off. But he did not. "I will take it upon myself to do it for $100,000 for a year," William replied. As he recalled, "Two or three gentlemen jumped up from the table and said we will do that."[88]

William's offer was an act of confidence in his authority as his father's agent, and he was soon punished for it. "There has never been any one act in my life that has so much met the disapprobation of Cornelius Vanderbilt as that act," William recounted. "He said the privileges I had granted was worth a half million of dollars a year to the Central R.R. Co." Considering the Commodore's past "disapprobation," this was saying a great deal. But Vanderbilt also accepted his son's power to act in this matter. Indeed, this negotiation reveals the maturation of their relationship.

"The $100,000 was a mere bagatelle," Vanderbilt remarked. "I did not care anything about it." The specific amount paid "should not be a subject of any difference between the two companies if we can only have some understanding among ourselves hereafter." But perhaps he went too far in making his point: he clearly wanted the maximum compensation possible for allowing the Central to treat the Hudson River Railroad as an extension of itself. Vanderbilt's company had numerous costs that he wished to shift, from the use of its engines and cars over the Central's tracks to the steep terminal expenses in Manhattan.

Eager to appease the Commodore, the rudderless Central board named a committee to balance the companies' accounts. The committee consisted of James Banker. He took the Central's treasurer, Edwin D. Worcester, to the Hudson River office on Thirtieth Street to see Vanderbilt. At the meeting, Worcester expected the Hudson River to pay the $97,000 it owed the Central for westbound freight. But the Commodore believed that the Central owed the Hudson River money, so he insisted on arbitrary deductions until the $97,000 debt disappeared. "I objected," Worcester recalled, "to which Mr. Vanderbilt said it did not make any difference at what rate they were put in."

"I said, 'Damn the thing, I don't care anything about it,'" Vanderbilt recalled. "That is the way I did, and that is the way I generally do." The whole thing was, he frankly admitted, "a kind of 'jumped' settlement." He and the Central directors had fixed a payment, so they fiddled with the accounts until the books absorbed the agreed-upon amounts. However, none of this was what the Vanderbilts wanted. "We would a great deal rather do the business, than to get the money and not do the business," William said. But at least the $100,000 and the other "jumped" amounts offered some compensation, and established the principle that they could not be taken for granted.[89]

But soon the Central would have a new president, one who would throw this hard-won compromise into chaos and replace respect with disdain. In November, Keep returned from Europe "with his coat-pockets full of London proxies," the *New York Times* reported.[90] He promptly called on Vanderbilt. Keep informed him that he and his allies would take control of the board in December, and he planned to assume the presidency. He had no intention of paying $100,000 to the Hudson River for nothing, as he saw it, and would only prorate passenger fares and freight charges.

"You may break if you please, but I will not do your work," Vanderbilt warned.

"We can live without the Hudson River Railroad," Keep replied. "We do not want the Hudson River Railroad."

After the struggles of the previous two years, Vanderbilt scorned this arrogance. "Mr. Keep, I do not care one rush who is elected President of the N.Y. Central road. There is one thing I do know, there is no party of men in the world who can manage its affairs more prejudicially to our interests than the last board of directors."[91]

Vanderbilt was wrong. Things were going to get much worse.

AS THIS BUSINESS INTRIGUE played out after the death of Dean Richmond, Vanderbilt spent an evening on politics. On August 29, he attended a dinner for President Andrew Johnson at Delmonico's on Fourteenth Street, thrown by the great capitalists of New York. Among those invited were Charles Morgan, Cornelius Garrison, August Belmont, and Peter Cooper, as well as Vanderbilt's circle of subordinates and sons-in-law— James Banker, Horace Clark, Augustus Schell, Daniel Allen, Frank Work, and Richard Schell—and William Vanderbilt.[92]

The dinner was billed not as a political event, but as an appropriate gesture to honor the president. In truth, politics suffused the evening. Johnson visited New York as part of his "swing around the circle," a speaking campaign designed to undermine congressional Republicans. He had broken with them in the spring in a fierce fight over the status of emancipated slaves and the nature of Reconstruction. Johnson, a longtime Democrat and a Southerner himself, had vetoed first an extension of the Freedmen's Bureau, and next a civil rights bill, which extended citizenship and some basic rights (but not the vote) to the freed people. Johnson argued that the latter bill would somehow discriminate against whites. In the face of rising violence across the South against blacks, however, his veto strengthened the radicals, who marshaled moderates to override it and pass the landmark Civil Rights Act of 1866. Johnson now launched an unprecedented effort to defeat the Republicans in the midterm elections.[93]

Vanderbilt most likely did not care much about the politics involved. He should have, though, because the dinner was a sign of how the political world was rotating beneath his feet. He still believed in the Jacksonian principles that he had embraced in the 1830s, in his battles on the Hudson and Long Island Sound: free competition, laissez-faire, limited government. In his youth, these beliefs were found on the radical side of the political spectrum. But the Civil War and its aftermath had put in motion a process that broke down this matrix. The federal government had taken on power to a previously unthinkable degree to defeat the rebellion. Then, in the turmoil and confusion of the postwar South, Congress found itself forced to intervene at the local level—the individual level—in ways that fell far outside the American political tradition. Before the war, the federal government had not reached down very far (except in the territories); it had delivered the mail, inspected steam engines, and helped to capture runaway slaves, but not much else. Now it taxed individuals, extended aid to freed people, defined citizenship, specified rights, prescribed penalties for violating those rights, and soon would impose direct military administration of most of the South. In this crisis, Americans awoke to the power of the central government.

The way was opening for a new political paradigm, in which those on the radical side would embrace government action to defend equality. At the moment, though, the older schools of politics remained alive. Most Republicans, in keeping with antebellum "free labor" ideology, championed "the small-scale competitive capitalism" (to use historian Eric Foner's words) that still defined life in the North. They saw the individual as the primary actor in an economy of farms, workshops, and small mercantile houses. But their philosophy could not account for changes sweeping the nation. For example, the union movement—bolstered by rising numbers of wage workers in big companies such as railroads— staged a convention in Baltimore that left orthodox thinkers scratching their heads. "The tendency of the assembly . . . is to the recognition and indeed creation of a special class known as working men," *Harper's Weekly* wrote. "Is such a tendency in this country wise, or is it even practicable?"[94] It was inevitable. The unionists looked to government for help, calling for legal limits on the working day. It would not be long before farmers followed their example. Vanderbilt's laissez-faire principles were becoming conservative without changing at all.

Personal and business matters kept him busy through the fall. On October 6, Sophia and grandson William K. Vanderbilt set sail for Europe. On October 8, the Commodore convinced Trinity Church to sell St. John's Park to the Hudson River Railroad. Once an elegant quadrangle of townhouses surrounding a gated park, dominated by St. John's Chapel at one end, it had been the model for Gramercy Park and the final home of Thomas Gibbons. It had fallen into decay, however, and offered a large, open space in lower Manhattan, close to the docks. As early as 1859, the railroad's management had eyed it as a location for a freight depot. Vanderbilt agreed to pay $1 million on behalf of the company—$400,000 going to the church, the rest to the lot owners.[95]

Vanderbilt attended to his affairs in an office at 25 West Fourth Street, near Greene Street, adjacent to his stables in the rear of his Washington Place lot. After so many years on Bowling Green, he finally had relinquished his desk there. "He comes in about nine o'clock," the *Boston Journal* wrote. "A digest of letters and papers is laid before him on a prepared sheet. Running his eye over the list, he dots down yes and no, and gives some brief direction to each." Always puffing on a cigar, he moved around his office in a light linen coat and carpet slippers. Wardell kept a desk in the outer chamber, the walls covered with railroad maps and photographs of Vanderbilt's steamships and railway depots. The Commodore's room was in the back. "Through his rear window could be continually heard the chafing of his thoroughbreds, eager for the five o'clock drive which the indefatigable old gentleman gives them every afternoon," a reporter for the *New York Herald* observed. After finishing whatever Wardell had prepared for his review, the *Journal* added, "he then goes out with some confidential friend to attend to what he calls business, which consists of going out to his stables and minutely examining his horses. After this he holds a levee [reception] in his office, and rides up to the Harlem and Hudson railroad."[96]

Famous for his expensive horses and his frugality in all other areas, Vanderbilt proved more generous than his reputation would suggest. In June, he had agreed to serve as a trustee of Horace Greeley's pet charity, the American Institute; in December, he served as a reference for the artist who had designed his congressional gold medal. But he cared little about whether he was seen as a public benefactor. "He does not go much to churches, and no one ever sees his name on a subscription paper, or ever will," the *Herald* later noted. "In his charities, which are numerous and liberal, he exhibits the reticence which marks his conduct as a man of business. He despises cant and humbug and pretentious show."[97] It was hard to imagine Vanderbilt ostentatiously putting his name on an institution of higher learning, as Daniel Drew did with a seminary.*

ON DECEMBER 12, 1866, the New York Central Railroad held its annual election in Albany. For weeks, rumors had flown about the fight for control. The winner was Keep, elected to the presidency by a new board largely consisting of his allies: Fargo, Corning, Azariah Boody, H. Henry Baxter, John H. Chedell, LeGrand Lockwood, and others. "The new regime may properly be called anti-Vanderbilt. All the Vanderbilt men in the old direction were thrown overboard," the *New York Herald* wrote. It was, the *New York Times* declared, a "revolution."[98]

On December 20, the new Central board revoked the agreement to pay $100,000 to the Hudson River Railroad. "We supposed they had got quite enough in their hands and we would not give them more," Keep later said. The Commodore recognized the crisis for what it was: the final battle in the long struggle between the two railroads. On December 29, he took William, Clark, Augustus Schell, and Charlick into a meeting with Keep, Corning, Baxter, and Boody, who had returned to New York from Albany. Again and again, William asked the same question: "Gentlemen, you have taken it upon yourselves to repudiate this contract, and to break up the connection under which the companies are running. We ask if you have anything to substitute in the place of it." Keep offered only to prorate the charges for whatever freight or passengers the Central deigned to provide. They talked fruitlessly for five hours.[99]

"I thought at that meeting there was no possible chance to do anything

---

* The seminary Drew endowed is now Drew University, in Madison, New Jersey.

with Mr. Keep," the Commodore recalled. "When we left I said to Mr. Corning, 'Get into my wagon and I will carry you up to the Fifth Avenue Hotel.' " He still respected Corning; Keep, on the other hand, he derided as "a shyster," and was heard to say "that he should never be recognized by gentlemen." Corning climbed up next to Vanderbilt, who held the reins and whipped his horses through the crowded New York streets. Vanderbilt said, "Mr. Corning, I am very sorry we cannot get along together in this matter."

"I am too," Corning replied. "If it was left to you and me we could fix it up in a little while."

"I believe we could," the Commodore said. The brief conversation told him all he needed to know. It was *not* left to Corning to fix it up. Clearly he had no power in the matter. Vanderbilt dropped his friend off at the hotel, certain that war was inevitable.[100]

On January 7, William received a notice from Worcester, the Central's treasurer, who said he was not authorized to pay the Hudson River's terminal charges. The Central also began to play with the accounts of the Albany bridge company, keeping for itself a certain amount of stock that should have been divided with the Hudson River.[101] William showed the note to his father. "This thing is getting very serious," the Commodore said. "Go to Albany. . . . Fix up some kind of arrangement with these people. I don't want to be compelled to split with them. Go to Albany."

William and Schell took the train to Albany the next morning, and arrived at half past one in the afternoon. They immediately went into a conference with the Central directors. William told them that he only wanted to do what was right. "Your father said that the other day," Keep replied, "but I have about made up my mind he does not know what is right and what is wrong."

The insult stunned Schell. He watched the reaction on William's face, under the great pyramids of whiskers that extended out and drooped from his cheeks. William "controlled himself," Schell recalled, and said "that he wished to avoid any personal difficulty, and he had come as a representative of the road to see if the matters in difference could not be fairly adjusted." Under this calm surface, William seethed. He thought to himself that if his father "was inclined at all to break his business connections with the N.Y. Central R.R. he had cause enough now."

William made one last proposal: to refer the dispute to arbitration. He said his father wished "to do nothing in the world that any man who walked the streets should not say was exactly right." At that, Azariah Boody leaped up and shouted, "There was no man in the world who could say that. Mr. Vanderbilt has not made a fair proposition." Keep coldly added, "We can settle our own business."

Vanderbilt equipped the *Vanderbilt* with a ram to destroy the Confederate ship *Virginia* and brought it to Hampton Roads, Virginia, where it bottled up the ironclad. He refitted it as a cruiser to search for the Confederate raider *Alabama* (note the cannons visible through gunports in this image) and sold it to the navy for one dollar. *Library of Congress*

Cornelius Vanderbilt as he appeared on a magazine cover in 1865. This image captures him just after he sold his last steamships and devoted himself to his growing railroad empire. *Library of Congress*

Confederate captain Raphael Semmes of the *Alabama* targeted Vanderbilt's Panama line, hoping to punish the Commodore for donating the *Vanderbilt* to the Union navy. On December 7, 1862, A. G. Jones, the captain of the Vanderbilt steamer *Ariel*, suspiciously watched the approach of the *Alabama* under a false U.S. flag. *Naval Historical Center*

Captain Jones attempted to escape the *Alabama*, but the *Ariel* was one of the slowest ships in the Vanderbilt fleet. But Semmes had been searching for the *Champion*, headed north with a cargo of gold; the *Ariel* was steaming south from New York, and had none. Semmes let it go after a few days. *Naval Historical Center*

In 1863, Vanderbilt took control of the struggling New York & Harlem Railroad, which had one key strength: it was the only steam railway to enter the center of Manhattan. Its trains ran down the surface of Fourth (later Park) Avenue to this station on Twenty-sixth Street, where they connected with the Harlem's horse-drawn streetcar line. *New York Central System Historical Society*

In keeping with steamboat and steamship tradition, locomotives were named in honor of leading officials of their companies. The *Commodore Vanderbilt* of the Hudson River Railroad was typical of those operated by Vanderbilt's lines. *Library of Congress*

After taking control of the Harlem, Vanderbilt bought its principal competitor, the Hudson River Railroad, which ran from Albany along the river to this freight depot at Chambers Street. The horse-drawn carts illustrate one of the railroad's strengths: it ran down the West Side, close to the piers that served the city's abundant shipping trade. *New York Central System Historical Society*

Horace F. Clark, one of Vanderbilt's sons-in-law, emerged in the 1850s as a trusted lieutenant. A prominent Democratic politician, he sat on the boards of Vanderbilt's railroads and became president of the Lake Shore & Michigan Southern, which Vanderbilt controlled. In that position he struck out on his own, and forged an alliance with Jay Gould. *Library of Congress*

Augustus Schell was Horace Clark's close friend and political ally, and served as grand sachem of Tammany Hall after Boss Tweed's downfall. He also sat on the boards of Vanderbilt's railroads. *Library of Congress*

The railroad bridge across the Hudson River at Albany was seen as a major feat of engineering when it was opened in 1866. It allowed a direct connection between Vanderbilt's lines and the New York Central Railroad. *Library of Congress*

Erastus Corning was one of New York State's leading businessmen and politicians. A resident of Albany, he rose to wealth as owner of an iron mill and president of the New York Central. Though Vanderbilt sometimes clashed with Corning, he liked and respected him. *Library of Congress*

Henry Keep became a major figure on Wall Street in partnership with financier LeGrand Lockwood. In December 1866, Keep led a takeover of the New York Central, then provoked Vanderbilt by revoking a hard-won agreement with the Hudson River Railroad. Vanderbilt closed the Albany bridge to train traffic in retaliation, cutting the Central's link to New York. Keep capitulated. *Library of Congress*

Jay Gould shared a birthday with Vanderbilt, making Gould exactly forty-two years younger. He proved to be Vanderbilt's most determined enemy. In 1867, Gould asked Vanderbilt for his help in throwing Daniel Drew off the board of the Erie Railway; in the end, Gould sided with Drew to defeat Vanderbilt's attempt to corner Erie stock. *Library of Congress*

James Fisk Jr. emerged as Jay Gould's closest ally on the Erie board. Often understimated because of his outrageous behavior, he proved to be Gould's capable partner after the latter took the Erie presidency in 1868. A rival for the affections of a mistress shot Fisk dead in a hotel lobby in 1871. *Library of Congress*

As vice president and later president of the Pennsylvania Railroad, Thomas A. Scott made a striking contrast with Vanderbilt. Scott was a professional executive who rose through the ranks of management. He pioneered the use of shell corporations and holding companies, and was Andrew Carnegie's mentor. *Library of Congress*

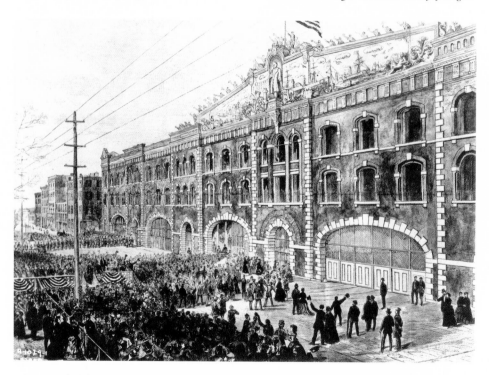

Vanderbilt negotiated the purchase by the Hudson River Railroad of St. John's Park, the model for Gramercy Park, located where the exit of the Holland Tunnel is now. The railroad built the St. John's Park Freight Depot, pictured here, on that site. This image depicts the unveiling on November 10, 1869, of a statue of Vanderbilt centered in a bronze relief that depicted his career. *New York Central System Historical Society*

The St. John's Park Freight Depot statue was designed by Ernst Plassman and paid for by a fund organized by Albert De Groot, a former employee who had grown rich with Vanderbilt's assistance. Twelve feet tall, it (and the reliefs on either side) cost a reputed $500,000. In the early twentieth century it was moved to the front of Grand Central Terminal, where it remains today. *New York Central System Historical Society*

As the richest man in America, Vanderbilt was often caricatured by the press, which cast a cynical eye on the wealthy. This cartoon mocks Vanderbilt by making an unflattering comparison between him and James Fisk, in their "watering" the stock of their railroads—increasing the number of shares, considered a grave misdeed in 1869. *Library of Congress*

Vanderbilt's consolidation of the New York Central and the Hudson River railroads pioneered the giant corporation in American history. This 1870 cartoon shows Vanderbilt racing his newly merged company against Fisk of the Erie. *Library of Congress*

In 1869, the Harlem Railroad began to build the continent's largest railroad station, the Grand Central Depot. The station was located on the north side of Forty-second Street, well above the built-up portion of New York, because of legal prohibitions on the use of steam locomotives below that point. Vanderbilt personally paid for much of the construction. This photograph shows the arched supports for the vast train shed, or "car house." *New York Central System Historical Society*

This engraving of Grand Central, completed in 1871, views it from the south, as most New Yorkers saw it. The depot anchored the rapid development of this district, and turned Forty-second Street into a major crosstown artery. Note the entrance on the far right for horse-drawn streetcars that rolled up Fourth Avenue from downtown. The depot was later rebuilt as Grand Central Station, and finally replaced by Grand Central Terminal on the same location. *New York Central System Historical Society*

The northern entrance of the Grand Central car house, shown here, opened onto Fourth Avenue. Because of complaints about the trains running on the surface of Fourth Avenue, Vanderbilt agreed to sink the tracks in an open cut. The cut was later covered over, and Fourth blossomed into Park Avenue. *New York Central System Historical Society*

This view shows the interior of Grand Central's car house, beneath the enormous arched glass roof. Note the horse-drawn streetcars on the far right, which entered the station through a southern entrance. *New York Central System Historical Society*

An express train for Chicago departs Grand Central. During the 1870s, the New York Central and the Pennsylvania competed to run the fastest train between New York and Chicago. The Pennsylvania, with a more direct route, usually won. But the Central possessed a nearly level route, by far the most economical. *New York Central System Historical Society*

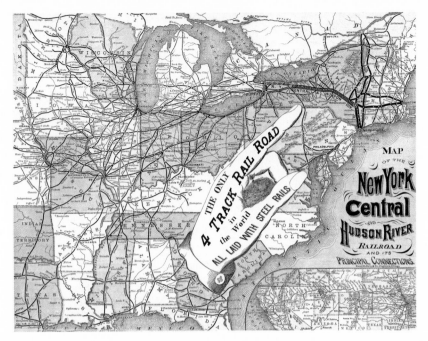

Four giant railroads, called the trunk lines, dominated traffic between the West and the Atlantic seaboard. Vanderbilt and his son William made the New York Central & Hudson River into the most profitable. A key strength, advertised here, was the unprecedented four-track line they built between Albany and Buffalo, at a time when many railroads had only one set of tracks. The four-track plan was Vanderbilt's brainchild. *Library of Congress*

Vanderbilt helped lift harness racing to social prominence in the 1850s, with his expensive horses and match races on the roads of rural upper Manhattan. The rising generation of Wall Street men chased the Commodore on Bloomingdale Road or Harlem Lane, shown here. Even after Vanderbilt (center-left foreground, with top hat and white cravat) turned eighty, he raced his expensive trotters on an almost daily basis. *Library of Congress*

Vanderbilt spent $14,000 on Mountain Boy, his finest horse and most prized posses-
sion, shown at right, racing its most famous rival, Lady Thorn. Mountain Boy began to
dominate American harness racing in 1867 and became a national celebrity. The horse
died in the epizootic of 1872, a loss that deeply affected Vanderbilt. *Library of Congress*

Starting in the 1830s, Vanderbilt went to the fashionable resort of Saratoga
Springs every summer. This photograph shows him (seated at right, with crossed
legs and top hat) on the veranda of the Congress Hall hotel in the early 1870s. He
took part in Saratoga's highly social environment, playing whist and attending
races. *New York Public Library*

Vanderbilt, shown here at about the age of eighty, impressed observers with his erect posture, physical energy, and youthful appearance. He acquired dignity with age, even winning praise for his courtly manners and fastidious dress. *Library of Congress*

Tennessee Claflin became Vanderbilt's magnetic healer, spiritualist medium, and possibly mistress. In 1870, she and her sister Victoria Woodhull claimed to have established the first female-run brokerage house on Wall Street with Vanderbilt's backing. There is no evidence that they conducted any trades or had Vanderbilt's support. *Library of Congress*

Victoria Woodhull used the fame of her purported brokerage house to take a leading role in the women's movement. Shown here addressing a committee of Congress (with her sister on her left), she declared herself a candidate for president in 1872. The sisters also launched *Woodhull & Claflin's Weekly*, devoted to spiritualism and radical causes. Though some have assumed that Vanderbilt supported the periodical, he did not. *Library of Congress*

Founder of the *New York Tribune*, Horace Greeley played a unique role in American public life. He befriended Vanderbilt's gambling-addicted son Corneil, and lent him tens of thousands of dollars. Greeley convinced Vanderbilt to serve as bondsman for the release of Jefferson Davis in 1867, which started him on the path toward his endowment of Vanderbilt University. *Library of Congress*

Vanderbilt's second wife, Frank Crawford Vanderbilt, was also his cousin. A native of Mobile, Alabama, Frank was a thirty-year-old divorcée when she gained the Commodore's acquaintance in 1868. A year later, they made a trip to Canada for a private wedding—after she signed a prenuptial agreement. A dignified woman with an aristocratic air, she brought her often-difficult husband fully into elite society. *Albany Institute of History and Art*

Vanderbilt's daughter Ethelinda married Daniel B. Allen, who served as a manager of his father-in-law's businesses for three decades. The Allens lived on Staten Island, not far from William H. Vanderbilt's farm. A permanent rift opened between the Commodore and the Allens in 1873 when Vanderbilt refused to save their son when his brokerage house failed. *Albany Institute of History and Art*

Vanderbilt's daughter Sophia married Canadian merchant Daniel Torrance, who ran his father-in-law's transatlantic line and served as vice president of the New York Central Railroad. Described by one nephew as "impulsive," Sophia criticized Frank behind her back. On his deathbed, Vanderbilt insisted that Sophia apologize and shake hands with Frank. *Albany Institute of History and Art*

Mary, another Vanderbilt daughter, married Nicholas B. La Bau, a lawyer and politician. Mary led the resistance to Vanderbilt's will, in which he left most of his estate to William. "Now don't be stubborn and give trouble," Vanderbilt told her on his deathbed. "I have left you all enough to live like ladies." Unsatisfied with $500,000 worth of bonds, she challenged the will, leading to a long court battle. *Albany Institute of History and Art*

When Seymour Guy painted *Going to the Opera* in 1873, William and his wife Maria had already begun to establish their large family in patrician society, as shown here by the fine art that William purchased on repeated trips to Europe. The Commodore cultivated William's oldest sons, Cornelius II and William K. *Biltmore Estate*

The Panic of 1873 posed the greatest crisis of Vanderbilt's career. His son-in-law Horace F. Clark had dangerously increased the debt of the Lake Shore & Michigan Southern Railroad, and had embroiled both it and a major bank, the Union Trust Company, in his personal stock speculations. The Union Trust had to close its doors in the face of a run (shown here) during the Panic. *Library of Congress*

Vanderbilt turned eighty in 1874. This engraving—made from a photograph taken for *Frank Leslie's Illustrated Monthly* in early 1876—shows him at rest in his house at 10 Washington Place. He holds a young descendant, likely a great-grandchild, demonstrating a warmth that outsiders rarely saw. *New York Central System Historical Society*

Vanderbilt's final illness began in May 1876, and he remained bedridden until his death on January 4, 1877. Though he was in agony for much of this period, his mind remained clear until very near the end. Here crowds are shown outside his double-wide house between Mercer and Greene streets, at 10 Washington Place, after word of his death. *Library of Congress*

Friends, family, and dignitaries crowded the Church of the Strangers on Mercer Street for Vanderbilt's funeral. Vanderbilt had purchased the church for Rev. Charles F. Deems, who ministered to fellow Southerners, or "strangers," in New York, including Frank Vanderbilt and her mother. Vanderbilt gave it to Deems partly out of his desire to bring North and South together after the Civil War. *Library of Congress*

Vanderbilt was buried in the family vault in the Moravian Cemetery on Staten Island. Years after his death, he would be reinterred in a lavish tomb constructed by William H. Vanderbilt, still in existence in the same cemetery. *Library of Congress*

Vanderbilt's daughter Mary sued to break his will, which left an estimated $95 million to William. This illustration shows Vanderbilt's personal doctor, Jared Linsly, testifying on the first day of the trial, which lasted more than two years. As soon as William settled the suit, he sold a controlling stake in the New York Central to a syndicate organized by J. P. Morgan and constructed an enormous mansion on Fifth Avenue, initiating the Vanderbilt family's Gilded Age extravagance. *Library of Congress*

This was the world that Vanderbilt made: New York City a few years after his death, when more than a million people crowded onto Manhattan. Described as an "overgrown seaport village" when he was a young man, it grew into the commercial and financial capital of North America, home to the greatest riches (and most desperate poverty) in the United States—a transformation that Vanderbilt helped lead. *Library of Congress*

Given Boody's eruption, it is curious to note that just prior to the meeting he had taken William aside and told him that he and Baxter both desired a settlement. It gave William some hope. He urged the board to confer with him and Schell in New York by January 14, after which their power to negotiate would expire. They left.[102]

In New York, William reported what had transpired, still optimistic that the negotiations would resume when the Central board came to New York. "They are humbugging you," the Commodore replied. "I'll tell you my opinion; when they come [to New York], they will keep away, they will never come nigh you. They are going to fool you and draw you along in this controversy through the winter, until spring comes and the river opens, and then they will tell you to go to the devil; that is their policy."

Vanderbilt was being bullied, and he didn't like it. But he had one great advantage. It was deep winter, and the river was frozen. He proposed that they use their ultimate weapon: to break off all connections with the New York Central. "They do not think that we dare break with them, but they will find themselves mistaken for once," he told his men. "We may as well break with those people tomorrow as at any time. I don't want to take two, three, or four days to do a thing that we can do in one."

"Don't do that," William replied. "Let it be. They will be here and we will have a meeting on Monday," January 14.

"Very well," Vanderbilt answered. "We will give them till that time, but they will not come."[103]

They never came. Late on January 14, the boards of both the Hudson River and the Harlem railroads voted to suspend relations with the New York Central as of January 18. No tickets or freight would be accepted from it; no trains would cross the Albany bridge. (Vanderbilt's lines would halt their own trains on the east side of the Hudson River.) "It would have this effect," William testified. "It would put the N.Y. Central road in a position that she could not go before the public and say she was a grand trunk line between New York and Buffalo." For the Central, it was apocalyptic.[104]

Notice of the impending break reached the Central directors on January 15. They immediately asked for the meeting that they had previously scorned. Now it was the Commodore's turn to display indifference. "I did not have the time," he blithely explained. "Life is not a bit too long for me, and I like to play whist; and I will not permit any business to come in and interfere with that."

As Vanderbilt enjoyed himself in the card rooms of the Manhattan Club, a howling blizzard swept down on the state. The heaviest snowfall in a decade piled up in enormous drifts; temperatures plunged below zero. "The present winter is to pass into the annals of the 'extraordinary,'" the

Albany Evening Journal remarked on January 18. Passengers were forced to trudge across the ice at Albany, or hire sleighs to carry them and their baggage over, in order to buy tickets directly from the respective lines. Freight from the west piled up at the Central's terminus. Shippers turned to the Erie and the Pennsylvania, but those lines had to use ferries to cross the Hudson into Manhattan, and the severe weather made this connection intermittent. In a season and an age when everything depended on the railroad, Vanderbilt had not only cut the Central off from New York, he had cut off New York from the country.[105]

It was a shocking example of a private company's power over the city, if not the nation itself. Vanderbilt, the *Brooklyn Eagle* wrote, "was placing the metropolis in a state of strict blockade, and cutting off its supplies. . . . We can imagine no act more criminal than this or more deserving of exemplary punishment." The *New York Herald* said, "Railroad corporations, whether ruled by boards or held within the grasp of a single individual, should not forget that they owe some consideration to the people who grant them special and valuable privileges, and to whose patronage and support they are indebted for their success." In the state senate, Henry C. Murphy of Brooklyn offered a bill to require connecting lines to carry through passengers and freight without breaking bulk, and to refer all disputes to the state engineer for arbitration. The assembly's Railroad Committee began hearing testimony on January 18.[106]

On February 5, the aged, erect figure of Cornelius Vanderbilt sat before this committee. His foes had testified first, excoriating him at length. His son and other Hudson River directors had followed, explaining the long history of their conflict with the Central and the details of the current crisis. But the assemblymen most wanted to hear from the Commodore himself. "Did you not take it for granted," one of them asked, "that the Central Railroad were legally bound to pay you a $100,000 annually?"

"When you talk about 'legally,' I suppose your next question will be: 'Why didn't you prosecute them?' " Vanderbilt replied. "It is not according to my mode of doing things, to bring a suit against a man that I have the power in my own hands to punish. . . . The law, as I view it, goes too slow for me when I have the remedy in my own hands." As he elaborated a few minutes later, "Let the other parties go to law if they want, but by God I think I know what the law is; I have had enough of it."

One of the committee members pointed out that the Commodore had personal friends on the Central board. "My personal friends, when they take such grounds as they did, I am afraid of. I am not afraid of my enemies, but, my God, you must look out when you get among your friends," he said. "No, sir, I never did any act in my life that I did with more reluctance than I did to assert my rights in that controversy with the N.Y. Central Railroad. But I would have asserted them if it had cost me half I was worth. It was not a matter of dollars and cents; it was a matter of principle."[107]

Vanderbilt's words later would be distorted into a sneer, one that mixed the essence of his speech with the caricature of him as a brute. "Law! What do I care about the law?" he would be quoted as saying. "Hain't I got the power?" This fabrication would have an enduring and misleading impact on his image. Over the course of his life, he had resorted to lawsuits many times; he found them inefficient, but he hardly spurned the courts. Far from a mere tyrant, he practiced patient and skillful diplomacy. Nor was his speech quite so crude—though he did say "damn" and "devil" far more often than was thought proper in the 1860s. But one point of both quote and misquote was the same: he had the power to punish.

The testimony of Vanderbilt and his men produced "a decided change in public sentiment, which had previously run altogether in favor of the Central management," the *Times* reported. For one thing, Vanderbilt had a chance to present himself in his own terms. "I have always served the public to the best of my ability," he remarked. "Why? Because, like every other man, it is to my interest to do so, and to put them to as little inconvenience as possible." More important, Vanderbilt and his men turned attention from the trivialities of business to the underlying problems: the fragmentation of the railway system that pitted connecting lines against each other, and the contradictory nature of railroads as both private businesses and public works. Clark and William pointed out that Senator Murphy's bill could strip a company of its power to defend itself against ill-treatment. How could society demand that private citizens provide the capital for the nation's railways, but leave them unable to protect their investments? Left unanswered was the question of how the public interest—and the public's interest in uninterrupted railway transportation was enormous—could be protected from disruptions caused by purely private disputes. The Central blockade contributed to a growing political conviction that railroads required regulation.

Vanderbilt voiced no worries. "If you could pass a law compelling men to take better care of their interests than their interests will compel them without the law, then it is well enough," he said. "I don't care what law the legislature makes in reference to railroads, provided it is general, and applies to all roads. For if I cannot exist upon the same terms with the rest of them, I will retire and go out of the business."[108]

By the time he said these words, the blockade had already ended. The demonstration of his ruthlessness had driven even Keep into a panic.

"What is to be done?" Keep telegraphed Corning on January 17, as soon as he received word of the blockade. He transferred all power to settle the matter to Corning, Boody, and Baxter, the three directors most open to a compromise. The trio took a carriage to Vanderbilt's office on West Fourth Street and began peace talks. "I will do Commodore Vanderbilt the justice to say that he was, during the negotiation . . . the most anxious man in the party to settle," Baxter said.[109]

On January 19, they agreed to a new contract. The Central committed to delivering as much through freight "from competing points" to the Hudson River as the Hudson River delivered to it. There would be no more empty cars returning from Albany. The Central also agreed to pay its share of the Hudson River's terminal charges. There would be no $100,000 payment, but William considered the Central's concessions to be worth twice that. On January 21, the *New York Herald* announced, "END OF THE RAILROAD WAR." Murphy's bill died, as did the assembly inquiry.[110]

In speaking to the assembly committee, Keep noted that Vanderbilt "claims to have had everything his own way, and I am afraid he has. I am very thankful that I have not been a party to it." This was a remarkable statement. He was president of the company, and yet he was not "a party to" its agreement? It was a sign that Vanderbilt had defeated him mentally, morally, emotionally, from the moment the great and unexpected blow fell. Keep gave Corning's committee responsibility for making peace, and then began to dump his New York Central shares. "Keep & Lockwood are large sellers. They have flooded the market with stock," John M. Davidson wrote to Corning on January 24. Vanderbilt, he recorded, had been out "on the road" driving his fast horses, "& said that he had instructed Wm never to notice any communications from Keep, that he was unworthy of notice, etc., etc." Tellingly, Vanderbilt advised his horse-racing friends to buy and hold Central stock.[111]

"Keep is cursed by all parties," Davidson wrote to Corning the next day. "The swearing against him by the stockholders is *terrible*. They talk of getting up a meeting requesting him to resign. This man, Mr. Corning, is a bad one, for the interests of your road. He has a worse reputation than Vanderbilt. The difference between the two is this: Keep will throw over the stockholders' interests by twisting the stock, while Vanderbilt will sustain stocks by holding them—for instance Hudson & Harlem." In all likelihood, Keep and Lockwood had been carrying their shares on narrow margins, and decided to cut their losses when the price fell during the blockade. As for Davidson, he joined the crowd in hurling his own Central shares into the flood.[112]

He should have paid attention to what Vanderbilt told his companions on the road. The Commodore's victory turned out to be more complete than he ever could have predicted. He not only had forced the Central to acknowledge his railroad's demands for justice, he had broken the spirit of its largest stockholders. As Central shares grew cheap and abundant, Vanderbilt saw an opportunity. He took it.

Chapter Sixteen

AMONG FRIENDS

On December 11, 1867, Cornelius Vanderbilt ascended to the presidency of the New York Central. Less than five years after he had taken control of the New York & Harlem, he presided over the state's most important railroad—one of the nation's four trunk lines—as well as the lines that connected it to Manhattan. This conquest marked the culmination of the third and most important phase of his empire building. The Central would be the bastion of his realm, much as Prussia would be to the German empire that Otto von Bismarck constructed a few years later. Only now would he move toward the creation of the gigantic corporation—and system—that would seal his place in history.

The press accordingly gave him a new title: the Railroad King.[1] It was a rank (or insult) often handed to railway presidents, but increasingly it stuck to Vanderbilt, who was so different from his peers. Unlike Drew, he did not go into a railroad to manipulate its stock; unlike Keep, he did not go in on borrowed money and sell out when overmatched; unlike J. Edgar Thomson, he was not a professional executive, hired by the stockholders. He used his own cash to buy large blocks of shares, moved into the management to stay, and brought along his eldest son and sons-in-law. (Clark was now joined by Daniel Torrance, who took office as vice president of the Central.) Vanderbilt never liked the title of king, but it looked very much like he was building a kingdom.

And yet, historians have often erred in accounting for this conquest. It has been written that he assumed all but formal control of the Central at the conclusion of the blockade in January 1867.[2] In fact, he moved slowly and cautiously into the great trunk line over the eleven months that followed. True, the disgusted Henry Keep promptly withdrew from active management, but there is no sign that Vanderbilt simply assumed his place.[3] To the contrary: on April 30, William wrote to James F. Joy, the president of the Michigan Central, to thank him for his help in clearing up a misunderstanding between the Hudson River and the New York Central—showing that Vanderbilt did not yet have even informal control of the larger line. But signs of growing influence, and stockholding, in the Central steadily accumulated.[4]

On July 25, Keep resigned the Central presidency, and was replaced by H. Henry Baxter. Eager to appease Vanderbilt, the directors voted to reconsider the Central's relations with the Hudson River Railroad and Daniel Drew's People's Line. Two days later, Erastus Corning's son overheard Vanderbilt advise a friend to buy Central stock. In August, the *New York Times* reported that the Central's new management had forged "a close alliance with the Vanderbilt roads." Ominously for Drew, the Central decided to "cut loose from all connection with the Hudson River steamboats."[5]

The latter statement would prove to be gravely portentous. The relationship between Vanderbilt and Drew had undergone a transformation of late, one that grew more dangerous with each passing month. Vanderbilt's acquisition of the Hudson River Railroad had broken their unwritten nonaggression pact—and their long-standing partnership—by pitting their interests against each other for the first time since their clash on the river three decades before. Drew's participation in the second Harlem corner had turned their rivalry into a matter of open combat. Vanderbilt's infiltration of the Central heightened tensions still further; as one newspaper reported, "Drew and Vanderbilt promise to fight it out on the Hudson River all summer."[6]

The summer of 1867 served as a mere skirmish before the battle to come. Vanderbilt's ascension to the presidency of the Central would spark a fight so fierce, so enormous, so outlandish, that history would record it as a formal noun: the Erie War.

EVEN BEFORE THE COMMODORE assumed control of the New York Central, his historical legacy as a railroad king began to take shape. He would be no Leland Stanford, no James J. Hill, building transcontinental lines through thousands of miles of unsettled plains and mountains; rather, he would be a creator of the invisible world, a conjurer in the financial ether. What made him powerful—and controversial—was not his riches alone, but his mastery of the corporate golem.

For his first magic trick, he took what was one and made it two. On March 30, 1867, the Hudson River shareholders (himself foremost among them) approved his plan to nearly double the stock by issuing new shares worth $6,963,900 at par value.[7] Called a stock dividend, it was similar to a stock split, an operation that would become common in the twentieth century. In the nineteenth century, it sparked outrage. Charles F. Adams Jr. typified the reaction of orthodox thinkers when he called the transaction an "astounding" act of "financial legerdemain."[8] It seemed to unhinge the value of stock from the world of the concrete and real. Even now, the economic mind shrank before abstractions. Economists, moralists, and financiers alike expected stock to represent the original cost of physical construction and real property, at a rate of $100 per share, the standard par value. Even the most sophisticated thinkers refused to accept that stock could be increased at will, or that the market alone should determine the value of a share. The construction-based par value provided a reassuring sense that one could indeed find the honest, *intrinsic*, value apart from day-to-day market fluctuations, much like the gold that backed pre-greenback banknotes.

Stock that did not reflect construction costs was derided as "fictitious capital," to use the formal term—or, more commonly, "watered stock," which called up the image of livestock encouraged to gorge on water before weighing and sale at the market. By contrast, new stock was *not* seen as diluting share value if it reflected actual construction or additional real estate. This thinking explains the curious fact that bonds were often convertible into stock: if used to buy cars and engines, purchase land, or finance construction, then they represented an increase of real capital.[9]

Vanderbilt used this conventional wisdom to justify his stock dividend. He distributed the new shares to existing stockholders on a one-for-one basis, but required them to pay 54 percent of the par value (or $54 each). This money went to pay for the purchase of St. John's Park for $1 million and the building of a freight depot in place of its trees and flowers. The remaining 46 percent represented construction and rolling stock that had been paid for previously through the sale of bonds, now to be retired. And the Commodore and his son managed to pay 8 percent dividends even after doubling the stock, which tamped down criticism. "They have shown so much of practical ability in bringing up the [Harlem] to an 8 percent investment," the *Times* wrote, "and of both ability and economy in making the Hudson River Road what is acknowledged to be . . . that this calculation was generally accepted as a sound opinion." Cynical observers on Wall Street saw a stockjobbing ploy behind every corporate decision, but the *Times* demurred. "Mr. Vanderbilt emphatically declared that he should keep his present large holdings . . . to the close of his days, or so long as he is permitted to participate in the management of the property."[10]

The Commodore also paid attention to the physical dimensions of his budding railroad system. In mid-1867, he realized that new construction would be necessary to integrate his two lines into Manhattan, to make the most efficient use of the strengths of each. The Hudson River had a level, double-tracked route with easy curves, allowing locomotives to pull more cars, use less fuel, and increase speed relative to other lines. It had access to the slips on the west side, convenient for freight handling. The Harlem possessed a portal in the center of Manhattan, which best served passengers. Vanderbilt planned a link between them close to the city: the Spuyten Duyvil Railroad, a short line that would curve along the Harlem River. The legislature chartered the company on April 24, and Vanderbilt took virtually all of the five thousand shares (later increased to a total of ten thousand, representing an investment of $1 million). Work would not begin until 1870, after a long struggle to secure the right of way, but the little line would prove to be an essential piece of Vanderbilt's kingdom.[11]

Of course, both these tangible and intangible creations remained within the parochial confines of New York. It was the presidency of the Central that would make Vanderbilt a national figure again, by giving him control of one of the four trunk lines that crossed the Appalachians. But the very success of the railroads over the past decade presented the trunk lines with a conundrum: the center of population and commerce had drifted far beyond their western termini (Buffalo for the Central, for example, and Pittsburgh for the Pennsylvania). They now depended heavily on connecting lines to such cities as Detroit, Cleveland, St. Louis, and Chicago. Managing their relations with these often quarrelsome connections posed a serious problem.

When it became clear to Vanderbilt that he would gain control of the Central at its annual election in December, he began to address this delicate matter of railroad statecraft. The Central had two routes to Chicago: the North Shore and the South Shore, named for their relationship to Lake Erie. On the North Shore, the Central connected via the Suspension Bridge over the Niagara River to the Great Western Railway of Canada, which used a ferry at Detroit to tie into the Michigan Central, which ran through to Chicago. On the South Shore, a chain of roads ran from Buffalo to Toledo; from there the Michigan Southern & Northern Indiana extended to Chicago. Vanderbilt invested in some of the South Shore lines and placed men on their boards of directors as these companies began a process of consolidation with each other that would not be complete for another two years. When he prepared a list of directors for the Central election coming in December, he included Amasa Stone Jr., an important South Shore railroad man from Cleveland.[12]

These steps worried the North Shore men, namely James F. Joy and the New England investors who had hired him to manage the Michigan Central. They believed that Vanderbilt, as president of the New York Central, probably would discriminate in favor of his South Shore connections, since that was where he had invested his own money. "I had seen by the NY papers that Vanderbilt probably had the control of the NY Cenl," Nathaniel Thayer, a Boston financier, wrote to Corning on November 26. "Two weeks ago Joy was in NY when Comodore [sic] V. sent for him." Vanderbilt had reassured Joy that he could "depend upon a perfectly fair course being taken, and that he knew we could injure the NY Cenl. more than they could us. We shall soon see however what course they will take—and must act accordingly."[13]

Joy shared Thayer's suspicions, even after his conference with the Commodore. William hurried to reassure him. "I think you have in some way received an impression that the management of this & NY Cent roads desire to run their trains regardless of the connecting roads," he wrote to Joy, under the letterhead of the Hudson River Railroad, "and I am most anxious to dispel any such ideas. I think we are fully aware of the importance of maintaining the most friendly relations with our connexions."[14]

The words speak for themselves. As always, the Commodore relied first on diplomacy. Aware of the intricately interwoven web of railroad interests, he carefully avoided alienating his partners, even at the expense of some of his own investments. In the end, the Michigan Central's executives would admit that he remained fair and impartial with them. It may well be that he invested in the South Shore lines because that route was more troublesome than the North Shore (in which he would have to deal with only two well-run companies). That persistent problem in the railroad system—fragmentation—created complications on the South Shore that would grow into a crisis, one that would force Vanderbilt to conquer yet again. But not until after he had gone to war with Daniel Drew one last time.

JOY AND THAYER'S WORRIES spoke to the paradoxical nature of Vanderbilt's reputation at this critical moment. On the eve of his ascension to power in the New York Central, he already stood as an icon of the best and the worst in the new corporate economy. R. G. Dun & Co. summed up the contradiction on July 2, 1867, in that five-word description quoted previously: "Good as gold but sharp." Good as gold, because none could deny Vanderbilt's "great skill, energy, experience, and business tact," as a Buffalo newspaper wrote. "He is a shrewd, far-seeing, and far-reaching man." Wall Street marveled at his accomplishment in turning the Harlem into a profitable, dividend-paying railroad. He won particular praise for his economical management. In the Harlem, he claimed to have reduced expenses by $1.6 million per year. In the Hudson River, he gave instructions to a similar end: "If we can do this business as cheaply as the boats, let us do it, and do it just as cheap as we can."[15]

His honesty attracted great admiration, for this was an era when even the best corporate officials routinely engaged in self-dealing, as they had since the first appearance of railroads in the 1830s. In the Pennsylvania— called by Azariah Boody "the most perfect road in this country"—the highly professional president and vice president, J. Edgar Thomson and

Thomas A. Scott, demanded kickbacks in the form of stock from outside contractors, such as sleeping-car and express companies. In the Central, Corning and other directors had ordered the company to purchase iron, goods, and services from their own firms. "The pecularity of Mr. Vanderbilt's railroad management," *Putnam's Monthly Magazine* wrote, "is that, instead of seeking to make money out of the road in contracts and side speculations, he invests largely in the stock, and then endeavors to make the road pay the stockholders." The only compensation he accepted as president of his roads was in dividends on his own shares. "I manage it [a railroad corporation] just as I would manage my individual property. That is my notion, and the way I think a railroad ought to be managed," he told the assembly committee in February. When he did manipulate share prices, he only drove them up.[16]

But he was sharp. In March 1866, the *American Phrenological Journal* saw "Firmness" and "Self-Esteem" in the high crown of his skull. "His will, self-reliance, and ambition to achieve success are *immense*." When he demonstrated those traits in the blockade of the Central, the non-phrenological press decided that they might not be so healthy for the public. "Mr. Vanderbilt is a bold, outspoken man, and, backed by immense private wealth, can afford to say and do things which ordinary and prudent railway people and even very respectable stockjobbers would hesitate to commit themselves," the *Times* wrote on February 7, 1867. "As the Colossus of Roads, he thinks as little of defying public opinion as when he used to snap his fingers at the world of California travel when he was dictator of steamship competition." The *Round Table* wrote of the blockade, "Mr. Cornelius Vanderbilt proceeded to show to what sublimity of insolence the chieftains of the railway banditti have attained. . . . Railway wars, according to the Vanderbilt view, are to be waged against the passengers."[17]

The enormous impact of this one man's decision to blockade the Central—even if it was short-lived—made him the personification of the unprecedented size and power of railroads. The Jacksonian fear of aristocracy and distrust of corporations reemerged in new form as the railroads became the only large-scale mode of transportation. Even before the blockade, the *Times* had singled out Vanderbilt for abuse in a scathing editorial, "The Tyranny of Corporations," that was about these larger changes. "There is no nation on earth where they are so utterly under the control and at the mercy of gigantic corporations and monopolies as in the United States," it claimed.

The tendency of power—of the modern aristocracy of capital—is toward disregard of individuals and individual convenience and comfort. We already begin to feel the first grindings of the approaching tyranny of capitalists or corporations. . . . Every public means of transit is in the hands of the tyrants of modern society—the capitalists. . . . Even the State Legislatures can barely hold their own against these powerful monopolies. They can bribe and bully and cajole, so as to squelch any bill directed against them.

In this essay, one can hear the writer straining to construct a new political matrix to account for conditions that antebellum Americans had only begun to glimpse in the 1850s. These words were heartfelt, but did not reflect a coherent critique of corporate power in a democratic society. The *Times* admitted, "It is no part of our present purpose to suggest a remedy. Indeed, we must frankly confess we see none."[18]

Inconclusive as this outcry may have been, it appeared in one publication after another, often in the context of an attack on Vanderbilt. On December 15, 1866, *Harper's Weekly* published an essay titled "King Corporation," arguing, "Some method must be devised of emancipating the country from the tyranny of these vast corporations." The *Cleveland Leader* wrote on January 21, 1867, "The tendency of great railroad corporations has been to become monopolies of the most unblushing and reckless character."[19]

On February 9, the *Round Table* published the lambasting of Vanderbilt quoted previously—but, unlike the *Times* or *Harper's*, it offered a solution: "Congress, under its power to regulate interstate commerce, is the only source whence effectual remedy can come." Of course: this was the obvious method, if Americans truly wished to regulate railroads. Generally speaking, the railroad (with the telegraph) was the first kind of company to straddle state lines, and it nearly monopolized interstate commerce. But neither the government nor the public was ready for federal regulation. Despite the expansion of federal power during the war, Washington still lacked a nonpartisan, professional civil service that could undertake such a vast and complex task as overseeing the railroads. Nor did the political will for it exist yet. But it was coming.[20]

None of this particularly mattered to the New York Central stockholders. The Vanderbilt they saw was the economical, energetic, far-seeing executive who promised to energize a leaderless trunk line. By the second week in November the Commodore had guaranteeed his success in the December election. To persuade the public—and his enemies—that he had widespread support, he and a party of socially prominent stockholders published a rather contrived exchange of letters. John Jacob Astor Jr., Edward Cunard, John Steward, and others in control of more than $13 million in stock formally asked Vanderbilt to lead the Central and enact "a thorough reformation in the management of its affairs." He accepted.

In reprinting the correspondence, the *New York Herald* offered a prag-matic commentary. "That the result aimed at will be beneficial to the stockholders of all the roads mentioned cannot be doubted," its financial writer said, "and although there is a look of monopoly about it, the practi-cal effect may be unobjectionable to the public."[21] For the stockholders, this was all that mattered. If Vanderbilt truly was becoming society's new tyrant, at least he made the trains run on time—and profitably.

But there was another trunk line in New York, one in which Daniel Drew reigned as treasurer. In taking the Central, Vanderbilt would come to the conclusion that he must drive Drew off the Erie board. It would be the costliest mistake he ever made.

THE YEAR 1867 WAS ONE OF momentous business for one Cornelius Vanderbilt—and of momentous personal developments for three Cor-nelius Vanderbilts: the Commodore; his benighted son; and his grandson, the oldest of William's four male children. "Handsome, serious, high-minded, industrious, efficient, and thorough," Louis Auchincloss des-cribes the grandson—Cornelius Vanderbilt Jr., as he was now known. He "got on well with his grandfather—no easy task." The well-educated scion of Staten Island had started out at the Shoe and Leather Bank in New York. After a certain period, the Commodore saw that he received a posi-tion at the banking and brokerage house of Kissam Brothers, and then he brought him in to work for the Harlem Railroad.[22]

The Commodore took a special interest in his namesake. Since young Cornelius was the presumed heir of the patriarch's presumed heir, this was natural enough, but the young man's name may have been a crucial factor. The aged founder of the family treasured those two words, Cornelius Vanderbilt. Throughout his life he had christened boats, ships, and chil-dren after himself until finally he ceased to produce them. The details of his beliefs about the power of words lie beyond detection, but it is signifi-cant that "name" is a synonym for reputation. He prized his "character," to use an old term, for honor, honesty, strength, and sagacity. The son who bore his name lacked all of those traits, to his bitter disappointment; but now he had a chance to reach down two generations, to build his dynasty by molding the character of another, better Cornelius.

On February 4, 1867, Cornelius Vanderbilt Jr. married Miss Alice Gwynne at the Episcopal Church of the Incarnation on Madison Avenue. The new Mrs. Vanderbilt came from a respectable family. She shared her husband's seriousness, his deep sense of responsibility to the family he was destined to lead. "One of Alice's nieces described her to me as 'pompous,' " Auchincloss writes, "but an old gentleman who had known her well insisted that, on the contrary, she had been . . . 'very definite and straightforward, with no airs at all.' Yet both descriptions might have been true, as they both might have been true of Queen Victoria. Alice's supposed pomposity might have consisted only in her concept of the role she deemed it her duty to fulfill." With the Commodore still very much in control of the clan, and William waiting to take his place, the young couple would have ample time to learn both the social and business roles laid out for them. And the Commodore soon accelerated his grandson's education. Three months after the marriage, he made Cornelius Jr. the treasurer of the Harlem Railroad, an enterprise that had a special place in the Commodore's heart.[23]

Cornelius Jeremiah resented his nephew's public appropriation of the designation "Cornelius Vanderbilt Jr." But self-loathing often manifests itself as bitterness toward others, just as helplessness can result in hatred of those who offer help. Corneil plunged to new depths after his discharge from the Litchfield asylum, writing bad checks and issuing fraudulent promissory notes. He often left Hartford to prowl his favorite gambling haunts in New York. In 1867, he stayed at the United States Hotel on Fulton Street, and befriended one of the proprietors, George N. Terry. The two men soon became very close friends.[24]

Corneil needed friends. For one thing, he was arrested on civil process for his unpaid checks. And, with more than $50,000 in debts (including $13,905 owed to Horace Greeley), he made plans to file for bankruptcy on October 1. As he explained in yet another pathetic letter to Greeley, he had pawned two gold watches, more than $2,000 worth of silver dinnerware, "a very costly bracelet & splendid set of *coral* belonging to my wife. She let me have them with her usual desire to please, and hardly dared to refuse my crazed, rascally demands. . . . God forgive me for taking advantage of such an ennobling disposition." To paraphrase the Book of James, repentance without works is dead; Corneil's was, as a doorknob.[25]

Just how dead could be seen in a letter he wrote to Nathaniel P. Banks, the Union general whom Corneil had besieged for money and favors in New Orleans. "I write to inform you that owing to the very weak condition of my mind for the last few years, I have become involved in a series of financial difficulties from which I can only obtain relief through bankruptcy," he told Banks, implying that he was a victim, preyed upon by others. "I take pleasure in stating that my general reconstruction has become an accepted fact by my relatives and friends. . . . My family will soon have an opportunity to display their magnanimity when matters of my personal honor are involved."[26] The words seem so bitter and so sarcastic, and were so false.

His anger at himself and all others now overwhelmed the oily solicitousness that usually flowed from his pen. After his bankruptcy proceedings, he wrote to William, "Your course toward me through the last four years has been unkind. . . . You perfectly ignored me in my dark and trying days and withheld from me every particle of your aid and encouragement." This was not true. Though William undoubtedly arched a censorious eyebrow at his younger brother's wastrel ways, he had supported his effort to reform himself in Litchfield. But Corneil was an addict. Typically, what had sparked his self-righteous outrage was William's refusal to give him money. "You promised me upon your honor that you would give me $150," Corneil wrote. "It appears that you are even now working underhandedly to injure me with my father at the very moment that I am gaining his confidence and respect."[27]

A decade later, Corneil's accusations would foster an image of William as a manipulator who schemed to influence his father behind the scenes. He was not. The Commodore came to his own harsh conclusions about his younger son without William's help, and Corneil had little hope of ever regaining his confidence and respect.

Curiously, Corneil's patron Greeley formed an intersection between the two episodes that most strongly marked the Commodore's own personal life in 1867. In recent months, the famous editor seems to have struck up a friendship with Vanderbilt. This was in spite of Corneil's debt, not because of it. Vanderbilt refused to pay it, and Greeley refused to ask.[28] Rather, Greeley needed help for something else, a mission that would become increasingly important to the Commodore, until it became his most cherished project: to heal the divide between North and South. The first step, Greeley thought, was to free Jefferson Davis.

Soon after Lee's surrender, the federal authorities had arrested Davis. They incarcerated him at Fortress Monroe, Virginia, month after month, year after year, without charges, without any sign that they might prosecute him. As early as June 1865, Davis's wife had written to Greeley to ask for help in at least bringing about a trial. Greeley sought advice, investigated Davis's connection to mistreatment of Union prisoners of war, and finally agreed to assist her. He secured the cooperation of leading Republicans, including Thaddeus Stevens and abolitionist Gerrit Smith, as well as such noted New York Democrats as Charles O'Conor, Augustus Schell, and Horace Clark. Greeley's editorials and lobbying piled pressure on President Johnson's administration. O'Conor, meanwhile, applied to the Supreme Court for a writ of habeus corpus, and Chief Justice Salmon P. Chase issued one on May 8, 1867. On May 13, army officers delivered Jefferson Davis to civil authorities. "The attorneys of the Government having announced that they were not prepared to prosecute at this term of the court, a motion was made to release the prisoner on bail," *Harper's Weekly* reported.

The bail was set at $100,000. At Greeley's request, Vanderbilt stood as one of the sureties for this huge amount; since he was the recent recipient of the congressional gold medal for his gift of the *Vanderbilt*, he made a politically (as well as financially) suitable guarantor, an emblem of national reconciliation. Clark and Schell represented him on the scene and signed the bond in his name. As for Davis, he quietly passed through New York after his release, taking a Hudson River Railroad train to Canada.[29]

Vanderbilt as healer: the role did not fit the caricature that defined his image, yet in the end it would leave a permanent imprint on the national landscape. More familiar was Vanderbilt as competitor, a part he played to immense public satisfaction in the fall of 1867. On September 30 he raced his prize horse Mountain Boy at the Fashion Course against the "fastest horses on the trotting turf." (Dexter, the unquestioned champion, recently had been purchased and retired from racing by Robert Bonner.) Driven by trainer Sam McLaughlin, Mountain Boy won the second heat in a best-of-five contest, but was edged out in the rest by Lady Thorn. McLaughlin insisted that the ground had worked against Mountain Boy, so Vanderbilt issued a challenge for another best-of-five against Lady Thorn at the Union Course for a wager of $2,500. The two horses met again exactly seven days later. "The interest created by this match in trotting circles was very great, and the betting was unprecedentedly heavy," the *New York Times* reported. Mountain Boy won easily.[30]

Vanderbilt exulted in the triumph. He and McLaughlin both publicly declared that Mountain Boy could defeat even the famous Dexter. Bonner declined to accept the challenge in a public letter to "My Dear Commodore," writing, "The good-natured contest between you and myself for the ownership of the fastest trotting horse in the world is attracting increased attention on account of the recent performances of Mountain Boy." Vanderbilt replied with his own letter to the press, claiming that Bonner had written "in a manner not in entire conformity with the rules of propriety." He disingenuously declared, "I have not been aware, Mr. Editor, that any strife has existed between Mr. Bonner and myself for the possession of the fastest horse." Of Mountain Boy, he said simply, "I thought him the best horse of his age I ever saw. . . . His performance speaks for itself. I think him the superior of Dexter."[31]

Newspapers nationwide reprinted this correspondence, demonstrating how famous Vanderbilt had become for his competitiveness and his horses. But Bonner offered a grim coda to the light-hearted exchange by bringing in bankrupt Corneil. "The disposition manifested in some quarters to hold the Commodore responsible for his son, where he has not signed for him, is, in our opinion, unjust," he wrote in his newspaper, the *Ledger*. "It is only fair towards the Commodore for us to say this; and we take pleasure in saying it, notwithstanding he manifested a little want of amiability—excusable, perhaps, in a man of his years—in replying to a good natured letter from us in a horse controversy into which he recently drew us." Corneil's bankruptcy, he noted, had left Greeley $13,905 poorer; he suggested that they stage a race between Dexter and Mountain Boy, "and offer the gate money to Mr. Greeley."[32]

On the face of it, this was a generous and reasonable suggestion, but there is no sign that the Commodore agreed. A man chooses his own friends, he believed; and when among friends, he must watch out for himself or accept the consequences.

THE GREAT ERIE WAR OF 1868 began almost invisibly. On a Sunday afternoon in the fall of 1867, Vanderbilt sat in his office with his longtime lawyer, Charles A. Rapallo, and honed a legal complaint against Daniel Drew. It laid out the details of Drew's famous 1866 bear campaign in Erie stock, and asked for an injunction to bar him from doing the same again. The papers were to be filed in the name of Frank Work, one of Vanderbilt's racing cronies. Reporters sometimes mistakenly referred to Work as Vanderbilt's nephew; he was not, though he was a partner in a brokerage house along with Samuel Barton, a real nephew who served as a director on the Hudson River and was one of Vanderbilt's favorites. But the error indicates how closely Work was identified with the Commodore.[33]

Shortly thereafter, most likely in the first week of October, Vanderbilt had occasion to explain the purpose of this planned injunction. One evening, in a private room of the Manhattan Club, he met with one of Drew's self-proclaimed enemies, the big-bearded, small-framed Jay Gould. A stock speculator as well as railroad executive, Gould told Vanderbilt that a clique had formed to seize control of the Erie Railway (as it was now formally called) and kick Drew off its board. Gould was a key, if low-profile, member of this group, assigned to obtain proxies for the cause. He had learned of the impending lawsuit against Drew, which made Vanderbilt a likely ally. Gould had come to ask for the proxy for Vanderbilt's ten thousand Erie shares.[34]

One of the clique's motives was obvious. During the war, Erie president Nathaniel Marsh had revitalized the recently bankrupt line. But his death in 1864 had left the railroad rudderless. Debt and mechanical breakdowns accumulated as Drew played on its weakness to manipulate the stock. The troubled line had enormous potential—if the "speculative director," as he was known, were removed.[35] And Gould's group had another purpose. The leader was a Boston financier named John S. Eldridge, president of the Boston, Hartford & Erie Railroad; Massachusetts had agreed to provide the line with $3 million to finish construction—if it could sell its bonds at 80. Eldridge wanted to take over the Erie to make the larger company buy his bonds.[36]

Tedious? Without a doubt. But out of such petty motives nation-shaking conflicts are born. And so are farces. The Erie War would fit both descriptions.

In that room in the Manhattan Club, the Commodore sat with Work and Richard Schell on either hand and frankly told young Gould that he didn't trust him. How could he know the clique would not "join hands" with Drew? So Gould agreed to give a bond, a financial penalty that he would pay if Drew were reelected to the board. As soon he finished the last stroke of his signature, Work handed over the proxy.

Vanderbilt then offered the reason why he "was anxious to defeat Drew," as Gould recalled—a reason that would be overlooked by posterity, but explains his role better than any other. It had nothing to do with the Erie itself, but was an indirect part of his still-unfolding campaign to take over the Central. He wished to halt the insidious effect on the money market of Drew's bear operations, an effect that destroyed credit and market values far beyond the borders of Erie stock certificates. The underlying cause was a grave weakness in the American financial system.[37]

As described earlier, the creation of a national bank system formalized the centralization of the U.S. financial structure in the city of New York.[38] With the restriction of gold to specialized uses (mostly in the import and export trade), the volume of money was ultimately pegged to the number of physical greenbacks authorized by Congress. To use the technical term, this was "high-powered money." All bank deposits and national banknotes were redeemable in greenbacks, so national banks were obligated to maintain a minimum reserve of them. The law required "country banks" to deposit reserves with national banks in designated cities, which in turn had to deposit their own reserves in New York. All year long, money flowed from the countryside toward New York, where banks loaned this surplus to stockbrokers. This was the money that brokers used to finance the purchase of securities on margin.

What went to New York did not stay in New York; like tourists from Topeka, those greenback reserves toured Wall Street and then went home again. In the fall, the harvest and shipping of foodstuffs to the seacoast—known as "the moving of the crops"—required a countermovement of currency to the countryside to accommodate the accompanying flurry of transactions. Country banks drew down their accounts in reserve cities; those banks drew down accounts in New York; and New York banks called in their loans to brokers. Stock trading slowed; prices tended to stall or fall. For this reason, Wall Street panics almost always occurred late in the year.

Economists call this problem "currency inelasticity," because the fixed quantity of high-powered money made it difficult to ease these seasonal fluctuations. Starting in the twentieth century, the Federal Reserve Bank would fine-tune the money supply on a daily basis, but in the nineteenth century there was no agency charged with such close supervision of the financial system. In fact, Treasury Secretary Hugh McCulloch determinedly made things worse. Believing that greenbacks were inflationary and literally an abomination—a violation of God's plan to make gold and silver the only money—he gradually withdrew greenbacks from circulation to enable the Treasury to redeem them in gold on demand. While orthodox policy by 1867 standards, it created deflationary pressure that was felt most strongly on Wall Street.

A man as cunning as Drew could see the vulnerabilities of this system, and he did not hesitate to deliberately manipulate it for personal gain. In early 1868, the *New York Evening Post* estimated the banks that belonged to the city's clearinghouse (including all the important ones) possessed a total greenback reserve of only $12 million, just 5 percent of their deposits and circulating notes. It was disturbingly easy for a few wealthy individuals to siphon much of that $12 million out of the system and cripple its ability to provide credit. This was done through a maneuver known as the "lock-up." A man (better yet, a group of men) with a large amount on deposit would draw certified checks against this sum. The bank was now obliged to keep those funds out of use until the checks were presented for payment. Then the perpetrator would take the checks to other banks and use them as collateral for loans, which he would take in the form of actual greenbacks; these he would lock up in a safe. Now he had removed from circulation far more money than was in his original account—and it was high-powered money. Banks, short of greenbacks, would call in loans to brokers, who would curtail trading on margin on Wall Street, causing stock prices to fall. A self-reinforcing credit crunch could ensue, as falling share values caused further reductions in loans against stock. The lock-up was a sawed-off shotgun of a financial weapon—devastating, imprecise, and likely to injure innocent bystanders.[39]

Vanderbilt accused Drew of carrying out a lock-up during his bear campaign of 1866, when he laid Erie low with his secret 58,000 shares. The chance that he might do it again posed a grave threat to Vanderbilt's campaign to conquer the Central.[40] The Commodore could afford to buy Central stock for cash, but he needed the support of a wide array of friends and allies who bought on margin and needed an easy money market to finance their purchases. More than that, Vanderbilt needed the perception that his rise to power was good for stockholders. If Drew sent the market tumbling, it would weaken the Commodore's reputation, one of his most valuable assets. And Vanderbilt faced one more worry: it was autumn. The moving of the crops was under way, and money was already tight. He had to forestall Drew's bear operations.

The explanation satisfied Gould, who went his silent way after the exchange of bond for proxy. With Vanderbilt's votes in hand, the Eldridge party looked certain to win the annual election on October 8, 1867. Drew knew he was beaten. On October 6, he called on Vanderbilt at home to beg for mercy. What Drew said is unknown, but the tight-lipped former cattle drover must have been at his most eloquent that night. Perhaps he cited their decades of friendship, the millions they had made together. Perhaps he reminded Vanderbilt of their bull campaign in Erie in 1854. They could do it again; and a rising market would help Vanderbilt conclude his operations in the Central.[41] Whatever he said, it worked.

Vanderbilt dispatched Richard Schell to fetch Eldridge and Gould and bring them to his house that evening. The Commodore explained that he had changed his mind—he wanted Drew to remain. "Some rather plain talk ensued," Gould dryly recalled. Finally they all settled on a deal. On October 8, Eldridge, Gould, and Work went onto the new Erie board along with a little-known broker named James Fisk Jr.; Drew was not elected. But one of the new directors promptly resigned, and the board named Drew to his place. Friendship had triumphed, with the help of a little trade.[42]

For Vanderbilt, everything seemed to work exactly as Drew promised in the days that followed. "These manipulators of Erie talk of putting the stock much higher," the *New York Herald* commented skeptically. The paper found Central's rising price to be still more remarkable—"ridiculous," to use the exact quote. "It is said that a certain would-be railway monopolist aspires to control it, and that he and his friends hold a large amount of the stock; but it is against the public interests that any one person should constitute himself a railway king." Drew led a pool to drive up the price of Erie, managing money contributed by Work, Richard Schell, Banker, and Steward. With the market rising, the Commodore duly conquered the New York Central in December. He little realized what treachery was in store for him.[43]

With Drew seemingly well in hand, Vanderbilt focused on reforming the management of the Central. "If I take possession of a railroad today," he explained a year later, "I send my men over it to examine it in every particular and all over. They report to me its condition, and then it is my business to see that it is kept up, equal in every respect to what it is then." This was a precise description of what he did upon taking command of the Central. On February 1, 1868, he dispatched Banker on an inspection tour with orders to examine the machine shops, ticket offices, and books kept by every office—"in fact look to every department of the company's property along its whole line." He wanted to save every shilling. As he told the treasurer, "Mr. Worcester, do everything just as you would do it if it was your own business. Vary from this only so far as the peculiar demands incidental to a corporation demand."[44]

Vanderbilt's reforms ranged from the petty to the profound. As on his other lines, he attacked the "monstrous" practice of handing out enormous quantities of free passes, restricting to himself and his vice president, Torrance, the privilege of granting them. He fired underperforming staff and eliminated patronage positions (including one held by Erastus Corning Jr.), in what one man called a "wholesale slaughter." He had William better coordinate traffic and running arrangements of the Harlem and the Hudson River. He halted the practice of using the company's money to buy stock in connecting lines. He also revoked an agreement, made when Keep and Fargo had run the board, to pay American Express $50,000 a year—a rather remarkable contract, since ordinarily express companies paid rent to railroads, not the other way around. He also fought to recover a grain elevator in Buffalo that Keep had leased to Fargo.[45]

Vanderbilt's most famous reform was the most superficial: he forbade brass ornamentation on all locomotives, to save the time spent polishing them. This one step attracted lengthy comment in newspapers and railroad journals. Clearly it sent a powerful signal that economy would be Vanderbilt's defining principle.[46]

These changes aroused bitter complaints. Impervious to them all, Vanderbilt continued to squeeze savings out of the Central. But he was never vindictive. Instead, he sought peace with the railroad's strategic partners. After all of the struggles over the previous four years, he wanted peace. According to John M. Davidson, Vanderbilt declared that "he did not wish to persecute, but rather, to forget, and heal old sores."[47]

AS 1868 BEGAN, VANDERBILT CONTINUED to participate in the bull campaign in the Erie, though it was the Central that really mattered to him. The brokers most closely identified with him were "the most steady buyers of NY Ctrl—they are buying for the Commodore's friends, who are all steadfast believers in the stock, even at these prices, for a long pull," one Wall Street denizen wrote on January 7. "Vanderbilt advises his *horse companions* to buy Central," Davidson wrote to Corning on January 14. "Told the noted driver [Dan] Mace yesterday to buy 500 shares, that he would make $25,000 in a short time." Erie tagged along, ascending to 76, its highest price since the previous summer.[48] Then, on January 22, it began to show "hesitation," according to the *New York Herald*. Something was amiss. Erie began to fall. Drew unexpectedly declared the pool operation complete and divided the profits.

Schell believed that Drew had cheated them. "There has been quite a quarrel going on for several days between Mr. Drew & Richd Schell," one financier wrote. Even as Drew had bought for the pool, for his own account he had "sold all his stock of Erie in the market, and gone largely short—in amount of nine millions of dollars. . . . Schell blows in a fearful manner—*public* & *private*—puffed up with his good fortune lately. He says that Erie will sell at *par* before next May, & threatens Mr. Drew with all kinds of prosecution & exposure." Schell informed Gould that the legal complaint against Drew—shelved as part of the peace accord—would be filed at last, unless Drew took 5,500 shares of Erie off his hands at 75 or (perhaps intending to expose the famously pious Drew as a hypocrite) paid $20,000 to the poor of New York. Drew declined.[49]

Vanderbilt's involvement in this pool is far from certain. The Commodore later claimed to have been a reluctant participant in the Erie campaign, and one insider reported, "Vanderbilt refuses to have any interest in Erie." After all, it was one thing to prevent Drew from ruining the money market; it was quite another to commit money into his hands. "There was a lot of people in the street that called themselves my friends, came up to me and pressed me very hard to go in with them," Vanderbilt later explained. "Damn your pools!" he said he replied. "It is altogether out of my line." Work and Richard Schell were in fact much more than Vanderbilt's puppets in this drama. They had pushed him to help them, not the other way around. Finally the Commodore had relented. "I had some loose money," he said. "If you want me to help you along with your Erie I will help you along," he recalled saying to them. "And they got me engaged in it, and I bought a pretty large amount of Erie."[50]

But then Drew cheated, and whether he cheated Vanderbilt directly or his friends mattered little to the outraged Commodore. More than that, Vanderbilt's strategic concerns may have motivated him to move against his treacherous old friend. The new Erie board negotiated to lay a third rail on the Michigan Southern's track, to allow the Erie's broad-gauge rolling stock to pass over its standard-gauge line to Chicago; and Michigan Southern already discriminated against the Central in favor of the Erie. It seems that honor and economics both impelled Vanderbilt to proceed with the long-threatened lawsuit.[51] On February 15, Work filed the complaint against Drew and his fellow Erie directors in New York's Supreme Court. (Despite the name, the Supreme Court was a trial, not appellate, court.) As mentioned earlier, it asked the court to halt Drew's trading in Erie stock and force the return of his secret 58,000 shares (which he had used to cheat the pool).[52]

Rapallo, as Work's attorney, filed the motion with the least respected, least honest, most notorious jurist in New York, Judge George G. Barnard. "Barnard," historian Allan Nevins wrote, "was an insolent, overbearing man of handsome face and figure who had for a time hypocritically posed as a reformer." He was not. Nor was he very, or even minimally, learned. "The court-room of Judge Barnard has been a place of amusement, where lawyers and others go to hear something 'good,' " the *New York Tribune* later wrote. "Every day his indecent sarcasms and vulgar jests keep his court-room crowded with laughing spectators." An ally of William Tweed, he had a reputation for being, as one newspaper wrote, "a most merchantable judge."[53]

Barnard issued an injunction against Drew that barred him from the stock market. Two days later, Rapallo appeared before him again, acting in the name of New York's attorney general, to ask that Drew be removed from the Erie board. Barnard delivered a temporary order to that effect.[54] With Drew thoroughly enjoined, Vanderbilt charged into the Erie china shop, determined to corner his old friend and punish him for his treachery. He gave orders to his brokers to buy all the Erie they could get.

Contemporaries and historians alike have concluded that the Commodore had "marked the Erie for his own," as Charles F. Adams Jr. famously wrote, in pursuit of "absolute control over the railroad system." Biographer Wheaton J. Lane claimed that Vanderbilt aimed at "ending competition between [the New York Central] and the Erie," by buying up the latter line.[55] Wasn't his course toward monopoly obvious, as he moved from Harlem to Hudson River to New York Central? The Erie was the closest and most troublesome of the trunk lines; it seemed a natural target.

The Commodore himself thought otherwise. "I never had any intention of taking possession of or having anything to do with the Erie road— I mean in the management of it," he later told a committee of the state assembly. "I never had the slightest desire; damn it! Never had time to. It is too big a thing!"[56]

Vanderbilt's words demand attention, for, flawed as he was, he was never a liar. And there is good reason to believe him. For one thing, he never launched a war of aggression in all his years as a railroad leader; always he practiced diplomacy first, fighting only as a last resort. For another, Vanderbilt was still mired in the process of taking over the Central, one of the largest and most important railroads in the United States; getting a grip on its levers of power proved to be a time-consuming task. Even a partial list of his work in February alone is imposing. On the 1st, he dispatched Banker on the inspection tour mentioned above; on the 6th, he wrote to President Andrew Johnson, complaining about the customs collector at the Niagara Suspension Bridge; on the 21st, he presided over a conference of the trunk lines to coordinate rates. All the while he fought resistance to his reforms by staff at all levels. "All the Assistant Supt. are doing their best to break the road down . . . because none of them like Mr. Torrance or the Commodore," one official wrote. "The way the road is now managed is most ridiculous in the extreme. . . . It is perfect confusion from one end to the other."[57] Soon afterward, a strike broke out in the Albany machine shops because Torrance had reduced the men's hours and wages, then restored the hours but not the wages. Vanderbilt himself had to intervene to settle it.[58] Seizing the Erie, in the midst of this enormous internal struggle, would have been too big a thing indeed. The surprising truth is that Vanderbilt fought one of the greatest business conflicts in American history purely out of a desire for revenge.

Drew's fellow Erie directors, unfortunately, could not see into the Commodore's heart. Their eyes were fixed instead on the stock certificates piling up in his safe, which made them fear that they would lose control of their railroad. Gould, Fisk, and Eldridge had come into the Erie in order to drive out Drew, but Vanderbilt's vengeance ironically forced them to rally around him and make his cause their own.

To defeat the attempted corner, they engaged in a stock-watering operation of unprecedented size and speed. In essence, they would drown Vanderbilt in new shares, created under cover of the law that permitted the conversion of bonds into stock. First, they approved an issue of $5 million in convertible bonds and sold them to Drew's broker. They also entrusted the "speculative director" with ten thousand new shares converted from the securities of a recently leased railroad, the Buffalo, Bradford & Erie. Then they established a fund of $500,000 in cash to pay for legal expenses—or what have you. On March 5, Erie attorney David Dudley Field approached a close friend of Barnard's and offered him $5,000 to convince the judge to modify his injunction; the friend declined, so Field placed the cash elsewhere. With these preparations made, Drew sold Erie short to Vanderbilt in massive quantities. He also took elaborate steps to have front men deliver the new shares in order to hide his hand from the courts.[59] The trap was set.

THE COMMODORE HAD NO CORONATION as railroad king—but New York's aristocrats acknowledged early on that he had founded a dynasty. On February 18, William's eldest girl, Louisa, married Elliott F. Shephard at the Episcopalian Church of the Incarnation, on Madison Avenue and Thirty-fifth Street. The chapel was jammed "by the fashionable denizens of Murray Hill, Fifth Avenue, and Madison Avenue," one newspaper reported. "The streets in the vicinity were lined with carriages for a quarter of a mile." Afterward the reception was held at William's new house on

Fifth Avenue. "For four hours the elite of the town flowed in and out, and it was altogether a splendid affair. The new home of Mr. Vanderbilt is the most elegant in its interior of any house in town." New York's ballrooms would not be barred to William's princeling children.[60]

Sadly, no one would confuse Ellen Vanderbilt with a princess. The respectable daughter of a prosperous New England merchant, she had married the son of one of the wealthiest men in the world, only to be thrown into poverty and disgrace. Yet she stood loyally by Corneil. Only Greeley shared her faith in her husband—in part because of his affection for her. "I but interest myself in the Commodore's good will to his son and namesake, but I know he cannot in any case leave you destitute, for he knows how nobly you have deserved his highest appreciation," he wrote her on March 8. "Even should he leave your husband nothing, he will leave a good income to you, and in that faith I rest content. . . . I know that he [the Commodore] has been sorely tried, and I can only hope that he will live to realize and put faith in his son's devotion."[61]

Ellen needed more than sympathy. The couple had emerged out of Corneil's bankruptcy penniless. In order to "commence housekeeping once more," she told Greeley, she needed money, though "I am really ashamed" to ask for more.[62]

Within the walls of 10 Washington Place, the fate of Corneil and Ellen remained a matter of dispute between Cornelius and Sophia. The Commodore simply didn't trust his son. He demanded that Corneil swear that he never again would borrow money; even then, he refused to help. "Father Vanderbilt is waiting to see us started, & in course of the summer he will be vastly more liberal than at present," Ellen wrote. "But he says we must get started first, & it certainly is strange he does not consider our extra wants & make some appreciation requisite. But he does not." The Commodore kept a close watch on his son's financial doings, as Ellen complained to Greeley. "I feel that you are in fact the only person on whom we can rely to keep our affairs from the world, & this is just the reason we ask you, as others would at present undoubtedly assist us, but father Vanderbilt would probably hear of it a day or two afterwards."

"Mother Vanderbilt," on the other hand, "aids us all in her power. She sent me last week a large quantity of linen, & other things, & says she shall continue to assist us as far as she is able. I think she has no patience with the Commodore for what she calls 'his stubborn inconsistency'!"[63] The divide between the two parents over their troubled son had continued—though, tellingly, it was no operatic feud. Sophia did not rage at her husband, just lost "patience."

If tension was muted between Mother and Father Vanderbilt, it was still tension. Sophia aided the bankrupt couple secretly, lest she arouse her husband's wrath. One did not defy his will lightly; already his power and forcefulness had become proverbial in American culture. On February 17, for example, a religious periodical sought to express the glory of Jesus Christ by equating the Son of God with Vanderbilt—"and none can get a pass on his railroad without respect and loyalty for the Bible." In the *New York Times* that same day, Albert DeGroot proposed a fund to build a life-size statue of the Commodore atop the mighty freight depot currently under construction in St. John's Park. "The public spirit, energy, and indomitable nerve of the great steamboat and railway king merits some such recognition," he wrote. Vanderbilt's admirers began to contribute as his detractors muttered that yes, he certainly had nerve.[64]

A FEW MORE STEPS, and the steel jaws would snap shut. With the secret new stock certificates rolling off the presses, the Erie directors prepared for war with Vanderbilt by withdrawing from the trunk line compact, which freed them to slash rates in competition with the Central. Drew secured a delay of his hearing before Barnard, and hurriedly distributed the fresh shares to his front men. On March 5, in the final piece of preparation, the Erie lawyers appeared in remote Broome County, New York, before Judge Ransom Balcom, who agreed to suspend Work from the Erie board and to bar him—and the New York State attorney general—from pursuing their lawsuits. The attorneys took advantage of a quirk in New York's judicial structure that gave every one of the thirty-three Supreme Court judges jurisdiction over the entire state, a flaw that fed rampant corruption in the legal system. "The New York community is not apparently unaccustomed to seeing one justice of its Supreme Court enjoining another," the *American Law Review* commented, "on the ground that his respected associate has entered into a conspiracy to use his judicial power in a stock-jobbing operation."[65]

A bewildering blizzard of lawsuits and injunctions began to snow paper across the desks of judges and lawyers across the state, giving Drew the legal cover to deliver giant blocks of new shares into Vanderbilt's hands. The courts and markets erupted in chaos: the price of Erie staggered, Richard Schell and the Erie lawyers obtained fresh injunctions, the New York Stock Exchange declared the new shares invalid, and the New York State Senate created a committee to investigate the imbroglio.

But Vanderbilt continued to buy, grimly determined to corner Drew. According to rumor, his entire fortune teetered on the brink as he fought to put up margins on millions of dollars' worth of questionable Erie stock (questionable, because the Erie board had not secured the approval of the shareholders to issue convertible bonds, as required by law). Supposedly he pressured banks to lend to him on the threat of selling off his Central stock and causing a general panic. If only half of the gossip was half true, he was in a desperate spot.

On March 10, with losses mounting, Vanderbilt suffered perhaps the most dangerous blow of all: Drew and the Erie board conducted a lock-up. "The Erie Company is understood to have drawn nearly the whole of the balance from its bankers in this city . . . including some of the proceeds of the recent sale of ten millions of convertible bonds," the *New York Herald* reported. The *Times* estimated that $5 million or $6 million in cash— formerly Vanderbilt's—had been withdrawn from the financial system (the Erie directors claimed $8 million), which forced bankers to call in loans, driving up interest rates and shaking down stock prices across the board.[66]

The farcical Judge Barnard decided that the farce must end. Despite the injunctions against his injunctions, he issued contempt citations for the entire Erie board. David Dudley Field, the railroad's esteemed chief attorney, advised that the distinguished directors go on the lam. "Anticipating a sudden visit by the officers of the law, a regular stampede took place Thursday morning [March 12] among the officials," the *New York Herald* reported, "each one lugging off an account book, desk, drawer, or as much of the red tape documents as could be grasped in the hurry of the moment." Carrying millions in greenbacks, bonds, and stocks, the officers of one of the largest corporations in the United States scampered aboard the ferry to Jersey City, where they crowded into Taylor's Hotel, a brick building with yellow doors hard by the ferry dock. "The proprietor was called for; a brief conference ensued, and the company passed to an upper room of the hotel, strict orders being given as to the admission of visitors."[67]

Gould and Fisk remained behind. On the evening of March 15, the officers tracked them to Delmonico's, where they were enjoying a luxurious meal. They dashed into the street, boarded a carriage, and rattled to the Canal Street dock. They secured an open boat and, with two hired hands, rowed into a dense fog that had settled on the Hudson. As they meandered the wide river, bellowing into the darkness, they heard a paddlewheeler bearing down on them. They clutched at the guardrails as their boat was swamped, and were hauled aboard. Soon after they joined their colleagues at Taylor's Hotel.

The desperate flight to New Jersey left the public agog. What had been merely a private (if outlandish) fight over a disreputable stock became a symbol of all that seemed wrong in post–Civil War America: public corruption, grasping monopolists, outsize corporations, and an utter disregard for morality. As Charles F. Adams Jr. would write, "The American people cannot afford to glance at this thing in the columns of the daily press, and then dismiss it from memory. It involves too many questions; it touches too nearly the national life."[68] *Harper's Weekly* wrote:

> The wealth and importance of the contesting roads; the prominence of the two men who control them and who direct this war; the singularity, not to say the illegality, of the judicial proceedings in the case; the amount of money involved in the quarrel; the numbers of brokers, bankers, and speculators engaged, pecuniarily, in it; the vigor and boldness of the effort to take possession of the Erie road; the not less bold maneuvre of a change of base to New Jersey soil—in short, all the circumstances of the rivalry make it one of the "stories of the street."[69]

Who was worse? Vanderbilt, who seemed to seek a monopoly of New York's railroads, or Drew and company, who defied both the law and business ethics with their stock watering and flight? Few saw any reason to choose between two sides of the same evil.

Crowds formed around the brick walls of "Fort Taylor," as the newspapers dubbed the hotel, amid rumors of a planned assault by hoodlums hired by Vanderbilt. A reporter for the *New York Herald* went in and found ten men seated for dinner in a special room—Drew, Eldridge, Gould, Fisk, and other directors and brokers. "Everyone appeared in good humor, and each seemed to relish a good joke which had just been told about Mr. Fisk, who was represented in one of the papers as armed to the teeth," the reporter wrote. "A good burlesque, on my soul; very good indeed, ha, ha," responded Fisk, who was described as "a gentleman with luxuriant tufts of hair and Dundreary mustache who sat at a corner of the table draining a glass."[70]

Fisk emerged as the public face of exiled Erie. Part clown, part generalissimo—"with shining buttons and studs and rings, and an immense shirt bosom, and a porcine carcass," as William Lloyd Garrison later described him—he was a gifted and often hilarious orator who declaimed freely to any reporter in his vicinity.[71] A former peddler and the son of a peddler, he once had rattled down the back roads of New England atop a wagon full of trinkets. He had joined a merchant house in Boston, helped Drew find a buyer for the Stonington steamboats, and made his way onto Wall Street, where he started a disreputable brokerage house, Fisk & Belden, with partner William Belden.

But Fisk was also shrewd. He seized on the image of Vanderbilt as a monarchical monopolist to win sympathy for their conjuring of stock and run from justice. He attributed to the Commodore alone the decade-old effort by the trunk lines to coordinate rates, and claimed that the result had diverted shipments of foodstuffs to Philadelphia and Baltimore instead of New York. "This struggle, then," he pronounced, "was in the interest of the poorer classes especially. Vanderbilt opposes the laying of the broad gauge track* [sic] on the Erie Railroad, which would secure such an abundance of provisions in the New York market from the West as to considerably reduce the current prices." When asked how long the directors would remain in New Jersey, he grandly declared, "We must throw personal comforts in the balance. Six weeks, six months, or six years are all equal to us in this sense. Just see and judge for yourself." It was bravado, yes, but he knew the importance of impressing the enemy with a sense of their determination. By contrast, Vanderbilt remained out of sight, turning away reporters.[72]

The legal comedy continued. Barnard appointed Vanderbilt's son-in-law—and Barnard's good friend—George A. Osgood as receiver for the proceeds of the enjoined stock. Then Osgood was enjoined by an Erie-friendly judge. At one point Osgood sprinted up his stoop and darted inside to avoid the service of papers, which were hurled at him and bounced off the door. New Jersey passed a law to make the Erie a corporation of the Garden State, offering the fugitives a home across the Hudson.

For all the laughter these events produced, the real battle now shifted to Albany. Vanderbilt's attorneys argued that Erie's convertible bonds were illegal, because the Erie's directors had not secured the required approval of two-thirds of the stockholders. A state senate committee began to consider a bill to legalize the enormous increase in stock, in the name of preventing a monopoly under Vanderbilt.[73]

Senator Abner C. Mattoon belonged to that committee. He had heard rumors that each side would spend up to a million dollars in the notoriously corrupt legislature to secure or kill the Erie bill. In the interests of justice—justice to himself—he visited Drew in New Jersey. Knowing the Erie directors' concern for the poor, Mattoon began to muse aloud about what little income legislators received. "We cannot go there and live upon what we get," he reflected sadly. Drew recalled, "The inference I drew was that he would take money if it was offered to him." Soon afterward Mattoon visited the other Erie directors in Taylor's Hotel. He told them that Vanderbilt's allies and attorneys were lobbying vigorously; soon Mattoon's committee would approve a report condemning one side or the other, most likely Erie. Mattoon, ever helpful, urged the exiled directors to send one of their number to Albany—preferably well funded.[74]

---

* The Erie already had a broad gauge. Presumably Fisk misspoke or was misquoted, and meant a third rail on the Michigan Southern.

The assignment fell to Jay Gould. If Fisk was the ideal spokesman at the besieged Fort Taylor, the discreet and cunning Gould made the perfect bribe-giver. "On March 30," writes biographer Maury Klein, "he left Jersey City with a suitcase full of greenbacks and a ready reserve of checkbooks. For three days he wooed legislators with a liberal supply of food, drink, and greenbacks." Now that Gould was in New York State, he was prey to Barnard's contempt citation. But his hearing was delayed, and Gould convinced the court officer who arrested him to serve as his bodyguard. "You may go with me," he said. "I will still be in your custody."[75]

The allegations of corruption remain impossible to verify in detail. A committee of the state senate later found solid evidence that a great deal of money had been paid in bribes by the Erie board—but it could not pin down who *received* the bribes. This is not surprising. Corruption had plagued government for decades, and a well-developed system had emerged to mask the dispersal of graft. Lobbyists who specialized in corruption were known as "strikers"; they acted as self-serving middlemen in transactions between legislators and wealthy men and corporations.

And yet, not all of what happened in Albany can be blamed on graft. Both sides of the dispute made serious arguments. The titanic watering of Erie stock struck many as illegal, not to mention immoral; and Vanderbilt's seeming attempt at monopolizing New York's trunk lines appalled others. William Cassidy, a Democratic newspaper editor, found himself confused as to the correct line to take in his editorials. "I have denounced the illegality of the overissue & the attempt to whitewash it; I will stand by that portion; but perhaps tis unwise to go further," he wrote to Samuel J. Tilden. "Our political capital is as important to us, as Vanderbilt's money to him." For honest legislators, the conundrum proved just as vexing. There is no way of knowing who voted out of conscience or calculation.[76]

Except, perhaps, for Senator Mattoon. On April 1, he gave the decisive vote in committee for a report that denounced the Erie board, declared Drew's conduct to be "disgraceful," and found that Eldridge, Gould, and Fisk were in collusion with him "in these corrupt proceedings." Gould later said that Mattoon's vote "astounded" him. He should have known better; to all appearances, it was a negotiating tactic. On April 18, after Gould had changed Mattoon's mind with crisp, green arguments, he reversed himself and voted with the senate majority in favor of the Erie bill. Vanderbilt's lobbyists abruptly withdrew from Albany. On April 20, the assembly passed the bill—which it had previously defeated—by 101 to 5, and the governor soon signed it. More than a legalization of the fresh Erie stock, the new law forbade any director of Vanderbilt's railroads from becoming a director of Erie. The Commodore had lost.[77]

Or had he? Vanderbilt appears to have pulled his forces back from the front line in Albany because he had begun to outflank the enemy in Manhattan. On April 6, Cassidy reported, "Last Sunday, Drew was at Vanderbilt's house; & yesterday the interview may have been renewed." Drew was able to visit his old friend because of a provision of New York law that gave a Sunday reprieve from arrest in civil cases. Drew later admitted, "I called on the Commodore two or three times. He always told me that I acted very foolish in going to Jersey City; I ought to have never left my home in the City." Drew sadly agreed with him. As Gould later observed, "He had got sick of New Jersey." Drew and Vanderbilt began to talk about a compromise.[78]

Drew conducted these talks without the knowledge of Eldridge, Gould, or Fisk, though they suspected that he was up to something. On Sunday, April 19, Drew offered to return Vanderbilt's money in return for the shares, saying something about wanting to take over the Erie himself. Fisk found out about the plan and immediately attached Drew's personal funds, which put a stop to the subterfuge. So Drew turned to Eldridge and convinced him to settle with the Commodore to end their exile. Soon the equally Jersey-weary Eldridge joined Drew on his secret visits to Vanderbilt.[79]

For the public, the Erie War ended suddenly and mysteriously. Even before the end of April, the Erie directors fearlessly returned to New York. Barnard spared them arrest, and the New York attorney general agreed to vacate the motion to suspend Drew from the board. But these doves of peace proved just as mysterious to two key Erie directors, Gould and Fisk. In Jersey City, the pair had forged a tight friendship, emerging as the most cunning and resilient opponents of Vanderbilt on the board. Recognizing this, Drew and Eldridge kept them in the dark as they negotiated terms.[80]

Frustrated, the two young men took a carriage early one June morning to 10 Washington Place and banged on the door. The servant showed them into the reception room, notified the Commodore, then sent them upstairs to the second-floor parlor. "Presently Mr. Vanderbilt sent for me to come into a little back room," Fisk testified. Gould waited in the parlor as Fisk went in. It seems that the flamboyant former peddler had made an impression on the Commodore—or perhaps Vanderbilt wished to see him separately as a negotiating tactic. Fisk found him sitting on his bed, putting on his shoes. "I remember those shoes on account of the buckles," Fisk later testified. "You see there were four buckles on that shoe, and I know it passed through my mind that if such men wore that kind of shoes I must get me a pair."[81]

Vanderbilt looked Fisk over sharply. "I had a very bad opinion of Mr. Fisk since I first knew him," he said later. "I thought he was a reckless man, and would do anything he undertook to accomplish a purpose."[82] But he was accustomed to dealing with enemies, even reckless ones. According to Fisk, Vanderbilt said that "several of the directors were trying to trade with him, and he would like to know who was the best man to trade with." Fisk proudly replied that Vanderbilt should trade with him, "if the trade was a good one." The Commodore ruefully said that he might be right. "Old man Drew was no better than a batter pudding, Eldridge was completely demoralized, and there was no head or tail to our concern," Fisk reported him saying. Fisk agreed.

Vanderbilt wanted to unload his 100,000 Erie shares, and demanded compensation for his losses. Eldridge had made a peace proposal that he had accepted, he said; according to Fisk, Vanderbilt argued that Gould and Fisk should "take hold of it. If we would advocate the settlement and pay his losses we should be landed in the haven where we were all desirious of being, where there was peace and harmony." Fisk said their talk grew momentarily heated.

> He said I must take the position of things as I found it. He would keep his bloodhounds on us and pursue us until we took his stock off his hands; he would be d——d if he would keep it. I told him I would be d——d if we would take it off his hands, and that we would sell him stock as long as he would stand up and take it. Upon this he mellowed down and said that we must get together and arrange this matter. I told him that we would not submit to a robbery of the road. . . . Well, he said, these suits would not be withdrawn until he was settled with.[83]

Soon after this interview, Gould and Fisk confronted Eldridge, who told them it was all over. "He was tired and worn out and had been driven away from home and wanted to get out of his troubles," Fisk recalled. "At last he had got the Commodore to settle on a price, and Schell and Work had fixed on their price, and if we would come in tomorrow we should be free and clear of all suits."

The two young men went to see Vanderbilt at his home one more time. The Commodore looked them over with respect. According to Gould, he told them that "Drew had no backbone, and if we had not come in he would have had it all his own way. . . . When we rose to come away he said to us, 'Boys, you are young, and if you carry out this settlement there will be peace and harmony between the two roads.' " Carry it out they did, but peace and harmony would prove elusive.[84]

The grand settlement was complex, and many of its details would elude contemporaries and historians alike. Of Vanderbilt's 100,000 Erie shares, he sold fifty thousand back at 80, for a total of $4 million. Except he did not actually sell it to the railroad. It was important to Vanderbilt that he technically sold the stock to Drew. As he said to Drew when they made the deal, "I must have an understanding about the matter. I will not sell the Erie Railroad anything; I will have nothing to do with it." Drew replied that he was buying the stock for himself. "I said that," Vanderbilt later explained, "because I had made up my mind the Erie Railroad had got under so many difficulties that I would have nothing to do with them."

If Vanderbilt did not sell his stock to the Erie, the Erie certainly bought it. After Drew made the original agreement, Eldridge arranged for the Erie to take the fifty thousand shares at 70, paying $3.5 million that went into Vanderbilt's hands (Drew himself paid the Commodore the remaining $500,000). The Erie also paid Vanderbilt $1 million for a sixty-day call on his remaining fifty thousand shares at 70 (that is, the Erie purchased the right to buy from Vanderbilt that quantity of stock at that price within two months). In addition to compensating Vanderbilt for his losses, this was a payment to keep the stock off the market, to give the company time to stabilize its finances. The Erie also compensated Frank Work and Richard Schell for their losses with a payment of $429,000, and paid Rapallo for his legal work with 250 Erie shares at 70. And, among other acts, the Erie also bought $5 million of Boston, Hartford & Erie bonds at 80 (accomplishing Eldridge's mission), released Drew from any claims, and settled his long-standing loan to the company. In July, Drew resigned as director and treasurer. In August, Vanderbilt carried out the final part of the agreement, buying $1,250,000 in Boston, Hartford & Erie bonds at 80. Eldridge resigned the presidency, leaving the Erie to Gould and Fisk.[85]

The Erie War proved to be the most serious defeat of Vanderbilt's railroad career. His corner had been thwarted, his attempt at revenge had failed, and his losses had been heavy—perhaps as much as $1 million, though they remain impossible to calculate. But it was not the defeat that the public imagined. Observers in Wall Street and the press saw him as a voracious monopolist, so they assumed that he had wanted the Erie itself, something he explicitly denied. Indeed, what is most striking is not the failure of his corner, but how he rallied on the brink of disaster and forced his enemies to restore much of what he had lost. Unfortunately, he could never recover his lost prestige. More serious than the hundreds of thousands that slipped from his fingers was the humiliation he had suffered at the hands of the upstart Fisk and Gould.

But even his costliest battles served as a reminder of his vindictiveness and his power. On May 19, R. G. Dun & Co. estimated his wealth at $50 million. He was "peculiar & eccentric in [character]," the agency reported, "a strong friend, a mostly bitter enemy." Drew, his oldest friend of all, would have agreed.[86]

ON MARCH 30, AS THE ERIE WAR approached its height, the United States
Senate convened as a court of impeachment for President Andrew Johnson. Most of the charges revolved around his violation of the Tenure of
Office Act, a constitutionally questionable law that limited his ability to
fire executive-branch officials without congressional approval. He had
deliberately flouted the law by sacking Secretary of War Edwin Stanton,
Commodore Vanderbilt's old friend.

The real issues driving the extraordinary trial were Johnson's personality and the nature of Reconstruction itself. Devotedly Jacksonian and vir-
ulently racist, Johnson wanted to quickly restore all-white governments
in the South. Rising violence against freed slaves drove Republicans on
Capitol Hill toward a far more expansive and direct federal role in recon-
structing the South. Johnson had thwarted them at every step, giving rise
to anger at his belligerence and sheer incompetence. Before the end of
May, the Senate acquitted Johnson on all counts, after failing to meet the
required two-thirds majority for a conviction by one vote. But congressional Reconstruction went forward. The South was divided into military
districts and put under the administration of army officers until new, more
racially just, state constitutions could be put into effect. In the old Confederacy, black voters, jurors, and officeholders appeared for the first time.[87]

In all this, Congress ventured into entirely unmapped terrain, not simply with respect to racial justice, but in terms of its own powers. The war
and continuing crisis in the South created a ferment on Capitol Hill,
opening up new possibilities. What else could the federal government do?
What *should* it do? The Republicans had been united in fighting the Civil
War, and one of the strongest arguments in favor of Radical measures
to aid freed slaves was that they had been the only consistently loyal population in the South during the conflict. But in other areas the party
remained deeply divided, and sometimes confused. On April 27, in the
midst of the impeachment trial, the House of Representatives ordered the
Committee on Roads and Canals to investigate whether Congress had
the power to regulate railroads. On June 9, the committee reported that
Gibbons v. Ogden had clearly established federal power over interstate
commerce, but the committee was not sure exactly what to do with railroads. "The question of the constitutional power of Congress to regulate
the rates of fare and charges for freight is one of very great importance
and of difficult solution," it hedged. The committee advised no action,
though it voiced a serious fear. "The great railroad corporations do possess the power and the will to absorb the lesser competing lines.... These
vast consolidated corporations have the power to crush out all competi-

tion and to fix upon such rates of fare and charges for the transportation of freight as they please to impose." But congressional interference was still too radical even for the Radicals.[88]

"We hope the question will not be allowed to drop into forgetfulness," the *Nation* responded. "The railroad corporations are already of immense power." In light of the negotiations to end the Erie War, the *Nation* thought that Vanderbilt and Drew might make an alliance "which puts for many important purposes the whole State of New York into their hands. It is plain that we need a different order of things from what we had when the Constitution was adopted, when railroads were unthought of."[89]

The Erie War proved to be a catalyst for rising anxieties over the place of the railroad corporation in a democratic society. In economic culture, railroads ran headlong against the deep Jacksonian belief that free competition was an essential component of democracy itself—that monopoly threatened free government. Their dual nature as both public works and private businesses presented a paradox: What was more important, to protect shareholders in their property rights, or to prevent a monopoly? Good management and returns on investment, or competition? When the Erie War brought this conundrum to a head, even business journals found themselves torn. The *Round Table* said, "It is very hard to understand why, if Mr. Vanderbilt does own a majority of the stock of the Erie Railway, he should not be allowed to manage it." On the other side, the *Merchant's Magazine* wrote, "While allowing that Erie would be sure of a more efficient head under his supervision than under its present and late control, yet it would be a matter of regret" if Vanderbilt added it to his empire. The *New York Times* awkwardly dodged the monopoly question when defending him: "It may be right that the amalgamation . . . of the Erie with the Central and other Vanderbilt lines should be prohibited . . . [but] nothing can justify or even extenuate the conduct of the [Erie] directors in creating ten millions of stock for speculative purposes, or in otherwise abusing their power."[90]

The *Times* editorial introduces the second current of anxiety surrounding railroads: the corruption of government. The tales of bribery that flowed out of Albany reinforced stereotypes of public officials on the take, acting as if they were retainers of wealthy corporations, not representatives of the people. After Jay Gould took over as president of the Erie, he allied the railroad explicitly with the Tweed ring, naming "Boss" Tweed himself to the board, along with his close associate Peter Sweeney.

The culmination of the Erie War, culturally speaking, would come in July 1869, with the publication in the *North American Review* of one of the most influential essays in American history: "A Chapter of Erie," by Charles F. Adams Jr.[91] (It would be reprinted in a collection, *Chapters of*

Erie, that included articles by Adams's brother Henry.) Ironic, incisive, and impressively researched, it combined a detailed account of the Erie War with an exploration of its broader meaning. "Freebooters have only transferred their operations to the land," he wrote. "It is no longer the practice of Governments and Ministries to buy legislators; but individuals and corporations of late not unfrequently have found them commodities for sale in the market. So with judicial venality."

Adams cogently expressed the anxiety that resulted from the combination of the corporation—that abstract entity feared since Jackson's day—with the size and wealth of the railroads. "Already our great corporations are fast emancipating themselves from the state, or rather subjecting the state to their own control," he wrote. It was the Commodore's mastery of this process that made him such a terrifying figure.

> In this dangerous path of centralization Vanderbilt has taken the latest step in advance. He has combined the natural power of the individual with the factitious power of the corporation. The famous "L'état, c'est moi" of Louis XIV represents Vanderbilt's position in regard to his railroads. Unconsciously he has introduced Caesarism into corporate life. He has, however, but pointed out the way which others will tread. . . . Vanderbilt is but the precursor of a class of men who will wield within the state a power created by it, but too great for its control. He is the founder of a dynasty.

Such power—concentrated in one man's hands through control of corporations—was only possible because of the centrality of the railroads to modern life. "As trade now dominates the world, and the railways dominate trade, his object has been to make himself the virtual master of all by making himself absolute lord of the railways."[92]

Adams's words captured a very real dilemma. American institutions and values stemmed from a largely rural, agricultural past in which businesses were limited in size and personal in nature. Corporations had arisen as a means of financing large public works without inflating the size and cost of government—yet they were also private property. This uncomfortable meeting of public and private aroused dark memories, particularly when focused on the person of Vanderbilt. "The country is not without experience of the dangers of intrusting so much power to an individual," one man wrote to the *Journal of Commerce*. "Nicholas Biddle and the United States Bank furnish a warning too well remembered by us who passed through the fearful ordeal caused by his abuse of power, to look with composure on the power possessed by this railroad king."[93] Of course, Jackson could control Biddle by vetoing the Bank of the United States charter and withdrawing federal deposits. In 1868 there was no such recourse with Vanderbilt. Small wonder that Adams compared him to Louis XIV.

And yet, this discussion points to a widely shared alertness to encroachments on democracy. It reflected a deep suspicion, even cynicism, about private power and public corruption. Adams and his contemporaries—and historians who followed them—were quick to believe the worst, whereas the truth was complicated and difficult to find. Even the transparently corrupt Tweed ring was a mechanism for controlling a huge, decentralized city through payoffs. "The term 'boss' applied to William Marcy Tweed or to John Kelly, his successor, is a measure of the mystery which surrounded their activities, not of their political omnipotence," writes historian Seymour J. Mandelbaum.

Journalists often claimed that railroads "bought" or "owned" state governments, but corrupt officeholders squeezed corporations as much as they obeyed them. Starting as early as the 1840s, politics had become a breeding ground for manipulators and lobbyists—those "strikers"—who abused the power of the state for the purpose of extortion. Horace Clark, for example, testified about the use of "pro-rata" bills in the state legislature to shake down railroads. Such a law would have set a single per-mile rate and prohibited discounts on through freight from competitive points; in theory, it would destroy a trunk line's ability to compete. "I think it is a fact that the introduction of those bills . . . has been done with a view to extract money from railroad companies," Clark said. "It is a very serious question for the railway managers to know what to do; and they do pay money, not to the members of the Legislature, for I don't believe that this money which is paid by a great corporation reaches members or is designed to, but goes to others who are preying upon the hopes and fears of men." The strikers knew that railroads would think it safer to give them money than to ignore them. Such payments, Clark claimed, "are not bribes but ransoms." Railroads feared government graft just as the public did, and suffered for it.[94]

Contemporaries and historians alike have carelessly lumped Vanderbilt together with Gould, Fisk, and the Erie board in their accusations of bribery. In fact, the state senate's investigation found little evidence of corruption by Vanderbilt and his agents, by contrast with the abundant proof that the Erie had poured out cash to judges and legislators. Indeed, Vanderbilt's lobbyists in Albany testified that he forbade them from buying votes (at least, not explicitly).[95] On close inspection, even the Commodore's relationship with the preposterous Judge Barnard proves to be more than a matter of graft. Little doubt exists as to Barnard's corruption, but there is no evidence that he simply took cash from Vanderbilt and did as he was told. Indeed, being a Tweed ally made him a foe of Horace Clark and Augustus Schell, who had started the Manhattan Club as a rival to the Tweed ring.[96] Even Vanderbilt's bitterest enemies never accused him of bribing Barnard; rather, they pointed out that the judge was a close friend of the Commodore's son-in-law and broker, George A. Osgood, and speculated in Erie. John M. Davidson socialized with Barnard and quoted his opinions about stocks, but his letters show that Barnard often talked down New York Central shares and took positions hostile to the Commodore. Temperamental and self-important, Barnard had his own agenda, if a dishonest one. In the Erie litigation, it simply coincided with Vanderbilt's.

These fine (but critical) details escaped opinion makers and newspaper-headline writers, let alone the public itself. "Exaggeration, misapprehension, and well-grounded allegations mingled together, and created a sense of crisis," writes Mark Summers, a historian of nineteeth-century corruption. This cynicism obstructed attempts to cure the underlying complaints. Regulation was the obvious method of keeping corporations answerable to democracy, and not the other way around—but why trust public officials to regulate if they were all on the take? The absence of a nonpartisan, professional civil service—still decades away—meant there was no easy answer. The power of the railroads gave rise to demands for a stronger government to control them, yet this same power aroused fears that they would simply corrupt a strong government, and grow still more powerful. As Adams wrote elsewhere, "Imagine the Erie and Tammany rings rolled into one and turned loose upon the field of politics."[97] Perversely, one lasting result of "A Chapter of Erie" was the doubt it cast on any solution to the problems it illuminated. And so the railroads grew still larger, and Vanderbilt more powerful.

THE VANDERBILT FAMILY SEEMED to be falling apart. In 1868, after the Commodore battled back from the brink of disaster in the Erie War, he found himself helpless to save his own loved ones. The first to go was the most vulnerable: Frances Lavinia, the invalid. Vanderbilt and Sophia buried their daughter in the family vault on Staten Island in the first week of June. The *Hartford Courant* took the occasion to report that the old man intended to "bequeath the great bulk of his property, now estimated at sixty millions of dollars, to his son William. . . . The Commodore has shown much interest in his relatives, particularly young men, and has put many of them . . . on the high road to wealth."[98]

With the family gathered in grief at 10 Washington Place, Corneil pulled his mother away from the others, "& held a long & important consultation," according to Ellen. "They both concluded it was best for him not to write his father again or in any way ask a favor at his hands." Sophia advised him to go on living quietly until January; if the Commodore did not assist him then, Corneil should take "a political position, or enter into some safe & respectable business," Ellen reported. In so many words, Sophia tried one last time to convince him to abandon his dreams of making a big score, of duplicating his father's success in one lucky strike.

"On coming home," Ellen wrote, "he seemed deeply impressed with his conversation with his mother & of his own accord assured me that he should not under any circumstances again trouble his father in any manner during the present year." She suffered for her husband's penance as much as his crimes. The couple no longer had a house or carriage, and lived in relative poverty. Even worse, Corneil sometimes turned against her in his frequent fits of self-hatred. When a close friend discussed Corneil's debts with her, he flared in anger at "this expose [sic] of my matters to *a woman*. . . . You certainly must know that I will stand no lecturing from any female." Ellen, he wrote, "has got nothing to do with my business, and . . . I am not in the least responsible to her." Yet still she defended him. "I fear you have a wrong impression in regard to his troubling his father," she told Greeley. "I know that for at least six months past he has neither personally nor by his letter asked his father a single favor, except that of recognition & this he immediately responded to satisfactorily. Cornelius has carefully avoided alluding to increase of allowance." Then she added a caveat, one that said everything about his habits and associates: "Whatever his friend may have solicited on his behalf is of course another matter."[99]

As ever, Vanderbilt declined to assist his son, convinced that it would be wasted until he reformed himself. Yet, as the *Courant* observed, he made extraordinary efforts for other young relatives. On June 27, he beseeched President Johnson to restore his grandson, Vanderbilt Allen, to the commission that the young officer had abandoned. The Commodore observed that he was departing from his "uniform practice" of never requesting public office for his friends, but, he wrote, "He is a promising young man and I am anxious to save his pride. . . . After the war was over feeling that the country could spare his services—*boy like*—[he] foolishly resigned his place to make a trip to Europe in July 1865. I want to get him reinstated." To Vanderbilt's disappointment, young Allen wanted to go into business. At least he took care of himself; the same could not be said for Jeremiah Simonson, the spendthrift nephew and master of the shipyard in Greenpoint. Vanderbilt sued him for $22,596.71 and won.[100]

In the third week of July, the Commodore traveled to Saratoga Springs as usual. He checked into the Union Hotel, a favorite of Daniel Drew. Sophia was not feeling well; in hopes of regaining her health, she went to Lebanon Springs, on the Massachusetts border southeast of Albany. There she was advised to return at once to New York, for her health was too frail. Rather than go to 10 Washington Place, where she would be alone with the servants, she stayed with her daughter Maria Louisa and son-in-law Horace Clark at their home in Murray Hill.

On August 6, a little more than two weeks after Vanderbilt went to Saratoga, he received a telegram that Sophia had collapsed with a stroke. Immediately he boarded a special train for Troy, and telegraphed an order to the Hudson River Railroad to ready a locomotive and car for him there, and to clear the track south. He found his car waiting for him, hitched to the *D. T. Vail*, driven by engineer S. F. Gregory Jr. The *Vail* roared down the rails at fifty miles an hour. "Gregory says that is the fastest he ever rode," the *Troy Times* reported, "and quite as fast as he thinks it safe to run."[101]

Sophia remained bedridden at the Clark house, and showed encouraging signs of recovery. Her husband, who had brought her so much, who had put her through so much, remained with her. He was there at one thirty in the morning on August 17, when she suffered a second stroke and died. As Greeley wrote in the *New York Tribune*, "She had lived nearly 74 years without incurring a reproach or provoking enmity."[102]

On August 19, Vanderbilt sat surrounded by family and flowers as mourners came to 10 Washington Place to pay their respects. They filed past a sleek rosewood casket, viewing Sophia's body through a lid that was glass from the bust upward. The pallbearers included Cornelius's closest cohorts, Marshall O. Roberts, Charles O'Conor, John Harper, Augustus Schell, and John Steward, and the couple's wider circle of friends— Alexander T. Stewart, William H. Bradford, and A. S. Halsted. The guests included Daniel Drew, Edwin D. Morgan (now a U.S. senator), and others of note. A short funeral service was held at ten thirty in the morning, after which the Commodore escorted his deceased wife down to Whitehall Slip and across the harbor to the family tomb.[103]

He returned to an empty house. Not literally empty, of course: the income tax assessor finally got a peek inside that year, and found an abundance of taxable possessions, including two fine watches, 468 ounces of silver dinnerware, and three carriages in the stables in the rear (in addition to $69,230 in taxable income, which did not include stock dividends).[104] Then, too, there was the staff of Irish-born servants. Not emotionally empty, either: the walls, floors, and cabinets abounded with mementos of their nearly fifty-five years together: paintings of each other, the gifts from their golden wedding anniversary. Each item served as a reminder of his loss.

The image of Vanderbilt as a man of force burns brightly in the historical eye, making it difficult to penetrate the glare to perceive a subtler vision behind it. He often comes across as having been abusive and domineering to his wife. The truth was more nuanced. Daniel Allen, for example, thought that Vanderbilt's notorious dispatch of Sophia to an asylum in 1846 was justified, that she required treatment. Ellen's letters never hinted at anger between her in-laws—and Corneil would have tried any parents' patience. Cornelius and Sophia grew rich together, traveled together, had children together, buried children together, attended the weddings of grandchildren together. They were a couple.

Perhaps the truth is not so nuanced after all: despite his shortcomings as a husband, Vanderbilt loved his wife. And her death left him alone. Of all the forms of stress that afflict human beings, one of the worst is loneliness, especially after the loss of a spouse. His unmarried sister Phebe recognized the emotional vacuum, and stepped in to supervise the maids, keep up the house, and keep up her brother.[105] He needed his sister in this hour; and through her, he glimpsed a future beyond his isolation and grief.

Chapter Seventeen

CONSOLIDATIONS

In time, all things came to the Commodore. Wealth, like mass, exerts a gravitational pull, attracting power, social recognition, and more wealth. With each fresh accumulation, its pull grows stronger. Vanderbilt was the biggest man in the biggest thing in America, the railroads, and so he drew to himself the leading figures in politics, society, and the economy. "Cornelius Vanderbilt is a man of power, unquestionably," the *Chicago Tribune* wrote. "Many fear, but few love him. . . . He is the railway king of America, and the great power of Wall Street. . . . He is so accurate a judge of men, so clear-sighted, so fertile of resource, so skilful an organizer of combinations, and the wielder of such an immense capital, that failure is next to impossible. . . . He is a foe even Wall Street stands in awe of."[1]

On April 18, 1868, in the midst of the Erie War, Vanderbilt beckoned to a thirty-year-old businessman from Ohio, a pious, long-faced oil refiner with a pinched mouth named John D. Rockefeller. Together with Henry Flagler, he had recently formed the Standard and Excelsior Oil Works in Cleveland. That put him at the forefront of one of the most important developments in the American economy. "Nothing in the history of this country," *Scientific American* had declared in 1865, "if we except the furor that followed the opening of the gold fields of California, has caused so much excitement in business circles as the rapid development of the petroleum oil interests."[2] The industry had fulfilled that excitement in the years that followed, as oil gushed out of wells in northwestern Pennsylvania to be refined into kerosene for the world's lamps. By 1868, petroleum products were a leading export, much of it shipped from New York.

Perhaps no other example better demonstrates the symbiotic relationship between railroads and industry. In part, the demands of the railroads themselves invigorated production. They consumed huge amounts of pig iron and coal, for instance; production of those commodities more than doubled in the decade after the Civil War. When Andrew Carnegie left the Pennsylvania Railroad in 1865, he invested in an iron mill, a bridge-building concern, a sleeping-car company, and other businesses that fed his former employer's voracious appetites—and helped turn Pittsburgh into a smoke-shrouded manufacturing center.[3] In addition, the railroads' craving for freight led them to radically cut rates, which encouraged new industries by lowering shipping costs. When petroleum took off in the 1860s, new lines sprang into existence to serve remote wellheads; trains clacked into the mushrooming drilling towns bearing iron, lumber, food-stuffs, and other supplies, and chuffed out hauling barrels of oil. Cleveland boomed with more than fifty refineries that clustered outside of town amid a forest of wooden tanks, pouring a waste product called gasoline into the Cuyahoga River, which caught fire regularly. The city began as a Lake Erie port, but now refiners could choose from the Pennsylvania, Erie, or Lake Shore railways to move their product for export.

When Vanderbilt took over the New York Central, he immediately inquired into its relations with the smaller lines being built into the oil region. That investigation naturally brought Rockefeller to his attention. Rockefeller and Flagler were to oil what the Commodore was to the rails: the great consolidators. They fought aggressively to bring their burgeoning industry under their own control; in so doing, they also worked to elevate Cleveland over Pittsburgh as a refining center (which they accomplished in 1869). That suited Vanderbilt's interests. Pittsburgh was the special preserve of the Pennsylvania, which currently carried the bulk of the oil traffic, but the Central connected to Cleveland through the standard-gauge Lake Shore Railway.[4]

Young Rockefeller often attended to his company's interests in New York at an office on Pearl Street, where he received the Commodore's request for a meeting at noon on April 18. He refused to go. "We sent our card by the messenger," Rockefeller wrote to his wife in Cleveland, "that Van might know where to find our office." The response showed Rockefeller's confidence; with so many routes to port, he knew the strength of his bargaining position. But the Commodore's gravity was too powerful to escape. In the afternoon, Rockefeller stopped by the St. Nicholas Hotel and saw his card in the hand of Amasa Stone Jr., a New York Central director from Cleveland. Stone explained that the Commodore had assigned him to secure the oil traffic. "We talked *business* to Amasa & guess he thinks we are rather prompt young men," Rockefeller wrote. At Stone's urging, he met with Vanderbilt that evening in the Manhattan Club, where they began a long, frustrating, but fruitful relationship.

The power of attraction worked both ways. Vanderbilt could be solicitous as well as commanding; Rockefeller himself wrote, "He is anxious to get our business, and said thought he could meet us on the terms."[5] Within the railroad industry, too, business logic demanded that the Commodore build close relationships with lines to the west. Previously freight from Chicago, Detroit, or Cleveland went by boat over the Great Lakes to Buffalo; now trains hauled most of it. The connecting lines needed to cooperate to coordinate schedules, set rates, divide costs, and allow freight to move without breaking bulk if at all possible. As early as May, William wrote to James F. Joy, chief executive of the Michigan Central and a broad network known as "the Joy roads," and asked him to meet with the Commodore. William assured Joy, "There is not the least disposition to make exactions. . . . You will find the right spirit here." On December 17, after months of negotiations, the Vanderbilts secured a comprehensive agreement for through traffic from the major western cities—Chicago, St. Louis, and Cincinnati—to New York and Boston. The signators met in the Commodore's office on West Fourth Street; they included Joy, for the North Shore lines (Michigan Central and Great Western of Canada), Chester W. Chapin for the Western (soon to be known as the Boston & Albany), and executives of the South Shore lines, as well as Vanderbilt himself. Diplomacy, cooperation, and consolidation were emerging as themes of his reign.[6]

As in business, so too in his personal life. When his sister Phebe stepped into his household after Sophia's death, she brought company. They were two visitors—reportedly his cousins—from Mobile, Alabama: a widow named Martha Crawford and her daughter, the twenty-nine-year-old Frank.[7] William H. Vanderbilt remembered meeting them on a Sunday evening in 1868 at Phebe's house, where they stayed as guests. The curiously named Frank was especially close to her mother; years before, Frank had married a John Elliott in Mobile, but refused to move out of her mother's house, and a divorce soon followed. Martha Crawford had brought her daughter north during Alabama's brutal summer to improve her health.

Vanderbilt found himself intrigued by Frank's Southernness, and much else. The child of a once-aristocratic family, she boasted the musical accomplishments expected of her social status, with a fine voice and skill at the piano. One observer described her as "quite a good-looking, though by no means beautiful, woman." Rather, Vanderbilt admired her immense dignity ("queenly," by one account) and her body (as much as could be seen under the dirigible dresses of the era).[8] He missed her when she and her mother went home in October. On the 24th, he received a letter from her, and put everything else aside to dictate a reply:

I am happy to hear that you and your dear mother arrived at home all straight, after so long a visit amongst—as it were—almost entire strangers to you previous to your leaving home. I hope you may continue to improve all the time—you in particular, until you will turn the scale when 125 pounds is on the opposite balance. This is weight enough for your beautiful figure. Please . . . accept of the kind wishes of Miss Phebe, Mrs. Osgood, Mrs. Dustan and family, William & all the rest as well as the subscriber.[9]

The haste of the letter, of course, spoke to his romantic interest—as did the way he turned the topic of her health into praise for her figure. She gave this grieving old man hope for the future.

What he intended to do in the future remained a mystery to those around him. Vanderbilt had more than one surprise in store for his family, and the world.

VANDERBILT RATHER LIKED his enemies. For decades, he had deftly switched from enmity to friendship, embracing Drew, Morgan, Garrison, Corning, and others once their wars ended. He never took business disputes personally. He made an exception for Jay Gould and Jim Fisk. He had admitted to them directly that they were the ones who had ensured his personal humiliation in the Erie War. Even worse, they broke the gentlemen's code of business combat. His other foes kept silent about secret business battles, but Fisk and Gould freely told the press every grimy detail, which infuriated the Commodore. He regarded Fisk as reckless, and didn't like the looks of Gould. "God Almighty has stamped every man's character upon his face. I read Mr. Gould like an open book the first time I saw him," Vanderbilt later said. "No man could have such a countenance as his, and still be honest."[10]

On November 15, 1868, Gould called on Vanderbilt. The younger man had taken office as the Erie's president, and it had strained his considerable capabilities to keep the troubled railroad afloat. The company had borrowed heavily against its own stock to pay off Vanderbilt; knowing this, Vanderbilt had sold his remaining fifty thousand shares in small batches on seller's option (retaining the right to decide when to deliver the stock). Then he delivered the entire lot on a single day, staggering the share price and nearly forcing the Erie into bankruptcy. Gould narrowly steered the Erie through this flood, but he now viewed Vanderbilt with deep suspicion.[11]

Gould asked the Commodore if he had anything to do with a lawsuit that would be filed the next morning by August Belmont, who represented foreign investors, demanding that the Erie be placed in receivership. Vanderbilt dismissed the notion. It was obvious he had nothing to do with it, he said; if he had a stake in the lawsuit, he would have sent the attorney Charles O'Conor into court.[12]

Unfortunately for Vanderbilt, O'Conor had more than one client. The next morning, he showed up at the courthouse as Belmont's counsel. Taking this as confirmation of Vanderbilt's role in the lawsuit, Gould and Fisk crafted a plan to undo the grand settlement of the Erie War. On December 5, Fisk rode a carriage through a howling storm to 10 Washington Place, and produced a carpetbag stuffed with fifty thousand Erie shares. Take them back, he demanded, and return the money paid for them—along with the $1 million "bonus" paid for the sixty-day call on the other fifty thousand shares. Vanderbilt threw him out. Gould then filed a lawsuit with the same demands.[13]

Vanderbilt had faced worse insults than those made in Gould's affidavits and Fisk's flamboyant orations, but these two men irritated him as no one ever had. On December 6, he sent a carefully worded letter to the *New York Times*, declaring all the assertions in the lawsuit to be false. "I have no dealings with the Erie Railway Company, nor have I ever sold that Company any stock or received from them any bonus," he wrote. Even the best historians have treated this as nonsense; Maury Klein, for example, calls it "a lame denial." In fact, it was literally accurate. Vanderbilt had insisted during the settlement that his sale of stock technically be to Drew, who contributed $500,000 to the purchase price; and Erie had paid $1 million not as a bonus, but for the sixty-day call. (Gould was not a party to the settlement talks, so his allegations may have been sincere.) But Vanderbilt walked a twisted path in trying to defend his honor without revealing the full story, and it led to a dead end. Fisk showed the press the two checks that comprised the $1 million payment, which seemed to prove his case. Rather than argue and fully expose the secret deal, Vanderbilt fell silent.[14]

Gould likely saw no direct profit in his lawsuit. Rather, it gave him leverage in future negotiations, and put stress on his enemy. The real fighting consisted of a rate war that had flared up in October, when Gould introduced what the press called "starvation prices." He also announced a planned line to the Niagara Suspension Bridge (to gain access to the North Shore route) and, most important, he opened secret talks with the South Shore lines for a connection to Chicago.[15]

In the end, the latter intrigue would prove to be the most consequential aspect of these hostilities, for it would force Vanderbilt into yet another war of conquest. In the meantime, the public spat announced to the world that he had survived the Erie War merely to acquire a new set of enemies—the most cunning and dangerous of his career.

BESET BY EXTERNAL FOES, Vanderbilt surely felt pressure to adopt a conservative domestic policy at the end of his first year as president of the New York Central. He did not. Instead he took two bold steps that startled contemporaries, and helped lay the foundation for the modern corporate economy.

The first revolved around the seemingly dry question of capitalization. Rumors had long circulated that he would issue new shares to existing stockholders. As early as January 9, John M. Davidson had told Corning, "I *think certain sure*, a stock dividend will be made on Central." But months had passed without one. In early December, brokers barely blinked at whispers that John Morrissey, Vanderbilt's prizefighting friend, was madly buying Central.[16]

On Friday, December 18, Central treasurer Edwin D. Worcester handed Vanderbilt a report. Its contents surprised him. He consulted his trusted son-in-law Horace Clark and began to track down directors for an immediate meeting. On Saturday evening, they assembled at Clark's house. The Commodore announced that Worcester had finished a six-month review of the line's construction accounts, which showed a remarkable increase in property over the previous several years. To represent it, Vanderbilt proposed an 80 percent stock dividend. For each one hundred shares held, a stockholder would receive scrip representing eighty new shares. (Stock was customarily bought or sold in blocks of one hundred shares.) Once converted into stock, the scrip would add $20 million at par value to the Central's existing $25 million stock capitalization. Vanderbilt recused himself from the vote, but his proposal passed without opposition.

Why issue scrip, and not actual stock? As Clark later explained, they were trying to distinguish themselves from the Erie by acting lawfully. The Central treated the scrip as if it were identical to stock, but the board would await explicit authorization from the legislature before converting it into shares. The scrip served another purpose as well: Judge Barnard recently had enjoined the board from issuing new stock; the use of this instrument dodged the order but performed the same function.[17]

The news drove the financial community into a frenzy. Not only did the Central prepare the way for nearly doubling its stock, from $25 million to $45 million, it also declared a semiannual dividend of 4 percent on both shares and scrip (amounting to $1.8 million). On Monday morning, Central shot up from 133 to 165. But not everyone in Vanderbilt's circle was pleased. He had given no prior warning to the board, except to Clark and Chester W. Chapin, who had designed and printed the scrip in advance. Many of his closest friends and one of his sons-in-law (most likely Osgood) complained about the secrecy. Vanderbilt replied, "You shan't speculate on us." He believed that some of his own directors had gone short on the stock; as he later explained, "I would not trust many of them." The surprise stock dividend caught them out, and delivered a sharp lesson in trying to profit off Vanderbilt's company.[18]

The sheer size of the issue aroused intense emotion, even among leading railroad men. James F. Joy and John M. Forbes considered it a "rascally abuse of stock dividends."[19] But why should a simple financial
transaction, conducted between the railroad and its existing shareholders,
arouse such outrage? The answer is that stock watering occupied the center of the national debate over the emerging new economy.

In part, the argument was pragmatic. The *New York Sun* wrote, "If the
road can really earn dividends on $45,000,000, it is all right to water the
stock." But the *Chicago Tribune* countered, "Its practical effect is to swindle
honest people who hold the stock as an investment. . . . The stock has been
watered to the point where no dividends can be made."[20] The Central
immediately declared a dividend, though, which seemed to refute that
complaint. Furthermore, Vanderbilt apportioned the new shares evenly
among the shareholders. By contrast, the Erie during its eponymous war
had thrown convertible bonds on the market; when these were converted
into stock, they diluted the stake of existing shareholders by reducing the
relative proportion of their holdings. And yet, the Commodore suffered
equally severe criticism.

For critics, the issue was not fairness, but the very nature of the corporate economy as envisioned on January 1, 1869—the date when the *North
American Review* published "Railroad Inflation," by Charles F. Adams Jr.
Though written prior to the December 19 meeting at Clark's house, this
essay made an argument against stock watering that reveals the persistence of a tangible understanding of the economic universe and a continuing resistance to abstractions.

To Adams, if a thing wasn't a thing, it was nothing. Wealth consisted
only of physical objects—goods, not services. "Transportation cannot add
to wealth," he wrote. For all the merchandise the railroad system carried,
"it never makes one ton two." Therefore, railroad revenue "constitutes a
tax on consumption"—essential, perhaps, but to be jealously watched.

Adams saw railroad dividends as a necessary evil. Like virtually everyone else, he did *not* consider them the simple division of profits among
stockholders. Rather, they were "interest on capital," a due return on the
amount originally invested in construction. Americans discussed the par
value of a railroad share as if it were money deposited in a savings account,
an account from which all interest must be drawn, and never allowed to
compound. Even the market value of the railroad's physical assets—its
"book value," or what it would bring if its property were sold—did not
enter into it; only the cost of construction mattered. And on this capital an
interest of about 6 to 10 percent was politically acceptable—indeed,
expected by investors and the broader public alike.

In this light, any increase of stock was a fraud unless it directly reflected money expended on new construction, and any dividend paid on those fraudulent shares was theft, fake interest paid on "fictitious capital." It was widely believed that stock watering caused railroad companies to raise their rates to pay the expected dividends on the excess stock, bleeding the public for the benefit of those who were in on this paper-certificate magic trick. Many railroad men feared that stock watering would call into question the validity of all corporate shares. Henry V. Poor, the leading chronicler of the industry, wrote, "Such enormous additions to the capital of companies, without any increase of facilities . . . threaten more than anything else to destroy the value of railway property as well as to prove most oppressive to the public."[21]

Did Vanderbilt argue against this logic? Did he make a case that share price should reflect earnings or growth or other factors, rather than initial construction costs? Did he declare that dividends should represent a division of profits—that competition determined his rates, not his need to pay dividends on "fictitious capital"? No, he emphatically did not. He *did* believe that the Central was worth far more than its existing par value; but he justified his actions by releasing a letter from major stockholders (ranging from Frank Work to John Jacob Astor II) that pleaded with him to increase the stock in order to represent prior real estate purchases and construction, made with money that should have been paid out as dividends. Whether Vanderbilt created the letter himself as political cover is irrelevant; the point is, he defended himself in terms that matched those of his critics. Indeed, Worcester testified that, at Vanderbilt's request, he had indeed conducted a six-month investigation of such prior expenditures. The Commodore pronounced himself "astonished" at how large a figure Worcester found. His insistence on the justice of all this would lead him into a bitter fight with the U.S. Treasury, in which his sincerity would become all too apparent.[22]

The future is made by those in the present. The acts that Vanderbilt performed out of the orthodox logic of his times undermined that very logic. A day was coming when the economic mind would relinquish the physical basis of stock price, the insistence on par value. A day was coming when the price of a share would be released to flap into the air, its height determined strictly by the market—the uplifts and downdrafts created by millions of buyers and sellers. A day was coming when dividends simply would mean the division of profits. Vanderbilt prepared the way for this time, and in practice he operated on many of its principles, though only on a subconscious level. He did not "concoct" a justification of the stock dividend, as one writer claims; he believed it. But sometimes actions really are more potent than words.[23]

The second dramatic step that the Commodore took as president of the

Central needed more time to mature, but its significance would be far more apparent to the public and historians alike. It would give his name to an era—the era of consolidations.

ON MARCH 3, 1869, a committee of the New York State Assembly settled into chairs in a private parlor on the third floor of the Fifth Avenue Hotel in Manhattan. They gathered to hear testimony regarding the New York Central's stock dividend. But the proceedings seemed peculiar to Hudson C. Tanner, the stenographer. "Everything was on the dead quiet," he wrote. No one was allowed in except the witnesses. They heard from Edwin Worcester, then Horace Clark. During Clark's testimony, the Commodore strode in, "wearing his traditional white choker, and appearing as innocent as a little, white lamb," Tanner snidely recorded. "All the members of the Committee were introduced to him, instead of his being introduced to the members of the Committee. That was, of course, due entirely to the respect which the Committee had for an old steamboat captain."

"Mr. Clark said it as he should say it," Vanderbilt told the committee when his turn to speak came. "I can do no better than he has done on that subject, only he talks a little too much! That is all the trouble. That is a general fault with lawyers." Obviously comfortable in front of his inquisitors—if not in outright command—he defended the $20 million scrip issue at length, engaged in banter with Clark, turned aside to question Worcester, and digressed into the tale of how he and Daniel Drew had saved the Harlem in 1857—all testimony that the committee politely struck from the published record, along with his occasional "damn."[24]

The committee duly reported a bill to the assembly to authorize the conversion of the scrip into stock. At the same time, a bill advanced to allow Vanderbilt to consolidate the Central with the Hudson River, to create a unified railroad from St. John's Park in Manhattan to the shores of Lake Erie. This second act would prove even more momentous than the enormous scrip dividend, for it would create a corporation on an unprecedented scale. Long envisioned as a practical matter (Dean Richmond had proposed the same thing years earlier), it promised to end the most troublesome fragmentation of the railroad system in New York, introduce greater efficiency, and reduce costs to shippers and consumers. More broadly, it represented the abandonment of the older, local purposes which had first brought railways into existence, as a truly national network emerged. No longer semipublic bodies, railroads now functioned entirely as business enterprises, operated for maximum profit, bought and sold in the market, managed as business logic would dictate. That logic led inexorably to consolidation. The day of the giant corporation had arrived.

On May 20, Governor Hoffman signed both bills into law. In one day Vanderbilt nearly doubled the capitalization of his largest company and opened the door to increase it another 50 percent by annexing the Hudson River. It would take the rest of the year before the consolidation would be complete, but the most difficult step—the political step—had been taken. And Hoffman signed another bill that would help Vanderbilt to make his mark in history: an act authorizing the Harlem Railroad to build, at Forty-second Street and Fourth Avenue, a grand, central depot.[25]

Vanderbilt immediately convened boards of directors and meetings of stockholders to approve the scrip dividend and the consolidation. He cast votes in his own name on 23,600 Central shares (one-tenth of the total voted). His son William voted seventeen thousand; his grandson Cornelius Vanderbilt Jr. seventeen thousand; and his grandson William K. Vanderbilt another ten thousand. Already the Commodore was laying the foundation for his dynasty, settling a large portion of his still-growing estate on the heirs of his heir.[26] Indeed, his family in general prospered. Another favorite grandson, Vanderbilt Allen, went into the railroad supply business at this time, forming the partnership Haven & Allen. Even Corneil partially righted himself that spring. On March 5, Horace Greeley approached the incoming administration of President Ulysses S. Grant to request a job for Corneil in the Internal Revenue Bureau. Corneil himself went to Washington to press his case (borrowing money from Greeley, of course). On May 1, he began work as superintendent of the bureau's Bonded Warehouse in New York under the collector, Joshua F. Bailey, with a salary of $175 a month.[27]

Everything seemed to go Vanderbilt's way. On February 1, the Harlem achieved such prosperity that he ceased to subsidize it with noncompetition payments from the Hudson River. In April, he closed a very old wound: the last reminder of Joseph L. White. Strong informed his diary, " 'Settlement' of the ancient suit of Nicaragua Transit Co. stockholders against that nefarious old Cornelius Vanderbilt, much talked of." The lawyers who had nursed the case for a dozen years absorbed most of the more than $400,000 that Vanderbilt agreed to pay; much of the rest went to speculators who had bought stockholders' claims for a penny on the dollar.[28]

His social life, too, took pleasurable turns. On May 25, he and his brother Jacob attended the opening day of the spring races at the Prospect Park Fairground in Brooklyn. They drove together through the gate, between carts piled with oranges, oysters, and other treats for sale, and made their way to the clubhouse, "its verandahs crowded with the beauty and fashion of the city, and from one of which the Fourteenth Regiment Band discoursed sweet music," the *Brooklyn Eagle* reported. Jake remained close to Cornelius; he often brought his trotters across from Staten Island on the ferry to race on Harlem Lane or Bloomingdale Road against his brother, snorting at the brokers who tried to curry favor with the Commodore by letting him win.[29]

Vanderbilt had hardly forgotten about Frank Crawford. No evidence speaks to when she came north again from Alabama; most likely it was not until the summer heat made Mobile unbearable. In the meantime, he acquainted himself with two most unusual sisters, Victoria Woodhull and Tennessee Claflin.[30] In late 1868, the pair appeared at 17 Great Jones Street, not far from Vanderbilt's home, and began to advertise themselves as "magnetic physicians and clairvoyants," according to the *New York Times*. "They charged $25 in advance for their services, advertised largely, and guaranteed wonderful cures." They attracted many clients, and for good reason. Emetics, bleeding, blistering, and mercury remained in the conventional doctor's arsenal; when fired at patients, they felt it. The role of unconventional healer, like that of spiritualist medium (or "clairvoyant"), remained one of the few professional roles largely reserved for women. Since femininity was seen as passive, women were thought to better serve as vessels for voices from the beyond, or invisible magnetic rays that passed through their hands into the patient.[31]

Victoria, at thirty-one, was a few years older than Tennessee (or Tennie C., as she preferred to be called). Both boasted striking features, with large eyes, dark hair, and full lips, though Tennie's face was softer, rounder, less angular. Victoria's marital status remained vague. At fifteen she had married Dr. Calvin Woodhull, whom she divorced, and had remarried a Union army veteran named James Harvey Blood (whom she later may have divorced and married again). Tennie, voluptuous and single, exuded sexuality. On one occasion, the *Herald* interrupted an account of a trial to observe "that Tenny C. displayed in the most aggravating way A WONDROUS SHIRT FRONT." In an age of strict social standards, her sensuality was an explosive weapon that she wielded as she chose, flirting with influential men in letters and conversation.[32]

Vanderbilt liked and trusted his primary doctor, Jared Linsly, but he didn't always like his treatments. Though he generally enjoyed abundant good health—he ate sparingly, drank little, and remained fit, alert, and active—he was an old man. He had been severely injured over the years in railroad and driving accidents, and felt the aches and pains that come with one's eighth decade. His daughter Mary La Bau obtained a "prescription" for him from a spiritualist healer named Tafts. Vanderbilt showed it to Linsly. "I think he was a believer in the efficacy of the medicine, and thought that the person [Tafts] could do him good," Linsly said. "He was relieved in his sufferings by being rubbed; that was as far as I supposed that he believed in magnetism."[33]

How and when Vanderbilt met Woodhull and Claflin remains unclear. Even less certain is his knowledge of their mysterious past. It does seem, though, that he felt particularly relieved when Tennie rubbed him. Soon the names of Woodhull and Claflin would be very publicly intertwined with that of Vanderbilt.[34]

ON FEBRUARY 24, 1869, the *New York Herald* reported that Vanderbilt had developed a "plan for a consolidation of all the railways connecting the Central with Chicago, thus . . . making but one corporation between New York City and the metropolis of the West." This project was to be carried out in the year ahead.[35]

The *Herald's* account struck many as obvious. The Commodore's seizure of the Harlem, the Hudson River, and the New York Central—and his announced plans for amalgamating the latter two lines—made it seem as if he would buy up and consolidate every connecting line between St. John's Park and Chicago. And reaching Chicago made all the difference. With a population soaring toward 300,000, this metropolis teemed with stinking stockyards, slaughterhouses, and factories. All this put it on the leading edge of changes in the economy. "Although Chicago lagged far behind Philadelphia and New York, the nation's leading manufacturing centers, in investment and output," notes historian Eric Foner, "a larger proportion of its labor force worked for firms with fifty or more employees." It was big in the biggest new thing: bigness.

Chicago had emerged as the commercial hub of the West. The wartime closing of the Mississippi had crimped the trade of its primary rival, St. Louis, which lacked a bridge across the great river. But Chicago captured the commerce of the region through a spider's web of rails that spread out from Cook County. Between 1860 and 1873, more than ten thousand miles of track were laid in the upper Mississippi states, putting 98.5 percent of all land in Illinois within fifteen miles of a railroad. Farmers in all but the most remote tracts of Minnesota, Wisconsin, Iowa, Missouri, Nebraska, and Kansas gained access to railheads, integrating them into national and international markets. The agricultural products of this region—the nation's primary export—moved to Chicago first on their way east for consumption or shipment overseas. To the trunk lines, nothing was more important than an untroubled connection to the Windy City.[36]

And yet, it is a mistake to assume that Vanderbilt thought it necessary to own the lines that connected the Central to Chicago if he were to capture their traffic. Admittedly there were great advantages to having a continuous line under one management: lower overhead, for example, and

greater efficiency in routing trains and handling freight. Still, the inefficiencies could be limited under agreements such as those signed by Vanderbilt and Joy in December 1868. Indeed, throughout Vanderbilt's reign
much of the Central's freight would come over Joy's Michigan Central
(via the Great Western of Canada), which was largely owned by New
England investors and maintained consistently healthy relations with the
Commodore.

More important, the New York Central had joined with its connecting railroads to establish cooperative fast-freight lines. In proportion to
mileage, member companies contributed cars, which were painted a uniform color. Each fast-freight line had its own management that solicited
freight, issued waybills, and fixed rates, but its profits were distributed to
the participating railroads. Often overlooked by historians, fast-freight
lines reduced the costs of through freight, even across separate railroads,
by eliminating the need to break bulk (that is, transfer freight from one
car to another) and increasing managerial efficiency. Finally, the Central
offered the best access to the nation's most important port (and to Boston). It was at least as necessary to western railroads as they were to it. In a
world without enemies, Vanderbilt would have felt no need to buy control
of his connections.[37]

But then there was Jay Gould. As Alfred D. Chandler Jr. wrote, "No
man had a greater impact on the strategy of American railroads." An
ambitious and farsighted chief executive, he embarked on an aggressive
effort to break the isolation of the Erie—with its unusual six-foot gauge—
by seizing connecting lines. He would fail in the end, but his campaign
forced his competitors, including Vanderbilt, to begin the process of constructing interregional railroad systems of mammoth proportions.[38]

Gould began by leasing the broad-gauge Atlantic & Great Western,
which added hundreds of miles to the Erie's network. Next he purchased
stock and proxies to get control of the Pittsburgh, Fort Wayne & Chicago
(the "Fort Wayne")—which happened to be the Pennsylvania Railroad's
primary connection to Chicago. This move jarred the Pennsylvania's
president and vice president, J. Edgar Thomson and Thomas A. Scott, out
of their complacency. Scott quickly secured a classification act from the
Pennsylvania legislature that rigged elections to the Fort Wayne board.
(As an indication of how thoroughly Scott dominated the state government, the bill was signed by the governor thirty-four minutes after it was
introduced.) On June 21, the Pennsylvania leased the Fort Wayne to forestall any further trouble.[39]

Gould turned to the fragmented South Shore lines, in which no one
party exerted dominance. This route had entered a turbulent period of
rapid consolidation, offering him the perfect opportunity to align it with

the Erie. In March, the Cleveland & Toledo merged with the Lake Shore Railway; in May, that line merged with the Michigan Southern & Northern Indiana, forming the Lake Shore & Michigan Southern Railway Company; in August, that line merged with the Buffalo & Erie (itself the product of an earlier consolidation). That made the Lake Shore (as it will now be called) a continuous line from Chicago to Buffalo, with branches to Detroit, Grand Rapids, and the oil regions of Pennsylvania.[40]

On May 31, Horace Clark and James Banker boarded a train to Cleveland for the Lake Shore & Michigan Southern's first stockholders' meeting. They had in their care the Commodore's interest in the new company—an interest, they soon learned, that faced strong opposition from LeGrand Lockwood. A banker, broker, and onetime treasurer of the New York Stock and Exchange Board, Lockwood wielded immense power in Wall Street. Short and rather fat, he had come to New York from Norwalk, Connecticut, at the age of eighteen, married a New York belle, and rapidly rose to riches—prominently displayed in a mansion he built in Norwalk for a reputed $750,000. With the half a million or more he earned each year, he traveled to Europe to purchase fine art and won acceptance in the most aristocratic parlors. He was also a close ally of Henry Keep and had suffered in Vanderbilt's blockade of the Central in January 1867.[41]

Fighting erupted in the first Lake Shore directors' meeting on June 2. In a series of close votes, Lockwood defeated Clark's attempt to control the election of the president. Finally they compromised on the neutral E. B. Phillips, with Lockwood as treasurer; Clark and Banker went on the executive committee. An uneasy peace settled over the divided board.[42]

In late June, Vanderbilt inspected the line for himself, a clear sign of his special concern with the Lake Shore. Accompanied by Phillips, he traveled the route to Chicago in a special train, in his first recorded visit to the city. "We understand the Commodore was well satisfied with the trip," the *Cleveland Herald* reported on June 22. In early July, he went to Saratoga as usual, staying at the rebuilt Congress Hall along with former president Millard Fillmore, Thurlow Weed, and former New York mayor George Opdyke. On July 12, he unexpectedly returned to Cleveland to consult with major Lake Shore stockholders. These movements left observers mystified. "I hardly know what to say about Central," one man wrote to Erastus Corning. "It is now my belief that the Commodore will in some way secure the Central of the *main line* to the *Pacific*."

Some of those closest to Vanderbilt had a more pessimistic view. In August, a story circulated that one of his daughters was seen teaching her own daughter to mend stockings; when asked why she would trouble herself with such a menial occupation, she replied, "There was no telling what a woman might be called upon to do in this country, or what fate awaited her, and she believed in instructing them [her daughters] in useful arts as a preparation for any reverse that might overtake them."[43]

Perhaps she knew that Gould and Lockwood were scheming to freeze Vanderbilt out of the Lake Shore. Over the summer, the two negotiated an alliance, with the aid of Fisk's skills as an entertainer. "The Erie clique," according to the *New York Herald*, "wined and dined the Michigan Southern party at the lower Delmonico's, and brought every argument to bear in favor of a union of the two lines." Gould and Lockwood settled on a plan, which they finalized on August 16 at a secret meeting in West Point. They agreed to a "running arrangement" to divert Lake Shore traffic to the Erie; even more important, they would lay a third rail on the Erie to open it to the Lake Shore's standard-gauge trains, funded by $5 million in Erie bonds, on which the Lake Shore would pay the interest. In return, Gould agreed to abandon his plans to build a broad-gauge line to Chicago. At a Lake Shore board meeting on August 19, the agreement steamed through with Lockwood's support over Clark's fruitless objection. Vanderbilt's only gain was the election of ally Amasa Stone Jr. to a vacant directorship.

At first, the consolidation of the South Shore lines had looked like the end of Vanderbilt's troubles. Instead, that critical route seemed to slip out of his hands before he could even grasp it. "The absorption of the line by the Erie will be the eventual result," the *Herald* wrote. "But the Commodore is fertile in resources."[44]

ON AUGUST 20, VANDERBILT SUDDENLY disappeared from Saratoga. He had been a fixture there, as usual, spending almost all of his time with Morrissey, until he vanished. He turned up later that day in Canada, when a locomotive pulling his private car chuffed into London, Ontario. The Commodore debarked and hurried into the Tecumseh Hotel, followed by a small party. He did not even stop to sign the register, but left that matter to Augustus Schell. He refused all calls and inquiries from the press. In his rooms, Schell produced a legal document, which Vanderbilt signed. Then a young woman signed as well. Her name was Frank Armstrong Crawford, and the document was a prenuptial agreement. She relinquished all claim on the Commodore's estate; when he died, she would receive $500,000 in first-mortgage bonds of the New York & Harlem Railroad. Except in comparison to Vanderbilt's estate, it was a vast sum for 1869; but comparisons to Vanderbilt's estate would be inevitable.[45]

At seven o'clock the next morning, a Saturday, Vanderbilt dressed in a plain black suit, the only sign of his wealth being the brilliant diamond studs in his shirt. The Canadians found him impressive. "He is a noble-looking gentleman, erect in figure, active in movement, intelligent in expression, and almost courtly in bearing," wrote a local reporter. "He is so well preserved, even amid all the cares and responsibilities of his position, that he looks to be not more than 61 or 62 years old." Vanderbilt entered a private parlor, where he saw Frank in a simple traveling dress, "wearing always a singularly happy expression of face."

A Methodist minister presided over the brief marriage ceremony. The handful of witnesses included Frank's mother, Martha, and brother Robert and his wife; Schell; James Tillinghast (superintendent of the New York Central); and only two others: Thomas Bragg, former Confederate attorney general, and his brother Braxton Bragg, one of the Confederate army's most senior generals. Frank had introduced Vanderbilt to the latter. Intelligent, impatient, and ridden with ulcers, Bragg had won a reputation during the Civil War for shooting privates until they obeyed his commands. A true believer in the rebel cause (he had peppered his orders with denunciations of "the Abolition tyrant"), he had shown some talent as a strategist, but his domineering personality had driven his subordinate generals into open revolt. Vanderbilt liked him. Perhaps he admired Bragg's technical competence as an engineer, or his full-bearded face, with his large, dark eyes under heavy brows. What he probably liked most about the general was the fact that so few others liked him, especially in the North. The Commodore mused openly about bringing Bragg into his railroads.[46]

The wedding over—and the American press and fashionable gossips safely avoided—Mr. and Mrs. Vanderbilt dashed back to their private railroad car for the journey east, accompanied by Schell, Tillinghast, and Frank's black maid, Nellie. The Bragg brothers and the Crawfords returned to the South separately. "I was completely overcome after leaving you all & poor Nellie tried to cheer me, but immediately burst into tears herself," Frank wrote to her "Ma" two days later. "I could not be sad long with such devoted attention as the Com showed me." The luxuries of the life of the Commodore—always "Com" to Frank—astonished her. "About 2 o'cl'k, the table was spread in our car, with the purest white cloths & silverware, & a delightful little dinner was brought in from the refreshment car—broiled chicken & chops, & everything *so clean & nice*," she wrote. "Mr. Schell & Tillinghast were so kind & attentive, & I begin to feel Schell belongs in part to me."

They spent that night at a hotel in Syracuse—the Vanderbilt, of course—hiding in ostentatiously appointed rooms from the crowds outside. "The Commodore was very lively indeed, and quite graceful and courteous in his attentions to his wife," the local press observed. Frank agreed. "Com. is so good," she wrote to her mother. "Says he loves me too much, it amounts to *worship*. He is up & down—can't stay away long."[47]

The next day they went to Saratoga Springs. At the hotel, the women in Vanderbilt's wide circle of friends swarmed around the rather over-whelmed Frank. "Mrs. Decker rushed in & such kissing & hugging us both," she wrote, "Mrs. Work, Harker, &c. I feel really gratified at the cordial warm reception given me." Most gratifying of all was the welcome from the Vanderbilt family. William and Maria, along with some of William's siblings, came straight in "and kissed me so cordially. They are glad their father married." One of them told her that the family "all thought favorably about the marriage." The musical Nicholas B. La Bau, a "nice little fellow," congratulated her as well—but his wife, the Com-modore's daughter Mary, did not. This devoted spiritualist comes across in the scant written record as prickly and defensive. She later remarked that she first met Frank and her mother a full year after the wedding. Other daughters proved equally cold. Emily Thorn recalled meeting Frank after the couple returned to the city, but could not recollect how much later, as she "did not feel interested enough to remember."[48]

Frank, unlike Vanderbilt, was uncomfortable at being the center of public attention. She did not want to leave their flower-stuffed rooms ("almost stifling with the perfume of tuberoses & heliotrope"). She knew she was a spectacle, and her clothes "old timey" and unfashionable. But the women insisted. "They all *made* me go down to dinner & tea & such staring & pulling on glasses & taking different & good views was most try-ing to stand," Frank wrote to her mother. Vanderbilt took her out for spins around the track in their double-top buggy, behind a fast new horse named Myron Perry. They drove out one day to the races to watch Moun-tain Boy defeat Lady Thorn, strolling onto the stand through curious onlookers. Vanderbilt's brother Jake strode up to them and exclaimed, "I must kiss the bride," much to Frank's embarrassment. "I was that day closely scrutinized by *thousands* of people. Mrs. Work says she could not help gazing too, seeing everybody else doing so, tho' she had seen me so often."

Frank's letters to her mother reveal many reasons why the Commodore fell in love with her. She was modest, scoffing at praise for her beauty by a toadying innkeeper. She admitted to being out of keeping with fashion, but she was also attentive to it. She exhibited grace, sociability, and a sense of fun (she thrilled to their fast drives and Mountain Boy's victory). She demonstrated a keen but unpretentious intelligence; as she was finishing one letter, William strode into the room, and the Commodore proudly insisted that Frank read her correspondence aloud to him. He even loved her masculine name, which she herself loathed.

But Frank also resonated with a contrarian aspect of Vanderbilt's per-sonality. She was an unrepentant Confederate. "Com. is proud of my being a rebel," she wrote. "Takes pains to tell it." At one point the seventy-two-year-old Alexander T. Stewart (Vanderbilt's primary rival for the title of richest man in America) sat down with Frank and argued with her about the virtues of General (now President) Grant. She debated "pleasantly of course—but I meant what I said." She found Stewart to be kind and talkative, as she did General Gordon Granger. Granger had led the Union forces that captured Mobile during the war. When he called on the newlyweds, he warmly remarked that he remembered when he had first met Frank. It seems that he had shown particular courtesy to the Crawfords during the occupation, and it proved to be a source of lasting gratitude from the Commodore.[49]

Vanderbilt's pride in his rebel wife speaks to his peculiar relationship with fashionable New York society. He had now grown so wealthy, so powerful, that the social aristocrats could hardly shut him out. As one observer wrote in 1870, "Even Vanderbilt *& others* are not ignored by gentlemen." Displaying a courtly bearing that belied his historical reputation as a vulgarian, he now dined with the Astors and mingled with the leaders of fashion at Saratoga, the Manhattan Club, or Jerome Park. Though he had always taken pride in being a man of honor, he may indeed have grown into the dignity generated by his tens of millions; where credit reporters had once derided him, they would soon record that he was considered "honorable & high toned." At the same time, he indulged in a proud independence of character as he levitated above the social strictures of the elite (later fictionalized by Edith Wharton, then a seven-year-old girl known as Pussy Jones). Amid Reconstruction's turmoil, he flouted gossips with his divorced Southern bride.[50]

But Frank's Southernness had another important attraction for Vanderbilt. He remained as patriotic now as when he had given his million-dollar steamship to the Union navy. That patriotism extended to the entire country after Appomattox. He demonstrated a growing interest in healing the wounds of the war. His friends and associates reinforced this impulse. Horace Greeley, Horace Clark, Augustus Schell, and Charles O'Conor all resisted what they saw as a harsh peace imposed on the South. Of course, when they thought about the South, they meant the white South; as elite members of wealthy New York society, they identified with the former planters who had gone bankrupt when the slaves went free. Regardless, Vanderbilt's desire to bring North and South together was sincere. It would be the ultimate consolidation.

ON SEPTEMBER 2, VANDERBILT RETURNED to face the crisis. Over the summer, LeGrand Lockwood, confident in his understanding with Gould, had purchased on credit $1.25 million worth of new Lake Shore stock, issued as part of the consolidation. Vanderbilt had bided his time. He had had personal matters to attend to, but the perfect time for his revenge would be the autumn, when the moving of the crops would squeeze the money market. Now he quietly issued contracts for sale of his own Lake Shore stock, along with the thousand shares held by the New York Central. Starting on Monday, September 13, cash began to grow scarce in New York. Vanderbilt struck.

"The whole course and tendency of prices have been reversed with magic-like power," the *New York Herald* reported on Saturday, September 19. It explained the next day, "The veteran Commodore indignantly tossed all his Lake Shore stock on the market and brought about a break in the stock which threatened the credit of his enemies and certainly entailed great losses upon them." Vanderbilt delivered all his stock on three successive days, collapsing Lake Shore from 107 to 75. This erased its value as collateral for the heavily leveraged Lockwood, leaving him "thoroughly frightened," as the *Herald* wrote. He begged for mercy. Vanderbilt gave none. Lockwood & Co., long one of the Wall Street's great houses, declared bankruptcy on October 1. "The veteran Commodore," the *Herald* noted, was "an unrelenting enemy."[51]

The waters in which he drowned Lockwood proved nearly fatal to himself. In striking down Lake Shore he inadvertently contributed to Black Friday, one of the greatest panics in American financial history. The immediate catalyst for the disaster lay in a breathtaking financial scheme crafted by Jay Gould. Well aware that the Gold Room served as a currency exchange, Gould wanted to drive down the price of greenbacks to make American exports cheaper overseas. The result would be a bounty for the railroads as more crops were shipped to the seaports in the fall. He brought Fisk into the plan, and the two of them lobbied President Grant to limit sales of government gold from customs duties collected in New York. The plot promised personal profit as well, provided Gould could properly time the sale of the massive amounts of gold he purchased in August and September.[52]

Gould and Fisk's attempt to corner the gold market played out in a field beyond Vanderbilt's immediate affairs, as they colluded with the president's brother-in-law, bribed the federal subtreasurer in New York, and even opened a gold account for First Lady Julia Grant. Their campaign did not go unopposed. Brokers who were bears in gold fought back mightily. Then Vanderbilt hammered the weak money market with his attack on Lake Shore stock. Gould and Fisk even accused the Commodore of carrying out a lock-up to make credit tight.[53] Fisk responded by flamboyantly bidding the gold premium up to heights not seen since the Civil War. The financial frenzy seemed to threaten the economy's stability, and rumors of Grant's involvement did not go unnoticed in the White House. Finally Grant decided to intervene. He ordered Treasury Secretary George Boutwell to sell a few million in gold. The signal this action sent mattered as much as the enormous quantity of greenbacks it sucked out of the market.

On September 24, the price of gold collapsed amid the worst panic since 1857. The radical rise and plunge in prices trapped many brokers; no less than fourteen Wall Street houses failed (not including those that were strictly gold dealers). In Fisk's oft-quoted phrase, "It was each man drag out his own corpse"—literally, in the case of a broker who shot himself to death. The problem for Vanderbilt was that the crashing market destroyed credit generally, carrying down stock prices across the board.[54]

On Friday evening he rushed home from a Central board meeting in Albany, where he had presided over the signing of the final consolidation agreement with the Hudson River Railroad. In the face of this crisis—a crisis he had helped make—he had to fight to protect his grip on his emerging giant, what soon would be called the New York Central & Hudson River Railroad. Most likely he lacked a clear majority of the stock without the support of friends and allies, including Augustus Schell and John Morrissey. At his urging, they had purchased large quantities; as the price fell, one of them was called "as terrified as a man can be." In a rare move, Vanderbilt put up a reported $2.5 million to meet their margin calls. Still more remarkably, he went in person to Wall Street to soothe the markets and sustain the price of Central.[55]

"I knew it, I knew it," an old broker said on the floor of the stock exchange, "the old rat (Vanderbilt) never forgets his friends." The Commodore very visibly set himself up at the Bank of New York at the corner of Wall and William streets, where his lieutenant James Banker provided him with "comfortable offices, upholstered as a Fifth Avenue drawing room," according to the *New York Sun*. From his nicely cushioned throne he issued orders to buy, and buy, and buy. A reporter asked Vanderbilt what he was up to; he replied, "Well, now really, sonny, I really cannot tell you anything. I don't care about forming opinions. *All we want is to protect ourselves.*"

The Commodore was being disingenuous. His presence on Wall Street had one purpose only, and that was to form opinions. Behind the scenes his situation grew desperate, as William revealed by paying a visit to Judge Barnard, who was considering various injunctions in the Erie's lawsuit against the Commodore. William pleaded with him to aid the Central. Barnard refused, saying "that his father and his gang had treated him badly," according to Barnard's friend, John M. Davidson. (It did not help the Vanderbilts' case that Barnard had sold all of his Central stock before the panic, and had no stake in the matter.) William replied that "his father was strong enough to take care of himself," Davidson wrote. "The Judge said *all right*, but he differed with him. Vanderbilt has struggled to save Central from falling."[56]

The Commodore, ever cool amid others' panic, projected pure strength. He strolled through the exchange to make his presence felt. "Central's coming up, Commodore," a young broker shouted. "Top o' the heap still, my boy," he replied. Soon the reason for his confidence leaked out: he had taken a large short-term loan from Baring Brothers in London, putting up as collateral an equal amount, at par, of New York Central stock. He bought back his Lake Shore shares (at radically reduced prices, of course), along with Lockwood's stake. And he very visibly purchased Central. He failed to keep the price above 200, where it had been before Black Friday, but he arrested its fall at 175, and brought it back to 184 in short order. On October 2, the *New York World* commented on his impact:

> The best men on the street all assert that had it not been for the Commodore coming to the rescue and sustaining his stocks, the panic on Tuesday and Wednesday of this week would have been a hundred fold greater than it was, and that nearly the whole street would have been ruined, and several of the banks have been obliged to succumb by the great decline that would have taken place in securities; that this decline would not have stopped with stocks, but have extended to government, State, and city stocks [i.e., bonds], and been universal and disastrous. To the prevention of this disaster, the brokers generally give the credit to Commodore Vanderbilt.[57]

In the drama of Black Friday—a morality play of Gould's greed, government corruption, and new economic intricacies that easily fell prey to manipulation—Vanderbilt appeared in the role of a hero: the man who saved the stock market, who prevented a panic from igniting a depression. Closer inspection reveals that a blood-chilling ruthlessness infused all his actions. To avenge himself upon Lockwood, and to bring the Lake Shore Railway into the Central's orbit, he had gambled with the economic health of the national economy. Well aware of the frailty of the financial market in the autumn (and of Gould and Fisk's gold-cornering scheme), he had pumped in still more pressure, taking the risk that Wall Street's boiler would explode. Along the way, he also endangered the fortunes of his friends and his own grip on his flagship corporation. He gambled all this on his confidence in his ability to singlehandedly sustain the market. The only thing more remarkable than his recklessness was his success. After contributing to one of history's great panics, he took his revenge, captured the Lake Shore, and rescued Wall Street.

To the American public, Black Friday suddenly illuminated, like a flash of lightning on a midnight floodplain, the way in which the new corporate and financial reality inundated the national landscape. The bankers and brokers of New York were no longer an oddity—an isolated batch of men who seemingly produced nothing but merely juggled bewilderingly abstract securities. Now, because of the railroads, corporations began to overshadow farmers, artisans, and merchants. Now, because of the increasing financial integration of the country, the fears and hopes of a few hundred men on Wall Street could shake the nation. More than any other man, the Commodore frightened or excited those few hundred, driving them as he willed. With the wave of one hand he created tens of millions in new wealth; with a wave of the other, he crushed his enemies; with cold-eyed calculation, he gambled with the lives of millions. The American people were fortunate that he gambled so well, but they had no say in how he placed his bets. Black Friday posed a great question: What was the place of a railroad king in a democracy of equals?

AFTER SURVIVING THE PRESENT, there remained the future—specifically, the future of the Lake Shore. Vanderbilt swept his enemies out and his lieutenants in: Lockwood resigned as treasurer and was replaced by James Banker, and another Lockwood ally resigned from the board to make room for Augustus Schell.[58] Clearly it was now Vanderbilt's property. But what would he do with it?

Lockwood's defeat prompted widespread speculation about a grand consolidation of the Lake Shore with the still-merging New York Central & Hudson River. Such a move would have been in keeping with the changing times. For example, the Pennsylvania Railroad responded to Gould's threats by creating a self-contained system extending from Philadelphia to New York, Chicago, St. Louis, and throughout the South. Its lease of the Fort Wayne was only the first step in the development of a highly sophisticated, centrally controlled network of subsidiaries and holding companies. Within five years, the Pennsylvania's managers would gain control of $400 million in assets and nearly six thousand miles of track—8 percent of the national total.[59]

But the Commodore balked at such an ambitious step as consolidating the Lake Shore into the Central. First, it is not clear that Vanderbilt had purchased an outright majority of Lake Shore stock. (It was hardly necessary to control the board.) Second, he and his lieutenants remained immersed in the immense task of merging the Central and the Hudson River. Third, the Lake Shore's finances were nowhere near as robust as those of Vanderbilt's other lines; to coalesce them before reforms could be enacted would scuff the gilt edges off Central stock.

Most important, Vanderbilt handled the Lake Shore gingerly because of his keen ear for politics, both the electoral variety and the realpolitik of railroad diplomacy. He fully grasped the public's worries over the rise of giant railroad corporations. A fresh consolidation would have been a vast undertaking, financially, legally, and especially politically, requiring legislation from each of the six states through which the line would run. And since he had no desire (and perhaps insufficient means) to buy *all* the lines that fed the Central traffic, he had to appease the executives of connecting lines; he could not afford to discriminate against them. To understand him as a railroad leader, it must always be remembered that he was first and foremost a diplomat.

Out of deference to both political and business sensitivities, he refused to treat the Lake Shore as a subsidiary of the Central. For example, he did not give it preference over the North Shore lines, which he did not control. Five years later, the Michigan Central's superintendent would applaud "the neutrality which *he* [the Commodore] has always professed and which up to this twine has been *pretty well* observed." Vanderbilt's battle with Lockwood, like all his railroad wars, had been one of self-defense (in this case, to block Gould), not an exercise in imperial conquest.[60]

The Commodore delegated command of the Lake Shore to Banker, Schell, and especially Horace Clark, who would take over as president at the next stockholders' meeting. They were more than puppets; they had agendas of their own, and Vanderbilt gave them latitude. "We have got some high-toned, honorable men in our board of directors, a set of men who are capable of thinking for themselves," he had said about Clark, Banker, and Schell in 1867. "And they might think very differently from me, and I would not blame them for expressing their opinions." As long as they managed the line wisely, cooperated in carrying through freight, and kept his enemies at bay, he would leave them to manage the railroad as they saw fit.

He should have remembered his own words about keeping an eye on your friends.[61]

"HOW I DO PITY YOU, Commodore Vanderbilt!" Mark Twain wrote. "You seem to be the idol of only a crawling swarm of small souls, who love to glorify your most flagrant unworthinesses in print; or praise your vast possessions worshippingly; or sing of your unimportant private habits and sayings and doings, as if your millions gave them dignity."

Twain's essay, "Open Letter to Com. Vanderbilt," appeared in March 1869 in *Packard's Monthly*, a new periodical devoted to fighting "the evils of the day."[62] Twain clearly saw Vanderbilt as evil. He ascribed to him a willingness to run down and kill pedestrians in his carriage. ("No matter,

I'll pay for them.") He pictured him as a creature of pure greed. ("You . . . rob yourself of restful sleep and peace of mind, because you need money so badly. I always feel for a man who is so poverty ridden as you.") He accused him of lacking all charity. ("*Do* go, now, and do something that isn't shameful.") Lest his point be missed, he added, "You observe that I don't say anything about your soul, Vanderbilt. It is because I have evidence that you haven't any."

And yet, what really irritated Twain was not the Commodore himself so much as the adoration of his ultra wealth. He complained of the praise for Vanderbilt that appeared in editorials, the tales that ran in the columns of miscellaneous chitchat. "No, sir; other men think and talk as brilliantly as you do, but they don't do it in the glare of seventy millions," he wrote, "so pray do not be deceived by the laudation you receive; more of it belongs to your millions than to you."

Twain saw a culture grown vulgar, selfish, materialistic, and corrupt, and he didn't like it. Like many of the Civil War generation, he viewed his times with a cynical eye and, underneath his ironic tone, a poignant sense that America had lost its virtue. (One of his most hilarious pieces of writing was an ironic attack on young Benjamin Franklin for having been so maliciously self-improving, "so that all other boys might have to do [the same] or else have Benjamin Franklin thrown up to them.") He did not attack Vanderbilt's fortune in its own right; rather, he went after the way it warped the rest of society—for it was corruption, not riches, that offended him. It is worth remembering that the novel he wrote with Charles Dudley Warner—the book that gave its name to this era, *The Gilded Age*—is not a satire of the wealthy, nor even of the extravagant lifestyles now associated with the title. The book's hero actually rises to fortune through expertise and hard work. Rather, Twain and Warner's villains are scurrilous adventurers who try to bilk the federal government with a pork-barrel project championed by a flagrantly corrupt senator.

At the opposite end of the social scale from Twain stood Henry and Charles Francis Adams Jr., yet they shared the same concerns. In their writings, they voiced an abiding belief in the scientific laws that governed economics, and argued that corruption in corporations and government prevented those laws from working properly.[63] Indeed, the key to understanding their critique is that it was infused with an almost Calvinist conviction that humanity is fallen. In "A Chapter of Erie," Charles wrote with alarm about the increasing size of giant railroad corporations, but his real complaint was not with corporations themselves, but the moral failings of the businessmen who misused them. "No acute moral sensibility has . . . for some years troubled either Wall Street or the country at large," he wrote. The natural laws of economics had been corrupted by "the legerdemain of paper financiering," he argued, as if corporations were not products of the human imagination, but of natural processes, as much as mountain ranges or spoon-billed sandpipers. They wished to remove the original sin, to rest economic values on the natural, the solid, the inanimate. With regard to currency, this meant an end to legal tender. Instead of the volume of high-powered money being set by Congress, they argued, it should be based on the supply of gold. With regard to the values of stocks, they wished to base them on construction costs, not the whims of stock-watering rascals such as Vanderbilt or Gould.

To the Adams brothers, the Commodore and his ilk were most dangerous when they spread their corruption into politics, as in Gould's alliance with Tweed. (Henry titled his own satirical novel *Democracy*, not *Capitalism*.) In "A Chapter of Erie," Charles wrote, "As the Erie ring represents the combination of the corporation and the hired proletariat of a great city, as Vanderbilt embodies the autocratic power of Caesarism introduced into corporate life . . . it, perhaps, only remains for the coming man to . . . put Caesarism at once in control of the corporation and of the proletariat."[64]

The phrase "the hired proletariat" speaks to the social prejudices that pervaded the Adams brothers' set, the liberal reformers—or the "best men," as they called themselves. Liberals such as E. L. Godkin (editor of the *Nation*), Charles Eliot Norton (editor of the *North American Review*), economist David A. Wells, historian Francis Parkman, and others scorned the poor and uneducated "dangerous classes" as vulnerable to Tweed and other manipulators. As Warner wrote, "All men are created unequal." The liberals recoiled from Reconstruction. Believing the worst tales about corruption in Southern state governments, they questioned black suffrage. They weren't sure all white men should vote. As Charles F. Adams Jr. proclaimed, "Universal suffrage can only mean in plain English the government of ignorance and vice."

In the same breath, they blasted the tycoons—Vanderbilt foremost among them—for one underlying, ultimate sin: they were uncultured. *The Education of Henry Adams* dismisses Vanderbilt and Gould by saying they "lacked social charm." But charm mattered, the Adamses thought; the tycoons' ignorance and lack of culture served as the fountainhead of their selfish defiance of natural economic laws. Twain later befriended one of the richest and most ruthless of all industrialists, Andrew Carnegie, in large part because Carnegie aspired to intellectual cultivation and literary accomplishment, and thus distinguished himself from his peers. The "best men" saw the corrupt poor and the corrupt robber barons (a term used in June 1868 by Edward Howland, and by Charles F. Adams Jr. in a private 1869 letter) as the twin causes of society's troubles. "An ignorant proletariat and a half-taught plutocracy," Parkman later wrote, had "risen like spirits of darkness on our social and political horizon."[65]

The worst fears of the liberal reformers seemed to come true on November 10, 1869, when half-taught Caesar and the ignorant plebeians met in a ceremony that rather resembled a coronation. New York's newspapers had given notice of the event, and the public came by the thousands—men and women, jostling and squeezing, stepping over curbs and clods of horse manure, pressing down the narrow streets of lower Manhattan toward the Hudson River. On Hudson Street they collided with a cordon of 250 policemen. Beyond the constables, a rope line divided the crowd from the invited ticket holders arrayed in front of an extended dais, beneath the long, low arches and massive brick walls of the new Hudson River Railroad freight depot. As a military band drummed and blared, the eyes of the crowd went to a detachment of twenty-five sailors who held a large canvas cover that flapped across the peak of the building's facade.

On the dais sat the leading men of the city, from Mayor A. Oakey Hall to Horace Greeley and August Belmont, along with two admirals, the U.S. district attorney, a bishop, Daniel Drew, and even Jim Fisk and Jay Gould. President Grant was expected, but sent his regrets. Vanderbilt occupied the center, smiling between the white shocks of his abundant sideburns, still a dominating presence at seventy-five.

The onlookers fell silent for a bishop's invocation. Then the sailors let go the cover and unveiled a twelve-foot bronze statue of the Commodore, which stood within the brackets of an enormous bronze relief depicting the icons of Vanderbilt's long career: sailboats, steamships, and trains. "At the same moment," the *New York Tribune* reported, a navy vessel "ran up the Commodore's pennant to the flagstaff; the band struck up a lively tune, and the crowd cheered with enthusiasm." Mayor Hall delivered a lengthy tribute. Vanderbilt was the richest man on the continent, Hall observed, but he did not fritter his wealth; he employed it "in public projects of startling conception that have kept employed almost armies of men." Vanderbilt, the mayor proclaimed, "is a remarkable prototype of that rough-hewn American character which asks no greater original capital than is afforded by that independence of thought . . . that irresistible resolution in executing great projects, which can carve the way of every humbly born American boy to national eminence." He was the equivalent of Benjamin Franklin, Andrew Jackson, and Abraham Lincoln. William Rose Wallace—the poet who wrote "The Hand That Rocks the Cradle Is the Hand That Rules the World"—then read an original, if abysmal, verse, beginning, "Mighty Monument to Conquest—so the Great Republic cries / Power orbed on her vast forehead, earnestness burning in her eyes."[66]

High praise indeed. Unfortunately, Mayor Hall was on his way to two indictments for corruption, ensuing public disgrace, and self-imposed exile abroad. "But there is something essentially laughable," E. L. Godkin noted in the *Nation*, "in the spectacle of a man's putting out his own cash to pay for civic honors to himself." He found it reminiscent of the decaying days of the Roman republic, in particular the story of how a group of citizens approached a nobleman with the news that the Senate had voted to erect a statue of him. The nobleman gravely replied that honor alone was enough—in fact, it was too much, so he would put up his own monument.[67]

Democracy must have its discontents, or it would not be democracy. Indeed, the liberal reformers formed only one channel of dissent against Vanderbilt and the corporate power he represented. The other would be a populist current that lifted up government regulation to counter the railroad monarchy. It would take longer to emerge, in large part because of the liberals' influence in intellectual circles and with the leadership of both political parties. The cynicism and social disdain of Godkin, Twain, and the Adams brothers created confusion, then and now, over the problems facing American society in 1869. Their attacks on corruption went beyond the Tweed ring, to the point of undermining black-elected governments in the South and giving credence to white supremacy. Their economic theories led them to lambast business practices that eventually would become standard. Most important, their distrust of popular government discredited regulatory measures that offered the only means of placing political limits on the power of large corporations.

They were right about many things, of course: political corruption was a real problem; the spoils system needed to be replaced by a professional, nonpartisan civil service; insider trading and other abuses wracked corporations; and no one could accuse Vanderbilt of being well educated. But prejudice cannot replace investigation. Vanderbilt, for example, did not pay for his monument, as Godkin believed. It was the brainchild of Albert De Groot, who once had worked on Vanderbilt's steamboats, enjoyed his patronage, and felt he "owed a debt of gratitude." He had planned the statue and relief, designed by Ernst Plassmann, and raised $500,000 from Vanderbilt's wealthy friends. De Groot claimed that the Commodore knew nothing about it until it was well under way.[68]

Even corrupt Mayor Hall had a point: Vanderbilt did devote his energy to constructing works of immense benefit to the public, building transportation infrastructure that would serve the city of New York for centuries. The St. John's Park freight depot was one example. Two historians of New York write, "The new terminal revolutionized the Lower West Side. An enormous complex of grain depots, stockyards, and stables arose along the waterfront." Like a "gigantic magnet," the confluence of rail and sea access at St. John's Park attracted "wholesalers, express companies, packing-box firms, and dry-goods commission merchants" from their old locations near the East River. More than two hundred new warehouses went up in the district in the late 1860s and early 1870s, leaving a mark that would last into the twenty-first century. And this was far from the only piece of Manhattan on which Vanderbilt would stamp his name. On November 15, the Harlem Railroad broke ground on Forty-second Street for what would be the largest railroad station in North America. They called it the Grand Central Depot.[69]

THE COMMODORE'S CRITICS would cluck their tongues once more on January 22, 1870. That day the *New York Herald* announced a sensation: Victoria Woodhull and Tennie C. Claflin had set themselves up as brokers and bankers on Wall Street. In doing so, the two sisters defied social expectations. "Were I to notice what is said by what they call 'society,' I could never leave my apartments except in fantastic walking dress or in ballroom costume," Claflin told a *Herald* reporter, "but I despise what squeamy, crying girls or powdered counter-jumping dandies say of me. I think a woman is just as capable of making a living as a man." She added, "I know as much of the world as men who are older. Besides, we have a strong back [i.e., backer]."

The reporter noticed a picture of Vanderbilt on the wall. "I have been told that Commodore Vanderbilt is working in the interest of your firm. It is stated that you frequently call at his office in Fourth street about business." Tennie replied, "I know the Commodore and frequently call to see him on business, but I am not prepared to state anything as to whether he is working with us."[70]

On February 4, the women formally opened Woodhull, Claflin & Co. at 44 Broad Street. Thousands of Wall Street men came calling, including Richard Schell, William R. Travers, Daniel Drew, and even the esteemed Jay Cooke, who admitted he was frankly curious. Edward H. Van Schaick visited several times, with a fresh haircut, hat, or coat on each occasion. They all found the women self-assured and forceful to a degree that surprised and unsettled them. Claflin said, "If I had engaged a little fancy store upon Broadway and sold ribbons and thread, it would have been perfectly proper. . . . No one would have remarked it. But because I have brains sufficient to carry on a banking house people are astonished."[71]

The reporters, brokers, and operators all asked, Who was the Co. in Woodhull, Claflin & Co.? A broker remarked that there was "something back of the movement." Claflin sharply responded: "Yes, there is something back of it. Commodore Vanderbilt is back of it." The sisters spoke his name more frequently with each passing day. On January 26, Woodhull had thanked journalist Whitelaw Reid for a favorable editorial. It "was entirely satisfactory to our best friend, the Commodore, who first called our attention to it as we were dining with him," she wrote. (Claflin sent Reid a note rife with sexual innuendo soon after.) "A rather free use has been made of the name of the veteran Commodore Vanderbilt as the aider and abettor, if not the full partner, of the firm," the *Herald* noted on February 9.[72]

Vanderbilt routinely alerted the press when his name was mistakenly attached to any operation. In this case, he kept silent—at first. As one broker asked, "What does Vanderbilt mean?"[73] The answer remains mysterious. One hint comes from the memoirs of Alva Vanderbilt Belmont, who married William K. Vanderbilt in 1875, and vividly recalled her first meeting with her husband's grandfather. "His manner was most overbearing, and the family more or less stood in great awe of him," she wrote. "I had never known what it was to be awed by anybody, and I think that for that reason he had a great deal of respect for me, and we became quite friendly."[74] He did not tolerate fools and had little respect for weak personalities. But a woman who stood her ground—in an age that idealized feminine frailty—impressed him. It was strength where he expected none. Woodhull and Claflin were nothing if not strong.

Then, too, there was his contrarian streak. If he relished his wife's outspoken loyalty to the Confederacy, he found far more controversial views in Woodhull and Claflin. They championed the cause of gender equality at a time when the twenty-two-year-old women's movement had won new prominence, as Elizabeth Cady Stanton, Susan B. Anthony, and others turned the debate over Reconstruction toward the question of women's rights. Woodhull and Claflin skillfully used the publicity of their Wall Street firm to promote the cause, and propel themselves into its leadership. More and more in the coming months, they would weave together various radical strands in American intellectual life, including Spiritualism, women's rights, workers' rights, and (most controversial of all) free love, that catchall phrase for any unconventional sexuality. In May 1870, the sisters began to publish *Woodhull & Claflin's Weekly*, which gave space to the ideas of such figures as Stephen Pearl Andrews, who would go on to join Karl Marx's International Workingmen's Association.[75]

Woodhull and Claflin hinted at other motivations that the Commodore might have had for supporting them. "At times I know and feel that I am under a spirit influence that I do not understand; and when in that condition I do see visions of future events," Claflin told a reporter later in 1870. "If you doubt it go and ask Commodore Vanderbilt! . . . Victoria and I both see visions." Years later, in the great trial over Vanderbilt's will, Susan A. King would testify that Claflin introduced her to the Commodore in 1870. He urged her to follow their advice to buy New York Central stock, for it would go up 22 percent in three months. "He said that Mrs. Woodhull was a spiritual medium, and while in a clairvoyant state, had told him so." Marie Antoinette Pollard would testify that she also called on him in 1870 to ask advice about the stock market. He replied, "Why don't you do as I do, and consult the spirits?"[76]

Claflin's sexual allure, it was said, was the most powerful motivation of all. A story would be put out that Vanderbilt was seen throwing his arm around Claflin; that he vainly boasted to her that women bought New York Central stock because his picture was on it; that he promised her a fortune in his will. It would be said that she asked Vanderbilt if he had not promised to marry her before he married Frank, and that he replied, "Certainly, but the family prevented it and otherwise arranged it." Joseph Treat, an acolyte of Woodhull and Claflin who turned against them, later wrote that he had heard from a friend of another sister of Claflin's that she had asked Vanderbilt how many sexual partners he had had, "and he said a thousand, to which she responded . . . that then she was only half as big a whore as he." Claflin, Treat wrote, suffered from a sexual disease, implying that Vanderbilt might have contracted it as well.[77]

This is scandalous stuff—irresistible to many writers over the years, who would abandon all skepticism to embrace or even inflate it with conjecture and outright invention. In reality, solid evidence of Vanderbilt's relationship with the sisters is lacking. The tales of Vanderbilt promising money to Claflin, boasting about his stock-certificate portrait, and having been forced to marry Frank, all came at the trial over his will, from the mouth of a lawyer who was paid to prove that Vanderbilt was not in his right mind.[78] The stories did not even come from a witness. They were merely declarations of what the counsel hoped to prove, and no such testimony was actually made. Even if Vanderbilt did say these things, they come across mostly as sexually charged banter with a woman who cultivated sensuality. The idea that he was forced to marry Frank at all, let alone by a family that had barely met her, flies in the face of direct documentation.

As for Treat's explosive account, it is hearsay of hearsay of hearsay, originating with Claflin herself, the most untrustworthy source of all. In 1871, she would proclaim her clairvoyant power in court—in order to soften an admission that she was a confidence artist. "To support this family I had to humbug people sometimes," she would say. Indeed, both Claflin and Woodhull proved to be accomplished liars who filled their interviews with the press with complete fabrications. Claflin claimed that she had studied law with her father. Woodhull said that they had made a fortune in real estate, and had operated quietly on Wall Street for years. They found themselves caught out in their lies in March, when creditors in Chicago, Claflin's most recent home, sued her for numerous unpaid debts. That led the *New York Sun* to report, "Commodore Vanderbilt, whom Miss Tennie claims to be her financial backer, denies all knowledge of her or her partner, Mrs. Woodhull."[79]

Were solid evidence to surface that Vanderbilt and Claflin had an affair between the death of Sophia and his marriage to Frank, it would not be a particularly startling discovery.* But the significance of their connection should not be exaggerated. There is no sign that Vanderbilt gave any support to the radical *Woodhull & Claflin's Weekly*, even though many writers have assumed that was the case. Rather, the sisters annoyed the business community with their efforts to bring in money for it. R. G. Dun & Co. would report in March 1871 that they "have obtained a quantity of [subscriptions] to their paper by dint of intrusive persistency, which has been as notorious as disagreeable. They have been accused of black mailing in their publication, which is believed by well posted parties." As to their "brokerage" house, it was a failure from the beginning—"no standing whatever," as R. G. Dun & Co. would put it. Vanderbilt denied being their partner in court, and the evidence supports him.[80]

But it *does* seem clear that Vanderbilt sought the sisters' visions. Dr. William Bodenhamer, a leading physician who would attend the Commodore on his deathbed, later testified that Vanderbilt confessed his belief in "clairvoyance." A deep accumulation of evidence suggests that he started to attend séances as early as 1864. In 1870, the high point of Spiritualism in American history, this was not unusual. Bodenhamer—who also testified to Vanderbilt's exceptionally clear mind, even when in intense pain—observed of his faith, "Many most intelligent and intellectual men in our country believe the same." It is doubtful that the Commodore made decisions based on the sisters' supposed revelations. Marie Antoinette Pollard, for example, was not a good witness: she was a felon, having shot a druggist in Baltimore, and couldn't identify Lambert Wardell, Vanderbilt's eternal gatekeeper. Even if she accurately quoted

---

* As mentioned previously, Edward Renehan Jr. claims in *Commodore: The Life of Cornelius Vanderbilt* (New York: Basic Books, 2007) to have discovered the privately held diary of Dr. Jared Linsly and that of sleeping-car manufacturer Webster Wagner, asserting that they show that Vanderbilt contracted syphilis in 1839 and began to show signs of dementia in 1868 (manifested in his backing of Woodhull and Claflin). Renehan claims that Vanderbilt descended into madness thereafter, and was used as a puppet by William for the rest of his life. In light of much contradictory evidence and subsequent developments, I must discount the validity of these sources and find Renehan's claims to be untenable. See the bibliographical essay, pages 581–4, for a full discussion.

Vanderbilt ("Why don't you do as I do, and consult the spirits?"), she took it as an attempt to put her off. "He was so gruff that I left," she said. Whenever Woodhull or Claflin were put on the spot in court, they would admit that they went to Vanderbilt for money and advice, not the other way around.[81]

The most likely explanation for his role in the sisters' scandalous, flamboyant adventures is simpler. It came from their mother—another unreliable witness, but with a believable story. He turned to them for magnetic healing, or rubbing, of his various aches and pains. He felt better, and perhaps took part in séances with them. He might have slept with Claflin, but ceased to before his second marriage. Impressed with the sisters' intelligence, allure, and forthrightness, he put their money into the stock market, and made a small fortune for them. Woodhull's husband, James H. Blood, who served as their writer, accountant, and impresario, suggested that they open a brokerage house with their new stake—perhaps only as a publicity stunt. Vanderbilt agreed to carry their stocks (as Woodhull later testified in court), though he would not spare them losses, and did not endorse or join their firm. He felt uncomfortable with their notoriety, and never gave them permission to use his name; but, fond of them still, he did not run very fast in the other direction.[82]

This scenario was eccentric enough, if not so satisfyingly outrageous as the myth. In the vast scope of Vanderbilt's affairs, from his extensive social circle to his various railroads to his new wife, Woodhull and Claflin were a minor diversion. But their notoriety, and his discomfort, would grow.

THE GREATEST ACCOMPLISHMENT of Vanderbilt's railroad reign culminated with surprisingly little fanfare. On January 27, 1870, he took part in the first stockholders' meeting of the New York Central & Hudson River Railroad. It was one of the largest corporations in American history—and his own special creation. He took office as president, of course, and made William his vice president. (Daniel Torrance had been the Central's vice president until consolidation.) To "equalize values," they set the stock of the company at $90 million (at the par value of $100 per share), an increase of 85 percent for the Hudson River and 27 percent for the Central, amounting to over $44 million in new shares. This figure astounded the public. As Charles F. Adams Jr. pointedly (and predictably) observed, twenty years earlier no corporation in the country had had a capitalization of more than $10 million. The new Central's semiannual 4 percent dividend on April 15 amounted to $3.6 million, "the very largest single dividend ever paid in this country by any one great corporation or state," the *New York Times* wrote.[83]

The Empire State had never seen anything like Vanderbilt's new empire. From St. John's Park to the shores of Lake Erie, its tracks stretched 740 miles in length, with branches fingering out another three hundred miles. It operated 132 baggage cars, four hundred locomotives, 445 passenger cars, and 9,026 freight cars. In 1870, the consolidating railroads carried some 7,045,000 passengers and 4,122,000 tons of freight. Though the number of employees remains uncertain, the payroll figures were vast: nearly $752,000 paid to engineers and firemen; $600,000 to porters, watchmen, flagmen, and switch tenders; $512,000 to conductors, baggagemen, and brakemen; and $185,000 for "general superintendence." These statistics speak to its vast economic displacement, which was rather that of a giant in a bathtub. No other enterprise in New York came close to these figures—not even its rival trunk line, the Erie, which was only three-quarters its size. The Central ran through all of the state's largest cities, with the exception of Brooklyn; in each, it was the single largest economic force, with its enormous payroll, voracious needs, and near monopoly on intercity transportation. Few businesses in the country, apart from a very few other railroads, boasted a capitalization as large as one-tenth that of the New York Central & Hudson River; and few if any factories represented investment equal to what it spent on fuel alone each year ($1,869,000).[84]

The New York Central & Hudson River (to be called simply the New York Central, or the Central, hereafter) was not an isolated phenomenon. The Pennsylvania Railroad in particular was building a vast integrated system from the Mississippi to the Atlantic. But it marked a decisive turn in economic history. By consolidating two companies of great size and financial health, it created a single behemoth on an unprecedented scale. This new entity, the giant corporation, would spread into manufacturing, as seen first in Standard Oil and later in other industries, beginning with a great wave of mergers from 1895 to 1904; eventually it would dominate every other sector of the economy as well. It would introduce economies of scale, lower prices, multiply productivity—and either crush out smaller businesses or set the terms of their existence. And it introduced bureaucratic management into American business. On the Central, Vanderbilt and son set about a program of rationalization that standardized procedures and introduced a departmental system of organization.[85]

The giant corporation would bring Americans of all stripes into its orbit with remarkable speed. A professional and managerial middle class began to emerge as the educated and skilled went to work as engineers, lawyers, technical experts, clerks, and middle managers for large companies. The ranks of permanent wage workers swelled, both within railroads and in the industries that fed their needs or expanded with the new markets they opened up. Labor prospered during the postwar boom, enjoying a 40 percent growth in average real income from 1865 through late 1873. Indeed, the rise of the large corporation had its counterpart in the expanding, increasingly militant union movement. Significantly, William H. Vanderbilt signed the first contract with the Brotherhood of Locomotive Engineers in the New York Central's history.

None of these changes were absolute, of course. Small producers, self-employed artisans, and other survivors of the old economy coexisted with the enterprises and unions of the new industrial, corporate economy. The outlook of social philosophers, labor organizers, economists, and businessmen alike remained rooted in the past. But the creation of the New York Central & Hudson River stands as a historical landmark, showing us where the era of big business—the Vanderbilt era—well and truly began.[86]

There is a double irony to all this. Vanderbilt had first marched onto the economic battlefield like a Viking warrior, storming the ramparts of corporations under the banner of the individual competitor. Now his flag fluttered from the greatest corporate fortress to date—one with a monopoly on rail transportation into Manhattan. He had put aside the sword in favor of statecraft. All he wanted was to be left alone to manage his realm. It was a task that demanded constant attention, even from a leader who tried to remain above matters of detail. As big as the Central was, Vanderbilt personally sustained it during the consolidation process, paying hundreds of thousands of dollars out of his own accounts to smooth its cash flow. The Harlem, too, announced it would issue twenty thousand shares to pay for the Grand Central Depot. Vanderbilt would buy them. Meanwhile William scheduled new trains to compete directly with the Hudson River steamboats, and began to re-lay tracks with steel rails (more expensive but far more durable than those of iron). Work began on a new double-track bridge at Albany. And Horace Clark joined in his father-in-law's diplomatic initiatives. On May 4, Clark took over the presidency of the Lake Shore, with Augustus Schell as vice president and Banker as treasurer; in short order they arranged with connecting roads for a passenger through line from Cincinnati, Louisville, and St. Louis, over the Central to New York.[87]

The second irony was that Vanderbilt would not be allowed to live in peace. Instead, his enemies forced him to fight once more. Those enemies were Jay Gould and Jim Fisk. In the end, their rivalry with Vanderbilt would loom above his larger but more sedate accomplishments, transforming the long-lived Commodore into one side of a matched set in American memory. But Vanderbilt himself bears some of the blame for history's overemphasis on his feud with Gould and Fisk. They angered him, embittered him, as no other enemies ever had or ever would. One

coldly unpredictable and lethally resourceful, the other predictably flamboyant and surprisingly shrewd, they refused to abide by the rules of combat that were so important to the Commodore. Again and again, they
provoked him into publicly overreacting despite the Erie's limited capacity for competition with the mighty Central.

In early 1870, Gould and Fisk reopened always-festering hostilities by
undercutting the rates set by the most recent trunk line rate agreement. In
May, Gould personally went to Chicago to cultivate livestock shippers,
traditionally loyal customers of the Central. These were the ordinary skirmishes of railroad competition, but Vanderbilt took everything that
Gould and Fisk did personally. On June 1, he declared that he would retal-
iate. Within a week, William slashed passenger fares by 25 percent (cutting the price of a ticket from Chicago to New York from $24.95 to $20);
ceased the practice of checking passengers through to the Erie from the
Great Western of Canada (the Central provided the only link); and
slashed livestock rates from Chicago to New York from $125 a car to
$100, and then $50, in response to Gould's grab for that traffic. Clark
showed a common front, declaring that the Lake Shore would cease to
cooperate with the Erie, leaving Gould dependent on the Fort Wayne, the
Pennsylvania's subsidiary, for a connection to Chicago. *Railroad Gazette*
wrote, "It will be a strange sight to see the Erie and the Pennsylvania
working together."[88]

On June 13, a reporter called at 10 Washington Place for an interview
about the "railroad war." Vanderbilt relished the opportunity to pour
scorn on Gould and Fisk. "We don't pay any attention to them; it would
be beneath us to have a row with them," he said. "You see, my son, there
are some disreputable fellows around this town who have got hold of a
railroad somehow or another, and are trying to run it. . . . To make it a little respectable they talked about a 'war' they'd hatched up with the Central, so as to make folks think that it amounted to something; but there's
nothing in it, nothing in it." The reporter said that Gould and Fisk
accused him of controlling the Lake Shore to their detriment. He replied,
"I don't know anything about it. The Lake Shore Line folks are all honest,
and I run the Central, but the Erie fellows are squealing about it, ain't
they? They can't do anything, nobody'll trust them, the Central has all the
traffic, and they have got none."

The reporter went off to see Gould and Fisk at Pike's Opera House, a
grand structure decorated with cut glass, carved woodwork, and ceiling
frescoes that Fisk had purchased for use as the Erie headquarters. Fisk
indulged in his own bluster. "He talks about us, and here we've had our
doors besieged for the last three days by his relatives, trying to effect a settlement of the affair amicably." When pressed on the fact that the Central

paid dividends and the Erie did not, he snapped, "That's so; we can't, until he sends back the $5,000,000 he took out of the Erie treasury when he left." Fisk's jab served as a reminder that Vanderbilt did, indeed, have a personal motive for the rate war, as the Erie's lawsuit against him continued to drag its slow way through Barnard's courtroom. But the two upstarts were already laying a trap for their wily opponent.[89]

About the time of this interview, Gould and Fisk secretly purchased some six thousand head of livestock in the West. Then, in late June, they announced that they were cutting the Erie's livestock rates to $1 per car. The move forced the Central to follow suit, as they knew it would. Shortly afterward, Gould and Fisk boasted to the press that they had shipped their livestock over the Central at these absurd rates, reaping a rich profit at the Commodore's expense. The Central instantly raised rates to $40 per car. It was one more example of why they irritated Vanderbilt so: they did not simply fight, they sought to humiliate him. And they succeeded.[90]

In July, Vanderbilt took Frank to Saratoga. They checked into the Congress Hall, along with William, the Schell brothers, and some of his other captains. "Mrs. Vanderbilt is admired more for her *hauteur* and modest dignity than for any dazzling beauty," the *New York Commercial* reported from the Springs. As for the Commodore, he was "as hale, hearty, and spry as ever," affectionate with Frank, relaxed and talkative with friends. Abstemious as always, he ate little and watered down his brandy.[91]

He was in good spirits at seven in the morning on August 10 when he went down to the Congress Spring for a draught of mineral water, along with William and Augustus Schell. There he happened across Jay Gould, seemingly by chance. They sat together on a bench, "but a few feet distant from the statue of Cupid," noted a reporter, who thought that Gould and the Commodore actually seemed warm with each other. Before they stood again, they had agreed on the basic outlines of a comprehensive settlement—one that William had discussed with Gould the previous evening. The Erie would withdraw its lawsuit against the Commodore, and both lines would work with the Pennsylvania to create a comprehensive rate agreement, "the same as though a single individual owned all three roads," as William wrote in a memorandum.[92]

The seemingly personal spat that had been going on between the Commodore and Gould and Fisk had national repercussions, forcing yet another realignment of the emerging interregional railway systems. The rate cutting between the Erie and the Central inevitably forced the Pennsylvania to slash prices as well, starting a conflict that would only be settled at a grand trunk line conference in New York in November. Indeed, this rate war demonstrated that the Central's greatest competition for traffic between Chicago and New York was with the Pennsylvania rather than the Erie. During the fight, the Central and the Pennsylvania both ran fast trains to Chicago, the first getting through in thirty hours, the latter in twenty-seven. They were a gimmick, but one that pointed to the relative advantages of each line. The Pennsylvania had a superbly constructed railroad, as well as a more direct route west, saving from forty-nine to sixty-one miles over the Central, depending on the connection to New York. The problem was, it did not have such a connection of its own. To reach New York Harbor, it relied on the United Companies of New Jersey—the old Camden & Amboy, still the state's railroad monopoly—which refused to cut prices, forcing the Pennsylvania to absorb rate-war losses. The Pennsylvania also suffered from heavy grades as its tracks climbed up and over the Appalachians. The Central, on the other hand, had an almost level route the entire way to Chicago, whether by the Lake Shore or North Shore lines. If not quite as short, it allowed locomotives to use less fuel and haul more cars, creating huge savings.

By launching a rate war in 1870, Gould prompted a scramble for control of track that lasted long after peace returned. The Pennsylvania entered into negotiations to lease the United Companies, which it succeeded in doing in 1871. The Central tried to block the Erie from building its own connection to the Niagara Suspension Bridge, until the courts forced it to relent. The New York & New Haven (soon to consolidate with the Hartford & New Haven, which would make Vanderbilt a major stockholder) leased the New England Shore Line, blocking the Erie's access to Boston. In December, the Central and the Lake Shore also made an exclusive contract to receive all the traffic of the Dunkirk, Warren & Pittsburgh, a new railroad being extended into Pennsylvania's oil region. Gould had thought to undermine his more robust rivals; instead he drove them to widen their already vast grip on the rail traffic between the West and the seaports.[93]

Even with these great affairs—and expenses—weighing on him, Vanderbilt may have found the strength to pick up one of the most massive companies outside of the railroad industry: Western Union, the giant telegraph monopoly. On October 12, 1870, five men closely identified with the Commodore moved onto its board of directors: Horace Clark, Augustus Schell, James Banker, Daniel Torrance, and John Steward. Western Union was a classic target for a Vanderbilt takeover: it possessed immense strengths, but needed reform. "With a magnificent income and a constantly increasing business, they found it impossible to pay regular dividends, and the value of the stock had declined to about one third its par value," an industry journal wrote. "The management of the company [will be] placed in the hands of new men. . . . It is intended to dispense with some of the sinecures . . . which have hitherto proved so lucrative to their holders." As was the case in all of the Commodore's takeovers, Clark and associates organized an executive committee and took radical steps to put Western Union's finances in order. And yet, their presence on the board hardly proved that Vanderbilt took a personal stake in the company, at least at this time. Wall Street was ever murky.[94]

For all of the Commodore's power—his cunning, his nerve, his strategic vision—some things remained beyond his control. The federal government had decided to tax the scrip dividend issued by the Central in 1868 at the standard 5 percent, for a total of $1,150,000. Vanderbilt claimed that the dividend represented earnings made before the income tax had been created, and should be exempt. In May he had sent Clark, Schell, and William to Washington to argue his case, to no avail.[95] On November 21 he went in person, taking Clark and Schell with him. The next day, he struck one observer in the Internal Revenue office as the "brightest and quickest" of the three. As Clark stated their case, Vanderbilt "did not hestitate to thunder out his opinion whenever he could get a word in edgeways, in a manner that would indicate he was used to driving everything before him."

As they got up to go, Vanderbilt said, "I am not very good at this kind of business. The last time I was here, it was on business. I said I could do better." He referred to his gift of the *Vanderbilt* to the navy. Even now, he took pride in the vessel. "Why, they never gave me my vessel back," he explained. Yes, he had made a gift of it, but the navy had abandoned it. "The finest ship ever built is now rotting at the wharves in San Francisco." He felt mistreated, and now felt a personal stake in the dividend-tax question above and beyond the money. "We'll make war if I don't get justice," he declared. The curious term "justice" speaks to his state of mind. This man of honor was accustomed to enforcing his idea of fairness on the world.[96]

"THIS IS VANDERBILT, probably the most powerful individuality in America," a reporter for the *Chicago Tribune* wrote in August 1870. "I saw him at Saratoga, sitting on the porch of the Congress Hall—a very tall, straight, graceful, and noticeable old man . . . surrounded by parasites—all of them coarser-looking men." The writer reflected that Vanderbilt was a fine name for a tycoon, especially one so dignified, so careful and honest with his corporate interests. "He is a member of society, a man of administration and not a thief. . . . On the other hand, what has this richest American done for any other motive than immediate gain?"[97]

At that moment, a fifty-year-old Methodist minister named Charles F. Deems was answering the question. Four years earlier, he had come from the South to New York, where he felt "the weight of Andersonville around his neck," his son wrote, in reference to the infamous Confederate prison camp. (That is to say, he felt ostracized because of Northerners' anger over Andersonville, rather than suffering guilt over its horrors.) He decided to establish a sanctuary for Southerners in Manhattan. On July 22, 1866, he began to rent the New York University chapel for weekly services. He called his flock the Church of the Strangers. One Sunday two new women attended, and became regular congregants: Frank Crawford Vanderbilt and her mother, who had moved into 10 Washington Place. In their chats with him, they strongly implied that he should call at the Vanderbilt home.[98]

In the year since the Commodore's second marriage, he had gradually curtailed his evenings at the Manhattan Club. Now and then he would have a party of friends over to his house to play whist or, more frequently now, euchre (a card game played by four people, teamed in pairs). His companions included Joseph Harker, Chester W. Chapin, and Cornelius Garrison, whom Vanderbilt had grown to like a great deal. But the aging Commodore came to prefer quiet evenings at home with his wife and his mother-in-law. He welcomed Deems, whom he had met briefly before the war, and the minister became a regular dinner guest.[99]

"The Commodore paid me special attention," Deems recalled. Over dinner or in the parlor afterward, often with Daniel Drew as a guest, Vanderbilt questioned Deems closely "about my preaching, my past history, and my expectations of the future." When the subject of "clerical beggars" came up—a sore point for Vanderbilt—Deems loftily pronounced to Frank that he delivered his sermons just a block from the Commodore's house, but he would never ask a dollar from him. Vanderbilt shot him "one of those steely looks of his which were very piercing and very subduing." Deems realized that he had sounded rather like a beggar as well, so he continued in a lighthearted tone, "For, if he has lived to attain his present age and has not got the sense to see what I need and the grace to send it to me, he will die without the sight!" They all laughed, and the subject lapsed.[100]

"I regarded him as an unscrupulous gatherer of money," Deems recalled. "The few interviews I had had with him after his marriage had modified my opinions of the man. I discovered fine points of which I had had no suspicion. But I was still a little afraid of him." One Saturday evening in July 1870, before Vanderbilt went to Saratoga, he called Deems up to a little office he kept next to his bedroom. He had heard that the minister was negotiating for the purchase of the Mercer Street Presbyterian Church for $50,000. "Doctor, I'll give you that church."

Deems flared indignantly. "There is not any man in America rich enough to have me for a chaplain."

"Doctor, I don't know what you mean. Lord knows I've got as little use for a chaplain as any other man you ever saw. I want to give you this church, and give it to you only. Now will you take it?"

"Commodore," Deems replied, "if you give me that church for the Lord Jesus Christ, I'll most thankfully accept it."

"Now, doctor, I would not give it to you that way, because that would be professing to you a religious sentiment I do not feel. I want to give you a church; that's all there is."

The two men stood up together. "Commodore, in whatever spirit you give it, I am deeply obliged, but I shall receive it in the name of the Lord Jesus Christ."

At the beginning of August, Vanderbilt wired Deems from Saratoga that negotiations for the purchase of the church were complete. He instructed the minister to see Lambert Wardell, who handed him a package containing $50,000 in cash.[101]

For a man so comfortable with financial abstractions, Vanderbilt was an extremely concrete thinker in other respects. He questioned Deems about his personal history and character, not his theology. As he remarked to the minister one summer evening, as Deems fanned himself in the heat, "Doctor, all you've said has had no more weight with me than that fan."[102] He focused on people, after studying them over a lifetime in business. He liked and trusted Deems, and that was what mattered. When the minister suggested a board of trustees for the church, Vanderbilt refused—he wanted to give the building to Deems, and only Deems. As far as his mission went, it was the outreach to Southerners, rather than the promise of salvation, that appealed to the Commodore. It planted the seed of a vastly larger project to heal the war-torn nation.

THERE WERE SOME FAMILY AFFAIRS that were in Vanderbilt's control, and some that weren't. The most amenable to control was the New York Central & Hudson River Railroad. As early as 1871, his grandson Henry Allen heard him boast that he had put the Central in such good condition that it could run itself. His sometimes truculent daughters were another matter. Mary La Bau snubbed Frank, and Sophia Torrance sniped at her father's wife behind her back. When Vanderbilt mentioned it to young Allen, a particular friend of Sophia's, Henry made excuses. "I said to him that he knew how impulsive Mrs. Torrance was, and often said things she didn't mean," Henry recalled. "He assumed a stern expression, as was usual with him when he was in earnest, and said, 'Oh, no! They've all been talking. Billy has told me enough.' "[103]

Frank did not need her husband's protection. Where he was fierce, she was elegant, dignified, and cultured. She dazzled patrician onlookers at the closing ball of the summer season in Saratoga in 1871. "Mrs. Commodore Vanderbilt," a society columnist wrote, "was dressed in exquisite taste. She had a white satin-striped grenadine; train trimmed with ruffles of the same, bound with white satin; full overskirt, looped, and trimmed with ruffles of the same; corsage high, with point-lace trimmings; and very rare diamonds." She promenaded at the clubhouse of the patrician Jerome Park with her husband at the opening of the fall races, and raised money for the Sisters of the Strangers, a volunteer group of aristocratic ladies, to which the Commodore contributed. Frank polished her husband's gold, as it were, until elite society began to forget that it had ever seen tarnish there.[104]

Ellen Vanderbilt did her best to rescue the reputation of her husband Corneil with the Commodore. The couple struggled, as always. Corneil lost his Treasury job after his supervisor absconded with thousands of dollars. The pair lingered in New York, borrowing money from Greeley. Ellen called at 10 Washington Place, alone. "I passed a very pleasant evening at the Commodore's & like Madame extremely," she wrote to Greeley. "William & his wife took tea with us. I spoke of your calling to see me & I never heard the Commodore speak in such rapturous terms of anyone as he did of you. He said you were the best man in New York, the fairest & squarest, the most honest of anyone he knew." It is striking that Vanderbilt should praise precisely those qualities that Corneil himself lacked.[105]

The Commodore could never bring himself to turn completely away from his son. When one of Ellen's sisters visited Vanderbilt in May 1871, she reported that, despite his being preoccupied and "miserable" with a flare-up of rheumatism, he questioned her closely about Corneil, showing great concern. Corneil went to visit his father at his office one morning, interrupting a meeting with other railroad executives. Vanderbilt told him to come back for lunch, and they spent much of the afternoon together. "He raised my salary [sic] a hundred dollars & gave me his check for $300," Corneil wrote to a friend, "and he said that he should do better as he became satisfied that I was continuing to improve." Clearly Vanderbilt loved his son, but, to use one of the Commodore's favorite words, he was no sucker.[106]

Corneil was always in over his head. But a crisis even overwhelmed Jacob Vanderbilt, the relative best equipped to take care of himself. On July 30, 1871, the Staten Island ferryboat *Westfield* exploded. Early reports put the death toll at ninety-three, with 113 injured. The Commodore himself had built the *Westfield*, which he had sold with all his ferryboats to the Staten Island Railroad, headed by Jacob, in 1863. To put it mildly, the city was outraged. A coroner's jury found criminal neglect, and a grand jury indicted Jacob for homicide. A long, difficult fight for Jacob's life ensued.[107]

As one relic of Vanderbilt's career fatally disintegrated, a lasting tribute to his life arose on Forty-second Street. On June 30, the *New York World* announced, "The great railroad depot erected by Commodore Vanderbilt at Forty-second Street is at last completed and ready for its occupants. This building . . . is a magnificent ornament to the city, and will doubtless prove a lasting monument to its builder. New York can now boast of the largest railroad depot in the country." It was the second largest in the world, a brick bastion with white iron trim, standing three stories high (160 feet to the top of the central tower), 240 feet wide, and 692 feet deep, extending north from Forty-second Street. A huge train shed, or "car house," stretched 650 feet long under an arched glass roof. The statistics of what went into the depot were staggering: eight million pounds of iron, ten million bricks, twenty thousand barrels of cement, plus eighty thousand feet of glass in the roof of the car house alone. Newfangled lights illuminated its vast interiors at night, and 75,000 feet of pipe carried steam to heat its expansive offices and waiting rooms.[108]

Vanderbilt paid for the construction out of his own bank accounts. Grand Central belonged to the Harlem Railroad, in which he, William, and William's sons now owned almost all the stock, and which had *not* been consolidated into the New York Central & Hudson River. In May, William presented figures to the board showing that his father had paid $2,027,146.51 in cash, taking about $1.5 million in stock in return and loaning the rest. (The final cost, including real estate, would be $6,419,118.10.) It formally opened on November 1, receiving about fifteen passenger trains each day and sending another fourteen up the quadruple track that ran over the surface of Fourth Avenue.[109]

The terminal had critics.* "The new 'Grand Central Depot' can only by a stretch of courtesy be called either central or grand," the *New York Times* groused—unfairly. For one thing, city and state law dictated how far downtown it could be placed; for another, it sat on the inner edge of the East Side, where the city grew fastest—growth that Grand Central would accelerate. The comprehensive street and sewage construction that Tweed had started provided the infrastructure for rapid development up to the Harlem River. The Commodore had seen the city expand from a mere town to a global metropolis during his lifetime; he had every reason to expect it to swell past his new depot, as the population increased from 942,292 in 1870 to 1,206,299 in 1880.[110]

---

* The old station on Twenty-sixth Street was sold, and became the first Madison Square Garden.

But the building was far from perfect. Though the car house was relatively free of engine smoke (locomotives unhooked from the cars before entering the shed and rolled off onto sidings, letting momentum carry the trains in), the lobby arrangements were peculiar. The New York Central, the Harlem, and the New York & New Haven each had separate waiting rooms; a passenger transferring from one railroad to another had to exit the building. In part, this was a design issue that the architects simply had not considered. But it also reflected the decentralized nature of Vanderbilt's empire. Rather like Spain under the Hapsburg kings, the Commodore's realm consisted of various railroad principalities united only by his own private estate. This reflected his often-overlooked sensitivity to public opinion, but the Harlem was also a property of great personal meaning to him. After rescuing the long-scorned company and raising it up to glory, he may well have resisted its consolidation into the Central out of purely sentimental motives.

Vanderbilt, that student of human nature, did not lend sentimentality to people as easily as he did to property. He had entrusted the Lake Shore to intelligent, independent men—Clark, Schell, and Banker—and they ran it in an independent but not always intelligent way. Though they supported the Commodore's fight with the Erie in 1870, they began to engage in their own stock market operations. After their experience with the Central stock dividend, they loudly hinted at a similar dividend on the Lake Shore. When they finally announced it in the summer of 1871, it turned out to be smaller than expected: $15 million at par value, one-third to be paid by shareholders to fund the double-tracking of the line. "The Lake Shore tactics have a more bungled look than the strategy adopted in New York Central," the *New York Herald* wrote. "Perhaps, after all, the venerable Commodore has been only letting his pupils try their hands at the game which he made so famous. In any view, the Lake Shore movement has lacked the brilliancy and Napoleonic skill displayed in the New York Central case."[111]

Then the Lake Shore suffered a staggering blow: the great Chicago fire of 1871. On October 7, according to the *Herald*, a woman named Scully on De Koven Street went out to tend to a sick calf in the darkness; her candle overturned in the hay. The ensuing conflagration proved so devastating that the *Herald* simply reported, "Chicago is wiped out." Wiped out with it was the Lake Shore depot, owned jointly with the Chicago, Rock Island & Pacific. The company estimated its share of rebuilding at $350,000.[112]

Still, the railroad declared 8 percent dividends that year, and the trio who ran it showed no lack of confidence. The newspapers identified Banker, still the vice president of the Bank of New York, as "the prime mover in all the current cliques and contrivances to move the Street, and the biggest man known around the brokers' offices." Wielding skills acquired in Vanderbilt's service, he managed the pooled funds of his allies. He affected an aristocratic lifestyle, and ordered a custom-built yacht.[113]

Augustus Schell and Horace Clark remained the senior partners. And, in 1871, they began to attain political power that they had not seen since 1860, as long-bubbling complaints over the flagrant corruption of Tweed-run Tammany boiled over into crisis. Tweed had softened opposition to his power by limiting taxes, which caused the city's indebtedness to rise from $30 million in 1866 to $90 million in 1871. In the latter year, the *Times* published evidence of Tweed's corruption in a series of spectacular articles. On September 4, a mass meeting assembled at Cooper Union and appointed a Committee of Seventy to return city government to the hands of safe, respectable men. The committee's attack was led by two Democratic allies of Clark and Schell, Samuel J. Tilden and Charles O'Conor, the latter appointed special prosecutor by the governor. They had Tweed arrested on October 26. The ring fell.[114]

"The first deadly breach made in Tammany was the foundation of the Manhattan Club," the *Times* reported. It identified Schell and Clark as leaders of the "silk-stocking sachems" of Tammany who "loved and revered its old traditions and its dignity, began to regard it as degenerate and degrading, and they seceded in a body." With Tweed gone, the old stalwarts took the Hall back. On December 30, the reformed Tammany elected Augustus Schell the new Grand Sachem by acclamation.[115]

If Banker led the trio on Wall Street and Schell in politics, Clark reigned as the railroad executive and chief strategist among Vanderbilt's "pupils." Talkative, nervous, and soft-fleshed, the Lake Shore's president finally achieved the wealth and power he had dreamed of since George Templeton Strong dismissed him as a vulgar climber twenty years earlier. Success only whetted his ambition. And his ambition would lead him into an alliance with the enemy whom Vanderbilt disliked more than any other.

Chapter Eighteen

DYNASTY

First pride, then the fall. More than a proverb, this formula seems to be a natural law. Readers of fiction, political pundits, and students of the business cycle all know that what goes up eventually reverses course—usually soon after a sense of invulnerability has set in. But there are different kinds of pride, and not all lead to destruction.

A circle of extremely proud men sat atop the railroad industry at the start of 1872: J. Edgar Thomson and Thomas A. Scott of the Pennsylvania, John W. Garrett of the Baltimore & Ohio, Jay Gould of the Erie, James F. Joy of the Michigan Central, Horace F. Clark of the Lake Shore, and, proudest of all, Cornelius Vanderbilt. When the time for a fall arrived, Vanderbilt alone would stand unbent and unbroken—though not uninjured. The key to his survival would be the nature of his pride. It never became complacency, and, great as he was, he paid heed to the world around him.

On January 12, 1872, for example, the Commodore received a delegation of the residents of Fourth Avenue, come to complain about the Harlem Railroad's new Grand Central Depot—or, rather, the increase in rail traffic down the surface of the avenue upon Grand Central's completion. More than a dozen trains a day ran in each direction, leading to fatal accidents. The noise, smoke, and danger of the trains had long been a grievance of uptown residents. Now the *New York Times* had turned their cause into a crusade. Backed by the *Times*'s daily editorials, they wanted the tracks buried in a tunnel and the train shed of the depot itself sunk below the surface of the avenue.[1]

A reporter for the *New York Herald* observed that the Commodore listened "attentively," and replied that "the great question was as to the best method of carrying out this proposed object. . . . It would certainly cost a heap of money." He named $5 million as the likely figure, and stated flatly that the railroad could not afford the entire cost. The owners of the real estate along the avenue shared an economic interest in this matter, he noted; sinking the tracks would increase the value of their lands. "When we get a piece of property, and we want to improve that piece of property, why, let each of us pay our proportion." (The fall of Tweed, he remarked elsewhere, made such a step possible, for the ring had blocked any such plan without a large payoff.)[2]

Two weeks later, Vanderbilt presided over a conference with the Citizens' Eastside Association in the offices of Grand Central and presented a plan that he had ordered from J. C. Buckhout, the railroad's chief engineer. It would leave the expensive car house exactly where it was, but sink the tracks below the surface of the avenue, starting at Forty-eighth Street, in an open cut, with overpasses at each intersection "so arranged that horses could not see approaching trains." At Ninety-seventh Street, where the terrain dropped into the Harlem Flats, a viaduct would run above the streets. Buckhout put the cost at $4 million (not far from Vanderbilt's original guess). The Harlem's directors, Vanderbilt said, "were not wedded to any particular plan, but were ready to adopt that which would be the most feasible, and best adapted to the interests of the community."

The conferences revealed the Commodore to be as mentally sharp as ever, not to mention politic. Though some on the committee grumbled about not getting everything they wanted, most agreed that the plan he presented was a reasonable compromise.[3]

Reasonable is a word that historians have rarely linked to the Commodore's name, but it defined his behavior as a railroad leader. He was especially reasonable in his attempts to cooperate with his fellow corporate titans. There was nothing new about that, of course. Adam Smith himself observed in *The Wealth of Nations*, "People of the same trade seldom meet together, even for merriment and diversion, but the conversation ends in a conspiracy against the public." As we have seen, formal and informal devices to control competition arose simultaneously with competition itself in American history. Among the railroad trunk lines, these efforts were particularly pronounced, leading to repeated attempts to erect highly structured cartels. Once constructed, railroads were there to stay, even if they went bankrupt. The fights between them could only be settled through takeovers or cooperation—and even the Commodore could not buy up every rival line. Nor did he want to. The companies most likely to slash prices were those in the most desperate condition.[4]

Vanderbilt, then, naturally grasped an opportunity to cooperate with the Pennsylvania in order to control one of the most lucrative kinds of freight. But the scheme that now unfolded spoke to something larger than the tension between competition and cooperation; it reflected the increasing concentration of power in the American economy. Four companies came together in this plot: the Central, the Pennsylvania, the Erie, and John D. Rockefeller's Standard Oil. Each was a giant in its industry, and Standard Oil was still growing rapidly, gobbling up its rivals. The symbolism of their conspiracy, far more than its actual impact on business, would turn it into one of the most notorious incidents in the rise of corporate capitalism in America.

On December 14, 1871, Vanderbilt was approached by Peter H. Watson, an executive of the Ashtabula & Franklin, a Lake Shore subsidiary that ran to the Pennsylvania oil fields. Watson invited the Commodore into a plan to divide the rail traffic in petroleum. They would do so through a shell corporation, the South Improvement Company (SIC). By far the largest refiner in the SIC would be Standard Oil. The plan had the following components: First, the SIC would provide the cars, pumps, tanks, and other equipment for shipping oil and kerosene. Second, the SIC would receive special rebates (as high as 50 percent) on freight charges. Third, the SIC would receive drawbacks from shipments made by other refiners—that is, a percentage of the money paid by outsiders would go to the SIC. Finally, the SIC's shipments would be split three ways, with 45 percent going to the Pennsylvania and 27.5 percent each to the Erie and the New York Central & Hudson River.[5]

The Pennsylvania's ingenious vice president, Thomas A. Scott, appears to have concocted the SIC, but it offered Vanderbilt multiple advantages. The provision of tanker cars, for example, would save the Central a great deal of money. Since tanker cars could be used for no other product, they rolled back to Cleveland or the oil region empty, a frustrating expense. The traffic division locked in the Pennsylvania's existing two-to-one advantage, but it also guaranteed the Central's share in the face of Scott's aggressive attempts to control oil shipments. Finally, it would add predictability and stability to the business produced by this rapidly growing and changing industry.

Watson, Rockefeller wrote to his wife on December 15, "saw Com. Vanderbilt last night & succeeded *admirably*, so that now we count surely on Clark, him, & W. H. Vanderbilt." This letter is telling: the Commodore conducted the talks without his son's involvement. William later testified that he had had nothing to do with the SIC negotiations, saying, "The contract was made and handed to me to sign." William had little affection for Rockefeller, who demanded special treatment by the railroads; in 1872, William would complain of the rising titan, "These oil men are sharp fellows & would like us to carry the oil for nothing." Seven years later, he would be heard to say that he "was disgusted with oil companies and oil men long ago." Historical caricatures notwithstanding, William struck many businessmen as less diplomatic than his famously imperious father (at this point in the Commodore's career, that is). "He has worked against me in petty ways," one man had complained of William in 1868, and behaved in a "dirty, contemptible manner." The superintendent of the Michigan Central would write in 1874, "He is ambitious, headstrong, and our experience shows to some extent unreliable & unfair." The Central's partners found the Commodore to be much more reasonable.[6]

The Pennsylvania legislature obediently chartered the SIC, as instructed by Scott. The forty-eight-year-old possessed one of the most brilliant minds of his times. With a head of thick, graying hair and writhing sideburns rather like those of the Commodore, he had a handsome face and large, engaging eyes—and served as mentor to Andrew Carnegie. Contemporaries called this witty, dapper man "Colonel Scott," in tribute to his service as assistant secretary of war early in the Civil War. The Pennsylvania's president, J. Edgar Thomson, relied heavily on him to craft the railroad's strategy.[7]

The cooperation between Vanderbilt and Scott was something of a paradox, for they represented contrary models of corporate executive. Vanderbilt exemplified the owner as manager—the amateur, the financier who purchased a majority of the stock and then took charge. By contrast, Scott and Thomson were professional executives who had risen through the ranks on their managerial merits. They owned relatively little stock, and ran the Pennsylvania on behalf of largely passive shareholders. As manager, not owner, Scott pioneered the art of operating through shell companies. With his skillful manipulation of the compliant state legislature, he created corporations for special purposes that were financed by the Pennsylvania but controlled by himself and Thomson. The Central's fast-freight lines were cooperative ventures with connecting lines, for instance, nothing more than management devices for efficient handling of through freight. The Pennsylvania's were distinct corporations, created by Scott, controlled by Scott, and paying dividends to Scott, with some left over for the railroad. Blandly dubbed "transportation" or "improvement" companies, Scott's shell corporations sometimes created managerial efficiencies, but always allowed him to personally control (and siphon money from) vast properties beyond the grasp of any individual stockholder.[8]

Scott and Vanderbilt forged divergent paths toward the future of the large enterprise in the American economy. Scott, along with Thomson, crafted the seemingly more sophisticated model, erecting holding companies to lease or purchase connecting lines far beyond the borders of Pennsylvania. Under his guidance, the Pennsylvania created a massive self-contained system that sprawled from the Mississippi River to the Atlantic seaboard, from the Great Lakes to the Gulf Coast. But the Commodore moved more cautiously. He pursued cooperation with his connections, and refrained from interfering in his son-in-law Clark's management of the Lake Shore. If Vanderbilt's decentralized strategy seems less advanced, it reflected his ever-astute calculations. He did not wish to alienate important partners, such as the Michigan Central. And he did not want to burden himself or the Central with financially unstable properties. As Scott aggressively acquired line after line, he found it more and more difficult to make them all pay; by contrast, Vanderbilt insulated the Central from the weaknesses of its connections—even from the Lake Shore, which he largely owned.[9]

Scott possessed great powers of mind, but he suffered from overconfidence. More and more, he began to overreach. Acting on his own account, he joined with his protégé Carnegie in 1871 to seize the Union Pacific in a complex operation, taking over as president. Already overworked, he gave little attention to his new duties. Carnegie quickly sold their shares at a profit, and the stockholders concluded to overthrow their absentee chief. In 1872, Scott began to promote the Texas & Pacific, a planned transcontinental road that increasingly weighed him down with debt and worry.[10]

As for the SIC, it soon collapsed under the weight of public outrage once the terms of its contracts were revealed. At a closed meeting on March 25 with angry refiners, officers of the participating railroads (including Scott and William H. Vanderbilt) abandoned it. The railroad men refused even to let Rockefeller into the room. But Rockefeller would go on with his conquest of the oil industry, and would press the railroads for further privileges and rebates, much to William's annoyance. And the Commodore would continue to look for cooperation with his competitors.

In the ensuing year, observers might wonder how he could harmonize the warring railroads when he could not even control his own house.[11]

EVERYBODY DIES—just not always in the right order. By all logic, Cornelius Vanderbilt should have gone before any of his many familiars who died in 1872. He turned seventy-eight that year, decades past life expectancy. He had survived fistfights, boiler explosions, a train wreck, heart trouble, Nicaraguan rapids, exposure to tropical diseases, Atlantic storms, and wagon smashes. Yet he endured as those younger than himself passed away. On February 24, LeGrand Lockwood fell dead at fifty-two, still in debt to the Lake Shore. Before that, on January 6, the "porcine carcass" of the thirty-eight-year-old Jim Fisk tumbled down the steps of the Grand Central Hotel, shot by Edward S. Stokes, and died soon after. "I cannot sufficiently give expression to the extent I suffer over the catastrophe," Jay Gould told the *New York Herald*. It was, perhaps, more than a coincidence that Gould lost control of the Erie Railway in just two months to an assault led by financier James McHenry. (Two years later, McHenry would recall that he offered control of the Erie to Commodore Vanderbilt, who declined, suggesting Peter H. Watson instead.) Lockwood and Fisk probably drew little of Vanderbilt's sympathy. In December, he would coldly testify at Stokes's trial, "I had a very bad opinion of Mr. Fisk since I first knew him."[12]

But death took friends and family as well as foes. On March 25, Ellen Vanderbilt died of pneumonia in West Hartford.[13] The loss of this self-sacrificing young woman struck Vanderbilt to the core. He received the news as he sat in his office at 25 West Fourth Street, talking with J. C. Smith, a railroad contractor. When he first had learned of his son's engagement to Ellen, he told Smith, he had gone to Hartford to meet her. He had taken her out in a carriage and recounted Corneil's many misdeeds. She had replied, "Commodore, isn't some of it your fault? Have you always treated him as you should?" At that, Vanderbilt related, he had looked around and said, "What a beautiful city"—because "he knew the thing was up."

What a rare burst of reflection, even self-criticism, the death of this young woman induced. It speaks to both the tenderness he felt for his daughter-in-law and the conflicting emotions that his tortured and torturing son aroused in him. On an evening soon after Ellen's death, Vanderbilt told Rev. Syndey A. Corey how he had approached her father, Oliver Williams, before the wedding and pestered him about her possessions. Williams naturally (and indignantly) had asked the reason for such questions. The Commodore had replied, "If your girl has silver and jewelry, and silk and satins, and fine shawls, and my son marries her, he will steal them away from her, pawn them, and gamble away the proceeds." Williams had said that Vanderbilt was giving his son a bad reputation. "I feel that it is due to your daughter," Vanderbilt had said. "It can't be as painful to you to hear as it is for me to say it."[14]

Corneil had been loosely moored at best since the death of his mother. The loss of his devoted wife set him almost literally adrift. He took up with George Terry, an unmarried hotel keeper whom Corneil considered "my dearest friend." The intensity of their relationship raises the question of precisely how intimate they were. Corneil once addressed a letter to "my darling George." On another occasion, he wrote, "Oh! George I cannot give you up. You must not desert me now, but must be brave & patient, and give me encouragement and hope for the future." In the full context of Corneil's prolific and effusive correspondence, however, such declarations turn out to be less than definitive evidence that their relationship was physical or romantic. It was an era when platonic male friends commonly wrote of their "affection" or "love" for one another—and

Corneil was particularly affectionate when he was asking Terry for money. Ellen had known Terry well, and had struggled together with him to save Corneil from his gambling addiction.[15]

But Terry and Corneil's relationship was certainly intimate. Both men later testified that, after Ellen's death, they became "almost constant companions, sleeping and eating and reading together almost all the time." In the spring, they departed for the West on a journey that would eventually take them to Japan. On June 25, Corneil wrote to Horace Greeley from Denver. "Having constantly employed myself roaming about the Colorado Country, I find myself much improved in health & my nerves more quiet and composed," he wrote. "I have just received quite an affectionate letter from the Commodore. He appears to take a deep interest in me just at present & begs me to do everything to regain my health. I have never known him quite so affectionate."[16]

This stubborn inconsistency by the Commodore was all too comprehensible. Ever a man who did not suffer fools, Vanderbilt felt impatience and scorn for Corneil's weaknesses; yet he unquestionably loved his son, and never quite gave up hope for him. Better parents than he have suffered contradictory emotions over their children.

It was, perhaps, for his son's sake that he assigned Chauncey M. Depew, the Harlem's attorney, to assist Corneil's patron that year. In one of history's ironies, Greeley ran for president as the nominee of the Liberal Republican Party, a breakaway formation of Republicans led by the "best men" who criticized Vanderbilt so fiercely. Depew, like so many who knew Vanderbilt well, recalled that he "took no interest in politics," but had great fondness for Greeley. "Mr. Greeley has been to see me and is very anxious for you to assist him," he told Depew. "If you can aid him in any way I wish you would." Depew obeyed. He helped organize the party in New York and ran for lieutenant governor. It was another point of divergence between the Commodore and William, who very publicly supported Grant in his bid for reelection.[17]

Vanderbilt's detachment from politics may have been a matter of personal taste, or it may have been a deliberate policy. His interests were constantly in play whenever the state legislature met in Albany, and every positive outcome (from Vanderbilt's perspective) was blamed on the Commodore's corruption. In the spring yet another pro-rata bill appeared, threatening to bar the Central from competitive pricing on through freight (condemned as "discrimination" by those who had to pay local rates). The bill went down to defeat because many believed, probably correctly, that it would divert commerce away from New York and into other seaports. Yet accusations of bribery by Vanderbilt as the cause of its demise proliferated.[18] Newspapers made the same charges regarding passage of the act that authorized the sinking of the Fourth Avenue tracks (a project known as the "Fourth Avenue Improvement"), because it required the city to pay half the cost. In fact, a serious theory stood behind this provision: the municipality would receive increased property taxes as real estate values rose, and the city as a whole would benefit from the new infrastructure.[19]

As Vanderbilt had written to Governor E. D. Morgan years before, he wished to avoid entangling his name with anything political, knowing what abuse would ensue. Yet he frequently mingled with political figures who were an integral part of New York's legal and business environment. One of them was Democratic lawyer Samuel J. Tilden, who had played a leading part in Tweed's downfall and would be elected governor in 1874. "I should like to have a little conversation with you," the Commodore wrote to him on May 20, 1872. "If you will do me the favor to stop at my office at your convenience—or at my house in the evening of any day that may suit you." The topic was the lease agreement that the Central and New York & New Haven would sign for the use of Grand Central, but the tone of the letter was light and familiar. He concluded, *"I am sure the ladies would be pleased to see the light of your countenance once more"* (italics in original), revealing that Tilden was a frequent guest at 10 Washington Place. (Tilden reviewed the lease, and sent his corrections to Vanderbilt personally.)[20]

On June 3, Vanderbilt stopped by the Murray Hill home of Horace Clark and encountered Grenville M. Dodge, the former Union general, congressman, and railroad engineer. The Commodore brought up the Central's ongoing dispute with the Internal Revenue Bureau over the tax on the scrip dividend of 1868, discussing it in detail. "He thinks the goverment [sic] has treated him *badly*," Dodge wrote to President Grant. "He feels the matter keenly." More interesting was Vanderbilt's attitude toward Grant. Dodge called Vanderbilt

a warm friend of yours. . . . Says if he should go to you about it at this time it would be misconstrued and he prefers to *pay*—that he should not do anythg [sic] that could hurt you in the campaign. . . . . My only reason for saying a word is the kindly feeling exhibited towards you by *Vanderbilt* and *Clark* and the *very evident* anxiety of former in the case—and his evident disappointment and surprise at the presnt [sic] action of Government.

This warm regard for Grant and Greeley alike reflected Vanderbilt's striking lack of partisanship—his attention to people, not ideology.[21]

Dodge mentioned one other telling aspect of this meeting: he met the Commodore at Clark's house by accident. Dodge had come to discuss with Clark an affair of their own—Clark's rise to the presidency of the Union Pacific, in which Dodge was a leading figure. It marked the full emergence of a starkly independent course for Clark—one that would push Vanderbilt to the brink of disaster.[22]

VANDERBILT'S FAMILY FLOURISHED financially under the arms of the patriarch, and as his offspring and sons-in-law gained strength, they struck out on their own. In 1871, Daniel Torrance had assumed the presidency of the Ohio & Mississippi as a personal project. William involved himself in the management of the Western Union Telegraph Company—perhaps in his father's interest, perhaps in his own.[23] In June 1872, grandson Vanderbilt Allen returned from Egypt. He had gone there (in defiance of the Commodore's wishes) to enroll in the army of the Khedive, the Turkish ruler of that principate. He came back as a Commander of the Order of the Mejidie, a recognition of his valor on the Nile. And his brother Harry formed a Wall Street firm with cousin Samuel Barton. Vanderbilt agreed to give Barton & Allen some of his business, provided they operated strictly on commission, and did not carry stocks or otherwise expose themselves to financial reverses. They agreed.[24]

Then they reneged. Instead, they followed the call of Augustus Schell, James Banker, and Horace Clark. In 1872, this trio abandoned all caution as they forged ahead with stock market speculations and railroad acquisitions on their own behalf. In February, they launched a bull campaign in Union Pacific stock. On March 6, Clark assumed the railroad's presidency, and brought Banker and Schell onto the board. Aha! the press collectively exclaimed—the rise of Clark shows that the Commodore now has control of the transcontinental railroad, and will divert its traffic onto the Central.[25] But no evidence points to Vanderbilt's involvement in the Union Pacific, as some contemporaries observed. "His friends assert that he is not engaged in the many plans set on foot by his ambitious son-in-law," remarked the *New York Herald* on March 7. Clark, Schell, and Banker all loaned money to the Union Pacific, but Vanderbilt did not—an important sign, considering how deeply he enmeshed his personal finances with the railroads he controlled. *Railroad Gazette* pointed out that control of the transcontinental line—a deeply troubled company, far from the classic target of a Vanderbilt takeover—would bring very little benefit to the Commodore's railroads. "The traffic, not large at best, must be pretty well divided before it reaches Chicago even, and a connection a hundred miles long in a State east of Chicago might easily give a more profitable traffic to the Lake Shore or the New York Central than the entire thousand miles of the Union Pacific."[26]

Vanderbilt, though, did engage in enterprises outside of his core railroad empire. In 1872, amid a general clamor for rapid transit through Manhattan, he proposed an underground railroad to run from city hall to Grand Central. He secured a charter for the New York City Rapid Transit Company, ordered a survey, prepared estimates of the cost, and finally concluded that it would not be profitable. Before letting the matter drop, he tried to sell the company to the Harlem Railroad. He recused himself from the vote, and the board declined. New York would have to wait for its subway.[27]

His role in this project had been entirely open, casting more doubt on any secret part in so big an affair as the Union Pacific. But Clark benefited from rumors that Vanderbilt was a member of the "Vanderbilt party," as the press called Clark, Schell, and Banker. The trio likely took advantage of their inside knowledge of Vanderbilt's moves on the stock market, for the Commodore often sent Banker handwritten instructions regarding his securities. On February 10, 1872, he wrote, "Wardell will hand you 1,000,000 of dollars worth of [New York Central] scrip. I wish you would have it exchanged in to stock in one certificate of 10,000 shairs in your name & sign it & give it [to] Wardell for me. I will tell you when I sea you the purpose. Let this be confidential."[28]

Vanderbilt increasingly expressed concern, perhaps even distress, as Clark struck out on his own. A banker later reported a discussion with Vanderbilt in 1872, in which he mentioned that he needed to see Clark. "Horace isn't up yet—he never gets up till about noon. But, if you want to see him very much, we'll go to his house and get the boy out of bed," Vanderbilt said. They drove to Murray Hill and, sure enough, Clark had worked late into the night and was still in bed. He hurried downstairs and began to consume an enormous breakfast as the callers watched. Vanderbilt said brusquely, "Horace, you eat too much. You keep bad hours, too. You can't stand it, my boy, strong and healthy as you are. If you don't stop this thing it will certainly kill you. I'd have been dead fifty years ago if I'd lived like you."[29]

When summer arrived, William set sail for Europe with his family, but Clark and Augustus Schell followed Vanderbilt to Saratoga, where the Commodore was seen each day on the Congress Hall veranda. "He wears light colored breeches, and a black coat, and a standing collar," a reporter observed. "He is tall and straight, and white whiskered." Vanderbilt drove Frank out to watch a medieval tournament, a recent fad. His daughter Ethelinda Allen wrote a warm letter from Newport to Frank, asking about "father's programme for the future." Would it be a trip to Niagara Falls, "or is he too comfortable to move?" Her question points to how deeply he rooted himself in Saratoga. Each evening he played cards for $5 to $25 a hand. One morning he came down from his room chuckling. He had gone to bed late, he explained to Edwin D. Worcester, and had seen the light on in Clark's room; going in, he found Clark, Schell, and two others playing cards. "What are you playing for?" he asked. "For fun," Clark answered. "The idea," Vanderbilt laughed, "of four grown-up men playing cards together at that time of night for fun!"[30]

Vanderbilt had serious problems that year. While he was at Saratoga, Frank's brother Robert L. Crawford was indicted for attempted murder. On the night of May 24, the police had banged on the door of 10 Washington Place, demanding access to Vanderbilt's stables. His coachman, James Ames, described by the *New York Times* as a "powerful, stalwart negro," had reportedly taken (or dragged, according to the *Times*) a drunk seamstress named Carrie Love into his bedroom in the stables. Vanderbilt himself let the police in, and a wild brawl ensued between Ames and the officers, who finally knocked out Ames and dragged him off. Bizarrely, Frank's brother Robert appeared at the police station. Crawford, who was on a visit from Alabama, acted as if Ames were the slave of a Southern planter before the war. "You dare not lock up Commodore Vanderbilt's coachman," he bellowed. The police finally tossed Crawford into the street, where he lurked until a detective emerged. Crawford produced a revolver and shouted his intention of killing the man. In a confused scuffle, he shot and severely wounded the detective. The initial press reports of the incident may have been exaggerated, since a jury swiftly acquitted Ames. Still, Crawford faced a long fight for exoneration and an eventual lawsuit by his victim.[31]

When the Commodore returned from Saratoga, he suffered a terrible loss. In October, an epizootic struck New York's forty thousand horses, afflicting them with disease. The *New York Herald* remarked on "the singular spectacle ... of a great city almost at a standstill; of thousands of persons, male and female, young and old, unable to reach their homes after a day of toil except on foot." Omnibuses, streetcars, carts, and drays sat in the streets, or "were dragged slowly around by horses more dead than alive." On November 15, thinking the worst had passed, Vanderbilt drove out behind Mountain Boy. Soon afterward the steed fell sick. Worcester came around to the Commodore's stables not much later, and Vanderbilt told him his finest horse was dead. He would rather have given a thousand shares of New York Central, he said sadly, than have that horse die. When Worcester later recounted this remark, William—knowing how much his father valued both money and the Central—could only say, "Whew!"[32]

The Commodore was in a grim frame of mind, then, when his name began to appear in the newspapers in the ensuing week. Horace Clark and Augustus Schell carried out a corner in Chicago & Northwestern Railroad stock, in alliance with none other than Jay Gould. As with the Union Pacific earlier in the year, the newspapers assumed that Vanderbilt was the mastermind of any operation involving Clark and Schell, and proclaimed a new alliance between Gould and the Commodore. In fact, Vanderbilt had no interest in acquiring the Northwestern, and he would never take part in its management. The linking of his name with the Union Pacific had been bad enough, but to be identified with Gould snapped his temper. On November 26, he dictated a "card" for the newspapers.[33]

> SIR: The recent corner in "Northwestern" has caused some considerable excitement in Wall street, and has called forth much comment from the press. My name has been associated with that of Mr. Jay Gould and others in connection with the speculation, and gross injustice has been done me thereby.
>
> I beg leave, therefore, to say, once and for all, that I have not had, either directly or indirectly, the slightest connection with or interest in the matter. I have had but one business transaction with Mr. Gould in my life. In July 1868, I sold him a lot of stock, for which he paid me, and the privilege of a call for a further lot, which he also settled. Since then I have had nothing to do with him in any way whatever; nor do I mean ever to have, unless it be to defend myself. I have, besides, always advised all my friends to have nothing to do with him in any business transaction. I came to this conclusion after taking particular notice of his countenance. The almost constant parade, therefore, of my name in association with his seems very much like an attempt to mislead the public, to my injury, and, after the publication of this, ignorance or misinformation can no longer be urged as an excuse for continuing this course.
>
> As for Wall Street speculators, I know nothing about them. I do not even see the street three times a year, and no person there has any authority to use my name, or to include me in any speculative operation whatever.
> C. VANDERBILT
> No. 25 West Fourth Street, Nov. 26, 1872[34]

The card shows the emotion and haste in which it was written. The claim that he had had only one "business transaction" with Gould was true only if the definition of a transaction was limited to stock trades, and excluded their relations as railroad presidents. Even then, Vanderbilt neglected the technicality he had insisted on in 1868, that his sale of stock at the end of the Erie War be to Drew and no one else. On the other hand, his denial of any role in speculation rings true; as Worcester would later report, since 1870 Vanderbilt had limited himself to strategic purchases of stock for investment or to control other companies.[35] As for his personal opinion of Gould—well, a lot of businessmen didn't like the look of him, let alone trust him.

When asked about the card by a reporter, Vanderbilt said, "The constant association of my name with that of Mr. Gould has injured me greatly." It made investors reluctant to buy the securities of his railroads, he claimed. He had seen one telegram from England that read, "What is the meaning of Vanderbilt's name being mixed up with Jay Gould's in this affair?" When pressed about Gould, he added:

> No man could have such a countenance as his, and still be honest. . . . I tell you, sir, God Almighty has stamped every man's character upon his face. I read Mr. Gould like an open book the first time I saw him. I did not like to express too strongly an opinion this morning, but if you wish to have it now I will give it to you. You have my authority for stating that I consider Mr. Jay Gould a damned villain. You can't put it too strongly.

As the reporter walked down the stoop into the rain, the Commodore shouted after him, "He is undoubtedly a damned villain, and you can say I said so."[36]

Vanderbilt's remarks apparently stung Gould, who proved equally petty. "The poor old Commodore is in his dotage," he told a reporter. "There is a class of rising financiers whom the old man hates. . . . While he in his second childhood is uptown amusing himself with his horses, and listening to the flatteries of sporting men, these young business men are rising into financial power which will far exceed the old Commodore's even in his palmiest days." Gould was wrong, of course. He would never achieve Vanderbilt's power, or even his absolute, unadjusted net worth.[37]

But this feud drew attention away from what truly made this moment so hurtful, and damaging, for the Commodore. Vanderbilt directed at Gould all the anger and frustration he felt at Clark and Schell's betrayal. The pair went so far as to bail Gould out of jail after he was arrested in a lawsuit at the height of the Northwestern corner. As *Railroad Gazette* observed, Gould "rarely worked with these men or men of their class, and . . . was thought to be hardly acceptable in their company."[38] Vanderbilt, that student of human nature in the business environment, must have known that this was a very bad sign. Such open defiance of his feelings suggested that Clark, in particular, had begun to think of himself as a great railroad manager and financier in his own right, as he took over the Union Pacific and cornered the Northwestern. As Vanderbilt knew all too well, first pride, then the fall.

ONE BY ONE, VANDERBILT'S old friends passed on. Erastus Corning had died in April 1872. Horace Greeley's wife died at the end of October, swiftly followed by Greeley's defeat in the presidential election and his own demise on November 29. It was publicly disclosed that Corneil owed nearly $46,000 to the editor, on promissory notes that were listed by the auditors of the estate under "items of doubtful value."[39]

More and more, Vanderbilt's legacy lingered in his mind as he rolled inexorably toward the same fate. The topic came up when he received a call from a Southern Methodist bishop named Holland N. McTyeire, who was married to a cousin of Frank's. The bishop had traveled to New York for treatment by Dr. William Bodenhamer. The Commodore liked him, and insisted that he stay at 10 Washington Place. McTyeire became a frequent guest. As Frank later wrote, Vanderbilt had high regard for his "noble Christian character & great executive ability"—the latter more important to him than the former, perhaps. Vanderbilt listened closely when McTyeire discussed how the Southern Methodists had received a charter for the Central University, to be erected somewhere in Dixie, where the destruction of the Civil War remained all too visible.

McTyeire returned to New York in March 1873, and called at Vanderbilt's home as usual. The Commodore took him aside and said that he would give $500,000 to endow the university. "It was a grateful surprise," McTyeire later remarked; wisely, he had never asked for any money, let alone such a vast sum as $500,000 represented in 1873. As the Commodore explained, it was his lifelong nationalism, his patriotism, that moved him. "It was a duty," Vanderbilt later quoted himself as saying, "that the North owed to the South, to give some substantial token of reconciliation which would be a benefit, and he wanted to do his individual share by founding an institution."[40]

Charles F. Deems testified under oath to hearing similar statements by the Commodore about his motives. Vanderbilt, he said, voiced a fear that "the greatness of his success would give an argument against education and its usefulness; that it had been secretly a life-long regret to him that he was not educated." But a desire to heal the divided nation was most important. "When the Commodore finally announced his purpose to make the gift, he said that he had this in mind during the Rebellion," Deems reported. "He spent a million of money in sending a vessel against the Southerners to show his views then, and he wanted to give the money after the war was over to show them that the men of the North were ready to extend the olive branch."[41]

Characteristically, Vanderbilt entrusted his gift to McTyeire as an individual. In a letter dated March 17, he placed several conditions on his gift: he specified that the university should be located in Nashville (as a major Southern city), and that the bishop should be the president, with the power to veto resolutions by the university board. McTyeire agreed, and the board swiftly accepted. Indeed, the Southern Methodists immediately decided to change the name from Central to Vanderbilt University.[42]

Vanderbilt had another project already under way to establish his legacy: the construction of two additional tracks on the Central between Albany and Buffalo (where its main feeders, the Lake Shore and the North Shore lines, converged). At the time, most railroads had only single-track lines, so even a complete double track was considered a great thing. The Lake Shore was considered an excellent road, yet it had only one track for part of its length. To construct a *quadruple* track over the distance of some three hundred miles loomed in the public mind as a monumental undertaking. Work began in 1872 through the simple device of extending sidings at various points along the line until they met. By the end of the year, seventy-five miles had been completed. To move the work along faster (and to consolidate existing debt), the New York Central board voted on January 11, 1873, to issue $30 million in bonds, plus another £2 million to be sold in London.[43]

"I had this design in mind when I went on the road three [sic] years ago," he told a reporter. "I got our best people together, and submitted a proposition to them. Suppose all the passenger trains were taken off, and the road given up entirely to freight? How much percent on the current expenses could we save in the transportation of freight?" The Central's freight haulage had risen dramatically since the Civil War. Freight receipts had climbed by 72 percent, despite the fact that freight *rates* had fallen by an average of 8 percent per year. In 1872, 203,351 freight cars passed over the line; in 1873, it would carry east 255 carloads in a single day, the largest total of any railroad to date. Passenger traffic, on the other hand, remained flat. "We have to run freight trains so rapidly to get them out of the way of the passenger trains that we frequently have to run thirty miles an hour," the Commodore explained. "But it uses up the rolling stock, knocking the cars to pieces without really carrying the freight any faster." Ten percent was the lowest estimate he received of the savings to be derived from running freight trains on separate tracks; Vanderbilt thought 15 percent.[44]

"Suppose, now, we should save 15 percent on $15,000,000 freight transportation. That would be $2,250,000," he lectured. "Now, suppose the new tracks cost $15,000,000, on which we should pay 7 percent, which would be $1,050,000. Now, if our business remained just as it is, the new tracks would give us a saving of $1,200,000 a year." It is significant that he made his calculations based on the railroad's current business. At the start of 1873, after years of rapid growth, such railroad executives as Scott and Clark banked on continued expansion; the older and wiser Vanderbilt did not. "I hope to seem them laid. I am getting pretty old, but I never had better health than now."[45]

On April 1, 1873, in a further step to put his empire in order, he leased the Harlem to the New York Central & Hudson River for an annual payment of 8 percent of the par value of its stock, the Harlem's now-customary dividend. It exemplified Vanderbilt's pattern: a slow but inexorable advance from financial control to coordination to centralization of the different components of his realm. Of all the Commodore's railroad vassals, only Clark's Lake Shore still ran its own affairs. As Vanderbilt Allen, Commander of the Order of the Mejidie, could have explained, it occupied a place rather like Egypt in the Ottoman Empire—owing allegiance to the sultan, but functionally independent. Not for long.[46]

NOW THAT THE CENTRAL had issued £2 million in bonds, they had to be sold to English investors. On March 3, 1873, Vanderbilt gave the job to James Banker. He had confidence in Banker's abilities, of course. He bombarded Banker with personal instructions for the disposition of millions of dollars worth of securities up to the moment of his departure for London. But Vanderbilt may have wished to banish Banker in order to halt the growing stock operations he conducted with Clark and Schell.[47]

His frustration with Clark in particular only had grown in the weeks following the Northwestern corner. In January, Vanderbilt again found his own name dragged into one of Clark's Wall Street operations, involving Western Union. Trading through George B. Grinnell & Co. (a firm in which Clark was a special partner), Clark's circle bulled the telegraph stock in January and February. That circle included Banker, Augustus and Richard Schell, and George A. Osgood. Osgood, too smart for his own good, told a reporter that "he would not allege that the Commodore was acting as the bone and sinew of the clique, for even if he were, it would not be wise to have the fact published as coming from him." The journalist reported the conversation to Vanderbilt, who became "indignant." Leaning back in his chair, the Commodore stretched out his arm and said, "My son, when the gang of stock speculators in Wall Street tell you a story about my connection to any enterprise but New York Central, Hudson, or Harlem, don't believe them. I have all I can do to tend to what I have on hand now, and if I had the Western Union Telegraph line I wouldn't want to be bothered with it." Vanderbilt was being a bit disingenuous himself; he may have had a large, perhaps even controlling, stake in Western Union, though he did not take part in its management, let alone in this attempted corner. More ominously, he now condemned his own sons-in-law as "the gang of stock speculators."[48]

"It is well known that several months ago Commodore Vanderbilt quarreled with his son-in-law, Mr. Horace F. Clark," the *New York Herald* reported that spring. "The reason of this was stated to be that the Commodore objected to his relative's speculating in Western [railroad] stock, particularly when they were fancy stocks."[49] This was more than a matter of personal pique. A subtle but profound shift in the economic winds could be felt, especially by so experienced an observer as Vanderbilt. In the judgment of English bankers, American railroads had overexpanded. As Junius S. Morgan wrote to Andrew Carnegie from England that spring, "Our market is at the moment over-supplied with American securities. . . . On the continent it is still worse." In London, Banker found it impossible to sell the Central's bonds, a matter of regret to Morgan's son in America, J. P. Morgan, precisely because the future of U.S. railroads looked so doubtful. "The kinds of bonds which I want to be connected with are those which can be recommended without a shadow of doubt, and without the least subsequent anxiety, as to payment of interest," J. P. Morgan wrote to his father on April 16. "I did feel exceedingly disappointed that we could do nothing with the New York Central. . . . It would do us all far more good to be connected with such a negotiation, even had the profit been small, than anything I have heard of for a long time."[50]

On the day that Morgan wrote these lines, the first tremor of the coming shock hit Wall Street—and it brought down the house of Barton & Allen. A squeeze in the money market led to a panic. When banks called in loans to Samuel Barton and Harry Allen, they could not pay. They had embroiled themselves too deeply in Clark and Schell's operations, especially in the Union Pacific, and Vanderbilt refused to save them. A reporter for the *Herald* asked Barton outright whether they were doing business for the Commodore. "None whatever, lately," he replied. Still, he felt wounded, after the long years in which Vanderbilt had taken a special interest in both himself and Allen. "If Mr. Vanderbilt had stuck by us, we shouldn't have failed," he said. "But he would not."[51]

Vanderbilt's stern refusal to rescue his relatives from their recklessness—which he had warned them against many times—split the clan. Daniel Allen took it personally, and broke off his long relationship with the Commodore. Expectations rose of a reckoning between Vanderbilt and Clark.[52] But fate intervened.

On June 19, Clark dropped dead at the age of fifty-eight. He had had heart disease—"rheumatism of the heart," as the press called it—and, after feeling unwell for some days, suffered a heart attack. On June 22, the Commodore and Frank led a parade of mourners into the Madison Square Presbyterian Church for the funeral, including William and his wife, Augustus Schell and his new spouse (married on March 25, with Clark playing a central role in the Quaker ceremony), and delegations from railroad boards from around the country. Afterward Clark was buried in Woodlawn Cemetery.[53]

Worcester rushed back from a trip to Buffalo for the funeral, and stopped to see Vanderbilt at his office on West Fourth Street. The Commodore told him to get into a carriage, remarking, "This is Mrs. Vanderbilt's coupé, and you must be careful not to soil it with your tobacco juice." As they drove to Grand Central, Vanderbilt became reflective. "Mr. Worcester, there's one thing you ought to inculcate upon your boys, and that is to be very economical." The source of his mood was an investigation he had launched into the Lake Shore's books. "Clark was foolish," Vanderbilt said. "This is a lesson teaching us to take care of ourselves."[54]

The full scope of that lesson unfolded over the summer. On July 2, the Lake Shore board (led by Schell and Banker, back from London) formally asked Vanderbilt to assume the presidency. He accepted, naming Amasa Stone as managing director. Though Stone took operational control of the company, the Commodore looked closely into its affairs, even traveling down the line to Toledo to inspect its condition. He voiced admiration of the railroad, and let it be known that he was buying its stock.[55]

In reality, he discovered that Clark had driven the company to the brink of annihilation. Counting on a continuing economic boom, Clark had gone on a reckless spending binge. As a financial columnist later wrote, "There was not a dollar in the treasury. Contracts for construction, equipment, 20,000 tons steel rail, &c., to the amount of $7,894,845, had been made and the work all commenced, with no provision whatever for meeting the large payments." Vanderbilt ordered an immediate halt to all construction, canceled all free passes, and ordered a new policy of frugality.[56]

The huge floating debt, amounting to $6,277,485, particularly worried him. Clark had paid for much of his new construction with high-interest call loans from banks, which could demand repayment at any moment. And to pay the most recent dividend—formally approved under Schell and Banker's direction on June 30, just before Vanderbilt took over— Clark had arranged for a call loan of $1,750,000 from the Union Trust Company, a financial institution in which he, Schell, and Banker were directors. "I am one of those men," Clark had said shortly before his death, "who believe it is the duty of the managers of a railroad to give to the stockholders each and every year a return." In following that policy, he had put at risk the Lake Shore itself.[57]

Worst of all, Vanderbilt discovered that Clark, Schell, and Banker had directly involved the Lake Shore in their stock speculations. The same tightening money market that brought Barton & Allen down had caught them short. Desperate to make good their margins, they, as directors of the Lake Shore, ordered themselves—as directors of the Union Trust— to transfer Lake Shore bonds, held as collateral for loans, to George B. Grinnell & Co. "As the story runs," the *New York Tribune* later reported, "when Commodore Vanderbilt became President of the Company he insisted that the transaction on the part of the Executive Committee was improper and illegal, and that the gentleman named should shoulder the load themselves."[58]

It took time to sort out such an enormous mess, so Vanderbilt followed his typical seasonal routine. He spent August in his usual haunt in Saratoga, the Congress Hall. There Frank completed her husband's long transformation from "illiterate & boorish" to "honorable and high-toned," in the words of R. G. Dun & Co. The press summarized this evolution in one remarkable sentence: "Commodore Vanderbilt led off in the opening ball at Saratoga." In September, he returned to New York and learned of the groundbreaking ceremony for Vanderbilt University in Nashville on September 16.[59]

On the afternoon of September 18, Vanderbilt drove out behind his fast trotters on his daily race through upper Manhattan. He whipped the team back into his stables at seven o'clock, and went up to his bedroom to change. A maid came up to tell him that a reporter from the *New York Herald* wished to see him. Vanderbilt received him in his second-floor sitting room, where Fisk and Gould had waited five years before. "Rising from his chair with the dignity of an old courtier, he politely invited the reporter to be seated. He then threw himself back in his capacious easy chair and turned his bright and penetrating eyes upon him," the reporter wrote. "You have heard today, Mr. Vanderbilt, I suppose," the journalist asked, "of the Wall Street panic?"

"No. I have only just come in from driving, and it is all news to me; but, after dinner, I shall see what the evening papers say."

The reporter explained that Jay Cooke & Co., one of the leading financial firms in the country, had fallen, crushed by the weight of millions in unmarketable Northern Pacific securities. It was autumn; the moving of the crops had begun; and the year's tight money market had turned anaconda. House after house had collapsed in Cooke's wake. Vanderbilt said he doubted things were really that bad. The reporter added, "I forgot to tell you . . . that Mr. Richard Schell has also had to suspend payment."

That brought Vanderbilt up short. "Well, there was no reason why Schell should have failed—wanted to be too rich too quick I suppose," he said. He asked if there was a rumor about the Pennsylvania (there was), and fell into thought. The reporter broke the silence by asking about "the cause of the rottenness in Wall Street." The Commodore, "giving one of his keen glances over his spectacles and speaking deliberately," delivered an astute impromptu lecture.

> I'll tell you what's the matter—people undertake to do about four times as much business as they can legitimately undertake. . . . There are a great many worthless railroads started in this country without any means to carry

them through. Respectable banking houses in New York, so called, make themselves agents for sale of the bonds of the railroads in question and give a kind of moral guarantee of their genuineness. The bonds soon reach Europe and the markets of their commercial centres, from the character of the endorsers, are soon flooded with them. . . .

When I have some money I buy railroad stock or something else, but I don't buy on credit. I pay for what I get. People who live too much on credit generally get brought up with a round turn in the long run. The Wall street averages ruin many a man there, and is like faro.[60]

Vanderbilt was clearly focused as he faced the greatest financial disaster of the century. He would need all his wits to survive.

"Vanderbilt is the only man who can come to our rescue and re-establish confidence," a broker remarked that evening. "I hope from the bottom of my heart that he will come down tomorrow, as he did on the occasion of Black Friday. . . . At the present moment there is a similar fight going on to break Vanderbilt's stocks—Lake Shore, New York Central, and Western Union." The failure of Richard Schell, long associated with the Commodore, gave the downward plunge added momentum. Almost instantly, New York Central dropped from 99½ to 94¾, Harlem from 126½ to 125, Lake Shore from 90½ to 86, Western Union from 88½ to 78. And they kept falling. Two days later, they would hit 89, 85, 79½, and 55¼ respectively. An enormous percentage of Vanderbilt's net worth evaporated. As of October 15, the New York Central's market value would shrink from its pre-panic level by $19 million, the Lake Shore's by $17.5 million, and Western Union's by $16.5 million.[61]

The crisis soon found its center in the Union Trust Company, the financial agent of Vanderbilt's railroads. Like other banks, it suffered a run—a sudden rush of depositors who demanded their money—which forced it to close its doors. Its president was in Europe and its secretary disappeared with an undetermined amount of cash. The bank's trustees called in the $1.75 million loan to the Lake Shore. But Vanderbilt and Amasa Stone had not had time to restore the railroad's finances, and it could not pay. The disastrous entanglements that Clark, Schell, and Banker had arranged between the Union Trust and the Lake Shore threatened both companies with bankruptcy.[62] If either went down, it would drag still more firms and financiers into failure, exacerbating the panic. The result might ruin Vanderbilt himself.

In one of the most painful moments of the Commodore's life, he faced the full repercussions of the greed—the treachery—of three of his most trusted lieutenants. In righteous fury, he forced them to face the consequences, demanding that Banker, Schell, and Clark's estate put in personal notes to repay the advances made to them against Lake Shore securities.

Banker and Schell knew it was nearly impossible for them to pay, and Clark's brokerage house, George B. Grinnell & Co., went bankrupt. But the real problem was the $1.75 million that the Lake Shore owed the Union Trust.

Outside the Union Trust's locked doors, Wall Street chattered nervously about the consequences if it should fail. Inside, its trustees anxiously reviewed the books. On September 20, the Commodore went in person to the bank's office, the *Herald* reported, "looking as placid and complacent, and smoking his cigar with as much nonchalance as though Central was being quoted at 200. . . . He and Mr. Worcester, the treasurer of the Central road, and several of the directors of the company were closeted together during the forenoon." The bank's trustees (including former Central director John V. L. Pruyn) had long left its affairs in the hands of Vanderbilt's lieutenants. Now they demanded that Vanderbilt personally pay the Lake Shore's debt. Pruyn—who was so distressed that he appears to have suffered a heart attack a few days later—was especially angry with the Commodore. But Vanderbilt declined to pay. He may have done that as a matter of principle, for he certainly was not individually responsible for the debt; but his refusal also may have been a sign of the precarious state of his own finances.[63]

On September 21, President Grant arrived in New York to assess the crisis. He set himself up in room 19 of the Fifth Avenue Hotel, where Wall Street's leaders begged him to inject liquidity into the markets by ordering the Treasury to issue the greenbacks it held in reserve. Vanderbilt sent up his card. He was conducted into room 19, where he made his own proposal. "I offered to extend relief to the financial community to the extent of $10,000,000," the Commodore related afterward. "I offered it in this way—to give $10,000,000 in as good securities as the government could give, provided the government would give $30,000,000." He suggested, in essence, a version of the open-market operations that the later Federal Reserve would conduct on a daily basis, in which it would fine-tune the supply of cash by buying and selling federal bonds. Grant turned down Vanderbilt's specific plan, but Treasury Secretary William A. Richardson did initiate a policy of buying bonds to nearly the amount he suggested. "I do not know what to say about the future," Vanderbilt said that night. "You say you newspaper people are in the dark yet, and don't know what to say about the result of all this panic. I am in the same state of doubt myself. I haven't the remotest idea of what the result will be. At present the outlook is very, very gloomy indeed."[64]

This public pessimism reveals how deeply the Panic of 1873 worried Vanderbilt. He had guarded his words all his life, knowing the impact they would have on friends, enemies, and the markets. Often he made a great show of unconcern, as on Black Friday in 1869 or during his recent visit to the Union Trust. But now there would be no fooling anyone about how bad the situation had become. The stock exchange shut its doors for ten days in a desperate attempt to halt the frenzy of fear. But the impact soon was felt far beyond Wall Street. "Factories and employers throughout the country are discharging hands, working half time, or reducing wages," George Templeton Strong wrote in his diary on October 27. "There is a prospect of a hard, blue winter."

The Panic of 1873 started one of the longest depressions in American history—sixty-five straight months of economic contraction. In the next year, half of America's iron mills would close; by 1876, more than half of the railroads would go bankrupt. Unemployment, hunger, and homelessness blighted the nation. "In the winter of 1873–74, cities from Boston to Chicago witnessed massive demonstrations demanding that authorities ease the economic crisis," Eric Foner writes. The irony is that the fall was far more severe because of the rapid rise of the previous decade. The expanding, increasingly efficient railroad network had created a truly national market. The fates of farmers, workers, merchants, and industrialists across the landscape were tied together as never before. New York had cast its financial net across the country, which meant that credit flowed to remote regions far more easily than before—but also that financial panics affected the entire nation. As Vanderbilt pointed out, railroad overbuilding was an underlying economic problem, and it was exacerbated by Wall Street's craze for railway securities. When the bubble burst, the consequences were felt across the country with devastating suddenness and severity.[65]

Even worse, the long boom had brought hundreds of thousands of workers into the industrial workforce without giving them any kind of cushion against a downturn. Even before the Panic, many had lived miserable lives. In New York, twenty-five thousand ironworkers lived close to their riverside foundries; lacking sufficient income to commute from healthier locations, they and their families jammed into the tenements that made Manhattan infamous. "Admixed with foundries and factories were reeking gasworks, putrid slaughterhouses, malodorous railyards, rotting wharves, and stinking manure piles," write two historians of New York, "which gave the working-class quarters their distinctively fetid quality." Diseases such as cholera swept Five Points, Corlears Hook, and other impoverished neighborhoods, leading to death rates as high as 195 out of every thousand. The closing of factory doors and slashing of wages in the Panic made a bad situation impossible for many. A "Work or Bread" movement swept the working poor; it would culminate in a protest by seven thousand unemployed workers in Tompkins Square in New York on

January 13, 1874. The police broke it up with ruthless force. Homeless and hopeless, many of the unemployed took to the road, giving birth to a new creature on the American landscape: the tramp.[66]

The tidal wave threatened to engulf even the mightiest of the mighty: the Pennsylvania Railroad and its gifted managers. After a period of rapid expansion, the railroad had accumulated a floating debt of $16 million, with a cash balance of only $4.4 million. J. Edgar Thomson personally made advances to save the company, but he himself was overextended. The disaster ruined his friendship with Scott, who was embroiled in the troubled Texas & Pacific. Scott's protégé Carnegie refused to help Scott, accusing him of "having acted upon his faith in his guiding star, instead of sound discretion." Many businessmen were guilty of just that crime in 1873.[67]

The storm swept away many of those closest to the Commodore. His son-in-law Osgood went bankrupt and was expelled from the Union Club. James Banker failed to pay his debts, amounting to some $750,000; Vanderbilt covered them (lest they drag the Lake Shore and the Union Trust down farther), in return for Banker's Fifth Avenue home and other real estate that would have brought $1.5 million in ordinary times. On October 27, Banker resigned the vice presidency of the Bank of New York in disgrace. Augustus Schell felt certain that he, too, would go under. Years later, Chauncey Depew would remember how he walked out the door of the Union Trust with Schell, who "had his hat over his eyes, and his head was buried in the upturned collar of his coat." As they walked past Trinity Church, Schell said, "Mr. Depew, after being a rich man for over forty years, it is hard to walk under a poor man's hat."[68]

In this deluge, it was all Vanderbilt could do to survive. The trustees of the Union Trust talked openly of forcing the Lake Shore into receivership. If that happened, it might start a chain reaction that would have potentially dire consequences for Vanderbilt's empire. Even though the Lake Shore was a separate corporation from the New York Central, both were strongly identified with the person of the Commodore. Should he fail to rescue the Lake Shore, the value of his other shares would sink still lower. Even worse, the Central's credit would likely suffer. Even a highly profitable railroad needed to borrow money on a regular basis to cover its immense expenses; if the Central found itself unable to sell its bonds, it might have to curtail operations, suspend dividends, and skip interest payments, spinning into a self-feeding cycle.

But the Union Trust needed Vanderbilt. For all the trustees' bluster, they knew as well as he did that bankrupting the Lake Shore would accelerate the economy's decline and gain them little in return. In the end, only Vanderbilt could save them, and only they could save Vanderbilt. The

Commodore saw his leverage. He applied all his force on that point, patiently negotiating as the weeks went by, waiting for the emotional tide of fear to subside. On October 24, he finally convinced the trustees to accept the railroad's notes, maturing at three, six, and nine months, to settle the loan.

There was a catch: the trustees insisted that Vanderbilt himself be responsible for repayment. Even now, after decades of economic growth and increasing financial sophistication, this one man towered above Wall Street as America's financial prince. For Vanderbilt, it was a test of his faith in his ability to save the Lake Shore. He agreed, putting up his personal Harlem shares as collateral for the railroad's notes.[69]

In Lake Shore board meetings, the Commodore insisted that Clark's estate and Augustus Schell settle their debts to the railroad, amounting to $1 million. Vanderbilt personally negotiated the terms, and secured full repayment over the next few months. (Because of these arrangements, Schell avoided bankruptcy.) And Vanderbilt loaned more than $1 million out of his own accounts to see the Lake Shore through its crisis. On April 18, 1874, the railroad paid off the last of its notes to the Union Trust.[70]

"Between the panic of September and the quieter days of January 1874, the Lake Shore Company was lifted over all its embarrassments, protected in all its obligations, by the strength of one man, cajoled at eighty years of age into taking the management of a road largely involved by extravagant outlays for construction," *Railroad Gazette* reflected. "At one time $6,000,000 of Mr. Vanderbilt's own private fortune in Harlem and New York Central stock was pledged for debts of the Lake Shore road. True, the road was one which could and did repay him; but his wealth was the only thing which enabled him to save it from going to protest." It was an accomplishment that said everything about Vanderbilt's negotiating skills and iron nerve. Impromptu newspaper interviews with the Commodore, comments by those who dealt with him, and the minutes of board meetings show him in full command as others nearly broke down in fear.[71]

In the aftermath of the Panic, Vanderbilt did more than survive. He laid the foundation for an integrated network of railroads that would become known as the Vanderbilt System. It would emerge slowly, as his empire absorbed lines weakened by the depression. William would carry the scheme to completion, but there can be little doubt that the Commodore himself envisioned it. In 1874, for example, he would develop a plan—without William's knowledge—to lease the Lake Shore to the New York Central; though the lease was never concluded, it spoke to his independent conclusion that his railroads required integration.[72]

He also decided to take an active role in the management of Western Union, in which he was reputed to hold a large, even controlling, share.

On October 8, he, William, and Edwin D. Worcester entered the tele-graph company's board. The executive committee now consisted of Van-derbilt, Worcester, Frank Work, Augustus Schell, William K. Thorn, and the not-yet-bankrupt James Banker (along with Alonzo B. Cornell, Harri-son Durkee, Norvin Green, Joseph Harker, and William Orton, who remained as president). William, interestingly, did not go into the execu-tive committee. The synchronization of the Panic with Vanderbilt's elec-tion to the Western Union board may have been more than a coincidence. If the Commodore took real estate from Banker in return for paying his debts, then he likely took stock as well—and Banker had been speculating heavily in Western Union. It may have been Vanderbilt's followers' fool-ishness that made him a leading force in the telegraph monopoly.[73]

Vanderbilt turned eighty on May 27, 1874. After amassing the greatest personal fortune in American history, he had protected it against the greatest financial crisis in American history. Now, at last, he could take on the role he had long envisioned for himself—letting his son and Amasa Stone serve as his prime ministers as he sat back on his throne, an attentive but retiring emperor. Of course, it was never quite that simple.

"THE GRANGER MOVEMENT?" Vanderbilt asked. "What the devil is that?"

The Commodore sat in his office at 25 West Fourth Street, with only Lambert Wardell standing guard outside. It was a September afternoon just a week before the Panic. He spoke to a reporter, who found him "looking strong and healthy enough to drive bears in Central down to the lowest point of despair, and seemed to be clear-headed enough, after all the summer at Saratoga." As usual, Vanderbilt had a cigar in his mouth and carpet slippers on his feet, wearing a linen jacket and gray pants as he leaned back in his armchair and threw a foot up on the table in front of him.

"The farmers' movement out west," the reporter said. He had come to ask for the Commodore's opinion of the Grangers, and was surprised at his ignorance.

"Well, I don't know anything about it. Haven't paid any attention to it."

The reporter explained that the movement—formally called the Patrons of Husbandry, which sprouted thousands of lodges, or "granges," in the Mississippi Valley in 1873—had arisen against the railroads. "They complain generally of high and exacting tariffs, too much special railroad legislation, and of various privileges enjoyed by railroads and used for pur-poses of extorting unfair prices from the farmers."

"They do, eh?" the Commodore said, as he tapped the ashes loose from his cigar. "Well, as to special legislation, I agree with them. If they are in favor of making only general railroad laws, I'll be willing to back 'em. Further than that, I don't care what the devil they do. The Central can hold its own."

"Then pray tell me if prices have been affected by the movement, prices of transportation."

"I don't know, really. The farmers complain of charges for local transportation or something or other of that sort. But I hardly ever attend closely to railroad matters nowadays. If the farmers are opposed to special legislation, all right. The Central can stand anything the other railroads will. Let 'em give us general railroad legislation, and after that I don't care what they do."[74]

At the most trivial level, this interview showed the nearly eighty-year-old Vanderbilt to be alert and engaged, consciously leaving to William and Stone the operational management of his lines. He only concerned himself with strategic and financial matters, as he would in minute detail when the Panic struck days later. But it also demonstrated the limitations of his own understanding of his role, now that he had become the railroad king. Ideological debates made no impression on him. He ignored all aspects of the reporter's description of the Grangers except for the issue of special legislation. And he placed even that point in the context of his competitive relationship with his rivals, rather than a larger philosophical discussion. His words bear repeating: "Further than that, I don't care what the devil they do. The Central can hold its own." He did not mean that it could hold its own against the Grangers, but against the Erie, the Pennsylvania, or the Baltimore & Ohio.

Vanderbilt dismissed these agrarian radicals with sentiments that had themselves been radical back in his youth. In his formative years, competition had been the stuff of individualism, the egalitarian battle cry. The Jacksonians had seen strong government as the bodyguard of the "aristocrats," as the creator of "special privileges" for the wealthy, best seen in state-chartered corporations. But two great developments had made antebellum politics obsolete: the rise of the railroads, and the Civil War.

The railroads posed a double, if not triple, conundrum. They could exist only as corporations, since they were too capital intensive, too long-lived, to be personal proprietorships or partnerships. As a result, they made the corporation a fact of life in America, which rendered the Jacksonian critique of special privileges almost irrelevant. But they remained hotly controversial, thanks to their sheer enormity (on a scale forged by Vanderbilt himself). No other force in society rivaled them. Charles F. Adams Jr. observed in 1869, "It is but a very few years since the existence of a corporation controlling a few millions of dollars was regarded as a subject of grave apprehension, and now this country already contains sin-

gle organizations which wield a power represented by hundreds of millions." Railroads virtually monopolized transportation, having eclipsed all
forms of domestic water transportation by the 1870s. "Railroads are the
greatest and most powerful monopoly on the face of the earth," one orator said. "They let the public feel their power in the fuel of their kitchens,
the bread of their bodies, the material for their houses." Everything and
everyone moved at prices set by the railroads—"a frightening life-or-
death power," as historian Irwin Unger wrote.[75]

Seemingly omnipotent to the general public, the railroads themselves
felt helpless to control rates. As discussed earlier, it was in their interest
to take traffic below cost rather than lose it, since such a large percentage
of their operating costs remained constant no matter how many trains
they ran. This led to ruinous rate wars over "competing points"—cities
served by more than one line. Railroads offered rebates to big shippers to
attract business, and cut through rates well below those paid on local
freight. But what the corporations saw as desperate discounting, western
farmers called "discrimination," as Vanderbilt himself noted. After all,
merchants, meatpackers, and millers, not farmers themselves, shipped
agricultural products over long distances. And, by separating pricing from
distance, rate discrimination represented yet another alarming way in
which the corporate system abstracted economic from physical reality.
For all these reasons, the Grangers lobbied state legislatures for pro-rata
rate regulation.

This lobbying speaks to the second great development of the era:
the Civil War, which broke the tradition of a weak and passive government. Wartime necessity is the great centralizer of power and sire of a
strong state. Soon after the conflict began, a quick succession of laws had
embroiled federal authorities in the national economy. They included the
Legal Tender Act, the National Bank Act, the chartering of the Union
Pacific, the income tax, the creation of the Secret Service. The war created a new paradigm in the American mind: the notion that an active government could serve as a counterweight to the railroads and other large
corporations. Of course, an alert historian of public policy will be quick to
note the many ways in which antebellum government *did* intervene in the
economy, from agricultural inspections to patent regulation. But what was
new was a willingness among radicals to have government intervene
against capital on behalf of farmers and labor—to redress the balance of
power between corporations and the rest of society.

"We hold that a State cannot create a corporation that it cannot thereafter control," a council of Missouri Grangers declared. Some went even
further: "The time would come when the management of the roads must
fall into the hands of the public—of the States," one radical suggested.[76]

And the Grangers were only one element in an emerging correlation of forces. The labor movement, for example, pushed hard for legal limits on working hours. In May 1872, some 100,000 laborers in New York—two-thirds of the city's industrial workforce—went on strike for eight weeks to demand an eight-hour day. And the populist Greenback Party arose in defense of the most basic federal intervention in the economy—legal-tender paper money.[77] Vanderbilt's laissez-faire beliefs had morphed from radical to conservative without him even noticing.

Yet the American economic mentality was not a ship at sea, turning in a body in one direction or another. It was more like the ocean itself, in which the new radicals comprised one of many currents. As we have seen, the liberals—an intellectual elite with their own agenda—criticized both large corporations and government activism. Where Jacksonians had resisted state action in order to preserve the equality of the common man, the liberals did so out of fear that an ignorant electorate and uncultured titans would violate immutable economic laws. Human beings were corrupt, they thought, so when human beings meddled with the natural forces of trade they inevitably wrought harm, whether in stock watering by overlords such as Vanderbilt or the issuing of paper money by Congress to please western farmers.

The liberals were not simply "the ideological vanguard of the city's economic elite," as historian Sven Beckert suggests. The liberals believed the market would solve all problems; many financiers did not. Though most wealthy New Yorkers did indeed want a return to the gold standard, Richard Schell argued that it defied economic reality. "I cannot get it through my head," he said, "that a great country like this should take for the basis of her wealth a commodity of which there are only eleven hundred millions worth in the world." (Many economists would eventually come to the same conclusion; John Maynard Keynes would famously call the gold standard a "barbarous relic.") And ruinous competition among the railroads transformed even the Commodore—the fiercest competitor of all—into an advocate of cartels. Over the coming decades, J. P. Morgan would make his mark on history by taming competition through financial coordination of rival companies. The corporate chieftains did lobby to keep government from regulating their industries, but they also imposed private regulation of their own making to tame the market in the name of stability and profit.[78]

As Vanderbilt entered his final years, it was not at all clear how these contradictory currents would resolve themselves into the new mainstream. The liberals won some battles, such as a return to the gold standard and civil-service reform (starting in 1878), which would slowly eliminate the spoils system. Agrarian radicals secured both "Granger laws" in western states that regulated railroad rates and the Bland-Allison silver act of 1878 (which expanded the money supply by adding silver). The Interstate Commerce Commission came in 1887, and the Sherman Antitrust Act in 1890. The courts, though, struggled with the implications of the changing economy. The Supreme Court allowed state regulation of the railroads in 1877, but hesitated to fully endorse the corporation's nature as a legal person. In the railroad tax cases of 1882, for example, the justices "looked through the corporation and saw the property of the shareholders," in the words of Gregory A. Mark. It took another four years until, in *Santa Clara County v. Southern Pacific Railroad*, the high court ruled that corporations were entitled to the same rights as natural persons under the Fourteenth Amendment.[79]

And yet, even before the Commodore's death it was clear that the forces he had helped to put in motion were remaking the economic, political, social, and cultural landscape of the United States. There was the transparently obvious: the dramatically improved transportation facilities that allowed Americans to fill in the continent; the creation of enormous wealth in new business enterprises; and the railroads' economic integration of the nation, bringing distant farms, ranches, mines, workshops, and factories into a single market, one that both lowered prices and dislocated older communities. (The new availability of western foodstuffs, for example, uprooted New England farmers.) And there was the less obvious, such as the emergence of a new political matrix in which Americans struggled to balance the wealth, productivity, and mobility wrought by the railroads and other industries with their anxiety over the concentration of vast economic power in the hands of a few gigantic corporations. Though government regulation would emerge slowly and fitfully—fiercely opposed by many—it would take its place at the center of politics in the decades ahead.

Still more subtle, and perhaps more profound, was a broad cultural shift as big business infused American life. An institutional, bureaucratic, *managed* quality entered into daily existence—what scholar Alan Trachtenberg calls the "incorporation of America," a cultural dimension of "managerial revolution" or "visible hand" that business historian Alfred D. Chandler Jr. identified. More and more, the national impinged upon the local, the institutional upon the individual, the industrial upon the artisanal, the mechanical upon the natural. Even time turned to a corporate beat. Time had always varied from town to town, or even by household; the young Jay Gould, for example, had helped families determine when the sun was at its height so they could set their clocks to noon. But the sun proved inconvenient for the schedules of nation-girdling railways. In 1883, writes Trachtenberg, these "distinct private universes of time" vanished when the railroads, "by joint decision, placed the country—without act of Congress, President, or the courts—under a scheme of four 'standard time zones.' "

By the end of the century, the industrial, corporate economy would color the answers to many of life's basic questions: Where to work? What to buy? From whom to borrow? How to go from here to there? The impact of big business would even be seen in Americans' choice of heroes, particularly the mythologization of Jesse James as an avenger of the small farmer against banks and railroads. In reality, he cast himself as a Confederate avenger against the victorious Union—but the wider nation wanted a champion of the individual against the faceless institution, and so it drafted James.[80]

In 1873, the railroads were the vanguard of these changes. They comprised by far the biggest industry, and boasted by far the largest corporations. At their forefront stood Cornelius Vanderbilt, child of the eighteenth century, master of the nineteenth, maker of the centuries to come. He never ceased to strive to rationalize his businesses, or to foster cooperation with his rivals. But he could not escape the legacy of the past, or the realities of economics. The irony is that the railroads suffered severely after the Panic of 1873 precisely because of the laissez-faire policies and culture that Vanderbilt himself had championed throughout his life. With the economy in shambles, railway companies battled each other ruthlessly to capture whatever traffic they could, sending prices spiraling downward. As the Commodore faced his final years, his empire fought to survive. Success would depend on how well he had constructed it.

VANDERBILT WAS A HARD MAN. Testifying in 1877, Edwin D. Worcester remembered many instances over the previous three years in which the Commodore had been brusque. He often said about his son Corneil, "He's a very smart fellow, but he has a cog out." But then, Worcester added, "I have heard him use that expression of 'having a cog out' about almost every man he knew, at some time or other." On another occasion after the Panic, Vanderbilt was sitting with Worcester in the offices at the Grand Central Depot when a Catholic priest walked in and returned $20 "which somebody had obtained wrongfully from the road." Vanderbilt handed the money to Worcester and instructed him to deposit it in the proper account. The priest lingered and talked about the poverty of his church; Worcester thought to himself that a reward of $10 might be in order, but the Commodore sat silent. Finally the priest left, and Vanderbilt said, "There's considerable good in religion after all."[81]

The Commodore was also more complex and contradictory than he has often been portrayed. This could be seen in December 1873, when George Terry called on him to ask for a loan to fund a new business in Toledo. Vanderbilt blamed Corneil's friends for exacerbating his weaknesses, and no friend was closer to him than Terry. Vanderbilt may have suspected that Terry was Corneil's lover; certainly he would have seen no particular reason to like him. But Vanderbilt patiently read through Terry's references, then looked up and asked, "Mr. Terry, if you go to Toledo, what will become of Corneil?" Terry suggested that Vanderbilt give his son a job. "He said that he must not be in too much of a hurry," Terry recalled, "and that everything would be right for him by and by."[82]

To the end, Corneil aroused conflicting feelings that Vanderbilt never resolved. "He said that if Cornelius J. had a little more sense he might be fit for business; if a little less, he could be put into a lunatic asylum out of harm's way, where he sometimes thought he properly belonged," Bishop McTyeire said later. "The Commodore spoke sadly of him, and thought he was not fully responsible for his actions." Then would come another bad debt, and Vanderbilt would flare in anger. Sydney Corey was at 10 Washington Place when a letter arrived, demanding payment for one of Corneil's bad checks, "which he read with expressions of disgust," Corey recalled. "He called his secretary, and dictated to him this letter in reply: 'DEAR SIR: . . . In reply I beg to say that there is a crazy fellow roaming over the land calling himself Cornelius J. Vanderbilt. If he has come in contact with you, don't trust him.' "[83]

On August 25, 1874, Corneil composed a bitter letter to his father. "One year ago I assured you that thereafter I should strive to do exactly right. . . . I told you, in fact, that I was determined to please you, and if I did not the fault should be yours, not mine," he wrote. But it was not so much his father's disapproval that upset Corneil as the elevation of William. "You have two sons," he continued, in his wordy style.

> Does the fact of your ostensible faith in the judgment, intelligence, and ability of your son William justify the conclusion that the combined intellect of your remaining children sinks to insignificance before his superior attainments, and does it preclude you from displaying a little hope over the reinvigorated intellect of your younger son, and tendering him a bit of charity in consideration of the sickness and disease that temporarily impaired his usefulness in times gone by?[84]

With each lie, each bad check, the Commodore's frustration grew. By May 1875, their alienation had grown to the point that Corneil would try to get a job on the New York Central for a friend of his by asking for help from Thurlow Weed. He knew that Weed had greater influence with his father or brother than he had.[85]

Cool and collected in business, Vanderbilt in his eighties often flared at his family, William included. A reporter later testified that, in 1874 or 1875, he made an unscheduled call on the Commodore—as so many reporters did—to ask about a rumor involving New York Central. The reporter said that he had spoken to William already, and repeated William's comments. "The Commodore got up angrily," the witness said. "Billy, Billy, he always tells more than he knows," Vanderbilt snapped.[86]

Despite such outbursts, Vanderbilt respected his son's abilities and relied on them heavily. As Wardell recalled, Vanderbilt "detested details," and relished his leisure hours as he passed into his ninth decade.[87] Vanderbilt and William must be viewed as a team, one that the father deliberately crafted. He had long intended for William to carry on the empire and perpetuate the family name, as reflected in the long history of his will, which changed little over the decades. William was, and always had been, the designated heir.

Charles A. Rapallo, Vanderbilt's longtime lawyer and a justice of the New York Court of Appeals since 1870, would attest that the Commodore drafted his final will on July 14, 1868. It was modified on January 9, 1870, to incorporate his prenuptial agreement with Frank, and amended again on January 16, 1874, to give Frank the use of 10 Washington Place for the rest of her life. Under its terms, Frank, Phebe Cross, Emily Thorn, Sophia Torrance, and Mary La Bau each would receive bonds with a face value of $500,000; Catherine Lafitte would receive the interest from $500,000 worth of bonds; Ethelinda Allen, the interest of $400,000; Eliza Osgood, the interest of $300,000; Cornelius J., the interest of $200,000. Frank also would get two thousand New York Central shares.[88]

In the 1870s, these were all vast sums. At the time, a skilled worker in New York might earn $400 to $600 per year—far less than 6 percent interest on $200,000 worth of bonds.[89] But these figures were dwarfed by the unspecified "residue" left to William. In the Commodore's mind, he was not rewarding one child at the expense of the others, but taking a necessary step to preserve what he had built. Henry N. Phillips remembered how Vanderbilt told him in the summer of 1874, "I have not been fool enough to get this thing together to have it scattered when I am gone. Not a single share will go upon the market after my death." At Saratoga in 1875, Vanderbilt said, "Harry, a million or two is as much as anyone ought to have." Phillips joked that there was an easy way to get rid of his excess money. "No, there ain't," Vanderbilt replied, "for what you have got isn't worth anything unless you have got the power; and if you give away the surplus you give away the control." Vanderbilt looked beyond his son to build a foundation for the dynasty's third generation, by assigning tens of thousands of Harlem and Central shares to William's four sons, Cornelius, William K., George W., and Frederick W. He also brought

William K. onto the Central board in place of the disgraced James Banker.[90]

The public recognized William H. Vanderbilt as the heir, and he assumed a place of distinction in aristocratic, fashionable circles well before his father's death. He joined the American Geographical Society of New York. He purchased expensive fine art, from European paintings to Japanese vases. He sent his sons to Yale and other leading universities. He rented expensive pews at the Episcopalian Church of St. Bartholemew. He went on the board of the company created to build the Brooklyn Bridge. When his son William K. married Alva Smith at a fashionable church in Murray Hill on April 25, 1875, the *New York Sun* proclaimed it "certainly the grandest wedding witnessed in this city for many years. . . . The blockade of carriages was immense, the line extending for twelve blocks north and south. The church presented an uncommonly brilliant scene." The Commodore and Frank attended, as did a roster of the city's elite, filling the guest book with such lofty names as Lorillard, Peabody, Cutting, and Morgan.[91]

As the Commodore intended, his son and grandsons moved smoothly toward the assumption of his throne. In June 1874, after Amasa Stone stepped down as managing director of the Lake Shore, Vanderbilt made William the vice president and operational manager of the railroad, just as he was on the Central. He did so "that in the event of his (the Commodore's) death Billy might succeed him without election," recalled Edwin D. Worcester. "This means a great deal, and I am afraid a great deal to our disadvantage," the superintendent of the Michigan Central wrote to James F. Joy. "He [William H. Vanderbilt] is ambitious, headstrong, and our experience shows to some extent unreliable & unfair." He feared that William would turn the Vanderbilt railroads into a truly integrated system, leaving the Michigan Central on the outside. The consolidation of the Vanderbilt empire and dynasty went hand in hand.[92]

William even adopted Vanderbilt's personal project, his eponymous school. Until virtually the moment of his death, the Commodore involved himself closely in the founding of Vanderbilt University. When Bishop McTyeire issued a draft upon Vanderbilt, also in June, the Commodore scolded him for making it "at sight," meaning payable immediately, and instructed him to make all such drafts "at three days," lest one arrive when he was out of town and his bankers refuse payment. "I mentioned it at the time to Frank," he wrote. "As it happened it made no kind of difference as I was on the spot. . . . My kindest regards to your dear Lady. From hearing Frank talk of her, I have almost got to loving her, so look out!" More substantively, he paid detailed attention to the university's needs, and gave further gifts (with conditions) until his donation amounted to just under

$1 million—mirroring his gift of the *Vanderbilt* to the Union navy, as he had intended. William began to give as well, and traveled to Nashville to inspect the university in September 1875, shortly before it formally opened on October 4. William later wrote to McTyeire, "It is my purpose to execute as far as I am able my Father's wishes. . . . Among the many things to which he gave thought and care, none was more important to him than the work he hoped would be accomplished by the Vanderbilt University."[93]

But Vanderbilt's obsession with building a dynasty wounded those who were not a part of his plans. In June 1875, for example, his daughter Emily Thorn and her husband, William, paid a visit to 10 Washington Place before they went on to Newport, the favorite summer resort of the younger generation. William H. Davidge, a onetime president of the Pacific Mail Steamship Company and a good friend of Vanderbilt's, was present. He remarked, "Commodore, you have got some nice grandchildren. I know Thorn's children and I hear about his daughters." Vanderbilt replied, "Yes, they are nice children, but they are not Vanderbilts." Emily, clearly upset, said, "Father, they are your grandchildren, nevertheless." At that, William Thorn recalled, "the old gentleman turned the subject." The exchange hurt the Thorns. Both vividly recalled it years later. Indeed, it has become an oft-told example of Vanderbilt's misogyny, of his egotistical fascination with his own name, as perhaps it was. But the Commodore may have been deliberately retaliating against his daughter for snubbing Frank after his wedding.[94] In any case, it clearly demonstrated how hard a man Vanderbilt could be.

J. EDGAR THOMSON DIED on May 27, 1874, and Thomas Scott assumed the presidency of the Pennsylvania Railroad. The Commodore met with Scott just two days later at a secret conference of the trunk lines at the Windsor Hotel on Fifth Avenue. With a sharp slackening of business in the aftermath of the Panic (and the onset of a depression), a sense of desperation had settled over the railroads, which began to slash rates to attract traffic, any traffic. William managed the Central's rates according to a principle his father had established on taking over the railroad: to follow, in self-defense, the cuts made by other lines, but not to initiate them. The Central had no reason to be the aggressor. With its rich local business in New York State, its cheap-to-operate line with low grades and few curves, and its four-track core between Buffalo and Albany, it found itself in the strongest competitive position of any trunk line. At the time of this conference, it boasted twice the passenger traffic of the Erie and 81 percent more than the Pennsylvania; and, though the Pennsylvania carried

10 percent more freight, the Central earned a significantly larger profit per ton, per mile.[95]

The conference had been arranged because no business needed cooperation more than the railroads, which could not relocate to escape or accommodate competitors. But the Commodore's character played a role as well. Over the decades, his personality had evolved in parallel with his changing material interests. He had earned his reputation as a ferocious competitor in steamboats, a business notoriously prone to warfare, due to the low start-up costs and the inherent mobility of the physical capital— the steamers—which allowed a proprietor to fight on one route after another. It was also a time in his life when New York's merchant aristocrats derided him as a boorish outsider. After devoting himself to railroads, however, he had consistently pursued peace, seeking industry-wide agreements (though he remained ready to fight when attacked). The transformation reflected the nature of the railroad business, but it also suited his late-life status. The elite now thought of him as an "honorable & high toned" gentleman, precisely the sort of man who sought dignified arrangements, not economic bloodletting.[96]

Af the end of this conference, though, the executives left the Windsor Hotel as divided as before, and prices fell still farther. "The trunk lines this year have been carrying a heavy traffic at very low rates," *Railroad Gazette* would summarize at the end of the 1874. For the efficient and profitable Central, the boost in traffic brought by low rates was not entirely a bad thing. Where other railroads' securities plunged in value, the Central's first-mortage bonds brought a 5 percent premium. But the prevailing prices cut margins to a minimum, so the Commodore and his son continued to seek peace in an attempt to bring order out of chaos.[97]

That summer Vanderbilt invited the presidents of the trunk lines and other important railroads to another conference, this one in Saratoga. On July 30 they met in his personal quarters. They arrived at a far-reaching agreement known as the Saratoga Compact. They would establish two bodies to regulate the industry's rates and traffic: a Western Bureau, consisting of the major trans-Appalachian companies, and a Trunk Line Commission for the East. The two boards would set rates, settle disagreements, and banish the costly use of commission agents, rebates, and drawbacks. Further meetings in New York on August 11 and in Chicago on September 2 worked out the details.[98]

It was a grand accomplishment—one that immediately foundered. Two lines, one weak and one powerful, refused to take part. The Grand Trunk Railway of Canada declined to enter the compact because of its competitive disadvantages. As a long, roundabout line between the West and the Atlantic, it could only attract business with absurdly low rates, and so declined any price-fixing arrangement. President John W. Garrett of the

Baltimore & Ohio, on the other hand, refused because of his competitive *advantages*. His was the shortest route between Chicago and a seaport (in this case, Baltimore), so he insisted on the right to set lower rates than the other trunk lines.[99]

Vanderbilt responded to this intransigence with patience and self-possession. On November 12, he and William stepped off a special train in Baltimore and went to Garrett's offices. There they met Thomas A. Scott and Hugh J. Jewett (the new president of the Erie). One observer described Garrett as "a portly figure" with a round face, "bluish-gray eye, and solid, unanxious tread and pace. . . . He had a hard, round head, a slow and gracious manner." His firm pate and rotund dignity may have reminded the Commodore of Erastus Corning or Dean Richmond; in any case, he impressed Vanderbilt, and the two got along well. "We have had a very pleasant interview in Baltimore, as pleasant a one as ever was held when so much capital was represented," Vanderbilt told the *Evening Post*. "I believe Mr. Garrett . . . to be a high-toned, honorable man, and that he is willing to concede to any equitable arrangement between all the parties, if the equities can be got at. As to the general principles of railroading, I find by conversation with him that President Garrett exactly agrees with me on all of them; or, in other words, I agree with him so far as he has expressed his views to me."

Alas, it was not up to these two alone to make the peace. An obstacle arose, and its name was Thomas A. Scott, whose sleight-of-hand approach to managing the Pennsylvania aggravated Garrett. (It also landed Scott in trouble with his own stockholders, who launched an investigation of his regime in 1874.) Garrett insisted on the abolition of Scott's independent fast-freight corporations, which funneled much of their profits to the Pennsylvania's president; not surprisingly, Scott refused. The result was a highly personal spat between the two, who traded public recriminations in early 1875.[100]

When the Pennsylvania and the Baltimore & Ohio fought, the New York Central could not avoid the resulting repercussions. A desultory rate war raged through 1875. William managed the rise and fall of prices, though his father remained informed and engaged. On June 23, the eighty-one-year-old Commodore gave a long interview to the *New York Times* in which he discussed communications with James Joy, the rate war, and the condition of the Lake Shore. He bridled when asked if he was selling Lake Shore short. "That is a lie!" he snapped. "You may say that he who tries to injure the property which he is managing for stockholders, and endeavors by any means to deteriorate its value, is a thief."[101] And yet, he remained close friends with Daniel Drew, the past master of deteriorating his own corporations' value.

The railroad war proved to be Vanderbilt's main point of interest in the management of Western Union, still run by William Orton. On November 17, 1875, Garrett wrote to the Commodore to inform him that the Baltimore & Ohio was ejecting Western Union from its line along that railroad in favor of Gould's upstart Atlantic & Pacific telegraph company. As Orton succinctly summarized the situation, "The competition between the Railroad Companies for Western business has caused the rivals of the New York Central to strike at the Western Union for the purpose of injuring the Commodore." Still, Vanderbilt, for the most part, was content to let Orton manage Western Union, as William did his railroads.[102]

This conflict would not end in a glorious victory. Rather, it offered a quiet affirmation of William's capable management and the Commodore's strategic gifts. As it dragged on through 1876, the New York Central continued to pay 8 percent dividends; in fact, the board made them automatic, issued on a quarterly basis. Even the Lake Shore resumed dividends. By glaring contrast, the Pennsylvania and the Baltimore & Ohio were forced to halt dividends altogether. Of all the competitive advantages that entered into this feat, the most important was the great infrastructure envisioned by the Commodore and completed by the end of 1874: the St. John's Park Freight Depot, the Grand Central Depot, the Fourth Avenue Improvement, a huge North River grain elevator, a double-track bridge at Albany, and especially the four-track line to Buffalo. The Central cut expenses by more than 20 percent on the freight traffic that now increased with the low rates. "This enormous gain is due chiefly . . . to the separate freight tracks, permitting a uniform moderate speed for freight trains," *Railroad Gazette* wrote at the end of 1876. The Commodore's calculations were proved correct.[103]

The rate war also led to Vanderbilt's last great acquisition: the Canada Southern Railway. Launched in 1871 by Daniel Drew and John F. Tracy as a rival to the Great Western of Canada, it was completed from Detroit to the Niagara Suspension Bridge in 1874, just as rates began to plummet. By the end of 1875 it was penniless, with $700,000 in floating debt, $1.4 million in unpaid bonds, and a workforce that received nothing but promissory notes for their wages. Indeed, it was in a far weaker condition than any company the Commodore had taken over in the past. But, given its strategic geographical location, its very weakness made it a threat. Left alone, it would likely fall into the hands of, or make an alliance with, the Grand Trunk, to the Central's injury. And it did possess a well-laid-out line with low grades. Vanderbilt opened negotiations with the Canada Southern directors to rescue their line, and they arrived at an agreement on December 18, 1875. He purchased 48,195 shares (of nearly 100,000 total) for $10 per share, with the right to acquire the remaining fifty thousand shares as they became available. By January 1, 1876, Vanderbilt owned a total of 85,000. On that day, he gave Worcester the stock certificates and ordered him to put ten thousand shares in the name of William; one thousand each in the name of William's sons William K. and Frederick; ten thousand in Worcester's own name; ten thousand in the name of Augustus Schell; and ten thousand in the names of several others. Worcester had each of these individuals endorse the certificates, then handed them back to the Commodore.[104]

Other business battles raged during these years, such as squabbles over the Wagner sleeping-car company (in which William owned much stock), pooling arrangements with the Fort Wayne, and the telegraph war with Gould's company. These were managed by William and Orton. From the Commodore's perspective, the storm that began in 1873 had come and gone (though the depression would continue to 1879). He had triumphed.[105]

VANDERBILT MADE A HABIT of facing eternity. Even after marrying the pious Frank, he occasionally tried to speak to the dead. Mary E. Bennett, a friend of the Commodore's, would recall how he took her to a séance in the fall of 1874. They sat at a table, two raps sounded, and the medium intoned, "This is for you, Commodore. It is from your wife."

"Business before pleasure," Vanderbilt said. "I want a communication from Jim Fisk. Give me some paper." He wrote a question for Fisk's ghost.

"Jim Fisk is here," the medium said. Vanderbilt asked a question aloud about the stock market, and the medium gave an answer.

"That can't be so," Vanderbilt said, "but I will watch and see if you are right or I am." At that, Bennett recalled, he began to joke with Fisk, "and asked him how he liked it on the other side. Fisk said he liked it pretty well, and told the Commodore he would find out soon enough, for he was pretty near the end of his line." Then Vanderbilt contacted Sophia and asked her for advice about Corneil.[106]

Bennett's account reveals Vanderbilt's ongoing interest in the world beyond—specifically his need to stay in contact with those who had died before him—and his continuing faith in his own sagacity, even in the face of the supernatural. The Commodore found the sessions with the dead comforting, but he kept his own counsel.

As for his most famous intermediaries with the spirit world, Victoria Woodhull and Tennie C. Claflin, he had turned against them years before. For a time after Vanderbilt's second wedding, it was rumored that John Morrissey relayed his messages to the sisters. But their notoriety grew, and with it the Commodore's disenchantment. One by one, their brokerage customers—most of them women who wanted to patronize a female-run firm—began to sue as the sisters' extravagant promises fell through. Whether they invested any money on the stock market at all was an open question. They and Col. Blood spent most of their time on *Woodhull & Claflin's Weekly*, "devoted to the interests of free love and the 'pantarchy,' whatever that may mean," the *Times* wrote. They became embroiled in lawsuits with their mother, herself a shady character, and were evicted from their fine townhouse on East Thirty-eighth Street. Woodhull briefly became a leading figure in the women's rights movement, and offered herself as a candidate for president in 1872. She and her sister were also indicted for sending obscene material through the mail that year, the fastidious federal authorities judging their radical weekly to fit the definition. Finally they launched a vicious attack on Vanderbilt in lectures and their newspaper, for he had spurned them. Called to testify on January 4, 1875, in yet another lawsuit against them by a duped investor, he said, "I have not had business relations with them as bankers or brokers. I do not recollect of any authority given by me to them to use my name in their business." By then, his connection with them had become a distant memory.[107]

Decay and death continued to claim Vanderbilt's friends. In March 1876, Daniel Drew went bankrupt. He had been battered repeatedly in stock market battles with Jay Gould, and never recovered from the Northwestern corner in 1872. His failure, one newspaper reported, "causes no special disturbance, as it would have done a few years ago. . . . The whole story of 'Uncle Daniel's' disasters is summed up in three words—he was tricky." *Railroad Gazette* remarked that Drew "has been a great railroad man in his way, which way has been almost entirely that of a speculator in railroad securities." This judgment was not entirely fair. Drew had been a great steamboat entrepreneur, and had helped start the Canada Southern, though that railroad proved to be a disaster for him, perhaps even the final blow. The real victims of his failure were his charities, especially Drew Seminary. He had endowed them with promissory notes which he could not pay. Vanderbilt said he was "sorry for Daniel Drew, whom he always advised to stop speculating and turn pious in real earnest."[108]

A reporter called on Drew, seeking his reflections on his rise and fall. "I had been wonderfully blessed in money-making; got to be a millionaire afore I know'd it hardly," he said. "I was always pretty lucky till lately, and didn't think I could ever lose very extensively. I was ambitious to make a great fortune like Vanderbilt, and tried every way I knew, but got caught at last. Besides that I liked the excitement of making money and giving it away." He should have quit Wall Street long ago, he mused, when he was worth $8-$10 million. "One of the hardest things I've ever had to bear has been the fact that I couldn't continue to pay the interest on the notes I gave to the schools and churches. And then my children ought to have been left with large fortunes, as they had a right to expect. The thought of these things at first came near killing me or driving me crazy, but I have got over the worst feelings now."

The reporter asked Drew who he thought were the richest men in New York. Alexander T. Stewart, he guessed, was worth $40 million, "but Vanderbilt was surely worth a hundred millions of money if he owned a dollar."[109] Stewart did not hold that fortune for much longer. He died on April 10. Three days after, the city saluted the department-store magnate with "an immense funeral," as the *New York Herald* described it, attended by the rich and powerful, including William H. Vanderbilt. The Commodore did not go to his friend's service. He was sick in bed himself.[110]

On April 14, Frank sent word to Dr. Linsly, asking him to come see the Commodore. Linsly found his patient in great distress. Vanderbilt's autopsy would show that he had an enlarged prostate—common in older men—which led in turn to cystitis, or an infection of the bladder, which was not draining properly. This condition was painful enough, but Vanderbilt also had terrible bowel disorders. He had anal stenosis, a constriction often caused by scar tissue—in his case, the result of surgery he had had decades earlier for hemorrhoids. In particular, he appears to have suffered from diverticulitis, another ailment that commonly afflicts the elderly, in which a pouch (diverticulum) forms in the lining of the colon and becomes infected and inflamed.[111]

Internal abdominal pain may well be the most unbearable of all. Vanderbilt loathed opiates, the only effective pain medication available. Even when he took them, they increased the constipation from his stenosis, which forced his waste into the infected pouch in his colon. The press reported, "His physical condition is rapidly going to pieces."

Unfortunately, Dr. Linsly was thrown from his carriage in a severe accident on April 15, and would remain bedridden for several weeks. Vanderbilt demanded an "electrical physician," William J. Bennett, who found the Commodore "howling like a wild beast with pain, so that he could be heard all over the house, calling upon God to relieve his sufferings and asking why the Lord persecuted him so much."[112] Vanderbilt's world had narrowed to the perimeter of his bed—to the surface of his skin—and it was aflame, with no hope of dousing the fire. He screamed; he exploded at those around him; he felt helpless after a lifetime in command.

Dr. William Bodenhamer would later talk about his treatment of Vanderbilt during the month when Linsly was bedridden. He spoke at length about Vanderbilt's faith in Spiritualism and his short-tempered explosions. He said that he explained to Vanderbilt that his enlarged prostate was likely the result of gonorrhea or "excessive venery"—too much sex. As for Vanderbilt's mental state, "I do not know that I ever did know a more clear-headed man under such suffering," Bodenhamer declared. "I never saw him when his mind was not clear. In my opinion, he was at all times capable of transacting any business he was accustomed to."[113]

Knowing the public impact of his illness, Vanderbilt pulled himself together to see a reporter in early May. He sat up in his sickbed and explained that he was recovering, though still weak, and he knowledgeably discussed the ongoing rate war. He explained that the New York Central "is placed on the defensive by all the other trunk lines—one road demanding the right to reduce fares because it is a longer route, and the other roads demanding the same right because they are shorter routes." The natural superiority of New York as a port, he said, gave the Central a critical advantage. All it had to do was defend itself. " 'In other words,' said he, as he turned to look through some letters just brought him, 'since I have been a railroad man it has always been my practice to let my opponents make the rates, and I follow them so long as they do not put the rate so high as to be an imposition on the public.' "[114]

A few days later, a reporter for the *New York Herald* called at 10 Washington Place. As a servant held the door open, the reporter saw Frank striding toward him when "the well known voice of the Commodore came rolling vigorously after her, saying, 'Tell the gentleman from the Herald that even my slight local disorder is now almost entirely removed. . . . Even if I were dying I could knock all the truth that there is in the wretches who start these reports out of them, and that, as vigorous as I am at present, I would, were they within easy reach, knock all the lies for hereafter out of them." Frank, now at the door, said "the Commodore's declaration was quite in accordance with her view of the case."[115]

William often came to consult with his father, as did Worcester. On one occasion, Worcester found the Commodore stretched out on a kind of bed set up over a bathtub—presumably so he could sit in steam—smoking a cigar. Vanderbilt said that he wished to establish a home for disabled employees, and endow it with $500,000 of second-mortgage Lake Shore bonds. He wanted it to serve New York Central workers first, and later those of the Lake Shore as well. He ordered Worcester to draw up a plan but keep it from William until he was finished. Also, Worcester recalled, "the Commodore said he did not want the lazy to be assisted by the institution."[116]

All the while, he suffered. At the end of May, Frank began to keep a diary, a grim record of his agony, his bowel movements (or lack of them), his fevers, his explosions, his despair, his love for her. "Regrets so any hard expressions he uses during the painful paroxysms," she wrote on June 4. "Com. strained *all* day. Had a natural passage from the bowels in the night," she wrote on June 17. "So tempted to temper & hard words. Dr.

says disease makes him so," she wrote on June 26. On days when he was feeling better, he laughed and joked and teased his nurse and doctors mercilessly.[117]

Often he received visits from his sister Phebe, who was close to the Crawfords. Speaking of Frank, he told her, "She has been so good to me, so true, so pure. I know she will never do dishonor to your *name*, Phebe. Say to my family too no matter how they do, they will always find her a Lady. . . . She may be like other women, but I have never detected any self-ishness in her." This combination of honest affection, keen searching of character, and harsh characterization ("like other women") was vintage Vanderbilt. As he told Frank after a particularly bad night, "Tho' my man-ner had been rough to you, there was always love beneath my rough exte-rior to protect you from all harm." His capacity for love did not contradict his famously domineering nature; it simply made him more complex. Frank wrote,

> He never lost the habit of controlg others. Lizzie his nurse was disposed to argue for what *she* thought would make him comfortable. He would say, "Quick quick Lizzie not a word but do the work." Asked for his spectacles & put them on with great deliberation & took Dr. Eliot's hand & examined his nails, ran his fingers over them very closely & carefully to see if they could possibly hurt him. His flesh was so sensitive. Dr. had trimmed his nails for-tunately.[118]

Both sides of his personality came out when dealing with his daughters. One day Martha Crawford asked if Frank really had to speak to Sophia Torrance, who had snubbed Frank so often. Some in the family said she should, Crawford said. "Who said so?" Vanderbilt asked. "*No*. She [Sophia] misused [Frank] & let her make the first advances." At his insis-tence, Sophia apologized and shook hands with Frank in his presence. On August 4, he spoke to Mary La Bau, who demanded that he redraw his will. "Now don't be stubborn & give trouble," he said. "I have left you all enough to live like ladies." Frank wrote, "When she began to argue that she was not stubborn, he merely waved his hand at her, as if he could not hear more."[119]

He frequently received visitors, ranging from old steamboat captains to Thurlow Weed. He sent telegrams to Bishop McTyeire. He read and crit-icized Worcester's lengthy report on the home for railroad workers. He listened to Frank, her mother, and Phebe sing. On September 12, Frank wrote, "He sent to the sitting room for me, kissed me, & asked me when I was going to the Centennial." The national centennial fair in Philadelphia was the great cultural event of the age. Vanderbilt said, "You ought to go one day at least, & come home at night." It took weeks before she was willing to leave his side, even for so short a time. When she read him the news of Braxton Bragg's death, he snapped, "Yes, I know about *that*." (Someone had told him earlier.) Frank wrote that he "remarked how well it [was] he had not taken him [Bragg] in his business as he once wished he had (that was when we were married). Head still so clear." His memory was sharp, she noted; he often corrected others, saying, "I don't forget what I remember."[120]

His condition rose and fell, his pain swelled and subsided. In August, he endured an unspecified operation. Frank could tell it was "*awfully pain-ful*. . . . It was heart-rending to witness his agony." The doctors felt certain that he would die in its aftermath, but he rallied. On September 27, she noted, "He agrees with Dr. Linsly. 'No cure.' Com seems oppressed but I played the piano for him & he revived wonderfully."[121]

Vanderbilt faced eternity. "He has queer dreams occasionally," Frank wrote. "He dreamed he had been away down to the bottom but was coming up again & that it took all the power of the steamer *Vanderbilt* to pull him out but she did." On October 5, he discussed business with Amasa Stone for half an hour, then met with Worcester. Afterward he called Frank to his bedside. "This morning he was trying to express himself to me about his soul & salvation & said for the first time, 'Why don't you talk to me?'" she wrote. "I did & afterwards read him some beautiful prayers & he would say amen & 'How sweet' & showed plainly he enjoyed & felt them." He actually prayed to Jesus for salvation. "I asked, 'Dear, is it because you love him or is it to be relieved of the pain?' He replied, 'To be candid—both.'" He turned to Linsly and said, "Dr., it may be selfish, but I would take Frank with me, if I could." He even said farewell to Corneil. After many refusals, he allowed him in for a last chat. "Poor unfortunate boy," he said. "You make good resolutions but are not able to keep them from here to Broadway."[122]

Almost every day during his long illness, the nation's leading newspapers published reports on Vanderbilt's condition, what he had eaten, how he had slept, what visitors said of his condition. This extraordinary attention underscored Vanderbilt's unique, self-made position in American society—the personification of the otherwise faceless corporations that increasingly overshadowed the land. But the death watch also prepared the public and the markets for his demise, assuring that there would be no collapse of his stock prices. Vanderbilt's long agony was his final gift to William.

On December 16, William attended a conference at the Windsor Hotel that ended the rate war on favorable terms. Two days later, he went to 10 Washington Place, along with Worcester and the auditor of the Lake

Shore. The Commodore spoke to them at length about the proper relationship of the Canada Southern to his other railroads.[123]

By this time, Vanderbilt's diverticulitis had resulted in a perforated colon. Fecal matter squeezed out of the intestine. Peritonitis set in.

At 9:12 a.m. on January 4, 1877, William sent a telegram to Bishop McTyeire at Vanderbilt University. "Father is very low. Be prepared for the worst." At 11:41 a.m., he sent a second telegram. "Commodore passed away at nine minutes to eleven this morning." At 9:55 p.m., he sent a third. "Father passed away at nine minutes of eleven o'clock this morning without a struggle, surrounded by his entire family," he wrote. "Dr. Deems offered up prayers a few minutes before, all of which he perfectly understood and responded acquiescence by motions. . . . Mrs. V. is very much depressed & we all feel very sad. A great loss which we hardly realize."[124]

EPILOGUE

They never learned his secrets. Starting on November 12, 1877, crowds of onlookers filled the seats in Surrogate Court, watching the lawyers of William H. Vanderbilt and Mary La Bau battle over the sanity of Cornelius Vanderbilt. The trial dragged on for week after week, month after month. The attorneys called as witnesses the great and the marginal, the convincing and the convicted, whose testimony was sometimes insightful, often salacious, and frequently misleading. The result was a bizarre, fragmented mosaic of true and false moments in the Commodore's life, lacking context, missing vast stretches of his activities or inner life. This image would harden in memory until it formed a kind of shield, blocking any deeper penetration of the man.[1]

The great will contest went on for two years, two months, and four days. At various points, Ethelinda Allen and Cornelius Jeremiah fought alongside their sister. In the end, William won, but he also doubled their shares of the estate. He gave Ethelinda Allen the interest on an additional $400,000 in U.S. bonds, for example, and added $200,000 to Corneil's trust fund. William retained control of their father's empire.[2]

William's words to McTyeire said everything about his father's death. Sons are notoriously prone to exaggerate the importance of their fathers, as are biographers with their subjects, yet few nineteenth-century businessmen equaled Vanderbilt in his impact on American history. A handful of rival candidates come to mind—John Jacob Astor, John D. Rockefeller Sr., Andrew Carnegie, J. P. Morgan, perhaps Jay Gould and Thomas A. Scott—but arguably none proved to be so influential at so fundamental a level over a period so formative or so long. His accomplishments bear repeating. With his role in *Gibbons v. Ogden*, he helped to transform the Constitution by tearing down state-erected barriers to trade and shattering the remnants of the eighteenth-century culture of deference. Vanderbilt epitomized the commercial, individualistic society that emerged in the early nineteenth century, and contributed to the creation of a culture in which competition was a personal, economic, and political virtue. With his leading part in the transportation revolution, he helped to shape

America's newly mobile society, and to foster long-distance trade and the early textile industry of New England. With the gold rush, Vanderbilt's impact on the geography of the United States grew even more marked. Since steamship travel via Central America was the primary channel of migration, commerce, and finance with the Pacific coast, his Nicaragua line and related ventures fed the growth of San Francisco and the state of California. He also sped the flow of high-powered money to Manhattan, feeding the boom of the 1850s. Indeed, all his enterprises contributed to the rise of New York as America's financial capital.

With the approach of the Civil War, the Commodore's influence on history continued undiminished. Though he transformed Nicaragua into a target for filibusters, he delivered the decisive blow against William Walker, one of the most dangerous international criminals of the nineteenth century, in the face of Washington's inaction and hostility. Vanderbilt played a significant role in the Union war effort—one perhaps best measured by the Confederates' failure to interrupt the shipment of gold from California. More important, he took on the role of railroad king as railways became central to American life. Step by step, he overcame the fragmentation of the system and built unprecedented new infrastructure. With his son as operational manager, he reduced costs and introduced new efficiency into long-distance transportation, helping to integrate the national economy and transform it into an industrial empire.

All this formed a legacy that would remain central to the United States into the twenty-first century—from its individualistic, opportunity-minded culture to its sprawling, continental scale to its dense transportation networks. And yet, he may have left his most lasting mark in the invisible world, by creating an unseen architecture which later generations of Americans would take for granted. The modern economic mind began to emerge in Vanderbilt's lifetime, amid fierce debate, confusion, and intense resistance. The imagined devices of commerce gradually abstracted the tangible into mere tokens, and then less than tokens. Money transformed from gold coin to gold-backed banknotes to legal-tender slips of paper and ledger entries of bank accounts. Property migrated from physical objects to the shares of partnerships to par-value stock to securities that fluctuated according to the market, that could be increased in number at will. Like a ghost, the business enterprise departed the body of the individual proprietor and became a being in itself, a corporation with its own identity, its own character, its own personhood.

Over the course of his career, Vanderbilt lived out the history of this abstraction, the invention of this imagined world. More than that, he took it to a new level by pioneering the giant corporation. By consolidating his New York lines into the New York Central & Hudson River Railroad, he constructed something larger than himself, not to mention virtually every other enterprise that had ever existed. It was a massive organization, one that served to depersonalize, to institutionalize, American business and life. It helped to lead the way to a future dominated by large enterprises possessing wealth and power that changed not only the economic land-scape, but the political one as well. A new matrix began to emerge, as radicals began to think of the state as the natural counterweight to the business corporation. This, too, is Vanderbilt's legacy.

The Commodore's life left its mark on Americans' most basic beliefs about equality and opportunity. He epitomized the Jacksonian ideal of every man being free to compete and rise on his merits, and that ideal remains a bright thread in the fabric of American thought. Yet his unprecedented wealth—and with it, unprecedented power—signaled that inequalities were exploding in size with the new corporate economy. Mark Twain's term "gilded age" came to stand for the extreme polarization of riches and poverty in the late nineteenth century, a polarization that Vanderbilt led. His life marks the start of the Era of Great Fortunes. And when he handed down the bulk of his fortune to one son and his sons, he created something that his fellow citizens had long thought to be the corrupt artifact of the aristocratic societies of Europe—that is, he started a dynasty. His example would be followed by Rockefeller and Ford and others. The inheritance of such fortunes had been roundly condemned in the early republic; indeed, early critics of the corporation feared that it would undermine the natural process by which estates were broken up upon death. Vanderbilt and the dynasts who followed him not only created a Gilded Age, they caused their fellow Americans to reexamine the place where opportunity and equality collided.

But Vanderbilt's admirers as well as his critics demand attention. On January 5, 1877, the directors of the U.S. railroads Vanderbilt had led as president—the New York & Harlem, the New York Central & Hudson River, and the Lake Shore & Michigan Southern—met and issued a joint tribute to their chief. It was hagiography, of course, but it spoke to how his followers saw him at the moment of his death. An excerpt:

> The truest monument to CORNELIUS VANDERBILT is the fact that he so organized his creation that the work will go on, though the master work-man is gone. . . .
> His career was a dazzling success. In an age and a country distinguished for their marvelous personal triumphs, his achievements rank among the most extraordinary and distinctive of all. Thoroughly practical and faith-fully wrought out, their splendor yet gives them the tinge of romance. . . .
> He was essentially the creator, not the creature, of the circumstances which he moulded to his purposes. He was the architect of his own fortune. Begin-

ning in a humble position, with apparently little scope of action and small promise of opportunity, he rose, by his genius, his indomitable energy and his clear forecast, to the control of vast enterprises involving millions of property and connected with the interests of millions of people. . . .

It is to his lasting honor that his uniform policy was to protect, develop, and improve the interests with which he was connected, instead of seeking a selfish and dishonorable profit through their detriment and sacrifice. The rights and welfare of the smallest stockholder were as well guarded as his own. In a period of crafty devices for sinister ends, he taught the way of success through legimate means. . . .

With all his brilliant success, his frank simplicity of character and habits remained unchanged. In the height of his rare fortune he was the same direct, provident, unostentatious man as before he had mounted to his large opportunities. The sterling qualities of his strong and commanding individuality were deeply appreciated by all who were associated with him. He was firm and true in his friendships.[3]

It was no wonder that the press devoted massive attention to his death. It was as if a head of state had died—the self-made chief executive of a country that he himself had invented, rather like a cross between George Washington and Genghis Khan. Generations had come of age in his shadow. At his funeral on Sunday, January 7, 1877, the great and powerful, past and present, came to salute him: Peter Cooper, Charles O'Conor, Thurlow Weed, Edwin D. Morgan, Cyrus W. Field, Daniel Drew, Marshall O. Roberts, Frank Work, William E. Dodge, and Augustus Schell, among many others. After a viewing of the body at 10 Washington Place and a ceremony at the Church of the Strangers, a line of carriages carried his casket down to Whitehall Slip, where he had first set foot in New York three-quarters of a century before. It crossed the harbor on the ferry he had created, to be buried in the family tomb.[4]

His children would agree that he was a hard man. They often suffered from his imperious manner, most pronounced when among his family. When his onetime friend John Morrissey heard of his death, he said, "Well, he died without making a bad debt or leaving a friend. See how all of them went to bed happily last night." Later Morrissey would declare, "I have known in the course of my life burglars, fighting men, and loafers, but never have I known such a bad fellow as Commodore Vanderbilt."[5]

But Morrissey was one of those who had hoped to get rich quickly and effortlessly from his association with Vanderbilt. So were all of the Commodore's bitterest enemies, including Joseph L. White and John M. Davidson. Most of those foes who met him in open combat—Cornelius Garrison, Charles Morgan, Marshall Roberts, William Aspinwall, Erastus Corning, and his quondam partner Daniel Drew—admired him, and socialized with him after their conflicts ended. It is a fact of human nature that one need not be nice to be liked and respected, and so it was with Vanderbilt. His fellow businessmen appreciated his forthrightness, capability, honesty, dignity, sense of honor, and force of personality. They felt that he had earned his pride in himself. More than that, they knew that Vanderbilt was as accomplished and patient as a diplomat as he was fierce and unrelenting as a competitor. More and more over the years, he sought compromise, common ground, accommodation. As a railroad leader, he fought each war of conquest only as a last resort, after repeated negotiations had failed.

The image of Vanderbilt as the man of force is powerful, so much so that it can easily be forgotten that he was a man, emotional and complicated. Here and there, his vulnerabilities and sensitivities poke through the cracks of the stony historical record. He was often difficult with both his wives, yet he loved and needed them. He was disgusted with Corneil's weaknesses, yet he agonized over his own inability to bring about his reformation, and he cherished Corneil's wife, Ellen, and her family. He was a difficult father for all of his sons. With his immense personal capabilities, he set an impossibly high standard. Even William suffered in his father's huge, dark shadow, yet Vanderbilt also respected William's decisions once he had given his son the authority to make them. The Commodore browbeat the younger generations of his clan, too, yet he gave his sons-in-law the highest positions of responsibility in his businesses, and repeatedly sought favors from presidents and associates for his nephews and grandsons.

His family loved him in return, as could be seen even in the pain he sometimes caused them. The Thorns, for example, felt wounded by the Commodore's remark that their children were not Vanderbilts—because his opinion mattered to them. Corneil, too, deeply loved his father. During the Commodore's final hours on his deathbed, Corneil wrote to George Terry, "I fear the time is at hand & God knows I regret it." But Corneil would not last much longer than his father. With his inheritance he reportedly repaid his debt to Greeley's estate, then managed to fall into bankruptcy once more. On April 2, 1882, with Terry in the next room, he put a revolver to his temple and shot himself to death. Frank followed on May 4, 1885, falling dead of a stroke at 10 Washington Place. Her letters and diary make clear that she loved her husband deeply; though more than four decades younger than he, she lasted barely eight years without him.[6]

The Commodore did value one family member more than the others in a most important respect. He intended to found a dynasty, and he planned for William to lead the next generation. The fortune he passed down largely to his eldest son is impossible to calculate. The press guessed that it was worth anywhere from $85 million to $115 million, based on the par value of what his holdings *might* have been in his railroads and Western Union. On the day that Vanderbilt died, Worcester—who handled many of his personal affairs—told a reporter, "About $100,000,000 is as near to a fair valuation as can be put upon the estate of Mr. Vanderbilt." Three problems make it impossible to find a more exact figure. First, the market value of his stock fluctuated. At the start of 1877, in the midst of the depression, it was low compared to recent years, though not at the absolute bottom; prices would rise as the economy improved. Second, up to almost the moment of Vanderbilt's death, he hid his shares under others' names, as his notes to James Banker and Worcester's testimony show. Worcester himself may not have known the full story. Finally, Vanderbilt transferred much of his wealth to William and his sons before his death. He gave all of his real estate, worth many millions, to William at about the time of his marriage to Frank, and transferred tens of thousands of railroad shares at various times. When William died on December 8, 1885, his estate was estimated at $200 million, and he was admired for doubling his inheritance in just a few years. In fact, there is good reason to believe that, had the Commodore lived eight years longer, and left his estate just as it was but kept it together as a single unit, his fortune would not have been worth much less than William's was when he died.[7]

How does $100 million or so translate into twenty-first-century dollars? These pages have not provided modern equivalent figures, in the conviction that historical dollar amounts cannot honestly be converted. They are irreducible facts that can be understood only in their contemporary context. The economy was not simply a balloon that inflated over time; in the nineteenth century it was lumpy, with partially integrated markets, uneven currency supplies in different regions, periods of rapid growth and dramatic increases in economic complexity, and long periods of deflation. At some point in the twentieth century, even the smallest, most remote communities in America would find themselves woven seamlessly into the national—even the international—financial system. This integration of all economic life into a single web, dominated by the Federal Reserve Bank, would prove to be the culmination of much of Vanderbilt's life of entrepreneurship and institution building. But it had not yet come into existence during his own time. Rural areas in the South and West frequently lacked access to banking; they were the areas most heavily dependent on cash, yet they were plagued with raw cash shortages. In 1876, the last full year of Vanderbilt's life, the comptroller of the currency reported that the combined total of all greenbacks, national banknotes, fractional currency, and gold and silver coin in circulation amounted to $900,676,194—just $19.77 for each of the estimated 45,550,000 citizens.

Even this figure is deceptively large, for national banknotes were concentrated in bank-rich regions, particularly the Northeast.[8]

On the other hand, these figures do provide some context for the scale of Vanderbilt's fortune. If he had been able to liquidate his $100 million estate to American purchasers at full market value (an impossible task, of course), he would have received about $1 out of every $9 in existence. If demand deposits at banks are included in the calculation, he still would have taken possession of $1 out of every $20. By contrast, *Forbes* magazine calculated in September 2008 that William Henry Gates III—better known as Bill Gates—was the richest man in the world, with a net worth of $57 billion. If Gates had liquidated his entire estate (to American buyers) at full market value at that time, he would have taken $1 out of every $138 circulating in the American economy.* Even this comparison understates the disparity between the scale of Vanderbilt's wealth and that of any individual in the early twenty-first century, let alone his own time. The calculation for 2008 uses the Federal Reserve's M2 figure, the most literal equivalent to the 1876 comptroller's report; the money supply in the far more complex modern economy is generally thought to include a far broader range of financial instruments, a tally referred to as M3.[9]

Vanderbilt cultivated William and William's sons as his heirs, instructing them to preserve the empire and perpetuate the dynasty. For an impious man, it was his greatest grasp at immortality, greater even than the creation of his university. But fathers rarely imprint themselves on their sons. No sooner had the trial over the Commodore's will ended in 1879 than William agreed to sell 250,000 shares of New York Central & Hudson River to a syndicate organized by banker J. P. Morgan. Morgan's consortium bought them at 120, for a total payout of $30 million. This was not a majority stake, and William and his sons retained a large percentage of the hundreds of thousands of remaining shares; but the family now worked closely with Morgan, who served as maestro of a banking syndicate that established interlocking directorates in the major railroads to tamp down the competition that had driven so many lines into bankruptcy. Morgan, together with William's sons, particularly Cornelius II, established a Board of Control that brought to fruition the great project started by the Commodore. Charles F. Adams Jr. would write in 1888, "The most perfect organization is that now known as the Vanderbilt system."[10]

William ostensibly sold out because a bill was pending in the legislature

---

* The *New York Times*, July 15, 2007, named Vanderbilt the second-wealthiest man in American history, relative to the size of the economy. Statistics for the nineteenth-century economy as a whole, however, are unreliable.

to bar any family from having majority control of the Central. Chauncey Depew, who knew Albany better than anyone, counseled in favor of the sale. But there is reason to think that William was simply worn out. He may have lacked his father's year-after-year resilience in the face of hostility. Where the Commodore had been calmest in the heat of battle, unleashing his temper largely at home, William seems to have been a kind father but, at times, a poor corporate diplomat. Even his ally Morgan wrote that he "irritated and harassed" other businessmen, and pursued "legal quibbles which would be disgraceful to any Bowery lawyer." Rather than slowly limit his role in business without giving it up, as his aging father had done, he retired to a life of luxury. He constructed twin mansions on Fifth Avenue between Fifty-first and Fifty-second streets, and filled them with fine art.[11]

His children followed suit, constructing their own Fifth Avenue palaces. In March 1883, William K. and Alva Smith Vanderbilt threw a costume ball that stood as one of the great extravagances of the Gilded Age. "I wish the Vanderbilts didn't retard culture so very thoroughly," Edith Wharton wrote to a friend. "They are entrenched in a sort of *thermopylae* of bad taste, from which apparently no force on earth can dislodge them." William H. Vanderbilt's mansion was eventually demolished (as was 10 Washington Place), though some of those built by William's children still remain, from the Breakers at Newport to the Biltmore in Asheville, North Carolina—monuments to an outrageous self-indulgence that the Commodore would have scorned, made possible by an enormous disparity in wealth that the Commodore pioneered.[12]

The story of the subsequent generations has no place here. Suffice it to say, as Louis Auchincloss does, "With the death of Cornelius II in 1899 at the age of only fifty-six, the Vanderbilt dynasty at the New York Central really came to an end." The family would play a role in the mighty corporation until its eventual merger with the Pennsylvania and the state takeover that soon followed, but "the sense of a family leader was gone."[13] The fortune was built on America's first great industry, but also the first industry to mature and fade, as the Commodore's descendants spent their money and enjoyed themselves. Descendants live on, but the family has drifted out of the main currents of history.

The Commodore himself remains. His statue still stands at the city gate, gazing down Park Avenue South from the front of Grand Central Terminal. In 1929, the railroad moved it from the top of the St. John's Park Freight Depot, which was slated for destruction, to its current location. The original Grand Central Depot had been rebuilt, then destroyed, and replaced in 1913 by the railroad palace that remains in use to this day. Trains rumble out of it, through the Park Avenue tunnel that dates to the

Fourth Avenue Improvement, along the curving track around the Harlem River that Vanderbilt originally built as the Spuyten Duyvil Railroad.[14] It is fitting that he should stand guard over the infrastructure he created, more grand and more central than it was even in his own time, so vitally important to the city that rose to greatness under his influence. His corporation has disappeared; his plans for a dynasty ultimately failed; but, as the directors of his railroads observed, "The work will go on, though the master workman is gone."

Acknowledgments

Shortly after 2:30 p.m. on October 15, 2003, I hurried my teenage niece and nephew into the Whitehall Terminal of the Staten Island Ferry. They had come to visit me in New York, where I had lived since 1986, and I thought we could do no better on their first day in town than to take the ferry. We just missed the 2:30 sailing, and had to wait half an hour to board the *Andrew J. Barberi*. Twenty minutes after we boarded, the *Barberi* smashed into a service pier on Staten Island. Now I had to shoo my niece and nephew out of the way of a mob of panicking commuters who were racing back from the bow. We were on the upper deck, and saw no carnage; it was not until we returned to Manhattan that we realized it had been a catastrophe, one that eventually cost the lives of eleven passengers. It was the deadliest transit accident in New York in more than a century.

From the moment of impact, I knew we had been caught in a historic event. As my nephew and I handed out life jackets—and as I scanned the deck to see if the *Barberi* was listing, and in danger of sinking—I thought to myself, *I've studied ferry disasters; now I'm in one.* We returned to Whitehall on the last ferry to run that day, where we gave our accounts to a crowd of reporters. It was peculiar to find myself delivering the sort of information I was consuming to write this book.

I had been at work on it for more than a year already, and was struck by the coincidence that I was writing a biography of the man who founded the Staten Island Ferry.* The 150 or so years between my subject and me matter far more, however. It is a gulf that requires immense effort to span, even in the imagination. Matters conscious and unconscious—grand political issues, meanings of words, social expectations, even the smell of the air—all must be reconstructed, but never can be completely. It is a literary and historical endeavor that cannot be carried out alone.

This book was the product of endless assistance: from archivists who ultimately hold the secrets, in disassembled pieces; from the scholars who

---

* The service Cornelius Vanderbilt started just before the Civil War to run in conjunction with the Staten Island Railroad, and later sold to the railway, is the lineal ancestor of today's ferry.

created the historiographical context and interpretive framework; from my editor and fellow writers who offered their insights; from institutions that gave financial and research support; and from family and friends, who offered not only emotional and material aid, but have shaped my personal understanding of humanity, the ultimate resource for any biographer.

First I must thank my wife, Jessica Stiles, who has supported and inspired me. Our meeting, long engagement, move to California, wedding, honeymoon, move to San Francisco, and birth of our first child all fall entirely within the brackets of my work on this book. I'm not sure she knew what she was in for. Her love, creativity, sensitivity, hard work, and fine talent as a writer have made it possible for me to complete this book, and I am grateful.

I must also thank the rest of my family, who have supported me unstintingly. I am grateful to my parents, Dr. Clifford and Carol Stiles, who always encouraged my interests, and even endured my decision to forgo an academic career after I had devoted years to graduate school. They have always been there for me. I must thank my sister Colleen Stiles for her creative assistance, and her son and daughter, Keegan and Kevyn Stokes, who survived the *Andrew J. Barberi* with me in 2003.

I include my wife's clans in my definition of family, and they offered abundant help before and after our move to California. I should single out my brothers-in-law Patrick and Kevin McKenna and sister-in-law Elizabeth McKenna, their parents, Susan and Michael McKenna, and my wife's grandparents, Jack and Ruth Kahoun. I owe a special debt to my grandmother-in-law, Elizabeth Frank, and her family, who let Jessica and me live for a year in the Frank home of the past sixty years, a house designed by Frank Lloyd Wright, where I wrote Part Two of this book. Friends and relatives of friends helped as well, especially Christina Wertz and Jeffrey Lerner, Kiki and Alex Beam, Woody Gilmartin, and Philip and Kathleen Brady. To all, thank you.

In acknowledging professional colleagues, I should begin with my editor, Jonathan Segal of Alfred A. Knopf, Inc. It is a great comfort to know that he won't publish a manuscript from me unless it's the best that I can make it. He sent this one back to me more than once for more work, and he was right to do so. I have profound respect for his literary judgment, not to mention gratitude for all he has done for me, and I'm honored to be on his list of authors. My agent, Jill Grinberg, brings an equal level of dedication to her work. She has remained a steadfast believer in my ability— or, at least, my potential—and has labored skillfully and hard to advance my career. I also have to thank Kirsten Wolf, another member of Jill Grinberg Literary Management, who has done so much to help me in the final year of work on this book.

There are a number of writers and historians who have given me their thoughts about this manuscript as it has progressed. David Hochfelder forwarded very useful details from the Western Union letterbooks. James McPherson, Richard Maxwell Brown, and Brenda Maddox supported my efforts to obtain a fellowship to support my work on this book (discussed below), and they have my deep gratitude. The late George Plimpton supported my application as well. We became acquainted with each other through my previous book, in which Plimpton's great-grandfather Adelbert Ames plays an important role, and I consider myself fortunate to have known him, however narrowly and briefly. My heartfelt thanks are due to Edward Countryman, Andrew Burstein, and Robert E. May, who commented on parts of various drafts. I must single out Joyce Appleby, Maury Klein, and Richard R. John for special thanks for looking over the entire manuscript. Each of them offered factual corrections, perceptive comments on my writing, and insightful criticism of my interpretations. To have distinguished historians labor through an uncut, unedited manuscript is a much-appreciated gift. I have benefited enormously from all the comments I have received; all failings of this book, however, are mine alone.

I believe very strongly in conducting my research myself. Unfortunately, I was forced to hire researchers for work at the Detroit Public Library and the University of Michigan, Ann Arbor. I must thank Ruth McMahon and Kristina Eden, respectively, for their fine work on my behalf there. They provided me with abundant material, though any oversight is my responsibility alone. I must also thank Frank Mauran of Providence, Rhode Island, who made available information from the ledger book of his ancestor, Oroondates Mauran. I wish to thank in particular Cristine Gonzalez, who assisted me as part of her Hertog Research Fellowship at Columbia University's School of the Arts. I never gave her much responsibility, I'm afraid, though she and her husband, Landon Hall, tracked down sources at the New-York Historical Society and photocopied them for me, and found valuable leads that I followed up. I was especially grateful for their labors after I arrived on the far side of the continent, copies in hand. I am indebted to the School of the Arts for the honor of working with a Hertog Fellow, especially one so talented.

Seemingly numberless archivists have assisted me generously and capably. I apologize for listing so many only by institution. My thanks go out to the staffs of the following, in no particular order: the California Historical Society; the Bancroft Library, University of California, Berkeley; the Huntington Library; the Newberry Library; the Manuscript Division of the Library of Congress; the National Archives in Washington, D.C., College Park, Maryland, and New York, New York; the Milton R. Perkins

Library, Duke University; Department of Special Collections, University Libraries, Wichita State University; Special Collections, Jean and Alexander Heard Library, Vanderbilt University; the American Antiquarian Society; the Watkinson Library, Trinity College, Hartford, Connecticut; the Baker Library, Harvard Business School; Carl A. Kroch Library, Cornell University; the Special Collections Research Center, Morris Library, Southern Illinois University, Carbondale, Ill.; Special Collections, University Libraries, University of Rhode Island; the Albany Institute of History and Art; the New York State Library; the Rockefeller Center Archives; the New York Municipal Archives; the New-York Historical Society; and the various libraries of Columbia University.

I must single out a few archivists who went above and beyond to help me as I spent weeks or months in their collections. Rebecca Rego Barry, late of Special Collections at Drew University, enthusiastically assisted me as I took the New Jersey Transit train to Madison, N.J., for so many snowy weeks in the winter of 2002–03. Joseph Van Nostrand and Bruce Abrams stand guard over the historical treasure trove of the Old Records Division of the New York County Clerk's Office, assisted by David Brantley, Robert Soenarie, Eileen McAleavey, and Annette Joseph. I would like to think we became friends as well as colleagues over the course of many months, as they guided me through the priceless collection of papers in their keeping. Bruce Abrams skillfully indexed this book.

I must conclude by singling out one institution in particular, which combined every form of assistance possible—financial, editorial, literary, historical, archival, emotional, even architectural. It is the New York Public Library (NYPL). I not only conducted years of research in the main research library on Fifth Avenue and Forty-second Street, I wrote much of the book there, in the Allen Room and the Center for Scholars and Writers (see below). It is one of America's great cultural institutions, and it is well served by its highly professional staff. I do a disservice to many by naming only a few, but I would like to single out, for their generous personal assistance, Wayne Furman of the Office of Special Collections (and thoughtful keeper of the Allen Room); Maira Liriano, Assistant Chief Librarian and Kate Cordes Librarian of the Milstein Division of United States History, Local History, and Genealogy; Alice C. Hudson, Chief of the Lionel Pincus and Princess Firyal Map Division; William Stingone, Charles J. Liebman Curator of Manuscripts in the Manuscripts and Archives Division; Kristin McDonough, Director of the Science, Industry, and Business Library; and David Ferriero, the Andrew W. Mellon Director and Chief Public Executive of the Research Libraries.

I wish to extend my special thanks to the NYPL's Dorothy and Lewis B. Cullman Center for Scholars and Writers. I could not have completed this book without the financial assistance of a fellowship at the center, 2004–05. For this award, I am grateful also to the Gilder Lehrman Institute of American History, which gave me the honor of being the first Gilder Lehrman Fellow in American History at the center. The center's staff, especially Pamela Leo and Adriana Nova, were exceptionally helpful. I am deeply indebted to Jean Strouse, the John and Sue Ann Weinberg Director of the center. A superb biographer, she both fostered a productive and collegial environment and offered specific advice on the early chapters of my manuscript. Finally, I thank my classmates of 2004-05. I hope they excuse me for singling out just a few whose insights, advice, or assistance I found particularly helpful: Hermione Lee, Jennifer Egan, Nathan Englander, Colum McCann, and Lisandro Perez. I admire them—and the other fellows of that year—for their character as much as their intellectual and artistic gifts.

T. J. S.

Bibliographical Essay

Cornelius Vanderbilt's life is truly an epic one. In length of activity, scope of action, and centrality to significant events, it looms larger than most others, at the very least. Unfortunately, his life and its impact have received little intensive study. The image of the Commodore that lingers in American memory is largely the creation of rumors reported as fact by the press, as well as tales told by outright fabulists, from his own time down to the present. I have found new information about every aspect of Vanderbilt's life (if only through sheer drudgery). Under the circumstances, I believe it is worthwhile to discuss previous biographies and the primary sources on which I have based my account. (This book was written before the 2008 financial crisis, and was not changed afterward.)

First, I should describe the method I have used to write this biography. I began by reading existing biographies and studies of the topics relevant to Vanderbilt's life, and combed through their notes to compile an initial list of primary sources. I examined those sources, and searched archival catalogs and online digitized collections, including the Proquest historical newspaper database and archives of congressional documents. (I examined every article obtainable through a Proquest search for "Vanderbilt" between 1810 and 1879, among many other searches—and learned just how much property was for sale on Brooklyn's Vanderbilt Avenue.) I visited archives, made photocopies and took notes, and saved thousands of electronic files. I also scrolled through microfilm and sifted through manuscript collections to search far beyond the specific citations on my list. (I surveyed every issue of *Railroad Gazette* for Vanderbilt's lifetime in the original printed form, for example.) I then created databases of my own, with an entry for notes and quotes from each relevant source, and wrote the initial draft of each chapter largely from the primary sources. I then went through the secondary sources again and revised my manuscript, incorporating other historians' information and interpretations (when not already cited in the text).

Just as important as the discovery of sources, of course, is their interpretation. It is famously said that the past is a foreign country; unfortunately, it is not always foreign enough. Nineteenth-century Americans spoke the same language as anyone who is now reading this sentence, but their vocabulary is deceptive in its familiarity. They imbued words with meanings that have long since disappeared, and they used expressions that, while familiar to historians, were built into a mental architecture that strikes the twenty-first-century mind as alien, even unsustainable. Terms such as "character," "monopoly," "competition," "stock watering," "par value," "intrinsic value," even "cash" must be understood in their original context, for they reflected a view of the world that is counterintuitive to us now and was constantly in dispute at the time. I have done my best to map this changing mental landscape over a rather long distance; authorities on any of the many periods covered here undoubtedly will find fault, and probably with cause. My motto is to research in terror, write with confidence, and publish with humility: terror, lest something escape me; confidence, lest the narrative seem weak and uncertain; and humility, because some sources and interpretations, not to mention perfect literary grace, always lie beyond the grasp of any writer.

Finally, I submitted drafts of my manuscript to some very generous academic historians. They include Joyce Appleby, Edward Countryman, Andrew Burstein, Robert E. May, Richard R. John, and Maury Klein. I owe them a great debt for correcting factual errors and misinterpretations, pointing out ideas I had not considered, and recommending further reading. But this book's failings are mine alone.

Cornelius Vanderbilt has not been well served by his biographers. Early writers based their works on—well, I don't know what. The newspapers freely embellished the rumors about Vanderbilt's life that came their way, as did the most influential account written before his death, by James Parton's *Famous Americans of Recent Times* (1867). This book is most useful as a description of how he was seen, not how he lived. Nine years after Vanderbilt's death, William A. Croffut published the lightweight volume *The Vanderbilts and the Story of their Fortune* (1886). This work has some value, for Croffut spoke to Charles F. Deems, William H. Vanderbilt's Staten Island field hands, and others for their firsthand accounts, but it is in no sense a scholarly work, and can best be used to give shading to accounts from solid sources.

The twentieth century brought only a small improvement. In 1927, novelist Arthur D. H. Smith published the heavily fictionalized *Commodore Vanderbilt: An Epic of American Achievement*, followed in 1941 by Wayne Andrews's *Vanderbilt Legend: The Story of the Vanderbilt Family*. Andrews offered endnotes, a rarity in books about Vanderbilt, though he based his work almost entirely on press accounts. As such, its main value is as a guide to newspaper stories about the Commodore.

In 1942 came the most important biography of Vanderbilt to date: Wheaton J. Lane's *Commodore Vanderbilt: An Epic of the Steam Age.* Lane, an authority on the history of transportation, adopted a serious approach to his subject, focusing overwhelmingly on his business career. He acquired access to business records and tracked down many examples of the relative handful of Vanderbilt's surviving letters. As a business historian, he wrote with none of the angry tone that emerged out of the populist and radical movements of the late nineteenth and early twentieth centuries—perhaps best exemplified by Gustavus Myers's *History of the Great American Fortunes* (1910), and Matthew Josephson's *The Robber Barons: The Great American Capitalists, 1861-1901* (1934). Lane placed Vanderbilt's business operations in their contemporary context, and revealed much about his historical significance.

Important as it is, this book also suffers serious flaws. As of this writing, it is nearly seven decades old. A great deal of historical research and analysis has been conducted in the interim, rendering Lane's account obsolete. His narrative of Vanderbilt's career through 1848 is gravely incomplete, particularly with reference to his involvement with Daniel Drew and in New England's early railroads. His discussion of the Nicaragua years fails to identify the great divide that opened early on between Vanderbilt and Joseph L. White, or the true nature of the relationship between the steamship magnates and William Walker. His narrative of Vanderbilt's creation of the New York Central empire better stands the test of time, but it, too, is incomplete, missing much of the Commodore's patient diplomacy and the extent to which Horace F. Clark operated on his own at the end of his life.

In terms of construction, Lane's book is a narrowly conceived piece of business history, paying limited attention to Vanderbilt's personal life, and often none at all to the larger historical context, such as the political and cultural issues that have occupied so much space in these pages. It segments Vanderbilt's different ventures by chapter, so that the reader is left without an understanding of his career's intensity as he engaged in multiple operations—and battled multiple foes—simultaneously. Finally, it frustratingly offers no endnotes. Rather, it provides bibliographic summaries for each chapter in the backmatter. Numerous quotes appear throughout the narrative without a clue as to what source they came from. Even worse, it frequently relies on unsourced and unreliable accounts, uncritically reprinting anecdotes and dialogue from Parton, Croffut, and Henry Clews, as well as obituaries and other apocryphal sources. That said, it remains the touchstone for any study of Vanderbilt's life.

Since Lane's work, there has been only one adult biography dedicated to the Commodore alone (as opposed to accounts of the Vanderbilt family as a whole). It is Edward J. Renehan Jr.'s *Commodore: The Life of Cornelius Vanderbilt* (New York: Basic Books, 2007). I had completed a draft of my own manuscript when this work appeared, and drew nothing from it; any similarities are entirely coincidental. I find *Commodore* to be a problematic work at best, based almost entirely on secondary sources, largely lacking annotation, and suffering numerous factual errors. I cannot verify many of the primary sources that Renehan does cite, and find that he mischaracterizes a number of those that I could locate.

Renehan writes that he discovered the privately held diaries of sleeping-car manufacturer Webster Wagner and Dr. Jared Linsly, Vanderbilt's personal physician. Renehan claims that Linsly's diary reveals that Vanderbilt contracted syphilis in 1839, began to suffer syphilitic dementia in 1868, and died of the disease. He further asserts, citing both these diaries, that William H. Vanderbilt used his father as a figurehead from 1868 on, treating the demented and uncomprehending Commodore as a puppet while William secretly ran his affairs.

I feel compelled to discount the validity of these diaries, and I find Renehan's assertions to be untenable. First, Renehan's claims are contradicted by an immense body of evidence, both medical and historical. There is no room here for a full discussion of the body of scientific knowledge of syphilis, but suffice it to say that Renehan's account conflicts with both recent medical literature and that written before effective treatment, when many patients were studied through the full life cycle of the disease. A doctor in 1839 would likely not have distinguished syphilis from gonorrhea and other sexually transmitted diseases, so any diagnosis would have meant little. Even if Vanderbilt did contract syphilis, he never developed syphilitic dementia, or "general paresis," to use the technical term (which only afflicted a small minority of syphilis victims). General paresis follows a well-documented course that is completely out of keeping with Vanderbilt's late-life history. Most important is the total lack of corroboration for Renehan's claims. Vanderbilt was a national celebrity, in the public eye on an almost daily basis; *no* observers noticed the distinctive abnormalities caused by general paresis, or even the loss of mental acuity. Both private and public records show him in full command of himself and his businesses, except as he chose to delegate to others. And William traveled to Europe more than once during his father's final decade, which he hardly would have done if he were secretly manipulating a demented father as his puppet.*

Second, Renehan has not allowed verification of his sources. I asked to

---

* General paresis is progressive, marked by wild behavioral aberrations and rapid loss of motor control. When untreated it leads to total paralysis and finally death within three or four years of its manifestation. Private letters, newspaper reports, and the directors' minutes of Vander-

examine his copy of the diaries, and offered to sign a written agreement to protect his right to first publication of any findings. He declined. When I asked the names of the owners, he refused to provide them. He claimed that he had promised each of them confidentiality, an arrangement I had never heard of before with holders of historic papers. He promised to contact them for me, but told me they were all very old. I heard no more from him.

Claims based on unauthenticated papers cannot be considered *information*. The most basic scholarly standards require that sources be available for scrutiny and verification by independent parties before they can be accepted. Renehan has chosen to make that impossible.

Finally, Renehan's credibility has been impeached by subsequent developments. In 2008, he pleaded guilty to two felonies, a federal charge of transporting stolen property across state lines, and a New York State charge of third-degree grand larceny, and was sentenced to eighteen months in federal prison. These criminal convictions stemmed from the theft of letters written by George Washington, Abraham Lincoln, and Theodore Roosevelt from the Theodore Roosevelt Association, during the period when Renehan was acting director of the organization. According to press reports, state and federal authorities believe that he forged a document to establish his ownership of the stolen letters, sold three of them through an auction house for nearly $100,000, and came under suspicion when he attempted to sell a fourth. (See *Newsday*, March 22, 27, April 21, June 14, September 20, 2008.) Renehan explained his conduct by claiming that he suffered from untreated bipolar disorder during this period, saying that he felt "invulnerable and answerable to no one." (See *Providence Journal*, May 29, 2008; also *New York Sun*, June 23, 2008.) Though his crimes do not pertain directly to *Commodore*, he committed them at the time he was writing that book. Together with the

---

bilt's railroads show him to have been active, in character, and intelligent up to his final illness, often presiding at meetings where William H. Vanderbilt was not present. See Deborah Hayden, *Pox: Genius, Madness, and the Mysteries of Syphilis* (New York: Basic Books, 2003), 29–37, 54–9, 317–8; Allan M. Brandt, *No Magic Bullet: A Social History of Venereal Disease in the United States since 1880* (New York: Oxford University Press, 1985), 9–13; Edward W. Hook III and Christina M. Marra, "Acquired Syphilis in Adults," *New England Journal of Medicine* 326, no. 16 (April 16, 1992): 1060–9; Catherine M. Hutchinson and Edward W. Hook III, "Syphilis in Adults," *Medical Clinics of North America* 74, no. 6 (November 1990): 1389–1454; Roger P. Simon, "Neurosyphilis," *Archives of Neurology* 42, no. 6 (June 1985): 606–13; John H. Stokes, *Modern Clinical Syphilology: Diagnosis, Treatment, Case Studies* (Philadelphia: W. B. Saunders, 1926), 906–7; Loyd [sic] Thompson, *Syphilis* (Philadelphia: Lea & Febriger, 1916), 58–9; H. Houston Merritt, Raymond D. Adams, and Harry C. Solomon, *Neurosyphilis* (New York: Oxford University Press, 1946), 3–4; D'Arcy Power and J. Keogh Murphy, eds., *A System of Syphilis*, vol. 4: *Syphilis of the Nervous System* (London: Oxford University Press, 1910), 259. For examples of William's travels to Europe, see *Chicago Tribune*, June 9, 1869, and the *New York Times*, July 4, 1872.

untenable nature of his claims for his sources, his insistence on keeping them secret, and his own description of his state of mind, this affair raises serious doubts about these purported diaries.

THIS BOOK RELIES ON numerous manuscript collections, many of which have never been cited in a Vanderbilt biography before. I will review only a few of the most significant, beginning with Part One of this book.

I am convinced that no history of American business in the first half of the nineteenth century (and perhaps the second half as well) that touches in any way on New York can be written without consulting the Old Records Division of the New York County Clerk's Office, 31 Chambers Street, 7th floor. It was central not only to my discovery of raw facts about Vanderbilt and his friends and allies, but also to the portrait I paint of America's emerging economic culture. I happened upon it by accident, and ended up spending many months conducting research there. I was helped by the highly professional archivists, Joseph Van Nostrand, Bruce Abrams, David Brantley, Robert Soenarie, Eileen McAleavey, and Annette Joseph, who have in their care the four-hundred-year legal history of New York City. Since legal papers find their way to the Old Records Division willy-nilly, the historian works alongside citizens in search of certified copies of divorce decrees from a few years before, lawyers seeking filings from long-running lawsuits, and the occasional private investigator. The papers I examined showed the inner workings of many of Vanderbilt's operations, from his takeover of the Staten Island Ferry in 1838 to conversations with angry passengers who had been stranded in Nicaragua. More than that, they revealed a time when insider trading, noncompetition deals, and market-division agreements were not only legal but sometimes enforced by the courts. Not all the documents are so rich; many are simple lawsuits over unpaid promissory notes. But it is worth the effort to find the gems.

Another essential collection, one that is already well known, is the Gibbons Family Papers at Drew University, Madison, New Jersey. This collection includes the largest number of letters in Vanderbilt's own hand, many of which were not cited by Lane or subsequent writers. It also sheds light on the crumbling culture of deference, and the failure of Thomas Gibbons's son William to come to grips with the competitive culture that his father and Vanderbilt had contributed to so notably. This episode is also illuminated by the Livingston Family Papers at the New-York Historical Society (NYHS).

My exploration of Vanderbilt's move into Long Island Sound, and his consequent assumption of the presidency of the Stonington railroad, owes much to the Comstock Papers at the American Antiquarian Society, Worcester, Massachusetts. But I relied in particular on the William D. Lewis Papers at the New York Public Library (NYPL). Lewis, an official of the Girard Bank of Philadelphia, was the trustee of the Stonington railroad, and often corresponded with its senior officers. It was a delight to read letters labeled "Burn This" or "Destroy Immediately"—a sign of the rare glimpse into the secret world of antebellum business afforded by these papers. They offer the most acute look at Vanderbilt in the 1830s and 1840s available (including a transcription of a conversation with him by the line's chief engineer), and illuminate the complex relationship between steamboat proprietors and early New England railroads.

In Part Two, covering Vanderbilt's Central America operations and Atlantic steamship line, I also drew heavily on the Old Records Division of the New York County Clerk's Office. I found invaluable the published correspondence of the State Department (as well as originals at the National Archives, College Park, Maryland) and the congressional reports that reprinted numerous primary sources related to the "transit question." The William L. Marcy and John M. Clayton collections at the Library of Congress contain many important letters, not only from Vanderbilt but from Joseph L. White as well, a figure long overlooked in histories of this period. The Baring Brothers archive, on file in microfilm at the Library of Congress, was invaluable to my understanding of the fate of the Nicaragua canal project, and I am grateful to the ING corporation for granting me permission to view it. The archive of R. G. Dun & Co., Baker Library, Harvard Business School, proved equal to its great reputation. By looking up reports for many of Vanderbilt's businesses, relatives, allies, and enemies, I was able to develop a much fuller picture of both Vanderbilt and his contemporaries.

Two little-used sources in particular allowed me to write a substantially new account of the activities of Vanderbilt, Cornelius K. Garrison, and Charles Morgan during William Walker's rule of Nicaragua. First, the files of the Costa Rican Claims Convention, housed at the National Archives, College Park, contain eyewitness testimony about the final campaign that brought Walker down, as well as a copy of the lengthy deposition of Joseph N. Scott, taken from the lawsuit *Murray v. Vanderbilt*. Second, the papers of lawyer Isaiah Thornton Williams, NYPL, contain extensive depositions from the lawsuits that sprouted out of the collapse of the Nicaragua transit. These depositions contain everything from discussions of relative fuel costs of the transit routes to the nature of Garrison's and Vanderbilt's relationships with Walker. In addition, the papers of H. L. Bancroft, held by the Bancroft Library, University of California, Berkeley, include important documents, including William Walker's own deposition in one of the transit lawsuits and an invaluable interview with Lambert Wardell. The Williams Family Papers at Trinity College, Hartford, shed important new light on a long-disregarded side of Vanderbilt's personality, as he fondly corresponded, often in his own hand, with his daughter-in-law's family. Finally, the miscellaneous NYHS manuscripts relating to Vanderbilt add significant details.

For Part Three, various congressional reports reveal Vanderbilt's role in the Civil War, as do the Stanton Papers at the Library of Congress and the well-worn but still-essential *Official Records of the War of the Rebellion*. To follow Vanderbilt's career as he moved into railroads, the New York Central Railroad papers in the PennCentral Collection, NYPL, is irreplaceable. This collection includes the directors' minutes for all the railroads that would eventually make up the Vanderbilt system, as well as financial records that show Vanderbilt's personal support for his corporations' finances. (It also sheds light on Vanderbilt's early involvement in railroads, as the minutes of the Long Island Railroad illustrate how his control of steamboats naturally led to his entrance onto the boards of connecting railways.)

The reports and testimony published by the New York State Assembly and Senate comprise another oft-cited but critical source. These prove particularly important for understanding Vanderbilt's relationship with the New York Central when he was head of the Harlem and Hudson River railroads. So, too, are the papers of Erastus Corning, Albany Institute of History and Art, Albany, New York. This rich collection builds an understanding of Vanderbilt as corporate diplomat. More than that, it includes many letters from John M. Davidson, a business partner of Corning's who played the stock market and mingled with such Tweed cronies as Judge Barnard, shedding abundant light on the dim world of Wall Street through 1870. Vanderbilt's notes to James H. Banker, NYHS, reveal his concern for secrecy when it came to the financial markets. The James F. Joy Papers, Detroit Public Library (with some copies at the University of Michigan, Ann Arbor), also offer insight into Vanderbilt's role as railroad chief, and are suggestive of how other railroad officials differentiated between the management styles of the Commodore and his son William. The Joy papers (along with those of Frank Crawford Vanderbilt) are the only case in which I was forced to resort to paid research assistants. I regret being unable to travel to conduct the research myself, and accept that much of importance may have been missed.

Some important collections also shed light on Vanderbilt's intimate world in the last period of his life. Frank Crawford Vanderbilt's letters, at the Detroit Public Library, and her diary, NYHS, paint a complex portrait of Vanderbilt as controlling, temperamental, and yet still loving. The many letters of Cornelius J. Vanderbilt and his wife, Ellen, to Horace Greeley, in the Greeley Papers, NYPL, illuminate the complicated relationship between the Commodore and his son. The Colt Family Papers, University of Rhode Island, contain the papers of George Terry, which include numerous letters from Cornelius J. Vanderbilt and legal documents related to his settlement with his brother William and his final bankruptcy. Numerous other collections, such as the Samuel J. Tilden Papers, NYPL, also offer occasional items that throw light on the Commodore as a man.

Finally, there is the abundant testimony of the Vanderbilt will case, much of it (but far from all) collected in scrapbooks and microfilm at NYPL. This is a treacherous source. Many of the witnesses and theories offered by the attorneys of Mary La Bau and Cornelius J. Vanderbilt were simply incredible. They claimed, for example, that William H. Vanderbilt hired someone to impersonate Corneil and engage in disreputable behavior. The notion is absurd, not because William was a saint, but because it was so unnecessary; and William proved willing to alter the will in the end. Unfortunately, the more outrageous claims of the testimony continue to color the imagination of writers who address the Commodore. So, too, do the self-serving assertions (and outright lies) told by Tennessee Claflin and Victoria Woodhull. I have found no evidence of Vanderbilt's *business* involvement with them (as opposed to medical or supernatural), except from the mouths of Woodhull and Claflin themselves. They were impressive individuals, no doubt—even admirable, as they brashly battled strictures on women. They were also veteran confidence artists who were pulling off the biggest con of their lives when they opened their "brokerage house," which is not known to have conducted any business on Wall Street.

The testimony of magnetic healers and the declamations of Woodhull and Claflin need not be dismissed in their entirety (Vanderbilt did hire such healers, and he did have a friendship with the sisters, especially Claflin), but they need to be treated skeptically, with an insistence on more evidence. The image of the Commodore has been shaped by prejudice from the early years of his life—when he drew sneers for his claim to be a man of honor—to the present, when he is often dismissed as a brutal, uncharitable vulgarian. The prejudice is in itself interesting, but it is no substitute for investigation.

Notes

ABBREVIATIONS

(The following is not a complete list of sources cited in the notes.)

MANUSCRIPT COLLECTIONS

AAS   American Antiquarian Society, Worcester, Mass.

ATC   *Accessory Transit Company v. Cornelius K. Garrison*, New York Superior Court, box 1, Isaiah Thornton Williams Papers, 1833–1918, Manuscript Division, New York Public Library

BB   Baring Brothers Archive, Manuscript Division, Library of Congress

BL   Bancroft Library, University of California, Berkeley

CRCC   Costa Rican Claims Convention of July 2, 1860, RG 76, National Archives, College Park, Md.

CFP   Comstock Family Papers, American Antiquarian Society, Worcester, Mass.

CV-NYHS   Cornelius Vanderbilt Papers, Misc. Manuscripts, New-York Historical Society

CV-NYPL   Cornelius Vanderbilt Papers, Misc. Files, Manuscript Division, New York Public Library

Duke   Rare Book, Manuscript, and Special Collections Library, Duke University, Durham, N.C.

ECP   Erastus Corning 1 Papers, Albany Institute for History and Art, Albany, N.Y.

EMSP   Edwin M. Stanton Papers, Manuscript Division, Library of Congress

GP   Gibbons Family Papers, Archives and Special Collections, Drew University, Madison, N.J.

GP-R   Gibbons Papers, Rutgers University, New Brunswick, N.J.

HL   Huntington Library, San Marino, Calif.

HGP   Horace Greeley Papers, Manuscript Division, New York Public Library

Hone ms.   Manuscript diary of Philip Hone, New-York Historical Society

JBP   James Buchanan Papers, Microfilm Copy, Columbia University

JFJP   James F. Joy Papers, Burton Historical Collection, Detroit Public Library

JFJP-2   James F. Joy Papers, Henry B. Joy Historical Research Collection, Bentley Historical Library, University of Michigan, Ann Arbor

JMC-P   John M. Clayton Papers, Manuscript Division, Library of Congress

LFP   Livingston Family Papers, New-York Historical Society

LOC   Manuscript Division, Library of Congress

LW Dictation   "Dictation Taken from the Lips of Lambert Wardell," H. H. Bancroft Notes on the Vanderbilt Family, Bancroft Library, University of California, Berkeley

MacDonald Lawsuit　*Charles J. MacDonald v. Cornelius K. Garrison and Charles Morgan,* New York Court of Common Pleas, box 42, Isaiah Thornton Williams Papers, 1833–1918, Manuscript Division, New York Public Library

NA　National Archives, Washington, D.C.

NA–CP　National Archives, College Park, Md.

NP　Neilson Papers, Rutgers University, New Brunswick, N.J.

NYCC　Old Records Division, New York County Clerk's Office, New York, N.Y.

NYCRR　New York Central Railroad Papers, PennCentral Collection, Manuscript Division, New York Public Library

NYHS　New-York Historical Society

NYMA　New York Municipal Archives

NYPL　Manuscript Division, New York Public Library

NYSL　Manuscripts and Special Collections, New York State Library

RG　Record Group

RGD　Records of R. G. Dun & Co., Baker Library, Harvard Business School ("NYC" indicates volumes for New York City, followed by volume and page numbers)

RWG　Richard Ward Greene Papers, American Antiquarian Society, Worcester, Mass.

SctDP　Deposition of Joseph N. Scott, *David Colden Murray v. Cornelius Vanderbilt,* fold. 1, box 1, Costa Rican Claims Convention of July 2, 1860, RG 76, National Archives, College Park, Md.

VFP　Vanderbilt Family Papers, New-York Historical Society

WFP　Williams Family Papers, Watkinson Library, Trinity College, Hartford, Conn.

WDLP　William D. Lewis Papers, Manuscript Division, New York Public Library

WLMP　William L. Marcy Papers, Manuscript Division, Library of Congress

GOVERNMENT DOCUMENTS

HsR　United States House of Representatives Report

HED　United States House of Representatives Executive Document

NYSAD　New York State Assembly Document

NYSSD　New York State Senate Document

OR　*The War of the Rebellion: A Compilation of the Official Records of the Union and Confederate Armies* (Washington, D.C.: Government Printing Office, 1880–1901), 128 vols.

OR Navy　*Official Records of the Union and Confederate Navies in the War of the Rebellion* (Washington, D.C.: Government Printing Office, 1894–1922), 30 vols.

SR　United States Senate Report

SED　United States Senate Executive Document

NEWSPAPERS

AltaC　*San Francisco Alta California*

ARJ　*American Railroad Journal*

AtlC　*Atlanta Constitution*

BE   *Brooklyn Eagle*
BG   *Boston Globe*
BM   *Bankers' Magazine and Statistical Register*
CT   *Chicago Tribune*
EP   *New York Evening Post*
HC   *Hartford Courant*
HW   *Harper's Weekly*
JoC   *New York Journal of Commerce*
LT   London *Times*
MM   *Merchant's Magazine;* also Hunt's *Merchant's Magazine*
NAR   *North American Review*
NBF   *New Brunswick Fredonian*
NR   *Niles' Register*
NYH   *New York Herald*
NYT   *The New York Times*
NYTr   *New York Tribune*
NYS   *New York Sun*
NYW   *New York World*
ProvJ   *Providence Journal*
PS   *Pittsfield Sun*
RT   *Railway Times*
RG   *Railroad Gazette*
SA   *Scientific American*
SEP   *Saturday Evening Post*
USMDR   *United States Magazine and Democratic Review*

PUBLISHED PRIMARY SOURCES

Fowler   William W. Fowler, *Ten Years in Wall Street* (Hartford: Worthington, Dustin, & Co., 1870)

Hone   Allan Nevins, ed., *The Diary of Philip Hone, 1828–1851* (New York: Dodd, Mead & Co., 1936)

Manning (3, 4, or 7)   William R. Manning, ed., *Diplomatic Correspondence of the United States: Inter-American Affairs, 1831–1860* (Washington, D.C.: Carnegie Endowment for International Peace), vol. 3 (1934); vol. 4 (1934); vol. 7 (1936)

Medbery   James K. Medbery, *Men and Mysteries of Wall Street* (Boston: Fields, Osgood, 1870)

Smith   Matthew Hale Smith, *Twenty Years Among the Bulls and Bears of Wall Street* (Hartford: J. B. Burr, 1870)

Soulé   Frank Soulé, John H. Gihon, and James Nisbet, *The Annals of San Francisco* (New York: D. Appleton, 1855)

Staten Island Church   Tobias Alexander Wright, ed., *Collections of the New York Records, Genealogical and Biographical Society,* vol. 4: *Staten Island Church Records* (New York: n.p., 1909)

Stonington Reports   *Annual Reports of the New York, Providence, and Boston Rail Road Company, 1833 to 1874* (Westerly, R.I.: 1874); copy in Library of Congress

Strong (1, 2, 3, or 4)   Allan Nevins and Milton Halsey Thomas, eds., *The Diary of George Templeton Strong* (New York: MacMillan, 1952), vol. 1: *Young Man in New York, 1835–1849,* vol. 2: *The Turbulent Fifties, 1850–1859,* vol. 3: *The Civil War, 1860–1865,* vol. 4: *Post-War Years, 1865–1875*

SECONDARY SOURCES

AHR	*American Historical Review*
Albion	Robert G. Albion, *The Rise of New York Port* (Boston: Northeastern University Press, 1984, orig. pub. 1939)
ANB	John A. Garraty and Mark C. Carnes, eds., *American National Biography* (New York: Oxford University Press, 1999)
Baughman	James P. Baughman, *Charles Morgan and the Development of Southern Transportation* (Nashville: Vanderbilt University Press, 1968)
BHR	*Business History Review*
Burns	E. Bradford Burns, *Patriarch and Folk: The Emergence of Nicaragua, 1798–1858* (Cambridge, Mass.: Harvard University Press, 1991)
Burrows & Wallace	Edwin G. Burrows and Mike Wallace, *Gotham: A History of New York City to 1898* (New York: Oxford University Press, 1999)
Confidence Men	Karen Halttunen, *Confidence Men and Painted Women: A Study of Middle-Class Culture in America, 1830–1870* (New Haven: Yale University Press, 1982)
Croffut	William A. Croffut, *The Vanderbilts and the Story of their Fortune* (New York: Belford, Clarke, 1886)
Folkman	David I. Folkman Jr., *The Nicaragua Route* (Salt Lake City: University of Utah Press, 1972)
Foner	Eric Foner, *Reconstruction: America's Unfinished Revolution, 1863–1877* (New York: Harper & Row, 1988)
Gunn	L. Ray Gunn, *The Decline of Authority: Public Economic Policy and Political Development in New York, 1800-1860* (Ithaca: Cornell University Press, 1988)
Heyl (1, 2, 3, 4, 5, or 6)	Erik Heyl, *Early American Steamers* (Buffalo: n.p.), vol. 1 (1953); vol. 2 (1956); vol. 3 (1964); vol. 4 (1965); vol. 5 (1967); vol. 6 (1969)
HAHR	*Hispanic American Historical Review*
JAH	*Journal of American History*
JEH	*Journal of Economic History*
JER	*Journal of the Early Republic*
JModH	*Journal of Modern History*
Kemble	John Haskell Kemble, *The Panama Route, 1848–1869* (Berkeley: University of California Press, 1943)
Klein	Maury Klein, *The Life and Legend of Jay Gould* (Baltimore: Johns Hopkins University Press, 1986)
Lane	Wheaton J. Lane, *Commodore Vanderbilt: An Epic of the Steam Age* (New York: Alfred A. Knopf, 1942)
McPherson	James M. McPherson, *Battle Cry of Freedom: The Civil War Era* (New York: Oxford University Press, 1988)
Morrison	John H. Morrison, *History of American Steam Navigation* (New York: Stephen Daye Press, 1959, orig. pub. 1903)
NYHis	*New York History*
NYHSQ	*New-York Historical Society Quarterly*
Stokes	I. N. Phelps Stokes, *The Iconography of Manhattan Island, 1498–1909* (New York: Robert H. Dodd, 1915–1928), vols. 1–6
Taylor	George Rogers Taylor, *The Transportation Revolution, 1815–1860* (New York: Rinehart, 1951)

WMQ *William and Mary Quarterly*
Wood Gordon Wood, *The Radicalism of the American Revolution* (New York: Vintage, 1993)

INDIVIDUAL AND COMPANY NAMES

AO	Aaron Ogden
AS	Augustus Schell
ATC	Accessory Transit Company
CFA	Charles Francis Adams Jr.
CM	Charles Morgan
COH	Charles O. Handy
CtP	Courtlandt Palmer
CJV	Cornelius J. Vanderbilt
CKG	Cornelius K. Garrison
CV	Cornelius Vanderbilt, 1794–1877
DDT	Daniel D. Tompkins
EC	Erastus Corning Sr.
EMS	Edwin M. Stanton
HFC	Horace F. Clark
HG	Horace Greeley
HR	Hudson River Railroad Company
HRR	New York & Harlem Railroad Company
JB	James Buchanan
JHB	James H. Banker
JMC	John M. Clayton
JLW	Joseph L. White
JMD	John M. Davidson
JRL	John R. Livingston
JWR	John W. Richmond
LS&MS	Lake Shore & Michigan Southern Railway Company
NYC	New York Central Railroad Company
NYC&HR	New York Central & Hudson River Railroad Company
TG	Thomas Gibbons
WG	William Gibbons
WGM	William Gibbs McNeill
WDL	William D. Lewis
WHV	William H. Vanderbilt
WLM	William L. Marcy
WmC	William Comstock

PART ONE CAPTAIN

One The Islander

1   *NYT,* November 13, 1877. For reporting on the opening of the trial, see almost any New York newspaper starting on this date.
2   *Annual Report of the Comptroller of the Currency* (Washington, D.C.: Government Printing Office, 1876), 45–69. I am including national, state, and private banks in calculating this figure, but I am leaving out savings banks. Even so, this figure somewhat exaggerates money stock, as it includes all coin and bullion, much of which was not in circulation. Note that the *New York Times,* July 15, 2007, calculated that Vanderbilt was the second-wealthiest figure in American history by comparing his estate to the size of the national economy. Such estimates are questionable, due to the poor quality of economic statistics in the nineteenth century.
3   CFA, "A Chapter of Erie," *NAR,* July 1869.
4   Mark Twain, "Open Letter to Com. Vanderbilt," *Packard's Monthly,* March 1869.
5   On the emergence of the term "business man," see Sven Beckert, *The Monied Metropolis: New York City and the Consolidation of the American Bourgeoisie, 1850–1896* (New York: Cambridge University Press, 2001), 256–7.
6   Isaac Lea to Horatio King, September 26, 1859, SED 45, 36th Cong., 1st sess., vol. 11; *NYT,* February 9, 1859.
7   See, for example, *NYH,* April 17, 1855.
8   Lane, 4–10; *Staten Island Advance,* June 29, 1907.
9   Burrows & Wallace, 50–89, 122–35; Michael Kammen, *Colonial New York: A History* (New York: Charles Scribner's Sons, 1975), 128–60, 241; Oliver A. Rink, "Before the English (1609–1664)," in Milton M. Klein, ed., *Empire State: A History of New York* (Ithaca: Cornell University Press, 2001), 21–3; Joyce D. Goodfriend, "Writing/Righting Dutch Colonial History," *NYHis* 80, no. 1 (January 1999): 5–28; Cathy Matson, *Merchants & Empire: Trading in Colonial New York* (Baltimore: Johns Hopkins Press, 1998), 4–10; Richard Middleton, *Colonial America: A History, 1607–1760* (Cambridge: Blackwell, 1992), 82–8; *NYH,* January 14, 1877.
10 Firth Haring Fabend, "The Synod of Dort and the Persistence of Dutchness in Nineteenth-Century New York and New Jersey," *NYHis* 77, no. 3 (July 1996): 273–300; Peter O. Wacker, "The Dutch Culture Area in the Northeast, 1609–1800," *New Jersey History* 104, nos. 1–2 (spring and summer 1986): 1–22; Martin Bruegel, *Farm, Shop, Landing: The Rise of a Market Society in the Hudson Valley, 1780–1860* (Durham: Duke University Press, 2002), 38; Goodfriend, 26; Rink, 61, 105–7.
11 Fabend; Wacker; Goodfriend, 26; Shane White, *Somewhat More Independent: The End of Slavery in New York City, 1770–1810* (Athens, Ga.: University of Georgia Press, 1991), 4–27, 189–90.
12 Fabend; Bruegel, 38; Rink, 61, 105–7; White, 4–27, 189–90; Edward Countryman, "From Revolution to Statehood (1776–1825)," in Klein, 229–305, esp. 248; Goodfriend, 26; Rocellus S. Guernsey, *New York City and Vicinity During the War of 1812–15* (New York: C. L. Woodward, 1889–95), 1:47–50; First Census of the United States, Richmond County, New York; Ira K. Morris, *Morris's Memorial History of Staten Island, New York,* vol. 2 (Staten Island: Ira Morris, 1900), 4–6; Burrows & Wallace, 51–89. As Allan Kulikoff notes, *The Origins of American Capitalism* (Charlottesville: University Press of Virginia, 1992), 30–3, it is important not to go too far in describing American agriculture as "subsistence farming." Early on, Northern farmers took part in both local and extended market exchanges. James A. Henretta, "The 'Market' in the Early Republic," *Journal of the Early Republic* 18 (spring 1998): 289–304, observes, "Clearly the United States economy during the

early republic was primarily a market-based, price-driven system. But . . . that economy also included elements of an older barter economy that was imbedded in the social structure of many communities." The Dutch-English contrast in market orientation must be considered relative, not absolute.

13 Numerous informal periauger ferries ran from Staten Island to New York (and often to New Jersey). CV's appears to have started in about 1800, competing with the Van Duzer family, which began to run boats across the harbor as early as 1788; Ira K. Morris, *Morris's Memorial History of Staten Island* (New York: Memorial Publishing, 1898), 1:391–5. *Periauger* was pronounced as well as spelled in various ways; the most common alternate was pettiauger (used in the New York Custom House registration books). The name appears to be related to "periagua" or "pirogue," a seagoing canoe common to Central and South America, first encountered by the Spanish in the sixteenth century. See Peter Kemp, ed., *The Oxford Companion to Ships and the Sea* (Oxford: Oxford University Press, 1976), 651.

14 The earliest published stories about CV's family and early life appeared in the 1850s. See *SA*, June 18, 1853; *HW*, March 5, 1859; *MM*, January 1865; James Parton, *Famous Americans of Recent Times* (Boston: Ticknor & Fields, 1867), 377–90; Lane, 9–13; Croffut, 10–17 (including the quote about Phebe Hand Vanderbilt); Bruegel, 54. Regarding Phebe's apparent career as a moneylender, see *Phebe Vanderbilt v. Charles M. Simonson et al.* April 17, 1844, file D-CH 177-V, Court of Chancery, NYCC. The best evidence that Phebe did indeed store her money in the clock is a reference to it in a poem by CV's son-in-law James M. Cross in 1863; see *Memorial of the Golden Wedding of Cornelius and Sophia Vanderbilt, December 19, 1863* (New York: Baker & Godwin, 1864), 27, copy at Duke.

15 Bruegel, 54–5; Duc de La Rochefoucauld-Liancourt, *Travels Through the United States of North America, the Country of the Iroquois, and Upper Canada, in the Years 1795, 1796, and 1797; with an Authentic Account of Lower Canada* (London: R. Phillips, 1799), 561–2.

16 Rochefoucauld-Liancourt, 230.

17 First Census of the United States; Taylor, 6–8; Walter Licht, *Industrializing America: The Nineteenth Century* (Baltimore: Johns Hopkins Press, 1995), xiii–xiv.

18 Rochefoucauld-Liancourt, quotes on 460, 462, 463, 474, 476; for his perceptive discussion of economics and Americans' attitudes toward commerce, see 439–76. John Lauritz Larson, *Internal Improvement: National Public Works and the Promise of Popular Government in the Early United States* (Chapel Hill: University of North Carolina Press, 2001), 37, stresses that the founding generation of the republic saw the need for transportation improvements. The trade ratios are imprecise at best, and reflect registered tonnage engaged in foreign and domestic trade; see Allan R. Pred, *Urban Growth and the Circulation of Information: The United States System of Cities, 1790–1840* (Cambridge, Mass.: Harvard University Press, 1973), 7, 104–9; Douglass C. North, *The Economic Growth of the United States, 1790–1860* (New York: Prentice-Hall, 1961), 24–35, 43, 250; Elisha P. Douglass, *The Coming of Age of American Business: Three Centuries of Enterprise, 1600–1900* (Chapel Hill: University of North Carolina Press, 1971), 39; Dorothy Gregg, "John Stevens: General Entrepreneur, 1749–1838," in William Miller, ed., *Men in Business: Essays in the History of Entrepreneurship* (Cambridge, Mass.: Harvard University Press, 1952), 121; Diane Lindstrom, *Economic Development in the Philadelphia Region, 1810–1850* (New York: Columbia University Press, 1978), 3–18; Kulikoff, 30–3; Countryman, 314. For key arguments in the debate over the emergence of capitalism in the American countryside, see Allan Kulikoff, "The Transition to Capitalism in Rural America," *WMQ*, 3rd ser., vol. 46, no. 1 (January 1989): 120–44; Henretta, "The 'Market' in the Early Republic," 289–304; Joyce Appleby, "The Vexed Story of Capitalism Told by American Historians," *Journal of the Early Republic* 21, no. 1 (spring 2001): 1–18; and Appleby, *Inheriting the Revolution: The First Generation of Americans* (Cambridge,

Mass.: Harvard University Press, 2000), 1–25, 56–90, 250–66. Appleby in particular argues forcefully and well that Americans embraced the market as a force of liberation.

19   Taylor, 6–8; Licht, xiii–xiv; Edmund M. Blunt, *Blunt's Stranger's Guide to the City of New-York* (New York: Edmund M. Blunt, 1817), 43; Guernsey, 1:133; John Lambert, *Travels Through Canada, and the United States of North America, in the Years 1806, 1807, and 1808* (London: C. Cradock, 1814), 2:55; David H. Wallace, ed., " 'From the Windows of the Mail Coach': A Scotsman Looks at New York State in 1811," *NYHSQ* 40, no. 3 (July 1956): 264–96.

20   Lambert, 2:49.

21   Albion, 19, 30, 220–1; Lambert, 2:63–4; Bayrd Still, "New York City in 1824: A Newly Discovered Description," *NYHSQ* 46, no. 2 (April 1962): 137–70.

22   Diary of John Adams, excerpted in T. J. Stiles, ed., *Founding Fathers* (New York: Berkley Publishing Group, 1999), 42; Wallace, "From the Windows."

23   Guernsey, 32–9, 47–8; Rochefoucauld-Liancourt, 227–30; Lambert, 2:56, 63; Burrows & Wallace, 359–60, 371–4; *Blunt's Stranger's Guide*, 34–41, 43, 45; Tyler Anbinder, *Five Points: The 19th-Century New York City Neighborhood That Invented Tap Dance, Stole Elections, and Became the World's Most Notorious Slum* (New York: Free Press, 2001), 14–15; Sean Wilentz, *Chants Democratic: New York City and the Rise of the American Working Class, 1788–1850* (New York: Oxford University Press, 1984), 25; Howard B. Rock, "A Delicate Balance: The Mechanics and the City in the Age of Jefferson," *NYHSQ* 43, no. 2 (April 1979): 93–114.

24   Taylor, 3–14; Ratner et al., 212–3; Robertson, 82–4; Nettels, 292–304; Naomi R. Lamoreaux, "Banks, Kinship, and Economic Development: The New England Case," *JEH* 46, no. 3 (September 1986): 647–67; Burrows & Wallace, 338; Douglass, 73–9; John Denis Haeger, *John Jacob Astor: Business and Finance in the Early Republic* (Detroit: Wayne State University Press, 1991), 62–6; Geoffrey Gilbert, "Maritime Enterprise in the New Republic: Investment in Baltimore Shipping, 1789–1793," *BHR* 58, no. 1 (spring 1984): 14–29; Janet A. Riesman, "Republican Revisions: Political Economy in New York after the Panic of 1819," 1–44, and Gregory S. Hunter, "The Manhattan Company: Managing a Multi-Unit Corporation in New York, 1799–1842," 124–46, in William Pencack and Conrad Edick Wright, eds., *New York and the Rise of American Capitalism: Economic Development and the Social and Political History of an American State, 1780–1870* (New York: New-York Historical Society, 1989); Wilentz, 23–35. Stuart M. Blumin notes the highly personal nature of the eighteenth-century urban economy in *The Emergence of the Middle Class: Social Experience in the American City, 1760–1900* (Cambridge: Cambridge University Press, 1989), 26.

25   Herman A. Krooss, ed., *A Documentary History of Banking and Currency in the United States* (New York: Chelsea House, 1965), 90, 1059.

26   Taylor, 56–7; Pred, 14, 20–77, 112–4; Licht, xv–xvii; Sidney Ratner, James H. Soltow, and Richard Sylla, *The Evolution of the American Economy: Growth, Welfare, and Decision Making* (New York: Basic Books, 1979), 105–7; Nathan Miller, *The Enterprise of a Free People: Aspects of Economic Development in New York State During the Canal Period, 1792–1838* (Ithaca: Cornell University Press, 1962), 67; Curtis P. Nettels, *The Emergence of a National Economy, 1775–1815* (New York: Holt, Rinehart & Winston, 1962), 292; Kulikoff, 30–3; W. T. Newlyn and R. P. Bootle, *The Theory of Money* (Oxford: Clarendon Press, 1978), 1–18; Leslie V. Brock, *The Currency of the American Colonies, 1700–1764: A Study in Colonial Finance and Imperial Relations* (New York: Arno Press, 1975), 2–37, 75–6; Jack Weatherford, *The History of Money: From Sandstone to Cyberspace* (New York: Crown, 1997), 112–36; Stanley Elkins and Eric McKitrick, *The Age of Federalism: The Early American Republic, 1788-1800* (New York: Oxford University Press, 1993), 235–6; Ross M. Robertson, *History of the American Economy*, 2nd ed. (New York: Harcourt, Brace & World, 1964), 82, 127–8,

144; Charles Sellers, *The Market Revolution: Jacksonian America, 1815–1820* (New York: Oxford University Press, 1991), 3–23. Lindstrom, 1, argues that household manufacturing peaked in 1815. Margaret G. Myers discusses bills of exchange and the personal nature of credit in *The New York Money Market*, vol. 1: *Origins and Development* (New York: Columbia University Press, 1931), 46–57. Robert E. Wright, *The Wealth of Nations Rediscovered: Integration and Expansion in American Financial Markets, 1780–1850* (New York: Cambridge University Press, 2002), 318–21, discusses the inherent problems with bills of exchange. Edwin J. Perkins, *American Public Finance and Financial Services, 1700–1815* (Columbus: Ohio State University Press, 1994), 261–73, discusses the transition from informal relationships to formal institutions in credit and finance, and the lack of interstate institutions. Bruegel offers an excellent discussion of book debt and personal relationships in trade, 42–3. On the shilling, Spanish money, and money of account in general, see *MM*, April 1852. The New York County Clerk's office abounds with lawsuits over unpaid promissory notes; see, for example, *Isaac Spencer Jr. v. Daniel Drew, Nelson Robinson, Robert W. Kelley, and Daniel B. Allen*, March 20, 1848, file 1848-951A, Court of Common Pleas, NYCC.

27 Fritz Redlich and Webster M. Christman, "Early American Checks and an Example of Their Use," *BHR* 41, no. 3 (autumn 1967): 285–302; Elkins and McKitrick, 114–61; Burrows & Wallace, 310–2; Myers, 1:8–17; Miller, 78–9. It should be stressed that Hamilton remained immersed in mercantilistic thinking; he sought to harness the merchant economy to the new federal government to enhance national power, and failed in his attempt to create a manufacturing sector through federal direction; see Wood, 262–4.

28 Thomas Cochran, "The Business Revolution," *AHR* 79, no. 5 (December 1974): 1449–66; Pauline Maier, "The Revolutionary Origins of the American Corporation," *WMQ*, 3rd ser., vol. 50, no. 1 (January 1993): 51–84; Shaw Livermore, "Advent of Corporations in New York," *NYHis* 16, no. 3 (July 1935): 245–98; Oscar Handlin and Mary F. Handlin, "Origins of the American Business Corporation," *JEH* 5, no. 1 (May 1945): 1–23; Morton J. Horwitz, *The Transformation of American Law, 1780–1860* (Cambridge, Mass.: Harvard University Press, 1977), 110–11; Gregory A. Mark, "The Personification of the Business Corporation in American Law," *University of Chicago Law Review* 54, no. 4 (autumn 1987): 1441–83; Naomi R. Lamoreaux, "Partnerships, Corporations, and the Limits on Contractual Freedom in U.S. History: An Essay in Economics, Law, and Culture," in Kenneth Lipartito and David B. Scilia, eds., *Constructing Corporate America: History, Politics, Culture* (Oxford: Oxford University Press, 2004), 29–65; Ronald E. Seavoy, "Laws to Encourage Manufacturing: New York Policy and the 1811 General Incorporation Statute," *BHR* 46, no. 1 (spring 1972): 85–95; Robert E. Wright, "Bank Ownership and Lending Patterns in New York and Pennsylvania, 1781–1831," *BHR* 73, no. 1 (spring 1999): 40–60; Nettels, 289–94; Douglass, 46; Bray Hammond, *Banks and Politics in America: From the Revolution to the Civil War* (Princeton: Princeton University Press, 1957), 146–7; James Willard Hurst, *The Legitimacy of the Business Corporation in the Law of the United States, 1780–1970* (Charlottesville: University of Virginia Press, 1970), 13–32. On the centrality of the financial sector, see especially Perkins and Wright, *Wealth of Nations*, who argue with great clarity that a financial revolution was central to the other revolutions in the American economy, including that in transportation.

29 Parton, 378; *NYT*, January 5, 1877; *NYTr*, January 5, 1877; Lane, 10–11. Regarding CV's strength and endurance, see the reminiscences of his assistant, LW Dictation. On New York City's role as the center of a large hinterland of market farming, see Countryman, 314.

30 For CV's early writing, see the following letters from CV to TG: February 2, 1819; February 24, 1819; January 5, 1820; November 16, 1821; March 1, 1822; November

4, 1822; all in GP; see also CV to JWR, n.d., RWG. A Staten Island historian speculated that CV "got his three months' education" at a Moravian academy; *Staten
Island Advance*, June 29, 1907.

31   Lane, 10n.

32   Lane, 11–14; Parton, 378; *NYT*, January 5, 1877; *NYTr*, January 5, 1877; *HW*, March
5, 1859; *MM*, January 1865.

33   *NYTr*, November 10, 1869; Paul A. Gilje, "On the Waterfront: Workers in New
York City in the Early Republic, 1800–1850," *NYHis* 77, no. 4 (October 1996):
395–426.

34   Lambert, 2:64.

35   This anecdote was often repeated in various forms in biographical material (see, for
example, Croffut, 17). This version is taken from a brief memorandum of a conversation with CV, written by an unknown party, in the VFP. The memorandum
reflects some confusion, as do most anecdotes (it refers to CV being sixteen in 1812),
but it appears to be the authentic record of a story told by CV himself.

36   V. S. Naipaul, *The Enigma of Arrival* (New York: Alfred A. Knopf, 1987), 77.

37   VFP; Croffut, 17; Lane, 13.

38   Croffut, 17–18; Lane, 13–14; Parton, 378–9; *NYT*, January 5, 1877; *NYTr*, January 5,
1877; *HW*, March 5, 1859; *MM*, January 1865.

39   *SA*, June 18, 1853.

40   Croffut, 17–18; Lane, 13–14; Parton, 378–9; *NYT*, January 5, 1877; *NYTr*, January 5,
1877; *HW*, March 5, 1859; *MM*, January 1865; *SA*, June 18, 1853.

41   Rochefoucauld-Liancourt, 587.

42   *HW*, March 5, 1859; *MM*, January 1865; John Komlos, "The Height and Weight of
West Point Cadets: Dietary Change in Antebellum America," *JEH* 47, no. 4
(December 1987): 897–927. CV was described as running a "packet" ferry in *EP*,
February 4, 1818.

43   *HW*, March 5, 1859; *MM*, January 1865; Parton, 376–80; Lane, 15–17; Croffut,
19–21; *Blunt's Stranger's Guide*, 207n, 223; Guernsey, 1:53. On CV's temper, see
NYTr, March 27, 1878; *NYW*, November 13, 14, 1877.

44   Burrows & Wallace, 409–23; Edward L. Beach, *The United States Navy: A 200-Year
History* (New York: Houghton Mifflin, 1986), 51–71.

45   Guernsey, 1:1–16, 120–3, 159–60, 218, 317–22; Burrows & Wallace, 409–5; W. E.
Apgar, "New York's Contribution to the War Effort of 1812," *New-York Historical
Society Quarterly Bulletin* 29, no. 4, 203–12.

46   Guernsey, 2:301–2; *MM*, January 1865; Parton, 380; *NYT*, January 5, 1877; *NYTr*,
January 5, 1877; *EP*, September 13, 1813.

47   *Staten Island Church Records*, 106; Parton, 381; Lane, 20–3.

48   Burrows & Wallace, 427–8; George W. Cullum, *Campaigns of the War of 1812–15
Against Great Britain* (New York: James Miller, 1879), 174–7.

49   Parton, 381–2; Lane, 18–19; Dorothy Kelly MacDowell, *Commodore Vanderbilt and
His Family* (Hendersonville, N.C.: privately printed, 1989), 22; Howard B. Rock, "A
Delicate Balance: The Mechanics and the City in the Age of Jefferson," *NYHSQ* 63,
no. 2 (April 1979): 93–114. Many boatmen were black; see the testimony of Joseph
Bonnington, July 1, 1820, GP, and "Thomas Gibbons against Isaac Morse," *Cases of
the Court of Errors of the State of New Jersey* (November Term, 1821), 253–71 (copy in
GP), a lawsuit involving a slave who escaped with the aid of a free black ferry captain
in 1818.

50   New York City Census, First Ward, 1816, NYMA.

51   Frances Trollope, *Domestic Manners of the Americans* (New York: Alfred A. Knopf,
1949), 369–70.

52   Wilentz, 23–60; Blumin, 20–65, quotes on 26, 32–3, 64; Lambert, 2:90, 100; Albion,
235–59. On the new assertiveness of the artisans in the Revolution, see especially Edward Countryman, *A People in Revolution: The American Revolution and Polit-*

ical Society in New York, 1760-1790 (Baltimore: Johns Hopkins University Press, 1981).

53 Pred; Perkins, 271–3, 350–62; Wright, *Wealth of Nations*, 18–25; Albion, 235–59; Guernsey, 2:512–14; Ross M. Robertson, *History of the American Economy*, 2nd ed. (New York: Harcourt, Brace & World, 1964), 82–4. The discussion of promissory notes reflects the author's work in contemporary collections; see, for example, almost any lawsuit from this period in the Court of Common Pleas, NYCC; TG to George Johnston, February 2, 1810 ("In money transactions in the city I have always had assurances that my paper would pass current"), and TG to David B. Ogden, June 1, 1816, GP.

54 Guernsey, 2:458–9, 483–94; Wilentz, 23.

55 Wilentz, 23; Albion, 9–15.

56 Lane, 22–5; Croffut, 26; Wilentz, 35; Morrison, 169; *EP,* November 20, 1812; *NYH,* January 5, 14, 1877; *NYW,* January 5, 1877; *NYT,* January 5, 1877. The cost estimate of a boat is based on the sale of a fully equipped twenty-seven-ton periauger for $750 to TG, John C. Hatfield to TG, July 17, 1817, GP. On the Chesapeake oyster schooners, and the role of Northern ships in the trade, see Geoffrey M. Footner, *Tidewater Triumph: The Development and Worldwide Success of the Chesapeake Bay Pilot Schooner* (Centreville, Md.: Tidewater Publishers, 1998), 213–25. The records of the New York Custom House, now with the National Archives, remain fragmentary at best, and the writings of earlier historians suggest that some have been lost. Morrison writes that the *Dread* was the first vessel registered under CV's name, but I could not find that enrollment record. On later enrollments of the *General Wolcott* and the *Dread,* see Enrollment Number 248, July 16, 1817, vol. 12139, and Enrollment Number 21, February 26, 1821, vol. 12148, Port of New York Certificates of Enrolment [sic], Bureau of Marine Inspection and Navigation, RG 41, NA. The *General Wolcott* entry notes that it was "rebuilt from an open boat," indicating CV's longer-range ambitions. For a reference to another of CV's periaugers, the *Thorn,* as a schooner, see *EP,* January 8, 1821.

57 *John De Forest and Cornelius Vanderbilt Jr. vs. Daniel Morgan,* April 5, 1817, file 1817-#337, Court of Common Pleas, and *Cornelius Vanderbilt and Cornelius Vanderbilt Jr. vs. Phineas Carman and Cornelius P. Wyckoff,* May 26, 1817, file 1817-#1261, Court of Common Pleas, NYCC; TG to Jonathan Johnston, November 24, 1817, GP; Morrison, 44. For background on the Mayor's Court, see Richard B. Morris, "The New York City's Mayor's Court," in Leo Hershkowitz and Milton M. Klein, eds., *Courts and Law in Early New York: Selected Essays* (Port Washington, N.Y.: National University Publications, 1978), 19–29.

58 Rochefoucauld-Liancourt, quotes on 460, 462, 463, 474, 476; for his perceptive discussion of economics and Americans' attitudes toward commerce, see 439–76. On the impact of the War of 1812 and the growth in banks, see Murray N. Rothbard, *The Panic of 1819: Reactions and Policies* (New York: Columbia University Press, 1962), 1–19. Janet A. Riesman discusses the intertwining of banking and American attitudes toward commerce and credit in "Republican Revisions," 1–44. Unquestionably the end of the war provided a boon to economic growth (see Albion and Taylor), but I agree with Daniel Walker Howe, *What Hath God Wrought: The Transformation of America, 1815-1848* (New York: Oxford University Press, 2007), 5, in disagreeing with the "market revolution" thesis popularized by Charles Sellers, *The Market Revolution: Jacksonian America, 1815-1820* (New York: Oxford University Press, 1991). For more arguments in the enormous debate over the emergence of capitalism, see Allan Kulikoff, "The Transition to Capitalism in Rural America," *WMQ,* 3rd ser., vol. 46, no. 1 (January 1989): 120–44; Henretta, 289–304; Appleby, "Vexed Story," 1–18; and Appleby, *Inheriting the Revolution,* 1–25, 56–90, 250–66.

59 Rochefoucauldt-Liancourt, 440; Appleby, "Vexed Story"; Appleby, *Inheriting the*

Revolution, 55–91; Kulikoff, "Transition"; Lambert, 2:26–7, 33. On the trip by sloop from New York to Albany, see Hone, 905; Lambert, 2:41–9; Taylor, 15–31.

60 Taylor, 56–7; Pred, 14, 20–77, 112–4.

61 For a fine survey of the issues of westward migration and transportation, see Howe, 211–22.

62 For a splendid view of Broadway in 1819, clearly depicting the fashions of the day, see Stokes, vol. 3, plate 85.

63 Enrollment Number 248, July 16, 1817, vol. 12139, Port of New York Certificates of Enrolment [sic], Bureau of Marine Inspection and Navigation, RG 41, NA.

64 Lane, 22–25; TG to Jonathan Johnston, November 24, 1817, GP; Morrison, 44. Elizabethtown is now known as Elizabeth. It has often been said that CV himself renamed the *Stoudinger* the *Mouse*, but it was advertised as the *Mouse* before CV took command; see *NBF*, November 13, 1817. Lane and Croffut depict CV on New Year's Eve pondering the growing importance of steam, then making a calculated decision to learn about it by working for TG. TG's letter to Johnston, however, demonstrates the fortuitous nature of his hiring of CV, as well as the fact that it took place more than a month before year's end.

Two The Duelist

1 TG to Jonathan Johnston, November 24, 1817, GP.

2 CV quoted in *Den D. Trumbull et al. v. Gibbons*, April 10, 1849, 22 NJ L 117, 16.

3 TG to Thomas Heyward Gibbons, September 15, 1786, *Georgia Gazette*, September 14, 21, 1786, TG to George Johnston, February 2, 1810, George Johnston to TG, May 22, 1812, Petition of James Field to the Honorable George Walters, 1783, WG to TG, January 23, 1785, TG to WG, January 27, 1785, Memorandum by WG, March 15, 1848, GP. See also Isaac Woodruff to TG, July 20, 1817, Isaac Woodruff Papers, NYHS. In 1819, TG was described as a man of "immense wealth" in *AO v. TG*, Supreme Court of Judicature of the State of New Jersey (February Term, 1819), 2 South. 5, 612–36, 1005–15.

4 Thomas Gamble, *Savannah Duels and Duellists, 1733–1877* (Savannah: Review Publishing & Printing, 1923), 41–4, 57–8; Carol S. Ebel, "Thomas Gibbons," *ANB*; see also George R. Lamplugh, *Politics on the Periphery: Factions and Parties in Georgia, 1783–1806* (Newark, Del.: University of Delaware Press, 1986).

5 For details on TG's many holdings in New Jersey and Georgia, see a copy of TG's will, Thomas Gibbons Papers, NYHS. TG described his move as a matter of climate and health; TG to Crawford Davison, June 1, 1818, GP. Various correspondence in the GP adumbrate the story of his illegitimate child, which he attempted to deny, against the advice of some of New York's leading attorneys. On New York's emerging role as creditor to Southern planters, see Philip S. Foner, *Business and Slavery: The New York Merchants and the Irrepressible Conflict* (Chapel Hill: University of North Carolina Press, 1941), 5–10; Albion, 95–121.

6 Joanne B. Freeman, *Affairs of Honor: National Politics in the New Republic* (New Haven: Yale University Press, 2001); Nancy Isenberg; *Fallen Founder: The Life of Aaron Burr* (New York: Viking, 2007), 255–404. See also Saul Cornell, *The Other Founders: Anti-Federalism and the Dissenting Tradition in America, 1788–1828* (Chapel Hill: University of North Carolina Press, 1999).

7 Bernard Bailyn, *The Ideological Origins of the American Revolution*, enlarged ed. (Cambridge, Mass.: Harvard University Press, 1992), 302; Frederic Cople Jaher, *The Urban Establishment: Upper Strata in Boston, New York, Charleston, Chicago, and Los Angeles* (Urbana: University of Illinois Press, 1982), 3, and, for an insightful discussion of the New York patricians before the Civil War, see 160–250. See also Wood.

8 Wood, 254–5, 269–70, 299–300; Martin Bruegel, *Farm, Shop, Landing: The Rise of a*

Market Society in the Hudson Valley, 1780–1860 (Durham: Duke University Press, 2002), 15–6, 36–8, 206; Stuart M. Blumin, *The Emergence of the Middle Class: Social Experience in the American City, 1760–1900* (Cambridge: Cambridge University Press, 1989), 64–5; John Lauritz Larson, *Internal Improvement: National Public Works and the Promise of Popular Government in the Early United States* (Chapel Hill: University of North Carolina Press, 2001), 9–10. See also Edward Countryman, "From Revolution to Statehood," in Milton M. Klein, ed., *The Empire State: A History of New York* (Ithaca: Cornell University Press, 2001), 242–56, 264–8, 295–7; Dixon Ryan Fox, *The Decline of Aristocracy in the Politics of New York* (New York: Columbia University Press, 1919), 58–65.

9   Countryman, "From Revolution," 242–68; Duc de La Rochefoucauld-Liancourt, *Travels Through the United States of North America, the Country of the Iroquois, and Upper Canada, in the Years 1795, 1796, and 1797; with an Authentic Account of Lower Canada* (London: R. Phillips, 1799), 587–8; Blumin, 58–64; Wood, 271–86. Particularly insightful is Gunn, esp. 70, 80–3. As Gunn writes, 83, New York before the end of the War of 1812 remained "a society in which public and private roles were virtually indistinguishable." An amusing illustration of the Jeffersonian view of elite rule in the election of 1800 can be found in Eric Homberger, *Mrs. Astor's New York: Money and Social Power in a Gilded Age* (New Haven: Yale University Press, 2002), 37. See also Edward Countryman's *A People in Revolution: The American Revolution and Political Society in New York, 1760–1790* (Baltimore: Johns Hopkins University Press, 1981), which analyzes the radicalism of the Revolution and the conservative reaction.

10 Countryman, "From Revolution," 369; Edward Countryman, *The American Revolution* (New York: Hill & Wang, 1985), 224–5; Joyce Appleby, *Capitalism and the New Social Order: The Republican Vision of the 1790s* (New York: New York University Press, 1984), 5, 14–5, 20–2, 46–50, 54–5, 88.

11 On Livingston's life, see especially Cynthia Owen Philip, *Robert Fulton: A Biography* (New York: Franklin Watts, 1985); Cynthia A. Kierner, *Traders and Gentlefolk: The Livingstons of New York, 1675–1790* (Ithaca: Cornell University Press, 1992); George Dangerfield, *Chancellor Robert R. Livingston of New York, 1746–1813* (New York: Harcourt, Brace, 1960); *EP*, February 26, 1802. Jaher, 160–96, discusses the intermingling of proprietary with mercantile wealth and the legal profession. Albion, 230–59, discusses the "merchant princes," noting the relative decline of the old families after 1815. I do not mean to suggest that British gentry or nobility did not engage in trade; I am specifically referring to the image in fiction. Washington quoted in Larson, 9.

12 Countryman, "From Revolution," 369; Countryman, *American Revolution*, 224–5; Appleby, 5, 46–55, 88. Gunn, 70, notes, "New York politics [had] a reputation for personalism and corruption unsurpassed in any other state." See also pages 1–22, 99–143. Appleby has elaborated on the rising opposition to mercantilism in other works, including "The Vexed Story of Capitalism Told by American Historians," *Journal of the Early Republic* 21, no. 1 (spring 2001): 1–18, and *Inheriting the Revolution: The First Generation of Americans* (Cambridge, Mass.: Harvard University Press, 2000). See also Bray Hammond, *Banks and Politics in America: From the Revolution to the Civil War* (Princeton: Princeton University Press, 1957), 145–7. The idea that the rise of a commercial society joined hands with political radicalism to undermine the culture of deference is central to Wood's thesis, 243–347. See also Kierner, 201–22, 236–8; Dorothy Gregg, "John Stevens: General Entrepreneur, 1749–1838," in William Miller, ed., *Men in Business: Essays in the History of Entrepreneurship* (Cambridge, Mass.: Harvard University Press, 1952), 121–6; Charles W. McCurdy, *The Anti-Rent Era in New York Law and Politics, 1839–1865* (Chapel Hill: University of North Carolina Press, 2001), 2–4; David Hackett Fischer, *The Revolution of American Conservatism: The Federalist Party in the Era of Jeffersonian Democracy* (New York:

Harper & Row, 1965), and Fox's much older, often challenged, but still useful *Decline of Aristocracy in the Politics of New York.* The most important discussion of the changing law regarding monopolies and government franchises is Morton J. Horwitz, *The Transformation of American Law, 1780–1860* (Cambridge, Mass.: Harvard University Press, 1977), xii–xv, 110–30. Also of interest is Pauline Maier, "The Revolutionary Origins of the American Corporation," *WMQ,* 3rd ser., vol. 50, no. 1 (January 1993): 51–84. As she notes, Adam Smith criticized corporations as vehicles of mercantilist monopoly; see, for example, book 1, chap. X, part II of *The Wealth of Nations.* On monopolies in American tradition, see Herbert Hovenkamp, "Technology, Politics, and Regulated Monopoly: An American Historical Perspective," *Texas Law Review* 62, no. 7 (April 1984): 1263–1312; Thomas P. Campbell Jr., "Chancellor Kent, Chief Justice Marshall, and the Steamboat Case," *Syracuse Law Review* 25 (1974): 497–534; W. Howard Mann, "The Marshall Court: Nationalization of Private Rights and Personal Liberty from the Authority of the Commerce Clause," *Indiana Law Journal* 38, no. 2 (winter 1963): 117–238; Albert S. Abel, "Commerce Regulation Before *Gibbons v. Ogden:* Interstate Transportation Enterprise," *Mississippi Law Journal* 18, no. 3 (May 1947): 335–80.

13 Larson discusses at length "a kind of state-level mercantilism" that drove the internal-improvement projects of the "monied gentry" (quote on 25). "New York's heritage of mercantilist ideology" is stressed by Nathan Miller, *The Enterprise of a Free People: Aspects of Economic Development in New York State During the Canal Period, 1792–1838* (Ithaca: Cornell University Press, 1962), 10–19.

14 The ensuing discussion of Livingston, Fulton, and the steamboat monopoly owes much to Maurice G. Baxter, *The Steamboat Monopoly: Gibbons v. Ogden, 1824* (New York: Alfred A. Knopf, 1972), 3–25; Philip, *Robert Fulton;* and Dangerfield, *Chancellor Robert R. Livingston.* For Livingston's own defense of a monopoly as a just reward for his public-spirited investment, see Dangerfield, 414. New York State first granted a steamboat monopoly to John Fitch, who committed suicide in 1798. I am grateful to Maury Klein for pointing out that Fitch, among others, was unaware of Watts's work on the steam engine.

15 Baxter, 3–25; Philip, 119–53, 194–219. Philip also notes Livingston's absurd engineering notions; see, for example, 208. See also Morrison, 20–33. Fulton and Livingston, who shared the New York monopoly, also won a monopoly on the Mississippi in 1811, which they were never able to enforce.

16 Baxter, 25–31; John Niven, *Martin Van Buren and the Romantic Age of American Politics* (New York: Oxford University Press, 1983), 11–13; Mann, 117–238; Gregg, 120–41; Thomas Campbell Jr., "Chancellor Kent, Chief Justice Marshall, and the Steamboat Case," *Syracuse Law Review* 25 (1974): 497–534. Ogden paid $600 to $800 a year, depending on the schedule; see Jonathan Dayton to TG, February 23, 1815, and Copy of Articles of Agreement between JRL and AO, May 5, 1815, GP. It should be noted that Ogden fought the New York monopoly by securing his own monopoly from the New Jersey legislature when he was the sitting governor. Fulton went to New Jersey to lobby the legislature (successfully) to rescind Ogden's grant, and then fell ill after he pulled his lawyer out of a crack in the ice on the Hudson. He died on February 24, 1815.

17 J. M. Trumbull to TG, November 18, 1814, TG to Mrs. Ann H. Gibbons, May 13, 1816, TG to AO, May 30, 1816, John M. Trumbull to Mrs. TG, August 14, 1818, GP; *AO v. TG,* Supreme Court of Judicature of the State of New Jersey (February Term, 1819), 2 South. 5, 612–36, 1005–15. See also Baxter, 3–15, 19–31, and Philip.

18 TG to AO, Copybook, September 25, 1814, TG to General Dayton, June 23, 1812, TG to Mrs. Ann H. Gibbons, May 13, 1816, TG to Ellet Tucker, January 3, 1816, TG to David B. Ogden, June 1, 1816, AO to TG, June 1, 1816, Jonathan Dayton to TG, February 23, 1815, TG to AO, August 4, 1815, Statement of Mrs. Trumbull, 1815, AO to TG, December 23, 1815, Jonathan Dayton to TG, 1816, TG to WG,

April 3, 1816, J. M. Trumbull to TG, November 18, 1814, TG to AO, May 30, 1816, GP; *AO v. TG*, Supreme Court of Judicature of the State of New Jersey (February Term, 1819), 2 South. 5, 612–36, 1005–15; *The State v. TG*, Supreme Court of Judicature of the State of New Jersey (February Term, 1818), 1 South. 4, 45–64; *EP*, September 22, 1818.

19 *EP*, February 4, 1818. The *EP* story referred to "Mr. Vanderbilt's packet ferry boat *Dread*," leaving the possibility that someone else commanded it; the narrative reflects my belief that this is extremely unlikely, given the storm, the skill with which the boat was handled, and the incident that followed at Sandy Hook, in which CV clearly piloted the *Dread* in person.

20 *EP*, February 27, 1818; *New York Commercial Advertiser*, February 27, 1818; *New York Daily Advertiser*, February 28, 1818. On the world of the countinghouses, see Albion, 260–86.

21 Lawrence & Sneden to TG, February 21, 1818, CV to TG, February 24, 1818, Thomas P. Allaire to TG, March 16, 1818, Alex B. Allaire to TG, March 19, 1818, TG to Brewster, Collector of the Port of Amboy, August 29, 1818, GP; Morrison, 41–5, 170; John H. Morrison, *History of New York Ship Yards* (New York: Wm. F. Sametz & Co., 1909), 22–49; Burrows & Wallace, 441–3; *Den D. Trumbull et al. v. Gibbons*, April 10, 1849, 22 NJ L 117, 17. On TG's afflictions, see, for example, TG to P. J. Munro, January 28, 1819, GP, in which TG wrote, "Old age is sensible of its weaknesses. And now I am severely afflicted with disease. I have been but twice beyond my front door for 4 weeks. And more than all this my eyes refuse their office. I am set down a stranger amidst a host of enemies." CV was seen as a leader of Staten Island's boatmen; see TG to Alderman Buckmaster, September 6, 1818, GP; and *Minutes of the Common Council of the City of New York, 1784–1831*, vol. 9 (New York: City of New York, 1917), 766 (copy in NYMA).

22 Memorandum of Agreement, June 26, 1818, GP; CV in Account with the Steamboat Bellona, July 1 to August 1, 1821, CV in Account with the Steamboat Bellona, August 1 to September 1, 1821, GP-R; W. J. Rorabaugh, *The Alcoholic Republic: An American Tradition* (New York: Oxford University Press, 1979).

23 On CV's own vessels, see Enrollment Number 248, July 16, 1817, vol. 12139, and Enrollment Number 361, December 22, 1820, and Number 21, February 26, 1821, vol. 12148, Port of New York Certificates of Enrolment [sic], Bureau of Marine Inspection and Navigation, RG 41, NA.

24 TG to John Randolph, March 20, 1816, TG to WG, November 19, 1816, TG to Peter Munro (Draft), January 21, 1819, GP.

25 TG to Seth D. Staples, May 11, 1822, Thomas Gibbons Papers, Misc. Files, NYPL. It is difficult to know why no commerce clause cases had come before, but the answer seems to lie in the fact that there was such little interstate commerce before the boom that followed the War of 1812.

26 Herbert A. Johnson, "*Gibbons v. Ogden* Before Marshall," in Leo Hershkowitz and Milton M. Klein, eds., *Courts and Law in Early New York* (Port Washington, N.Y.: National University Publications, 1978), 105–13; Aaron Burr, "Of the Validity of the Laws Granting Livingston & Fulton the Exclusive Right of Using Fire and Steam to Propel Boats or Vessels," Document GLC06183, Gilder Lehrman Institute of American History, NYHS.

27 Philip, 200, 229–30, 252, 289–94, 315; Dangerfield, 415–7; Charles H. Rhind, Accounts of the North River Steam Boat Company, December 2, 1819, JRL to Robert L. Livingston, September 9, 1821, LFP. Regarding the North River's profits, it must be remembered that accounting remained primitive, and the company did not calculate depreciation; see Thomas Cochran, "The Business Revolution," *AHR* 79, no. 5 (December 1974): 1449–66. For an idea of how large these sums were, $100,000 represented the total capital investment of James P. Allaire's extensive steam engine works, one of the largest employers in New York with as many as one hundred workmen; James P. Allaire to TG, January 10, 1822, GP.

28 Memorandum of General Dayton, October 16, 1815, Memorandum of WG, December 5, 1817, GP. On Livingston's New Brunswick line, see *NBF,* November 6, 1817. For a description of the *Atalanta,* see *EP,* June 1, 1822.

29 On the entanglements of DDT, TG, CV, AO, and the Livingstons, see TG to AO, December 10, 1818, WG Memorandum, December 11, 1818, AO to TG, December 12, 1818, TG to Peter Jay Munro, December 27, 1818, TG to Peter Jay Munro, January 21, 1819, TG to Peter Jay Munro, January 28, 1819, CV to TG, February 2, 1819, CV to TG, February 24, 1819, James P. Allaire to TG, January 4, 1818, DDT to TG, May 21, 1818, GP; *Gibbons v. Ogden,* Court of Errors, January 1820, 17 Johns., 488–510; Agreement of DDT, Adam Brown, and Noah Brown, October 11, 1817, Staten Island Papers, NYHS; DDT to Edward P. Livingston, October 5, 1818, LFP. On DDT himself, see Niven, 11–29, 76–7; Ray W. Irwin, *Daniel D. Tompkins: Governor of New York and Vice President of the United States* (New York: New-York Historical Society, 1968), 213–33. In various court records, it appears that JRL sold to DDT the rights to steam to Staten Island (see *JRL v. DDT,* June 1, 1820, New York Court of Chancery, 4 Johns. Chancery, 413–32); his frequent complaints, however, suggest that he had been pressured into it; see JRL to Robert L. Livingston, September 9, 1821, LFP.

30 Rachel Stevens to R. Stevens, October 12, 1819, Stevens Family Papers, New Jersey Historical Society (copy in GP).

31 TG to AO, October 31, 1817, TG to Peter Jay Munro, October 3, 1818, GP; *AO v. TG,* December 4, 1819, file O-109, Court of Chancery, NYCC; *Ogden v. Gibbons,* 4 Johns. Chancery, 150, and *Gibbons v. Ogden,* Court of Errors, January 1820, 17 Johns., 488–510; *NBF,* November 3, 1817; *EP,* September 22, 1818; Johnson, "*Gibbons v. Ogden* Before Marshall." See also Baxter.

32 Sworn statements of John G. Dusenberry, June 21, 1819, DDT to TG, July 14, 1819, James Ward to TG, October 22, 1819, GP; In the Matter of Vanderbilt, July 1, 1819, New York Court of Chancery, 4 Johns. Chancery, 57–62; Affidavit of CV, *AO v. TG,* December 4, 1819, file O-109, Court of Chancery, NYCC; Johnson, "*Gibbons v. Ogden.*"

33 Allan R. Pred, *Urban Growth and the Circulation of Information: The United States System of Cities, 1790–1840* (Cambridge, Mass.: Harvard University Press, 1973), 143–77; Margaret G. Meyers, *The New York Money Market,* vol. 1: *Origins and Development* (New York: Columbia University Press, 1931), 3–9; Sidney Ratner, James H. Soltow, and Richard Sylla, *The Evolution of the American Economy: Growth, Welfare, and Decision Making* (New York: Basic Books, 1979), 121–4, 222–6; and see especially Diane Lindstrom, *Economic Development in the Philadelphia Region, 1810–1850* (New York: Columbia University Press, 1977). CV to TG, February 2, 1819, CV to TG, February 24, 1819, TG to JRL, April 22, 1819, Agents of the Union Line to TG, June 14, 1819, Articles of Agreement, April 22, 1822, GP; *Gibbons v. Ogden,* Court of Errors, January 1820, 17 Johns., 488–510.

34 On JRL's New Brunswick line, see *NBF,* November 6, 1817. His monopoly was immensely unpopular in New Brunswick; see Petition from Citizens of New Brunswick, February 26, 1819, Sworn statements of John G. Dusenberry, June 21, 1819, TG to Isaac Pierson, Samuel Tooker, Edmund Smith et al., May 13, 1822, GP. The complicated tactical maneuvering of this struggle defies description, as TG sought ways around the injunctions that barred his boat from New York. For example, JRL actually sought injunctions against both AO and TG, because the two had come to a temporary arrangement to connect with one another, since New Brunswick was the natural destination of passengers from New York, but AO was barred from going there under the terms of his license. In addition, DDT subdivided the rights he had purchased from the monopoly, and sold TG the right to travel between Staten Island and New Jersey, which allowed the *Bellona* to connect to the *Nautilus.* Affidavit of Wm. B. Jacques, April 27, 1819, Proposed Agreement between TG and JRL, drafted by Livingston, April 1, 1819, JRL to TG, April 21,

1819, TG to JRL, April 22, 1819, Agreement between DDT and TG, May 13, 1819, GP; DDT to Edward P. Livingston, October 5, 1818, LFP. See also Affidavit of CV, *AO v. TG*, December 4, 1819, file O-109, Court of Chancery, NYCC.

35 *NBF*, September 30, 1819; CV to TG, January 5, 1820, TG to Daniel Webster, December 13, 1819, GP; Johnson, *"Gibbons v. Ogden,"* 109–11; Robert V. Remini, *Daniel Webster: The Man and His Time* (New York: W. W. Norton & Co., 1997), 201. An excellent summary of the legal conflict appears in Andrew J. King, ed., *The Papers of Daniel Webster: Legal Papers, 3: The Federal Practice, Part I* (Hanover, N.H.: University Press of New England, 1989), 255–9. TG also sought a repeal of the monopoly in the state legislature, but Martin Van Buren declined an offer of $100 to push the cause; TG to William Price, March 1, 1819, James Ward to TG, October 22, 1819, TG's memorandum with John W. Patterson, March 18, 1819, GP.

36 *New York Daily Advertiser*, February 7 and 8, 1820; *New York Commercial Advertiser*, February 7, 1820; *EP*, February 7, 1820; Lane, 39; P. J. Staudenraus, *The African Colonization Movement, 1816–1865* (New York: Columbia University Press, 1961), 55–8. For CV's address, see TG to CV, January 25, 1821, GP.

37 "The New Jersey Monopolies," *NAR*, April 1867, 428–76 (see esp. 434); *TG v. JRL* and *TG v. AO*, 1 South. 6, 236–300; Affidavit of CV, July 24, 1820, GP. It should be noted that the flurry of injunctions did not cease. The legal conflict was staggeringly complicated, but the general thrust was that the *Bellona* was regularly allowed to run to New York.

38 On the *Bellona*'s connection to the city, and the Philadelphia route, see *NBF*, May 11, November 9, 1820; *EP*, January 3, April 29, November 25, 1820; Anne Royall, *Sketches of History, Life, and Manners in the United States* (New Haven: n.p., 1826), 239; entry for May 22, 1824, Samuel S. Griscom Diary, May to June 1824, NYHS; Frances Trollope, *Domestic Manners of the Americans* (New York: Alfred A. Knopf, 1949), 335–6. Philip Hone, in a diary entry for March 13, 1832, recorded that the steamboat passage between New York and New Brunswick took four and a half hours; Hone, 58.

39 Enrollment Number 53, October 10, 1818, Perth Amboy Custom House Enrollments, 1818–1821, vol. 2169, Custom House Records, RG 41, NA. For illustrations of early steamboats, see Morrison, and the five volumes of Erik Heyl's very useful work. An excellent capsule description of steamboat patterns in the East and the development of the industry can be found in Taylor, 56–61.

40 *NBF*, March 11, 1819; Memorandum Signed by TG and John Lisle, March 5, 1819, Roster of *Bellona* crew, October 1828, John Hunt Receipt, September 1, 1818, Inventory of Bellona Articles, December 19, 1825, J. & S. Fischer Receipt, August 22–9, 1821, George H. Cooper Receipt, August 31, 1821, Receipt of John Hutchings, May 31, 1822, GP-R; Archibald Douglass Turnbull, *John Stevens: An American Record* (New York: Century Company, 1928), 443; Trollope, 335.

41 Enrollment Number 361, December 22, 1820, New York Custom House Enrollments, November 14, 1820, to May 29, 1821, vol. 12148, RG 41, NA; *SA*, June 18, 1853; *EP*, March 8, 1820, January 8, 1821; Heyl, 2:27–8; Heyl, 5:41–2; Agreement for Sale of the *Mouse*, March 18, 1820, GP.

42 TG to Peter Jay Munro, December 27, 1818, TG to Peter Jay Munro, January 21, 1819, TG to Peter Jay Munro, January 28, 1819, CV to TG, February 2, 1819, CV to TG, February 24, 1819, James P. Allaire to TG, January 4, 1818, GP.

43 CV to TG, December 25, 1820, Nath. Shuff & Co. to TG, December 25, 1820, TG to Isaac Brown, copy by CV, January 5, 1821, CV to TG, January 13, 1821, Isaac Brown to TG, January 21, 1821, TG to D. B. Ogden, February 15, 1821, Receipt of William Wirt, February 27, 1821, Receipt of Daniel Webster, February 28, 1821, TG to Daniel Webster, April 2, 1821, GP; CV to TG, January 25, 1821, CV-NYHS; *Gibbons v. Ogden*, March 8, 1821, 6 Wheaton, 448–50. See also Daniel Webster to TG, May 9, 1821, GP.

44 Lane writes that CV now moved to a house on Renwick Street in New York, citing an agreement between CV and J. S. Watkins & Brothers, February 13, 1821, and an agreement with David Fenton and J. S. & L. S. Watkins, February 13, 1821, CV-NYPL. However, the signature on these papers does not match that of CV, and there was at least one other Cornelius Vanderbilt in New York at the time, as shown by NYCC records. For a convenient listing of CV's progeny, see Dorothy Kelly MacDowell, *Commodore Vanderbilt and his Family* (Hendersonville, N.C.: n.p., 1989), 22.

45 Charles H. Rhind, Accounts of the North River Steam Boat Company, December 2, 1819, JRL to Robert L. Livingston, September 9, 1821, LFP; Robert Montgomery Livingston to AO, October 3, 1820, Aaron Ogden Papers, Rutgers University. Dangerfield, 414, discusses Chancellor Livingston's calculations that there was a limit on the traffic to Albany.

46 *In the Supreme Court of the United States between Cornelius Vanderbilt and John R. Livingston* (New York: Edwin B. Clayton, 1823), copy in GP; Paul A. Gilje, *The Road to Mobocracy: Popular Disorder in New York City, 1763–1834* (Chapel Hill: University of North Carolina Press, 1987), 275–7; A. E. Costello, *Our Police Protectors: History of the New York Police from the Earliest Period to the Present Time*, 2nd ed. (New York: n.p., 1885), 92–3, 98.

47 D. O. Price to TG, October 27, 1821, GP.

48 CV in Account with Steamboat Bellona, August 1, 1821, GP-R; Memorandum of Agreement between TG and Lawrence & Sneeden, October 16, 1821, CV to TG, November 16, 1821, GP; *NBF,* November 9, 1820.

49 Lane, 37; Firth Haring Fabend, "The Synod of Dort and the Persistence of Dutchness in Nineteenth-Century New York and New Jersey," *NYHis* 77, no. 3 (July 1996): 273–300; CV to TG, March 1, April 12, 1822, Abraham DeGraw to TG, June 22, 1822, Thomas Hill Rental Receipt, November 1, 1822, GP; Copy of TG's Will, October 26, 1825, Thomas Gibbons Papers, NYHS; TG to ?, March 12, 1822, GP-R; MacDowell, 22. It appears from DeGraw's letter that TG initially rented, or planned to rent, the building to DeGraw, but CV occupied it before the end of 1822. For CV's salary, see CV in Account with Steamboat Bellona, August 1, 1821, GP-R. Details about the education of the children emerged during the trial over CV's will; see the testimony of Daniel B. Allen, *NYS,* November 13, 1877.

50 *EP,* March 28, 1822; James P. Allaire to TG, January 11, 1822, Petition of the Ship-Builders of the City of New-York, February 1, 1822, Statement of Isaac Brown, June 21, 1822, Instructions to Mr. Parkman, August 6, 1822, TG to AO, March 22, 30, 1822, GP. On the state of New York–Philadelphia trade during this time, see *Trenton Federalist,* August 26, 1822.

51 Countryman, "From Revolution," 369–75; Wood, 268–70, 287–305; Donald B. Cole, *Martin Van Buren and the American Political System* (New York: Oxford University Press, 1984), 88–98; Cynthia A. Kierner, "Patrician Womanhood in the Early Republic: The 'Reminiscences' of Janet Livingston Montgomery," *NYHis* 73, no. 4 (October 1992): 389–407; see especially Fischer.

52 R. M. Livingston to TG, June 14, 25, 27, August 31, 1822, WG to TG, September 8, 1822, GP.

53 *EP,* August 26, 31, November 5, 1822; Memorandum of TG, September 18, 1822, William B. Jaques to TG, September 12, 1822, WG to TG, September 8, 1822, Memorandum of TG, November 27, 1822, GP.

54 CV to TG, November 4, 1822, GP; Countryman, "From Statehood," 369; Gunn, 26–8; Wood, 325–47; Andrew Burstein, *America's Jubilee* (New York: Alfred A. Knopf, 2001), esp. 34–5. See also Burstein's *Sentimental Democracy: The Evolution of America's Romantic Self-Image* (New York: Hill & Wang, 1999), which examines "the Americanization of sensibility," and *Confidence Men,* 56–60, 94. Bruegel is also very illuminating on the penetration of the market into the private sphere. A reference to

CV as an "economic man" appears in Edward J. Renehan Jr., *Commodore: The Life of Cornelius Vanderbilt* (New York: Basic Books , 2007), but I wrote this passage in 2003, several years before Renehan began work on his book.

55 CV to TG, March 1, November 4, 1822, Robert Arnold to TG, May 23, 1822, GP.

56 TG also claimed that CV had plotted to cheat a Griswold, probably a stage operator or boatman, by running directly to South Amboy; TG to WG, December 12, 1822, GP; Lane, 40; *Den D. Trumbull et al. v. Gibbons*, April 10, 1849, 22 NJ L 117. Regarding CV's partnership with Allaire in the *Fanny*, see Conference abt. Fanny, undated memorandum, GP; *EP*, March 31, April 1, 1822; *NYS*, November 13, 1877. Though CV would later be renowned for his harness racing, the horses discussed by TG almost certainly were Thoroughbreds, as harness racing remained an informal sport with inexpensive horses; see Melvin L. Adelman, "The First Modern Sport in America: Harness Racing in New York City, 1825–1870," *Journal of Sport History* 8, no. 1 (spring 1981): 5–32.

57 CV to TG, April 1, 1823, TG to WG, April 4, 1823, GP; *New York Daily Advertiser*, March 31, 1823.

58 CV to WG, March 25, 1823, GP.

59 *JRL v. CV*, December 28, 1822, file L J-1822-V-18, Supreme Court Judgments, NYCC.

60 Lane, 34–5, 40–1; TG to WG, May 2, 4, 5, 17, 1823, GP.

61 James Day and Jacob Vanderbilt appear in the November 1823 receipts in GP-R. Regarding the New Brunswick dock maneuver, see CV to TG, April 11, 1823, GP. The two CV letters quoted (cited in Lane, 34–5, 40–1) no longer appear in the GP, and appear to have been lost, misfiled, or stolen. As will be deduced, CV's parents had had a second son named Jacob.

62 Baxter, 37–9; King, 270; for a marvelous portrait of the now-forgotten Wirt, see Burstein, *America's Jubilee*, 34–58.

63 Wood, 287–305; Donald B. Cole, *Martin Van Buren and the American Political System* (New York: Oxford University Press, 1984), 88–98; Cynthia A. Kierner, "Patrician Womanhood in the Early Republic: The 'Reminiscences' of Janet Livingston Montgomery," *NYHis* 73, no. 4 (October 1992): 389–407; Baxter, 23–31; TG to WG, January 23, 1823, CV to TG, January 22, 1823, William Talmage to TG, January 20, 1823, *In the Supreme Court of the United States, Between Cornelius Vanderbilt and John R. Livingston* (New York: Edwin B. Clanton, 1823), GP; JRL to Robert L. Livingston, December 15, 1823, LFP.

64 Statement of Interview between Walter Livingston and WG, January 27, 1824, GP.

65 Baxter, 40; Remini, 8–9.

66 See especially Horwitz, 110–34, and Appleby, *Inheriting the Revolution*, 56–8, 88–9. Appleby powerfully argues that economic and political liberalization were linked, though I would stress that the link between government intervention and elite politics was most marked at the state level in the case of New York; see Miller, 10–19. Some of Hamilton's federal policies democratized the economy in ways that he did not intend, as women and artisans bought shares and took loans; see Robert E. Wright, "Bank Ownership and Lending Patterns in New York and Pennsylvania, 1781–1831," *BHR* 73, no. 1 (spring 1999): 40–60.

67 Baxter, 40–57, 70–1, 80; Remini, 202–8; King, 270–91; 9 Wheaton U.S. 1; *EP*, March 5, 1822; see also *NR*, March 27, 1824.

Three A Tricky God

1 Receipt of Thomas Richards from Capt. Vanderbilt for Steamboat *Thistle*, March 31, 1824, Receipt of Blossom, Smith, & Demon to Steamboat *Thistle*, April 14, 1824, GP-R; Enrollment Number 16, *Thistle*, April 3, 1824, Perth Amboy Custom

House, Certificates of Enrollment, 1824–26, vol. 2196, Bureau of Marine Inspection and Navigation, RG 41, NA; *EP,* April 23, 1824; Wheaton J. Lane, *From Indian Trail to Iron Horse: Travel and Transportation in New Jersey, 1620–1860* (Princeton: Princeton University Press, 1939), 203.

2   *EP,* March 13, 1823, March 5, 16, 18, 26, 1824; *NBF,* March 11, 1824; *NR,* March 27, 1824; *New York Daily Advertiser,* March 6, 8, 1824; Maurice G. Baxter, *The Steamboat Monopoly: Gibbons v. Ogden, 1824* (New York: Alfred A. Knopf, 1972), 70–1, 80.

3   Leonard W. Levy, *Seasoned Judgments: The American Constitution, Rights, and History* (New Brunswick, N.J.: Transaction, 1995), 439; R. Kent Newmeyer, *John Marshall and the Heroic Age of the Supreme Court* (Baton Rouge: Louisiana State University Press, 2001), 269–71, 302–15; Jean Edward Smith, *John Marshall: Definer of a Nation* (New York: Henry Holt, 1996), 481. On the erosion of state franchises and "exclusionary privileges of first entrants" in American law, see Morton J. Horwitz, *The Transformation of American Law, 1780–1860* (Cambridge, Mass.: Harvard University Press, 1977), 34, 110–39. On the popular enthusiasm for laissez-faire, see the works of Joyce Appleby, such as "The Vexed Story of Capitalism Told by American Historians," *JER* 21, no. 1 (spring 2001): 1–18. In *Capitalism and the New Social Order: The Republican Vision of the 1790s* (New York: New York University Press, 1984), Appleby explicitly argues that the free market came to be seen as a natural force. For a contemporary discussion along these lines of *Gibbons v. Ogden* and monopolies, see *Workingman's Advocate,* August 16, 1834.

4   Baxter, 61–133, discusses the evaluations of the decision and its many legal consequences, and includes the Beveridge quote. See also Albert J. Beveridge, *Life of John Marshall,* vol. 4 (Boston: Houghton Mifflin, 1947, orig. pub. 1919), 445–8; Charles Warren, *The Supreme Court in United States History,* vol. 2 (Boston: Little, Brown, 1922), 58–86, John Randolph quoted on 71. See also G. Edward White, *The Marshall Court and Cultural Change: 1815–35* (New York: Macmillan, 1988). To understand Marshall's decision in the larger legal context of the era, one must consult Horwitz's discussion of the emerging acceptance of competition and the declining primacy of state franchises, 109–39.

5   John Lauritz Larson, *Internal Improvement: National Public Works and the Promise of Popular Government in the Early United States* (Chapel Hill: University of North Carolina Press, 2001), 80, notes that the Erie Canal so solidified New York's position that the city captured railroads, instead of having railroads divert trade elsewhere.

6   The registration figures compare 1825 with typical prior years (the 1825 number reflects the number of vessels built in 1824, after *Gibbons v. Ogden*). See Bureau of Navigation, *Merchant Steam Vessels of the United States, 1807 to 1856* (Washington, D.C.: United States Department of Commerce, 1931), 5–7. *NR* cited in Smith, 481.

7   Baxter, 62–8, 70; Paul G. E. Clemens, "Aaron Ogden," *ANB.* For an inside look at the rising tensions between JRL and his nephews, see the correspondence between Charles H. Rhind and Robert L. Livingston, April 26, July 16, 31, September 4, 1824, LFP. On the transformation of the old patricians, see David Hackett Fischer, *The Revolution of American Conservatism: The Federalist Party in the Era of Jeffersonian Democracy* (New York: Harper & Row, 1965), and Wood, 325–47.

8   Bill of Jacob Wyckoff to TG, March 1, 1824, TG in Account with CV, September 1, 1824, Statement of the Union Line Way-Bills on the Noon Line, 1826 and 1827, GP-R.

9   *EP,* April 29, May 17, 19, 1824; CV to TG, April 30, 1824, GP; Anne Royall, *Sketches of History, Life, and Manners in the United States* (New Haven: n.p., 1826), 239; Harlan I. Halsey, "The Choice Between High-Pressure and Low-Pressure Steam Power in America in the Early Nineteenth Century," *JEH* 41, no. 4 (December 1981): 723–44. In slightly more than a decade, on March 14, 1836, Philip Hone was able to write in his diary: "The loss of life from steamboat explosions, railroad

accidents, falling walls, etc. has gotten to be a matter of every-day occurence, and no longer occasions surprise or excites sympathy." And yet his frequent comments on deadly steam disasters shows how troubling they were to Americans; Hone, 203, 261.

10 William Benedict, *New Brunswick in History* (New Brunswick, N.J.: n.p., 1925), 178; CV to TG, April 27, 1824, GP; *EP,* May 27, 1824. On the New Brunswick investors behind the ferry business, see the NP. CV's insight is all the more remarkable because corporations at this time were thought of as a kind of partnership in which ownership and management were one and the same. See, for example, Gregory A. Mark, "The Personification of the Business Corporation in American Law," *University of Chicago Law Review* 54, no. 4 (autumn 1987): 1441–83; Naomi R. Lamoreaux, "Partnerships, Corporations, and the Limits on Contractual Freedom in U.S. History: An Essay in Economics, Law, and Culture," in Kenneth Lipartito and David B. Scilia, eds., *Constructing Corporate America: History, Politics, Culture* (Oxford: Oxford University Press, 2004), 29–65.

11 *New York Daily Advertiser,* June 4, 1824; *EP,* June 5, 1824; Sam S. Griscom, "Journal of a Tour thro N. Jersey, Penn and N. York with occasional remarks on the people, Literary characters Ladies Institutions &c. &c. &c.," 1824, NYHS. For details on the *Legislator'*s company, the Exchange Line, and transportation across New Jersey in general at this time, see Lane, *From Indian Trail,* 200–5.

12 Anne Royall, *Sketches,* 239: On the speed between New York and Philadelphia, see *NR,* December 10, 1825.

13 *John Adams, Treasurer of New York Hospital, v. CV,* June 27, 1826, file 1826-20, Court of Common Pleas, NYCC. See also *Minutes of the Common Council of the City of New York, 1784–1831,* vol. 9 (New York: City of New York, 1917), for a reference to the *Legislator'*s owners requesting permission to extend the Marketfield Street dock (the one shared by the two boats) on June 21, 1824; CV filed a petition opposing the request on July 1. The dock was constructed in 1808 by none other than AO; see AO to Peter Dobbs, August 23, 1808, Aaron Ogden Papers, Misc. Files, NYPL.

14 *EP,* June 3, 1825.

15 Andrew Burstein, *America's Jubilee* (New York: Alfred A. Knopf, 2001), 3, 8–14; A. Levasseur, *Lafayette in America in 1824 and 1825; or, Journal of Travels in the United States,* vol. 1 (New York: White, Gallagher & White, 1824), 8–10. For another fine study of this transition between generations, see Joyce Appleby, *Inheriting the Revolution: The First Generation of Americans* (Cambridge, Mass.: Harvard University Press, 2000).

16 Benedict, 270.

17 Burstein, *America's Jubilee,* 50. Cornelius Jeremiah was born in 1830, the first George Washington in 1832, the second (the first died in infancy) in 1839; Verley Archer, *Commodore Cornelius Vanderbilt, Sophia Johnson Vanderbilt, and Their Descendents* (Nashville: Vanderbilt University, 1972), iv.

18 See the correspondence for 1824 and 1825 in GP; for examples of the Union Line recordkeeping, see the GP-R; see also the toll books of the Trenton and New Brunswick Turnpike Company, folds. 9B and 10, box 3, NP. CV's testimony appears in *Den D. Trumbull et al. v. Gibbons,* April 10, 1849, 22 NJ L 117, 16.

19 On Gibbons's death, see the Account Book, 1826, GP; *EP,* May 17, 1826. On the completion of the canal and subsequent celebrations, see Burrows & Wallace, 429–32; Edward Countryman, "From Revolution to Statehood (1776–1825)," in Milton M. Klein, ed., *Empire State: A History of New York* (Ithaca: Cornell University Press, 2001), 229–305. On the deaths of Adams and Jefferson and the Jubilee celebrations, see Burstein, *America's Jubilee,* 228–86.

20 *Den D. Trumbull et al. v. Gibbons,* April 10, 1849, 22 NJ L 117, 16, 32–3. For evidence of CV's ongoing management of Union Line business, see GP-R and the

Trenton and New Brunswick Turnpike Company Toll Books, folds. 9B and 10, box 3, NP. For insight into WG, see WG to CV, March 14, 1832, WG to George Jenkins, June 30, 1827, WG to James Parker, October 26, 1827, WG to George Jenkins, October 30, 1827, WG to Elias Van Arsdale, November 15, 1827, WG to Robert L. Stevens, October 26, 1828, WG to Robert Baylies, November 23, 1828, WG to E. A. Stevens, November 30, 1828, WG to William Halsted, December 2, 1828, WG to Phineas Withington, January 30, 1829, WG to E. Hall, February 6, 1829, WG to Robert L. Livingston, February 18, 1829, WG to Thomas J. J. Lefevre, Matthew C. Jenkins, and James T. Watson, February 23, 1829, GP. On Americans' still-emerging views of corporations, see Pauline Maier, "The Revolutionary Origins of the American Corporation," *WMQ*, 3rd ser., vol. 50, no. 1 (January 1993): 51–84; Naomi R. Lamoreaux, "Partnerships, Corporations, and the Limits on Contractual Freedom in U.S. History: An Essay in Economics, Law, and Culture," in Kenneth Lipartito and David B. Scilia, eds., *Constructing Corporate America: History, Politics, Culture* (Oxford: Oxford University Press, 2004), 29–65.

21 *EP,* August 27, 1825, June 2, 1826 (the description of the *Emerald* appears in a Union Line ad); Robert T. Thompson, *Colonel James Neilson: A Business Man of the Early Machine Age in New Jersey, 1784–1862* (New Brunswick, N.J.: Rutgers University Press, 1940), 269–72; entries for August 1828, May 3–6, 1829, Farm Diary, box 14, NP.

22 *EP,* November 6, 1826; *SEP,* November 11, 1826; Entries 162 and 252, April 28, 1826, Abstracts Licenses Enrolled, July 1, 1825, to December 31, 1829, vol. 13041, New York Custom House Records, RG 41, NA.

23 *NYT,* November 13, 1877; *NYW,* November 13, 1877. On CV's continuing obsession with horses, see WG to Samuel B. Parkman, March 16, 1827, GP.

24 *NYW,* November 13, 14, 1877.

25 Alexis de Tocqueville (George Lawrence, trans.), *Democracy in America* (New York: HarperCollins, 1988, orig. pub. 1966), vol. 2, part 3, chap. 6, 580.

26 *CV v. Patrick Rice,* November 26, 1827, file 1827-#1360, Court of Common Pleas, *Patrick Rice v. CV,* November 26, 1827, file 1827-#1671, Court of Common Pleas, NYCC.

27 *NBF,* July 29, 1829 (which shows Jacob Vanderbilt as captain of the *Citizen*); *New-York and Richmond Free Press,* July 6, 1833; Entry 37, July 10, 1828, Enrollments, 1818–1821, vol. 2169, Perth Amboy Custom House Records, RG 41, NA; subscriber list, New Brunswick Coal Association, Rariton Coal Mining Company, fold. 47, box 4, NP. For CV's dealings with William Gibbons, see citations from GP, next endnote.

28 Lane, 52; *EP,* July 8, 1828; *NBF,* July 29, 1829; *New-York and Richmond Free Press,* July 6, 1833; Entry 37, July 10, 1828, Enrollments, 1818–1821, vol. 2169, Perth Amboy Custom House Records, RG 41, NA; WG to CV, March 14, 1832, WG to George Jenkins, June 30, 1827, WG to James Parker, October 26, 1827, WG to George Jenkins, October 30, 1827, WG to Elias Van Arsdale, November 15, 1827, WG to Robert L. Stevens, October 26, 1828, WG to Robert Baylies, November 23, 1828, WG to E. A. Stevens, November 30, 1828, WG to William Halsted, December 2, 1828, WG to Phineas Withington, January 30, 1829, GP. On the view of corporations as trade-restricting organizations, see Maier, "The Revolutionary Origins of the American Corporation," and WG to E. Hall, February 6, 1829, WG to Robert L. Livingston, February 18, 1829, WG to Thomas J. J. Lefevre, Matthew C. Jenkins, and James T. Watson, February 23, 1829, GP. Lane, 49, repeats a tale popularized by Croffut, 34, that CV decided to leave the line to become an independent operator, to Gibbons's protest; when CV refused an offer to become his partner in the Union Line, Gibbons then sold the boats. For early renderings of this story, see *HW,* March 5, 1859, and *MM,* January 1865. The Gibbons Papers show there is no truth to it.

29 Lane, 49; *NBF,* July 29, 1829; *Trenton Emporium and True American,* July 11, 1829 (which appears to show that the *Emerald,* which had been sold and rebuilt, now operated on the Delaware). CV began to pay tolls on the Trenton and New Brunswick Turnpike for the Dispatch Line as early as May 1829; see the Trenton and New Brunswick Turnpike Company Toll Book, fold. 11, box 3, NP.

30 The *Gazette* story was quoted in the *SEP,* May 2, 1829. On the heavy-handed ways of captains and the shifty world of the waterfront, see a story about freelance porters in *EP,* September 23, 1824. CV did not move out of New Brunswick until some time in 1830, contrary to Lane's account; see the farm diary and James Neilson to George Able, January 28, 1830, fold. 17, box 3, NP. CV's ownership of bank stock is notable, a sign of his interest in investment opportunities and ease with banks and corporations; but it should be noted that New York was far in advance of the rest of the country in abandoning exclusive practices in both lending and stock ownership, with women and artisans trading shares and receiving loans (though bank chartering remained highly political). See Robert E. Wright, "Bank Ownership and Lending Patterns in New York and Pennsylvania, 1781–1831," *BHR* 73, no. 1 (spring 1999): 40–60; Naomi R. Lamoreaux, "Banks, Kinship, and Economic Development: The New England Case," *JEH* 46, no. 3 (September 1986): 647–67; Naomi R. Lamoreaux and Christopher Glaisek, "Vehicles of Privilege or Mobility? Banks in Providence, Rhode Island, During the Age of Jackson," *BHR* 65, no. 3 (autumn 1991): 502–27.

31 David R. Johnson identifies 1830 as a turning point in the response to professional criminals, in *Policing the Urban Underworld: The Impact of Crime on the Development of the American Police, 1800–1887* (Philadelphia: Temple University Press, 1979), 12–15, 41–3. Allan Stanley Horlick, *Country Boys and Merchant Princes: The Social Control of Young Men in New York* (Cranbury, N.J.: Associated University Presses, 1975), 45, 26, 89.

32 Appleby, *Inheriting the Revolution,* 1–2; William Austin, *Peter Rugg, the Missing Man* (Worcester: Franklin P. Rice, 1882, orig. pub. 1824), 52–3.

33 Royall, 243–4; Patricia Cline Cohen, *The Murder of Helen Jewett: The Life and Death of a Prostitute in Nineteenth-Century New York* (New York: Alfred A. Knopf, 1998), 62. On the expansion of New York, see Burrows & Wallace, 429–528; Countryman, in Milton Klein, 295–316; Eric Homberger, *The Historical Atlas of New York City: A Visual Celebration of Nearly 400 Years of New York City's History* (New York: Henry Holt, 1994), 68–72.

34 Daniel Walker Howe, *What Hath God Wrought: The Transformation of America, 1815–1848* (New York: Oxford University Press, 2007), 525–42. As L. Ray Gunn notes, 39, "Wherever its influence was felt, the transportation revolution literally remade society"; see also 19, 23–56. See also Martin Bruegel, *Farm, Shop, Landing: The Rise of a Market Society in the Hudson Valley, 1780–1860* (Durham: Duke University Press, 2002), 159; Wood, 305–47; *EP,* May 17, 1826. For the "Yankee principle" quote, see *New York Illustrated Magazine of Literature and Art,* September 20, 1845. An excellent summary of the impact of the transportation revolution on local economies, and the subsequent rise of manufacturing for national markets in New England, is provided by Douglass C. North, *The Economic Growth of the United States, 1790–1860* (New York: W. W. Norton & Co., 1966), 156–76. On the relative lack of immigration in the 1820s, see Tyler Anbinder, *Five Points: The 19th-Century New York City Neighborhood That Invented Tap Dance, Stole Elections, and Became the World's Most Notorious Slum* (New York: Free Press, 2001), 42–3, who notes, "Immigration increased enormously after 1830. . . . The foreign-born population expanded from 9 percent of the city's total in 1830 to 36 percent in 1845."

35 Bray Hammond, *Banks and Politics in America: From the Revolution to the Civil War* (Princeton: Princeton University Press, 1957), 145; William R. Taylor, *Cavalier and Yankee: The Old South and American National Character* (New York: George Braziller,

1961), 47–8; Trollope, 302, 352, 370. The emphasis on being "smart" is also noted by Clifford Browder, *The Money Game in Old New York: Daniel Drew and His Times* (Lexington, K.Y.: University Press of Kentucky, 1986), 38–9. On the New England migration to New York, see Edward K. Spann, *The New Metropolis: New York City, 1840–1857* (New York: Columbia University Press, 1981), 7; Horlick, 69–72; and Dixon Ryan Fox, who observes in *Yankees and Yorkers* (New York: New York University Press, 1940), 198, "It is safe to say that by 1830 the Yankee strain was becoming predominant in New York blood." On February 14, 1835, Philip Hone attended a meeting called to organize "a regular Knickerbocker society" to counter the influence of New Englanders; Hone, 148–9. On the impact of the decline of traditional authority and new geographical mobility on culture, see *Confidence Men*, esp. 1–15, 19–23. P. T. Barnum dedicated his book, *The Life of P. T. Barnum, Written by Himself* (New York: Redfield, 1855), to "the universal Yankee nation, of which I am proud to be one." In understanding the rise of the Yankee stereotype, it is worth quoting Gunn again, 27, "Traditional community values declined and were replaced by those of the marketplace. Informal, face-to-face relationships gave way to more formal and impersonal modes of human interaction."

36   Lane, 50–1; Lane, *Indian Trail*, 196–201; George Henry Preble, *A Chronological History of the Origin and Development of Steam Navigation, 1543–1882* (Philadelphia: L. R. Hamersly, 1883), 58–9; *NBF*, July 29, 1829; *Trenton Emporium and True American*, July 11, 1829; Trenton and New Brunswick Turnpike Company Toll Book, fold. 11, box 3, NP; Abstracts of Licenses Enrolled, January 1, 1830, to September 30, 1832, vol. 13044, New York Custom House Records, RG 41, NA. The *Bellona* cost CV around $15,000; see WG to E. Hall, February 6, 1829, GP.

37   On the Stevens family, see in particular Dorothy Gregg's excellent study, "John Stevens: General Entrepreneur, 1749–1838," in William Miller, ed., *Men in Business: Essays in the History of Entrepreneurship* (Cambridge, Mass.: Harvard University Press, 1952), 120–52. Robert L. Stevens introduced, among other things, the skeleton beam, a false bow, a hull-stiffening truss, and the placement of engines on platforms over the water; see Morrison, 29, 37–9, 48–51, 66. Hone visited Hoboken on May 21, 1831; Hone, 42. On the impending termination of the Citizen's Line, see WG to E. A. Stevens, November 30, 1828, GP.

38   "The New Jersey Monopolies," *NAR*, April 1867, 428–76; Lane, *Indian Trail*, 302–4; Gregg, 150–2. A fine survey is in Taylor, 74–90, esp. 89 and 101. For contemporary discussions of the Camden & Amboy monopoly, see *Workingman's Advocate*, August 16, 1834, and *NYH*, April 1, 1837.

39   Lane, 51–2; *HW*, March 5, 1859.

40   On WG's anxiety about the railroad, see WG to Robert L. Stevens, January 16, 1829, and WG to Robert Baylies, February 2, 1829, GP. Details of CV's previously unknown Sawpits venture appear in *Charles Hoyt v. John Brooks Jr.*, May 8, 1833, file BM 2163-H, Court of Chancery, NYCC; see also an advertisement in the *EP*, June 15, 1831, which notes that the *Fanny* also worked as a towboat, and *SEP*, April 23, 1831. Contrary to Lane's account, CV moved to New York from New Brunswick between January and September 1830; see James Neilson to George Able, January 28, 1830, and Farm Diary, fold. 17, box 3, NP, and entry for September 19, 1830, Hiram Peck Diary, NYHS. On the location of Sawpits, I am indebted to Alice C. Hudson, chief of the Map Division at the New York Public Library. See, for example, Joseph R. Bien, *Atlas of Westchester County, New York* (New York: Julius Bien, 1893), plate 47. On CV's address at this time, see Croffut, 279.

41   Frances Trollope, *Domestic Manners of the Americans* (New York: Alfred A. Knopf, 1949, orig. pub. 1832), 301. Many historians discuss the commercialization of American society during this period, including Gunn, 23–56; Wood, 325–69; Maier, 51–84; Appleby, *Inheriting the Revolution*, 56–89.

42   Entries for August 3, 11, September 17, 19, 21, October 13, 29, November 19, 1830,

July 18, 1831, Hiram Peck Diary, NYHS. On Captain Brooks's relationship to CV, see *Charles Hoyt v. John Brooks Jr.*, May 8, 1833, Court of Chancery, BM 2163-H, NYCC. It is possible that Peck was writing of a different Vanderbilt, as later he specified "Captain C. Vanderbilt"; however, the reference to Captain Brooks, among other hints, strongly suggests that he meant CV in these entries. Lorena S. Walsh discusses the evolving domestic life of middling Americans during this period, including diet, hygiene, and table manners, in "Consumer Behavior, Diet, and the Standard of Living in Late Colonial and Early Antebellum America, 1770–1840," in Robert E. Gallman and John Joseph Wallis, eds., *American Economic Growth and Standards of Living before the Civil War* (Chicago: University of Chicago Press, 1992), 217–61. On the new social dilemma of the untrustworthiness of one's fellow Americans, see especially *Confidence Men*, 31–53.

43 On Cornelius J. Vanderbilt's birth, see *Richmond County Advance*, April 15, 1882. On the children's lingering resentment, see, for example, *NYS*, November 13, 1877; *NYW*, November 13, 14, 1877; *NYTr*, March 28, 1878.

44 On the life of Jackson, see Robert V. Remini, *The Life of Andrew Jackson* (New York: Penguin, 1988). For an insightful account of Jackson's personality, see Andrew Burstein, *The Passions of Andrew Jackson* (New York: Alfred A. Knopf, 2003).

45 Entry for *General Jackson*, November 2, 1830, Abstracts of Licenses Enrolled, January 1, 1830, to September 30, 1832, vol. 13044, New York Custom House Records, RG 41, NA; Heyl, 2:97–8; *EP*, June 8, 1831; *New York Commercial Advertiser*, June 20, 1831; *SEP*, June 11, 1831; Lane, 53–5. Lane mistakenly reads the *EP* article to mean that Jacob Vanderbilt himself had run to Peekskill for two years, whereas the Custom House records show that he enrolled as the *General Jackson*'s captain in November 1830.

46 *EP*, June 8, 9, 11, 14, 15, 1831; *SEP*, June 11, 1831; *New York Commercial Advertiser*, June 20, 1831; *Workingman's Advocate*, June 18, 1831; entry for June 8, 1831, Hone, 42–3; *New York Illustrated Magazine of Literature and Art*, September 20, 1845. For a useful summary of steamboat explosions during this era (including one on the *Bellona*, killing two, in 1825), see *The American Almanac and Repository of Useful Knowledge*, 1835.

47 *SEP*, June 25, 1831.

48 *SEP*, April 23, 1831; *Charles Hoyt v. John Brooks Jr.*, May 8, 1833, Court of Chancery, BM 2163-H, NYCC.

49 *SEP*, April 23, June 25, 1831; *Charles Hoyt v. John Brooks Jr.*, May 8, 1833, Court of Chancery, BM 2163-H, NYCC; entry for *Cinderella*, October 19, 1831, Abstracts of Licenses Enrolled, January 1, 1830, to September 30, 1832, vol. 13044, New York Custom House Records, RG 41, NA; Lane, 53; *New York Gazette* quoted in the *Workingman's Advocate*, September 10, 1831.

50 CFA, "A Chapter of Erie," *NAR*, July 1869; Henry Clews, *Fifty Years in Wall Street* (New York: Irving Publishing, 1908), 121; Smith, 131; Fowler, 127. It should be noted that this book will not cite the often-cited *Book of Daniel Drew*, a 1910 publication which purports to be a secret autobiography. I agree with Drew's biographer, Clifford Browder, who argues it is a fraud; see Browder's *The Money Game in Old New York: Daniel Drew and His Times* (Lexington: University Press of Kentucky, 1986). The *Book of Daniel Drew* was a hoax, and should be shunned by historians. Drew's son denounced the book on its publication, and declared that he had never seen his father write anything more than his signature; *NYW*, April 25, 1910.

51 *Walter Blair v. Daniel Drew*, March 10, 1831, file 1831-#87, Court of Common Pleas, and *Fitz G. Halleck v. Daniel Drew*, March 15, 1820, file 1820-#479, Court of Common Pleas, NYCC. Drew's overlordship of the livestock market is demonstrated by a report he sent to the *New York Farmer* for its 1831 issue.

52 *HW*, March 5, 1859; *EP*, August 12, 1831; Heyl, 3: 337–8. On Drew, see Browder, esp. 32–9, and J. M'Clintock, "Daniel Drew, Esq. of New York," *Ladies' Repository*,

September 1859. See entries for *Water Witch*, September 20, 1831, May 26, 1832, and *Fanny*, June 14, 1831, Abstracts of Licenses Enrolled, January 1, 1830, to September 30, 1832, vol. 13044, New York Custom House Records, RG 41, NA.

53 *Charles S. De Forest v. Tunis Egbert, Francis Perkins, Preston Sheldon, and Helmus M. Wells*, March 5, 1852, box SI-68, Supreme Court, Richmond County, NYMA; entries for July 5, September 12, 15, 18, Hiram Peck Diary, NYHS; *NR*, July 28, 1832; *EP*, January 17, May 1, 2, 1832; *NYS*, November 14, 1877; *NYW*, November 14, 1877.

54 Entries for July 5, September 12, 15, 18, Hiram Peck Diary, NYHS.

55 *Charles Hoyt v. John Brooks Jr.*, May 8, 1833, Court of Chancery, BM 2163-H, NYCC; Heyl, 5: 293–4.

56 *EP*, June 12, 13, and 15, 1833; Trollope, 345; *American Turf Register and Sporting Magazine*, December 1833; Hone, 42. On CV's manner, see the testimony of Dr. Jared Linsly, *NYS*, November 14, 1877. On New York's new elite, see Burrows & Wallace, 452–72.

57 *Ariel*, April 16, 1831; *NR*, September 28, 1833. On December 18, 1832, Hone found it worth recording that the Camden & Amboy was complete; Hone, 85. On the early craze for railroads, see especially Taylor, 74–94.

58 John H. White Jr., *The American Railroad Passenger Car* (Baltimore: Johns Hopkins University Press, 1978), 3–6, 8; *EP*, November 9, 11, 13; *NR*, September 28, November 16, 1833; *Hazard's Register*, November 16, 1833; *NYS*, November 14, 1877; *NYW*, November 14, 1877. On early locomotives used by the Camden & Amboy (including, most famously, the John Bull), see John H. White Jr., *American Locomotives: An Engineering History, 1830–1880* (Baltimore: Johns Hopkins University Press, 1968).

Four Nemesis

1 In addition to other sources cited below, see *NYT*, August 7, 1876.

2 *NYW*, November 14, 15, 1877; *NYS*, November 14, 15, 1877.

3 Daniel Walker Howe, *What Hath God Wrought: The Transformation of America, 1815–1848* (New York: Oxford University Press, 2007), 373–95; see also Charles Sellers, *The Market Revolution: Jacksonian America, 1815–1846* (New York: Oxford University Press, 1991), 313–32. Historians long debated whether Jackson and Jacksonian Democrats favored entrepreneurial capitalism or desired a primitive agrarian economy. The Consensus School claimed that Americans across the political spectrum were essentially in agreement that a market economy was good, as best argued by Bray Hammond in the still-valuable *Banks and Politics in America from the Revolution to the Civil War* (Princeton: Princeton University Press, 1957), 326–457. Other scholars from the same era depicted Jackson as a forefather of New Deal policies; see especially Arthur M. Schlesinger Jr., *The Age of Jackson* (Boston: Little, Brown, 1950), 74–131. A later wave of scholarship claimed that Jacksonians resisted the market economy; see especially John Ashworth Sellers, *"Agrarians" and "Aristocrats": Party Political Ideology in the United States, 1837–1846* (New Jersey: Humanities Press, 1983), and, with more specific focus, Sean Wilentz, *Chants Democratic: New York City and the Rise of the American Working Class* (New York: Oxford University Press, 1984). More recent scholarship has to some degree returned to the view that Jacksonians favored a market economy, though with greater subtlety than the Consensus School. See in particular Michael J. Connolly, *Capitalism, Politics, and Railroads in Jacksonian New England* (Columbia: University of Missouri Press, 2003), as well as John M. McFaul, *The Politics of Jacksonian Finance* (Ithaca: Cornell University Press, 1972), 1–15, and Peter Temin, *The Jacksonian Economy* (New York: Norton, 1969). I am very much in agreement with Howe, 364, who writes, "Eco-

nomic enterprise generally became controversial only when government became involved." For sources that document Jackson's financial policies, and his personal hostility to banking, see Herman E. Krooss, ed., *Documentary History of Banking and Currency in the United States* (New York: Chelsea House Publishers, 1965), 982–93, 1055.

4   The literature on Jacksonianism is vast. Unfortunately, even some of the best historians display a tendency to frown on Jacksonians as regressive or reactionary; see, for example, John Lauritz Larson's otherwise superb discussion in *Internal Improvement: National Public Works and the Promise of Popular Government in the Early United States* (Chapel Hill: University of North Carolina Press, 2001), 149–93, esp. 150, 192. In my claim that both Jacksonians and anti-Jacksonians favored markets, entrepreneurship, and development, I am in agreement with Howe, esp. 364, 501, and Connolly, 14. James L. Huston, *Securing the Fruits of Labor: The American Concept of Wealth Distribution, 1765–1900* (Baton Rouge: Louisiana State University Press, 1998), 83–151, offers a very insightful discussion of American economic culture (the "republican theory of wealth distribution," as he calls it), stressing that the antebellum economy was dominated by horizontal expansion and small producers, despite the attention given to industrialization. Sean Wilentz, *The Rise of American Democracy: Jefferson to Lincoln* (New York: W. W. Norton, 2005), 438, argues, "The Jacksonians opposed large government not because it burdened business but because they believed it was a creature of the monied and privileged few. . . . They aimed not to liberate private business interests from a corrupt government, but to liberate democratic government from the corrupting power of exclusive private business interests." This was unquestionably true, but they clearly wished to liberate individuals as economic actors from the unfair advantages of the wealthy "aristocracy"; laissez-faire was both an economic means to a political end and a desired economic end state. One of the most influential books to this day remains Marvin Meyers's *The Jacksonian Persuasion: Politics and Belief* (Stanford: Stanford University Press, 1960), which argues, 7–15, that the Whigs and the Democrats were "fraternal twins" in their faith in the market economy, but that Democrats conjured up "moral plots" to rally their followers. I believe that Meyers, as insightful as he is, fails to appreciate how seriously Jacksonians took the threat that government action might give rise to a privileged class.

5   "President Andrew Jackson's Veto Message Regarding the Bank of the United States, July 10, 1832," in *A Compilation of the Messages and Papers of the President* (New York: Bureau of National Literature, 1897); Daniel Webster in Krooss, 787–8.

6   Sellers, 324, 336; Huston, 134; William M. Gouge, *A Short History of Paper Money and Banking in the United States* (Philadelphia: T. W. Ustick, 1833), 42, 833–4; Gregory A. Mark, "The Personification of the Business Corporation in American Law," *University of Chicago Law Review* 54, no. 4 (autumn 1987): 1441–83; Naomi R. Lamoreaux, "Partnerships, Corporations, and the Limits on Contractual Freedom in U.S. History: An Essay in Economics, Law, and Culture," in Kenneth Lipartito and David B. Scilia, eds., *Constructing Corporate America: History, Politics, Culture* (Oxford: Oxford University Press, 2004), 29–65. For insight into the Jacksonian hatred of the artificial, see Lawrence Frederick Kohl, *The Politics of Individualism: Parties and the American Character in the Jacksonian Era* (New York: Oxford University Press, 1989), 35–8. Wilentz, *Rise of American Democracy*, 440–1, argues that hard-money Jacksonians were emphatically not economic primitivists who "aimed at turning back the clock," and often were as sophisticated as their opponents. There is a great deal of truth to this, yet I believe that Wilentz downplays their discomfort with economic abstractions. Even corporate figures had difficulty grasping them, as will be seen in later chapters of this book. However, I agree with Wilentz's argument, 511, 513, that Jacksonians envisioned a commercial economy of agricultural small producers, and distrusted speculation and credit.

7   *EP,* August 28, 1834; James Willard Hurst, *The Legitimacy of the Business Corporation in the Law of the United States, 1780–1970* (Charlottesville: University Press of Virginia, 1970), 30–43.

8   Huston, 134, 251–5; Pauline Maier, "The Revolutionary Origins of the American Corporation," *WMQ,* 3rd ser., vol. 50, no. 1 (January 1993): 51–84; *EP,* August 28, 1834; Gouge, 41–2. Ashworth notes correctly that Democrats embraced self-interest, Adam Smith, and laissez-faire, but argues incorrectly, in my view, that they could be summarized as "anti-entrepreneurial" and agrarian (e.g., 21, 51). Naomi R. Lamoreaux shows (as my own research does as well) that early corporations only slowly took on the characteristics cited here; see "Partnerships, Corporations, and the Limits on Contractual Freedom in U.S. History." The abstraction of economic reality and the cultural shock it induced is one of my central themes. On this topic, see Daniel J. Boorstin, *The Americans: The Democratic Experience* (New York: Random House, 1973), 414–6, who discusses "a new mystery, a new unintelligibility" of corporations—"this new metaphysic of property," as he calls it. Boorstin, however, focuses on the late nineteenth century, whereas I believe this was felt decades earlier. Joseph A. Schumpeter discusses the "evaporation of the substance of property" in *Capitalism, Socialism, and Democracy* (New York: Harper &Brothers, 1942), 156–8.

9   Krooss, 1026–7; Huston, 252; A. B. Johnson, "Advantages and Disadvantages of Private Corporations," *MM,* December 1850, 626–31 (italics added); Gouge, 42. Taylor, 242, offers an excellent brief discussion of the controversy over corporations, as does Kohl, 66, 96, and Ashworth, 79. The law also insisted on the centrality of the persons behind corporations; see Mark, "Personification." Meyers, 11, astutely notes, "Americans were boldly liberal in economic affairs, out of conviction and appetite combined, and moved their world in the direction of modern capitalism. But they were not inwardly prepared for the grinding uncertainties, the shocking changes, the complexity and indirection of the new economic ways."

10 Burrows & Wallace, 571–5; *EP,* November 13, 1833; *NYW,* November 14, 1877; Sellers, 332–7; Hone, 110–2. See also *NR,* November 2, 1833.

11 Howe, *What Hath God Wrought,* 537–36, esp. 582–84; Daniel Walker Howe, *The Political Culture of the American Whigs* (Chicago: University of Chicago Press, 1979), esp. 9–20, 181; Amy Bridges, *A City in the Republic: Antebelleum New York and the Origins of Machine Politics* (New York: Cambridge University Press, 1984), 19–24; Meyers, 12–5; Michael A. Bernstein, "Northern Labor Finds a Southern Champion: A Note on the Radical Democracy," in William Pencak and Conrad Edick Wright, eds., *New York and the Rise of American Capitalism: Economic Development and the Social and Political History of an American State, 1780–1870* (New York: New-York Historical Society, 1989), 147–67. As L. Ray Gunn notes in "The Crisis of Distributive Politics: The Debate over State Debts and Development Policy in New York, 1837–1842," Pencak and Wright, 168–201, the Democratic Albany Regency made active use of the state to promote development. Ashworth offers an astute interpretation of the Whig orientation, 54–68, and the Federalist legacy, 117–8. My view that many Whigs were suspicious of competition will be developed over the succeeding chapters.

12 *NYW,* November 14, 1877; *EP,* August 30, 1834, February 10, 1837. On CV's address at this time, see Croffut, 279.

13 *EP,* August 30, 1834, September 10, 1833; *Albany Argus,* March 15, 1834; *Charles Hoyt v. John Brooks Jr. and Others,* May 8, 1833, file BM 2163-H, Court of Chancery, and *James Ingham and James Leslie v. CV,* December 15, 1834, file 1834-#756, Court of Common Pleas, NYCC. On the *Water Witch,* see also *New York Illustrated Magazine of Literature and Art,* September 20, 1845.

14 Robert Stevens's brother, John C. Stevens, remained a member of the association. See Articles of Agreement between Robert L. Stevens and John C. Stevens, Anthony N. Hoffman, et al., December 1, 1832, fold. 13, box 34, Stevens Family

Papers, New Jersey Historical Society, Newark, N.J. The agreement was made with Anthony N. Hoffman, Michael Van Beuren, Smith Cutter, James Mason (owners of the *Ohio*, the *Constellation*, and the *Constitution*), Alsop Weed, Griffith P. Griffith, Le Grande Cannon (owners of the *Erie* and the *Champlain*), James A. Stevens (owner of the *Albany*), and Robert Dunlop (owner of the *DeWitt Clinton*).

15 *Albany Argus*, March 15, 1834, November 23, 1835, April 16, 1836; Gunn, 30; Martin Bruegel, *Farm, Shop, Landing: The Rise of a Market Society in the Hudson Valley, 1780–1860* (Durham: Duke University Press, 2002), 159–63; Morrison, 46, 68. CV's account appeared in a front-page advertisement in *EP*, August 30, 1834.

16 *EP*, August 30, 1834.

17 *EP*, August 28 and 30, 1834. On Leggett's new control of the *Post* and the Locofoco faction of Democrats with which he was aligned, see Burrows & Wallace, 518–22, 606–9, 621–5; Wilentz, *Chants Democratic*, 145, 235; Ashworth, 94–6. Connolly notes in his introduction that Jacksonian Democrats distinguished between enterprising businessmen, whom they favored, and "capitalists," another word for stock-jobbing speculators, whom they condemned.

18 *Albany Argus*, July 17, 1834; *New-York Mirror*, September 27, 1834.

19 *Albany Argus*, July 17, September 2, 1834; *New-York Mirror*, September 27, 1834; entries for September 14, 16, 1834, Hone ms.; Heyl, 5:203–5. Morrison, 68, reports that racing steamboats made "flying landings," putting passengers in a boat attached to a line and then sheering off, giving the passengers seconds to get out of the boat at the dock before the line yanked it away. Hone's description casts doubt on this, though landings were clearly rushed. The *Albany Argus*, October 23, 1835, reported that the *Champlain*, on the fastest-ever trip between New York and Albany, lost an average of two minutes for each landing, enough for a hurried stop at a pier.

20 *Albany Argus*, September 2, 3, 1834; *Albany Evening Journal*, November 7, 1834, March 27, 1835.

21 *NYH*, May 3, 1839; *NYT*, February 9, 1859. As will be seen, Daniel Drew adopted the People's Line name in June 1835 and began his own attack on the monopoly, eventually becoming its chief. See *Cincinnati Mirror*, May 16, 1835, and advertisements in the *Albany Argus* and *Albany Evening Journal* through 1835.

22 *EP*, June 4, 1835, January 20, 1840; *NYTr*, March 7, 1878; *New York Review*, July 1838.

23 *EP*, June 4, 1835, January 20, 1840; *NYTr*, March 7, 1878; *New York Review*, July 1838; Heyl, 5:167–9. Bishop and Simonson's shipyard was at the foot of Walnut Street; John H. Morrison, *History of the New York Ship Yards* (New York: Sametz & Co., 1909), 59. For Charles Simonson's marriage to Mary Vanderbilt, Cornelius's oldest sister, see *Staten Island Church Records*, 174. For an excellent account of steamboat and steamship construction, and an explanation of "hog" and "sag" problems, see Cedric Ridgely-Nevitt, *American Steamships on the Atlantic* (Newark, Del.: University of Delaware Press, 1981), 105–6.

24 The most forceful advocate of the notion that cotton drove the American economy is Douglass C. North, *The Economic Growth of the United States, 1790–1860* (New York: W. W. Norton, 1966), 66–74; see also 102, 113–7, 122–9 (quote on 129). On the "cotton triangle" between New York, Southern ports, and Europe, see Philip S. Foner, *Business and Slavery: The New York Merchants and the Irrepressible Conflict* (Chapel Hill: University of North Carolina Press, 1941), 6–14; Albion, 95–121. Wilentz, *Chants Democratic*, notes, 108, "the rising dominance of antebellum New York over American trade and finance is still staggering to contemplate."

25 For a capsule history of the rise of manufacturing in Massachusetts, see Kinley J. Brauer, *Cotton Versus Conscience: Massachusetts Whig Politics and Southwestern Expansion, 1843–1848* (Lexington: University of Kentucky Press, 1967), 8–11, and Taylor, 229–49. Banker William D. Lewis of Philadelphia wrote to James N. Paige and James K. Mills, two commission merchants of Boston, December 1839, "The South

& West require a certain quantity of your fabrics. The two greatest points of distribution are New York & this city," fold. 6, box 2, WDLP. New York also took large shipments of boots, shoes, and hats from New England; on March 18, 1842, WmC wrote to COH that "a large proportion of the freight is shoes and straw bonnets," fol. vol. 2, CFP. On the rise of finished textile manufacturing in New York, see Wilentz, *Chants Democratic,* 107–16.

26   Larson , 225–9. For more on early railroads and government attitudes toward them, see Taylor, 72–101. Alfred D. Chandler Jr. and Stephen Salsbury note that, as of 1850, only forty-one factories had a capitalization of $250,000 or more, though railroads routinely were capitalized at over a million dollars; "The Railroads: Innovators in Modern Business Administration," in Bruce Mazlish, ed., *The Railroad and the Space Program: An Exploration in Historical Analogy* (Cambridge, Mass.: MIT Press, 1965), 128–30. See also Edward Chase Kirkland, *Men, Cities, and Transportation: A Study in New England History, 1820–1900,* vol. 1 (Cambridge, Mass.: Harvard University Press, 1948), 111–4, 223–58; *MM,* December 1846.

27   Entry for April 11, 1836, Hone ms. Kirkland notes, 244, that in 1835, when the Boston & Providence was completed, four of its seven directors (including its president) were New Yorkers, and that 97 percent of its stock was held outside of Boston, most of it in New York. Hone noted in his diary on June 17, 1835, "A majority of the board are citizens of New York"; Hone ms. For details of the specie and bank bills carried by a typical Long Island steamboat, see a report on the loss of the *Lexington* in the *EP,* January 18, 1840, and stories about thefts, *ProvJ,* September 21, 1836, and *NYH,* October 3, 1836.

28   Kirkland, 121–6, 244; Morrison, 270; *ProvJ,* June 16, 1836; *EP,* January 20, 21, 24, 1840; Heyl, 2:139, 5:167–9. On the cost of the *Lexington,* see also CtP to WDL, April 22, 1838, fold. 2, box 2, WDLP.

29   *EP,* June 4, 1835, January 21, 1840; *New York Review,* July 1838; Kirkland, 1:23, 244; Morrison, 270; *Statement by the Boston and Providence Rail Road Corporation in Explanation of their Proceedings in Relation to Steamboats* (Boston: John H. Eastburn, 1838); *A Replication to a "Statement by the Boston and Providence Rail Road Corporation in Explanation of their Proceedings in Relation to Steamboats"* (n.p., n.d.). To put the *Lexington's* speed in context, see Taylor, 71, who notes, "The average rate of speed even of the faster steamboats before the Civil War was seldom greater than fifteen miles an hour."

30   Entry for June 17, 1835, Hone ms.; Kirkland, 1:23–4, 243–5; *BE,* April 21, 1842. The *Lexington* was also listed as a connecting boat to the railroad to Boston from New York in J. H. Colton, *Guide to Burr's Map of New York and Steam-Boat, Stage, Railroad, and Canal Register, &c., &c., &c., for the year 1835* (New York: J. H. Colton, 1835), 33. On the rise of Connecticut as a manufacturing state, see *MM,* December 1846. On fares, see *ProvJ,* April 8, May 28, October 4, 1836.

31   *ProvJ,* July 2, 1836.

32   *EP,* January 21, 1840; *ProvJ,* July 2, 1836; Charles Dickens, *American Notes for General Circulation* (New York: Penguin, 2000, orig. pub. 1842), 88. On interior accommodations of steamboats, see Kirkland, 1:24; *ProvJ,* October 13, 1836; and entry for April 11, 1836, Hone ms.

33   *ProvJ,* June 15, 1836; *JoC,* October 25, 1837; WmC to COH, July 31, 1841, fol. vol. 2, CFP; Edwin L. Dunbaugh, *Night Boat to New England, 1815–1900* (Westport, Conn.: Greenwood Press, 1992), 28–9, 41–2; *Nestor Houghton v. CV,* August 10, 1837, file BM V016-H, Court of Chancery, NYCC. The $74,000 price was equal to the net profits of the ferry for the preceding four and a half years. The purchasers, John H. Smith, Edward Kellogg, George Gault, Nestor Houghton, George Lockwood, Robert T. Haws, and Ephraim Corning, paid $10,000 in cash, plus six-, ten-, and eighteen-month promissory notes at 6 percent interest. CV agreed to supervise the installation of new boilers, and received free passage for himself and his family

on the boats. The agreement specified that the boats could not be run on the North River above New York, where CV had a line, but CV might have intended to prevent another conflict with the Hudson River monopoly.

34 *ProvJ*, June 15, September 21, October 3, 4, 12, 13, 1836, March 20, 22, 1837; *EP*, March 21, 1837.

35 Entry for April 11, 1836, Hone ms.; *New-York Mirror*, November 12, 1836; *ProvJ*, July 14, 1837.

36 CV to JWR, November 1836, RWG; Kirkland, 276–9.

37 *ProvJ*, January 23, 1837; JWR to CV, January 24, 1837, CV to JWR, January 30, 1837, CV to John Whipple, April 8, 1837, RWG; *Statement by the Boston and Providence Rail Road Corporation; A Replication;* Kirkland, 276–9.

38 *NYW*, November 14, 1877; *NYS*, November 13, 14, 1877; *NYTr*, March 28, 1878. On CV's new address, see the return address on CV to JWR, November 1836, RWG. It was then a respectable neighborhood, despite its proximity to Corlears Hook; see *NYT*, January 11, 1886.

39 Hone, 185–9; Burrows & Wallace, 596–8.

40 Burrows & Wallace, 598–602; Peter Temin, "The Jacksonian Economy," in Edward Pessen, ed., *The Many-Faceted Jacksonian Era: New Interpretations* (Westport, Conn.: Greenwood Press, 1977), 102–13; North, 198–201; Sellers, 338.

41 *NYH*, October 5, 1836; Burrows & Wallace, 529–41; Patricia Cline Cohen, *The Murder of Helen Jewett: The Life and Death of a Prostitute in Nineteenth-Century New York* (New York: Alfred A. Knopf, 1998), 61, 66, 104–5. A reference to businessmen playing whist about this time appears in J. R. Ingersoll to WDL, May 7, 1841, fold. 2, box 1, WDLP.

42 Burrows & Wallace, 567–9; Walter Licht, *Working for the Railroad: The Organization of Work in the Nineteenth Century* (Princeton: Princeton University Press, 1983), 9; *James Guyon and CV v. Moulton Bullock, James W. Otis, and Jonathan Prescott Hall*, March 16, 1838, file BM 1404-G, *CV v. John Martineau and Eliza, His Wife, and Anna B. Cook, Executrix of Richard M. Cook, Deceased*, September 13, 1839, file D CH 100-V, *CV v. John W. De Grauw and Jane, His Wife, Walter N. DeGrauw, John J. Stephens, and Others*, May 30, 1839, file D CH 104-V, Court of Chancery, NYCC. I speculate that he made other loans since these are only known because the borrowers defaulted; repaid loans do not appear in surviving records.

43 Sellers, 344; Hone, 228; North, 198–201. Temin sharply disputes the impact of Jackson's policies, though they undoubtedly contributed to the atmosphere of uncertainty.

44 *NYS*, November 13, 1877; *NYT*, November 14, 1877; JWR to CV, January 24, 1837, RWG.

45 *Nestor Houghton v. CV*, August 10, 1837, file BM V016-H, *James Guyon and CV v. Moulton Bullock, James W. Otis, and Jonathan Prescott Hall*, March 16, 1838, file BM 1404-G, *CV v. John Martineau and Eliza, His Wife, and Anna B. Cook, Executrix of Richard M. Cook, Deceased*, September 13, 1839, file D CH 100-V, *CV v. John W. De-Grauw and Jane, His Wife, Walter N. DeGrauw, John J. Stephens, and Others*, May 30, 1839, file D CH 104-V, Court of Chancery, NYCC; Hone, 247.

46 *ProvJ*, March 17, 20, 22, 1837; *EP*, March 21, 1837; *NYH*, April 1, 1837; Hone, 250.

47 Strong, 1:16–7.

48 *NYH*, April 1, 1837; Hone, 256; Taylor, 341–5.

49 The *New York Courier and Enquirer* noted, as quoted in the *ProvJ*, May 13, 1837, "The banks *will not* discount under present circumstances freely to good and safe men. They are afraid of each other. . . . Nearly every transaction is for cash." CV accumulated specie because it appears that passengers largely paid in coin. In part, this was because of his low fares—most banknotes were for denominations higher than a dollar (though "shinplasters," small-denomination banknotes, did proliferate during the panic). Comstock, it should be noted, complained that the Transporta-

tion Company's clerks were accepting too much "bad money" (WmC to COH, July 17, 1841, fol. vol. 2, CFP), but coin seems to have been demanded in most cases. *NYH*, June 13, 1845, observed that "railroad tickets . . . must be paid in specie."

50   For Allen's new office, see an ad in *NYH*, July 1, 1837. For details on his management of daily routine, see a lawsuit filed by a merchant who regularly shipped goods to customers in Connecticut by way of the *Cleopatra, Joseph Tobey v. CV,* October 15, 1839, file 1839-1291, Superior Court, NYCC.

51   *NYT*, February 6, 1910; LW Dictation.

52   *NYH*, July 1, 1837; *EP*, July 15, 1837.

53   *JoC*, October 25, 1837; *Norfolk Herald* quoted in *JoC*, November 30, 1837. Phillpot Woolfe was fare collector for the Staten Island Ferry in 1838; testifying in court in 1847 about Oorandates Mauran, the company president, he said, "We always understood him to be the general agent as well as the president. That is what we call 'Commodore.' His word was will there." See *Oliver Vanderbilt v. the Richmond Turnpike Company,* July 17, 1848, file 1848-1238, Superior Court, NYCC. JWR to CV, January 24, 1837, RWG. Elihu Bunker, a pioneer in the steamboat trade, was given the title "Commodore" in the press; *ProvJ*, June 15, 1836; Moses Beach, *Wealth and Pedigree of the Wealthy Citizens of New York City,* 3rd ed. (New York: New York Sun, 1842), 5.

Five Sole Control

1   *NYS*, March 9, 1878; *NYTr*, June 26, 1878; *NYT*, March 9, 1878. The descriptions of WHV and CJV appear in the *NYS*, November 15, 1877.

2   Alfred D. Chandler Jr., "Patterns of American Railroad Finance, 1830–50," *BHR* 28, no. 3 (September 1954): 248–63; Stonington Reports, 12, 22; WGM, Memorandum of Interview with C.V. in Relation to Steamers, November 14, 1840, fold. 1, box 3, WDLP; Edward Chase Kirkland, *Men, Cities, and Transportation: A Study in New England History, 1820–1900,* vol. 1 (Cambridge, Mass.: Harvard University Press, 1948), 246–8, 258. On early stockholder anxiety over the company's debts, see Alexander Hamilton to WDL, January 1, 1838, fold. 2, box 2, WDLP. Hone took the Stonington soon after its opening, and highly approved of it; Hone, 358. Lane, who has a weakness for repeating unsubstantiated anecdotes, includes the claim that CV hated railroads, 58–9, 73, following Croffut, 71.

3   *EP*, January 22, 1840; *JoC*, November 30, 1837.

4   *NYS*, November 13, 1877, December 9, 1885; *NYW*, November 14, 15, 1877; LW Dictation.

5   *NYTr*, December 9, 1885; Morrison, 54; Clifford Browder, *The Money Game in Old New York* (Lexington: University Press of Kentucky, 1986), 42–4. Two letters clearly show that Drew had become a dominant figure in the Hudson River monopoly: Jonas C. Heartt [Troy] to CtP, September 10, 1840, CtP to Jonas C. Heart, September 12, 1840, fold. 8, box 2, WDLP. I am making a judgment that CV and Drew made an agreement to invest in each other's businesses based on evidence relating to numerous shared enterprises over the next three decades, as will be shown below.

6   *NR*, November 2, 1833; *New York Courier and Enquirer* quoted in *ProvJ*, May 13, 1837; *New-Yorker*, March 31, 1838; *NYS*, December 9, 1885; *NYTr*, December 9, 1885. For detailed examples of the sort of financial transactions that Drew, Robinson & Co. engaged in, see *Daniel Drew v. Bates Cooke,* September 8, 1840, file BM 1233-D, Court of Chancery (a case involving Drew's demand that the state of New York's safety fund sell bonds in order to redeem notes of the Millers' Bank), *Isaac Schuyler v. Daniel Drew, Nelson Robinson & Co.,* October 27, 1841, file BM S-476, Court of Chancery, *Isaac Spencer Jr. v. Daniel Drew, Nelson Robinson, Robert W. Kelley, and Daniel B. Allen,* March 20, 1848, file 1848-#951A, Court of Common Pleas,

NYCC. CV's investment in the People's Line, and the relationship between the various steamboat proprietors on the Hudson, is detailed in *Curtis Peck v. Daniel Drew*, January 7, 1850, file PL-1850-P-3, Supreme Court Pleadings, NYCC. When the People's Line reorganized as a joint-stock association in 1843, CV held $11,500 out of $360,000 in the company's shares; Drew owned $108,500. Though this case does not confirm CV's earlier involvement, circumstantial evidence points to his participation as early as 1838. For additional commentary on William's place in Drew, Robinson & Co., see a letter from CJV to CV, August 25, 1874, quoted in *New York Sunday News*, January 6, 1878, Vanderbilt Will Trial Case Clippings, NYPL.

7 *Boston Advertiser and Patriot*, quoted in *Maine Farmer*, July 31, 1838; Frederick Gardiner to Charles Gill, September 6, 1838, Rare Book and Manuscript Collections, Carl A. Kroch Library, Cornell University.

8 CtP to WDL, March 26, 30, April 1, 4, 1838, fold. 2, box 2, WDLP.

9 Entry for Courtland Palmer in James Grant Wilson and John Fiske, eds., *Appleton's Cyclopedia of American Biography* (New York: D. Appleton, 1887–89); CtP to WDL, April 18, 22, 26, May 3, 1838, fold. 2, box 2, WDLP; LW Dictation; Stonington Reports, 13.

10 CtP to WDL, January 9, 1839 (misdated 1838), June 6, 1838, fold. 2, CtP to WDL, November 22, 1838, fold. 3, box 2, CtP to WDL, August 13, 28, September 5, October 1, 22, 1838, Richard M. Blatchford to WDL, December 15, 1838, fold. 4, box 2, CtP to WDL, February 11, 1839, Joseph Cowperthwait to WDL, January 10, 1839, fold. 5, box 2, CtP to WDL, July 16, 1839, fold. 6, box 2, WDLP; Stonington Reports, 15–7; *EP*, January 20, 21, 1840.

11 CtP to COH, July 28, 1841, fold. 5, box 3, WDLP; WmC to COH, July 31, 1841, fol. vol. 2, CFP. The full sentence reads, "I had no confidence in him at the time the *Lexington* was purchased, and so stated."

12 *Richmond Turnpike Company v. Oliver Vanderbilt*, July 24, 1841, file BM 4-42, Court of Chancery, and *Oliver Vanderbilt v. the Richmond Turnpike Company*, July 17, 1848, file 1848-#1238, Superior Court, NYCC. These sources provide the quotations and incidents in the paragraphs that follow.

13 Enrollment No. 387, Port of New York Certificates of Enrolment [sic], vol. 12150, October 4, 1819, to February 26, 1820, Bureau of Marine Inspection and Navigation, RG 41, NA; *NYH*, January 3, 1839; *Richmond Turnpike Company v. Oliver Vanderbilt*, July 24, 1841, file BM 4-42, Court of Chancery, and *Oliver Vanderbilt v. the Richmond Turnpike Company*, July 17, 1848, file 1848-#1238, Superior Court, NYCC; *Petition of C. Vanderbilt for Confirmation of Letters Patent, Issued April 3, 1816* (New York: S. S. Chatterton, 1852), NYPL.

14 *ProvJ*, November 3, 1837; Hone, 261; *BE*, April 21, 1842; *NR*, May 17, 1845; John Ashworth, *"Agrarians" and "Aristocrats": Party Political Ideology in the United States, 1837–1846* (New Jersey: Humanities Press, 1983), 151–65. The key work to consult in regard to this point is Gunn, 112–3, 141.

15 *Richmond Turnpike Company v. Oliver Vanderbilt*, July 24, 1841, file BM 4-42, Court of Chancery, NYCC; *Richmond Turnpike Company v. Oliver Vanderbilt*, July 11, 1842, file L.J.-1842-N-66, Supreme Court Law Judgments, NYCC; *Petition of C. Vanderbilt*. On Westervelt, see RGD, NYC, 544:13.

16 *NYT*, January 4, 1882.

17 Hone, 403.

18 Francis J. Grund, *Aristocracy in America* (London: Richard Bentley, 1839), 20–4.

19 Dickens, 267–8.

20 Hone, 410; Moses Beach, *Wealth and Pedigree of the Wealthy Citizens of New York City*, 3rd ed. (New York: New York Sun, 1842), 3, 7, 12, 17. Beach relied on rumors to make estimates of his subjects' wealth, placing CV's at $250,000, Drew's at $200,000, Mauran's at $150,000, Hone's at $100,000, and John Jacob Astor's at $14 million. In the case of CV, this estimate is certainly much below his actual wealth; his

steamboats alone were likely worth substantially more. On Jacksonian attitudes toward entrepreneurship and stockjobbing, see Michael J. Connolly, *Capitalism, Politics, and Railroads in Jacksonian New England* (Columbia: University of Missouri Press, 2003), 1–19. Karen Halttunen is particularly enlightening on the moral meaning given the phrase "self-made man" in a society that had lost the traditional rules of conduct under the culture of deference; *Confidence Men*, 15–25.

21 CtP to WDL, August 11, 1841, fold. 5, box 3, WDLP; Hone, 415.

22 *NYT*, February 2, 1885.

23 *Liberator*, December 8, 1837. For Thorn (sometimes spelled "Thorne") as CV's attorney, see *Richmond Turnpike Company v. Oliver Vanderbilt*, July 24, 1841, file BM 4–42, Court of Chancery, NYCC.

24 *NYT*, January 4, 1882; *NYTr*, March 7, 1878; *Ladies' Companion*, February 1840; Hone, 453; *SEP*, January 18, 25, 1840; *EP*, January 20, 21, 25, 1840. On the *Lexington* tragedy, see almost any newspaper from the northeastern states from January 18 through 25, 1840, and Edwin B. Dunbaugh, *Night Boat to New England, 1815–1900* (Westport, Conn.: Greenwood Press, 1992), 60–4.

25 R. M. Whitney to WDL, November 12, 1840, fold. 1, box 3; CtP to WDL, August 4, 1841, fold. 5, box 3; WGM, "Memorandum of Interview with C.V. in relation to *Steamers*," November 14, 1840, fold. 1, box 3; WDLP; Kirkland, 121.

26 CtP to WDL, October 22, 1835, fold. 1, box 2; CtP to WDL, October 21, 1840, fold. 1, box 3; E. R. Biddle to WDL, May 9, 1844, fold. 5, box 4; J. Sherman to WDL, September 7, 1840, CtP to WDL, September 10, 1840, CtP to WDL, September 12, 1840, Jonas C. Heartt to CtP, September 10, 1840, CtP to Jonas C. Heart, September 12, 1840, fold. 8, box 2; CtP to WDL, January 24, 1841, fold. 2, box 3; WDLP. CtP remarked to WDL, "Our transfer clerk is not permited [sic] in any case to transfer stocks, unless the parties transfering [sic] have it in their names & it is never done"; CtP to WDL, October 5, 1840, fold. 1, box 3, WDLP.

27 *MM*, May 1840. On the cultural ramifications of, and sources of, the confidence man, see Halttunen's fine study. I am hardly the first to comment on the relationship between the new commercial world and Melville's fiction; see, for example, Steve Fraser, *Every Man a Speculator: A History of Wall Street in American Life* (New York: HarperCollins, 2005), 67–9. I wrote this commentary without reference to other works, however.

28 *NYT*, December 9, 1885; *NYTr*, April 13, 1878. In addition to a previous home at 173 East Broadway, CV owned a three-story brick "dwelling house" at 165 East Broadway, which he rented out in the early 1840s; *CV v. Henry N. Caldwell*, March 4, 1845, file 1845-#1669, Court of Common Pleas, NYCC.

29 *State of Indiana v. Daniel Drew, Nelson Robinson, Eli Kelly, Milton Stapp, William S. Dunham, and David Leavit*, August 20, 1841, file BM 19-I, Court of Chancery, NYCC; *NYH*, September 9, 1841; Larson, *Internal Improvement: National Public Works and the Promise of Popular Government in the Early United States* (Chapel Hill: University of North Carolina Press, 2001), 210–7, 226, 229, 233. Drew and Robinson sold far more than the canceled bonds without proper authorization; the *Herald* put the total at $629,000.

30 *NYT*, December 9, 1885; *NYTr*, April 13, 1878.

31 WGM to WDL, November 13, 1840, fold. 1, box 3, WDLP; Stonington Reports, 21–6.

32 Grund, 7–8; *EP*, January 25, 1840; *SEP*, June 1, 1839; *Army and Navy Chronicle*, April 25, August 1, 1839. The interview that follows is recorded in WGM to WDL, November 13, 1840, fold. 1, box 3, WDLP.

33 WGM to WDL, November 13, 1840, fold. 1, box 3, WDLP.

Six Man of Honor

1 Karl Marx, "The Eighteenth Brumaire of Louis Bonaparte," in Robert C. Tucker, ed., *The Marx-Engels Reader*, 2nd ed. (New York: W. W. Norton & Company, 1972), 594–617.

2 Chase Kirkland, *Men, Cities, and Transportation: A Study in New England History, 1820–1900*, vol. 1 (Cambridge, Mass.: Harvard University Press, 1948), 234–7, 246–9; CtP to WDL, August 12, 1841, fold. 5, box 3, WDLP. The William D. Lewis Papers offer abundant accounts of the turmoil within the corporation and deep resentment among the railroad's officers at the New Jersey Steam Navigation Company.

3 CtP to WDL, March 14, 1840, fold. 7, box 2, CtP to WDL, May 8, 1841, fold. 4, box 3, Courtland Palmer to WDL, July 3, 1841, fold. 5, box 3, WDLP; WmC to COH, May 8, 1841, fol. vol. 2, CFP; Edwin L. Dunbaugh, *Night Boat to New England, 1815–1900* (Westport, Conn.: Greenwood Press, 1992), 68–73. WmC wrote, "No doubt his object is to be bought off." Dunbaugh's book is generally useful, but due to his lack of research into correspondence of the different companies' officers he misses much of the maneuvering and payoffs behind the placement of boats on different routes.

4 Morrison, 328; Dunbaugh, 68–73; Francis B. C. Bradlee, *Some Account of Steam Navigation in New England* (Salem: Essex Institute, 1920), 89; CtP to WDL, May 19, 1841, WGM to CtP, June 7, 1841, CtP to WDL, June 18, 1841, fold. 4, box 3, CtP to WDL, August 4, 1841, fold. 5, box 3, WDLP; WmC to COH, June 24, 1841, fol. vol. 2, CFP. On CV's connection to the Hartford & New Haven Railroad, see an advertisement in *EP*, May 6, 1840.

5 WmC to COH, July 17, 29, 31, 1841, fol. vol. 2, CFP; CtP to WDL, August 4, 1841, fold. 5, box 3, WDLP.

6 WmC to COH, July 29, 1841, January 19, 26, 1842, fol. vol. 2, CFP; CtP to WDL, July 28, 1841, fold. 5, box 3, WGM to WDL, November 29, 1842, fold. 8, box 3, WDLP; *BE*, April 21, 1842. For reflections on the ongoing debate over corporations, see James Willard Hurst, *The Legitimacy of the Business Corporation in the Law of the United States, 1780–1970* (Charlottesville: University Press of Virginia, 1970), 30–43.

7 CtP to WDL, September 23, 1841, fold. 5, box 3, and December 16, 1841, fold. 6, box 3, WDLP; *ProvJ*, September 3, 13, 1842.

8 For an idea of how fuel costs loomed over other categories, see CtP to WDL, November 9, 1840, fold. 1, box 3, WDLP. This letter gives the monthly figure for fuel expenditures for a steamer to Stonington at $2,600, far above the next largest item ("wear & tear," at $1,000). On the unusual reliance on tips and incidental charges on this route, see an amusing complaint in the *Anglo–American*, September 11, 1847. For the quotations and other details, see WmC to COH, July 17, 29, 31, 1841, January 19, 26, February 2, 10, 23, March 1, 18, 19, April 12, 18, 19, May 19, 1842, fol. vol. 2, CFP.

9 WmC to COH, July 17, 29, 31, 1841, January 19, 26, February 2, 10, 23, March 1, 18, 19, April 12, 18, 19, May 19, 1842, fol. vol. 2, CFP; CtP to WDL, January 18, February 18, March 3, 6, 19, 29, June 26, 1842, WGM to WDL, April 9, 1842, fold. 7, box 3, WDLP. CV's maneuvers did not draw traffic away from the Hartford & New Haven, because that railroad did not yet have a through connection to Boston.

10 *Hugh McLaughlin v. CV*, December 12, 1843, Judgements, 1838–1848, box SI-66, Staten Island Court Papers, NYMA.

11 Meeting of February 16, 1842, Minute Book of the Elizabethport and New York Ferry Company, box 4, Central Railroad Company of New Jersey Papers, Hagley Museum and Library, Wilmington, Del.

12 *NYH*, September 22, 1841, October 24, 1842; Lane, 71; WmC to COH, August 29, 1842, fol. vol. 2, CFP; WGM to WDL, October 20, 1842, fold. 8, box 3, WDLP; Morrison, 328; Bradlee, 89–95. CV continued to call his line "Vanderbilt's Independent Line" through the end of September; *ProvJ*, September 13, 1842; *EP*, September 27, 1842.

13 Minutes for March 1, July 29, 1844, Minute Book of the Elizabethport and New York Ferry Company, box 4, Central Railroad Company of New Jersey Papers, Hagley Museum and Library, Wilmington, Del.; *Anglo-American*, June 22, 1844 (which shows Daniel Allen also selling tickets for steamboats to the Norwich Railroad at 34 Broadway).

14 *ARJ*, September 1844, February 20, 27, 1845; Long Island Railroad Company Directors' Minutes Book 1, 325, 344–50, 354, Long Island Railroad Company Directors' Minutes Book 2, 1, box 305, PennCentral Collection, NYPL. *ARJ*, February 27, 1845, discussed CV's sale of the three steamboats to the Long Island Railroad, and noted, "the former successful and experienced proprietor of these boats has taken a large interest in the company and participated in its management."

15 *Anglo-American*, April 19, 1845; meeting of April 8, 1845, Long Island Railroad Company Directors' Minutes Book 2, 16–7, box 305, PennCentral Collection, NYPL; CtP to WDL, April 16, 1843, fold. 2, box 4, WDLP. Immediately after completion, the Long Island Railroad did connect to the Stonington; however, director Elihu Townsend warned Lewis about a change that "seems to alter the state of feeling so far as relates to the former association"; Elihu Townsend to WDL, August 21, 1844, fold. 6, box 4, WDLP.

16 WGM to WDL, January 7, 1843, CtP to WDL, January 23, 1843, fold. 1, box 4, S. Jaudon & Co. to WDL, April 5, 1843, fold. 2, box 4, Richard M. Blatchford to WDL, July 23, 1843, WDL to H. G. Stebbins, July 31, 1843, fold. 3, box 4, WDLP; Stonington Reports, 32–9.

17 *New York, Providence, and Boston Rail Road Company v. Elisha Peck, Richard M. Blatchford, James Foster Jr., Henry G. Stebbins, Matthew Morgan, Samuel Jaudon, and William S. Wetmore*, January 3, 1848, file PL-1848-N-4, Supreme Court Pleadings, NYCC.

18 Samuel R. Brooks to WDL, October 9, 1845, fold. 6, box 4, WDLP; Stonington Reports, 41; WmC to COH, April 18, 19, 1842, fol. vol. 2, CFP. Though WmC's report was made three years earlier, its truth regarding the events of 1845 and 1846 were clearly born out. For contemporary evidence of Drew's partnership with Newton in Hudson River steamboats, see *Daniel Drew and Isaac Newton v. New York and Erie Rail Road Company*, September 10, 1842, file 1842-#331, Superior Court, and *Caleb F. Lindsley and George E. Cock v. Daniel Drew and Isaac Newton*, March 20, 1848, file 1848-#951A, Court of Common Pleas, NYCC (the latter referring to an incident in 1846); also entries for August 1846, pages 336–6, in vol. 2 of the William D. Murphy Account Books, NYHS.

19 *Curtis Peck v. Daniel Drew*, January 7, 1850, file PL-1850-P 3, Supreme Court Pleadings, NYCC; *Curtis Peck v. Daniel Drew*, January 31, 1848, file PL-1848-P 256, Supreme Court Pleadings, NYCC.

20 *Nelson Robinson, Robert W. Kelley, and Daniel B. Allen v. Daniel Drew and Isaac Newton*, June 27, 1848, file PL-1848-R, and *Nelson Robinson, Robert W. Kelley, and Daniel B. Allen v. Daniel Drew and Isaac Newton*, November 2, 1848, file PL-1848-R 2, Supreme Court Pleadings, NYCC.; Medbery, 312; Edmund Clarence Stedman, *The New York Stock Exchange* (New York: Stock Exchange Historical Company, 1905), 104. Interestingly, the court filings cited here make clear that manipulation of the road's traffic and its stock price were part of the initial investment plan.

21 *Boston Daily Advertiser*, July 3, 1845. For full sources for my analysis of CV's operation, see the next endnote.

22 *NYH*, July 4, September 26, 1845; *Boston Daily Advertiser*, July 3, 1845; *NYTr*, Octo-

ber 2, 1845, September 29, 1847; Stonington Reports, 46–50; Lane, 75. CV, it appears, rallied support among Drew and others by promising to challenge the legitimacy of the corporation's bonds, even though they represented a 50 percent reduction of the original debt. The argument used in court was that the original bonds were usurious and thus invalid, which would invalidate the compromised debt as well. The case never reached a decision. See *NYH*, cited above, and *New York, Providence, and Boston Rail Road Company v. Elisha Peck, Richard M. Blatchford, James Foster Jr., Henry G. Stebbins, Matthew Morgan, Samuel Jaudon, and William S. Wetmore*, January 3, 1848, file PL-1848-N-4, Supreme Court Pleadings, NYCC.

23 *ARJ*, October 10, 1846; *Seventeenth Annual Report of the Board of Directors to the Stockholders of the Hartford & New Haven R. R. Co.* (Hartford: Case, Tiffany, 1852); *HC*, September 10, 1846.

24 *NYH*, July 4, September 26, 1845, September 30, 1847; *NYTr*, October 2, 1845, September 29, 1847; Stonington Reports, 46–50. Regarding the dates of Drew's takeover of the Navigation Company: on August 7, 1846, WmC wrote a letter to COH; on August 17, he wrote to R. E. Lockwood, Drew's secretary, asking him to show the letter to Drew; fol. vol. 2, CFP.

25 *NYTr*, October 31, 1844.

26 Daniel Walker Howe, *What Hath God Wrought: The Transformation of America, 1815–1848* (New York: Oxford University Press, 2007), esp. 570–612; Sean Wilentz, *The Rise of American Democracy: Jefferson to Lincoln* (New York: W. W. Norton, 2005), 530–3; Howard Bodenhorn, "Bank Chartering and Political Corruption in Antebellum New York: Free Banking as Reform," in Edward L. Glaeser and Claudia Goldin, eds., *Corruption and Reform: Lessons from America's Economic History* (Chicago: University of Chicago Press, 2006), 231–57; Richard R. John, "Private Enterprise, Public Good? Communications Deregulation as a National Political Issue, 1839–1851," in Jeffrey L. Pasley, Andrew W. Robertson, and David Waldstreecher, eds., *Beyond the Founders: New Approaches to the Political History of the Early Republic* (Chapel Hill: University of North Carolina Press, 2004), 329–54; Richard R. John, *Spreading the News: The American Postal System from Franklin to Morse* (Cambridge, Mass.: Harvard University Press, 1999), 94–9, 242–3. Richard R. John stresses the pragmatic and nonpartisan considerations behind antebellum policy making; see Richard R. John, "Ruling Passions: Political Economy in Nineteenth-Century America," in Richard R. John, ed., *Ruling Passions: Political Economy in Nineteenth-Century America* (University Park, Penn.: Pennsylvania State University Press, 2006), 1–20.

27 Howe, 648–743; *NYTR*, November 1, 1844.

28 *NYTr*, October 31, November 1, 1844. On the dates, nature, and impact of Irish immigration, see Tyler Anbinder, *Five Points: The 19th-Century New York City Neighborhood That Invented Tap Dance, Stole Elections, and Became the World's Most Notorious Slum* (New York: Free Press, 2001).

29 Elliott J. Gorn, *The Manly Art: Bare-Knuckle Prize Fighting in America* (Ithaca: Cornell University Press, 1986), 69–79; Anbinder, 156–7, 159, 201–6; Burrows & Wallace, 633–5; Edward K. Spann, *The New Metropolis: New York City, 1840–1857* (New York: Columbia University Press, 1981), 24; *NYT*, May 14, 1845, February 4, 1849.

30 *NYT*, January 5, 1877. An example of how the press followed Yankee Sullivan is in *NYH*, May 14, 1845, as well as its story of February 4, 1849.

31 *NYH*, June 13, August 15, 1845, August 15, 1846; Grund, 212, 214. Halttunen's observations in *Confidence Men* (esp. 6–23, 93–4) of the disruptive impact of the market, the anonymity of Jacksonian society, and the importance of behavior in establishing gentility underscore the point I am trying to make about the artificiality of social status. On the *NYH*'s mixture of "fawning" and "exposé" in its high-society coverage, see Burrows & Wallace, 525–7, 640. The idea that Jacksonian America experienced a great deal of social mobility was attacked by Edward Pessen; see espe-

cially *Riches, Class, and Power Before the Civil War* (Lexington, Mass.: D. C. Heath, 1973). However, Frederic Cople Jaher, *The Urban Establishment: Upper Strata in Boston, New York, Charleston, Chicago, and Los Angeles* (Urbana: University of Illinois Press, 1982), 160–250, illustrates the extreme instability of the upper stratum following the end of the culture of deference. Pessen's point is well taken here, as many of the antebellum wealthy came from prosperous backgrounds. However, not all belonged to the old aristocratic families of the eighteenth century; the old aristocracy disappeared as a functional category, breaking the grip of a select group of families on wealth and power. Eric Homberger, *Mrs. Astor's New York: Money and Social Power in a Gilded Age* (New Haven: Yale University Press, 2002), 3, is interested in the period that followed the downfall of the culture of deference, in the ways in which a highly unstable social elite sought to write and enforce rules of status. As my discussion will show, this issue pertains to my analysis as well, but I am more concerned with the new distinction between a *fashionable* elite and a *functional* one.

32 *NYH*, March 2, 1840; Homberger, 135–42.

33 Book of Minutes 1, July 30, 1844, to March 18, 1891, box 1, New York Yacht Club Library and Archives, New York, NY.

34 Burrows & Wallace, 625–8, 635–8; Spann, 36–9, 55, 117, 132–3.

35 "The Islets of the Gulf," *Graham's American Monthly Magazine of Literature, Art, and Fashion*, January 1847; Dickens, 89, 91.

36 *BE*, June 5, 1845; *NYH*, July 2, 8, 19–21, 1845; *NYTr*, July 22, 1845; *BE*, June 5, 1845; Meetings of September 29, 1845, and October 10, 1846, Minute Book of the Elizabethport and New York Ferry Company, box 4, Central Railroad Company of New Jersey Papers, Hagley Museum and Library. It should be noted that the Richmond Turnpike Company's charter expired on April 1, 1844. On January 29, 1844, before the corporation formally dissolved, Mauran and CV assigned to themselves all of its property and leases, and continued the business as the Staten Island Ferry. See *People of the State of New York v. CV, Anthony Bird, Stephen Williams, Elias Butler, Jacob Van Cleef, and Jacob Arnold*, November 22, 1851, Supreme Court, Richmond County, box SI-68, NYMA.

37 *Liberator*, March 24, 1848; *NYT*, January 5, 1877; Eric Homberger, *The Historical Atlas of New York City* (New York: Henry Holt, 1994), 78, and *Mrs. Astor's New York*, 111–9.

38 *Phebe Vanderbilt v. Charles M. Simonson and His Wife, John K. Vanderbilt and Charles M. Simonson Junior, Executors, and Mary Simonson, Executrix of the Last Will and Testament of Cornelius Simonson, Deceased, and John K. Vanderbilt*, April 27, 1844, file D CH-177-V, Court of Chancery, *Jacob H. Vanderbilt and John Vanderbilt v. the People of the State of New York*, May 10, 1844, file PL-1844-P-424, Supreme Court Pleadings, *People of the City of New York v. Jacob H. Vanderbilt*, December 19, 1844, file 1844-771, Court of Common Pleas, NYCC; *NYT*, December 19, 22, 1877; *NYW*, November 14, 1877; *NYS*, November 14, 1877. CJV later testified that his first seizure came at the age of seven; *NYS*, December 22, 1877.

39 *NYW*, November 14, 1877; *NYS*, November 13, 14, 1877; *NYT*, November 13, 14, 1877.

40 *NYH*, August 15, September 7, 1846. See also *SA*, August 27, 1846; *NYTr*, June 1, August 15, 27, 1846; *MM*, September 1846; *ProvJ*, November 30, 1846. CV charged the Norwich Railroad about $160,000 for the *Atlantic*.

41 *NYW*, November 14, 1877; *NYS*, November 13, 14, 1877; *NYT*, November 13, 1877.

42 *ProvJ*, November 28, 30, December 2, 1846; *ARJ*, December 5, 1846; *Liberator*, December 4, 1846; *NYH*, November 29, 30, December 10, 1846.

43 *NYH*, June 2, 1847; *SA*, March 27, 1847; *HC*, September 10, 1846; Morrison, 312–3, 328; Heyl, 6:73–7.

44 Morrison, 312–3; WDL to CtP, March 6, 1843, fold. 1, box 4, WDLP.

45 Morrison, 312–3; *NYH*, September 5, 9, 1846, June 1, 1847; *EP,* June 1, 1847; *NYTr,* June 2, 1847.

46 *A Sketch of the Events of the Life of George Law* (New York: J. C. Derby, 1855); entry for George Law, *DAB; ARJ,* April 11, 1846; *David S. Manners and Lydia Roberts, Administrators of Samuel Roberts, Deceased, v. George Law and Arnold Mason,* March 18, 1854, file 1854-2117, Superior Court, NYCC; *Curtis Peck v. Daniel Drew,* file PL-1850-P 3, January 7, 1850, Supreme Court Pleadings, NYCC; Heyl, 2:185–6. He also served for a year as a director of the Long Island Railroad, starting in 1843; see Long Island Railroad Company Directors' Minutes Book 1, 274, 318, Penn-Central Collection, NYPL. Law actually owned the *Oregon* with A. P. St. John; see a lawsuit regarding the sinking and raising of the *Oregon* at Hell Gate, *Russell Sturgis v. George Law and Alanson P. St. John,* March 27, 1850, 1850-922, Superior Court, NYCC.

47 Morrison, 312–3; *NYH,* June 1, 2, 4, 1847; *EP,* June 1, 2, 1847; *NYTr,* June 2, 1847; *SA,* June 25, 1847; *Anglo-American,* June 5, 1847. On the telegraph, see *ARJ,* January 2, 1847. Lane, 76–7, eager as always to repeat undocumented anecdotes, reverses the reasons for the defeat, claiming that CV prevented a slackening of speed.

48 Hone, 801; *NYH,* June 26, 1847.

49 *Oliver Vanderbilt v. Richmond Turnpike Company,* July 17, 1848, file 1848-#1238, Superior Court, NYCC; Stonington Reports, 44–54; *EP,* November 18, 1848; Long Island Railroad Company Directors' Minutes Book 2, 41–3, 64, box 305, PennCentral Railroad Collection, NYPL. *ARJ,* August 5, 1848, quoting the *Hartford Times,* referred to the *Commodore* as a "magnificent and agile steamer."

50 *ARJ,* February 5, 1848; *Liberator,* March 24, 1848.

PART TWO COMMODORE

Seven Prometheus

1 *Memoirs of General William T. Sherman* (New York: Da Capo Press, 1984), 1:39–41.

2 Sherman, 1:39; John F. Marszalek, *Sherman: A Soldier's Passion for Order* (New York: Free Press, 1993), 4, 61–7.

3 Sherman, 1:40–1.

4 Strong, 1:272, 302, 341. The "rosewood and red satin" observation is Strong's. Karen Halttunen writes, in *Confidence Men,* 187, that "personal rituals of self-congratulation," a new "social formalism" seen in "the parlor theatrical" among the wealthy, started to emerge in the 1850s; obviously they emerged even earlier in New York.

5 *HC,* March 9, 1848; RGD, NYC, 374:1, entry dated May 26, 1853. The Mercantile Agency, founded in 1841 by Lewis Tappan, became R. G. Dun & Co. in 1859. Though the records of the firm, held at Harvard Business School's Baker Library, are titled R. G. Dun & Co., the company will be called the Mercantile Agency until 1859 in this narrative. See James D. Norris, *R. G. Dun & Co., 1841–1900: The Development of Credit Reporting in the Nineteenth Century* (Westport, Conn.: Greenwood Press, 1978). In all R. G. Dun & Co. citations, the bracketed words are simply expanded from abbreviation in the original (for example, "very" for "vy.").

6 On the aristocratic nature of CV's neighborhood, especially Astor Place and Lafayette Place, see Eric Homberger, *Mrs. Astor's New York: Money and Social Power in a Gilded Age* (New Haven: Yale University Press, 2002), 104–19.

7 *SA,* June 17, 1848; *Independent,* December 7, 1848; Stonington Reports, 44–54.

8 *New York Evangelist,* March 27, 1851; entry for March 7, 1848, Hone ms.

9 Stonington Reports, 52–8; *NYT,* September 23, 1852; *Curtis Peck v. Daniel Drew,* January 7, 1850, file PL-1850-P 3, *Curtis Peck v. Daniel Drew,* January 31, 1848, file

　　　PL-1848-P 256, and *Nelson Robinson, Robert W. Kelley, and Daniel B. Allen v. Daniel Drew and Isaac Newton,* June 27, 1848, file PL-1848-R, Supreme Court Pleadings, NYCC; RGD, NYC, 366:251, 300C.

10　RGD, NYC, 374:1, 341: 184; Medbery, 312; Minutes of the New York Stock and Exchange Board, vol. 4: 1851–1858, 248, New York Stock Exchange Archives. Decades later, Drew testified that he had often seen CV at Robinson's office; *NYW,* March 9, 1878. Medbery's excellent account vividly and clearly describes practices on the early stock exchange; see especially pages 21–8. On the cultural impact of commercial abstractions, see *Confidence Men,* 6–7.

11　For an excellent summary of the emergence of the corporation in antebellum America, see Gunn, 49.

12　For an important discussion of the vagueness and permeability of the distinction between corporations and partnerships, see Naomi R. Lamoreaux, "Partnerships, Corporations, and the Limits on Contractual Freedom in U.S. History: An Essay in Economics, Law, and Culture," in Kenneth Lipartito and David B. Scilia, eds., *Constructing Corporate America: History, Politics, Culture* (Oxford: Oxford University Press, 2004), 29–65. Gregory A. Mark notes that nineteenth-century courts refused "to recognize a corporate personality separate from the summed interests of the individuals who made up the corporation"; see "The Personification of the Business Corporation in American Law," *University of Chicago Law Review* 54, no. 4 (autumn 1987): 1441–83.

13　This discussion derives from a full reading of the evidence presented throughout this book. My interpretation of the profound shift in culture produced by the corporation and other commercial abstractions is informed by James L. Huston, *Securing the Fruits of Labor: The American Concept of Wealth Distribution, 1765–1900* (Baton Rouge: Louisiana State University, 1998), but I differ with his conclusion that "nothing that occurred in the years 1765 to 1880 drastically revised the revolutionary heritage" (149). I believe that the emergence of the business corporation, and the corresponding reaction, did drastically revise the revolutionary heritage, and did so long before "industrialization" fully arrived. In a broader cultural sense, Halttunen captures this anxiety over the hidden—an anxiety closely tied, I believe, to the emergence of commercial abstractions. Joseph A. Schumpeter discusses the "evaporation of the substance of property" in *Capitalism, Socialism, and Democracy* (New York: Harper & Brothers, 1942), 156–8.

14　Morton J. Horwitz, *The Transformation of American Law, 1780–1860* (Cambridge, Mass.: Harvard University Press, 1977), 136–7; Adam Smith, *The Wealth of Nations* (New York: Modern Library, 2000), book 1, chap. 6, 70.

15　John Lauritz Larson, *Internal Improvement: National Public Works and the Promise of Popular Government in the Early United States* (Chapel Hill: University of North Carolina Press, 2001), 225–55, esp. 243. See also Daniel Walker Howe, *What Hath God Wrought: The Transformation of America, 1815–1848* (New York: Oxford University Press, 2007), 557–69.

16　Soulé, 172, 174, 202, 214; H. W. Brands, *The Age of Gold: The California Gold Rush and the New American Dream* (New York: Doubleday, 2002), 62.

17　Sherman, 46.

18　Ibid., 56–60.

19　*MM,* April 1847.

20　Entries for March 22, September 6, 1848, Minute Book of the Elizabethport and New York Ferry Company, box 4, Central Railroad Company of New Jersey Papers, Hagley Museum and Library; *Petition of C. Vanderbilt for Confirmation of Letters Patent, Issued April 3, 1816* (New York: S. S. Chatterton, 1852), NYPL. On joint real estate holdings, see, for example, *Oroondates Mauran and CV v. Morris Woolf,* May 11, 1843, file 1843-#814, Court of Common Pleas, NYCC. I am indebted to Mr. Frank Mauran of Providence, Rhode Island, for information from Oroondates Mauran's account books.

21 *NYW,* November 14, 1877; entry for March 23, 1845, Strong, 1:257.
22 Polk quoted in T. J. Stiles, *Jesse James: Last Rebel of the Civil War* (New York: Alfred A. Knopf, 2002), 24; Strong, 1:337; Brands, 70.
23 Strong, 1:344; James G. King to Messrs Baring Bros. & Co., January 22, 1849, reel 41: Letters Received from New York, BB; James P. Delgado, *To California by Sea: A Maritime History of the California Gold Rush* (Columbia: University of South Carolina Press, 1990), 19, 27; *NYH,* April 19, 1849.
24 My guess that Daniel B. Allen created the scheme is based on the fact that he took the largest number of shares (three). See *Daniel B. Allen, Jeremiah Simonson, William McLean, Alexander H. Britton, WHV, Nathaniel Hayward, Henry Anderson, John Peck, and the Said Daniel B. Allen, Jacob H. Vanderbilt, and James Brady, Trustees of the California Navigation Company of New York, v. James H. Fisk and CV,* January 24, 1851, file PL-1851-A 17, Supreme Court Pleadings, NYCC. I will use the spelling "Corneil" for the diminutive for Cornelius J., as this was the spelling his wife later used; see *NYW,* December 22, 1877.
25 *NYTr,* March 28, 1878.
26 Larson, 240; John G. B. Hutchins, *The American Maritime Industries and Public Policy, 1789–1914* (Cambridge, Mass.: Harvard University Press, 1941), 358–63; Leonard D. White, *The Jacksonians: A Study in Administrative History, 1829–1861* (New York: Macmillan, 1954), 458. White notes, 450, that enthusiasm for federal subsidies for steamships that could be converted to naval use predated Polk's administration.
27 Kemble, 3, 7–19; Joseph B. Lockey, "A Neglected Aspect of Isthmian Diplomacy," *AHR* 41, no. 2 (January 1936): 295–305. For a review of federal subsidies for steamships overall during this period, see Hutchins, 348–68. Richard R. John notes in *Spreading the News: The American Postal System from Franklin to Morse* (Cambridge, Mass.: Harvard University Press, 1999), 94–9, 242–3, that the Post Office Department had long subsidized stagecoach lines, to the extent of hundreds of thousands of dollars per year; in 1845, though, Congress cut off such subsidies. As John's work makes clear, the Post Office is no small exception to the rule that the federal government largely left the economy alone prior to the Civil War. Though it had its critics in the Locofoco movement, essentially all parties embraced its expansive role, and the Democrats made it a tool of party building (see 213–4, 236–40). In size and in scale of corruption, however, the steamship subsidies appear to have dwarfed the stagecoach subsidies.
28 Mark W. Summers, *The Plundering Generation: Corruption and the Crisis of the Union, 1849–1861* (New York: Oxford University Press, 1987), 134; Kemble, 14–5, 19–20, 22–5; SED 50, 32nd Cong., 1st sess., vol. 8; SR 292, 36th Cong., 2nd sess., vol. 1; *Theodosius F. Secor and CM v. George Law,* May 22, 1861, file 1861-832, Superior Court, NYCC; *Western Journal of Civilization,* September 1852. The federal subsidies, and Sloo's assignment of his rights, were much more complicated than perhaps is suggested by this brief description. For example, the navy supervised construction of the vessels, which were on call for national service; and Sloo actually assigned his rights to a trusteeship run by Law, Roberts, and a representative of Sloo's interests. Sloo was to receive 10 percent of the annual profits of the five ships on the Atlantic.
29 *Theodosius F. Secor and CM v. George Law,* May 22, 1861, file 1861-832, Superior Court, NYCC; RGD, NYC, 342:300D; *A Sketch of Events in the Life of George Law* (New York: J. C. Derby, 1855).
30 *Curtis Peck v. Daniel Drew,* January 31, 1848, file PL-1848-P 256, Supreme Court Pleadings, NYCC. See also Summers's descriptions of Law's government dealings, 37, 159–60, and *NYT,* March 13, 1852.
31 Strong, 1:272, 348, 2:253; *NYT,* January 19, 1875; see also Moses Beach, *Wealth and Pedigree of the Wealthy Citizens of New York City,* 3rd ed. (New York: New York Sun, 1842), 3.
32 *NYT,* January 19, 1875; *New York Observer,* January 21, 1875.

33   Folkman, 14. On published accounts of the Nicaragua route, see, for example, *MM*, March 1847.

34   Ephraim George Squier, *Nicaragua: Its People, Scenery, Monuments, and the Proposed Interoceanic Canal* (New York: D. Appleton, 1856), 81, 98–9, 107; Orville W. Childs, *Report of the Survey and Estimates of the Cost of Construction of the Inter-Oceanic Ship Canal* (New York: William C. Bryant, 1852), 5.

35   Report of Robert Mills, HsR 145, 30th Cong., 2nd sess., vol. 2.

36   The quotes and descriptions of San Francisco are from Soulé et al., 214–26, 243–4; other information from *Daniel B. Allen, ors., v. James H. Fisk and CV,* January 24, 1851, file PL-1851-A 17, Supreme Court Pleadings, NYCC; *NYH*, December 29, 1877. See also Kevin Starr, *Americans and the California Dream, 1850–1915* (New York: Oxford University Press, 1973), 49–63, and Delgado, 75–81.

37   Soulé et al., ibid.; *Daniel B. Allen, ors., vs. Fisk, ibid.; NYT,* December 29, 1877.

38   *EP,* June 4, 1847; *CT,* February 11, 1861; *NYT,* December 27, 1855, February 4, 1861; Folkman, 16–7. The Mercantile Agency first reported on JLW in December 1853; see RGD, NYC, 374:97.

39   Minutes for March 24, 1849, Minute Book of the Elizabethport and New York Ferry Company, box 4, Central Railroad Company of New Jersey Papers, Hagley Museum and Library; JLW to JMC, March 29, 1849, vol. 3: Letters Received, January 15 to March 29, 1849, JMC-P.

40   JLW to JMC, April 3, 1849, vol. 4: Letters Received, March 30 to May 11, 1849, JMC-P; JMC to Ephraim G. Squier, May 1, 1849, HED 75, 31st Cong., 1st sess., vol. 10; Folkman, 17–8; Richard W. Van Alstyne, "British Diplomacy and the Clayton-Bulwer Treaty, 1850–60," *JModH* 11, no. 2 (June 1939): 149–83.

41   Groesbeck later testified that he had been Drew's broker since about 1848; *NYH*, March 26, 1868. He also stated that he had known Drew since about 1842; *NYT,* April 24, 1868.

42   Dispatch dated April 16, 1849, Manning, 3:316.

43   Manning, 3:360–5; HED 75, 31st Cong., 1st sess., vol. 10; *Terms of Contract Between the State of Nicaragua and the Atlantic & Pacific Ship Canal Company: Proposed by the Commissioners of the State of Nicaragua, at the City of León, in the State of Nicaragua, on the 27th Day of August, 1849* (New York: William C. Bryant & Co., 1849), copy in NYPL. The rival firm signed an agreement on March 14, 1849, but it was never ratified; see Squier, 262, 268. Interestingly, the rival firm attempted to sell its contract to CV's company; JLW to JMC, August 22, 1849, vol. 6: Letters Received, August 15 to October 20, 1849, JMC-P.

44   Burns, 2–7, 34–5, 39, 59, 67; Squier, 136–8.

45   Burns, 147–8, 156, 158, 161–2; Mary Wilhelmine Williams, ed., "Letters of E. George Squire to John M. Clayton, 1849–1850," *HAHR* 1, no. 4 (November 1918): 426–34; Manning, 3:534. See also Squier, 262, 268.

46   *USMDR*, November-December 1849.

47   Burns, 161–2; Richard W. Van Alstyne, "British Diplomacy and the Clayton-Bulwer Treaty, 1850–60," *JModH* 11: no. 2 (June 1939): 149–83; *USMDR*, November–December 1849.

48   Manning, 7:49.

49   Robert A. Naylor, "The British Role in Central America Prior to the Clayton-Bulwer Treaty of 1850," *HAHR* 40, no. 3 (August 1960): 361–82; Richmond F. Brown, "Charles Lennox Wyke and the Clayton-Bulwer Formula in Central America, 1852–1860," *The Americas* 47, no. 4 (April 1991): 411–45; G. F. Hickson, "Palmerston and the Clayton-Bulwer Treaty," *Cambridge Historical Journal* 3, no. 3 (1931): 295–303; Mario Rodriguez, "The 'Prometheus' and the Clayton-Bulwer Treaty," *JModH* 36, no. 3 (September 1964): 260–78; Squier, 263. For Squier's views of Chatfield, see Mary Wilhelmine Williams, ed., "Letters of E. George Squire to John M. Clayton, 1849–1850," *HAHR* 1, no. 4 (November 1918): 426–34; Manning,

3:534. The Nicaraguans communicated to the canal company their plans to move against the British in San Juan del Norte; see JLW to JMC, August 22, 1849, vol. 6: Letters Received, August 15 to October 20, 1849, JMC-P.

50 George L. Bernstein, "Special Relationship and Appeasement: Liberal Policy towards America in the Age of Palmerston," *Historical Journal* 41, no. 3 (September 1998): 725–50; Jasper Ridley, *Lord Palmerston* (London: Constable, 1970), 273.

51 *PS*, December 6, 1849; *National Era*, December 27, 1849; Richard W. Van Alstyne, "British Diplomacy and the Clayton-Bulwer Treaty, 1850–60," *JModH* 11, no. 2 (June 1939): 149–83; Mario Rodriguez, "The 'Prometheus' and the Clayton-Bulwer Treaty," *JModH* 36, no. 3 (September 1964): 260–78; JLW to Sir Henry Lytton Bulwer, New York, January 16, 1850, vol. 8: Letters Received, January 1 to April 9, 1850, JMC-P.

52 Allan Nevins, *The Ordeal of the Union*, vol. 1: *Fruits of Manifest Destiny, 1847–1852* (New York: Charles Scribner's Sons, 1947), 221, 255; JMC to [John J.] Crittenden, February 10, 1850, Clayton Misc. Mss., NYHS. On JLW's belief that he dictated the resulting treaty, see *NYH*, June 25, 1850. For insight on the political fever of the moment, see diary entry for January 26, 1850, Strong, 2:5. For Whig attitudes toward "British encroachments and aggressions in Central America," see *American Review*, February 1850.

53 Kemble, 36–9, 46–50.

54 Stonington Reports, 53. One possible reason for CV's loss of interest in the Stonington was the completion in 1848 of a continuous rail connection between Boston and New York, when the New York & New Haven connected to the HRR. Though the Stonington still offered faster and more comfortable transportation between the two cities, it was already clear that railroads had a tendency to drive out steamboats; see Thomas C. Cochran, *Railroad Leaders, 1845–1890: The Business Mind in Action* (New York: Russell & Russell, 1965, orig. pub. 1953), 23.

55 RGD, NYC, 374:193; *BE*, May 1, 1850; *NYTr*, October 1, 1850; Heyl, 6:259. On the organization and elaboration of the canal company and its successors, see *NYTr*, March 26, 1852. CV did not complete purchase of the shipyard until April 8, 1850, when he mortgaged the property for $43,680; *New York Life Insurance & Trust Co. v. CV, Freeman Campbell and Mary Ann, His Wife, Rutherford Moody and Eunice P., His Wife, Jacob J. Van Pelt and Sarah, His Wife, and Jay Jarvis, President of the Citizen's Bank*, September 25, 1855, file PL 1855-N14, Supreme Court Pleadings, NYCC. For a discussion of the steamships first built for the California business, see Cedric Ridgely-Nevitt, *American Steamships on the Atlantic* (Newark, Del.: University of Delaware Press, 1981), 103–14.

56 *NYH*, December 14, 1849.

57 Allan Pred, *Urban Growth and City-Systems in the United States, 1840–1860* (Cambridge, Mass.: Harvard University Press, 1980), 150.

58 *NYH*, December 17, 1849; Baughman, 6–9, 12–3, 44–63; *Theodosius F. Secor and CM v. George Law*, May 22, 1861, file 1861-832, Superior Court, NYCC. See also Squier's report on the progress made by the canal company, Manning, 3:510.

59 *NYTr*, January 5, 1850; *NYH*, January 9, March 10, 1850.

60 CM's reluctance to discuss his affairs was a subject of comment in the newspapers. See, for example, a transcription of an amusingly unenlightening interview, *NYT*, July 31, 1857.

61 CV to Hamilton Fish, February 7, 1850, vol. 18, Hamilton Fish Papers, LOC. For a reference to Robert Kelly, see Strong, 2:173.

62 *NYH*, February 22, 1850.

63 *NYH*, February 24, 1850; *NYTr*, April 24, May 25, 1850; *Charter and Act of Incorporation of the American Atlantic and Pacific Ship Canal Company and Treaty of Protection Negociated Between the United States and Great Britain* (New York: Globe Job, 1850), copy in NYPL; George L. Bernstein, "Special Relationship and Appeasement: Lib-

eral Policy towards American in the Age of Palmerston," *Historical Journal* 41, no. 3 (September 1998): 725–50; G. F. Hickson, "Palmerston and the Clayton-Bulwer Treaty," *Cambridge Historical Journal* 3, no. 3 (1931): 295–303; Burns, 178–9. JLW even irritated Bulwer; see JLW to Sir Henry Lytton Bulwer, February 25, 1850, vol. 8: Letters Received, January 1 to April 9, 1850, JMC-P.

64 Ephraim G. Squier to JMC, May 8, 1850, quoted in Mary Wilhelmine Williams, ed., "Letters of E. George Squire to John M. Clayton, 1849–1850," *HAHR* 1, no. 4 (November 1918): 426–34. JLW let it be known in the United States as well that he had drafted the treaty himself; see *NYH*, June 25, 1850.

65 *NYTr*, April 25, October 1, 1850; *BE*, May 1, 1850; see also entries for June 22 and July 10, 1850, William D. Murphy Account Books, vol. 3: 1849–1851, NYHS; *NYH*, July 9, 12, 1850.

66 *CV v. Jesse P. Wilson*, March 19, 1856, file 1856-2735, Superior Court, and *CV v. Mark Wadleigh and Calvin E. Knox*, June 24, 1857, file LJ-1857-W-173, Supreme Court Judgments, NYCC; entry for November 7, 1850, William D. Murphy Account Books, vol. 3: 1849–1851, NYHS; *RT*, September 19, 1850; Stonington Reports, 58.

67 Nevins, 1:333–5; Strong, 2:17.

68 *NYTr*, October 1, 1850. For a ship-by-ship review of all of CV's operations on the Atlantic, see Cedric Ridgely-Nevitt, *American Steamships on the Atlantic* (Newark, Del.: University of Delaware Press, 1981), 222–49.

69 Richard W. Van Alstyne, "British Diplomacy and the Clayton-Bulwer Treaty, 1850–60," *JModH* 11, no. 2 (June 1939): 149–83; Mario Rodriguez, "The 'Prometheus' and the Clayton-Bulwer Treaty," *JModH* 36, no. 3 (September 1964): 260–78.

70 Ralph W. Hidy, "The Organization and Functions of Anglo-American Merchant Bankers," *JEH* 1 (Supplement: *The Tasks of Economic History*) (December 1941): 53–66; Ralph W. Hidy, "The House of Baring and American Trade," *Bulletin of the Business Historical Society* 9, no. 5 (October 1835): 71–5.

71 JLW and H. L. Routh to Baring Brothers, Rothschild & Sons, Finlay Hodgson & Co., Capel & Co., Sir J. H. Pelly, George Peabody, Esq., London, July 21, 1852, vol. 10: Letters Received, January 1851 to August 1853, JMC-P; Baring Brothers to Thomas W. Ward, October 15, 1850, reel 63: Letterbook, April 1848 to April 1851, BB.

72 JLW and H. L. Routh to Rothschild & Sons, July 17, 1852, vol. 10: Letters Received, January 1851 to August 1853, JMC-P; *LT*, October 15, 16, 1850.

73 Baring Brothers to Thomas W. Ward, October 15, 1850, reel 63: Letterbook, April 1848 to April 1851, BB.

74 Ibid., and James G. King to Messrs Baring Bros. & Co., October 29, 1850, reel 41: Letters Received from New York, BB. On August Belmont and New York society, see Eric Homberger, *Mrs. Astor's New York: Money and Social Power in a Gilded Age* (New Haven: Yale University Press, 2002), 174–8.

75 Edward Harold Mott, *Between the Ocean and the Lakes: The Story of Erie* (New York: Ticker Publishing, 1908), 460; entry for February 3, 1849, Hone ms.

76 James G. King to Messrs Baring Bros. & Co, October 29, 1850, reel 41: Letters Received from New York, BB.

77 *NYH*, November 15, 1850; *Farmers' Cabinet*, October 31, 1850.

Eight Star of the West

1 *Zion's Herald and Wesleyan Journal*, October 8, 1850; Strong, 2:15–16.

2 *New York Evangelist*, January 3, 1850; *SA*, January 5, 1850; *Zion's Herald and Wesleyan Journal*, October 8, 1850.

3 McPherson, 64–77; Strong, 2:21–2.

4   *Littell's Living Age*, November 2, 1850.
5   SED 50, 32nd Cong., 1st sess., vol. 8; LW Dictation.
6   *NYH*, December 26, 27, 1850; entry for December 26, 1850, Joseph N. Allen Diary (Allen Diary), BL. See also *LT*, January 21, 1851.
7   See Allen's obituary, *NYT*, March 15, 1883.
8   Allen Diary; Ephraim George E. Squier, *Nicaragua: Its People, Scenery, Monuments, and the Proposed Interoceanic Canal* (New York: D. Appleton, 1856), 56, 72–4; *Harper's New Monthly Magazine*, December 1854. On CV's selection of Punta Arenas, see *NYH*, August 15, 1854.
9   Allen Diary. The *Orus* would soon be wrecked on the river; as a result, the vessel that CV piloted on this occasion has regularly been misidentified as the *Director*. See Lane, 92, and Folkman, 26. However, the Allen Diary makes clear that the *Director* was already on the lake.
10 Allen Diary; *HW*, March 5, 1859; *SA*, February 8, 1851; *NYH*, January 22, 1851.
11 Allen Diary; *NYTr*, March 21, 1851.
12 Squier, 136–8; Allen Diary.
13 Allen Diary; *NYTr*, March 21, 1851.
14 Allen Diary; *NYTr*, February 10, 1851; *NYH*, February 1, 27, 1851.
15 Allen Diary.
16 John Guthrie, *A History of Marine Engineering* (London: Hutchinson Educational, 1971), 17, 44, 60; Cedric Ridgely-Nevitt, *American Steamships on the Atlantic* (Newark, Del.: University of Delaware Press, 1981), 69, 98–101, 105–6, 153, 223; *LT*, March 18, 1851.
17 *NYH*, February 23, 1851; *LT*, March 18, 1851; *SA*, March 29, 1851. A Darius Davison supposedly accepted the bet; no more was ever heard of him.
18 SED 50, 32nd Cong., 1st sess., vol. 8; *Congressional Globe*, January 17, 1851.
19 *NYH*, March 6, 1851.
20 *NYT*, February 7, 1856; SED 50, 32nd Cong., 1st sess., vol. 8. Law also became a heavy investor in Aspinwall's Panama Railroad, the largest buyer of the company's bonds; see *NYTr*, June 16, 1851. For Law's efforts to improve the speed of the mail delivery under such threats as Vanderbilt's, see George Law to N. K. Hall, July 21, 1851, SR 326, 35th Cong., 1st sess., vol. 2. For details on the U.S. Mail and Pacific Mail assets and operations, see SR 292, 36th Cong., 2nd sess., vol. 1.
21 Daniel T. Rodgers, *The Work Ethic in Industrial America, 1850–1920* (Chicago: Chicago University Press, 1974), 19, notes, "As late as 1850 the centers of manufacturing remained the home and workshop."
22 RGD, NYC, 316:48, 81.
23 Heyl, 1:123, 219, 307, 331; *NYTr*, February 10, 25, May 27, 1851; *LT*, June 30, July 16, 23, 1851; P. T. Barnum, *Struggles and Triumphs; or, Forty Years' Recollections of P. T. Barnum* (Buffalo, N.Y.: Warren, Johnson, 1873), 362–3; John A. Butler, *Atlantic Kingdom: America's Contest with Cunard in the Age of Sail and Steam* (Washington, D.C.: Brassey's, 2001), 177–8. Tonnage figures tend to vary by source, and should be viewed as approximate.
24 *LT*, August 28, 1851; *AltaC*, August 31, September 2, 1851; Folkman, 29–30.
25 *LT*, August 28, 1851; *AltaC*, August 31, September 2, 1851; Folkman, 29–30. A debate raged over the Nicaragua route in the San Francisco newspapers in early September. Rabe's fellow passenger, Harris T. Fitch, found the crossing entirely satisfactory, and said that Rabe's complaints only started after he was forced to pay for the second half of his journey to California.
26 *NYTr*, August 1, 1851. Diplomat John Bozman Kerr confirmed that in July 1851 the Nicaraguan government was discussing a plan to annul the charter of the canal company; Manning, 4:265.
27 Burns, 43, 47; *NYTr*, September 5, 6, 24, October 7, 1851; Manning, 4:228–9, 235.
28 *NYTr*, October 7, 9, 1851. The bribe figure is from *NYTr*, December 2, 1851. Newspaper reporters in the mid-nineteenth century were not particularly exacting, but

these accounts fit with other reports of White's methods. See also White's testimony, *NYH*, October 17, 1856.

29 *Compilation of Executive Documents and Diplomatic Correspondence Relative to a Trans-Isthmian Canal in Central America*, vol. 2 (New York: Evening Post Printing, 1900), 714–7; Manning, 4:235–6; *NYTr*, September 5, 1851. Kerr's official correspondence is rife with racial judgments of the Nicaraguans; on March 15, 1852, for example, he wrote of "the ill-blood against each other, natural to mixed races"; Manning, 4:267.

30 *NYTr*, September 26, 1851.

31 *NYT*, November 15, 1851; *NYTr*, October 9, December 15, 1851; Manning, 4:256–7, 266–7; *James H. Quimby v. CV*, November 21, 1855, file 1855-1313, Court of Common Pleas, NYCC. On CV's percentage as ATC agent, see JLW's explanation in *George S. Salls v. CV*, November 17, 1856, file 1855-#1226, Court of Common Pleas, NYCC.

32 Soulé, 359–64, 379–85.

33 *MM*, December 1854; *NYT*, July 3, 1860; *Memoirs of William T. Sherman* (New York: Da Capo, 1984, orig. pub. 1875), 95–105, 118–24; Soulé, 626–30; Kemble, 71, 152–3, 206; Richard Maxwell Brown, *Strain of Violence: Historical Studies of American Violence and Vigilantism* (New York: Oxford University Press, 1975), 123–40.

34 James P. Delgado, *To California by Sea: A Maritime History of the California Gold Rush* (Columbia: University of South Carolina Press, 1990), 76–7.

35 CV to Jonas Winchester, October 15, 1851, Winchester Papers, California Historical Society. It is reported by two of William C. Ralston's biographers that CV asked him in 1851 to investigate a railroad proposed by a group of Californians; see David Lavender, *Nothing Seemed Impossible: William C. Ralston and Early San Francisco* (Palo Alto: American West, 1975), 58, and Julian Dana, *The Man Who Built San Francisco: A Study of Ralston's Journey with Banners* (New York: Macmillan, 1936), 41.

36 *People of the State of New York v. Cornelius Vanderbilt, Anthony Bird, Stephen Williams, Elias Butler, Jacob Van Cleef, and Jacob Arnold*, November 22, 1851, New York Supreme Court, box SI-68, NYMA; *NYT*, March 16, 21, 1853, February 12, 1855; Lane, 71.

37 *A Sketch of Events in the Life of George Law* (New York: J. C. Derby, 1855), 46; Kemble, 46–52, 55.

38 Kemble, 46, 54–7. As Kemble shows, the mail monopoly was immensely lucrative. In July 1850, Pacific Mail paid a dividend of 50 percent ($50 per share, with the par value of each share being $100). CV's competition cut fares from a high of $300 for first cabin to as low as $80.

39 *CV v. the New York and Staten Island Steam Ferry Company, William B. Townsend, George Law, John J. Boyd, Levi Cook, Robert C. Wetmore, Jeptha B. Parks, John Burgher, David Marfleet, Gottlieb Kiesele, and Henry M. Western*, August 23, 1851, New York Supreme Court, fold. 10, box 1, Ferry and Railroad Collection, Staten Island Institute of Arts & Sciences; *CV v. George Law and Others*, August 16, 1851, file CV-V-20, Supreme Court Pleadings, NYCC. The report of retaliation was published three decades later in an obituary of Jeremiah Simonson, *NYT*, February 13, 1887, which claimed that Simonson led the attack on Law's pier.

40 SR 326, 35th Cong., 1st sess., vol. 2; *LT*, October 25, 1851; Lane, 97; Kemble, 61.

41 *NYT*, November 27, 1851; Folkman, 33–4. Kemble, 61, who displays a clear bias in favor of Pacific Mail, shows that workers on the Panama route genuinely believed that the Nicaragua route was much worse. It was not, at least until the completion of the Panama Railroad in 1855. For an example of passengers publicly protesting conditions on the Nicaragua route, see *AltaC*, January 15, 1852. See also the testimony in *James H. Quimby v. CV*, November 13, 1854, file 1854-#1242, Court of Common Pleas, NYCC, and *James H. Quimby v. CV*, November 21, 1855, file 1855-#1313, Court of Common Pleas, NYCC.

42 *LT*, December 4, 1851.

43 *NYTr*, October 23, 1851.

44 LW Dictation; *LT,* December 4, 1851; *NYTr,* December 2, 1851.

45 *LT,* December 4, 1851; *NYTr,* December 2, 1851.

46 *LT,* January 2, 1852; Manning, 7:420; Mario Rodriguez, "The 'Prometheus' and the Clayton-Bulwer Treaty," *JModH* 36, no. 3 (September 1964): 260–78.

47 CV quoted in Rodriguez, "The 'Prometheus' and the Clayton-Bulwer Treaty"; Mary Wilhelmine Williams, *Anglo-American Isthmian Diplomacy: 1815–1915* (New York: Russell & Russell, 1965), 119–20.

48 SED 6, 32nd Cong., 1st sess., vol. 4; *LT,* December 17, 1851, January 2, 1852.

49 *LT,* December 17, 30, 1851, January 2, 1852; *NYT,* December 17, 1851, February 14, 1852; SED 6, 32nd Cong., 1st sess., vol. 4; SED 30, 32nd Cong., 1st sess., vol. 7; Manning, 7:73–4; *NYH,* December 6, 1851; Williams, 120–2.

50 *LT,* January 29, 1852; Manning, 7:448; Richmond F. Brown, "Charles Lennox Wyke and the Clayton-Bulwer Formula in Central America, 1852–1860," *The Americas* 47, no. 4 (April 1991): 411–45; Williams, 120–3. Rodriguez, in "The 'Prometheus' and the Clayton-Bulwer Treaty," notes that one reason the British recoiled so quickly is that the cabinet received a report that Greytown had become largely American in population, which made the dispute something of an internal U.S. affair.

51 *New York Evangelist,* August 28, 1873; *HC,* June 7, 1851; entry for August 4, 1851, Strong, 2:60. For evidence of Clark's early law practice, see Horace F. Clark to Lauristen Hall, July 20, 1839, Hall Papers, HL, and HFC Misc. File, NYPL. See also the entry for Charles Antonio Rapallo, *National Cyclopedia of American Biography* (New York: James T. White & Co., 1904). HFC's name appears in a list of Democratic leaders, *USMDR,* June 1851. I am indebted to Maira Liriano of the New York Public Library for finding the wedding date, which had long eluded me; see *EP,* April 7, 1848. For a vivid description of a typical fashionable New York wedding, see *Eclectic Magazine,* July 1850.

52 *CT,* June 21, 1873. For an earlier and more elaborate version of this story, see Medbery, 160–1.

53 *NYT,* December 22, 29, 1877; *Charles H. Wright v. Cornelius Vanderbilt Jr.,* January 21, 1856, file LJ-1856-V-100, Supreme Court Judgments, NYCC; *NYTr,* March 28, 1878. A reference to CJV's poor health appears in John P. Hale to Charles Sumner, March 18, 1854, Gilder Lehrman Institute of American History, NYHS.

54 *NYW,* November 13, 14, 1877.

55 Croffut, 58–9.

56 *NYH,* December 6, 7, 1851.

57 This information about CV's office and operations can be found in one thick file, *James H. Quimby v. CV,* November 21, 1855, file 1855-#1313, and *George S. Salls v. CV,* November 17, 1856, file 1855-#1226, both Court of Common Pleas, NYCC. See also Heyl, 1: 219. On Robert Schuyler, see *United States Magazine of Science, Art, Manufactures, Agriculture, Commerce,* July 15, 1854.

58 Senate Journal, 32nd Cong., 1st sess., January 27, 1852; *National Era,* March 4, 1852; *NYT,* February 5, 19, March 10, 29, 1852; *Farmer's Cabinet,* March 18, 1852; *BE,* February 26, 1852; Heyl, 1:307, 407, 413.

59 *A Sketch of Events in the Life of George Law* (New York: J. C. Derby, 1855), 46; F. N. Otis, *Isthmus of Panama: History of the Panama Railroad and of the Pacific Mail Steamship Company* (New York: Harper & Brothers, 1867), 33; *NYT,* April 6, May 19, 21, 1852.

60 *NYT,* February 7, 1856; MacDonald lawsuit. CV also collected 20 percent of the $35 Accessory Transit fare, as JLW explained in *George S. Salls v. CV,* November 17, 1856, file 1855-#1226, Court of Common Pleas, NYCC. For other commentary on the bitterness of the Law-CV rivalry, see *NYT,* July 19, 1852. CV himself noted that faster shipments of specie resulted in savings in interest payments; CV to WLM, October 10, 1853, vol. 43: Letters Received, September 28 to October 24, 1853, WLMP.

61 *NYT,* March 13, 1852.

62 *NYT,* March 31, 1852; *James H. Quimby v. CV,* November 21, 1855, file 1855-#1313, Court of Common Pleas, NYCC; *George S. Salls v. CV,* November 17, 1856, file 1855-#1226, Court of Common Pleas, NYCC.

63 *NYT,* July 7, 15, August 20, 1852; *Liberator,* July 9, 1852; *National Era,* July 15, 1852; *NYTr,* August 20, 1852; *BE,* February 26, 1853.

64 *NYTr,* March 30, April 3, August 13, 1852; Orville W. Childs, *Report of the Survey and Estimates of the Cost of Construction of the Inter-Oceanic Ship Canal* (New York: William C. Bryant, 1852); *NYH,* April 1, 1852; JLW and H. L. Routh, Commissioners of the American Atlantic & Pacific Ship Canal Co., to Baring Brothers, Rothschild & Sons, Finlay Hodgson & Co., Capel & Co., Sir J. H. Pelly, George Peabody, Esq., London, July 21, 1852, reel 9: Letters Received, 1849 to November 1853, BB.

65 *NYTr,* August 23, 1852.

66 *NYTr,* August 24, 25, 1852. The share total comes from testimony by company secretary Isaac Lea, *James H. Quimby v. CV,* November 21, 1855, file 1855-#1313, Court of Common Pleas, NYCC.

67 Joshua Bates to Baring Brothers, July 23, 1852, reel 9: Letters Received, 1849 to November 1853, BB. JLW's statements on his return were clearly fraudulent, so I believe my conclusion concerning his actions have a sound basis. My assumption that CV was not in on JLW's plan, however, is based on indirect evidence: his vocal hatred for JLW, which will be seen shortly, and the timing of his attack on the ATC stock, coming so soon after JLW's return. The newspapers published an accurate account of the mission to London in December; *NYT,* December 3, 1852.

68 *NYT,* April 6, 1855.

69 *NYT,* August 27, 1852; *NYH,* April 6, 1855.

70 *NYT,* March 29, August 27, 1852; *NYTr,* June 2, 1852; *NYH,* April 6, 1855; Manning, 4:266.

71 *NYT,* September 14, 18, 1852; RGD, NYC, 341:184; Medbery, 312. Decades later, Daniel Drew testified that he had often seen CV at Robinson's office; *NYW,* March 9, 1878.

72 *NYT,* September 18, 1852, April 6, 1855; *NYH,* April 6, 1855. For an excellent account of nineteenth-century Wall Street, in particular purchasing on margin, see Medbery, 53–61.

73 *EP,* November 17, 1852; *NYH,* November 18, 1852; *NYTr,* August 20, 1852, January 3, 6, 1853; *NYT,* November 19, 1852; Manning, 4:35–6, 325–7; *Compilation of Executive Documents and Diplomatic Correspondence Relative to a Trans-Isthmian Canal in Central America,* vol. 2 (New York: Evening Post Printing, 1900), 818–9.

74 *NYT,* October 4, 1852.

75 *NYT,* April 6, May 8, 1855; *NYTr,* September 27, 1852. To follow the history of these negotiations as they played out in the press, see *NYT,* September 25, 28, 1852; *NYTr,* September 25, 27, 1852. For the quote on Allen, see RGD, NYC, 343:316.

76 *NYT,* November 10, December 24, 1852. For a reference to "sick Transit," see *NYTr,* June 7, 1852.

77 *NYTr,* December 28, 1852, January 7, 1853; *NYH,* December 29, 30, 1852; *NYT,* December 30, 1852.

78 *NYH,* December 29, 1852; *NYT,* December 30, 1852.

79 *NYT,* December 30, 1852, February 15, 1853; *BE,* February 26, 1853.

Nine North Star

1 LW Dictation; *National Era,* April 6, 1854.

2 *NYH,* April 6, 1855.

3 *NYS,* November 13, 1877.

4   *NYT,* April 6, 1855.
5   *NYTr,* March 30, 1878.
6   John Overton Choules, *The Cruise of the Steam Yacht* North Star (New York: Evans & Dickerson, 1854), 17–8.
7   CV to Hamilton Fish, February 15, 1853, vol. 32, Hamilton Fish Papers, LOC.
8   *NYT,* January 21, February 15, 1853; *NYTr,* February 15, 1853. As a further sign of CV's closeness to CM, one source describes a fancy ball that CM hosted in 1852, attended by the family of CV's son-in-law William K. Thorn; David Lavender, *Nothing Seemed Impossible: William C. Ralston and Early San Francisco* (Palo Alto: American West, 1975), 60.
9   *ATC v. CKG,* September 13, 1858, file 1858-#53, Superior Court, NYCC; Deposition of Theodore A. Wakeman, MacDonald Lawsuit.
10 *BE,* February 26, 1853.
11 *NYTr,* March 18, 1878.
12 *NYT,* March 16, 21, May 20, 1853, February 12, 1855; *William McClean v. Minthorne Tompkins, the Staten Island and New-York Ferry Company, and Others* [inc. George Law and Sarah A., His Wife, HFC], Papers on Appeals: July 14, 1856, and November 3, 1856, Supreme Court, Second Judicial District, fold. 5, box 2, Ferry and Railroad Collection, Staten Island Institute of Arts & Sciences; RGD, NYC, 374:1; *Petition of C. Vanderbilt for Confirmation of Letters Patent, Issued April 3, 1816* (New York: S. S. Chatterton, 1852), NYPL.
13 *NYTr,* March 18, 1878. Note also that CV sold to Van Pelt extensive property on the East River, apparently the grounds on which the Simonson shipyard stood. See *New York Life Insurance & Trust Co. v. CV, Freeman Campbell and Mary Ann, His Wife, Rutherford Moody and Eunice P., His Wife, Jacob J. Van Pelt and Sarah, His Wife, and Jay Jarvis, President of the Citizen's Bank,* September 25, 1855, file PL 1855-N14, Supreme Court Pleadings, NYCC. Personal wealth was extraordinarily difficult to ascertain. My statement that the $11 million figure sounds accurate is based on a close examination of surviving evidence of CV's business transactions during this period. My belief that this would make him one of the wealthiest men in the country is based on an extensive reading of the RGD reports, as well as other sources.
14 *NYH,* April 29, 1853; *NYT,* March 11, 1853; *SA,* April 30, May 7, 1853. See also *CT,* May 4, 1853, and a quotation from the *New York Illustrated News,* April 9, 1853, in Choules, 18.
15 *NYTr,* June 2, 1852.
16 Quoted in *The Knickerbocker,* July 1853. See also Choules, 18–22.
17 *SA,* May 7, 1853.
18 *NYT,* April 15, May 13, 1853.
19 Choules, 28.
20 *Circular,* May 21, June 1, 1853; *NYT,* May 21, 1853; *SA,* May 28, 1853; Choules, 25–6; Richard Schell to WLM, May 21, 1853, vol. 37: Letters Received, May 14–30, 1853, WLMP.
21 Choules, 26; *NYT,* May 21, 1853; *Spirit of the Times,* June 25, 1853.
22 See CV's letter to this effect, *NYH,* September 28, 1853.
23 JLW to WLM, April 25, 1853, vol. 35: Letters Received, April 22 to May 2, 1853, WLMP.
24 *NYH,* May 28, 30, 1853.
25 *NYT,* July 21, 1853.
26 RGD, NYC, 341:184; Medbery, 312. RGD may have had its dates wrong; in July, Robinson was reported as the head of the "bull clique" in Erie; *NYH,* July 29, 1853.
27 *NYT,* March 16, 1852; *National Magazine,* March 1853; Tyler Anbinder, *Five Points: The 19th-Century New York City Neighborhood That Invented Tap Dance, Stole Elections, and Became the World's Most Notorious Slum* (New York: Free Press, 2001), 67–8, 245–9.

28 *NYH,* July 29, 1853.

29 *NYH,* June 17, 1853; *Spirit of the Times,* June 25, 1853; *NYT,* September 24, 1853.

30 Quotation in *Spirit of the Times,* June 25, 1853; Choules, 30, 245. The letter quoted in *Spirit of the Times* names no author, but some of the language is identical to that of Choules's book.

31 *CT,* June 21, 1853. For other coverage, see in particular press coverage in late June and early July, such as *Spirit of the Times,* June 25, July 2, 1853. On the *North Star's* tour in general, see Choules, passim.

32 Choules, 47, 49–51; Muriel E. Hidy, *George Peabody: Merchant and Financier, 1829–1854* (New York: Arno Press, 1978), 356. CV attempted to return the favor to Peabody, inviting him and other notables for a jaunt aboard the *North Star.* Also, though CV brought his own gold, Peabody facilitated his financial transactions in England. See George Peabody to CV, June 13, 1853, ser. I, letterbook 42, mss. 181, George Peabody Papers, Peabody Essex Museum, Salem, Mass.

33 Choules, 51, 56, 118, 145, 222–4, 241–3, 247–8, 262, 322. Powers's fee was named in *PS,* September 8, 1853.

34 RGD, NYC, 374:1; Choules, 32, 71.

35 LW Dictation; Croffut, 108.

36 Choules, 82, 103; Croffut, 108.

37 Choules, 324.

38 Choules, 351.

39 Croffut, 68–9.

40 Choules, 348–50.

41 *NYT,* August 12, 1853. *NYT* only referred to CM as "the Vanderbilt agent." The Nicaragua line was still known as the Vanderbilt line. The other plausible candidates, Daniel Allen and CKG, were in Europe and California, respectively.

42 *NYT,* August 12, 1853; *NYTr,* September 13, 1855; *Spirit of the Times,* August 11, 1849.

43 *NYT,* September 24, 1853; *NYH,* September 24, 1853.

44 *NYT,* January 5, 1877. Lane believed the letter was real and reprinted it without caveat, 109. Lane also wrote that CKG joined CM in ousting CV; as I will discuss in Chapter Ten, I believe that this was not the case. In this I am contradicting virtually every historical account of this episode.

45 *NYH,* September 28, 1853. In assessing CV's dispute with the ATC, Folkman, 53–5, concludes that CV was in the wrong—that he had pocketed roughly $500,000 during his agency. Simple theft was out of keeping with CV's personality or methods, whereas blatant lying was the hallmark of JLW. The numbers reported by the *NYH* during the airing of this argument cannot be trusted. The ATC later paid CV to settle the dispute—hardly the step to be expected from the victim of a half-million-dollar theft.

46 *NYTr,* September 30, 1853; *NYH,* October 27, 28, November 3, 1853. For CM's office, see an ad in the *NYT,* December 17, 1855. A curious debate arose in the *NYH,* October 31–November 2, 1853, over whether the ATC legally could own the steamships CV had sold it. Only a few papers from the lawsuit survive; see, for example, *CV v. ATC,* January 12, 1854, file PL 1854-V9, Supreme Court Pleadings, NYCC.

47 *Circular,* July 8, 1854; *NYT,* July 4, 1854; *USDM,* July 15, 1854; *HC,* July 10, 1854. On the loss of the *Independence,* see *AltaC,* April 1, 1853, and a report from the *San Francisco Whig,* reprinted in the *LT,* May 13, 1853.

48 *NYT,* October 12, 1853; *EP,* quoted in the *HC,* October 17, 1853; RGD, NYC, 341:184. Drew was not new to transactions with the Erie Railroad. As early as February 10, 1842, he and Isaac Newton supplied a steamboat connection to the Erie's terminus at Piermont; see *Daniel Drew and Isaac Newton v. New York & Erie Rail Road Co.,* September 10, 1842, file 1842-#331, Superior Court, NYCC.

49 LW Dictation.

50 *CV v. ATC*, January 12, 1854, file PL 1854-V9, Supreme Court Pleadings, NYCC; *NYH*, December 2, 7, 8, 1853; *NYTr*, December 9, 1853.

51 *NYH*, January 6, 7, 1854.

52 *NYT*, January 17, 23, 1854; *NYH*, November 11, 18, 1853. William Thorn held a mortgage on half the value of the *Uncle Sam* and *Yankee Blade*, for $130,000 advanced to Mills; I am assuming that Thorn, as CV's son-in-law, served as his agent in this matter. See RGD, NYC, 374:118.

53 Allan Nevins, *Ordeal of the Union*, vol. 2: *A House Dividing, 1852–1857* (New York: Charles Scribner's Sons, 1947), 50–1; CV to WLM, October 10, 1853, vol. 43: Letters Received, September 28 to October 24, 1853, WLMP.

54 Allan Nevins, *Ordeal of the Union*, vol. 1: *Fruits of Manifest Destiny, 1847–1852* (New York: Charles Scribner's Sons, 1947), 39–40, 160.

55 Joseph L. Williams, Washington, to James N. Reynolds, New York, January 23, 1854, quoted in HsR 2, 36th Cong., 2nd sess., vol. 1; *NYT*, January 17, 1854. For an example of Williams's lobbying, see *NYT*, July 26, 1852.

56 *NYT*, January 17, 1854.

57 Joseph L. Williams, Washington, to James N. Reynolds, New York, March 21, 1854, quoted in HsR 2, 36th Cong., 2nd sess., vol. 1; Croffut, 109.

58 JLW to WLM, February 22, 1854, vol. 48: Letters Received, February 6 to March 15, 1854, WLMP.

59 When Nicaragua threatened to tax specie shipments, for example, Marcy intervened; Manning, 4:395–7.

60 Folkman, 49, 54–9.

61 *NYT*, March 14, May 18, 1854.

62 *NYT*, July 25, 29, 1854; *NYH*, April 26, 1853; July 25, 1854; Folkman, 63–7; James M. Woods, "Expansionism as Diplomacy: The Career of Solon Borland in Central America, 1853–1854," *The Americas* 40, no. 3 (January 1984): 399–415; Nevins, *House Dividing*, 365–6. The destruction of Greytown followed on earlier conflicts with the municipality; on February 21, 1853, the town's authorities led a mob in an attack on Punta Arenas, which destroyed some of the ATC buildings. See SED 8, 33rd Cong., 1st sess., vol. 4; *Harper's New Monthly Magazine*, December 1854; *NYT*, March 16, April 14, 1853; *LT*, March 30, 1853; *National Era*, April 7, 1853. The outbreak of the Crimean War, and the fact that Greytown was largely American in population, muted the British response to the destruction of the town; see George L. Bernstein, "Special Relationship and Appeasement: Liberal Policy towards America in the Age of Palmerston," *Historical Journal* 41, no. 3 (September 1998): 725–50.

63 *CV v. William C. Moon*, June 7, 1854, file L J-1854-M-398, Supreme Court Judgments; *CV v. Reuben C. Stone*, September 12, 1854, file L J-1854-S-19, Supreme Court Judgments; *CV v. John C. Thompson and Minthorne Tompkins*, September 26, 1854, file J L-1854-T-172, Supreme Court Judgments; *CV v. Spring Valley Shot & Lead Manufacturing Company*, April 21, 1855, file L J-1855-S-206, July 26, 1855, file L J-1855-S-208, May 2, 1855, file L J-1855-S-212, Supreme Court Judgments; all NYCC. See also Loan Agreement from CV to Mary Parmelisa M. Van Winkle, April 1, 1854, CV-NYPL; LW Dictation. On Vanderbilt's openness to callers, see Smith, 123–4.

64 John P. Hale to Charles Sumner, March 18, 1854, Gilder Lehrman Institute of American History, NYHS; Henry Clews, *Fifty Years in Wall Street* (New York: Irving Publishing Company, 1908), 375–6; McPherson, 121–30.

65 *NYS*, December 19, 1877; *NYTr*, March 30, 1878.

66 *NYW*, November 14, 1877; *NYT*, May 31, 1854; *NYTr*, March 28, 1878. For Clark's settlement of the *North America* lawsuits, see a set of 128 cases with identical outcomes, such as *George J. Lathrop v. CV and Daniel Drew*, May 4, 1854, file L.J. 1854-v-131, Supreme Court Law Judgments, NYCC.

67 *EP* quoted in the *NYT*, June 1, 1854; *NYT*, July 7, 1854; *NYTr*, March 30, 1878.

CJV had gone to an asylum before, on his return from California. He later testified that CV had him arrested; *NYW*, December 20, 1877.

68 *NYS*, December 19, 1877, March 2, 1878.

69 Strong, 2:178; Smith, 169–70. Halttunen writes, *Confidence Men*, 166, "In the 1850s and 1860s, polite hypocrisy was achieving cultural legitimacy."

70 *EP* quoted in *HC*, July 3, 1854; *BM*, July 1854.

71 *NYT*, July 4, 1854; *EP*, quoted in *HC*, July 7, 1854.

72 *United States Magazine of Science, Art, Manufactures, Agriculture, Commerce*, July 15, 1854; *NYT*, July 6, 1854; *EP*, quoted in *HC*, July 7, 1854; *Circular*, July 8, 1854.

73 *United States Magazine of Science, Art, Manufactures, Agriculture, Commerce*, July 15, 1854; Strong, 2:178–9; *PS*, July 13, 1854.

74 *NYT*, February 3, 1855; *CV v. HRR*, July 16, 1858, file LJ-1858-N-41, Supreme Court Judgments, NYCC. See also entry for June 9, 1857, Directors' Minutes, HRR, reel 27, box 242, NYCRR. See also CV's letter to the *HC*, August 3, 1854.

75 *BM*, March 1856; *HC*, August 13, 1857; Smith, 171. See also *NYT*, March 11, 1856, and *New York Observer and Chronicle*, March 27, 1856.

76 *Indianola Bulletin* quoted in *Texas State Gazette*, May 27, June 17, 1854; *San Antonio Ledger*, June 15, 1854. See also *Texas State Gazette*, July 29, 1854; Baughman, 81. See also James P. Baughman, "The Evolution of Rail-Water Systems of Transportation in the Gulf Southwest, 1836–1890," *Journal of Southern History* 34, no. 3 (August 1968): 357–81.

77 *NYT*, July 18, 1854, February 7, 1856, July 12, 1860; *Home Journal*, April 8, 1854; RGD, NYC, 342:300. Kemble, 88, mistakenly places the time of Law's departure from the company in March 1853. Roberts also stood as the Whig candidate for mayor in 1852; *NYT*, October 30, 1852.

78 RGD, NYC, 374:118. The song, "Humbug Steamship Companies," is quoted in Kemble, 68; see also 69–71.

79 *NYH*, August 30, 31, September 1, 1854; *NYTr*, November 11, 21, 1855; *JoC*, November 21, 1855; *NYT*, February 7, 1856; *AltaC*, October 2, 1854; RGD, NYC, 374: 118; Folkman, 56–7.

80 *NYTr*, December 25, 1854.

81 *Weekly AltaC*, October 7, 1854.

Ten Ariel

1 LW Dictation.

2 For a complaint about the Staten Island Ferry, see *NYT*, February 12, 1855.

3 The story of the Erie is an oft-told tale. See John Steele Gordon, *The Scarlet Woman of Wall Street: Jay Gould, Jim Fisk, Cornelius Vanderbilt, the Erie Railway Wars, & the Birth of Wall Street* (New York: Weidenfeld & Nicolson, 1988), 94–107; Edward Harold Mott, *Between the Ocean and the Lakes: The Story of Erie* (New York: Ticker Publishing, 1908); CFA, "A Chapter of Erie," *NAR*, July 1869.

4 Mott, 105, 114–5; Alfred D. Chandler, *The Visible Hand: The Managerial Revolution in American Business* (Cambridge, Mass.: Harvard University Press, 1977), 81–94.

5 *NYH*, August 30, 31, 1854; *NYT*, September 5, 1854. On the lack of distinction between a corporation and its members and officers, see Naomi R. Lamoreaux, "Partnerships, Corporations, and the Limits on Contractual Freedom in U.S. History: An Essay in Economics, Law, and Culture," in Kenneth Lipartito and David B. Scilia, eds., *Constructing Corporate America: History, Politics, Culture* (Oxford: Oxford University Press, 2004), 29–65.

6 RGD, NYC, 341:184; *Daniel Drew and Isaac Newton v. New York & Erie Rail Road Co.*, September 10, 1842, file 1842-#331, Superior Court, NYCC.

7 *NYH*, August 30, 1854.

8   *NYT*, August 30, September 4, 5, October 16, 1854; *PS*, September 7, 1854; RGD, NYC, 340:13; Mott, 115, 125.

9   *NYT*, October 4, 1854; *NYH*, February 13, 1855.

10 John Steele Gordon, *A Thread Across the Ocean: The Heroic Story of the Transatlantic Cable* (New York: Walker & Company, 2002), 18–27; CV to Cyrus W. Field, [December 2?], 1855, Cyrus W. Field Collection, Morgan Library.

11 Croffut, 113.

12 John A. Butler, *Atlantic Kingdom: America's Contest with Cunard in the Age of Sail and Steam* (Washington, D.C.: Brassey's, 2001), 206–8. On the *Arctic* sinking, see *NYT*, October 12, 1854, and press coverage in general surrounding this date. The Collins Line was formally called the New York & Liverpool United States Mail Steamship Company.

13 *NYH*, quoted in *LT*, January 1, 1855.

14 *EP*, quoted in *NYT*, February 2, 1855; Croffut, 109–10. As noted above, CV estimated his own fortune at $11 million at the beginning of 1853. On wages, see *NYT*, August 9, 1858.

15 *NYT*, March 9, 1855.

16 Mark W. Summers, *The Plundering Generation: Corruption and the Crisis of the Union, 1849–1861* (New York: Oxford University Press, 1987), 104–6, 262; John G. B. Hutchins, *The American Maritime Industries and Public Policy: 1789–1914* (Cambridge, Mass.: Harvard University Press, 1941), 348–58.

17 Summers, 104–6, 262; Hutchins, 348–58; Butler, 175–6; *Western Journal of Civilization*, September 1852; *NYH*, February 28, 1855; *National Era*, March 8, 1855; Benjamin B. French to Henry F. French, September 5, 1852, reel 5, Benjamin B. French Papers, LOC; David Budlong Tyler, *Steam Conquers the Atlantic* (New York: D. Appleton-Century Company, 1939), 209–10. For a thorough discussion of the Collins Line's steamships, see Cedric Ridgely-Nevitt, *American Steamships on the Atlantic* (Newark, Del.: University of Delaware Press, 1981), 147–71.

18 My discussion is informed by John Lauritz Larson's analysis of the early fights over the transcontinental railroad, *Internal Improvement: National Public Works and the Promise of Popular Government in the Early United States* (Chapel Hill: University of North Carolina Press, 2001), 243–55.

19 *Circular*, February 8, 1855; *SA*, February 10, 1855.

20 For a review of these events, see T. J. Stiles, *Jesse James: Last Rebel of the Civil War* (New York: Alfred A. Knopf, 2002), 48–55; McPherson, 145–62.

21 *NYT*, February 16, 1855.

22 *NYT*, February 28, 1855; *NYTr*, March 9, 1855; Lane, 144–6.

23 *NYTr*, March 3, 1855.

24 *NYT*, March 2, 6, 1855.

25 *NYTr*, March 8, 1855. Croffut, 108, quotes Wardell as saying, "In dictating a letter to a clerk I never saw his equal."

26 David Herbert Donald, *Lincoln* (New York: Simon & Schuster, 1995), 154–61.

27 *NYT*, March 9, 1855.

28 *Circular*, April 5, 1855; *National Era*, April 5, 1855; Butler, 211–2. Vanderbilt exchanged another ship, the *Granada*, for the *North Star*; see *NYT*, February 7, 1856. On Torrance, see RGD, NYC, 341:167.

29 James Maurice to Jefferson Davis, February 7, 1855, James Maurice to General Joseph G. Totten, February 15, 1855, George W. Vanderbilt to Jefferson Davis, February 19, 1855, entry 214, reel 200, U.S. Military Academy Application Papers, Microfilm Publication M688, NA. See also George W. Cullum, *Biographical Register of the Officers and Cadets of the U.S. Military Academy at West Point, N.Y.*, vol. 2 (Boston: Houghton, Mifflin, 1891), 766–7; George W. Vanderbilt's index number is 1885.

30 *NYT*, March 24, 1855; *NYW*, December 20, 1877.

31 *NYH*, March 16, 1855; *NYT*, March 16, 17, 1855.

32 *NYW*, November 14, 1877; *NYT*, April 4, 1855.

33 *NYT*, January 18, May 29, August 7, 1855.

34 *NYT*, November 30, 1852, March 29, April 18, 1854.

35 *NYH*, March 4, 5, June 2, 1855.

36 *NYH*, April 17, 1855.

37 LW Dictation.

38 The notion of a highly partisan and politically engaged public has been challenged by Glenn C. Altschuler and Stuart M. Blumin, *Rude Republic: Americans and Their Politics in the Nineteenth Century* (Princeton, N.J.: Princeton University Press, 2000), who find that ordinary life was filled with ordinary life, not politics. In particular, they argue that the rise of mass politics alienated the wealthier and better educated voters—that "respectable people" found politics to be a "dirty trade," 84–5. This corrective is well taken, but clearly politics remained an important part of the culture in which CV was situated.

39 *NYT*, April 26, May 1, 1855, February 7, 1856.

40 *Circular*, April 5, 1855; *National Era*, April 5, 1855; *BE*, April 13, 1855; *NYH*, May 17, 1855; *SA*, June 23, 1855.

41 *LT*, August 1, 1855; *SA*, May 19, 1855.

42 Butler, 215–20; *Littell's Living Age*, May 15, 1858; *MM*, September 1858; Ridgely-Nevitt, 128–39, 156–7, 163.

43 *NYTr*, September 13, October 15, November 21, 1855; *NYT*, November 21, 1855; *Littell's Living Age*, December 8, 1855.

44 *NYH*, November 28, 30, 1855.

45 *JoC*, November 22, 1855; *NYTr*, November 27, 1855.

46 Even the extremely elitist George Templeton Strong deemed Marshall O. Roberts an example of "decent, well-bred men"; Strong, 3:424.

47 *NYTr*, December 17, 24, 1855; *NYH*, December 24, 1855; *NYT*, February 7, 1856. Aspinwall apparently had been unhappy with how Pacific Mail had been run in 1855, and wished to make reforms of his own; *NYT*, July 19, 1855. On November 6, 1855, the Mercantile Agency (which estimated Aspinwall's estate at about $2 million) noted that he was not thought to be actively engaged in business, though he did maintain a large interest in Pacific Mail.

48 *NYTr*, November 29, 1855; *NYT*, November 29, 1855; Citizens of Granada, Nicaragua, "Petition to General William Walker to Commute Death Sentence of General Ponciano Corral," November 7, 1855, Papers Concerning the Filibuster War, BL; entry for November 8, 1855, Diary, John Hill Wheeler Papers, LOC; Manning, 4:487; Burns, 199. Accessory Transit agent Joseph Scott noted that Walker dismissed the Nicaraguans from the service after his victory, SctDP; Burns, 199–200. Walker himself admitted Corral's popularity; see William Walker, *The War in Nicaragua* (Tucson: University of Arizona Press, 1985, orig. pub. 1860), 134–40. For a very useful discussion of the historiography of Walker in Nicaragua, see Ralph Lee Woodward Jr., "William Walker and the History of Nicaragua in the Nineteenth Century," *Latin American Research Review* 15, no. 1 (1980): 237–40. Woodward, however, writes in error that the completion of the Panama Railroad made the Nicaragua route uncompetitive. As already shown, it was highly competitive, both in the perceptions of businessmen involved in the California trade and in such objective measurements as speed of passage, economy of operation, and number of passengers.

49 Robert E. May, *The Southern Dream of Caribbean Empire: 1854–1861* (Athens: University of Georgia Press, 1989), 79; Commodore Hiram Paulding to James C. Dobbin, January 22, 1856, roll 96: Home Squadron, June 30, 1855, to December 17, 1856, Letters Received from the Secretary of the Navy from Commanding Officers of Squadrons, 1841–1886, Microfilm Publication M89, NA. See also H. W. Brands,

The Age of Gold: The California Gold Rush and the New American Dream (New York: Doubleday, 2002), 383–4. For a full biography of Walker, see Albert Z. Carr, *The World and William Walker* (Westport, Conn.: Greenwood Press, 1963). As May notes, 81n., Carr's book "is sparsely annotated, and much of Carr's psychological interpretation seems intuitive to the extreme." Stephen Dando-Collins's *Tycoon's War: How Cornelius Vanderbilt Invaded a Country to Overthrow America's Most Famous Military Adventurer* (New York: Da Capo, 2008) is likewise unreliable, with some fictionalized scenes.

50 Robert E. May, *Manifest Destiny's Underworld: Filibustering in Antebellum America* (Chapel Hill: University of North Carolina Press, 2002), 1–16; McPherson, 103–16; May, *Southern Dream*, 79–85, 119–21; Carr, 1–11, 36, 56, 63–4. May argues effectively that, despite enthusiasm for territorial expansion, U.S. presidents did not condone filibustering, and actively opposed it. See, for example, "The Slave Power Conspiracy Revisited: United States Presidents and Filibustering, 1848–1861," in David W. Blight and Brooks D. Simpson, eds., *Union and Emancipation: Essays on Politics and Race in the Civil War Era* (Kent: Kent State University Press, 1997), 7–28. On the broader cultural significance of filibustering, see May's article, "Young American Males and Filibustering in the Age of Manifest Destiny: The United States Army as a Cultural Mirror," *JAH*, December 1991, 857–86. I am indebted to Professor Lisandro Perez of Florida International University for information on the Cubans of New York and their role in filibustering expeditions. The literature on filibustering is extensive. In addition to May's important books, see, for example, Amy S. Greenberg, *Manifest Manhood and the Antebellum American Empire* (New York: Cambridge University Press, 2005), which depicts filibustering as the result of a crisis of masculinity in America; and William O. Scroggs, *Filibusters and Financiers: The Story of William Walker and his Associates* (New York: Macmillan Company, 1916), an account that remains highly influential. Philip S. Foner, *Business and Slavery: The New York Merchants and the Irrepressible Conflict* (Chapel Hill: University of North Carolina Press, 1941), 121, notes the enthusiasm for seizing Cuba in the business community, led by August Belmont.

51 McPherson, 103–16; Manning, 4:267–8, 424; Hiram Paulding to My Dear Cal, January 19, 1856, Hiram Paulding Papers, LOC.

52 Walker, 27; C. W. Doubleday, *Reminiscences of the "Filibuster" War in Nicaragua* (New York: G. P. Putnam's Sons, 1886), 164.

53 Walker, 106–27; HED 103, 34th Cong., 1st sess., vol. 11; SED 68, 34th Cong., 1st sess., vol. 13; Burns, 197–8; Carr, 1–36. As will be discussed, newspapers at the time assumed that the ATC deliberately aided Walker; direct evidence, however, shows that Walker coerced the company at every step, starting with the commandeering of *La Virgen* to capture Granada. See, for example, SctDP. On Walker's early military blundering, see Doubleday, 120–30; *National Era*, August 2, 1855. Walker, 51–65, managed to convince himself that he was a genius despite his failures.

54 Walker, 149–50, quote on 151–2. On Walker's reaction to CKG's failure to respond, see Deposition of Parker H. French, ATC Lawsuit. On French, see Deposition of Parker H. French, ATC Lawsuit; *NYT*, December 18, 26, 1855; May, *Southern Dream*, 98n. Joseph Scott witnessed Law's sale of rifles to French in New York; SctDP.

55 Deposition of Edmund Randolph, Deposition of Alexander P. Crittenden, MacDonald Lawsuit; Deposition of Parker H. French, ATC Lawsuit; May, *Southern Dream*, 98; May, *Manifest*, 121. See also *AltaC*, October 21, 1855. Walker, 146, supports the account given here, writing, "Before leaving San Francisco Walker had tried to ascertain the wishes of the Transit Company concerning the introduction of Americans into Nicaragua. . . . The agent of the company in California stated that his principals had instructed him to have nothing to do with such enterprises as he supposed Walker to contemplate." Commodore Paulding would report that Acces-

sory Transit remained neutral, writing, "The Transit Company acted in good faith pursuing their business with a singleness of purpose. . . . Their impunity in conducting their business depended upon their acquiescence when there was power to command obedience"; Commodore Hiram Paulding to James C. Dobbin, January 22, 1856, roll 96: Home Squadron, June 30, 1855, to December 17, 1856, Letters Received by the Secretary of the Navy from Commanding Officers of Squadrons, 1841–1886, Microfilm Publication M89, NA. Note, too, that when one naval officer traveled to Granada in May to consult with the Conservative government about preventing Walker's landing in Nicaragua, Accessory Transit provided him with free passage on a lake steamboat; Commander T. Baily to James C. Dobbin, May 28, 1855, Letter Books of U.S. Naval Officers, March 1778 to July 1908: Correspondence of Rear Admiral William Mervine, July 1836 to August 1868, vol. 3, entry 603(15), RG 45, NA.

56　Soulé, 744–7; Baughman, 73; David Lavender, *Nothing Seemed Impossible: William C. Ralston and Early San Francisco* (Palo Alto: American West, 1975), 17, 21–39; *NYT,* October 20, 1851. Every secondary source I have consulted names CM and CKG as coconspirators during the 1853–54 conflict, even though no primary source evidence supports this conclusion. It appears to be an extrapolation based on their later partnership.

57　*AltaC,* April 11, 1853; Deposition of Nicholas Laning, ATC Lawsuit; Deposition of Theodore A. Wakeman, Deposition of Benjamin F. Voorhees, MacDonald Lawsuit; Lavender, 58–60.

58　Dialogue and details of this conversation are taken from the depositions of Edmund Randolph, Alexander P. Crittenden, and John W. Bent, MacDonald Lawsuit.

59　Depositions of Edmund Randolph, Alexander P. Crittenden, John W. Bent, Benjamin F. Voorhees, and Edward J. C. Kewen, MacDonald Lawsuit; *NYT,* November 21, 1855. Randolph's partner in the transit-flipping scheme was Alexander P. Crittenden, who spoke to CKG about the proposal repeatedly; see William Walker to Alexander P. Crittenden, October 25, 1855, MacDonald Lawsuit.

60　Commodore Hiram Paulding, USS *Potomac,* Havana, to James C. Dobbin, January 22, 1856, roll 96: Home Squadron, June 30, 1855, to December 17, 1856, Letters Received by the Secretary of the Navy from Commanding Officers of Squadrons, 1841–1886, Microfilm Publication M89, NA; Walker, 150.

61　CV to WLM, March 26, 1856, HED 103, 34th Cong., 1st sess., vol. 11; Deposition of Edmund Randolph, San Francisco, January 11, 1859, MacDonald Lawsuit. Contrast my version of CKG's actions with that of Scroggs, *Filibusters and Financiers,* and "William Walker and the Steamship Corporation in Nicaragua," *AHR* 10, no. 4 (July 1905): 792–811. Scroggs crafted the accepted version of these events, arguing that it was CM and CKG's "plan" to convince Walker to annul the charter and give them the rights to carry passengers across Nicaragua. Abundant evidence not consulted by Scroggs, and a closer analysis, points to the version given here.

62　John H. Wheeler to WLM, December 15, 1855, Manning, 4:496: *NYT,* March 15, 1856; Walker, 146–8. Historians as well as contemporary reporters have ignored Walker's own declaration that the armed force dispatched by White convinced him to destroy the company. It is, in fact, the most satisfying explanation for his actions. By revoking the corporate charter, he endangered his lifeline to the United States, and made a powerful enemy; but, as an extreme reaction to White's small armed force, it is in keeping with Walker's loathing of treachery and obsession with power. Scroggs mentions the force, but only in the context of the Pierce administration's attitude toward the company; see "William Walker and the Steamship Corporation."

63　Deposition of Edmund Randolph, San Francisco, January 11, 1859, Deposition of John W. Bent, New York, July 3, 1858, MacDonald Lawsuit; Walker, 150–2. Interestingly, Walker wrote that Alexander Crittenden and Randolph led him to believe that CKG wanted him to cancel the ATC charter, whereas Crittenden, Randolph, and French all testified that CKG resisted this action. The most likely explanation is that Crittenden and Randolph misled Walker to secure his cooperation.

Eleven Vanderbilt

1 *BE*, December 8, 1855; *NYT,* December 11, 1855; *NYT,* December 11, 1855; *New York Courier and Enquirer,* reprinted in the *LT,* December 29, 1855; *NYH,* January 1, 1856. For a detailed analysis of the *Vanderbilt* (and all of CV's other Atlantic steamships) see Cedric Ridgely-Nevitt, *American Steamships on the Atlantic* (Newark, Del.: University of Delaware Press, 1981), 222–49.

2 RGD, NYC, 374:1. CV would later claim that he spent between $800,000 and $900,000 on the *Vanderbilt;* see HsR 2, part 2A, 37th Cong., 2nd sess., vol. 2.

3 *NYTr,* December 17, 24, 1855; *NYH,* December 24, 1855; *NYT,* February 7, 1856.

4 *National Era,* January 10, 1856.

5 On the administration's attitude toward Walker and French, see *NYT,* December 14, 15, 1855; *NYH,* November 25, 1856; WLM to John H. Wheeler, November 8, 1855, Manning, 4:74. On the Crampton affair, see WLM to J. F. Crampton, August 27, 1855, vol. 80: Private Letterbook, WLMP; *NYH,* December 25, 1855; *NYT,* November 17, 1855, May 21, 1856; *SEP,* May 24, 1856.

6 *NYH,* December 24, 25, 1855, May 9, 1856; *NYTr,* December 24, 25, 1855; *NYT,* December 25, 1855; *LT,* January 8, 1856.

7 *NYH,* December 24, 25, 1855, May 9, 1856; *NYTr,* December 24, 25, 1855; *NYT,* December 25, 1855; *LT,* January 8, 1856. Scott, a careful man, searched the *Northern Light* for arms with McKeon, offering more proof that the company was not secretly supporting Walker, beyond its special emigrant rate. No arms were found on the ship; later it became clear that arms were being shipped down in sailing vessels; *NYTr,* February 7, 1857. Scott also testified that emigrants to California typically went heavily armed, often with revolvers and rifles, and so many weapons were probably carried to Nicaragua by individual filibuster recruits. On the Irish and Five Points, see Tyler Anbinder, *Five Points: The 19th-Century New York City Neighborhood That Invented Tap Dance, Stole Elections, and Became the World's Most Notorious Slum* (New York: Free Press, 2001), 42–50, 67–80, 111–40.

8 *NYTr,* January 7, 8, 24, 1856; *NYH,* January 7, 8, 10, 1856; *NYW,* November 14, 1877; *David Colden Murray, Receiver of the ATC, v. CV,* November 3, 1859, file PL 1859-M V74, Supreme Court Pleadings, NYCC.

9 *NYTr,* January 7, 8, 26, February 9, 1856; *NYH,* January 8, 10, 25, 1856; entry for January 21, 1856, Senate Journal, 34th Cong., 1st sess.; William Walker, Response to Interrogatories, *Charles MacDonald v. CKG and CM,* July 26, 1858, Papers Concerning the Filibuster War, BL; *David Colden Murray, Receiver of the ATC, v. CV,* November 3, 1859, file PL 1859-M V74, Supreme Court Pleadings, NYCC; CV to WLM, March 17, 1856, HED 103, 34th Cong., 1st sess., vol. 11. On CV's hostility toward Walker, see Wheeler's statement in Memorial Presented by David Colden Murray, fold. 1, box 1, CRCC.

10 *NYTr,* January 7, 8, 26, February 9, 1856; *NYH,* January 8, 10, 25, 1856; entry for January 21, 1856, Senate Journal, 34th Cong., 1st sess.; William Walker, Response to Interrogatories, *Charles MacDonald v. CKG and CM,* July 26, 1858, Papers Concerning the Filibuster War, BL; *David Colden Murray, Receiver of the ATC, v. CV,* November 3, 1859, file PL 1859-M V74, Supreme Court Pleadings, NYCC; CV to WLM, March 17, 1856, HED 103, 34th Cong., 1st sess., vol. 11; Depositions of O. M. Wozendraft and Edward J. C. Kewen, MacDonald Lawsuit.

11 *NYTr,* February 14, 19, 23, March 5, 11, 12, 1856; *NYT,* March 6, 1856.

12 *NYTr,* March 14, 1856; *NYH,* March 14, 18, 1856; *NYT,* March 14, 15, 25, 1856. A

dispute erupted on Wall Street over whether CM's short sales were legal, given the revocation of the charter; see entries for March 14, 18, 1856, Minutes of the New York Stock and Exchange Board, vol. 4: 1851–1858, 247, New York Stock Exchange Archives.

13   *NYTr*, March 15, 17, 1856; HED 103, 34th Cong., 1st sess., vol. 11; *NYH*, October 16, 1856; *NYT*, March 20, 1856; *Congressional Globe*, March 17, 1856.

14   *LT*, April 8, 1856; *NYT*, March 18, 24, 26, 1856; *NYTr*, March 29, 1856; *CT*, March 28, 1856; HED 103, 34th Cong., 1st sess., vol. 11. See McPherson, 103–16, and Robert E. May, *The Southern Dream of Caribbean Empire: 1854–1861* (Athens: University of Georgia Press, 1989).

15   *NYT*, March 17, 1856; *David Colden Murray, Receiver of the ATC, v. CV*, November 3, 1859, file PL 1859-M V74, Supreme Court Pleadings, NYCC; *NYH*, March 31, 1856; *NYTr*, October 15, 1856. Though the subsidy was usually attributed to Pacific Mail alone, the *Independent*, February 11, 1858, reported that 75 percent was paid by Pacific Mail and 25 percent by U.S. Mail, a ratio that corresponds to other joint operations. Though the *Times* later would condemn the noncompetition payment, on March 18, 1856, it said in approving tones that it assumed such a "bonus" would be paid.

16   Memorial of David Colden Murray, CRCC; Mary Wilhelmine Williams, *Anglo-American Isthmian Diplomacy: 1815–1915* (New York: Russell & Russell, 1965), 211–2. Regarding Cross's mission, see a letter from Cross, September 6, 1856, in a newspaper clipping in the Scrapbook, John Hill Wheeler Papers, LOC. Birdsall was identified as "superintending engineer" in *NYH*, October 16, 1856. On Birdsall's mission, see Manning, 4:556.

17   *New York Express*, in *CT*, May 12, 1856; Heyl, 6:79–80.

18   Walker, 188–9; May, *Manifest Destiny's Underworld*, 201–5. Both Walker and Edmund Randolph said that they thought steamship service to Nicaragua would continue without interruption, but that Cross's coup disrupted the line on the Pacific for six critical weeks; Deposition of Edmund Randolph, MacDonald Lawsuit.

19   Published letter from Cross, September 6, 1856, Scrapbook, John Hill Wheeler Papers, LOC; Folkman, 78–9. CKG's contract as agent expired March 31, 1856; *ATC v. CKG*, September 13, 1858, file 1858-#53, Superior Court, NYCC. On the ATC steamships on the Pacific, see *NYH*, December 1, 1856.

20   SctDP; see also CV to WLM, March 17, 1856, HED 103, 34th Cong., 1st sess., vol. 11. For more on Scott, see *NYT*, December 27, 1855; entry for November 8, 1855, Diary, John Hill Wheeler Papers, LOC.

21   Shortly before the *Orizaba* incident, Captain Tarleton had allowed a sailing ship to unload 160 filibusters, along with rifles, ammunition, and artillery; see Commodore Hiram Paulding to James C. Dobbin, June 16, 1856, with accompanying documents, roll 96: Home Squadron, June 30, 1855, to December 17, 1856, Letters Received by the Secretary of the Navy from Commanding Officers of Squadrons, 1841–1886, Microfilm Publication M89, NA; Manning, 4:556–7; SED 68, 34th Cong., 1st sess., vol. 13; SctDP; May, *Manifest Destiny's Underworld*, 245. On the arming of the Costa Ricans by the British, see *AltaC*, June 2, 7, 1856; *NYT*, June 5, 1856. For a description of the rebuilt Greytown, see *NYT*, March 27, 1857. See also Jasper Ridley, *Lord Palmerston* (London: Constable, 1970), 457, on British reluctance to take direct action against Walker.

22   *NYT*, May 19, 20, 21, 1856; *SEP*, May 24, 1856; May, *Southern Dream*, 89.

23   Burns, 70, 201; *NYT*, May 15, 16, 1856; May, *Southern Dream*, 101–3. Williams, *Anglo-American Isthmian Diplomacy*, 211–2, argues that intelligence of British shipments of arms to Costa Rica led to the recognition. Though this is an overstatement, the discovery certainly gave added urgency to the decision.

24   Even Scroggs, who argued that the ATC supported the filibusters, wrote in

"William Walker and the Steamship Corporation" that "the government officers had no means of distinguishing the filibuster from the passenger. Moreover it seems that the recruits were never organized on a military basis until they were beyond the jurisdiction of the United States." Yet Scroggs expected the company to know the difference between emigrant and filibuster!

25 Thomas W. Ward to WLM, April 18, 1856, SED 68, 34th Cong., 1st sess., vol. 13.

26 Manning, 4:536–41. Walker's version appears 214–28, 231; Burns, 203.

27 T. J. Stiles, *Jesse James: Last Rebel of the Civil War* (New York: Alfred A. Knopf, 2002), 46–55; McPherson, 145–61.

28 *MM*, December 1854; *NYT*, July 3, 1860; *Memoirs of William T. Sherman* (New York: Da Capo, 1984, orig. pub. 1875), 95–105, 118–24; Kemble, 71, 152–3, 206; Richard Maxwell Brown, *Strain of Violence: Historical Studies of American Violence and Vigilantism* (New York: Oxford University Press, 1975), 123–40.

29 Sherman, 95–105, 118–24; Brown, 123–40; *NYT*, March 27, June 27, 1857; *National Era*, July 3, 1856; Deposition of Benjamin F. Voorhees, MacDonald Lawsuit. See also Leonard L. Richards, *The California Gold Rush and the Coming of the Civil War* (New York: Alfred A. Knopf, 2007), 5–6, 26–33, 184–6. The Pierce administration expressed "alarm" but also a need for "extraordinary circumspection" with regard to the vigilance committee, and declined to intervene; see James C. Dobbin to Commodore William Mervine, August 2, 1856, Letter Books of U.S. Naval Officers, March 1778 to July 1908: Correspondence of Rear Admiral William Mervine, July 1836 to August 1868, vol. 4, entry 603(15), RG 45, NA. For commentary on gang violence in contemporary New York elections, see *NYTr*, June 7, 1852.

30 Deposition of Edmund Randolph, Deposition of Alexander P. Crittenden, MacDonald Lawsuit; *NYT*, July 15, 16, 28, 1856, March 20, 1857; *NYH*, November 21, 1856; Baughman, 81. Walker officially transferred the transit rights and property to CM and CKG in a decree signed August 26, 1856; *SEP*, October 4, 1856.

31 HsR 2, 36th Cong., 2nd sess., vol. 1; *NYT*, March 6, 1852, April 23, 25, 1886; LW Dictation.

32 Medbery, 312–3; entry for March 24, 1856, Minutes of the New York Stock and Exchange Board, vol. 4: 1851–1858, New York Stock Exchange Archives; RGD, NYC, 366:251.

33 Strong, 2:282; *David Colden Murray, Receiver of the ATC, v. CV*, November 3, 1859, file PL 1859-M V74, Supreme Court Pleadings, NYCC; CV to John Hawes, August 4, 1856, fold. 12, box 1, Ms 82-01, Panama Collection, Department of Special Collections, University Libraries, Wichita State University; *NYH*, July 16, September 15, October 16, December 1, 1856; *NYT*, June 3, 6, 12, August 22, 1856; *NYTr*, October 16, November 4, 1856.

34 *NYT*, May 6, June 3, 6, 1856; *NYH*, July 16, 1856; *NYTr*, October 15, 1856; *David Colden Murray, Receiver of the ATC, v. CV*, November 3, 1859, file PL 1859-M V74, Supreme Court Pleadings, NYCC.

35 *NYT*, November 21, 1857; Ridgely-Nevitt, 163–9.

36 *NYT*, April 16, July 21, 24, 30, 1856; January 21, July 23, 1856, Senate Journal, 34th Cong., 1st sess.; Benjamin B. French to Henry F. French, September 5, 1856, reel 7, Benjamin B. French Papers, LOC; David Budlong Tyler, *Steam Conquers the Atlantic* (New York: D. Appleton-Century Company, 1939), 236–8.

37 Burns, 198, 202; *NYT*, March 17, April 17, May 30, 1856; Walker, 190, 197-210; SED 68, 34th Cong., 1st sess., vol. 13.

38 *CT*, September 6, 1856; *NYH*, September 6, 7, 1856. As discussed previously, social concerns over the difficulties of assessing character had grown up in the collapse of the culture of deference, and the rise of an individualistic, commercial society; see in particular *Confidence Men*. Amy S. Greenberg, in "A Gray-Eyed Man: Character, Appearance, and Filibustering," *Journal of the Early Republic* 20, no. 4 (winter 2000):

673–99, and *Manifest Manhood and the Antebellum American Empire* (New York: Cambridge University Press, 2005), goes so far as to argue that "the American reception of William Walker's Nicaragua adventures was shaped by a national conflict over the relationship between character and appearance." I would argue that this "conflict" may have led Walker's supporters to cast about for a way to put his unimpressive appearance in a positive light, but it in no way determined the public's response to him.

39 RGD, NYC, 374:1.

40 *NYT,* November 22, 1856; *NYH,* November 21, 25, 1856; SctDP; Francisco Calcagno, *Diccionario Biográfico Cubano* (New York: Ponce de León, 1878), 302; William O. Scroggs, "William Walker's Designs on Cuba," *Mississippi Valley Historical Review* 1, no. 2 (September 1914): 198–211; Scroggs, *Filibusters,* 217–8; May, *Southern Dream,* 106. One of Goicouria's letters stated, in the passive voice, that someone had offered him $250,000 for the transit rights. The press assumed that this offer came from CV (*NYT,* November 24, 1856), and historians have followed suit (see, for example, Baughman, 82). This is possible (perhaps simply as a feint), but I doubt it. For one thing, Goicouria mentioned CV by name elsewhere in the same letter; why leave out his name with regard to the offer? And such an offer would have been out of keeping with CV's consistent course, to oppose Walker and restore the original company to possession. Further, there is every indication that he believed Walker would soon be driven from power. Finally, CV explicitly denied that Goicouria was his "agent" (*NYH,* November 25, 1856), or that he had ever supported Walker, a statement supported by Goicouria himself (*NYT,* March 24, 1857) and the pro-filibuster U.S. minister to Nicaragua, John N. Wheeler (see his sworn deposition in CRCC).

41 *NYT,* November 22, 1856; *NYH,* November 21, 25, 1856; SctDP; Calcagno, 302; Scroggs, "William Walker's Designs on Cuba," 198–211; Scroggs, *Filibusters,* 217–8; May, *Southern Dream,* 106. Walker, 256–66, offers a lengthy defense of his reestablishment of slavery.

42 *NYH,* November 25, 1856; *HW,* May 23, 1857; *NYTr,* February 7, 1857.

43 *NYH,* October 15, 1856.

44 Burns, 203–5, 213–5. Michel Gobat emphasizes, in *Confronting the American Dream: Nicaragua Under U.S. Imperial Rule* (Durham: Duke University Press, 2005), 21–41, Walker's revolutionary role in displacing old power structures and remaking Nicaraguan society, and his support from both local elites as well as peasants and Indians. He did not, for example, press Nicaraguans into armed service, as had traditionally been done. However, such incidents as the hanging of Byron Cole and the slaughter of Walker's wounded on Ometepe demonstrate widespread, violent discontent with filibuster rule.

45 *HW,* January 31, 1857; May, *Manifest Destiny's Underworld,* 200–3. Walker, 301, wrote that not until Charles Henningsen arrived in October 1856 did he have an officer qualified to train the men in the use of the Minié rifle or artillery.

46 Walker, 287–94, 301–12; Manning, 4:576; Scroggs, *Filibusters,* 255.

47 *HW,* May 23, 1857; *NYTr,* January 14, 1857; *NYH,* January 25, 1857.

48 Walker, 367–71; Charles Henry Davis to Commodore William Mervine, March 4, 1857, Correspondence of Rear Admiral William Mervine, July 1836 to August 1868, vol. 4, Letter Books of U.S. Naval Officers, March 1778 to July 1908, entry 603 (15), RG 45, NA.

49 *NYT,* January 28, 1857; *HW,* January 31, 1857; *NYTr,* December 20, 21, 22, 1855.

50 SctDP.

51 Scroggs, "William Walker and the Steamship Corporation," makes precisely this point about Vanderbilt's strategy.

52 Statement of U.S. Commissioner B. F. Rexford, In the Matter of David Colden Murray, Receiver of the ATC, CRCC; *NYH,* January 26, 1857.

53 *NYT,* January 29, June 11, July 4, 1857; Juan R. Mora to Sylvanus M. Spencer, December 3, 1856, Memorial of David Colden Murray, CRCC. Historians have consistently reported that an Englishman, W. R. C. Webster, commanded Spencer's expedition as CV's chief agent; see, for example, Lane, 129, and Folkman, 88. In fact, Webster appears to have been a confidence man who promoted this idea (see, for example, *NYT* and *NYH,* January 29, 1857). CV refused to pay drafts that Webster issued; and Webster appears nowhere in the extensive investigations of the CRCC. I therefore conclude that, as per the *NYT* reporting cited, Webster was a fraud.

54 *NYH,* January 29, 1857; *NYT,* January 29, March 27, 1857; Affidavit of Sylvanus M. Spencer, July 25, 1860, Affidavit of George F. Cauty, August 9, 1858, Statement of B. Squire Cottrel, January 26, 1858, CRCC; Walker, 342–3.

55 Marriage Certificate, November 26, 1856, WFP; *HC,* November 28, 1856; *NYS,* December 19, 1877. On Vanderbilt's feelings toward the Williams family, see CV to Ezekiel Williams Jr., February 12, 1857, and CV to Oliver Williams, May 5, 1860, WFP.

56 *Texas State Gazette,* November 29, December 6, 1856; *NYT,* December 11, 16, 1856, January 16, 1857.

57 *NYH,* January 16, 1857.

58 Statement of B. Squire Cottrel, January 26, 1858, CRCC; SctDP. Cottrel places these events one day earlier; I am following Scott, whose account agrees with contemporary newspaper reports.

59 SctDP.

60 SctDP; Deposition of William W. Wise, CRCC; *NYT,* March 5, 1857.

61 *NYH,* January 26, 1857; *NYTr,* January 26, 1857; *NYT,* March 5, 1857; Deposition of William W. Wise, CRCC.

62 *NYTr,* January 26, 1857; *NYH,* January 25, 1857; Deposition of William W. Wise, CRCC.

Twelve Champion

1 *NYTr,* January 27, 1857.

2 "The Experience of Samuel Absalom, Filibuster," *Atlantic Monthly,* December 1859; HED 24, 35th Cong., 1st sess., vol. 7; Walker, 371–84. Walker admitted to the demoralization of his men. A filibuster force landed at Greytown and tried to fight its way through, but a Costa Rican ruse held them off at Castillo Viejo until Mora could send reinforcements; then Goicouria arranged for a steamship to pick up the retreating filibusters at Greytown; *NYH,* April 30, 1857; Manning, 7:703–4. *NYT,* December 24, 1856, and *NYTr,* June 1, 1857. Goicouria was now on the ATC payroll, taking a total of $15,000 from it; see *David Colden Murray, Receiver of the ATC, v. CV,* November 3, 1859, file PL 1859-M V74, Supreme Court Pleadings, NYCC. Note also that Charles J. MacDonald asked the U.S. Navy to intervene to recover the steamboats for CKG and CM; C. J. Macdonald to Captain Charles Henry Davis, U.S. Sloop of War *St. Mary's,* February 23, 1857, Affidavit of C. J. Macdonald, February 23, 1857, Letter Books of U.S. Naval Officers, March 1778 to July 1908: Correspondence of Rear Admiral William Mervine, July 1836 to August 1868, vol. 4, entry 603(15), RG 45, NA.

3 *NYH,* May 29, 1857; Charles Henry Davis to Commodore William Mervine, March 4, 19, 1857, Letter Books of U.S. Naval Officers, March 1778 to July 1908: Correspondence of Rear Admiral William Mervine, July 1836 to August 1868, vol. 4, entry 603(15), RG 45, NA; Walker, 419–28; Burns, 206; William O. Scroggs, *Filibusters and Financiers: The Story of William Walker and his Associates* (New York: Macmillan, 1916), 286–301.

4   *NYH*, May 29, 1857; *Atlantic Monthly*, December 1859. For newspaper coverage of Spencer's raid, see any New York newspaper starting January 16, 1857, especially *NYT*, January 28, 1857. For examples of the "war of the commodores" reporting, see *NYH*, November 29, 1856, January 27, 1857; *NYT*, March 17, 1857.

5   Manning, 4:719, 768; *NYH*, January 28, 1858.

6   *LT*, February 23, 1857.

7   CM's letter quoted in Baughman, 83; RGD, NYC, 316:83, 1G; Deposition of Benjamin F. Voorhees, MacDonald Lawsuit; *Texas State Gazette*, March 7, 1857; *NYTr*, March 9, 1857.

8   *HW*, April 4, 1857.

9   *HW*, March 5, 1859.

10   Francis Gerry Fairfield, *The Clubs of New York* (New York: Henry L. Hinton, 1873), 151.

11   *NYH*, April 9, 1857; CV to Ezekiel Williams Jr., February 12, 1857, WFP. Letters in Vanderbilt's own hand are rare after 1837, when first Daniel Allen and then Lambert Wardell assumed the physical chore of putting pen to paper.

12   *HC*, March 11, 1857; *NYW*, December 20, 1877.

13   *NYTr*, March 9, 1857; McPherson, 174–8.

14   Sean Wilentz, *The Rise of American Democracy: Jefferson to Lincoln* (New York: W. W. Norton, 2005), 699–702; McPherson, 156, 161–3; Kenneth M. Stampp, *America in 1857: A Nation on the Brink* (New York: Oxford University Press, 1990), 47–9.

15   *NYH*, February 14, 1858; *NYT*, September 8, 1857, July 2, 1858; *USMDR*, December 1857; Stampp, 72, 76; Jerome Mushkat, *Tammany: The Evolution of a Political Machine, 1789–1865* (Syracuse, N.Y.: Syracuse University Press, 1971), 264, 267–9, 300, 303, 315; Francis Schell, *Memoir of the Hon. Augustus Schell* (New York: privately printed, 1885). For more on Wood, see Burrows & Wallace, 831–41. For a story showing Clark and Schell practicing law together, see *NYT*, March 21, 1854. As political allies, see *NYT*, October 5, 1854, June 23, 1857, April 6, 1858. For more commentary on violence in New York elections, see *NYTr*, June 7, 1852. For insight into the many ways the collector of the port could profit from his position, see SR 227, part 1, 42nd Cong., 2nd sess., vol. 4.

16   *Washington Evening Star*, December 6, 1858; JB to Alexander Dimitry, November 1, 1859, reel 50, JBP.

17   *David Colden Murray, Receiver of the ATC, v. CV*, November 3, 1859, file PL 1859-M V74, Supreme Court Pleadings, NYCC; *NYT*, May 5, 1857; *NYH*, May 6, 21, 1857.

18   SctDP; Sylvanus M. Spencer Deposition, David Colden Murray Memorial, fold. 1, box 1, CRCC. On Webster, see *NYT*, January 29, June 3, 11, July 4, 1857. Not only did CV repudiate Webster, but Webster's name appears nowhere in the extensive investigations of the CRCC.

19   *NYT*, August 30, 1855.

20   Burns, 4, 42, 221; *NYT*, August 26, 1857, April 24, July 1, 1858; *NYH*, March 1, 1858.

21   *CT*, December 11, 1857, February 28, 1859; HED 47, 35th Cong., 1st sess., vol. 9; John A. Butler, *Atlantic Kingdom: America's Contest with Cunard in the Age of Sail and Steam* (Washington, D.C.: Brassey's, 2001), 220; Cedric Ridgely-Nevitt, *American Steamships on the Atlantic* (Newark, Del.: University of Delaware Press, 1981), 137–8.

22   *National Era*, April 23, 1857; *CT*, April 24, 1857; *NYT*, April 28, May 6, 1857; *HC*, May 14, 1857; *SA*, June 6, 1857; *Albany Evening Journal*, quoted in *NYT*, June 11, 1857. *NYT*, June 15, 1857, lists Mrs. C. Vanderbilt as one of the Americans registered with a bank in Paris.

23   *HC*, May 14, 1857; *LT*, June 4, 1857.

24   On the speed of crossing, see *Liberator*, July 17, 1857; *NYT*, July 15, 21, August 3, 25, 1857. For the bankruptcy of the Bremen line, see *National Era*, July 2, 1857; *CT*,

December 11, 1857; HED 47, 35th Cong., 1st sess., vol. 9; Ridgely-Nevitt, 137–9. For an astute analysis of CV's method, see *NYT,* October 26, 1857.

25 Thomas C. Cochran, *Railroad Leaders, 1845–1890: The Business Mind in Action* (New York: Russell & Russell, 1965, orig. pub. 1953), 22–3.

26 *NYT,* January 21, 1857; *CV v. HRR,* July 16, 1858, file LJ-1858-N-41, Supreme Court Judgments, NYCC.

27 Directors' Minutes, June 15, 24, 1857, HRR, reel 27, box 242, NYCRR (cited hereafter as HRR Minutes). I do not mean to say that CV's only contact with the HRR was through the Schuyler fraud; the same source shows, in the list of voters at the annual stockholders' meeting, April 22, 1853, that CV owned 1,500 shares of stock, out of 50,897 total, at a time when Robert Schuyler was president. For details of the dispute, and the HRR's refusal to accept CV's terms, see the HRR Minutes, July 18, 19, 20, 1854. There is a fine summary of these events in a *NYTr* report quoted in *HC,* August 15, 1876.

28 *NYT,* May 20, 1857; *NYH,* May 20, 1857; According to the HRR Minutes, CV owned 1,001 shares (alongside Clark's three hundred), yet he won 79,124 votes, the most of any candidate; Report of the Inspectors of Election, May 19, 1957, see entry for May 18, 1858, HRR Minutes. See also Hudson C. Tanner, *"The Lobby" and Public Men from Thurlow Weed's Time* (Albany: George MacDonald, 1888), 226. Tanner claimed to be quoting unpublished minutes of CV's testimony before a committee of New York's legislature that he took as official stenographer, material that was suppressed in official publications. Given the close correlation between Tanner's account and the minutes of the HRR, I believe he wrote truthfully. Tanner later swore before Congress that the suppressed testimony was given on March 3, 1869, to a committee of the New York State Assembly, reported in NYSAD 142, 92nd sess., 1869; see *NYTr,* March 6, 1871. I accept Tanner's account in *"The Lobby"* as accurate.

29 Entries for June 15, 24, 1857, HRR Minutes. I am extrapolating a figure of $6.5 million, based on the commissions reported in the minutes and CV's comment in Tanner, 226, that he and Drew took a commission of one-half of 1 percent on their endorsements.

30 Entries for June 24, 25, 1857, HRR Minutes; Tanner, 224.

31 Tanner, 225–6.

32 September 9, 1857, HRR Minutes.

33 *NYH,* June 17, 1857; *Farmer's Cabinet,* June 25, 1857.

34 *BE,* June 22, 1857; *NYH,* quoted in *National Era,* July 23, 1857; JB to Isaiah Rynders, September 14, 1859, reel 50, JBP. The *BE* and the *NYH* said that JB told CV nothing; the latter part of the *NYH* report suggests that he did, as does a letter from CV to General José María Cañas, August 5, 1857, in Manning, 4:638. Robert E. May observes that historians have "unfairly stigmatized" Buchanan as a supporter of filibustering; "The Slave Power Conspiracy Revisited: United States Presidents and Filibustering, 1848–1861," in David W. Blight and Brooks D. Simpson, eds., *Union and Emancipation: Essays on Politics and Race in the Civil War Era* (Kent: Kent State University Press, 1997), 7–28. It was thought that CM and CKG were helping Walker; in fact, they purchased a transit contract from Webster that led nowhere; *NYT,* July 31, 1857; *AltaC,* September 16, 1857; Kemble, 77.

35 *NYT,* August 26, December 19, 1857, April 24, July 1, 1858; *NYH,* March 1, 1858, May 2, 1859; Manning, 4:594–5, 623n, 625–6, 637–8; *HW,* November 21, 1857; CV to JB, October 20, 1857, roll 33, JBP; Folkman, 94–8; Burns, 4, 42, 221. A distinctly irritated secretary of state wrote that CV was "deserving of censure" for his attempts to prevent the recognition of Yrisarri; Lewis Cass to Mirabeau B. Lamar, January 2, 1858, Diplomatic Instructions of the Department of State, 1801–1906: Central American States, vol. 15, May 29, 1833, to July 25, 1858, roll 27, Microfilm Publication M77, NA-CP.

36   SED 13, 35th Cong., 1st sess., vol. 1; Robert E. May, *The Southern Dream of a Caribbean Empire: 1854–1861* (Athens: University of Georgia Press, 1989), 113.

37   Strong, 2:211; Burrows & Wallace, 666–70.

38   *NYH*, June 17, 1857, *Liberator*, July 17, 1857; Burrows & Wallace, 836–41.

39   Stampp, 214–7, 221; Burrows & Wallace, 846–7; McPherson, 188–91; Tanner, 226.

40   *NYH*, January 1, 1858; Strong, 2:351.

41   *NYT*, September 3, 19, 1857; RGD, NYC, 342:290.

42   Strong, 2:355–6; *NYT*, October 6, 1857.

43   RGD, NYC, 316:81.

44   This dialogue is taken from Tanner, 225–30.

45   Tanner, 225–30; October 21, 1857, HRR Minutes; *NYTr* in *HC*, August 15, 1876. The crisis largely involved the coupons of the first-mortgage bonds, which the company lacked the funds to pay.

46   Tanner, 225–30; RGD, NYC, 340:47. As mentioned earlier, Tanner's quotation strikes me as accurate. It closely fits the HRR Minutes and RGD, which records a mortgage to Drew issued on September 30, 1857. I believe this unpublished testimony was given on March 3, 1869, to a committee of the New York State Assembly; see NYSAD 142, 92nd sess., 1869, in which CV and Horace Clark testified that CV took the bonds at a 50 percent discount.

47   November 11, 20, 28, 1857, January 30, February 10, 1858, HRR Minutes. On the HRR's improved condition in 1858, see *NYH*, May 19, 1858; NYSAD 142, 92nd sess., 1869.

48   *HW*, November 21, 1857. For a discussion of Thanksgiving's spread, see *JoC*, November 30, 1837.

49   *NYH*, February 23, 1868; *CT*, January 13, 1867, February 11, 1868.

50   *HW*, November 28, 1857. For more information about CV's racing and the carriages of the wealthy, see *NYH*, June 18, December 5, 1859; Melvin L. Adelman, "The First Modern Sport in America: Harness Racing in New York City, 1825–1870," *Journal of Sport History* 8, no. 1 (spring 1981): 5–32. Adelman notes that Thoroughbred racing was considered a sport of the older, aristocratic elite, and that harness racing—both formal and informal—was championed by a rising wealthy class that lacked social pedigree. On Frank Work's role as CV's broker, see *NYS*, March 7, 1878.

51   SED 13, 35th Cong., 1st sess., vol. 1; *NYT*, December 28, 1857; Strong, 2:378–9; May, *Southern Dream*, 113–25; Folkman, 95–6.

52   *NYH*, January 28, March 1, 1858; Manning, 4:660–1; Burns, 221–4. Webster tagged along with Allen, to his apparent annoyance. On the attitude of the Nicaraguans toward the White contract, see *NYH*, April 28, 1858.

53   Pacific Mail had stopped its subsidy during the operation of CKG and CM's Nicaragua line, but resumed when they suspended operations. *NYH*, February 4, 5, 1858; *NYT*, February 6, March 27, April 21, 1858; *Independent*, February 11, 1858; Kemble, 78, 92.

54   *NYT*, April 10, 1858; *National Era*, April 15, 1858; SctDP; *ATC v. CKG*, September 13, 1858, file 1858-53, Superior Court, NYCC. A year later, the receiver for Accessory Transit asked for the decision to be set aside "on the ground of collusion between Vanderbilt and Garrison"; *NYT*, September 26, 1859.

55   RGD, NYC, 374:97; *NYT*, March 14, 18, 1854, April 28, 1858; *CV v. JLW*, November 7, 1860, file 1860-#985, Superior Court, NYCC. On White's private opera box, see *NYH*, December 25, 1855.

56   *HW*, March 8, 27, 1858; *NYH*, April 2, 1858; *NYT*, May 26, 27, 1858; Cedric Ridgely-Nevitt, *American Steamships on the Atlantic* (Newark, Del.: University of Delaware Press, 1981), 169–70.

57   *David Colden Murray, Receiver of the ATC, v. CV*, November 3, 1859, file PL 1859-M V74, Supreme Court Pleadings, NYCC.

58 *NYT,* March 27, July 1, 5, 1858.

59 *NYH,* May 30, 1858; *NYT,* June 28, July 15, 16, 31, 1858; SctDP; Manning, 4:686; Burns, 231. See also Cyril Allen, "Felix Belly: Nicaraguan Canal Promoter," *HAHR* 37, no. 1 (February 1957): 46–59, to understand the role of Felix Belly, a French canal promoter who intrigued against CV.

60 McPherson, 163–7.

61 *NYT,* July 2, 1858. See also *CT,* March 22, 1858; *NYT,* February 9, 1858.

62 Daniel E. Sickles to JB, September 29, 1857, roll 33, JBP. For more on JB's coldness toward CV because of his hostility to Clark, see *NYT,* September 2, 1858.

63 *BE,* August 18, 1858; *NYT,* April 6, July 2, September 2, 1858.

64 Burrows & Wallace, 847–51; *NYT,* August 9, 13, 1858.

65 Strong, 2:411–3; *NYT,* January 28, September 6, 7, 27, October 7, 1858.

66 *NYT,* October 15, 29, 30, 1858; *National Era,* November 4, 1858; Strong, 2:419.

67 *NYH,* September 5, October 5, 1859; *Washington Evening Star,* December 6, 1858; *NYH,* September 5, 1859; *NYTr,* September 8, 1859; SED 45, 36th Cong., 1st sess., vol. 11; Kemble, 83.

68 *NYT,* June 11, December 13, 1858; *Washington Evening Star,* December 13, 1858; Manning, 4:862.

69 *NYT,* June 2, 1860; *HW,* February 12, 19, March 5, 1859; *NYH,* April 29, 1859; *LT,* March 2, 1859; *PS,* July 28, 1859. There are signs of an early start to negotiations with Samuel L. M. Barlow, a prominent figure in Pacific Mail; see CV to Samuel L. M. Barlow, May 7, 1859, BW box 30 (47), Samuel L. M. Barlow Collection, HL; CV to John T. Wright and William S. Freeman, October 19, 1859, CV-NYHS.

70 *New York Observer and Chronicle,* April 7, 1859; *NYT,* November 28, 1859; *NYH,* September 10, October 3, 1859, January 1, 1860; *NYTr,* September 7, 1859; Pacific Mail Steamship Co., *Proceedings in Connection with Negotiations with C. Vanderbilt, November 30th, 1859* (New York: G. F. Nesbitt & Co., 1859), copy in BL; Kemble, 83–5. Though incorporated in April, the Atlantic & Pacific Steamship Company advertised for stock subscriptions in *NYT,* September 23, 1859, and was mistakenly derided as simply an attempt to drive down the Pacific Mail share price.

71 *Washington Evening Star,* December 6, 1858; *NYH,* September 5, 1859; *NYTr,* September 8, 1859; SED 45, 36th Cong., 1st sess., vol. 11; Kemble, 83. CV's correspondence with Holt appears in SED 45.

72 CV to Pliny Miles, June 8, 1859, NYSL.

73 CV to JB, August 30, 31, November 1, 1859, reel 38, JB to Alexander Dimitry, November 1, 1859, reel 50, JBP.

74 SED 45, 36th Cong., 1st sess.; *NYT,* September 27, October 13, 1859; *NYH,* October 3, 1859; *HW,* September 24, 1859; October 1, 1859. On CV's purchase of CKG's stake, see *NYT,* October 10, 1859; *NYH,* October 10, 1859; *CT,* October 14, 1859; *NYTr,* March 2, 1860. CKG continued to serve as agent until Vanderbilt's new agents arrived from New York; CV to John T. Wright and William S. Freeman, October 19, 1859, CV-NYHS. Kemble, 93, reported that an examination of Pacific Mail's books showed that it lost money.

75 *NYH,* October 5, 6, 7, 1859; *CT,* October 8, 1859; *NYT,* October 25, 1859; SED 45, 36th Cong., 1st sess., vol. 11; SED 44, 41st Cong., 3rd sess., vol. 1.

76 *HW,* December 18, 1858.

77 *NYH,* October 17, 1859.

78 *NYH,* July 10, 1859; *HW,* October 1, 1859; Strong, 2:454.

79 *NYH,* December 5, 1859. On the symbolic nature of the CV-Bonner rivalry, and the social implications of the rise of trotting, see Adelman, "The First Modern Sport."

80 *HW,* February 26, 1859.

81 Burrows & Wallace, 697–705, 845–6, 849–51 (*Harper's* quoted on 697).

82 Burrows & Wallace, 847–51; *NYT,* August 9, 13, 1858.

83 *NYH,* March 5, 1879; *NYTr,* March 18, 1878; *NYW,* November 14, 1877. William's

love of driving fast horses would later be well publicized; see, for example, *NYS*, January 26, 1878.

84 *NYH*, March 5, 1879; *NYT*, April 6, 1857, August 20, 1860; NYSAD 75, February 15, 1861.

85 *HW*, September 3, 1859; SED 2, part 2, 36th Cong., 1st sess., vol. 2.

86 CV to Oliver Williams, May 5, 1860, WFP.

87 McPherson, 206; Strong, 2:473–4.

88 McPherson, 200–1; *CT*, December 19, 1859.

89 Letters and excerpts from minutes reprinted in Pacific Mail Steamship Co., *Proceedings*.

90 *NYH*, December 1, 1859. For discussions of these negotiations in the press, see the New York newspapers for November 26 through December 5, 1859. On the vagueness of distinctions between shareholders and corporations, see Naomi R. Lamoreaux, "Partnerships, Corporations, and the Limits on Contractual Freedom in U.S. History: An Essay in Economics, Law, and Culture," in Kenneth Lipartito and David B. Scilia, eds., *Constructing Corporate America: History, Politics, Culture* (Oxford: Oxford University Press, 2004), 29–65; Gregory A. Mark, "The Personification of the Business Corporation in American Law," *University of Chicago Law Review* 54, no. 4. (autumn 1987): 1441–83.

91 SctDP.

92 *NYTr*, January 30, February 2, 1860; *NYT*, January 25, 1860; HFC to Samuel L. M. Barlow, January 16, 1860, BW box 36 (14), Samuel L. M. Barlow Collection, HL.

93 *NYTr*, February 16, 17, 21, 29, 1860; *NYH*, August 12, 1859, February 16, 17, 20, March 1, 1860; *Seventh Annual Report of the Pacific Mail Steamship Company, May 1861* (New York: G. F. Nesbitt & Co., 1861); *Proceedings in Connection with Negotiations with C. Vanderbilt*, BL; CV to Samuel L. M. Barlow, February 20, 1860, BW box 36 (14), Samuel L. M. Barlow Collection, HL; Kemble, 93–7.

94 Kemble, 93–7; *NYTr*, February 29, 1860.

95 *CT*, July 12, 1858. With five thousand shares with a par value of $100 each, CV owned one-eighth of the forty thousand shares of Pacific Mail, with a total par value of $5 million; NYSAD 210, 90th sess., 1867.

96 *NYT*, June 23, July 3, 4, 9, 10, November 15, December 8, 1860; *NYH*, June 30, July 11, 12, September 13, October 17, 1860; *RT*, January 7, 1860; Edward Harold Mott, *Between the Ocean and the Lakes: The Story of Erie* (New York: Ticker Publishing, 1908), 129–36. Congress did retroactively pay him $175,000 for his service during the remainder of 1860, followed by payments of $61,249.99 and $113,750 in 1861, and finally $58,725 for the rest of his career in steamships to California, making a total federal subsidy to CV of $596,224.99 for the California mail; SED 44, 41st Cong., 3rd sess., vol. 1.

97 Manning, 4:762; *HW*, October 13, 1860; Cyril Allen, "Felix Belly: Nicaraguan Canal Promoter," *HAHR* 37, no. 1 (February 1957): 46–59.

98 *NYT*, February 4, 1861.

99 *NYT*, November 9, 1859. The paper reprinted the article at issue on October 18, 1859. It was full of errors and innuendo; it claimed, for example, that Walker would depart for Central America on the *Philadelphia*, saying it was one of Vanderbilt's "mail steamers." It was not.

100 *NYT*, May 26, 1858.

101 Burrows & Wallace, 679.

102 *HW*, February 19, 1859.

103 *HW*, March 5, 1859.

104 For an example of CV's approach to management of a geographically sprawling enterprise, see his instructions to his San Francisco agents, CV to John T. Wright and William S. Freeman, October 19, 1859, CV-NYHS. Richard Franklin Bensel, *Yankee Leviathan: The Origins of Central State Authority in America, 1859–1877* (New

York: Cambridge University Press, 1990), argues that the failure of the federal government to develop bureaucratic regulatory competence turned Northern capitalists in an antistate direction. James L. Huston, *Securing the Fruits of Labor: The American Concept of Wealth Distribution, 1765–1900* (Baton Rouge: Louisiana State University, 1998), 144–9, argues that only after 1880 did Americans abandon their belief in the essentially horizontal nature of the economy, and abandon older Jacksonian mental constructs. As early as 1859, however, we see public intellectuals struggling with the problem of bigness, in the form of CV. My discussion of CV's role is informed by John Lauritz Larson, *Internal Improvement: National Public Works and the Promise of Popular Government in the Early United States* (Chapel Hill: University of North Carolina Press, 2001).

105 *NYT*, December 27, 1858; *HW*, January 9, 1859.
106 Leo Tolstoy, *The Sebastopol Sketches* (London: Penguin, 1986), 152.

PART THREE KING

Thirteen War

1 *NYT*, October 24, 1878. For a single-source overview of much (but not all) of the trial, see Vanderbilt Will Trial Case Clippings, NYPL.
2 For an illustration of the courtroom, see *Frank Leslie's Illustrated Newspaper*, December 1, 1877, Vanderbilt Will Trial Case Clippings, NYPL. For Allen's testimony, see almost any New York newspaper for November 13, 1877, including the *NYT.*
3 Strong, 3:56–7.
4 McPherson, 212–33, 236.
5 *Staten Island Church*, 232. For a description of CV's house, see *NYT*, January 5, 1877. Annotations in the margin of the U.S. census in 1870 show 10 Washington Place was between Mercer and Greene streets, farther west than the same address today.
6 Joseph Conrad, *Nostromo: A Tale of the Seaboard* (London: Wordsworth Editions, 2000), 59.
7 *Phebe Vanderbilt v. Charles M. Simonson et al.*, April 17, 1844, file D-CH 177-V, Court of Chancery, NYCC; Croffut, 111. For two examples from the 1860s of writers who stressed CV's love for his mother, see *MM*, January 1865, and James Parton, *Famous Americans of Recent Times* (Boston: Ticknor & Fields, 1867), 377. CV's reverence for his mother can be seen in the family stories told at his golden wedding anniversary, and in his deathbed comments; see *Memorial of the Golden Wedding of Cornelius and Sophia Vanderbilt, December 19, 1863* (New York: Baker & Godwin, 1864), 27, Duke, and entry for July 12, 1876, Mrs. Cornelius Vanderbilt Diary, 1876–1878, Misc. Microfilms, reel 72, NYHS.
8 Conrad, 45–6.
9 NYSAD 75, 84th sess., 1861; NYSAD 125, 87th sess., 1864; HsR 2, part 2, 37th Cong., 2nd sess., vol. 2; *NYT*, August 25, 1860, June 21, 1862; *NYH*, September 13, 1860, August 3, 1871.
10 *NYH*, November 7, 1860; McPherson, 234–5.
11 *CT*, December 19, 1860; McPherson, 250–7.
12 Ernest A. McKay, *The Civil War and New York City* (Syracuse, N.Y.: Syracuse University Press, 1990), 3, 33, 37, 45; Sven Beckert, *The Monied Metropolis: New York City and the Consolidation of the American Bourgeoisie, 1850–1896* (New York: Cambridge University Press, 2001), 96.
13 McPherson, 262–75.
14 Strong, 3:114, 118; McKay, 55.
15 McPherson, 274; McKay, 69; Strong, 3:123–4, 127; *NYT*, April 28, 1861.
16 Strong, 3:133; McPherson, 442–3.

17 William C. Jewett to Abraham Lincoln, April 11, 1861, Abraham Lincoln Papers, LOC.

18 *OR Navy*, ser. 1, vol. 1: 8; *OR* ser. 1, vol. 53: 675; *NYT*, April 28, 1861; McPherson, 315–6.

19 *NYH*, April 26, 1861; Beckert, 116.

20 Beckert, 117; Mark R. Wilson, "The Politics of Procurement: Military Origins of Bureaucratic Autonomy," in Richard R. John, ed., *Ruling Passions: Political Economy in Nineteenth-Century America* (University Park, Penn.: Pennsylvania State University Press, 2006), 44–73; McPherson, 312–3; Foner, 23. For a comprehensive study of mobilization and procurement, see Mark R. Wilson, *The Business of Civil War: Military Mobilization and the State, 1861–1865* (Baltimore: the Johns Hopkins University Press, 2006).

21 LW Dictation.

22 HsR. 2, part 2, 37th Cong., 2nd sess., vol. 2. On the ubiquity of ship brokers, see the testimony of Ambrose Snow, SR 75, 37th Cong., 3rd sess., vol. 1.

23 *NYTr*, June 24, August 14, 1861; *NYH*, August 15, 1861.

24 HsR 2, part 2, 37th Cong., 2nd sess., vol. 2; *OR Navy*, ser. 1, vol. 4: 361.

25 HED 78, 38th Cong., 2nd sess., vol. 13; HsR 2, part 2, 37th Cong., 2nd sess., vol. 2. The charge of unfair charter prices has been made by, among others, Cedric Ridgely-Nevitt, *American Steamships on the Atlantic* (Newark, Del.: University of Delaware Press, 1981), 241.

26 George W. Cullum, *Biographical Register of the Officers and Cadets of the U.S. Military Academy at West Point, N.Y.*, vol. 2 (Boston: Houghton, Mifflin, 1891), 766–7 (George's entry number, or "Cullum number," in this authoritative guide is 1885); *Senate Journal*, March 28, 1861; Proceedings of the General Court Martial of Lt. George W. Vanderbilt, May 29, 1861, Records of the Office of the Judge Advocate General (Army), RG 153, NA.

27 Cullum, 766–7; Proceedings of the General Court Martial of Lt. George W. Vanderbilt, May 29, 1861; *NYT*, June 6, 1861. For an example of an unreliable account of George (described as capable of lifting nine hundred pounds), see *NYTr*, January 5, 1877.

28 McPherson, 324; Strong, 3:203.

29 McPherson, 373–6.

30 Howard K. Beale, ed., *Diary of Gideon Welles*, vol. 1: *1861–March 30, 1864* (New York: W. W. Norton & Co., 1960), 60–5, 473–4; McPherson, 374–6.

31 *OR* ser. 1, vol. 9: 31.

32 Welles Diary, 473; *OR Navy*, ser. 1, vol. 7: 123.

33 *OR* ser. 1, vol. 9: 31. A decade later, William B. Dinsmore hired the Pinkertons to capture Jesse James and his colleagues after the Gads Hill, Missouri, train robbery; see T. J. Stiles, *Jesse James: Last Rebel of the Civil War* (New York: Alfred A. Knopf, 2002), 249–52.

34 CV to William H. Seward, May 3, 1866, in SED 46, 39th Cong., 1st sess., vol. 2.

35 *NYT*, November 24, 1870; CV to William H. Seward, May 3, 1866, in SED 46, 39th Cong., 1st sess.

36 *JoC*, March 22, 1862; John Niven, ed., *The Salmon P. Chase Papers*, vol. 1 (Kent: Kent State University Press, 1993), 336–8; *OR* ser. 1, vol. 14: 25–6.

37 *OR* ser. 1, vol. 8: 642, vol. 14: 29; *JoC*, March 22, 1862; LT, May 5, 1862.

38 CV to EMS, March 31, 1862, reel 2, EMSP. Goldsborough's orders appear in *OR Navy*, ser. 1, vol. 7: 144–5. See also the report to Stanton by Assistant Secretary of War P. H. Watson, March 28, 1862, *OR* ser. 1, vol. 14: 46.

39 *OR* ser. 1, vol. 14: 477; *Battles and Leaders of the Civil War*, vol. 1 (New York: Century Co., 1887), 707.

40 *Salmon P. Chase Papers*, 1:338; *OR* ser. 1, vol. 14: 157; Doris Kearns Goodwin, *Team of Rivals: The Political Genius of Abraham Lincoln* (New York: Simon & Schuster, 2005), 436–9.

41 McPherson, 445.

42 McPherson, 444; Stiles, 168–9. The extent of the government's role in the suspension of gold payments is disputed by historians, but certainly it played a role. See Stuart Banner, "The Origin of the New York Stock Exchange, 1791–1860," *Journal of Legal Studies* 27, no. 1 (January 1998): 113–40; Robert P. Sharkey, *Money, Class, and Party: An Economic Study of Civil War and Reconstruction* (Baltimore: Johns Hopkins University Press, 1959), 15–28; James K. Kindahl, "Economic Factors in Specie Resumption, 1865–1879," in Stanley L. Engerman and Robert W. Fogel, eds., *The Reinterpretation of American Economic History* (New York: Harper & Row, 1971), 468–79; Irwin Ungter, *The Greenback Era: A Social and Political History of American Finance, 1865–1879* (Princeton: Princeton University Press, 1964), 13–7; Milton Friedman and Anna Jacobson Schwartz, *A Monetary History of the United States, 1867–1960* (Princeton: Princeton University Press, 1963), 3–14. See also Esther Rogoff Taus, *Central Banking Functions of the United States Treasury, 1789–1941* (New York: Columbia University Press, 1943), 57–64.

43 Herman E. Krooss, ed., *Documentary History of Banking and Currency in the United States* (New York: Chelsea House Publishers, 1965), 1315–6.

44 McPherson, 445–7; Sharkey, 28–50; McKay, 122; Fowler, 153–4.

45 Krooss, 2085–6; Taus, 79, 85–6, 102, 112; Richard Franklin Bensel, *Yankee Leviathan: The Origins of Central State Authority in America, 1865–1877* (New York: Cambridge University Press, 1990), 262–74, 287–8; Richard Sylla, "Federal Policy, Banking Market Structure, and Capital Mobilization in the United States, 1863–1913," *JEH* 29, no. 4 (December 1969): 657–86. Stuart Banner, "The Origin of the New York Stock Exchange," argues that by 1860 the New York Stock & Exchange Board was already the premier stock exchange in the United States, effectively setting prices nationwide.

46 Entry for August 22, 1861, David Mitchell Turnure Journal, NYHS; Bensel, 168–9.

47 McPherson, 442–53; Bensel, 150–78; John Jay Knox, *A History of Banking in the United States* (New York: Augustus M. Kelley, 1969, orig. pub. 1903), 91–104. Boston merchant Amasa Walker, for example, duplicated McCulloch's remarks; see Bensel, 282.

48 McPherson, 447; Fowler, 73–5, 156–7; Bensel, 152, 162. Foreign coins were actually legal tender in the United States until 1857; Krooss, 1059.

49 *NYH*, January 20, 1869.

50 Since imports were paid in gold, the gold premium represented a kind of tariff. In states that thrived on international commerce, such as New York, leading businessmen favored a return to gold-based currency, as opposed to those in manufacturing centers, such as iron-and-coal-producing Pennsylvania, who competed with English imports. Railroad managers, who imported British rails, favored a gold standard and low tariffs. See Stanley Cohen, "Northeastern Business and Radical Reconstruction: A Re-Examination," *Mississippi Valley Historical Review*, 46, no. 1 (June 1959): 67–90.

51 *HC*, September 19, 1861; *Seventh Annual Report of the Pacific Mail Steamship Company, May 1861* (New York: G. F. Nesbitt & Co., 1861); *Report of the President to the Stockholders, Pacific Mail Steamship Company* (n.p.: 1868); CV to Chester Arthur, October 8, 1861, reel 1, Chester A. Arthur Papers, LOC; *CT*, November 11, 1861; Directors' Minutes, May 15, 1861, HRR, reel 27, box 242, NYCRR; NYSAD 100, 85th sess., 1862. The War Department's chartering of CV's transatlantic steamers, particularly the *Vanderbilt*, led him to discontinue the European line; see RGD, NYC 341:167.

52 Beckert, 135–6; McKay, 141; Fowler, 54, 57, 73; *Harper's New Monthly Magazine*, April 1865.

53 RGD, NYC 375:200a4; *SA*, November 15, 1862; *RT*, June 7, 1862.

54 Andrew Shuman to William H. Seward, August 9, 1861, Walter H. Gaines and Henry S. Rowland to Abraham Lincoln, December 21, 1862, Franz Sigel to Abraham Lincoln, March 17, 1863, Abraham Lincoln Papers, LOC; John D. Hayes, ed.,

Samuel Francis Du Pont: A Selection from his Civil War Letters, vol. 1: *The Mission, 1860–1862* (Ithaca: Cornell University Press, 1969), 112; Frames 237 and 244, Annual List, 1862, District 6, Division 3, Annual Lists, 1862–3, District 1, New York, roll 65, Internal Revenue Assessment Lists for New York and New Jersey, 1862–1866: Microfilm Publication M603, NA. On the problem of dividends in tax reporting, see Rufus S. Tucker, "The Distribution of Income Among Taxpayers in the United States," *Quarterly Journal of Economics* 52, no. 4 (August 1938): 547–87.

55 *Atlantic Monthly*, May 1868; *Forest and Stream*, August 28, 1873.

56 RGD, NYC 374:1; Strong, 3:21.

57 Burrows & Wallace, 877–81. Melvin L. Adelman argues that the rise of the respectability of harness racing reflected the rise of a new elite in New York; see "The First Modern Sport in America: Harness Racing in New York City, 1825–1870," *Journal of Sport History* 8, no. 1 (spring 1981): 5–32.

58 Beckert, 115–9, 136–7; Fowler, dedication page. Fowler also dedicated it to Salmon P. Chase and George S. Boutwell, secretaries of the treasury. His dedication to CV reads, "who has aided so powerfully to foster the steam industries of the nation on land and water." For an overview of this period, see Burrows & Wallace, 872–82.

59 McPherson, 314–6, 546–7; Charles G. Summersell, ed., *The Journal of George Townley Fullam* (Tuscaloosa: University of Alabama Press, 1973), 4–14.

60 SED 71, 37th Cong., 2nd sess., vol. 6.

61 *HW*, May 3, 1862; *OR* ser. 1, vol. 14: 365–6; HsR 28, 41st Cong., 2nd sess., vol. 1.

62 *OR* ser. 3, vol. 2: 525.

63 *OR Navy*, ser. 1, vol. 1: 538.

64 SR 75, 37th Cong., 3rd sess., vol. 1. These quotes come from CV's testimony before Congress a few months later, on December 30, 1862. Regarding the dates of these conversations, Banks reported on November 1 that he left Washington on October 27; *OR* ser. 3, vol. 2: 712–3. See also James G. Hollandsworth Jr., *Pretense of Glory: The Life of General Nathaniel P. Banks* (Baton Rouge: Louisiana State University Press, 1998), 83–8.

65 SR 75, 37th Cong., 3rd sess., vol. 1.

66 Nathaniel P. Banks to CV, November 3, 1862, CV to Nathaniel P. Banks, November 3, 4, 1862, cont. 24, Nathaniel P. Banks Papers, LOC; CV to EMS, January 24, 1863, reel 4, EMSP; SR 75, 37th Cong., 3rd sess., vol. 1; *OR* ser. 3, vol. 2: 712–3.

67 SR 75, 37th Cong., 3rd sess., vol. 1; Senate Misc. Doc. 27, 37th Cong., 3rd sess., vol. 1. CV has been criticized for not personally inspecting all of the scores of vessels chartered for the expedition. But as *CT*, January 15, 1863, justly noted, he went by the insurance underwriters' ratings, which he would have relied on if he had chartered the ships for his own use. CV had earlier testified, "I seldom go aboard of ships unless to go somewhere"; HsR 2, Part 2, 37th Cong., 2nd sess., vol. 2. On the censure resolution, see Senate Journal, January 21, 27, 29, 1863.

68 *NYTr*, December 5, 1862.

69 McPherson, 624. For a report from aboard ship on the expedition, see *NYTr*, December 29, 1862.

70 Raphael Semmes, *Memoirs of Service Afloat During the War Between the States* (Baton Rouge: Louisiana State University Press, 1996, orig. pub. 1868), 529–30; Fullam Journal, 60–1.

71 *NYT*, December 28, 1862.

72 George Willis Read, ed., *A Pioneer of 1850: George Willis Read, 1819–1880* (Boston: Little, Brown, 1927), 130–2; *NYT*, December 28, 1862; *Frank Leslie's Illustrated Newspaper*, January 10, 1863.

73 Semmes, 535; Fullam, 66; *NYT*, December 28, 1862; *Frank Leslie's Illustrated Newspaper*, January 10, 1863; *LT*, January 14, 1863; *CT*, December 31, 1862; *OR Navy*, ser. 1, vol. 1: 782–3.

74 *NYT*, December 29, 1862.

75 *OR Navy*, ser. 1, vol. 1: 604–5.
76 Semmes, 672, 737; HED 1, part 2, 38th Cong., 2nd sess., vol. 2; McPherson, 547. The *Vanderbilt*, though much sought after by navy officers, had problems peculiar to its adaptation to naval service. At the end of commercial voyages, the jet condensers that allowed it to boil seawater ordinarily would be cleared of scale formed by boiling brine; under continuous use, scale buildup and corrosion became a serious problem; Cedric Ridgely-Nevitt, 244–5.
77 Senate Journal, July 17, 1862; SED 30, 37th Cong., 3rd sess., vol. 1; Cullum, 766–7. For reports of the other George W. Vanderbilt, see *OR* ser. 1, vol. 21: 59, vol. 27, part 1: 981–2. In CV's obituaries and elsewhere, it would be claimed that George fell sick during the Corinth campaign in early 1862. No direct evidence supports the story. *NYS*, December 9, 1885, claimed that George had consumption, but the accuracy of this report is impossible to assess.

Fourteen The Origins of Empire

1 *NYTr*, February 6, 1879. See also *NYH*, October 3, 1869.
2 Sven Beckert, *The Monied Metropolis: New York City and the Consolidation of the American Bourgeoisie, 1850–1896* (New York; Cambridge University Press, 2001), 146–9.
3 SR 75, 37th Cong., 3rd sess., vol. 1; *CT*, January 13, 1863.
4 NYSAD 19, 90th sess., January 18, 1867.
5 *RG*, January 12, 1877.
6 *RG*, January 12, 1877.
7 These changes are often located at the very end of the nineteenth and beginning of the twentieth centuries, when they took full hold on the economy as a whole, but they would be well under way before the end of CV's life. See Gregory A. Mark, "The Personification of the Business Corporation in American Law," *University of Chicago Law Review* 54, no. 4 (autumn 1987): 1441–83; Naomi R. Lamoreaux, "Partnerships, Corporations, and the Limits on Contractual Freedom in U.S. History: An Essay in Economics, Law, and Culture," in Kenneth Lipartito and David B. Scilia, eds., *Constructing Corporate America: History, Politics, Culture* (Oxford: Oxford University Press, 2004), 29–65; Alan Trachtenberg, *The Incorporation of America: Culture and Society in the Gilded Age* (New York: Hill & Wang, 1982), 4–6, 57–8.
8 Alfred D. Chandler, *The Visible Hand: The Managerial Revolution in American Business* (Cambridge, Mass.: Harvard University Press, 1977), 1–12, 79–121; Trachtenberg, 3–10.
9 For examples of this thinking among contemporaries and later writers, see Henry Clews, *Twenty-Eight Years in Wall Street* (New York: Irving Publishing, 1888), 110, and Edward J. Renehan Jr., *Commodore: The Life of Cornelius Vanderbilt* (New York: Basic Books, 2007), 239.
10 For a portrayal of CV's plans as a long-laid campaign, see the highly influential "A Chapter of Erie," *NAR*, July 1869, 30–106, in which CFA writes, "His object has been to make himself the virtual master of all by making himself absolute lord of the railways." I may be accused here of misrepresenting CFA and the historiography; CFA, like many historians, hedges on CV's thinking. My point is merely to represent the general tenor of the depictions of CV's method. See, for example, Fowler, 494–5.
11 This observation reflects a broad investigation of CV's life. See also Chauncey M. Depew, *My Memories of Eighty Years* (New York: Charles Scribner's Sons, 1922), 228–9.
12 CV to Edwin D. Morgan, February 16, 1863, fold. 2, box 13, Edwin D. Morgan Papers, NYSL.
13 LW Dictation.

14   *NYH*, January 20, 1869. On railroads' size relative to other enterprises, see Alfred D. Chandler Jr., ed., *The Railroads, the Nation's First Big Business: Sources and Readings* (New York: Harcourt, Brace & World, 1965), 43. On the value of Harlem shares, see NYSAD 175, 86th sess., 1863.

15   NYSAD 175, 86th sess., 1863; NYSAD 19, 90th sess., 1867; NYSAD 114, 90th sess., 1867; *NYH*, March 25, 1863.

16   See HFC's testimony in NYSAD 19, 90th sess., January 18, 1867. See also Lane, 188–9; *NYT*, June 30, 1858, April 15, 1859; Directors' Minutes, May 4, 1859, HRR, reel 27, box 242, NYCRR; Alvin F. Harlow, *The Road of the Century: The Story of the New York Central* (New York: Creative Age Press, 1947), 166; Edward Hungerford, *Men and Iron: The History of the New York Central* (New York: Thomas Y. Crowell, 1938), 120–6. For a precise description of a journey (albeit a customized one) from the depot north, showing how the horses hauled cars to Forty-second Street, see *NYT*, July 6, 1865.

17   Fowler, 199–201, 203–5.

18   Hudson C. Tanner, *"The Lobby" and Public Men from Thurlow Weed's Time* (Albany: George MacDonald, 1888), 230.

19   NYSAD 175, 86th sess., February 17, 1863, shows that the Harlem had unusually high revenues and expenses per ton/mile, making it a ripe target for reform.

20   NYSAD 19, 90th sess., January 18, 1867.

21   It is nearly impossible to accurately estimate how many shares anyone—least of all CV—held in the 1860s and '70s. As will be seen, CV routinely transferred shares he owned into the names of others to disguise his holdings. Both press reports and WHV's testimony suggest that, by the end of the events described at least, CV owned half of the company's shares, not including those held by allies and family members. See *HW*, July 11, 1863; NYSAD 19, 90th sess., January 18, 1867. These reports, however, came later; on May 18, 1863, CV voted only 8,801 out of more than 114,000 shares (and 88,978 voted) at the annual stockholders' meeting and election; Directors' Minutes, May 18, 1863, HRR, reel 27, box 242, NYCRR.

22   McPherson, 323–4; Mark Wahlgren Summers, *The Era of Good Stealings* (New York: Oxford University Press, 1993), 16–23.

23   *HW*, July 11, 1863; Burrows & Wallace, 917.

24   RGD, NYC 342:300D. See also Smith, 294, for an amusing description of Law.

25   *NYH*, March 26, 1864. For examples of reports that name Law, see *NYTr*, April 24, 1863; Strong, 3:313; *NYT*, April 25, 1863. See also Lane, 191–2.

26   Strong, 3:313; *NYTr*, April 24, 1863; *NYH*, April 24, 1863; *HW*, July 11, 1863. In truth, money-driven attempts to build a Broadway railroad (and the belief that corrupt railroad men had bought the legislature) had been a regular feature in Albany in recent years; see *NYH*, January 1, 1860.

27   Burrows & Wallace, 835–8; Ernest A. McKay, *The Civil War and New York City* (Syracuse: Syracuse University Press, 1990), 230–3.

28   *NYH*, April 22, 24, 1863; *HW*, July 11, 1863; Fowler, 205; see also *NYH*, April 24, 1863; Directors' Minutes, April 22, 23, 1863, HRR, reel 27, box 242, NYCRR.

29   *NYH*, April 24, 25, 1863; *NYT*, April 25, 1863; Strong, 3:313.

30   CV to EC, May 13, 1863, fold. 3, box 81, ECP.

31   Ibid.; Directors' Minutes, May 18, 19, 29, 1863, HRR, reel 27, box 242, NYCRR. The new board was seen as "the Vanderbilt ticket"; *PS*, May 28, 1863. The HRR minutes show that CV voted only 8,801 of the 88,978 shares represented at the stockholders' meeting (about 114,000 existed). HFC had 1,350, AS had two thousand, and JHB had three thousand, all of which really might have been CV's property, held in their names. To achieve victory, then, CV drew upon the support of men who controlled many more shares, such as A. B. Baylis with 19,970, and Henry G. Stebbins (JLW's onetime partner) with 10,650, though they may have been holding shares for CV as well.

32   Directors' Minutes, May 18, 19, 29, 1863, HRR, reel 27, box 242, NYCRR.

33 *NYH*, April 22, 24, May 11, 1863; *HW*, July 11, 1863.
34 *HW*, July 11, 1863; *NYH*, June 26, 1863. Henry Clews, *Fifty Years in Wall Street* (New York: Irving Publishing, 1908), 111, and Fowler, 206–8, repeat similar versions of this story.
35 *NYH*, June 26, 1863; LW Dictation.
36 *NYH*, June 26–9, July 13, 1863.
37 *HW*, July 11, 1863.
38 Ibid.; *NYH*, July 1–5, 1863; *Independent*, July 2, 1863; Strong, 3:328.
39 At the election of 1864, CV voted 29,607 shares; Directors' Minutes, May 17, 1864, HRR, reel 27, box 242, NYCRR. As ever, it is impossible to know how many he really owned. On February 5, 1867, CV refused to tell a committee of the state legislature how much Harlem stock he owned, but his son William put the total at about half of the total number of shares; NYSAD 19, 90th sess., 1867.
40 Strong, 3:329–30.
41 Seymour J. Mandelbaum, *Boss Tweed's New York* (New York: John Wiley & Sons, 1965), 58, 66–70.
42 Summers, *Good Stealings*, 16–29, and throughout; Mark Wahlgren Summers, " 'To Make the Wheels Revolve We Must Have Grease': Barrel Politics in the Gilded Age," *Journal of Policy History* 14, no. 1 (2002): 49–72; Seymour J. Mandelbaum, *Boss Tweed's New York* (New York: John Wiley & Sons, 1965), 46–75. Glenn C. Altschuler and Stuart M. Blumin argue in *Rude Republic: Americans and Their Politics in the Nineteenth Century* (Princeton, N.J.: Princeton University Press, 2000), 8 (see also 84–5), that the "uncomfortably disreputable associations and activities" of mass party politics that rose in the 1830s alienated elites.
43 Clews, 111; Fowler, 124; Medbery, 92–3, 98. Lane, 193, accepts that Drew fought CV in the 1863 corner.
44 RGD, NYC 366:300c.
45 Clifford Browder, author of *The Money Game in Old New York: Daniel Drew and His Times* (Lexington: University Press of Kentucky, 1986), a poorly sourced and unsatisfying biography of Drew, argues, 101–2, that Drew did not take part in the Harlem corner of 1863. I believe he is correct. Edmund Clarence Stedman, in *The New York Stock Exchange* (New York: Stock Exchange Historical Company, 1905), 174, observed that Drew "is said" to have opposed CV in the corner, but he appears to be simply citing Clews.
46 *OR* ser. 3, vol. 3: 1083; J. C. Buckhout to CV, February 11, May 23, 1864, Engineer's Office Letterbook, HRR, 1864, box 19, NYCRR.
47 McKay, 216–29.
48 McKay, 195–210, 216; Burrows & Wallace, 887–99. Maps in Burrows & Wallace, 891, and *NYH*, July 20, 1863, show no fires in the vicinity of CV's home.
49 Burrows & Wallace, 896. On HFC and AS's continuing political prominence, see Strong, 3:101, 513.
50 Jay Gould to EC, August 20, 1863, fold. 5, box 38, ECP.
51 Klein, 15, 27–54, 72–3; RGD, NYC 347:737. Klein's biography remains definitive.
52 George Rogers Taylor and Irene D. Neu, *The American Railroad Network, 1861–1890* (Cambridge, Mass.: Harvard University Press, 1956), 2–29.
53 *NYT*, November 24, 1854; NYSAD 114, 90th sess., 1867; NYSAD 38, 103rd sess., 1880.
54 See the testimony of Edwin D. Worcester, HFC, AS, and Robert L. Banks, NYSAD 19, 90th sess., 1867. The importance of local freight to the Central can be seen from a chart provided in testimony by Worcester before Congress: in 1862, through freight amounted to 777,000 tons, local 610,000; in 1863, through 824,000, local 624,000; and local surpassed through in 1864, 790,000 to 766,000 through. Due to lesser mileage on local freight, the earnings from through freight were more than double. See SR 307, part 2, 43rd Cong., 1st sess., vol. 3, 158.
55 Julius Grodinsky, *Railroad Consolidation: Its Economics and Controlling Principles* (New

York: D. Appleton and Company, 1930), 29–31; Alfred D. Chandler Jr., ed., *The Railroads; The Nation's First Big Business: Sources and Readings* (New York: Harcourt, Brace & World, 1965), 10, 159–60.

56   Irene D. Neu, *Erastus Corning: Merchant and Financier, 1794–1872* (Ithaca: Cornell University Press, 1960), 1–13, 43, 161–4; Harlow, 19, 112; Hungerford, 72–3, 93; *NYT,* April 10, 1872; JMD to EC, February 1, 1867, fold. 3, box 89, CV to EC, September 15, 1863, HFC to EC, September 21, 1863, fold. 3, box 82, ECP.

57   Strong, 3:416; Fowler, 178; Smith, 252–3. See also RGD, NYC 349:983, which notes Jerome was considered to be of good character, "& reputed very strong."

58   Jay Gould to EC, November 28, 1863, fold. 7, box 38, Watts Sherman to EC, October 22, 1863, fold. 3, box 82, ECP; Directors' Minutes, October 20, 1863, HR, oversize vol. 247, NYCRR; Neu, *Corning,* 173–4. For an example of a nearly contemporary HR complaint to the NYC, see Samuel Sloan to EC, March 17, 1864, copied in Executive Committee Minutes, March 24, 1864, HR, oversize vol. 249, and cited in Directors' Minutes, March 18, 1864, NYC, vol. 3, box 34, NYCRR.

59   CV to EC, November 12, 1863, fold. 7, box 38, Watts Sherman to EC, December 7, 1863, fold. 2, box 39, ECP; Smith, 379.

60   Watts Sherman to EC, October 22, 1863, fold. 3, box 82; JHB to EC, November 11, 19, 1863, CV to EC, November 12, 1863, fold. 7, box 38; all in ECP. See also Corning's testimony in NYSAD 19, 90th sess., 1867.

61   *NYH,* November 19, 1863, in *NYT,* November 28, 1863. Jerome, who owned a controlling interest in *NYT,* appears to have pushed it to attack the Central's management, calling it the Democratic ring that ran New York (see Jay Gould to EC, November 28, 1863, JHB to EC, fold. 7, box 38, ECP). The notion that the Central under EC and Richmond "was itself the Democratic political organization," as argued by Thomas C. Cochran, *Railroad Leaders, 1845–1890: The Business Mind in Action* (New York: Russell & Russell, 1965, orig. pub. 1953), 25, is a historical truism that deserves reexamination. Unquestionably EC and Richmond were leaders of the state's Democratic Party, and used their power in the railroad to gain influence. But even cynical contemporaries admitted that they did not control the government. See, for example, the *Nation,* April 18, 1867. And John V. L. Pruyn objected to directors being chosen because of their political affiliations (in this case, Republican); see entry for November 10, 1864, John V. L. Pruyn Journal, box 2, John V. L. Pruyn Papers, NYSL.

62   CV to EC, November 20, 1863, fold., box 38, ECP.

63   JHB to EC, November 20, 1863, fold. 7, box 38, Leonard W. Jerome to CV, enclosed in CV to EC, December 5, 1863, fold. 2, box 39, ECP.

64   *NYT,* December 3, 1863.

65   *CT,* December 8, 1863; *NYT,* December 9, 1863; *NYH,* December 9, 1863.

66   *NYH,* December 13, 1863; entry for December 11, 1863, Pruyn Journal; Richard M. Schell to EC, December 11, 1863, fold. 2, box 39, ECP.

67   CV to EC, December 25, 1863, fold. 2, box 39, ECP; Neu, *Erastus Corning,* 177–8. In relation to this, see CV to Samuel L. M. Barlow, March 6, 1860, BW box 36 (14), Samuel L. M. Barlow Collection, HL.

68   For a precise description of 10 Washington Place, see *NYT,* January 5, 1877. In the 1870 U.S. census, CV had five servants resident at 10 Washington Place, all born in Ireland.

69   This account of CV's golden wedding celebration is from *NYTr,* December 21, 1863, and *Memorial of the Golden Wedding of Cornelius and Sophia Vanderbilt, December 19, 1863* (New York: Baker & Godwin, 1864), copy in Duke. The *Memorial* identifies Ann S. Stephens as the author of the *Tribune* story.

70   Smith, 409; RGD, NYC 343:316; Certificate of Incorporation, November 27, 1863, Certificate of Increase of the Capital Stock, October 5, 1866, Atlantic Mail Steamship Company, NYCC. Allen and Garrison did not appear as the original

incorporators; they were JHB, Edward A. Quintard (Charles Morgan's son-in-law), Edward Mott Robinson, Samuel G. Wheeler, Charles A. Gould, and William Barton Allen (son of Daniel Allen). Once in operation, both Allen and Cornelius Garrison served as directors, with their headquarters at 5 Bowling Green, CV's old office. See also *CT*, July 20, 1864. On Osgood, see Smith, 409; *NYT*, May 4, 1867; *NYH*, March 19, 1868.

71 *NYTr*, December 21, 1863.

72 *NYS*, December 19, 22, 1877; *NYH*, December 27, 1877, in Vanderbilt Will Trial Case Clippings, NYPL; *NYTr*, March 13, 18, 1878; Ellen W. Vanderbilt to HG, March 19, 1868, reel 2, HGP. It appears that CJV had bad checks outstanding that very evening; see HG to Hanson A. Risley, March 27, 1864, Hanson A. Risley Papers, Duke. Note also that he had resumed his practice of befriending leading politicians, notably Schuyler Colfax, who became speaker of the house in 1863, with CJV claiming to have helped secure him the post; Willard H. Smith, *Schuyler Colfax: The Changing Fortunes of a Political Idol* (Indianapolis: Indiana Historical Bureau, 1952), 182–5.

73 *NYS*, December 9, 1885; NYSAD 75, 84th sess., 1861; NYSAD 175, 86th sess., 1863; NYSAD 125, 87th sess., 1864. In 1863, WHV owned five carriages and 160 ounces of silver plate, indications of his prosperity; Annual List, May 1, 1863, Collection District 1, Division 21, New York, New York, District 1: Annual Lists, 1862–3, roll 38, Internal Revenue Assessment Lists for New York and New Jersey, 1862–1866, Microfilm Publication M603, NA. He had no income listed, suggesting he earned the bulk of his income through corporate dividends, which were taxed at the source.

74 *Memorial of the Golden Wedding*; *NYTr*, January 5, 1877; Dorothy Kelly MacDowell, *Commodore Vanderbilt and His Family: A Biographical Account of the Descendants of Cornelius and Sophia Johnson Vanderbilt* (n.p., 1989), 22.

75 *NYS*, December 9, 1885; *NYT*, February 4, 1864. January 1, 1864, is usually stated as George's death date. The *NYT* report on George's funeral gives December 31; as it was the account closest in time to the event, and had other telling details, I am accepting December 31.

76 *NYT*, February 4, 1864; *NYS*, December 15, 1877; *NYTr*, November 2, 1878; *NYH*, March 5, 1879; Frontis, Directors' Minutes, HR, oversize vol. 248, NYCRR; NYSAD 19, 90th sess., 1867; *NYS*, December 9, 1885.

77 SED 46, 39th Cong., 1st sess., vol. 2.

78 NYSAD 19, 90th sess., 1867; *CT*, February 25, 1866. James A. Ward discusses the nation-state metaphor for railroads in *Railroads and the Character of America, 1820–1851* (Knoxville: University of Tennessee Press, 1986).

79 A mysterious bill to consolidate the Harlem and the New York Central drove this commentary; *NYT*, February 6, 1864; *RT*, February 13, 1864; *NYH*, February 25, 1864.

80 Directors' Minutes, January 27, 1864, HRR, reel 26, box 242, NYCRR; J. C. Buckhout to CV, February 11, 1864, Engineer's Office Letterbook, HRR, 1864, box 19, NYCRR; *RT*, May 14, 1864; *NYT*, April 16, 1864, March 19, 1866; Lane, 208–15; Alvin F. Harlow, *The Road of the Century: The Story of the New York Central* (New York: Creative Age Press, 1947), 164, 180. Harlow argues that CV's action in participating in the creation of the Athens railroad was "inexplicable." It makes perfect sense, however, if CV was not yet the hidden power in the HR when the Athens project was conceived.

81 Smith, 265–7; Fowler, 162–4; RGD, NYC 265:237.

82 Executive Committee Minutes, April 11, 1863, HR, oversize vol. 249; Directors' Minutes, June 8, 1863, HR, oversize vol. 247; both NYCRR.

83 The basic story told by Clews, 107–9, appeared much earlier in *Harper's New Monthly Magazine*, April 1865. In *Harper's*, however, the management of the Hudson

corner was contrasted with CV's handling of the Harlem corners, rather than attributed to CV himself.

84   Clews, 107–9; NYSAD 19, 90th sess., 1867. Even Lane, 208–11, who readily accepts most of Clews's anecdotes, expresses doubts about CV's role in the HR corner. Tellingly, CV abandoned the double-tracking of the HR after he took control of the HRR.

85   *NYH*, October 19, 30, 1863; Lane, 195. It is clear from *NYH*, September 7, 1863, that the purchase of the stage lines had never been effected.

86   Directors' Minutes, March 12, 1864, HRR, reel 26, box 242, NYCRR; *NYT*, March 17, 1864; *NYH*, March 25, 26, April 30, 1864; Lane, 195–6.

87   Browder, 66.

88   *NYH*, April 21, 1864; Lane, 194–8. Fowler, 350–4, not only claims that Drew was a bear in Harlem, but also provides an excellent account of calls. Browder, 103–6, agrees that Drew took a bear position in Harlem in 1864.

89   Fowler, 351. See also Clews, 107–9; *BM*, May 1864.

90   *CT*, April 9, 1864; *Zion's Herald and Wesleyan Journal*, April 13, 1864; Strong, 3:430. On the Sanitary Commission, see McPherson, 480–3.

91   Fowler, 284–6; *NYT*, April 16, 1864.

92   *NYH*, April 17, 19, 21, 1864; *EP* in *CT*, April 23, 1864; *NYT*, April 22, 1864; Medbery, 241; Fowler, 71–4, 260, 354, 364–5; Robert P. Sharkey, *Money, Class, and Party: An Economic Study of Civil War and Reconstruction* (Baltimore: Johns Hopkins Press, 1959), 51–2. For a recollection of the impact of Chase's act on the corner, see *NYTr*, August 5, 1876.

93   *NYH*, April 30, May 15, June 3, 1864; *NYT*, May 5, 12, 18, 1864. See also the reminiscences of a Wall Street insider, *NYTr*, August 5, 1876. Lane, 196–8, repeats Clews's fanciful version, complete with dialogue that may be regarded as fiction. Medbery, 159–60, gives an excellent description of the workings of a corner, explicitly citing this one as an example.

94   Lane, 198–9; *NYT*, April 22, 23, May 18, 1864; *NYH*, April 30, 1864; Fowler, 355–6. It will be noted that I am relying more freely on Fowler, even though, like Clews, his version of events necessarily relied on rumor. Fowler wrote much sooner after the events quoted, and was generally far more reliable than Clews. Still, I give credence to his account only when he offers personal information or is confirmed by other sources.

95   Clews, 116.

96   Directors' Minutes, May 17, 18, 1864, HRR, reel 26, box 242, NYCRR.

97   Directors' Minutes, June 13, 14, 1864, HR, oversize vol. 247; Executive Committee Minutes, June 14, July 6, 1864, HR, oversize vol. 249; all NYCRR.

98   *CT*, July 20, 1864; *United States Service Magazine*, August 1864. On July 1, Congress ceased to pay CV for mail service to California; SED 44, 41st Cong., 3rd sess., vol. 1.

99   *NYH*, May 2, 1878; Smith, 178–85.

100   *NYT*, July 9, 1865, June 26, 1866; *CT*, August 12, 1866; Smith, 180.

101   *CT*, September 6, 1860, September 23, 1866; *PS*, August 11, 1864; *NYT*, July 9, 1865; Smith, 183. Lane, 199, and Medbery, 163–4, claim that Morrissey went against CV in the second Harlem corner; Fowler, 355, says the opposite. Fowler seems more likely to be right. *NYT*, July 9, 1865, reports that the Saratoga track, with CV as a key backer, was in operation with Morrissey as a manager in 1864, hinting that Morrissey's attempt to ingratiate himself with CV dated to the aftermath of the first Harlem corner.

102   *NYS*, December 22, 1877.

103   HG to Hanson A. Risley, February 16, March 27, 1864, Hanson A. Risley Papers, Duke.

104   CJV to HG, September 7, 1864, reel 2, HGP.

105 HG to Abraham Lincoln, September 21, 1864, Abraham Lincoln Papers, LOC. HG was correct that CV was a leading purchaser of federal bonds; see, for example, a report of his purchase of $300,000 in 5-20 bonds in early 1865, HED 52, 39th Cong., 2nd sess., vol. 8.

106 HG to William P. Fessenden, October 4, 1864, HG, E. D. Morgan et al. to William P. Fessenden, October 10, 1864, HG to William P. Fessenden, December 1, 1864, Gilder Lehrman Institute of American History, NYHS; HG to Hanson A. Risley, October 12, Hanson A. Risley Papers, Duke.

107 HG to Abraham Lincoln, November 23, 1864, Abraham Lincoln Papers, LOC.

108 Directors' Minutes, September 6, October 4, 1864, HR, oversize vol. 247, NYCRR.

109 Medbery, 161–2, gives a story circulating in Wall Street in 1870 that CV had tested WHV by trying to trick him into short-selling Hudson River stock at a time when he was planning to drive the price up; WHV, however, saw through the ploy, and purchased Hudson River instead. Though Lane tells the tale as well, it was simply one more rumor circulating around CV. There is no good evidence that he tried to undercut his son, on whom he increasingly relied.

Fifteen The Power to Punish

1 W. L. Garrison to Wife, September 5, 1864, William Lloyd Garrison Papers, Rare Books and Manuscripts Department, Boston Public Library.

2 *NAR*, April 1867; Foner, 462; Alfred D. Chandler Jr., ed., *The Railroads; The Nation's First Big Business: Sources and Readings* (New York: Harcourt, Brace & World, 1965), 3, 9.

3 William Cronon, *Nature's Metropolis: Chicago and the Great West* (New York: W. W. Norton & Co., 1991), 23–93; Edward Chase Kirkland, *Men, Cities, and Transportation: A Study in New England History, 1820–1900*, vol. 1 (Cambridge, Mass.: Harvard University Press, 1948), 496; George Rogers Taylor and Irene D. Neu, *The American Railroad Network, 1861–1890* (Cambridge, Mass.: Harvard University Press, 1956), 57, 67–75; Maury Klein, *Unfinished Business: The Railroad in American Life* (Hanover, N.H.: University Press of New England, 1994), 9–16; Alfred D. Chandler Jr., *The Visible Hand: The Managerial Revolution in American Business* (Cambridge, Mass.: Harvard University Press, 1977), 91.

4 Sven Beckert, *The Monied Metropolis: New York City and the Consolidation of the American Bourgeoisie, 1850–1896* (New York; Cambridge University Press, 2001), 145–9; Chandler, *Visible Hand*, 81–94; Chandler, *The Railroads*, 43; Foner, 20, 461; NYSAD 114, 90th sess., February 20, 1867. For bank reports, see *BM* throughout this period.

5 Annual Report, February 11, 1865, HR Annual Reports, oversize vol. 241, NYCRR; Thomas C. Cochran, *Railroad Leaders, 1845–1890: The Business Mind in Action* (New York: Russell & Russell, 1965, orig. pub. 1953), 63–4, 83, 84–6, 474–5; Alfred D. Chandler Jr., "The Railroads: Pioneers in Modern Corporate Management," *BHR* 39, no. 1 (spring 1965): 16–40; Alfred D. Chandler Jr. and Stephen Salsbury, "The Railroads: Innovators in Modern Business Administration," in Bruce Mazlish, ed., *The Railroad and the Space Program: An Exploration in Historical Analogy* (Cambridge, Mass.: MIT Press, 1965), 127–62; Chandler, *Visible Hand*, 94–121.

6 NYSAD 19, 90th sess., 1867. For an example of CV's guidance to his distant agents during his steamship years, see CV to John T. Wright and William S. Freeman, October 19, 1859, CV-NYHS.

7 NYSAD 19, 90th sess., 1867; LW Dictation. For examples of CV's scrutiny and direction, see J. C. Buckhout to CV, May 23, 1864, Engineer's Office Letterbook, HRR, 1864, box 19, NYCRR; *RT*, September 30, 1865.

8 Railroad track nationwide grew by less than a thousand miles per year during the

war; the rate of construction would more than double within twelve months of Appomattox. Chandler, *The Railroads,* 13, 43; Executive Committee Minutes, February 16, 1865, HR, oversize vol. 249, Directors' Minutes, February 7, 1865, HR, oversize vol. 248, NYCRR; NYSAD 19, 90th sess., 1867; Edward Hungerford, *Men and Iron: The History of the New York Central* (New York: Thomas Y. Crowell, 1938), 196–8. In Missouri, among other states, local counties issued bonds to fund local railroads, which often went bankrupt and were absorbed by larger lines; T. J. Stiles, *Jesse James: Last Rebel of the Civil War* (New York: Alfred A. Knopf, 2002), 230–9.

9 Beckert, 136–7, 148; James A. Ward, *J. Edgar Thomson: Master of the Pennsylvania* (Westport, Conn.: Greenwood Press, 1980), 93–6; Chandler, *Visible Hand,* 90–4, 105.

10 Executive Committee Minutes, February 16, 1865, HR, oversize vol. 249, NYCRR; NYSAD 19, 90th sess., 1867.

11 *MM,* January 1865.

12 *NYT,* December 9, 1864.

13 Strong, 3:409, 565.

14 Henry Clews, *Fifty Years in Wall Street* (New York: Irving Publishing, 1908), 3–7, 110. For an example of how this mistaken notion that CV hated trains has taken hold in popular thinking, see John Steele Gordon, *An Empire of Wealth: The Epic History of American Economic Power* (New York: HarperCollins, 2005), 212.

15 Cochran, 178–9; John V. L. Pruyn Journal, April 28–30, 1864, box 2, John V. L. Pruyn Papers, NYSL (to be referred to hereafter as "Pruyn Journal").

16 *NYT,* August 28, 1866; *CT,* August 30, 1866; Pruyn Journal, November 10, 1864; Directors' Minutes, August 29, 1866, NYC, vol. 4, box 34, NYCRR; Cochran, 178–9; Hungerford, 193–4. For examples of EC's need for transcriptions of Richmond's letters, see fold. 5, box 38, ECP.

17 Stiles, 141–2. For insight into the trunk line diplomacy that would ensue in 1865, see Dean Richmond to J. Edgar Thomson, June 22, 1865, J. Edgar Thomson to Dean Richmond, September 15, 1865, J. Edgar Thomson to Samuel J. Tilden, August 13, 1865, fold. 3, box 6, Samuel J. Tilden Papers, NYPL.

18 Another factor in their relationship was the railroads' co-ownership of the Albany bridge, which required a further infusion of $400,000 for completion; Pruyn Journal, November 10, 1864, December 12, 1866; NYSAD 19, 90th sess., 1867; Directors' Minutes, February 7, 1865, HR, oversize vol. 248, NYCRR. For more evidence of JHB's role as CV's messenger at this time, see CV to Edwin D. Morgan, February 7, 1865, CV to Edwin D. Morgan, June 4, 1866, fold. 2, box 13, Edwin D. Morgan Papers, NYSL.

19 NYSAD 19, 90th sess., 1867.

20 Ibid. The fast steamboats of the People's Line remained reasonably competitive in terms of speed with the HR passenger trains, which averaged twenty-five to thirty miles per hour, including stops; see HR Annual Reports, oversize vol. 241, NYCRR.

21 NYSAD 19, 90th sess., 1867.

22 Ibid.; Chauncey M. Depew, *My Memories of Eighty Years* (New York: Charles Scribner's Sons, 1922), 37.

23 NYSAD 19, 90th sess., 186.

24 *NYT,* February 10, 1865.

25 McPherson, 838–40, 845–6.

26 Strong, 3:573–5.

27 McPherson, 847–9; Philip H. Sheridan, *Personal Memoirs of P. H. Sheridan,* vol. 2 (New York: C. L. Webster, 1888), 195–7; John B. Gordon, *Reminiscences of the Civil War* (New York: Charles Scribner's Sons, 1904), 441.

28 Pruyn Journal, April 15, 18, 1865; McPherson, 853.

29 McPherson, 854.

30 McPherson, 853. As McPherson also notes, 484–9, disease was far more deadly to

soldiers than enemy weaponry. On the social response to the war, see David W. Blight, *Race and Reunion: The Civil War in American Memory* (Cambridge, Mass.: Harvard University Press, 2001); and Drew Gilpin Faust, *This Republic of Suffering: Death and the American Civil War* (New York: Alfred A. Knopf, 2008).

31 Strong, 4:25; *NYTr*, September 25, 1878; Faust, 180–5; Anne Braude, *Radical Spirits: Spiritualism and Women's Rights in Nineteenth-Century America* (Boston: Beacon Press, 1989), 2–6.

32 *NYTr*, October 16, 24, 1878; *NYS*, November 14, 1877.

33 Directors' Minutes, June 6, 1865, HR, oversize vol. 248, NYCRR.

34 Directors' Minutes, June 12, 13, 1865, HR, oversize vol. 248, Executive Committee Minutes, December 8, 1865, May 5, 1866, HR, oversize vol. 249, NYCRR; *RT*, August 19, 1865. See also Directors' Minutes, December 6, 1864, HR, oversize vol. 247, NYCRR, and *HW*, August 12, 1865.

35 Directors' Minutes, April 26, 1865, Michigan Southern and Northern Indiana Railroad Company, reel 67, box 243, NYCRR; Medbery, 176–7; Fowler, 176, 256–60. CV reportedly held $7 million in Erie bonds; *CT*, January 10, 1865.

36 Pruyn Journal, June 19, 20, 21, 1865.

37 *NYH*, August 23, 1865; Hungerford, 196; NYSAD 19, 90th sess., 1867.

38 Lib to Cornele, n.d., Family Record, WFP.

39 CV to Oliver E. Williams, September 2, 1865, WFP.

40 *PS*, October 26, 1865; *NYS*, December 19, 1877. Harlem Lane later became St. Nicholas Avenue; *NYT*, October 2, 1872.

41 *NYH*, November 21, 1865; *Atlantic Monthly*, May 1868. Apart from a horse named Commodore Vanderbilt, there was no sign that CV attended these events.

42 *NYTr*, February 6, 1879; John Y. Simon, ed., *The Papers of Ulysses S. Grant*, vol. 16 (Carbondale: Southern Illinois University, 1988), 79–80. WHV had already met Grant, having escorted him in a Harlem Railroad train to Albany in July, and was an admirer of the general; *NYT*, July 6, 1865.

43 *Round Table*, November 25, 1865; *NYT*, September 7, 1871; Francis Gerry Fairfield, *The Clubs of New York* (New York: Henry L. Hinton, 1873), 138–43; *HW*, July 11, 1868.

44 Fairfield, 138–43; LW Dictation. CV resigned from the New York Yacht Club on February 13, 1850; Book of Minutes, box 1: July 30, 1844, to March 18, 1891, New York Yacht Club Library and Archives.

45 *NYTr*, February 26, December 5, 1867; *New York Observer and Chronicle*, November 23, 1865; Depew, 14–5.

46 *NYH*, December 14, 1866. In January 1867, Henry Keep would testify, "We suppose that Mr. Vanderbilt has managed the N.Y. Central for the last two years, through men in his interest." See NYSAD 19, 90th sess., 1867. Keep was wrong, but the quote demonstrates how Banker was perceived.

47 *NYS*, December 22, 1877.

48 *NYS*, December 19, 27, 1877, March 13, 1878, *NYTr*, March 6, 1878.

49 CJV to HG, February 26, n.d., reel 3, HGP. This letter, though dated without a year, was written from Litchfield, Conn.; as will be seen, CJV went into the asylum in Litchfield in December 1865, showing that this letter must have been written in 1866.

50 *NYS*, December 27, 1877; *NYW*, December 22, 1877.

51 *NYS*, December 27, 1877; CJV to HG, February 26, n.d., reel 3, HGP.

52 *NYS*, December 27, 1877; *Henry S. Thatcher and George Buckland v. CJV*, April 2, 1867, LJ-1867-V-192, Supreme Court Law Judgments, NYCC.

53 *NYS*, December 19, 1877.

54 CJV to HG, February 26, n.d., reel 3, HGP.

55 *HW*, March 17, 1866; *SA*, July 6, 1867.

56 *NYT*, January 25, 1866; *Commercial and Financial Chronicle*, January 27, 1866.

57 Smith, 119; RGD, NYC 374:1.
58 *NYT*, March 19, 1866; NYSAD 19, 90th sess., 1867.
59 *RT*, August 3, 1867.
60 NYSAD 19, 90th sess., 1867.
61 Strong, 4:77; McKay, 218–9; Beckert, 173; Burrows & Wallace, 986–8.
62 Directors' Minutes, June 25, 1866, HRR, reel 27, box 242, NYCRR. At the annual election on May 15, CV personally voted 60,647 of the 75,560 shares represented. Tobin voted 31,500, and WHV 10,600.
63 NYSAD 19, 90th sess., 1867.
64 *NYH*, January 20, 1869; SED 46, 39th Cong., 1st sess., vol. 2.
65 *HW*, January 6, September 15, 1866; *Nation*, June 5, 1866.
66 *NYH*, May 30, June 1, 1866; *NYT*, May 29, 30, June 4, 1866; *American Law Review*, October 1868; *Frank Work v. Daniel Drew, John E. Eldridge, Alexander Drew, Homer Ramsdell, J. C. Bancroft Davis, Henry Thompson, Dudley Gregory, Frederick A. Lane, George Gravel, James Fisk Jr., Jay Gould, and William Skidmore*, July 24, 1868, file PL-1868-W-25, Supreme Court Pleadings, NYCC; CFA, "A Chapter of Erie," *NAR*, July 1869. On the law that created the additional shares, see *RT*, May 7, 1864.
67 *CT*, January 10, 1865.
68 JMD to EC, June 1, 1866, fold. 5, box 88, ECP; NYSAD 19, 90th sess., 1867.
69 *Buffalo Freight Convention*, May 2, 1866, *Proceedings of the Railway Meeting Held at the St. Nicholas Hotel, New York, May 22d and 23d, 1866, called by the Vice President of the Erie Railway Company, in pursuance of a resolution passed at Buffalo, May 2d, 1866*, Erie Railway Company Collection, Baker Library, Harvard Business School; Chandler, *Visible Hand*, 123. Chandler, it should be noted, wrote generally of the cartels the railroads repeatedly formed over this period.
70 NYSAD 19, 90th sess., 1867.
71 This conversation is taken from HFC's testimony, NYSAD 19, 90th sess., 1867.
72 Testimony of HFC, NYSAD 19, 90th sess., 1867. After taking over as president of the Central in 1864, Richmond had pushed to include more Republicans in the Central board, to improve the chances of convincing the Republican-dominated legislature to increase the legal limit on passenger fares. That bill failed. Pruyn protested the move as tending to bring politics into the railroad's management; Pruyn Journal, November 10, 1864.
73 HFC and CV testimony, NYSAD 19, 90th sess., 1867. On the proposed consolidation or lease, see also *NYTr*, July 26, 1866; *NYH*, December 14, 1866.
74 NYSAD 19, 90th sess., 1867. On the proposed consolidation or lease, see also *NYTr*, July 26, 1866; *NYH*, December 14, 1866.
75 *CT*, October 14, 1866; *RT*, July 13, August 3, 1867.
76 NYSAD 19, 90th sess., 1867.
77 *NYTr*, August 11, 1866.
78 *NYH*, July 1, 1865, May 30, 1866.
79 *BE*, July 17, 1866; *CT*, October 24, 1867.
80 Fowler, 242–3.
81 *NYH*, December 14, 1866; *HW*, January 11, 1868; JMD to EC, June 18, 1866, fold. 5, JMD to EC, June 19, 1866, fold. 3, box 88, ECP; Stiles, 249–51. See also *NYH*, July 15, 1865; Pruyn Journal, December 12, 1866.
82 *EP*, July 31, in *CT*, August 3, 1869; Fowler, 255–6; *HW*, January 11, 1868. For more background on Keep's campaigns, see Edmund Clarence Stedman, ed., *The New York Stock Exchange* (New York: Stock Exchange Historical Company, 1905), 190–4.
83 G. C. Davidson to EC, July 1866?, fold. 3, box 88, ECP.
84 *NYT*, December 19, 1866, would note that Keep returned from England "with his coat-pockets full of London proxies."
85 NYSAD 19, 90th sess., 1867.
86 *NYT*, August 28, 1866; *NYTr*, in *CT*, August 30, 1866; Directors' Minutes, August 29, 1866, NYC, vol. 4, box 34, NYCRR.

87　*BE*, November 19, 1866; Directors' Minutes, September 27, 1866, NYC, vol. 4, box 34, and Executive Committee Minutes, September 22, 1866, HR, oversize vol. 249, NYCRR; *CT*, October 14, 1866; NYSAD 19, 90th sess., 1867.

88　See the testimony of the parties cited in NYSAD 19, 90th sess., 1867. The information and quotes that follow are taken from the same source, until otherwise noted.

89　All of the foregoing is from NYSAD 19, 90th sess., 1867.

90　*NYT*, December 19, 1866.

91　Testimony of CV, NYSAD 19, 90th sess., 1867.

92　"Dinner to the President of the United States, in Honor of His Visit to the City of New York, August 29, 1866, at Delmonico's, Fifth Avenue and Fourteenth Street," fold. 4, box 6, Samuel J. Tilden Papers, NYPL; Foner, 264–5. For an attack on the capitalists (including "the Vanderbilts") for their tribute to Johnson, see *NYT*, September 7, 1866.

93　Foner, 243–51.

94　Foner, 235; *HW*, September 15, 1866. Given that this is a biography, and not a study of economic ideology, I am restricted to a schematic discussion. Given the enormous changes of this era, both political parties lost much of the cohesion in their economic views, leading to complexities to which I cannot do justice here.

95　*NYT*, October 7, 1866; Strong, 4:108–9; *NYT*, October 13, 1866; Directors' Minutes, May 13, 1859, NYC, vol. 2, box 33, NYCRR.

96　*Boston Journal*, in *BE*, November 19, 1866; *NYH*, September 10, 1873; *AtlC*, October 21, 1875. I am mixing in these later reports in the belief that they are consistent with the contemporary reporting in the *Journal* story, reprinted in *BE*.

97　HG to EC, June 8, 1866, fold. 3, box 88, ECP; CV to Edwin D. Morgan, December 28, 1866, fold. 2, box 13, Edwin D. Morgan Papers, NYSL; *NYH*, October 3, 1869; *HW*, November 23, 1867.

98　*NYT*, December 12, 19, 1866; *NYH*, December 14, 1866; Directors' Minutes, December 12, 1866, NYC, vol. 5, box 34, NYCRR.

99　Directors' Minutes, December 20, 1866, NYC, vol. 5, box 34, NYCRR; testimony of Robert L. Banks, Henry Keep, WHV, NYSAD 19, 90th sess., 1867.

100　The conversation is from CV's testimony, NYSAD 19, 90th sess., 1867. For CV's remarks on Corning and Keep, see JMD to EC, February 1, 1867, fold. 3, box 89, ECP.

101　Testimony of WHV and HFC, NYSAD 19, 90th sess., 1867.

102　Testimony of WHV, CV, and AS, NYSAD 19, 90th sess., 1867.

103　Testimony of AS and CV, NYSAD 19, 90th sess., 1867.

104　Directors' Minutes, January 14, 1867, HR, oversize vol. 248, Directors' Minutes, January 14, 1867, HRR, reel 26, box 242, NYCRR; testimony of WHV, NYSAD 19, 90th sess., 1867. See also *NYH*, January 15, 1867.

105　Testimony of CV, NYSAD 19, 90th sess., 1867; *Albany Evening Journal*, January 18, 1867; *NYT*, January 19, 1867; *NYH*, January 18, 19, 20, 1867. For the impact of the blockade on the Central's business, see also the testimony of Harlow W. Chittenden, NYSAD 19, 90th sess., 1867. The Central attempted to send through freight by a roundabout route, using the Housatonic Railroad, but experienced great difficulties arranging it.

106　*BE*, January 21, 1867; *NYH*, January 17, 19, 1867.

107　Testimony of CV, NYSAD 19, 90th sess., 1867.

108　*NYT*, January 23, 1867; *NYT*, January 23, 1867.

109　Henry Keep to EC, January 17, 1867, fold. 3, box 89, ECP; Directors' Minutes, January 17, 1867, HR, oversize vol. 248, NYCRR; testimony of H. Henry Baxter, NYSAD 19, 90th sess., 1867.

110　Testimony of WHV, NYSAD 19, 90th sess., 1867.

111　Testimony of Henry Keep, NYSAD 19, 90th sess., 1867; JMD to EC, January 24, 1867, fold. 3, box 89, ECP. See also *NYT*, January 25, 1867.

112　JMD to EC, January 25, 1867, fold. 3, box 89, ECP.

Sixteen Among Friends

1   For a reference to CV as "the Railroad King of New York," see *CT,* December 16, 1867. For references to "railroad kings" in a general sense, see *Albany Evening Journal,* January 21, 1867.

2   See, for example, CFA, "A Chapter of Erie," *NAR,* July 1869; Alfred D. Chandler Jr., *The Visible Hand: The Managerial Revolution in American Business* (Cambridge, Mass.: Harvard University Press, 1977), 149.

3   Keep delegated to EC authority to manage relations with CV—for example, to equalize sleeping-car income with the HR, "and make such other arrangements" as might be in the interests of the company; Directors' Minutes, February 15, 1867, NYC, vol. 5, box 34, NYCRR.

4   WHV to JFJ, April 30, 1867, box 3, JFJP-2.

5   *NYT,* June 29, August 7, 1867; *RT,* July 13, 1867; Directors' Minutes, July 25, August 22, 1867, NYC, vol. 5, box 34, NYCRR; Erastus Corning Jr. to EC, July 27, 1867, fold. 2, box 89, ECP.

6   *Flag of Our Union,* June 22, 1867.

7   Testimony of HFC, NYSAD 142, 92nd sess., 1869; *NYT,* April 4, 1867; Proceedings of the Stockholders' Meeting, March 30, 1867, Directors' Minutes, HR, oversize vol. 248, NYCRR.

8   CFA, "The Railroad System," in CFA and Henry Adams, *Chapters of Erie and Other Essays* (New York: Henry Holt, 1871), 403.

9   Recent historical and popular literature does a poor job of explaining why stock watering was considered such an abuse in the nineteenth century. (Of course, I simply may not have read widely enough.) For example, John Steele Gordon, *The Scarlet Woman of Wall Street: Jay Gould, Jim Fisk, Cornelius Vanderbilt, the Erie Railway Wars, and the Birth of Wall Street* (New York: Weidenfeld & Nicholson, 1988), 87, writes that it was seen as "cheating the stockholders by diluting their equity," which misses the real complaint, and does not touch the underlying thinking that made it such a politically sensitive subject. See CFA, "The Railroad System," 398–413. For an enlightening discussion between CV's executives and state legislators on the problem of "fictitious capital," see NYSAD 142, 92nd sess., 1869. Stock watering was a focus of the famous Hepburn Committee, NYSAD 38, 103rd sess., 1880. For a contemporary attack on the "great evil" of "fictitious capital," see *BM,* August 1869. See also Montgomery Rollins, "Convertible Bonds and Stocks," *Annals of the American Academy of Political and Social Science* 35, no. 3 (May 1910): 97–110. Fowler, 24–5, is especially good at expressing the wonder his contemporaries felt for the abstraction of corporate finance.

10 *HC,* March 18, 1867; *NYT,* April 4, 1867.

11 Spuyten Duyvil & Port Morris Railroad Company Minutes Book, vol. 1, box 39, NYCRR; *NYT,* April 21, 1870. When Daniel Drew had operated the Upper Bull's Head Tavern on Third Avenue, it had been the primary north-south route to the city; see *Walter Blair v. Daniel Drew,* March 10, 1831, Court of Common Pleas, file 1831-87, and *Fitz G. Halleck v. Daniel Drew,* March 15, 1820, Court of Common Pleas, file 1820-479, NYCC.

12 *RT,* July 13, 1867; *NYT,* May 20, August 29, September 11, 1867; Directors' Minutes, December 11, 1867, NYC, vol. 5, box 34, NYCRR. On the Great Western's third rail (it had been built to a gauge of 5'6") and the creation of a through line on the North Shore, see Directors' Minutes, November 8, 1866, NYC, vol. 5, box 34, NYCRR; *CT,* January 9, 1867.

13 Nathaniel Thayer to EC, November 26, 1867, fold. 8, box 39, JMD to EC, December 7, 1867, fold. 2, box 90, ECP; Directors' Minutes, December 11, 1867, NYC,

vol. 5, box 34, NYCRR. On Joy, see Alfred D. Chandler Jr. and Stephen Salsbury, "The Railroads: Innovators in Modern Business Administration," in Bruce Mazlish, *The Railroad and the Space Program: An Exploration in Historical Analogy* (Cambridge, Mass.: MIT Press, 1965), 152; Julius Grodinsky, *Transcontinental Railway Strategy, 1869–1893: A Study of Businessmen* (Philadelphia: University of Pennsylvania Press, 1962), 5–6.

14 WHV to JFJ, January 29, 1868, JFJP. See also WHV to JFJ, May 14, 1868; Memorandum of Agreement, December 17, 1868; and H. E. Sargent to JFJ, May 16, 1874; all in JFJP; Notice of NYC&HR, October 1, 1874, Document Summary, box 5, JFJP-2. WHV used back channels to reassure Joy as well, speaking to Samuel Sloan of the Vanderbilts' desire to treat the North Shore lines fairly; Samuel Sloan to JFJ, August 30, 1867, JFJP.

15 RGD, NYC 374:1; *Buffalo Express*, in *CT*, December 16, 1867; *NYT*, October 15, 1866; testimony of CV, NYSAD 19, 90th sess., 1867. For high praise for his Harlem management, from a very skeptical source, see the *Nation*, March 26, 1868. See also praise from the *RT*, September 30, 1865, for CV's emphasis on safety.

16 Testimony of Azariah Boody and CV, NYSAD 19, 90th sess., 1867; *Putnam's Monthly Magazine*, February 1868. For a splendid illustration of corruption in the Pennsylvania, see David Nasaw, *Andrew Carnegie* (New York: Penguin, 2006), 59–63.

17 *American Phrenological Journal*, March 1866; *NYT*, February 7, 1867; *Round Table*, February 9, 1867.

18 *NYT*, November 10, 1866.

19 *HW*, December 15, 1866; *Cleveland Leader*, January 21, 1867.

20 *Round Table*, February 9, 1867.

21 *NYH*, November 14, 1867.

22 Louis Auchincloss, *The Vanderbilt Era: Profiles of a Gilded Age* (New York: Charles Scribner's Sons, 1989), 37; *The Way Bill*, March 1887.

23 Auchincloss, 38; *CT*, February 3, 1867; Directors' Minutes, May 23, 1867, HRR, reel 26, box 242, NYCRR.

24 *NYS*, December 22, 1877, February 27, 1878; *NYW*, December 20, 1877; *NYTr*, February 27, 1868, February 6, 1879; *Henry S. Thatcher and George Buckland v. CJV*, April 2, 1867, file L.J.-1867-V-192, *George R. Pecker v. CJV*, April 2, 1867, file L. J-1867-V-100, Supreme Court Law Judgments, NYCC.

25 *New York Ledger* in *CT*, November 19, 1867; CJV to HG, September 28 n.d., reel 3, HGP.

26 CJV to Nathaniel P. Banks, October 27, 1867, cont. 40, Nathaniel P. Banks Papers, LOC.

27 Letter quoted in *NYS*, December 27, 1877.

28 *SEP*, April 4, 1873.

29 *NYT*, April 27, 1867; *New York Observer and Chronicle*, May 16, 1867; *NYH*, May 22, 1867; *HW*, June 1, 1867; *NYTr*, January 24, 1876.

30 *NYT*, October 1, 8, 1867.

31 *CT*, October 18, 24, 1867; *NYT*, October 19, 22, 1867.

32 *New York Ledger*, in *CT*, November 19, 1867.

33 For the original complaint, see *Frank Work v. Daniel Drew, John E. Eldridge, Alexander Drew, Homer Ramsdell, J. C. Bancroft Davis, Henry Thompson, Dudley Gregory, Frederick A. Lane, George Gravel, James Fisk Jr., Jay Gould, and William Skidmore*, July 24, 1868, file PL-1868-W-25, Supreme Court Pleadings, NYCC. The account given here of the complaint and CV's interaction with Jay Gould, to follow, comes from an overlooked deposition later filed by Gould; *CT*, March 30, 1868. For an influential source that calls Work CV's nephew, see CFA, "A Chapter of Erie," *NAR*, July 1869. Work himself made no claim to any relation to CV; see his testimony in the will trial, *NYS*, March 7, 1878. On Samuel Barton's role in the HR, see Direc-

tors' Minutes, June 10, 1867, HR, oversize vol. 248, NYCRR. For his partnership with Work, see a notice in *NYT,* February 19, 1866. For evidence that CV specially favored Barton, see CV to Samuel L. M. Barlow, March 6, 1860, BW Box 36 (14), Samuel L. M. Barlow Collection, HL.

34 *CT,* March 30, 1868. According to Gould's lieutenant and bodyguard, G. P. Morosini, Gould joined the Eldridge clique through contact with lawyer Frederick A. Lane and broker James Fisk Jr.; G. P. Morosini, "Jay Gould and the Erie Railway," NYHS.

35 Klein, 77; Edward Harold Mott, *Between the Ocean and the Lakes: The Story of Erie* (New York: Ticker Publishing, 1908), 141.

36 *NYT,* December 14, 1865, June 10, 1867; *PS,* August 13, 1868; Edward Chase Kirkland, *Men, Cities, and Transportation: A Study in New England History, 1820–1900,* vol. 2 (Cambridge, Mass.: Harvard University Press, 1948), 34–40. Kirkland notes that Adams stressed the need for the Boston, Hartford & Erie in his article on Boston for the *NAR.*

37 *CT,* March 30, 1868.

38 The discussion of the financial system that follows is largely based on the same sources cited in the discussion of the introduction of the greenback in Chapter Thirteen. See in particular Richard Franklin Bensel, *Yankee Leviathan: The Origins of Central State Authority in America, 1865–1877* (New York: Cambridge University Press, 1990), 239–80, esp. 264–77; Richard Sylla, "Federal Policy, Banking Market Structure, and Capital Mobilization in the United States, 1863–1913," *JEH* 29, no. 4 (December 1969): 657–86; Esther Rogoff Taus, *Central Banking Functions of the United States Treasury, 1789–1941* (New York: Columbia University Press, 1943), 65–9; and also George A. Selgin and Lawrence H. White, "Monetary Reform and the Redemption of National Bank Notes, 1863–1913," *BHR* 68, no. 2 (summer 1994): 205–43.

39 *EP* in *CT,* March 28, 1868; Fowler, 508; Smith, 56–7; Bensel, 239–40, 254–74.

40 In Gould's affidavit, quoted above, he said CV had told him that "Mr. Drew was bearing stocks, and was mainly instrumental in producing money stringency which took place just previous; that Drew had several millions on deposit, and knowing that Mr. Vanderbilt and his friends were carrying a large amount of stock, never offered assistance"; *CT,* March 30, 1868.

41 Ibid.; Klein, 79.

42 *CT,* March 30, 1868; *NYH,* October 9, 1867; Klein, 79.

43 *NYH,* October 9, 1867. *NYH,* October 12, 1867, refers to the operations of "the Erie clique," and the *Albany Evening Journal,* quoted in *CT,* December 10, 1867, observed the broad upward movement in railroad stocks, including Erie. In Gould's affidavit quoted in *CT,* March 30, 1868, as elsewhere, he names the members of the pool.

44 *NYH,* January 20, 1869; CV to JHB, February 1, 1868, CV-NYHS; SR 307, part 2, 43rd Cong., 1st sess., vol. 3, 137.

45 *NYTr,* August 5, 1876; Directors' Minutes, December 11, 1867, Executive Committee Minutes, December 12, 20, 21, 26, 1867, January 20, February 11, 1868, NYC, vol. 3, box 34, NYCRR; *Circular,* February 10, 1868; *NYH,* January 20, 1869; JMD to EC, December 28, 1867, fold. 2, box 90, JMD to EC, July 2, 1868, fold. 8, box 39, ECP. For a recollection of CV's elimination of sinecures, including EC Jr., see *NYTr,* August 5, 1876. For an account of the costs of free passes see *RRG,* July 6, 1872. The elimination of free passes created some problems; drovers, for example, usually traveled for free with their cattle, and when the Central stopped that practice the Erie captured much of the livestock business temporarily; see S. H. Dubois to EC, March 7, 1868, fold. 8, box 39, ECP. For a useful summary of CV's rationalization of the Central, see Alfred D. Chandler Jr., "The Railroads: Pioneers in Modern Corporate Management," *BHR* 39, no. 1 (spring 1965): 16–40.

46 *RT,* February 8, 1868; *NYT,* February 9, 1868; *SA,* February 15, 1868.

47 *BE,* January 15, 1868; JMD to EC, December 28, 1867, fold. 2, box 90, JMD to EC, July 2, 1868, fold. 8, box 39, ECP.

48 John D. Prince to JMD, January 7, 1868, JMD to EC, January 7, 14, 1868, fold. 8, box 39; JMD to EC, January 8, 1868, fold. 5, box 90, ECP; *NYT,* January 11, 1868.

49 *NYH,* January 23, 1868; *NYT,* December 1, 1868; *CT,* March 30, 1868; S. W. Harned to EC, February 14, 1868, fold. 5, box 90, ECP.

50 S. W. Harned to EC, February 14, 1868, fold. 5, box 90, ECP; NYSAD 142, 92nd sess., 1869. The stenographer, Hudson C. Tanner, later testified that the assembly committee before whom CV spoke these words suppressed some of his comments (reproduced here) to delete his profanity and generally clean up his comments; *NYTr,* March 6, 1871. Schell is quoted in HR 31, 41st Cong., 2nd sess., vol. 1.

51 Klein, 81; *NYH,* February 20, 23, 1868; H. E. Sargent to JFJ, April 8, 1868, Telegram, Document Summary, box 5, JFJP-2. On March 7, a New York Central official reported, "4 out of 6 of the stock cars that comes down the Lake Shore Road [Michigan Southern's eastern connection] goes over the Erie Road in consequence of a nefarious arrangement"; S. H. Dubois to EC, March 7, 1868, fold. 8, box 39, ECP.

52 *Frank Work v. Daniel Drew, John E. Eldridge, Alexander Drew, Homer Ramsdell, J. C. Bancroft Davis, Henry Thompson, Dudley Gregory, Frederick A. Lane, George Gravel, James Fisk Jr., Jay Gould, and William Skidmore,* July 24, 1868, file PL-1868-W-25, Supreme Court Pleadings, NYCC.

53 Strong, 4:263n; *NYTr,* March 25, 1872, in *HW,* April 13, 1872; *Zion's Herald,* March 26, 1868. On Tweed, Barnard, and the role of the city's courts, see Seymour Mandelbaum, *Boss Tweed's New York* (New York: John Wiley & Sons, 1965), 57–8, 66–7, 83; Burrows & Wallace, 837.

54 See the complaint against Barnard by James Fisk's partner, William Belden, *NYH,* March 12, 1868. On Barnard's closeness with Osgood, see *NYH,* March 19, 31, 1868. For some of the many letters from JMD to EC on Barnard and the stock market, see those for December 28, 1867, fold. 2, box 90; February 11, 27, 1868, fold. 8, box 39; August [n.d.], August 23, 1869, fold. 1, box 94; all in ECP. For a timeline of the Erie litigation, see *American Law Review,* October 1868. Barnard actually rebuked Rapallo at one point as he presented the motion to remove Drew; *NYT,* February 22, 1868.

55 CFA, "A Chapter of Erie," *NAR,* July 1869; Lane, 243.

56 NYSAD 142, 92nd sess., 1869; *NYTr,* March 6, 1871.

57 CV to JHB, February 1, 1868, CV-NYHS; CV to Andrew Johnson, February 6, 1868, in Paul H. Bergeron, ed., *The Papers of Andrew Johnson,* vol. 13, *September 1867–March 1868* (Knoxville: University of Tennessee Press, 1996), 534–5; *NYT,* February 18, 22, 1868; S. H. Dubois to EC, March 7, 1868, fold. 8, box 39, ECP.

58 *CT,* March 19, 1868; *RT,* March 21, 1868.

59 *NYT,* March 4, April 24, 1868; NYSSD 52: *Report of the Select Committee of the Senate, Appointed April 10, 1868, in Relation to Passage of Certain Railroad Bills* (Albany: Argus Company, 1869), 1–6, 107; *American Law Review,* October 1868; *NYH,* April 9, 1868; Klein, 81–2.

60 *NYT,* February 20, 1868. The wedding description is from the *New York Mail* in *Flake's Bulletin,* March 3, 1868.

61 HG to Ellen Williams Vanderbilt, March 8, 1868, WFP.

62 Ellen W. Vanderbilt to HG, March 19, 1868, reel 2, HGP.

63 Ibid.

64 *Circular,* February 17, 1868; *NYT,* February 17, March 17, 1868.

65 *NYH,* March 7, 10, 25, 1868; *American Law Review,* October 1868.

66 *American Law Review,* October 1868; *NYH,* March 12, 15, 25, April 3, 1868; *NYT,*

March 12, 1868; NYSSD 52, 1–6. Those interested in the fine details of this tangle of legal actions, see John Steele Gordon, *The Scarlet Woman of Wall Street: Jay Gould, Jim Fisk, Cornelius Vanderbilt, the Erie Railway Wars, and the Birth of Wall Street* (New York: Weidenfeld & Nicolson, 1988), 164–73. Henry Clews reported the rumors about Vanderbilt forcing banks to lend, in *Fifty Years in Wall Street* (New York: Irving Publishing, 1908), 139, as did Croffut, 91.

67 *NYH*, March 14, 15, 21, 1868; *CT*, March 24, 1868. Drew later testified that Field had advised the flight to New Jersey; *NYT*, November 30, 1869.

68 CFA, "A Chapter of Erie."

69 *HW*, April 11, 1868.

70 *NYH*, March 15, 1868.

71 W. L. Garrison to Wife, May 24, 1871, William Lloyd Garrison Papers, Rare Books and Manuscripts Department, Boston Public Library.

72 *HW*, October 16, 1869; *NYH*, March 15, 19, 1868; Klein, 80–3.

73 *NYH*, March 16, 19, 20, 1868; *CT*, March 24, 25, 1868; Klein, 83.

74 NYSSD 52, 11, 50, 111–2; *NYH*, March 21, 25, 1868; Klein, 84.

75 Klein, 84.

76 NYSSD 52, 1–11; *NYH*, April 2, 1868; *NYT*, April 2, 1868; William Cassidy to Samuel J. Tilden, April 6, 1868, fold. 6, box 6, Samuel J. Tilden Papers, NYPL.

77 NYSSD 52, 9–11; Klein, 84–5.

78 William Cassidy to Samuel J. Tilden, April 6, 1868, fold. 6, box 6, Samuel J. Tilden Papers, NYPL; Klein, 83; *NYT*, November 30, 1869, March 17, 1870.

79 *CT*, April 29, 1868; *HC*, November 30, 1869; *NYTr*, April 27, 1868, in *CT*, April 30, 1868; *NYT*, March 17, 18, 1870. Drew testified, as reported in the *NYT*, November 30, 1869, that he intended to take CV's shares in order "to get control of the Erie Road—get these people out of it."

80 *NYTr*, April 27, 1868, in *CT*, April 30, 1868; *NYT*, April 28, 1868.

81 The ensuing conversation is largely drawn from Gould and Fisk's testimony, *NYT*, March 16, 18, 19, 1870. Gordon, relying on Clews, claims that Fisk burst into CV's bedroom; the account I am citing, given by both Fisk and Gould under oath, shows CV called Fisk in.

82 *CT*, January 1, 1873.

83 *NYT*, March 16, 17, 18, 1870.

84 Ibid.

85 *NYH*, July 11, 1868, November 21, 30, 1869; *BE*, August 25, 1868; *NYS*, November 28, 1872; Klein, 85–6. A somewhat different version of this settlement would be laid out in an affidavit by Gould, *NYH*, December 1, 1868. However, since Gould was suing CV at the time, he oversimplified, and (not having been in on all the negotiations) he made errors. CV's court testimony on November 20, 1869, shows that his deal was technically with Drew, though the Erie paid most of the money; also, CV said he had sold the shares at 80, not 70 as Gould claimed. Drew's testimony, *NYT*, November 30, 1869, *HC*, November 30, 1869, tends to confirm CV's account. This is important, as will be seen, for CV later claimed that he had not sold his shares to the Erie, a claim that historians have scoffed at; see, for example, Klein, 91.

86 RGD, NYC 374:10. As will be discussed later, estimates of CV's wealth can be no better than guesses, often wild ones.

87 Foner, 333–6.

88 *RT*, April 25, 1868; HsR 57, 40th Cong., 2nd sess., vol. 2.

89 *Nation*, June 25, 1868.

90 *Round Table*, April 4, 1868; *MM*, April 1868; *NYT*, April 4, 1868. A fine explanation of the divided public opinion appears in the *Nation*, March 26, 1868.

91 On the writing and importance of this essay (for which Adams was only paid $150), see Edward Chase Kirkland, *Charles Francis Adams, Jr., 1835–1915: The Patrician at Bay* (Cambridge, Mass.: Harvard University Press, 1965), 40–1, 77.

92　CFA, "A Chapter of Erie." For two excellent accounts of the "liberals," as the Adams brothers and their cohorts came to be called, see John G. Sproat, *"The Best Men": Liberal Reformers in the Gilded Age* (New York: Oxford University Press, 1968), and Thomas K. McGraw, *Prophets of Regulation: Charles Francis Adams, Louis D. Brandeis, James M. Landis, Alfred E. Kahn* (Cambridge, Mass.: Belknap Press, 1984). The liberal reformers will be discussed further later in the text.

93　Letter to the *JoC*, in *NYT*, March 6, 1868.

94　Mandelbaum, 58; *Testimony Taken Before the Special Committee of the Assembly . . . in the Matter of the Erie Railway Investigation* (1873), 764, Erie Railway Company Collection, Baker Library, Harvard Business School. For an important article on railroads and corruption, see Richard White, "Information, Markets, and Corruption: Transcontinental Railroads in the Gilded Age," *JEH* 90, no. 1 (June 2003): 19–43. White's discussion, while perceptive, treats the corruption of financial information as a new phenomenon of the Gilded Age, whereas it arose as early as corporations themselves; this book has shown examples as early as the 1830s. Nor is it generally true that "profit came less from selling goods and services than from financial maneuvering involving the securities of the firms"; CV's railroads paid 8 percent annual dividends on a stock capitalization that eventually amounted to roughly $100 million. The use of shell companies in the transcontinentals, seen in Crédit Mobilier, was pioneered by the Pennsylvania Railroad; and, as Mark Wahlgren Summers points out in *The Era of Good Stealings* (New York: Oxford University Press, 1993), 46–54, Crédit Mobilier provided Union Pacific with a necessary means of financing itself, as Congress unrealistically prohibited it from selling its securities below par.

95　NYSSD 52, 1–11.

96　Francis Gerry Fairfield, *The Clubs of New York* (New York: Henry L. Hinton, 1873), 138–44. It was reported that Tweed and his ally Peter Sweeney were blackballed when they applied to become members of the Manhattan Club; *NYT*, October 16, 1869.

97　Summers, 61. My statement of this paradox is to some extent a rephrasing of Summers's own conclusion. For another view of the causes of the diminishing of free-labor ideology, see Sven Beckert, *The Monied Metropolis: New York City and the Consolidation of the American Bourgeoisie, 1850–1896* (New York: Cambridge University Press, 2001), 176–7.

98　*HC*, June 11, 1868.

99　Ellen W. Vanderbilt to HG, June 19, 1868, reel 2, HGP; CJV to George Terry, June 12, 1871, fold. 24, box 59, ser. 13, Colt Family Papers, Special Collections, University Libraries, University of Rhode Island

100　CV to Andrew Johnson, June 27, 1868, in Paul H. Bergeron, ed., *The Papers of Andrew Johnson*, vol. 14 (Knoxville: University of Tennessee Press, 1997), 278, 279n; *AtlC*, October 6, 1871; *CV v. Jeremiah Simonson*, August 13, 1868, file L. J. 1858-S-574, Supreme Court Law Judgments, NYCC.

101　*NYT*, July 19, August 18, 1868; *NYTr*, August 18, 1868; *Troy Times*, August 15, in *NYT*, August 18, 1868. On Drew's stays at the Union Hotel, see *NYT*, August 11, 1865.

102　*NYTr*, August 18, 1868. See also *CT*, August 30, 1868. Previous biographers have written that CV remained in Saratoga until Sophia died; the evidence shows otherwise.

103　*NYTr*, August 20, 1868.

104　1868 Annual Income Tax List, Collection District 6, Division 12, page 249, box 429, New York Tax Assessment Lists, 1867–1873, RG 58, National Archives, New York, N.Y.

105　*NYH*, March 5, 1879.

Seventeen Consolidations

1   *CT*, October 11, 1868.
2   *SA*, January 2, 1865.
3   Foner, 460–2; Joseph Frazier Wall, *Andrew Carnegie* (University of Pittsburgh Press, 1989), 188–306.
4   John D. Rockefeller to Laura S. Rockefeller, April 19, 1868, fold. 270, box 36, RG 1.2, Rockfeller Archives Center, Sleepy Hollow, N.Y.; Directors' Minutes, February 11, 1868, NYC, vol. 5, box 34, NYCRR; Ron Chernow, *Titan: The Life of John D. Rockefeller, Sr.* (New York: Random House, 1998), 98–115. Chernow dates the letter from Rockefeller cited here as August 19, 1868; I read it differently, but the difference is insignificant. On railroads and the oil business, see Rolland Harper Maybee, *Railroad Competition and the Oil Trade, 1855–1873* (Mount Pleasant, Mich.: Extension Press, 1940), esp. 207, 223–4, 238–46, 254–5, 263–9, 280.
5   John D. Rockefeller to Laura S. Rockefeller, April 19, 1868, fold. 270, box 36, RG 1.2, Rockfeller Archives Center, Sleepy Hollow, N.Y.; Directors' Minutes, December 11, 1867, NYC, vol. 5, box 34, NYCRR.
6   WHV to JFJ, May 14, 1868; Memorandum of Agreement, December 17, 1868; JFJP; *CT*, December 21, 1868.
7   Prenuptial Agreement, CV and Frank Armstrong Crawford, August 20, 1869, CV-NYHS. (Martha was sometimes mistakenly called Mary in newspaper accounts.) In the trial over CV's will, the opposing counsel would claim that CV put Frank and Martha up in a house in New York before Sophia's death, and dashed away from her funeral to see them, but he offered no evidence to support this; *NYTr*, March 30, 1878.
8   *NYT*, May 5, 1885; *NYH*, August 25, 1869, March 5, 1879; *Toronto Christian Guardian* in *NYT*, September 11, 1869.
9   CV to Frank Armstrong, October 24, 1868, CV-NYHS. On CV's pride in her Southernness, see Frank A. Vanderbilt to Ma, August 26, 1869, CV-NYHS.
10 *NYS*, November 27, 1872. CV's comments should not be seen as idiosyncratic. Phrenology remained a mainstream system of reading one's inner state from the surface; and, as John F. Kasson observes in *Rudeness & Civility: Manners in Nineteenth-Century Urban America* (New York: Hill & Wang, 1990), "Etiquette books express this intense new interest in reading character from appearances."
11 *NYS*, November 28, 1872; testimony of Jay Gould, NYSAD 142, 92nd sess., 1869.
12 *NYS*, November 28, 1872; *NYT*, March 18, 1870; Klein, 90–1. On O'Conor, see *HW*, June 1, 1867; *CT*, February 29, 1868, August 7, 1872. For rumors that CV colluded in the Belmont lawsuit, see *CT*, November 22, 1868.
13 *NYT*, December 1, 1868, March 18, 1870; *HC*, December 7, 1868; Klein, 91.
14 *NYT*, December 7, 1868; *CT*, December 15, 1868; Klein, 91.
15 *NYTr*, in *RT*, October 10, 1868; J. Edgar Thomson to J. F. Lavien, April 27, 1868, Thomas A. Scott to Samuel J. Tilden, May 4, 1868, fold. 6, box 6, Samuel J. Tilden Papers, NYPL; *HC*, December 7, 1868; Klein, 92–3.
16 JMD to EC, January 8, 1868, fold. 5, box 90, ECP; *BE*, November 30, 1868; *NYH*, December 3, 5, 22, 1868.
17 *NYH*, January 20, 1869; NYSAD 142, 92nd sess., 1869; Directors' Minutes, December 19, 1868, NYC, vol. 3, box 34, NYCRR; Hudson C. Tanner, *"The Lobby" and Public Men from Thurlow Weed's Time* (Albany: George MacDonald, 1888), 218–23; *NYS*, December 22, 1868, in *Flake's Bulletin*, December 31, 1868.
18 *NYH*, December 22, 1868, January 20, 1869; NYSAD 114, 90th sess., 1867; NYSAD 142, 92nd sess., 1869; Directors' Minutes, December 19, 1868, NYC, vol. 3, box 34, NYCRR; Tanner, 216–7. In yet another lawsuit, Judge Ingraham issued

an injunction barring the payment of any dividend on the scrip; Edward Hungerford, *Men and Iron: The History of the New York Central* (New York: Thomas Y. Crowell, 1938), 219.

19 John M. Forbes to Green, January 8, 1869, Letterbooks, vol. 5, C. B. & Q. Collection, Newberry Library, Chicago.

20 *NYS*, December 22, 1868, in *Flake's Bulletin*, December 31, 1868; *CT*, January 21, 1869. In the ultimate pragmatic response, the New York Stock Exchange threw up its hands and allowed trading in the scrip; Minutes for December 21, 22, 1868, February 27, 1869, New York Stock & Exchange Board Minutes: 1867–1871, New York Stock Exchange Archives.

21 *NAR*, January 1869; Henry V. Poor, *Manual of the Railroads of the United States for 1869–70*, quoted in *BM*, August 1869. See also a description of Central dividends as "exorbitant interest on all this manufactured and fictitious capital and cost," in *RT*, June 19, 1869, and *RRG*, June 4, 1870.

22 NYSAD 142, 92nd sess., 1869; Tanner, 221–2.

23 John Steele Gordon, *The Scarlet Woman of Wall Street: Jay Gould, Jim Fisk, Cornelius Vanderbilt, the Erie Railway Wars, and the Birth of Wall Street* (New York: Weidenfield & Nicholson, 1988), 224.

24 NYSAD 142, 92nd sess., 1869; Tanner, 215–30.

25 *NYH*, April 9, 27, May 21, 1869.

26 Directors' Minutes, June 11, 1869, HR, oversize vol. 248; Directors' Minutes, June 9, 30, 1869, NYC, vol. 3, box 34; all in NYCRR; *RT*, June 19, 1869. In *Isaac Jenks v. New York Central*, the lawsuit in which Barnard issued his injunction, Jenks said that a close friend of CV's told him that CV owned (directly and indirectly) 130,000 shares of Central; *NYH*, January 22, 1869.

27 RGD, NYC 364:100Q; *NYT*, March 20, 23, 1870, August 9, 1872; Promissory Note, March 17, 1869, Misc. Papers, Cornelius Vanderbilt Jr., NYPL; *NYS*, December 20, 1877.

28 Executive Committee Minutes, February 1, HR, oversize vol. 249, NYCRR; Strong, 4:244; *BE*, April 21, 1869.

29 *BE*, May 26, 1869; Smith, 263, 271.

30 For my portrait of Woodhull and Claflin, I will rely wherever possible on primary sources. I am informed by Mary Gabriel, *Notorious Victoria: The Life of Victoria Woodhull, Uncensored* (Chapel Hill, N.C.: Algonquin Books of Chapel Hill, 1998), Louis Beachy Underhill, *The Woman Who Ran for President: The Many Lives of Victoria Woodhull* (Bridgehampton, N.Y.: Bridge Works Publishing, 1995), and the essays of Helen Lefkowitz Horowitz, "Victoria Woodhull, Anthony Comstock, and Conflict over Sex in the United States in the 1870s," *JAH* 87, no. 2 (September 2000): 403–34, and "A Victory Woodhull for the 1990s," *Reviews in American History* 27, no. 1 (1999): 87–97. By contrast, Barbara Goldsmith's *Other Powers: The Age of Suffrage, Spiritualism, and the Scandalous Victoria Woodhull* (New York: Alfred A. Knopf, 1998), strikes me after close investigation as unreliable. I have consulted some sources cited by other writers (for example, the Victoria Woodhull-Martin Papers at the Boston Public Library) that I will not cite because I found them to contain nothing reliable or useful.

31 *NYTr*, March 21, 1878; *NYT*, February 6, 1870; Anne Braude, *Radical Spirits: Spiritualism and Women's Rights in Nineteenth-Century America* (Boston: Beacon Press, 1989), 23, 145–8; Stiles, 32. See also Robert C. Fuller, *Alternative Medicine and American Religious Life* (New York: Oxford University Press, 1989).

32 *NYH*, May 16, 17, 1871; *NYTr*, May 17, 1871; Horowitz, "Victoria Woodhull, Anthony Comstock"; *NYH*, February 22, 1871. For an example of Tennie's flirting by letter, see Tennie C. Claflin to Whitelaw Reid, February 6, 1870, reel 192, Reid Family Papers, LOC.

33 *NYS*, November 14, 1877; see also *NYW*, November 14, 1877. I have never seen or

found a source for claims by Edward J. Renehan Jr. and Goldsmith that CV drank heavily, chewed tobacco, and spat on his hosts' carpets. Indeed, such tales fly in the face of all evidence, such as the LW Dictation, the diary of Frank Crawford (see next chapter), or various press accounts.

34 *NYTr*, March 21, 1878.

35 *NYH*, February 24, 1869.

36 William Cronon, *Nature's Metropolis: Chicago and the Great West* (New York: W. W. Norton & Co., 1991), 23–93; George H. Miller, *Railroads and the Granger Laws* (Madison: University of Wisconsin Press, 1971), 6–16; George Rogers Taylor and Irene D. Neu, *The American Railroad Network, 1861–1890* (Cambridge, Mass.: Harvard University Press, 1956), 74; Foner, 464.

37 Taylor and Neu, 68–74; Edward Chase Kirkland, *Men, Cities, and Transportation: A Study in New England History, 1820–1900*, vol. 1 (Cambridge, Mass.: Harvard University Press, 1948), 501–3. An excellent history of fast-freight lines and trunk line competition appears in Maybee, 114–22, 131–35. For a discussion of the forces driving consolidation, see Julius Grodinsky, *Railroad Consolidation: Its Economics and Controlling Principles* (New York: D. Appleton and Company, 1930). Curiously, Alfred D. Chandler Jr. confuses fast-freight lines with express companies, in *The Visible Hand: The Managerial Revolution in American Business* (Cambridge, Mass.: Harvard University Press, 1977), 127–8, 129, 145, 153, 210. As noted in *RRG*, May 7, 1870, the Michigan Central drew freight from a vast network controlled by Joy, which CV could not ignore.

38 Chandler, *Visible Hand*, 148–51.

39 *Cincinnati Gazette* in *NYH*, February 10, 1869; Klein, 93–4; Maybee, 141–2, 150–60, also 51, 101–11.

40 *RRG*, May 14, 1870; Articles of Agreement of Consolidation, April 6, 1869, LS&MS, reel 65, box 243, NYCRR; *Toledo Commercial*, April 7, 1869, in *CT*, April 9, 1869; *First Annual Report of the President and Directors of the Lake Shore & Michigan Southern Railway Company, to the Stockholders, for the Fiscal Year Ending December 31, 1870* (Cleveland: Fairbanks, Benedict & Co, 1871), copy in Baker Library, Harvard Business School.

41 *NYH*, June 2, 1869; *RRG*, May 14, 1870; Fowler, 221; *New World*, June 18, 1842; *BM*, June 1862, March 1872; *HC*, February 22, 1865; *New York Observer and Chronicle*, November 21, 1867; *Flag of Our Union*, July 25, 1868; *New York Observer and Chronicle*, February 29, 1872.

42 Directors' Minutes, June 2, 3, 1869, LS&MS, reel 65, box 242, NYCRR.

43 *Cleveland Herald*, June 22, 1869, in *NYT*, June 27, 1869; *BE*, July 10, 1869; *NYH*, July 15, 1869; E. C. Deavan to EC, August 2, 1869, fold. 1, box 94, ECP; *NYT*, August 11, 1869.

44 *NYH*, August 18, 27, 1869; Running Arrangement and Narrow Gauge Contract between the Erie Railway Company and the LS&MS, August 16, 1869, and Directors' Minutes, LS&MS, August 18, 19, 1869, reel 65, box 242, NYCRR.

45 E. C. Deavan to EC, August 19, 1869, fold. 1, box 94, ECP; Prenuptial Agreement, CV and Frank Armstrong Crawford, August 20, 1869, CV-NYHS; *London Free Press*, August 23, 1869, in *NYT*, August 25, 1869; *Syracuse Journal*, August 23, 1869, in *NYH*, August 25, 1869.

46 Marriage Certificate, August 21, 1869, CV-NYHS; McPherson, 516–7, 676; Mrs. Cornelius Vanderbilt Diary 2, 1876–1878, Misc. Microfilms, reel 72, NYHS; *London Free Press*, August 23, 1869, in *NYT*, August 25, 1869; *Toronto Christian Guardian* in *NYT*, September 11, 1869.

47 *London Free Press*, August 23, 1869, in *NYT*, August 25, 1869; *Syracuse Journal*, August 23, 1869, in *NYH*, August 25, 1869; Frank A. Vanderbilt to Ma, August 23, 1869, CV-NYHS.

48 *NYH*, August 25, 1869; Frank A. Vanderbilt to Ma, August 23, 1869, CV-NYHS; *NYTr*, March 30, 1878; *NYS*, March 6, 1878.

49 Frank A. Vanderbilt to Ma, August 23, 26, 1869, CV-NYHS; *NYT,* August 24, 1869; *HW,* September 11, 1869.

50 RGD, NYC 374:1, 10; JMD to EC, April 2, August 12, 1870, fold. 1, box 95, ECP.

51 *NYH,* September 2, 18, 19, 20, 30, October 1, 2, 1869; New York Stock and Exchange Board Minutes: 1867–1871, October 1, 1869, New York Stock Exchange Archives. See also JMD to EC, October 1, 1869, fold. 3, box 94, ECP.

52 This narrative of the gold market panic of 1869 relies primarily on Klein, 100–15, still the single best account. See also William S. McFeely, *Grant: A Biography* (New York: W. W. Norton, 1981), 320–31; Kenneth D. Ackerman, *The Gold Room: Jay Gould, Jim Fisk, and Black Friday, 1869* (New York: Carroll & Graf, 1988); and Julia Grant's and Boutwell's memoirs, excerpted in T. J. Stiles, ed., *Robber Barons and Radicals* (New York: Berkeley Publishing Group, 1997), 217–9.

53 McFeely, 320–31; JMD to EC, October 2, 1869, fold. 3, box 94, ECP.

54 Klein, 100–5.

55 Directors' Minutes, September 23, 1869, HR, oversize vol. 248, vol. 3, box 34, NYCRR; JMD to EC, October 1, 1869, fold. 3, box 94, ECP. The account of the panic that follows is largely derived from the following newspaper accounts: *NYS,* September 27, 1869, in *CT,* September 30, 1869; *NYT,* September 30, 1869; *NYH,* September 18, October 1, 2, 3, 18, 1869; *NYTr,* September 25, 1869; *NYW,* October 1, 2, 4, 1869; see also JMD to EC, September 23, 24, 30, October 4, 16, 20, 1869, fold. 2, JMD to EC, October 1, 1869, fold. 3, box 94, ECP.

56 JMD to EC, September 23, 24, 30, October 4, 16, 20, 1869, fold. 2, box 94, ECP. For commentary on the fear that CV could not control the Central's stock price, see RGD, NYC 342:262.

57 *NYW,* October 2, 1869. The press reported that CV borrowed $10 million against HR stock, but letters in BB suggest the loan was much smaller, with NYCRR stock as collateral. See S. G. Ward to Baring Brothers, October 2, 1869, reel 37, and (in code) Duncan to Baring Brothers, October 5, 1869, reel 42, BB. For further commentary on Vanderbilt's role in stemming the panic, see Medbery, 156; JMD to EC, October 1, 1869, fold. 3, box 94, ECP. Other quotes and information can be found in the newspaper issues listed previously.

58 *NYH,* October 13, 1869; *CT,* October 15, 1869; Directors' Minutes, October 4, 5, 14, 15, 23, 1869, Finance Committee Minutes, October 16, 23, 24, November 4, 1869, LS&MS, reel 65, box 242, NYCRR.

59 Chandler, *Visible Hand,* 151–7.

60 H. E. Sargent to JFJ, May 16, 1874, JFJP; NYSAD 19, 90th sess., 1867. For a discussion of the Michigan Central and other "Joy Roads," see *RRG,* June 11, 1870. Chandler, *Visible Hand,* 157–9, recognizes this cautious policy, noting, "The Commodore did little to integrate the operations of that road [the Lake Shore] with those of the New York Central"—though he mistakenly writes that James H. Devereux managed it after 1873.

61 H. E. Sargent to JFJ, May 16, 1874, JFJP; NYSAD 19, 90th sess., 1867.

62 Mark Twain, "Open Letter to Com. Vanderbilt," *Packard's Monthly,* March 1869; Victor Fischer and Michael B. Frank, eds., *Mark Twain's Letters,* vol. 4 (Berkeley: University of California Press, 1995), 125n.

63 John G. Sproat, *"The Best Men": Liberal Reformers in the Gilded Age* (New York: Oxford University Press, 1968), 6.

64 Sproat, 144–5; CFA, "Railroad Inflation," *NAR,* January 1869. Examples of editorials that follow Adams's critique abound; see, for example, *Nation,* June 30, 1870.

65 Warner quoted in Sproat, 255; see also 46–7, 205–6; *Galaxy Magazine,* June 1868; Joseph Dorfman, *The Economic Mind in American Civilization,* vol. 2 (New York: Viking, 1946), 23; Henry Adams, *The Education of Henry Adams* (New York: Penguin, 1995), 229; T. J. Stiles, *Jesse James: Last Rebel of the Civil War* (New York: Alfred A. Knopf, 2002), 220; Parkman quoted in Foner, 489–90; see also 488–511. I am interpreting the basis of Twain's friendship with Carnegie from David Nasaw, *Andrew*

Carnegie (New York: Penguin, 2006), 645–6, 691–2, 722–3. Social prejudice deeply informed the influential writings of CFA. His biographer observes, "It is hard to see how Adams's way of making a fortune greatly differed from that he censured. He borrowed and he gambled on the price of stocks, sometimes outrageously"; Edward Chase Kirkland, *Charles Francis Adams, Jr., 1835–1915: The Patrician at Bay* (Cambridge, Mass.: Harvard University Press, 1965), 77. For other uses of the term "robber baron," see *RRG*, November 13, 1875.

66 *NYT*, November 11, 1869; *NYTr*, November 10, 11, 1869. On the statue, see *NYT*, September 2, 8, 1869.

67 *Nation*, November 18, 1869; Jerome Mushkat, "Hall, A(braham) Oakey," in Kenneth T. Jackson, ed., *The Encyclopedia of New York City* (New Haven: Yale University Press, 1995), 517.

68 *NYT*, September 2, 8, 1869; *CT*, November 25, 1871; *HW*, February 3, 1872; Directors' Minutes, November 3, December 16, 1869, HRR, reel 27, box 242, NYCRR.

69 Burrows & Wallace, 944–5; *CT*, November 25, 1871; *HW*, February 3, 1872; Directors' Minutes, November 3, December 16, 1869, HRR, reel 27, box 242, NYCRR.

70 *NYH*, January 22, 1870.

71 *NYH*, February 6, 1870; *NYS*, February 7, 8, 1870.

72 *NYS*, February 8, 1870; *NYH*, February 9, 1870; Victoria Woodhull to Whitelaw Reid, January 26, 1870, Tennie C. Claflin to Whitelaw Reid, February 6, 1870, reel 192, Reid Family Papers, LOC. See also *NYH*, February 3, 1870, in *CT*, February 8, 1870.

73 *NYH*, February 6, 1870.

74 "Memoir of Alva Murray Smith Vanderbilt Belmont," Matilda Young Papers, Duke.

75 Helen Lefkowitz Horowitz, "A Victoria Woodhull for the 1990s," *Reviews in American History* 27, no. 1 (1999): 87–97, and "Victoria Woodhull, Anthony Comstock, and Conflict over Sex in the United States in the 1870s," *JAH* 87, no. 2 (September 2000); Mary Gabriel, *Notorious Victoria: The Life of Victoria Woodhull, Uncensored* (Chapel Hill, N.C.: Algonquin Books of Chapel Hill, 1998), 92; see also Amanda Frisken, *Victoria Woodhull's Sexual Revolution: Political Theater and the Popular Press in Nineteenth-Century America* (Philadelphia: University of Pennsylvania Press, 2004); Burrows & Wallace, 981–5; Foner, 446–9, 472–4.

76 *NYS*, September 25, 1870; *NYH*, May 17, 1871; *NYTr*, May 17, 1871; October 16, 1878.

77 *NYS*, November 14, 1877; Joseph Treat, *Beecher, Tilton, Woodhull, and the Creation of Society: All Four of Them Exposed, and if Possible Reformed, and Forgiven, in Dr. Treat's Celebrated Letter to Victoria C. Woodhull* (New York: n.p., 1874), Rare Books and Manuscripts Department, Boston Public Library.

78 CV revised his will on January 9, 1870, providing $500,000 in securities for his wife and daughters, with no mention of Claflin or Woodhull; *NYH*, March 5, 1879. Edward J. Renehan Jr., *Commodore: The Life of Cornelius Vanderbilt* (New York: Basic Books, 2007), claims that John J. Ogden testified in court to the points made here, as reported in *NYT*, March 2, 1878. Renehan is wrong; the source he cites clearly shows that the lawyer made claims for what Ogden would say, but the testimony was prevented by the Surrogate, who declared, "I don't see that the conversation is any evidence of unsoundness of mind. It might be a question of taste."

79 *NYH*, January 22, February 13, 1870; *NYS*, March 26, 1870. One of the would-be witnesses by whom the lawyers offered to prove that CV had put his arm around Claflin, kissed her, and performed other scandalous acts was her father, Buck Claflin, whom even the sympathetic Goldsmith acknowledges to have been a confidence artist. He did not actually testify to the allegations; *NYTr*, March 21, 1878. The other purported witness was John J. Ogden, but he, too, did not speak to it in court; *NYS*, March 2, 1878; *NYH*, March 2, 1878.

80 RGD, NYC 349:1062.

81 *NYTr*, October 16, 1878; *NYT*, January 5, 1875, August 7, 1876, December 8, 1877.

Bodenhamer testified, "His mind was clear and his perception good as long as I knew him. . . . I do not know that I ever did know a more clear-headed man under such suffering [in his final illness]. I never saw him when his mind was not clear. In my opinion he was at all times capable of transacting any business he was accustomed to"; *NYT,* December 8, 1877. Bodenhamer is a particularly credible witness, because he clearly did not shade his testimony to cast Vanderbilt in a favorable light. He was a leading medical authority, and the author of *The Physical Exploration of the Rectum* (New York: William Wood, 1870).

82 *NYH,* June 8, 1871; *NYT,* January 5, 1875.

83 Directors' Minutes, January 27, 1870, NYC&HR, vol. 1, box 93, NYCRR; *NYT,* February 12, 28, March 4, April 10, 1870; NYSAD 38, 103rd sess., 1880, 20–1; CFA, "Railway Problems in 1869," *NAR,* January 1870. See also RGD, NYC 342:262. The *NYT* included state bond interest payments in its calculation.

84 NYC&HR Annual Report, December 16, 1870, Annual Reports Folder, box 34, NYCRR; NYSAD 161, 91st sess., 1868; Chandler, *Visible Hand,* 154.

85 Walter Licht, *Working for the Railroad: The Organization of Work in the Nineteenth Century* (Princeton: Princeton University Press, 1983), 18–9.

86 Chandler, *Visible Hand,* 81–121, 145–56; Licht, 27; Foner, 461–88; Burrows & Wallace, 966–87.

87 *CT,* March 4, May 5, 6, 1870, January 13, 1871; *RRG,* May 7, June 4, 1870, June 28, 1873; *NYTr,* October 30, 1869; *NYTr,* in *RRG,* May 21, 1870; *NYT,* May 25, 27, 1870; *RT,* June 18, 1870; JMD to EC, May 9, August 12, 1870, fold. 1, box 95, ECP; New York Stock and Exchange Board Minutes: 1867–1871, May 14, 1870, New York Stock Exchange Archives; Executive Committee Minutes, March 10, 13, 1870, NYC&HR, vol. 1, box 93, NYCRR.

88 *NYH,* June 8, 1870; *CT,* June 7, 8, 11, 1870; *NYT,* June 7, 8, 1870; *RRG,* May 14, June 11, 1870; Klein, 96.

89 *NYTr,* June 14, 1870, in *CT,* June 16, 1870; *NYT,* March 16, 1870; Klein, 92.

90 *NYTr,* June 29, 1870; *CT,* July 2, 4, 6, 1870; *RRG,* July 2, 1870; see also *HC,* June 13, 1870; *NYH,* June 19, 1870. These newspaper reports make clear that the Erie initiated the cut to $1 per car, often ascribed to the Central by historians.

91 *NYT,* July 1, 15, 1870; *New York Commercial,* in *CT,* August 2, 1870.

92 The press reports of this encounter named Richard, not Augustus, Schell, but I think this was a mistake. Richard played no part in the Central's management, but the Schell at this meeting pressed for a compromise. *NYS* in *CT,* August 13, 23, 1870; *Albion,* August 20, 1870; *NYT,* August 23, October 29, 1870; *NYS,* November 28, 1872.

93 *RRG,* July 2, November 19, 26, December 3, 17, 24, 1870; *Circular,* July 25, 1870; *The Stockholder,* in *RRG,* September 17, 1870; *HC,* November 26, 1870, July 19, 1871; Directors' Minutes, July 6, 1871, Dunkirk, Warren & Pittsburgh Railroad Company, reel 58, box 242, Directors' Minutes, May 3, 1871, LS&MS, reel 65, box 243, NYCRR; Edward Chase Kirkland, *Men, Cities, and Transportation: A Study in New England History, 1820–1900,* vol. 1 (Cambridge, Mass.: Harvard University Press, 1948), 372–5.

94 *NYT,* October 13, 1870; *The Telegrapher,* in *RRG,* October 29, 1870. CV would imply (though not explicitly state) that he had no stake in Western Union, in *NYT,* January 21, 1873. Norvin Green, then a vice president of Western Union, later testified before Congress, "In 1869 Commodore Vanderbilt and his friends came in. Horace Clark . . . and Mr. Schell and a number of leading men came into the company and organized an executive committee, suspended dividends, and introduced some new features." See SR 577, 48th Cong., 1st sess., vol. 1, 2238. Historians have generally taken this as proof of CV's leading role. See, for example, Julius Grodinsky, *Jay Gould: His Business Career, 1867–1892* (Philadelphia: University of Pennsylvania Press, 1957), 150. However, Green seems to have been speaking casually; he misdated this event by a year (among other factual errors he made in his testimony),

and may have been making the offhand connection between CV and HFC that most observers made at the time. I am not fully convinced that CV did in fact invest in Western Union at this time. See also SR 1262, 48th Cong., 2nd sess., vol. 1, 948-9.

95   *CT*, May 5, 6, 1870; *RRG*, May 7, June 4, 1870; *NYTr*, in *RRG*, May 21, 1870; *NYT*, May 25, 27, 1870; *RT*, June 18, 1870.

96   *NYT*, November 23, 24, 1870.

97   *CT*, August 29, 1870. CV's defenders often wrote that he engaged in secret charity, disdaining public approbation; see a letter to the editor, *NYS*, September 24, 1870.

98   Edward M. Deems and Francis M. Deems, *Autobiography of Charles Force Deems and Memoir by his Sons* (New York: Fleming H. Reveli, 1897), 194, 196, 205; *NYTr*, October 24, 1878; *NYT*, September 2, 1870, August 3, 1874.

99   *NYTr*, January 15, 1877; Deems, 206-7.

100   Deems, 207-8.

101   Deems, 208-14; Charles F. Deems to Mrs. Vanderbilt, August 6, 1870, Mrs. F. A. Vanderbilt Papers, Burton Historical Collection, Detroit Public Library; *HC*, August 5, 1870; *NYT*, September 2, 1870.

102   CV was quoted by Edwin D. Worcester, *NYTr*, February 13, 1879.

103   *NYS*, December 15, 1877.

104   *CT*, September 3, 1871; *NYT*, October 15, November 2, 1871, August 3, 1874; *NYT*, January 5, 1877.

105   *NYT*, March 20, 23, 1870; *NYS*, December 20, 1877; Ellen W. Vanderbilt to HG, October 18, 1871 [?], reel 3, HGP.

106   Cornelius J. Vanderbilt to George Terry, May 12, 1871, fold. 24, and Cornelius J. Vanderbilt to George Terry, n.d., fold. 26, box 59, ser. 13, Colt Family Papers, Special Collections, University Libraries, University of Rhode Island.

107   *NYH*, August 3, 1871; *NYT*, August 3, 18, September 3, 16, 1871.

108   *NYW*, June 30, 1871, in *RRG*, July 8, 1871; *RT*, August 12, 1871; *HW*, February 3, 1872; Burrows & Wallace, 944.

109   Directors' Minutes, May 16, 1871, Lease Agreement, November 17, 1872, HRR, reel 27, box 242, NYCRR; NYSSD 41, February 28, 1872. The taking of land for the depot, under the state authorization of 1869, resulted in extended, tedious legal complications; *RT*, July 23, 1870.

110   *NYT*, November 17, 1871; Burrows & Wallace, 929-31, 943-5.

111   *NYH*, July 28, 1871; *Second Annual Report of the President and Directors of the Lake Shore & Michigan Southern Railway Company, to the Stockholders for the Fiscal Year Ending December 31, 1871* (Cleveland: Fairbanks, Benedict & Co, 1872), Baker Library, Harvard Business School.

112   *NYH*, October 20, 1871; *RRG*, October 28, 1871; *Second Annual Report of the . . . Lake Shore.*

113   *CT*, May 6, 1871; *NYT*, April 25, 1871; *BM*, March 1872.

114   *NYT*, September 7, 1871; Seymour J. Mandelbaum, *Boss Tweed's New York* (New York: John Wiley & Sons, 1965), 76-86; Burrows & Wallace, 1008-11. The Samuel J. Tilden Papers in the New York Public Library collections show frequent correspondence with AS.

115   *NYT*, September 7, December 30, 1871; *CT*, August 7, 1872. As a sign of just how close AS and HFC were, HFC served as the equivalent of best man in AS's Quaker wedding in 1873; *CT*, March 27, 1873.

Eighteen Dynasty

1   *NYH*, January 13, 1872; *NYT*, October 17, 19, November 16, 17, 18, 22, 1871, December 12, 1871. For a count of the number of trains that ran on Fourth Avenue, see WHV's testimony, NYSSD 41, February 28, 1872. For earlier complaints about

the noise and danger of the trains on Fourth Avenue, see Jonas P. Sevy to Corporation Counsel, July 27, 1868, Jonas P. Sevy to Corporation Counsel, July 27, 1868, box 1216, Mayor John T. Hoffman Correspondence, Mayors' Papers, NYMA.

2   *NYH*, January 13, 1872.

3   *NYT*, January 27, 1872.

4   Adam Smith, *The Wealth of Nations* (New York: Modern Library, 2000), book 1, chap. 10, part 1, 148; Alfred D. Chandler Jr., *The Visible Hand: The Managerial Revolution in American Business* (Cambridge, Mass.: Harvard University Press, 1979), 137.

5   John D. Rockefeller Sr. to Laura S. Rockefeller, December 15, 1871, fold. 270, box 36, Record Group 1.2, Rockefeller Archives Center, Sleepy Hollow, N.Y.; Ron Chernow, *Titan: The Life of John D. Rockefeller, Sr.* (New York: Random House, 1998), 133–8; Edward Harold Mott, *Between the Ocean and the Lakes: The Story of Erie* (New York: Ticker Publishing, 1908), 467–70; Rolland Harper Maybee, *Railroad Competition and the Oil Trade, 1855–1873* (Mount Pleasant, Mich.: Extension Press, 1940), 244–6, 253, 263–4, 280, 282, 285–305.

6   John D. Rockefeller Sr. to Laura S. Rockefeller, December 15, 1871, fold. 270, box 36, Record Group 1.2, Rockefeller Archives Center, Sleepy Hollow, N.Y.; *NYT*, August 22, 28, 1879; WHV to J. H. Devereaux, July 2, 1872, and John D. Rockefeller to J. H. Devereux, December 7, 1872, fold. 19, box 1, New York Central Railroad Collection, Albany Institute for History and Art, Albany, N.Y.; H. E. Sargent to JFJ, May 16, 1874, JFJP; JMD to EC, June 3, 1868, fold. 8, box 39, ECP; Chernow, 110–7. Rolland Harper Maybee, *Railroad Competition and the Oil Trade, 1855–1873* (Mount Pleasant, Mich.: Extension Press, 1940), is an excellent study of the economics of oil traffic for railroads, and the advantages of the SIC.

7   *CT*, April 3, 1872; NYSAD 38, 103rd sess., 1880, 40–1; *HW*, July 12, 1873; *RRG*, June 13, 1874; Maybee, 101–10, 165–72, 182–8, 286; James A. Ward, *J. Edgar Thomson: Master of the Pennsylvania* (Westport, Conn.: Greenwood Press, 1980), 95–6, 140–51; Scott Reynolds Nelson, *Iron Confederacies: Southern Railways, Klan Violence, and Reconstruction* (Chapel Hill: University of North Carolina Press, 1999), 71–94; Chandler, *Visible Hand*, 151–6. On Scott's role as mentor to Carnegie, see David Nasaw, *Andrew Carnegie* (New York: Penguin, 2006), 55–85.

8   Nasaw, 59–60, 61–3, 105–112; Nelson, 138–62; Maybee, 101, 114, 133–8, 286. Nasaw writes, 122, that Scott "followed the standard financing practices of the time and established improvement companies," whereas Scott had pioneered the form. Ward, 150, notes that Scott, for example, organized the Pennsylvania Company, a subsidiary corporation that owned or leased the Pennsylvania's western connections.

9   Chandler, *Visible Hand*, 145–87. Chandler astutely discusses these divergent patterns of system building, but fails to appreciate the defensive advantages of CV's decision not to integrate his lines. As noted, CV not only insulated his companies from each other's ailments, but also shielded himself from political outrage at his expanding reach.

10   Maury Klein, *Union Pacific: Birth of a Railroad, 1862–1893* (Garden City, N.Y.: Doubleday, 1987), 286–7; Nasaw, 122–4. Citations of "Klein" below refer to *Jay Gould*.

11   *NYT*, March 22, 26, 1872; Chernow, 141–2.

12   *NYH*, January 7, 9, 1872; *HW*, January 20, 1872; *NYT*, May 2, 1874; *New York Observer and Chronicle*, February 29, 1872; *BM*, March 1872; *CT*, January 1, 1873; Klein, 121–5. The phrase "porcine carcass" is from William L. Garrison to Wife, May 24, 1871, William Lloyd Garrison Papers, Rare Books and Manuscripts Department, Boston Public Library.

13   *CT*, April 1, 1872; *NYTr*, June 15, 1878; Family Record, WFP.

14   Both Smith and Corey testified to their conversations during the will trial; *NYTr*, June 15, 1878.

15   Cornelius J. Vanderbilt to George Terry, April 12, 20, May 14, 1871, fold. 24, box 59, ser. 13, Colt Family Papers, Special Collections, University Libraries, Univer-

sity of Rhode Island. In making these generalizations, I am drawing on a reading of the full contents of folds. 23–26, box 59, ser. 13, in this collection.

16 *NYS*, December 19, 22, 1877; *NYT*, December 29, 1877; *NYTr*, February 27, 1878; *CT*, January 13, 1873; CJV to HG, June 25, 1872, reel 3, HGP.

17 Chauncey M. Depew, *My Memories of Eighty Years* (New York: Charles Scribner's Sons, 1922), 91–2; Foner, 501–10; *NYT*, April 16, 1872.

18 *NYT*, March 15, 1872; *CT*, April 5, 1872; *NYH*, April 18, 20, 22, 1873.

19 *NYT*, April 11, 16, 19, 20, 23, 1872; *NYH*, April 23, 24, May 3, 1872.

20 CV to Samuel J. Tilden, May 20, 1872, Samuel J. Tilden to CV, June 14, 1872, fold. 8, box 7, Samuel J. Tilden Papers, NYPL.

21 Grenville M. Dodge, Philadelphia, to U. S. Grant, June 6, 1872, in John Y. Simon, ed. *The Papers of Ulysses S. Grant*, vol. 23 (Carbondale: Southern Illinois University, 2000), 163.

22 Klein, *Union Pacific*, 287–90.

23 WHV to Edwin D. Morgan, April 17, June 14, 1872, fold. 3, box 13, Edwin D. Morgan Papers, NYSL; *NYT*, March 21, 1871. It was generally believed that CV had bought control of Western Union by 1872; see Gardiner G. Hubbard, "In the Matter of the Postal Telegraph Bill," April 22, 1872, Baker Library, Harvard Business School.

24 *NYT*, June 26, 1872, April 17, 1873, March 12, 1898; *CT*, April 17, 1873; *NYH*, April 17, 1873; *NYS*, April 18, 1873. Paul H. Bergeron, ed., *The Papers of Andrew Johnson*, vol. 14 (Knoxville: University of Tennessee Press, 1997), 278–9n.

25 *NYH*, February 24, March 7, 1872; *NYTr*, October 3, 1873.

26 *NYH*, March 7, 1872; *RRG*, June 28, 1873; HsR 78, 42nd Cong., 3rd sess., vol. 2. See also *RRG*, March 16, 1872.

27 *NYH*, April 23, 1872; *BG*, May 31, 1872, January 29, 1873; *NYT*, April 11, 16, May 9, September 7, 1872, November 1, 1873; *RT*, October 12, 1872; *CT*, December 12, 1872; *New York Evangelist*, July 8, 1875; Executive & Finance Committee Minutes, May 2, 1873, HRR, reel 26, box 242, NYCRR.

28 CV to JHB, February 10, 1872, CV-NYHS. See also CV to JHB, March 1, 3, 1873, May 22, n.d., same collection.

29 *CT*, July 6, 1873.

30 *NYT*, July 4, 1872; *CT*, August 4, 1872; *New York World* in *CT*, August 21, 1872; *NYTr*, February 13, 1879; Ethelinda Vanderbilt Allen to Frank Armstrong Crawford Vanderbilt, July 20, 1872, CV-NYHS. Chivalric tournaments were especially popular with Southerners; see T. J. Stiles, *Jesse James: Last Rebel of the Civil War* (New York: Alfred A. Knopf, 2002), 224.

31 *AtlC*, May 26, July 17, 1872; *CT*, May 27, 1872, April 26, 1873; *BG*, May 27, 1872; *NYT*, May 31, June 7, 1872. CV later made Crawford an agent and director of the NYC&HR.

32 *NYT*, October 29, 1872; *NYH*, October 30, 1872; *CT*, November 17, 1872; *SA*, November 30, 1872; *NYTr*, February 13, 1879; James P. McClure, "The Epizootic of 1872: Horses and Disease in a City in Motion," *NYH* 79, no. 1 (January 1998): 5–22; Burrows & Wallace, 948.

33 *NYT*, November 21, 1872; *NYH*, November 23, 1872; *CT*, November 23, 25, 27, 1872; *New York Commercial Advertiser*, in *CT*, December 1, 1872; *Commercial and Financial Chronicle*, November 30, 1872; *RRG*, November 30, 1872; Klein, 129–32.

34 *NYH*, November 27, 1872.

35 *NYT*, January 5, 1877.

36 *NYS*, November 27, 1872.

37 *NYS*, November 28, 1872.

38 *RRG*, November 30, 1872.

39 *NYT*, April 10, 1872; *NYH*, November 30, 1872; *CT*, March 4, 1873; *SEP*, April 4, 1873.

40 Mrs. Frank A. Vanderbilt to Chancellor Garland, n.d., Mrs. F. A. Vanderbilt Papers, Burton Historical Collection, Detroit Public Library; *New York Sun* in *AtlC*, May 5, 1876; *NYTr*, November 21, 1878; CV to H. N. McTyeire, March 17, 1873, Resolutions of Board Accepting the Gift of Commodore Vanderbilt to Central University, March 26, 1873, CV to G. C. Kelly, March 31, 1873, H. N. McTyeire to CV, May 21, 1873, CV to H. N. McTyeire, May 26, 1873, Correspondence of Cornelius and William H. Vanderbilt, NYPL. CV's correspondence with McTyeire verifies that McTyeire came to New York to be treated by Bodenhamer; see H. N. McTyeire to CV, July 31, 1873, Correspondence of Cornelius and William H. Vanderbilt, NYPL.

41 *NYTr*, October 24, 1878.

42 Mrs. Frank A. Vanderbilt to Chancellor Garland, n.d., Mrs. F. A. Vanderbilt Papers, Burton Historical Collection, Detroit Public Library; *New York Sun* in *AtlC*, May 5, 1876; *NYTr*, November 21, 1878; CV to H. N. McTyeire, March 17, 1873, Resolutions of Board Accepting the Gift of Commodore Vanderbilt to Central University, March 26, 1873, CV to G. C. Kelly, March 31, 1873, H. N. McTyeire to CV, May 21, 1873, CV to H. N. McTyeire, May 26, 1873, Correspondence of Cornelius and William H. Vanderbilt, NYPL. CV's correspondence with McTyeire shows that he took a close personal interest in the progress and the financing of the university. In the letter of May 26, for example, he gave instructions to McTyeire on how to date the drafts on him so that they would be properly paid.

43 *RRG*, November 2, 1872; Executive Committee Minutes, January 11, 1873, NYC&HR, vol. 1, box 93, NYCRR. The minutes of this meeting show CV in full command, as he presented negotiations he had conducted for the lease of a grain elevator in Buffalo.

44 *NYS* in *CT*, January 14, 1873; *RRG*, February 8, August 9, 1873; HED 46, part 2, 44th Cong., 2nd sess., vol. 13.

45 *NYS* in *CT*, January 14, 1873.

46 Board of Directors' Minutes, April 1, 2, 1873, NYC&HR, vol. 2, box 93, Lease Agreement, April 1, 1873, HRR, reel 27, box 242, NYCRR. On a prior reorganization of the New York Central & Hudson River, see *RRG*, December 30, 1871.

47 CV to JHB, March 1, 3, 1873, CV-NYHS; Executive Committee Minutes, March 3, 1873, NYC&HR, vol. 1, box 93, Directors' Minutes, March 3, 1873, LS&MS, reel 65, box 243, NYCRR; *NYT*, March 10, 1873.

48 *NYT*, January 20, 21, February 7, 1873; *HC*, July 4, 1873.

49 *NYH*, April 17, 1873.

50 J. S. Morgan to Carnegie, quoted in Nasaw, 144; J. P. Morgan to Junius Spencer Morgan, April 16, 1873, J. P. Morgan Letterpress Books, vol. 1, Department of Literary and Historical Manuscripts, Morgan Library.

51 *NYH*, April 17, 18, 1873; *NYT*, April 17, 1873; CV to Samuel L. M. Barlow, March 6, 1860, BW box 36 (14), Samuel L. M. Barlow Collection, HL.

52 RGD, NYC 343:316 *NYW*, November 14, 1877.

53 *NYT*, June 20, 21, 22, 23, 1873; *HW*, July 12, 1873.

54 *NYTr*, February 13, 1879.

55 Directors' Minutes, June 30, July 2, October 10, 1873, LS&MS, reel 65, box 243, NYCRR; *CT*, July 17, 18, 1873; *NYH*, July 17, 1873; *BG*, July 17, 1873.

56 *NYW* in *Railway World*, April 17, 1875; *CT*, July 17, 1873; *Cleveland Leader* in *CT*, July 24, 1873; *Fourth Annual Report*. On Amasa Stone, see *Magazine of Western History*, December 1885.

57 *New York World* in *Railway World*, April 17, 1875; *NYTr*, September 22, 23, 1873; *Fourth Annual Report; Testimony Taken Before the Special Committee of the Assembly . . . in the Matter of the Erie Railway Investigation* (1873), Erie Railway Company Collection, Baker Library, Harvard Business School, 716.

58 *CT*, October 25, 1873; *NYTr*, October 25, 1873.

59   *NYT,* July 1, 1873; *AtlC,* August 5, September 21, 1873; *HW,* October 11, 1873; RGD, NYC 374:1, 10; H. N. McTyeire to CV, July 31, 1873, Correspondence of Cornelius and William H. Vanderbilt, NYPL.

60   *NYH,* September 19, 1873.

61   *NYH,* September 19, 21, 1873; *NYTr,* September 19, 1873; *HW,* November 1, 1873. The pre-panic market capitalization figures are based on average stock prices in the weeks preceding the collapse.

62   Entries for September 18, 19, 22–27, 1873, John V. L. Pruyn Journal, box 2, John V. L. Pruyn Papers, NYSL.

63   *NYH,* September 21, 22, 23, 1873; *NYTr,* September 22, October 3, 1873; entries for September 22–27, 1873, October 4, 9, 1873, Pruyn Journal.

64   *NYH,* September 22, 1873; *CT,* September 23, 1873; Joseph Dorfman, *The Economic Mind in American Civilization,* vol. 3, *1865–1918* (New York: Viking, 1949), 15; Esther Rogoff Taus, *Central Banking Functions of the United States Treasury, 1789–1941* (New York: Columbia University Press, 1943), 68–71.

65   Strong, 4:498; Foner, 512–4; Jean Strouse, *Morgan: American Financier* (New York: Random House, 1999), 150–7.

66   Burrows & Wallace, 991, 1022–34.

67   Nasaw, 151–5; Strouse, 150–7; James A. Ward, *J. Edgar Thomson: Master of the Pennsylvania* (Westport, Conn.: Greenwood Press, 1980), 202–15.

68   *NYH,* October 15, 1873; *NYTr,* October 24, 1873; *NYT,* October 29, 1873; *CT,* April 11, 1874, November 14, 1882; Chauncey M. Depew, *My Memories of Eighty Years* (New York: Charles Scribner's Sons, 1922), 353.

69   Entry for October 9, 24, 1873, Pruyn Journal; *NYT,* October 28, 1873. Lest there be any confusion about which Vanderbilt negotiated with the trustees, Pruyn's journal specifies that CV proposed the final settlement, confirming press accounts.

70   *NYT,* October 28, 1873; Executive Committee Minutes, December 17, 1873, Directors' Minutes, April 18, 1874, LS&MS, reel 65, box 243, NYCRR; Depew, 354.

71   *RRG,* May 16, 1874. See also *NYW,* April 9, 1875, in *Railway World,* April 17, 1875. It should be noted that the LS&MS minutes show that WHV was not present at some meetings over which his father presided, and that CV took an active part in all the meetings—presenting, for example, the results of his negotiations with Schell. See Executive Committee Minutes, December 17, 1873, Directors' Minutes, April 18, 1874, LS&MS, reel 65, box 243, NYCRR.

72   Edwin D. Worcester testified on the lease plan, and WHV's lack of knowledge of it; *NYS,* December 15, 1877.

73   *NYTr,* February 13, 1879; *HC,* October 9, 1873; *RRG,* October 18, 1873; Western Union Telegraph Company Annual Report, 1873, Baker Library, Harvard Business School; Klein, *Gould,* 196–205.

74   *NYH,* September 10, 1873.

75   Irwin Unger, *The Greenback Era: A Social and Political History of American Finance, 1865–1879* (Princeton: Princeton University Press, 1964), 203; *CT,* April 1, 1873. See also *RRG,* April 19, 1873, and the still-important Robert P. Sharkey, *Money, Class, and Party: An Economic Study of Civil War and Reconstruction* (Baltimore: Johns Hopkins Press, 1959).

76   *CT,* April 1, 1873; *Nation,* May 1, 1873; Stiles, 232. See also George H. Miller, *Railroads and the Granger Laws* (Madison: University of Wisconsin Press, 1971).

77   Stiles, 170–1; Unger, 195–327; Richard Franklin Bensel, *Yankee Leviathan: The Origins of Central State Authority in America, 1859–1877* (New York: Cambridge University Press, 1990), 303–65; Foner, 480–2; Sven Beckert, *The Monied Metropolis: New York City and the Consolidation of the American Bourgeoisie, 1815–1896* (New York: Cambridge University Press, 2001), 192.

78   Beckert, 190 (see also 191–2); Schell quoted in Unger, 48, also 195–327. During Andrew Johnson's administration, one conservative banker, steeped in hard-money

orthodoxy, compared a return to the resumption of specie payments to death—necessary for eternal salvation, but to be resisted to the end; Dorfman, 4–5. On railroad cartels and attempts to cooperate, see Chandler, *Visible Hand*, 122–87; Jean Strouse, *Morgan: American Financier* (New York: Random House, 1999), 195–9.

79 Gregory A. Mark, "The Personification of the Business Corporation in American Law," *University of Chicago Law Review* 54, no. 4 (autumn 1987): 1441–83. See also Naomi R. Lamoreaux, "Partnerships, Corporations, and the Limits on Contractual Freedom in U.S. History: An Essay in Economics, Law, and Culture," in Kenneth Lipartito and David B. Scilia, eds., *Constructing Corporate America: History, Politics, Culture* (Oxford: Oxford University Press, 2004), 29–65. On the post–Civil War struggles of the Supreme Court to account for the new corporate age, see Michael A. Ross, *Justice of Shattered Dreams: Samuel Freeman Miller and the Supreme Court during the Civil War Era* (Baton Rouge: Louisiana State University Press, 2003), 176–254. Miller had long criticized the "money power," and in 1877 voted with the 7–2 majority in *Munn v. Illinois*, which accepted the constitutionality of Granger laws. The justices were products of their time. As Ross writes, 254, "Throughout his judicial career, Miller clung to the Republican ideology of the 1850s, an ideology that became impracticable as a result [of] the nation's postwar economic transformations."

80 Alan Trachtenberg, *The Incorporation of America: Culture and Society in the Gilded Age* (New York: Hill & Wang, 1982), 59–60, 79–86; Stiles, 376–95; see also Chandler, *Visible Hand*.

81 *NYS*, December 15, 1877; *NYT*, December 15, 1877.

82 *NYT*, December 29, 1877.

83 *NYTr*, November 21, June 15, 1878.

84 *New York Sunday News*, January 6, 1878, Vanderbilt Will Trial Case Clippings, NYPL.

85 Cornelius [J.] Vanderbilt to Thurlow Weed, May 28, 1875, Thurlow Weed Papers, NYHS.

86 *NYTr*, March 13, 1878.

87 LW Dictation; *Independent*, August 13, 1874.

88 *NYH*, March 5, 1879; *NYTr*, January 9, 1877.

89 Beckert, 220.

90 *NYTr*, January 9, 1877, February 6, 1879; *RRG*, June 20, 1874.

91 *NYT*, November 8, 1872, June 2, 1874, December 16, 1875; *Journal of the American Geographical Society of New York*, February 17, 1875; *CT*, January 25, 1876; *AtlC*, February 20, 1876; *NYS*, in *Atlanta Constitution*, April 25, 1875.

92 *NYT*, February 15, 1879 (this account mistakenly substitutes "president" for the correct "vice president"); *NYT*, December 15, 1877; Directors' Minutes, May 6, June 16, August 8, 1874, LS&MS, reel 65, box 243, NYCRR; H. E. Sargent to JFJ, May 16, 1874, JFJP. Sargent named the rivalry between WHV and HFC as one reason for the Central's prior neutrality between the North Shore lines and the Lake Shore, a statement supported by Amasa Stone Jr., *NYT*, November 23, 1878.

93 CV to H. N. McTyeire, June 15, 1874, WHV to Bishop H. N. McTyeire, February 24, 1877, H. N. McTyeire, "Last Words Before Leaving for the Ecumenical Conference in London," June 28, 1881, Correspondence of Cornelius and William H. Vanderbilt, NYPL; CV to H. N. McTyeire, March 24, 1874, fold. 23, box 2, John James Tigert IV Papers, Special Collections, Jean and Alexander Heard Library, Vanderbilt University; *CT*, September 3, 1875; *NYH*, October 5, 1875. See also CV to H. N. McTyeire, July 13, 1874, CV to H. N. McTyeire, December 2, 1875, F. A. P. Barnard to CV, June 29, 1876, NYPL; Charles F. Deems to CV, October 2, 1875, Mrs. F. A. Vanderbilt Papers, Burton Historical Collection, Detroit Public Library; *Nashville American*, June 17, 1876, in *NYT*, June 20, 1876.

94 *NYW*, December 13, 1877; *NYS*, March 6, 1878.

95 *CT,* May 29, 30, 1874; *RRG,* March 21, April 11, June 13, 1874. For a review of the impact of the depression over the course of 1874, see *RRG,* December 26, 1874. For explicit statements by both CV and WHV that CV set the nonaggression policy, see *CT,* May 10, 1876, *NYT,* June 16, 1876.

96 RGD, NYC 374:1.

97 *RRG,* July 6, December 26, 1874.

98 *CT,* August 3, 1874; *RRG,* August 8, 15, September 12, 1872.

99 *CT,* October 16, 22, 1874; *RRG,* October 31, November 21, 1874.

100 HC, November 13, 1874; *CT,* November 6, 1874; *RRG,* September 24, November 14, 21, 1874; *NYT,* November 13, 18, 1874; *EP* in *NYT,* November 18, 1874; *NYH,* February 18, March 27, 1875.

101 *NYT,* June 24, 1875. During the year, CV traveled to Cleveland for the LS&MS annual meeting and took part in discussions with Scott and Garrett; see Directors' Minutes, May 5, 1875, LS&MS, reel 65, box 243, NYCRR; *CT,* May 5, 1875: *NYT,* May 6, 1875; *RRG,* May 8, 1875; *NYH,* June 9, 1875; *CT,* June 9, 14, 1875; *RRG,* June 19, 26, July 3, 1875. WHV, however, clearly took operational leadership; see, for example, *NYH,* December 26, 1875.

102 I am grateful to Prof. Richard R. John of the University of Illinois at Chicago and David Hochfelder, Edison Papers, Rutgers University, for providing summaries of these two letters (John W. Garrett to CV, November 17, 1875, and William Orton to CV, November 19, 1875). They appear in fold. 1, box 200B, subser. 1, ser. 4, Western Union Telegraph Company Collection, Archives Center, National Museum of American History, Smithsonian Institution, Washington, D.C. Orton quote from William Orton to Edwin D. Morgan, May 12, 1876, fold. 9, box 10, Edwin D. Morgan Papers, NYSL.

103 Board of Directors' Minutes, September 9, 1874, NYC&HR, vol. 2, box 93, Directors' Minutes, October 1, 1874, LS&MS, reel 65, box 243, NYCRR; NYSAD 38, 103rd sess., 1880, 15, 25; *RRG,* December 15, 22, 29, 1876; *NYT,* December 17, 1876; Edward Hungerford, *Men and Iron: The History of the New York Central* (New York: Thomas Y. Crowell, 1938), 249–54.

104 Directors' Minutes, June 7, 1871, June 3, 1874, December 18, 1875, Canada Southern Railway Company, reel 68, box 242, NYCRR; *Railway World,* January 1, February 5, 1876; *NYW,* November 15, 1877; *NYTr,* February 13, 1879.

105 Directors' Minutes, July 1, 1875, LS&MS, reel 65, box 243, NYCRR; J. W. Brooks to JFJ, April 13, 1875, Telegram, C. J. Brydges to JFJ, April 21, 1875, Joseph Hickson to JFJ, October 13, 1875, JFJP; *CT,* September 18, 1875; *NYT,* October 15, 1875, August 29, 1879; *NYW,* November 15, 1877; Klein, 196–203.

106 *NYTr,* October 16, 1878; *NYH,* October 16, 1878; see also *NYTr,* April 10, 1878.

107 On Morrissey, see *CT,* July 25, 1870. On lawsuits against them, see *NYH,* February 22, 1871. On their court battle with their mother, see *NYTr,* December 15, 1871, in *CT,* December 18, 1871; *NYT,* May 17, 1871; *NYH,* May 16, 17, 1871. For the quote regarding pantarchy and their status as brokers, see *NYT,* March 31, 1872; also RGD, NYC 349:1062. On their eviction, see *NYH,* June 8, 1871. CV's testimony quoted in *NYT,* January 5, 1875. See also Helen Lefkowitz Horowitz, "Victoria Woodhull, Anthony Comstock, and Conflict over Sex in the United States in the 1870s," *JAH* 87, no. 2 (September 2000): 403–34, and "A Victoria Woodhull for the 1990s," *Reviews in American History* 27, no. 1 (1999): 87–97; Mary Gabriel, *Notorious Victoria: The Life of Victoria Woodhull, Uncensored* (Chapel Hill, N.C.: Algonquin Books of Chapel Hill, 1998), and Louis Beachy Underhill, *The Woman Who Ran for President: The Many Lives of Victoria Woodhull* (Bridgehampton, N.Y.: Bridge Works Publishing, 1995). Barbara Goldsmith, in *Other Powers: The Age of Suffrage, Spiritualism, and the Scandalous Victoria Woodhull* (New York: Alfred A. Knopf, 1998), makes several claims without citing sources—or citing them incorrectly. Two of the most important claims, and perhaps most likely, are that Woodhull and Claflin's mother

tried to blackmail CV in early 1871, prompting him to cut the sisters off (272–3); and that, upon CV's death, WHV came to see them, and they assured him that they had seen no signs of CV's being of unsound mind (430–1). Claflin appears to have attempted to extort money out of WHV during the trial over CV's will, colluding with the challenging attorney, Scott Lord, and threatening a lawsuit on the incredible claim that CV stole money from her; see Tennie C. Claflin to Father, c. 1877 (which includes a copy of a letter from Claflin to WHV), fold. 3, box 4, Tennessee Claflin Cook Family Correspondence, Victoria Woodhull-Martin Papers, Special Collections Research Center, Morris Library, Southern Illinois University, Carbondale, Ill.

108   *Independent*, March 16, 1876; *RRG*, March 17, 1876; *NYH*, March 24, 1876; *BG*, April 24, 1876; *CT*, March 17, 1876.
109   *BG*, April 24, 1876.
110   *NYH*, April 11, 14, 1876.
111   *NYW*, November 15, 1877; *NYS*, November 17, 1877.
112   *NYT*, August 7, 1876; *NYW*, November 15, 1877; *AtlC*, April 30, 1876; *NYH*, March 9, 1878.
113   *NYT*, December 8, 1877.
114   *CT*, May 10, 1876.
115   *NYH*, May 11, 1876.
116   *NYT*, December 15, 1877.
117   Mrs. Cornelius Vanderbilt Diary 2, 1876–1878, Misc. Microfilms, reel 72, NYHS (cited hereafter as "Diary 2"). Curiously, she left two parallel diaries with overlapping information. Frank may have made a second record at the time, or she may have copied her original at a later date, leaving out potentially embarrassing revelations, as the primary difference is that only one diary has any references to magnetic healers, who came in to rub CV periodically.
118   Entries for June 4, 19, 1876, Mrs. Cornelius Vanderbilt Diary, 1876–1878, Misc. Microfilms, reel 72, NYHS (cited hereafter as "Diary 1").
119   Entries for August [?]11, September 3, 1876, Diary 2; entry for August 4, 1876, Diary 1; see also *NYT*, March 7, 1878.
120   Entries for September 12, 27, 28, October 9, 1876, Diary 2; see multiple telegrams in 1876 to McTyeire, fold. 24, box 2, John James Tigert IV Papers, Special Collections, Jean and Alexander Heard Library, Vanderbilt University.
121   Entry for August 3, 1876, Diary 1; entries for August 8[?], September 27, 1876, Diary 2.
122   Entries for June 24, August 8, October 4, 1876, Diary 1; entry for October 5, 1876, Diary 2. Corneil mistakenly blamed Frank and Martha Crawford for turning him away; *NYS*, December 22, 1877.
123   *NYH*, December 17, 1876; *NYTr*, February 13, 1879.
124   *NYS*, November 17, 1877; Telegrams, WHV to Bishop H. N. McTyeire, January 4, 1876, 9:12 a.m., 11:41 a.m., 9:55 p.m., fold. 24, box 2, John James Tigert IV Papers, Special Collections, Jean and Alexander Heard Library, Vanderbilt University.

Epilogue

1   For examples of especially questionable witnesses, see *NYTr*, October 2, 1878; *NYH*, March 5, 1879.
2   A history of the contest appears in *NYH*, March 5, 1879; see also *New York Sunday News*, December 23, 1877, Vanderbilt Will Trial Case Clippings, NYPL; *NYTr*, March 21, 1878; *NYT*, April 8, 1880. It was widely believed that WHV eventually gave Corneil a total of $1 million; RGD, NYC 392:2938.
3   Board of Directors' Minutes, January 5, 1877, NYC&HR, vol. 2, box 93, NYCRR.

4 *NYH*, January 8, 1877; *HW*, January 27, 1877. CV's remains would later be removed to the present family tomb, in the same cemetery, constructed by WHV.

5 *NYH*, May 2, 1878.

6 CJV to George Terry, fold. 26, box 59, ser. 13, Colt Family Papers, Special Collections, University Libraries, University of Rhode Island; Family Record, WFP; *Richmond County Advance*, April 15, 1882; *NYT*, April 3, 1882, May 5, 1885.

7 *NYT*, December 8, 1885. The Colt Papers include voluminous documents related to CJV's final bankruptcy.

8 *Annual Report of the Comptroller of the Currency: December 4, 1876* (Washington, D.C.: Government Printing Office, 1876), 45–69; Richard Franklin Bensel, *Yankee Leviathan: The Origins of Central State Authority in America, 1859–1877* (New York: Cambridge University Press, 1990), 268–74. The population estimate for 1876 is extrapolated from census data for 1870 and 1880.

9 *Forbes*, September 17, 2008; "Money Stock Measures," November 13, 2008, Federal Reserve Statistical Release, http://www.federalreserve.gov/releases/h6/current/. The Federal Reserve has ceased to publish M3 statistics.

10 CFA to George E. Crocker, August 7, 1888, Charles Francis Adams Papers, Rare Books and Manuscripts Department, Boston Public Library; Jean Strouse, *Morgan: American Financier* (New York: Random House, 1999), 195–9; Alfred D. Chandler Jr., ed., *The Railroads; The Nation's First Big Business: Sources and Readings* (New York: Harcourt, Brace & World, 1965), 45; Alfred D. Chandler Jr. and Stephen Salsbury, "The Railroads: Innovators in Modern Business Administration," in Bruce Mazlish, *The Railroad and the Space Program: An Exploration in Historical Analogy* (Cambridge, Mass.: MIT Press, 1965), 127–62. Strouse's excellent account is marred by one error: she writes of the New York Central as a family-owned company and of Morgan taking it public, whereas it always was a publicly traded corporation in which the Vanderbilts simply owned a majority of the stock.

11 Strouse, 198–9; *NYS*, December 9, 1885.

12 Strouse, 224–5.

13 Louis Auchincloss, *The Vanderbilt Era: Profiles of a Gilded Age* (New York: Charles Scribner's Sons, 1989), 41. For a fine portrait of the successive generations of the Vanderbilt family, see Arthur T. Vanderbilt II, *Fortune's Children: The Fall of the House of Vanderbilt* (New York: Morrow, 1989).

14 *NYT*, March 19, 2006.

Primary Source Bibliography

UNPUBLISHED PRIMARY SOURCES

Albany Institute for History and Art, Albany, New York
    Erastus Corning I Papers
    New York Central Railroad Collection
American Antiquarian Society, Worcester, Massachusetts
    Comstock Family Papers
    Richard Ward Greene Papers
Baker Library, Harvard Business School, Boston, Massachusetts
    Erie Railway Company Collection
    Records of R. G. Dun & Co.
    Western Union Telegraph Company Collection
Bancroft Library, University of California, Berkeley, California
    Joseph N. Allen Diary
    H. H. Bancroft Collection
        H. H. Bancroft Notes on the Vanderbilt Family
        Papers Concerning the Filibuster War
Bentley Historical Library, University of Michigan, Ann Arbor, Michigan
    James F. Joy Papers, Henry B. Joy Historical Research Collection
Rare Books and Manuscripts Department, Boston Public Library, Boston, Massachusetts
    Charles Francis Adams Papers
    William Lloyd Garrison Papers
    Victoria Woodhull-Martin Papers
Butler Library, Columbia University, New York, New York
    James Buchanan Papers, Microfilm Copy
California Historical Society, San Francisco, California
    Winchester Papers
Carl A. Kroch Library, Rare and Manuscript Collections, Cornell University, Ithaca, New York
    Frederick Gardiner to Charles Gill, September 6, 1838
Detroit Public Library, Detroit, Michigan
    Burton Historical Collection
        James F. Joy Papers
        Mrs. F. A. Vanderbilt Papers
Archives and Special Collections, Drew University, Madison, New Jersey
    Gibbons Family Papers
Rare Book, Manuscript, and Special Collections Library, Duke University, Durham, North Carolina
    "Memoir of Alva Murray Smith Vanderbilt Belmont," Matilda Young Papers
    Hanson A. Risley Papers
Gilder Lehrman Institute of American History, New-York Historical Society, New York, New York

Aaron Burr, "Of the Validity of the Laws Granting Livingston & Fulton the Exclusive Right of Using Fire and Steam to Propel Boats or Vessels"
John P. Hale to Charles Sumner, March 18, 1854
Horace Greeley to William P. Fessenden, October 4, 1864
Horace Greeley, E. D. Morgan et al. to William P. Fessenden, October 10, 1864
Horace Greeley to William P. Fessenden, December 1, 1864
Hagley Museum and Library, Wilmington, Delaware
 Central Railroad Company of New Jersey Papers
Huntington Library, San Marino, California
 Samuel L. M. Barlow Papers
 Lauriston Hall Papers
Manuscript Division, Library of Congress, Washington, District of Columbia
 Chester A. Arthur Papers
 Nathaniel P. Banks Papers
 Baring Brothers Archive, Microfilm Copy
 John M. Clayton Papers
 Hamilton Fish Papers
 Benjamin B. French Papers
 Abraham Lincoln Papers
 William L. Marcy Papers
 Hiram Paulding Papers
 Reid Family Papers
 Edwin M. Stanton Papers
 John Hill Wheeler Papers
Department of Literary and Historical Manuscripts, Morgan Library, New York, New York
 Cyrus W. Field Collection
 J. P. Morgan Letterpress Books
National Archives, College Park, Maryland
 Diplomatic Instructions of the Department of State, 1801–1906: Central American States, vol. 15, May 29, 1833–July 25, 1858, Microfilm Publication M77
 Costa Rican Claims Convention of July 2, 1860, Record Group 76
National Archives, Washington, District of Columbia
 Letters Received by the Secretary of the Navy from Commanding Officers of Squadrons, 1841–1886, Microfilm Publication M89
 Internal Revenue Assessment Lists for New York and New Jersey, 1862–1866, Microfilm Publication M603
 U.S. Military Academy Application Papers, Microfilm Publication M688
 Custom House Records, Bureau of Marine Inspection and Navigation, Record Group 41
 Letter Books of U.S. Naval Officers, March 1778–July 1908, Record Group 45
 Records of the Office of the Judge Advocate General (Army), Record Group 153
National Archives, New York, New York
 New York Tax Assessment Lists, 1867–1873, Record Group 58
Old Records Division, New York County Clerk's Office, New York, New York
 John De Forest and Cornelius Vanderbilt Jr. vs. Daniel Morgan, April 5, 1817, file 1817-#337, Court of Common Pleas
 Cornelius Vanderbilt and Cornelius Vanderbilt Jr. vs. Phineas Carman and Cornelius P. Wyckoff, May 26, 1817, file 1817-#1261, Court of Common Pleas
 Aaron Ogden v. Thomas Gibbons, December 4, 1819, file O-109, Court of Chancery
 Fitz G. Halleck v. Daniel Drew, March 15, 1820, file 1820-#479, Court of Common Pleas
 John R. Livingston v. Cornelius Vanderbilt, December 28, 1822, file L J-1822-V-18, Supreme Court Judgments
 John Adams, Treasurer of New York Hospital, v. Cornelius Vanderbilt, June 27, 1826, file 1826-#20, Court of Common Pleas

Cornelius Vanderbilt v. Patrick Rice, November 26, 1827, file 1827-#1360, Court of Common Pleas

Patrick Rice v. Cornelius Vanderbilt, November 26, 1827, file 1827-#1671, Court of Common Pleas

Walter Blair v. Daniel Drew, March 10, 1831, file 1831-#87, Court of Common Pleas

Charles Hoyt v. John Brooks Jr., May 8, 1833, file BM 2163-H, Court of Chancery

James Ingham and James Leslie v. Cornelius Vanderbilt, December 15, 1834, file 1834-#756, Court of Common Pleas

Nestor Houghton v. Cornelius Vanderbilt, August 10, 1837, file BM V016-H, Court of Chancery

James Guyon and Cornelius Vanderbilt v. Moulton Bullock, James W. Otis, and Jonathan Prescott Hall, March 16, 1838, file BM 1404-G, Court of Chancery

Cornelius Vanderbilt v. John W. De Grauw and Jane, His Wife, Walter N. DeGrauw, John J. Stephens, and Others, May 30, 1839, file D CH 104-V, Court of Chancery

Cornelius Vanderbilt v. John Martineau and Eliza, His Wife, and Anna B. Cook, Executrix of Richard M. Cook, Deceased, September 13, 1839, file D CH 100-V, Court of Chancery

Joseph Tobey v. Cornelius Vanderbilt, October 15, 1839, file 1839-#1291, Superior Court

Daniel Drew v. Bates Cooke, September 8, 1840, file BM 1233-D, Court of Chancery

Richmond Turnpike Company v. Oliver Vanderbilt, July 24, 1841, file BM 4-42, Court of Chancery

State of Indiana v. Daniel Drew, Nelson Robinson, Eli Kelly, Milton Stapp, William S. Dunham, and David Leavit, August 20, 1841, file BM 19-I, Court of Chancery

Isaac Schuyler v. Daniel Drew, Nelson Robinson & Co., October 27, 1841, file BM S-476, Court of Chancery

Richmond Turnpike Company v. Oliver Vanderbilt, July 11, 1842, file L.J.-1842-N-66, Supreme Court Law Judgments

Daniel Drew and Isaac Newton v. New York and Erie Rail Road Company, September 10, 1842, file 1842-#331, Superior Court

Oroondates Mauran and Cornelius Vanderbilt v. Morris Woolf, May 11, 1843, file 1843-#814, Court of Common Pleas, NYCC

Phebe Vanderbilt v. Charles M. Simonson and His Wife, John K. Vanderbilt and Charles M. Simonson Junior, Executors, and Mary Simonson, Executrix of the Last Will and Testament of Cornelius Simonson, Deceased, and John K. Vanderbilt, April 27, 1844, file D CH-177-V, Court of Chancery

Jacob H. Vanderbilt and John Vanderbilt v. the People of the State of New York, May 10, 1844, file PL-1844-P-424, Supreme Court Pleadings

People of the City of New York v. Jacob H. Vanderbilt, December 19, 1844, file 1844-#771, Court of Common Pleas

Cornelius Vanderbilt v. Henry N. Caldwell, March 4, 1845, file 1845-#1669, Court of Common Pleas

New York, Providence, and Boston Rail Road Company v. Elisha Peck, Richard M. Blatchford, James Foster Jr., Henry G. Stebbins, Matthew Morgan, Samuel Jaudon, and William S. Wetmore, January 3, 1848, file PL-1848-N-4, Supreme Court Pleadings

Curtis Peck v. Daniel Drew, January 31, 1848, file PL-1848-P 256, Supreme Court Pleadings

Isaac Spencer Jr. v. Daniel Drew, Nelson Robinson, Robert W. Kelley, and Daniel B. Allen, March 20, 1848, file 1848-#951A, Court of Common Pleas

Nelson Robinson, Robert W. Kelley, and Daniel B. Allen v. Daniel Drew and Isaac Newton, file PL-1848-R, June 27, 1848, Supreme Court Pleadings

Oliver Vanderbilt v. the Richmond Turnpike Company, July 17, 1848, file 1848-#1238, Superior Court

Nelson Robinson, Robert W. Kelley, and Daniel B. Allen v. Daniel Drew and Isaac Newton, file PL-1848-R 2, November 2, 1848, Supreme Court Pleadings

Curtis Peck v. Daniel Drew, January 7, 1850, file PL-1850-P-3, Supreme Court Pleadings, NYCC

Russell Sturgis v. George Law and Alanson P. St. John, March 27, 1850, 1850-922, Superior Court

Daniel B. Allen, Jeremiah Simonson, William McLean, Alexander H. Britton, William H. Vanderbilt, Nathaniel Hayward, Henry Anderson, John Peck, and the Said Daniel B. Allen, Jacob H. Vanderbilt, and James Brady, Trustees of the California Navigation Company of New York v. James H. Fisk and Cornelius Vanderbilt, January 24, 1851, file PL-1851-A 17, Supreme Court Pleadings

Cornelius Vanderbilt vs. George Law and Others, August 16, 1851, file CV-V-20, Supreme Court Pleadings

Cornelius Vanderbilt v. Accessory Transit Company, January 12, 1854, file PL 1854-V9, Supreme Court Pleadings

David S. Manners and Lydia Roberts, Administrators of Samuel Roberts, Deceased, v. George Law and Arnold Mason, March 18, 1854, file 1854-#2117, Superior Court

George J. Lathrop v. Cornelius Vanderbilt and Daniel Drew, May 4, 1854, file LJ-1854-V-131, Supreme Court Law Judgments

Cornelius Vanderbilt v. William C. Moon, June 7, 1854, file L J-1854-M-398, Supreme Court Judgments

Cornelius Vanderbilt v. Reuben C. Stone, September 12, 1854, file L J-1854-S-19, Supreme Court Judgments

Cornelius Vanderbilt v. John C. Thompson and Minthorne Tompkins, September 26, 1854, file J L-1854-T-172, Supreme Court Judgments

James H. Quimby v. Cornelius Vanderbilt, November 13, 1854, file 1854-#1242, Court of Common Pleas

Cornelius Vanderbilt v. Spring Valley Shot & Lead Manufacturing Company, April 21, 1855, file L J-1855-S-206, Supreme Court Judgments

Cornelius Vanderbilt v. Spring Valley Shot & Lead Manufacturing Company, July 26, 1855, file L J-1855-S-208

Cornelius Vanderbilt v. Spring Valley Shot & Lead Manufacturing Company, May 2, 1855, file L J-1855-S-212, Supreme Court Judgments

New York Life Insurance & Trust Co. v. Cornelius Vanderbilt, Freeman Campbell and Mary Ann, His Wife, Rutherford Moody and Eunice P., His Wife, Jacob J. Van Pelt and Sarah, His Wife, and Jay Jarvis, President of the Citizen's Bank, September 25, 1855, file PL 1855-N14, Supreme Court Pleadings

James H. Quimby v. Cornelius Vanderbilt, November 21, 1855, file 1855-#1313, Court of Common Pleas

Charles H. Wright v. Cornelius Vanderbilt Jr., January 21, 1856, file LJ-1856-V-100, Supreme Court Judgments

Cornelius Vanderbilt v. Jesse P. Wilson, March 19, 1856, file 1856-#2735, Superior Court

George S. Salls v. Cornelius Vanderbilt, November 17, 1856, file 1855-#1226, Court of Common Pleas

Cornelius Vanderbilt v. Mark Wadleigh and Calvin E. Knox, June 24, 1857, file LJ-1857-W-173, Supreme Court Judgments

Cornelius Vanderbilt v. New York and Harlem Railroad Company, July 16, 1858, file LJ-1858-N-41, Supreme Court Judgments

Accessory Transit Company v. Cornelius K. Garrison, September 13, 1858, file 1858-#53, Superior Court

David Colden Murray, Receiver of the Accessory Transit Company, v. Cornelius Vanderbilt, November 3, 1859, file PL 1859-M V74, Supreme Court Pleadings

Cornelius Vanderbilt v. Joseph L. White, November 7, 1860, file 1860-#985, Superior Court

Theodosius F. Secor and Charles Morgan v. George Law, May 22, 1861, file 1861-#832, Superior Court

Certificate of Incorporation, November 27, 1863, Atlantic Mail Steamship Company

Certificate of Increase of the Capital Stock, October 5, 1866, Atlantic Mail Steamship Company

Henry S. Thatcher and George Buckland v. Cornelius J. Vanderbilt, April 2, 1867, file LJ-1867-V-192, Supreme Court Law Judgments

George R. Pecker v. Cornelius J. Vanderbilt, April 2, 1867, file LJ-1867-V-100, Supreme Court Law Judgments

Frank Work v. Daniel Drew, John E. Eldridge, Alexander Drew, Homer Ramsdell, J. C. Bancroft Davis, Henry Thompson, Dudley Gregory, Frederick A. Lane, George Gravel, James Fisk Jr., Jay Gould, and William Skidmore, July 24, 1868, file PL-1868-W-25, Supreme Court Pleadings

Cornelius Vanderbilt v. Jeremiah Simonson, August 13, 1868, file LJ-1858-S-574, Supreme Court Law Judgments

New Jersey Historical Society, Jersey City, New Jersey

Stevens Family Papers

New-York Historical Society, New York, New York

Thomas Gibbons Papers

Samuel S. Griscom. "Journal of a Tour thro N. Jersey, Penn and N. York with occasional remarks on the people, Literary characters Ladies Institutions &c. &c. &c.," 1824

Philip Hone Diary

Livingston Family Papers

Misc. Manuscripts

    John M. Clayton

    Charles O. Handy

    Cornelius Vanderbilt

Misc. Microfilms

    Mrs. Cornelius Vanderbilt Diary, 1876–1878, reel 72

    Mrs. Cornelius Vanderbilt Diary 2, 1876–1878, reel 72

G. P. Morosini, "Jay Gould and the Erie Railway"

William D. Murphy Account Books

Hiram Peck Diary

Staten Island Papers

David Mitchell Turnure Journal

Vanderbilt Family Papers

Thurlow Weed Papers

Isaac Woodruff Papers

New York Municipal Archives, New York, New York

John T. Hoffman Correspondence, Mayors' Papers

New York City Census, 1816

Staten Island Court Papers

Hugh McLaughlin v. Cornelius Vanderbilt, December 12, 1843, Supreme Court, Richmond County, box SI-66

Charles S. De Forest v. Tunis Egbert, Francis Perkins, Preston Sheldon, Helmus M. Wells, March 5, 1852, Supreme Court, Richmond County, box SI-68

People of the State of New York v. Cornelius Vanderbilt, Anthony Bird, Stephen Williams, Elias Butler, Jacob Van Cleef, and Jacob Arnold, November 22, 1851, Supreme Court, Richmond County, box SI-68

Manuscript Division, New York Public Library, New York, New York

Horace Greeley Papers

William D. Lewis Papers

Misc. Files

    Horace F. Clark

    Thomas Gibbons

    Aaron Ogden

Augustus Schell
Cornelius Vanderbilt
Cornelius Vanderbilt Jr. [Cornelius J. Vanderbilt]
PennCentral Collection
   Annual Reports, Directors' and Executive Committee Minutes, Ledgers, and Letter-
      books, Canada Southern, Dunkirk, Warren & Pittsburgh, Hudson River, Lake
      Shore, Lake Shore & Southern Indiana, Long Island, Michigan Central, Michi-
      gan Southern & Northern Indiana, New York & Harlem, New York Central,
      New York Central & Hudson River, and Spuyten Duyvil Railroads
Samuel J. Tilden Papers
Correspondence of Cornelius and William H. Vanderbilt
Vanderbilt Will Trial Case Clippings
Isaiah Thornton Williams Papers
New York State Library
   Edwin D. Morgan Papers
   John V. L. Pruyn Papers
   Cornelius Vanderbilt to Pliny Miles, June 8, 1859
New York Stock Exchange Archives, New York, New York
   Minutes of the New York Stock and Exchange Board
New York Yacht Club Library and Archives, New York, New York
   Book of Minutes No. 1
Newberry Library, Chicago, Illinois
   Chicago, Burlington, and Quincy Collection
Peabody Essex Museum, Salem, Massachusetts
   George Peabody Papers
Rockefeller Archives Center, Sleepy Hollow, New York
   John D. Rockefeller I Correspondence, Record Group 1.2
Rutgers University, New Brunswick, New Jersey
   Gibbons Papers
   Nielson Papers
   Aaron Ogden Papers
Staten Island Institute of Arts and Sciences, Staten Island, New York
   Ferry and Railroad Collection
Archives Center, National Museum of American History, Smithsonian Institution, Wash-
   ington, D.C.
   Western Union Telegraph Company Collection
Special Collections Research Center, Morris Library, Southern Illinois University, Carbon-
   dale, Ill.
   Victoria Woodhull-Martin Papers
Watkinson Library, Trinity College, Hartford, Connecticut
   Williams Family Papers
Special Collections, University Libraries, University of Rhode Island, Providence, Rhode
   Island
   Colt Family Papers
Special Collections, Jean and Alexander Heard Library, Vanderbilt University, Nashville,
   Tennessee
   John James Tigert IV Papers

GOVERNMENT PUBLICATIONS

Annual Report of the Comptroller of the Currency. Washington, D.C.: Government Printing
   Office, 1876.
Bureau of Navigation. *Merchant Steam Vessels of the United States, 1807 to 1856.* Washington,
   D.C.: United States Department of Commerce, 1931.

Minutes of the Common Council of the City of New York, 1784–1831. Vol. 9. New York: City of New York, 1917.

New York State Assembly Document 75. 84th sess., 1861.

New York State Assembly Document 100. 85th sess., 1862.

New York State Assembly Document 175. 86th sess., 1863.

New York State Assembly Document 125. 87th sess., 1864.

New York State Assembly Document 19. 90th sess., 1867.

New York State Assembly Document 114. 90th sess., 1867.

New York State Assembly Document 210. 90th sess., 1867.

New York State Assembly Document 142. 92nd sess., 1869.

New York State Assembly Document 38. 103rd sess., 1880.

New York State Senate Document 52: *Report of the Select Committee of the Senate, Appointed April 10, 1868, in Relation to Passage of Certain Railroad Bills.* Albany: Argus Company, 1869.

Official Records of the Union and Confederate Navies in the War of the Rebellion. Washington, D.C.: Government Printing Office, 1894–1922. 30 vols.

United States House of Representatives Executive Document 75. 31st Cong., 1st sess., vol. 10.

United States House of Representatives Executive Document 103. 34th Cong., 1st sess., vol. 11.

United States House of Representatives Executive Document 24. 35th Cong., 1st sess., vol. 7.

United States House of Representatives Executive Document 47. 35th Cong., 1st sess., vol. 9.

United States House of Representatives Executive Document 1. Part 2, 38th Cong., 2nd sess., vol. 2.

United States House of Representatives Executive Document 78. 38th Cong., 2nd sess., vol. 13.

United States House of Representatives Executive Document 52. 39th Cong., 2nd sess., vol. 8.

United States House of Representatives Report 145. 30th Cong., 2nd sess., vol. 2.

United States House of Representatives Report 2. 36th Cong., 2nd sess., vol. 1.

United States House of Representatives Report 2. Part 2, 37th Cong., 2nd sess., vol. 2.

United States House of Representatives Report 28. 41st Cong., 2nd sess., vol. 1.

United States House of Representatives Report 31. 41st Cong., 2nd sess., vol. 1.

United States House of Representatives Report 78. 42nd Cong., 3rd sess., vol. 2.

United States Senate Executive Document 6. 32nd Cong., 1st sess., vol. 4.

United States Senate Executive Document 50. 32nd Cong., 1st sess., vol. 8.

United States Senate Executive Document 8. 33rd Cong., 1st sess., vol. 4.

United States Senate Executive Document 68. 34th Cong., 1st sess., vol. 13.

United States Senate Executive Document 13. 35th Cong., 1st sess., vol. 1.

United States Senate Executive Document 2. Part 2, 36th Cong., 1st sess., vol. 2.

United States Senate Executive Document 45. 36th Cong., 1st sess., vol. 11.

United States Senate Executive Document 30. 37th Cong., 3rd sess., vol. 1.

United States Senate Executive Document 71. 37th Cong., 2nd sess., vol. 6.

United States Senate Executive Document 46. 39th Cong., 1st sess., vol. 2.

United States Senate Executive Document 44. 41st Cong., 3rd sess., vol. 1.

United States Senate Executive Document 46. Part 2, 44th Cong., 2nd sess., vol. 13.

United States Senate Journal.

United States Senate Misc. Document 27. 37th Cong., 3rd sess., vol. 1.

United States Senate Report 326. 35th Cong., 1st sess., vol. 2.

United States Senate Report 292. 36th Cong., 2nd sess., vol. 1.

United States Senate Report 75. 37th Cong., 3rd sess., vol. 1.

United States Senate Report 307. Part 2, 43rd Cong., 1st sess., vol. 3.

United States Senate Report 577. 48th Cong., 1st sess., vol. 1.

United States Senate Report 1262. 48th Cong., 2nd sess., vol. 1.

United States Census. Washington, D.C.: Government Printing Office.

The War of the Rebellion: A Compilation of the Official Records of the Union and Confederate Armies. Washington, D.C.: Government Printing Office, 1880–1901. 128 vols.

PUBLISHED PRIMARY SOURCES

Annual Reports of the New York, Providence, and Boston Rail Road Company, 1833 to 1874. Westerly, R.I.: 1874.

Barnum, Phineas T. *The Life of P. T. Barnum, Written by Himself.* New York: Redfield, 1855.

Beach, Moses. *Wealth and Pedigree of the Wealthy Citizens of New York City,* 3rd ed. New York: New York Sun, 1842.

Beale, Howard K., ed. *Diary of Gideon Welles.* Vol. 1. New York: W. W. Norton & Co., 1960.

Bergeron, Paul H., ed. *The Papers of Andrew Johnson.* Vol. 13, 14. Knoxville: University of Tennessee Press, 1996, 1997.

Blunt, Edmund M. *Blunt's Stranger's Guide to the City of New-York.* New York: Edmund M. Blunt, 1817.

Calcagno, Francisco. *Diccionario Biográfico Cubano.* New York: Ponce de León, 1878.

Charter and Act of Incorporation of the American Atlantic and Pacific Ship Canal Company and Treaty of Protection Negociated Between the United States and Great Britain. New York: Globe Job, 1850.

Childs, Orville W. *Report of the Survey and Estimates of the Cost of Construction of the Inter-Oceanic Ship Canal.* New York: William C. Bryant, 1852.

Choules, John Overton. *The Cruise of the Steam Yacht North Star.* New York: Evans & Dickerson, 1854.

Clews, Henry. *Fifty Years in Wall Street.* New York: Irving Publishing, 1908.

———. *Twenty-Eight Years in Wall Street.* New York: Irving Publishing, 1888.

Colton, J. H. *Guide to Burr's Map of New York and Steam-Boat, Stage, Railroad, and Canal Register, &c., &c., &c., for the year 1835.* New York: J. H. Colton, 1835.

Compilation of Executive Documents and Diplomatic Correspondence Relative to a Trans-Isthmian Canal in Central America. Vol. 2. New York: Evening Post Printing, 1900.

A Compilation of the Messages and Papers of the President. New York: Bureau of National Literature, 1897.

Depew, Chauncey M. *My Memories of Eighty Years.* New York: Charles Scribner's Sons, 1922.

Dickens, Charles. *American Notes for General Circulation.* New York: Penguin, 2000, orig. pub. 1842.

Doubleday, C. W. *Reminiscences of the "Filibuster" War in Nicaragua.* New York: G. P. Putnam's Sons, 1886.

Fairfield, Francis Gerry. *The Clubs of New York.* New York: Henry L. Hinton, 1873.

First Annual Report of the President and Directors of the Lake Shore & Michigan Southern Railway Company, to the Stockholders, for the Fiscal Year Ending December 31, 1870. Cleveland: Fairbanks, Benedict & Co, 1871.

Fowler, William W. *Ten Years in Wall Street.* Hartford: Worthington, Dustin & Co., 1870.

Gordon, John B. *Reminiscences of the Civil War.* New York: Charles Scribner's Sons, 1904.

Gouge, William M. *A Short History of Paper Money and Banking in the United States.* Philadelphia: T. W. Ustick, 1833.

Hayes, John D. ed. *Samuel Francis Du Pont: A Selection from his Civil War Letters.* Vol. 1. Ithaca: Cornell University Press, 1969.

King, Andrew J., ed. *The Papers of Daniel Webster: Legal Papers.* Vol. 3, part 1. Hanover, N.H.: University Press of New England, 1989.

Kroos, Herman A., ed. *A Documentary History of Banking and Currency in the United States.* New York: Chelsea House, 1965.

Lambert, John. *Travels Through Canada, and the United States of North America, in the Years 1806, 1807, and 1808.* Vol. 2. London: C. Cradock, 1814.

Levasseur, A. *Lafayette in America, in 1824 and 1825: or, Journal of Travels, in the United States.* New York: White, Gallagher & White, 1829.

Manning, William R., ed. *Diplomatic Correspondence of the United States: Inter-American Affairs, 1831–1860.* Vols. 3, 4, 7. Washington, D.C.: Carnegie Endowment for International Peace, 1934, 1934, 1936.

Medbery, James K. *Men and Mysteries of Wall Street.* Boston: Fields, Osgood, 1870.

Memorial of the Golden Wedding of Cornelius and Sophia Vanderbilt, December 19, 1863. New York: Baker & Godwin, 1864.

Nevins, Allan, ed. *The Diary of Philip Hone, 1828-1851.* New York: Dodd, Mead & Co., 1936.

Nevins, Allan, and Milton Halsey Thomas, eds. *The Diary of George Templeton Strong,* Vols. 1, 2, 3, 4. New York: MacMillan, 1952.

Niven, John, ed. *The Salmon P. Chase Papers.* Vol. 1. Kent: Kent State University Press, 1993.

Otis, F. N. *Isthmus of Panama: History of the Panama Railroad and of the Pacific Mail Steamship Company.* New York: Harper & Brothers, 1867.

Pacific Mail Steamship Company. *Proceedings in Connection with Negotiations with C. Vanderbilt, November 30th, 1859.* New York: G. F. Nesbitt & Co., 1859.

———. *Seventh Annual Report of the Pacific Mail Steamship Company, May 1861.* New York: G. F. Nesbitt & Co., 1861.

Petition of C. Vanderbilt for Confirmation of Letters Patent, Issued April 3, 1816. New York: S. S. Chatterton, 1852.

Read, George Willis, ed. *A Pioneer of 1850: George Willis Read, 1819–1880.* Boston: Little, Brown, 1927.

A Replication to a "Statement by the Boston and Providence Rail Road Corporatin in Explanation of their Proceedings in Relation to Steamboats." N.p., n.d.

Report of the President to the Stockholders, Pacific Mail Steamship Company. N.p.: 1868.

Rochefoucauld-Liancourt, Duc de La. *Travels Through the United States of North America, the Country of the Iroquois, and Upper Canada, in the Years 1795, 1796, and 1797; with an Authentic Account of Lower Canada.* London: R. Phillips, 1799.

Royall, Anne. *Sketches of History, Life, and Manners in the United States.* New Haven: n.p., 1826.

Schell, Francis. *Memoir of the Hon. Augustus Schell.* New York: Privately printed, 1885.

Semmes, Raphael. *Memoirs of Service Afloat During the War Between the States.* Baton Rouge: Lousiana State University Press, 1996, orig. pub. 1868.

Seventeenth Annual Report of the Board of Directors to the Stockholders of the Hartford & New Haven R. R. Co. Hartford: Case, Tiffany, 1852.

Sheridan, Philip H. *Personal Memoirs of P. H. Sheridan.* Vol. 2. New York: C. L. Webster, 1888.

Sherman, William T. *Memoirs of General William T. Sherman.* New York: Da Capo Press, 1984, orig. pub. 1875.

Simon, John Y., ed. *The Papers of Ulysses S. Grant.* Vols. 16, 23. Carbondale: Southern Illinois University, 1988, 2000.

A Sketch of the Events of the Life of George Law. New York: J. C. Derby, 1855.

Smith, Matthew Hale. *Twenty Years Among the Bulls and Bears of Wall Street.* Hartford: J. B. Burr, 1870.

Squier, Ephraim George. *Nicaragua: Its People, Scenery, Monuments, and the Proposed Interoceanic Canal.* New York: D. Appleton, 1856.

Soulé, Frank, John H. Gihon, and James Nisbet. *The Annals of San Francisco.* New York: D. Appleton, 1855.

Statement by the Boston and Providence Rail Road Corporation in Explanation of their Proceedings in Relation to Steamboats. Boston: John H. Eastburn, 1838.

Summersell, Charles G., ed. *The Journal of George Townley Fullam*. Tuscaloosa: University of Alabama Press, 1973.

Tanner, Hudson C. *"The Lobby" and Public Men from Thurlow Weed's Time*. Albany: George MacDonald, 1888.

Terms of Contract Between the State of Nicaragua and the Atlantic & Pacific Ship Canal Company: Proposed by the Commissioners of the State of Nicaragua, at the City of León, in the State of Nicaragua, on the 27th Day of August, 1849. New York: William C. Bryant & Co., 1849.

Tocqueville, Alexis de. George Lawrence, trans. *Democracy in America*. New York: Harper-Collins, 1988, orig. pub. 1966.

Treat, Joseph. *Beecher, Tilton, Woodhull, and the Creation of Society: All Four of Them Exposed, and if Possible Reformed, and Forgiven, in Dr. Treat's Celebrated Letter to Victoria C. Woodhull*. New York: n.p., 1874.

Trollope, Frances. *Domestic Manners of the Americans*. New York: Alfred A. Knopf, 1949.

Twain, Mark. "Open Letter to Com. Vanderbilt." *Packard's Monthly*, March 1869.

Walker, William. *The War in Nicaragua*. Tucson: University of Arizona Press, 1985, orig. pub. 1860.

Wallace, David H., ed. " 'From the Windows of the Mail Coach': A Scotsman Looks at New York State in 1811." *NYHSQ* 40, no. 3 (July 1956): 264–96.

Williams, Mary Wilhelmine, ed. "Letters of E. George Squire to John M. Clayton, 1849–1850." *Hispanic American Historical Review* 1, no. 4 (November 1918): 426–34.

Wright, Tobias Alexander, ed. *Collections of the New York Records, Genealogical and Biographical Society*. Vol. 4: *Staten Island Church Records*. New York: n.p., 1909.

LAW REPORTS

New Jersey Law Reports
Southard's New Jersey Supreme Court Reports
Johnson's New York Chancery Reports
Johnson's New York Reports
Wheaton's United States Supreme Court Reports

NEWSPAPERS AND PERIODICALS

Albany Argus
Albany Evening Journal
Alta California
American Almanac and Repository of Useful Knowledge
American Law Review
American Railroad Journal
Anglo-American
Ariel
Army and Navy Chronicle
Atlantic Monthly
American Phrenological Journal
Banker's Magazine and Statistical Register
Boston Daily Advertiser
Boston Globe
Brooklyn Eagle
Chicago Tribune
Cincinnati Mirror
Circular
Cleveland Leader

Commercial and Financial Chronicle
Congressional Globe
Eclectic Magazine
Farmer's Cabinet
Flag of Our Union
Flake's Bulletin
Forest and Stream
Frank Leslie's Illustrated Newspaper
Georgia Gazette
Graham's American Monthly Magazine of Literature, Art, and Fashion
Harper's New Monthly Magazine
Harper's Weekly
Hartford Courant
Home Journal
Independent
Hazard's Register
Journal of the American Geographical Society of New York
Ladies' Companion
Ladies' Repository
Liberator
Littell's Living Age
London *Times*
Maine Farmer
Magazine of Western History
Merchant's Magazine (also *Hunt's Merchant's Magazine*)
Nation
National Era
New Brunswick Fredonian
New York and Richmond Free Press
New York Commercial Advertiser
New York Courier and Enquirer
New York Daily Advertiser
New York Evangelist
New York Evening Post
New York Farmer
New York Herald
New York Illustrated Magazine of Literature and Art
New York Illustrated News
New York *Journal of Commerce*
New-York Mirror
New York Observer
New York Observer and Chronicle
New York Review
New York Sun
New York Times
New York Tribune
New York World
New-Yorker
Niles' Register
North American Review
Packard's Monthly
Putnam's Monthly Magazine
Pittsfield Sun
Providence Journal

Railroad Gazette
Railway World
Railway Times
Richmond County Advance
Round Table
Saturday Evening Post
Scientific American
Spirit of the Times
Staten Island Advance
Texas State Gazette
Trenton Emporium and True American
Trenton Federalist
United States Magazine and Democratic Review
United States Magazine of Science, Art, Manufactures, Agriculture, Commerce
United States Service Magazine
Washington Evening Star
Washington Post
Way Bill
Western Journal of Civilization
Workingman's Advocate
Zion's Herald and Wesleyan Journal

Index

ALSO BY T. J. STILES

"So carefully researched, persuasive, and illuminating that it is likely to reshape permanently our understanding of its subject's life and times."
—The New York Times Book Review

JESSE JAMES

Last Rebel of the Civil War

In this brilliant biography, T. J. Stiles offers a new understanding of the legendary outlaw Jesse James. Although he has often been portrayed as a Robin Hood of the Old West, in this groundbreaking work Stiles places James within the context of the bloody conflicts of the Civil War to reveal a much more complicated and significant figure. Raised in a fiercely pro-slavery household in bitterly divided Missouri, at age sixteen James became a bushwhacker, one of the savage Confederate guerrillas that terrorized the border states. After the end of the war, James continued his campaign of robbery and murder into the brutal era of Reconstruction, when his reckless daring, his partisan pronouncements, and his alliance with the sympathetic editor John Newman Edwards placed him squarely at the forefront of the former Confederates' bid to recapture political power. With meticulous research and vivid accounts of the dramatic adventures of the famous gunman, T. J. Stiles shows how James resembles not the apolitical hero of legend, but rather a figure ready to use violence to command attention for a political cause—in many ways, a forerunner of the modern terrorist.

Biography/978-0-375-70558-8